CANADIAN WOMEN

A History

CANADIAN WOMEN

A History

Third Edition

GAIL CUTHBERT BRANDT
Renison University College/University of Waterloo

NAOMI BLACK
York University

PAULA BOURNE
Ontario Institute for Studies in Education/University of Toronto

MAGDA FAHRNI
Université du Québec à Montréal

NELSON / E D U C A T I O N

NELSON / EDUCATION

Canadian Women: A History, Third Edition
by Gail Cuthbert Brandt, Naomi Black,
Paula Bourne, and Magda Fahrni

Vice President,
Editorial Director:
Evelyn Veitch

Editor-in-Chief,
Higher Education:
Anne Williams

Executive Editor:
Laura Macleod

Senior Marketing Manager:
Amanda Henry

Developmental Editor:
Theresa Fitzgerald

Photo Researcher:
Kristiina Paul

Permissions Coordinator:
Kristiina Paul

Content Production Manager:
Claire Horsnell

Production Service:
KnowledgeWorks Global Ltd.

Copy Editor:
Colleen Ste. Marie

Proofreader:
Jayaprakash

Indexer:
Kevin Broccoli

Senior Production Coordinator:
Ferial Suleman

Design Director:
Ken Phipps

Managing Designer:
Franca Amore

Interior Design:
Peter Papayanakis

Cover Design:
Martyn Schmoll

Compositor:
KnowledgeWorks Global Ltd.

Printer:
RR Donnelley

Library and Archives Canada
Cataloguing in Publication Data

Main entry under title:

Canadian women : a history /
Gail Cuthbert Brandt ... [et al.].
— 3rd ed.

Previous editions written by
Alison Prentice ... [et al.].
Includes bibliographical
references and index.
ISBN 978-0-17-650096-2

1. Women—Canada—History.
2. Women—Canada—Social
conditions. I. Cuthbert Brandt,
Gail

HQ1453.C356 2010   305.40971
C2010-903901-7

ISBN-13: 978-0-17-650096-2
ISBN-10: 0-17-650096-0

Cover Photo Credits:

Top left: Women roller skating. John Boyd fonds, John Boyd numbered photographs Women roller skating, Sarnia, 1909, 1741. Archives of Ontario, C 7-3. **Bottom left:** Elsa Sillanpaa using a washing machine, Sault Ste. Marie, ON, 1927. Archives of Ontario/F 1405. **Centre:** Aboriginal group awaiting arrival of the future king of England, George V, during a royal visit to Calgary, 1901. William James Topley / Library and Archives Canada / PA-012122. **Top right:** Mission Specialist Julie Payette arrives at KSC. NASA Kennedy Space Center (NASA-KSC), ID: KSC-99PP-0445. **Bottom right:** Kathleen Carter and Geraldine Carter working in a Christmas ornament factory, Toronto, 1944. York University Libraries, Clara Thomas Archives & Special Collections/ Toronto Telegram fonds, image no. ASC06634.

For our daughters—Nicole and Andrea Brandt, Susanna Eve, Alexandra Bourne, and Beatrice Astrid Estok; and our granddaughters—Toby Louise Dewar, Sarah Laurel Rosenbaum, Gemma and Megan Bourne, and Cecily and Eloise Bourne Melnychuk.

Contents

PART FOUR

1960 TO THE PRESENT *429*

List of Figures and Tables

LIST OF FIGURES AND TABLES

Preface

We had two main reasons for writing a third edition of *Canadian Women: A History*. First, there has been ongoing demand for a synthesis that encompasses the major demographic, economic, social, and political realities of Canadian women over the course of some 500 years. Although the second edition, published in 1996, has been technically out of print for the past few years, some college and university instructors across Canada have continued to order it in special print runs. As well, many have repeatedly asked about the possibility of a revised edition. The more important reason for writing this third edition has been the remarkable outpouring since 1996 of historians' research concerning women and gender. In developing this third edition, we have been motivated by a strong desire to acknowledge and to share as much as possible the approaches and findings of this scholarship.

As was the case for the second edition, it has been a challenge to capture the depth and variety of so much new material within a single volume. Incorporating recent findings in the field of Canadian women's history has led us well beyond trying to splice fragments into the 1996 text. We have, in fact, done a considerable amount of reassessing, rewriting, and reorganizing. In this edition, Part Four now begins in 1960, rather than with the Second World War, and covers the last half of the twentieth century and the first decade of the twenty-first. At the same time, we have decided to adhere to the organizing principle used in both of the previous editions. Each section begins with a brief introduction to the general historical trends of the time period covered by the chapters in that section so that readers with little knowledge of Canadian history can contextualize the discussion of women's experiences. We then follow with an examination of women's work and material culture before moving on to analyze women's demographic characteristics, their family lives, and their involvement in public culture and politics. We have also tried to remain faithful to our practices of balancing scholarly analysis with individual stories and writing in a readily accessible style. In this way, we continue our commitment to producing a work that can find an audience beyond the confines of the postsecondary classroom.

With this edition we have sought to take advantage of new technologies while meeting both professional and amateur historians' traditional interest in primary documents. We have chosen a variety of such documents to further elucidate the themes of each section and to illustrate the diversity of sources and viewpoints that merit consideration. Our publisher has posted this material at http://www.canadianwomen3e.nelson.com.

The complex and lengthy task of preparing this revised edition has reinforced our conviction that such a project is best undertaken by a highly collaborative and committed team. We hope that our readers find the finished product as stimulating and enlightening as we found the process of creating it.

A book of this nature is truly a collaborative effort and we have many individuals we wish to thank, more than we can officially acknowledge here. It goes without saying that we are deeply indebted to all of the scholars whose work we have drawn on. We thank them for their inspiration and their insights. We would also like to thank Laura Macleod, Executive Editor at Nelson Education, for her enthusiastic endorsement of the idea of a third edition, and Alison Prentice, Wendy Mitchinson, and Beth Light—members of the writing team for the previous editions—for their permission to proceed, even though they were unable to participate this time. We are grateful as well for the patient assistance of Theresa Fitzgerald, who served as our developmental editor, and for the detailed comments on an earlier draft we received from the reviewers engaged by Nelson Education: Margaret Conrad, University of New Brunswick; Linda Ambrose, Laurentian University; Jacqueline Gresko, Douglas College; and Denyse Baillargeon, Université de Montréal. We would also like to thank Colleen Ste. Marie for her careful copy editing of our manuscript.

Significant support came from other individuals. We are especially indebted to Jennifer Brown, Canada Research Chair in Aboriginal Peoples and Histories at the University of Winnipeg, for generously sharing her time and insights. Other individuals whose advice we sought include Louise Carbert (Dalhousie University), Jean-Philippe Garneau (Université du Québec à Montréal), Lorna Marsden (York University), and Patricia McCormack (University of Alberta). We would also like to acknowledge the important work done by our research assistants: Jacinthe Archambault, Ted Boniface, Stephanie Friel, Valérie Poirier, and Lindsay Van Wyck.

Finally, we would like most warmly to thank our families and friends for their understanding when we were often preoccupied with the preparation of this manuscript. To Bernd Brandt, Pat Rosenbaum, and Larry Bourne, we owe a special debt of gratitude for their unfailing love and support.

Introduction

_____

In the 1970s, as a renewed and newly visible feminism raised questions about the place of women in Canadian society, there was a growing awareness that the fact of gender made women's lives profoundly different from the lives of men. Convinced that women had a history, even if it was barely present in the standard studies, some historians began to take up the challenge of finding women in Canada's past. In the context of the women's movement and of a general broadening of historical inquiry, Canadian women's history blossomed. By the mid-1980s, enough research had been undertaken that a group of us could write a general history of women in Canada: our first edition. In the middle of the 1990s, when we wrote the second edition, new research, perspectives, and questions already demanded a more complex and nuanced account. Now, a decade into the new millennium, we, as practitioners of women's history, are all too aware that generalizations about the experience of women in the past risk missing key differences structured by social class, race, ethnicity, religion, sexuality, and bodily condition. Like all historians, we must also confront epistemological challenges that call into question the very notion of *experience*, along with the possibility of truly knowing the past.

This new edition of *Canadian Women: A History* includes the years since the last edition was completed, that is, the years between 1995 and 2009. In addition, this version attempts throughout to integrate the wealth of new material and interpretations that historians of women have produced since our second edition. We found this a difficult task for a number of reasons. To begin with, it was, of course, impossible to assimilate all the accumulated research on a topic as vast as the history of Canadian women over the course of more than four centuries. Furthermore, the very idea of a comprehensive historical narrative or even, more modestly, of a synthesis such as this one has been profoundly shaken. Although from the start we called our work "a" history of Canadian women, we have had to face the challenges posed by those linguistic and poststructuralist turns of the 1980s and 1990s that interrogated the categories and linear narratives central to Western forms of knowledge. The central concept of *women* itself has been called into question by scholars from several disciplines, including historians. As they have pointed out, it is important to be aware of the fluid and mutable nature of gendered identities as well as the significance of other identities that intersect with gender and sometimes trump it.[1] Finally, the years since the publication of the second edition of this book have been marked by debates over the relative merits of women's history (the study of those identified as women) as compared to gender history (the study of how gender, as a category of analysis, operated historically to construct persons and phenomena as masculine or feminine). In Canada, at least, many historians manage to reconcile the two approaches without too much apparent difficulty; we hope to do the same.[2]

The present volume is thus a considerably updated version of a work first conceived and published in the 1980s. We continue to endorse the validity of women's history and we also attempt throughout to keep in mind the theoretical and methodological challenges posed to historians of women in the intervening years. This edition was written by a slightly different team. To our regret, three of the original authors (Prentice, Mitchinson, Light) did not feel they could participate; the group finally comprised three of the original team (Cuthbert Brandt, Black, Bourne) and one welcome new addition (Fahrni). Though we were no longer in close geographical proximity, we reviewed, discussed, and agreed on all that is to be found here.

Much that we learn from conventional history remains problematic for the history of women. The very language used has often failed to describe women's experience. A particularly basic and yet complex set of problems surrounds the concept of what is considered productive work. For example, the generally accepted census definition of *occupation* omits unpaid work that women have always done, such as housework, child care, care of the elderly and the sick, and community service or social work. Even less recognized has been the reproductive work women do in the family, both in bearing and acculturating children and in providing emotional stability and support. These omissions have stemmed directly from the failure to treat unpaid work with the same respect as work for pay. In addition, much of women's paid work, from taking in sewing or boarders to doing housework or child care for others, has gone unrecorded. We have tried to uncover and discuss the different kinds of unpaid work, and to describe at the same time the intricate connections between them and women's involvement in paid employment in different times and places in Canada.

An additional set of problems emerges with the generally accepted definitions of *culture* and *politics*. By using the term *culture* anthropologically, our aim has been to move beyond high culture to a concept that encompasses ways of thinking and acting, ways of being in the world and seeing the world. We have also attempted to explore the question of whether or not a separate women's culture has existed at different times or among various groupings of women, and how such a culture or cultures might have changed over the years. We have had similar questions about women's politics. Officially excluded from the politics of state during much of Canada's history, Canadian women focused on diverse and sometimes conflicting goals of their own. Political scientists now believe that attempts to influence political systems from the outside are themselves political. Can women therefore be said to have had a politics separate and distinct from that of men?

If accepted definitions of *work, culture,* and *politics* have been problematic, so, too, have been the periods into which Canadian history has traditionally been organized. Is it appropriate, for the purposes of dividing Canadian women's history meaningfully, to follow the usual practice of focusing on major constitutional events such as Confederation? Or would events more directly affecting women's lives, such as the adoption of married women's property laws, make better markers? Neither alternative seems genuinely satisfactory, yet this was an issue that we had to resolve in the writing of this text. Books, after all, have to be divided into sections and chapters, however seamless the fabric of life may be in the real world. Since events of all kinds influence the lives of human beings, we have tried to construct a chronology that takes into account the interaction of the technological, economic, and social, as well as the political, religious, and cultural dimensions of women's experience.

After much discussion, we were able to agree upon turning points particularly relevant to the history of women in Canada. The first is the transition from a pre-industrial to an industrial society in the mid-nineteenth century, marked for us by the establishment in the 1840s of a cotton mill in the eastern townships of Quebec. The first corporate industrial venture in Canada, it was the beginning of an industry that was to employ large numbers of women. For convenience, we use the last year of that industrializing decade, 1850, as our first historical marker. The second turning point we selected is 1918, the end of the First World War. The Great War, that cataclysm for women as well as for men, nevertheless saw the achievement of two major goals that had been fought for by the women's movement in Canada: Prohibition and, at the federal level, women's suffrage. This was the end of an era: the worlds of the pioneer, the gentlewoman, and the Victorian lady receded from sight and gave way to those of the flapper and the so-called working girl. In this third edition of *Canadian Women: A History*, which, as mentioned, covers a longer period of time than previous editions, we have chosen a third turning point: 1960. The creation of Canadian Voice of Women for Peace (VOW) in 1960 can be seen as the beginning of the renewed feminism of the late twentieth century. That same year, the federal government approved the sale of the hormonal birth control pill, eventually making available for women a reliable form of contraception that allowed them greater control over their bodies and sexuality. From that date, we take our account up to the end of 2009, 50 years later.

We need to ask, however, whether even our own new chronological markers were relevant for women who lived on the margins of Canadian society. What did industrialization, the achievement of Prohibition and the vote, or the availability of the Pill mean to women living on Canada's more isolated resource frontiers or on Aboriginal reserves? Such changes may not have had the same meaning and impact for women of colour, for lesbians, or for poor or immigrant women as they did for women who were white, heterosexual, middle-class, and Canadian-born. We have tried to be particularly attentive to the lives of those women most remote from the centres of political or economic power. This effort has not been easy since most of these women did not leave written records. And even those women who did record their lives wrote from inside worlds that were not much like our own; as the British novelist L.P. Hartley famously wrote, "The past is a foreign country: they do things differently there."[3] The voices of women in the past are thus difficult to hear and a challenge to interpret; historians of women have even more reason than other historians to read sources against the grain, putting them to uses other than those for which they were originally intended.

Inevitably, as we learn more about the lives of girls and women in Canada's past, we come to question even the earlier formulations advanced by women's historians. For instance, for over 40 years now, the convention has been to speak of two waves of feminism. In this interpretation, the first wave took place in the late nineteenth and early twentieth centuries. At that time, organized women deployed—sometimes simultaneously—arguments such as the importance of women's maternal role or the necessity of securing rights equal to those enjoyed by men to demand the vote and full civil rights, including married women's entitlement to their own property and earnings. This first wave of feminist activism was followed, after a hiatus, by a second wave, beginning in the 1960s and 1970s. This time, feminist demands ranged from legalizing access to contraception and abortion to criminalizing marital rape to applying pay equity. Most recently, some speak of a third wave of feminism, beginning in the 1990s and articulated especially by young women. These young women reassert women's specificity while insisting that feminism must explicitly recognize a broad spectrum of ethnic, racial, and sexual diversities. Over the course of the past few years, however, some historians of women have suggested that the waves metaphor does not accurately describe the history of Canadian feminism. It is evident that a number of women engaged in feminist politics spanned the so-called waves: we think, for example, of Thérèse Casgrain and Agnes Macphail, who were still active in the post–Second World War years. Nor does the characterization of the successive periods of activism seem accurate. For some time now, researchers have provided evidence of women's collective mobilizations during the interwar and immediate postwar periods. Their activism was concerned with peace and social conditions and was often centred on the family and the household. Long-established women's groups clearly continued to press on with their ambitious goals for reform.

As is the case for all historians, we have had to pay careful attention to our own cultural, political, and personal locations as women writing in Canada in the early twenty-first century. It is therefore incumbent on us to describe our shared perspective, the point of view that has necessarily affected what we have selected as important and how we have interpreted or reinterpreted the past. We all identify ourselves as feminists. There are many definitions and, more important, many versions of feminism. But underlying all is the commitment to increasing women's autonomy and collective power in a world where these have generally been less than men's. A feminist perspective recognizes that women's situations and experiences are distinct from those of men. Nor is the category "women" a homogeneous one. Increasingly, feminist scholars follow the lead of activists and insist upon the importance of differences among women, deriving from their experiences of race, class, ethnicity, religion, bodily condition, and sexual orientation. Finally, a feminist perspective insists that women should not be judged as inferior by male standards or in comparison with men.

That said, we certainly do not deny the value of comparisons. How women have fared, compared to men, must be a central question in women's history—hence the attention given by those working in the field to the question of women's status and to the possible existence of separate spheres for women and men in any given time or place. Whether we were considering Aboriginal hunting-and-gathering communities or Victorian households and non-domestic workplaces, we have had to make judgments about how separate the so-called domestic (or private) and public spheres really were. How did their separation or non-separation affect the degree of authority men and women exercised over their own lives, as well as in their respective communities? Certainly, the nature and meaning of public and private life have shifted in Canada over the years. It seems clear that much of the work of education, as well as a good deal of economic production, at first took place in the home. These activities were only gradually removed from private life as they became part of an emerging public world from which women were, in theory, largely excluded. How and why this occurred and with what results—and how this process was eventually modified—are questions that we try to address in this book.

Also intriguing are the possible demographic or ideological influences on women's authority and their ability to control their work and their lives. For example, have women been more in command of their situations when they were relatively scarce and therefore presumably especially valuable? When fewer numbers of women married, and did so later in their lives? In addition, questions of relative power have to be examined in the context of broader social structures and of prevailing ideologies. How have particular groups of women been devalued or empowered at particular times and places? As feminists focusing on the experiences of women, we also recognize the power of ideas and feelings, of social and political movements, and of identities other than gender in fixing or altering how people react to the economic and demographic conditions they both help to create and encounter.

We take the position that the material conditions of people's lives are the most important among the many factors influencing them. Yet we would not limit such influences to the economic, for we are convinced that women's bodies are an important part of the material bases of their lives. In all cultures, the lives of the childbearing portion of the community will be greatly influenced by the fact of that childbearing and by the ideologies and practices surrounding it. Biology, however, is more variable than we have been led to believe; for instance, biological clocks respond to factors such as climate and food supply so that the age of puberty can vary widely from one place or time to another. When we consider such issues, we return to economic configurations and material culture. An important component of both is technological change. The technology of birth control has had dramatic potential to alter women's lives. But a host of other technologies have been important as well. From the sewing machine to the automatic washing machine to the Internet, how have women initiated or responded to technological transformations, and how have new technologies changed women's daily work?

In Canada, moreover, all questions of analysis and interpretation must be considered in the context of the country's immense size and considerable diversity. Our definitions of both *Canadian* and *women* are ecumenical. We include as women all those who have considered themselves or were seen by others to be women; we include as Canadian all those who lived or are living in the territory that now comprises present-day Canada. And we adopt these working definitions while recognizing that some women—for instance, Aboriginal women, new immigrants, and many *Québécoises*—would not choose the term "Canadian woman" as their primary or even as any way of identifying themselves. Moreover, we must recognize that all significant events in the history of this country affected different groups of women to varying degrees and in different ways. One of the recurrent themes of the women's movement in Canada has been the quest for a single, unified voice—a quest that has been successful only on very rare occasions, if at all. In this, the Canadian women's movement no doubt resembles women's movements elsewhere. Indeed, as well as examining Canadian specificities, a synthesis such as this one might serve as the basis for future explorations of the ways in which the lives of women in Canada—their daily experiences as well as their shared activism—were often similar to those of women in the United States, Great Britain, and France.

Often faced with enormous difficulties, sometimes treated with the most cruel injustice in communities that were for the most part decidedly patriarchal, Canadian women struggled to survive, to contribute to their society, and to make their lives meaningful. We study their lives because women have been integral to Canada's history. Who they were and what they did made all the difference.

Notes

1. Joan Scott, "Gender: A Useful Category of Historical Analysis," in Joan Scott, *Gender and the Politics of History* (New York: Columbia UP, 1988), 28–50; Denise Riley, *"Am I That Name?": Feminism and the Category of "Women" in History* (London: Macmillan, 1988).

2. Kathryn McPherson, Cecilia Morgan, and Nancy M. Forestell, "Introduction: Conceptualizing Canada's Gendered Pasts," in Kathryn McPherson, Cecilia Morgan, and Nancy M. Forestell, eds., *Gendered Pasts: Historical Essays in Femininity and Masculinity in Canada* (Toronto: University of Toronto Press, 2003 [1999]), 2. See also Joy Parr, "Gender History and Historical Practice," *Canadian Historical Review* 76, 3 (September 1995): 354–76. For an early Canadian debate on the merits of women's history versus those of gender history, see the exchange in *Left History*: Joan Sangster, "Beyond Dichotomies: Reassessing Gender History and Women's History in Canada," *Left History* 3, 1 (Spring/Summer 1995): 109–21; Karen Dubinsky and Lynne Marks, "Beyond Purity: A Response to Sangster" and Franca Iacovetta and Linda Kealey, "Women's History, Gender History and Debating Dichotomies," *Left History* 3, 2 and 4, 1 (Fall 1995/Spring 1996): 205–37.

3. L.P. Hartley, *The Go-Between*, ed. Douglas Brooks-Davies (London: Penguin Books, 1997 [1953]), 5.

PART ONE

BEGINNINGS TO THE
MID-NINETEENTH CENTURY

"The Dancing Woman," drawn by Shanawdithit in 1829, the year she died. She was the last recorded surviving member of the Beothuk people of Newfoundland.

Source: From James P. Howley, *The Beothuks or Red Indians: the Aboriginal Inhabitants of Newfoundland* (Cambridge: University Press, 1915) 248. Original drawing in the Newfoundland Museum, St. John's, Newfoundland.

Aataentsic, according to the Hurons, was the great mother who fell from a hole in the sky. It was for the pregnant Aataentsic that the great tortoise ordered other swimming creatures to gather soil from the bottom of the ocean and pile it on his back so that she could land safely. In this way the earth was created. Aataentsic then gave birth to humanity. Ojibwa elders tell of Spirit Woman, mother of all the birds, animals, and fish of the world, while the Blackfoot and Wet'suwet'en speak of Old Woman. A modern rendering of Nuu'chah'nulth legend tells us of Copper Woman, the awe-inspiring figure who created the first man from her own mucus. With her humour as well as her strength, Copper Woman inspired her daughters to heroic feats of survival in an environment that was often hostile and always challenging.

Our knowledge of powerful mythic figures like Aataentsic, Spirit Woman, Old Woman, and Copper Woman is inspiring but vague. What about our knowledge of Canada's founding women, the women of early Aboriginal and colonial cultures? Certainly, even in the remote worlds of Canada's indigenous peoples, tracings of women's lives can be discovered, and archeologists, anthropologists, and historians continue to piece scraps of evidence together into larger studies that are of absorbing interest and that inspire considerable debate. Agreement on the character or meaning of women's lives in pre-industrial societies remains elusive for a number of reasons. To begin with, it is an immensely long time from the earliest records of Canada's past to the transitional years of the mid-nineteenth century. In addition, we are also considering a great many different peoples under the heading of "founding cultures." And, as with all history, new ideas and interpretations continue to challenge older ones.

Consider the Aboriginal cultures that Europeans encountered when they first came to the northern parts of North America. In the fifteenth and sixteenth centuries, the rich fisheries of the east and west coasts supported a great number of indigenous societies, some of them very populous, while in the region that was to become Ontario, agriculture sustained as many as 30 000 people. Anthropologists estimate that the Aboriginal population of the area that now constitutes Canada numbered about 350 000 at that time. These figures are striking when we realize that the people of New France probably numbered no more than 70 000 by the middle of the eighteenth century. Moreover, at the time of contact with Europeans, the indigenous peoples of what was to become Canada belonged to 12 separate language families and spoke a much larger number of languages.

Students of the early Aboriginal peoples have also identified several different major regional economies. The hunting-and-gathering cultures in the north and east differed not only from each other and from the partly agricultural economies of the St. Lawrence River valley, but also from the buffalo-centred cultures on the plains. And these stood in considerable contrast again to the salmon- and whale-based economies of the Pacific west coast, and to the Inuit culture of the Arctic regions based on the hunting of sea mammals, polar bears, and caribou. Perhaps the one major factor that Aboriginal economies had in common was their dependence on the ecosystem in which they were located, and the intricate and reciprocal relationships they established with their various natural environments.

We know that Europeans reached the shores of North America as early as the eleventh century, and Norse legends, as well as the presence of tools for spinning and sewing in a Viking archeological site in Newfoundland, inform us that women were among these early visitors. Gudrid and Freydis, according to the eleventh-century Vinland sagas, actually gave birth to children in the "New World." It was not until the sixteenth century, however, that European incursions into Aboriginal territory began in earnest. The first arrivals were chiefly fishermen and traders who did not linger. Nevertheless, there is considerable evidence that by the late 1500s the development of trade on the east coast was altering Aboriginal economies. Gradually, as European goods were introduced, Aboriginal women had to adapt to new forms of change. Some of the clothing and utensils they had once manufactured, for example, could now be purchased with furs. Settled communities were forced to move as the trade animals became depleted in any given region. In addition, the spread of European diseases, such as measles and smallpox, decimated many Aboriginal populations.

Another result of the newcomers' arrival was the development of the Europeanized versions of Aboriginal names. We use them in some chapters of our book since this is how Aboriginal groups were identified in historical documents, and referred to by most Canadians, during the time periods covered by those chapters. In later chapters, we use the more authentic names now preferred by Aboriginal groups, and we provide a list of correspondences between the two naming practices on p. 618.

French-speaking European women first began to arrive in North America in the seventeenth century. Like the Aboriginal women they encountered, they were an amazingly diverse group. The France from which they sailed was ruled by a monarchy intent on extending its administrative control over a fragmented and fractious realm. From his palace at Versailles, Louis XIV (the Sun King) and his advisers sought to enhance the glory of France by laying claim to much of the North American continent. But mercantilist dreams of prosperous colonies shipping valuable resources to the mother country and importing its manufactured goods could be realized only if this vast territory were populated by French colonists. Steeped in the religious zeal of the Counter Reformation, which sought to revitalize the Roman Catholic Church through a renewed spirituality and increased discipline, the court at Versailles also viewed colonization as a means of spreading the Catholic faith.

Populating the French colonies was a slow and difficult process. Very soon, the inhabitants of New France were embattled on nearly all sides, first by the Iroquois and then by the British, who were locked in a deadly struggle with the French for empire. Of the French colonies that developed in the northern half of the continent, Acadia had the longest history of French presence, enjoyed the best relations between the French and local Aboriginal peoples, but suffered the most from the consequences of the Franco-British conflict. Despite prolonged war with the Iroquois throughout much of the seventeenth century, it was the colony called Canada, situated on the banks of the St. Lawrence River, that became the economic and administrative centre of New France. A third major population centre developed in the eighteenth century around the fortress of Louisbourg, located on present-day Cape Breton Island.

In all three colonies, the arrival of French women signalled an official intention to create permanent European settlements. The women and men who came to New France brought with them the varying ideals, ambitions, and anxieties of their metropolitan patrons. French merchants sought to transform fish and fur into handsome profits, colonial administrators struggled to reproduce the political and social structures of Bourbon

France in the wilderness, and nuns and priests devoted their lives to imposing a particularly austere and mystical brand of French Catholicism on Aboriginals and colonists alike. The first groups of permanent settlers in Canada also included soldiers and the *filles du roi*, mostly young, marriageable women sponsored by the French state to populate the struggling colony. The resulting cultures reflected all of these forces as well as the diverse origins and circumstances of the settlers. The Acadians, for example, were so varied in their backgrounds that they not only spoke different dialects but also in the Old World had lived in communities ruled by differing laws, customs, and religious traditions. The more numerous *Canadiens* hailed from Paris and the surrounding Île de France, as well as from coastal ports. In both colonies, there was initially considerable intermarriage between the French and the Aboriginal populations. In addition, Canada's first blacks were brought as slaves to Acadia, the St. Lawrence River valley, and Louisbourg in the latter part of the seventeenth century. Finally, the settlers' experiences varied, depending on their social rank and where they lived. Life among the upper classes in Quebec was marked by relative comfort and sophistication, features largely absent from the lives of the *habitants* struggling to carve farms from the forest.

A variety of populations and a continuing intermingling of peoples characterized the great migrations of the eighteenth and early nineteenth centuries. Women immigrated to British-controlled areas as soldiers' and fishermen's wives and daughters, and also as farmers and businesswomen. They arrived from the British Isles and the American colonies both before and especially after the British Conquest of New France. Women also came as Loyalists and as so-called late Loyalist migrants of European, African, and Aboriginal origin, gravitating to British North America during and after the American Revolution. These migrants were uniform neither in their languages, which included Gaelic and German as well as the dominant English, nor in their customs or possessions.

Fixing borders for these founding peoples is as complex a process as attempting to delineate their cultures. Boundaries between indigenous groups were often fluid to begin with, and major shifts occurred in their territories as they relocated in response to the demands of the fur trade, the vagaries of war, the devastations of disease or famine, or their own changing economic or political requirements and agendas. To further complicate the picture, the borders established by both the French and their British successors were short-lived. Acadia endured as part of New France only until 1713; the Acadians themselves were finally uprooted in the Great Deportation or Expulsion of 1755–1762, when their British rulers scattered men, women, and children along the coasts of North America and Europe. Despite continuous warfare, New France survived in the St. Lawrence River valley until the British Conquest was completed in 1760; Canada was finally ceded to the British Crown by the Treaty of Paris in 1763. Yet British rule did not end the strife. The American Revolution (1776–1783), the cataclysm that set so many Loyalists on the road north, broke the peace, as did, to a much smaller extent, the eighteenth-century fur trade wars. It was not until the War of 1812 was over and the nineteenth century was well into its second decade that the six colonies then comprising British North America—Newfoundland, Nova Scotia, New Brunswick, Prince Edward Island, and Lower and Upper Canada—began to assume relatively stable boundaries. Even then, Upper and Lower Canada had still to endure the traumatic events of the

Rebellions of 1837–1838. Indeed, throughout most of its history British North America, like New France before it, was regularly on military alert.

Canada's early women, therefore, lived amid extraordinary conflict and change. War and the effects of war were important factors in their lives. Of equal significance was the mercantile nature of their societies. The Aboriginal peoples drew the Europeans into their world while, at the same time, they were gradually drawn into the staple economies that the European intruders generated. The quest for furs would eventually become the driving force of many Aboriginal women's lives; in fact, without their labour, the fur trade would not have flourished as it did. European women were also crucial to the inshore fishery and to the economies that subsequently developed around the production of lumber and wheat. In addition, both Aboriginal and European women were active in subsistence hunting and gathering, in farming, in craft production, and in local commerce. Most of the economies in which they participated were family-based: women and men alike laboured for the subsistence or improvement of the family or of larger family groupings, such as clans. Generally, labour in colonial society was quite sharply divided along the lines of gender, although women frequently took on men's work, particularly when the adult males in their families were absent.

The problems historians face in analyzing women's roles in pre-industrial economies are multiple. An outstanding one is trying to determine the implications of the sexual division of labour for the status of women in such societies. How rigid was that division? Did women's designated work give them power, or did it tend to exclude them from authority? How, indeed, do we define *power* and *choice* in these economies, particularly in Aboriginal societies? Did women's work help to support a separate, gender-based culture that was different from that of men? If so, how did this cultural identity manifest itself among women?

Equally problematic are the concepts of change and difference and how they can be documented. What, in fact, was the impact of contact with Europeans on the experiences, roles, and status of the Aboriginal women who inhabited the regions that were to become Canada? How, in turn, did the "New World" affect the lives of European women immigrants to New France and British North America? And what of the many women of mixed descent, who often became the women "in between" two cultures? In addition, even within these larger groupings, there are often significant variations of region, race, religion, ethnicity, and class, and of urban and rural settings, that must be considered in any assessment of how women lived in this pre-industrial period of Canada's history.

If the contemporary sources for making these assessments are often mere scraps, it is true that the scraps are sometimes marvellous. Jesuit missionaries writing back to France, fur traders keeping track of what was going on in their trading territories for company officials or for friends at home, male travellers of different nationalities writing for a variety of publics—all often had fascinating things to say about women in the "New World." For the lives of Aboriginal women particularly, historians have to rely almost entirely on the evidence of these men, and such evidence must be treated with great caution, filtered as it was through individuals who shared neither the race nor the sex of the people they were describing.

Recently there has been a flourishing of interdisciplinary scholarship about Aboriginal women produced by Aboriginal as well as non-Aboriginal researchers. This research, undertaken by historians, anthropologists, historical geographers, and Native Studies specialists, provides the basis for more detailed and nuanced analyses of the historical experience of Aboriginal women. A particularly fruitful area has been the examination of women's relationship to colonization and of Aboriginal women's agency, as well as their challenges, in the contact zones where they encountered European colonialism. This research has also provided valuable insights into how British imperialism was fashioned and re-fashioned on the basis of race and gender. Most of this literature, however, focuses on the period after 1850, when sources such as government and missionary reports, women travellers' diaries, photographic records, and artifacts created by Aboriginal women become much more plentiful. For earlier years, including the pre-contact period, we are still left with many gaps in our knowledge. The temptation to use modern anthropological findings and extrapolate to firm conclusions about the women of our more remote past is to be avoided. On the other hand, the studies by contemporary anthropologists are valuable guides to the historian trying to understand the beliefs or social configurations that might have influenced women in earlier times. Often it is only with the most imaginative use of fragmentary sources that we are able to construct a picture of those worlds that perhaps we have not quite lost. Increasingly, some analysts are successfully turning to the oral tradition of Aboriginal societies to obtain a deeper understanding of those societies' own view of their history and to take into account different perspectives on the roles and status of Aboriginal women.

For European women, the sources are more plentiful, but are still scattered and problematic. Convent women writing the annals of their convents are wonderful sources for New France, but their focus is largely, although certainly not exclusively, on the lives of their communities. Notarial records and censuses generated during the French regime have proven rich sources for historians of women, as have some groups of family business records. By the eighteenth century, the diaries and letters of laywomen begin to supplement these sources, along with accounts by travellers. But if by the nineteenth century such records prove exceptionally rich for British North America, by that time there is much less quantitative material. The superb parish, census, and notarial records of New France were to some extent carried on in Quebec and Lower Canada under British rule, but are not to be found in great profusion elsewhere for the post-Conquest years. The New Brunswick, Nova Scotia, and Upper and Lower Canada censuses of 1851, however, provide a wealth of information for the end of the period covered by Part One. And scattered other local surveys, coupled with what may be gleaned from individual, family, and parish records, as well as from the court records and newspapers that are increasingly being examined by historians help us reconstruct the lives of women, especially in the first half of the nineteenth century.

CHAPTER ONE

The First Women

Thanadelthur, an eighteenth-century Chipewyan woman, was both a survivor and a peacemaker. She was also one of the few Aboriginal women of the European contact era whose individual lives we can document through written and oral sources.[1] She and a female companion were captured in 1713 by Crees, long-standing enemies of the Chipewyan. Both managed to escape from their captors, but neither could complete the long journey back to their own peoples. Narrowly avoiding the death by starvation that was the fate of her friend, Thanadelthur succeeded in making contact with Hudson's Bay Company (HBC) traders at York Fort. The Fort's governor, James Knight, recognizing the young woman's value as a potential link between the traders and her fur-wealthy people, quickly purchased her from her Cree captors. The eventual result was a peace mission between the Cree and Chipewyan, ostensibly led by a Company man. However, as recorded in Knight's journal, its success owed much to the work of Thanadelthur herself. When the mission seemed doomed to failure owing to mounting hostility and fear on both sides, Knight's narrative tells us, it was Thanadelthur whose courage and determination carried the day. By turns, she persuaded both sides to continue the talks and harangued them until they were finally "forced . . . to ye peace." The HBC trader who accompanied Thanadelthur admired her spirit. It was "Divellish," he reported. If but 50 of her people had the same "Carriage and Resolution," no other "Indian tribe" would stand a chance in Chipewyan country.

In the few years that Thanadelthur survived after her arrival at York Fort, she became so valuable to James Knight as an interpreter and envoy that he despaired when, in the bad winter of 1717, she became ill and he was unable to nurse her back to health. "She was one of a Very high Spirit and of the Firmest Resolution that ever I see any Body in my Days," Knight wrote in his log, calling her a person "of very great Courage & forecast." Since we learn this version of Thanadelthur's history not from her or from her own people but, in this account, from the pen of an outsider, the words are not easy to interpret.[2] Did James Knight really see her as the powerful figure his final description implied: a woman of courage and resolution whose role was so important to his mission that he hardly knew how he would replace her? And what relationship is there between Knight's words and the reality of Thanadelthur's life? We cannot answer any of these questions definitively, but Chipewyan oral traditions enrich our understanding of Thandelthur's story. In those narratives Thanadelthur is known as a "stolen woman" much prized for her beauty and intelligence and captured by Crees. The oral tellings corroborate Knight's account of her escape from her Cree captors and the subsequent successful peace mission. They suggest, however, that her primary motivation for undertaking the mission was not so much to benefit the traders as to assist her own people. This goal she accomplished by helping, at least for a time, to put an end to the conflicts between the Chipewyans and the Crees and opening up trade opportunities between her people and the Hudson's Bay Company traders.[3] But in the end, even this version does not necessarily represent Thanadelthur's own perspective on her story.

We can only speculate about what the events of Thanadelthur's life meant to her. Did she understand her situation as an envoy among three peoples jockeying for position in a world that may once have been the exclusive territory of her own people? Or was she simply trying to return to her family? Although such questions are ultimately impossible to answer, Thanadelthur's story is instructive. First, it suggests something of the power that at least some indigenous women appear to have had when the host peoples of North America first encountered European intruders on their territory. At the same time, it suggests the fragility of that power, especially in periods of conflict and upheaval. Aboriginal women, who may have had considerable authority in their own communities as traders or as interpreters between peoples, were nevertheless vulnerable when men were on the warpath. Second, Thanadelthur was on the move. Seasonal movement was normal for hunting-and-gathering groups, while European contact and the fur trade brought new dimensions and additional travelling. Women acting as traders and negotiators, women travelling with their trader husbands, women captives escaping and seeking refuge—many women might have had tales to tell like Thanadelthur's.

Other Aboriginal women would see similar extraordinary changes occurring in their lifetimes. The Beothuk of Newfoundland numbered around 2 000 when they first encountered European explorers in 1500. By the early nineteenth century they were virtually extinct, the result of disease and violent contact with Europeans and other Aboriginal groups. In fact, in 1829 the last known Beothuk died, a woman called Shanawdithit. The large palisaded Iroquoian villages that Cartier had seen in his explorations of the St. Lawrence River valley in the 1540s were abandoned, most likely because their inhabitants had been decimated due to epidemic diseases, by the time Champlain came to this region seven decades later. And it was not many years after the beginnings of French settlement in Canada that those Huron who had once been so numerous north of Lake Ontario were almost entirely destroyed by disease and war. From an early-seventeenth-century population that might have reached 30 000, the Huron were reduced by the 1650s to refugees who were scattered in several directions, including Quebec, while some Huron women and children were adopted into Iroquoian communities.[4] Yet despite the disruption of their societies, there were survivors—and adapters—and they appear in the records.

The questions that we are bound to ask about Aboriginal women are important, but hard to answer. What were women's lives like before the coming of the Europeans? And how did women react to the changes European trade and settlement brought? The groups whose cultures have been studied with such questions in mind include the Micmac of Nova Scotia; the Montagnais and Naskapi of Labrador and Quebec among the eastern Algonquian linguistic groups; and the Huron and the Iroquois of the Great Lakes region. Much of our information for these groups dates from the seventeenth century, although some is more recent. For the eighteenth and nineteenth centuries, we can also draw on studies looking at women and gender roles among the Chipewyan (of the Athapaskan language family), the Cree, who were also Algonquian, the Carrier of the northwest, and the peoples belonging to the Eyak-Athapaskan, Salish, and Haida language groups of the west coast.[5] (See Figure 1.1 for a map of Aboriginal groups in and near Canada at the time of contact.) Useful as well for all periods are various studies that are not focused on women or on gender roles specifically but that do nevertheless allude to them in passing. From the work that has been done to date, it is possible to examine women's roles in the economic lives of their communities and, in some cases, to also catch glimpses of their status and spiritual power in both the pre-contact and early contact periods.

Figure 1.1   MAP: ABORIGINAL GROUPS IN AND NEAR CANADA AT TIME OF CONTACT

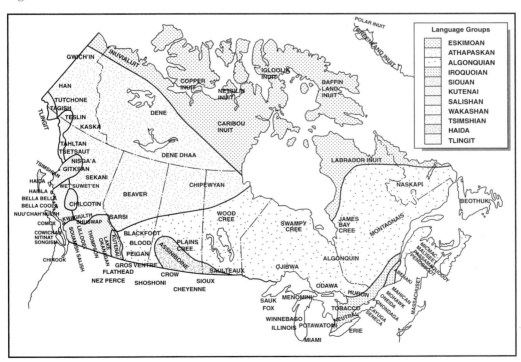

Sources: Alan D. Macmillan, *Native Peoples and Cultures of Canada* (Vancouver: Douglas & McIntyre, 1988); John Price, *Indians of Canada: Cultural Dynamics* (Scarborough, Ont.: Prentice-Hall, 1979).

ABORIGINAL WOMEN'S WORK

Most historians and anthropologists agree that all North American Aboriginal communities organized their work along age and gender lines. They disagree, however, about the significance of gendered work roles and the extent to which important economic contributions can be translated into social authority.[6] In general, women in Aboriginal communities did work that was compatible with the task of looking after small children. This work did not require "rapt attention," as hunting did; it could be easily interrupted and resumed. It did not place children in danger, and it did not require mothers and children to go very far from home. This situation applied even when "home" was a movable encampment. Women generally remained close to the camp; men moved farther afield on land or sea to hunt animal food that could not be obtained in any other way.[7]

Within such limits, Aboriginal women's work in northern North America varied according to the resources of the region and the group. In the opinion of many early European observers, Aboriginal women led incredibly hard lives in their marginal subsistence economies. They particularly pitied women in those groups that were dependent on hunting and gathering in the northern forests and tundra or who lived in the plateau between the Rocky Mountains and the west coast and subsisted chiefly on salmon and roots. By contrast, some observers found Aboriginal women in agricultural economies or coastal fishing economies living amid relative ease and plenty.

Europeans were struck by the fact that women did most of the planting and harvesting in agricultural communities; but it was the opinion of at least one eighteenth-century British American woman that this work was relaxed and convivial. A white woman who had been taken captive by the Seneca and adopted into the tribe, Mary Jemison seems to have found much to approve of in the lives of Iroquois women.[8] Agricultural work was not only the responsibility of these women but was also under their control. Iroquois and Huron men cleared the land, but the maize (corn), beans, and squash were grown, stored, and distributed entirely by teams of women organized by leaders chosen by the women themselves. Among the Iroquois, the meat brought home from the hunt went to the wife's household to be distributed by her according to Iroquois rules of hospitality, which dictated that all members of the community as well as all visitors should be fed. The wealth of the community consisted chiefly of its cleared land but also included the food stored and controlled by the women.[9]

The relative ease with which women's agricultural work was performed depended on a variety of factors, including the climate and the quality of the land, but according to Mary Jemison the labour of Iroquois women was rarely "severe." Even though they had "all the fuel and bread to procure, and the cooking to perform," she noted, their work was "probably not harder" than that of those white women who had these articles provided for them. More importantly, "their cares" were neither so numerous nor so great as those of white women: "In the summer season, we planted, tended and harvested the corn, and generally had all our children with us; but had no master to oversee or drive us, so that we could work as leisurely as we pleased."[10]

Working in the Fields, Jesuit Missionary Claude Chauchetière's (1645–1709) drawing of a springtime scene in the vicinity of Kahnawake. The woman in the foreground uses an Aboriginal hoe to heap up earth into hillocks where corn will be planted, and a woman or girl nearby is climbing a tree to gather birds' eggs.

Source: © Archives départementales de la Gironde, H 48

Jemison's observations cover only the time in which she lived among the Seneca at the turn of the eighteenth century and the particular region in Pennsylvania where they lived. Moreover, captivity narratives, presenting the experiences of European women carried off by Aboriginals, were sufficiently numerous in Jemison's time to constitute a literary genre and so must be treated cautiously as historical evidence.[11] But other evidence suggests similar working patterns among the agricultural peoples of the lower Great Lakes region generally. Earlier Iroquois and Huron women were also in charge of their communities' farming; Iroquoian people of the Great Lakes and St. Lawrence valley had been growing squash, sunflowers, maize, and beans for at least 1 000 years before the arrival of Europeans. Indeed, it is the cultivation of the protein-rich maize and beans that is believed to account for the large Iroquoian populations that the first Europeans encountered.

The Montagnais and Naskapi were among the non-agricultural, hunting-and-gathering peoples encountered by the French in the St. Lawrence River valley. Their communities varied in size depending on the season. In summer, many families gathered at larger lakes and waterways for fishing and social activities. In wintertime they broke up into hunting bands of one or two families that went into the bush in search of game. As was the case among the Huron and Iroquois, Montagnais and Naskapi women's work was different from the men's; the Jesuit observers of New France noted that each sex knew the role of the other and that they did not "meddle" with each other's work. Women did, however, participate in fishing and in trapping of small animals, such as rabbits. They were certainly involved in transporting larger animals, preparing hides, and manufacturing clothing from them. But their main economic role was as gatherers of shellfish and other foods; they generally supplied more than half of their people's diet through this work. Montagnais and Naskapi women, like the women of the agricultural Huron and Iroquois, were also in charge of the distribution of the food they gathered as well as of the products of the hunt and fishery.[12]

Some European male observers, however, thought that Chipewyan and Cree women of the northwest had very hard lives. Hudson's Bay Company trader Andrew Graham, who wrote about the Swampy Cree in the late eighteenth century, found that in these groups, "all drudgery and domestic duty is performed by the women. They pitch and unpitch the tent, cut fire-wood, dress the victuals. . . . The women also catch fish, hares, fetch all the water used in the tent, knit the snow-shoes, and make the clothes." Graham observed that the women waited on the men when the latter returned from the hunt, and that they worked as hard as ever when pregnant.[13] Alexander Mackenzie, writing in 1802, had similar things to say about Cree women. He found that they were "in the same subordinate state with those of all other savage tribes" and that they worked extremely hard: "They are . . . subject to every kind of domestic drudgery . . . so that when the duties of maternal care are added, it will appear that the life of these women is an uninterrupted succession of toil and pain. This, indeed, is the sense they entertain of their own situation."[14]

Such statements should be weighed against the observers' background and gender. Although European men were astounded at the heavy work performed by Aboriginal women, the relatively few European women who wrote about Aboriginal peoples seemed to say far less about this subject. Marie de l'Incarnation of the Ursulines, for example, wrote a great deal about the people she encountered in New France, but she said nothing about extraordinary labour performed by Aboriginal women. Were Graham and Mackenzie comparing the Aboriginal women they observed to European women servants or agricultural labourers, or, more likely, to women of their own relatively privileged class? Or were they comparing the lives of migratory Aboriginals, both male and female, with the more settled lives of most Europeans? In some cases, they were comparing women's work to that of Aboriginal men—who, if they refused to participate in the fur trade in any consistent way, appeared lazy to Europeans, whose major focus was on the trade.[15]

Aboriginal men probably viewed women's labour in a different light entirely. Samuel Hearne quoted a Chipewyan chief, Matonabbee: "Women were made for labour," the chief had apparently told him; "one of them can carry, or haul, as much as two men can do." Their work was so important, in fact, that there was "no such thing as travelling any considerable distance, or for any length of time, in this country, without their assistance."[16]

Certainly, the Aboriginal women of northern North America worked very hard. Plains women not only participated in communal hunts, they collected food essential to communal welfare if the buffalo hunt failed; they also dried, pounded, and mixed berries with fat and buffalo or other meat to make pemmican. They prepared hides and stitched them into carrying bags and tipis. The labour of dressing a single buffalo hide took a minimum of three days if a woman had no other preoccupations; a tipi made from buffalo skins could require up to 20 hides.[17]

Nearly everywhere, Aboriginal women made the moccasins and the leather or woven clothes their people wore, netted the snowshoes that were indispensable to winter travel, and gathered gum and prepared birchbark, spruce, or cedar fibres to make canoes. In many migrant communities, women were the carriers; in nearly all, they pitched the tents and broke camp when travelling. In coastal, riverside, and lakeside communities, women prepared and cured fish and gathered shellfish, as well as berries and the plant materials that they dried and made into baskets, fishnets, and various articles of clothing. Similarly, Inuit women were involved in many tasks connected with hunting for caribou, seals, whales, and other mammals—and with preparing food and domestic items, including clothing, from them. If contemporary evidence reflects older traditions, the women were also occasionally involved in the hunt itself.[18] The work of Aboriginal women, in other words, was essential.

The tasks women performed depended on the characteristics of their environments. The annual Micmac cycle took the people from the seal fishery on the coast in January to hunting beaver, otter, moose, bears, and caribou inland in February and March; spring sent them to the river mouths to fish and hunt waterfowl and eggs, while in summer they gathered berries and nuts. In the fall, the people withdrew from the shoreline to catch spawning eels in the rivers and, once again, to hunt the larger animals. The sexual division of labour among the Micmac, as described by an observer in 1612, seems to have meant that the women performed nearly every task within this seasonal cycle while the men focused exclusively on hunting and warfare:[19]

> The [women] besides the onerous role of bearing and rearing the children, also transport the game from the place where it has fallen; they are the hewers of wood and drawers of water; they make and repair the household utensils; they prepare the food; they skin the game and prepare the hides . . . sew garments . . . catch fish and gather shellfish for food; often they even hunt; they make the canoes . . . set up tents.[20]

Among the Micmac, preparing those hides and sewing those garments amounted to more than simple tanning and stitchery, for they developed five different techniques of working with dyed porcupine quills.[21]

Among women everywhere, birthing (as well as the care of young children) was women's work. Travellers and especially traders with the inland communities commented on the ease with which mothers gave birth to their children. On the western shore of Hudson Bay, Andrew Graham noted how few of the symptoms that "afflict the delicate European" were experienced in either pregnancy or childbirth by Aboriginal women, "their pains being very light and soon over." Graham went on to give further details about motherhood among the Cree. Women giving birth while travelling, he claimed, simply dropped behind, brought forth "the little stranger . . . and carrying it on their backs, proceed[ed] to overtake their companions as if nothing had happened." He noted that children were "solely under the direction of the mother . . . being always esteemed the maternal property."[22]

Europeans greatly admired the wooden cradles in which infants were often tied and strapped to their mother's back. Packed in moss and soft deer hides, babies seemed conveniently cared for in these cradles, which were sometimes decorated with beautiful designs. Mothers nursed infants for at least two or three years, and this practice contributed to a relatively low birth rate. Women living in their own communities rarely seem to have had more than three or four children, which must have increased both their mobility and their productivity.[23]

Micmac Woman and Child. Elizabeth Ladds (1837–1922) painted this watercolour of a Micmac woman and child in dress typical of the period.

Source: Mi'kmaq Woman and Child, watercolour by Elizabeth Ladds, c. 1865. History Collection, Nova Scotia Museum, (N-4430), NSM 24.4.4. Courtesy of the Nova Scotia Museum – Ethnology Collection

THE QUESTION OF WOMEN'S AUTHORITY

Looking at the cultural and social roles of Aboriginal women through the eyes of such European recorders is a complex exercise that often tells us as much about the observers as about the observed. European observers' interest in and admiration for Aboriginal women's control of their children and the apparent ease with which the women bore and cared for children is a clue, perhaps, to a certain unease. What women controlled, men did not; this situation gave European male observers pause. In addition, white women of their own acquaintance were cast in a somewhat unfavourable light, as comparatively delicate or incompetent.

There is evidence, both from contemporary anthropology and the historical record, that gathering-and-hunting economies—such as those of the Micmac, Montagnais, and Naskapi—as well as agricultural economies—such as those of the Iroquois and Huron—were relatively egalitarian communities in which women enjoyed considerable power in several crucial areas: relative autonomy in sexual life and marriage; significant participation in the religious or ceremonial lives of their people; and some degree of influence in group decision-making.[24] There was no rigid distinction in these societies between the private or domestic sphere and public life. To the extent that decision-making and religious ceremonies were part of the larger communal world, they were in some sense distinct from the immediate concerns of the family. Yet women were often involved in both, despite their largely separate and distinct economic roles.

All Aboriginal societies appear to have ritually secluded young women at the time of their first menstruation, and to have regarded menstruating women as powerful or even dangerous (as, indeed, did some seventeenth-century Europeans).[25] Marriage customs varied, depending on the community; gradually, they changed as a result of contact, although it is not always clear how and when. Women among the Montagnais, Naskapi, Iroquois, and Huron were evidently as free as men were in their choice of a spouse, although among the latter two, mothers often arranged marriages. There was considerable sexual freedom among adolescents, and both young women and young men might initiate sexual encounters outside restricted categories of kin, such as members of their own clan. Nor did the Iroquois and Huron or the Montagnais and Naskapi believe that marriage entailed a lifetime commitment. Persons of either sex had a right to be satisfied with their unions; divorce was apparently easy. This circumstance was particularly so because women had control over their children and, in the case of the Iroquois and Huron, exercised control over domestic space. Polygamy, practised among the Montagnais and Naskapi (as among many west coast groups), especially when females outnumbered males, provided husbands for women who might otherwise not have had them. However, this practice diminished under missionary pressure. Iroquois, Huron, Montagnais, and Naskapi welcomed children, male and female, with great delight, and female children were considered a boon.

Prior to and in the early days of contact, a young Montagnais or Naskapi man often joined the household and hunting band of his wife, at least temporarily, thus supporting the wife's family in a subsistence economy in which skilled hunters were valuable and added to a family's strength. The unpredictability and difficulty of Montagnais and Naskapi existence appear to have favoured a subtle and inclusive approach to decision-making, taking the needs and wishes of all group members into consideration before a consensus was reached. In fact, women's role in such decision-making equalled men's, according to seventeenth-century observers. Indeed, Jesuits who came into contact with these groups reported that Montagnais and Naskapi women enjoyed "great power" in their communities. "A man may promise you something," one recounted, "and if he does not keep his promise, he thinks he is sufficiently excused when he tells you his wife did not wish to do it." The Jesuit recorders of Montagnais and Naskapi life did not approve, and said as much.[26]

The Iroquois and the Huron were matrilocal: that is, husbands generally resided with the households of their wives. In addition, they were matrilineal: to the extent that where there was either property or a chieftainship to inherit, inheritance was through the female line. Reports about the detailed role of women in Huron or Iroquois government are inconsistent. It does seem true, however, that at tribal councils, only male speakers were usually heard. But it is clear that leading Iroquois women also exercised considerable power in selecting chiefs by bequeathing the names of deceased chiefs related to them. Because women could demand to be given captives to replace male relations who had died, they also sometimes exercised the power of life or death over prisoners. Since familial relations were central to Aboriginal societies, the control that women exercised in the running of the longhouses is also particularly significant. The Iroquois respected the "matrons" or clan mothers who ran the houses they lived in, and this power was reflected in their higher councils. There is also evidence that Iroquois women, in isolated instances, engaged in warfare along with the men. The increase in European settlements and rivalries, which forced Iroquois men to travel farther and farther afield in the interest of the hunt, trade, and diplomacy, placed even greater power in the hands of women. Specifically, the changing conditions of colonialism may have led some Aboriginal women to take on new or expanded roles. During the smallpox epidemic of 1640, for example, a Huron woman defied tradition and spoke out at an important tribal assembly in order to denounce the Jesuits for spreading disease among the people.[27]

Women's authority was also reflected in the ceremonial and spiritual lives of indigenous peoples. Among the Montagnais and Naskapi and the Inuit, not just men but also women, especially those who were postmenopausal, could be shamans or people with special religious powers. In Igloolik in recent times, the people told of a female shaman called Itijjuak, who could not sew, cook, or have children but who was loved and cared for by her two husbands and others, who brought food, clothing, and children to her. She was a powerful healer in her community.[28] Among the Iroquois, women had a significant role in the management of communal religious ceremonies and festivals and, certainly, control over their own female ceremonial life. Women's dreams and foretellings were considered as important as men's and gave women influence. This situation was also true for the Ojibwa. Eighteenth-century Ojibwa women were observed conducting a six- or seven-day ceremony designed to assist their men who were away at war, a ceremony that ended when the women divined (correctly, it later turned out) that the warriors had won their battle.[29] In a later period, Blackfoot women were recorded as having similar powers of mediation between the natural and spiritual worlds. Senior medicine women were central figures in the vital communal ritual of the sun dance. In this role, they embodied Elk-Woman and Woman-Who-Married-Morning-Star, the mythical heroines who brought ceremonial dress, the sacred digging stick, and the prairie turnip to the Blackfoot people.[30]

The Roman Catholic priests who first conducted missions among Canada's Aboriginal peoples were appalled by such female power, steeped as the missionaries were in a patriarchal tradition. The early priests carried on intense campaigns to change the relations between the sexes, which they clearly felt were disruptive of all "natural" authority. The Jesuits complained about the lack of male control over women and, in the case of the Montagnais and Naskapi, connected it with their casual attitudes toward authority. The priests preached that wives should obey their husbands, that sexually exclusive monogamy should prevail, and that there should be no divorce. For one thing, they argued, women's sexual permissiveness confused the laws of lineage and inheritance. How could a man know which of his wife's children were his own? At least one Jesuit critic was rebuked for expressing this doubt about Montagnais and Naskapi mores. "Thou hast no sense," was the Aboriginal man's response. "You French people love only your own children; but we love all the children of our tribe."[31]

The zeal of seventeenth-century French missionaries to alter gender relations among the Aboriginals they were attempting to convert was provoked also by the number of informal unions that were occurring between French traders and Aboriginal women. From the Jesuit perspective, it was important that these marriages be "regularized" and that the children be raised according to French and Catholic cultural traditions. Indeed, the government of New France offered financial incentives for Aboriginal girls to be taught French housekeeping skills in order to facilitate such marriages, in the hope that the resulting couples would abandon the forest and settle down to populate the country.[32] The Jesuits made similar efforts to change male/female relations among the Huron. In both cases, the aim was essentially the same: male control of women's sexuality. The alteration of gender relations in these communities was considered essential if the Aboriginal people were to be brought under the control of both the Roman Catholic church and the French state. Hierarchical government could work only when hierarchy permeated the entire culture.[33] The French were also disconcerted by matrilineal societies, in which fathers and husbands had less authority over a woman's children than maternal uncles had.

In broad outline, Cree and Chipewyan ways of life were very similar to those of the Montagnais and Naskapi. All were gatherers and hunters, and what we know of Thanadelthur suggests that some Chipewyan women might have considerable autonomy and power. But there is also evidence of greater parental control over marriage among northwestern groups, as marriageable young women could lose sexual autonomy to become pawns in trading alliances or intertribal rivalries. Among the Chipewyan, for example, women sometimes had no choice at all when it came to a husband; fur traders told stories of seeing Chipewyan men wrestle each other for a wife, who became the possession of the winner. Among the Carrier of British Columbia, widows were required to participate in arduous mourning rituals, and a young widow became the virtual slave of her in-laws for a period following the death of her spouse. When communities were at war, captured Aboriginal women could also be enslaved by their captors as may have been the case for Thanadelthur.[34]

The Hudson's Bay Company, unlike the French companies that sent their agents into the woods from the seventeenth century on, was at first reluctant to countenance any intimacy between Aboriginal women and HBC employees. This was not an attitude that could last. It quickly became apparent that a knowledgable female companion not only fostered trade relations but was essential to any man who intended to travel great distances or to live for any time in fur trade country. Thus, many employees of both the Hudson's Bay and the North West companies, like the *coureurs du bois*, not only travelled into Aboriginal country in the course of their work but also formed relationships there. Indeed, marriages between Aboriginal women and traders became commonplace rather than the exception. Although commonly referred to as marriages "according to the custom of the country," these unions varied in form and status. Some lasted briefly while, in a number of instances, traders developed long-term relationships with Aboriginal women, whom they married according to a diverse range of Aboriginal customary rites. These women often became known as "country" wives. Fur trader George Nelson, for example, had two such marriages, both to Ojibwa women: the first, in 1804, lasted only nine months; the second, in 1808, continued for 23 years until his wife's death.[35] Significantly, Hudson's Bay Company Chief Factor James Douglas wrote in 1842 not only of the practical nature of traders' alliances with Aboriginal women but also of their psychological value.

If these alliances were important to the traders, they were no less so to the women and their relatives. West coast evidence suggests that marriages conducted with a view to cementing trade alliances were frequent among Aboriginal elites. And European traders found that marriages were sometimes even initiated by Aboriginal women, possibly in league with their families. The story of Alexander Henry's encounter with an Ojibwa woman illustrates the point. Returning from New Year's festivities, Henry found the young woman in question in his rooms. When he asked her to leave, she refused, so Henry went buffalo hunting. We do not know whether or not her father, an Ojibwa chief, initially instructed this young woman to pursue Alexander Henry. But her tactics succeeded, and she and Henry went on to have three daughters and a son.[36]

When they occurred, such marriage alliances created a reciprocal social bond, which in turn was intended to consolidate economic relations. Traders, as a result of their marriages to Aboriginal women, were supposed to be drawn into Aboriginal kinship circles; Aboriginal families, in return for access to their women, expected unhindered access to the trading posts and their provisions. Nor did these families permit their daughters to marry indiscriminately. The Flathead of the Pacific Northwest, for example, would allow marriages only with traders whom they particularly esteemed, and the evidence generally suggests that, by the end of the eighteenth century, parental consent was essential for unions between young Aboriginal girls and traders. A voyageur, recalling his experience, was adamant on the importance of such consent: a man ran the risk of getting his "head broken" if he took an Aboriginal girl without her parents' permission. Some bride price was customary; among plains people, blankets, guns, or utensils might be offered. It is clear that traders followed Aboriginal custom in these matters. Bride price represented, in essence, a repayment to the daughter's family for sacrificing her valuable economic services.[37]

While there was no exchange of vows, there was ritual: for example, a pipe might be smoked and a celebratory dance held; the bride might be lectured by her relatives on her new duties. In some cases, the trader visited the home of his bride, and her relatives ceremonially accompanied her to her new home. Similar customs prevailed when Aboriginal men and women were married, either within their own communities or to members of neighbouring bands or nations. And Aboriginal intermarriage did take place, perhaps increasingly as European or other intrusions pushed Aboriginal peoples from their former territories or when warfare resulted in the captivity of women. There is clear evidence of extensive intermarriage, for example, between the Ojibwa and the Cree. Both also intermarried with the Assiniboine, as some Cree and Ojibwa moved onto the plains and became involved in the buffalo economy in the eighteenth century.[38]

The special circumstances of women on the west coast add considerable complexity to any discussion of the relative power and autonomy of Aboriginal women in precontact and early contact societies, for west coast cultures tended to have considerable material property and to be rank-differentiated. In fact, early traders reported three classes within these cultures: nobility and upper-class, commoners, and slaves. Women of the upper classes had considerable economic power. For example, the Haida of the Queen Charlotte Islands, who were matrilineal like the Iroquois and the Huron of the Great Lakes, evidently passed all property through the female line. Older Haida women, like their Tlingit and Tsimshian neighbours, were active traders, often berating men who had given away too much or otherwise failed to trade wisely. The power to trade was likely based, at least in part, on women's roles in domestic life and food production and distribution.[39]

However, marriages among the Haida appear to have been arranged by men, particularly when they involved the nobles or upper classes, although arranged marriages could also be true for commoners. The mother might be consulted, but her brother and the father made the final decision. Moreover, a bride was expected to accept the authority of her husband, and a widow was required to take a new husband selected by her husband's relatives. Women's subordinate status in marriage was reflected in their limited access to political power: women *could* be chiefs (and the number of female chiefs increased after the introduction of European diseases decimated the Haida in the late nineteenth century), but in general chiefs were male, and female participation in political activity was restricted.

Because of menstrual and reproductive taboos, the presence of Haida women was thought dangerous to men who were hunting or fishing, and women were evidently completely excluded from male work of this kind. In the crafts and arts, weaving was the work of women; carving was strictly reserved for men. Yet despite the fact that the dominant trade role was played by men, trade deals often seem to have required a wife's consent, and women also participated in Haida ceremonial activities. They were involved in the famous feasts known as potlatches that were so important to the wealthy Haida; in fact, mothers held potlatches for their daughters at puberty.[40] And, while women were barred from the more important dances at Haida ceremonies, they could become shamans.[41]

The behaviour of a Vancouver Island Clayoquot woman in connection with the landing of a whale illustrates her importance as a partner, although not necessarily an equal partner, in her husband's work. She was observed coming to her husband's boat and performing certain ritual actions, following which she gave a speech. In her speech she told everyone "that she and her husband had observed strict preparatory rituals for eight moons, had slept in separate beds, and prayed for strength and power." Clearly, this woman's actions were vital to the hunt, even as she was excluded from it.[42]

Women seem to have had less authority, however, in the patrilineal groups, such as the Salish. At the time of contact at least, all important property in this group appears to have been held by men and was passed on from father to son. Women married men chosen by their parents and, upon marriage, went to live in the villages of their husbands. If there was a divorce, the children generally remained with the father. Although some women did go on quests for guardian spirits, their journeys were not long ones. Possibly because they were not hunters, they were considered to have less need for spirit helpers than men had. Community decision-making, in general, belonged to men, and women appear to have been excluded from the governing councils of at least some Salish peoples. In addition, because west coast communities were hierarchical societies, some lower-status Aboriginal women (i.e., commoners) in the west probably had very little control over their lives. This was of course the case for slaves, who did exist among some communities at the time the Europeans arrived. European imperialism brought increased trade and wealth, but it also brought greater reason for slavery and polygamy, at least on the west coast. Wives and slaves were pressed into dressing the sea otter pelts that were required in increasing numbers for the coastal fur trade, and this development may well have altered the social structure and lowered the status of Aboriginal women in the Pacific coast region.[43]

Much less is known about the Inuit peoples of the seventeenth, eighteenth, and early nineteenth centuries. The first Europeans to make contact and record their impressions came in the nineteenth century to search for a Northwest Passage to China or fish on the coasts of what is now Labrador. Inuit women were hired by the explorers to make the warm clothing required for survival in such a cold climate and their status was, to some extent, enhanced by this responsibility. But, generally, relations between Inuit and intruders were poor. When Moravian missionaries came to the area in the mid-eighteenth century, one of their goals was to foster better relations. The governor over the region was persuaded to send a woman, Mikak, to London, in the hope that she would be impressed with Britain's power and would influence her people to stop harassing the fishing fleets. Mikak obliged. What resulted from her mission, we do not know; what is clear from this story is that the governor assumed that Mikak had significant influence among her people.[44]

Mikak, the Inuk woman whose visit to London in 1769 was intended to ease Inuit/European relations in eighteenth century Labrador. The portrait was painted by John Russell.

Source: Photo courtesy Institut und Sammlung fur Völkerkunde der Universität Göttingen. Photo: Harry Haase, Institute of Ethnology, University of Goettingen

ABORIGINAL WOMEN'S PERSPECTIVES

How did Aboriginal women regard the Europeans, whose patriarchal culture encroached so powerfully on their own? As far as we can tell, the reactions of Aboriginal women varied enormously, according to the time and place.

As the Jesuits reported, missionaries did not always succeed in altering the marriage and social patterns of the peoples they had hoped to convert. Montagnais wives, for example, regularly ran away from husbands who attempted to impose their Christian will on them.[45] And clearly more than one Montagnais husband came to the conclusion that the Jesuits had no sense. Yet, gradually, the missionaries did begin to influence the lives of those Aboriginals who were attracted more or less permanently to French settlements. In the seventeenth century, at the Aboriginal settlement of Sillery, near Quebec, where Aboriginal families who had been converted to Christianity were engaged in farming, the French authorities gave the land to the men of that Aboriginal settlement, who were made "captains" by their benefactors. These newly created officials handed out government charity to families in need. Unmarried women were strictly controlled, and any wife who disobeyed her husband was beaten.

Some Aboriginal women met the Jesuits on their own ground, however. Kateri Tekakwitha, an Iroquois orphan who fled to the "praying town" of Kahnawake in the 1670s, was one of a number of Aboriginal women who dedicated themselves to virginity and self-mortification, spiritually empowering concepts that made sense in an Iroquois cultural framework as well as in a French Catholic one. Saintly powers were attributed to Tekakwitha soon after her death in 1680 at the young age of 24.[46] We cannot know just what the Catholic faith meant to Kateri or to other Aboriginal women, but we do know that the structures of Catholicism opened up new opportunities for some. They acted as catechists—that is, instructing other converts—and frequently served as godparents to each other's children and grandchildren, thereby creating a Catholic kin network linking Aboriginal fur trading families across North America. And, contrary to the view that Catholicism subordinated all Aboriginal women to men, some, at least, used their faith as a basis to challenge tribal elders, negotiate their own marriage terms, and generally resist the imposition of patriarchal authority.[47] Salish women of the western Plateau region provide an example of how Aboriginal women recast the Jesuit missionaries' view of the Virgin Mary to reflect their own cultural and spiritual beliefs. They worshipped her as a warrior woman for her power, strength, and ability to protect, and they rejected the missionaries' promotion of her as an example of female submissiveness.[48]

The Jesuits did less well among those Montagnais and Naskapi—who stayed away from French settlements—and among the Huron, whom they attempted to convert in Huronia itself. When the Aboriginals were on their own turf, the system of economic and social dependency that developed at Sillery and other villages that were close to French administrative centres could not be duplicated. Many Huron, already settled agriculturalists with their own complex systems of land use and inheritance, resisted the encroachment of the missionaries. Indeed, it may well have been Huron women who were at the core of the resistance. A Huron man who adopted Christianity could

Kateri Tekakwitha painting by the Jesuit missionary Claude Chauchetière, between 1682 and 1693.

Source: Painted by Father Chauchetière between 1682–1693.

find himself ostracized and ejected from the longhouse by his mother-in-law. Until the 1640s, when the Huron were dispersed by Iroquois incursions, the traditional family-oriented systems of production continued to guarantee to women, as to men, access to the necessities of life.[49] From a material perspective, provided that one was not starving or defeated in battle, there was little temptation for Aboriginal women to adopt the missionaries' culture, which offered so little and threatened so clear a loss of status. But after the dispersal of the Huron, some women of the remaining Huron communities found spiritual satisfaction in Christianity. Khionrea, who had been renamed Thérèse by Marie de l'Incarnation, was eventually captured by the Iroquois and married to a Mohawk. But she retained her new Christian beliefs and by 1653 "was the mistress of the several families of her Iroquois long-house, still praying to her Christian God and leading others publicly in prayer." Another Huron woman, Cécile Gannendaris, whose story was recorded by the Sisters of the Quebec Hospital, taught the Huron language to Jesuit priests and was an eloquent preacher of Christianity to her own people.[50] The impact of European religion on Aboriginal women was ambiguous and variable, but as European trade and settlement increased, so did missionaries' influence.

And as trade with Europeans increased in scope and importance, it was also increasingly difficult for Aboriginal women to resist the influence of the white traders. Often, trade altered gender relations for the worse within Aboriginal societies. After the horse was introduced onto the plains through Aboriginal networks, for example, men's hunting work was made easier, but the number of hides women had to prepare probably increased. The more a woman's community depended on trade with Europeans, the more difficult it was to maintain independent traditions and customs. Furthermore, if marriage to a trader was a possibility, the temptation for some Aboriginal women must have been considerable. Their belief in the interconnectedness of kinship and trade made such relationships not only normal but desirable. The fur traders certainly claimed that Aboriginal women regarded marriage to white men as preferable to marriage within their own tribes. Cree women were reported to consider it an honour to be chosen as a trader's wife. Such perceptions were reinforced by traders' confused notions about both the workload and the status of Aboriginal women in their own societies. To European men, the burden of Aboriginal women's work appeared enormous; such women, they felt, could only welcome the relative comfort of life within the trading forts.[51]

When the women married European men and moved into the trading posts, their material circumstances and their leverage with Aboriginal and white men alike probably did improve, at least initially. As North West Company (NWC) trader George Nelson pointed out, Aboriginal women had a particular interest in keeping the peace, and there is no doubt that, for a time, intermarriage between fur traders and Aboriginals did promote better relations between the two groups. Through their marriages, Aboriginal women could gain significant power: the power to create or destroy friendly relations by their influence and good offices with both sides.[52] Moreover, these women provided an important informal labour pool at fur trading posts, as was the case at the Hudson Bay Company outpost of Île-à-la-Crosse in Northern Saskatchewan. Here their work in the fisheries was crucial to the well-being of company employees, for whom fish was a dietary staple. When Mrs. Kirkness, an Aboriginal wife considered to be a particularly skilled fisher, left her husband and moved to an NWC post, HBC officials appealed to her to return to her husband, claiming that the loss of her services was "potentially devastating." Evidently Mrs. Kirkness's personal confidence and self-assurance were sufficient to overcome the company pleas, and she remained at the NWC settlement.[53]

In general, fur traders' wives did enjoy a life that was physically easier than life in a migratory band. They had the benefit, perhaps illusory, of clothing made from imported textiles, and company servants did some of the heavy work that Aboriginal women customarily did, such as carrying goods and hauling firewood and water. Although domestic tasks were never given over entirely to others by traders' Aboriginal wives, they were able to become more sedentary and spend more time making moccasins, snowshoes, and other family goods. Altogether, the material improvement may have seemed very great indeed. The "country" wife's access to European goods, moreover, generally extended to members of her family and band, who already benefitted from the good trade relations that her marriage had helped cement. There is ample evidence that many fur trade marriages were loving and life-long arrangements, and some traders wrote about their Aboriginal and mixed-descent families with great affection and warmth.[54] Recent research into mixed-descent families in Île-à-la-Crosse show how the kinship networks initially established by fur traders' Cree wives in their maternal land created a stable community for subsequent generations. These Cree wives retained their Aboriginal attitudes and beliefs about family and social life and influenced the development of a Métis culture that was essentially an Aboriginal culture.[55] Further research into the roles played by "semiautonomous female headed family units" promises to help our understanding of the emergence of Métis identity.[56]

But there was a negative side. During the eighteenth century, some traders saw the capture and abuse of a rival's wife as a weapon in the ongoing struggle between different interests for mastery of the trade. Traders' Aboriginal wives were also subject to new diseases. They bore more children and had them closer together; fur traders' families, in the early to mid-nineteenth century at least, were large—from eight to twelve children, compared to the four typically born to the average Cree woman. This trend surely took a physical toll. Childbirth itself appears to have been more difficult for traders' Aboriginal wives. Unlike their counterparts in Aboriginal society, many "country" wives were subject to their husbands in raising their children, and these husbands' views on discipline and education could be very different from their own. Wives of officers, for example, had to face sending children, especially sons, to boarding schools or to paternal relatives, sometimes as far away as Great Britain, for their education, and often these absent children died.[57]

By 1815, mixed-descent families represented a sizable portion of the population in the Upper Great Lakes region.[58] However, in the early nineteenth century, the arrival in fur trade country of missionaries and European wives brought about a decline in the incidence of traders taking Aboriginal spouses. Even before this, traders who wished to return to Europe or to the east had often engaged in a practice that came to be known as "turning off" their Aboriginal wives. At one time such women had been able to return to their Aboriginal communities with pride, and they and their children had been welcomed; but this was to be less and less the case, and was probably not an option at all for mixed-descent women. Some wives were turned over to new trader husbands, but others found themselves abandoned, belonging to neither white nor Aboriginal worlds.[59]

Such women were probably still better off than those Aboriginal and mixed-descent women who, as European men moved into their territories in greater and greater numbers, found themselves involved in prostitution. The sexual freedom of women in many, if not all, Aboriginal communities was misinterpreted by Europeans. One trader noted that Cree girls were rarely virgins by age 13 or 14. Another trader claimed that "fornication" could hardly be considered a vice among the Aboriginals; according to him, the practice was accepted as "normal."[60] Coupled with the sale of alcohol to Aboriginal men and women, prostitution and venereal diseases took their tragic toll. Seventeenth-century accounts of the Nova Scotia Micmac point to considerable prostitution, drunkenness, and wife-beating. A French traveller saw women who had fallen into "a melancholy so black and profound that they became immersed wholly in a cruel despair." The result, he said, was sometimes suicide.[61]

Yet not all Aboriginal women were victims, and, while some cultures were vastly changed or destroyed, more remarkable are the many that survived. Many women and communities wove a careful and resourceful path among the options that were open to them, adapting where possible and surviving as best they could. Most Aboriginal women who came into intimate contact with white men did so as their tribally sanctioned so-called "country" wives, following the customs of their own peoples, and gaining at least short-term benefits by their actions. On the east coast, Micmac women were examples of those who managed to rescue something of their former lives. Although four out of five of their quill-working techniques were lost during the seventeenth century, by the late eighteenth and early nineteenth centuries, Micmac craftswomen had developed new techniques for working quills on birchbark, and there was a new flowering of their art, which developed considerable economic importance.[62]

Finally, the vast majority of Aboriginal women, such as the Montagnais and Naskapi and the Huron before their defeat and dispersal, probably followed a more resistant path, holding on to their cultures and customs and adapting slowly to change. Most of the Huron perished in the seventeenth century during wars with the Iroquois. But by the nineteenth century, Aboriginal groups who recognized the damage wrought in their societies by European intrusion retreated where they could, and some at least managed to avoid the tragedies that befell the Beothuk, who were completely extermi-nated, and other groups such as the Huron, who were decimated. In 1838, in a remote part of what was to become the Yukon Territory, Hudson's Bay Company trader, Robert Campbell, met a 35-year-old "Nahany Chieftainess" whose commanding pres-ence and energy created a lasting impression on him. For perhaps several more gen-erations, women of her region would remain isolated enough to continue their lives relatively untouched by European ways. By then, at least some Aboriginal women must have understood the threat. In 1850, in the Similkameen and Okanagan areas of the territory that was to become British Columbia, a prophet travelled through the country urging the Aboriginal people to fight white encroachment and to keep their own traditions. This prophet told them to "retain their old customs and not to adopt any of the ways of the white man" because to do this would poison their spirit. The prophet was a woman.[63]

If male observers often referred to the dreariness of Aboriginal women's lives, the British feminist Anna Jameson put forward a different opinion when she encountered Aboriginal communities in Upper Canada and adjacent regions in the 1830s. Jameson was aware of and called attention to European men's castigations of Aboriginal societies for their enslavement and oppression of women. Yet whatever the lot of the Aboriginal woman, Jameson pointed out, at least she was not in a "false position":

> When we speak of the drudgery of the women, we must note the equal division of labour; there is no class of women privileged to sit still while others work. Every squaw makes the clothing, mats, moccasins, and boils the kettle for her own family. . . . Compare her life with that of a servant-maid of all work, or a factory girl,—I say that the condition of the squaw is gracious in comparison, dignified by domestic feelings, and by equality with all around her. . . . The personal property, as the clothing, mats, cooking and hunting apparatus, all the interior of the wigwam . . . seems to be under the control of the woman. . . . The corn she raises, and the maple sugar she makes, she can always dispose of as she thinks fit—they are hers.[64]

In all indigenous societies, women's work was essential to the survival of family and community. Among gatherers and hunters, women supplied a major share of the diet. Should we then conclude that Aboriginal societies were egalitarian on the whole, at least as far as male/female relations were concerned? Perhaps it is unwise to put our query in these terms. These societies did not share European notions of individual economic rights. In small gathering-and-hunting bands, where decision-making was often communal, women do seem to have shared power with men. In the Iroquois and Huron agricultural communities, matrons (the leading women in charge of the longhouses) appear to have enjoyed great authority, both in their own realms of production, distribution, and child care, as well as in the larger decision-making processes of the group. Among the northwestern and western Aboriginal peoples, however, the situation was more complicated. High-status women of certain families could be chieftains, but many women were relatively powerless.

The history of Aboriginal women continues to be explored; perhaps much of it is permanently lost to us. But where history is lost, legend and story, archaeology, and language analysis come to our aid. Stories told by contemporary Aboriginal and mixed-descent women about the heroines of their mythic past emphasize their ingenuity and practical skills.[65] The Blackfoot tell of "this world's dawn," when the women and the men travelled separately, the women living by their skill near their own buffalo jump in the foothills of Alberta. Two versions of the story agree that it was the men who thought they would benefit by joining up with the women but that it was the women who chose the husbands they wanted from the group. "Old Man" had been contemptuous of "the leader of the women" in one version; in another, he cheated and tried to get the best woman for himself. In both versions, he ended up an outcast and alone, transformed into a tree; in both versions, women's power is remembered and validated.[66]

Notes

1. James Knight, the Hudson's Bay Company Governor at York Fort (now known as York Factory), wrote at some length about Thanadelthur in his journal, referring to her as "the slave woman." Knight's use of the term "slave" has led to considerable confusion. He may have meant it fairly literally when he applied it to Aboriginal people such as Thanadelthur whom he ransomed from other Aboriginals, and from whom he apparently expected in return some degree of service, compliance, and goodwill. It is also possible that Knight was simply trying to render the Cree word for *captive*. What is certain is that Thanadelthur was not a member of the Slave Nation as some have suggested but probably Chipewyan. The Chipewyans were Dene, usually identified as "Northern Indians" by Knight and other Hudson's Bay Company traders. The Slave or Slavey Indians, after whom Great Slave Lake was named, were another Dene people who lived west of the Chipewyans.
2. Sylvia Van Kirk, "Thanadelthur," *The Beaver* (Spring 1974): 40–45.
3. Patricia A. McCormack, "The Many Faces of Thanadelthur: Documents, Stories and Images," in Jennifer S. H. Brown and Elizabeth Vibert, eds., *Reading Beyond Words: Contexts for Native History* (Peterborough, ON: Broadview Press, 2003), 329–64. For more information

on "stolen woman" stories in Aboriginal narratives, see Julie Cruikshank, *The Stolen Woman: Female Journeys in Taglish and Tutchone* (Ottawa: National Museums of Canada, 1983).

4. R. Cole Harris, ed., *Historical Atlas of Canada* (Toronto: University of Toronto Press, 1987) vol. 1, plate 12; Margaret Conrad and James Hiller, *Atlantic Canada: A Concise History* (Toronto: Oxford Press, 2006), 18–19, 98; Somer Brodribb, "The Traditional Roles of Aboriginal Women in Canada and the Impact of Colonization," *Canadian Journal of Aboriginal Studies* 4, 1 (1986): 85–103; Karen Anderson, "A Gendered World: Women, Men, and the Political Economy of the Seventeenth Century Huron," in Heather Jon Maroney and Meg Luxton, eds., *Feminism and Political Economy: Women's Work, Women's Struggles* (Toronto: Methuen, 1987), 125; for information about the adoption of women and children, see Daniel K. Richter, *The Ordeal of the Longhouse: The Peoples of the Iroquois League in the Era of Colonisation* (Raleigh: University of North Carolina Press, 1992), 73.

5. For the distribution of tribal and linguistic groups at the time of contact, see the map on page 9. For more detail on Aboriginal peoples prior to and at the time of contact, see Harris, ed., *Historical Atlas of Canada* vol. 1, plates 2–18, 33–35, and 57–69.

6. See Elisabeth Tooker, "Women in Iroquois Society," in Wendy Mitchinson et al., eds., *Canadian Women: A Reader* (Toronto: Harcourt Brace, 1996), 19–32; and Georges E. Sioui, *For an Amerindian Autohistory* (Montreal and Kingston: McGill-Queen's University Press, 1992), 17.

7. Judith K. Brown, "A Note on the Division of Labor by Sex," *American Anthropologist* 72, 5 (October 1970): 1073–78.

8. Brown, "Note on the Division of Labour," 1076.

9. Judith K. Brown, "Economic Organization and the Position of Women Among the Iroquois," *Ethnohistory* 17, 3–4 (Summer/Fall 1970): 151–67; Karen Anderson, "Commodity Exchange and Subordination: Montagnais-Naskapi and Huron Women, 1600–1650," *Signs* 11, 1 (Autumn 1985): 48–62.

10. Brown, "Note on the Division of Labour," 1076. The document is reproduced in James Axtell, ed., *The Indian Peoples of Eastern America: A Documentary History of the Sexes* (New York: Oxford University Press, 1981), 138–39.

11. June Namias, *White Captives: Gender and Ethnicity on the American Frontier* (Chapel Hill: University of North Carolina Press, 1993).

12. Eleanor Leacock and Jacqueline Goodman, "Montagnais Marriage and the Jesuits of the Seventeenth Century: Incidents from the Relations of Paul Le Jeune," *Western Canadian Journal of Anthropology* 6, 3 (1976): 77–91; Leacock, "Women in Egalitarian Societies," in Renate Bridenthal and Claudia Koonz, eds., *Becoming Visible: Women in European Society* (Boston: Houghton-Mifflin, 1977), 11–35; Leacock, "Class, Commodity, and the Status of Women," in Ruby Rohrlich-Leavitt, ed., *Women Cross-Culturally: Change and Challenge* (The Hague: Mouton, 1975), 601–16; Leacock, "Montagnais Women and the Jesuit Program for Colonization," in Mona Etienne and Eleanor Leacock, eds., *Women and Colonization: Anthropological Perspectives* (New York: Praeger, 1980), 25–42; Leacock, with a new introduction by Christine Ward Gailey, "Women's Status in Egalitarian Society," in Rebecca Kugel and Lucy Eldersveld Murphy, eds., *Native Women's History in Eastern North America before 1900* (Lincoln and London: University of Nebraska Press, 2007), 77–106.

13. Glyndwr Williams, ed., *Andrew Graham's Observations on Hudson's Bay, 1767–91* (London: Hudson's Bay Record Society, 1969), 177–78.

14. W. Kaye Lamb, ed., *The Journals and Letters of Sir Alexander Mackenzie* (Cambridge, U.K.: Published for the Hakluyt Society at Cambridge Press, 1970), 135; for information on the topic

of the "squaw drudge" see David D. Smits, "The 'Squaw Drudge'?: A Prime Index of Savagism," *Ethnohistory* 29, (1982): 281–306; Sylvia Van Kirk, *"Many Tender Ties": Women in Fur Trade Society, 1670–1870* (Winnipeg: Watson and Dwyer, 1980), 17–21. Throughout this chapter, except where specifically noted, discussion of women in the fur trade draws on Van Kirk's work.

15. Natalie Zemon Davis, "Iroquois Women, European Women," in Margo Hendricks and Patricia Parker, eds., *Women, "Race," and Writing in the Early Modern Period* (London: Routledge, 1994), 243–58; Elizabeth Vibert, *Traders' Tales: British Fur Traders' Narratives of the Encounter with Plateau Peoples, 1807–1846* (Norman, OK: University of Oklahoma Press, 1996).

16. Van Kirk, *"Many Tender Ties,"* 18.

17. Mary Jane Schneider, "Women's Work: An Examination of Women's Roles in Plains Arts and Crafts," and Alan M. Klein, "The Political Economy of Gender: A 19th Century Plains Indian Case Study," both in Patricia Albers and Beatrice Medicine, eds., *The Hidden Half: Studies of Plains Indian Women* (Lanham, N.Y.: University Press of America, 1983), 198, 149; Vibert, *Traders' Tales.*

18. Loraine Littlefield, "Women Traders in the Maritime Fur Trade," in Mitchinson et al., eds., *Canadian Women: A Reader*, 6–19; and Barbara Bodenhorn, "'I'm Not the Great Hunter, My Wife Is': Inupiat and Anthropological Models of Gender," *Études/Inuit/Studies* 14, 1–2 (1990): 59–61.

19. Ellice B. Gonzalez, *Changing Economic Roles for Micmac Men and Women: An Ethnohistorical Analysis* (Ottawa: National Museums of Canada, 1981), espec. 15; Andrew Hill Clark, *Acadia: The Geography of Early Nova Scotia to 1760* (Madison: University of Wisconsin Press, 1968); Virginia P. Miller, "The Decline of Nova Scotia Micmac Population, A.D. 1600–1850," *Culture* 2, 3 (1982): 107–20.

20. Gonzalez, *Changing Economic Roles*, 18.

21. Ruth Holmes Whitehead, *Micmac Quillwork: Micmac Indian Techniques of Porcupine Quill Decoration, 1600–1950* (Halifax: Nova Scotia Museum, 1982).

22. Williams, ed., *Andrew Graham's Observations*, 177.

23. Van Kirk, *"Many Tender Ties,"* 21, 86.

24. Karen Anderson, in her *Chain Her by One Foot: The Subjugation of Women in Seventeenth-Century New France* (London: Routledge, 1991), argues the case for Huron women's power in the political realm prior to and in the early days of contact; Elisabeth Tooker, in "Women in Iroquois Society," and Natalie Zemon Davis, in "Iroquois Women," take a more nuanced view, with Tooker especially seeing little evidence for the argument.

25. Davis, "Iroquois Women," 249.

26. Leacock, "Montagnais Women," 26–27.

27. Roland Viau, *Femmes de personne. Sexes, genres et pouvoir en Iroquoisie ancienne* (Montréal: Boréal, 2000); Davis, "Iroquois Women," 253.

28. Bernard Saladin d'Anglure, "Penser le 'féminin' chamanique, ou le 'tiers sexe' des chamanes inuit," *Recherches amérindiennes au Québec* 18, 2–3 (automne 1988): 24–25.

29. Davis, "Iroquois Women," 248–49; Peter S. Schmalz, *The Ojibwa of Southern Ontario* (Toronto: University of Toronto Press, 1991), 52.

30. Alice B. Kehoe, "The Shackles of Tradition," in Albers and Medicine, eds., *Hidden Half*, 68; Kehoe, "Old Woman Had Great Power," *Western Canadian Journal of Anthropology* 6, 3 (November 1976): 72–74.

31. Leacock, "Montagnais Women"; Leacock and Goodman, "Montagnais Marriage," 80–82.

32. Dickason, *Canada's First Nations*, 169–72.

33. See Anderson, *Chain Her*, for an elaboration of this argument.

34. Van Kirk, *"Many Tender Ties,"* 24–25; Van Kirk, "Toward a Feminist Perspective in Aboriginal History," *Occasional Paper* No. 14 (Toronto: Centre for Women's Studies in Education, OISE, 1987), 7.

35. Jennifer S. H. Brown, "Partial Truths: A Closer Look at Fur Trade Marriage," in Theodore Binnema, Gerhard J. Ens and R. C. Macleod, eds., *From Rupert's Land to Canada* (Edmonton: The University of Alberta Press, 2001), 59–80.

36. Van Kirk, *"Many Tender Ties,"* espec. chaps. 2 and 4; Margaret Whitehead, "'A Useful Christian Woman': First Nations' Women and Protestant Missionary Work in British Columbia," *Atlantis* 18, 1–2 (Fall/Winter 1992; Spring/Summer 1993): 153; Barry M. Gough, ed., *The Journal of Alexander Henry The Younger, 1799–1814, v. 1* (Toronto: The Champlain Society, 1988).

37. Van Kirk, *"Many Tender Ties,"* chap. 2; Whitehead, "'A Useful Christian Woman,'" 162–63 n. 117; Carolyn Podruchny, *Making the Voyageur World: Travelers and Traders in the North American Fur Trade* (Toronto: University of Toronto Press, 2006), chap. 8.

38. Susan R. Sharrock, "Crees, Cree-Assiniboines, and Assiniboines: Interethnic Social Organization on the Far Northern Plains," *Ethnohistory* 12, 2 (Spring 1974): 8.

39. Littlefield, "Women Traders," 173–85.

40. The potlatch was a festival or ceremony practised among peoples of the Pacific Northwest coast. Families or hereditary leaders hosted a feast for their guests, to whom they gave gifts. Family status was raised by who distributed the most resources so hosts demonstrated their wealth and prominence by giving away goods. This practice was condemned by Europeans because it was contrary to their notions of capitalism, accumulation, industry, and economy. For more information on potlatches, see Tina Loo, "Dan Cranmer's Potlatch: Law as Coercion, Symbol, and Rhetoric in British Columbia, 1884–1951," *Canadian Historical Review* 73, 2 (1992).

41. Marjorie Mitchell and Anna Franklin, "When You Don't Know the Language, Listen to the Silence: An Historical Overview of Aboriginal Indian Women in B.C.," in Barbara K. Latham and Roberta J. Pazdro, eds., *Not Just Pin Money: Selected Essays on the History of Women's Work in British Columbia* (Victoria: Camosun College, 1984), 17–35.

42. Jan Gould, *Women of British Columbia* (Saanichton: Hancock House, 1975), 13–14.

43. Mitchell and Franklin, "When You Don't," 24.

44. Dickason, *Canada's First Nations*, 226–27; Robert McGhee, *The Last Imaginary Place: Human History of the Arctic World* (Toronto: Key Porter Books, 2004), 241; William H. Whiteley, "Mikak," *Dictionary of Canadian Biography* (Toronto: University of Toronto Press, 1979) vol. 4, 536–37.

45. Leacock and Goodman, "Montagnais Marriage," 82–88.

46. Cornelius J. Jaenen, *Friend and Foe: Aspects of French–Amerindian Cultural Contact in the Sixteenth and Seventeenth Centuries* (Toronto: McClelland and Stewart, 1976), 76; Nancy Shoemaker, "Kateri Tekakwitha's Tortuous Path to Sainthood," in Nancy Shoemaker, ed., *Negotiators of Change: Historical Perspectives on Aboriginal American Women* (New York: Routledge, 1995), 49–71; Henri Béchard, "Tekakwitha," *Dictionary of Canadian Biography* (Toronto: University of Toronto Press, 1966) vol. 1, 635–36; Allan Greer, *Mohawk Saint: Catherine Tekakwitha and the Jesuits* (New York: Oxford University Press, 2005). In 1980 the Roman Catholic Church beatified Tekawitha, the final stage before canonization as a saint. She is now known as Blessed Catherine Tekakwitha, and her feast day is celebrated annually on April 17. She is likely to become the first North American Aborginal woman saint.

47. Susan Sleeper-Smith, *Indian Women and French Men* (Amherst: University of Massachusetts Press, 2001); Sleeper-Smith, "Women, Kin and Catholicism: New Perspectives on the Fur Trade," in Kugel and Eldersveld Murphy, eds., *Native Women's History*, 234–74.

48. Laura Peers, "'The Guardian of All': Jesuit Missionary and Salish Perceptions of the Virgin Mary," in Brown and Vibert, eds., *Reading Beyond Words*, 217–36.

49. Anderson, "Commodity Exchange," 62.

50. Davis, "Iroquois Women," 254–56; Dominique Deslandres, *Croire et Faire: Les missions françaises au XVIIe siècle (1600–1650)*, (Paris: Fayard, 2002), chap. 24.

51. Dickason, *Canada's First Nations*, 169–72.

52. Van Kirk, *"Many Tender Ties,"* 76.

53. Brenda MacDougall, "Wahkootowin: Family and Cultural Identity in Northwestern Saskatchewan Metis Communities," *Canadian Historical Review*, 87, 3, (September 2006): 451–53.

54. Van Kirk, *"Many Tender Ties,"* espec. chap. 4; for a discussion of some divergences between the way Hudson's Bay Company men treated their Aboriginal wives and offspring as compared to those of the North West Company, see Jennifer S. H. Brown, *Strangers in Blood: Fur Trade Company Families in Indian Country* (Vancouver: University of British Columbia Press, 1980).

55. MacDougall, "Wahkootowin," 431–62.

56. Jennifer S. Brown, "Women as Centre and Symbol in the Emergence of Métis Communities," in Kugel and Murphy, eds., *Native Women's History*, 65–76.

57. Van Kirk, *"Many Tender Ties,"* chap. 4; Jennifer S. H. Brown, "Ultimate Respectability: Fur Trade Children in the 'Civilized World,'" *The Beaver* (Winter 1977): 4–10 and (Spring 1978): 48–55; Brown, "Presbyterian Métis of St. Gabriel Street, Montreal," in Jacqueline Peterson and Jennifer S. Brown, eds., *The New Peoples: Being and Becoming Métis in North America* (Winnipeg: University of Manitoba Press, 1985), 195–206.

58. Jacqueline Peterson, "Many Roads to Red River: Métis Genesis in the Great Lakes Region," in Peterson and Brown, eds., *The New Peoples*, 37–71; on the various trajectories of Aboriginal women and their descendants, see Heather Devine, *The People Who Own Themselves: Aboriginal Ethnogenesis in a Canadian Family, 1660–1900* (Calgary: University of Calgary Press, 2004).

59. Van Kirk, *"Many Tender Ties,"* chaps. 5–10.

60. Van Kirk, *"Many Tender Ties,"* chap. 1; Mitchell and Franklin, "When You Don't," 25–26.

61. Whitehead, *Micmac Quillwork*, 24.

62. Whitehead, *Micmac Quillwork*, chap. 3.

63. Douglas Sanders, "Indian Women: A Brief History of Their Roles and Rights," *McGill Law Journal* 21, 4 (Winter 1975): 656.

64. Mrs. [Anna] Jameson, *Winter Studies and Summer Rambles in Canada* (London: Saunders and Otley, 1838; reprinted, Toronto: Coles Canadiana Collection, 1972) vol. 3, 305, 308.

65. See Marilyn Ravicz, Diane Battung, and Laura Baker, "Rainbow Women of the Fraser Valley: Lifesongs through the Generations," in Latham and Pazdro, eds., *Not Just Pin Money*, 37–52.

66. Kehoe, "Old Woman," 68; Richard G. Forbis, "The Old Women's Buffalo Jump, Alberta," *National Museum of Canada Bulletin* No. 180, Anthropological Series No. 57 (Ottawa: Department of Northern Affairs and National Resources, 1962), 61.

CHAPTER TWO

Women in New France

On June 25, 1669, just one year after her marriage, a young woman in the advanced stages of pregnancy appeared before the Sovereign Council, the highest judicial body in the colony of Canada. Marie Bourgois had come to charge her husband and her father-in-law with denying her the necessities of life. In her moving appeal for support, she reminded the councillors that she was "a poor woman who had left her father and her mother and her relatives to come to this country."[1] Like Marie Bourgois, many of the women who made the arduous voyage to New France left behind the comforts of family, friends, and familiar surroundings, only to encounter disappointment and deprivation in a strange and often inhospitable land. Most, however, persevered and took satisfaction in the re-rooting of family and society in the "New World." Some came from the rural peasantry, others from bourgeois families of French coastal towns, and others still from the more sophisticated commercial and administrative centres of Paris and Versailles. We have only to think of the nuns, with their mixture of wealthy aristocrats and women with few or no economic resources, to realize the complexities of character and circumstance that marked the lives of French women who came to North America.

LES PIONNIÈRES

While many of the women who migrated to New France in the seventeenth century were married women or daughters who came with their families, hundreds of single women and widows also tackled the voyage, either alone or in the company of more distant relations. The trip from French Atlantic ports, such as La Rochelle, to Quebec could take anywhere between six and twelve weeks, with boats typically departing from France in April or May. Marie (Guyart) de l'Incarnation, the founder of the Ursuline convent at Quebec, described her first voyage to North America in 1639 in letters that she sent back to France. Guyart boarded ship in Dieppe at the beginning of May with

Figure 2.1 NEW FRANCE

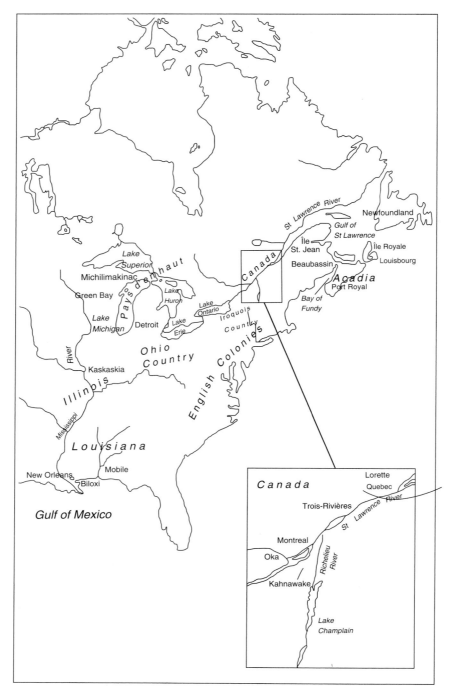

Source: Based on Allan Greer, *The People of New France* (Toronto: University of Toronto Press, 1997).

two other Ursuline nuns and several nuns belonging to the religious order known as the *Hospitalières*. Once the boat had set sail, these women, along with the other passengers, faced many hazards, including Spanish marauders, storms, and seasickness. Safely arrived in Quebec, Guyart wrote in a letter to one of her brothers back in France that she and her travelling companions had "suffered great travails during three months' navigation through storms and tempests which obliged us, instead of the thirteen hundred leagues of the crossing, to journey more than two thousand. We were within a hair's breadth of shipwreck, but the One that commands the winds and the seas preserved us with his all-powerful finger."[2] Despite the arduous nature of this voyage, some women came to New France and then went back. Marie Joly, for example, was a Parisian widow who came to Canada with her cousin. In Quebec she contracted a marriage with Antoine Damiens of Rouen, only to return to France and settle in La Rochelle.[3] Many of the single women came with the intention to marry immediately; others came as *engagées* or indentured servants, and had to delay marriage; still others, for whom the religious mission was paramount, came intending to devote their lives to God.

The first married European woman to remain in New France permanently was Marie Rollet, the spouse of the apothecary and farmer Louis Hébert. She established a household in Quebec with her husband in 1617 and lived there with her family until his death, when she joined the farming household of her daughter and son-in-law. Rollet was of more humble origins than Hélène Boullé, the 22-year-old gentlewoman who accompanied her husband, the explorer Samuel de Champlain, to Canada in 1620. Hélène Boullé was a wealthy woman: she had been officially married to Champlain at age 12, and by the time she embarked for Quebec her dowry had already paid for the outfitting of one of her husband's earlier expeditions. There must have been a considerable gulf between Madame de Champlain's aristocratic Parisian upbringing and what she found in North America, but we know little about her except that she had a brother who was in her husband's service and who may have given her some companionship during her stay in Canada. She spent four years in the colony, devoting at least some of her time to performing charitable works among the Aboriginal peoples, and then returned to France, eventually to retire to an Ursuline convent that she had founded and endowed.[4]

In sharp contrast to the aristocratic Hélène Boullé, some of the early female colonists were outcasts of French society, recruited from the slums, brothels, and prisons of French ports by unscrupulous representatives of the fur trade monopoly. As part of its contract with the French authorities, the fur trade company known as the *Compagnie des Cent-Associés*, or Company of One Hundred Associates, was required to send a specified number of settlers each year to New France. However, there was little enthusiasm for this project since colonists were an unnecessary and expensive investment for those whose primary interest was securing beaver pelts from the Aboriginal peoples. Consequently, little attention was paid to the physical or moral qualities of those the company sent out.[5] No doubt it was the initial scarcity of so-called respectable unmarried white women in the colony that led Champlain to favour the establishment of a new "founding race," to be produced as a result of relationships between French men and Aboriginal women. However, the civil and religious authorities in France did not share his enthusiasm for marriages between Aboriginal peoples and Europeans, and moved instead to assert more control over the selection of emigrants.

The authorities' efforts to enhance the reputation of the colony and its female inhabitants were greatly aided by women caught up in the zeal of the Catholic Counter-Reformation. Inspired by what they read in the *Relations,* which were the letters written by Jesuit missionaries and sent back to France, pious French women soon saw in North America another and especially fertile field for their spiritual endeavours.[6] These French women were not unique, for similar feelings inspired the Puritans of New England. They *were* unusual, however, in two important respects. First, a remarkable number of them came to New France independently as single women or as members of female religious communities. Second, the all-female institutions they founded played a vital role in the material, social, and spiritual development of their colony. Similar charitable and social institutions were not created in Britain's American colonies until at least the eighteenth century, and even then few, if any, welfare establishments in those colonies were run by women.[7]

In 1639 the *Hospitalières* arrived in the vicinity of Quebec. The two sisters who directed Quebec's first medical mission, Marie Grunet and Marie Forrestier, were responding to a need outlined in the 1635 *Relations* of Father Lejeune, and their first thought was for the Huron community then living at Sillery, outside the fortress of Quebec. In 1644, the Sillery mission was abandoned as a result of the wars with the Iroquois; the hospital nuns then moved into the citadel, a small wooden structure, and made the French population the focus of their care. By 1658, the sisters had acquired a larger building, boasting eight doors and eight windows. While the hospital normally held 10 beds, in times of epidemic it could accommodate up to 20. By 1672 the *Hôtel-Dieu,* as the hospital was called, had expanded to two halls—one for women and one for men—and also included a small chamber for wealthier patients.[8]

The Ursulines also came to Quebec in 1639 expecting to devote themselves to the Aboriginal peoples, only to have these expectations crushed when many of their Aboriginal charges proved resistant to what the Ursulines believed was their civilizing mission. The strict discipline of the convent school was alien to homesick Aboriginal girls, who, with the aid of their parents, slipped away to the forest. Soon the principal function of the Ursuline convent was to educate the daughters of the French colonists.

The Ursuline Marie (Guyart) de l'Incarnation had nurtured a religious vocation through adolescence, marriage, motherhood, widowhood, and a 10-year business involvement in the mercantile household of her brother-in-law. Her faith eventually led Marie de l'Incarnation to enter a convent in Tours, but not before she had learned much in the management of her brother-in-law's business affairs that would be of practical value in her future work in New France. Indeed, the creation of a convent school in Quebec involved far more than an understanding of the management of children. She had to assure the community's finances, which were only partly organized by her patron and chief fundraiser, a widow named Madame de la Peltrie; she had to oversee the construction of the first convent and then of a second one when the first was destroyed by fire; and she had to deal with the complicated matter of provisioning her community in the midst of the wars waged between the French and the Iroquois. Held in high regard by the colony's civil authorities, Marie de l'Incarnation was often consulted on matters of public policy. She was also prepared to confront the powerful first bishop of New France, Montmorency de Laval, when it appeared he wanted to change the Ursulines' constitution of 1647.[9] Somehow, while she governed the Quebec Ursulines and ran a boarding school for Amerindian and French girls, this astounding woman also found time to write not only several religious works in Aboriginal languages and in French, but also some 13 000 letters to her son and to others in France who were interested in her "New World" mission.[10]

The lives of the women who founded religious communities in the mission called Ville Marie (Montreal) were no less demanding. In one way these women were even more unusual than the nuns of Quebec, for neither of the two key figures in the Montreal context were at first members of established orders. Jeanne Mance was a single woman in her mid-thirties when she came to Canada in 1641. She first settled in Quebec, in order to study the organization of the *Hôtel-Dieu* there and to learn the Huron language; only then did she move on to Ville Marie to found its first medical dispensary. As an entrepreneur and organizer, she must have had few equals. Her efforts included three trips back to France to raise money and to search out an order of nuns to staff the new mission, and a major battle with the bishop of Quebec for the right to bring a second nursing order to New France. The hospital nuns of *Saint-Joseph de la Flèche* were installed by permission of the French king against the will of Bishop Laval, who would have preferred to send a detachment of the sisters already established in the hospital at Quebec.[11]

Laval also fought with the *Congrégation de Notre-Dame*, which was the creation of another laywoman, Marguerite Bourgeoys, who joined Paul de Chomedey de Maisonneuve's Montreal mission as an educator. She eventually felt the need for assistants in her educational work and returned to France to find like-minded women. The result was a secular community, founded in 1671, that was to become the *Congrégation*. The creation of an order of religious women who did not remain behind convent walls

Jeanne Mance (1606–1673), founder of Montreal's *Hôtel-Dieu* and one of the first European women to settle in New France.

Source: Bibliothèque et Archives nationales du Québec, Centre d'archives de Québec, P1000, S4, D83, PM28-1.

but, rather, lived and worked in the community was truly remarkable for this period. The teachers of Bourgeoys's new order came into conflict not only with the bishop of Quebec but also with the larger church and its rules because these teachers preferred not to wear distinctive habits, nor to take solemn public vows, nor to cloister themselves; they argued that their guide and teacher was none other than the Virgin Mary, who had remained in the world without benefit of formal vows or, presumably, distinctive dress. She had nevertheless fulfilled her religious destiny, and so would they.[12]

At first, religious communities shared with the fur trading monopoly—the *Compagnie des Cent-Associés*—the task of recruiting brides for French soldiers and traders wishing to settle in the "New World." It was generally the nuns who took charge of the single women who came to the colony with the intention of marrying, until these *filles à marier* found husbands. However, when royal officials assumed direct control of the colony in 1663, they became actively involved in promoting the immigration of single women. Between 1643 and 1663, only 230 unmarried female immigrants had made their way to New France; in the next decade, nearly 800 marriageable women (mostly single, but including a certain number of young widows), known as the *filles du roi* (daughters of the king), arrived. Interested parties—such as Jean Talon, the *intendant* or chief civil administrator of New France during the early years of royal government—wanted to be sure that the young women selected to enjoy the king's bounty were indeed going to be useful immigrants. Talon specified that the women destined for Canada should be in no way "disgraced by nature" or have anything "repulsive about their exterior persons." He also demanded that "they should be healthy and strong for country work, or at least that they have some inclination to work with their hands." Fears were expressed by others that women brought up in cities like Paris might not adapt well to conditions in New France. Yet they had little choice but to adapt. It has been estimated that only half of all immigrants to New France remained for the rest of their lives, but of the single women who came to be married there, nine out of ten became permanent settlers. Especially once married, women had fewer options for geographic mobility than the men of the colony.[13]

The social origins of the *filles du roi* were diverse. However, more than 30 percent were recruited from the *Hôpital-Général* in Paris, an institution that harboured women who had become pregnant out of wedlock, as well as orphans and abandoned children. Two-thirds of these immigrants had not yet attained adulthood before their fathers died and only one-third were able to sign their own names. Many were clearly young women whose parents or remaining parent could not arrange good marriages for their daughters. In fact, most of the *filles* were of humble origins, with only eight known to have been of noble birth.[14] Three sisters, Françoise, Marie-Madeleine, and Marie Raclot, not only had good dowries for the time but were accompanied to New France by their father in 1671. The latter stayed in the colony only long enough to sign the marriage contracts of two of his daughters. Aged 18, 17, and 15 when they came to New France, the Raclot sisters settled in the vicinity of Trois-Rivières with the husbands they had acquired within a few months of their arrival.[15]

Most of the *filles*, like the inmates of the *Hôpital-Général* and the Raclot sisters, came from Paris or from other relatively large towns, and many must have been ill-prepared for the new lives that awaited them in this colonial society built largely upon the fisheries, the fur trade, and agriculture. Of those whose ages were recorded, most were between 12 and 25, but a significant one of every four of these women was older. The main interest of these *filles*, once in Canada, was reportedly a practical one: to find husbands who had already built houses or cabins on their land. A full 40 percent married within just two months of their arrival, and the fact that some 11 percent entered into more than one marriage contract before going through with the final religious ceremony suggests not only a healthy respect for their own self-interest, but a willingness to take advantage of their major trump card: the scarcity of unmarried European women in New France. The women were promised substantial dowries by the king, according to their station, to assist them and their husbands in setting up their households; no doubt these dowries added to their considerable bargaining power. One source values the "king's gift" at between 100 and 500 *livres* (French currency), with further disbursements for practical items that would be needed either immediately in the way of clothing or equipment (including 100 sewing needles) or, later, in the way of household goods. The Raclot sisters, for example, received gifts from the king in addition to the dowry of 1000 *livres* each was given by her father. It appears, however, that the sisters were part of a fortunate minority since only one-third of the women actually received the promised dowry amounts.[16]

Between 1663 and 1673, at least 770 *filles du roi* came to New France to join the approximately 1200 men and women colonists who had arrived earlier. In Montreal, by 1681, more than two-thirds of the 161 women immigrants were *filles seules*—women who were neither nuns nor servants and yet had come to the colony alone.[17] After the special push of the 1660s and 1670s and until the 1750s, the French colonies welcomed an average of fewer than 50 new arrivals a year; and fewer than one in five of these were women. Altogether, immigrants numbered fewer than 10 000 for the entire French regime. In the eighteenth-century trading and military fortress of Louisbourg, where the immigrants came mostly from the bourgeois and artisan classes, women were never more than one-tenth of the immigrants or one-third of the total population. In New France as a whole, women were also very much a minority at first. But by 1760, the nearly 70 000 people who made up the total European population of New France were almost equally divided between men and women.[18] The key role played by the natural increase in population highlights the central importance of reproduction, and thus of women, in the young colony.

MARRIAGE AND FAMILY

Most of the women who came to New France married. As in comparable English colonies of the period, the rates of marriage and remarriage were very high. The story of Anne Le Sont of Trois-Rivières, while perhaps atypical, is nevertheless instructive. The employer of this middle-aged *engagée* had prevailed upon her to sign a life contract in November 1655, and took her to court when she married Jean Desmarais soon after her arrival. The affair was settled in Anne's favour but only after she issued a suitable apology for her "insulting words" and on payment of the plaintiff's costs. Perhaps more typical was the case of the young *engagée* Judithe Rigeault, who, when she married a soldier and master tailor named François le Maître, still owed a portion of the five years she had contracted to serve Madame Le Neuf de la Poterie. Once again a court case ensued, and once again the financial obligations of both parties had to be worked out before a settlement could be reached.[19]

Anne Le Sont was much older than the average bride when she married, but this might not have been her first marriage. In general, servants who came out to New France on their own appear to have married in their early twenties.[20] But even this was older than average for girls who were born in the colony in the seventeenth century, for at first the average age at which women married in New France was very low compared to typical marriages in western Europe at this time. Young people were not supposed to marry until puberty, but there is evidence that occasionally girls as young as 12 and 13 embarked on matrimony during the initial period of colonization, when European men vastly outnumbered European women. Estimates of average age at first marriage have varied depending on the period or region studied. For rural families before 1700, the average was 19.6 for women and 27.3 for men. A different pattern has been uncovered for mid-eighteenth-century Sorel, however. By this time, the numbers of European men and women had almost evened out; indeed, the average age at first marriage was 22.4 for women and 26.6 for men. For New France as a whole, the average age for those contracting marriage for the first time has been placed at 22 for women (three years younger than was typical in France itself) and 27 for men. And relatively large groups of people delayed marriage: some 18 percent of men and women did not marry until they were 30 or older; 6 percent were 40 or older.[21]

However, the royal administration gave explicit encouragement to early marriages in New France. A seventeenth-century statute provided that men marrying at 25 or younger and women marrying by 20 were entitled to a bonus of 20 *livres* from the Crown; a further law imposed fines on the parents of young people who failed to marry by the required age. Colonial authorities publicly complained about young men becoming *coureurs du bois* or fur traders rather than settling down, and also discouraged persons of either sex remaining celibate. The married state was officially encouraged for both sexes, as was the production of children. Religious authorities also cooperated: in the case of the *filles du roi*, for instance, the Church dispensed with the requirement that banns be published before a marriage could be celebrated.[22] Certainly, the state's fundamental goal in sponsoring female immigration and rewarding early marriage was to promote population growth. If New France was to survive and prosper, increasing the population was considered a vital necessity for obtaining the workers and soldiers essential to mercantilist economies. And for individual couples, having children was equated with wealth: children were workers, first and foremost for their own families.

For much of the seventeenth century, economic factors and the unequal numbers of European men and women probably had the most effect on age at marriage and the high rates of marriage and remarriage. They even affected the season of marriage, which, before 1680, was typically early autumn, following the arrival of the ships from France and the harvest. Later on, when the sexes were more equal in number, January and early February became the most popular season for weddings, although October and November were frequent choices as well.

The relatively young age at which women in New France married and the high rates of remarriage almost certainly helped boost the average number of children per marriage, as did the fact that spouses lived slightly longer than they did in Europe. In eighteenth-century Acadia, for example, four out of five marriages were "complete" in the sense that both spouses survived to the end of the wife's childbearing years. And although infant mortality was high in New France—approximately one in four children died before reaching his or her first birthday—surviving children were probably healthier than those in the Old World. So, too, were adults. For all these reasons, it is not surprising that women in Canada gave birth to eight or nine children on average in the early years (and then seven on average from 1700 on), and that, taking into account children lost to illness or accidents, the average completed family was 5.65 children per couple (compared to 4.5 in France at this time). Studies indicate that relatively large families were characteristic of other European colonists in North America in the seventeenth and eighteenth centuries because good food was generally available and European diseases not so rampant, at least among white populations. Still, the numbers of children born and surviving seem to have been particularly high in New France.[23]

Were these marriages happy? While historians have few ways of peering into seventeenth- and eighteenth-century relationships between men and women, evidence exists that some women in New France were prepared to seek a way out of intolerable marital situations. The *Coutume de Paris*, New France's civil law, provided for the option of legal separation with respect to property or with respect to property and bed and board. Legal separation did not nullify the marriage; nor did it allow the separated spouses to remarry. It did, however, permit the spouses to cease living together. Historians have found that it was much more common for women than for men to request a legal separation and that requests for separation often came from women of the urban upper and middle classes. Women requesting legal separations justified their initiative by pointing to the alcoholism or irresponsibility of their spouse, or to their physical or emotional mistreatment at his hands. Separations were very difficult to obtain; and when they were granted, the separated woman often found herself in a precarious financial state. That some women requested such separations, regardless, hints at the degree of unhappiness of some marriages in New France.[24]

Childbirth in New France was a major social event. Women gave birth at home, assisted by midwives, and often in the presence of a large group of people—certainly with relatives and perhaps the priest very close at hand. The event frequently took place at the home of the new mother's parents, and birth was accompanied by important rituals: the baptism, which took place as soon as possible after the birth, and a *repas de baptême*, a festive meal to repay and thank the assistants. A new mother might have women friends stay for a week to help after her child was born; she would also usually have her own mother's assistance for at least a month.[25]

In the colony, the seasons influenced the rhythms of childbirth. Historians have discovered that conception tended to occur in the winter and spring, and that there were slight differences between Montreal and Quebec in this seasonal timing. The church had an influence as well: there were fewer conceptions during the seasons of Advent and Lent, when the population was expected to focus on religious duties and to refrain from the pleasures of the body.[26]

Unfortunately, childbirth was dangerous, and the maternal mortality rate was significant; the death rate for women aged 15 to 49 years was higher than that for men in the same age classification. When the mother did survive childbirth, and if her marriage was unbroken by the death of her husband, she was likely to have a child every two to three years. Prolonged breastfeeding did reduce the likelihood of more frequent conceptions, but one social group deviated from this trend—the nobility. By the eighteenth century, noblewomen in Canada were sending 60 to 70 percent of their newborns to a wet nurse, and consequently they experienced shorter intervals between births. The infant mortality rate for the nobility also climbed dramatically as a result of this practice, so that while 73 percent of noble infants survived to 20 years and beyond in the seventeenth century, less than 40 percent of those born between 1735 and 1765 did so.[27]

If women faced the real possibility of death in childbirth, men ran the risk of dying from work-related accidents. Widowhood was thus a life stage known by many—perhaps most—women, at least for a time. Under the *Coutume de Paris*, widows gained full legal capacity, providing them with a measure of legal autonomy unknown to married women in New France. Yet we should be careful not to assume that this sudden acquisition of legal capacity was always perceived to be a new-found "liberty." To many widows, particularly those who had not participated in the affairs of property and capital while their husbands were alive, it might have seemed a burden greater than they could shoulder. Even for those women unfazed by the intricacies of their new legal capacity, their male relatives, including, occasionally, their own sons, challenged, and sometimes limited, their new legal freedom. Moreover, upon the death of their husband, widows also lost the family's principal breadwinner. Yet, while young children could seem an overwhelming responsibility to women newly widowed, older children might constitute a source of support, both emotional and material. Furthermore, widows frequently relied upon extended kin—mothers, daughters, nieces, sons, sons-in-law, and nephews—for practical aid. Marie-Catherine Peuvret, the *seigneuresse* of Beauport, was widowed in 1715 at the age of 48 upon the death of her husband, Ignace Juchereau Duchesnay. Peuvret had given birth to 17 children; at the time of her husband's death, 11 of them had survived, ranging in age from 2 to 31. Peuvret, known thereafter as "the widow Duchesnay," never remarried, and she alone assumed the management of her substantial properties and financial assets. Evidence exists, however, that until her death in 1739, Peuvret had to wage a constant battle against neighbouring seigneurs and other local leaders, as well as against various male relatives belonging to her own elite family or to that of her deceased husband, all of whom wished to have a say in how Peuvret managed her affairs.[28]

In a society where both men and women were often widowed much younger than today, remarriage was a common phenomenon although, as in other pre-industrial societies, widowers remarried more frequently than did widows. The study of one cohort of widows and widowers in the city of Quebec between 1710 and 1744 demonstrates that while 42 percent of the widows remarried, 68 percent of the widowers did so. Age at widowhood was a major determinant of the likelihood of remarriage: while a full 80 percent of women widowed under the age of 30 remarried, only 59 percent of women widowed in their thirties did so. This percentage dropped to 42 percent for women, like Peuvret, widowed in their forties, while not one woman in the cohort who was over the age of 50 when she was widowed remarried. By contrast, almost 90 percent of men widowed in their twenties and thirties remarried; 80 percent of men widowed in their forties remarried; and among men who were over the age of 50 when they lost their spouse, almost one in four remarried despite their advancing years.[29]

WORK

Marriage and, especially, children meant work for women, since the labour of childbirth and child-rearing was particularly hard in the difficult pioneer conditions in both town and country in New France. Yet, as they grew up, many children could eventually lighten a woman's workload. Older children, for example, minded younger ones, and, when they were old enough, girls helped with all the tasks of the household, garden, farm, or workshop that fell to women. These tasks were many and of significant value; few households, farms, or businesses could run without the work of women.

Women spent much of their time on the production of food. Soups, stews, roasts, and bread were standard fare and were cooked mostly in open fireplaces. Rural women probably laboured as much at the outdoor tasks involved in food production as they did at the work of preparing the food for the table, including butchering, curing, and drying meat; performing the various tasks of the dairy and the poultry yard; and growing vegetables and fruit. In the Lower Richelieu valley by the eighteenth century, women typically grew squash, onions, cabbages, and tobacco in their gardens. Travellers in Acadia commented on the large variety of vegetables that were grown, including "cabbages, beets, onions, carrots, chives, shallots, turnips, and all sorts of salads." Even urban women kept cows and poultry and had vegetable gardens when they could, although most produce and grains were generally purchased from the surrounding countryside.[30]

Women in New France also shared in the work of their husbands. At certain busy times of the year, farm women worked in the fields; artisans' and merchants' wives were frequently skilled assistants to their spouses. Both rural and urban women often kept the accounts and managed the servants or apprentices, if there were any. Owing to the periodic absences of their husbands, soldiers' and traders' wives sometimes had to take complete charge of their households, farms, and businesses. Existing notarial records clearly indicate the extensive responsibilities and legal powers that these women assumed in such situations.[31] Women also occasionally found that the fur trade or the wars or both had arrived on their very doorsteps. The famous 14-year-old Madeleine de Verchères was only one of many women who fired a gun, or took over when men were absent, in skirmishes with enemies. Indeed, Madeleine's own mother had defended the fort at Verchères from Iroquois attack in 1690, two years before her daughter was called upon to do so. In subsequent centuries, Madeleine de Verchères would become a symbol of the fortitude and valour of New France's European women, defending the young colony against attacks from without.[32] Likewise, in the early days of Acadia, Françoise-Marie Jacquelin de la Tour spent a good part of the first four years of her marriage travelling back and forth between France, New England, and her husband's fort at the mouth of the St. John River, working to defend his precarious position in the Acadian trade. Finally settled in Fort La Tour during one of his absences, she not only took charge of its defence but was forced to witness the execution of nearly all of its men after its capture. Madame de la Tour herself did not survive this defeat by many weeks; she died at Fort La Tour in 1645.[33]

Although not all came to grief in such a traumatic way, most seventeenth-century women of New France probably experienced warfare first-hand. The early eighteenth century brought somewhat more peaceful times as the colonists faced fewer conflicts with the Iroquois, but by the mid-eighteenth century a series of European wars affected the young colony. The most recent historical scholarship on this period calls into question the long-held belief that the people of New France were a fierce "warrior people," imbued with a military ethos. Nonetheless, it is clear that the military establishment was essential to the colony's economy (second only to the fur trade, perhaps, in importance) as well as to its social and political structures. The administration of the colony was organized along military lines. Military commissions had a positive impact on social status, and helped to link the elite of New France to governing structures in France. Military troops from France constituted an important part of the colony's population and infused a considerable amount of money into the local economy. All men between the ages of 16 and 60 were, after 1669, organized into militia units, and militia captains played a key role in local governance. One might well ask whether such a militarized, and thus masculine, environment left women much political and social room to maneuver. What is certain is that wars and military skirmishes, involving both Aboriginal peoples and European powers, were frequent: as one historian has written, with the exception of the years between 1666 and 1684, "war was the norm in New France."[34] This recurrent military activity took men away from their homes and left women responsible both for their own domestic labour and, often, the agricultural labour of their sons and husbands. For some women, it also meant the permanent loss of a husband, a brother, or a son. Both European and Aboriginal women were affected by the periodic absence of the men of their families that war entailed. But Iroquois women often accompanied military expeditions, such as those integral to the Seven Years' War, during which they carried out necessary domestic tasks and even, occasionally, participated in active warfare.[35]

The eighteenth century brought economic development. In seventeenth-century Canada, few if any women had the time or the facilities for spinning or weaving. Except for Aboriginal-style clothing made of leather, most apparel and fabrics for bedding and the like had to be imported, and early wills suggest how few clothes even the most prosperous colonists possessed. Despite the scarcity of local materials, clerics and upper-class visitors to the colony commented on women's "idleness," and they urged the authorities to establish a textile industry. The women themselves maintained that more pressing work took up their time. But in the eighteenth century, women did begin to be involved in the production of spun and woven goods. Acadian women learned many crafts from their Micmac neighbours: birchbark household utensils and leather moccasins were only a few of the items they adopted as their own. Yet it is important to stress how few farms or communities in North America were entirely self-sufficient. Goods like needles, metal pots, and farm tools had to be imported, as did fancier items, such as silk fabrics and dress shoes. The movement of both goods and people was considerable in New France.[36]

FEMMES FAVORISÉES? WOMEN'S OPTIONS

The status of women in New France has been the subject of vigorous debate among historians. Some have suggested that the colony's women were *femmes favorisées*, that is, women who enjoyed a favourable position compared both to their counterparts in Europe at the time and to North American women in subsequent historical eras.[37] Other historians have disputed this claim, arguing that much-celebrated "founding mothers," such as Jeanne Mance, Marie de l'Incarnation, and Marguerite Bourgeoys, were exceptional, and that most European women in New France were subject to constraints similar to those imposed upon women elsewhere in the world. These historians argue that the church, the state, the law, morals, and social customs were all shaped by patriarchy and affected areas of women's lives ranging from family to work.[38] Moreover, non-European women—Aboriginals, or African slaves, for instance—faced an even more imposing number of restrictions. In order to ascertain the status of women in New France, it is essential to understand their position in the social, legal, and political systems in place, as well as the possibilities open to them in the world of work.

Like the society of France, that of New France was hierarchical, and stratified both by gender and class. A woman's social position was determined first by that of her father, and subsequently by that of her husband. Individual privileges were determined by one's social ranking (*ordre*); and family and group interests, not individual rights, were paramount. Because New France was fashioned according to the absolutist principles of the seventeenth-century French monarchy, there were no representative institutions or democratic forms of government in the colony. The small group of women who reached the age of majority—set at 25 years—without marrying were deemed to have the same legal status as men in all but one respect: they could not be appointed to public office. As in France, the law was harsh in some respects, but it did provide a measure of protection to married women. Women of the upper and middle classes were sometimes able to play influential (albeit seldom official) roles in trade, political life, and medicine. Finally, the missionary church provided opportunities for religious women, especially those in leadership roles, to organize their own lives.

The women of New France did appear to have enjoyed relative freedom of choice in marriage. Among rural women in particular, there appears to have been little interference from either parents or clergy in the selection of a partner, although the church was anxious to prevent the marriage of people who were too closely related, and parental permission was officially required.[39] Moreover, historians have pointed out the importance of informal community control in eighteenth-century rural Quebec: the behaviour of individuals was subject to the scrutiny and condemnation of the parish priest, but also to that of neighbours.[40] There may have been less freedom of choice among social elites, where parents exerted considerable pressure on their sons to choose mates who would bring wealth into the family in the form of a dowry and, later, an inheritance. Because New France was a patriarchal, patrilineal society, a wife adopted her husband's social position: the daughter of a noble family who married a commoner lost her noble status, as did her children, while the daughter of a commoner who married a nobleman became a member of the nobility, and her children were also considered noble.[41]

All marriages were subject to the rules laid down in the *Coutume de Paris*. Under this law, married women had a status inferior to that of their husbands and were "severely restricted in their rights and prerogatives." The law clearly regarded the man as the head of the household. Widows sometimes could not even exercise guardianship over their own children. But the same law did afford some important economic protection both to married women and to widows. Spouses were seen to have mutual obligations toward each other. The community of property that came into being at a marriage imposed some legal restrictions on the husband: whatever property his wife brought into the marriage, he was to administer with care, and he could not dispose of it without his wife's permission. Furthermore, he was to use whatever property the couple acquired after marriage to support his wife and children: indeed, any property acquired after marriage belonged equally to both spouses. On the death of her husband, the widow could choose to continue the community of property or, if the debts exceeded the assets, to renounce it and with it any accumulated debt. By virtue of her dower rights, the widow was entitled to receive half the income generated by the communal property until her own death.[42]

Because of the complexity of the laws governing matrimony, it is not surprising that a significant proportion of marriages—indeed, as many as 95 percent in some regions of France—involved written contracts. Studies of seventeenth-century Canadian marriages indicate that about 65 percent of marriage partners drew up such contracts, while by the eighteenth century, approximately 80 percent did so.[43] Often signed by dozens of witnesses, these contracts also provide a fascinating glimpse of the social networks surrounding brides and grooms, as well as evidence of their social standing in their communities. Although unions among the wealthier classes were arranged with economic or political interests in mind, they nevertheless crossed boundaries between the landed aristocracy, the merchant class, and the military.[44]

Considerable information also survives regarding the pensions of older women and widows. If a woman chose to give up her farm or her household to a son or daughter (or to another person) in return for her subsistence, the *pension alimentaire* usually contained very specific provisions. The widow Thibeault, who lived in the Richelieu valley in 1760, was to be provided with heat, light, clothing, and houseroom, according to the arrangement she made with her family. Her annual allotment of food included 16 *minots* (bushels) of flour, 1/4 *minot* of salt, and 120 pounds of salt pork. Another widow's pension specified that she should be provided with two pairs of French shoes every year.[45] It is hard to know how to interpret these documents. Did such arrangements mean security and comfort for aging widows? Or were they last-ditch attempts to defend women against relatives whose goodwill could not be counted on? Whatever the answer, at least the notarized pensions of New France did provide a modicum of support to women who otherwise might have had none.

Changing inheritance practices were also important determinants of the status of girls and women in seventeenth- and eighteenth-century New France. The *Coutume de Paris* allowed for family land to be divided equally among the heirs: girls as well as boys. From around 1740 onward, however, the system of equal division was increasingly replaced by the practice of *donation*, or the deeding of the land to one sole heir, with that fortunate heir having to compensate the other heirs (usually siblings) in the form of money or household goods. Daughters appear to have been the chief losers in this transition: usually deprived of their share of the family land, they were compensated in cash, tools, or other goods but often had to wait years for this compensation. If and when they were compensated in cash, the money was likely to be invested in their spouse's land.[46]

Some women played a significant role in the commercial life of New France. Relatively ordinary women operated taverns and illegal as well as legal trading operations. A few exceptional women appear to have been extraordinarily successful. The introduction of the textile industry to early eighteenth-century Canada is, in fact, credited to Agathe de Saint-Père, Madame de Repentigny, of Montreal. Left to manage a family of 10 stepsisters and stepbrothers after the death of her mother, Agathe de Saint-Père married Legardeur de Repentigny in 1685 and produced 8 children of her own. Children evidently did not take up all her time, however, for Agathe de Saint-Père was heavily involved in the buying and selling of contracts, fur trade licences, and land. Soon Madame de Repentigny was also experimenting with textiles because of continuing shortages in the colony. At first she worked with indigenous fibres, such as bark, cottonweed, and buffalo hair; by 1705, her productions had already caught the king's attention. But it was the sinking of a supply vessel that was the catalyst for her most daring experiment. Madame de Repentigny ransomed nine English weavers who were being held captive by the Aboriginal allies of the French, had looms manufactured, engaged apprentices to learn the craft, and turned her home into a workshop to make "linen, drugget, twilled and covert-coating serge." Soon there were more than 20 looms in Montreal, and an independent manufactory had been created.[47]

Marie-Anne Barbel is another woman known to have been active in the commercial world of New France. At first Barbel must have been much taken up with childbirth and child-rearing: she had 14 children altogether, although only 5 survived to adulthood. But she must also have been actively involved in the business affairs connected with the shop that her husband, Jean-Louis Fornel, ran in Quebec between 1723 and 1737. In the late 1730s, Fornel became increasingly involved in entrepreneurial activity and exploration. When he departed in 1743 on a major expedition to explore the Baie des Esquimaux, Fornel left his Quebec business affairs in the hands of his wife. When her husband died two years later, Marie-Anne Barbel did not dissolve the community of property established at her marriage. Instead, she took sole charge. She continued a business partnership with two other entrepreneurs in a fishing concession, fought lawsuits with the government in connection with that concession and another, and traded for furs in Tadoussac. She also bought and sold properties, quarrelled with the Jesuits over a piece of land, and established a brickworks. Not all of Barbel's undertakings, however, were successful. The widow Fornel managed to establish only two of her five children in marriages (one of which failed), and she was not among the top-ranking "notables" of New France. On the other hand, this enterprising businesswoman was able to pay off all her debts, and she supported herself, three unmarried children, and the fourth daughter (who had separated from her husband and returned to the family) in relative comfort until her death at age 90.[48]

Other cases have been recorded of widows who were actively involved in the commercial life of New France; perhaps it was this possibility of exercising some autonomy over their own affairs that led upper-class widows, particularly those over the age of 30, to remarry less often and after a longer interval than widowers of the same class. Or perhaps, as we have seen, so-called older widows—especially those over the age of 40, who were more likely to have dependent children—were simply less attractive than younger women to men seeking mates and children of their own.[49]

Women were not allowed to hold any public office in New France other than that of midwife. However, as wives and mistresses, or through other relationships, a few women did exert some political influence. Marie-Madeleine Maisonnat, an Acadian woman married to a British officer in Port Royal after its transfer to the British Crown in 1713, was said to have had influence in military circles there, which she used to help her fellow Acadians. And in eighteenth-century Canada, as the French regime was drawing to a close, at least two important government officials were thought to have been under the sway of women. Madame Péan was reputedly the mistress of the powerful *intendant* François Bigot, attracting him to her salon every evening and thereby becoming the envy of the entire capital. In another example, the wife of Governor Vaudreuil became so influential at a certain point that petitioners began to go directly to her rather than to the governor.[50]

Women of humbler backgrounds occasionally participated in protest that we might consider political. In 1714, when Monseigneur de Saint-Vallier attempted to redraw parish boundaries near Saint-Léonard, outside Montreal, the local population protested vigorously. The officer sent by the bishop to look into the protests "was attacked by a crowd of women, who threatened to kill him and throw his body into the swamp."[51] Some years later, in the difficult period just before the fall of Quebec in 1759, women were involved in public demonstrations protesting the food shortages caused by the war with England. The first of these protests occurred in December 1757. Governor Vaudreuil, away from Quebec on business in Montreal, had just ended the distribution of bread, substituting a ration of horsemeat and beef that was to be available at a reduced price. A group of women made their way to the governor's Montreal residence, demanding bread and expressing their repugnance at the idea of eating horsemeat. Vaudreuil responded by arranging for the women to be taken on a tour of the butchery in order to assure them that all was in order, but also by threatening to throw the women in jail and to hang half of them if they rioted again. Although the ringleaders were to have been arrested, none were, probably because the authorities were more concerned about restive soldiers. In Quebec the following April, continuing food shortages again brought women out into the streets, this time to call on the lieutenant-general of the police. The arrival of ships evidently alleviated the misery for a time; by the winter of 1758–59, however, rumours of further rationing of bread produced a final protest. On this occasion, some 400 women marched to the palace of the *intendant*, demanding redress. Their protest was successful. Wheat was brought to Quebec from Lachine, and the *intendant* promised an increase in the bread ration.[52]

We do not know whether women participated in the more formally constituted popular assemblies that were occasionally held at the local community level in New France. But their participation in the protest of 1714 and in the food riots of the 1750s is significant. When their own interests were at stake—the borders of their parish, food for their households—they did not hesitate to take to the streets in an effort to force the hand of both church and state. By doing so, they were following a long tradition of women's street demonstrations, in France and elsewhere.

Women also played a vital role in medicine in the colony. Experienced older lay-women were often the leading healers of their communities, and acted as midwives at births. The midwife especially was an important community figure, whose office—sometimes an elective one—was strongly supported and, as time went on, to some extent controlled by the church. By the early 1700s, each territory had an official midwife; by the middle of the century, four midwives in New France were being paid salaries by the French state. Midwives' knowledge was passed on from generation to generation, often, although not always, from mothers to daughters or to daughters-in-law. The women who performed this role were by no means impoverished or unskilled. On the contrary, most were educated and respected members of their communities, with above-average wealth.[53]

As nuns, women were actively involved in both the religious life and the secular life of the colony. While the most important male religious orders—the Jesuits and the Sulpicians—remained closed to individuals born in New France, the women's religious orders actively recruited within the local population: by 1690, the majority of nuns were Canadian-born. Interestingly, nearly one out of every five noblewomen who reached age 15 became a nun, compared to just under 4 percent of all *Canadiennes* born before 1739. Convent life was particularly attractive for educated women because it allowed them to exercise their administrative skills, and their work affected a great many people. Quebec's *Hôtel-Dieu*, for example, admitted some 3297 men and 1765 women in the decade between 1689 and 1698 alone. Men probably predominated because they were more susceptible to accidents and military injury, while both sexes suffered from seasonal sickness and from epidemics. Patients of both sexes were usually young, and the hospital's death rate was low. Indeed, by all accounts Quebec's *Hôtel-Dieu* was a far more pleasant place than European hospitals of the same era, or than North American hospitals were later to become.[54]

A study of the financial dealings of the sisters who ran the *Hôpital-Général*, a Quebec almshouse founded in 1701, regarding some property left to the nuns by a

An ex-voto (offering made as a token of gratitude or devotion) to Sainte Anne, depicting Madame Riverin and her children, 1703.

Source: Courtesy of Musée de Sainte Anne

generous bishop, shows a group of women deeply aware of their economic interests and prepared to defend them. The battle over the bishop's property lasted 15 years and did not, in the end, result in a settlement very favourable to the convent. On the other hand, the nuns followed the complexities of the case (a good part of which were unravelled in France) assiduously; they refused to act hastily and defended themselves from accepting financial burdens that might have been insurmountable. They saw their battle, moreover, as a fight for justice and for the rights that were due them. Their efforts show that although they were cloistered, these women had frequent contacts with the outside world and were much involved in the property struggles that were so characteristic of their times.[55]

Financial problems were endemic to all religious orders throughout the history of New France. Convent women made extraordinary efforts to raise money for their communities, however, and some had notable success. Their leaders made frequent fundraising journeys to France. Often, the women themselves secured the loans or gifts; often, they were also the ones who gave. Nuns also supported themselves through extra work. In Louisbourg, for example, the teaching sisters made bedding and straw mattresses for the barracks in order to earn much-needed cash; elsewhere, the nuns sold embroidery or raised funds through other crafts.[56]

Not only were convent women involved in managing their communities, they also engaged in the intellectual and spiritual currents of their times. Mère Sainte-Hélène of Quebec's *Hôtel-Dieu* corresponded with physicians in France who were willing to send her medical supplies and who were also interested in the medicinal herbs and remedies discovered in New France. Marie Morin is considered to be the first writer born in Canada. Her *annales* of Montreal's *Hôtel-Dieu* are an absorbing account of the nuns' struggles for daily survival in the face of poverty and natural disasters, such as fires, and of the early years not only of the convent but also of Montreal.[57]

Not all women in New France enjoyed the privileges of female members of religious orders. Many women in New France, as elsewhere, were poor. Some were the victims of abuse. Marie Boucher, who applied for a legal separation with respect to bed and board and with respect to property from her husband, Nicolas Vernet, claimed that he physically mistreated her; witnesses testified that Boucher had to leave her house at night in order to escape his beatings.[58] In the *annales* of Louisbourg's *Congrégation de Notre-Dame*, we read of a woman and her children who were taken in by the sisters because she had been repeatedly beaten by her husband. In another instance, the parishioners of St-Esprit on Cape Breton Island petitioned the colonial authorities to imprison and then deport a man who regularly beat his wife and children. They appear to have dispensed their own rough justice by giving him a sound thrashing before turning him over to the authorities. However, far too many abused wives were left to their own devices; tragically, some were murdered by their husbands.[59] Domestic servants were frequently subjected to the sexual advances of the male members of the household in which they were engaged. If they became pregnant, they were likely to lose their employment; in a desperate effort to avoid detection, some resorted to abortion, infanticide, or abandoning their newborn.[60]

There were also slaves in New France, although they constituted a very small proportion of the total population: one historian has identified just over 3600 slaves in French

Canada between the late seventeenth century and the early nineteenth century. In New France, slavery was a primarily urban phenomenon, particularly present in Montreal, Louisbourg, and, to a lesser extent, in Quebec and Trois-Rivières. Slaves could be found in the possession of merchants, colonial officials, military officers, and religious authorities, such as bishops. In Louisbourg, a port town integrated into the Atlantic trade network, over 90 percent of the slaves were Black—some from the French West Indies, some from French West Africa. In the St. Lawrence Valley, by contrast, the majority of slaves were Aboriginal, particularly before the British Conquest of 1760, although a significant minority were of African descent. In Louisbourg, slaves, both men and women, worked as household servants. The women among them cleaned, cooked, and cared for children. In the St. Lawrence Valley, Aboriginal slaves worked in domestic service, in agriculture, and in the fur trade. Men (particularly young men and boys) initially predominated among the Aboriginal slaves owned by French colonists, but over the course of the eighteenth century this tendency was reversed and women increasingly constituted the majority of Aboriginal slaves.[61]

One female slave who has attracted a great deal of attention from historians of New France is Marie-Josèphe-Angélique. In 1734, Montreal slave Angélique, born in Portugal of African descent, was accused of setting fire to her owner's house after her owner, Madame Thérèse de Couagne, the widow Francheville, had threatened to sell her. The fire had spread, destroying the *Hôtel-Dieu* hospital and 45 houses near the rue Saint-Paul in fewer than three hours. Angélique, a young woman then in her twenties, was apprehended, tried, tortured, and finally condemned and publicly hanged before the ruins of the houses destroyed by the fire. Her dead body was then burned, and her ashes scattered in the wind. There is no consensus among historians as to whether or not Angélique was guilty. Some argue that she probably did set fire to Thérèse de Couagne's house, and thus view her story as a tale of slave resistance to cruel and arbitrary treatment. Other historians suggest that Angélique was innocent, that the fire was accidental, and that the guilty verdict reflected the racism and sexism of the judicial system and of eighteenth-century society.[62] Further evidence of the exploitation of Aboriginal and African slaves is suggested by the story of Marie-Louise, an African slave in Louisbourg who gave birth to seven illegitimate children during the 18 years she was owned by a local merchant.[63]

It is clearly impossible to speak about the women of New France as a single, undifferentiated entity or to generalize about their position in society. Some female members of religious orders and a few extraordinary businesswomen evidently had more opportunities than others to develop their skills, to communicate in the world, and to achieve their goals. But like women of humbler circumstance (of French, Aboriginal, and African background), they lived in a society that imposed legal, social, and moral restrictions upon women. Recent work by historians has scrutinized the factors once thought to have "favoured" women in New France and found many of them to be illusory. The supposed demographic advantage enjoyed by European women in the colony (that is, their relative scarcity) was short-lived and varied by region; the advantages enjoyed by nuns did not significantly alter the status of laywomen; and husbands' ability to delegate legal authority to their wives in their own absence does not appear to have been exploited more often in New France than elsewhere.[64]

EDUCATION

Originally, the educational mission of the French religious women who came to North America was to both teach and convert the Aboriginal children. Marie de l'Incarnation of the Ursulines learned two Aboriginal languages and translated religious tracts for the use of her pupils and their families, but the results were disappointing. Her students resisted acculturation to a way of life that seemed unnatural and alien to them. Some Aboriginal girls were assimilated to the extent of marrying French men, but few were willing to stay in the Quebec convent for more than a very short time. Gradually, the Ursulines modified their ambitions, turning their attention to the French-Canadian girls growing up in the colony. As in France, the order developed boarding schools chiefly for the daughters of the well-to-do, combining them with day schools for poorer children. By the time of the British Conquest, there were two Ursuline schools, one in Quebec and a second in Trois-Rivières. The convent in Quebec usually had about 12 boarders at any given time. Since most children attended school for only a year or so, one can argue that the brief but all-enveloping education provided by the sisters influenced more girls than would at first seem likely from such a small number. Indeed, there is reason to believe that, if we include the day school, nearly all the girls who lived in Quebec came at least for a time to the Ursulines to be taught.[65]

The other great teaching order of New France was the *Congrégation de Notre-Dame*, founded by Marguerite Bourgeoys in Montreal. The *Congrégation* focused all its attention at first on the creation of schools for the female children of the poor. The order expanded more rapidly than the Ursulines, founding schools in at least 12 different missions, although not all of them survived. By 1760, the *Congrégation de Notre-Dame* could count a total of 70 sisters in its various convents in New France—twice the number of any other order.[66] Other religious orders also founded schools for girls, but none achieved the reputation in education of either the *Congrégation* or the Ursulines during the French regime. That reputation was based on their success in preparing girls for their First Communion (a preparation that involved learning to read and write and to recite an appropriate catechism) and in teaching girls domestic arts (or, as Marie de l'Incarnation put it, "all sorts of work proper to their sex").[67]

The convent schools of New France in the seventeenth and eighteenth centuries shared with all schools of their time a growing emphasis on regularity and discipline. Because the schools were small and because pupils stayed for relatively short periods, there was perhaps little of the regimentation and rigidity we associate with educational institutions today. Yet the nuns themselves espoused the regular life, and days in school were ordered by the ringing of bells. French nuns, Marie de l'Incarnation included, sometimes found their French-Canadian pupils almost as undisciplined as the Aboriginal ones, and the taming of this wild spirit became a major goal of their schooling. Proper manners and the ability to hold a conversation were both intended results of convent instruction, particularly for Ursuline boarders. The gracious and lively manners of urban *Canadiennes* noted by eighteenth-century travellers may have owed something to this training.

Girls in rural areas, unless their parents could afford to send them to board at a convent school, were less likely to have such an intense training in the social graces, and even Montreal girls were said to be less sophisticated than their Quebec counterparts. Yet rural women were not without formal schooling. In the villages, institutions known as *petites écoles* were run at first by the missionaries and later by parish priests or by lay male teachers under the priests' direction. We can deduce that girls attended such schools, as the 1727 ordinance issued by the bishop of Quebec proclaimed that unmarried lay teachers should not teach members of the opposite sex. As in the convents, girls in the *petites écoles* were taught to read, to recite their catechism, and possibly to write. That these schools were not always conducted according to the ideal is suggested by the promulgation of regulations concerning them. In addition to the rule regarding unmarried lay teachers, there were rules instructing priests to make sure that teachers were moral individuals, to supervise what went on in the schools, and to make sure that parents sent their children. There were at least 29 schools of this type by the end of the French regime, a number that may seem very small for a total population of nearly 70 000; but when we recall that most children attended only briefly in order to prepare for First Communion, it is possible that this schooling also reached a substantial number of girls—at least among those who lived in a region that had such a school.[68]

The people who came to New France were, on average, more likely to be able to read and write than those who remained in France—probably because so many came from urban centres. There was initially some falling off in literacy in the North American colony; a study of seventeenth-century Canadian parish registers suggests that there were many people, both male and female, who did not learn to read or write in the early years. But eighteenth-century parish registers from Louisbourg and Trois-Rivières indicate that more than half the brides married in these communities could sign their names.[69] Although the formal schooling of most women was brief and oriented to religion and domestic learning, some women enjoyed a measure of literary culture in New France; a few may even have been considered learned. Religious women like Sister Morin and Sister Cuillerier, Morin's successor in writing the *annales* of Montreal's *Hôtel-Dieu*, perhaps had special opportunities—and a special need—for literary culture. But upper-class laywomen were not all that far behind. Elisabeth Bégon, the wife of an eighteenth-century Trois-Rivières governor, had enough leisure to write at considerable length of the salons that fashionable women attended and of the dances they held; she also wrote about the condition of the St. Lawrence River as the seasons changed, and about her grandchildren. A single letter by Marie-Angélique Hamel regarding the marriage of her son has been preserved; it suggests that some women of humbler circumstance put pen to paper when the occasion required it.[70]

For girls who did not attend school or acquire a literary training, service was probably the dominant form of education. Girls who were put into service were sometimes bound out as young as age four; their contracts specified that they would stay with their master or mistress until they were married or otherwise provided for. The contracts also specified, somewhat vaguely, that the arrangement was for their well-being and *bon avancement*. A study of the contracts of domestics suggests, in fact, that binding girls into service was a way of providing for them when a natural parent was unable to do so. Formal instruction was a major part of a contract only when it was a question of apprenticeship to a trade, such as that of *couturière*, or seamstress. In such cases, the person bound was usually a young woman in her late teens or early twenties, the instruction was paid for, and the period of apprenticeship was only one or two years.[71]

All girls, whether they served in the households of others or lived at home with their own families, learned the multiple and time-consuming tasks of house and farm work from the older women with whom they lived. They began to learn from the earliest possible age—gathering eggs, holding yarn, stirring the pot, milking, spinning, and looking after animals and babies—while older women supervised or did other work. Most of their learning was directed toward their becoming competent assistants in the households of their elders, and eventually managers of their own.

CONTINUITY, CHANGE, AND THE BRITISH CONQUEST

Settlements along the St. Lawrence and its tributaries, in Louisbourg and in Acadia, began to have a sense of permanence as succeeding generations of French inhabitants took root. The "New World" communities that had been dominated by the fisheries, the fur trade, and the religious mission, and subject to continual warfare, had been replaced by a society based on agriculture and small industries. But the impression of stability was in part deceptive, for the final years of New France were hardly peaceful or static. The Acadians' relatively quiet existence was rudely shattered in 1755 when the British began to force on them the long exodus known as "*le Grand Dérangement*" or the "Expulsion." Many Acadian women were separated from their families and had their lives permanently disrupted. Some were sent to England; some ended up in France; many were scattered along the shores of the eastern seaboard of North America. A few, remarkably, managed to go into hiding and stay near their homes or to return to Nova Scotia later on.[72] War with the English affected the people of Canada as well. War meant blockades and food shortages, and, ultimately, bombardments, raids, and the loss of lives. The presence of troops encouraged prostitution, and the shortage of goods encouraged smuggling. In the war's last years, Canada as well as Acadia suffered much privation and dislocation.

Throughout the eighteenth century, French-Canadian clerics protested what they perceived as a moral decline. Like the Protestant clergy of New England, they found the world less pure than it had seemed in the early period of religious faith and missionary fervour. Priests no doubt complained about women's low necklines, frivolous dresses, and attendance at dances precisely because the material circumstances of women in eighteenth-century New France were better than those of their seventeenth-century mothers and grandmothers, and such extravagances were now possible. But moral attitudes had possibly also shifted. In Montreal, penalties for serious offences like adultery were less severe in the eighteenth century than they had been in the seventeenth.[73]

Increasing numbers of illegitimate or abandoned children might suggest a society in which social controls were not as powerful as they once had been; or they might simply be proof of better record-keeping by a more established state and church. Concern for orphans had a great deal to do with the development of a new women's religious community, founded just before the Conquest. The order of the Sisters of Charity (or Grey Nuns, as they came to be called) came into being in the 1740s and received official sanction from the king in 1753. Founded by Marguerite d'Youville, the *Soeurs de la Charité de l'Hôpital-Général* of Montreal had as their original focus the general care of the sick and the poor. But the problem of abandoned infants led to the admission of the hospital's first foundling in 1754, and soon more than 20 babies a year were finding their way to the Grey Nuns' door. The infant death rate at the hostel was extremely high—80 percent in the first decade—and would eventually match the even higher rates that were typical of similar foundling hospitals in Europe.[74] Evidently the institution was able to do little more than stem the tide of infanticide during difficult times by giving some measure of care and baptism to infants who otherwise would have died even sooner after birth. In New France, as elsewhere in the western world, the presence of foundling hospitals, with their high death rates, indicated the continuing—or perhaps growing—presence of hardships that institutional efforts were inadequate to alleviate. The founding of the Grey Nuns occurred at a time of growing awareness that the existing religious orders of New France were not attracting recruits. Some critics believed that the authorities were effectively limiting the numbers of women entering the religious life by insisting more than they had in the past on the payment of large dowries to the convents. It was pointed out in support of lower dowries that girls in New France loved liberty too much to be attracted to religious life in large numbers, and that the government need not fear the wholesale abandonment of marriage and child-rearing if convent entry were made easier. A genuine social problem existed, moreover, among women who did not find husbands and whose families could not afford the high cost of their entry into the convent. The dowries were finally lowered, although women did not flock into the convents as a result.[75]

Membership in a female religious order represented an alternative to marriage and motherhood for women. But most women still married, and most women's lives revolved

Marguerite d'Youville and other Montreal-dwellers in front of the fire that ravaged the town on May 17, 1765, painted by Soeur Marie-du-Rédempteur, s.g.m.

Source: Soeurs Grises de Montréal: Marguerite d'Youville et l'incendie du 17 mai 1765. 1974.A.106

around the demands of family reproduction and production. By the eighteenth century, this was especially true, although a European population that was more evenly balanced in terms of men and women may have meant later marriage on average for women than had been typical in the seventeenth century.

The marriages of a woman whose life spanned the years before and after the Conquest tell us something of how ordinary women arranged their affairs in mid-eighteenth-century French Canada. Félicité Audet first appears in the records in 1761. A widowed domestic servant with one child, Félicité married Théophile Allaire—himself a widower with one surviving child—in 1761. In the six years they lived together, Félicité and Théophile had three additional children; in 1767, Théophile died and Félicité and her family were left with a farm of 60 *arpents* (acres), 33 of which were still bush; a bed; three chairs; a bureau; and a sideboard. Félicité married once again and had three more children, but this marriage ended in a separation. According to the settlement that was arranged with her third spouse, she kept from this marriage 60 *arpents* of land, a bed, a cow, and a pig. She was also allotted half a *minot* (bushel) of grain, along with one of the children of this final union. When we last hear of her, Félicité is selling her land in order to buy another farm and a loom so that she can earn her living.[76]

It is hard to know how typical Audet's three marriages were, but her life appears to have been typical of women's lives in New France in that it focused on material realities, such as cows and pigs, husbands and children, three chairs and a sideboard. The state helped to determine the material conditions of her life, especially if there were shortages because of war. And the church impinged on her life as well. Her children would have been baptized shortly after they were born; she herself may have gone to the parish priest to undergo the traditional purification ritual of churching at some point following each birth.

An eighteenth-century *Canadien* couple in their Sunday clothes.

Source: Collection Gagnon, Bibliothèque de la ville de Montréal.

We can only guess what the impact of the British Conquest of 1760 might have been on Félicité Audet. We know that, among the elite and governing families of Louisbourg, Montreal, and Quebec, many women were forced to return to France. Others stayed on and no doubt wondered how they would cope under the new regime. The lingering of many Scottish and English names in French-Canadian families to this day indicates that some women followed the path of Marie-Madeleine Maisonnat, whom we saw earlier in this chapter: instead of marrying French soldiers, they married English ones. The role of women in the transmission of language and culture is suggested by the fact that most of their descendants consider themselves French-Canadians, not English-Canadians. By replacing Paris with London as the colony's metropole, the Conquest irrevocably altered the political and, in some ways, the economic context in which French-Canadian and Aboriginal women lived. The sprawling colony of New France was reduced to the smaller Province of Quebec, and then, in 1791, to the even smaller Lower Canada. But patriarchy was as evident post-Conquest as it had been under the French regime, and many of the other institutions that had shaped the lives of women in New France in fundamental ways either remained intact, or were reinstated not long after the Conquest: French civil law, the Catholic Church, and the seigneurial system.

Notes

1. Silvio Dumas, *Les filles du roi en Nouvelle-France. Étude historique avec répertoire biographique* (Québec: Société historique de Québec, 1972), 114–15.

2. Kenneth Banks, *Chasing Empire Across the Sea: Communications and the State in the French Atlantic, 1713–1763* (Montreal and Kingston: McGill-Queen's University Press, 2002), 71; Joyce Marshall, ed. and trans., *Word from New France: The Selected Letters of Marie de l'Incarnation* (Toronto: Oxford University Press, 1967), 65–69.

3. Raymond Douville and Jacques Casanova, *Daily Life in Early Canada*, translated by Carola Congreve (London: George Allen and Unwin, 1968), 27.

4. Ethel M. G. Bennett, "Marie Rollet," and Marie-Emmanuel Chabot, O.S.U., "Hélène Boullé," *Dictionary of Canadian Biography* (Toronto: University of Toronto Press, 1966), vol. 1, 578, 110.

5. D. Owen Carrigan, *Crime and Punishment in Canada: A History* (Toronto: McClelland and Stewart, 1991), 247.

6. On the importance of women to Catholic missions in New France, see Allan Greer, "Colonial Saints: Gender, Race, and Hagiography in New France," *William and Mary Quarterly*, 3rd series, 57, 2 (April 2000): 336.

7. Micheline Dumont-Johnson, "Les communautés religieuses et la condition féminine," *Recherches sociographiques* 19, 1 (janvier/avril 1978): 80.

8. François Rousseau, "Hôpital et société en Nouvelle-France: L'Hôtel Dieu de Québec à la fin du XVIIe siècle," *Revue d'histoire de l'Amérique française* 31, 1 (juin 1977): 29–30.

9. Marie-Emmanuel Chabot, "Marie Guyart de l'Incarnation, 1599–1672," in Mary Quayle Innis, ed., *The Clear Spirit: Twenty Canadian Women and Their Times* (Toronto: University of Toronto Press, 1966), 36; Natalie Zemon Davis, *Women on the Margins: Three Seventeenth-Century Lives* (Cambridge, MA: Harvard University Press, 1995), 63–139.

10. Le collectif Clio, *L'histoire des femmes au Québec depuis quatre siècles*, édition entièrement revue et mise à jour (Montréal: Le Jour, Éditeur, 1992), 48; Marshall, ed. and trans., *Word from New France*; Dom Guy Oury, *Marie de l'Incarnation, 1599–1672*, 2 vols. (Québec: Presses de l'Université Laval, 1973).

11. Le collectif Clio, *L'histoire des femmes au Québec*, 48–49, 52; Soeur Marguerite Jean, "L'État et les communautés religieuses féminines au Québec, 1639–1840," *Studia Canonica* 6, 1 (1972): 166.

12. Le collectif Clio, *L'histoire des femmes au Québec*, 52, 54–55; Hélène Bernier, ed., *Marguerite Bourgeoys* (Montréal: Fides, 1958).

13. Dumas, *Les filles du roi*, 70 [our translation]; Le collectif Clio, *L'histoire des femmes au Québec*, 60.

14. Yves Landry, *Les filles du roi au XVIIIe siècle: Orphelines en France, pionnières au Canada* (Montréal: Leméac, 1992), 258–59. For an abridged discussion of the characteristics of the *filles du roi*, see Landry, "Gender Imbalance, *les filles du roi*, and Choice of Spouse in New France," in Bettina Bradbury, ed., *Canadian Family History: Selected Readings* (Toronto: Copp Clark Pitman, 1992), 14–32.

15. Dumas, *Les filles du roi*, chap. 2; "Les soeurs Raclot," *Nos Ancêtres* 4 (1983).

16. Douville and Casanova, *Daily Life*, 32; Dumas, *Les filles du roi*, 320–21; Landry, *Les filles du roi*, 75–76.

17. Louise Dechêne, *Habitants et marchands de Montréal au XVIIe siècle* (Montréal: Plon, 1974), 45.

18. Jacques Henripin, *La population canadienne au début du XVIIIe siècle*, Institut national d'études démographiques: Travaux et documents, Cahier 22 (Paris: Presses universitaires de France, 1954); A. J. B. Johnston, *Religion in Life at Louisbourg, 1713–1758* (Montreal and Kingston: McGill-Queen's University Press, 1984), 5.

19. Yves Landry et Jacques Légaré, "Le cycle de vie familiale en Nouvelle-France: méthodologie et application à un échantillon," *Histoire sociale/Social History* 17, 33 (May 1984): 7–20; Isabel Foulché-Delbosc, "Women of Three Rivers: 1651–63," in Susan Mann Trofimenkoff and Alison Prentice, eds., *The Neglected Majority: Essays in Canadian Women's History* (Toronto: McClelland and Stewart, 1977) vol. 1, 16–18.

20. Foulché-Delbosc, "Women of Three Rivers," 18.

21. Landry et Légaré, "Le cycle de vie," 11; Allan Greer, *Peasant, Lord, and Merchant: Rural Society in Three Quebec Parishes, 1740–1840* (Toronto: University of Toronto Press, 1985), 51; John Bosher, "The Family in New France," in B. M. Gough, ed., *In Search of the Visible Past* (Waterloo: Wilfrid Laurier University Press, 1975), 1–13.

22. See Henripin, *La population canadienne*, 90; P. A. Leclerc, "Le mariage sous le régime français," *Revue d'histoire de l'Amérique française* 13/14 (1959–60): 230–46, 374–406, 525–43; Landry, "Gender Imbalance," 19.

23. Naomi Griffiths, "The Acadians," *Dictionary of Canadian Biography* (Toronto: University of Toronto Press, 1979), vol. 4, xvii–xxxi; Henripin, *La population canadienne*, 49–53; Robert V. Wells, "Quaker Marriage Patterns in Colonial Perspective," *William and Mary Quarterly*, 3rd Series, 24 (July 1972): 41–42; Roderic Beaujot and Kevin McQuillan, *Growth and Dualism: The Demographic Development of Canada* (Toronto: Gage, 1982), 6–9.

24. Sylvie Savoie, "Women's Marital Difficulties: Requests of Separation in New France," *The History of the Family* 3, 4 (1998): 473–85.

25. Hélène Laforce, *Histoire de la sage-femme dans la région de Québec* (Québec: Institut québécois de recherche sur la culture, 1985), 30–64.

26. Hélène Rioux, "Les amours québécoises au XVIIIe siècle," *Histoire* 11 (avril 1979): 71; Beaujot and McQuillan, *Growth and Dualism*, 9.

27. Lorraine Gadoury, *La noblesse de Nouvelle-France: Familles et alliances* (Lasalle: Hurtubise HMH, 1992), 120–29, 142–46.

28. Josette Brun, *Vie et mort du couple en Nouvelle-France. Québec et Louisbourg au XVIIIe siècle* (Montreal and Kingston: McGill-Queen's University Press, 2006), 70–76; Benoît Grenier, *Marie-Catherine Peuvret. Veuve et seigneuresse en Nouvelle-France, 1667–1739* (Sillery: Septentrion, 2005), esp. 16–17, 20–23, 93–105.

29. Josette Brun, "Gender, Family, and Mutual Assistance in New France: Widows, Widowers, and Orphans in Eighteenth-Century Quebec," in Nancy Christie and Michael Gauvreau, eds., *Mapping the Margins: The Family and Social Discipline in Canada, 1700–1975* (Montreal and Kingston: McGill-Queen's University Press, 2004), 41.

30. Greer, *Peasant, Lord, and Merchant*, chap. 2; Andrew Hill Clark, *Acadia: The Geography of Early Nova Scotia to 1760* (Madison: University of Wisconsin Press, 1968), 165.

31. Josette Brun, "Les femmes d'affaires dans la société coloniale nord-américaine: le cas de l'Île Royale, 1713–1758," Université de Moncton, thèse de maîtrise ès arts, 1994, 103–104.

32. Colin Coates and Cecilia Morgan, *Heroines and History: Representations of Madeleine de Verchères and Laura Secord* (Toronto: University of Toronto Press, 2002).

33. George MacBeath, "Françoise-Marie Jacquelin," *Dictionary of Canadian Biography* vol. 3 (1974), 308–313; vol. 1 (1966), 383.

34. The idea of the military ethos of New France was articulated most notably by W. J. Eccles: see, for instance, his essay, "The Social, Economic, and Political Significance of the Military Establishment in New France," in Eccles, ed., *Essays on New France* (Toronto: Oxford Press, 1987), 110–24. The quotation is from page 114 of this essay. Parts of Eccles' thesis have recently been called into question by Louise Dechêne, *Le peuple, l'État et la guerre au Canada sous le régime français*, edition prepared by Hélène Paré, Sylvie Dépatie, Catherine Desbarats, and Thomas Wien (Montreal: Boréal, 2008). Dechêne questions the notion that the typical French-Canadian had a warrior mentality, but she does acknowledge that war played a central role in daily life in New France.

35. D. Peter MacLeod, *Les Iroquois et la Guerre de Sept Ans* (Montreal: VLB Éditeur, 2000 [original English-language edition 1996]), 26–27.

36. Robert-Lionel Séguin, "La canadienne au XVIIe et XVIIIe siècles," *Revue d'histoire de l'Amérique française* 13, 4 (Mars 1960): 492–508; Clark, *Acadia*, 165, 168, 176–77, 377–78, 243; Foulché-Delbosc, "Women of Three Rivers," 25; Griffiths, "The Acadians," xix–xxi; Greer, *Peasant, Lord, and Merchant*, 14.

37. Jan Noel, "New France: Les femmes favorisées," in Alison Prentice and Susan Mann Trofimenkoff, eds., *The Neglected Majority: Essays in Canadian Women's History* vol. 2 (Toronto: McClelland & Stewart, 1985): 18–40; Noel, *Women in New France*, CHA Booklet No. 59 (Ottawa: Canadian Historical Association, 2001).

38. Micheline Dumont, "Les femmes de la Nouvelle-France étaient-elles vraiment favorisées?" *Atlantis* 8, 1 (1982): 118–24; and, most recently, Brun, *Vie et mort du couple en Nouvelle-France*, esp. 3–4, 97–98.

39. Greer, *Peasant, Lord, and Merchant*, 49–51; Leclerc, "Le mariage," 375–76.

40. Ollivier Hubert, "The Invention of the Margin as an Invention of the Family: The Case of Rural Quebec in the Eighteenth and Nineteenth Centuries," in Christie and Gauvreau, eds., *Mapping the Margins*, esp. 186–93.

41. Gadoury, *La noblesse*, 92–103.

42. Yves F. Zoltvany, "Esquisse de la Coutume de Paris," *Revue d'histoire de l'Amérique française* 25, 3 (décembre 1971): 366–83; Allan Greer, *The People of New France* (Toronto: University of Toronto Press, 1997), 69–71.

43. Landry, "Gender Imbalance," 19.

44. Dechêne, *Habitants et marchands*, 419; Louis Lavallée, "Les archives notariales et l'histoire sociale de la Nouvelle-France," *Revue d'histoire de l'Amérique française* 28, 3 (décembre 1974): 388–89; Johnston, *Religion in Life*, chap. 5; Cameron Nish, *Les bourgeois-gentil-hommes de la Nouvelle-France, 1729–1748* (Montréal: Fides, 1968), chap. 10.

45. Greer, *Peasant, Lord, and Merchant*, 34.

46. Sylvie Dépatie, "La transmission du patrimoine au Canada (XVIIe–XVIIIe siècle): qui sont les défavorisés?" *Revue d'histoire de l'Amérique française* 54, 4 (Printemps 2001): 558–70.

47. Madeleine Doyon-Ferland, "Agathe de Saint-Père (Legardeur de Repentigny)," *Dictionary of Canadian Biography* vol. 3, 580–81.

48. Liliane Plamondon, "Une femme d'affaires en Nouvelle-France: Marie-Anne Barbel, veuve Fornel," *Revue d'histoire de l'Amérique française* 31, 2 (September 1977): 165–86; Brun, "Les femmes d'affaires," 22; Gadoury, *La noblesse*, 81–2.

49. Brun, *Vie et mort du couple en Nouvelle-France*, 36–40.

50. Hector J. Hébert, "Marie-Madeleine Maisonnat (Winniett)," *Dictionary of Canadian Biography* vol. 3, 421; Douville and Casanova, *Daily Life*, 201; Noel, "New France: Les femmes favorisées," 25–6.

51. Greer, *The People of New France*, 36.

52. Noel, "Les femmes favorisées," 32; Terence Crowley, "Thunder Gusts: Popular Disturbances in Early French Canada," *Historical Papers/Communications historiques* (1979): 19–20.

53. Laforce, *Histoire de la sage-femme*, 138–200.

54. Gadoury, *La noblesse*, 64–67; Rousseau, "Hôpital et société," 36–47.

55. Micheline D'Allaire, "Les prétensions des religieuses de l'hôpital-général de Québec sur le palais épiscopal de Québec," *Revue d'histoire de l'Amérique française* 23, 1 (June 1969): 53–67.

56. Micheline Dumont-Johnson, "History of the Status of Women in the Province of Quebec," in Royal Commission on the Status of Women in Canada, *Cultural Tradition and Political History of Women in Canada*, Study No. 8 of the RCSW (Ottawa: Information Canada, 1971), 6; Johnston, *Religion in Life*, 96.

57. Antonio Drolet, "Quelques remèdes indigènes à travers la correspondance de Mère Sainte-Hélène," in Yolande Bonenfant et al., *Trois siècles de médecine québécoise*, Cahiers d'histoire No. 22 (Quebec: Société historique de Québec, 1972); Soeur Morin, "Annales de l'Hôtel-Dieu de Montréal," *Mémoires de la société historique de Montréal* vol. 12 (1921).

58. Savoie, "Women's Marital Difficulties," 477.

59. A. J. B. Johnston, "Women as Victims in 18th-Century Cape Breton: Violence at Home and in the Street," paper presented to the French Colonial Historical Society, Montreal, May 1992, 20–24; Carrigan, *Crime and Punishment in Canada*, 203, 247.

60. Marie-Aimée Cliche, "Unwed Mothers, Families and Society during the French Regime," in Bradbury, ed., *Canadian Family History*, 42–45.

61. Marcel Trudel, *L'esclavage au Canada français*, abridged edition (Montreal: Les Éditions de l'Horizon, 1963); Marcel Trudel, *Deux siècles d'esclavage au Québec* (Montreal: Éditions Hurtubise HMH, 2004); Kenneth Donovan, "Slaves and Their Owners in Île Royale, 1713–1760," *Acadiensis*, 25, 1 (Autumn 1995): 3–32; Brett Rushforth, "Savage Bonds: Indian Slavery and Alliance in New France" (PhD thesis, University of California at Davis, 2003), 81–84; Brett Rushforth, "'A Little Flesh We Offer You': The Origins of Indian Slavery in New France," *William and Mary Quarterly* 60, 4 (2003): 777–808.

62. André Vachon, "Marie-Joseph-Angélique," *Dictionnaire biographique du Canada*, http://www.biographi.ca/009004-119.01-e.php?&id_nbr=973&interval=20&&PHPSESSID=s9m8 b1e62v5ij9ibvecdcsahj2; Marcel Trudel, *L'esclavage au Canada français: histoire et conditions de l'esclavage* (Quebec: Les Presses de l'Université Laval, 1960), 226–29; André Lachance, *Crimes et criminels en Nouvelle-France* (Montreal: Boréal Express, 1984); Afua Cooper, *The Hanging of Angélique: The Untold Story of Canadian Slavery and the Burning of Old Montreal* (Toronto: Harper Collins, 2006). The most detailed treatment by far is that of Denyse Beaugrand-Champagne, *Le procès de Marie-Josèphe-Angélique* (Outremont: Éditions Libre Expression, 2004).

63. Johnston, *Religion in Life*, 8, 93; Johnston, "Women as Victims," 10; Donovan, "Slaves and Their Owners," 30.

64. Brun, *Vie et mort du couple en Nouvelle-France*, 3-4.

65. Nadia Fahmy-Eid, "L'éducation des filles chez les Ursulines de Québec sous le régime français," in Nadia Fahmy-Eid and Micheline Dumont, eds., *Maîtresses de maison, maîtresses d'école: Femmes, famille et éducation dans l'histoire du Québec* (Montreal: Boréal Express, 1983), esp. 66–67. For an English translation, see "The Education of Girls by the Ursulines of Quebec during the French Regime," in Wendy Mitchinson et al., *Canadian Women: A Reader* (Toronto: Harcourt Brace, 1996), 33–49.

66. Johnston, *Religion in Life*, 91. See also Johnston, "Education and Female Literacy at Eighteenth-Century Louisbourg: The Work of the Soeurs de la Congrégation de Notre Dame," in J. Donald Wilson, ed., *An Imperfect Past: Education and Society in Canadian History* (Vancouver: Centre for the Study of Curriculum and Instruction, University of British Columbia, 1984), 48–66.

67. Fahmy-Eid, "L'éducation des filles," 53.

68. Andrée Dufour and Micheline Dumont, *Brève histoire des institutrices au Québec de la Nouvelle-France à nos jours* (Montreal: Boréal, 2004), 28–31.

69. Johnston, *Religion in Life*, 107; Allan Greer, "The Pattern of Literacy in Quebec, 1745–1899," *Histoire sociale/Social History* 11, 22 (November 1978): 299.

70. Soeur Morin, "Annales"; Ghislaine Légendre, ed., "Relation de Soeur Cuillerier," *Écrits du Canada français* 42 (Montreal 1979); Elisabeth Bégon, *Lettres au cher fils: Correspondance d'Elisabeth Bégon avec son gendre, 1748–1753* (Montreal: Hurtubise, 1972); Douville and Casanova, *Daily Life*, 202–16.

71. Francine Barry, "Familles et domesticité féminine au milieu du 18e siècle," in Fahmy-Eid et Dumont, eds., *Maîtresses de maison*, 223–36.

72. See Griffiths, "The Acadians"; Naomi E. S. Griffiths, *From Migrant to Acadian: A North American Border People 1604–1755* (Montreal and Kingston: McGill-Queen's University Press, 2005).

73. André Morel, "Réflexions sur la justice criminelle canadienne au 18e siècle," *Revue d'histoire de l'Amérique française* 29, 2 (September 1975): 241–53.

74. Peter Gossage, "Foundlings and the Institution: The Case of the Grey Nuns of Montreal," paper presented to the Canadian Historical Association, Winnipeg, 1986.

75. On dowries, see Dechêne, *Habitants et marchands*, 478; Jean, "L'État," 166–68.

76. Greer, *Peasant, Lord, and Merchant*, 25–28, 55–56.

CHAPTER THREE

"Plenty of Work": Women's Waged and Unwaged Labour in British North America

The fall of New France in 1760 ushered in a century of extraordinary change in North America. While the last decades of the French regime were hardly static, the advent of British government in the French-occupied territories combined with subsequent economic and political events in Europe and in the Thirteen Colonies to the south to produce a century of almost continuous political and military upheaval. One profound effect was a vast movement of peoples. A second was a rapid increase in the number of people of European origin living in the territory that would become Canada. (See Figure 3.1.) Single men predominated among the first arrivals to the British North American colonies. But if Britain wanted them to remain and her colonies to be settled, it was apparent that women were required. Indeed, an early comment on the Newfoundland experience by a British naval officer suggests just how important women were to permanent settlement. "Soe long as there comes noe women," this gentleman remarked in 1694, the people are not "fixed."[1] Women's work in its many forms—reproductive, productive, and social—was necessary to the development of colonial society. In fact, in a pre-industrial economy based on household production, the labour of women and children was essential. By bearing and raising children, women made a direct contribution to solving labour shortages that hampered initial economic progress. Moreover, the products of women's labour—items surplus to the family's immediate needs and able to be bartered or sold—frequently enabled pioneer families to accumulate much-needed capital. And as capital accumulated in the countryside, local economies diversified and urban centres developed.

By the middle of the nineteenth century, new industries appeared that, in turn, depended on women for a major part of their workforce. The early stirrings of industrial and urban development gradually affected family patterns, and daughters as well as sons increasingly sought remunerative work outside the home. At the same time, the household economy continued to prevail, and a daughter's wages were a vital part of the family subsistence—hence the view that a workingman was indeed injured if he was deprived of his daughter's earnings. Although the single woman's right to an independent living

Figure 3.1 BRITISH NORTH AMERICA, 1791

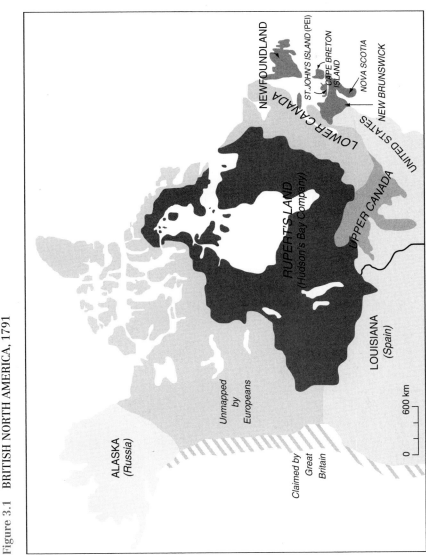

Source: Based on *Canadian Geographical Society,* Historical Maps of Canada, 1791 (http://www.canadiangeographic. ca/mapping/ historical_maps/1791.asp).

was an idea whose time had not yet come, the single woman's obligation to work for her family did nevertheless enable her to move toward employment in the new public sphere that was coming into being.

Many women in British North America performed various forms of labour simultaneously, for the boundaries of what constituted work were fluid: one form of work frequently overlapped another. While there were many similarities across British North America in the labour girls and women were called upon to perform, the exact nature of their work varied according to their age, marital status, and where they lived. Race, class, and ethnicity also greatly influenced the nature, quantity, and experience of women's work.

THE NEW MIGRANTS

The first large-scale influx of English-speaking migrants into British North America followed the establishment of Halifax in 1749 as a British garrison and the expulsion of the Acadians six years later. Between 1759 and 1768, some 8 000 New England planters (settlers) arrived in Nova Scotia, which at that time encompassed much of what is now New Brunswick and Prince Edward Island. In the late eighteenth century, families also began making their way from colonies such as New York and Pennsylvania to the new British province of Quebec, whose boundaries for most of the late eighteenth century continued to include much of present-day Ontario and vast tracts of the Ohio and Mississippi river valleys to the south and west. This migration, which included Quaker and Mennonite pacifists, preceded the American Revolution (1776–1783) that would eventually result in the birth of the United States of America. Despite the pacifist leanings and religious concerns of some of these American migrants, the chief motivation of most was the quest for new land and new opportunities.

Nor were economic motives absent in the vast Loyalist influx into the eastern and northern British colonies that was precipitated by the American Revolution itself. Like the movements that preceded it, this influx, too, was largely a migration of families and included the Abenaki, members of the Iroquois Confederacy (mainly Mohawk), black slaves and former slaves, and migrants of German and Dutch origin, as well as women and men of Anglo-Celtic backgrounds. These peoples were followed in turn by another generation of American migrants, the "Late Loyalists," whose motives seem to have been overwhelmingly economic. Then, economic and political upheaval in the British Isles following the end of the Napoleonic wars in 1815 and famine in Ireland in the late 1840s, brought yet another great movement of people, chiefly of English, Irish, and Scottish families. This influx for the most part occurred after the American migration, reaching its peak in the 1830s and 1840s. Between 1825 and 1845, some 450 000 Irish alone arrived in British North America.

While most women migrated as members of families, included in all of these movements were female immigrants travelling without families: domestics, schoolmistresses, and businesswomen seeking a living in partnership with other women or alone. In the

1840s, at the invitation of the Bishop Ignace Bourget of Montreal, new groups of French nuns arrived in Canada East (Quebec) to staff the Catholic educational and charitable institutions the bishop was creating to reinvigorate the Roman Catholic mission in the "New World." They, in turn, were followed by Irish and American nuns, who set up schools and hospitals in other parts of British North America.[2]

Immigrants and native-born alike often lived in many different places before they settled permanently. Marie-Henriette Lejeune, for example, born in Rochefort of Acadian parents who had been deported to France after the fall of Louisbourg in 1758, became part of an Acadian population that has been described as "constantly expanding and moving." By 1764, she was back in North America and living with her family on the island of Miquelon; but by 1766, the family had once again been forcibly moved to Cape Breton. Returning to Miquelon in 1777, the Lejeune family found themselves once again deported to France. By then 16, Marie-Henriette married another displaced Acadian, a widower with children to raise. However, by 1786, she was back on Cape Breton, widowed and remarried, this time to a cousin. Her third and last marriage was to a member of the MacDonald's Highlanders, a regiment disbanded in 1783. Living with her husband James Ross for a time in Little Bras d'Or on Cape Breton, Marie-Henriette made her final home in the North East Margaree Valley. By this time a skilled midwife and healer, she was remembered by her descendants as "Granny Ross."[3]

The Acadians may have travelled more than most colonists, but others moved about as well. Countless Loyalists and other migrants used the Maritime provinces or the old province of Quebec (later known as Lower Canada) as staging grounds for migrations farther west. Some black Loyalists in Nova Scotia gave up on the Americas entirely and sought a better life in Sierra Leone, where they nevertheless continued to be known as Nova Scotians.[4] Later, many Maritimers decided that the prospects were better in the eastern United States than at home, and migrant French Canadians began to colonize new parts of British North America or strike out for the towns and factories of New England.

In the early 1800s, Scottish settlers under the leadership of Lord Selkirk planted the Red River colony in a small corner of Rupert's Land, in what would later be the province of Manitoba. Since French-Catholic mixed-descent families settled in the region as well, religious women were not far behind; in 1844, a contingent of Grey Nuns established the first women's religious community in the Canadian West to teach and to care for the sick. Another small group of white women helped initiate the pioneer era in what was eventually to become the province of British Columbia. Their voyages by sea from the British Isles were often of six or seven months' duration, rounding Cape Horn and eventually bringing them to the new settlements that were being created in Hudson's Bay Company territory on the west coast.[5]

Who were these women, who left the relative comforts of home and parted from family and friends for what were often gruelling and extraordinarily long journeys into unknown and inhospitable environments? Did any common themes mark their passage or characterize their lives? One thing they certainly had in common was the migration experience. Sometimes this was an experience the women themselves might not have chosen; many migrated because of political or economic choices made by fathers or husbands, or more remotely by distant landholders, military men, or governors. Loyalist records

Engraving showing the cramped and unhealthy interior of a ship transporting British emigrants to North America, 1851.

Source: Library and Archives Canada/C-006556

reveal such forced moves with particular poignancy,[6] but many other women must also have migrated unwillingly. For those who emigrated from the British Isles in the 1820s and 1830s, especially those who travelled in steerage, surviving the six- to eight-week voyage was itself a major challenge. Cheap-fare passengers were crammed, along with their baggage and food supplies, into dingy ship holds built to carry lumber and other cargo. Common problems they encountered included insufficient rations, spoiled food, chronic seasickness, rats, and deadly diseases, such as cholera and typhus, contracted in the close and unhygienic quarters.

Not all women migrants spent months at sea, for many were overland migrants. Nor did all of them walk for more than 1 300 kilometres as did the women who trekked from York Factory to Red River between 1812 and 1820.[7] But many did have extraordinary experiences as immigrants; most must have found their lives enormously changed. For those who were refugees or were forcibly displaced or were fleeing from slave hunters, moving was definitely traumatic. Some came with a fair share of the world's goods, but others arrived with very little or with nothing. However they came, they brought traditional skills and knowledge of women's ways and women's work; but they also had to adapt to new ways of doing things in the communities they encountered or founded in British North America.

The story of Sarah McGinnis illustrates both the mobility and the need to adapt. Born in the upper Mohawk River valley in present-day New York State to a first-generation family of German immigrants in 1713, Sarah, who had "prevailed upon her parents" to let her live for long periods among the Mohawks, married an Irish fur trader and had produced four children by the time she was widowed at 42. Continuing to operate the family fur trading post, the widow McGinnis was in her sixties when the American Revolution swept away all she possessed and forced her to head north. She watched as her property and goods were sold at public auction, and spent time imprisoned with her family in conditions so bad that her granddaughter ultimately died from the treatment she received. When she and her family escaped, Sarah McGinnis had to abandon a son "who was out of his senses and bound in chains . . . and who was later burnt alive." Then began the long odyssey that would eventually take the widow McGinnis to Canada. During the revolutionary war, at the age of 64, she wintered in Mohawk country at the request of British authorities and played a key role in keeping the Mohawk–British alliance intact. She also spent brief periods in Niagara and Montreal, in the latter case in great poverty. Her ultimate journeys took her first to Carleton Island, then to Ernestown, and finally to Fredericksburgh (all at the eastern end of Lake Ontario), where she died in 1791 at the age of 78.[8]

Frequent moves, insufficient food, and the loss of possessions—or, worse, the loss of family members: these were the lot of many migrants. American Patriots not only plundered the house of Filer Dibblee of Long Island but also turned his wife, Polly, and their five children "naked into the Streets." "Plundered and stripped" two more times before they made their way to New Brunswick, the Dibblee family discovered that a safe arrival in British territory did not mean the end of their troubles. Filer, who had spent six months in prison during the war, succumbed to despair during the first year in Saint John and committed suicide; not long afterward, the widow and her children were burned out of their log-cabin home twice in one year. In a letter to a brother in England, Polly expressed her gratitude for gifts of clothing that he had sent and recounted some of her trials as a prelude to a request for further aid:

> I assure you, my dear Billy, that many have been the Days since my arrival in this inhospitable Country, that I should have thought myself and Family truly happy could we have "had Potatoes alone—" but this mighty Boon was denied us—! I could have borne these burdens of Loyalty with Fortitude had not my poor Children in doleful accents cried, Mama, why don't you help me and give me Bread?[9]

Polly Dibblee wondered about the value of loyalty to a British Crown whose material assistance, at that stage, had been wholly insufficient; she also worried about the effect the news of her condition would have on her mother, who remained in the United States. At the time of writing (November 1787), she had not had the courage to inform her American relatives of her difficulties.

All Loyalist women suffered the loss of familiar surroundings, communities, and homes; many took on new and unfamiliar roles during the long absences of husbands, fathers, and brothers who were fighting the revolutionary war. Often they endured abuse at the hands of hostile Patriots; a few even lost the support of their parental families, who disagreed with the course taken by sons or sons-in-law. All were forced, at some point, to migrate, frequently under terrible conditions. Some did not make it to the end of their journey.[10] Nor did migrants' troubles necessarily end with their arrival in British North America. And if it was hard to be Sarah McGinnis or Polly Dibblee, how much harder must it have been to be Peggy Qwynn, a black Loyalist who arrived in Nova Scotia only to be judged by the official recipient of her petition for assistance "not a free woman [who] must be delivered to her owner."[11]

During the War of 1812, some 2 000 slaves, who had escaped from Maryland and Virginia when the British occupied Chesapeake Bay, made their way north to so-called freedom—only to encounter much hardship and considerable prejudice in their new Nova Scotia and New Brunswick homes, as had other black migrants, both slave and free, before them.[12] The government of Upper Canada did pass legislation prohibiting the importation of new slaves in 1793, and the last recorded slave sale in Halifax appears to have occurred in 1820. Owning slaves, however, continued to be legal until 1834, when the British government abolished slavery in its colonies. In the 1850s, thousands more black refugees made their way to Canada West (Ontario) during the fugitive slave movement via the Underground Railroad and created communities in what was to become southwestern Ontario. Some came with their families, but the circumstances of their migration forced others, including women and mothers with young children, to leave family members behind. This was the situation of Louisa Pipkins of Yorkville, who was still making inquiries and trying to get her four children out of the United States three years after her own escape with her husband in 1853. The Pipkins children were already scattered, living with three different families in North Carolina and Virginia. Some black women went back themselves for their children. A Mrs. Armstrong, disguising herself as a man in order to travel more easily, returned to Kentucky for the seven youngsters she had been forced to leave behind when she had escaped in 1842. She brought out five and arranged with friends for the escape of the other two.[13]

Even migrants whose travels were precipitated by immediate causes other than war or oppression could suffer privation and loss. The experiences of Catharine Parr Traill and Susanna Moodie, the sisters who were two of Canada's most famous gentlewomen immigrants from the British Isles in the 1830s, were punctuated by traumas and tragedies. Both wed Scottish half-pay officers who were ill-equipped to deal with the harsh realities of pioneer life and who were constantly in debt. Catharine nearly succumbed to cholera in Montreal before she was able to set out for her homestead near Peterborough, and in the ensuing years lost several homes to fire. In winters, there was often not enough food, and Catharine's four school-aged children could not go to school because their clothes were in rags and they had no shoes. Susanna also lost a farmhouse to fire, endured attacks of intermittent fever, and suffered the drowning of a son.

In her famous account of pioneer life, *Roughing It in the Bush*, Susanna portrayed the rigours of backwoods life with particular flair. She told a tale of constant struggle, albeit a struggle laced with humour as well as dogged determination. As a gentlewoman, Moodie was unprepared for much of the relentless manual work she had to do on her bush farm, which she managed on her own for two long winters. She nevertheless persevered, and in the end even admitted to contemplating her own "well-hoed ridge of potatoes" with considerable satisfaction. Moodie was fortunate in having the knowledge and skill to take up her pen as well as her hoe. She won a government post for her husband by her petitions to the governor and, as an experienced author, was able to supplement the family income through her published writings in a period when a certain number of women were able to earn money through their writing. Finally, as a result of both initiatives, the Moodies were able to leave the trials of backwoods life behind them. They moved to Belleville, where Susanna and Captain Moodie could more easily pursue work to which they felt better suited. Nonetheless, financial success continued to elude them, and after her husband's death in 1869, the 66-year-old Susanna had no home to call her own. She spent the next 16 years shuffling between the homes of her adult children, dependent on their willingness and capacity to support her.[14]

Not all pioneer stories are as well-documented as the Moodie story, nor are they all tales of worry and woe. An upper-class woman recorded in her 1789 diary an encounter with one of her domestic servants, Nancy, who had married a disbanded soldier after the American revolutionary war and settled with him on a farm in the St. Lawrence valley. The former mistress was impressed with what she saw. Already Nancy and her husband had exchanged a small farm for one that was double its size, and were in the process of developing their new acreage and raising a fine family of three children. Asked if she was happy, Nancy replied, "Yes, perfectly so." She worked hard, "but it was for herself and the children [. . .] Her husband took care of the Farm and she of the family, and at their leisure hours she wove Cloth, and he made and mended shoes for their neighbours for which they were well paid, and every year they expected to do better and better."[15]

Also hopeful of bettering their lot were the women who migrated on their own. Many followed relatives who had gone before them, but some women seem to have been entirely independent of close family connections. For example, 16 unattached women over 12 years of age were among the 448 Scottish Highlanders who immigrated in 1802 as an organized group to Glengarry, Upper Canada, where they joined other clan members who had earlier reached the area by various routes.[16] Such women immigrants might find their way into the countryside, but more often they would find work in urban centres like Fredericton, Halifax, Montreal, or York (Toronto), swelling the numbers of single women who were already moving into these communities from rural British North America. By 1851, such centres were reporting disproportionate numbers of young women living in their midst. Most of these women took work as servants in urban households; others established themselves as teachers; still others set up dressmaking establishments, shops, or other businesses. Whatever their means of support, these single women, too, were participating in the high degrees of mobility and change that characterized the lives of British North American women.[17]

Not all, however, adapted easily to the changes in their world. Change was particularly difficult if it brought in its wake a clash of cultures. Molly Brant, Mohawk matron and spouse of Sir William Johnson, the British Superintendent of Indian Affairs, and her sister-in-law, Catharine Adonwentishon, head of the prestigious Mohawk Turtle clan and wife of Chief Joseph Brant, had to choose between two paths: acculturation to the British way of life in North America or a return to Mohawk ways. In the end, neither choice was clear-cut. Molly always spoke Mohawk and dressed in the Mohawk style, but her daughters all married members of the Upper Canadian elite. She saw out her days in Kingston, where three of her daughters had settled. In contrast, Catharine, the daughter of an Irish father and a Mohawk mother, found life uncomfortable in her husband Joseph Brant's lavish establishment in Burlington. Five of her seven children married Mohawks and settled in the Mohawk community at Grand River. When Joseph died, Catharine, too, returned to Grand River to live.[18] Other Aboriginal women continued to be a valuable source of aid for newly arrived white women by sharing with them their survival and midwifery skills and their knowledge of traditional medicines. Catherine Parr Traill, for example, adopted deerskin moccasins for walking in the snow and used a herbal remedy recommended by her Aboriginal neighbours to treat her children's diarrhea. In return, Aboriginal women used their contacts with their white neighbours to barter their handicrafts for items such as blankets, pots, and European dress goods.[19]

Aboriginal women suffered increasing hardship, however, as their communities were forced to retreat from the pressure of colonial development. The military and fur trade worlds of which they had been so important a part were ending with the coming of white women. In the northwest, Aboriginal women who had married traders did not necessarily fare better than their counterparts in the east, nor than those Aboriginal women who had remained with their tribal communities in the rapidly changing conditions of the nineteenth century.[20] Following the arrival of white women and missionaries in fur trade country in the early and mid-nineteenth century, some traders began to feel encumbered by their Aboriginal "country" wives. When they retired to eastern British North America or to Britain, these men often turned their Aboriginal spouses over to others, or abandoned them. Some, like Hudson's Bay Company governor Sir George Simpson, not only "turned off" their Aboriginal wives but also insisted on bringing their new British wives west. Frances Simpson's experience indicates, however, that life in the northwest was not necessarily any happier for white women. Only 18 when she arrived as the new bride of Simpson, who was her cousin and already in his mid-forties, Frances valiantly tried to adjust to the alien environment of Red River society. In the end, however, her health failed and she was compelled to return home to England after only a few years.[21]

Despite their own problems and insecurities, women like Frances Simpson constituted a threat to Aboriginal "country" wives. They represented a civilized world that fur traders increasingly wanted. And when Aboriginal wives were abandoned, whole families suffered. The children of mixed-descent marriages might be left with their mothers, sent off to boarding school, or put into trades; few were fully integrated into their fathers' new families.[22] Of course, by no means were all "country" wives or their children abandoned. Many fathers continued to care for their mixed-descent offspring; others attempted to move their wives and families into the little European worlds that they were establishing in centres like Red River and Victoria. This was the experience of Amelia Douglas, the part-Cree wife of Vancouver Island's first governor. A practical woman who had once saved her husband's life from a knife-wielding attacker, Amelia was the mother of 13 children, 7 of whom died in infancy. First in Fort Vancouver and then in Victoria, she had to endure the insults of the new white settlers, who felt she was beneath them. Amelia Douglas probably found her new world ridiculously artificial as well as unpleasantly prejudiced, but she learned to deal with her new official role with good humour, turning some of the duties connected with it over to her daughters. She also drew on her Aboriginal heritage to the end, inviting other First Nations and mixed-descent men and women into her home, and telling Aboriginal legends to her grandchildren. The paths of most mixed-descent women were no doubt far more difficult. They could rarely go back to their mothers' bands, and they were often unwelcome in white society. Truly women "in between," some were not fully accepted in either world.[23] The most tragic stories of all were those of Aboriginal women who faced the obliteration of their cultures and, in one case, the extinction of their people.

In the north and west, the Athapaskans and coastal peoples like the Haida still had some time and sufficient space to maintain their distinctive cultures, but this was

Women baking in a Métis camp, Pembina area, Manitoba, 1859.
Source: Glenbow Archives NA-1406-27

not the case in the Atlantic colonies. The Micmac of Nova Scotia and the Beothuk of Newfoundland had been suffering from economic and social dislocation and enduring the ravages of European-introduced diseases since at least the 1500s. During the late eighteenth and early nineteenth centuries, these groups experienced death by slow starvation. Some of the Micmac migrated to Newfoundland; others survived by moving onto reserved lands or developing a tourist trade in crafts that the women managed to preserve or revive. The Beothuk, despite last-ditch efforts on the part of colonial philanthropists to save them, finally dwindled to one woman, Shanawdithit. This young Beothuk was taken captive. When she learned to communicate with her captors, she was able to tell them about the final days of her people: how they had hidden from white Newfoundlanders, who seemed to be hunting them even into their last retreat in the interior; how they had watched from the woods as white men returned the body of one of their number to their camp; and how, finally, all but Shanawdithit herself had died. This last Beothuk woman succumbed to tuberculosis in 1829.[24]

REPRODUCTIVE WORK

In British North American society, most people considered marriage to be a means to enhance their economic security, as well as a social responsibility. In their minds, marriage and motherhood were intrinsically linked to womanhood.[25] The majority of women in British North America probably embarked on marriage in their early twenties. The 1851 census for Canada East and West, for example, gave the average age at first marriage for females as 23. In Hamilton, by contrast, marriage was considerably delayed. Only 40 percent of the city's women were married by the age of 22; by the age of 25, only 60 percent were wed. Among those older than 25, the percentage of women who were married gradually rose. Nevertheless, 17 percent of Hamilton's 30-year-old women remained unmarried in 1851.[26]

Late marriage is often correlated with few children, and it may well be that British North American women—especially urban women—were somewhat less fertile than the women of New France. But it is also true that these pre-industrial women still produced large families in comparison to average family sizes of later periods. Estimates of the numbers of children born to typical British North American families vary according to the date, the locality, and the data available, but all indicate substantial average birth rates. A study of eighteenth-century Quebec reveals an average of more than eight births per woman and an average family size of more than five per completed family—that is, children born to women during their years of fertility—while similar figures are given for Peel County, Canada West, in 1851. Mid-nineteenth-century French-Canadian women in two Prescott County townships in Canada West also had an average of more than seven children by the time they reached the end of their childbearing years; English-Canadian mothers in this sample were only slightly less fertile, with an average of about six. Here, age at marriage might have made the difference, for English-Canadian women in these townships tended to marry a few years later than their French-Canadian counterparts. Rural living also clearly made a difference. The average number of children in all of the households in the city of Hamilton when the census was taken in 1851 was fewer than three; where heads of household were in their forties, it was fewer than four. Yet for all of British North America, the average number of children born to families in 1851—slightly more than seven—was still remarkably high.[27]

However, numbers can tell us only so much. The childbearing stories of Anne Powell and her daughter Mary illustrate the high fertility of early nineteenth-century upper-class women and the stresses that could accompany it. Anne gave birth to nine children, of whom one died in infancy and another died at the age of 9. Her daughter Mary Jarvis had ten deliveries altogether. The first child was stillborn, but all the others survived birth. After Mary's sixth confinement, a female relative and a friend moved in for a period to provide extra help. Mary took comfort in this support and in the competence of her domestic servants, but she was still tired, and she missed her mother and sister, who were in England. "I was sadly harassed with work," she wrote to her mother. "I have been very sick. . . . My illness was caused I believe by want of rest and too much fatigue before I had quite recovered from my confinement." For her part, Catharine Parr Traill gave birth to nine children, two of whom died in infancy: she bore her first child at the age of 31, and her last at the age of 46. Her sister, Susanna, went through seven difficult pregnancies in eleven years, ending her childbearing when she was 40 years old.[28]

Affluent women such as Anne and Mary Powell could rely on the help of domestic servants and female relatives to take on many of their household responsibilities during their pregnancies; women of the urban labouring class or those who lived in rural areas did not usually have this advantage. If they were fortunate enough to have a neighbour or a relative close by, these female supports would often be on hand to assist them during childbirth, particularly if an experienced midwife were not available. While doctors were becoming more numerous as the nineteenth century progressed, few women outside those belonging to the urban elites had access to their services or could afford them. Mary O'Brien, a pioneer wife and mother who was wealthy enough to have permanent assistance in her own home most of the time, was able to help a neighbour give birth in her isolated Upper Canadian community in the 1830s. She also helped the new mother cope with the postpartum depression that followed. Assistance was not always forthcoming, however. O'Brien wrote to relatives in England of her own feat of "cheating the doctor" by giving birth attended only by her husband and children on the occasion of at least one of her confinements. High rates of both maternal and infant mortality belied the prevailing messages about the joy that women would experience upon embracing motherhood. It is estimated in Upper Canada, for example, that at least one child in every family would die before reaching the teen years.[29]

A woman's security was also frequently jeopardized by the loss of her spouse. The census for Hamilton, Canada West, indicates that nearly one-quarter of the women over 40 and one-third of the women over 50 were widows in 1851.[30] In comparable urban centres, the large number of women of marriageable age compared to the number of men probably reduced the likelihood of remarriage for many. Furthermore, given the risks of childbirth, many widows who could support themselves perhaps preferred not to remarry. Early widowhood would interrupt the childbearing potential of women, and the decision not to remarry would curtail it. The cumulative effect of such individual decisions may help explain the relatively small family sizes in an urban community like Hamilton, with its large number of widows.

All studies of British North American communities indicate that, in most places and times, the majority of households consisted of nuclear families; that is, they were composed of the conjugal couple and their children. In Hamilton and the predominantly rural community of Peel County, Canada West, for example, the proportions of all households that were described as simple—that is, composed solely of nuclear families—at mid-century were 79 and 56 percent, respectively. But it is also clear that over time and as a result of a variety of circumstances households expanded and contracted. In Hamilton and Peel, more than one in ten households were extended by the presence of relatives in 1851; the same year in Moncton, New Brunswick, nearly one-quarter of all households were multiple—that is, they contained more than one conjugal couple. This high proportion, compared to other British North American localities, is attributed to the press of population resulting from a ship-building boom in mid-century Moncton.[31]

Examination of the Hamilton census has shown that extended families were often headed by young couples, suggesting that many young parents had extra adults on hand at the time when help with first-born and young children would have been most welcome. The evidence indicates as well that in some communities it was the more prosperous families that were able to accommodate relatives in their households, if only because they had larger houses and therefore more space.[32] But it is also true that the majority of families may well have been in this extended category at one time or another. Studies of less prosperous communities have yielded evidence that it was not always or only the very well-off who shared their households. For example, among the families living on Campobello Island, New Brunswick, where fishing was the main occupation, 26 percent of all households were extended by the presence of at least one relative in 1851.[33]

Nevertheless, wealthier families probably found it easier to expand when the occasion demanded it. The Jarvis family of Prince Edward Island is a case in point. Large enough, first of all, to accommodate at least three servants, the Jarvis home also became the residence of visiting friends and relatives for various periods during the life of its patriarch, the colony's Chief Justice Edward Jarvis. When his first wife, Maria, died in 1841, Edward's 20-year-old daughter, Mary, took over the running of the household for a while, but at her own marriage she relinquished this task. In 1843, an unmarried aunt was briefly in residence; in the same year Edward married a second wife, Elizabeth Gray. Elizabeth died in childbirth in 1847, leaving several young children of her own in addition to Maria's offspring, who still remained at home. At this point Edward welcomed into his household a second unmarried relation, who evidently continued the domestic management of his household until his death in 1852.[34]

It seems safe to suggest that women who were bearing and raising children and managing households in this period of Canadian history were less likely than is the case today to be working at these tasks single-handedly. If they did not have female relatives on hand to help out, a substantial number had servants or live-in helpers. A study of early nineteenth-century household service in Montreal and Quebec, for example, shows that 20 percent of Quebec households had at least one servant in 1818. In mid-century Hamilton, about one-quarter of the families had a resident domestic.[35] The continuing prevalence of large families, especially in the countryside, also meant that older daughters were often on hand to help with the housework and the younger children. Frances Stewart, who settled on the Otonabee River near Peterborough with her husband and children in 1833, relied entirely on her daughters when "asthma and weakness" affected her health in 1843.[36]

Childbearing, child-rearing, and helping other families with these tasks constituted a large part of women's work. Susanna Moodie wrote of walking miles on a winter day to take food to a woman who had been abandoned by her husband and who, with her children, was starving. Moodie considered her mission of charity both an obligation and a necessity.[37] The charitable tradition was handed down from mother to daughter. Ann Racey, a Loyalist brought to Canada as a small child, settled near what was to become Hamilton, Canada West, and worked among the neighbouring Iroquois; her daughter, Jane O'Reilly, helped nurse the sick in the cholera epidemic that struck the province in 1832.[38] By helping one another and the needy, and by attempting to improve the environment for their families, women were involved in community-building from the beginning.

DOMESTIC AND NON-DOMESTIC EMPLOYMENT

The other major part of women's labour was what women called their domestic employments. Older women usually managed such work—and, of course, did a great deal of it. In general, however, it was the province of younger women of almost all classes and conditions to perform service tasks in the household and farmyard. Thus, girls and young women did a great deal of the carding and spinning and various kinds of other work, both inside and outside the household. This was true whether they were daughters, domestic servants, or slaves. Girls and young women also did a lot of watching—minding small livestock or, even more routinely, younger children.

Frances Stewart's description of her daughters' work is a particularly apt illustration of young women's work. All three of her girls were under 16 years of age when Frances outlined their tasks in a letter to a friend. Work such as fetching and carrying or knitting could begin when a child was as young as five or six:

> Anna Marie is the general overseer of the household concerns, who makes all the preserves and pickles, cakes, etc. She also has the care of Johnny, the third boy, who is now five years old. . . . Ellen mends all the stockings for the little boys and repairs their clothes. She has the care of George in particular who is three; besides this she is manager and caretaker of the poultry. In spring she attends to the sowing and raising of plants and nurseries of young apple trees. Bessie is in charge of Charlie, the infant, she is always busy and can make most of her own underclothes and knits.[39]

Domestic servants were mostly young and, increasingly during the 1800s, more often young women than young men. In early nineteenth-century Montreal and Quebec, some 5 to 8 percent of the population were servants, and two-thirds of them were women. In Hamilton, in 1851, three out of ten girls aged 13 to 16 were servants in the homes of people who were not their relatives; 40 percent of all 17- to 20-year-olds were in domestic service.[40] Young female domestic servants played a central role in household production, whether they were newly arrived immigrants or a neighbour's daughter. For most, domestic service was a fairly short stage in their life cycle, something they did prior to their own marriage to support themselves or to provide a bit of extra income for their birth families. In addition to her room and board, a live-in female helper in Upper Canada between 1815 and 1840 earned $3 to $4 a month, an amount considerably lower than that paid to male help.[41]

As the colonies developed, the demand for live-in domestics increased but wages generally did not. This situation no doubts reflects the fact that very few women saw domestic service as an occupation; rather, they viewed their work as helping out. They were often considered, both by themselves and by their employers, to be part of their employer's family. In all but the most affluent households, they took their meals with the rest of the family and fully participated in the joys and sorrows of family life. Emigrant British gentry women frequently railed against the so-called Yankee practice of social levelling, and sought to replicate the class system of the mother country in their own homes. Lucy Peel, the young mistress of a comfortable home she and her husband occupied near Sherbrooke in 1833, wrote to her sister about her difficulty in getting her domestic helpers to wear servants' caps: ". . . none of the servants in this country wear caps . . . however, mine is preparing some and I made my first woman Sarah use them, I have no idea of giving way to such people." Sarah represented another group of women who sought to support themselves through domestic service; she was an Irish widow who had "put out" her own two children to the care of others so that she could provide live-in service for the Peels. When one child fell seriously ill, she left Lucy's employ to look after him.[42]

Whether they were servants, mothers, unmarried aunts, or daughters, the work that women did depended to a considerable extent on the occupations of the men who headed the households in which they lived. For example, the work of Frances Stewart and her daughters was determined in large part by the fact that they lived on a farm; but not all women lived in the countryside or occupied themselves solely with farm or housework. Eliza Ruggles, a Nova Scotian orphan who was disinherited by her Upper Canadian stepmother when she insisted on marrying a Methodist clergyman in the 1830s, helped her husband with his school for black children. Eventually, their mission to the black community took the couple to the United States and then to Africa. Eliza lost her three children and her husband in the course of this work, and later embarked on a second life as the wife of a Nova Scotian farmer. She gave birth to three more children and lived to tell her seven grandchildren about her missionary days.[43]

Eliza Ruggles's life was unusual, but she was not the only woman who travelled with a missionary husband. Methodist wives sometimes accompanied itinerant-preacher husbands on their travels, and, among the Bible Christian and Primitive Methodists, some of these missionary wives were also preachers in their own right. Frances Calloway and her husband William were Bible Christian itinerants in Prince Edward Island between 1846 and 1851. More commonly, wives made possible the work of itinerant clergymen by taking charge of both household and church activities during their husbands' absences.[44] For her part, Phillis George, a black woman married to a Baptist minister, faced not only the problem of feeding her three children despite serious food shortages in Shelburne, Nova Scotia, but also ongoing racial violence. In a riot perpetrated by a gang of disbanded soldiers, the George house was overturned; a few weeks later, a white mob beat Phillis's husband, David George, and forced him into a swamp. The family retreated to Birchtown, a nearby black community, but even there attacks by whites on the black inhabitants continued for more than a month. The Georges were among the black Loyalists of Nova Scotia who eventually sought refuge in Sierra Leone.[45]

The wives and daughters of fur traders were also involved with their husbands' and fathers' work. Thérèse Schindler and Madeleine La Framboise, Métis sisters, accompanied their spouses in the trade; both also became independent traders themselves when widowed.[46] Other wives went to sea with husbands who were mariners. The Englishwoman Frances Hornby Barkley was with her new husband on the voyage of discovery that took them to the Pacific northwest and the coast of what was to become British Columbia in 1787. She journeyed there again with him in the 1790s. Similar voyages were also part of the tradition and practice of Maritime women. Indeed, Maritime women "regularly accompanied" sea captain husbands and fathers on their voyages well into the late nineteenth and early twentieth centuries.[47]

If women like Eliza Ruggles and Frances Calloway, the sisters Schindler and La Framboise, or Frances Barkley travelled in order to play their part in the family, other women worked with their husbands closer to home. On Newfoundland's northeast coast, sometime in the eighteenth century, women's presence marked the transformation of the cod fishery from an industry pursued by migrant fishermen to one dependent on residents, as family workers began to replace the male servants hired by the companies. While women's domestic work continued to be important, that labour had to be accommodated to the rhythm of the fishery. Women played a key role by cleaning, salting, spreading the salted fish out on flakes (raised platforms), and turning it often to prevent it from becoming sunburned. Since the quality of the cure determined the price paid for the cod, women's skill in preparing the fish was critical.[48] Ephraim Tucker, an American travelling up the coast of Labrador for his health in the summer of 1838, was astonished at how constantly the women worked, noting that they engaged

> in the hard and laborious toils of fishing with as much zeal and activity as the males. When the salmon and trout fishing commences, the women and children employ themselves assiduously in the sport, and are often out night and day while the season of this fishery lasts. At the fish stands, while the cod fishery is in the full tide of operation, the women are seen among the most constant and dextrous in dressing the fish, thrown up by the fishermen. Some of these females will dress two or three thousand fish in a single day.[49]

Women on farms were no less involved in family business. As the women of New France had before them, British North American farm wives and daughters took charge of the poultry and barnyards and the growing of vegetables and fruit in addition to their household tasks. They were involved in food production at two levels: tending, growing, and gathering food; and salting, drying, or otherwise preserving it, as well as preparing dairy products, such as butter and cheese—all this in addition to cooking meals for large families and for regular farm servants or temporary hired labour. The husbands, brothers, and fathers of farm women were frequently away: off in the lumber shanty, rafting the potash down the river, or taking the wheat to market. At such times women took over all the responsibilities of the farm. The letters of Robert to Eliza Hoyle, of Lacolle, Lower Canada, demonstrate a husband's expectation that his wife should be able to handle everything in the absence of her male partner. In addition to looking after his three offspring from a previous marriage as well as her own children, during Robert's endless sojourns on business in Quebec and Stanstead Eliza received detailed instructions from him regarding not only the conduct of the farm and the mill, but also the collection of his debts.[50] Other pioneer diaries and letters tell the same story: a frequently absent husband; wife and children—as well as servants, if there were any—growing vegetables and fruits, looking after animals, and occupying themselves with the production of the family's basic food.

Many women, like the former servant Nancy, may also have been occupied in spinning or weaving if they had time left over. Although men eventually dominated professional weaving, women produced homespun flax and wool; some spun and wove for their neighbours as well as for their own families. This work was particularly intense in Lower Canada in the early nineteenth century. The evidence is contradictory about how widespread weaving actually was; it is clear, however, that in turn-of-the-century Lower Canada, rural women were chiefly the weavers. Lists of equipment taken from inventories of the household effects of deceased persons indicate that in the region around Quebec, only 30 percent of households possessed looms but around 80 percent had spinning wheels. In many families, it would seem, women did all their own spinning but had their wool and linens woven by others, or went to a neighbour's home to weave.[51]

Painting illustrating the domestic manufacture of straw hats in Quebec. After a painting by Cornelius Krieghoff, 1852.

Source: Library and Archives Canada/C-11224

Whether they bought or wove fabric, most rural women knitted and sewed, manufacturing most or all of their families' clothing. And it was women's subsistence work as well as the production of goods for sale—spun wool, woven goods, butter, cheese, and the like—that made possible the accumulation of capital in many farm families.[52]

Mary Morris Bradley of New Brunswick left the following description of her subsistence labour after nine months of marriage to her first husband in 1790. "I had the privilege of two cows' milk," she reported.

> One my husband brought home, and the other my father gave me; so that by an exchange of milk with my mother, I made plenty of cheese and butter for our use. We raised potatoes sufficient for the family, and for fatting our pork; so that with these necessaries of life, milk and butter, potatoes and pork, with but little bread, we lived; excepting particular occasions, I made little use of tea and sugar.[53]

The reminiscences of this New Brunswick housewife also demonstrate the way in which British North American women's work in the home could make the difference to a family's survival. In the first year of their marriage, Bradley's husband got into debt over a lumber transaction, with the following result:

> Just at this critical time, it occurred to me, I will commence the business of weaving. Accordingly, I set up my loom, and notified the neighbours, and I soon had plenty of work. I took my pay in such trade as was suitable for our family's use, which made payment easy for my customers. I soon got into the way of helping ourselves greatly. My labor was hard; but I was favoured with a good constitution, and I felt much encouraged and truly thankful for such a providential opening.[54]

Providential or not, Mary Bradley's weaving evidently saved the day. By 1805, the Bradleys were able to move into Saint John. Here Mary and her husband kept a grocery store and

Acadian woman from Chezzetcook, Nova Scotia, with basket of eggs and hand-knit woollen socks, 1859.

Source: In F.S. Cozzens "Acadia; or a month with the Blue-noses," 1859. Nova Scotia Archives and Record Management. NSARM Photo Collection: People - Acadian French Women

rented out part of their house, eventually paying off the mortgage and enjoying the "great blessing" of owning "a comfortable home." Many other women in New Brunswick made substantial contributions to their household incomes well into the late nineteenth century by manufacturing homespun cloth and knitting mittens, socks, underwear, and other warm clothing for men who laboured in the lumber camps and fisheries.[55]

Similarly, Catharine Parr Traill and Susanna Moodie frequently engaged their many talents to save their families from eviction and hunger. When writing did not produce sufficient income, Catharine turned her hand to teaching, nursing, midwifery, selling eggs, and raising geese for their down. For her part, Susanna worked late into the night hand-painting tree fungus for sale in Peterborough, and writing articles for various literary magazines "by the uncertain light of old rags dipped in pork lard and stuffed into the mouth of a bottle." When Catharine could not afford tallow for candles, she resorted to burning pine knots to provide light for her writing.[56]

Plain and fancy sewing provided another avenue of remunerative work that could be done in one's own household or in the homes of other women on a rotating basis. Indeed, by the middle of the nineteenth-century, sewing had replaced weaving as a major source of income. "Seamstress" is, in fact, one of the few employments that emerges clearly on mid-nineteenth-century census returns as a woman's occupation. In Canada East and West, 553 women were listed as seamstresses in the census of 1851.[57] Far more women than these 553 were undoubtedly making their livings this way as the fashion trade expanded in British North America. Townswomen of the period not only wanted dresses, shawls, and cloaks, but also increasingly demanded corsets, hats, and gloves. The hat industry alone created substantial employment for women. Mrs. Jones and Miss Rose Anne Osbourne moved from Quebec to York, Upper Canada, in 1828 in order to set up

Nineteenth-century engraving contrasting the toil of old-fashioned hand sewing to the ease of modern machine sewing. Engraving by John Henry Walker.

Source: McCord Museum M930.50.8.469

"a Millinery, Bonnet and Dressmaking Shop"; Mrs. Caffrey of Brockville advertised her "inexpensive silk, straw and leg horn bonnets" in her local paper in 1832; and Mrs. M. A. Sterritt, a black businesswoman in Chatham, solicited customers in 1855 for her dresses, cloaks, and children's wear by advertising in the *Provincial Freeman*.[58]

Some urban housekeepers turned their homes into inns or shops; others took in sewing or laundry. In the eighteenth and nineteenth centuries, doing laundry was probably one of women's most physically demanding jobs. Hauling water, lifting water-soaked fabrics, heating irons, stirring, rinsing, and wringing were only some of the steps that might have been involved. A study of the process at its most elaborate, as it would have been done in a wealthy household in the first half of the nineteenth century, outlines some 10 steps altogether, including scrubbing especially dirty clothes on a washboard; adding blueing compound to prevent linens from turning yellow; starching; and putting large items through long wooden rollers known as "mangles" to wring out the water and flatten them.[59]

An examination of eighteenth-century Nova Scotia civil litigation records has revealed women traders, innkeepers, retailers, and others who earned their livings in business; while many of these litigants were widows and single women, others were married women whose work supported families or supplemented other family income.[60] Rose Fortune, a black Nova Scotian, was among the more enterprising examples of a nineteenth-century businesswoman. Fortune set herself up as a carter to move baggage from ship to shore in Annapolis Royal in the 1820s, eventually creating a transport business that was to remain in her family for 125 years. She established a second related business, providing a wake-up service to travellers so that they would not miss their ships. She also appointed herself as a police constable to keep unruly local youth under control, an activity that has earned her, by some accounts, the designation of the first policewoman in Canada.[61]

A much more typical remunerative occupation that women shared with men was school teaching. In the eighteenth century and the first half of the nineteenth, it was relatively easy for women to teach because most schools were domestic affairs. Indeed, the word *school* referred more to the teacher and her pupils than to whatever housing a school might have. The schoolmistress advertised her skills in the instruction of reading and writing, or of sewing, French, or fine arts, and waited at home for her pupils—as indeed did the vast majority of schoolmasters. When the teacher moved, so did her school; her pupils came on an irregular basis, attending only when they could be spared from

A sketch of Rose Fortune, who began a family cartage business in Annapolis Royal, Nova Scotia, around 1825. The business continued to support her descendants until 1960.

Source: Black Cultural Centre for Nova Scotia

their tasks at home. As the numbers of towns and newspapers expanded in British North America, so did the ads and the schools—which, like farming, fishing, or fur trading, were often family enterprises. A widow and her daughters, a husband and wife, or two sisters might set up a school together; the combinations varied, as did the subjects offered and the clientele. What is certain is that these domestic or private schools often taught quite large numbers of children and were important educational resources in their communities, as well as vital sources of income for the schoolmistresses and their families.[62]

Angélique and Marguerite Nolin are just one of many examples of sisters who taught. After their father died (sometime in the 1820s), these young mixed-descent women were persuaded to set up a school in Red River in 1829 by the Roman Catholic bishop of the region, Joseph-Norbert Provencher. The record does not supply details about the content of their lessons, but their pupils were undoubtedly the Métis children of French-Canadian fur traders and their Aboriginal wives, whose families had started to settle in the Red River area. The Nolins' knowledge made it possible for the priest in the area to translate texts into Ojibwa. In this way, they were representative of a number of Aboriginal and Métis women during this period who taught their languages to missionaries and helped with translations of various religious works.[63]

It was also in the 1820s that Kate Andrews opened a "private school" in the "ample basement flat of her . . . commodious residence" in Liverpool, Nova Scotia, shortly after her second marriage. Her chronicler notes that the schoolmistress was self-educated:

> By conversation with broadly educated persons with whom she came in contact, by perusal of books and periodicals, as well as by practical definite study, she had informed herself on many subjects. Her reading manner was delightful, her calligraphy elegant in style. With this acquired knowledge, and her art in needlework, she at length felt well equipped for imparting instruction to the children of the town.

The school, which was mainly for day pupils but always had a few boarders as well, moved with its teacher when she moved house. It continued for some 50 years, touching nearly every family in the community for three or four generations. Kate taught with the assistance of a servant and later that of a niece. "Gentility" as well as the three Rs and needlework constituted the curriculum.[64]

There were many such schools in British North America by the early decades of the nineteenth century. Some catered to the well-to-do; others had a fairly representative clientele of pupils. Anne Langton, an Upper Canadian spinster who taught school two days a week in the rural household that she managed for her brother and elderly parents, saw her work as charity toward the local poor. But more often than not, domestic schools provided women with a livelihood or with a way to supplement the family income. Eliza Thresher, a painter and watercolourist married to artist George Thresher, supplemented the family income by operating a school for young ladies in Halifax between 1821 and 1823. With the help of her daughters, she taught drawing and painting. After the family moved to Charlottetown, in 1830, she opened another school in which a number of subjects were taught.[65]

As we have illustrated, the transition from domestic to public employment was a subtle one for women, and one example of this transition can be seen in the changes in women's involvement in public education. A first step was taken when a few British North American married women, who had been teaching in their own homes, applied for and received certification as teachers eligible to receive the newly available provincial school grants; their household schools thus became public schools by virtue of this new source of income, although they continued to conduct their teaching at home. The more typical process in the nineteenth century, however, was in the reverse direction: the school itself moved out of domestic space and into public space—the tax-supported school-house—and the teacher moved with it. Initially the distance was not great. Most publicly employed schoolmistresses were young unmarried women or widows who taught in a schoolhouse not far from home. Often they taught only in the summer, when male teachers were less available and the pupils tended to be younger. But by mid-century, women were teaching in winter schools, too.[66]

Women of African origin were deeply involved in teaching in British North America for the deep-seated racism of the time resulted in blacks in many regions having to organize their own schools. In Brindley Town, Nova Scotia, the black Loyalist teacher Joseph Leonard was assisted by his daughter, who taught sewing to the girls in the school; in Preston, the black school was entirely under the direction of Mrs. Catherine Abernathy.[67] When the fugitive slave migration brought a new African-American population to Canada West, women teachers were among these migrants as well. One was Mary Miles Bibb, born in 1820, who had graduated from the Massachusetts State Normal School; she had taught in elementary schools in Boston and Albany, as well as in an African-American high school in Cincinnati, before her marriage to fellow abolitionist Henry Bibb.[68] In 1850, the Bibbs came to Sandwich, Canada West, where Mary Bibb helped found the Windsor Anti-Slavery Society, assisted other migrants through the Refugee Home Society, and also found time to work on her husband's newspaper, the *Voice of the Fugitive*. More important, she offered the first formal education for black children in Sandwich township, first in her own home and subsequently in a schoolhouse. Following the Bibbs' move to Windsor in 1852, Mary established another school that welcomed both black and white pupils. An abolitionist traveller writing about Canada West in 1861 felt that his readers would already know about Mary Bibb's work and so did not feel called upon to describe it in detail, but his admiration was obvious: "Her labours during the lifetime of Mr. Bibb, in connection with him, for the fugitives, and her exertions since, are too well known for me to make mention here. Mrs. [Bibb] Cary has a private school with about 40 pupils, mostly of the better class of Windsor."[69] Following the death of her first husband, Mary Bibb had married the brother-in-law of another famous black abolitionist and teacher, Mary Ann Shadd—later Mary Shadd Cary. Like Bibb, Shadd Cary taught in a number of places in Canada West before she returned to the United States during the Civil War to serve as a recruiting officer for the Union forces.[70]

By 1851, almost one-fifth of teachers in publicly supported elementary schools in Canada West were women, and in Nova Scotian parish or common schools the proportion was about the same. But in New Brunswick, almost half the teachers were women by mid-century; in Canada East, the proportion who were women was higher still, reaching 69 percent by 1859. The trend toward women teaching in public schools did not necessarily originate in cities, however. Although urban schools were beginning to be interested in employing female teachers as assistants, even at mid-century their numbers were still tiny. A study of teachers in central Canada during the middle of the nineteenth century suggests that rural poverty and the lure of resource industries for young men explain in part the preferential hiring of young women in the common schools. In addition, as rural school trustees and commissioners candidly admitted, female teachers could be got for "half the price"; when local funds to match the government grant for salaries were pitifully small, male teachers were simply beyond the community's reach.[71] In some regions, however, even the population's poverty did not result in the hiring of many women. In Newfoundland, school inspectors in the mid-1840s turned up a total of only four Roman Catholic and nine Protestant women teachers in the whole colony, and it was clear that both inspectors shared a preference for school*masters*.[72]

As well, some schoolmasters railed against the advent of the woman teacher. They and later commentators contended that female teachers, being less educated, less experienced, and less attached to the work force than were their male counterparts, accepted low wages and prevented teaching from becoming a suitable profession for men. However, many rural women teachers in Lower Canada in the late 1830s had comparable levels of education and experience to those of male teachers and did consider teaching to be their chosen career. It was the substantial reduction of government subsidies to local school boards, better opportunities for males in other professions, and a significant increase in the amount of teaching undertaken by religious orders that led men to desert primary teaching in that colony.[73] Increasingly, public-school teaching became an occupation for girls who sought employment immediately after their own schooling was over.

Perhaps the most difficult to document of women's vocations in the pre-industrial era was also one of the most important: the vocation of healer or midwife. Part of the problem of documentation is no doubt the fact that healing and midwifery were arts practised to some degree by all women in caring for their families and helping their neighbours. Probably most women who were literate kept records of medicinal remedies for use when their families became ill; the non-literate learned from watching and helping older relatives, and passed the treatments on orally to younger generations. But as there had been in New France, so in British North America there were also women who were renowned and sought-after for their knowledge of herbs and for their midwifery skills. The importance of the woman healer to her community is illustrated by the story of Elizabeth Doane, an eighteenth-century immigrant to Nova Scotia. A thrice-married mother of 11, Doane migrated from New England to Nova Scotia before the American Revolution, settling in the town of Barrington. Her knowledge of herbs, surgery, and midwifery was so highly prized by her neighbours that when her husband considered returning to New England in 1770 because his business was not prospering, 35 petitioners supported Elizabeth Doane's request for a land grant from the town proprietors so that she could build a house and stay.[74]

Elizabeth Innes, a New Brunswick midwife, kept a diary but began it only on her sixtieth birthday. The diary recorded cures for rheumatism and a recipe for plastering a weak joint, as well as the various deaths, accidents, and other calamities that occurred in her family and neighbourhood. Under the heading "Nursing," she noted that in her time she had nursed "168 women in their Confinement and 150 Labour." One of the first midwives in Elgin, an African-Canadian settlement near Chatham, Ontario, was Julia Laison; in gratitude for her services, several mothers named their daughters Julia.[75]

Catharine Parr Traill, Elizabeth Doane, Mary Bradley, Elizabeth Innes, Mrs. Caffrey, or Julia Laison may have made little distinction between their housework and their other activities. While most of their domestic employments were unpaid, such activities as weaving, millinery, dressmaking, laundry, school teaching, and midwifery could and did bring in income—income that was often essential. Nearly all of this work nevertheless took place in "domestic space." Christiana Morris, born in Nova Scotia in 1804, married a Micmac man who died shortly after their marriage. To support herself and two children she took into her home, she relied on her exquisite quillwork, which was based on traditional Micmac handicrafts. She won a number of prizes for her work at provincial exhibitions, and was given a grant of land in appreciation for a pair of moccasins she made for Queen Victoria. This land enabled her to engage in livestock production and market gardening and ensured her a more stable income.[76]

Art was another way for women, both those who were professionally trained and those who were amateurs, to earn at least a partial income. When Agnes Moodie Fitzgibbon found herself a widow at the age of 32 with five young children to support, she decided to publish an illustrated volume of Canadian wildflowers, using a manuscript prepared by her aunt, Catharine Parr Traill. Traill had made a name for herself as a talented amateur botanist by sending specimens of Canadian plants to scientists in England. Unable to find a Toronto printer capable of producing finely engraved lithographs, Agnes etched her own intricate designs onto a block of limestone and printed a total of 5 000 copies of her drawings, each of which she painstakingly hand-coloured with the help of her three eldest daughters.[77]

Countless were the women, also, who ran small inns or taverns in their homes, or who accepted lodgers. Taking in boarders was an especially vital occupation for townswomen. For example, the census for Hamilton, Canada West, records that 29 percent of all households in that community contained boarders in 1851.[78] Since a woman who took in boarders often provided a laundry service as well as meals for her lodgers, the work involved was far from minimal. Like domestic service, weaving, laundry, and sewing—and even teaching and healing—keeping boarders was an expansion of women's traditional role, a way women could respectably earn their livings or assist in the maintenance of their families without straying very far from either their homes or their communities' expectations. Widows, on the other hand, might take on their husbands' businesses in other, less traditionally female occupational areas. In mid-nineteenth century Upper Canada, widows held 4 percent of tavern licences, and ran some of the colony's most prosperous drinking establishments. While married women could not legally own their own property at this time, many ran public houses and inns on their husband's behalf and often relied on their daughters to assist in cooking, cleaning, and other domestic tasks required to keep the enterprise running.[79]

Prostitution was another, if not respectable, way of earning money. British North America had many military installations, and there is no doubt that prostitution was a form of employment for some women in the ports and garrison towns. Taverns and brothels in urban centres, such as Halifax, Quebec City, Montreal, and York, attracted

An advertisement appearing in the *St. Andrew's Standard*, July 21, 1838, for Mrs. Elizabeth Atherton's hotel and livery stables located in Saint Stephen, New Brunswick.
Source: St. Andrews Standard of July 21, 1838. University of New Brunswick.

a steady stream of soldiers, sailors, and local residents. Lack of education, racial and ethnic discrimination, and few opportunities for alternative paid employment combined to increase the likelihood that members of certain groups of women—for example, Irish immigrant, Aboriginal, and black—would have to rely on prostitution to support themselves. Many sex trade workers were homeless vagrants for whom the brothel offered a place to live and to socialize with other women, as well as to eke out a living. When Margaret Delany was arrested in a raid on a Montreal bawdy house in 1841, she was allowed to stay behind to mind her five children, who lived in the house with her. In some instances, prostitution was a family affair, involving mothers, daughters, and sisters. "Prostitute" and "Keeper of house of ill-fame" were among the occupations that appeared on the 1851 census returns for Hamilton, suggesting that one census taker at least was thinking in terms of permanent labels or identities.[80]

Interestingly enough, "Widow" and "Spinster" were also designated occupations on the census. In the latter case, the term had evolved over the centuries from designating a woman who spun wool and therefore could earn her own living, to one who remained single beyond the normally accepted age of marriage for women. In both cases, this specification presumably reflected the understanding that a woman's marital status had an effect on what she did. Certainly, a woman who had lost her husband would have been anxious to have remunerative employment of some kind, unless she had been provided for by her family prior to her widowhood. Women who did not marry also increasingly needed paid work. We know that many widows and single women either sought or created employment for themselves.

Yet if the word "Wife" was occasionally to be found in the column for occupations on the census, this column was generally left blank opposite the names of married women. Did most census takers believe, therefore, that wives did not work? Or was their work so taken for granted that it did not need to be itemized on the census? Perhaps the answer lies in the fact that wives' roles were too diverse and variable to be easily pinned down. An additional answer is to be found in the perception, increasingly powerful as we move into the nineteenth century, of a growing gulf between two newly defined worlds: the personal, domestic world of women and the family, where it was assumed that traditional female work would and should continue to go on; and a newly developing public world, from which wives and children were most appropriately excluded. Work or employment that could be dignified by the title of an occupation would increasingly be seen as belonging to the latter sphere, the sphere governed and occupied chiefly by men. The mid-nineteenth century was still a period when extraordinary numbers of people in British North America—perhaps the majority—had more than one occupation. To identify men or women by a single profession or kind of work, as the census did, was itself a move toward altering people's perceptions of what they did with their lives and who they were.

Men's occupations expanded in number and began to move out of the household; in some cases, they became specialized, full-time vocations. Women's domestic employments began to seem, in contrast, rather limited, unspecialized, and poorly remunerated.[81] Yet in British North America, this was largely an urban phenomenon and one that was not noticeable until the middle decades of the nineteenth century. Probably relatively few British North American women were greatly affected by the new attitudes toward women's work that were developing in England and New England, where things were patently changing far more rapidly.

Nevertheless, upper- and middle-class emigrants from New England and England could not and did not leave their belief in the ideology of "domestic" or "true" womanhood behind when they came to British North America. They adhered to the ideology as best they could, aligning themselves with those in the colonies who seemed sympathetic and who shared their belief that every woman was supported by a father, a brother, or a husband. Two of Anne Powell's three daughters did not marry, but there was no question of either woman being allowed to work for her living—despite Anne's own history of employment in a millinery shop in Boston, where she had been set up in business by her eminently successful businesswoman aunt in the 1780s. Of the two unmarried daughters, Anne and Elizabeth, only Elizabeth successfully adapted to the pursuit of good works and ornamental dependency that was considered appropriate for a respectable single woman in the Powell circle in the early 1800s. Daughter Anne clearly craved something different, but was not permitted to found the school that she coveted and thus seek a life of her own. In an ill-fated attempt to escape from what eventually became an unbearable situation at home, Anne finally lost her life in a shipwreck off the coast of Ireland in 1822.[82]

In the upper-middle-class and affluent circles of families like the Powells, traditional class prejudice began to share mental space with a new ideology of domesticity that—in theory, at least—emphasized the differences between women and men more than the differences between the classes. As a result of its pervasive stress on differences between the sexes, considered to run the gamut from physical to intellectual and even spiritual, this system of beliefs increasingly called for the creation and maintenance of separate spheres of activity for women and men for the good of society. But in the world of British North America, this ideology denied what the vast majority of women, even those in the urban middle classes, actually experienced: the absolute necessity of work and sometimes of hard labour in the household, on the farm, or wherever they lived, to keep body and soul together and to keep the family going. This ideology also denied the vital contribution British North American women made to family and community economies by their reproductive and productive labour. In the former category, they had babies and raised children; they also fed, clothed, cared for, and otherwise reproduced the paid labour force. In the second category, they did work that not only was essential to the survival of their families but that often made all the difference to the family's ability to accumulate capital as well.

The vast majority of British North American women were probably beyond the reach of the disabling beliefs that so negatively affected the life of Anne Powell's daughter Anne. If women were not supposed to engage in productive or remunerative work, most British North American women did not know it. Or, if they thought that this was the case, they were soon disabused of the notion. Even Susanna Moodie disciplined herself "to learn and practice all the menial employments which are necessary to a good settler's wife." She admired Canadian women, who possessed the "excellent practical abilities" that were so essential on the frontier, and eventually prided herself not only on her neat rows of potatoes but also on her ability to bring in some much-needed cash through her literary and artistic productions. Finally, Susanna Moodie learned that chaos and difficulty did not last forever and could even be productive of good. Indeed, she found that it was when their situation appeared most desperate that they "were on the threshold of a new state of things, which was born out of that very distress."[83]

Notes

1. Marilyn Porter, "'She Was Skipper of the Shore-Crew': Notes on the History of the Sexual Division of Labour in Newfoundland," *Labour/Le Travail* 15 (Spring 1985): 109.
2. Diane Bélanger et Lucie Rozon, *Les religieuses au Québec* (Montréal: Libre Expression, 1982), 294; Roberto Perin, *Ignace de Montréal* (Montréal: Boréal Express, 2008); Sister Maura, *The Sisters of Charity, Halifax* (Toronto: Ryerson Press, 1956).
3. Elva E. Jackson, "The True Story of the Legendary Granny Ross," *Nova Scotia Historical Quarterly* 8, 1 (1988): 42–61; Naomi Griffiths, *From Migrant to Acadian: A North American Border People, 1604–1755* (Montreal and Kingston: McGill-Queen's University Press, 2005).
4. James W. St. G. Walker, *The Black Loyalists: The Search for a Promised Land in Nova Scotia and Sierra Leone, 1783–1870* (Toronto: University of Toronto Press, 1992).
5. Beth Light and Alison Prentice, eds., *Pioneer and Gentlewomen of British North America, 1713–1867* (Toronto: New Hogtown Press, 1980), 1–12; Elisabeth de Moissac, "L'éducation à

la Rivière Rouge (1844–1870): Les Soeurs Grises," *Canadian Catholic Historical Association, Report* (1948–49): 39–45; Jan Gould, *Women of British Columbia* (Saanichton, B.C.: Hancock House, 1975), chap. 2; Adele Perry, *On the Edge of Empire: Gender, Race and the Making of British Columbia, 1849–71* (Toronto: University of Toronto Press, 2001).

6. Janice Potter-Mackinnon, *While the Women Only Wept: Loyalist Refugee Women in Eastern Ontario* (Montreal and Kingston: McGill-Queen's University Press, 1993).

7. Elizabeth Jane Errington, *Emigrant Worlds and Transatlantic Communities: Migration to Upper Canada in the First Half of the Nineteenth Century* (Montreal and Kingston: McGill-Queen's University Press, 2007), 74–110; L. Lee, "The Myth of Female Equality in Pioneer Society: The Red River Colony as a Test Case," University of Manitoba, M.A. Thesis, 1978, 14.

8. H. C. Burleigh, "A Tale of Loyalist Heroism," *Ontario History* 42, 2 (1950): 91–99; Potter-Mackinnon, *While the Women*, espec. 50–51, 108, 150–52.

9. Wallace Brown, *The Good Americans: The Loyalists in the American Revolution* (New York: Morrow, 1969), 140–41, 206.

10. Potter-Mackinnon, *While the Women*, espec. chaps. 2–4.

11. Beatrice Ross Buszek, "'By Fortune Wounded': Loyalist Women in Nova Scotia," *Nova Scotia Historical Review* 7, 2 (1987): 54.

12. W. A. Spray, "The Settlement of the Black Refugees in New Brunswick, 1815–1836," in P. A. Buckner and David Frank, eds., *Atlantic Canada Before Confederation: The Acadiensis Reader* (Fredericton: Acadiensis Press, 1985); Sylvia Hamilton, "Naming Names, Naming Ourselves: A Survey of Early Black Women in Nova Scotia," in Peggy Bristow, co-ord., et al., *"We're Rooted Here and They Can't Pull Us Up": Essays in African Canadian Women's History* (Toronto: University of Toronto Press, 1994), 13–40.

13. Adrienne Shadd, "'The Lord Seemed to Say "Go"': Women and the Underground Railroad Movement," and Peggy Bristow, "'Whatever You Raise in the Ground You Can Sell It in Chatham': Black Women in Buxton and Chatham, 1850–65," in Bristow et al., *"We're Rooted Here,"* espec. 53–54, 81–82, 96.

14. Susanna Moodie, *Roughing It in the Bush or Life in Canada* (London, 1852; Virago Press edit., 1986), espec. 342; Charlotte Gray, *Sisters in the Wilderness: The Lives of Susanna Moodie and Catharine Parr Traill* (Toronto: Penguin, 1999); Elizabeth Hopkins, "A Prison-House for Prosperity: The Immigrant Experience of the Nineteenth Century Upper Class British Woman," in Jean Burnet, ed., *Looking into My Sister's Eyes: An Exploration in Women's History* (Toronto: Multicultural History Society of Ontario, 1986); Marian Fowler, *The Embroidered Tent: Five Gentlewomen in Early Canada* (Toronto: Anansi, 1982); Carl Ballstadt, Elizabeth Hopkins, and Michael Peterman, eds., *Susanna Moodie: Letters of a Lifetime* (Toronto: University of Toronto Press, 1985).

15. Diary of Anne Powell, Diaries Collection, Public Archives of Ontario.

16. Marianne McLean, *The People of Glengarry: Highlanders in Transition, 1745–1820* (Montreal and Kingston: McGill-Queen's University Press, 1991), espec. 139–41.

17. See, for example, D. Suzanne Cross, "The Neglected Majority: The Changing Role of Women in 19th Century Montreal," in Susan Mann Trofimenkoff and Alison Prentice, eds., *The Neglected Majority: Essays in Canadian Women's History* (Toronto: McClelland and Stewart, 1977) vol. 1, 66–86; Michael B. Katz, *The People of Hamilton, Canada West: Family and Class in a Mid-Nineteenth-Century Canadian City* (Cambridge, Mass.: Harvard University Press, 1976), 265; Jane Errington, "Single Pioneering Women in Upper Canada," *Families* 31, 1 (February 1992): 5–19.

18. Gretchen Green, "Molly Brant, Catharine Brant, and Their Daughters: A Study in Colonial Acculturation," *Ontario History* 81, 3 (September 1989): 235–50.

19. Gray, *Sisters in the Wilderness*, 108–9.

20. Sylvia Van Kirk, "'Women in Between': Indian Women in Fur Trade Society in Western Canada," *Historical Papers/Communications historiques* (1977): 30–47; Van Kirk, "'What If Mama Is an Indian?': The Cultural Ambivalence of the Alexander Ross Family," in John Foster, ed., *The Developing West* (Edmonton: University of Alberta Press, 1983), 125–36; Van Kirk, *"Many Tender Ties": Women in Fur Trade Society, 1670–1870* (Winnipeg: Watson and Dwyer, 1980), espec. chap. 8.

21. Sylvia Van Kirk, "The Impact of White Women on Fur Trade Society," in Trofimenkoff and Prentice, eds., *Neglected Majority* vol. 1, 27–48; Van Kirk, *"Many Tender Ties,"* chap. 8.

22. See Jennifer S. H. Brown, "Ultimate Respectability: Fur Trade Children in the 'Civilized World,'" *The Beaver* (Winter 1977), 4–10 and (Spring 1978), 48–55.

23. Van Kirk, *"Many Tender Ties,"* 111–13, 156, 208–9, and 237; John Adams, *Old Square Toes and His Family: The Life of James and Amelia Douglas* (Victoria, B.C.: Horsdal & Schubart, 2001), 30, 215; Van Kirk, "'Women in Between'"; Gould, *Women of British Columbia*, chap. 2.

24. Ingeborg Marshall, "Disease as a Factor in the Demise of the Beothuck Indians," *Culture* 1, 1 (1981): 71–77; Virginia P. Miller, "The Decline of Nova Scotia Micmac Population, A.D. 1600–1850," *Culture* 2, 3 (1982): 107–20; Ruth Holmes Whitehead, "Christina Morris: Micmac Artist and Artist's Model," *Material History Bulletin* 3 (Spring 1977): 1–14; Keith Winter, *Shananditti: The Last of the Beothucks* (North Vancouver: J. J. Douglas, 1975). On peoples of the northwest who managed to remain relatively isolated and escape the worst aspects of cultural conflict, see Julie Cruikshank, "Becoming a Woman in Athapaskan Society: Changing Traditions on the Upper Yukon River," *Western Canadian Journal of Anthropology* 5, 2 (1975): 1–14; Robin Ridington, "Stories of the Vision Quest among Dunne-Za Women," *Atlantis* 9, 1 (Fall 1983): 68–88.

25. Elizabeth Jane Errington, *Wives and Mothers, Schoolmistresses and Scullery Maids: Working Women in Upper Canada, 1790–1840* (Montreal and Kingston: McGill-Queen's University Press, 1995), 25–26.

26. Ellen M. Thomas Gee, "Marriage in Nineteenth-Century Canada," *Canadian Review of Sociology and Anthropology* 19, 3 (August 1982): 315–20; Katz, *People of Hamilton*, 271–72.

27. Jacques Henripin, *La population canadienne au début du XVIII siècle*, Institut nationale d'études démographiques: Travaux et documents, Cahier No. 22 (Paris: Presses universitaires de France, 1954); David Gagan, *Hopeful Travellers: Families, Land, and Social Change in Mid-Victorian Peel County, Canada West* (Toronto: University of Toronto Press, 1981), 70–73; Chad Gaffield, "Canadian Families in Cultural Context: Hypotheses from the Mid-Nineteenth Century," *Historical Papers/Communications historiques* (1979), espec. graph 4; Katz, *People of Hamilton*, 34, 233; Roderic P. Beaujot and Kevin McQuillan, "Social Effects of Demographic Change: Canada 1851–1981," *Journal of Canadian Studies* 21, 1 (Spring 1986): 57–59.

28. Katherine M. J. McKenna, *A Life of Propriety: Anne Murray Powell and Her Family, 1755–1849* (Montreal and Kingston: McGill-Queen's University Press, 1994), espec. 197; Gray, *Sisters in the Wilderness*, 103.

29. Audrey Saunders Miller, ed., *The Journals of Mary O'Brien* (Toronto: Macmillan, 1968); Errington, *Wives and Mothers*, 53–79.

30. Katz, *People of Hamilton*, 255.

31. Katz, *People of Hamilton*, 223; Gagan, *Hopeful Travellers*, 64–65; Sheva Medjuck, "Family and Household Composition in the Nineteenth Century: The Case of Moncton, New Brunswick, 1851–1871," *Canadian Journal of Sociology* 4, 3 (Summer 1979): 275–86.

32. Katz, *People of Hamilton*, 249, 255.

33. F. K. Donnelly, "Occupational and Household Structures of a New Brunswick Fishing Settlement: Campobello Island, 1851," in R. Chanteloup, ed., *Labour in Atlantic Canada* (Saint John: Social Service Monographs, 1981) vol. 4, 55–63; Katz, *People of Hamilton*, 250. See also Gagan, *Hopeful Travellers*, 65–67.

34. J. M. Bumsted, "The Household and Family of Edward Jarvis, 1828–1852," *The Island* 14 (Fall–Winter 1983), 22–28.

35. Claudette Lacelle, "Les domestiques dans les villes canadiennes au XIXe siècle: Effectifs et conditions de vie," *Histoire sociale/Social History* 15, 29 (May 1982): 181–207; Katz, *People of Hamilton*, 27.

36. Frances Stewart, *Our Forest Home, Being Extracts from the Correspondence of the Late Frances Stewart*, compiled and edited by her daughter, E. S. Dunlop (Toronto, 1889), 78–79.

37. Moodie, "The Walk to Dummer," *Roughing It in the Bush*, 446–82.

38. Elsie Gregory MacGill, *My Mother the Judge: A Biography of Helen Gregory MacGill* (Toronto: Peter Martin Associates, 1981), 6, 9, 32.

39. Stewart, *Our Forest Home*, 80–81.

40. Lacelle, "Les domestiques"; Katz, *People of Hamilton*, 260, 270.

41. Errington, *Wives and Mothers*, 113–14.

42. J. I. Little, ed., *"Love Strong as Death": Lucy Peel's Canadian Journal, 1833–36* (Waterloo, ON: Wilfrid Laurier University Press, 2001), 73.

43. Leone Banks Cousins, "Woman of the Year—1842: The Life of Eliza Ruggles," *Nova Scotia Historical Quarterly* 6, 4 (December 1976): 349–76.

44. Elizabeth Gillan Muir, *Petticoats in the Pulpit: The Story of Early Nineteenth-Century Methodist Women Preachers in Upper Canada* (Toronto: United Church Publishing House, 1991), 75; Marilyn Färdig Whiteley, *Canadian Methodist Women, 1766–1925: Marys, Marthas, Mothers in Israel* (Waterloo, ON: Wilfrid Laurier University Press, 2005), 37–59.

45. Sylvia Hamilton, "Our Mothers Grand and Great: Black Women of Nova Scotia," *Canadian Woman Studies/Les cahiers de la femme* 11, 3 (Spring 1991): 46; Walker, *Black Loyalists*, 48–49 and chap. 5.

46. John E. McDowell, "Madame La Framboise," *Michigan History* 56, 3 (Winter 1972): 271–86; McDowell, "Thérèse Schindler of Mackinac: Upward Mobility in the Great Lakes Fur Trade," *Wisconsin Magazine of History* 61 (Winter 1977–78), 125–43.

47. W. Kaye Lamb, "The Mystery of Mrs. Barkley's Diary," *British Columbia Historical Quarterly* 6, 1 (1942): 31–59; Margaret Conrad, "Recording Angels: Private Chronicles of Maritime Women, 1800–1950," in Alison Prentice and Susan Mann Trofimenkoff, eds., *The Neglected Majority: Essays in Canadian Women's History* (Toronto: McClelland and Stewart, 1985) vol. 2, 41–60.

48. Sean T. Cadigan, *Hope and Deception in Conception Bay: Merchant–Settler Relations in Newfoundland, 1785–1855* (Toronto: University of Toronto Press, 1995), 64–70; Porter, "She Was Skipper," 105–23. See also Phillip McCann, "Class, Gender and Religion in Newfoundland Education, 1836–1901," *Historical Studies in Education/Revue d'histoire de l'éducation* 1, 2 (Autumn 1989): 180–81.

49. Ephraim W. Tucker, *Five Months in Labrador and Newfoundland during the Summer of 1838* (Concord: 1838), 119–20.

50. Françoise Noël, *Family Life and Sociability in Upper and Lower Canada, 1780–1870: A View from Diaries and Family Correspondence* (Montreal and Kingston: McGill-Queen's University Press, 2003), 107–8.

51. David-Thiery Ruddel, "Consumer Trends, Clothing, Textiles and Equipment in the Montreal Area, 1792–1835," *Material History Bulletin* 32 (Fall 1990): 45–64. See also Judith Buxton-Keenleyside, *Selected Canadian Spinning Wheels in Perspective: An Analytical Approach* (Ottawa: National Museums of Canada, 1980), 285; Jan Noel, "'Femmes Fortes' and the Montreal Poor in the Early Nineteenth Century," in Wendy Mitchinson et al., eds., *Canadian Women: A Reader* (Toronto: Harcourt Brace, 1996), 68–85.

52. Marjorie Griffin Cohen, "The Decline of Women in Canadian Dairying," in Prentice and Trofimenkoff, eds., *Neglected Majority* vol. 2, 61–83.

53. Conrad, "Recording Angels," 44–45.

54. Conrad, "Recording Angels," 44.

55. Judith Rygiel, "Thread in Her Hands—Cash in Her Pockets": Women and Domestic Textile Production in 19th-Century New Brunswick," *Acadiensis*, 30, 2 (Spring 2001): 56–70.

56. Gray, *Sisters in the Wilderness*, 175, 137, 181.

57. *Census Reports of the Canadas*, 1851: Upper Canada vol. 1, 520; Lower Canada vol. 1, 546.

58. Errington, *Wives and Mothers*, 204, 202; Bristow, "Whatever You Raise," 104.

59. Christina Bates, "Blue Monday: A Day in the Life of a Washerwoman, 1840 . . . " *Canadian Collector* (July/August 1985), 44–48.

60. Julian Gwyn, "Female Litigants in the Civil Courts of Nova Scotia, 1749–1783," paper presented to the Atlantic Canada Studies Conference, Fredericton, May 1994.

61. Hamilton, "Naming Names," 26.

62. For a discussion of domestic schools and their teachers in Upper Canada, see Susan E. Houston and Alison Prentice, *Schooling and Scholars in Nineteenth Century Ontario* (Toronto: University of Toronto Press, 1988), chap. 3; Jane Errington, "Ladies and Schoolmistresses: Educating Women in Early Nineteenth-Century Upper Canada," *Historical Studies in Education/Revue d'histoire de l'éducation* 6, 1 (Spring 1994): 71–96; and Errington, *Wives and Mothers*, chap. 9.

63. Donald Chaput, "The 'Misses Nolin' of Red River," *The Beaver* (Winter 1975), 14–17; Carole Gerson, "Women and Print Culture" in Patricia Lockhart Fleming, Gilles Gallichan, and Yvan Lamonde, eds. *History of the Book in Canada*, I (Toronto: University of Toronto Press, 2004), 356.

64. Grace McLeod Rogers, "Kate Andrews, Schoolmistress," *Maritime Advocate and Busy East* 32 (1942), 5–10.

65. H. H. Langton, ed., *A Gentlewoman in Upper Canada: The Journals of Anne Langton* (Toronto: Clarke, Irwin, 1950); "Thresher, Eliza W.," Canadian Women Artists History Initiative, http://cwahi.concordia.ca, 1.

66. For Ontario, see Houston and Prentice, *Schooling and Scholars*, chaps. 2 and 3; for Quebec, see Andrée Dufour, *Tous à l'École: État, communautés rurales et scolarisation au Québec de 1826 à 1859* (Montréal: Éditions Hurtubise HMH Ltée, 1996), 209–19.

67. Walker, *Black Loyalists*, 80–84; Hamilton, "Our Mothers," 46.

68. Afua Cooper, "Black Women and Work in Nineteenth-Century Canada West: Black Woman Teacher Mary Bibb," in Bristow et al., *"We're Rooted Here,"* 143–70; and Cooper, "The Search for Mary Bibb: Black Woman Teacher in Nineteenth-Century Canada West," *Ontario History* 83, 1 (March 1991): 39–54.

69. Cooper, "Black Women," 157–58.

70. Adrienne Shadd, "300 Years of Black Women in Canadian History: Circa 1700–1980," *Tiger Lily* 1, 2 (1987), 7; Bristow, "'Whatever You Raise,'" 98, 105–107. See our Chapter 4 for more on Shadd Cary's work in Canada.

71. Alison Prentice, "The Feminization of Teaching," in Trofimenkoff and Prentice, eds., *The Neglected Majority* vol. 1, 49–65; Marta Danylewycz, Beth Light, and Alison Prentice, "The Evolution of the Sexual Division of Labour in Teaching: A Nineteenth Century Ontario and Quebec Case Study," *Histoire sociale/Social History* 16, 31 (May 1983): 81–109; and Marta Danylewycz and Alison Prentice, "Teachers, Gender, and Bureaucratizing School Systems in Nineteenth Century Montreal and Toronto," *History of Education Quarterly* 24, 1 (Spring 1984): 75–100.

72. Phillip McCann, "Class, Gender and Religion in Newfoundland Education, 1836–1901," *Historical Studies in Education/Revue d'histoire de l'éducation* 1, 2 (Fall 1989): 186.

73. Andrée Dufour, "Les institutrices rurales du Bas-Canada: incompétentes et inexpérimentées?" *Revue d'histoire de l'Amérique française* 51, 4 (printemps 1998): 527, 539, 547–48.

74. Phyllis R. Blakely, "And Having a Love for People," *Nova Scotia Historical Quarterly* 5, 2 (June 1975): 165–75. See also Ivy Lynn Bourgeault, Cecilia Benoit, and Robbie Davis-Floyd, eds., *Reconceiving Midwifery* (Montreal and Kingston: McGill-Queen's University Press, 2004), espec. chap. 1.

75. Elizabeth W. McGann, ed., *Whispers from the Past: Selections from the Writings of New Brunswick Women* (Fredericton: Fiddlehead/Goose Lane Editions Ltd., 1986), 145–50; Bristow, "Whatever You Raise," 92.

76. "Morris, Chistiana," Canadian Women Artists History Initiative, http://cwahi.concordia.ca, 1.

77. Gray, *Sisters in the Wilderness,* 293–94; "Fitzgibbon, Agnes Dunbar Moodie," Canadian Women Artists History Initiative, http://cwahi.concordia.ca, 1.

78. Katz, *People of Hamilton*, 222.

79. Julia Roberts, *In Mixed Company: Taverns and Public Life in Upper Canada* (Vancouver: UBC Press, 2009), 153–56; Errington, *Wives and Mothers*, 192–98.

80. Judith Fingard, *The Dark Side of Life in Victorian Halifax* (Porters Lake, Nova Scotia: Pottersfield Press, 1989); Mary Anne Poutanen, "Bonds of Friendship, Kinship, and Community: Gender, Homelessness, and Mutual Aid in Early-Nineteenth-Century Montreal," in Bettina Bradbury and Tamara Myers, eds., *Negotiating Identities in 19th- and 20th- Century Montreal* (Vancouver: UBC Press, 2005), 29; Katz, *People of Hamilton*, 348.

81. In the list of occupations for Hamilton, 21 appear to be clearly women's; men's occupations numbered several hundred (Katz, *People of Hamilton*, appendix two).

82. McKenna, *Life of Propriety*, chap. 9.

83. Moodie, *Roughing It in the Bush*, espec. 296 and 342.

CHAPTER FOUR

Women and the Public Order

British North Americans lived in a society regulated by popular custom and belief, by social hierarchy, by the rules of churches (where these existed), and, of course, by government and law. Colonial officials, magistrates, military or trading company officers, and large landowners as well as priests and other clergy wielded formal political, economic, and social power. These authority figures were all men, and their range of activity was wide. As the economies of the British North American colonies moved into the early stages of urbanization and industrialization in the 1840s, an emerging middle class composed of businessmen, industrialists, and professionals joined the ranks of men who directed the destinies of their communities.

Sometimes men in authority enforced unwritten codes. Respectability was one such code to which women, in particular, were expected to adhere. For a woman, respectability required that she dress and conduct herself in a modest, chaste, and genteel manner. Women who did not conform to this norm often paid a heavy cost for their transgressions. Such was the case at Fort Detroit in the 1780s, when Pierre Frechette, the local priest, simply expelled two "disreputable" women from his parish. He reported to his bishop that he had forced the badly behaved Madame Moisseau to leave Simon's Mill; Madame Tourangu he had likewise "chased away." In another case, in the winter of 1834, Father Timothy Browne, the parish priest in Ferryland, Newfoundland, succeeded in hounding a pregnant Peggy Mountain out of the community, despite the fact that she had successfully sued her husband for desertion and had obtained a court order for him to support her and her unborn child. The priest's campaign to have her ostracized was so successful that her only refuge was an unheated jail cell, where she gave birth to a daughter who survived only a few hours. Shortly after recovering from childbirth, Peggy was put on ship for Saint John's.[1]

These were not isolated or atypical events. Two other women who got into trouble with British North American authorities, in part because they had disguised themselves as men, illustrate the gradual encroachment of more formal regulation. One, known to history as the "Orkney lad," had come by sea to the northwest in 1806 disguised as a

Hudson's Bay Company servant (possibly in order to be with the father of her expected child); her identity was discovered only when she gave birth. Isabel Gunn was then no longer allowed to do the work of a company servant and was instead given employment as a washerwoman. Although she managed to stay in Rupert's Land for three years, Gunn was finally shipped back to Scotland by company authorities, who were enforcing a code that discouraged white women from entering or living in fur trade country at that time. Some 15 years later, Mary Palmer seems to have aggravated her disobedience of the law by cross-dressing: she was arrested in Halifax for causing a disturbance on the streets one night while wearing an officer's uniform. But although Mary had to spend the night in the watch house and appear before the magistrate in the morning, she got away with a reprimand, a small fine, and a warning.[2]

Female crime in British North America was generally minor in character. The offenders were chiefly young illiterate women who got into trouble with the law for vagrancy, drunkenness, theft, or prostitution. Yet the law could sometimes be severe, as the punishment of an eighteenth-century Halifax servant proved. She had misplaced some household silver, probably when cleaning it. After her trial and execution for theft, the missing goods were found outside, where they had been covered with snow.[3]

In the British colonies and in Hudson's Bay Company territory, women of all conditions, ranks, and stations found their lives increasingly affected by church regulation, by British law, or by new legislation passed by colonial legislatures. Some of these regulations and laws perpetuated traditional sexual inequalities or divisions of labour, or extended them to the new public world that men were in the process of creating. There is evidence, for example, that female vagrants, especially those convicted of sexual misdemeanours, were singled out as middle-class male elites sought to assert more control over public spaces. In fact, between 1810 and 1847, authorities in Montreal made over 2 500 arrests of women accused of vagrancy, compared to just over 1 300 arrests of men. Moreover, the punishments magistrates meted out to women convicted of this crime were often harsher than those they imposed on men charged under the same offence. A study of cases appearing between 1834 and 1850 before the Board of Police in Prescott, a community located in what is now the province of Ontario, also concludes that town officials increasingly used this body to assert more control over labouring class women and to impose a gendered, middle-class moral code.[4]

Women were not without recourse in the public sphere, however. Canada's first comic novel, Frances Brookes's *The History of Emily Montague*, an account of manners and morals as Brookes experienced them in Quebec in the early days of British rule, reveals a community in which upper-class women (English or French) exercised considerable social power, if no official authority.[5] The extent of this power—and the various forms of agency or resistance practised by non-elite women—is not easy to assess. But historians are finding increasing evidence on which to base discussions of women's place in the emerging public worlds of British North America, and to question the impact of the seemingly pervasive cult of domesticity on the lives of ordinary women.[6] Through their daily toil, their visible presence in public spaces, their organizational activities, and their individual acts, women ensured that the boundaries between public and private remained fluid and the interactions between them and men, multiple and complex.

REGULATING WOMEN

Jane Beaver and her husband, Herbert—the Hudson's Bay Company chaplain—complained bitterly of many things they found wrong with Fort Vancouver on the Columbia River in the late 1830s. But their greatest grief was the country marriages between traders and Aboriginal women. Due to their pressure, several couples, including James and Amelia Douglas, who had already been spouses for eight years and parented six children, were married for a second time according to the rites of the Church of England by Herbert Beaver; the church thus sought to regulate a custom that had been in place for two centuries.[7]

Church authorities no doubt found reason to complain in other parts of British North America about casual attitudes to marriage. Owing to the shortage of persons authorized to marry them officially, many couples lived together without benefit of religious rites. As the clergy became more numerous, efforts were made to alter this state of affairs, and accounts abound of couples from Newfoundland to the west coast whose several children were present at their weddings. One traveller to Canada West in 1842 met an informant who was proud of the fact that when she had married, her daughter had already been two years old. He claimed that Canadian girls preferred this practice and that Canadians considered ridiculous the "correcter feelings on this subject, of females from the old country." What this traveller either did not know or did not remember is that the high value placed on fertility and child labour in rural Europe had long been the source of similar attitudes. In Canada, too, as he himself was quick to point out, children were "so valuable a possession" that bringing "two or three into the world in this irregular fashion, instead of being a bar to marriage, proves . . . an additional attraction, making the young lady a species of heiress." It followed that the producer of Canadian children was highly valued. "After marriage," the traveller went on, the Canadian "makes an active industrious wife, but expects from her husband much deference, and even that he should wink at occasional frailties."[8]

For the most part, British North Americans appear to have believed in companionate marriage and in the importance of love and mutual respect between prospective marriage partners. Given the fact that courtship often took place within familiar networks of family and friends, most young people chose marriage partners within their own race, class, and religion. Parents of substantial material means had the most reason to influence their child's choice of a spouse, but even they do not appear to have favoured arranged marriages.[9] In urban centres young women met men in formalized situations, at balls and parties in wintertime, and at various meetings connected with their churches. Young men requested permission to call or were invited to young women's homes. Taking a young woman for a drive, if one was wealthy enough to command a sleigh or a carriage, was a customary way to pay her court; if not, taking her for a walk, or accompanying her home from an event, was another. Tradition has it that in the County of Beauce on the south shore of the St. Lawrence, when a girl was ready for courting, her brother took her to church and escorted her to a similarly minded group of young women who stood apart from their families.[10] In the countryside, the process of daily life brought the sexes together, despite the gendered divisions

Round dancing in Quebec at the beginning of the nineteenth century. Painting by George Heriot.
Source: Library and Archives Canada, Acc. No. 1989-479-2

of labour that generally prevailed. Although work was hard and time for courting and lovemaking may have seemed limited, people appear to have had a relatively open approach to sexuality, albeit one in which men had greater power and freedom than women. Respectable courting went on more or less under the watchful eyes of the young woman's elders.

There was a clear sense of family involvement when a decision to marry was made. Rebecca Byles of Halifax, for example, discussed her engagement with relatives before she accepted her future husband's proposal in 1785. More than four decades later, Mary Gapper O'Brien hesitated for some time over her proposed marriage in Upper Canada, consulting parents and siblings on both sides of the Atlantic to make sure that her services, as the one remaining unmarried daughter in the family, could be spared. In many parts of British North America, community surveillance of marriage was to be expected. This informal regulation sometimes erupted into the traditional wedding-night rioting known as the charivari. Young male revellers, often in disguise, besieged the newlyweds in their home, banging pots and pans, shouting, and demanding gifts. A charivari might happen when one spouse was much older than the other, when the bride or groom may have remarried before what was deemed an appropriate length of time, when the union was an interracial one, or when some members of the community thought that the marriage challenged existing social norms.[11]

In Quebec, the French Civil Code—and thus French marriage law—continued after the British takeover, and remained in effect in the St. Lawrence colony of Lower Canada

A country walk, such as this one depicted around 1810, might provide an opportunity for courtship or private conversation. Painting by James Pattison Cockburn.

Source: Library and Archives Canada, Acc. No. 1970-188-321 W.H. Coverdale Collection of Canadiana

after new boundaries were put in place in 1791. As revised on a number of occasions between the Conquest and 1795, the law of Quebec and then Lower Canada required the agreement of both parties, the publication of banns, and a ceremony performed by an Anglican or Catholic priest for the marriage to be legal. The wedding also had to be witnessed and registered with the civil authorities. Eventually it became a little easier to get legally married: between 1827 and 1845, clergy from other religious denominations were given the power to officiate.

While the French provision for the "community of property" continued to be operative, both the francophone and anglophone propertied classes were beginning to favour separation of property. In 1844, for example, Lydie Clément, daughter of a Montreal master shoemaker, and Hubert Langlois, a merchant in the same city, initially signed a contract to put all of their goods into a system of community of property. One day later, however, the same notary who had drawn up the contract was summoned to cancel that agreement and write another specifying that each spouse would maintain separate property. Clearly, at least one of the parties had had second thoughts about merging his or her assets. Lydie and Hubert were among a declining number of couples who were entering into such contracts: whereas before 1820, between 60 and 90 percent of couples in Quebec or Lower Canada signed marriage contracts, in the city of Montreal after that date, the proportion dropped sharply among both Protestants and Catholics. In fact, by the 1840s in Montreal, 12 percent or less signed such contracts before they married. Those who did so were mainly members of the wealthy classes, who had real property to be concerned about.[12] In cases where there was no marriage contract, couples were considered to be living under a *communauté légale* or *coutumier*. This regime did not provide them the same degree of control over what property was to be considered communal, nor how it would be treated if debts were incurred or when one spouse died.

Elsewhere in British North America, British common law governed marriage. To paraphrase the dictum of William Blackstone, England's most influential jurist, in common law the husband and wife were considered one person—and that person was the husband. In a patriarchal, patrilineal society in which private property featured largely, ensuring that one's heirs were indeed legitimate was a key concern. The wife's property and person, therefore, came entirely under the control of her husband: consequently, a husband could not be charged with raping his wife; a wife could not sue her husband or testify against him in court. He was entitled to her sexual services and could use the courts to seek compensation from anyone having sexual relations with her, encouraging her to leave him, or providing her sanctuary if she did leave him.

The families of well-to-do women sometimes attempted to protect them by drawing up marriage contracts similar to those used in Lower Canada, in order to keep brides' funds and inheritances safe from unscrupulous or incompetent husbands. But contracts do not seem to have been concluded in great numbers by English-speaking British North Americans, suggesting that few women had such protection.[13] All the same, despite the discriminatory and oppressive legal framework, there is a growing body of evidence that married women, especially those of the labouring classes, took advantage of lower civil courts to initiate suits against their husbands. In some cases, they were successful in securing judgments against them for offences such as desertion, spousal violence, and "breaking the peace". Mrs. Ann Black, who appeared some 15 times before Prescott's Board of Police between 1839 and 1851, laid charges against her husband after he called her bad names and struck her during a heated argument over her relations with soldiers stationed at Fort Wellington. He was found guilty and fined 25 shillings.[14]

Under British common law, a married woman had the right to dower—a lifetime interest in one-third of her husband's property. In Lower Canada, however, the Registry Act of 1841 eliminated the automatic right to dower, which was seen as an obstacle to commercial transactions. Dower complicated the transfer of land title since purchasers might discover, perhaps years after they acquired it, that a property was encumbered by a widow's dower rights. Since dower was based on land ownership, as urbanization proceeded and the proportion of the population that was without property grew, only wealthier women were able to benefit from dower rights. Even when and where it was operative, dower became effective only upon the death of the husband. Evidence gathered from civil court cases in Nova Scotia in the latter half of the eighteenth century reveals that widows were both plaintiffs and defendants in actions relating to the estates of their late husbands. Despite the male-dominated nature of the legal system, some widows with sufficient economic resources used the courts to advance their interests.[15]

Although a woman was guaranteed some support during widowhood, no law protected her economic interest in the case of marriage breakdown. Women who separated from their husbands lost their legal right not only to the use of whatever property the family had accumulated, but also to the custody of their children. And at a time and in a place where children's labour was extremely valuable, the loss of their children constituted more than an emotional loss to those women who endured such separations.[16] Divorce was possible, but not easy, and the law varied from colony to colony. There were several attempts to establish divorce courts in Upper and Lower Canada between 1833 and 1859, but these failed; in the Canadas, divorce had to be obtained through a special act of the legislature that was difficult and costly to achieve. Only in the Maritimes were there provisions for divorce courts. In Nova Scotia, the legislature granted the governor and council the authority to hear divorce cases in 1758; it took a subsequent law to settle the grounds, but these were fairly extensive and included impotence, adultery, and cruelty, as well as kinship within the prohibited degree, and bigamy. This relatively liberal legislation may have had some relation to initial shortages of women; it is also true that the Nova Scotia law was probably influenced by the New England planters, that is, the settlers who were moving into the colony in the mid-eighteenth century and diluting the power of the Anglican establishment. New Brunswick passed a law similar to Nova Scotia's in 1791, but the grounds for divorce were slightly different, as cruelty was not included. In the 1830s, Prince Edward Island introduced a law identical to New Brunswick's; with some amendments, it received royal assent in 1836. Yet despite the more liberal laws and divorce courts, divorce remained unusual even in the Maritime colonies.[17]

Women's lack of economic protection in marriage and the difficulty of divorce were hard enough. But even more damaging to some women was the common law's assumption of the husband's right to control his wife's person, which included control over her earnings as well as a veto over the possibility of her working for wages outside the home, control over the location of the household, the right to "confine" her to it under certain conditions, and even the right to mete out what was considered a reasonable amount of physical punishment. Of course, not everyone accepted the subordination that the law and legal marriage rites prescribed. An Upper Canadian traveller told the story of a bride who simply walked out of the church when she discovered that the wedding ceremony required that she promise to obey; she chose to join those couples who lived as husband and wife without benefit of clerical or legal intervention in their affairs.[18]

Public protest against the injustice of British laws regarding marriage began to be heard early in the nineteenth century. In 1826, the *Novascotian* reprinted a letter, originally sent to an English newspaper, that was deeply critical of the laws governing marriage. Its author demanded legal changes in three areas: to prevent husbands squandering their wives' property; to give widows better access to the estates of their deceased husbands; and to prevent or stop domestic violence. Yet despite attempts to bring about reform of the married women's property law in Nova Scotia and despite evidence of concern elsewhere, change in this and other areas was slow to come.[19] In the meantime, women coped as best they could. Ann Melvin, a mid-nineteenth-century Upper Canadian woman, was married to a man who would not permit her to go out of the house without his leave. She wrote to her sister in 1851 that she would rather live "in some Desert on bread and water" than remain married, but her offer to take the children away and "work out" to support them was scorned by the man who had become her jailor. Some wives in such untenable situations, especially women with economic resources, managed to arrange for legal separations, and to survive by moving back to parents or finding homes with friends. Others acted more precipitously. Advertisements in which husbands announced their refusal to pay debts incurred by runaway wives were by no means unusual in British North American newspapers. They testify to the fact that some women dealt with their unhappy marriages by simply walking out the door and down the road.[20]

The ad that Charles Wright placed in the Nova Scotia *Gazette and Weekly Chronicle* on September 13, 1775, described his wife's behaviour and also illustrated his concern for his patriarchal rights. Hannah Wright, the ad claimed, had "been very remiss in her duty" toward her husband and children, "living in idleness and such like vicious acts and practices, as tend wholly to subvert all kind of family order and Government." Hannah had evidently not only kept bad company but had carried off and sold a large part of the household furniture before she finally "eloped" from his "bed and board." Wright intended to prosecute anyone who harboured his wife, and declared that he would pay no debts that she contracted. On the other hand, he was willing to repay to "all good people" any money advanced on the furniture, should they return it in the same condition that it was in when taken away.[21]

Probably the most common response to a problematic marriage was endurance, or even transformation of personal unhappiness into just another hardship to be conquered. Mary Morris Bradley of New Brunswick, whose weaving made such an important contribution to the economic success of her first marriage, sought solace in religion when she found her husband overbearing and unkind. Fortunately, after her first husband died, her second choice made her happier. Similarly, the diary of Sarah Welch Hill, an English woman who settled near Port Hope in 1843, contained numerous references to her husband's "unbearable" temper. Despite her note that "we cannot live in the way we do, think we had better part," it was only the death of her husband a decade later that brought Sarah relief from his tirades.[22]

Although the movement to reform the marital property provisions under English law did not result in change in the first half of the nineteenth century, in other areas affecting women, legal change—while not necessarily *reform*—did occur in British North America. Altered laws relating to infanticide, abortion, seduction, and rape reveal much about the changing politics of male–female relations.

Early British North American law on infanticide exactly duplicated an English statute from the seventeenth century. Under English common law, child murder was a felony punishable by death. But if a newborn were dead, it was difficult to establish why it had died or even whether it had been born alive. The law on infanticide therefore made it a crime, also punishable by death, to conceal the birth of a so-called bastard, illegitimate children being the most likely to be simply done away with. What is intriguing about these brutal laws on infanticide is their ineffectiveness. At first the laws applied only to illegitimate births, and the cases that were heard applied only to unmarried women; very few were convicted. When Angélique Pilotte, a 20-year-old Aboriginal servant, was given the death sentence for "concealment," there was a public outcry and, later, a royal pardon. Pilotte's defenders pointed out that the defendant knew nothing of Christianity and was guilty only of the "invariable custom of Indian women to retire and bring forth their children alone and in secret."[23]

In 1803, with a view to obtaining convictions where they had failed in the past, the English lawmakers decided that the ordinary rules of murder trials were to apply to infanticide; if there was an acquittal, a verdict of concealment could be substituted, now punishable by imprisonment for a maximum of two years. The British North American colonies followed suit, all passing similar laws between 1810 and 1840. Further legislation increased the scope of the law to include married women in the 1830s and 1840s; in New Brunswick and Nova Scotia, accomplices were also made subject to the law in 1849 and 1851, respectively. There were still very few convictions, however, suggesting that the courts had some compassion for the women—who, it must have been clear, were often victims themselves.[24]

Prior to 1803, under British law, abortion had been legal before quickening—that is, at any stage before the fetus's movements were felt. Then, in 1803 British legislation criminalized all abortion but still maintained the distinction between abortion before and after quickening. The latter was punishable by death, the former by lesser sentences such as imprisonment or transportation; the criminal in both cases was the abortionist. Most British North American colonies gradually enacted similar legislation in the first decades of the nineteenth century, with New Brunswick the first. By 1837, British legislators had abolished the distinction between the time before and after quickening but had reduced the maximum sentence to three years. This time British North American legislators, with the exception of Newfoundland, did not follow the British model in its entirety, tending to be more severe. New laws were passed in both Canada West and New Brunswick in the 1840s that also eliminated the distinction, but maximum sentences remained harsh: imprisonment for life in Canada West, and for 14 years in New Brunswick. In 1849 and 1851, respectively, New Brunswick and Nova Scotia shifted ground substantially: in a move that was unprecedented, except in the State of New York, they made it a criminal offence for the woman herself to obtain an abortion at any stage of her pregnancy.[25]

One reason for the increasing criminalization of abortion was the growth of doctors' opposition to the procedure. In 1832, the human ovum was discovered. Until then, the association between menstruation and reproduction was only speculative. Since doctors no longer thought of quickening as the start of life, they were increasingly reluctant to interfere with what they now thought of as a continuous process that began with conception. At the same time, abortions continued to be performed because it remained difficult to diagnose pregnancy before quickening made it unmistakable. Earlier in a pregnancy, remedies aimed at regulating or re-establishing menstruation were not easily distinguishable from remedies aimed at producing abortion, either by medical assistants or by the women concerned.[26]

Rape, like abortion and infanticide, came under the criminal code, and was punishable by death; the related crime of seduction was a civil offence. In both cases, it was not the woman who was held to be the victim, but her father. We know little about the enforcement of the law with regard to rape in British North America, although some Upper Canadian cases reported between 1824 and 1850 suggest that violent resistance had to be proved—and even then the all-male juries were reluctant to convict. Two convicted rapists were sentenced to death during this period; a number of others were given prison sentences of varying lengths.[27]

Infinitely more numerous than rape trials were the lawsuits generated by the unique Upper Canadian law of 1837 dealing with seduction. Under common law, seduction had been a crime against masters as well as parents, the offence being that it deprived a young woman's master or father of her services during the pregnancy and childbirth that resulted from an illicit relationship. The 1837 law may have recognized a new situation: young unmarried women who had emigrated before their parents and worked as servants were particularly vulnerable to the attentions of the men who were in fact their masters. It was thus fathers, not masters, who needed to be defended against the so-called ruin of their chaste daughters, and they needed this protection even if their daughters were no longer living at home. The law also recognized that it was not merely the loss of services per se that was at issue but, as the attorney-general of Upper Canada put it, "the wound given to parental feelings, the disgrace and injury inflicted upon the family of the person seduced." Except in Prince Edward Island, where an 1852 statute allowed the woman herself to sue, the injury to the women seems to have been ignored in seduction legislation. In contrast to the punitive rape law, the law on seduction was frequently called upon in the colonies.[28]

The existence of the tort of seduction entrenched in civil law a father's right to his daughter's services. In addition, the new statute stated that his property interests took precedence over her sexuality and reputation. Certainly, it denied in a fundamental way the autonomy of the woman concerned. Indeed, all of the laws affecting sexuality, marriage, and motherhood might be regarded as evidence of new kinds of intrusions into women's lives, as male lawgivers attempted to reinforce or reinterpret traditional male controls over, as well as their protection of, women in a changing world. In the 1840s, when criminal law came under the jurisdiction of the two Canadas, another British statute, this time the law with respect to abduction, was altered. The ancient British law had criminalized the abduction of a propertied daughter against her father's wishes; the Canadian version applied to all daughters, but distinguished between the majority of women (to whom the law applied only until they were 16) and heiresses (who were covered until the age of 21).[29]

How did women react to these laws? Anna Jameson, the British writer who visited Upper Canada in the 1830s, expressed what might be described as a feminist reaction to the 1837 seduction legislation. It was only a passing comment, but she seemed to imply that women needed less to be protected by their fathers and the law than to be equal and held responsible for their own persons and acts.[30] To achieve such equality and responsibility, however, women needed to be able to earn an independent living. This would gradually come to mean the right to enter the public sphere and seek employment outside the home.

BEYOND THE HOUSEHOLD

With the development of publicly supported education systems across British North America in the 1840s, thousands of young women found in teaching that opportunity to enter the world of paid employment, even if only for a brief period of time. Less numerous than the female teachers employed in public-supported elementary schools, but highly influential all the same, were the women teachers who worked in the larger

Protestant and Roman Catholic academies. Many elite Protestant families sent their daughters to the Lower Canadian convent schools that the sisters of the *Congrégation de Notre-Dame* and the Ursulines continued to operate in the late eighteenth and early nineteenth centuries. Some of the new Protestant institutions may well have been created in response to the obvious attraction of these influential Catholic schools. Protestant and Catholic schools for young ladies differed very little in their educational offerings: both emphasized the genteel arts, strict timetables, and social supervision. In religion-based schools, and even in the co-educational academies, girls were offered basic instruction in English or French; arithmetic, geography, and perhaps history; and a wide variety of the practical as well as the ornamental arts. Generally unavailable to girls were such subjects as higher mathematics or classical languages, subjects that educators tended to define as masculine. In the same way, in the public schools that girls attended and that were more often co-educational, girls could be denied access to advanced mathematics. In elementary schools, wherever female teachers were employed, girls were nearly always taught sewing in addition to the three Rs.[31]

Whether they were in public schools or domestic schools, Protestant academies or Catholic convent schools, women participated in varying degrees in a female culture that increasingly valued learning. Women were taught what was considered suitable to their sphere, and by the middle of the nineteenth century this was much expanded from what had been made available to most women of previous generations. Those women who were aware of the growing international agitation for female improvement believed that a more advanced education was essential to fit women for their vital and enhanced educational role as mothers and teachers.

Mary Electa Adams was affected by this movement. The daughter of Loyalists who had settled first in Lower Canada, then in Upper Canada, Mary Electa was educated by her parents until, at the age of 17, she was sent to Vermont's Montpelier Academy. There she was admitted to the study of the classics and advanced mathematics. After a year at Montpelier, the young scholar returned to Upper Canada to study at the Cobourg Ladies' Seminary, founded when girls were excluded from the Upper Canada Academy when it became Victoria College and a school for boys only. The Seminary offered a diploma thought suitable for young ladies: the M.L.A. or "Mistress of Liberal Arts." Adams obtained the diploma and then remained at the Seminary to teach until it moved to Toronto, where it reopened as the Adelaide Academy in 1847. By 1849 Adams had embarked on a career of her own in the administration of girls' academies. She went from the Picton Lady's Academy in Prince Edward County, Canada West, to Michigan, and then to New Brunswick, where she was "Lady Preceptress" of the women's department of Mount Allison College in the 1850s before returning to Canada West to head first the Wesleyan Female College in Hamilton, then an academy of her own known as Brookhurst, and, finally, the Ontario Ladies College in Whitby.[32]

The educational impulse took women in two somewhat contradictory directions. On the one hand, it led to an expansion of all-female institutions, like those with which Mary Electa Adams was associated. This was particularly true in Roman Catholic Canada East, where seven new female religious communities were established between 1842 and 1851, four of them dedicated to the provision of schooling for

A photograph taken in the 1850s of Mary Electa Adams, first Preceptress of Mount Allison Ladies' College, New Brunswick.

Source: Mount Allison Archives. Picture Collection. 2007.07/254

girls or for poor children. English-speaking convents devoted to education were also established in centres like Halifax and Toronto at mid-century. Like the larger female academies and the smaller girls' parish schools, these institutions took girls and women out of the private household but remained all-female enclaves. They provided forums where women could exercise power but only by separating both teachers and students from the public world.[33]

The alternative route, which affected far more British North American women in the long run, was the move into co-educational public schooling, where women worked and learned in closer proximity to men. This avenue was made more accessible for women by their admission to most of the normal schools, which were opened by the governments of nearly every British North American colony in the 1840s and 1850s for training teachers. In French Canada, the normal schools remained strictly male institutions, and the training of women teachers was undertaken by female religious orders, most notably the *Congrégation de Notre-Dame* and the Ursulines. Indeed, convent women had been engaged in the formal training of teachers in Lower Canada since the 1830s. But elsewhere in British North America, women moved into the same institutions and buildings as the men. Their position was by no means the same as that of their male counterparts, however. In Toronto, when women were admitted to the newly founded normal school in 1848, they were much younger on average than the male teachers being trained there; they were also less advanced in their preparation, for many of the men had already taught school. Finally, the women were treated differently, were streamed into lower levels of teacher certification, and were more strictly supervised. Moreover, interaction between male and female students was largely forbidden. Martha Hamm Lewis, who successfully petitioned the governor for permission to attend New Brunswick's all-male normal school in Fredericton in 1849, was required to wear a veil when attending the school. She also had to arrive in class before the arrival of her fellow students, and leave well after the men had left.[34]

Interpreting what educational innovation meant for British North American women in the first half of the nineteenth century is a subtle exercise. As mid-nineteenth-century observers recognized and the early normal schools demonstrated, simply admitting girls to boys' schools or colleges could be problematic. Should young men and women study the same things together? Or should they be in separate departments studying different things? The latter was the solution chosen by most of the early co-educational academies. Government-funded grammar schools in Canada West, on the other hand, often admitted girls and offered them a curriculum almost the same as that offered to boys.[35]

In the end, no solution really worked in the context of a society in which educational norms were established with young men's needs in mind, and in which the worlds of men and women seemed to be drifting apart. The more rapid advancement of education for boys and young men put girls and young women at a disadvantage, as the first colleges and universities were exclusively male institutions. Advanced formal education was increasingly replacing apprenticeship for men who were preparing for professional roles. If this was so, what, then, was the purpose of such education for women—who, those in authority believed, were properly excluded from the learned professions? The new medical schools founded for men in the 1830s and 1840s did not admit women; nor did the law schools. Nor could women train for the ministry. The established denominations placed great emphasis on learning and on a proper training in theology at a college or university for their priests and ministers, an ideal in which women had no place.[36]

Women preachers were not unknown in British North America, however, at least among the more radical sects. In the great religious revival known as the Second Awakening, which swept across North America in the late eighteenth and early nineteenth centuries, women and children were active participants. Protracted revival meetings engulfed communities for weeks, and prayer meetings went on day and night; both appeared to provide release and even leading roles for the young and female members of communities, whose lives were normally more constrained. With its emphasis on conversion and the importance of so-called exhortation—providing personal testimony of the power of the Holy Spirit in reordering one's life—religious revivalism encouraged more permanent ministries among women. As well, Bible Christian and Primitive Methodists, Universalists, and some Wesleyan Episcopals briefly supported women missionaries. Elizabeth Dart Eynon, for example, came to the Cobourg area in the 1830s with her recently converted husband, John Hicks Eynon; both were itinerants in that region for several decades, often travelling and preaching separately. Mary Narraway Bond, described as perhaps the "most successful woman preacher in the entire history of the Maritimes," established a meeting house with her husband in the labouring class community of Sand Point near St. John, New Brunswick, after arriving from England around 1820. For nearly 30 years, she preached regularly and led a mixed-race Sabbath school in what became known as Mrs. Bond's Chapel. Perhaps the most vibrant-sounding of the Methodist women preachers was the American Ellen Bangs, who "exhorted like a streak of red-hot lightning" on the Niagara circuit at the turn of the century.[37]

More numerous were the women who led class meetings, that is, weekly small groups of Methodists that often brought together adherents of both sexes and various age groups. Another American, Barbara Heck, is credited with founding the first Methodist class after she and her husband fled to Upper Canada during the American Revolution. Ann Jane Robinson led a class meeting, comprising both men and women, in St. Stephen, New Brunswick, from 1841 until she died in 1853 and was succeeded by her son. In some cases, women led class meetings for as long as 50 years, and the role of class leader was one that they were able to carry on into the latter part of the nineteenth century.[38]

The woman preacher, however, was increasingly regarded as an anomaly and even as a threat to the respectability of Protestant denominations that were becoming more established and hierarchical in structure. By the middle of the nineteenth century, women who exhorted or preached in public violated the social construction of the ideal woman as modest and silent. Even evangelical sects had begun to adopt more conservative notions about the need for a professionally trained ministry—and women called to preach rarely had access to the kind of education church leaders had in mind. Preaching women, moreover, were probably associated with what was referred to as religious enthusiasm, itself identified by many British North Americans as a Yankee import and a danger to the dignity and safety of the imperial state. In the end, women remained largely excluded from the evangelical ministry, as they did from the other learned professions.[39]

Still, Protestant women often kept the faith alive during the initial settlement period when few officially sanctioned male religious leaders were available, and there is evidence that some lay Roman Catholic women also played this role. Prior to the arrival of Catholic priests in Newfoundland in the late eighteenth century, Catholic midwives reportedly performed certain post-natal religious rituals, while other women sometimes presided over the administration of marriage contracts. As the Catholic male hierarchy established itself, there was an insistence on orthodoxy and the elimination of such practices. Moreover, Bishop Michael Fleming arranged for the introduction of two female religious orders—the Presentation sisters in 1833, and the Sisters of Mercy in 1842—so that Catholic girls would no longer be corrupted by attending co-educational schools. Rather, they would be educated in convent schools to protect "that delicacy of feeling and refinement of sentiment which form the ornament and grace of their sex."[40]

Perhaps Quaker women were most successful in creating an equal space for themselves in the public conduct of religion. Members of the Society of Friends arriving in British North America brought with them the tradition of the separate women's meeting, in which women's concerns were discussed and validated. The minutes that survive of the Quaker women's meeting in Norwich, Upper Canada, show no deference whatsoever toward the men's meetings. They reveal, rather, that women used their meeting to discuss issues, such as marriage and children's education, that the whole community regarded as vitally important.[41]

While women found quasi-public roles in education and religion, they also challenged and subverted the separate-spheres ideology and the meaning of domestic space through the act of writing. Literate women of British North America were far more involved in writing for publication than has previously been acknowledged. Through these writings, educated women sought influence in the worlds outside their families and familiar communities. To the extent that they were successful in getting their words into print, they introduced the idea of women's voices—and women's authority—into the realm of public discourse.[42] A particularly striking example is that of Mary Ann Shadd Cary, the first woman to publish and edit a newspaper in Canada. Born into a free black family in Delaware that was involved in the Underground Railway, Shadd Cary moved to Canada West in 1851 where she published *The Provincial Freeman* between 1853 and 1859, successively in Windsor, Toronto, and Chatham. She was a strong voice for the anti-slavery movement, as well as for temperance, moral reform, and self-reliance, and for the integration of blacks on an equal basis with whites.[43]

Women authors were often seeking to augment their incomes through their writing, but only a few (chiefly those who had already established writing careers before they came to the colonies) were successful for any length of time. Publishing was an expensive proposition, and authors frequently had to secure advance subscriptions before they could see their works in print. Many women began writing with private circulation only in mind, but were encouraged by friends to publish their works for the enjoyment and edification of larger audiences. This was the case for poet and schoolmistress Deborah How Cottnam of Nova Scotia and New Brunswick, and for romantic novelist Julia Beckwith Hart. Born in New Brunswick, Hart was running a boarding school in Kingston when she published her novel, *St. Ursula's Convent or the Nun of Canada*, in 1824. It was the first work of fiction produced by a writer born in British North America and the first novel to be published there. Nonetheless, both Julia Hart and Mary Eliza Herbert, who founded a literary periodical called *The Mayflower* in mid-century Halifax, had to face patronizing criticism and, in Herbert's case, condemnation of her efforts as unsuitable for the "parlour or boudoir." At least one teacher in the 1820s had pedagogy in mind for her writing. She used the subscription method of raising funds in advance to publish her treatise, *Mrs. Goodman's First Step in History, Dedicated to the Young Ladies of Canada*. Through this publication, she hoped to "cultivate the mind, improve the temper" and create an appetite for history in young women.[44] By the 1850s, whether or not respectable women should seek remuneration for their writing—or even a public voice in the first place—was proving controversial, as ideology about women's proper sphere hardened in British North America. Nevertheless, women wrote and began to make the point that women had something to say and needed to be heard.

And, sometimes tentatively, sometimes unabashedly, their ideas were political. In Pictou, Nova Scotia, Jane McPhail attempted to rouse her community to support her campaign against slavery and capital punishment, circulating her copy of *Uncle Tom's Cabin*, and sending Micmac crafts to bazaars to support the abolitionist cause in Boston. In Lower Canada, "Adelaïde" tried to influence opinion in a letter to the *Patriote* journal *La Minerve*, arguing for a recognition of the French-Canadian nation as one that promoted equality between the sexes. Her concern was that married women, who had previously continued to use their own parental family names to sign contracts, were beginning to sign with their husbands' names, a practice that she felt might undermine women's equality.[45]

GOVERNMENT AND POLITICS

If barring women from the learned professions and from the training that led to them along with attempting to exclude women from public discourse were among the notable forms of discrimination in British North American history, another was barring women from direct participation in government. Men were active in politics in growing numbers as the imperial authorities established elected assemblies in the British North American colonies and introduced franchises based on increasingly generous property qualifications. The franchise was exercised, in this period before the secret ballot, in public election meetings—rowdy and highly contentious events that could last several days. At first it was not entirely clear what women's position might be under the rapidly changing political conditions of British North America. New Brunswick regulations specifically excluded women from voting in 1785 but a law passed there 10 years later had no provision regarding women. In the other colonies, the laws with respect to voting were similarly non-specific. People simply assumed that most women would not exercise the franchise. According to one constitutional historian, women had not voted in British elections "for centuries," although there was no formal legal restraint.[46]

Yet, intriguingly, it appears that propertied women were not fully aware of their supposed exclusion. There is clear evidence that women voted occasionally in New Brunswick and Nova Scotia, and exercised the franchise somewhat more frequently in Lower Canada. Six women, in fact, are recorded as voting in Windsor Township in Nova Scotia in a 1793 election, while another five voted in Amherst Township in 1806. In the latter case, the loser of the election challenged the women's votes, all of which had been cast for the winner, but the House of Assembly disallowed his petition. A study of the Lower Canadian poll books that remain available to us discovered that there were more than 900 women voters in various elections between 1791 and 1849. In addition, a nineteenth-century history of the Papineau family described Montreal women voting in the election of 1809, noting particularly one "elderly lady, long a widow, but not-withstanding her age, still fresh and vigorous." When she was asked for whom she wished to vote, "she answered with a voice strong and filled with emotion 'For my son, M. Joseph Papineau, for I believe that he is a good and faithful subject.'" Evidently there was no protest, and the voter's son, Louis-Joseph Papineau, was elected for the East Ward of Montreal.[47]

Women in Bedford township and the borough of Trois Rivières exercised the franchise in the election of 1820. The Bedford case was disputed, however, because the votes of 22 married women had duplicated the votes of their husbands on the same properties. The Assembly declared that the election was void, and that voting by wives was illegal whether or not the husbands voted. Clearly, the notion of an individual franchise was meaningless to these early nineteenth-century legislators. It was property that voted, as represented by male heads of families. By the late 1820s, the question of women at elections had begun to arouse more extensive controversy. In 1828, the election of the previous year in Quebec Upper Town was called into question because a widow had been refused permission to vote. Petitioners called this a lapse of justice, declaring that "it would be impolitic and tyrannical to circumscribe [woman's] efforts in society,—to say that she shall not have the strongest interest in the fate of her country, and the security of her common rights." Pointing out that women were responsible for rearing and educating men, they added that "widows exercise, generally, all the rights of men, are liable to most of the same duties towards the State, and can execute them as well."[48]

Public opinion and the views of British North American legislators and their imperial governors were moving inexorably in the other direction, however. In that same 1828 election in the borough of William Henry, a counter-petition claimed that there had been a miscarriage of justice because "many women" had been permitted to exercise the franchise. In the debate, one of the two members for Quebec Upper Town based his objection to women's participation in politics on historical tradition: "It was incontrovertibly the practice of all representative governments, both ancient and modern, to exclude women from any share therein," he explained; therefore, he could not "decide in favour of the ladies."[49] Reformers in the colonies did not take up votes for women as a serious political cause for any length of time, however. Louis-Joseph Papineau and other Lower Canadian Reformers evidently espoused the idea in the 1820s, but a violent by-election in Montreal West in 1832 changed Papineau's mind. Men and women alike were intimidated, he claimed; three people were killed, and women were being "drawn to the hustings by their husbands or their guardians, often against their wills." Papineau finally concluded that such scenes were against the "public interest, decency, and the natural modesty of the sex." It has been suggested that he was also responding to the fact that, unlike his mother, the majority of qualified female property-holders in Lower Canada were anglophones who could not be expected to support his party.[50] In 1832, as part of an act concerning controverted elections, the Assembly of Lower Canada included a measure specifically prohibiting the exercise of the franchise by women; the Reform Act in Britain made the same provision in the same year. The Canadian law was disallowed by the British authorities for reasons unrelated to its content, but there seems to be no further record of women going to the polls in Lower Canada.

Something of the flavour of male attitudes to the idea of women voting comes through in an account of an election that took place in Nova Scotia before women's official exclusion. The incident was a hot contest in Annapolis County, reported in the *Novascotian* of December 3, 1840, by a supporter of the Reform party. He had gone into Annapolis in the middle of the election to see what the Tories there were doing and found that they were up to mischief:

> Getting all the old women and old maids, and everything in the shape of petticoats to be carried up to the hustings the next and last day to vote for [the Tory candidate] Whitman. As it was 9 o'clock in the evening no time was to be lost. I . . . rode all Tuesday night, and roused up every farmer; and what was the result, they harnessed up their horses, went off, and each one by ten of the clock, was back with a widow or a fair young fatherless maid, to vote against the Tory women from Annapolis Royal. They found out that we should outnumber them, and at last we had the satisfaction of seeing them return to Annapolis without voting.[51]

It is not clear, in the end, if any of these Nova Scotia women actually managed to exercise the franchise. What is clear is that the attempt of women to vote was finally dismissed as no more than a partisan "manoeuvre" or perhaps, at the most, an occasion for a clever story. In 1844, shortly after the union of Upper and Lower Canada, seven women evidently managed to vote in Canada West, and the election was upheld. But in 1849 a Reform government finally passed a law excluding women from the franchise in both of the Canadas. Prince Edward Island and New Brunswick had passed similar laws in 1836, and Nova Scotia would do so in 1851.[52]

While women in British North America were gradually disenfranchised, it would be wrong to imply that they played no political or public roles whatever. On the contrary, the women of the colonial political elites—and even women who were not in the official governing classes—sometimes had considerable influence, particularly in times of stress. In New Brunswick, for example, Lois Paine prevailed upon her husband, who was a member of the legislature, to get up a petition for the founding of a "Provincial Academy of the Arts and Sciences." He did what she asked in 1785; the result was a land reserve that would eventually support the creation of the University of New Brunswick. Probably Molly Brant was the most effective female political actor during the American revolutionary war. The third wife of the British Indian agent Sir William Johnston, and the sister of the Mohawk chief Joseph Brant, Molly Brant was a leading matron of her extensive and important tribe. She exerted a steady influence on her people and helped persuade them to continue their support for the Six Nations' alliance with the British. When the war forced the Mohawk to abandon their ancestral territories in New York State for a new home in Upper Canada, she continued to work for the best possible conditions for their settlement.[53]

Other examples exist of women's involvement in war. Laura Secord won fame for warning British officers of an impending American attack during the War of 1812. There are various accounts of her act, but it appears that Secord walked the entire day and partway through the evening of June 22, 1813, behind enemy lines and for a distance of some 30 kilometres to carry her message. As a result, the entire American detachment of about 400 men was captured. The British officer in charge later described the event and his indebtedness to Secord: "The weather on the 22d was very hot and Mrs. Secord whose person was slight and delicate . . . no doubt was much exhausted by the exertion she made coming to me." He added that, since Secord and her family were "entire Strangers" to him before June 22, her "exertions . . . could have been made for public motive only." He therefore recommended her to the "favourable consideration" of the provincial government. But no reward was forthcoming, and Secord was left to live in poverty with the husband she had earlier saved from death in battle. In 1828, finally, he—not she—was rewarded with a series of local offices. Left with nothing after her husband's death in 1841, Laura Secord taught school in her home in Chippewa until, at age 85, she received a small reward of her own from the Prince of Wales. Military officers recorded the bravery of other women during the War of 1812, but their individual acts received even less official recognition than did Secord's. Mrs. Defield of Lundy's Lane, for example, reportedly kicked the sword out of the hand of an American militiaman about to stab a British officer and subsequently confiscated it, thereby saving the grateful officer's life. Her daring exploit, accomplished while protecting the young child she had been holding in her arms, received, however, only a brief and completely inaccurate mention in a colonial newspaper. The various contributions of other women to the British cause, such as providing intelligence about American troop movements or freeing captives, generated no publicity whatsoever.[54]

There was, however, another kind of politics in which the wives of military and government officials in British North America's capital cities were active. Heavily involved in establishing social relations that defined rank and could cement (or destroy) political alliances, elite women could unofficially play powerful roles, making or breaking the political careers of their male relatives or enemies, or promoting the political goals of their choice. For example, women were intensely involved in the social rounds of Upper Canada's capital in the 1790s and early 1800s, choosing to call on certain ladies but not on others. Their choices were not without political impact. And in Nova Scotia, many a lawyer appears to have advanced his political career by marrying into the local elite. Wives were also not wholly silent or inactive in the reform movements that began to affect the colonies in the 1820s and 1830s. In Toronto, Isabel Mackenzie, the wife of Upper Canada's most famous rebel, was later characterized by her son-in-law as a more ardent opponent of the ruling Family Compact than William Lyon Mackenzie himself, during the period when he was becoming enmeshed in the movement that would lead to the 1837–1838 Rebellions in the Canadas.[55]

The Rebellion in Lower Canada offers the historian a fascinating case study in attitudes toward women's roles in politics, as well as changing historical interpretations of those roles. Some appraisals of this event have produced evidence of women's

A portrait of Laura Secord executed by Mildred Peel (Lady Ross) in 1904. Peel, a successful sculptor and painter, received a gold medal for painting excellence at a Paris salon. She did several commissioned works for the Ontario Legislature, and painted the official portrait of Liberal premier George Ross, whom she subsequently married.

Source: PEEL, Mildred, Laura Secord [Loyalist, heroine of War of 1812]. Archives of Ontario, AC619796

participation in the Patriot cause. Women, for example, formed the *Association des dames patriotiques du comté des Deux-Montagnes* in the summer of 1837 and became involved in a campaign to boycott the goods of British merchants. Soon women in Montreal joined the movement, pledging to wear only French-Canadian homespun clothing and to avoid all but the most necessary purchases of imported materials. Individuals and groups of women also made flags, manufactured armaments, lent their homes for meetings, and even carried arms. Cordelia Lovell, a Lower Canadian who wrote to her sister about her alarm at the deteriorating political situation in November 1837, wondered if her sister would think she had become a *politicienne*. She assured her that she had not, but that on the other hand it was not possible to avoid politics altogether. The political question preoccupied everyone and was "the subject of all conversation."[56]

An analysis of the Rebellion suggests that Patriot rhetoric was, however, far from supportive of the idea of women's intrusion into the world of politics, espousing, rather, the increasingly dominant myth of separate spheres. Misogynous verbal attacks on Queen Victoria were accompanied, in this rhetoric, by the notion that assertive women produced effeminate men; and the latter, Patriots argued, were susceptible to tyranny. This assessment argues that the evidence of active female participation in the Rebellion itself is slight, and that the most assertive individual women were, in fact, pro-government.[57]

After the fighting was over, women did what they could to assist imprisoned rebels and win better treatment or reprieves for them, or to influence the climate of opinion in favour of the defeated rebels. In 1838, Eugénie Saint-Germain petitioned Lady Colborne, the wife of the governor, begging that her husband be spared from death for his part in the Rebellions. Her pleas had no effect; under the law, neither Madame Saint-Germain nor Lady Colborne was in a position to exercise genuine political power, despite their membership in the elite circles of their respective societies. For such women, power was, at the most, influence on those who were in a position to make decisions. During his exile in the United States in 1839, Louis-Joseph Papineau wrote to his friend Louis Perrault about the passionate defence of the rebel cause by Perrault's mother. She had exerted such an influence that an important American official had written to England, attempting to explain the extent of nationalist feeling in Lower Canada and urging a more moderate policy toward the Patriots.[58] But it is not clear what such efforts gained, and the aftermath of rebellion meant grief for many women. When, for example, Isabel Mackenzie followed her husband, William Lyon Mackenzie, into exile in December 1837, she had to leave five daughters under the age of 11; she did not see them again until navigation reopened the following spring. William's depressions, the death of one child, the birth of three more, and the necessity of moving house almost yearly made it all the more difficult for Isabel to endure their 12-year exile.[59]

Women's political involvement could take forms other than indirect influence or actions for or against men's rebellions. For instance, rural women in Prince Edward County in the early nineteenth century were both leaders and participants in physical confrontations with wealthy landowners and their agents in order to protect their family's property. One of them, a pregnant, board-wielding Isabella MacDonald drove away an armed officer who had come to collect back rents from his tenants.[60] Fighting for one's own liberty, taking flight from oppression, or supporting others who were refugees were also political acts. At least two black women went to court in Nova Scotia in the late eighteenth century in an attempt to claim their freedom from abusive masters who had unlawfully treated them as if they were slaves. They were just two among the substantial number of eighteenth-century Nova Scotia women, the court records reveal, who were willing to sue in order to obtain justice. The women of the Underground Railroad, which brought runaway slaves to Canada after an imperial statute abolished slavery in all British territories in 1834, usually worked in clandestine ways, but when necessary their actions could be overt.[61] Anna Jameson, for example, reported the excitement that developed among both white and black inhabitants of the Districts of Gore and Niagara when Upper Canadian authorities were preparing to deliver an escaped slave to his former owner. Because the man had stolen a horse to effect his escape, he was considered a felon; and by an agreement between the British and American governments, all felons had to be extradited. Drawing upon older traditions of popular political action, a black mob assembled and began to riot when the man was led out of jail; in the ensuing melee, he escaped. What fascinated Jameson was "the conduct of the women":

> They prevailed upon their husbands, brothers, and lovers, to use no arms, to do no illegal violence, but to lose their lives rather than see their comrade taken by force across the lines. They had been most active in the fray, throwing themselves fearlessly between the black men and the whites. . . . One woman had seized the sheriff, and held him pinioned in her arms; another . . . held [one of the artillerymen] in such a manner as to prevent his firing.[62]

A woman had, in fact, been the mob's leader. A former slave from Virginia who had been treated well by her owners, she had nevertheless run away when her master died and it appeared that she would be sold. Anna Jameson asked to meet this black leader and was impressed by her passion as well as her courage. She expressed a fiery determination to live where she could be safe. If her people could not be safe on British ground, the woman told Jameson, she would go "to the end of the world" to find a country where they could be.

Still another form of politics was the use of petitions. Loyalist women used petitions in their attempts to win compensation for their losses or assistance in times of particular distress. One such petitioner was Sally or Sarah Ainse, an Oneida or possibly a Shawnee Loyalist trader who signed "eight petitions and half as many letters" between 1789 and 1808, claiming legal entitlement to extensive lands on the Thames River. In the end, however, the Executive Council of Upper Canada refused to recognize that the land had been deeded to her by the Chippewa. And petitioning did not stop with the Loyalists. A study of New Brunswick women petitioners of the mid-nineteenth century found widows continuing the tradition of asking for compensation for family services rendered to the state; schoolmistresses who petitioned to receive the school grant for their teaching; and widows petitioning to promote their business interests after the death of husbands.[63]

Nor were the petitioners of government the only women to use this form. In 1846, Barbe Desroches, a New Brunswick midwife, organized a petition in support of a priest she preferred to his rival in the village of Saint-Antoine; she threatened to withdraw her services as midwife from those who failed to sign. Desroches presented her petition to the bishop in person and appears to have won the day. The defeated priest was outraged but powerless. Barbe Desroches, he wrote, intended to "hold the keys" of the church when it was built. Indeed, so powerful was this "wicked woman" that it was she, he maintained, who governed "the whole village" of Saint-Antoine. Similarly, there is evidence women were among parishioners in Lower Canada who petitioned bishops for the removal of priests they accused of improper conduct.[64]

Recent historical studies of women's use of public space, even as they were being denied access to formal political power, also demonstrate the many ways in which women continued to participate in community affairs. For her part, Eliza Grimason, a well-known and wealthy tavern keeper in Kingston, actively campaigned on behalf of local provincial candidate John A. Macdonald, even though she could not exercise the ballot herself. She hosted Tory functions and attended election strategy meetings held in her hotel. There is also evidence that women of various classes used taverns and inns for their own social and business purposes, and in doing so, they ensured that public houses were far from being male-only public spaces.[65]

FORMALIZING COLLECTIVE ACTION

Women were not powerless. Nor were they cut off from each other. Pioneer women were, however, lonely in British North America because farms were often isolated and travel was difficult. But as quickly as they could, women attempted to re-establish their traditional patterns of female sociability and cooperation. Thus, quilting and sewing bees, cooperative cooking for festivals, all-female gatherings to attend a birth, and long-term visiting by aunts, sisters, mothers, daughters, and female friends continued to reinforce women's sense of community and common interest in a world in which, as a sex, some may have perceived themselves as increasingly set apart.

New outlets in religious work offered opportunities for individual expression as well as for collective action. Very few Protestant women could become itinerant preachers, class leaders, or settled ministers. But many more were able to immerse themselves in the Sunday-school movement that had begun in the Maritime colonies and had spread to the Canadas by the early nineteenth century. Young middle-class women wanting useful religious work found it in teaching poor children the three Rs and giving Bible lessons at Sunday schools, which often lasted for the whole day. Other women led prayer groups, such as the Maternal Association of Milltown/St. Stephen, founded in 1836 as a support group for mothers. For Roman Catholic women, the revival of religious life and the expansion of convents provided important opportunities for individual choice and socially useful work. Francophone sisters continued to run the hospitals that had served Montreal and Quebec for generations and to care for foundlings. Furthermore, their work in all fields grew; by 1825, there were four times as many nuns as priests in the city of Montreal, as increasing numbers of women chose the religious path.[66]

Women turned to social activism when they saw around them what seemed to be increasing levels of social distress and crime as migration and economic dislocation wrought major changes in town and country. It is unclear whether the growing numbers of people arrested and jailed in the nineteenth century represent real increases in criminal activity or a growing unwillingness in urban centres to tolerate public drunkenness, prostitution, and vagrancy. But there is no doubt that in some localities more women were being jailed. In many jails, young and old, petty criminals and the mentally disturbed mixed with members of both sexes who had committed serious crimes.[67] Protestant and Roman Catholic women alike responded to such problems by banding together to create new charitable and religious associations to address the problems of unwed mothers, starving families, or orphaned children, or to try to reform their communities in ways that would make them better places for women and children. In this way they continued and extended the well-established traditions of mutual assistance and care for the needy. In small communities, informal home visiting continued to seem adequate to meet the needs of the poor and destitute; in larger centres, women began to move toward more formal solutions and organized efforts.

By the middle decades of the nineteenth century, Protestant women's benevolent or missionary societies had sprung up in nearly every major town or city. The Prince Town Female Society for Propagating the Gospel and Other Religious Purposes was founded by Presbyterian women in Prince Town, or Malpeque, Prince Edward Island, in 1825, and included among its missions the distribution of Bibles to the isolated families of fishermen in the colony. In their report for 1828, the women of the Zoar Methodist Church in Halifax recorded that they had made and distributed 300 garments to the city's needy that year. In Montreal, three Church of Scotland women banded together with their friends in 1815 and founded the Female Benevolent Society to give aid to the distressed immigrants of the city. In Upper Canada, furthermore, Hamilton's Ladies' Benevolent Society was, like its Montreal counterpart, interdenominational and devoted to visiting and distributing assistance to the poor.[68] Many of the new associations involved women ministering to women, but some had children as their special care. The Montreal Protestant Orphan Asylum, for example, a foundation of the Female Benevolent Society, came into existence in 1832. Efforts to convert Aboriginal communities—especially Aboriginal women—to Christianity led Protestant women in Upper Canada to form missionary societies in order to raise funds to support such activities. Their efforts to assist what they called the "degraded Indian woman" by recruiting her into a Christian sisterhood and transforming her into a neat and pious homemaker reveal a great deal about colonial ideas and discourses relating to religion, race, and gender.[69]

Black women in Canada West developed their own organizations as part of the anti-slavery movement and to meet the needs of both the established African-Canadian community and recently arrived African Americans. Serving the needs of poor black women in Toronto between 1840 and the 1860s, the Queen Victoria Benevolent Society was founded by Ellen Abbott, a free African American and former domestic servant from Baltimore. Other societies founded by Canada West black women included the Ladies Coloured Fugitive·Association, the Ladies Freedman's Association, and the Daughters of Prince Albert. The latter was a burial society that also cared for the poor and the sick.[70]

The need for such charities demonstrates that British North American society, for all its increasing idealization of motherhood and family, was a challenging world for many women and children. Unmarried mothers and poor widows did not fit the view of the family that was emerging in the third and fourth decades of the nineteenth century, nor did the few women who chose not to marry and instead attempted to live independently. Women's activity outside the household, although it continued, was increasingly viewed with disfavour. Even the Protestant and Catholic women's associations that tried to alleviate the poverty and distress they saw around them sometimes ran into male opposition. In French Canada, in fact, the Church discouraged laywomen's organizations and channelled women's efforts into the development of religious orders. One group of laywomen under the direction of Emélie Gamelin had sick and destitute women as its special concern in a charity that dated from 1828; it was transformed into the Sisters of Providence in 1843. The French-Canadian women who gathered around Montreal widow Rosalie Cadron-Jetté in the early 1840s ministered to unwed mothers. Persuaded by the city's Bishop Ignace Bourget that their work could best be accomplished if she and her assistants were bound by religious vows, this 50-year-old midwife became the founder and first superior of the *Soeurs de la Miséricorde*, a community devoted at first to assisting unmarried mothers, and later to caring for their "orphaned" children as well.[71]

Eventually, some women began to recognize that their charitable and educational efforts, for all their worthwhile character, were superficial remedies in a social system that required more radical attention to the causes of social distress. As a result, many sought to bring about a fundamental reform of society by embracing the temperance movement. The consumption rate of alcohol in British North America was very high, and drunkenness was a widespread phenomenon, especially among men. Inevitably, wives and children were the ones who suffered when men drank away their wages and became abusive while drunk. The first recorded temperance society was created by Mrs. John Forbes in Russelltown, Lower Canada in 1822, shortly after she set up the area's first Sunday School.[72]

By the 1840s, women, girls, and youth often represented the majority of those attending temperance meetings, and Protestant women were among the most active temperance advocates. In 1841, the Ladies' Committee of the Montreal Temperance Society undertook a successful fundraising effort to support the first travelling temperance lecturer. Female temperance workers also canvassed neighbourhoods to secure individual abstinence pledges, sold subscriptions to temperance publications, and prepared food for temperance meetings. By mid-century, they were assuming more visible roles. In 1847, the Saint John Ladies' Total Abstinence Society petitioned the New Brunswick legislature, asking for a ban on "strong drink," the evil that this group identified as the source of much of the city's social dislocation. Four years later, in Hamilton, Canada West, Miss Maria Lamas gave a temperance lecture to a large assembly in the Methodist Episcopal Church. According to one newspaper account,

> [i]t is rather a novel thing for a female to be engaged in this cause, as a public lecturer, but we can see no valid objection to it. We do not know who could better describe the sad scenes occasioned by intemperance than those who have been its innocent victims.[73]

Lay women's involvement in church life and voluntary associations thus afforded them ample opportunity to extend their activities and their influence well beyond their

Temperance Pledge: a mid-nineteenth-century engraving by John Henry Walker.

Source: McCord Museum M930.50.3.197

individual homes. In their own way, then, women were active participants in the nation-building process and in the development of an engaged and virtuous citizenry. Through their bazaars and benevolent societies, they raised substantial amounts of money that funded the building and maintenance of church structures, missionary activities, temperance campaigns, and charitable projects. These activities encouraged the development of social relations among women as they frequently gathered in same-sex organizations. However, they also brought women into mixed-sex organizations, where women and men worked together for common causes, such as temperance, social improvement, and moral reform. Paradoxically, then, women's very devotion to their Christian duty as nurturing mothers protecting the sanctity of the home became the justification for their increased involvement in public matters. These "citizen-mothers" were already laying a strong foundation for the social and political activism of the generations of women who would follow them.[74]

Notes

1. Beth Light and Alison Prentice, eds., *Pioneer and Gentlewomen of British North America, 1713–1867* (Toronto: New Hogtown Press, 1980), 213–14; Willeen Keough, "The Riddle of Peggy Mountain: Regulation of Irish Women's Sexuality on the Southern Avalon, 1750–1860," *Acadiensis* 31, 2 (Spring, 2002): 38.

2. Sylvia Van Kirk, *"Many Tender Ties": Women in Fur-Trade Society, 1670–1870* (Winnipeg: Watson and Dwyer, 1980), 175–77; Malvina Bolus, "The Son of I. Gunn," *The Beaver* (Winter 1971), 23–26; Light and Prentice, eds., *Pioneer and Gentlewomen*, 215–16.

3. Jim Phillips and Allyson N. May, "Female Criminality in 18th-Century Halifax," *Acadiensis* 31, 2 (Spring 2002): 71–96; D. Owen Carrigan, *Crime and Punishment in Canada: A History* (Toronto: McClelland and Stewart, 1991), 444.

4. M. A. Poutanen, "Regulating Public Space in Early-Nineteenth Century Montreal: Vagrancy Laws and Gender in a Colonial Context," *Histoire sociale/Social History* 35, 69 (May 2002): 35–58; Katherine M. J. McKenna, "Women's Agency in Upper Canada: Prescott's Board of Police Record, 1834–1850," *Histoire sociale/Social History* 36, 72 (November 2003): 347–70.

5. Frances Brookes, *The History of Emily Montague* (London, 1769; Toronto: McClelland and Stewart, 1961).

6. See, for example, Cecilia Morgan, *Public Men and Virtuous Women: The Gendered Languages of Religion and Politics in Upper Canada, 1791–1850* (Toronto: University of Toronto Press, 1996).

7. Van Kirk, *"Many Tender Ties,"* 154–57; John Adams, *Old Square Toes and His Family: The Life of James and Amelia Douglas* (Victoria, B.C: Horsdal & Schubart, 2001), 44.

8. Light and Prentice, eds., *Pioneer and Gentlewomen*, 120.

9. Françoise Noël, *Family Life and Sociability in Upper and Lower Canada, 1780–1870: A View from Diaries and Family Correspondence* (Montreal and Kingston: McGill-Queen's University Press, 2003), 19–20, 58, 273–74.

10. Peter Ward, "Courtship and Social Space in Nineteenth Century English Canada," *Canadian Historical Review* 68, 1 (March 1987): 35–62; Madeleine Ferron et Robert Cliche, *Les Beaucerons, ces insoumis: Suivi de Quand le peuple fait la loi* (La Salle, QC: Hurtubise, 1982), 279–80. See also Peter Ward, *Courtship, Love, and Marriage in Nineteenth-Century English Canada* (Montreal and Kingston: McGill-Queen's University Press, 1990).

11. Audrey Saunders Miller, ed., *The Journals of Mary O'Brien* (Toronto: Macmillan, 1968), 84, 88–89; Ward, *Courtship*, 137; Bryan D. Palmer, "Discordant Music: Charivaris and Whitecapping in Nineteenth-Century North America," *Labour/Le Travail* 3 (1978): 5–62.

12. Bettina Bradbury et al., "Property and Marriage: The Law and the Practice in Early Nineteenth-Century Montreal," *Histoire sociale/Social History* 26, 51 (May 1993): 9–39.

13. Constance B. Backhouse, "Married Women's Property Law in Nineteenth-Century Canada," in Bettina Bradbury, ed., *Canadian Family History: Selected Readings* (Toronto: Copp Clark Pitman, 1992), 320–59; and Backhouse, *Petticoats and Prejudice: Women and Law in Nineteenth-Century Canada* (Toronto: Osgoode Society, 1991).

14. McKenna, "Women's Agency," 370, 368; see also Keough, "The Riddle of Peggy Mountain," 61, 64–65.

15. Bradbury et al., "Property and Marriage," 13–14; Julian Gwyn, " Female Litigants before the Civil Courts of Nova Scotia, 1749–1801," *Histoire sociale/Social History* 36, 72 (November 2003): 311–46.

16. Rosemary Ball, "'A Perfect Farmer's Wife': Women in 19th Century Rural Ontario," *Canada: An Historical Magazine* 3, 2 (December 1975), 2–21.

17. Constance B. Backhouse, "'Pure Patriarchy': Nineteenth Century Canadian Marriage," *McGill Law Journal* 31, 2 (March 1986): 264–312; Backhouse, *Petticoats*, chap. 6; B. Hovius, *Family Law* (Toronto: Carswell, 1987), 110; Kimberley Smith Maynard, "Divorce in Nova Scotia, 1750–1890," in Philip Girard and Jim Phillips, eds., *Essays in the History of Canadian Law*

Vol. 3: The Nova Scotia Experience (Toronto: University of Toronto Press, 1990), 232–72; Wendy Owen and J. M. Bumsted, "Divorce in a Small Province: A History of Divorce on Prince Edward Island from 1833," *Acadiensis* 20, 2 (Spring 1991): 86–104.

18. Light and Prentice, eds., *Pioneer and Gentlewomen*, 119.

19. Philip Girard, "Married Women's Property, Chancery Abolition, and Insolvency Law: Law Reform in Nova Scotia, 1820–1867," in Girard and Phillips, eds., *Essays in the History of Canadian Law Vol. 3*, espec. 80–92.

20. Light and Prentice, eds., *Pioneer and Gentlewomen*, 125–26, 163–64; Margaret Conrad, "Recording Angels: Private Chronicles of Maritime Women, 1800–1950," in Alison Prentice and Susan Mann Trofimenkoff, eds., *The Neglected Majority: Essays in Canadian Women's History* (Toronto: McClelland and Stewart, 1985) vol. 2, 41–60.

21. Light and Prentice, eds., *Pioneer and Gentlewomen*, 163.

22. Conrad, "Recording Angels," 44–45; Kathryn Carter, ed., *The Small Details of Life: Twenty Diaries by Women in Canada, 1830–1996* (Toronto: University of Toronto Press, 2002), 73.

23. Constance B. Backhouse, "Desperate Women and Compassionate Courts: Infanticide in Nineteenth-Century Canada," *University of Toronto Law Journal* 34, 4 (Fall 1984): 450–52; also Backhouse, *Petticoats*, chap. 4.

24. Backhouse, "Desperate Women"; Backhouse, *Petticoats*; Marie-Aimée Cliche, "L'infanticide dans la région de Québec, 1660–1969," *Revue d'histoire de l'Amérique française*, 44, 1 (été 1990): 31–59.

25. After 1841, Upper Canada became Canada West. Constance B. Backhouse, "Involuntary Motherhood: Abortion, Birth Control and the Law in Nineteenth Century Canada," *Windsor Yearbook, Access to Justice 3* (1983): 61–130; and Backhouse, *Petticoats*, chap. 5.

26. Richard A. Leonardo, *History of Gynecology* (New York: Froben, 1944), 255.

27. Ruth A. Olson, "Rape—An 'Un-Victorian' Aspect of Life in Upper Canada," *Ontario History* 68, 2 (June 1976): 75–79; Backhouse, *Petticoats*, chap. 3.

28. Constance B. Backhouse, "The Tort of Seduction: Fathers and Daughters in Nineteenth Century Canada," *Dalhousie Law Journal* 10, 1 (June 1986): 50; Backhouse, *Petticoats*, chap. 2; Martha J. Bailey, "Servant Girls and Upper Canada's Seduction Act: 1837–1946," in Russell Smandych, Gordon Dodds, and Alvin Esau, eds., *Dimensions of Childhood: Essays on the History of Children and Youth in Canada* (Winnipeg: Legal Research Institute of the University of Manitoba, 1991), 159–82. Bailey's interpretation takes issue with the view of Backhouse (and the apparent assumption of Anna Jameson, noted in this chapter on page 107) that young women servants were in any position to defend themselves and act autonomously.

29. Backhouse, "Tort of Seduction"; Backhouse, *Petticoats*; Bailey, "Servant Girls"; and Karen Dubinsky, *Improper Advances: Rape and Heterosexual Conflict in Ontario, 1880–1929* (Chicago: University of Chicago Press, 1993), 81.

30. Light and Prentice, eds., *Pioneer and Gentlewomen*, 208–10.

31. Susan Houston and Alison Prentice, *Schooling and Scholars in Nineteenth-Century Ontario* (Toronto: University of Toronto Press, 1988), chap. 3; Johanna Selles-Roney, "'A Realm of Pure Delight': Methodists and Women's Education in Ontario, 1836–1925," University of Toronto, Ed.D. Thesis, 1993, chap. 1; Elizabeth Smyth, "'A Noble Proof of Excellence': The Culture and Curriculum of a Nineteenth Century Ontario Convent Academy," in Ruby Heap and Alison Prentice, eds., *Gender and Education in Ontario: An Historical Reader* (Toronto: Canadian Scholars' Press, 1991), 273–94.

32. Elsie Pomeroy, "Mary Electa Adams," *Ontario History* 41, 3 (1949): 106–17; Alison Prentice, "Scholarly Passion: Two Women Who Caught It," in Alison Prentice and Marjorie R. Theobald,

eds., *Women Who Taught: Perspectives on the History of Women and Teaching* (Toronto: University of Toronto Press, 1991), 258–83.

33. Diane Bélanger et Lucie Rozon, *Les religieuses au Québec* (Montréal: Libre Expression, 1982), annexe 2, 294–315; Sister Marthe Baudoin, "The Religious of the Sacred Heart in Canada, 1842–1980," *Canadian Catholic Historical Association Study Sessions* 48 (1981), 43–60; Sister Maura, *The Sisters of Charity, Halifax* (Toronto: Ryerson Press, 1956); Smyth, "'Noble Proof.'"

34. Jeanette Létourneau, *Les écoles normales de filles au Québec* (Montréal: Fides, 1981), espec. chaps. 1 and 2; Alison Prentice, "'Friendly Atoms in Chemistry': Women and Men at Normal School in Mid-Nineteenth Century Toronto," in David Keane and Colin Read, eds., *Old Ontario: Essays in Honour of J. M. S. Careless* (Toronto: Dundurn Press, 1990), 285–317; Light and Prentice, eds., *Pioneer and Gentlewomen*, 216–18.

35. R. D. Gidney and W. P. J. Millar, *Inventing Secondary Education: The Rise of the High School in Nineteenth-Century Ontario* (Montreal and Kingston: McGill-Queen's University Press, 1990).

36. For Ontario, see R. D. Gidney and W. P. J. Millar, *Professional Gentlemen: The Professions in Nineteenth-Century Ontario* (Toronto: University of Toronto Press, 1994).

37. G. A. Rawlyk, *Ravished by the Spirit: Religious Revivals, Baptists and Henry Alline* (Montreal and Kingston: McGill-Queen's University Press, 1984), espec. 76–79, 120–28; Jean Bannerman, *Leading Ladies: Canada 1639–1867* (Galt, ON.: Highland Press, 1967), 25; Elizabeth Gillan Muir, "Dent, Elizabeth (Eynon)," *Dictionary of Canadian Biography* (Toronto: University of Toronto Press, 1985) vol. 8, 200–1; Gillan Muir, "Beyond the Bounds of Respectable Behaviour: Methodist Women Preachers in the early Nineteenth Century," in Gillan Muir and Marilyn Färdig Whiteley, eds., *Changing Roles of Women within the Christian Church in Canada* (Toronto: U of T Press, 1995), 170; D. G. Bell, "Allowed Irregularities: Women Preachers in the Early 19th Century," *Acadiensis* 30, 2 (Spring 2001): 14–16. See also Gillan Muir, *Petticoats in the Pulpit: The Story of Early Nineteenth-Century Methodist Women Preachers in Upper Canada* (Toronto: United Church Publishing House, 1991).

38. Hannah M. Lane, "'Wife, Mother, Sister, Friend': Methodist Women in St. Stephen, New Brunswick, 1861–1881," in Janet Guildford and Suzanne Morton, eds., *Separate Spheres: Women's Worlds in the 19th-Century Maritimes* (Fredericton: Acadiensis Press, 1994), 111–12; Marilyn Färdig Whiteley, *Canadian Methodist Women, 1766–1925: Marys, Marthas, Mothers in Israel* (Waterloo, ON: Wilfrid Laurier University Press, 2005), 74–94.

39. For a discussion of the various factors leading to the demise of women preachers by the mid-nineteenth century, see Bell, "Allowed Irregularities," especially 34–39.

40. Keough, "The Riddle of Peggy Mountain," 48–49, 68.

41. Cecilia Morgan, "Gender, Religion, and Rural Society: Quaker Women in Norwich, Ontario, 1820–1880," *Ontario History* 82, 4 (December 1990): 273–88.

42. Anne Innis Dagg, "Canadian Voices of Authority: Non-Fiction and Early Women Writers," *Journal of Canadian Studies* 27, 2 (Summer 1992): 107–23.

43. Jane Rhodes, *Mary Ann Shadd Cary: The Black Press and Protest in the Nineteenth Century* (Bloomington: Indiana University Press, 1998).

44. Carole Gerson, "Women and Print Culture," in Patricia Lockhart Fleming, Gilles Gallichan and Yvan Lamonde, eds., *History of the Book in Canada, I* (Toronto: University of Toronto Press, 2004), 354–60; Douglas Lockhead, "Introduction" to Julia Catherine Beckwith Hart, *St. Ursula's Convent or the Nun in Canada* (Ottawa: Carleton University Press, 1991); Gwendolyn Davies, *Studies in Maritime Literary History, 1760–1930* (Fredericton: Acadiensis Press, 1991), 71–87.

45. Davies, *Maritime Literary History*, 78–79; Allan Greer, *The Patriots and the People: The Rebellion of 1837 in Lower Canada* (Toronto: University of Toronto Press, 1993), 207.

46. Elspeth Tulloch, *We, the Undersigned: A Historical Overview of New Brunswick Women's Political and Legal Status, 1784–1984* (Moncton: New Brunswick Advisory Council on the Status of Women, 1985), 3; John Garner, *The Franchise and Politics in British North America 1755–1867* (Toronto: University of Toronto Press, 1969), 156.

47. Tulloch, *We, the Undersigned*, 3–4; Bradbury et al., "Property and Marriage," 13; Brian Cuthbertson, *Johnny Bluenose at the Polls: Epic Nova Scotian Election Battles, 1758–1848* (Halifax: Forma Publishing Company, 1994), 9; William Renwick Riddell, "Woman Franchise in Quebec a Century Ago," *Royal Society of Canada, Proceedings and Transactions* Series 3, 22 (1928), 87–88.

48. Garner, *Franchise*, 157, 88–89; Light and Prentice, eds., *Pioneer and Gentlewomen*, 211–13.

49. Garner, *Franchise*, 155, 156–58.

50. Bettina Bradbury, "Women at the Hustings: Gender, Citizenship, and the Montreal By-Elections of 1832," in Mona Gleason and Adèle Perry, eds., *Rethinking Canada. The Promise of Women's History*, 5th ed., (Toronto: Oxford University Press, 2006); Greer, *The Patriots*, ch. 7.

51. Cuthbertson, *Johnny Bluenose*, 142.

52. Garner, *Franchise*, 155.

53. Tulloch, *We, the Undersigned*, 5; Pearson Gundy, "Molly Brant—Loyalist," *Ontario History* 45, 3 (1953); Helen Caister Robinson, "Molly Brant: Mohawk Heroine," in Phyllis R. Blakeley and John N. Grant, eds., *Eleven Exiles: Accounts of Loyalists of the American Revolution* (Toronto: Dundurn Press, 1982); Jean Johnston, *Wilderness Women: Canada's Forgotten History* (Toronto: Peter Martin Associates, 1973).

54. Ruth Mackenzie, "Laura Ingersoll (Secord)," *Dictionary of Canadian Biography* (Toronto: University of Toronto Press, 1976) vol. 9, 405–7; John S. Moir, "An Early Record of Laura Secord's Walk," *Ontario History* 51, 2 (Spring 1959): 105–8; Cecilia Morgan, "'Of Slender Frame and Delicate Appearance': The Placing of Laura Secord in the Narratives of Canadian Loyalist History," *Journal of the Canadian Historical Association*, n.s., 5 (1994): 195–212; Colin M. Coates and Cecilia Morgan, *Heroines and History: Representations of Madeleine de Verchères and Laura Secord* (Toronto: University of Toronto Press, 2002), espec. chap. 5; Morgan, *Public Men and Virtuous Women*, 41–43.

55. Katherine M. J. McKenna, "The Role of Women in the Establishment of Social Status in Early Upper Canada," *Ontario History* 83, 3 (September 1990): 179–206; McKenna, *A Life of Propriety: Anne Murray Powell and Her Family* (Montreal and Kingston: McGill-Queen's Press, 1994), espec. chap. 3; Cuthbertson, *Johnny Bluenose*, 10; Nancy Luno, "Domestic History: Following the Paper Trail of the W. L. Mackenzie Family," paper presented to the Ontario Women's History Network, Toronto, February 1994.

56. Marcelle Reeves-Morache, "La canadienne pendant les troubles de 1837–1838," *Revue d'histoire de l'Amérique française* 5, 1 (juin 1951–52): 99–117; Francis Back, "L'étoffe de la liberté: politique textile et comportements vestimentaires du mouvement patriote," *Bulletin d'histoire politique* 10, 2 (hiver 2002): 58–71.

57. Greer, *Patriots*, 190–218.

58. See Light and Prentice, eds., *Pioneer and Gentlewomen*, 165–66; Greer, *Patriots*, 353.

59. Nancy Luno, *A Genteel Exterior: The Domestic Life of William Lyon Mackenzie* (Toronto: Toronto Historical Board, 1990).

60. Rusty Bitterman, "Women in the Escheat Movement: The Politics of Everyday Life on Prince Edward Island," in Janet Guilford and Suzanne Morton, eds., *Separate Spheres: Women's*

Worlds in the 19th Century Maritimes (Halifax: Acadiensis Press, 1994), 24. For a discussion of Newfoundland women's resort to violence to protect their family's property from court officials and others, see Sean Cadigan, *Hope and Deception in Conception Bay: Merchant–Settler Relations in Newfoundland, 1785–1855* (Toronto: University of Toronto Press, 1995), 72–80.

61. Gwyn, "Female Litigants," 340–43; Adrienne Shadd, "'The Lord Seemed to Say "Go"': Women and the Underground Railroad Movement," in Peggy Bristow, co-ord., et al., *"We're Rooted Here and They Can't Pull Us Up": Essays in African Canadian Women's History* (Toronto: University of Toronto Press, 1994), 41–68. For a discussion of decisions by the courts of New Brunswick relating to enslaved women, see D. G. Bell, "Slavery and the Judges of Loyalist New Brunswick," *The University of New Brunswick Law Journal/Revue de droit de l'Université de Nouveau Brunswick*, 31 (1982): 20–25.

62. Light and Prentice, eds., *Pioneer and Gentlewomen*, 191–96.

63. Patricia Kennedy, "Voices in the Shadows," *The Archivist* 20, 1 (January/February 1993): 2–4; Gail G. Campbell, "Disfranchised but Not Quiescent: Women Petitioners in New Brunswick in the Mid-19th Century," in Guildford and Morton, eds., *Separate Spheres*, 39–66.

64. Tulloch, *We, the Undersigned*, 5; Christine Hudon, *Prêtres et fidèles dans le diocèse de Saint-Hyacinthe, 1820–1875* (Sillery: Septentrion, 1996).

65. Julia Roberts, *In Mixed Company: Taverns and Public Life in Upper Canada* (Vancouver and Toronto: UBC Press, 2009), 156, chap. 7.

66. Allan Greer, "The Sunday Schools of Upper Canada," *Ontario History* 67, 3 (September 1975): 169–84; Marguerite Van Die, "'A Woman's Awakening': Evangelical Belief and Female Spirituality in Mid-Nineteenth Century Canada," in Wendy Mitchinson et al., eds., *Canadian Women: A Reader* (Toronto: Harcourt Brace, 1996), 49–68; Elizabeth W. McGann, ed., *Whispers from the Past: Selections from the Writings of New Brunswick Women* (Fredericton: Fiddlehead/Goose Lane, 1986), 106–9; Rawlyk, *Ravished by the Spirit*, 124–27; Marta Danylewycz, *Taking the Veil: An Alternative to Marriage, Motherhood and Spinsterhood in Quebec, 1840–1920* (Toronto: McClelland and Stewart, 1987); Jan Noel, "'Femme fortes' and the Montreal Poor," in Mitchinson et al., eds., *Canadian Women: A Reader*, 68–85.

67. On crime and the perception of crime in this period, see John Weaver, "Crime, Public Order and Repression," *Ontario History* 78, 3 (September 1984): 191–92.

68. J. T. McNeil, *The Presbyterian Church in Canada 1875–1925* (Toronto: General Board of the Presbyterian Church in Canada, 1925), 140, 142; Halifax Woman's Christian Temperance Union (1890), 40; Haley P. Bamman, "The Ladies' Benevolent Society of Hamilton, Ontario: Form and Function in Mid-Nineteenth Century Urban Philanthropy," in Michael B. Katz and Paul H. Mattingly, eds., *Education and Social Change: Themes from Ontario's Past* (New York: New York University Press, 1975).

69. Noel, "'Femmes fortes'"; Whitely, *Canadian Methodist Women*, 102, 139–40; Cecilia Morgan, " Turning Strangers into Sisters? Missionaries and Colonization in Upper Canada," in Marlene Epp, Franca Iacovetta, Frances Swyripa, eds., *Sisters or Strangers? Immigrant, Ethnic, and Racialized Women in Canadian History* (Toronto: University of Toronto Press, 2004), 23–48.

70. Robin Winks, *The Blacks in Canada: A History* (Montreal and Kingston: McGill-Queen's University Press, 1971), 328–29; Shirley J. Yee, *Black Women Abolitionists: A Study in Activism, 1828–1860* (Knoxville: University of Tennessee Press, 1992), 80; Karolyn Smardz Frost, "Communities of Resistance: African Canadians and African Americans in Antebellum Toronto," *Ontario History* 99, 1 (Spring 2007): 61.

71. Le Collectif Clio, *L'histoire des femmes au Québec depuis quatre siècles* (Montréal: Éditions Le Jour, 1992), 124; Danylewycz, *Taking the Veil*, 20, 47; D. Suzanne Cross, "The Neglected

Majority: The Changing Role of Women in 19th Century Montreal," in Trofimenkoff and Prentice, eds., *Neglected Majority* vol. 1, 79.

72. Jan Noel, *Canada Dry: Temperance Crusades before Confederation* (Toronto: University of Toronto Press, 1995), 99.

73. Noel, *Canada Dry,* 13–17 and chap. 7; Maritime Woman's Christian Temperance Union, Annual Report (1890), 40.

74. Jill Vickers, "In Search of the Citizen-Mother: Using Locke to Unravel a Modern Mystery," http://www.cpsa-acsp.ca/paper-2003/vickers.pdf.

PART TWO

THE MID-NINETEENTH CENTURY TO THE END OF THE GREAT WAR

Woman with prairie chicken, Southern Alberta, circa 1915.

Source: Glenbow Archives NA-4658-25

Historians have been fascinated by the period that stretches from the middle of the nineteenth century to the end of the Great War. The tremendous changes that occurred in those years laid the groundwork for Canadian society as we know it. In l867, the colonies of Canada East and Canada West, New Brunswick, and Nova Scotia joined in Confederation; in the decades that followed, the political goal of a Dominion from sea to sea was achieved. During the same era, the burgeoning women's groups that existed across the country began to unite in more formalized associations; in the National Council of Women of Canada, they formed a single umbrella organization that joined in the unifying and expansionist impulses of the nascent national community.

The background to these events was the nation's continuing economic development. With the completion of the transcontinental railway system from the Atlantic to the Pacific in 1885, the staple economy expanded into the new pioneer areas of the north and west. In the settled regions, household production gave way to the beginnings of a factory system that co-existed with artisan workshops and the putting out of industrial work into workers' homes. The vast forest, mineral, and hydro-electric resources of central British Columbia, Ontario, and Quebec helped fuel this development, as did foreign capital from Great Britain and increasingly from the United States. By the end of World War I, a full-blown industrial society had emerged, albeit with strong remnants of the earlier economic systems still in place in various regions and locales.

The two decades following Confederation saw a boom in the Maritime economy, and it appeared that the provinces of New Brunswick and Nova Scotia in particular would benefit from industrialization. But the boom was not to continue, and by the early decades of the twentieth century the eastern regions had lost ground to the more industrially developed southern regions of Quebec and Ontario. Westerners, too, had complaints about the distribution of economic benefits—specifically, the effects of the 1879 Conservative National Policy. The high protective tariffs integral to that plan had the result of filling the coffers of eastern banks and enriching central Canadian industrialists at the expense of agricultural producers.

As well, a massive growth in Canada's population accompanied and contributed to the economic changes that were underway. From approximately 2.5 million people in 1851, the population grew to nearly 9 million by 1921. However, population growth was not even; during the economic recession of the 1880s and early 1890s, hundreds of thousands of Canadians left the country to seek their fortunes elsewhere. Nevertheless, as a result of a high birth rate, the population did increase, and by 1900 the exodus had been stemmed.

Industrial development was predicated on cheap labour, and, increasingly, capitalists relied on thousands of immigrants, especially those from non-English countries, to satisfy the country's needs. Labour was an especially scarce commodity in the northern and western regions of the country. As a result, officials of the Canadian Pacific Railway relied extensively on workers recruited from eastern and southern Europe and from China to lay the rails across the Canadian shield, over the Prairies, and through the mountains of British Columbia. In the forests, mines, and factories, immigrant labourers and native-born working-class Canadians also endured harsh and unsafe working conditions and low pay, with little public acknowledgment of their plight or appreciation of their efforts. Yet immigrants continued to come, a testimony to the even harsher realities of the societies they were leaving behind.

By the turn of the century, new immigrants were flooding into Canada, not only from Great Britain and the United States—the two nations from which Canada had always attracted settlers—but now also from all parts of the European continent. Much smaller numbers also came from some parts of Asia and the West Indies. As a result, Canadians of British origin decreased from 60 percent of the population in 1871 to 55 percent in 1921; and those of French origin, from 31 percent to 28 percent. The host community sometimes displayed overt hostility to immigrants from non-English speaking countries, and there was considerable discussion and debate about how best to assimilate them. Nonetheless, many Canadians could see the benefits of a growing population, and the federal government continued to encourage immigrants, including young women (whom officials viewed as potential childbearers), to settle here. Many of the immigrants were attracted by the offer of free homestead land in the region west of Ontario. Not only did these newcomers help open up and develop this area, but their presence was strongly felt since the host community was so small. In 1901, the foreign-born share of the population of British Columbia, the Northwest Territories, and Manitoba was 26, 30, and 15 percent, respectively. For the country as a whole, in comparison, it was only 3 percent.

The native-born population was also very mobile between 1851 and 1911, as thousands from the country's settled areas headed northward and westward. In Quebec, religious and political leaders debated whether it was better to stop the exodus of hundreds of thousands from the province to New England by creating new agrarian-based communities in the northern part of the province or by establishing a French-Canadian Catholic presence in the West. For the greatly diminished Aboriginal populations, there was little choice about where they should go. The rapid expansion of the white population into western Canada meant treaties, reserves, the loss of their traditional way of life, residential schools, and increased death rates. At the time of Confederation, it is estimated that only 100 000 to 125 000 Indians, 10 000 Métis and 2 000 Inuit inhabited the new Dominion. Only after 1901 did the Aboriginal population start to increase again.

In 1876, with the introduction of the Indian Act, the federal government formally regulated who could be considered a status Indian and how those who met the official definition would live out their lives. The act's assumptions regarding women were profoundly patriarchal; a double standard based on gender was integral to both the act and its application.

The gender composition of the Canadian population also changed. Due to the massive movement of young men to the Prairies, the Northwest Territories, and the United States in pursuit of greater economic opportunities, women of marriageable age in the original British North American provinces outnumbered men in the same age range. In Manitoba and British Columbia, on the other hand, the 1881 and 1891 censuses revealed that men significantly outnumbered women. At the same time as new regions were being settled, many Canadians and immigrants moved into urban areas. In 1851, more than four-fifths of the British North American population lived in rural regions. By 1901, the proportion of rural dwellers had declined to two-thirds and by 1921 the number of rural and urban Canadians was about equal. Women continued to lead this shift in the population because they moved to the cities for employment opportunities that the rural areas could not offer them. Consequently, women outnumbered men in most cities, just as men tended to form the majority in rural and frontier areas.

The grand themes for the nation as a whole during this period have been identified as urbanization and industrialization. Only local studies, though, can reveal how people actually integrated change into their lives. Canadians experienced urban or industrial development differently since the pace varied depending on region, class, race, ethnicity, and gender. Women participated fully in the economic transformation of Canada in all regions. Indeed, without them, it is unlikely that the transformation would have occurred at all. Besides bearing the children who would form the workforce of the future, women themselves provided a cheap and efficient labour force. Most of their work continued to be unpaid, absorbed into the family economy, but it was vital. Women also provided much of the labour on which the nation's first industrial establishments, such as textile, clothing, and food manufacturers, depended. Like men, women were active participants in the change process, not the passive victims of economic, political, or demographic forces utterly beyond their control.

The tremendous changes in the demographic and economic makeup of Canada gave many Canadians a sense that they were part of a modern and developing nation. The economy was evolving from one that stressed the ownership of land to one that emphasized industrial development and wage labour, and society was moving from one in which individuals derived prestige from their parentage to one that placed value on what they themselves did. These changes in turn led Canadians to call for some adjustments in their institutions. One example was the franchise, which was gradually changed to almost universal manhood suffrage. The general enfranchisement of women, however, continued to be denied until after the outbreak of World War I; indeed, the Dominion Franchise Act that governed the federal franchise between 1885 and 1898 specified that for the purposes of voting, a *person* was defined as a "male person, including an Indian and excluding a person of Mongolian or Chinese race." It took nearly half a century of determined struggle on the part of women activists and their allies to secure votes for women.

Canada's expansion, industrialization, and rapid urbanization resulted in densely populated areas that accentuated the cities' problems of poor sanitation and contagious disease. The concentration of factories in certain sections of the larger industrial centres created pollution and filth in the areas surrounding them. Drunkenness, delinquency, prostitution, and other crimes were seen as social problems and appeared to be worsening. Nor was life in the rural areas idyllic. Many farmers' sons and daughters were lured to cities by the prospect of paid employment, a trend that resulted in rural depopulation in some regions and a sense of an agrarian lifestyle under siege.

Canadians responded to these problems in various ways. Individually and collectively, they sought solace and solutions in their religious faith. Institutional religion became an even more potent force in the late nineteenth century. One's religious affiliation influenced nearly every aspect of life: where one went to school, whom one married, and, often, where one could get a job. Even in death, religion—or the lack of it—determined one's final earthly resting place. Within the Protestant churches, a vigorous, generally white and middle-class reform movement developed; thousands of Canadian women were active in it. For many Protestant women, the temperance movement provided an important cause around which their efforts could coalesce as they sought to improve conditions for women and children in particular.

The existing women's organizations expanded the range of their activities during these years. Improved transportation and communication networks began to overcome the vast distances of Canada's geography, and some women developed an enlarged sense of common identity. The growth of a female paid workforce in education, health, business, and industry also strengthened a spirit of sisterhood and increased the potential for organization. The isolation of rural women often made getting together difficult; nonetheless, their efforts to counter this isolation led to an enhanced awareness of shared experiences and problems and, ultimately, to the creation of their own organizations.

At the same time, the women's movement responded to the nationalism and imperialism of the era, sharing in a patriotic concern both to protect the country's stability and future vitality, and to maintain and reinforce strong links with the British empire. Most English Canadians hoped that the territorial expansion of Canada would lead to a glorious future for the nation at the centre of the British empire, and the more imperialistic among them pressured the Canadian government into supporting the British in the 1899 Boer War in South Africa. Anglo-Celtic women who shared these aims formed the Imperial Order Daughters of the Empire to look after the graves of those Canadian soldiers who had fallen on foreign battlefields. Such women were also enthusiastic supporters of Empire Day celebrations in the various schools throughout English-speaking Canada. These patriotic activities reached their zenith during World War I. The more extreme imperialist and nationalist attitudes could shade into nativism or racism, which at times invoked eugenics, the science of improving the so-called Anglo-Saxon race through controlled breeding. English-speaking Canadians worried about the growing numbers of non-English-speaking immigrants and the high birth rate of French Canadians. Anglophone women activists frequently shared these anxieties.

At the opposite end of the ideological spectrum, some women embraced pacifism, viewing it as a natural expression of women's nurturing role. French-Canadian women in particular had reason to be opposed to war; unlike their anglophone sisters, they did not identify with British imperialist dreams of grandeur. French Canadians proudly asserted that their loyalty was undivided, and that their identity was rooted solidly in Canadian soil. Any affinity they had once had with Great Britain was largely destroyed as English-Canadian imperialists invoked their belief in the superiority of the Anglo-Saxon race, and of all things British, to justify their attacks on French-Canadian rights outside Quebec. School crises in New Brunswick, Manitoba, the Northwest Territories, and Ontario and the violent reactions of English Canadians to the two Riel uprisings (1869–1870 and 1885) as well as the ongoing debate over the status of the French language underscored anglophone intentions to limit the French presence to Quebec. There, the response of the influential clerical and nationalist elites was a turning inward, a concentration on *la survivance*.

A key element in the French-Canadian strategy for survival has been dubbed "the revenge of the cradle"—an emphasis on encouraging large families to offset the tide of immigration that was swelling the ranks of non–French Canadians. This strategy was, of course, dependent on the labour of women, and it reinforced an ideology that exalted women's role in the home. Historical demographic evidence indicates, however, that the traditional view—that Quebec society at this time was composed of very large families—is misleading. It was only after 1871 that Quebec's birth rate surpassed that of Ontario, and only one in five Quebec women born in the late nineteenth century gave birth to more than 10 children. The Anglo-Protestant reform movement that was intended to accord most women increased economic and eventually political rights was generally unacceptable in Quebec. Nonetheless, as elsewhere in Canada, French-Canadian Catholic women did organize, and they challenged the constraints on their activities. They, too, concentrated on initiating social reforms in response to the problems generated by industrialization and urbanization.

Contemporary historians, including historians of women, have studied this period of our history more than any other period. As a result, we have been able to draw on a wealth of secondary literature that reflects rich primary sources. The number of newspapers and magazines expanded dramatically during these years. So did interest in women: in fact, the proper sphere of women was an obsession for Victorian and Edwardian Canadians, and they delighted in writing about it. Women were told what it meant to be a woman and the proper way to behave. At mid-century, religious authorities were the most significant voice in this discussion. However, new experts appeared in the wake of Charles Darwin's evolutionary theory and a questioning of the literal truth of the Scriptures arising from critical analysis of the Bible. Science in particular gained an aura of authority in the late nineteenth century, and those who invoked it, such as physicians, could bask in its reflected glory.

More reliable than the stereotypes in the written materials produced by male pundits are the records generated by women themselves: their actions, their words, and their artifacts. Diaries and letters were generally written by educated women, however, and by no means reflected the lives of all. This is true as well of the abundant records belonging to women's groups of this period. The evidence of material culture that has come down to us—the kitchen utensils, the new household appliances, the dresses—is also from relatively affluent homes. Not all women could afford to save things or not wear them out before additional purchases were made. Yet these items are important, for they allow us to get closer to individual women and to flesh out impressions based on more impersonal data.

The evidence of individual lives can be supplemented by that contained in census returns and other quantifiable data. Comprehensive censuses of the British North American colonies, first taken in 1851, were repeated at 10-year intervals thereafter. In Catholic parishes, manuscript census returns augment the continuing parish records. In non-Catholic communities, the census returns are often the only source of demographic data; they enable us to estimate the age at which women married, the number of children they had, and their life expectancies. From birth intervals, we can even infer whether or not they used birth control.

It is from many kinds of evidence that we are now able to piece together a picture of women's experience in the second half of the nineteenth century and in the early decades of the twentieth. We know about women's public activities, their involvement in the paid labour force, and their participation in myriad women's organizations. Still, it is much easier for historians to document the unpaid labour and organizational activities of upper- and middle-class white women who left behind journals and letters, than it is to reconstruct the lives and work of Aboriginal and black women and women of the labouring classes, many of whom were illiterate. However, manuscript censuses, newspapers, parish registers, factory inspector reports, and even police records provide valuable, if fragmentary, glimpses into the many kinds of activities that non-elite girls and women engaged in, during this period. Such documents also make it possible to discern how women's work, and attitudes toward it, changed as the various regions that constituted Canada evolved from pioneer economies into more advanced commercial and industrial societies.

Historians interested in gender relations have frequently described the creation of an ideology of separate spheres, clearly visible by the mid-nineteenth century, as both indicating and contributing to a growing inequality between women and men. According to this set of beliefs, men naturally possessed traits—such as strength, competitiveness, and rationality—needed to succeed in the public sphere of economics and politics, while women—represented as delicate, virtuous, and nurturing—should restrict their energies to the domestic realm of home and family. It is difficult to know how much individual women internalized this ideal concept of their gender. To what degree did they perceive contradictions between the popular perceptions of women and the reality of their own lives? And how did they respond? The relevance of such a gender belief system, and the nature of the response to it, undoubtedly varied considerably depending on the class, race, and ethnic group to which a woman belonged, or even on the geographical location in which she found herself. For Aboriginal, black, poor immigrant, or working-class women, the ideal of "the lady" may have been far removed from their everyday reality. Nonetheless, the construct of virtuous womanhood increasingly influenced the economic, social, political, and legal structures in which their lives unfolded. The many ramifications and contestations of the separate spheres ideology continue to provide historians ample opportunity to undertake fascinating and important research.

CHAPTER FIVE

Industrial Capitalism and Women's Work

In his annual report for 1906, A. W. Vowell of the British Columbia Indian Superintendent's Office observed the following:

> The Indian women, it may be remarked, are also money earners to no inconsiderable extent. During the canning season and at the hop fields they find profitable employment; they engage extensively in the manufacture of baskets, which they dispose of profitably to the tourists and others; they cure and dress deer and caribou skin, out of which they make gloves and moccasins, and they frequently find a market for dressed skins intact, they being useful for many purposes; mats from the inner bark of the cedar and rags are also made . . . [1]

Vowell added that Aboriginal women sold berries to Euro-Canadians, were employed "doing chores and laundry work for white neighbours," and now used "sewing and knitting machines" to help with the fabrication of their children's clothing.

This long list of women's productive activities at the dawn of the twentieth century spoke to the impact of both colonialism and industrial capitalism on the Aboriginal peoples of British Columbia. Seasonal waged labour, the production of handicrafts and clothing for tourists, travellers, hunters, and traders,[2] paid domestic labour in the homes of others, foraging for berries to preserve and to sell: all of these forms of work were integrated into a cash economy. They reflected both the changes in Métis and Aboriginal women's work effected over the course of the nineteenth and early twentieth centuries and the ways in which, more generally, pre-industrial forms of production persisted under industrial capitalism.

Between 1851 and 1921, years during which Canada experienced the industrial revolution, the working lives of all women were marked by both dramatic changes and long-standing continuities. Increasingly, young women in rural areas sought work

Aboriginal women mending a birchbark canoe at the North West Angle, Kenora District, Ontario, 1872.

Source: Library and Archives Canada/PA-074670

off the farm. For most of the period, the major paid employment for women was the traditional one: domestic service. Yet after 1850, women began to move into new areas of wage labour: with industrialization and the growth of secondary industry, thousands of women found paid work within labour-intensive manufacturing enterprises. Moreover, by the turn of the twentieth century, the service sector of the economy was expanding rapidly; it afforded many women additional employment opportunities in fields such as teaching, nursing, clerical, and sales. Indeed, by the First World War, there were more women holding down white-collar jobs than there were women engaged in manufacturing. The Great War and accompanying crises, such as the Halifax Explosion of 1917 and the influenza pandemic of 1918–1920, created new, short-term demands for women's work, both waged and volunteer. Throughout this period, the work that women did was remarkably varied, not only at any one time but over an individual woman's life cycle. Women's labour, both paid and unpaid, fundamentally shaped the development of the economy and of society.

For all women, there was tension between the ideal of the woman at home and the reality of women's work—whether inside or outside the home. From the mid-nineteenth century on, some Canadians protested the constraints and poor conditions faced by working women. They rarely spoke with a united voice; for example, middle-class women were often oblivious to the particular needs of working-class women. Nonetheless, some women began to recognize common problems and a common cause. Their collective efforts and the increased visibility of women's employment outside the home prompted public awareness of the new realities of women's lives.

MIGRATION

The settler experience did not disappear with the emergence of industrial capitalism; thousands of Canadians of European background continued to move into areas of the country that had not long before been populated largely by Aboriginal peoples. For many women, the opportunities afforded by migration outweighed its disadvantages; but for others, giving up a home in a settled part of the country was not easy. Alice Bailey, for example, a young woman of Irish descent, was married in Ingersoll, Ontario, on February 26, 1908. Shortly thereafter, she and her husband, Thomas, buoyed by the dream of owning their own farm, set out for Saskatchewan. In the little log house they built on their homestead, Alice subsequently bore two daughters; but, worn out by the hard work of pioneer life, she died of consumption when she was only 29. Other women refused to move, like Rebecca Ells of Port Williams, Nova Scotia, who with her son ran a mixed commercial farm while her husband went off to the Klondike for 12 years.[3] Others did not want to move, but had no choice. This was the situation of Mrs. Carmichael of Sunnyside, New Brunswick. Her husband insisted on selling the family farm and moving farther north. Her daughter recalled her mother's tears and her initial refusal to sign away her share of the farm. But in the end, seeing no alternative, she signed and the family made its move.[4]

By the late nineteenth and early twentieth centuries, single women were also moving west. Some went on their own or with migration agencies; some were motivated by the high wages offered to domestic servants in a labour-scarce region; others were attracted by matrimonial offers. One such woman, the bride-to-be of a Mountie, made the trip out west. But when she arrived in town, her prospective groom, unbeknownst to her, was looking her over from a distance. Deciding that she did not suit his needs, he sent a message to her and paid her way home.[5]

Immigrants from other countries also continued to move to Canadian farms. Between 1901 and 1921 alone, 644 089 men and women came from the British Isles and 246 125 from the United States.[6] Although Canadian customs and environments must have seemed very different to these immigrants, at least there was a shared language. Women who came from countries whose language was neither English nor French had more to contend with. Between 1901 and 1921, some 500 000 immigrants entered Canada, principally from continental Europe. The women among them often felt they had little choice in moving. For example, Ida Bronowoski left Poland to join her 20-year-old husband in Canada because "I hear lots in Poland come from Canada, they talk. Man stay in rooms there, he forget wife and kids. I not trust."[7] One of the largest groups of non-Anglo-Saxon immigrants to arrive during this period were the Ukrainians. From fewer than 6 000 in 1901, their numbers swelled to more than 75 000 just 10 years later. The influx of Ukrainian women to the Prairie provinces, particularly Alberta, was a source

URGENT!

Thousands of nice girls are wanted
in THE CANADIAN WEST.

Over 20,000 Men are sighing for what they
cannot get-WIVES ! Shame !

Don't hesitate-COME AT ONCE.
If you cannot come, send your
sisters.

So great is the demand that anything in skirts
stands a chance

No reasonable offer refused
They are all shy but willing.
All Prizes! No Blanks.

Hustle up now Girls and don't miss
this chance. Some of you will never
get another.

———

Special Application Card from

An advertisement directed at unmarried women, urging them to move to the Canadian West.

of great concern to local women's organizations there, appalled as they were by what they perceived to be the low status of women immigrants and the "abomination of child marriages among the Galicians [Ukrainians]."[8]

In addition to the language barrier, women from non-English-speaking or non-western countries often had to cope with cultural, racial, or religious hostility. Racist policies were integral to the shaping of this white settler society and kept women of colour from the Caribbean and Asia from entering Canada in any significant numbers during these years. Governments and many citizens alike reasoned that if Asian women were kept out, the residence in Canada of male migrants from China, Japan, and India would remain only temporary. Most Canadians believed that those they referred to as Orientals could not be assimilated. From 1886 until 1923, when they were barred as permanent settlers, nearly all Chinese wishing to come to Canada had to pay a head tax. Beginning in 1904, the fee was set at the very high level of $500. This measure effectively kept female immigration to a minimum since most Chinese men could not afford to bring their wives, and most single women did not have the resources to pay for themselves. Only Chinese women who had non-Chinese husbands or who were the wives of Chinese clergymen or merchants were exempt from the tax. As a result, many of the women who did immigrate were slave girls brought in by Chinese businessmen, who claimed them as either wives or daughters. These young women were bought from their impoverished parents in China to work as domestic servants, waitresses, or prostitutes in British Columbia.[9] Paradoxically, as recent work has shown, fears of interracial sexuality could sometimes fuel calls for the admission of female migrants of colour: the immigration

Mrs. Louie and her children, British Columbia, c. 1900.
Source: Image B-04145 courtesy of Royal BC Museum, BC Archives

of women from Asia would, some commentators hoped, prevent intimate relationships from developing between Euro-Canadian women and Asian men.[10]

Women from all cultures often experienced dire poverty in the course of their immigration. In the spring of 1905, Ottilia Tetzlaff Doering, pregnant with her eighth child, left Russia for Canada with her husband and seven children. En route, the wagon in which all their possessions were packed caught fire; only a samovar (a metal container traditionally used to heat and boil water) survived. During the ocean voyage, on what was essentially a cattle boat, Ottilia became ill and would have died but for the captain's taking the entire family into his quarters. With only 50 cents to their name on arrival, the family accepted the help of an immigrant aid committee, which provided fare to Manitoba. There, Ottilia's husband ran church services and taught, her sons worked as farm labourers, and her daughters worked as kitchen helpers. Eventually the family saved enough to build a log house on a homestead in Chevlin, but Ottilia died of tuberculosis a few years later and did not see the fruits of these collective efforts.[11]

At least Ottilia had a family with whom to share her trials. Single women of all groups lacked even that comfort, although their willingness to move suggests an independence and strength that would serve them well. Not all single women, however, moved freely: we have only to think of the thousands of young home girls sent to Canada from various agencies in Great Britain. In the last decades of the nineteenth century and the first decade of the twentieth, dozens of British charitable agencies, led by social reformers, including Thomas John Barnardo, Maria Rye, and Annie Macpherson, organized the emigration of over 80 000 so-called surplus children—approximately one-third orphaned, all poor—from the working-class districts of British cities to Canadian farms, particularly those in southern Ontario and Manitoba. Once in Canada, these child emigrants, ranging in age from toddlers to adolescents, were hired out as indentured labour: the boys were given placements as agricultural labourers; the girls, as household help. Many were placed in remote, recently settled areas, where they were, at best, lonely and, at worst, vulnerable to physical and emotional exploitation.[12]

Migration to agricultural or northern frontiers, however, was not the only migration of the era. Women also left rural areas to seek their fortunes in the cities, pushed by the difficulties or loneliness of country life and pulled by new economic opportunities. By the turn of the century and increasingly afterward, columnists writing in farm newspapers acknowledged this rural exodus. They blamed it on the harshness of farm life for young people, and especially for young women, who felt they had no prospects on the farms, particularly in the less prosperous regions. Few wanted to end up as one 40-year-old farm woman did—upon her father's death, left with only a cow and 100 dollars to show for her lifelong work on the farm, when each of her three brothers had inherited a 320-acre farm. At least the cities offered women a chance to work for pay. Soon women were moving to urban centres in massive numbers. By 1871, in fact, women in Montreal outnumbered men in every age category. Nor was Montreal an anomaly. By 1921, women between the ages of 15 and 29 outnumbered men of the same age range in most urban centres in Canada.[13]

Migration to and between cities was the experience of both immigrant women and Canadian-born women. Despite the fact that government policy encouraged immigrants to settle in agricultural regions, many chose cities or towns instead. The average rate of increase in the urban population after mid-century was 34 percent per decade. Moreover, many urban Canadians were transients in the decades after the middle of the century: in the centres that have been studied, 50 to 75 percent of city residents in a given year cannot be traced ten years later. For women, the cities of Canada offered significant work opportunities. Indeed, between 1891 and 1901, women in the paid labour force increased by 41 959 or 21.4 percent, and most of these employed women worked in urban centres—big cities such as Montreal, Toronto, or Hamilton, but also small industrial towns, such as Paris, Ontario, or Valleyfield, Quebec.[14]

WOMEN'S WORK IN RURAL AREAS

Women in rural regions and on the frontier continued to perform labour-intensive work for little or no pay. In fact, Russian Mennonite women newly arrived in Manitoba found that their work had increased: they laboured in the fields for the first year or so, something they had not done in the old country.[15] Labour on the farm continued to be gender-specific, although women participated in farm work far more than men contributed to domestic work. Women scrubbed clothes on scrub boards, hauled water from the creek or the well, cooked on wood stoves, and made most of the family's clothes. In addition, they grew vegetables, gathered fruit, preserved and baked, and looked after their children. The domestic work of women was seldom easy. Susan Dunlap's diary of 1866–68, written when she was a young girl in Stewiacke, Nova Scotia, details the household chores performed by her sister, her mother, and her. These included churning butter; washing, picking, and carding fleeces; spinning; weaving; and "pulling, setting, breaking, hackling, and scutching . . . of the flax." Even Christmas Day was not free from labour. In 1866 Susan wrote, "Christmas day and a rainy one. Mother and Mary scoured fifty skanes [skeins] of filling. Mother spun 2 skanes. Mary made Howard's cap. Aunt Ellen was over. Mother stitched a sack [dress] for Mary." These chores not only saved money but also, in some families, generated income. The butter Susan churned every day, for example, was sold and the money used to help support the family.[16]

In the 1890s, Micmac women in the Maritimes continued to bring in money with their basket work, and this money tended to be the most dependable source of family income. In addition, many of these women were doing most of the work on their farms. As the Indian agent in 1893 noted, "those Indians living on the reserve have done much more planting this spring than at any time previous, the women doing a large part of the work while the men are employed on the streets [in Yarmouth] at good pay."[17] Halfway across the continent, Dominko Roshko and her mother, pioneering in early twentieth-century southern Manitoba, dug seneca roots and sold them at 35 cents a pound for medicinal purposes, or traded them for supplies. The money these women earned helped their families to survive and also stimulated the economy. But selling their produce could be more difficult for Aboriginal women. Those on Prairie reserves were encouraged by the Indian agents to be agricultural producers and to sell their surplus eggs and butter as white women did. However, each woman on the reserve needed the permission of the agent to do so—permission that was not always forthcoming. Newfoundland women, too, had difficulty participating directly in the market economy. Caught up with subsistence production tied to the fishery, they had little time to produce other goods for purchase or trade.[18] Market-oriented or not, women needed ingenuity in order to survive. In 1884, when her hens and a rooster were killed by a mink and her one remaining hen froze its foot, Harriet Neville fashioned an artificial leg and foot for it out of whalebone, wire, and a kid glove. The hen went on to raise several clutches of chicks.[19]

Although farm women, particularly pioneer women, continued many of the work patterns of their mothers and grandmothers, change did occur during the second half of the nineteenth century. When farms became prosperous, the money that women generated was no longer as necessary for survival, although it often continued to represent a regular source of income for their families. Those women who continued to bring in money welcomed it for the independence it gave them, and the chance it gave them to buy things for their families and homes without feeling that they were robbing the farm. At the same time that the farm's financial needs were shifting, large-scale and centralized production often took over some of the work that traditionally had been women's, such as spinning and weaving, and making cheese and butter. In 1864, the first cheese factory in Ontario opened. By 1900, there were 200 cheese factories in Oxford County alone; as a result, the share of cheese produced on Ontario farms declined steadily. At the same time, milk production increased to meet factory demand, and care of the growing dairy herds passed from the hands of the farm women into the hands of their husbands and farm labourers. In general, there was a decline in skilled work for farm women and a resulting decline in the money they were able to earn, leaving these women with little visible or recognized economic input, and little money of their own. Yet when specifically asked whether the development of cheese factories had altered their financial position, Ontario farm women in 1903 said it had not: their focus was on how their lives related to others, how the family worked together, the family's well-being, as well as the farm economy's well-being.[20]

Many farmers acknowledged the work women did; in rural areas it was well known that bachelors were less successful at farming than were married men because the work that wives and children did remained so essential. Indeed, in the early 1860s, the Agricultural Association of Upper Canada stated explicitly that "a good wife" was "indispensable" to a farmer.[21] After having seen first-hand the work that women performed in early twentieth-century Saskatchewan, settler Georgina Binnie-Clark could only concur with this judgment. She believed that she owed one important debt to her life on the Prairie: "a fair appreciation" of her own sex.[22] Yet few farm wives received tangible recognition. Farmers were notorious for purchasing new equipment for the barn or fields but refusing to buy anything for the house. Nor did the government of Canada recognize the work that farm women did: in the census, farm wives—like other wives who worked in their homes—were listed as having "no occupation."[23]

In the English-speaking provinces, according to both custom and the common law, a farm wife had little or no legal claim to family property that had been acquired partly as a result of her labour. The land was owned by her husband, and he had the right to sell it at any time unless she was protected by dower right—that is, that part of her husband's property that the law guaranteed a widow for life. Increasingly, Canadian men viewed the buying and selling of land, including the family farm, as a way to get ahead,

Doukhobor women winnowing grain in what would later become Saskatchewan, 1899.

Source: Library and Archives Canada / C-008891

and saw dower right as an anachronistic holdover from an earlier time when agricultural property seldom changed hands. The hostility to dower was particularly strong in the Northwest Territories (a vast administrative region that included what are today the Prairie provinces, along with parts of current-day Ontario and Quebec), where the right was abolished in 1886.[24]

Even if the land was not sold, a woman who outlived her husband often found her position tenuous. Frequently, widows found that the farm had been left to a son, and that they had little beyond their dower portion and some form of limited maintenance. Sometimes even this much was conditional on the wife's good behaviour—in particular, her willingness to remain a widow. In Richibucto, New Brunswick, in 1856, a widow discovered that her husband's will specified that she would lose her right to the use of the family property if she remarried.[25] Control from the grave continued in many farming regions well into the twentieth century, as Lucy Maud Montgomery observed in connection with her grandmother in 1905:

> Uncle John and Prescott have been using grandmother shamefully all summer. In short, they have been trying to turn her out. . . . Grandfather's absurd will put her completely in their power—the power of selfish, domineering men eaten up with greed. Grandmother told them she would not leave the home where she had lived and worked for sixty years and since then Uncle John has never spoken to her or visited her.[26]

The legal rights of widows in Aboriginal communities were also tenuous. The 1884 revisions to the Indian Act insisted that widows had to be "of moral character" in order to inherit. Indian agents also were reluctant to allow widows property unless there was a son to inherit from the mother. Those married to white men without benefit of clergy were particularly vulnerable. In 1878 a young South Peigan woman, Awatoyakew, also known as Mary Brown, was living with Nicholas Sheran. When he died, neither she nor the two sons she had had with Sheran received anything from his estate. His sister—who became the administrator of Sheran's estate and knew of Mary and her sons—claimed that her brother had been a bachelor. Mary returned to her own people, and Sheran's sister placed the two boys in a Catholic orphanage. In some Aboriginal cultures, inheritance practices encouraged extreme self-denial on the part of women.[27] In 1888, for instance, an elderly Inuit woman whose health had been declining for several years decided to follow the custom of her people, and asked her son to abandon her on an island to die. What prompted her to this decision was not only her failing health but the knowledge that if she died in her son's home he, by custom, would have to throw away his clothes. His wife had already died that year; the mother decided that her son could not afford to lose a second set of clothes.

In Quebec, widows' dower rights had traditionally been protected by French civil law and, more specifically, by the Custom of Paris. Beginning in the 1830s, however, dower rights were increasingly viewed as archaic, particularly by capitalists interested in land speculation and the transaction of real estate unencumbered by the obligations of dower. The Lower Canadian Civil Code of 1866 confirmed this ideological shift by requiring married couples to register dower rights if they did not wish to lose them. It appears that as the nineteenth century advanced, fewer and fewer married women registered their dower rights, perhaps because they did not realize that they needed to. By the final third of the nineteenth century, dower rights had largely fallen into abeyance in Quebec.[28]

Widows' relative lack of financial control over their future added to the decline in status that they frequently experienced. Often, the widow was no longer the mistress of her own house but, like Lucy Maud Montgomery's grandmother, a guest of her son and daughter-in-law, or of other younger family members. Nor were her daughters any better off. Women rarely inherited family farms—and when they did, their portions of estates were usually smaller than those given to their brothers. The idea of women farming on their own did not appeal to Victorian public opinion—nor to Victorian legislators, for that matter, as the 1872 Dominion statute governing public lands made clear: only women with dependent children were permitted to homestead on their own. At least one woman is known to have disguised herself as a man when, after her husband died, she decided to carry on with the couple's scheme to raise horses on the Prairies. It is possible that she did so in order to get access to public land; for the most part, women who wanted to be farmers had to accumulate enough capital to purchase land that had already been developed.[29]

Few farm women sought public recognition for their work. Their reward was the well-being of their families, even if they personally did not always have an equal share of the material benefits. Many delighted in living close to nature and building something for the future. One woman captured this faith in the following terms: "I no longer utter a mental protest against the prairie as a final resting place. Our western life is too real, too vital to waste time in gloomy speculation. It is enough that you are alive and can take your chances in the great future that lies just at hand."[30]

Knowing that they were working for the good of their families helped offset the loneliness felt by many women in farming and rural communities. In the older, more prosperous farming districts, roads and railways gradually made access to and from rural areas easier, and speeded the delivery of mail. Yet even in such communities, women could be isolated: they generally had too little leisure time to enjoy contact with neighbouring friends and kin. In the outport villages of Newfoundland and in other remote regions, women could be cut off from their friends and relatives; in the case of frontier towns dependent on single resources, such as mining and lumbering, the problem for women was the sense that they were living in a largely masculine environment. Those on Prairie homesteads were among the most isolated: neighbours were not close, and women were often hundreds, if not thousands, of kilometres from extended family members and childhood friends. Johanne Fredericken, for example, who came from Denmark in 1911 to join her husband homesteading in Saskatchewan, described the implications of this isolation: "Everything depends on the mother, one cannot share the responsibility with the shoemaker, tailor and baker, school or priest, and therefore, one stands by oneself poor and powerless."[31] As a sympathetic male commentator noted in 1913, the isolation of the frontier was difficult for all, but "especially for the women to whom the little amenities of social intercourse mean so much."[32]

It was an isolation not all could tolerate. While many women coped reasonably well, helped by husbands and children, newly made friends, and a belief in their contribution to the future, heartbreaking stories abound of women whose physical and mental health broke down. Letitia Youmans noted in her 1893 autobiography that farm women seemed to be particularly numerous in one Ontario asylum—because, according to the superintendent's laconic observation, of "hard toil and monotonous mode of living."[33]

As a result, many women worked vigorously to decrease their isolation and to improve their situations by maintaining ties with friends and family from whom they were separated, and by creating new relationships with other women in their adopted communities, especially with those of the same religious, racial, or ethnic origin. Together they ensured that there were schools for their children and occasions when people could meet and socialize. Women were often the chief supporters of institutional religion and were, therefore, among the first to encourage the establishment of churches in isolated areas. In mid-nineteenth-century Quebec, for instance, Catholic women petitioned church authorities for the creation of new parishes, which provided not only a church and a parish priest, but the framework for institutional and social life. Across Canada, rural women thus sought to improve their quality of life and preserve cultural traditions. Unfortunately, their efforts in this direction were not without victims, for they often excluded those who could not or would not conform. Aboriginal women were among those who suffered from the community-building efforts of English-speaking settlers in the west, convinced as the latter were of the superiority of their own culture.[34]

WOMEN'S WORK IN THE URBAN HOME

Farm women's lives, while undergoing important transformations, maintained a strong continuity with the past. The work performed in the home by urban women, on the other hand, changed more dramatically in this period. Industrialization had the effect of accentuating the division between paid and unpaid work, with most paid work now being performed outside the home. There was an increasing acceptance of the idea that it was the husband's responsibility to bring home a family wage—one that would support both the worker and his family—and the wife's, to see to it that the wage covered the needs of the family. Some women became involved in the network of home manufacture created by the "putting out" system. Employers avoided the necessity of renting or buying factories and passed on overhead costs to workers, employing subcontractors or middlemen who distributed work to women in their homes. In the garment trade, for instance, the employer might sell or rent sewing machines to home workers; he often deducted the cost of the needles, thread, or material from the women's wages. Domestic manufacture was paid by the piece, so that it was the worker, not the employer, who absorbed the cost of low production because of faulty equipment, crowded or difficult working conditions, or irregular demand. Many women with families were willing to put up with this situation. They could make some money without leaving home, and even their small children could be conscripted to accomplish simple parts of the work. In towns and cities, women could also earn an income by taking in laundry or boarders. The money earned by such work might come in irregularly, but it was often crucial for the continued well-being of the family.[35] Yet because the income generated by women in the home was not as visible as wages earned outside it, few Canadians recognized the important role that women's earnings played in a family's survival. Certainly, the government did not. Its statistics on women's employment never acknowledged this kind of income, with the result that the percentage of women in paid employment was greatly underestimated.

Even more significantly, official statistics did not acknowledge the unpaid work that women did and its contribution to the country's wealth and prosperity. And women continued, of course, to work extremely long hours at the traditional tasks associated with housekeeping, child-rearing, and general family management. As the family's survival increasingly required cash, managing its funds became an important part of women's work. Many working-class women stretched the family budget by keeping gardens; raising animals, such as cows and pigs; making their own soap; and (once glass bottles became reasonably priced), canning their own fruits and vegetables. Some even stinted on their own food intake to ensure that the principal breadwinner was sufficiently fed. Women also assisted their husbands through their savings. They saved on medical costs by using Balm of Gilead (made from the gum of the balsam tree) for blisters, mustard plasters for colds, poultices made from milk and bread for boils, baking soda for bites, cold tea leaves for burns, salt water for sore throats, and senna tea for constipation.[36]

For urban women, however, the character of housekeeping and child care was gradually changing. For public health reasons, municipal bylaws gradually ended the keeping of the pigs, cows, and hens that had been so important to the traditional household economy. And as children spent more time at school and as families became smaller, fewer children were at home to help with household chores or to mind younger siblings. At the same time that married women faced shortages of domestic help, new technological developments contributed to the mechanization of housework. The application of technology to domestic work had the potential to change household routines radically. Yet while the women portrayed in advertisements had at their disposal a team of servants using carpet sweepers and washing machines, few of these ideal women, with both servants and the money necessary to purchase new appliances, in fact existed.

By the end of the nineteenth century, all women had to contend with new, elevated standards of cleanliness and efficiency. The recently discovered germ theory of disease propagation made dirty clothes or a dirty house seem tantamount to family neglect, as public health nurses and doctors tied childhood illness and high infant mortality rates to mothers' ignorance of the need to keep their households and children clean.[37] The introduction of the hand-powered washing machine in the 1890s made washing easier, so laundry could be done more often. There seemed little or no excuse for soiled clothing or linens; unfortunately, so-called labour-saving technology combined with new standards could actually mean an increase in the housekeeper's workload. These new standards could be particularly oppressive for poor urban families: not only could they not afford the new household technology, but dirt was endemic in the working-class districts of Canada's growing industrial and commercial cities and towns. Technology was thus a double-edged sword, rather than the simple progress that manufacturers claimed it to be.[38]

Sometimes, new household technology even replaced women's traditional lore and experience, especially when new consumer goods also replaced the products that women had once made themselves. As stores distributing mass-produced goods proliferated, and as store-bought became the standard by which to measure home-made products, such as bread and dresses, the items women used to make for their families in the home were increasingly replaced by factory-produced goods. As a result, women's work in the home declined in variety, although not in intensity. The noted feminist Nellie McClung recalled seeing her first ready-made dress, which a "daring" Manitoban woman had ordered from Montreal. She and other women waited with bated breath to see this new phenomenon, and were pleasantly surprised when it turned out to be attractive.[39] More women of all classes entered a changed world—a world in which it was possible to be consumers of goods they had not produced themselves and in which "it was wonderful to imagine everything coming from a store."[40] But shopping carefully and effectively was itself work, as was accumulating the cash necessary to buy the new goods that seemed increasingly indispensable.

OLD AND NEW KINDS OF EMPLOYMENT

Domestic service continued to be the single most important paid employment for women in Canada; in 1891, 41 percent of all women considered to be working were employed in this area. But it was work that increasing numbers of Canadian-born women spurned. As early as 1868, the *Globe* reported that "our working women dread household service, and hundreds would perhaps rather famish than apply at a servants' agency."[41] Domestics tended to be young girls—immigrants, more often than not—with little or no training. For many immigrant women, such as the Irish of the nineteenth century and the eastern Europeans of the early twentieth century, the income earned as a domestic servant allowed them to put down roots in Canada while they looked for better work—or a husband. And the demand for servants was so great that the federal government and many women's organizations encouraged British and European domestic servants to come to Canada. That said, domestic service provided an entry into the Canadian paid workforce not only for European women, but also for many Canadian farm girls. It was a job for which they were considered ideally suited since they were familiar with household work and with conditions in Canada. From their parents' point of view, the occupation sometimes seemed preferable to others, since it at least took place in a family environment. Above all, domestic service was considered suitable for women because it prepared them for their eventual role as housewives. Government officials and private employers alike encouraged Aboriginal women to become domestics; Micmac women in Nova Scotia at the turn of the century, for instance, were excluded from industrial employment in towns and considered suited only for domestic work. Most whites also deemed domestic service especially suitable for black women, although this attitude did not translate into any support for the immigration of black domestics. When an immigration scheme to bring West Indian domestics to Montreal from Guadeloupe began in 1911, it was quickly stopped due to the vocal opposition of white Canadians.[42]

Domestic work was only as good as the mistress for whom one worked. Since there were no employment standards to govern either work or living conditions, both could be very bad. "Living in" meant that one did not have to pay for room and board, but employers of live-in servants were known to hold back wages to ensure that their employees would remain. Some domestics had to spend entire days bent over the washtub; others were given next to no time off, and few servants had any privacy. Life could also be lonely, since few families could afford more than one servant, and differences of class, age, race, and ethnicity frequently prevented warm servant–mistress relationships.[43] Not all domestics were willing to play a subservient role, however. Nellie McClung recounted the story of a servant girl who was told that she must take a bath on her day off at the YWCA—not in the family tub. Her response was, "No bath, no work."[44]

Perhaps the most serious problem of the domestic servant, if she was far from the protection of friends or family, was her vulnerability to sexual exploitation. Olive Savariat, a 17-year-old domestic in the Clarenceville, Quebec, home of James Collins in the early 1860s, was a servant made pregnant by her employer. Olive's story ended tragically in her employer's barn, where she died as a result of an abortion he had arranged.[45] In an atypical case that nonetheless reveals the risks run by servants, Carrie Davies, an 18-year-old servant of Charles Albert Massey, a scion of the wealthy Toronto family, shot and killed her employer in 1915 because of his sexual advances. Davies did not escape trial, but about 1 000 sympathetic supporters contributed to her defence fund, and the jury acquitted her. Davies's reaction was extreme, but the law certainly did not provide much protection for women like her: between 1880 and 1930, not one Toronto employer charged by a domestic with rape or indecent assault was convicted.[46]

The more typical response of the exploited servant, whatever the form of exploitation, was simply to leave. The turnover rate in domestic service was very high as domestics searched for better positions or left to get married. For this reason, up to one-third of Canadian employment agencies specialized in women workers.[47] For a domestic, it was better to leave than to be fired since all servants depended to some extent on personal

An African-Canadian nanny with her white charges in Guysborough, Nova Scotia, at the turn of the twentieth century.

Source: Attributed to William H. Buckley Collection, ca 1900. Nova Scotia Archives and Records Management, Buckley Family fonds. 34.4.6 (N-6066), no. 1985-386/216

references. Most domestics lived in the homes of their employers; if they lost their jobs, they also lost their homes. As a result, servants who were dismissed by their employers were in an extremely insecure position. Those who had lost their virginity and might therefore have difficulty making a respectable marriage were particularly vulnerable to the overtures of madams and pimps who offered them lodgings and companionship. The same was true of some immigrant women, far from family and friends. For many, then, prostitution was one of the few options available for earning a living, especially in regions where there were few employment opportunities for women. Especially at risk were Chinese women, some of whom had been specifically brought to Victoria's Chinatown to be prostitutes or servants without pay. At risk also were Aboriginal women: a national scandal broke out in 1886 when some employees of the federal Indian Affairs Department were charged with trafficking in Aboriginal women.[48]

One of the positive features of domestic service that government and women's organizations liked to stress was the level of remuneration. At the turn of the century, in western Canada, so-called general servants made from $10 to $20 monthly. In the east, they could earn $8 to $14 per month (except for black domestics there, who made much less).[49] Wages paid to white servants were comparable to, and in some cases higher than, those earned by women in other occupations because domestics did not have to pay for room and board.

With the development of Canadian industry after mid-century, young women were increasingly employed in factories or at piecework in the home. In fact, by 1871, women and children constituted 42 percent of the industrial workforce in Montreal and 34 percent in Toronto. Many young women continued to live at home while they were working at paid employment; many periodically left paid work to attend to the needs of their household.[50] Women played a particularly important role in the Canadian textile industry. Girls entered the mills as young as 11 and 12 in the 1880s, and at 13 and 14 at the turn of the century. Some textile companies actively recruited experienced female workers from abroad. Penmans Limited, located in Paris, Ontario, was the country's largest knit-goods manufacturer: in the early twentieth century, it hired recruiting agents and placed advertisements in British newspapers in order to attract skilled female hosiery workers from the English east midlands.[51] In the Quebec cotton industry in 1908, almost half the operatives were women.

Indeed, so tied to the industry were Quebec women that when jobs were scarce, a veritable exodus occurred to the mill towns of New England. Single women and men were often the first to go; as they became established, other family members followed. Married Franco-American women working in New England mill towns could count on networks of family and neighbours to help with child care. In 1909 alone, more than 10 000 people left Quebec for the United States in search of jobs.[52] This exodus worried the Catholic Church and the Quebec government, who were concerned about *la survivance* of French culture within the larger English milieu of North America. Neither priests nor politicians wanted to see future childbearers leaving the province. However, Quebec was not the only province to see many of its energetic young people leave. Between 1881 and 1921, more than 165 000 Maritime women also left Canada to try their luck in the more industrialized and more lucrative job markets on the eastern seaboard of the United States. And jobs did seem easy to get. When Ada Williams left her fishing village in Nova Scotia for Boston in 1907, she quickly gained employment in a box factory and, when laid off, had no difficulty finding another job, this time in an ice-cream parlour.[53]

By 1901, women represented 25 percent of the Canadian workforce engaged in manufacturing and mechanical work; in 1921, they still constituted 24 percent of a much-expanded industrial labour force.[54] Factory work was hard and involved long hours, despite the introduction of protective legislation applying to women and adolescents who were employed in industrial establishments. In 1884, Ontario became the first province to pass such a law; it set the age at which young women could begin factory work at 14 (for young men, the age was set at 12). The hours that women, girls, and youths could work were limited to 10 per day or 60 per week, with an hour provided each day for a noon meal. Employers could apply for, and often received, special permits that enabled them to work their employees up to 72 hours per week for a maximum of 6 weeks each year. Concern for women's safety and especially for their reproductive potential was reflected in the portion of the law that prohibited their being employed in situations in which their health might be permanently damaged; however, the principal onus was placed on the worker to protect herself. For example, rather than requiring employers to install guards on dangerous machines, the law stipulated that women workers should wear hairnets to prevent themselves from being scalped.

Similar protective legislation applicable to factory work was passed by the Quebec Assembly in 1885. However, it took the government of Ontario two years to set up a system of factory inspectors to enforce its 1884 legislation; and the government of Quebec, three years before it appointed its first factory inspector. By the 1890s, both governments had appointed female factory inspectors to visit those manufacturing establishments that employed large numbers of women and children; but as late as 1913 there were only two badly overworked female factory inspectors in each province. In 1913, women in Ontario and Quebec factories still routinely worked 55–60 hours a week and up to 70 hours in rush seasons.[55] But at least the hours were defined and at the end of the working day the time remaining was a worker's own. Factory work usually provided the opportunity to talk and make friends with other women. In the factory, and during free time after work, a young woman was able to meet young men and perhaps develop a relationship that would lead to marriage and the establishment of her own home.

The hierarchical work relations of factories, however, proved as potentially abusive as those in domestic service. When the Royal Commission on the Relations of Capital and Labor reported in 1889, it described the case of Georgiana Loiselle, an apprentice in a Montreal cigar factory. When this young woman refused to make another hundred cigars, her employer attempted to spank her; she fell to the ground, where he pinned her and struck her with a cigar mold. However, it was not the beating that concerned the Commission, but the propriety of "a man placing a girl of eighteen in that position."[56] The entry of women into the industrial workforce engendered concern about immorality, the future of the family, and even the future of "the race." Ironically, this concern in turn created new employment opportunities for at least a few women. After 1910, many cities in Canada appointed women police officers to work on morality squads to help protect the thousands of young women arriving in the city in search of work.[57]

Whatever concerns women might have had about their relations with men in the workplace, they continued to seek industrial jobs. Many working-class families depended on the wages of their children, whether girls or boys. In 1891, more than 7 000 females under the age of 16 were employed in industrial establishments. Unfortunately, women's ability to contribute to the family income was limited by the comparatively poor wages they received. According to early twentieth-century census returns, average earnings for women in central and eastern Canada, where most female industrial workers were situated, remained at 55 to 60 percent of male earnings. Moreover, neither male nor female earnings kept pace with inflation. In 1901, a Toronto woman was working for the equivalent of 2 cents per hour; and as late as 1921, factory women in Montreal received only half the wages men did.[58] One of the reasons for this large discrepancy was that women were employed on piecework more often than men. Since employers based piecework rates on the output of the fastest workers, the less speedy—that is, the majority—earned less than a living wage.

In fact, most female workers barely made a living wage. In 1889, the Ontario Bureau of Industries provided a cost-of-living analysis for women workers without dependants. Average annual earnings were calculated to be $216.71, and average annual costs to be $214.28, leaving a grand surplus of $2.43! Female workers with dependants faced a yearly deficit of $14.23.[59] Not only did women receive less pay than men, but their wage-earning patterns were also different. A study of working women in three Nova Scotia communities—Sydney Mines, Yarmouth, and Amherst—in 1921 revealed that women's earnings gradually increased over their work lives, peaking at age 30, after which they declined. Men's wages increased significantly after age 20, peaking between 31 and 40 and only gradually declining after age 50. Women's pay, then, did not improve greatly with time nor with the introduction of new technology. Although machines did away with brute strength as a prerequisite for many jobs, sexual stereotypes remained. Women who worked machines were not identified as skilled operatives, as their brothers were, but only as unskilled workers who were "alert" and "nimble" (and were paid accordingly less).[60]

At the same time that industrial work was opening up for women, there was a transfer of domestic skills from the home into society. For example, women found employment as laundresses in commercial laundries, as waitresses in restaurants, and as cooks. But the work tended to be hard and poorly paid. Women who worked the Labrador fishery as cooks, for instance, received one-third the wages paid to men doing the same work. Some women, however, were able to take advantage of opportunities. Julia Hernandez and her sister, African-Americans attracted by the Fraser River gold fever, went to British Columbia, where Julia found a job as a cook that paid her $100 a week.[61]

Other new areas of work, chiefly for white women with some minimal level of education, emerged in the clerical and retail sectors. For all of the nineteenth century and even in the early decades of the twentieth century, clerical work was still considered men's work. When the Bank of Nova Scotia in St. John's, Newfoundland, hired a woman stenographer in 1898, it was described as an "'experiment' . . . courageously and gallantly undertaken."[62] But women gradually found openings. In 1901, only 1 in 20 female workers was a clerical worker, and women accounted for only one-fifth of all clerical workers; 10 years later, approximately 1 in every 10 gainfully employed women was a clerical worker, and one-third of all such workers were female.[63]

Clerical work at first seemed to offer considerable opportunity for upward mobility, and was valued as clean, white-collar work. And some women were indeed able to launch innovative careers by taking advantage of the need for clerical workers. For instance, Mary Frances Forbes, a student at Dalhousie University in 1896–97, eventually made a career for herself as principal of the Forbes Shorthand School in Halifax.[64] Then, when the typewriter was introduced, women quickly made it their own, opening up a new area of employment for themselves. When Cora Hind first moved to Winnipeg, she created a job for herself as a "lady typewriter" by renting a typewriter and teaching herself how to work it. She moved on to journalism and a career as a wheat crop forecaster. Gwen Cash was hired in 1917 by the Vancouver *Daily Province* "upon promising to learn typing."[65] However, for most women, access to office work would prove less fulfilling. Clerical work, once an avenue to learning the business, gradually became routinized and mechanized, characterized as women's work, and without prospects for advancement. Women did not replace male clerical workers so much as they filled a need for a new type of office worker. Secretarial work, while requiring special skills, was not always recognized as skilled labour, although in the years 1901 to 1921 those women in higher-status clerical jobs, such as stenographers and bookkeepers, were paid on a par with women teachers and nurses.[66]

Retail work grew quickly in the late 1890s with the re-emergence of economic prosperity. Women were preferred to men as sales personnel because they were considered to be more polite to the customers, particularly since by then women were increasingly the purchasers of household goods. Even more to the point, women sales clerks accepted low wages compared to men. By 1921, one in every four clerical and sales workers was a woman.[67] Such jobs were seen as a step up for many young working-class women: as sales clerks, they could at least work in a cleaner environment than women in factories. Their work was less isolating than domestic service, less menial, and more respectable. It brought working-class women into contact with the manners and mores of middle-class customers, and held out the promise of upward mobility through marriage. But in reality, the pay was low; the hours were long (often longer than in a factory); and the physical strain was high, as sales clerks were required to stand for hours on end. Such jobs, too, required a certain outlay of money for clothing. Owing in large measure to pressure from women's organizations concerned about the long hours that shop girls were on their feet—and the possible negative effects on their capacity to bear children—some provincial governments introduced legislation setting minimum standards for women working in the retail trade. By 1897 Ontario had amended its original Shops' Regulation Act (1888) to limit women's employment to the hours between 7:00 a.m. and 6:00 p.m., and to require employers to provide seats for sales clerks to use when they were not working.[68]

WOMEN IN THE PROFESSIONS AND IN BUSINESS

By the last few decades of the nineteenth century, the occupation that engaged the most women, after domestic service, was teaching. Indeed, the number of women teachers became so great that they were largely responsible for the high percentage of individuals designated professionals in turn-of-the-century census returns. In 1901, for example, almost half of those individuals were women, and well over 80 percent of these women were teachers. After that date, the percentage of professionals who were lay teachers decreased, because the census began to incorporate nurses and religious workers (many of whom were also teachers) in the professional category.

In truth, however, teaching lacked the attributes of a profession. Lay teachers, whether women or men, did not control entry into their field, nor did they make the regulations that controlled their workplace; they had little choice regarding the curriculum or the books used in their classrooms, and they were increasingly subject to an extraordinary degree of regulation by their local school boards, as well as by provincial school authorities.[69] The status of a teacher was thus ambiguous; the occupation might represent upward mobility for a farm girl, but not for a middle-class girl. Who was classified as a teacher was equally unclear. In the 1891 aggregate census, religious women who taught were classified as "Non-productive" (along with "Indian Chiefs," paupers, asylum inmates, and students).[70]

As public schooling expanded after mid-century, educational systems provided women with increasing opportunities for both work and training. There were a greater number of normal schools, and some provinces also provided model schools, which were authorized to give temporary teaching certificates. By the early twentieth century, the development of secondary schooling in some provinces and the continuation of private schooling provided additional opportunities. Overall, the need for teachers vastly increased, and employing women continued to be the solution for school boards that were hard-pressed for funds. In addition, educators and trustees alike were convinced that women made ideal assistants in schools where the senior grades and the schools as a whole were controlled by men. Not all school boards, however, agreed with this approach. Catholic boards in Quebec obtained higher provincial grants if they hired male teachers; and in 1903, the board in Victoria, British Columbia, determined "that in the interests of tactful discipline and the cultivation of strength and character in the boys," they should hire more male teachers. Partly for this reason, the feminization of teaching occurred later in British Columbia than in other provinces.[71] Nevertheless, at the turn of the century, women dominated the profession numerically: in 1901, three-quarters of all those engaged in the educational profession in Canada were women. In 1920, women constituted 83 percent of elementary-school teachers.[72] In Quebec, the second half of the nineteenth century bore witness to both the feminization and the clericalization of teaching staff. In 1857, 67 percent of Quebec teachers were women; by 1900, this proportion had reached 87 percent. Moreover, a growing proportion of teachers were nuns and religious brothers. Montreal Archbishop Ignace Bourget recruited teaching orders from France in the 1840s and 1850s and also encouraged the founding of new Canadian religious communities. By 1894, there were 21 female teaching orders in Quebec, regrouping almost 2 500 teaching sisters. By 1901–1902, almost 30 percent of female teachers in Quebec were nuns.[73]

The conditions of work may gradually have improved in some urban centres over time, but many teachers in rural areas continued to teach all ages in one classroom. Given the deeply rooted belief that women teachers were best supervised by men, it is somewhat ironic that they were entrusted with complete responsibility in rural schools, although it is true that the trustees were never very far away. Rural teachers boarded with students' families and so, like domestics, had little or no privacy. Indeed, the parallel with domestic service can be taken further: many teachers had to do the cleaning in their schools and, in the early years, even perform light duties for the families with whom they boarded. Still, teaching was a respectable job that provided some upward mobility and a modicum of financial security for women who needed to work in order to support themselves or their dependants. A western Canadian remembered that when he started school, the women teachers of his community exuded authority. They had been to normal school in Brandon, Manitoba, and the fact that they had done so and were teaching meant "that they had been out in the great world, had met its demands and had proved themselves. They were, even after only a year, professionals and knew their job. It was an unusual thing for students, encountered only, and that rarely, in the local doctor and the local lawyer."[74]

But there were limits to women teachers' prestige. Women continued to be paid less than men, even when equally qualified. In Toronto in 1870, the average salary for a woman teacher was $220–$400 per year; a man earned $600–$700. In rural areas of Ontario, the average pay for women and men teachers was $187 and $260, respectively.[75] Astonishingly, many women were able to save enough money from teaching to further their education and their careers. Dr. Elizabeth Margaret MacKenzie from Prince Edward Island taught for three years before attending the Dalhousie Medical School, from which she graduated in 1900.[76] Certainly there was little room for advancement within the teaching profession itself. A few women did become principals and even inspectors; in the Catholic school systems in Quebec and elsewhere in Canada, where the sexes were segregated and many of the teachers were nuns, there were far more opportunities for such administrative positions. But overall, promotions were rare. And those that did occur were certainly the preserve of the unmarried career teacher. Indeed, as the occupational structure of teaching changed in the second half of the nineteenth century, so did the employment prospects for married women in schools. Gradually, schools taught by married couples or married women working with sisters or daughters disappeared; more and more often, women teachers lost their jobs if they married.

The higher up the educational ladder one went, in fact, the scarcer women teachers became. Grammar-school teachers—and, later, high-school teachers—usually possessed a university degree, a requirement that posed a barrier for women, as did the assumption that older pupils needed a male teacher to guide them. In 1900, only 17 percent of secondary-school teachers in Ontario were women, although by 1920 this proportion had increased to 51 percent. Concern about this situation led one educator to opine, "if women receive the same pay as men, men will not go into the profession."[77]

Barriers to women's employment as university teachers were greater than at any other level of the educational system. In 1901, of the 857 professors listed in the census, only 47 were women. One of the most successful was scientist Carrie Derick, who received her B.A. from McGill in 1890 and her M.A. in 1896. She also studied at leading institutions in the United States, Great Britain, and Germany. In 1891 she was the first woman appointed to McGill's academic staff when she became a demonstrator in botany; in 1912, she became the first woman in Canada to be named a full professor. Her own struggle for recognition within the academic world led Derick to an active involvement in the women's movement, and to her assertion that "the professions should be open to men and women alike. It is just a question of the survival of the fittest."[78]

Like teaching, nursing had an ambiguous and changing status. For generations, religious nursing orders had enjoyed the support and appreciation of those they had laboured among. When Soeur Sainte-Thérèse, a pharmacist in the Red River settlement, was recalled by her order to Bytown (Ottawa) in 1859, Louis Riel's father had her kidnapped and returned to the settlement. In Dawson (Yukon), the Sisters of Saint Ann not only worked in St. Mary's Hospital, but provided financial assistance for health services as well. In fact, at the turn of the century, two of their members covered 475 miles in 28 days, collecting money from miners for support of the hospital: they raised $10 000.[79] In Quebec, in particular, female religious orders such as the Grey Nuns continued to play a key role in nursing through the second half of the nineteenth century and well into the twentieth.

Unlike nursing sisters, however, lay nurses in the mid-nineteenth century were not held in high esteem. Hospitals were designed for the poor and destitute; the nurses who worked in them were essentially servants who were unable to find employment elsewhere. However, by the latter part of the century, Florence Nightingale's campaign to make nursing respectable began to have an impact in Canada, and with the opening of the first training school in St. Catharines in 1874, nursing began a new era—although change could be slow. By the first decade of the twentieth century, there were 70 training schools in Canada, all attached to hospitals. The young nurses-in-training were used as a source of cheap labour in the hospitals, where, indeed, they constituted the principal hospital labour force; they took their classes in between their regular duties, which could last from 7:00 a.m. to 7:00 p.m. In return for their work in the hospital, nursing students were housed and taught and received a small stipend. As long as hospitals continued to depend on nursing students as their labour force, the only work for graduates was private-duty nursing, which shared many of the inconveniences and unattractive aspects of domestic service. Moreover, maintaining a reputation for respectability was difficult for nurses—the only women workers, aside from prostitutes, with an intimate knowledge of and contact with the bodies of male strangers. In fact, nurses' uniforms, which signalled their specialized occupational identity, were also an attempt to downplay their sexuality.[80]

Nurses did make various attempts to change their situation. Some tried to expand their area of expertise: the Victorian Order of Nurses (VON) was formed in 1897 with the intention of allowing some of its members to act as midwives. The medical profession opposed this proposal so vigorously, however, that it never became a reality. Nonetheless, the VON created a model national public health nursing service, dedicated to sending trained nurses to people's homes, particularly in sparsely populated communities. In Alberta, trained nurses were legally permitted to assist in births in 1919, but only in remote areas where a physician was not available.[81] Doctors were also hostile when nursing education seemed to take a professional turn. As one physician put it, in 1906, nurses ought to forgo scientific study and return to the "gentle touch."[82] Municipal public health nurses, who emerged as a separate group in the early twentieth century, were more successful in exerting their power, perhaps because they tended to work in teams and were able to control their work with little interference from doctors. As a result, they were also able to develop an *esprit de corps* that gave them a sense of worth and identification with their calling. School nurses, too, had more control over what they did than did hospital or private-duty nurses.[83]

While teaching and nursing remained the largest professions to attract women, others gradually opened up, although not without a struggle. Jennie Trout and Emily Howard Stowe, the two women most responsible for advancing medical training for women in Canada, were both trained as physicians in the United States since no medical school in Canada in the 1860s and mid-1870s would accept women. Women had traditionally been healers, and caring for the sick was not a departure from women's traditional sphere—but being highly educated to do so and being paid for it were. When they had finished their training and returned to Canada, Trout and Stowe pushed for the admission of women to medical schools. The major obstacle to medical training for women was the problem of co-education, particularly when the subject was the human body. In fact, so antagonistic were Canadians to the idea of allowing women into existing medical schools that two separate women-only training facilities were established in 1883. The Kingston Women's Medical College was affiliated with Queen's University, and Woman's Medical College, Toronto, was affiliated with the University of Toronto and with the University of Trinity College. Beginning in 1890, women in Quebec were also able to study at the Faculty of Medicine established by Bishop's University. In 1895, that institution graduated Regina Lewis-Landau, the first Jewish woman to gain a medical degree in Canada. But the required education was only the first barrier women had to face in their quest to practise medicine; few hospitals would provide women with the opportunity to gain clinical experience. To be admitted to the Quebec College of Physicians and Surgeons in 1903, Dr. Irma Levasseur, who had trained in the United States, had to win authorization through a private member's bill in the legislature. Even once licenced, women doctors were unlikely to attract enough patients to make private practice economically viable.[84]

Despite the obstacles, many of these early women physicians went on to distinguished careers. In the early years, some women doctors chose to leave Canada and become medical missionaries. Maud Menten, who graduated with a medical degree in 1911 from the University of Toronto, travelled to Germany, where, with Dr. Lenore Michaelis, she studied the properties of enzymes; together they devised the Michaelis–Menten Equation, which provided a theoretical framework for further studies and research on enzymes.[85]

Law degrees came later than medical degrees, perhaps because there was no equivalent in the legal profession to the image of woman as healer. In *The Canada Monthly* in 1872, the distinguished journalist and former academic Goldwin Smith argued that the physical attraction between the two sexes made it highly improper for women to be admitted to the bar. In his words, this physical attraction "would be present when a female advocate rose to address male jury men and judges; and perhaps the class of women who would become advocates would not be those least likely to make an unscrupulous use of their power of appealing to emotions subversive of the supremacy of justice."[86] As a result of this kind of attitude, Clara Brett Martin, the first woman trained in law in Canada and in the British Empire, had to face much opposition. An exceptionally bright student, Martin graduated at 16 in 1890 from Trinity College with an honours degree in mathematics. The following year she applied for admission as a student to the Law Society of Upper Canada, but was rejected on the grounds that the society's regulations restricted admission to "persons"—and, since women were not legally persons, they were ineligible to study law. This decision failed to dampen Martin's determination. Championed by Dr. Emily Stowe and the Dominion Women's Enfranchisement Association, she succeeded in having a bill passed by the Ontario legislature making it possible for women to study law.

Martin's victory owed much to the personal support she received from Sir Oliver Mowat, the premier and attorney general. Under pressure from the suffragists to enfranchise women, Mowat appears to have supported Martin as a way of appeasing the suffrage forces without succumbing to their more controversial demand. By 1892, Martin was able to pursue her studies, but throughout her student years she endured the taunts and ridicule of male classmates, teachers, and the press. Before graduating in 1895, she decided to petition the Law Society for admission as a barrister. She received extensive public support, including from Lady Aberdeen, the wife of the governor general, and from the recently formed National Council of Women of Canada, of which Lady Aberdeen was president. Premier Mowat again brought pressure to bear on the Law Society. Finally the society grudgingly amended its regulations, thereby allowing Clara Brett Martin to become, in 1897, a fully fledged member of the legal profession. In recent years, however, Martin has been criticized for her anti-Semitism—a reminder that efforts to achieve gender equality could coexist with ethnic and racial prejudice and that real women were much more complex than portraits of so-called heroines often acknowledge.[87] In Quebec, women aspiring to careers in the law were not as successful. Although the first woman in that province to graduate with a law degree did so in 1914, women there were not allowed to practise law until 1941.[88]

Isabel Grant, an honours mathematics graduate from Dalhousie University, became, in 1911, the federal government's first woman actuary and insurance expert. Family lore has it that she applied for the job using her initials, and when her application was accepted and she reported for work, her employers were shocked when a woman appeared.[89]

Other occupations that opened up to women did not need the intensive training required by law, medicine, and accountancy. The rapid growth of the Salvation Army in the 1880s in English Canada necessitated the recruitment of preachers; 56 percent were women, who challenged Victorian stereotypes of womanhood by marching in the streets. Their largely working-class origin and following may have made it easier to flout convention, as did the fact that the work they did was for others, not themselves. As well, between 1881 and 1921, the Woman's Missionary Society of the Methodist Church hired more than 300 women to be missionaries both at home and abroad.[90]

Women also entered journalism. When Cora Hind applied for a job on the *Free Press* in Winnipeg in 1881, she met with shocked disbelief on the part of the editor. "It would never do to have a woman in the newspaper business," he argued; it was a business "marked by hard, rough work, late hours, and sometimes involved meeting not quite nice people."[91] Nevertheless, some women were attracted to this work that was a bit daring and different and that offered them a public vehicle for their thoughts. Many papers, in fact, exploited the fact that women were major consumers of reading material by writing columns for and about their sex. Some of these columns were short-lived, but others, like Francis Beynon's in the *Grain Growers' Guide*, became an essential part of their paper's popularity. One of Canada's best-known female journalists was "Kit" Coleman, whose "Women's Kingdom" page in the Toronto *Mail* helped boost the circulation of that paper.

Her work, however, went beyond the women's page. In 1898, she made her way to Cuba to cover the Spanish-American War; in 1906, she described the aftermath of the San Francisco earthquake.[92] Finally, by 1904, women journalists were sufficiently numerous that they were able to set up the Women's Press Club.

Some women even helped establish and edit newspapers. One of the earliest was Mary Ann Shadd, who established, published, and edited the *Provincial Freeman* in the mid-1850s—first in Windsor, then in Toronto—to publicize the plight of African-Canadians and to give them a voice. When she moved to Chatham in 1856, Shadd resigned the editorship and bade farewell to her readers, writing that "we have worked . . . through difficulties such as few females have had to contend against."[93] Two other influential women were editors of widely read women's magazines: Joséphine Marchand of *Le coin du feu*, 1893–1899, and Robertine Barry of *Le journal de Françoise*, 1902–1909.[94] Sara McLagan published the Vancouver *World* after her husband's death, thereby becoming the first woman to both own and publish a newspaper in Canada. Finally, some women made their living or supplemented the family income with their novels and poetry. Félicité Angers (Laure Conan) was the first French-Canadian woman novelist; Margaret Marshall Saunders was the first person in Canada to sell one million copies of a book (her 1894 novel *Beautiful Joe*).[95] With the publication of *Anne of Green Gables*, moreover, L. M. Montgomery became not only one of Canada's most beloved writers, but an international literary figure.

The visual and performing arts also attracted women, at both the amateur and the professional levels, although women musicians seldom played professionally except when there were not enough men to fill orchestra positions. Pauline Johnson, an Ontario woman of mixed Iroquois and European ancestry, was celebrated during her lifetime for her original poetry and her essays. She was also a performer: she presented her poems and dramatic monologues in schools, drawing rooms, church halls, and private salons, and on public stages in Canada, the United States, and Britain. Praised for her beauty and elaborate dress, she was, in addition, viewed by her white audiences as a representative of a "Vanishing Race."[96] Emma Lajeunesse from Chambly, Quebec, took the late-nine-teenth-century opera world by storm under the name Madame Albani; when she retired in 1896, she had performed 43 starring roles. Beyond the few who won acclaim, however, most went unpraised. Canadians tended to view the stage as not quite respect-able and associated actresses with dancehall girls. Among those active, nevertheless, was Pauline (Lightstone) Donalda, daughter of a Jewish immigrant family in Montreal, who made her debut in France but never sang in Canada; she helped establish the Montreal Opera Company in 1937. Another was Elizabeth Ann Thomas Johnson, a well-known African-Nova Scotian singer of spirituals in the late nineteenth century. Then there was Emma Scott Raff, who helped found the little-theatre movement in Canada through the Margaret Eaton School of Literature and Expression in Toronto.[97] Canadian-born actresses such as Marie Dressler and Mary Pickford found success in the United States as moving-picture stars, and Margaret Anglin had a noted career there on the stage. All three became household names.[98]

Women visual artists also had difficulty achieving public recognition and supporting themselves with their art. The great Emily Carr, for example, gave drawing lessons, raised animals, and ran a boarding house for a number of years because she needed the money to continue her painting. Mary Riter Hamilton, whose realistic scenes of World War I won her acclaim from the French government, was ignored in her own country.[99] By the 1860s, at least 20 women were working in professional photography in Ontario alone. While in 1894, women were admitted to the newly formed Toronto Camera Club, they were prohibited from using the darkroom until 1943.[100]

Finally, some women were self-employed and ran their own businesses. Self-employed women often worked from their own homes and thus blurred the boundaries between private and public spheres. These women kept hotels and taverns, ran their own millinery and dressmaking businesses, operated their own private schools, or ran their own ranches. Brothels were often female-owned and operated: madams not only managed their female labour force and the male clientele, but also dealt with local authorities and saw to the upkeep of the house, the provision of food, and the sale of alcohol.[101] Census returns often did not distinguish between those who worked for someone else and those who worked for themselves; the extent of any entrepreneurial endeavour is thus difficult to trace. It was often difficult for women on their own to gain access to capital or credit, although by the end of the century this situation had improved. And there were startling success stories. For example, Belinda Mulrooney, a poor Irish girl from Pennsylvania, made her way to the Klondike in 1897 on a steamship, working as a stewardess. In the exceptional circumstances of boomtown Dawson, in the middle of the Klondike Gold Rush, she ran a lunch counter, started a contracting business, and later opened a roadhouse. She then built the elegant Fairview Hotel in Dawson and subsequently became part owner of a mining company and a telephone syndicate.[102]

WOMEN WORKERS ORGANIZE FOR CHANGE

Generally speaking, women workers had little power to improve their working conditions. Yet some did become involved with unions or form their own associations; they were also involved in protests and strikes. In the textile and garment trades, for example, unions had to come to terms with the presence of large numbers of women workers. The Knights of Labor, a unique union organization that originated in the United States in the late nineteenth century, believed that most workers—skilled or unskilled, male or female, regardless of their craft—should be organized. The notable exception to the Knights' inclusiveness were certain immigrant workers, notably those from Asia.[103] As a way of attracting women workers to the union, the Knights held socials that brought together female and male workers. They also asked Leonora Barry, who was the general investigator of women's work and wages for the Knights in the United States, to come to Toronto to help organize female workers. These efforts met with some success. In 1884, Local Assembly 3040 of the Knights was formed among the woollen-mill operatives in Hamilton, and it included women within its ranks. The women later broke away and formed the exclusively female Excelsior Local Assembly 3179, led by Katie McVicar. McVicar was a young, single worker who was devoted to improving the lot of women workers. She stressed the need for organized labour to change its usual recruiting techniques to meet the needs of women, who were unlikely to participate in mass rallies or to be swayed by vague promises of improved conditions. Unfortunately, her untimely death at age 30 robbed the union movement of one of its most effective female leaders. In 1885, another women's local, the Hope Local Assembly, was established in Toronto, primarily by garment workers.[104] The Knights were a short-lived phenomenon whose impact in provinces other than Quebec greatly diminished after 1890. By 1902 the Knights had been reduced to a mere remnant in Quebec also.

The majority of women workers were not members of trade unions; nonetheless, on many occasions they demonstrated a high degree of militancy, devotion to working-class solidarity, and commitment to advancing their own economic interests. In 1880 in Hochelaga, Quebec, for example, female weavers initiated a strike to protest an increase in the work week. Although the strike included some men, the Montreal *Gazette* reported that the men "were not so nearly demonstrative as the women."[105] White-collar workers, however, were in a different situation. The public perceived their work as more respectable and less onerous, and so it was with surprise that Toronto citizens faced a strike by 400 Bell telephone operators in 1907. In fact, the job of a telephone operator was fatiguing and stressful; it could even be dangerous, for severe electric shocks on the long-distance lines gave some workers convulsions. The strike began when the company decided to increase the hours of work and eliminate overtime. The workers protested and eventually went out on strike on January 31. The women's solidarity during the strike was impressive—as was public support for them, since the telephone monopoly had earned little sympathy. William Lyon Mackenzie King, the deputy minister of labour, intervened in the strike and persuaded the women to go back to work in return for a public inquiry. Most of the testimony at that inquiry supported the workers, and Bell agreed to a settlement that reduced their hours of work. Take-home pay, however, remained inferior to what it had been under the overtime system.[106]

In 1912, almost 1 000 workers from the T. Eaton Co. department store's factory in Toronto, many of them women, went out on strike to protest the firing of some co-workers. The strike spread to Montreal, and sympathetic garment workers in Kingston, Ontario, threatened to strike firms that did business with Eaton's. In addition, women in Toronto's immigrant Jewish community ran an effective boycott of Eaton's goods. However, gender was not always a predictor of support: during the 1911 strike of Jewish cloak-makers and shirt-makers at the Toronto Puritan factory, women were on both sides of the picket line. Even among the most isolated of female workers, there were attempts at organization. In British Columbia, a group of domestic workers established the Home and Domestic Employees Union in 1913 to work toward obtaining a nine-hour day and minimum wages. Given the enormous obstacles the union had to confront in its attempt to organize domestics, most of whom worked alone in individual households, it is not surprising that within two years, the Union had dissolved.[107]

Despite their militancy, women did not play a major role within the union movement in these years. This absence was partly because of the practical problems involved in organizing them. Even women who worked in manufacturing were frequently employed in such small shops dispersed around the city that they were difficult to bring together. For example, in 1891 more than 2 000 Toronto women worked in either dressmaking or tailoring, but they were divided among 614 different workplaces.[108] In addition,

Millinery workroom, T. Eaton Co., Toronto, 1904.
Source: Used with the permission of Sears Canada Inc. F 229-308-0-1819-3, Archives of Ontario

unions were generally restricted to workers who were considered skilled, of whom few were women. The work performed by women, whatever its characteristics, was usually labelled unskilled. As well, unions during this period were very fragile and vulnerable, and were convinced that they had more than enough to do trying to organize male workers. Women workers presented union organizers with additional problems: compared to men, women had high turnover rates, since many left their jobs when they married. In addition, female wage earners often had family or domestic obligations that prevented them from attending union meetings in the evenings.

Of equal significance, however, was the ambivalence or outright hostility many union members and leaders felt toward the idea of women working in the public labour force. In 1898, for example, the Trades and Labour Congress, the largest grouping of organized labour, declared its support for the "abolition . . . of female labor in all branches of industrial life such as mines, factories, workshops, etc."[109] By the turn of the century, many male workers saw women as competitors for their jobs, even though statistics indicated that women and men workers seldom performed the same kind of work. Even when both sexes worked in the same industry, a closer examination indicates that the separation of the sexes into specific job categories was maintained. Indeed, in the cotton industry, while female and male operatives worked alongside each other in the weave rooms, other departments were overwhelmingly composed of either female or male workers. Ring spinners looked after a stationary frame on which the cotton yarn was drawn onto spindles by means of a ring travelling around a small circular track; such spinners were almost exclusively female, since manual dexterity was the principal requirement for the successful ring spinner. Mule spinners, by contrast, were always male, since the mule-spinning frame was a large, complex machine with a moving carriage, a machine that

162

was considered too difficult for women to operate. Not surprisingly, this job and that of loom fixer, another exclusively male occupation, constituted the highest-paying manual work in the mills.

Male workers also believed that women workers caused wages to be low. If the only way to counteract this influence was to bring women into a union, it would sometimes be done—but often more for the benefit of the male members than for the female ones. As the *Palladium of Labor* pointed out in 1894, "place the sexes upon equal pay for the same kind of service and man has the advantage."[110] Indeed, insistence on economic equality with men in the workforce often cost women their jobs. This seemed to be the case in the cigar industry of late-nineteenth-century Toronto. As one commentator explained, "in Toronto there are very few women employed in cigar-making. The reason being that all the employés [*sic*] belong to a union which insists on all workers being paid alike, and the employers prefer to employ men, because they are likely to remain longer in the business."[111]

The intersection of class and gender, then, was complex and highly charged. Underlying much of the uneasiness toward women workers was the growing belief, in the latter half of the nineteenth century, in the idea of the family wage. Workers believed that if a family wage were paid to men, women would not need to seek paid employment, and they could then remain in their proper sphere—the home. This belief, of course, assumed that most women had a male protector. It overlooked the fact that many women had dependants of their own for whom they were responsible, while others simply wanted to work outside the home. Working men also saw the workplace as morally dangerous for women.[112] Even labour radicals did not question the accepted norms of gender relations.

Women continued, however, to enter the paid workforce—especially the service sector and the new or growing so-called women's professions—in massive numbers. In these areas, poor working conditions and low pay often brought women together in an effort to improve their situations. The first associations of women teachers were formed in towns and cities, where it was easier both to organize and to see the extent to which women were discriminated against compared to the men who taught in the public schools. Eight women created the original Women Teachers' Association of Toronto in 1885; teachers in Montreal and in several smaller Ontario cities soon followed suit. Teachers were ambivalent about their organizing efforts, caught as they were between an image of professionalism and the realities of their working conditions and their pay. In Toronto, for example, the more radical members of the Women Teachers' Association considered affiliating with the Trades and Labour Council in the early 1900s; caution won out and the affiliation never happened. Energies went, rather, into campaigns for better wages and working conditions, and into making connections with other groups. In 1918 the various Ontario groups formed the Federation of Women Teachers' Associations of Ontario and began the long process of building a province-wide organization. In the same year, the Saskatoon Women Teachers' Association was formed by 15 teachers. Campaigning for better contracts, equal pay for equal work, and the retention of married women teachers, they, too, demonstrated an awareness of women's disadvantages in the labour force and of the need to organize in order to seek improvement.[113]

Catholic teachers were also struggling to improve their lot. In Montreal, the Catholic association for laywomen teachers and the Protestant women teachers' association combined forces to fight for improvements in Quebec teachers' pension pay, which was manifestly unfair to women. They made some headway, but eventually Joséphine Samson became so frustrated with the grievances of the Catholic teachers in particular that she initiated a campaign of her own, which she finally carried to the office of the prime minister. It would be a gross miscarriage of justice, Samson argued, if Catholic women teachers should end their days "having only black bread to eat" because they had taught practically for free. It was galling to think that two other categories of retired teachers would do better: male teachers and, even, Protestant women teachers would be able to eat "white bread" as pensioners because their salaries had been greater than those paid to the Catholic women. In Quebec urban centres, the majority of women teachers were members of religious orders, and they perhaps had a greater sense of control over their conditions of work. On the other hand, teaching sisters were not immune from the interference of school officials and bishops. In Halifax the Sisters of Charity came into conflict with their new archbishop in 1876 when he attempted to prevent the attendance of the laity at the graduation exercises of Mount Saint Vincent Academy, and to institute other reforms not to the liking of the teaching sisters. A deputation to Rome eventually succeeded in having the order placed under the authority of their friend, the bishop of Antigonish. In Montreal, the sisters of the *Congrégation de Notre-Dame* fought a battle with a Catholic school commission that was perennially short of money and seemed to believe that nuns did not need to be paid a living wage for their work.[114]

Nurses also organized to improve their working conditions. In 1905, for example, the Alumnae Association of the Toronto General Hospital School of Nursing inaugurated a journal called *The Canadian Nurse*, which concerned itself with such issues as the need for registration. Nurses believed that registration would attest to their training and skill, thus raising their status in the eyes of other professionals and the public.[115] From 1912 on, the Canadian National Association of Trained Nurses, formed originally to affiliate with the International Council of Nurses in 1897, struggled to obtain registration laws in the various provinces.

WOMEN'S PAID AND UNPAID WORK IN TIMES OF NATIONAL CRISIS

Canada's involvement in the First World War had important repercussions for women's work, not all of them positive. Among those women whose ethnic background was the same as that of the enemy, such as German- and Italian-Canadians, some found that holding onto a job was difficult. Others found themselves placed in internment camps along with their husbands.[116] For most women workers, however, the war created opportunities—especially after 1915, when the recruitment of thousands of young men into the armed forces resulted in serious labour shortages. Daisy Phillips of Athalmer, British Columbia, expressed the consequences to her sister: "Fancy all the men having to go at a moment[']s notice without time to make arrangements but I suppose the women will just carry on as best they can. . . . [T]hat is the other part of our Duty if we cannot fight."[117] As Canada increased its agricultural exports to hard-pressed Britain, women were called upon to assume an even larger part of farm work. During the summer months, farm wives and daughters were aided in their efforts by hundreds of female students housed in camps and hostels run by the Young Women's Christian Association. In 1917 and 1918, there were more than 2 000 young women in these camps in Ontario alone. They worked at every job: "besides picking and packing fruit, [they] handled horses, pitched hay, drove motor trucks to market and sold the fruit[,] . . . took charge of chicken houses, worked in canning factories, put handles on baskets, [and] hoed for ten hours a day."[118] Not all farmers were convinced, however, that young women should do such heavy work. One even worried about whether a woman could carry a ladder. Government officials also expressed concern about work in the canning factories, since the Anglo-Celtic women who took those jobs had to "mix so much with foreigners."[119]

Urban working women also saw their employment opportunities change. Although many continued to enter domestic service, still the largest employer of women, new jobs opened up as the wartime economy moved into full gear after 1916. The most widely publicized were in the munitions industry, since before the entry of the United States into

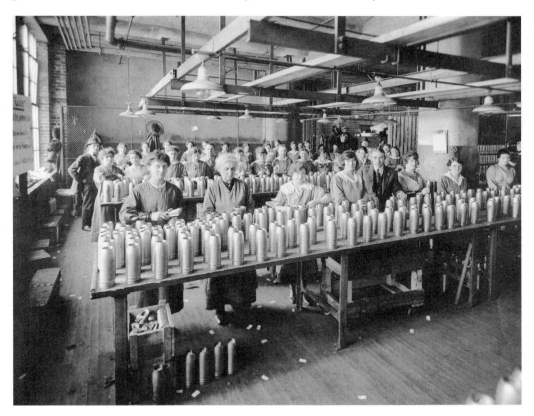

Women war workers in the Northern Electric Co. Ltd. factory, Montreal, around 1916.
Source: Canada. Dept. of National Defence / Library and Archives Canada / PA-024627

the war in 1917, Canada was a major supplier of munitions to Great Britain. To meet its commitment to supply arms, the Canadian government actively recruited female workers for the munitions factories, and by 1917 more than 35 000 women in Ontario and Quebec were producing shells for the Allies. Although the munitions manufacturers paid wages well above those earned by women in traditional occupations, female munitions workers in 1917 earned only 50 to 83 percent of what their male co-workers earned.[120] In addition, the wartime emergency was used to justify extremely long hours (13 to 14 hours a day) and deplorable working conditions. It is important to note that the proportion of married women working in industry increased in these years. In 1921, for example, 22 percent of the female munitions workers in the Montreal area were married, although married women made up only 2 percent of all gainfully employed women.[121]

The brief but impressive economic boom and the manpower shortage engendered by the war enabled women to move into areas of employment normally reserved for men. In Montreal alone, more than 2 300 women were employed by the railways and by the steel and cement industries in jobs formerly held by men only. As well, that women were becoming telegraph messengers was headline news.[122] And in October 1917, Maude Chart made history in Kingston by becoming the first street-railway "conductorette" in Canada; soon all male conductors in Kingston had been replaced by women.

The insatiable demand for men to serve overseas—a demand that resulted in conscription late in 1917—also facilitated the entry of women into white-collar work previously performed by men. Between 1911 and 1921, the number of female clerical workers nearly tripled (rising from 33 723 to 90 577); by 1921, they accounted for nearly 42 percent of all clerical workers and for more than 18 percent of all paid women workers in Canada. In English-speaking Canada, even the most renowned bastions of

Women boat-builders at the end of the First World War in Baddeck, Nova Scotia, 1918.
Source: Canada. Dept. of National Defence / Library and Archives Canada / PA-024363

male clerical work, the banks, were motivated by a combination of male-labour short-ages and increased task specialization to hire women as tellers and clerks. In 1916, more than 40 percent of the clerks employed by the Bank of Nova Scotia in Ontario were women, compared to fewer than 10 percent five years earlier.[123] Women also continued to replace male teachers at the elementary and secondary-school levels. In Alberta, for example, there were 630 more women teachers in 1916 than there had been in 1914.[124] Racial and ethnic barriers to securing white-collar jobs remained entrenched, however.[125]

The armed services also recognized the potential of women's work, but only as nurses. In 1885 during the Riel Rebellion, at the invitation of the minister of militia and defence, seven Church of England nursing sisters had travelled to the Northwest Territories to tend the wounded. The South African War presented Canadian nurses with another opportunity to serve in battlefield hospitals, and in 1901 the Canadian Nursing Service was created as a part of the Canadian Army Medical Corps (CAMC). At the onset of the First World War, nurses rushed to serve in the CAMC. In the end, 2 504 military nurses were actively involved in overseas duties; 46 died while in the service of their country.[126] Most of these 2 500 nurses were Canadian-born, anglophone, unmarried, in their mid-twenties, of lower-middle-class backgrounds, with several years of nursing experience. In applying to join the CAMC, they acted out of patriotism but also out of a desire for adventure and, not least, the hope of consolidating their professional status. Employed on the western, eastern, and Mediterranean fronts, these women received rapid training in military nursing, sometimes onboard the ships that took them to Europe. Once overseas, nurses were employed in work that was physically and emotionally demanding, and they carried out their many and varied duties under difficult circumstances, often caring for their patients in tents and huts. Clare Gass, a professional nurse originally from Nova Scotia who had undertaken her training at the Montreal General Hospital from 1909 to 1912, served at No. 3 Canadian General Hospital (McGill) on the northeastern coast of France, some 40 miles behind the front lines in Flanders. In June 1915, 28-year-old Gass wrote this in her diary:

> Some of these new patients have dreadful dreadful wounds. One young boy with part of his face shot away both arms gone & great wounds in both legs. Surely Death were merciful. Many head cases which are heart-breaking, & many many others. The men are all so good & patient. & so grateful for even the smallest attention. These are the horrors of war. but they are too horrible. Can it be God's will or only man's devilishness. It is too awful. Our boy with both his arms gone is only twenty years old.[127]

Major Margaret Macdonald, another professionally trained nurse originally from rural Nova Scotia, became Matron-in-Chief of Canada's military nurses during the Great War and the highest-ranking female military officer in the British Empire. For Macdonald, supervising Canada's overseas military nursing was above all a professional duty and an opportunity to put her expertise and long experience (including nursing duty in the Spanish-American and the South African wars) to work. No doubt it also satisfied her desire for autonomy and personal achievement, all the while contributing to a cause in which she believed: that of the British Empire.[128]

The dedication and heroism of the wartime nurses contributed a great deal to enhancing the status of the nursing profession. On the home front, women without the qualifications of trained nurses worked through the Red Cross and the St. John Ambulance Association. In fact, inspired by the British example, Canada's St. John Ambulance Association trained almost 2 000 female volunteers as Voluntary Aid Detachment (VAD) nurses. Canadian VADs were generally unmarried women in their twenties and thirties, largely Anglo-Celtic and middle-class. A significant proportion of them—motivated, it appears, by patriotism or by a desire for adventure—gave up salaried jobs as teachers or clerical workers, for example, in order to become VAD nurses. These women helped doctors and trained nurses in military hospitals during the war, but also put their skills and experience to use during such wartime home-front disasters as the Halifax Explosion of December 1917 and the influenza pandemic of 1918–1920. The flu pandemic, in particular, heightened awareness of the shortage of trained nurses across Canada, since many of them had been siphoned off for the war effort; as a result, the efforts of religious nursing sisters and of public-spirited volunteers were crucial to caring for influenza victims.[129]

Women's new work during the war had been considered to be part of the war effort—as men had assumed military responsibilities, so, too, had women but on the domestic front, as supporters of the soldiers. During, as prior to, the war, the vast majority of paid female workers were young, single women. Dominant ideologies of femininity were thus not radically altered.[130] But the war established, once and for all, the propriety of women working for wages before marriage, even when the young woman belonged to the middle class. Moreover, owing to the terrible casualties among the young men of Canada, many women could not expect to marry. With these women in mind, the Women's War Conference of February 1918, which had been convened by the federal government to ensure women's continued support for the war effort, passed resolutions in favour of equal pay for equal work, technical training, and a minimum wage for women.[131]

Although it was difficult for many Canadians to accept with equanimity the idea of the working woman, they could not ignore the entry of thousands of (mostly young and unmarried) women into the workforce between the mid-nineteenth century and the end of the Great War; indeed, the wartime propaganda that punctuated the very end of this period highlighted the importance of women's paid employment. Some of women's unpaid labour continued to resemble that carried out in earlier decades, as did some of their ways of earning cash. In other ways, however, industrialization had fundamentally restructured women's work in both cities and rural areas. A small but important group of women were already making lifelong careers for themselves: they represented the New Woman of the late nineteenth and early twentieth centuries. More typical were the many women who worked for wages only during the years between leaving school and marriage. The example of Alma Drouin helps us to understand the ways in which women in this period—and young women in particular—moved across national borders and in and out of jobs in an effort to support themselves and their families and, sometimes, as part of a strategy of social mobility. The second daughter of a working-class Franco-American family in New Hampshire, Alma Drouin studied with the *Soeurs de l'Assomption de la Sainte-Vierge* in Nicolet, Quebec, before moving to Montreal in 1917 at the age of 20. There, she boarded with members of her extended family and took advantage of the many pleasures that Montreal had to offer to young, sociable women, including new opportunities for commercial leisure, such as moving pictures, dance halls, and amusement parks. She was also one of the thousands of young women who took up white-collar work in the early-twentieth-century Canadian city, staffing sales counters at Murphy's department store and Birks' jewellers before obtaining a secretarial position in the advertising department of Imperial Tobacco. Alma Drouin's experience of waged work in Canada ended in the fall of 1918 when she returned to New England; as for most young women of the period, her experience of paid work ended definitively a few years later when she married.[132]

Notes

1. Cited in John Lutz, "Gender and Work in Lekwammen Families, 1843–1970," in Kathryn McPherson, Cecilia Morgan, and Nancy M. Forestell, eds., *Gendered Pasts: Historical Essays in Femininity and Masculinity in Canada* (Toronto: University of Toronto Press, 1999), 94.

2. Sherry Farrell Racette, "Sewing for a Living: The Commodification of Métis Women's Artistic Production," in Katie Pickles and Myra Rutherdale, eds., *Contact Zones: Aboriginal and Settler Women in Canada's Colonial Past*, ed. (Vancouver: University of British Columbia Press, 2005), 17–46.

3. Margaret Conrad, "'Sunday Always Makes Me Think of Home': Time and Place in Canadian Women's History," in Veronica Strong-Boag and Anita Clair Fellman, eds., *Rethinking Canada: The Promise of Women's History* (Toronto: Copp Clark Pitman, 1986), 72.

4. Beth Light and Joy Parr, eds., *Canadian Women on the Move, 1867–1920* (Toronto: New Hogtown Press and OISE Press, 1983), 169–70.

5. Linda Rasmussen et al., eds., *A Harvest Yet to Reap: A History of Prairie Women* (Toronto: Women's Press, 1976), 26.

6. Canada, Dominion Bureau of Statistics, *Origin, Birthplace, Nationality and Language of the Canadian People* (Ottawa: King's Printer, 1929), 42.

7. Dominion Bureau of Statistics, *Origin*, 42; Carolyn Moore, *Our Land, Too: Women of Canada and the Northwest 1860–1914* (Whitehorse: Government of the Yukon, 1992), 18.

8. F. H. Leacy, ed., *Historical Statistics of Canada*, 2nd ed. (Ottawa: Statistics Canada, 1983), A110–53; Howard Palmer, *Patterns of Prejudice: A History of Nativism in Alberta* (Toronto: McClelland and Stewart, 1982), 39.

9. Tamara Adilman, "A Preliminary Sketch of Chinese Women and Work in British Columbia, 1858–1950," in Barbara K. Latham and Roberta J. Pazdro, eds., *Not Just Pin Money: Selected Essays on the History of Women's Work in British Columbia* (Victoria: Camosun College, 1984), 54–57; Michiko Midge Ayukawa, *Hiroshima Immigrants in Canada, 1891–1941* (Vancouver: UBC Press, 2008).

10. Enakshi Dua, "Exclusion through Inclusion: Female Asian Migration in the Making of Canada as a White Settler Nation," *Gender, Place and Culture* 14, 4 (August 2007): 445–66.

11. Information provided by Ottilia Doering's great-granddaughter, Bonnie Shettler.

12. Joy Parr, *Labouring Children: British Immigrant Apprentices to Canada, 1869–1924* (Montreal and Kingston: McGill-Queen's University Press [1980], 2nd edition, 1994).

13. Rasmussen et al., eds., *Harvest*, 22; Paul Phillips and Erin Phillips, *Women and Work: Inequality in the Labour Market* (Toronto: James Lorimer, 1983), 6; Leacy, ed., *Historical Statistics*, A94–109.

14. Warren E. Kalbach and Wayne W. McVey, *The Demographic Bases of Canadian Society*, 2nd ed. (Toronto: McGraw-Hill Ryerson, 1971), 136; Emily Nett, "Canadian Families in Social–Historical Perspective," *Canadian Journal of Sociology* 6, 3 (Summer 1981): 245; *Census of Canada* (1921) vol. 4, xiv.

15. Royden K. Loewen, *Family, Church, and Market: A Mennonite Community in the Old and the New Worlds, 1850–1930* (Toronto: University of Toronto Press, 1993), 101.

16. G. G. Campbell, "Susan Dunlap: Her Diary," *Dalhousie Review* 46, 2 (Summer 1966): 218–19.

17. Ellice B. Gonzalez, *Changing Economic Roles for Micmac Men and Women: An Ethnohistorical Analysis* (Ottawa: National Museums of Canada, 1981), 86, 91.

18. Anne B. Woywitka, "Homesteader's Woman," *Alberta History* 24, 2 (Spring 1976): 21; Pamela Margaret White, "Restructuring the Domestic Sphere—Prairie Indian Women on Reserves: Image, Ideology and State Policy 1880–1930," McGill University, Ph.D. Thesis, 1987, 132; Linda Kealey, "Introduction," in Kealey, ed., *Pursuing Equality: Historical Perspectives on Women in Newfoundland and Labrador* (St. John's: Institute of Social and Economic Research, Memorial University, 1993), 9.

19. Harriet Neville, "Pioneering in the North-West Territories, 1882–1905," *Canada: An Historical Magazine* 2, 4 (June 1975), 29.

20. Sarah Kolasiewicz, "Outstanding Women of Oxford County," *Canadian Women's Studies/Les cahiers de la femme* 3, 1 (1981): 50–1; Marjorie Griffin Cohen, "The Decline of Women in Canadian Dairying," in Alison Prentice and Susan Mann Trofimenkoff, eds., *The Neglected Majority: Essays in Canadian Women's History* (Toronto: McClelland and Stewart, 1985) vol. 2, 71–83; Terry Crowley, "Mechanization, Proletarianization, and the Gendered Division of Labour: The Rural Crisis in Late Nineteenth-Century Ontario Reconsidered," paper presented to the Canadian Historical Association, Charlottetown, 1992, 13–14.

21. Beth Light and Alison Prentice, eds., *Pioneer and Gentlewomen of British North America, 1713–1867* (Toronto: New Hogtown Press, 1980), 160.

22. Susan Jackel, "Introduction" to Georgina Binnie-Clark, *Wheat and Woman* (Toronto: University of Toronto Press, 1979), xvii.

23. Light and Parr, eds., *Canadian Women on the Move*, 189–90.

24. Anita Penner, "Emily Murphy and the Attempt to Alter the Status of Canadian Women, 1910–31," Carleton University, M.A. Thesis, 1979, 46.

25. Nanciellen Davis, "'Patriarchy from the Grave': Family Relations in 19th Century New Brunswick Wills," *Acadiensis* 13, 2 (Spring 1984): 95.

26. Mary Rubio and Elizabeth Waterson, eds., *Selected Journals of L. M. Montgomery* Vol. 1 (1889–1910) (Toronto: Oxford University Press, 1986), 310.

27. Jo-Anne Fiske, "Child of the State Mother of the Nation: Aboriginal Women and the Ideology of Motherhood," *Culture* 13, 1 (1993): 18; Alex Johnston, "Nicholas and Marcella Sheran: Lethbridge's First Citizens," *Alberta History* 31, 4 (Autumn 1983): 1–10.

28. Jean-Philippe Garneau, "Quebec Civil Law," in *The Oxford Companion to Canadian History* (Toronto: Oxford UP, 2004), 524–25; Collectif Clio, *Histoire des femmes au Québec depuis quatre siècles*, 2e éd. (Montréal: Le Jour, 1992), 164–69.

29. "How the Chamberlains Found Canada," *Women's Work in Western Canada* (Canadian Pacific Railway, 1906), 63–66; Georgina Binnie-Clark, *Wheat and Woman* (Toronto: William Heinemann, 1914).

30. Rasmussen et al., eds., *Harvest*, 60.

31. Jorgen Dahlie, "Learning on the Frontier: Scandinavian Immigrants and Education in Western Canada," *Canadian and International Education* 1, 2 (December 1972): 64.

32. Light and Parr, eds., *Canadian Women on the Move*, 168.

33. Letitia Youmans, *Campaign Echoes: The Autobiography of Letitia Youmans* (Toronto: William Briggs, 1893), 81.

34. Christine Hudon, *Prêtres et fidèles dans le diocèse de Saint-Hyacinthe 1820–1875* (Sillery: Septentrion, 1996); Sylvia Van Kirk, "The Impact of White Women on Fur Trade Society," in Susan Mann Trofimenkoff and Alison Prentice, eds., *The Neglected Majority: Essays in Canadian Women's History* (Toronto: McClelland and Stewart, 1977) vol. 1, 27–48.

35. Bettina Bradbury, "The Fragmented Family: Family Strategies in the Face of Death, Illness and Poverty, Montreal, 1860–1885," in Joy Parr, ed., *Childhood and Family in Canadian History* (Toronto: McClelland and Stewart, 1982), 109–28; Bradbury, "Pigs, Cows and Boarders: Non-Wage Forms of Survival among Montreal Families 1861–1891," *Labour/Le Travail* 14 (Fall 1984): 9–48; see also Bradbury, *Working Families: Age, Gender, and Daily Survival in Industrializing Montreal* (Toronto: McClelland and Stewart, 1993).

36. Light and Parr, eds., *Canadian Women on the Move*, 27; Rasmussen et al., eds., *Harvest*, 70.

37. Nancy Tomes, *The Gospel of Germs: Men, Women, and the Microbe in American Life* (Cambridge, Mass.: Harvard University Press, 1998).

38. See Ruth Schwartz Cowan, *More Work for Mother: The Ironies of Household Technology from the Open Hearth to the Microwave* (New York: Basic, 1983).

39. Nellie McClung, *The Stream Runs Fast* (Toronto: Thomas Allen, 1945), 47.

40. Light and Parr, eds., *Canadian Women on the Move*, 61.

41. Ian Davey, "Educational Reform and the Working Class: School Attendance in Hamilton, Ontario, 1851–1891," University of Toronto, Ph.D. Thesis, 1975, 175.

42. White, "Restructuring the Domestic Sphere," 149; Gonzalez, "Changing Economic Roles," 94; Marlene Epp, "West Indian Domestics to Canada in 1911: A Study of Discrimination in Immigration," paper presented to the Canadian Historical Association, Victoria, 1990, 1.

43. Phillips and Phillips, *Women and Work,* 12; Magda Fahrni, "'Ruffled' Mistresses and 'Discontented' Maids: Respectability and the Case of Domestic Service, 1880–1914," *Labour/ Le Travail* 39 (Spring 1997): 69–97; Lorna R. McLean and Marilyn Barber, "In Search of Comfort and Independence: Irish Immigrant Domestic Servants Encounter the Courts, Jails, and Asylums in Nineteenth-Century Ontario," in Marlene Epp, Franca Iacovetta and Frances Swyripa, eds., *Sisters or Strangers? Immigrant, Ethnic, and Racialized Women in Canadian History* (Toronto: University of Toronto Press, 2004), 133–60.

44. McClung, *The Stream Runs Fast*, 259.

45. Peter Gossage, "Absorbing Junior: The Use of Patent Medicines as Abortifacients in Nineteenth Century Montreal," *The Register* 3, 1 (March 1982): 2–3.

46. Genevieve Leslie, "Domestic Service in Canada, 1880–1920," in Janice Acton, Penny Goldsmith, and Bonnie Shepard, eds., *Women at Work: Ontario 1850–1930* (Toronto: Canadian Women's Educational Press, 1974), 94; Carolyn Strange, "Wounded Womanhood and Dead Men: Chivalry and the Trials of Clara Ford and Carrie Davies," in Franca Iacovetta and Mariana Valverde, eds., *Gender Conflicts: New Essays in Women's History* (Toronto: University of Toronto Press, 1992), 177.

47. Robin John Anderson, "Domestic Service: The YWCA and Women's Employment Agencies in Vancouver, 1898–1915," *Histoire sociale/Social History* 25, 50 (November 1992): 308.

48. Tamara Adilman, "A Preliminary Sketch of Chinese Women and Work in British Columbia, 1858–1950," in Gillian Creese and Veronica Strong-Boag, eds., *British Columbia Reconsidered: Essays on Women* (Vancouver: Press Gang, 1992), 314; Lori Rotenberg, "The Wayward Worker: Toronto's Prostitute at the Turn of the Century," in Acton et al., eds., *Women at Work,* 33–69; Constance B. Backhouse, "Nineteenth-Century Canadian Prostitution Law: Reflection of a Discriminatory Society," *Histoire sociale/Social History* 18, 36 (November 1985): 387–423.

49. Agnes Calliste, "Race, Gender and Canadian Immigration Policy: Blacks from the Caribbean, 1900–1932," *Journal of Canadian Studies* 28, 4 (Winter 1993–94): 132.

50. Phillips and Phillips, *Women and Work*, 8; Bradbury, *Working Families*, 142.

51. Joy Parr, *The Gender of Breadwinners: Women, Men, and Change in Two Industrial Towns, 1880–1950* (Toronto: University of Toronto Press, 1990), espec. chap. 1.

52. Albert Faucher, "Explication socio-économique des migrations dans l'histoire du Québec," in Normand Séguin, *Agriculture et colonisation au Québec* (Montréal: Boréal Express, 1980), 114; Jacques Rouillard, *Ah les États! Les travailleurs canadiens-français dans l'industrie textile de la Nouvelle-Angleterre* (Montréal : Boréal, 1985); Bruno Ramirez, *On the Move: French-Canadian and Italian Migrants in the North Atlantic Economy, 1860–1914* (Toronto: McClelland & Stewart, 1991); Bruno Ramirez with Yves Otis, *Crossing the 49th Parallel: Migration from Canada to the United States, 1900–1930* (Ithaca: Cornell University Press, 2001); Yukari Takai, *Gendered Passages: French-Canadian Migration to Lowell, Massachusetts, 1900–1920* (New York: Peter Lang, 2008).

53. Light and Parr, eds., *Canadian Women on the Move*, 100–1; Betsy Beattie, "'Going Up to Lynn': Single, Maritime-Born Women in Lynn, Massachusetts, 1879–1930," *Acadiensis* 22, 1 (Autumn 1992): 65–86.

54. Ceta Ramkhalawansingh, "Women during the Great War," in Acton, Goldsmith, and Shepard, eds., *Women at Work*, 281.

55. Bob Russell, "A Fair or a Minimum Wage? Women Workers, the State, and the Origins of Wage Regulation in Western Canada," *Labour/Le Travail* 28 (Autumn 1991): 70–71; Wayne Roberts, "Honest Womanhood: Feminism, Femininity and Class Consciousness among Toronto Working Women 1893–1914," in R. Douglas Francis and Donald B. Smith, eds., *Readings in Canadian History: Post Confederation*, 2nd ed. (Toronto: Holt, Rinehart and Winston, 1986), 240; Terry Copp, *The Anatomy of Poverty: The Condition of the Working Class in Montreal 1897–1929* (Toronto: McClelland and Stewart, 1974), 45.

56. Susan Mann Trofimenkoff, "One Hundred and Two Muffled Voices: Canada's Industrial Women in the 1880's," *Atlantis* 3, 1 (Fall 1977): 67–68.

57. Carolyn Strange, *Toronto's Girl Problem: The Perils and Pleasures of the City, 1880–1930* (Toronto: University of Toronto Press, 1995); Tamara Myers, "Women Policing Women: A Patrol Woman in Montreal in the 1910s," *Journal of the Canadian Historical Association*, New Series, 4 (Ottawa, 1993): 229–45.

58. *Census of Canada* (1891), 186; Phillips and Phillips, *Women and Work*, 22; Wayne Roberts, *Honest Womanhood: Feminism, Femininity and Class Consciousness among Toronto Working Women, 1893–1914* (Toronto: New Hogtown Press, 1976), 37; J. T. Copp, "The Conditions of the Working Class in Montreal, 1897–1920," in Francis and Smith, eds., *Readings in Canadian History*, 2nd ed., 227.

59. Rotenberg, "The Wayward Worker," 48–49.

60. D. A. Muise, "The Industrial Context of Inequality: Female Participation in Nova Scotia's Paid Labour Force, 1871–1921," *Acadiensis* 20, 2 (Spring 1991): 19; Roberts, "Honest Womanhood," 242.

61. Roberts, *Honest Womanhood*; Linda Cullum and Maeve Baird with the assistance of Cynthia Penney, "A Woman's Lot: Women and Law in Newfoundland from Early Settlement to the Twentieth Century" in Kealey, ed., *Pursuing Equality*, 116; Sherry Edmunds-Flett, "The Family and Community Life of British Columbia's 19th Century African-Canadian Women," paper presented to the Canadian Historical Association, Charlottetown, 1992, 10.

62. Barbara Hansen, "A Historical Study of Women in Canadian Banking, 1900–1975," *Canadian Women's Studies/Les cahiers de la femme* 1, 2 (Winter 1978/79): 17.

63. Ramkhalawansingh, "Women during the Great War," 280–81.

64. Judith Fingard, "College, Career, and Community: Dalhousie Coeds, 1881–1921," in Paul Axelrod and John G. Reid, eds., *Youth, University and Canadian Society: Essays in the Social History of Higher Education* (Montreal and Kingston: McGill-Queen's University Press, 1989), 26–50.

65. Kennethe M. Haig, "E. Cora Hind," in Mary Quayle Innis, ed., *The Clear Spirit: Twenty Canadian Women and Their Times* (Toronto: University of Toronto Press, 1966), 120–41; Gwen Cash, *Off the Record: The Personal Reminiscences of Canada's First Woman Reporter* (Langley, B.C.: Stagecoach, 1977), 12.

66. Graham Lowe, "Class, Job, and Gender in the Canadian Office," *Labour/Le Travail* 10 (Autumn 1982): 20, 28; Lowe, *Women in the Administrative Revolution* (Toronto: University of Toronto Press, 1987).

67. Phillips and Phillips, *Women and Work*, 25.

68. Linda Bohnen, "Women Workers in Ontario: A Socio-Legal History," *University of Toronto Faculty of Law Review* 31 (1973): 47; Susan Porter Benson, *Counter Cultures: Saleswomen, Managers, and Customers in American Department Stores, 1890–1940* (Champaign, IL: University of Illinois Press, 1988).

69. Alison Prentice and Marta Danylewycz, "Teacher's Work: Changing Patterns and Perceptions in the Emerging School Systems of Nineteenth- and Early Twentieth-Century Central Canada," *Labour/Le Travail* 17 (Spring 1986): 65.

70. *Census of Canada* (1921), vol. 4, 6–7; Elizabeth Smyth, "Teacher Education within a Community of Religious Women in Nineteenth Century Ontario: The Teaching Sisters of the Congregation of the Sisters of St. Joseph, Toronto 1851–1911," paper presented to the Canadian Historical Association and the Canadian Society of Church History, Kingston, 1991, 29.

71. J. Donald Wilson, Robert M. Stamp, and Louis-Philippe Audet, eds., *Canadian Education: A History* (Scarborough: Prentice-Hall, 1970), 317; Jean Barman, "Birds of Passage or Early Professionals? Teachers in Late Nineteenth-Century British Columbia," *Historical Studies in Education/Revue d'histoire de l'éducation* 2, 1 (Spring 1990): 18; Alison Prentice, "Mapping Canadian Women's Teaching Work: Challenging the Stereotypes," in Alison Mackinnon, Inga Elgqvist-Saltzman and Alison Prentice, eds., *Education into the 21st Century: Dangerous Terrain for Women?* (London: Falmer Press, 1998), 31–36.

72. Patrick Harrigan, "The Development of a Corps of Public School Teachers in Canada, 1870–1980," *History of Education Quarterly* 32, 4 (Winter 1992): 489.

73. Andrée Dufour and Micheline Dumont, *Brève histoire des institutrices au Québec de la Nouvelle-France à nos jours* (Montréal: Boréal, 2004), 62–63.

74. W. L. Morton, "Furrow's End," *Journal of Canadian Studies* 21, 3 (Fall 1986): 29.

75. Elizabeth Graham, "Schoolmarms and Early Teaching in Ontario," in Acton, Goldsmith, and Shepard, eds., *Women at Work*, 194.

76. Saskatoon Women's Calendar Collective, "Medical Women of Prince Edward Island," in *Herstory* (Sidney, B.C.: Gray's Publishing, 1981), 12.

77. Susan Gelman, "The 'Feminization' of the High Schools? Women Secondary School Teachers in Toronto: 1871–1930," *Historical Studies in Education/Revue d'histoire de l'éducation* 2, 1 (Spring 1990): 123–25, 129.

78. Margaret Gillett, *We Walked Very Warily: A History of Women at McGill* (Montreal: Eden Press, 1981), 227, 306; see also Alison Prentice, "Bluestockings, Feminists, or Women Workers? A Preliminary Look at Women's Early Employment at the University of Toronto," *Journal of the Canadian Historical Association*, New Series 2 (1991): 231–61.

79. Sr. Marie Bonin, "The Grey Nuns and the Red River Settlement," *Manitoba History* 11 (Spring 1986): 13; Sister Margaret Cantwell, *North to Share: The Sisters of Saint Ann in Alaska and the Yukon Territory* (Victoria: Sisters of Saint Ann, 1992), 87–88.

80. Susan Mann, ed., *The War Diary of Clare Gass, 1915–1918* (Montreal and Kingston: McGill-Queen's University Press, 2000), xviii–xix; Kathryn McPherson, "'The Case of the Kissing Nurse': Femininity, Sexuality, and Canadian Nursing, 1900–1970," in McPherson, Morgan, and Forestell, eds., *Gendered Pasts*, 179–98; Kathryn McPherson, *Bedside Matters: The Transformation of Canadian Nursing, 1900–1990* (Toronto: Oxford University Press, 1996).

81. Judi Coburn, "'I See and Am Silent': A Short History of Nursing in Ontario," in Acton, Goldsmith, and Shepard, eds., *Women at Work*, 150.

82. Colin Howell, "Reform and the Monopolistic Impulse: The Professionalization of Medicine in the Maritimes," *Acadiensis* 11, 1 (Autumn 1981): 20.

83. Heather MacDougall, "'Guides, Philosophers and Friends': The Development of Public Health Nursing in Toronto, 1907–1932," paper presented to the Canadian Historical Association, Winnipeg, 1986, 1–2; Kari Dehli, "'Health Scouts' for the State? School and Public Health Nurses in Early Twentieth-Century Toronto," *Historical Studies in Education/ Revue d'histoire de l'éducation* 2, 2 (Fall 1990): 247–64.

84. A. A. Travill, "Early Medical Co-Education and Women's Medical College, Kingston, Ontario, 1880–1894," *Historic Kingston* 30 (January 1982), 86; Micheline Dumont-Johnson, "History of the Status of Women in the Province of Quebec," in Royal Commission on the Status of Women in Canada, *Cultural Tradition and Political History of Women in Canada*, Study 8 of the RCSW (Ottawa: Information Canada, 1971), 29; Elizabeth Hearn Milner, "Bishop's Medical Faculty 1871–1905: Its Jewish Dean, Aaron Hart David, and Its Jewish Students," *Canadian Jewish Historical Society Journal* 6, 2 (Fall 1982): 74; see also Veronica Strong-Boag, "Canada's Women Doctors: Feminism Constrained," in Linda Kealey, ed., *A Not Unreasonable Claim: Women and Reform in Canada, 1880s–1920s* (Toronto: Canadian Women's Educational Press, 1979), 109–29.

85. Strong-Boag, "Canada's Women Doctors," 109–29; Heather Fawcett, "Not Just Stackers of Bones: The History of Chiropractic in Canada," unpublished paper, University of Waterloo, 1992.

86. A Bystander, "The Woman's Rights Movement," *The Canada Monthly* (March 1872), 255.

87. Constance B. Backhouse, "'To Open the Way for Others of My Sex': Clara Brett Martin's Career as Canada's First Woman Lawyer," *Canadian Journal of Women and the Law* 1, 1 (1985): 1–41. On Martin's anti-Semitism, see Backhouse, "Clara Brett Martin: Canadian Heroine or Not?" *Canadian Journal of Women and the Law* 5, 2 (1992): 263–79; Lita-Rose Betcherman, "Clara Brett Martin's Anti-Semitism," *Canadian Journal of Women and the Law* 5, 2 (1992): 280–97; Brenda Cossman and Marlee Kline, "'And If Not Now, When?': Feminism and Anti-Semitism beyond Clara Brett Martin," *Canadian Journal of Women and the Law* 5, 2 (1992): 298–316; Lynne Pearlman, "Through Jewish Lesbian Eyes: Rethinking

Clara Brett Martin," *Canadian Journal of Women and the Law* 5, 2 (1992): 317–50; Backhouse, "Response to Cossman, Kline, and Pearlman," *Canadian Journal of Women and the Law* 5, 2 (1992): 351–54; Betcherman, "Response to Cossman, Kline and Pearlman," *Canadian Journal of Women and the Law* 5, 2 (1992): 355–56.

88. Dumont-Johnson, "History," 28–29; Gilles Gallichan, *Les Québécoises et le Barreau. L'histoire d'une difficile conquête, 1914–1941* (Sillery: Septentrion, 1999).

89. Fingard, "College, Career, and Community."

90. Lynne Marks, "Working-Class Femininity and the Salvation Army: Halellujah Lasses in English Canada, 1882–1892," in Strong-Boag and Fellman, eds., *Rethinking Canada*, 189–90; Rosemary R. Gagan, "More than 'A Lure to the Gilded Bower of Matrimony': The Education of Methodist Women Missionaries, 1881–1925," *Historical Studies in Education/ Revue d'histoire de l'éducation* 1, 2 (Fall 1989): 239–59.

91. Isabel Bassett, *The Parlour Rebellion: Profiles in the Struggle for Women's Rights* (Toronto: McClelland and Stewart, 1975), 154.

92. Barbara Freeman, "'Every Stroke Upward': Women Journalists in Canada, 1880–1906," *Canadian Woman Studies/Les cahiers de la femme* 7, 3 (Fall 1986): 44–45. See also Marjory Lang, *Women Who Made the News: Female Journalists in Canada, 1880–1945* (Montreal and Kingston: McGill-Queen's University Press, 1999).

93. Peggy Bristow, "'Whatever You Raise in the Ground You Can Sell It in Chatham': Black Women in Buxton and Chatham, 1850–65," in Peggy Bristow, co-ord., et al., *"We're Rooted Here and They Can't Pull Us Up"*: Essays in African Canadian Women's History (Toronto: University of Toronto Press, 1994), 105; Paula Giddings, *When and Where I Enter: The Impact of Black Women on Race and Sex in America* (New York: Bantam, 1984), 69.

94. Mary Jean Green, "The Literary Feminists in the Fight for Women's Writing in Quebec," *Journal of Canadian Studies* 21, 1 (Spring 1986): 129.

95. Our thanks to Margaret Conrad for this information.

96. Daniel Francis, *The Imaginary Indian: The Images of the Indian in Canadian Culture* (Vancouver: Arsenal Pulp Press, 1992), 118–19; Elizabeth Loosley, "Pauline Johnson" in Innis, ed., *Clear Spirit*, 74–90; Carole Gerson and Veronica Strong-Boag, "Championing the Native: E. Pauline Johnson Rejects the Squaw," in Pickles and Rutherdale, eds., *Contact Zones*, 47–66; Veronica Strong-Boag and Carole Gerson, *Paddling Her Own Canoe: The Times and Texts of E. Pauline Johnson (Tekahionwake)* (Toronto: University of Toronto Press, 2000).

97. K. Linda Kivi, *Canadian Women Making Music* (Toronto: Green Dragon, 1992), 19–24. The information on Johnson comes from the Black Cultural Centre for Nova Scotia and from Heather Murray, "Making the Modern: Twenty Five Years of the Margaret Eaton School of Literature and Expression," *Essays in Theatre/Études théâtrales* 10, 1 (November 1991), 39.

98. Carol Budnick, "The Performing Arts as a Field of Endeavour for Winnipeg Women, 1870–1930," *Manitoba History* 11 (Spring 1986), 51.

99. Maria Tippett, *Emily Carr: A Biography* (Toronto: Oxford University Press, 1979), 118–19; Angela E. Davis, "Mary Riter Hamilton: Manitoba Artist 1873–1954," *Manitoba History* 11 (Spring 1986): 23–25.

100. Laura Jones, "Rediscovery," *Canadian Woman Studies/Les cahiers de la femme* 2, 3 (1980): 5–6; Diana Pedersen and Martha Phemister, "Women and Photography in Ontario, 1839–1929: A Case Study of the Interaction of Gender and Technology," *Scientia Canadensis* 9, 1 (June 1985), 34.

101. Rhonda L. Hinther, "The Oldest Profession in Winnipeg: The Culture of Prostitution in the Point Douglas Segregated District, 1909–1912," *Manitoba History* 41 (2001): 2–13.

102. Peter A. Baskerville, "She Has Already Hinted at 'Board': Enterprising Urban Women in British Columbia, 1863–1896" *Histoire sociale/Social History* 26, 52 (November 1993): 224; Peter Baskerville, *A Silent Revolution? Gender and Wealth in English Canada, 1860–1930* (Montreal and Kingston: McGill-Queen's University Press, 2008); Laurie Alberts, "Petticoats and Pickaxes," *Alaska Journal* 7, 3 (Summer 1972): 146–59; Charlene Porsild, *Gamblers and Dreamers: Women, Men, and Community in the Klondike* (Vancouver: UBC Press, 1998).

103. David Goutor, "Constructing the 'Great Menace': Canadian Labour's Opposition to Asian Immigration, 1880–1914," *Canadian Historical Review* 88, 4 (December 2007): 549–76; David Goutor, "Drawing Different Lines of Color: The Mainstream English Canadian Labour Movement's Approach to Blacks and the Chinese, 1880–1914," *Labor: Studies in Working-Class History of the Americas* 2, 1 (2005): 55–76.

104. Gregory S. Kealey and Bryan D. Palmer, *Dreaming of What Might Be: The Knights of Labor in Ontario, 1880–1900* (New York: Cambridge University Press, 1982), 106.

105. Jacques Ferland, "When the Cotton Mills 'Girls' Struck for the First Time: A Study of Female Militancy in the Cotton and Shoe Factories of Quebec (1880–1910)," paper presented to the Canadian Historical Association, Winnipeg, 1986, 18–19.

106. Joan Sangster, "The 1907 Bell Telephone Strike: Organizing Women Workers," *Labour/Le Travail* 3 (1978): 109–30.

107. Ruth Frager, "Sewing Solidarity: The Eaton's Strike of 1912," *Canadian Woman Studies/Les cahiers de la femme* 7, 3 (Fall 1986): 96–97; Frager, *Sweatshop Strife: Class, Ethnicity, and Gender in the Jewish Labour Movement of Toronto, 1900–1939* (Toronto: University of Toronto Press, 1992), 92–93; Star Rosenthal, "Union Maids: Organized Women Workers in Vancouver, 1900–1915," *BC Studies* 41 (Spring 1979): 50.

108. Roberts, "Honest Womanhood," 243.

109. Margaret E. McCallum, "Keeping Women in Their Place: The Minimum Wage in Canada 1910–25," *Labour/Le Travail* 17 (Spring 1986): 37; Christina Burr, "'Defending Art Preservative': Class and Gender Relations in the Printing Trades Union, 1850–1914," *Labour/Le Travail* 31 (Spring 1993): 47–74.

110. Cassie Palamar, "The Treatment of Issues Affecting Women by the Knights of Labor in the *Palladium of Labor*, 1883–86," unpublished paper, Ontario Institute for Studies in Education, 9.

111. Ruth Frager, "No Proper Deal: Women Workers and the Canadian Labour Movement, 1870–1940," in Linda Briskin and Lynda Yanz, eds., *Union Sisters: Women in the Labour Movement* (Toronto: Women's Press, 1983), 52.

112. A. M. Givertz, "Considering Race and Class in the Regulation of Sexuality and the Prosecution of Sexual Assault in Hamilton, Ontario, 1880–1929," paper presented to the Canadian Historical Association, Ottawa, 1993, 13.

113. Prentice and Danylewycz, "Teacher's Work," 76; Alison Prentice, "Themes in the Early History of the Women Teachers' Association of Toronto," in Paula Bourne, ed., *Women's Paid and Unpaid Work: Historical and Contemporary Perspectives* (Toronto: New Hogtown Press, 1985), 97–121; Pat Staton and Beth Light, *Speak with Their Own Voices: A Documentary History of the Federation of Women Teachers' Associations of Ontario and the Elementary Public School Teachers of Ontario* (Toronto: FWTAO, 1987), chap. 3; Apolonja Maria Kojder, "In Union There Is Strength: The Saskatoon Women Teachers' Association," *Canadian Woman Studies/Les cahiers de la femme* 7, 3 (Fall 1986): 82–84; Harry Smaller, "Gender and Class: State Formation and Schooling Reform in 1880s Toronto," in Elizabeth Smyth and Paula Bourne, eds., *Women Teaching Women Learning* (Toronto: Inanna Publications, 2006), 131–57.

114. Ruby Heap and Alison Prentice, "'The Outlook for Old Age Is Not Hopeful': The Struggle of Female Teachers over Pensions in Quebec, 1880–1914," *Histoire sociale/Social History* 26, 51 (May 1993): 91; P. B. Waite, *The Man from Halifax: Sir John Thompson Prime Minister* (Toronto: University of Toronto Press, 1985), 61–65; Marta Danylewycz, *Taking the Veil: An Alternative to Marriage, Motherhood and Spinsterhood in Quebec, 1840–1920* (Toronto: McClelland and Stewart, 1987), 95.

115. Margaret Street, *Watch-Fires on the Mountains: The Life and Writings of Ethel Johns* (Toronto: University of Toronto Press, 1973), 43.

116. Cash, *Off the Record*, 19.

117. Charles W. Humphries, "Keeping the Home Fires Burning: British Columbia Women and the First World War," paper presented to the Canadian Historical Association, Charlottetown, 1992, 4.

118. Mary Quayle Innis, *Unfold the Years: A History of the Young Women's Christian Association in Canada* (Toronto: McClelland and Stewart, 1949), 80.

119. Margaret Kechnie, "'This Is Not a Paying Job': The Farmerette Movement in Ontario during the Great War," paper presented to the Canadian Historical Association, Ottawa, 1993, 17.

120. Ramkhalawansingh, "Women during the Great War," 279; see also Joan Sangster, "Mobilizing Women for War," in David Mackenzie, ed., *Canada and the First World War: Essays in Honour of Robert Craig Brown* (Toronto: University of Toronto Press, 2005).

121. Ramkhalawansingh, "Women during the Great War," 276.

122. Ramkhalawansingh, "Women during the Great War," 275; Shirley Tillotson, "'We May All Soon Be "First-Class Men"': Gender and Skill in Canada's Early Twentieth-Century Urban Telegraph Industry," *Labour/Le Travail* 27 (Spring 1991): 110.

123. Graham S. Lowe, "Women, Work and the Office: The Feminization of Clerical Occupations in Canada, 1901–1931," in Strong-Boag and Fellman, eds., *Rethinking Canada*, 109–14.

124. John Herd Thompson, *The Harvests of War: The Prairie West, 1914–1918* (Toronto: McClelland and Stewart, 1978), 110.

125. Ruth A. Frager and Carmela Patrias, *Discounted Labour: Women Workers in Canada, 1870–1939* (Toronto: University of Toronto Press, 2005), 71–74.

126. G. W. L. Nicholson, *Canada's Nursing Sisters* (Toronto: Hakkert, 1975), 4, 98.

127. Mélanie Morin-Pelletier, *Briser les ailes de l'ange. Les infirmières militaires canadiennes (1914–1918)* (Montreal: Athéna, 2006); Mann, ed., *The War Diary of Clare Gass*. The quotation from Clare Gass's diary can be found in Mann, ed., 26.

128. Susan Mann, *Margaret Macdonald: Imperial Daughter* (Montreal and Kingston: McGill-Queen's University Press, 2005).

129. Linda J. Quiney, "Borrowed Halos: Canadian Teachers as Voluntary Aid Detachment Nurses during the Great War," *Historical Studies in Education/Revue d'histoire de l'éducation* (Spring 2003): 79–99; Linda J. Quiney, "'Filling the Gaps': Canadian Voluntary Nurses, the 1917 Halifax Explosion, and the Influenza Epidemic of 1918," *Canadian Bulletin of Medical History* 19, 2 (2002): 351–73; Magda Fahrni, "'Elles sont partout': les femmes et la ville en temps d'épidémie, Montréal, 1918–1920," *Revue d'histoire de l'Amérique française* 58, 1 (Summer 2004), 67–85.

130. Kori Street, "More Than Bombs and Bandages: Women Who Served on the Homefront during the Great War," paper presented to the Canadian Historical Association, Charlottetown, 1992, 2, 7, 8.

131. Margaret McCallum, "Keeping," 34.

132. Magda Fahrni and Yves Frenette, "'Don't I long for Montreal': L'identité hybride d'une jeune migrante franco-américaine pendant la Première Guerre mondiale," *Histoire sociale/Social History* 41, 81 (May 2008): 75–98.

CHAPTER SIX

Woman's Sphere

Sarah A. Curzon, a nineteenth-century journalist and playwright, was distressed by the Canadian government's failure to recognize the contribution of Laura Secord to her nation's sovereignty. Responding to the debate over pensions for veterans of the War of 1812, she took up her pen in 1876 and wrote a play focusing on Secord's heroic deeds. In her preface to "Laura Secord, the Heroine of 1812," Curzon lamented the injustice of showering so much attention on the male heroes of the war: "To save from the sword is surely as great a deed as to save with the sword; and this Laura Secord did, at an expense of nerve and muscle fully equal to any that are recorded of the warrior." In the play itself, Curzon had Colonel Fitzgibbon, the officer who made his military reputation as a result of Secord's warning, deliver the moral that Canadians ought to draw:

> Men, never forget this woman's noble deed.
>
> Armed, and in company, inspirited
>
> By crash of martial music, soldiers march
>
> To duty; but she alone, defenseless,
>
> With no support but kind humanity
>
> And burning patriotism, ran all our risks,
>
> Of hurt, and bloody death, to serve us men,
>
> Strangers to her save by quick war-time ties.
>
> Therefore, in grateful memory and kind return,
>
> Ever treat women well.[1]

With these words and by her play, Curzon acknowledged the link between her generation and Secord's, a link that many educated, middle-class Canadian women of her time felt profoundly. For all their sense that they were living in a new era, they recognized how close they still were to the women before them.[2]

It was true that women were increasingly entering the labour market. But they tended to do so when they were single and young, working for pay between the ages of 15 and 24. In 1891, in fact, only 11 percent of women over 15 were employed, according to the official record of the census; by 1911, that figure had risen to a mere 14 percent.[3] What such statistics ignored, of course, were the thousands of women who toiled in their own homes as their mothers and grandmothers had done before them. These same statistics also failed to acknowledge women's work alongside their husbands—for example on family farms or within Aboriginal communities—in hunting, fishing, and trapping.

That women were crucial to the household had been evident in those earlier days when the household and the paid workforce were less sharply separated. In the mid-nineteenth century, as some women moved into an identifiable, non-domestic world of work for pay, the family and women's role in the home seemed threatened. In response, nineteenth-century ideologues promoted the concept of separate spheres for women and men and, most significantly, prescribed a highly idealized domestic and maternal role for women. Clergymen, doctors, and other so-called male experts had much to say about the nature of womanhood and about what the ideal woman should or should not do. Notions of appropriate behaviour were, however, culturally specific, as the following Aboriginal examples illustrate. Cree women in the James Bay area were expected to learn the same survival skills as their male counterparts and, until the end of the nineteenth century, a few Kaska women in the Yukon could cross the gender divide and for all social and economic purposes become male. Among the Innu Naskapi, in the area around Fort McKenzie—a Hudson's Bay Company fort in Quebec—gender roles remained relatively fluid and uninfluenced by the intrusion of commercial interests. For some Inuit women, conforming to their cultural norm might result in ceremonial partner exchange. And in Haida culture, girl offspring were actually preferred because they ensured the continued expansion of their family in the future.[4]

Women were not silent on the subject of the ideology of woman's proper sphere. In the second half of the nineteenth century, a growing number of women, mostly drawn from the middle class, began to propose solutions to what was increasingly identified as the "woman question" or the "woman problem." Many argued that education was the way to improve women's condition, but two different directions were proposed. One sought a more practical training geared to the reality of women's work in the home, and led to the domestic science movement; the other demanded access to higher education and to the professions, and led to the movement of small numbers of women into universities. Another burning issue was women's reproductive behaviour. Since motherhood was so inextricably linked to the image of the ideal woman and the continuation of "the race," it was with consternation that many realized that women were apparently abandoning this role and having fewer children.

THE IDEALIZATION OF DOMESTICITY

Many Victorian Canadians embraced an ideology that saw women as the embodiment of purity, and as both physically and financially dependent. Home was a woman's proper sphere. In 1851 the *Voice of the Fugitive*, a newspaper predominantly directing its words to the black population of southwestern Ontario, instructed women about their importance: "The most powerful and beneficial of the influences ordinarily at work in the formulation of human character is that of woman. . . . Man in life is what he is, to a great extent by the power of woman. His infancy being committed to her charge and his childhood spent in her society."[5] Woman, the ideal proclaimed, was man's equal, but *equal* did not mean "identical." Women were different, and from this difference complementary roles and responsibilities naturally evolved. As the Reverend Robert Sedgwick explained to a group of young men in 1856,

> Woman is the equal of man, alike in the matter of intellect, emotion, and activity, and . . . she has shown her capabilities in these respects. . . . It would never do, however, from these premises, to draw the conclusion that woman . . . is bound to exert her powers in the same direction and for the same ends as man. This were to usurp the place of man—this were to forget her position as the complement of man, and assume a place she is incompetent to fill, or rather was not designed to fill.[6]

Two decades later, another commentator could only concur: "Woman's first and only place is in her home," this writer explained. "She is destined by Providence to make her home . . . a cloister wherein one may seek calm and joyful repose from the busy, heartless world. . . . The land she governs is a bright oasis in the desert of the world's selfishness."[7] Since most women married and indeed expected to make home and children their main concerns, the ideal was not completely divorced from reality. If it had been, it would not have been so powerful. What was new and confining about the ideal of domesticity was the increasingly sharp distinction it made between the domestic world of women and the public world of men, the growing emphasis it placed on the mothering role, and the negative reactions that greeted most deviations from the norm.

Several groups of men were heavily involved in public discussion of the question of woman's proper sphere. Among the first to take up the issue were clergymen like Robert Sedgwick. Clerics continued to preach and write on women's place and possibilities throughout the latter part of the nineteenth century and into the twentieth century. Within the Roman Catholic church, there were two possible roles for women: wife and mother, or member of a religious order. For members of religious communities, a variety of paths was possible, since the church fostered and supported contemplative orders like the Carmelites as well as more active ones involved in teaching or social work. What the church frowned on, however, were communities of laywomen who had not taken any formal vows and were therefore outside of church control. In fact, women who tried to organize communal life for charitable purposes were urged to take permanent vows and bring their associations under church control. Catholic religious orders expanded phenomenally, as a result, between the middle of the nineteenth century and the first two decades of the twentieth century; existing orders established many new foundations and saw their numbers mushroom, while across the country, at least two dozen new orders of women religious came into being during this period.[8] These orders were responding to the needs not just of the church but of the women who entered them. But male clerics continued to see themselves as the proper interpreters of women's roles, both inside and outside the convent. In their view, women were naturally separate and different from men, as a French-Canadian priest explained in 1918:

> Equality, whatever it is before God, in no way implies the parity of roles in society. One forgets that woman, by her very sex, by her physical structure and her moral qualities, by her tastes, talents, and tendencies, absolutely differs from man, and that this radical difference between the sexes results in no less a difference in their duties.[9]

Protestant clergymen of all denominations also felt called upon to pronounce on women's proper roles and duties. Whereas earlier in the century some sects had encouraged women to speak out at meetings or even to preach, by the third quarter of the nineteenth century the practice was condemned. However, women's roles as Sunday School teachers and fundraisers were not only permitted but indeed encouraged, and many women embraced the opportunity to engage in these activities outside their domestic spheres. At the same time, all faiths emphasized women's place as in the home, where they were expected to raise good Christian families. So-called bad mothers were increasingly held responsible

Hazel Purdy of Bear River, Nova Scotia, having tea with her dolls, circa 1896.

Source: E. R. Redden, photographer: Armstrong-Archibald Collection #20 33.4.6 (N-1346). Public Archives of Nova Scotia.

for delinquent children, whether drunken sons or fallen daughters. By the early twentieth century, the leading Methodist reformer J. S. Woodsworth had no doubt that mothers who went out to work were to blame for a good deal of "truancy and juvenile crime."[10]

Physicians were a second group of men who had much to say on the subject of women and their roles. In an era when religious faith was being challenged and when physicians were working very hard to upgrade their profession and gain control of health care, the voice of doctors was an increasingly powerful one. Like clergymen, they wrote in the popular press, but they also wrote a great deal for each other in the medical press. Physicians tended to emphasize women's physical frailty, reflected in every aspect of the biological life cycle. Such weakness began with puberty. This difficult and mysterious stage appeared to heighten the physical, mental, and emotional differences between the two sexes. A pubescent woman's energies evidently became so concentrated on the development of her reproductive system that there was little energy left for anything else—certainly not for higher education or for sports. Some doctors warned that the woman who did continue her studies during this crucial stage might well damage her reproductive system forever, as her vital energies would go to her brain instead of to her uterus. Medical experts encouraged girls to engage in appropriate physical activity, but the sports recommended were very different from those recommended for their brothers: walking was good for girls; running was not.[11]

Unlike Euro-Canadian society, Aboriginal culture continued to acknowledge the power of menstruating women and treated puberty as a time for young women to learn about their culture and traditions. Where Aboriginal women were able to maintain their traditions, the practice of having pubescent girls withdraw to menstrual huts continued well into the twentieth century. Among the Wet'suwet'en, the period of retreat could last from a few months to several years. The young women observed dietary restrictions and were not to gaze into the faces of others in the community. They were visited and taught by the older women of their communities. At the end of their seclusion, a ceremony celebrated their reintegration into society.[12]

Among non-Aboriginals, even when a woman passed the precarious age of puberty, her reproductive system continued to control every aspect of her being. "Woman exists for the sake of the womb," declared a popular health manual of the 1890s.[13] Doctors also believed that the complexity of a woman's reproductive system made her especially subject to disease. This condition placed women at risk throughout their lives, and this risk permitted the medical profession to speak out on a number of topics. Women were urged, for example, to cast off their corsets and wear clothing that was both more comfortable and more healthy, and less likely to damage their childbearing capacity. While physicians acknowledged woman's sexuality, they interpreted it in their own way. They comforted themselves by arguing that women's sexuality existed to encourage conception, and they developed fascinating theories about the relationship between sexual excitement and its results. The *Canadian Practitioner* of 1886, for example, republished a review from an American journal that solemnly informed its readers that "at the generation of male offspring the mother must be in a higher state of excitement than the father. And, conversely, at the generation of female offspring the father must be in a higher state of such excitement than the mother."[14] In general, doctors believed that a woman's sex drive was not nearly as strong as a man's, and that it was a woman's responsibility to keep both under control since men could not. Nor should women attempt to avoid the repercussions of their sexuality. If they remained virgins or practised birth control, they risked physical breakdown.

Even after the childbearing years were over, medical experts thought that a woman's reproductive system continued to exert its unremitting control. Menopausal women were thought to be irrational and liable to "every form of neurasthenia, neuralgia, hysteria, convulsive disease, melancholia," and even insanity.[15] Doctors believed women in general to be highly susceptible to emotional disorders, particularly hysteria. Their belief in reflex action—the tendency of healthy parts of the body to be weakened by diseased parts—persuaded some doctors that certain cases of insanity in women could be reversed by curing them of their gynecological disorders. As a result, hundreds of women believed to be insane were given gynecological operations, from simple curettage or cleansing of the supposedly diseased surface to complete hysterectomies. A middle-aged woman who was subjected to "curettage and amputation of the cervix" in the London, Ontario, insane asylum in 1898 had been diagnosed as suffering from a "subinvoluted uterus and cystic and hypertrophied cervix" as well as a perineum that was "slightly torn." She reported that her husband neglected and abused her and consorted with other women. According to her file, her insanity took the form of pyromania: she "gathers anything she can and burns it." Whatever the relationships between the various aspects of her case, the operation was declared to have been a success and the patient was discharged.[16]

Operating on women judged insane was an extreme approach. More typically, physicians avoided discussing the causes of women's emotional disabilities. They argued that women were simply weaker and less emotionally stable than men and needed to be both protected and controlled. Yet at the same time, many asserted that because women were more moral and less sexually excitable, they should be able to control themselves—and men. Such contradictory views also permeated the pronouncements of lawmakers and jurists, who routinely differentiated between the sexes and made judgments, both overt and implicit, about women's capabilities and roles. Their views had practical as well as ideological force: adolescent girls were more likely to be convicted of moral rather than criminal offences, for example, and received longer sentences than boys did in the new reformatories that were being set up for young offenders. Concern over the need to regulate female sexuality also led magistrates and legislators to be more willing to incarcerate adult women than men for what were viewed as moral offences. An 1871 statute stipulated five years' imprisonment for Quebec women convicted of vagrancy for a second time; no such law applied to men.[17]

Canadian divorce law continued to embody the double standard. In 1857, the British Matrimonial Causes Act was adopted in the province of Canada and similar laws were in effect in most of the other British North American colonies. Typically, a husband might win a divorce if his wife was proven to have committed adultery. It was still the case, however, that a wife could obtain a divorce only if her husband was proven guilty of adultery coupled with desertion without reason, extreme cruelty, incest, or bigamy, or if he was convicted of raping another woman or of sodomy.[18] In general, the law seemed to be saying that men needed some freedom and that women should be content with their lot in the home, no matter what their circumstances. No transgressions were permitted. In Quebec the new civil code of

1866 declared that marriage for Roman Catholics was dissoluble only by death. The code did allow for the possibility of legal separation, but this provision did not allow for remarriage.

Laws governing Aboriginal women also reflected the view that a woman's place was with her husband and her identity was defined by her husband's. The Indian Act of 1869 eliminated Indian women's official status if they married non-status men, but marriage to a status man conferred that status on his non-Aboriginal wife and their children. There were practical reasons to be concerned about what happened when status Indians married. White husbands of Indian women, who could be expected to join their wives on the reserves, were a potential threat to the resources of various bands. White wives of Indian men did not, it was believed, constitute such a threat, and consequently on marriage they were granted Indian status. While the government did acknowledge the validity of Aboriginal marriages between Aboriginals according to their own customs, it refused to sanction traditional practices with respect to divorce.[19] Because harmony in relationships and respect for each other's needs were paramount, instances of divorce were rare. In some cases, however, abusive or adulterous husbands would be banished, and the wife of a banished husband was allowed to remarry.

The double standard in many provinces regarding divorce also applied to the status of married women. After the 1870s, a woman could sue her husband but only for damages to her property, not to her body. Ontario judges continued to cite an 1844 court decision that had stated that it was a wife's duty "to conform to the tastes and habits of her husband, to sacrifice much of her own comfort and convenience to his whims and caprices, [and] to submit to his commands." If the husband was violent, it was the wife's role "to endeavour . . . to induce a change and alteration" in his behaviour.[20] Wives who attempted to sue for divorce after repeated beatings were chastised for failing to leave after the first beating— they were held to have condoned their husbands' actions. On the other hand, wives who did leave after only one or two beatings were chastised for being insufficiently patient with their husbands. Nonetheless, in what can be seen as an act of resistance, many women resorted to the courts in an effort to curb their husbands' violence. And in both murder and assault cases where wives were the victims, judgments often suggested that the women involved were somehow themselves to blame for inciting their husbands to these acts.[21] The wife's disability and the double standard extended beyond her husband's death. In any province that provided relief for widows, the woman was deprived of her right to that relief if she had committed adultery.[22] And for all the increasing emphasis on motherhood and the importance of this role for women, women did not have equal guardianship rights over their children. Only unwed mothers had rights over their children, but even those rights could be trumped. For example, an 1859 Canada West statute prevented the prosecution of any man who abducted a child, if he "claim[ed] to be the father."[23]

The courts, in general, lacked sympathy for women who deviated from the domestic ideal. Prostitutes, not their clients, were viewed as the criminals. They, after all, were the ones who made the money. Nor were the courts particularly sympathetic to women who were the subjects of men's violence outside marriage. It was still rare for rapists to be prosecuted, and even more rare for them to be convicted. Non-English-speaking immigrant women were especially vulnerable since the courts and the press often treated sexual assault against them as simply "the outcome of a row among foreigners."[24] The treatment of Aboriginal women corresponded to prevailing Victorian racial discourses of sexuality that viewed Aboriginal women as agents of men's ruin and white women as agents of men's salvation. This view was clearly illustrated in the 1863 Red River (now Winnipeg) trial of the Reverend Corbett, accused of sexually assaulting his servant, Maria Thomas, a 16-year-old of mixed descent, and subjecting her to several unsuccessful abortion attempts. The court dismissed the assault charge on the grounds that Maria was a common prostitute but found Corbett guilty of procuring an abortion. Subsequent newspaper accounts depicted Maria as a "fallen woman" and Corbett's English wife as a symbol of respectable Victorian womanhood.[25]

As in an earlier period, the courts in British North America were reluctant to find women guilty of infanticide, but the reason for this leniency was the demeaning view that women were uninformed and therefore morally incapable. Newfoundland courts, on the other hand, were much harsher in sentencing women. The view of women as morally incapable also emerged when women turned their violence against themselves. Coroners and jurors investigating female suicide in British Columbia were convinced that respectable European women would resort to suicide only if they were insane. By contrast, those not deemed respectable, such as Aboriginal or immigrant women, were considered sane. Their situation or culture was blamed for the suicides.[26]

A good deal of what late-Victorian Canadians said about women suggested that they were to be feared rather than protected. At the very least, a woman outside what was considered her place was a woman who had placed herself in danger—or a woman who did not deserve protection and invited ridicule. In late nineteenth-century Saint John, for example, a group of working-class male workers calling themselves the "Polymorphians" joined in public processions and celebrations dressed as females to parody women and, occasionally, men whom they saw as deviating from the separate spheres' norm. Their targets included hen-pecked husbands and women who had the temerity not to stay at home. In 1882 the group constructed a float that ridiculed the women of Loch Lomond, a nearby black settlement, for making and selling brooms in order to help support their families. The Polymorphians attacked these women as unladylike because they participated in trade.[27] As a Halifax feminist noted at the time, "so persistently [are women workers] ignored by the advocates of 'women's proper sphere,' we are forced to the conclusion that female wage earners are not to be ranked as women." But staying in the home provided little protection: even there, women could find themselves at risk of attack by relatives and friends.[28]

WOMEN'S LIVES

For most married women the centre of their world was indeed the home, and for many the home was a base of power and influence, not merely a refuge. Women were responsible for maintaining family rituals, remembering family events and family history, and for celebrating occasions as a reminder of family connections.[29] They recognized the importance of their ties to other women, particularly the relationships between sisters and between mothers and daughters. As a young girl in boarding school in the late 1870s, Margaret Marshall Saunders, who later became a successful author, wrote to her mother in Halifax explicitly about her feelings: "I do not believe a child ever loved her mother as much as I love you. I would be willing to die to ensure your happiness, my darling. I hope the dear Lord Jesus will keep you safely till I come back."[30] There was a sense that family obligation fell more on women than on men, and that this was appropriate. It seemed right that they should help to care for younger siblings or for their parents as they aged. When Elizabeth Smith wanted to enter medical school in 1877, her best friend, Maud Rankin, tried to dissuade her because of the duty she owed her parents. "Lay aside those silly thoughts and you will be a better woman," Rankin urged. "I know that you are wishing to do something grand something that will carry your name on to further ages . . . but are you neglecting no home duties . . . ? Lizzie your first duty lies there, you never can repay your father and mother for all they have done for you."[31] While Smith did leave home for medical school, Jessie McQueen left her teaching position in British Columbia to return to Nova Scotia to care for her aging parents; not until she was free of family responsibilities did she return to B.C. and to teaching.[32] But the role of the helping daughter, sister, or aunt was not one that all enjoyed. At times, caring for parents delayed or prevented any chance a woman had to lead a full life of her own. In her personal recollections, suffragist and labour advocate Alice Chown had much to say about the constraints on women. Only after the death of her widowed mother, when Alice was 40, did she finally have some control over her own fate:

> During the next few months I shall have all the struggle for life and breath that an infant has, for I shall be breaking away from all the old walls that have surrounded me, from all the old environments that have enfolded me, that have kept me hidden from life and have forced me to live only through others.[33]

Chown celebrated her liberation by throwing herself into labour politics. Other women, forced almost against their will into domesticity, reacted more dramatically. Flora McPhee, for example, was a single woman who had made her life in Montreal but was called home to Campbellville, Ontario, in the early twentieth century to nurse her mother, who then treated her like a servant. When her mother died, McPhee, free at last, expressed her rebellion by going out to the barn and chopping "into little pieces the old spinning wheel and loom. . . . She said she needed kindling." What she really needed, according to her niece, "was to destroy the symbols of her bondage."[34]

When many single women admitted that they coveted domesticity, they usually meant married domesticity. And they expected more than just a home of their own. By this time, love was becoming the measure of a successful marriage, and many women's diaries and letters testify to its reality in their lives. As always, marriage also represented a sense of place, of creating a family of one's own, and of shaping and controlling the next generation. In the words of a rare woman banker quoted in the 1915–16 *Journal of the Canadian Bankers' Association*, "When the opportunity offers the most successful banking women amongst us will cheerfully retire to her own hearthstone, preferring the love of a husband and little children to thousands a year and a seat in the council of the mighty!"[35] Indeed, professional single women were sometimes the most vociferous promoters of the domestic ideal. Many were sure that the employment of the married woman outside the home meant that her family would suffer. In her 1910 "Report on Infant Mortality in Toronto," Dr. Helen MacMurchy took these sentiments to their ultimate conclusion: "Where the mother works," she stated, "the baby dies."[36] Certainly, most women agreed about the importance of the family and of their own role in keeping it together. They argued that, as the family went, so went the nation. So focused were women on their role as mothers that Nellie McClung felt she could safely declare that "every normal woman desires children."[37]

Unfortunately, to the extent that they accepted their role as the exclusive moral guardians of children and the family, women left themselves open not only to the barbs of male moralists and clergymen when their children transgressed, but also to feelings of guilt and self-blame. Even those women considered to be good mothers puzzled over how best to train their children. Indeed, one Victorian mother, who kept a running diary of her child's development, recorded a constant state of worry over her daughter's moral health. How was she to train her daughter and ensure that she would "grow up a good woman?"[38] Women were also not above blaming each other. In 1911, the Presbyterian Woman's Home Missionary Society criticized Eastern European immigrant women for lacking the ideals and morals needed to raise their children as proper, Christian Canadians.[39]

Despite the primacy of family for most, however, women did not define themselves solely by their familial roles and obligations. Victorian and Edwardian women also saw themselves increasingly as individuals in their own right, with obligations and friendships outside the family. As in previous generations, they helped out family members and neighbours in need, and participated in a variety of benevolent and voluntary causes, most of which focused on helping other women and children. Women formed friendships through the numerous organizations and clubs that they developed during this era. One reason unmarried working-class women gave for preferring factory work to domestic service was the opportunity it gave them to make female friends. The telephone, when it was initially introduced, was first seen as an aid to business. However, women quickly added a social dimension to the new instrument, using it to keep track of friends and relatives. In rural areas in particular, the party line became a way for many women to participate in community life.[40]

The respectability of romantic friendships between women began to erode in the late nineteenth century. Such relationships were now deemed pathological and became the object of societal opposition and censure. In a small village in Quebec in the 1880s, a teacher named Elizabeth Hébert was persecuted because of her intimate friendship with an older woman in the community; she lost her position as a result, but was "exonerated" in the hearing that the Quebec Department of Public Instruction held at her request.[41]

Family and close friendships do not constitute the total picture, however. For many women—perhaps for most of the women who put their thoughts on paper during this period—religion played a significant role in their lives. Even when women did not leave a record, we know from other contemporary accounts that faith gave meaning to their existence and was the foundation for their work in the larger world. In 1878, medical student Elizabeth Smith thanked God in her diary for her religion: "It is my rock of strength—it has never failed me yet—it never will."[42] Other women—particularly those newly emigrated to the country—found special comfort in their religion in a strange

Quilting bees facilitated friendship and socializing for women. The women who made this quilt were from the Balmoral area near Red Deer, Alberta.

Source: Red Deer and District Museum and Archives, P125-c-5-4

and often uninviting land. Still others found in religion the route to collective action, for women frequently outnumbered men in their congregations and saw themselves as the special carriers of the Christian message. Laura Haviland, for example, was a Quaker for whom religious faith led to a mission to former American slaves. In addition to helping fugitive slaves escape the United States, she set up a Christian Union church for blacks in the Puce River area of Canada West in the early 1850s. Black women were crucial to their own black churches—filling the membership rolls, raising money, teaching, and even physically helping to construct the building. Women were also the majority of those attending Salvation Army meetings, although they were more reluctant than men to give public testimony about their faith, thus conforming to expected gender roles. Women were particularly active in the Protestant Social Gospel movement at the turn of the century, a movement with links to earlier evangelicalism and devoted to the establishment of God's Kingdom on earth and thus to the reform of the temporal world. To work for social reform seemed to the women in the Social Gospel movement a logical extension of their maternal obligations; in this context, they developed many new roles. Toronto's first settlement house, Evangelia House, opened in 1902: women students from the university supported it and found some employment opportunities there. In Manitoba, Beatrice Brigden was hired in 1913 by the Methodist church to work with girls, and became a travelling lecturer on sex, hygiene, and young women's social problems.[43]

Catholic women similarly found their roles expanding through their work in the Church. Between 1851 and 1911, the number of nuns in the province of Quebec increased from 650 (representing just over 1 percent of single women over the age of 20) to 13 579 (or 9 percent). In English Canada, several religious orders were introduced—at mid-century, the Sisters of Charity in Halifax and the Loretto Sisters and Sisters of Saint Joseph in Toronto and Hamilton; and in the early 1860s, the Ursulines in Chatham and the Sisters of Providence in Kingston. Through the Church, nuns could find and maintain a status in society outside of marriage. Outlets for Catholic laywomen also increased. In the 1860s, devotional organizations dominated by women developed. Two of the largest in Toronto were the Sodality of the Blessed Virgin Mary and the Association of the

Group of women in front of the YWCA boarding house in Toronto circa 1913–1917.

Source: William James / Library and Archives Canada / PA-126710

Children of Mary. These groups, which appealed to all classes of women, were characterized by an emotional intensity that focused on Mary and on the saying of the rosary; the groups gave new meaning and authority to these women's role in the home. After the 1890s, laywomen found more in the church than an individual source of strength, as they joined with nuns to further Christian education or supported the sisters' social activism.[44]

Jewish women from eastern Europe played an important but subordinate role in their religion, but in their case this circumstance was offset by an acceptance of their active participation in the marketplace. They were seen as more practical and more worldly than men; in their case, the domestic ideology was not played out in the same way it was for many other Canadian women.[45]

Although women were generally very active participants in organized religion, they were not necessarily unquestioning believers. Henriette Dessaulles, who grew up in the village of St. Hyacinthe in the 1870s, became critical of the Catholic church from an early age: she went to confession but learned to tell the priest only what she wanted him to know. And when he criticized her friendship with a young man, Henriette rejected his opinion out of hand. Dessaulles was also critical of the conformity to rules and formalized ritual that she found among the nuns at her convent school and in the Church generally. Similarly, in 1910, Lucy Maud Montgomery made it clear that church attendance for her was part of a social ritual and a way of focusing on her own spiritual development. It did not signify acceptance of the formalized doctrine that her church espoused, even though she was engaged to a minister.[46]

Nor did Victorian women necessarily accept prevalent views of themselves as purely spiritual beings. Privileged young women who had the leisure to do so engaged in a variety of physical activities, and revelled in the opportunities they had for play. In their diaries they wrote about the pleasure they derived from walking, riding, playing hockey, curling, skating, dancing, and, at the end of the century, from the new craze of bicycling. In 1893, the *Brampton Conservator* felt that the idea of a woman riding a bicycle was novel and important enough to report. Miss Lillie Roberts had "the proud distinction of being Brampton's first lady bicyclist," the newspaper noted. "The graceful appearance she presents while passing through the town on her wheel will no doubt lead others to take up the healthy pastime." For many women, the bicycle represented increased mobility and independence. Predictably, some men disapproved, among them the trustees of the Toronto Public School Board when one of the city's teachers was seen riding in public.[47] Opportunities for team sports were also increasing. By the 1890s, there were lawn tennis and curling championships for women, and in 1903 a women's rink from Quebec City defeated a men's curling team from Scotland. Sport reformers who had encouraged women to participate in moderate physical activity to promote health became concerned about the competitive nature of team sports and the physical strength they required. By the early twentieth century, they had altered their emphasis to focus on proper behaviour and appearance for women engaged in sports.[48]

Women's fashions of the time called attention to their bodies. At mid-century, the bustle accentuated the hips; then and later, corsets emphasized not only the hips but the breasts as well. In looking back on the buttoned gloves they wore, one woman recalled that "[b]oy friends, then known as sweethearts, would tenderly stroke the small

Young women enjoying hockey practice at Diamond Park, Edmonton, 1916.
Source: Provincial Archives of Alberta, A2972

area of flesh exposed between those buttons, sending delicious thrills through maidenly breasts."[49] Because the dictates of fashion could interfere with physical activity, when dress increasingly interfered with what women wanted to do, they altered it. Women began to adopt new and more comfortable clothing as they started to bicycle, play tennis, and swim. For example, they sometimes wore bloomers or a divided skirt for bicycling. The shirtwaist, a blouse that was slightly more comfortable and plainer than the fitted bodice, reflected the impact of the working girl on the fashion industry. The shirtwaist had the additional advantage of being inexpensive because it required less measuring and sewing and could be mass-produced.

If sports and fashion generated debate, women's sexuality generated even more. Control seemed necessary to most women who wrote on the subject, since it was women who paid the price of sexual pleasure in the fact of childbirth. Women gained moral stature and a certain amount of domestic power through affirming their sexual purity, and some were willing to carry that image into public life. Social purity advocates were particularly concerned about the fate of naive young girls attracted to urban centres and susceptible to the sexual entreaties of immoral men. These advocates and churches and women's groups all feared that the "unprecedented freedom" such girls experienced would lead to problems. Young immigrant girls were thought to be especially at risk. Working men, too, believed that young women were vulnerable to attacks from wealthy men. *The Palladium of Labor* in 1885 asked, "Would you not 10 000 times rather your beautiful daughter had a dagger put through her heart or a bullet through her brain, than she should be doomed to die in agony of suffering brought on by being forced to submit to inhuman, diabolical outrages, to the nature it is impossible even to allude."[50]

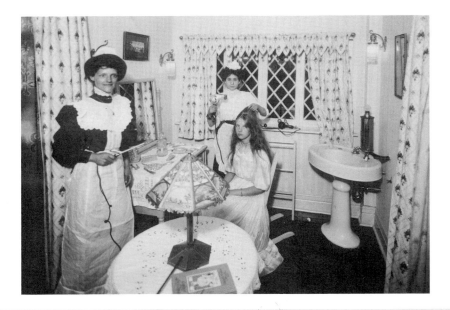

Manitoba hairdressers using electric curling irons around 1915.

Source: Provincial Archives of Manitoba, Industry, Commerce, Hairdresser 1, N231

The Woman's Christian Temperance Union (WCTU) was more pragmatic; in 1894, the Ontario WCTU threatened to publish the names of prostitutes' clients so that mothers could protect their daughters from such men. At times women resorted to violence when men transgressed sexual norms. In a 1909 tragic case of domestic violence, Annie Robinson, who lived outside of Sudbury, Ontario, had to face the fact that her husband had committed incest with their two daughters. Her response was infanticide—she killed the two infants born from this abuse.[51]

Sexually transmitted diseases, such as gonorrhea and syphilis, were associated with prostitution and also became a topic of public discussion in this period. Indeed, the danger from venereal disease was very real, and it gradually became another subject that women were willing to discuss. Some physicians in the late nineteenth century estimated that 15 percent of gynecological disorders, including sterility, were the result of women having contracted sexually transmitted diseases from their husbands, who had acquired them before or outside of marriage. The Haven, a Toronto charity, provided shelter for young women who had contracted venereal disease; its members refused to give in to public pressure to stop doing so.[52] In 1917, the National Council of Women urged "a Dominion campaign for the study and control of sexually transmitted diseases."[53]

The concern about the dangers of sexuality and the belief in the need for control over sexual feelings were part of a larger moral panic created by social change. There is ample evidence, however, that Victorian women did have sexual feelings.[54] In her old age, the poet Elsa Gidlow recalled how, as a young woman living in Montreal, she had fallen in love with her "best friend," Frances, and had written "about her eyes like bits of smiling skys on a sunny day, her red-gold hair and graceful body." So limited was her own knowledge about sexuality, however, that it was only later that she realized she was a lesbian.[55] Lucy Maud Montgomery poured out her feelings about an early love in her diary on April 8, 1898. Looking back on her passion for Herman Leard, a man with little education and few prospects, she recalled that she had loved him "with a wild, passionate, unreasoning love that dominated my entire being and possessed me like a flame—a love I could neither quell nor control—a love that in its intensity seemed little short of absolute madness. Madness! Yes!" But she controlled the madness, for, as she concluded, Herman had been "impossible, viewed as a husband."[56] Montgomery eventually chose to marry someone she deemed more suitable—someone who, she believed, could provide her with the kind of home and family life she wanted.

Similarly, Ellen Smallboy, a Cree woman from the James Bay area, chose her husband, Simon, because he was a good hunter. Although many girls were after him, Ellen proved her worth: "Just before I married him, I killed four otters and ten martens, and when I came in with the fur it was worth $50. Then I went back to my traps and got a couple of beavers. That is why I could get a good husband, because he knew I could help him."[57] For most young women, then, courtship was now occurring outside the boundaries of the home and family; they made their own decisions about whom to marry, although they still sought parental blessing.[58]

For many racial and ethnic groups, marriage itself proved particularly problematic. As Christian missionaries imposed their ideology of monogamous marriage and the prohibition of polygamy and divorce on Aboriginal communities, the number of impoverished Aboriginal single women and mothers increased. Also, during this period racist immigration laws designed to keep Canada, particularly British Columbia, a white settler society, also severely restricted marriage opportunities for Chinese, Japanese, and Indian immigrants.

In 1885, a head tax or immigration fee was imposed exclusively on Chinese immigrants. At that time there were only 55 married Chinese women living in British Columbia; they made up a mere a 1.2 percent of the total Chinese population in the province. Initially the tax was set at $50 and then raised to $100 in 1900 and $500 in 1903. Few Chinese men could afford to pay the tax to bring their existing or future wives to Canada. Consequently, most wives remained in China, where, in addition to the hardship of being separated from their husbands, they had to raise their children by themselves.

For Japanese picture brides, there was no courtship but only an exchange of photographs before they arrived in Canada. Some found that their husbands were much older than the men portrayed in the youthful pictures they had sent and that their spouses were far less successful than they had claimed. Many of these women, who had been well-educated and had worked as teachers and nurses in Japan, ended up working in isolated fishing villages, on lonely farms, or in remote logging camps. Under these adverse conditions, they strove to educate their children in the Japanese language and culture. When living conditions became too difficult, some sent their children back to Japan to be raised by family members.

The first two women from India migrated to Canada in 1912. Kartar Kaur and Harman Kaur were denied entry to Canada when they arrived in Vancouver with their husbands, both of whom were legally in Canada and therefore allowed to re-enter the country. The husbands successfully challenged the deportation ruling against their wives, and the case, referred to as the "Hindu Woman's Question," generated a public debate as to whether women from India should be allowed to enter Canada.[59]

The domestic ideal might depict a woman with a man to protect her, but the vast majority of women—pioneer and working-class women especially—probably took the idealization of their situation with a grain of salt. Certainly farm women, such as those in Alberta, seldom romanticized their positions as wives. When reflecting on their marriages later in life, they tended to focus on the economic nature of these partnerships.[60] Francis Beynon, a columnist for the *Grain Growers Guide*, used this platform to chastise farmers who took advantage of their wives' good will and self-sacrifice. Clearly, the domestic ideal was irrelevant to women who were not married: in 1916 more than 20 percent of women in Winnipeg between the ages of 35 and 64 were single, widowed, or divorced.[61] Women's testimony before various government commissions also spelled out the harsh conditions under which many married and single women in paid employment worked and lived.

The domestic ideal also had little to offer a woman like Mary Gorman, who never really had a chance to achieve it. Born in 1858 in Ontario to a mother who was a

An elaborate wedding party in Nova Scotia at the turn of the century.
Source: McCord Museum VIEW-7654

prostitute, Mary had few advantages and certainly little if any chance to learn the codes of Victorian respectability. Arrested at the age 9 for being drunk and disorderly, she served 30 days at hard labour. By the time she was 10 she had been convicted at least three times and served more time at hard labour. From 10 to age 14, she worked as a servant but was also convicted four more times. When she was 14, she was listed as a prostitute in the jail records, which also noted that she was illiterate.[62] For this young girl, the cult of domesticity was irrelevant; life in Victorian Canada was ugly and even brutal.

THE QUEST FOR EDUCATION

That Mary Gorman's illiteracy was noted was symptomatic of the nineteenth-century attention to education. Everywhere the socially concerned were promoting improved and more regular schooling for both sexes as a solution to many of the social ills of their time. Educators were another group who spoke at length about the differences between men and women, focusing on the kind of training appropriate to each.

Educational reformers believed that more systematic school attendance, in state-supported institutions designed to uplift as well as to inform, had the potential to prevent the social, economic, and moral ruin of girls like Mary Gorman. Governments worked to achieve the aims of educational reform by legislating free schooling and compulsory school attendance, along with programs designed to improve what went on in schools. By 1905, all provinces except Quebec and the colony of Newfoundland had laws requiring young children (initially those between the ages of 7 and 12) to attend school for certain minimum periods. Although some families resisted, many parents saw the economic and social value of schooling, and were motivated to send their children to school more regularly and for longer periods. Attendance continued to be sporadic and geared to the requirements of the family rather than the school, but gradually more young people attended classes for more months of the year and stayed in school for more years altogether. By 1911, Canadian girls and boys typically spent almost eight years in classrooms.

Nevertheless, in the same year, only 44 percent of all 15-year-old girls were attending school.[63] Old patterns of girls' school attendance—or non-attendance—persisted, especially in rural or isolated areas. Many working-class and immigrant families who needed their girls at home also retained traditional practices, such as rotating school attendance among their daughters. Where younger women had access to jobs, as they did in towns with textile mills or food-processing plants, working-class girls tended to leave school early.

Attendance also varied according to race, ethnicity, and class.[64] In parts of the country, despite black parents' struggles to gain access for their children to elementary schools, black children had to attend separate black schools, which often lacked money, equipment, and well-trained instructors.[65] British immigrant children who came to Canada through such organizations as the Barnardo Homes were less likely to attend school than Canadian-born children. In 1896, a young woman who had migrated to southern Ontario through another child immigration agency, Annie Macpherson's House of Industry, was made an apprentice and evidently obtained no schooling whatever. She wrote back to the House, saying that she was ashamed of her poor writing: "The people you let take me and raise as their child they would not sent me to school and mistreat me. . . . I run away when I was 15 year old I wish I could see you."[66]

Beyond the elementary level, access to education was uneven and varied. After mid-century, there were still many small private schools for girls, along with a number of grammar schools, academies, and colleges that either admitted girls or were designed for them alone. But in the co-educational institutions, girls were often treated as second-class citizens. In the 1860s a debate developed in Ontario over the conditions under which girls could attend state-subsidized grammar schools: the government eventually decided that female students who were not studying the classics were worth only half the subsidy paid for male students.[67] Supporters of grammar schools, however, were aware that girl students were needed to make the schools an economic success, and advocates of a woman's intellectual equality with that of a man's furnished these supporters with a theory that would allow the schooling of girls without changing the grammar-school curriculum. By 1871, as a result, Ontario had a new system of secondary education that was more accessible to girls; but not many secondary schools in any province were free, and few parents could afford to subsidize the additional costs of their daughters' attendance even when a school was free.

In all provinces, the number of teacher-training institutions increased, as did the number of young women who attended them. Known as normal schools, these schools opened up to women the prospect of superior or better-paid teaching jobs and the chance to save money to further their education in other fields. Still, the normal schools contributed to the doctrine of separate spheres in their unequal treatment of the sexes. In Toronto in the 1880s, for example, a separate training institute was founded for men who would go on to teach in the secondary schools; in the early twentieth century, the creation of a Faculty of Education associated with the University of Toronto (later the Ontario College of Education) was also motivated by the concern to foster an elite corps of male secondary-school teachers. As well, in Quebec, all Roman Catholic teacher education continued to be segregated by gender.

Girls' academies, while often providing an excellent grounding in academic and cultural areas, varied in quality. Many considered their primary task to be the training of young ladies. Such goals did not necessarily negate good scholarly training, and the calendars of some of these colleges reveal a rigorous academic program. Denominational schools such as those run by the Methodist church were seen as an "investment in the education of young women [that] paid dividends in a stable family and church membership." Many girls' academies seemed designed, however, to keep particular groups of girls apart from the less respectable parts of society. In Victoria, for example, white parents initially refused to send their daughters to the convent run by the Sisters of Saint Ann because the classes integrated Aboriginal, black, and white pupils. The sisters, fearing competition from other private schools, agreed to segregated classes. The All Hallows School for Girls in Yale, British Columbia, which had once taught Aboriginal and white students together, was by 1891 advertising its strict separation of the two groups.[68]

In English Canada, public elementary schools initially appeared to make no distinction between the sexes as far as curriculum was concerned, but separate playgrounds, school entrances, and seating in classrooms made it clear that boys and girls needed to be kept apart. In urban schools, which were largely taught by female instructors, the male principals and superintendents provided a model of masculine authority that was not lost on the children who attended. Then, at the high-school level, differing curricula for young men and young women reinforced the separate sphere for women. Only the former were encouraged to take the classics or the more advanced mathematics required for university entrance and the professions. When physical education was introduced, it also was segregated, with the girls engaged in calisthenics and excluded from the rougher games of boys, while the latter were also given military drill.

Finally, the latter years of the nineteenth century witnessed the beginning of a new educational campaign to provide practical training in the schools for both young men and women. Gradually, public secondary schools took over from private colleges the commercial courses that were so popular with middle-class families. In response to the rapidly changing commercial workplace at the turn of the century, the business curriculum also became increasingly gendered, as boys enrolled in subjects like accounting, while girls were steered into stenography and typing. In both elementary and secondary schools, boys were offered manual training and girls, domestic science.[69]

There were at least two fundamental motives behind the domestic science movement. On the one hand, there was the problem of girls like Mary Gorman, who so clearly and tragically lacked any kind of schooling and who required some practical training. On the other hand, there was the housewife and mother, who increasingly laboured alone without any servants and could use trained help. To make a point, some middle-class women exaggerated the repercussions of not having adequate help. When faced by the lack of domestic help, one newspaper columnist named Gwen questioned, "Why should we women be forced to give up our homes, why should we be forced to neglect our children, our sewing and our requisite rest and recreation?"[70] Young girls were reluctant, however, to choose domestic service if they could find paid work elsewhere; too often, those who did go into service seemed poorly educated or socially unsuited to the work.

Commentators offered two solutions to the servant shortage. One was to encourage the government of Canada to bring over immigrant women to replace the dwindling pool of Canadian-born domestics. The second and more innovative project was to improve the status of domestic work through domestic science education. Young women would then be attracted to domestic service, it was argued, because the work would be considered educated, professional work. At the same time, those trained in domestic science would be properly prepared for their future roles and more capable of managing their own households and families.

Needlework had always been taught in girls' schools. Quebec's convent schools had been renowned since the seventeenth century for teaching fine embroidery and other kinds of needlework.[71] But the way sewing was taught began to change toward the end of the nineteenth century, as the domestic science movement took hold. Teachers were now given detailed and often rigid instructions about the needlework lessons they were to teach. By the early twentieth century, classes in the new subject of domestic science were formally established in most school systems, and cooking and nutrition were added to the subjects girls studied. By 1903, advanced training in domestic science was being provided at the Macdonald Institute in Guelph, Ontario;

later it was made available at the University of Toronto, and at McGill (Macdonald College in Ste. Anne de Bellevue), Acadia, and Mount Allison universities. In 1905–06, fewer than 6 percent of the girls in elementary school took formal domestic science classes in Ontario cities; by 1920–21, the figure had risen to 70 percent. In rural schools, however, the figure remained below 7 percent. Although in some rural locations local Women's Institutes offered short courses in home economics to adult women, the impressive expansion of domestic science classes was largely an urban and school-based phenomenon.[72]

These courses were not popular with everyone. The supporters of domestic science education argued that with more young women entering the workforce, daughters who would no longer learn household skills from their mothers had to be trained in scientific and hygienic ways. But these courses emphasized woman's domestic role to the exclusion of all others, and critics complained about their lack of intellectual content as well as about their remoteness from some girls' realities. Domestic science courses promoted the latest technology—technology that girls rarely found in their homes—and also subtly undermined the work women had traditionally done and the way students or their mothers still did it. The emphasis was on what women were doing wrong, not on what they were doing right. And as governments sponsored lectures and organized leaflet campaigns designed for adult learners, mature farm women and housewives joined schoolgirls as recipients of the messages of the domestic science movement. Many women were grateful that someone was taking enough interest in what they were doing to proffer advice, and they certainly enjoyed the excuse to meet and chat with other women. Rural women, in particular, valued Women's Institute meetings as a means of establishing friendships and breaking down the physical and emotional isolation they frequently endured. But, as with other mature women, they felt their own wisdom and experience were often ignored. As one woman complained to the *Grain Growers' Guide* in 1916, such educational programs seemed designed "for very young schoolgirls." She had more than one question to ask: "Does this program speak to your head and intellect? Does this program give us a larger field than the usual 'women's yard'? Always suggestions about housework, knitting, and the main woman's destination 'preparing of dainty side-dishes and salads'. Kitchen, kitchen, and again kitchen!"[73] In reform institutions for delinquent females and in industrial schools on the Prairies, the inmates, mostly Aboriginal, found their education dominated by hands-on domestic training—they were expected to do the housework, sew, knit, mend, and wash, with the "washing for the school only taking a little over two one half days per week." On reserves, moreover, Aboriginal women were encouraged to learn so-called domestic skills, meaning the skills of white homemakers; their teachers were often the unpaid wives of the Indian agents.[74]

The most vociferous and lengthy debate in education was over the question of women at university. When New Brunswick's Mount Allison University granted a B.Sc. degree to Grace Annie Lockhart in 1875, it was the first university in the British empire to graduate a woman.[75] Nova Scotia's Acadia University soon followed. Other universities in the country were not as open to change but eventually yielded to pressure as more women acquired the necessary entrance qualifications. Young women desperately wanted the chance to learn. Quebec's Maude Abbott, for example, who eventually became a renowned doctor and medical researcher, wrote in her diary in 1884 about her "selfish" desire to go to school:

> I do so long to go. And here I go again, once begun dreaming of the possibilities and I become half daft over what I know will never come to pass. Oh, to think of studying with other girls! Think of learning German, Latin, and other languages in general. Think of the loveliness of thinking that it entirely depended on myself, whether I got on and that I had the advantages I have always longed for.[76]

Such women would not be denied, and their campaigns for advanced schooling initiated a wide-ranging discussion on a woman's role in society and the kind of education she needed.

Some, however, ridiculed the idea of the educated woman. In 1872, in one example, a writer in the *Christian Guardian* snidely remarked that "very intellectual women are seldom beautiful; their features, and particularly their foreheads, are more or less masculine."[77] Others were concerned about the more serious effects of educating women. Dominion statistician George Johnson announced in the 1890s that the decline in the birth rate was "due to the spread of education which enables females to become better wage earners and therefore less interested in marriage."[78] Johnson's perception was not inaccurate—about half of the 392 women who studied at Dalhousie University between 1885 and 1900 remained single, a high figure compared to the 10 percent of the whole female population that did not marry.[79]

Most Canadians who wrote on the subject supported higher education for women—as long as women were educated separately and differently from men. But the question of separate facilities remained an issue of critical importance. Many feared that it was dangerous to educate young women and men in the same classrooms during the years when they were reaching sexual maturity. In 1895, when female students at the University of Toronto joined male students in a strike against the administration, critics of co-education

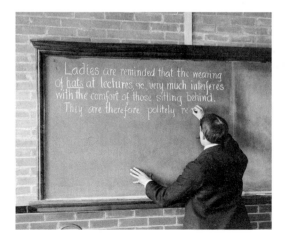

This admonition to women students was being written in one of the classrooms at McGill University, circa 1912.

Source: Evans, Nevil Norton/Library and Archives Canada / PA-122876

described such defiant behaviour on the part of the women as being a step, if only a small one, toward sexual impropriety.[80] Although there were some attempts to found ladies' colleges, few succeeded in establishing themselves as university-level institutions. One of the institutions that came closest to success in English Canada was Mount Saint Vincent Academy in Halifax. Established by the Sisters of Charity in 1873, it was recognized by the government in 1895 as a teacher-training school for the members of that order. By 1915 many of the teaching sisters had obtained advanced degrees, and the Academy, in association with Dalhousie University, was permitted to offer university-level courses for a degree that the latter would confer. In Quebec, the Sisters of the *Congrégation de Notre-Dame* also moved into higher education for women when they founded the *École d'enseignement supérieur* (later the Collège Marguerite Bourgeoys) in 1908.[81]

Heavy costs prevented the development of other colleges for women; but, at the same time, the expensive operating costs at the universities, along with a shortage of qualified male students, were partly responsible for the fact that women were finally admitted to those once exclusively male halls of learning. The progress of women's acceptance was slow, however. In the case of McGill, women's higher education began in 1857, when the new McGill Normal School admitted both men and women. In 1870, a meeting of Montreal citizens convened by the McGill Board of Governors unanimously adopted a resolution to extend university benefits to women as soon as possible; the following year, the Ladies' Educational Association was formed to provide lectures for women and to look into the establishment of a women's college connected with the university. The founding of a high school for girls by the Protestant Board of School Commissioners in Montreal was a necessary first step. Girls at that school took exams that McGill considered equivalent to matriculation or successful completion of high school, but they were still not permitted to enter the university. Only in 1884, when Donald Smith gave McGill a substantial sum earmarked for the higher education of women, did the university finally open its doors to them. Even then, McGill was reluctant, and for many years the university did all it could to educate its women students, nicknamed "Donaldas," separately and differently from the men.[82]

The three Rs, domestic science, art, music, and literature were generally accepted as appropriate subjects for women. Few objected to women's training to be teachers or to be better wives and mothers. But opposition was acute to the idea of women entering the medical or law schools, which would suggest that women actually intended to be doctors and lawyers. Emily Howard Stowe, along with Jennie Trout, did the most to break down the barriers to the entry of women into medicine in Canada. Born in 1831 in Norwich, Upper Canada, the eldest daughter of a Quaker family, Emily Howard was raised to believe in religious freedom and the equality of women. Like so many young women of her era, she began teaching school when she was 15. But like no others in her period that we know of, she also had the audacity to apply for admission to the University of Toronto. Her application rejected, Howard continued to teach and save money so she could attend the Normal School in Toronto, from which she graduated in 1854 with a first-class certificate. Armed with her certificate, Emily Howard captured a job as the principal of a Brantford elementary school, and thus became the first Canadian woman to hold such a position in the public-school system. Two years later she married, and by 1863 she was the mother of a daughter and two sons. When her husband contracted tuberculosis, she determined to become a physician. After returning to teaching to support her family and to earn the money she would require for further study, she was again denied admission to the University of Toronto. Undeterred, this tenacious woman finally earned her degree from the New York Medical College for Women in 1867.[83]

But this was not the end of Emily Stowe's battle. When she tried to establish a practice, she found herself at odds with the provincial requirement that all doctors obtain a licence from the College of Physicians and Surgeons of Ontario; for doctors who had trained outside the province it was necessary to attend a series of lectures given by a provincial school of medicine and then be examined by the College. The problem was that no medical school in Ontario yet admitted women. Finally, in the 1870s, Stowe was allowed to attend the necessary courses at the medical school of the University of Toronto, but she refused to submit to the required examination. Instead, she practised without a licence until 1880, when she finally received provincial accreditation. Jennie Trout, who attended the courses with Stowe, did take the exams and so became the first licenced woman physician in Canada.

The first women actually admitted as students to Canadian medical schools did not necessarily have better experiences. When Elizabeth Smith and a handful of women colleagues attended medical lectures at Queen's in the 1882–83 session, some of the male medical students staged a revolt and threatened to transfer to another school. This and other hostile behaviour, on the part of the professors as well as that of the male students, took its toll. The women felt excluded. As Smith put it, her early medical school experience was like going through a "furnace fiery & severe."[84]

Similar resistance was encountered across the country: some universities refused to admit women altogether, while others denied their entry to particular faculties. Nevertheless, by 1900, 11 percent of college and university students in Canada were women, and by 1919–20 the percentage had risen to 14. The majority of women students were concentrated in the undergraduate faculties of arts and education, but some found their way into other faculties; a few even braved graduate study. Access to graduate study was not assured, however, even for top students. Elizabeth Laird graduated first in her mathematics and physics class at the University of Toronto in 1896, but the scholarship for graduate work abroad for the top student was denied her and awarded to the male student who came second. Evidently, the terms of the scholarship specified a "he" and not a "she." Laird did eventually receive a scholarship from Bryn Mawr, an American college for women, which allowed her to pursue graduate work both there and in Germany. Then, in 1903, Emma Baker became the first woman to gain a Ph.D. (in philosophy) from a Canadian university when she graduated from the University of Toronto.[85]

Despite their limited numbers and despite the fact that, for many, higher education for women was accepted only reluctantly and with a view to reinforcing women's traditional roles, the new graduates began to alter women's public image. Certainly there was now evidence that women were capable of advanced learning and of taking on the professional work that such learning could lead to. Bigoted views could still be openly expressed, however. In Quebec, a vice-rector at Laval University warned of the dangers of failing to measure out knowledge according to "the nature and scope" of young girls' minds, and of what would happen if women students were not immunized against "stupid pride or ambition." This cleric believed that higher education might easily be the means of launching such young women "on a disastrous course . . . no longer preparing them to be generous and devoted companions of man, but rather his inhibiting and, in all instances, misunderstood rivals." In another example of such bigotry, the news that the first graduate of the new *Congrégation de Notre-Dame* college for women had come first in the 1911 Quebec provincial examinations was deliberately kept quiet, as were similar "compromising incidents."[86]

But women proved in their university work that they were the intellectual equals of men. They also proved that educated women could marry and have children, even if they did so less frequently than other women. After all, half of Dalhousie's women graduates had in fact married. A university education also opened up new careers and employment possibilities to women. While a woman lawyer or doctor was still atypical in 1920, she was no longer an anomaly. The first generation of women graduates themselves had a sense that they were special. They formed long-lasting friendships with each other and established local University Women's Clubs, the first in Toronto in 1903. In 1919, representatives from the Ottawa, Toronto, Winnipeg, Regina, Edmonton, and Victoria clubs met in Winnipeg for the inaugural meeting of the Canadian Federation of University Women.

CHILDBEARING AND CHILD-REARING

Women graduates provided a new dimension to the concept of womanhood but did not change its underlying premises. Women continued to be seen in terms of their destinies as wives and mothers. Indeed, on one level, the world of women was remarkably stable: the majority of women married and had children. But on another level, women's lives were dramatically altered as the timing of family events changed. The age at which women experienced puberty, for example, was dropping in the western world. Canadian evidence is not available, but according to British studies, attainment of sexual maturity fell from about 16 at mid-century to around 15 by the 1890s.[87] At the same time, the average age at first marriage was rising—a factor that contributed to the declining birth rate. Later marriage shortened the total number of years that a woman might bear children, and also resulted in the bypassing of several years of potentially high fertility. To illustrate, in 1851, the average age at first marriage for women was 23; by 1871, it was over 25, and by 1891 it had risen to 26. (See Table 6.1 for a breakdown of average age at marriage by province.) The economic recession of the 1880s was a possible related cause for this increase.[88] Although the average age at first marriage for women declined again in 1921 to just over 24, it still remained higher than it had been in the middle of the nineteenth century.[89] In addition, fewer women in fact married; in Canada, the percentage of single women between the ages of 45 and 49, which was 8 in 1851, rose to 11 by 1921.[90]

Fertility rates for legitimate births began a slow but progressive decline in the late nineteenth century. Whereas in 1851 a woman who had come to the end of her child-bearing years would have borne on average 7 children, by 1921 the average had dropped to 3.54. (See Table 6.2.) This general decline in fertility rates was in part a result of older

Table 6.1   AVERAGE AGE AT FIRST MARRIAGE AND SEX RATIOS, 1851–1891

	Average Age at Marriage		Number of Men Aged 20–49 per 100 Women Aged 17½–47½
	Men	Women	
1851			
Quebec	25.4	23.7	89.1
Ontario	26.7	22.4	103.7
1861			
Nova Scotia	28.8	26.8	85.2
Quebec	26.5	24.7	91.9
Ontario	27.2	23.9	97.5
1871			
Nova Scotia	29.4	26.6	87.0
New Brunswick	28.8	26.0	90.8
Quebec	26.9	25.3	86.0
Ontario	28.4	25.0	92.5
1881			
Prince Edward Island	30.1	26.9	88.1
Nova Scotia	29.8	25.9	89.0
New Brunswick	29.4	25.4	91.4
Quebec	26.7	24.9	87.5
Ontario	28.0	25.3	91.4
Manitoba	28.3	20.1	147.7
British Columbia	29.3	20.0	173.7
1891			
Prince Edward Island	31.1	27.9	89.6
Nova Scotia	30.1	26.4	92.0
New Brunswick	29.4	26.3	90.8
Quebec	27.5	25.3	89.1
Ontario	29.3	26.6	91.9
Manitoba	29.8	23.8	134.7
British Columbia	32.7	22.3	231.2

Source: Ellen M., Thomas Gee, "Marriage in Nineteenth-Century Canada," *CARS/Canadian Review of Sociology/revue Canadienne de Sociologie* 1982, 30(3), 311–325. Copyright © 1982 Blackwell Publishing Ltd. Reproduced with permission of Blackwell Publishing Ltd.

married women limiting the number of children they had; married women under 25 continued to have high rates of fertility. To be sure, the number of children women bore varied according to region, religion, ethnicity, and class. In the 1850s and 1860s, Nova Scotia's was the highest birth rate of all, but in subsequent decades, the newly settled Prairie region had a higher birth rate than the older provinces. Quebec maintained a high birth rate until the period toward the end of the century, at which time its birth rate also began a long, steady decline. More generally, as the 1871 census showed, women

Table 6.2   AVERAGE NUMBER OF CHILDREN BORN TO EVER-MARRIED WOMEN,
BY MOTHER TONGUE, 1896–1921

Period of Birth of Women (Approx.)	English	French	Other	All Languages
Before 1896	3.23	6.37	4.70	4.04
1896–1901	2.90	5.58	3.81	3.65
1901–1906	2.69	5.05	3.46	3.39
1906–1911	2.58	4.61	3.17	3.15
1911–1916	2.68	4.33	3.03	3.11
1916–1921	2.87	4.13	2.92	3.19

Source: A. Romaniuc, *Fertility in Canada: from Baby-Boom to Baby-Bust* (Ottawa: Statistics Canada, 1984), p. 16; Statistics Canada, Fertility, Cat. No. 93-321 (Ottawa: Minister of Industry, 1993), Table 4, pp. 113–16.

of Scottish origin and women of French-Canadian origin had higher marital fertility rates than women of Irish or German backgrounds—who, in turn, had higher rates than women of English origin. As for Aboriginals, between 1900 and 1910, their birth rate increased, but after that it, too, decreased slowly but steadily.[91]

Some groups may have delayed marriage as a deliberate strategy for limiting family size, and some Canadians were also intentionally limiting the sizes of their families by using birth control. Coitus interruptus or withdrawal was probably the most widespread birth control method used during this period. But many others were also known. Advertisements in late-nineteenth-century newspapers attest to the use of condoms, which became less expensive than they had been previously when rubber was vulcanized at mid-century. Condoms, however, were associated with prostitution and the prevention of sexually transmitted diseases and were, therefore, not deemed respectable. Abstinence from sexual intercourse was another method of birth control that couples practised. Sex manuals, widely distributed by the Methodist Church publishing house, recognised too frequent childbearing as a problem but condemned the use of any birth-control device. Instead, the manuals advocated abstinence and provided information on what it erroneously thought was the safe period of the menstrual cycle. Some women shared information about how to prevent pregnancy through the use of herbs or the insertion of vaginal sponges or pessaries, often homemade. One recipe that a young woman actually passed on to her mother called for cocoa butter, tannic acid, and boric acid.[92] It has been suggested that the declining birth rate in other countries in this period could be construed as evidence of a kind of domestic feminism, as married women achieved a greater measure of control over their bodies and over an important area of their lives through insisting on the use of birth control.[93] This phenomenon may well have been true for some Canadian women.

Not all birth control methods were reliable, however, nor were all men cooperative. Women frequently faced unwanted pregnancies, and many sought abortions. As with birth control, women's traditional knowledge included ways of inducing miscarriage using herbs. Among the Nuu-chah-nulth of the west coast in the 1870s, women mashed the roots of "a three-leaved plant" in water and drank the infusion once or twice a day to induce abortion.[94] Elsewhere, a variety of home remedies were known, although they were not necessarily effective or safe. These ranged from jumping off a hay wagon, taking excruciatingly hot baths, or drinking carbolic acid or a mixture of turpentine and sugar, to even more dangerous methods involving the insertion of instruments like scissors or knitting needles to bring on miscarriage. Scores of patent medicines were thinly disguised abortifacients, among them Dr. Holloway's Pills, which were advertised as being designed to cure "female irregularities."[95] Throughout the period, women who could afford to do so also sought the services of abortionists. In Toronto "Mamma [Lyyli] Anderson" ran an abortion service as well as a hostel and job exchange for Finnish domestic servants.[96]

While abortion before quickening had once been legal and had not been regarded by the society at large as a moral problem, the practice was increasingly condemned over the course of the nineteenth century. Everywhere in the western world, moral and legal barriers were gradually raised against it. Nativists of British origin worried about what they and other middle-class moralists referred to as the race suicide of the Anglo-Saxon population. The logical outcome of such thinking was to condemn not just abortion but all methods of birth control. In 1892, Section 179 of the Criminal Code of Canada read as follows:

> Everyone is guilty of an indictable offense and liable to two years' imprisonment who knowingly, without lawful excuse or justification, offers to sell, advertises, publishes an advertisement of or has for sale or disposal any medicine, drug or article intended or represented as a means of preventing conception or causing abortion.[97]

This law remained unchanged until 1969.

The birth rate continued to decline, however, particularly among the middle class in urban centres.[98] By 1921, the fertility of urban couples was approximately 20 percent lower than that of rural couples, perhaps because children were not as useful in the urban economy, where family costs were higher. Child labour laws, compulsory education laws, and parents' changing attitudes to children all conspired to make large families seem impractical, if not irresponsible, even for the working classes. Farm families also experienced pressures to limit their fertility as the future on the land, especially in older settled regions, began to seem less promising than it had in the past.[99] The decline of the family as a unit of economic production accounts for the variation in fertility patterns by region. It was in Ontario, an early industrialized province, that the rate first plummeted most sharply; in Nova Scotia, the rate dropped between 1871 and 1891, when industrialization first became a major factor there. Elsewhere the decline came later; for cultural reasons, the decline was especially delayed in Quebec. (Table 6.3 shows the number of children born to ever-married women who have reached the end of childbearing)

A further reason for declining family size was the more positive factor of declining infant mortality rates. Many couples still experienced the tragedy of children dying young. But by 1920, infant mortality had decreased significantly (to approximately 102 deaths per 1 000 population, compared to 184 per 1 000 in 1851).[100] However, the decline in the birth rate pre-dates—by at least a generation—the decline in infant mortality. Thus we

Table 6.3   SIZE OF COMPLETED FAMILIES, FOR WOMEN BORN BEFORE 1922

Period of Birth of Women (Approx.)	0	1	2	3	4	5	6+	Average Number of Children Per Married Woman
Prior to 1876	12.83	9.23	11.08	10.86	9.99	8.65	36.89	4.818
1877–1886	13.20	11.16	13.46	12.31	10.38	8.16	31.01	4.398
1887–1896	12.31	12.36	15.44	13.32	10.55	7.96	27.77	4.167
1897–1901	12.62	14.11	17.31	13.85	10.30	7.52	24.04	3.795
1902–1906	15.48	14.99	19.04	14.40	9.90	6.81	19.38	3.385
1907–1911	15.25	15.76	21.32	14.92	9.76	6.56	16.43	3.154
1912–1916	13.12	15.12	22.48	16.82	10.85	6.75	14.87	3.110
1917–1921	11.77	13.14	22.41	17.96	12.24	7.66	14.83	3.189

Source: A. Romaniuc, *Fertility in Canada: From Baby-Boom to Baby-Bust* (Ottawa: Statistics Canada, 1984), p. 31.

know that the expectation that more children would live can only be part of the cause of family limitation. Declining infant mortality did mean that fewer women would undergo the heartbreak of losing a child and living with the loss, as did one woman who, eight years after the death of her son, wrote in her diary: "Oh how I miss him yet—that dear sweet face—but God knows best and I am sure he is better off—But O I miss him all the time."[101]

For women, a positive result of the decline in fertility was the reduced physical toll of childbearing, which in turn increased women's average life expectancy. However, childbirth remained a major cause of death among women of childbearing age, and puerperal fever continued to be common, despite the medical knowledge that it was preventable with the use of antiseptic techniques as simple as doctors and nurses washing their hands. In 1921 the Canadian maternal mortality rate was 4.7 per 1 000 live births, a rate higher than that experienced in most other western countries.[102]

Physicians argued that their scientific expertise and access to medical technology justified their increasing control of childbirth, and that it made the process safer. In 1874, the medical journal *The Canadian Lancet* explicitly called for women's gratitude to the male medical profession:

> But if woman could only be made intimately acquainted with the truth, that the cultivation of obstetrics by men has been to their advantage by immense odds over what could have been expected of its continued practice by women, what a debt of gratitude would the sex be sensible of owing to man.[103]

While most women accepted such arguments, believing that doctors' scientific knowledge was more valuable than the experiential wisdom of midwives and grandmothers, for many, the daily reality of their lives precluded following medical prescriptions about diet and rest during pregnancy. Issues of race and class dominated some of the medical literature around childbirth as physicians argued that, while Aboriginal women could give birth virtually anywhere, the more "civilized" white woman required medical assistance.[104] Childbirth came to be regarded more as a medical rather than a natural phenomenon, and as a matter for a woman together with her physician rather than with midwives, women friends, and families. Midwives did continue to practise in remote regions, among many immigrant groups, and within Aboriginal communities. While midwives' expertise varied, some were highly trained as was the case with Icelandic midwives. Within Aboriginal communities, midwives served lengthy periods of apprenticeship and were held in high regard.[105] But in urban centres, doctors were taking control of childbirth. Almost all births, however, still took place in the home. Only the unmarried or the very poor gave birth in hospitals, or lying-in homes, where infant mortality rates were shockingly high, although by the second decade of the twentieth century, medical authorities were beginning to persuade other women that hospitals were the safest places to give birth.

Child-rearing began to change as well. For much of the nineteenth century, there was typically a 40-year span between the birth of a woman's first child and the departure of the last one from home.[106] Smaller families did not alter this situation; the tendency for children to stay in the home longer and marry later initially meant little change in the number of years that women devoted to children at home. Now mothers had to cope with the newly defined period of adolescence in their children, as earlier puberty and later marriage resulted in young people who were sexually mature but still unmarried, living at home, and economically dependent. For most Canadians, the onset of puberty began to be seen as a problem, as there was less work for the young to do on the farm, in the home, and in the public labour force, and schooling extended longer into the teenage years.

Mothers also found that the state was increasingly intervening in how they raised their children. Public health officers could enter their homes and examine their children; moreover, truant officers enforced compulsory education. Unwed mothers were likely to be treated particularly invasively; according to one analyst, they were viewed as "a distinct class of social classification, laden with assumptions of race, class, gender and other social distinctions" and, as such, subjected to the harshest scrutiny.[107]

Yet motherhood was more than birthing, coping with adolescence, and putting up with others telling a woman how to care for her family. Carrie Best, a black Nova Scotian, tells a story about her mother: at the end of World War I there was a race riot in New Glasgow, Nova Scotia; fearing for her son, who had not returned home from work, Best's mother went out at night, walked through an angry crowd, and brought her son home to safety.[108] Many women had to raise their families alone. Some were deserted by husbands, but many others were widowed at a young age and often had to rely on the support of older children. Among the Haida, a young widow was expected to remarry within her husband's lineage, whereas a widower was under no obligation to his wife's family once he had given a mortuary potlatch for his wife.[109]

About older women, regardless of their culture, we know very little. Perhaps this is because so much emphasis was placed on woman as mother; when a woman stopped being able to bear children, she became less visible. We do know that there was a great difference in life expectancy among people over 60. At mid-century, men outlived women at this age level, but by the end of the century this trend had reversed. Some old-age homes were built to cater to paying customers. Evidence suggests that in the late nineteenth century, however, more elderly women than elderly men were able to avoid institutions through some form of family co-residency. These women could still make contributions to the household, such a helping with child care, and so were welcomed. Those poorer women who were not welcome were dependent on charity or the poorhouse to look after them in their old age. When Newfoundland in 1911 introduced the first state-run old age pension program, only men could receive it. In Aboriginal cultures, by contrast, older women were particularly esteemed; in some cases their status increased, since they now had access to areas of endeavour, such as hunting, previously prohibited during their pre-menopausal years.[110]

What many women experienced, then, was, on the one hand, greater opportunity to educate themselves for wider roles, but, on the other hand, an intensification of the motherhood role. Books devoted to advising women on child care proliferated, along with storybooks for children. While the number of children might have been fewer, the task of raising them became more complex. Where women had once seen raising children as part of the many things they did, it now seemed their most important responsibility, and one that, according to the prescriptive literature, belonged chiefly to them. The tensions produced by this new vision were multiple, but three were particularly important. First, women were told that they bore the responsibility for their children's lives, but the reality was that more and more of their children's time was in fact controlled by schools. Second, women were to take responsibility for the young but, at the same time, their real sphere was the supposedly separate one of the home. The public world, the world that affected all their children and in which their grown sons would have to spend their working lives, was controlled by men. Finally, increasing numbers of women were educated or had a period of employment outside the home. But how much of what they learned at school or at work had bearing on their future lives as wives and mothers is questionable.

It was to these realities and conditions that late-nineteenth-century and early twentieth-century women responded as they increased their demand for a voice in the public realm. Many of them were already "voting with their wombs" by having fewer children as they recognized the complexities of child-rearing in the new industrial age. Drawing on the powerful ideology of separate spheres and on a culture of womanhood that celebrated not only the home but also the bonds between women, they now proclaimed that as mothers and the managers of families or as single professional women they had both the need and the right to influence what went on in the world outside the home.

Notes

1. Anton Wagner, ed., *Women Pioneers: Canada's Lost Plays* (Toronto: Canadian Theatre Review Publications, 1979) vol. 2, 94–5, 136–37.
2. Colin M. Coates and Cecilia Morgan, *Heroines and History: Representations of Madeleine de Verchères and Laura Secord* (Toronto: University of Toronto Press, 2002).

3. Paul Phillips and Erin Phillips, *Women and Work: Inequality in the Labour Market* (Toronto: James Lorimer, 1983), 8.

4. Regina Flannery, *Ellen Smallboy: Glimpses of a Cree Woman's Life* (Montreal and Kingston: McGill-Queen's Press, 1995); Evelyn Blackwood, "Sexuality and Gender in Certain Native American Tribes: The Case of Cross-Gender Females," *Signs* 10, 1 (Autumn 1984): 27–42; Danielle Desmarais, Carole Levesque et Dominique Raby, "La contribution des femmes naskapies aux travaux de la vie quotidienne à l'époque de Fort McKenzie," *Recherches féministes* 7, 1 (1994): 39; G. Oosten Jaarich, "Male and Female in Inuit Shamanism," *Études/Inuit/Studies* 10, 1–2 (1986): 119; Margaret B. Blackman, *A Haida Woman* (Vancouver: Douglas and McIntyre, 1982), 26.

5. Peggy Bristow, "'Whatever You Raise in the Ground You Can Sell It in Chatham': Black Women in Buxton and Chatham, 1850–65," in Peggy Bristow, co-ord., et al., *"We're Rooted Here and They Can't Pull Us Up": Essays in African Canadian Women's History* (Toronto: University of Toronto Press, 1994), 84.

6. Ramsay Cook and Wendy Mitchinson, eds., *The Proper Sphere: Woman's Place in Canadian Society* (Toronto: Oxford University Press, 1976), 9.

7. "Woman's Sphere," *The Harp* (December 1874), 25.

8. Diane Bélanger et Lucie Rozon, *Les religieuses au Québec* (Montréal: Libre Expression, 1982), 294–319, annexe 2; Michel Thériault, *The Institutes of Consecrated Life in Canada* (Ottawa: National Library of Canada, 1980).

9. Cook and Mitchinson, eds., *Proper Sphere*, 86–87 [our translation].

10. Michael Owen, "Keeping Canada God's Country: Presbyterian Perspectives on Selected Social Issues 1900–1915," University of Toronto, Ph.D. Thesis, 1984, 114; Marguerite Van Die, "'The Marks of a Genuine Revival': Religion, Social Change, Gender, and Community in Mid-Victorian Brantford, Ontario," *Canadian Historical Review* 79, 3 (September, 1998): 524–63.

11. Wendy Mitchinson, "'All Matters Peculiar to Woman and Womanhood'": The Medical Context for Women's Education in Canada in the First Half of the Twentieth Century," in Elizabeth M. Smyth and Paula Bourne, eds., *Women Teaching Women Learning: Historical Perspectives* (Toronto: Inanna Publications and Education Inc., 2006), 158–73.

12. Jo-Anne Fiske, "Gender and Politics in a Carrier Indian Community," University of British Columbia, Ph.D. Thesis, 1989, 109–11; Fiske, "Pocahonta's Granddaughters: Spiritual Transition and Tradition of Carrier Women of BC," *Ethnohistory* 43, 4 (Fall 1996): 663–82; Margaret B. Blackman, "The Changing Status of Haida Women: An Ethnohistorical and Life History Approach," in Donald A. Abbott, ed., *The World as Sharp as a Knife: An Anthology in Honour of Wilson Duff* (Victoria: British Columbia Provincial Museum, 1981), 67; Edward Sapis, "A Girl's Puberty Ceremony among the Nootka Indians," Royal Society of Canada, *Proceedings and Transactions* Series 3, 7 Part 2 (1930), 67.

13. M. L. Holbrook, "Parturition without Pain," in George Napheys, *The Physical Life of Woman* (Toronto: 1890), 312.

14. *Canadian Practitioner*, reprinted from *N.Y. Med. Recorder* (January 1886), 43.

15. J. Thorburn, *A Practical Treatise of the Diseases of Women* (London: 1885), 192–93; Wendy Mitchinson, "Causes of Disease in Women: The Case of Late 19th Century English Canada," in Charles G. Roland, ed., *Health, Disease, and Medicine: Essays in Canadian History* (Toronto: Clarke, Irwin, 1984), 381–95.

16. Wendy Mitchinson, "Gynecological Operations on Insane Women, London, Ontario, 1895–1901," *Journal of Social History* 15, 3 (Spring 1982): 467–84; Public Archives of Ontario,

Case Files of London Ontario Asylum for the Insane, Case No. 4269, E.F.; see also Wendy Mitchinson, *The Nature of Their Bodies: Women and Their Doctors in Victorian Canada* (Toronto: University of Toronto Press, 1991).

17. Constance B. Backhouse, "Nineteenth-Century Canadian Prostitution Law: Reflection of a Discriminatory Society," *Histoire sociale/Social History* 18, 36 (November 1985): 416–17; Joan Sangster, *Female Delinquency in English Canada* (Toronto: Between the Lines, 2002); Tanya Woloschuk, "A Promise of Redemption: The Soeurs du Bon Pasteur and Delinquent Girls in Winnipeg, 1911-1948," *Manitoba History* 51 (February 2006): 16–19.

18. Linda Silver Dranoff, *Women in Canadian Life: Law* (Toronto: Fitzhenry and Whiteside, 1977), 62, 64.

19. Sally Weaver, "The Status of Indian Women," in Jean Leonard Elliott, ed., *Two Nations, Many Cultures: Ethnic Groups in Canada* (Scarborough: Prentice-Hall, 1983), 58–59; Douglas Sanders, "Indian Women: A Brief History of Their Roles and Rights," *McGill Law Journal* 21, 4 (Winter 1975): 663.

20. Erin Breault, "Educating Women about the Law: Violence against Wives in Ontario, 1850–1920," University of Toronto, M.A. Thesis, 1986, espec. 39.

21. Bernadine Dodge, "Gendered Discourses: Women and the Law in Ontario, 1850–1900," University of Toronto, Ph.D. Dissertation, 1993, chap. 6; Judith Fingard, "The Prevention of Cruelty. Marriage Breakdown and The Rights of Wives in Nova Scotia, 1880–1900," in Janet Guildford and Suzanne Morton, eds., *Separate Spheres: Women's World in the 19th-Century Maritimes* (Fredericton, New Brunswick: Acadiensis Press, 1994), 211–31; Lori Chambers and John Weaver, "'The Story of Her Wrongs': Abuse and Desertion in Hamilton 1859–1892," *Ontario History* 93, 2 (2001): 107–26; Chambers and Weaver, "Alimony and Orders of Protection: Escaping Abuse in Hamilton and Wentworth, 1837–1900," *Ontario History* 95, 2 (2003): 113–35.

22. Dranoff, *Women in Canadian Life: Law*, 58.

23. Dranoff, *Women in Canadian Life: Law*, 20–23.

24. Constance B. Backhouse, "Nineteenth Century Canadian Rape Law 1800–92," in David Flaherty, ed., *Essays in the History of Canadian Law* (Toronto: Osgoode Society, 1983) vol. 2, 200–47; A. M. Givertz, "Considering Race and Class in the Regulation of Sexuality and the Prosecution of Sexual Assault in Hamilton, Ontario 1880–1929," paper presented to the Canadian Historical Association, Ottawa, 1993, 38.

25. Erika Koenig-Sheridan, "'Gentlemen, This is no Ordinary Trial': Sexual Narratives in the Trial of the Reverend Griffith Owen Corbett, Red River, 1863," in Jennifer S. H. Brown and Elizabeth Vibert, eds., *Reading Beyond Words: Contexts for Native History* (Peterborough, ON: Broadview Press, 2003), 365–84. For more information on the dominant representations of Aboriginal and white women in the late nineteenth century, see Sarah Carter, *Capturing Women: The Manipulation of Cultural Imagery in Canada's Prairie West* (Montreal and Kingston: McGill-Queen's University Press, 1997).

26. Susan Johnston, "'Mother Was Never Very Happy': Women and Suicide in Late Nineteenth-Century British Columbia," unpublished paper, University of Victoria, 1988, 52–54; Marie-Aimée Cliche, "L'infanticide dans la region de Québec (1660–1969)," *Revue d'histoire de l'Amérique francaise* 44, 1 (1990): 31–59; Linda Cullum and Maeve Baird with the assistance of Cynthia Penney, "A Woman's Lot: Women and Law in Newfoundland from Early Settlement to the Twentieth Century," in Linda Kealey, ed., *Pursuing Equality: Historical Perspectives on Women in Newfoundland and Labrador* (St. John's: Institute of Social and Economic Research, Memorial University, 1993), 111; Kirsten Johnson Kramer, *Unwilling Mothers,*

Unwanted Babies: Infanticide in Canada, (Vancouver: University of British Columbia Press, 2005).

27. Bonnie Huskins, "The Ceremonial Space of Women: Public Processions in Victorian Saint John and Halifax," in Guildford and Morton, eds., *Separate Spheres*, 151.

28. Sharon Myers, "'Not to Be Ranked as Women': Female Industrial Workers in Turn-of-the-Century Halifax," in Guildford and Morton, eds., *Separate Spheres* 176; Karen Dubinsky, *Improper Advances: Rape and Heterosexual Conflict in Ontario, 1880–1929* (Chicago: University of Chicago Press, 1993).

29. Jeanne Kay, "Landscapes of Women and Men: Rethinking the Regional Historical Geography of the United States and Canada," *Journal of Historical Geography* 17, 4 (October 1991): 446; Jenny Cook, "Bringing the Outside In: Women and the Transformation of the Middle-Class Maritime Canadian Interior, 1830–1860," *Material History Review* 38 (Fall 1993): 36–46. For more information on the daily domestic and social lives of many middle-class women of this period, see Frances Hoffman and Ryan Taylor, *Much to Be Done: Private Life in Ontario from Victorian Diaries* (Toronto: Natural Heritage/Natural History Inc., 1996) and Kathryn Carter ed., *The Small Details of Life: 20 Diaries by Canadian Women in Canada, 1830–1996* (Toronto: University of Toronto Press, 2002).

30. Karen Sanders, "Margaret Marshall Saunders: Children's Literature as an Expression of Early Twentieth-Century Social Reform," Dalhousie University, M.A. Thesis, 1978, 20.

31. Maud Rankin to Elizabeth Smith, September 1877. Elizabeth Smith Shortt Papers, Doris Lewis Rare Book Room, University of Waterloo.

32. Jean Barman, *Sojourning Sisters: The Lives and Letters of Jessie and Annie McQueen* (Toronto: University of Toronto Press, 2003).

33. Alice Chown, *The Stairway* (Boston: Cornhill, 1921), 11.

34. Janet McPhee, "The Campbellville Chronicles," unpublished paper, 1987.

35. Barbara Hansen, "A Historical Study of Women in Canadian Banking, 1900–1975," *Canadian Women's Studies/Les cahiers de la femme* 1, 2 (Winter 1978/79): 18.

36. Michael Piva, *Conditions of the Working Class in Toronto—1900–1921* (Ottawa: University of Ottawa Press, 1979), 125.

37. Veronica Strong-Boag, "Introduction," to Nellie McClung, *In Times Like These* (Toronto: University of Toronto Press, 1972), 22.

38. Alison L. Prentice and Susan E. Houston, eds., *Family, School and Society in Nineteenth-Century Canada* (Toronto: Oxford University Press, 1975), 267.

39. Owen, "Keeping Canada God's Country," 85.

40. Gail Cuthbert Brandt, "Organizations in Canada: The English Protestant Tradition," in Paula Bourne, ed., *Women's Paid and Unpaid Work: Historical and Contemporary Perspectives* (Toronto: New Hogtown Press, 1985), 79–96; Michèle Martin, *"Hello, Central?": Gender, Technology, and Culture in the Formation of Telephone Systems* (Montreal and Kingston: McGill-Queen's University Press, 1991), chap. 6.

41. Karen Duder, "The Spreading Depths: Lesbian and Bisexual Women in English Canada, 1910–1965," University of Victoria Ph.D. Thesis, 2001, 111; John Abbott and Alison Prentice, "Policy, Gender and Conflict: Teachers and Inspectors in Ontario and Quebec in the 1870s and 1880s," paper presented to the Canadian History of Education Association, Halifax, October 1986.

42. Elizabeth Smith, *"A Woman with a Purpose": The Diaries of Elizabeth Smith 1872–1884*, edited and with an introduction by Veronica Strong-Boag (Toronto: University of Toronto Press, 1980), 22.

43. Robin Winks, *The Blacks in Canada: A History* (Montreal and Kingston: McGill-Queen's University Press, 1971), 243; Shirley J. Yee, "Gender Ideology and Black Women as Community Builders in Ontario, 1850–70," *Canadian Historical Review* 75, 1 (March 1994): 63–65; Lynne Marks, "The 'Hallelujah Lasses': Working-Class Women in the Salvation Army in English Canada, 1882–92," in Franca Iacovetta and Mariana Valverde, eds., *Gender Conflicts: New Essays in Women's History* (Toronto: University of Toronto Press, 1992), 79; Sara Z. Burke, "Science and Sentiment: Social Service and Gender at the University of Toronto, 1888–1910," *Journal of the Canadian Historical Association*, New Series 4 (1993): 80–82; Burke, *Seeking the Highest Good: Social Service and Gender at the University of Toronto, 1888–1937* (Toronto: University of Toronto Press, 1996); Cathy James, "A Passion for Service: Edith Elwood and the Social Character of Reform," in Smyth and Bourne, eds., *Women Teaching*, 105–30; Beatrice Brigden, "One Woman's Campaign for Social Purity and Social Reform," in Richard Allen, ed., *The Social Gospel in Canada* (Ottawa: National Museums of Canada, 1975), 36–62.

44. Marta Danylewycz, *Taking the Veil: An Alternative to Marriage, Motherhood and Spinsterhood in Quebec, 1840–1920* (Toronto: McClelland and Stewart, 1987), 134–37; Christine Lei, "The Educational Work of the Loretto Sisters in Ontario, 1847–1900," in Elizabeth M. Symth, ed., *Changing Habits: Women's Religious Orders in Canada* (Ottawa: Novalis Publishing Inc., 2007), 172–90; *The Canadian Encyclopedia* (Edmonton: Hurtig, 1985) vol. 1, 341; Brian P. Clarke, *Piety and Nationalism: Lay Voluntary Associations and the Creation of an Irish-Catholic Community in Toronto, 1850–1895* (Montreal and Kingston: McGill-Queen's University Press, 1993), chap. 6.

45. Ruth A. Frager, *Sweatshop Strife: Class, Ethnicity and Gender in the Jewish Labour Movement of Toronto, 1900–1939* (Toronto: University of Toronto Press, 1992), 150–53.

46. Henriette Dessaulles, *Hopes and Dreams: The Diary of Henriette Dessaulles, 1874–1881*, translated by Liedewy Hawke (Willowdale, Ont.: Hounslow, 1986), espec. 64; Mary Rubio and Elizabeth Waterson, eds., *Selected Journals of L. M. Montgomery Vol. 1 (1889–1910)* (Toronto: Oxford University Press, 1986), 263.

47. Jean Cochrane, Abby Hoffman, and Pat Kincaid, *Women in Canadian Life: Sports* (Toronto: Fitzhenry and Whiteside, 1977), 25–27; Honora M. Cochrane, ed., *Centennial Story: Board of Education for the City of Toronto, 1850–1950* (Toronto: Thomas Nelson, 1950), 173.

48. Cochrane, Hoffman, and Kincaid, *Women in Canadian Life: Sports*, 25–27; Michael J. Smith, "Graceful Athleticism or Robust Womanhood: The Sporting Culture of Women in Victorian Nova Scotia, 1870–1914," *Journal of Canadian Studies* 23, 1–2 (Spring/Summer 1988): 133; M. Ann Hall, *The Girl and the Game: A History of Women's Sport in Canada*, (Peterborough, ON: Broadview Press, 2002).

49. Gwen Cash, *Off the Record: The Personal Reminiscences of Canada's First Woman Reporter* (Langley, B.C.: Stagecoach, 1977), 13.

50. Givertz, "Considering," 10–11, 20; Carolyn Strange, *Toronto's Girl Problem: The Perils and Pleasures of the City, 1880–1930* (Toronto: University of Toronto Press, 1995).

51. Dubinsky, *Improper Advances*, 104.

52. *Dominion Medical Monthly and Ontario Medical Journal* (February 1897): 146–47; John R. Graham, "The Haven, 1870–1930: A Toronto Charity's Transition from a Religious to a Professional Ethos," *Histoire sociale/Social History* 25, 50 (November 1992): 296.

53. Jay Cassel, *Venereal Disease in Canada, 1838–1939* (Toronto: University of Toronto Press, 1987), 156. See also Suzann Buckley and Janice Dickin McGinnis, "Venereal Disease and Public Health Reform in Canada," *Canadian Historical Review* 63, 3 (September 1982): 337–54.

54. Mariana Valverde, *The Age of Light, Soap and Water: Moral Reform in English Canada, 1885–1925* (Toronto: McClelland and Stewart, 1991).

55. Elsa Gidlow, "Casting a Net: Excerpts from an Autobiography," *The Body Politic* (May 1982), 27–30; "Elsa Gidlow: Memoirs," *Feminist Studies* 6, 1 (Spring 1980): 107–27; Elsa Gidlow, *Elsa: I Come With My Songs* (San Francisco: Booklegger Press, 1986) 47–58.

56. Rubio and Waterson, eds., *Selected Journals*, 209–10.

57. Flannery, *Ellen Smallboy*, p. 26.

58. Peter Ward, *Courtship, Love, and Marriage in Nineteenth-Century English Canada* (Montreal and Kingston: McGill-Queen's University Press, 1990).

59. Adele Perry, "Metropolitan Knowledge, Colonial Practice, and Indigenous Womanhood: Missions in Nineteenth-Century British Columbia," in Katie Pickles and Myra Rutherdale, eds., *Contact Zones: Aboriginal and Settler Women in Canada's Colonial Past* (Vancouver: University of British Columbia Press, 2005), 109–30; Sarah Carter, "Creating 'Semi-Widows' and 'Supernumerary Wives': Prohibiting Polygamy in Prairie Canada's Aboriginal Communities to 1900," in Pickles and Rutherdale, eds., *Contact Zones, 131–159;* Harry Con, et al., *From China to Canada; A History of the Chinese Communities in Canada* (Toronto: McClelland and Stewart, 1982), 18; Peter S. Li, *The Chinese in Canada* (Toronto: Oxford University Press, 1988) 58–60; Tomoko Makabe, *Picture Brides: Japanese Women in Canada* (Toronto: University of Toronto Press, 1995); Enakshi Dua, "Racializing Imperial Canada: Indian Women and the Making of Ethnic Communities," in Marlene Epp, Franca Iacovetta and Frances Swyripa eds., *Sisters or Strangers? Immigrant, Ethnic, and Racialized Women in Canadian History* (Toronto: University of Toronto Press, 2004), 71–85.

60. Eliane Leslau Silverman, "Women's Perceptions of Marriage on the Alberta Frontier," in David C. Jones and Ian MacPherson, eds., *Building beyond the Homestead* (Calgary: University of Calgary Press, 1985), 55.

61. Mary Horodyski, "Women and the Winnipeg General Strike of 1919," *Manitoba History* 11 (Spring 1986): 29.

62. Backhouse, "Nineteenth-Century Canadian Prostitution Law," 404–5.

63. Frederick Elkin, *The Family in Canada* (Ottawa: Vanier Institute of the Family, 1964), 113; Jean Barman, "Youth, Class and Opportunity in Vancouver," paper presented to the Canadian Historical Association, Vancouver, 1983, 5.

64. Ian Davey, "Educational Reform and the Working Class: School Attendance in Hamilton, Ontario, 1851–1891," University of Toronto, Ph.D. Thesis, 1975, 134–35.

65. Claudette Knight, "Black Parents Speak: Education in Mid-19th Century Canada West," *Ontario History* 89, 4 (1997): 269–85.

66. Joy Parr, *Labouring Children: British Immigrant Apprentices to Canada, 1869–1924* (Montreal and Kingston: McGill-Queen's University Press, 1980), 109.

67. Marion V. Royce, "Arguments over the Education of Girls—Their Admission to Grammar Schools in This Province," *Ontario History* 67, 1 (March 1975): 1–13.

68. Donna Varga Heise, "Gender Differentiated Teacher Training: The Toronto Normal School, 1877–1902," University of Toronto, M.A. Thesis, 1987; R. D. Gidney and W. P. J. Millar, *Inventing Secondary Education: The Rise of the High School in Nineteenth-Century Ontario* (Montreal and Kingston: McGill-Queen's University Press, 1990); Susan Gelman, "Women Secondary Teachers: Ontario, 1871–1930," University of Toronto, Ph.D. Thesis, 1994, chap. 3; Dunham Ladies' College *Calendar* (1883–84), 7; Johanna M. Selles, *Methodists and Women's Education in Ontario, 1836–1925,* (Montreal and Kingston: McGill-Queen's University Press, 1996) 4; Jacqueline Gresko, "Gender and Mission: The Sisters of Saint

Ann in British Columbia," in Elizabeth Smyth, ed., *Changing Habits: Women's Religious Orders in Canada* (Ottawa: Novalis Publishing Inc., 2007), 277–78; Jean Barman, "Separate and Unequal: Indian and White Girls at All Hallows School, 1884–1920," in Jean Barman Yvonne Hébert, and Don McCaskill, eds., *Indian Education in Canada Vol. 1: The Legacy* (Vancouver: University of British Columbia Press, 1986), 114.

69. Nancy S. Jackson and Jane S. Gaskell, "White Collar Vocationalism: The Rise of Commercial Education in Ontario and British Columbia, 1870–1920," in Ruby Heap and Alison Prentice, eds., *Gender and Education in Ontario: An Historical Reader* (Toronto: Canadian Scholars' Press, 1991), espec. 174–85.

70. Patricia E. Roy, *A White Man's Province: British Columbia Politicians and Chinese and Japanese Immigrants, 1858–1914* (Vancouver: University of British Columbia Press, 1989), 180.

71. Joyce Taylor Dawson, "A Note on Research in Progress: The Needlework of the Ursulines of Early Quebec," *Material History Bulletin* 5 (Spring 1978): 73–80.

72. Barbara Riley, "Six Saucepans to One: Domestic Science vs. the Home in British Columbia 1900–1930," in Barbara K. Latham and Roberta J. Pazdro, eds., *Not Just Pin Money: Selected Essays on the History of Women's Work in British Columbia* (Victoria: Camosun College, 1984), 168, 100; Marta Danylewycz, Nadia Fahmy-Eid, et Nicole Thivierge, "L'enseignement ménager et les 'home economics' au Québec et en Ontario au début du 20e siècle: Une analyse comparées," in J. Donald Wilson, ed., *An Imperfect Past: Education and Society in Canadian History* (Vancouver: Centre for the Study of Curriculum and Instruction, University of British Columbia, 1984), 109; Margaret C. Kechnie, *Organizing Rural Women: The Federated Women's Institutes of Ontario, 1897–1919* (Montreal and Kingston: McGill-Queen's Press, 2003), 93–109.

73. Linda Ambrose, "'What Are the Good of Those Meetings Anyway?': Early Popularity of the Ontario Women's Institutes," *Ontario History* 97, 1, March 1995: 1–19; Linda Rasmussen et al., eds., *A Harvest Yet to Reap: A History of Prairie Women* (Toronto: Women's Press, 1976), 132.

74. Pamela Margaret White, "Restructuring the Domestic Sphere—Prairie Indian Women on Reserves: Image, Ideology and State Policy 1880–1930," McGill University, Ph.D. Dissertation, 1987, 114–19, 131–41, 171–72; Woloschuk, "A Promise of Redemption," 18–19.

75. Beth Light and Alison Prentice, eds., *Pioneer and Gentlewomen of British North America, 1713–1867* (Toronto: New Hogtown Press, 1980), 82.

76. Hugh Ernest MacDermot, *Maude Abbott: A Memoir* (Toronto: Macmillan, 1941), 10.

77. *Christian Guardian* (October 30, 1872), 346.

78. Alan A. Brookes, "The Golden Age and the Exodus," *Acadiensis* 11, 1 (Fall 1981): 67.

79. Judith Fingard, "College, Career, and Community: Dalhousie Coeds 1881–1921," in Paul Axelrod and John G. Reid, eds., *Youth, University and Canadian Society: Essays in the Social History of Higher Education* (Montreal and Kingston: McGill-Queen's University Press, 1989), 26–50.

80. Sara Z. Burke, "Women of Newfangle: Co-education, Racial Discourse and Women's Rights in Victorian Ontario," *Historical Studies in Education* 19, 1 (2007): 111–33; Sara Z. Burke, "New Women and Old Romans: Co-education at the University of Toronto, 1884–95," *Canadian Historical Review* 80, 2 (June 1999): 221.

81. Sister Theresa Corcoran, SC, *Mount Saint Vincent University: A Vision Unfolding, 1873–1988* (Lanham, MD: University Press of America, 1999); Sister Maura, *The Sisters of Charity, Halifax* (Toronto: Ryerson Press, 1956), 24, 34, 77–78; Danylewycz, *Taking the Veil*, 146.

82. Donna Ronish, "The Development of Higher Education for Women at McGill University from 1857 to 1907," McGill University, M.Ed. Thesis, 1972; Paula J. S. LaPierre, "Separate or Mixed: The Debate over Co-Education at McGill University," McGill University, M.A. Thesis, 1983; Margaret Gillett, *We Walked Very Warily: A History of Women at McGill* (Montreal: Eden Press, 1981).

83. Catherine L. Cleverdon, *The Woman Suffrage Movement in Canada*, 2nd ed. (Toronto: University of Toronto Press, 1974), chap. 2; Deborah Gorham, "Singing Up the Hill," *Canadian Dimension* 10, 8 (June 1975): 29; Carlotta Hacker, *The Indomitable Lady Doctors* (Toronto: Clarke, Irwin, 1974), chap. 2; Veronica Strong-Boag, "Canada's Women Doctors: Feminism Constrained," in Linda Kealey, ed., *A Not Unreasonable Claim: Women and Reform in Canada, 1880s–1920s* (Toronto: Canadian Women's Educational Press, 1979), 109–30; J. E. Thompson, "The Influence of Dr. Emily Howard Stowe on the Woman Suffrage Movement in Canada," *Ontario History* 54, 4 (December 1962): 253–66.

84. A. A. Travill, "Early Medical Co-Education and Women's Medical College, Kingston, Ontario, 1880–1894," *Historic Kingston* 30 (January 1982), 72.

85. *Canada Year Book* (1918–19); *Report of the Royal Commission on the Status of Women in Canada* (Ottawa: Information Canada, 1970), 68; John A. Reid, "The Education of Women at Mount Allison, 1854–1914," *Acadiensis* 12, 2 (Spring 1983): 38; Alison Prentice, "Three Women in Physics," in Elizabeth Smyth, Sandra Acker, Paula Bourne and Alison Prentice, eds., *Challenging Professions: Historical and Contemporary Perspectives on Women's Professional Work,* (Toronto: University of Toronto Press, 1999), 121–25.

86. Danylewycz, *Taking the Veil*, 146–47.

87. Peter Laslett, "Age at Menarche in Europe since the Eighteenth Century," in Theodore K. Rabb and Robert I. Rotberg, eds., *The Family in History: Interdisciplinary Essays* (New York: Harper and Row, 1971), 29.

88. Ellen M. Thomas Gee, "Marriage in Nineteenth-Century Canada," *Canadian Review of Sociology and Anthropology* 19, 3 (August 1982): 315.

89. Ellen M. Thomas Gee, "Female Marriage Patterns in Canada: Changes and Differentials," *Journal of Comparative Family Studies* 11, 4 (Autumn 1980): 460.

90. Gee, "Marriage in Nineteenth-Century Canada," 315; Gee, "Female Marriage Patterns," 460.

91. Lorne Tepperman, "Ethnic Variations in Marriage and Fertility: Canada, 1871," *Canadian Review of Sociology and Anthropology* 11, 4 (November 1974): 331; A. Romaniuc, *Fertility in Canada: From Baby-Boom to Baby-Bust* (Ottawa: Statistics Canada, 1984), 19; Jacques Henripin, *Trends and Factors of Fertility in Canada* (Ottawa: Federal Census Bureau, 1972), 39; Roderic P. Beaujot and Kevin McQuillan, "Social Effects of Demographic Change: Canada 1851–1981," *Journal of Canadian Studies* 21, 1 (Spring 1986): 57–59; Danielle Gauvreau, Diane Gervais, and Peter Gossage, *La Fécondité des Québécoises 1870–1970. D'une exception à l'autre* (Montréal: Boréal, 2007), espec. chaps. 1–3.

92. Terry Chapman, "Women, Sex, and Marriage in Western Canada, 1890–1920," *Alberta History* 33, 4 (Fall 1985), 8; Michael Bliss, "'Pure Books on Avoided Subjects': Pre Freudian Sexual Ideas in Canada," in Michiel Horn and Ronald Sabourin, eds., *Studies in Canadian Social History* (Toronto: McClelland and Stewart Limited, 1974), 326–47; Eliane Leslau Silverman, *The Last Best West: Women on the Alberta Frontier, 1880–1930* (Calgary: Fifth House Ltd., 1998), 80–85; Rasmussen et al., eds., *Harvest*, 72.

93. Daniel Scott Smith, "Family Limitation, Sexual Control, and Domestic Feminism in Victorian America," *Feminist Studies* 1 (Winter/Spring 1973): 40–57.

94. Gilbert Malcolm Sproat, *The Nootka: Scenes and Studies of Savage Life* (1868), West Coast Heritage Series (Victoria: Sono Nis Press, 1987), 169.

95. Peter Gossage, "Absorbing Junior: The Use of Patent Medicines as Abortifacients in Nineteenth Century Montreal," *The Register* 3, 1 (March 1982), 6; Silverman, *The Last*, 85.

96. Varpu Lindström-Best, *Defiant Sisters: A Social History of Finnish Immigrant Women in Canada* (Toronto: Multicultural History Society of Ontario, 1988), 81.

97. Angus McLaren and Arlene Tigar McLaren, *The Bedroom and the State: The Changing Practices and Politics of Contraception and Abortion in Canada 1880–1980* (Toronto: Oxford University Press. 1997), 19.

98. Henripin, *Trends*, 81.

99. Joy Parr, "Hired Men: Ontario Agricultural Wage Labour in Historical Perspective," *Labour/ Le Travail* 15 (Spring 1985): 91–103.

100. Beaujot and McQuillan, "Social Effects," 59.

101. Margaret Conrad, "'Sunday Always Makes Me Think of Home': Time and Place in Canadian Women's History," in Veronica Strong-Boag and Anita Clair Fellman, eds., *Rethinking Canada: The Promise of Women's History* (Toronto: Copp Clark Pitman, 1986), 74.

102. Beth Light and Joy Parr, eds., *Canadian Women on the Move, 1867–1920* (Toronto: New Hogtown Press and OISE Press, 1983), 112.

103. *The Canadian Lancet* 7 (October 1874), 57.

104. Wendy Mitchinson, *Giving Birth in Canada, 1900–1950* (Toronto: University of Toronto Press, 2002); Denyse Baillargeon, *Un Québec en mal d'enfants. La Médicalisation de la maternité, 1910–1970* (Montréal: Boréal, 2004).

105. Lesley Biggs, "Rethinking the History of Midwifery in Canada," in Ivy Lynn Bourgeault, Cecilia Benoit and Robbie Davis-Floyd, eds., *Reconceiving Midwifery* (Montreal and Kingston: McGill-Queen's Press, 2004), 17–45; Biggs, "In Search of Gudrun Goodman: Reflections on Gender, 'Doing History' and Memory," *Canadian Historical Review* 87, 2 (June 2006): 293–316.

106. Light and Parr, eds., *Canadian Women on the Move*, 153.

107. Karen Bridget Murray, "Governing 'Unwed Mothers' in Toronto at the Turn of the Twentieth Century," *Canadian Historical Review* 85, 2 (June 2004): 265.

108. Carrie Best, *That Lonesome Road* (New Glasgow, N.S.: Clarion Publishing, 1977), 43–44.

109. Lorna R. McLean, "Single Again: Widow's Work in the Urban Family Economy, Ottawa, 1871," *Ontario History* 83, 2 (June 1991): 127–50; Blackman, "Changing Status," 68.

110. F. H. Leacy, ed., *Historical Statistics of Canada*, 2nd ed. (Ottawa: Statistics Canada, 1983), A78–93; Tom Belton, "Homes for the Aged in Ontario, 1870–1920," unpublished paper, University of Waterloo, 1986; Teresa A. Bishop, "Peel Industrial Farm and House of Refuge: A Case Study in Institutional Development," University of Toronto, M.A. Thesis, 1982, 35–75; Stormie Elizabeth Stewart, "The Elderly Poor in Rural Ontario: Inmates of the Wellington County House of Industry, 1877–1907," paper presented to the Canadian Historical Association, Charlottetown, 1992, 9, 14; Suzanne Morton, "Old Women and Their Place in Nova Scotia, 1881–1931," *Atlantis,* 20,1 (Fall-Winter 1995): 21–38; Cynthia R. Comacchio, *The Infinite Bonds of Family: Domesticity in Canada, 1850–1940* (Toronto: University of Toronto Press, 1999), 30–32; Megan J. Davies, *Into the House of Old: A History of Residential Care in British Columbia* (Montreal and Kingston: McGill-Queen's Press, 2003), 30–35; James G. Snell, "The Newfoundland Old Age Pension Programme, 1911–1949," *Acadiensis* 23, 1 (Autumn 1993): 86–109.

CHAPTER SEVEN

The "Woman Movement"

For Canada's nineteenth-century women reformers, the impulse for social change often began with a personal experience. Letitia Youmans recalled how, as a child, she saw the rotting body of a local drunkard, "swarming with worms" after he had lain dead and unmissed for several days. "This was my first impressive temperance lesson," she wrote, "and I still look back to it with horror."[1] While not all women activists could recall such an early and searing awakening, all could, like Youmans, document a growing awareness of needs and problems in the industrializing society surrounding them. They coupled these societal concerns with a growing dissatisfaction with the constraints of their own prescribed roles. And cooperation with and for other women often led to the identification of shared problems.

The female activists who attempted to change the society in which they lived were the objects of public criticism and even abuse. The arguments they used in response to this criticism were the basis of the "woman movement" and incorporated the two perspectives that continue to be influential today. The first of these, and the most characteristic of Canadian feminism, was maternal or social feminism, an ideological current premised initially on woman's role as guardian of the home. The precise relationship between maternalist beliefs and feminist activism, in Canada and abroad, has been much debated in recent years.[2] Yet most historians agree that at the centre of this dimension of the women's movement was the idea that women's specific experience and values would allow them to ensure the well-being, not just of their families, but of the country. Indeed, how could they care for their families unless conditions were improved across the nation? And they came to believe that, unless women had the same political rights as men, and particularly the right to vote, society would never be reformed as they wished.

At the same time, a version of feminist beliefs often called equal-rights or equity feminism focused more directly on arguments of simple justice. This viewpoint stressed how much women resembled men, and how unjust it was that they should have fewer rights. As human beings, women were endowed with souls and abilities, but they were barred by custom and law from participating in public life. In such a context, the vote became the symbol of citizenship. A number of women had the property qualifications that would have let them vote if they had been men. Yet assemblies of men, elected by other men, continued to decide what women might or might not do. It was infuriating, quite apart from noble ideals for reforming society. Throughout most of the nineteenth century, however, the vote remained a radical cause that respectable women hesitated to endorse, in part because many respectable, otherwise reasonable men found the idea outrageous.[3]

While the arguments these activist women used can be labelled, the women themselves cannot. Most of them accepted both types of feminist arguments, emphasizing one or the other as seemed most useful or appropriate, apparently without feeling any contradiction. Most of them would have been reluctant to adopt the term *feminist*, which at that time meant a quite extreme degree of commitment to women's issues. They preferred instead to speak of what was then called the woman movement; in this, many kinds and groups of women could and did cooperate.

The woman movement was not unique to Canada. Similar ideas and reform movements were present in other western societies. Leading feminists toured each other's countries and read each other's publications, and there is evidence of considerable cross-fertilization of ideas and transnational borrowing of tactics and strategies.[4] Indeed, by the early twentieth century, there existed four important international organizations of women with which Canadian women were actively involved: the International Council of Women, founded in 1888; the International Alliance of Women (formerly the International Woman Suffrage Alliance), established in 1904; the *Union internationale des ligues féminines catholiques*, founded in 1910; and the Women's International League for Peace and Freedom, which grew out of the violence and bloodshed of the Great War. These associations were an acknowledgment of the fact that middle-class, educated women in various western countries had common experiences and aspirations. To be sure, the aims and demands of these associations also reflected the nature of their membership: that is, elite, white, Christian women whose children, if they had them, tended to be already grown.[5] By the end of the nineteenth century, then, Canadian women were aware that the woman question was a topic of discussion abroad as well as at home.

In Canada, the strongest international influences came from England and other parts of the British Empire, such as New Zealand and Australia, as well as from the United States. The feminism that developed in Canada in this period was thus not surprisingly strongly rooted in an outlook that was British, often imperialist, and Protestant.[6] This outlook existed alongside a burgeoning feminism among French-speaking Catholic women, particularly in Quebec, and as we shall see, often proved alienating to francophone feminists. These divergent strands of feminism were part of what made the nineteenth-century women's movement in Canada both similar to and different from its counterparts elsewhere in the Empire. Although a national umbrella organization, the National Council of Women of Canada, eventually played a significant role, the Canadian women's movement derived its success from the diversity and strength of many organizations rather than from a single unified or national force. Moreover, tactics involving deliberate flouting of the law were never used in Canada, and only a few of the Canadian leaders approved of the attacks on property and politicians organized by the British militants. The traditional methods of the disenfranchised—petitions, lobbying, publicity, and private efforts at influence—remained their preferred weapons. Finally, in Canada, winning the franchise did not become the obsessive goal it did in some other countries. This was particularly the case in Quebec, where feminist efforts were often focused on reforming the Civil Code, in addition to securing the vote.

THE POLITICS OF WOMANHOOD

For most women in Canada—Protestant, Catholic, and Jewish—religious faith was the underpinning for their activism, just as it was the underpinning for their work in charitable associations. Women's politics, like all Canadian politics in the latter half of the nineteenth century, then, were heavily influenced by religion.

After 1850, evangelicalism—the belief that the world could be perfected by individual moral behaviour and efforts and that a rejuvenated Christian social order could be achieved—became a key component of Protestant conviction. A central tenet held individuals responsible to Christ, to themselves, to their families and friends, and to the extended society. Evangelicals attributed moral superiority and redemptive power to Christian women, and especially to mothers. This understanding both motivated and justified Protestant women's involvement and expanding role first in church-based organizations and later in wider-ranging activities on behalf of the family and society.[7] In the Maritimes, for example, Protestantism stimulated the growth of church societies with local women's auxiliaries. As the local Protestant churches joined together into larger national organizations, their proselytizing efforts expanded to include overseas missions in such areas as the West Indies, India, China, and Japan. The male-controlled missionary societies refused, however, to sponsor women missionaries. In Canso, Nova Scotia, Baptist women led by Hannah Maria Norris formed the first separate female missionary society in 1870; similar local groups then grew rapidly. Norris was a teacher active among the poor; in fact, she learned the Micmac language in order to work with them. Converted from Congregationalism as an adult and baptized in the cold waters of Canso harbour in March 1869, she applied to go to "Burmah" as a missionary. When the Baptist Foreign Mission Board rejected her application, she turned to the women of the church, who established the first female fundraising society. Soon there were 32 Baptist Woman's Missionary Aid societies, and, with their guarantee of financial support, Hannah Maria Norris sailed for Burma, where she served for 42 years, married a fellow missionary, and raised three children.[8]

The women's missionary societies grew rapidly and were successful in all the Protestant denominations. A Baptist board was formed for Quebec and Ontario in 1876. By 1885, there were 123 Baptist Woman's Missionary Aid societies in small towns and villages across the Maritimes, operating under a central regional board after 1884. Presbyterian women in Quebec established a Ladies' Auxiliary (1864), which became the Ladies' French Evangelization Society (1875), and then in 1882 became part of the Montreal Woman's Missionary Society for Home, French and Foreign Work. The Presbyterian Woman's Foreign Missionary Society, with a Western Division for Ontario, Quebec, and the western provinces, and an Eastern Division for the Maritimes, was established in 1876. Methodist women created a similar association in 1881. In 1885, seven Anglican women approached the Domestic and Foreign Missionary Society to offer the services of women as an auxiliary. The Anglican women did not secure independence from their general missionary society until 1911.[9]

Women's roles in these new societies differed significantly from their earlier ones in church auxiliaries. They now raised funds for their own organizations, funds that they controlled. The amount of money raised was truly remarkable, considering that most of it came from women themselves through weekly pledges, special collections, donations, and the sale of literature and reports. In 1899, Presbyterian women from the Western Division collected no less than $45 513 from 21 000 members; in 1900, Baptist women collected $10 000 in the Maritimes alone; in 1901, Methodist women raised more than $50 000.[10] With this money, the societies supported female missionaries throughout the world, and by 1899 the Western Division of the Presbyterian Woman's Foreign Missionary Society was supporting 17 women in India and 4 in China. Many of the early women missionaries trained as teachers or doctors specifically for this work; in fact, one of the first three women who graduated from the Kingston Women's Medical College, Dr. Elizabeth Beatty, went to India under the sponsorship of the Presbyterian Woman's Foreign Missionary Society.[11]

Female missionaries increased the overseas effort at little cost to the churches. They were valuable to the missions because they had access to women in cultures where there were many taboos relating to contact between women and men who were unrelated. Canadian missionary women's educational and medical work also benefitted many individual women. For example, in central India they established local dispensaries and clinics that provided valuable health-care services, while mission medical schools trained Indian women doctors. On the other hand, the imposition of western and Christian values often caused social and cultural alienation among those they served. Similar problems occurred as a result of the activities of the home-based women missionaries among Aboriginal and immigrant women.[12] Religious ideology and deep personal spirituality inspired missionary society women; at the same time, their activities also had significant institutional consequences. They challenged men's control of important work both at home and abroad. Most did not see themselves as part of a larger women's movement. Nevertheless, coordinating female missionary societies' activities provided many women with their first chance to develop leadership and administrative skills. Their societies were the first large-scale women's organizations in which women were able to act independently and to develop confidence in their own abilities.

Unlike the female missionary societies, the Woman's Christian Temperance Union (WCTU) was from the very start strongly identified with Canadian women's causes and concerns at home. It began as a women's group and closely guarded its independence from male intrusion, allowing men to be honorary members but not to vote. Yet there were similarities between the women's missionary movement and the temperance movement. Both were deeply Christian and drew heavily on smaller communities for their members; both provided a valuable training in public speaking and in parliamentary procedure. And both were crucial to the development of the women's movement in Canada—in English Canada in particular.

Letitia Youmans founded the first Canadian local of the WCTU in Picton, Ontario, in 1874. Although a women's temperance society called the Ladies' Prohibition League had been established early the same year in Owen Sound, Ontario, by Mrs. R. J. Doyle, Youmans is rightly regarded as the pioneer organizer of Canadian women's temperance activities. A former ladies' academy teacher who, at the age of 23, married a widower with eight children, Youmans was inspired to form the Picton local after attending the founding meeting of the American WCTU. As a Methodist Sunday-school teacher, she had earlier been horrified by the harm caused by alcohol among her students' families; in response, she had started a non-denominational temperance group for children. Youmans progressed from local community involvement to leadership at the provincial and national levels, eventually becoming first president of both the Ontario and the Dominion Unions, in 1877 and 1883, respectively.[13]

Letitia Youmans was also one of a number of Canadian women activists who earned a considerable international reputation. She was prominent in the World WCTU, whose founder, Frances Willard, wrote of how Youmans had been "loved and honored" in the United States as well as Canada, and how her powerful voice "electrified . . . her American sisters."[14] It obviously electrified Canadians also, for by 1891 there were more than 9 000 members of WCTU locals in Canada. While Ontario claimed over 4 000 dues-paying members, the participation rate of women in British Columbia was proportionally even higher.[15]

At its beginning stages, the WCTU focused on the evils associated with alcohol consumption (and to a lesser degree, tobacco consumption); temperance was a pressing moral and religious issue. Most members were convinced that government intervention was necessary and that only complete prohibition could save society from crime, male violence, family breakdown, political corruption, and immorality. For WCTU women, the beliefs and the cause they espoused grew out of their evangelical roles and perspectives as middle-class wives and mothers, and their acknowledged responsibility to convert sinners and to protect the family from the results of male intemperance and moral weakness.[16] Most members had seen the tragic results of drunkenness, even if less horrific than Letitia Youmans's tale of a maggot-infested corpse; Youmans herself recounted many more commonplace episodes of family disruption and domestic violence. Practical concern for the victimized wives and children led the organization to a truly radical departure from women's traditional charitable works among the needy.

Until the 1890s, the WCTU directed its energies toward membership recruitment, individual temperance pledges, and petitions asking various levels of government to adopt prohibition. These were formidable tasks. Thousands of signatures testify to the endless hours of trudging from door to door. Attending and addressing public meetings was also a triumph for many women, who faced audiences that were unaccustomed to and frequently hostile to the idea of women speaking in public. The members of the Picton, Ontario, WCTU were typical as they presented their first prohibition petition to the all-male town council. Fearing that their appearance would be regarded as "bold . . . and unwomanly," they met and prayed before entering the council chamber "with palpitating hearts." When the mayor insisted that the ladies should defend their own petition instead of having a council member do so, they "looked at each other in blank despair." But Letitia Youmans rose to the challenge and aroused the room with an

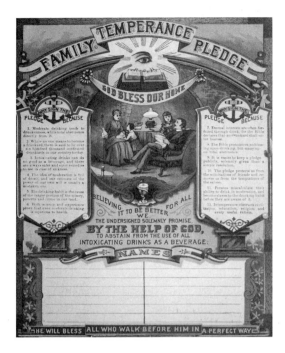

A family temperance pledge, signed by both adults and children.

Source: Hulton Archive/Stringer/Archive Photos/Getty Images

account of "the suffering families, the freezing in the snow-drift under the influence of drink, and the amputations resulting therefrom."[17]

Through their Evangelical Departments, local WCTU members ministered to "needy" groups, especially women and children, establishing homes for prostitutes and reading rooms, and visiting the elderly, the ill, and the imprisoned.[18] Members also sought to have temperance teaching materials used in both Sunday and public schools, and tried to influence doctors to cease prescribing liquor as medicine. Gradually, as all these activities proved unfruitful, the WCTU became convinced that the major obstacle to the achievement of its goal was women's political powerlessness.[19] From religion-based ideas that men were morally weak and women were morally strong, WCTU members forged the demand that women exercise more practical power within both the family and society. This conviction was increasingly shared by other women activists, some of whom focused more directly on women's rights.

The WCTU was less successful in Quebec than in most of the English-speaking provinces. To be sure, in the nineteenth century, temperance became an issue for politicized middle-class women (and men) in Quebec as elsewhere in the country. Quebec's first francophone female novelist, Félicité Angers, who wrote under the pen name Laure Conan, was a devout Catholic and an ardent advocate of temperance. She supported the cause through writings such as *Aux Canadiennes: le people canadien sera sobre si vous le voulez*, published in 1913.[20] Both Protestant and Catholic temperance associations existed in Quebec; the most important of these was Montreal's *Ligue antialcoolique*. But most of these associations advocated moderation in alcohol (and tobacco) use, not prohibition. Quebec Catholics were wary of state intervention in areas related to individual morality. Moreover, numerically speaking, the single most important group of Quebec Protestants were Anglicans, who were much less influenced by the social gospel than Methodists were, for instance, and were thus less receptive to the message advocated by the WCTU. Another reason for the WCTU's limited success in Quebec may have been that it did not always devote the effort necessary to translating and transmitting its message in French.[21]

Nonetheless, Catholicism, too, shaped social reform efforts in this period. During the second half of the nineteenth century, the charitable works undertaken by Catholic laywomen in Quebec were to some degree marginalized by the growth and institution-alization of the Catholic Church and its female religious orders from the 1840s until the end of the century. Old orders expanded and new ones were founded in an effort to manage the familial and individual consequences of urbanization and industrialization. These orders also cared for the physically and mentally ill, the disabled, the homeless, the destitute, the orphaned, and those, such as unmarried mothers, considered delinquent or deviant by the broader society. Albine Gadbois, for example, was born in 1830 on the banks of the Richelieu River. At the age of 17, she became a novice with the Sisters of Providence in Montreal. She took her vows two years later, assuming the name Soeur Marie de Bonsecours, and began her lifelong work as a teacher, more precisely a teacher of deaf children. She founded the *Institution des Sourdes-Muettes de Montréal* for young deaf girls in 1851. For over 20 years, until her death in 1874, Soeur Marie ran her insti-tution and sought continually to keep abreast of the latest pedagogical approaches to teaching deaf children, travelling periodically to study in New York, Germany, Belgium, France, and England.[22] Other religious sisters were able to apply their skills and experi-ence in Latin America, the Yukon, and the Canadian West by travelling abroad as mem-bers of Catholic missionary orders.[23] Thus, until the very end of the nineteenth century, in Catholic circles it was primarily nuns, rather than laywomen, who were faced with actively tackling the social problems that Protestant women were addressing in their benevolent and missionary societies or through the WCTU. There is intriguing evidence that some nuns and laywomen fashioned feminist alliances to address the problems and inequities confronting women in Quebec society. But the primary responsibility for the care of the needy resided with the nuns, and their efforts in social and political reform always remained under the control of male-dominated church hierarchies.[24] Not surpris-ingly, convent women for the most part immersed themselves in the necessary work on the ground, caring for the poor, the ill, and the troubled, rather than pressuring different levels of government to pass social reform legislation.

THE PURSUIT OF CIVIL AND POLITICAL RIGHTS

In Quebec, the 1866 Civil Code provided a modicum of protection for married wom-en's property, even though married women in Quebec suffered from legal incapacity. In the common-law provinces, the second half of the nineteenth century saw a number of changes in married women's property law. The first known shift occurred in 1851, when New Brunswick passed An Act to Secure to Married Women Real and Personal Property Held in Their Own Right. This legislation stated that a married woman's property, whether acquired before or after marriage, was her own separate property and, as such, was exempt from responsibility for her husband's debts and liabilities. Married women were not, however, given the right to sell or otherwise dispose of their assets. The motivation behind this early legislation appears to have been primarily economic in nature. From the late 1840s to 1851, New Brunswick experienced a financial crisis that resulted in many business failures and bankruptcies. Under the existing British common law, which gave total control over a wife's property to her husband, creditors could and did seize it to repay debts accumulated by the husband. The 1851 statute was therefore intended to protect this separate property and to preserve at least some family assets in times of economic emergency.[25]

Between 1852 and 1857, three groups of women petitioned the legislature of Canada West, requesting the passage of a married women's property act giving them some degree of freedom from control of their property by their husbands. These are the first records we know of women going to the legislature on behalf of their own property rights. Anne Macdonald "and other ladies" made the appeal in 1852, Elizabeth L. Hawley "and others" petitioned in 1856, and Elizabeth Dunlop "and others" did the same the next year. We know little about the petitioners, though Elizabeth Dunlop, at least, was apparently active in women's issues; her name appears on the list of prominent women attempting to incorporate the Toronto Magdalen Asylum and Industrial House of Refuge in 1858, in order to provide assistance to prostitutes and unmarried mothers.[26] These sources show that, by the 1850s, some Canadian women were increasingly concerned about their economic dependence and had organized to seek remedies. And they seem to have produced results. The 1856 petition had asked for legislation like that in New York State. In 1859 an Upper Canadian law without any British precedent recognized a married woman's right to own property. Although she could not sell it, her consent was now required if her husband wished to make the sale. Like the earlier New Brunswick measure, the Ontario legislation was, in part, designed to insulate a married woman's property from seizure by her husband's creditors. In Ontario, there was also concern for cases where drunken or improvident husbands would dispose of women's earnings, savings, or other assets, and the Women's Rights petition supporting the measure noted specifically "the injury sustained by women of the lower classes," whom common law deprived "of all pecuniary resources."[27] The drafts of the law even included permission for married women to retain their earnings. But a more moderate version was passed, and judicial interpretations tended, in practice, to restrict women's right to manage or get benefits from their property. In 1872 an Ontario statute—this time following a previous British one—gave married women control over their own earnings.[28]

At approximately the same time as the earliest-known groups of women were presenting petitions relating to married women's property, there is the first evidence of public interest in women's rights. The Toronto *Provincial Freeman* reported in 1855 that Lucy Stone, the well-known American feminist, "held forth to crowded audiences on the subject of 'WOMAN'S RIGHTS.'" Editor and abolitionist Mary Ann Shadd was encouraged that "in Toronto, with the strong attachment to antiquated notions respecting woman and her sphere, so prevalent, she was listened to patiently, applauded abundantly, and patronized extensively."[29] There was, in fact, an early association between the anti-slavery movement and the budding women's rights movement. For example, in 1858, the 91 black members of Halifax's Cornwallis Street Baptist Church sponsored and attended two lectures: one by an escaped slave who was raising money for refugee slaves in Dresden, Ontario; the other by a former member of the British regiment on the subject of the "Rights of Women."[30]

In 1871, Susan B. Anthony, the renowned American suffragist, gave a series of lectures to enthusiastic audiences in Victoria, British Columbia. She "thundered out, night after night" that the local women were "meek, milk and water and had no rights of their own."[31] Although there is no record of a British Columbia woman's suffrage organization during the 1870s, a bill supporting the provincial vote for women was introduced into the provincial legislature in 1872. It received the support of only two members. British Columbia women property-holders did receive the municipal franchise in 1873, however, becoming the first women in Canada to be granted the right to vote after their mid-century exclusion from the franchise. Moreover, the right was given to both married and unmarried women. In January 1875, three eligible women, organized by the doughty widow Silvestria Theodora Smith, actually voted in the municipal election in spite of "jibes and catcalls."[32]

Only in 1876, it seems, was an organization formed explicitly to address women's lack of access to the political process, when a small group of women founded the Toronto Women's Literary Club. Although historians have long argued that the group's name suggests that its founders felt the need to disguise its major political objectives, recent scholarship has demonstrated the ways in which these women's desire for a liberal education was intimately linked to their desire for access to the political realm. Far from being simply a pretext, the literary and educational aims of the TWLC were part and parcel of their political goals; indeed, a liberal education was seen as necessary preparation for participation in public life. The dynamic leader of the Toronto Women's Literary Club, Dr. Emily Howard Stowe, had confronted women's exclusion from the public realm in her own struggles to enter the medical profession. Along with other Literary Club members, she was concerned about women's educational and professional rights, the inadequate protection of women in the workplace, married women's property rights, and the need to acquire the vote. The Club facilitated the discussion of these topics; although small, it became an important catalyst for reform. Its educational program was enhanced in 1881 when one of its members, the witty and urbane Sarah Curzon, became associate editor of *Canada Citizen*, a weekly temperance newspaper, and started a regular column outlining the Club's activities and urging the adoption of woman suffrage.[33]

The Club's members must have been pleased when, in 1882, an Ontario law gave the right to vote on municipal bylaws to spinsters and widows with the requisite property qualifications, even though the full municipal franchise and eligibility to hold office were still denied to women. In spite of, or perhaps because of, the partial character of this victory, the Literary Club decided to publicly proclaim its adherence to the suffrage cause, adopting the following motion on February 1, 1883: "That in view of the end for which the Toronto Women's Literary Club was formed, having been attained, viz., to foster a general and living public sentiment in favor of women suffrage, this Club hereby disband, to form a Canadian Woman Suffrage Association."[34] To implement this motion, a quite remarkable turnout of 130 women and men attended a meeting in the Toronto City Council Chamber and agreed to organize the Canadian Women's Suffrage Association, as well as a Toronto local named the Toronto Women's Suffrage Association; both endorsed equal suffrage as their major aim.

Discussions of female suffrage, and of suffrage more generally, took place at all levels of government in the 1880s. For four months in 1885, members of the House of Commons debated the content of a federal franchise law, the first for the new Dominion since the Canadian Confederation of 1867. These debates reveal much about conceptions of citizenship in this late-nineteenth-century white settler society. Should women, unmarried or married, be entitled to the vote? What about Aboriginal peoples? Or immigrants from Asia? The debates reveal a not insignificant degree of support among some politicians for the enfranchisement of some women. Indeed, the original bill (Bill 103) proposed that the vote be given to spinsters and widows of European origin who possessed the requisite property qualifications. Prime Minister John A. Macdonald himself stated this in the House:

> There is one question, however, in this Bill in which, personally, I may be considered to be interested, and that is women's franchise. I have always and am now strongly in favor of that franchise. I believe that it is coming as certainly as came the gradual enfranchisement of women from being the slaves of men until she attained her present position, almost the equal of man. I believe the time is coming, although we are not any more than the United States or England quite educated up to it, I believe the time will come, and I shall be very proud and glad to see it, when the final step towards granting women the full enfranchisement is earned in Canada.

Not only did Macdonald support the enfranchisement of unmarried women and widows proposed in Bill 103, he also went on record as personally supporting the enfranchisement of married women, a much more controversial proposal at the time. Yet despite the support voiced by the prime minister and certain members of the Liberal Opposition, the 1885 Franchise Act ultimately excluded all women from the category of persons; this law also denied the franchise to residents of Canada belonging to "the Mongolian or Chinese race" and to most of the country's Aboriginal peoples.[35]

Despite this failure at the federal level, the mid-1880s did see additional gains in Ontario in the quest for equality with men. For example, women were admitted to the University of Toronto (1884), and medical colleges for women were established in both Toronto (1883) and Kingston (1883). In 1884, the full municipal franchise was extended to unmarried women with the appropriate property qualifications, although they did not obtain the right to hold public office, and married women were once again excluded. That same year, however, Ontario passed a Married Women's Property Act giving married women the right not only to own separate property but also to deal with it—i.e., rent or sell it—without their husbands' consent. In addition, married women were for the first time allowed to enter into contracts with respect to their separate property.[36] In 1897, the Ontario law would be amended to permit a married woman to sign a contract whether or not she owned property, a provision that was a crucial condition of carrying on business independently. For many years, historians have argued that few married women actually owned property and that the impact of Married Women's Property Laws such as these was, therefore, limited.[37] However, recent scholarship suggests that Married Women's Property Acts in fact had far-reaching effects on women's capacity to participate in the "affairs of capital." Indeed, one historian argues that the series of Married Women's Property Laws passed in the common-law provinces in the last half of the nineteenth century in fact "enabl[ed] economic agency" on the part of unmarried as well as married women.[38] Moreover, it was not just in Ontario that women secured concrete gains in these years. In Montreal, for example, unmarried women and widows, both property-owners and tenants, were granted the right to vote in municipal elections in 1887, and the 1880s saw the municipal vote extended to propertied spinsters and widows in various municipalities across the country.[39]

Public service often led women to a deeper involvement in the political questions of the day. This development was facilitated by the movement toward more extensive organizational structures. In 1885 the national WCTU formalized an effective nation-wide structure. Moreover, the evangelical reform impulse had generated other socially concerned groups; by the 1890s, they, too, had been transformed into national organizations. An especially important example is the Young Women's Christian Association (YWCA), while the Girls' Friendly Society, an Anglican organization very much like the YWCA, was also prominent at this time. Both provided reception centres, shelters, and educational programs for single working-class women.[40] The varied objectives of these organizations capture the dynamism of the women's movement; together, they provided a range of opportunities for women who wished to expand their concerns beyond the home. Membership in such groups appealed to women at different stages of their life cycles. Those with young families and little free time tended to join local organizations focused on issues affecting children. As their family responsibilities diminished, women involved themselves with broader issues at the provincial and national levels. Letitia Youmans, for instance, waited until all of her stepfamily was grown before becoming heavily involved in the public domain. But she was unusual in having not just the approval but the active support of her husband, who eventually accompanied her on temperance lecture tours.

The YWCA, the Girls' Friendly Society, the missionary societies, and the WCTU all took a maternal or social feminist stance, imbued with a strong sense of Christian morality. The WCTU was the first of these groups to articulate both a social feminist perspective and the need for equal political rights in order to achieve its main objective. In Victoria, British Columbia, the local WCTU unsuccessfully petitioned for the provincial vote in 1883 and repeated the process with the same result in 1885. On the east coast, the Nova Scotian WCTU locals succeeded in pressuring their legislators to introduce a municipal suffrage bill in 1884. The bill failed, but three years later unmarried women were at last granted the municipal franchise; New Brunswick women had obtained this right the previous year. These suffragist initiatives of WCTU locals were always tied to

Inside the Ottawa Home for Friendless Women, 1895. Notice the young children in the basket on the table and the elderly woman in the forefront of the picture.

Source: William James Topley/National Archives of Canada/PA-027434.

evangelical goals. For some the evangelical vision was more compelling than the reform goals. Indeed, as Ontario WCTU President, Mrs. Chisholm, told annual-meeting listeners in 1887,

> I have sometimes feared . . . when all our efforts were turned to the legal side of the question, we were in danger of forgetting to be as earnest as before with the gospel part of our work. Therefore, I would urge again upon our Unions that more attention be paid to evangelistic work and more time given to gospel temperance meetings . . . the stated object of which shall be not only to induce men and women to sign the pledge but to take the first step in a new and better life.[41]

Pragmatism more than unquestioning adherence to any particular feminist philosophy probably guided most women activists. Between 1884 and 1893, the Woman's

228

Christian Temperance Union continued its educational and social service programs and intensified political activities through its national, provincial, and local organizations. In 1891 it formally endorsed woman suffrage at all levels of government. Repeated petitions, delegations to provincial and federal governments, and demands for plebiscites kept the question of votes for women before the public. This tireless work played a crucial role in bringing Canadians to accept the notion of political rights for women.

The Toronto-based Canadian Women's Suffrage Association, in the meantime, seems to have been relatively inactive in the second half of the 1880s, after a very energetic and effective first year. There are a number of possible explanations for this hiatus. Activists may have been temporarily satisfied with the real, though limited, gains that women had made. The leaders may well have felt the need to rest, to recharge their energies, and to plan future directions for the movement; Emily Stowe and her daughter Augusta Stowe-Gullen were both heavily involved in their professional lives at this time. In addition, according to Stowe, the presence of men sapped the organization of its vitality: "We admitted the opposite sex as members and the effect was demoralizing. The old idea of female dependence crept in and the ladies began to rely on the gentlemen rather than upon their own efforts."[42] Whatever the reason for the lull, the Canadian Women's Suffrage Association entered into a renewed phase of activity in 1889. Meeting in Emily Stowe's home, members agreed to engage Dr. Anna Howard Shaw, the eloquent American suffragist and preacher, to address a Toronto public meeting. The enthusiasm generated by this event led to the creation of a renewed and more effective suffrage organization, the Dominion Women's Enfranchisement Association (DWEA). Stowe was elected the group's first president.

Immediately after its founding, the DWEA took action, along with the Toronto WCTU, to support passage of a suffrage bill for Ontario sponsored by John Waters, an opposition member of the provincial legislature. Waters had introduced proposals to enfranchise women every year beginning in 1885, some aimed at extending the municipal franchise to married women, others at giving the provincial vote to unmarried women; it was clear that his efforts needed organized support. But although Emily Stowe was described as addressing legislators "in a style that would have done justice to an Oxford lecturer," the bill was defeated; Stowe commented tartly that she wished Attorney-General Mowat, who had voted against woman suffrage, had been "less the politician and more the Christian."[43] During its first year, the DWEA also mounted a lecture series to increase public knowledge about and sympathy for its causes, bringing Dr. Shaw back and ending with a stirring presentation by Susan B. Anthony. The success of this series convinced the DWEA that it could command broader support; it hired an American organizer to establish branch associations, and in 1890 it held its first national convention. A number of Canadian delegates from outside Ontario attended, as did several representatives of the American movement, but only a few branches were organized. The DWEA's national aspirations remained elusive. Like the earlier Canadian Women's Suffrage Association, it was Toronto-based, was directed and dominated by Toronto members, and never fully succeeded in the difficult task of organizing a nation-wide suffrage group.[44]

THE 1890S: CONSOLIDATION

In the 1890s the women's movement continued to pursue other political goals. Toronto feminists celebrated a notable success in 1892, when three women won election to the Toronto School Board as trustees. Arguing that education was of particular interest to women because of their maternal role, movement activists had evidently persuaded a larger public that women should participate in school management. The right was of particular interest to women teachers, who felt that female trustees would understand their problems and work harder to improve their conditions of work. One of the first women trustees was Augusta Stowe-Gullen. As a young woman she had participated in the discussions of the Toronto Women's Literary Club; she later became the first woman doctor to graduate from a Canadian medical college and the first woman staff member of the recently established Toronto Woman's Medical College. A founding member of the DWEA, she followed her mother as its president in 1903.[45]

The 1890s also witnessed a general broadening of middle-class women's reform aspirations and activities. The DWEA was one of the women's groups that supported Clara Brett Martin's struggle to become a lawyer. The passage of the 1892 Ontario statute permitting women to study and practise law in the province was greatly assisted by the cooperative efforts of mainstream women's groups; such cooperation was now more than ever characteristic of the women's movement. The flowering of reform interest led, in 1893, to the establishment of the National Council of Women of Canada (NCWC), an umbrella group that comprised representatives from national women's organizations. Affiliated Provincial and Local Councils of Women (LCWs) served likewise as umbrella groups for organizations operating within their communities, usually including branches of national women's groups, such as the YWCA, as well as local societies, such as women teachers' associations. The NCWC's major objective was to encourage and support the extension of women's domestic roles into the larger society, as its constitution made clear:

> We, Women of Canada, sincerely believing that the best good of our homes and nation will be advanced by our own greater unity of thought, sympathy, and purpose, and that an organized movement of women will best conserve the greatest good of the Family and State, do hereby band ourselves together to further the application of the Golden Rule to society, custom and law.[46]

The founder of Canada's National Council of Women was the indefatigable Lady Ishbel Marjoribanks Gordon, Countess of Aberdeen. Lady Aberdeen was elected president of the International Council of Women during its Congress at the Chicago World Fair in 1893. An enthusiastic and energetic supporter of reform causes, Lady Aberdeen was well known to many Canadian women reformers for her work on behalf of British women and children. She first visited Canada with her husband in 1890 and helped found the Aberdeen Association to provide reading materials for isolated settlers. Lady Aberdeen came to Canada for a longer stay when her husband was appointed governor

A meeting of the National Council of Women at Rideau Hall (the governor general's residence in Ottawa), 1898.

Source: Topley Studio / Library and Archives Canada / PA-028034

general in 1893. The Victorian Order of Nurses, first proposed by the Vancouver Local Council of Women, also benefitted from the sponsorship of Lady Aberdeen. This organization, established in 1897, provided visiting nurses for areas not served by trained medical help. Lady Aberdeen held the dual presidency of the Canadian and International Councils of Women until her husband's tour of duty in Canada ended in 1898. Devoting both time and money to the National Council's development, she remained a staunch supporter of its activities until the 1920s.[47]

Aware of the potential divisiveness of political and religious differences, Lady Aberdeen, with difficulty, got agreement at the outset that Canada's National Council would avoid activities or positions that allied it with any particular creed or political organization. Although personally sympathetic to woman suffrage, she refrained from publicly endorsing it so as not to alienate more conservative women. Largely through her influence, the National Council also adopted silent instead of spoken prayer in the hope of attracting Catholic, Jewish, and other non-Protestant women's groups while still remaining acceptable in an overwhelmingly Protestant society. Seven urban Jewish women's groups affiliated with the NCWC through locals in Hamilton, Montreal, and Toronto before the turn of the century, but they made up only three percent of the locals' membership. Although Catholic women constituted some five to ten percent of the membership, they also failed to join the NCWC in large numbers. Despite its official constitution as a non-sectarian organization, the NCWC and the majority of its members promoted and followed the strongly held religious beliefs of the Protestant middle-class majority. In the 1890s, especially at the Local Council level, religious or broadly defined moral or spiritual societies dominated the membership and policy development.[48] As with other women's groups, the impulse to convert people and to improve society under-scored the work of NCWC members and contributed substantially to the rapid spread of Local Councils.

But the decision against audible prayer so alienated the Methodist, Presbyterian, and Congregational women's missionary societies that they did not affiliate—nor did they accept the invitation to attend the NCWC's second annual meeting in 1895 as fraternal observers.[49] The NCWC's public non-denominational stance also lost it the immediate support of the Dominion Woman's Christian Temperance Union (WCTU), the largest nationally organized women's reform association at the time. Although the WCTU was officially non-denominational, its members believed that their Union and its causes were essentially and rigorously Christian, as their name stated. For them, silent prayer was an unacceptable denial of the need for an explicit religious commitment. The Dominion WCTU consequently refused to affiliate with the newly formed National Council, as did other Christian women's associations (including the National YWCA). As it turned out, however, the National YWCA eventually did affiliate in 1914, and the Dominion WCTU also did so in 1921; some local branches of the YWCA and the WCTU joined Local Councils of Women even earlier.[50] The early hostility between the Dominion WCTU and the National Council reflected in part the different origins of the two groups' leaders: the WCTU tended to draw on small communities and the middle- or lower-middle-class; the National Council, on the other hand, was led by upper-middle-class women from small towns and cities. Lady Aberdeen herself disapproved of some aspects of the WCTU, noting acidly in her journal, "They train their younger women to be so pain-fully aggressive and self-asserting on all matters & on all occasions. They are essentially *American*."[51]

Although the National Council had difficulty encompassing all women's groups, its organizational structure did create a nation-wide network for organized women's activities and communication. Within six years of its founding, in fact, seven Dominion-wide societies affiliated: the Victorian Order of Nurses, the Girls' Friendly Society, the Dominion Women's Enfranchisement Association, the Dominion Order of King's Daughters, the Lady Aberdeen Association for Distribution of Literature to Settlers in the West, the Women's Art Association of Canada, and the National Home Reading Union. Also, within six years, 23 Local Councils were set up in towns and cities from Charlottetown to Victoria. For example, the Winnipeg LCW, founded in 1894, affili-ated members of the Children's Home, the Women's Hospital Aid Society, the Central Woman's Christian Temperance Union, the Free Kindergarten, the Woman's Christian Union, the Young Women's Temperance Union, and the Lady Aberdeen Association.[52]

Once the basic structure was in place, local and national resolutions determined Local Council programs. Members discussed, studied, and recommended reforms relating to such diverse areas as dental and medical health, "pernicious" literature, truancy, prostitution, and the traffic in women and children (the so-called white slave trade), the provision of recreational facilities, and immigration policy. In some instances, they set up standing committees to examine a cluster of related concerns, as with the important committees on laws for the protection of women and children, and issues related to public health.[53]

For rural women, however, physical isolation created sets of problems and responses that were different from those of city women. Concern for their children, for themselves, and for other rural women, and a sense that rural problems also demanded political solutions drew rural women into new organizations focusing on their own particular needs. Such was reportedly the case for Adelaide Hoodless, whose youngest child died as a result of drinking impure milk. Galvanized to action, she determined to eradicate this common cause of infant mortality. Working initially through the YWCA in Hamilton, Ontario, Hoodless concentrated on the need for educational programs dealing with nutrition and sanitation. She soon became an influential advocate of public-school domestic science courses, pure-milk legislation, and the public health movement. Already familiar with the activities of the Farmers' Institutes, a government-supported organization aimed at male agriculturalists and designed to improve agricultural practices, Hoodless told an audience of Wentworth County women that they, too, needed an organization to promote their interests; she proposed an affiliated institute to foster homecraft and educated motherhood. Spurred on by this suggestion, the women established in February 1897 the Women's Institute of Saltfleet (Stoney Creek) as a separate, rather than an affiliated, organization. Its stated objectives were ambitious and optimistic, emphasizing the role of science in the home: "to promote that knowledge of household science which shall lead to the improvement in household architecture with special attention to home sanitation, to a better understanding of economics and hygienic value of foods and fuels, and to a more scientific care of children." Their goal was "raising the general standards of health of our people."[54] Although Hoodless was made honorary president of this first Women's Institute, she did not become involved in its work, concentrating instead on promoting school-based domestic science.

The Women's Institutes (WIs) spread slowly at first, hampered by the problems of organization within isolated rural communities and by the lack of money to hire qualified resource people. In 1900 there were still only three branches. Convinced by women's assiduous lobbying of the advantages that would accrue to rural society, the Ontario provincial government agreed to provide assistance in organizing WIs, including cash subsidies for hiring lecturers and demonstrators to teach courses in hygiene, nutrition, cooking, home nursing, and sewing. The response was overwhelming, and by 1903 there were 52 branches throughout Ontario, with a dues-paying membership of over 4 000. As their popularity suggests, the WIs met important needs for rural women. They also played a significant role in the early development of continuing education for adults, as branches extended their initial concerns beyond the farm home itself, seeking to improve rural schools, introduce preventive health measures for children, and set up cultural programs for both men and women in their communities.[55]

Other women reformers shared the Women's Institutes' interest in improving household management and child-rearing practices in accordance with Anglo-Canadian and middle-class standards. The National Council of Women had already resolved in 1894 to lobby for domestic science courses in the schools, an initiative designed not only to further women's education as so-called proper wives and mothers, but also to provide better-trained domestics for those who could afford them.[56] Similarly, during the 1890s the Woman's Christian Temperance Union expanded its plan for a "moral society" to include domestic science education and manual training.

All women's organizations of this period had an expanding and diverse range of reform interests. The WCTU, for instance, initiated what were referred to as social purity campaigns in the hope of ridding society of such perceived evils as prostitution and gambling, both of which all too often accompanied excessive drinking. Some carried such programs further, worrying about the effects of nude art or even of allowing young women and men to dance together in modern dances such as the waltz. Members urged mothers to protect their daughters from temptation for their own sake and in society's interest. By 1900 the WCTU boasted 26 different departments organized around separate issues but united in the belief that social reform could be achieved through female activism. Yet Prohibition remained a primary goal. The federal government's refusal to enact temperance legislation, however, prompted the WCTU to pursue its suffrage campaign with increased vigour.

THE TACTICS OF REFORM

Endorsement of suffrage as the means of achieving Prohibition quickly became part of the platform of the Manitoba WCTU, organized in the early 1890s by a committed group of Winnipeg women. This innovative group—which included Dr. Amelia Yeomans, journalist Cora Hind, and Mrs. J. A. McClung, a temperance advocate who was the future mother-in-law of Nellie McClung—staged the first mock Parliament in 1893, with the women taking roles for and against suffrage. The event forcefully demonstrated the absurdity of much of the opposition to female suffrage and received favourable publicity in the local press, as did a similar 1896 mock Parliament staged by the DWEA in cooperation with the Ontario WCTU. While these tactics did not result in legislation, they did serve to draw attention to the suffrage cause. In Manitoba, the renewal of publicity, fired by WCTU disillusionment with the negative legislative response to a Prohibition petition, led to the founding of the Manitoba Equal Franchise Club in 1894. The crucial factor in the founding of this, the first English-speaking suffrage organization west of Ontario, was the appointment of Yeomans as the provincial president of the DWEA. The Winnipeg-based club provided information and public education about women's political rights, although it cannot be described as having exerted a lasting influence.[57]

The Icelandic community in Manitoba generated one of the earliest expressions of pro-suffrage opinion. An Icelandic population was firmly established in the province by the 1890s, but it remained isolated from the Anglo-Saxon majority by its different

E. Cora Hind (1861–1942), Manitoba feminist, reformer, journalist, and teacher.

Source: (N978) Provincial Archives of Manitoba

language and culture. Another major distinction between the two communities was the role and status of women. The cultural, economic, and political participation of Icelandic women drew not only on a solid community base, but also on a long tradition of equal rights for women, including the right to vote. An active Icelandic Women's Society existed in Winnipeg as early as 1881. In that year, the Society staged a full-length play and held a tombola—a type of lottery—and other fundraising activities. The results were impressive. Records detail donations of $65 to the newspaper *Franfar*, $122 to school work by the Progressive Society, $87 to pay the tuition of two women attending a convent school, and $50 toward erecting a monument to Passion Hymn author Reverend Hallgrimur Pétursson. At the end of the year, $150 remained in reserve. One generous teacher, Gudrun Jonsdottir, contributed half her monthly wages of $15 to support the school work. Also under the Society's auspices, a regular column, written by various Icelandic women, began publication on January 16, 1890, in the newspaper *Heimskringla*. Not all Icelandic men supported the women's initiative: one critic called the articles "nonsense" and condemned the paper for their publication.[58]

Determined to secure in Canada the status that they had enjoyed before emigrating, Icelandic women mounted a sustained campaign. They formed suffrage associations, petitioned the legislature, and, in 1890, staged a debate on suffrage at the Icelandic settlement in Argyle. Margret J. Benedictsson became a major force in the Icelandic suffrage movement. Born in Iceland in 1866, and orphaned at age 13, she learned to care for herself. She emigrated in 1887 to North Dakota but subsequently moved to Winnipeg, where she studied shorthand and typing at business college. Between 1898 and 1910, Benedictsson and her husband, Sigfus, published a magazine called *Freyja* (Woman); its articles advocated political, social, legal, and economic equality for women. In 1908, Benedictsson founded an Icelandic suffrage association, *Tilraum* (Endeavour), in Winnipeg. A second society, *Sigurvon* (Hope of Victory), worked in Gimli from 1910. Despite a shared concern for temperance and contacts with the Manitoba Equal Franchise Club, Icelandic feminists remained relatively separate from the wider women's movement. Certainly, Benedictsson's outspoken views on women's rights tended to set her apart from many suffrage supporters.[59]

The difficulties of building a strong common front among women of different cultural backgrounds are further illustrated in the Quebec case. While the mainstream Manitoba suffrage activists appear to have made little effort to communicate or cooperate with Icelandic women, the very active Montreal Local Council of Women initially consisted of associations of both French-speaking and English-speaking women. It strongly supported suffrage from the outset. Local Council women struggled valiantly, if largely unsuccessfully, to open the professions and higher education to women, to effect urban reforms, and to abolish legal discrimination against women. Eventually, however, the francophone Catholic women involved in the Montreal Local Council came to find its British Protestant values unacceptable. Influenced by the Catholic feminism then developing in France and elsewhere in Europe, in 1907 Marie Lacoste Gérin-Lajoie, Caroline Dessaulles Béique, and Joséphine Marchand-Dandurand, all prominent leaders in French-Canadian society, founded a separate, explicitly francophone and Catholic

Marie Lacoste Gérin-Lajoie (1867–1945), Quebec feminist, self-taught legal expert, and founder of the *Fédération nationale Saint-Jean-Baptiste*.

Source: La femme canadienne-française. Almanach de la langue française. Montréal: Éditions Albert Lévesque, 1936, p. 46.

women's organization: the *Fédération nationale Saint-Jean-Baptiste* (FNSJB). All three of these women were born into upper-middle-class families and were socially and politically well connected; all were well educated, or at least well read; and all three married ambitious professional men, active in law and politics.

Organized along lines similar to the Montreal Local Council of Women and often collaborating with it on such matters as temperance, the *Fédération nationale Saint-Jean-Baptiste* linked the few existing French-speaking laywomen's groups and established three areas of concern—charity, education, and economics. Under the latter heading, the FSNJB sought to improve the plight of working women, and fostered the establishment of associations for store employees, factory workers, office employees, servants, teachers, and businesswomen. These associations also acted as mutual aid societies and provided members with religious support as well as technical and homemaking courses. The FNSJB could also frequently count upon the support of female Catholic religious orders—a support that these French-Canadian lay activists might not have enjoyed had they remained within the Local Council of Women. While the need for political rights was recognized by FNSJB members, who encouraged women to exercise those municipal rights that they had obtained, escalating opposition by the Catholic Church inhibited full support for suffrage.[60] Nonetheless, the "maternalist" outlook and activities of the FNSJB made it an association of its time, and many of its principles, including Catholic social action, were perfectly in keeping with the Christian feminism present in turn-of-the-twentieth-century Europe.[61]

An 1889 newspaper illustration of a Lady Bountiful distributing coupons to a working-class family in Montreal. The coupons could be exchanged for food or other household necessities.

Source: Une Visite chez les Pauvres, *Le Monde illustré*, no. 254 (16 mars 1889), p. 364. Courtesy of Bibliothèque nationale du Québec.

The role of religion in relation to women's public activities was also evident in the Maritime provinces. There, Protestantism provided the major outlet for female energies; women perhaps felt less need for involvement in reform causes, such as a major campaign for the vote, that would take them beyond the church. The relatively slow pace of industrialization and urbanization and the resulting small size of the urban middle class also likely limited the range of causes adopted by activist wives and daughters. Nevertheless, temperance, prostitute "rescue and prevention," and child welfare caught the attention of urban reformers in Nova Scotia, where WCTU locals actively supported suffrage from their formation in the early 1880s through the mid-1890s.[62] Leaders of the Halifax WCTU organized a Local Council of Women in 1893, which continued support for the cause. Their zeal and work for the franchise is shown by the annual doubling of pro-suffrage petition signatures from 3 000 in 1893 to between 6 000 and 7 000 the next year, and more than 12 000 names in 1895.[63] After 1895, interest in suffrage apparently waned in the midst of a wave of anti-feminist propaganda, much of it emanating from the Roman Catholic archbishop of Halifax. The evidence suggests that Halifax feminists did not abandon the suffrage question, but instead avoided confrontation by pragmatically shifting their emphasis toward achievable social reform goals (such as the organization of a branch of the Victorian Order of Nurses). These tactics enabled the Halifax Local Council to attract support, and eventually—in 1910, when progress appeared more likely—once again to endorse suffrage.[64]

Suffrage was also a topic on the mind of a New Brunswick–born Acadian woman teaching in Nova Scotia. Between 1895 and 1898, Emilie Carrier LeBlanc, under the pseudonym "Marichette," wrote a series of 13 letters about the lives and aspirations of Acadian women to *L'Evangéline*, the major French Maritime newspaper. An avowed supporter of temperance and of women's education, in a February 1895 letter Marichette addressed the question of the female franchise, punning on the Latin word *suffrager* to describe the suffering of Acadian women impatiently awaiting enfranchisement. And in March 1895 she supported women's claim to the vote with a witty and impertinent version of God's creation of Eve: "When He was making woman, He found Adam, 'le boss' of all men, dozing with the sun shining on his belly, too lazy to work in his garden. He ripped out Adam's brain and took the best stuff out of it and made woman, who has saved man from disaster." For Marichette, women were superior to men, and should have "worn the pants and governed the country."[65] Evidently her stance provoked *L'Evangéline*'s readers, editors, or owners, for within two months the paper editorially opposed woman's suffrage and announced its intention not to publish favourable views from other writers on the question. However, owing to Marichette's popularity, the newspaper did continue to publish her letters, in spite of their controversial content.[66]

The only recorded separate women's suffrage association to exist in the Atlantic region before World War I, the Women's Enfranchisement Association of New Brunswick, was organized in 1894 and articulated equal rights arguments to advance its cause. The provincial WCTU remained the major pro-suffrage supporter, basing its position on a social-feminist perspective that focused on women's special nurturing and domestic roles. These ideological differences prevented a close relationship between the two groups, while the Saint John Local Council of Women refused to support suffrage for any reason. The Women's Enfranchisement Association attempted to cooperate with both the Local

Council, of which it was an affiliate, and the WCTU. Increasingly frustrated by the Local Council's unwillingness to endorse woman suffrage, the Women's Enfranchisement Association developed its own political agenda. Between 1899 and 1902, it expressed support for equal pay for equal work and argued that there was a need for more collectivist approaches to social life, as well as for equality between men and women. The alienated Local Council responded by being outspokenly critical of such ideas at its 1902 annual meeting—a stance that precipitated the withdrawal of the Enfranchisement Association. That withdrawal, though it proved only temporary, was nevertheless evidence of the way in which feminist forces could disagree.

During the early 1890s, WCTU members campaigned for suffrage in Newfoundland as well. The issue was debated twice in the legislature and defeated on both occasions. The narrow base of evangelical support limited WCTU activities in this province, where suffrage did not re-appear as an issue until after World War I. In Prince Edward Island, even women active in the WCTU showed little interest in the question of suffrage. By 1900, the province had already adopted Prohibition; evidently, less radical tactics had succeeded in achieving WCTU members' most cherished goal.[67] The situation in British Columbia was very different. There suffrage and temperance reform remained closely linked. Until the formation of the Political Equality League in 1910, the only formal voice petitioning and supporting bills in the cause of suffrage was that of the anti-liquor lobby. In this respect British Columbia resembled Manitoba and Ontario, where temperance women continued to be the primary suffrage agitators between 1896 and 1905.

By the end of the nineteenth century, organized middle-class women had demonstrated their ability to perceive and respond to social problems in distinct ways. Although disagreements existed between individual women and between women's groups, a measure of unity was fashioned at the community, provincial, national, and even international levels. The WCTU, missionary societies of various denominations, and suffrage organizations affiliated formally or linked themselves informally with other organizations, such as the YWCA, Women's Institutes, and the NCWC, to take advantage of the power that came with organization and to break down the isolation of women in their homes. Together they moulded a lobby committed to reform.

The work of enrolling members and of developing organizations that dominated these years taught women the techniques of public speaking and of pressure politics. Although the provincial and federal franchises had yet to be won, a number of other political efforts bore fruit. Women became eligible to be elected to school boards, and could vote in municipal elections in many jurisdictions. Between 1872 and 1907, Married Women's Property Laws were passed in all the common-law provinces except Alberta.[68] In these provinces, a married woman's personal property, including her earnings, were at last her own.

Laws were also passed to help deserted wives. In Newfoundland, such legislation dated from 1872, and in 1888 Ontario followed suit, pegging assistance at $5 per week. Wives who left husbands who were cruel or who refused to support them were not eligible for the assistance because they, rather than the husbands, had technically deserted. Still, such laws were a beginning, and between 1900 and 1911, Manitoba, British Columbia, and Saskatchewan also passed laws designed to help women who had been abandoned by their husbands.

The legislation that women reformers lobbied for and won was designed to uphold the family and to protect women. This protection, however, did not extend to married Aboriginal women. In fact, under the 1876 Indian Act and its 1884 revisions, the federal government took away their property rights on reserves and severely restricted the inheritance right of widows.[69] For various categories of Euro-Canadian women, however—those who were married, those who had been deserted, those with earnings—the new laws constituted progress. They were also proof that organized women could indeed have a positive influence.

Activist groups never represented all Canadian women, but for those involved, they did provide a foundation for action and sisterhood. Although few organizations attempted to forge alliances across race, ethnic, or class lines, most were not completely unresponsive to the concerns of women different from their own members. For their part, some women excluded from these groups developed or joined organizations that better served their own communities. For instance, on the west coast, the Vancouver Island Committee of Coloured Ladies raised funds to assist former slaves. In Amherstburg, Ontario, the Black Women's Home Missionary Society was founded in 1882. Like other missionary associations, the Society afforded its members leadership opportunities and training and enabled some to undertake overseas conversion work in Africa.[70]

Despite differences in focus and size, and in the race, ethnicity, and class position of members, all of these organizations politicized, to some degree, longstanding concerns involving other women, children, the family, the church, and the community. By continuing to address these problems, reform-minded women found a respectable, acceptable rationale for their increasingly political activities and for the expansion of their fields of endeavour.

Notes

1. Letitia Youmans, *Campaign Echoes: The Autobiography of Letitia Youmans* (Toronto: William Briggs, 1893), 42.
2. Seth Koven and Sonya Michel, eds., *Mothers of a New World: Maternalist Politics and the Origins of Welfare States* (New York: Routledge, 1993); Molly Ladd-Taylor, *Mother-Work: Women, Child Welfare, and the State, 1890–1930* (Champaign, IL: University of Illinois Press, 1995); Theda Skocpol, *Protecting Soldiers and Mothers: The Political Origins of Social Policy in the United States* (Cambridge, MA: Belknap Press of Harvard University Press, 1992); Linda Kealey, ed., *A Not Unreasonable Claim: Women and Reform in Canada, 1880s–1920s* (Toronto: Canadian Women's Educational Press, 1979).
3. Naomi Black, *Social Feminism* (Ithaca, NY: Cornell University Press, 1989).
4. Deborah Gorham, "English Militancy and the Canadian Suffrage Movement," *Atlantis* 1, 1 (Fall 1975): 83–112; Gorham, "WSPU Deputation to Prime Minister Borden, 1912," *Atlantis* 5, 2 (Spring 1980): 188–95; Ian Tyrrel, *Women's World, Women's Empire: The Woman's Christian Temperance Union in International Perspective* (Chapel Hill: University of North Carolina Press, 1991); Margot I. Duley, *Where Once Our Mothers Stood We Stand: Women's Suffrage in Newfoundland 1890–1925* (Charlottetown: Gynergy books, 1993), 55–57, 77–78.

5. Nancy Forestell, "Mrs. Canada Goes Global: Canadian First Wave Feminism Revisited," *Atlantis* 30, 1 (2005): 7–20; Leila J. Rupp, *Worlds of Women: The Making of an International Women's Movement* (Princeton: Princeton UP, 1997).

6. Mariana Valverde, "'When the Mother of the Race is Free': Race, Reproduction, and Sexuality in First-Wave Feminism," in Franca Iacovetta and Mariana Valverde, eds., *Gender Conflicts: New Essays in Women's History* (Toronto: University of Toronto Press, 1992), 3–26; Vron Ware, *Beyond the Pale: White Women, Racism and History* (London; New York: Verso, 1992), espec. Part Three, "Britannia's Other Daughters: Feminism in the Age of Imperialism," 117–66; Janice Fiamengo, "Rediscovering our Foremothers Again: Racial Ideas of Canada's Early Feminists, 1885–1945," in Mona Gleason and Adele Perry, eds., *Rethinking Canada: The Promise of Women's History*, 5th edition (Don Mills: Oxford UP, 2006), 144–62.

7. Sharon Anne Cook, *'Through Sunshine and Shadow': The Woman's Christian Temperance Union, Evangelicalism, and Reform in Ontario, 1874–1930* (Montreal and Kingston: McGill-Queen's University Press, 1995), espec. 7–14.

8. E. C. Merrick, *These Impossible Women: The Story of the United Baptist Woman's Missionary Union of the Maritime Provinces* (Fredericton: Brunswick Press, 1970), 13–16.

9. Wendy Mitchinson, "Aspects of Reform: Four Women's Organizations in Nineteenth Century Canada," York University, Ph.D. Thesis, 1977, 69, 76.

10. Wendy Mitchinson, "Canadian Women and Church Missionary Societies," *Atlantis* 2, 2 (Spring 1977): 60–62.

11. Carlotta Hacker, *The Indomitable Lady Doctors* (Toronto: Clarke, Irwin, 1974), 68–69.

12. Ruth Compton Brouwer, *New Women for God: Canadian Presbyterian Women and India Missions, 1876–1914* (Toronto: University of Toronto Press, 1990); Rosemary R. Gagan, *A Sensitive Independence: Canadian Methodist Women Missionaries in Canada and the Orient, 1881–1925* (Montreal and Kingston: McGill-Queen's University Press, 1992); Margaret Whitehead, "'A Useful Christian Woman': First Nations' Women and Protestant Missionary Work in British Columbia," *Atlantis* 18, 1–2 (Fall/Winter 1992; Spring/Summer 1993): 142–66; Michael Owen, "'Lighting the Pathways for New Canadians': Methodist and United Church WMS in Eastern Alberta, 1904–1940," in Catherine A. Cavanaugh and Randi R. Warne, eds., *Standing on New Ground: Women in Alberta* (Edmonton: University of Alberta Press, 1993), 1–18; Valverde, "'When the Mother of the Race Is Free,'" 10–11.

13. Wendy Mitchinson, "The Woman's Christian Temperance Union: A Study in Organization," *International Journal of Women's Studies* 4, 2 (March/April 1981): 143–56.

14. Frances Willard, "Introduction," in Youmans, *Campaign Echoes*, 18; Suzanne M. Marilley, "Frances Willard and the Feminism of Fear," *Feminist Studies* 19, 1 (Spring 1993): 130–31.

15. Mitchinson, "Woman's Christian Temperance Union," 148–49.

16. Cook, *'Through Sunshine and Shadow,'* 13.

17. Youmans, *Campaign Echoes*, 106–7.

18. Cook, *'Through Sunshine and Shadow,'* 49–50, 147–53.

19. Wendy Mitchinson, "The WCTU: For God, Home and Native Land: A Study in Nineteenth-Century Feminism," in Kealey, ed., *A Not Unreasonable Claim*, 155.

20. Laure Conan, *Aux Canadiennes: le people canadien sera sobre si vous le voulez* (Québec: Imprimerie commerciale, 1913).

21. Jarrett Rudy, "Unmaking Manly Smokes: Church, State, Governance, and the First Anti-Smoking Campaigns in Montreal, 1892–1914," *Journal of the Canadian Historical Association*, New Series, 12 (2001): 95–114; Micheline Dumont, *Le féminisme québécois raconté à Camille* (Montréal: Éditions du remue-ménage, 2008), 21, 42–43.

22. Huguette Lapointe-Roy, *Charité bien ordonnée. Le premier réseau de lutte contre la pauvreté à Montréal au 19e siècle* (Montréal : Boréal, 1987); Jean-Marie Fecteau, *La liberté du pauvre. Crime et pauvreté au XIXe siècle québécois* (Montréal : VLB Éditeur, 2004); Micheline Dumont-Johnson, "Des garderies au XXIXe siècle: Les salles d'asile des Soeurs Grises à Montréal," *Revue d'histoire de l'Amérique française* 34, 1 (juin 1980): 27–55; Anne de la Durantaye, "Albine Gadbois (Soeur Marie de Bonsecours) (1830–1874)," in Maryse Darsigny et al., eds., *Ces femmes qui ont bâti Montréal* (Montréal : Les Éditions du remue-ménage, 1994), 93–95.

23. Dumont, *Le féminisme québécois raconté à Camille*, 15.

24. Jan Noel, "'Femmes Fortes' and the Montreal Poor," in Wendy Mitchinson et al., eds., *Canadian Women: A Reader* (Toronto: Harcourt Brace, 1996), 68–85; Marta Danylewycz, *Taking the Veil: An Alternative to Marriage, Motherhood, and Spinsterhood in Quebec, 1840–1920* (Toronto: McClelland and Stewart, 1987), espec. chap. 5.

25. Constance B. Backhouse, "Married Women's Property Law in Nineteenth-Century Canada," in Bettina Bradbury, ed., *Canadian Family History: Selected Readings* (Toronto: Copp Clark Pitman, 1992), 329–30.

26. Communication from Mary Jane Mossman.

27. *The Globe* (January 9, 1857), 1.

28. Backhouse, "Married Women's Property Law," 330–42; Lori Chambers, *Married Women and Property Law in Victorian Ontario* (Toronto: The Osgoode Society for Canadian Legal History and University of Toronto Press, 1997), chaps. 5 and 6.

29. Jim Bearden and Linda Jean Butler, *Shadd: The Life and Times of Mary Shadd Cary* (Toronto: NC Press, 1977), 160–61.

30. Allen P. Stouffer, "Towards a Redrawing of Nova Scotia Black History: A First Look at Mid Nineteenth Century Halifax," paper presented to the Canadian Historical Association, Ottawa, 1993, 5.

31. Elizabeth Forbes, *Wild Roses at Their Feet: Pioneer Women of Vancouver Island* (Vancouver: Evergreen, 1971), 27–28.

32. Forbes, *Wild Roses*, 7; Michael H. Cramer, "Public and Political—Documents of the Woman's Suffrage Campaign in British Columbia, 1871–1917: The View from Victoria," in Barbara Latham and Cathy Kess, eds., *In Her Own Right: Selected Essays on Women's History in B.C.* (Victoria: Camosun College, 1980), 79–100.

33. Edith M. Luke, "Woman Suffrage in Canada," *Canadian Magazine* 5 (1895), 330; Heather Murray, "Great Works and Good Works: The Toronto Women's Literary Club, 1877–1883," in Veronica Strong-Boag, Mona Gleason, and Adele Perry, eds., *Rethinking Canada: The Promise of Women's History*, 4th edition (Don Mills: Oxford UP, 2002), 103–20.

34. Luke, "Woman Suffrage in Canada," 330.

35. Veronica Strong-Boag, "'The Citizenship Debates': The 1885 Franchise Act," in Robert Adamoski, Dorothy E. Chunn, and Robert Menzies, eds., *Contesting Canadian Citizenship: Historical Readings* (Toronto: Broadview Press, 2002), 69–94.

36. Linda Silver Dranoff, *Women in Canadian Life: Law* (Toronto: Fitzhenry and Whiteside, 1977), 45–59; Backhouse, "Married Women's Property Law," 341; Chambers, *Married Women and Property Law in Victorian Ontario*, chap. 8.

37. For instance, Chambers, *Married Women and Property Law in Victorian Ontario*, 4, 12, 184.

38. Peter Baskerville, *A Silent Revolution? Gender and Wealth in English Canada, 1860–1930* (Montreal and Kingston: McGill-Queen's University Press, 2008). The quotations are from pages 9 and 14.

39. Dumont, *Le féminisme québécois raconté à Camille*, 33–34; Paul-André Linteau, *Histoire de Montréal depuis la Confédération*, 2e édition (Montréal: Boréal, 2000), 121; Strong-Boag, "'The Citizenship Debates'," 73.

40. Diana Pedersen, "'Keeping Our Good Girls Good': The YWCA and the 'Girl Problem' 1870–1930," *Canadian Woman Studies/Les cahiers de la femme* 7, 4 (Winter 1986): 20–24; Josephine P. Harshaw, *When Women Work Together: A History of the Young Women's Christian Association in Canada, 1870–1966* (Toronto: Ryerson Press, 1966); Mary Quayle Innis, *Unfold the Years: A History of the Young Women's Christian Association in Canada* (Toronto: McClelland and Stewart, 1949); Pedersen, "Providing a Woman's Conscience: The YWCA, Female Evangelicalism, and the Girl in the City, 1870–1930," in Mitchinson et al., eds., *Canadian Women: A Reader*, 194–210.

41. Annual Report of the Woman's Christian Temperance Union, Ontario (1887), 40.

42. Joanne Emily Thompson, "The Influence of Dr. Emily Howard Stowe on the Woman Suffrage Movement in Canada," *Ontario History* 54, 4 (December 1962), 259.

43. Thompson, "Influence," 260–61.

44. Catherine L. Cleverdon, *The Woman Suffrage Movement in Canada*, 2nd ed. (Toronto: University of Toronto Press, 1974), 22–26.

45. Hacker, *Indomitable Lady Doctors*, 26–35.

46. Veronica Strong-Boag, *The Parliament of Women: The National Council of Women of Canada 1893–1929* (Ottawa: National Museums of Canada, 1976), 81.

47. Strong-Boag, *Parliament of Women*, 131–46; N. E. S. Griffiths, *The Splendid Vision: Centennial History of the National Council of Women of Canada, 1893–1993* (Ottawa: Carleton University Press, 1993), 13–47, 65.

48. Beverly Boutillier, "Gender, Faith and the Ideal of Female Unity in Late Victorian Canada: The National Council of Women and the Silent Prayer Debate of 1895," unpublished paper, 1994, 7, 26 n. 14, 8.

49. Boutillier, "Gender," 28 n. 26.

50. Mitchinson, "Woman's Christian Temperance Union," 152–53; Strong-Boag, *Parliament of Women*, 78–79; Griffiths, *Splendid Vision*, 13–15.

51. J. T. Saywell, ed., *The Canadian Journal of Lady Aberdeen* (Toronto: University of Toronto Press, 1960), 258.

52. Griffiths, *Splendid Vision*, 14.

53. Griffiths, *Splendid Vision*, 13–47.

54. Ruth Howes, "Adelaide Hoodless," in Mary Quayle Innis, ed., *The Clear Spirit: Twenty Canadian Women and Their Times* (Toronto: University of Toronto Press, 1966), 114.

55. Terry Crowley, "Madonnas before Magdalenes: Adelaide Hoodless and the Making of the Canadian Gibson Girl," *Canadian Historical Review* 67, 4 (December 1986): 520–47; "The Origins of Continuing Education for Women: The Ontario Women's Institutes," *Canadian Woman Studies/Les cahiers de la femme* 7, 3 (Fall 1986): 78–81; Linda Ambrose, "'What Are the Good of Those Meetings Anyway?': Explaining the Early Popularity of the Ontario Women's Institutes," *Ontario History* 87, 1 (Spring 1995): 1–19.

56. Robert Stamp, "Teaching Girls Their 'God Given Place in Life': The Introduction of Home Economics in the Schools," *Atlantis* 2, 2, part 1 (Spring 1977): 18–34.

57. Cleverdon, *Woman Suffrage Movement*, chap. 3.

58. W. J. Lindal, *The Icelanders in Canada* (Ottawa/Winnipeg: National Publishers/Viking Printers, 1967), 160–61; Hrund Skulason, "The Battle of the Sexes," *Icelandic Canadian* (Winter 1975), 47.

59. Mary Kinnear, "The Icelandic Connection: *Freyja* and the Manitoba Woman Suffrage Movement," *Canadian Woman Studies/Les cahiers de la femme* 7, 4 (Winter 1986): 25–28.

60. Yolande Pinard, "Les débuts du mouvement des femmes à Montréal, 1893–1902," in Marie Lavigne et Yolande Pinard, eds., *Travailleuses et féministes: Les femmes dans la société québécoise* (Montréal: Boréal Express, 1983), 194–96; Le Collectif Clio, *L'histoire des femmes au Québec depuis quatre siècles*, 2e édition (Montréal: Le Jour, 1992), 361; Marie Lavigne, Yolande Pinard, and Jennifer Stoddart, "The *Fédération nationale Saint-Jean-Baptiste* and the Women's Movement in Quebec," in Kealey, ed., *A Not Unreasonable Claim*, 71–88.

61. Karine Hébert, "Une organisation maternaliste au Québec: la Fédération nationale Saint-Jean-Baptiste et la bataille pour le vote des femmes," *Revue d'histoire de l'Amérique française* 52, 3 (printemps 1999) : 315–44; Karine Hébert, "Le maternalisme, une solution féministe à la Crise? La réponse de la Fédération nationale Saint-Jean-Baptiste," *Bulletin d'histoire politique* 9, 2 (2001): 52–62; Dumont, *Le féminisme québécois raconté à Camille*, 30–47.

62. Margaret Conrad, "Recording Angels: Private Chronicles of Maritime Women, 1800–1950," in Alison Prentice and Susan Mann Trofimenkoff, eds., *The Neglected Majority: Essays in Canadian Women's History* (Toronto: McClelland and Stewart, 1985) vol. 2, 41–60; Judith Fingard, "The Prevention of Cruelty, Marriage Breakdown, and the Rights of Wives in Nova Scotia, 1880–1900," *Acadiensis* 22, 2 (Spring 1993): 87.

63. Luke, "Woman Suffrage in Canada," 335–36.

64. Ernest Forbes, "The Ideas of Carol Bacchi and the Suffragists of Halifax," *Atlantis* 10, 2 (Spring 1985): 119–26.

65. Pierre M. Gérin et Pierre Gérin, "Une femme à la recherche et la défense de l'identité acadienne à la fin du XIXe siècle, Marichette," *La revue de l'Université de Moncton* 11 (mai 1978): 22 [our translation].

66. Elspeth Tulloch, *We, the Undersigned: A Historical Overview of New Brunswick Women's Political and Legal Status, 1784–1984* (Moncton: New Brunswick Advisory Council on the Status of Women, 1985), 43; Pierre M. Gérin et Pierre Gérin, "Qui êtes-vous Marichette?" *Cahiers de la société historique acadienne* 8, 4 (décembre 1977): 165–72; Gérin et Gérin, "Une femme," 17–26.

67. Tulloch, *We, the Undersigned*; Duley, *Where Once*, 14–38; Cleverdon, *Woman Suffrage Movement*, chap. 6.

68. Susan Altschul and Christine Carron, "Chronology of Some Legal Landmarks in the History of Canadian Women," *McGill Law Journal* 21, 4 (Winter 1975): 476–94; Backhouse, "Married Women's Property Law," 337–45.

69. Jo-Anne Fiske, "Child of the State Mother of the Nation: Aboriginal Women and the Ideology of Motherhood," *Culture* 13, 1 (1993): 18.

70. Adrienne Shadd, "300 Years of Black Women in Canadian History: Circa 1700–1980," *Tiger Lily* 1, 2 (1987): 9–10; Shirley J. Yee, "Black Women as Community Leaders in Ontario, 1850–70," *Canadian Historical Review* 85, 1 (March 1994): 53–73; Sherry Edmunds-Flett, "'Abundant Faith': Nineteenth-Century African-Canadian Women on Vancouver Island," in Catherine A. Cavanaugh and Randi R. Warne, eds., *Telling Tales: Essays in Western Women's History* (Vancouver: University of British Columbia Press, 2000), 261–80.

CHAPTER EIGHT

The Dawn of the Century of Feminism[1]

> Many of the statesmen of the Anglo-Saxon race, who stand higher than
> their fellows, and scan the political horizon, see in the distance the sure
> coming of the enfranchisement of women. [. . .] Canadian women them-
> selves, until lately, have taken very little interest in this movement, and
> a few years ago, were, as a whole, antagonistic to it. However, at the
> present time almost every Canadian woman, who is at all interested in
> questions of the day dealing with education, philanthropy, or social life,
> is in favor of some form of woman franchise, either school, municipal,
> or parliamentary. This rapid change of opinion and its causes make an
> interesting study.

So wrote Henrietta Muir Edwards—feminist, activist, and one of the founders of the
National Council of Women of Canada—in 1900. Her confident reflections were published in a report entitled *Women of Canada: Their Life and Work*, produced by the
National Council of Women for the Paris International Exposition held that year. Funded
by the federal government, this was the first published coast-to-coast portrait of Canadian
women.[2]

As well as documenting women's status, roles, and conditions in both English Canada
and Quebec, *Women of Canada* set an agenda for mainstream women's reform activities
in the years to come. Its program for change was not stated in so many words; it was
implied by the careful chronicling of achievements and remaining challenges. Introducing
this survey of the organizations in which the Canadian woman "realizes the power of a
corporate life," the compilers signalled their confidence in organized, activist women. The
book reviewed women's group activities and problems in the legal and political realms,
the professions, trades and industries, education, literature, the arts, the churches, charitable and reform work, and social life. The biases of *Women of Canada* were those of the

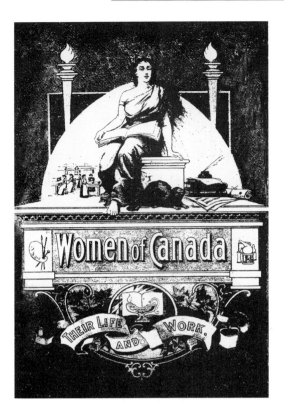

The front cover of the National Council of Women's report on the situation of women across Canada, published in 1900.

Source: Courtesy of the National Council of Women of Canada

individuals who made up the mainstream women's movement; they were also a reflection of the particular moment in which the book was published, during the South African War and at the height of popular imperialist sentiment. The brief historical sketch that opens the book ends with this sentence:

> In the 18th century Loyalist women relinquished their homes for love of a United British Empire; at the end of the 19th century their steadfast spirit animates the Women of Canada, who stand ready to make an even greater sacrifice to maintain the integrity of that Empire.[3]

Nonetheless, the book attempted to take into account all the women of Canada. The specificities of politics, education, and culture in Quebec, along with that province's Civil Code, received a great deal of attention, and a French-language version of the report, entitled *Les femmes du Canada. Leur Vie et leurs Oeuvres*, was published simultaneously.[4] Some attention was paid to non-Anglo-Celtic immigrants and to Aboriginal peoples; the book included a short essay by Mohawk poet Pauline Johnson (whose Mohawk name was Tekahionwake). What *Women of Canada* provided, essentially, were insights into the leadership of the mainstream Canadian women's movement and the themes that would dominate it over the next two decades.

The dawning of the new century stimulated many Canadians to assess—formally and informally—the country's past, present, and future. After half a century of collective endeavours, the time was propitious for Canadian women to reflect on their progress. Judging by sheer numbers and diversity of activities, women's organizations were a great success. Female reform groups representing a wide range of causes were thriving in urban and rural communities throughout the country. Alongside them existed a rich mosaic of women's cultural and artistic organizations dedicated to personal and communal improvement. Yet the optimism voiced by many Canadians at the start of the new century was not shared by everyone. While some suffragists believed that the tide of public support and legislative debate on the vote had turned in their favour, and that female enfranchisement was imminent, others expressed concern about the rising anti-suffrage voice and the conservatism of provincial and federal legislators.

THE FLOWERING OF THE WOMEN'S MOVEMENT

The vast majority of organized women belonged to local groups, frequently developed by local women themselves and devoted to improving the quality of community life. This was particularly so in the frontier areas of the nation. Mrs. McNeil of Leslieville, Alberta, is a case in point. When the McNeils arrived in Leslieville in 1907, most of the residents were preoccupied with homesteading. The determined Mrs. McNeil, convinced that her community needed a non-denominational church building, set about organizing local women. The women held a series of community bees at which the menfolk constructed the building while the women did finishing work, such as plastering and painting; the women also supplied the meals. When interest lagged at various stages of the construction, Mrs. McNeil rose to the occasion, one time mailing cards around and another, posting a placard that read "WANTED—1,000 men for a worthy cause! Payment— Virtue is its own reward." Mrs. McNeil got her church built, and the women's group continued as a spiritual, educational, and fundraising force in the community.[5]

Women's auxiliaries like the one in Leslieville proliferated across the country and became the mainstays of many churches, schools, and other community activities. Depending on their denominational affiliation, the women called themselves sewing circles, ladies' aids, mothers' meetings, or guilds. While designed to tend to the social and spiritual needs of their members, these groups also engaged in charitable work and did much to advance the material circumstances of their communities. Aboriginal women in Split Lake, Manitoba, for example, formed an Anglican auxiliary in 1913 to supply equipment necessary for their church and to cooperate with other women's auxiliaries in local and international mission work. Lara Bjarnason brought the pressing need for a home for the aged to the Ladies Aid of the First Icelandic Lutheran Church in Winnipeg early in 1901. The members began fundraising; by 1916, they had purchased a building and opened the Betel home in Gimli. Similarly inspired to serve their community's need, the Daughters of Israel in Saint John, New Brunswick, created and maintained the mikvah (ritual bath for women). Nova Scotian black women in the

Halifax Baptist church constituted themselves informally in 1917 as the "Women at the Well," with the purpose of supporting education for their community. In 1918, the African Baptist Association passed a resolution calling on every local church to organize a Ladies Auxiliary. And the Ladies Auxiliaries worked tirelessly to raise money for the Nova Scotia Home for Coloured Children.[6]

Already by 1900, clubs promoting social interests—the arts, handicrafts, drama, music, history—had been established in such great numbers as to occupy one-tenth of the 442 pages in *Women of Canada*. The founders in most cases had a particular interest or expertise in the arts and sought to extend their enjoyment and knowledge to other women in the community. A variety of cultural interests occupied Anna Leonowens, for instance, during the decade she spent in Halifax. A former teacher in the court of Siam (her story became the basis for Margaret Landon's book *Anna and the King of Siam*, and later for the musical *The King and I*), Leonowens organized a Shakespeare Club for young women as well as a book club, was a director of Halifax's Victoria School of Art and Design, and played a key role in the city's Local Council of Women.[7] By 1920, all major Canadian centres—and many of the smaller communities, as well—could take pride in a host of women's clubs devoted to the various arts and crafts.

In the first two decades of the new century, some Canadian women became more active in their professional organizations. As they made progress in such fields as teaching, journalism, social work, and public health, and began to make advances in medicine and law, their involvement in political reform also intensified. Toronto's female teachers, for example, formed a separate teachers' franchise club in 1909. Activity aimed at gaining the franchise also grew within the National and Local Councils of Women, culminating in the National Council's endorsement of suffrage at its 1910 annual meeting. The Council's philosophy evolved after 1900, and the organization less frequently justified its public involvement by citing the benefits of women's influence.[8] New and expanded suffrage undertakings, including visits by American and British suffrage leaders, also brought energy to the movement. The Dominion Women's Enfranchisement Association (DWEA) changed its name in 1907 to the Canadian Suffrage Association. One of the earliest groups to affiliate with it was the Icelandic Suffrage Association. In 1909, the Canadian Suffrage Association collaborated with the Woman's Christian Temperance Union (WCTU) in a monster demonstration at the Ontario legislature. A vigorous new group of progressive and professional members were attracted to the cause, along with members of the Toronto Local Council of Women, most of whom were wives of the city's leading businessmen.[9]

An unorthodox new participant in the Toronto movement, Flora MacDonald Denison, quickly made her voice heard. Born in 1867, she had spent her childhood and youth in impoverished circumstances. As a young woman, MacDonald taught school, worked for a Toronto insurance company, and then worked as a journalist in Detroit. After her marriage to Howard Denison in 1892 and the birth of a son, the family returned to Toronto, where Flora Denison worked first as a dressmaker, then as a *modiste* (fashion designer) for Simpson's, and eventually opened her own dressmaking business. By 1898, Denison was also writing for *Saturday Night*, frequently drawing on her experiences and observations of the sweated needle trades for her articles. In 1903, Denison met Dr. Emily Stowe, who introduced her to the Toronto women's movement and encouraged her to become actively involved in it. Within three years, Flora Denison held the post of secretary of the DWEA and was appointed the official Canadian delegate to attend the third World Conference of the International Woman Suffrage Alliance in Copenhagen. Denison increasingly expounded on her view of a widely democratic, egalitarian feminism. However, she adopted a position that was intensely critical of capitalist society and orthodox Christianity, a position that most women found unacceptable.[10] Denison's democracy did not, that said, extend to Canada's recent male immigrants. She labelled them "illiterate and often the scum of the earth" and complained that "in a few years they will be empowered to vote and make laws for the women of our land." In the use of such nativist stereotypes, Denison voiced opinions current among reformers that were openly used to press for women's rights.[11]

The majority within the small Canadian suffrage movement wanted to continue the cautious route of petitioning, issuing pamphlets, public speaking, and letter-writing campaigns. They argued for restraint and for the pursuit of other reforms in times of anti-suffrage hostility, moving toward more active pressure only when public sentiment seemed less hostile to female enfranchisement. By contrast, some of the new members, particularly Denison, increased tension by advocating more militant strategies for getting the vote. They were impressed by and sympathetic to the arguments, slogans, and strategies adopted by the Women's Social and Political Union founded in Manchester, England, in 1903. Led by Emmeline Pankhurst and her daughters, Christabel and Sylvia, the "suffragettes," as they were eventually labelled, conducted a militant campaign for votes for women: their tactics included heckling politicians, chaining themselves to fences, breaking shop windows, and resorting to arson. Like the majority of Canadian suffrage supporters, Flora MacDonald Denison initially rejected the tactics of the British suffragettes, labelling them "unwomanly" in a 1906 interview. However, the International Woman Suffrage Alliance conference that same year, which she attended, changed her mind. Speaking on her return, she explained:

> I am inclined to think that the press has woefully exaggerated the behaviour of the women who are not lunatics or fanatics, but earnest women anxious and willing to sacrifice themselves that the race may be benefitted and moved nearer to an ideal civilization of cooperative brotherhood and sisterhood.[12]

Denison's column in the *World* regularly and sympathetically reported the activities of the British suffragettes, and in 1909, Denison helped arrange for Emmeline Pankhurst to speak in Toronto. In 1913, at the height of the Women's Social and Political Union campaign of violence, Denison changed the name of her column to "Stray Leaves from a Suffragette's Notebook," becoming one of the very few Canadian women to identify herself publicly as a suffragette. The hostility engendered by Denison's open espousal of the British suffragettes' militant tactics led to a split in the Toronto movement. In 1912, members of the Toronto Local Council of Women founded a competing franchise organization, the Equal Franchise League. Unlike Denison, this group of women argued for the vote not as a natural right but as a means of achieving other necessary reforms. A letter in

Denison's papers suggests that some may also have been uneasy with her working-class background and connections.[13]

Hostilities and tensions among reformers were not new, however. Unity among women could be difficult to achieve, for reasons related to class, religion, race, ethnicity, rural or urban location, and philosophical and personal differences. The influx of large numbers of non–Anglo-Celtic immigrants, especially after 1896, heightened nativist concerns. The larger families, non-Protestant backgrounds, and higher birth rates of the newcomers often met with xenophobic reactions, as did immigrants' supposedly lenient attitudes toward alcohol. Some women activists were, in fact, strongly attracted to eugenics, which, at its most extreme, advocated selective breeding of the fittest and compulsory sterilization for those considered inferior.[14] Their aim was the "regeneration" of the "Anglo-Saxon" race, a cause that could only alienate those belonging to other groups.[15] Yet only a minority of reformers thoroughly supported eugenics; its premise that heredity determined all was contrary to their belief in social change and Christian perfection. Most hoped that, through education, conversion to Protestantism, and improvement of their social environment, immigrants' problems—or the problem of the immigrant—could be overcome.

Aggressive Protestant evangelical missions directed at converting the youth of Toronto's Jewish community in the first decade of the century sparked an immediate response. Ida Siegel organized a Hebrew Ladies Sewing Circle in 1906, the same year that the Presbyterian Jewish mission opened. Initially conceived to provide girls in the Ward (a working-class district of Toronto) with sewing skills and to distribute the clothing they made to the poor, the Sewing Circle soon expanded its efforts to counter the successful recreational programs of the Protestant missions. For example, the ladies organized a picnic for children on Centre Island and drew 200 participants. The next year, the largely East European group again enlarged its interests to include education, medical care, domestic assistance, and food for new mothers and infants—activities reflected in their new name: Hebrew Ladies' Maternity and Child Welfare Society. Expansion of the sewing school and girls' club continued, and in 1912 the institution added a library for those who wished to read in English. By then called the Jewish Endeavour Sewing School, it held classes after regular school hours and taught girls not only sewing but also Jewish religion, history, and Zionism. In 1913, 200 elementary-school girls attended.

The energetic Ida Siegel also arranged additional efforts through the local public school. She won permission for a Jewish girls' club to meet Saturday afternoons at the school. Siegel played on community concerns about idle children shoplifting in nearby department stores, and initiated the club's program to teach young Jewish girls values at an age earlier than the formal religious education available within the East European community. Members of a mothers' club also began to learn about child welfare issues. While all these efforts fostered Jewish cultural and religious identity, they also facilitated adaptation to Canadian life. Group leaders and teachers served as role models, and the groups provided a safe environment in which the participants could develop familiarity with English.[16]

Resistance to the evangelizing activity of the Methodist Woman's Missionary Society took a different form at the Chinese Rescue Home, founded in 1887 in Victoria, British

Columbia, to rescue, convert, and "civilise" Victoria's Chinese prostitutes or "slave girls." Over time, the Chinese clients developed strategies that enabled them to use the home only for services they valued—namely, child care and education. This shift led the mission to redefine its role and redirect its energies to concentrate on providing such services. The change in the institution's primary role was acknowledged when, in 1908, the WMS constructed a new building and named it the Oriental Home and School.[17]

Other groups of women who were excluded from mainstream associations or who were made to feel unwelcome there sometimes chose to form their own organizations. In Montreal, for example, African-Canadian women began to meet informally in 1900 for mutual support and friendship, the first known example of organized black women's solidarity in that community. Although the census recorded only 191 African-Canadians in Montreal in 1901, by 1902 the women had formalized their organization as the Coloured Women's Club of Montreal.[18] The members recognized that social agencies in the city were ignoring or overlooking the hardships and problems suffered by black families, especially by new arrivals from the West Indies. The Coloured Women's Club initiated a number of relief and benevolent services, providing warm clothing for newly arrived families, introducing them to the existing black community, and suggesting strategies for dealing with discrimination.[19]

In other instances, women had to decide whether their interests were best served in freestanding women's associations or in auxiliaries to male associations. Among the participants in the women's congress held at the annual Saskatchewan Grain Growers' Association (SGGA) convention in 1913, for example, "there was a great discussion as to whether they should become Homemakers' Clubs or evolve an organization of their own. The preponderance of opinion was that they should become a part of the farm people's organization and so strengthen the hands of all concerned."[20] In the end, they decided to create a Women's Section of the 10 000-member-strong SGGA, rather than join the Homemakers' Clubs, which were not exclusively farm-based. Violet McNaughton, who began organizing Women's Grain Growers Clubs after the convention, summed up the farm women's feelings about the Homemakers' Clubs: "They are doing splendid work, but are distinctly a women's organization; also, being under the government or university control, [they] are much restricted in their topics."[21] Despite the decision to organize separately within the SGGA, the new Women's Grain Growers Clubs developed a cooperative relationship with the Homemakers' Clubs.

A similar organizational perspective developed in Alberta. In a 1916 letter to McNaughton, Irene Parlby, president of the United Farm Women of Alberta (UFWA), an auxiliary of the United Farmers of Alberta (UFA), commented on the differences from the Women's Institutes:

> Their [Women's Institutes] line of work to tell you the truth does not interest me very much—there is too much of the housekeeping business about it, and . . . I think the farm women want to be taken out of their housekeeping troubles and made to realize there are other things of interest in the world, and that they do their housework all the better for thinking of outside affairs.[22]

Parlby's comments notwithstanding, the Alberta Women's Institutes (AWIs) attracted many women by offering them a reprieve from the isolation of farm life. Activities that extended beyond the domestic included educational programs designed to improve farm management and to expand their knowledge of political issues and legislation affecting women and children. Although some Alberta women joined both organizations, more opted for the AWI, which by 1920 comprised 265 institutes with a total membership of 13 150. At its peak in 1921, the UFWA counted 309 locals representing 4 536 women. Differences from the UFWA not noted by Parlby accounted for the AWI's larger numbers. First of all, it was open to all rural and urban women, while the UFWA restricted membership to wives and daughters of farmers. And the AWI was officially non-partisan, whereas the UFWA was the women's branch of the United Farmers, who formed the government in Alberta from 1920 to 1935.[23]

While the WIs accommodated city and farm women, rural/urban differences in various locales divided female social reformers. In response, the Winnipeg Political Equality League was founded in 1912 and subsequently renamed the Manitoba Political Equality League in 1913. Like its predecessor, the Manitoba Equal Franchise Club, it did not attract many members among rural women or women belonging to ethnic minorities. Rather, it appealed to urban Social Gospellers, who believed that the church should play a major role in eradicating the problems of cities, and saw women as an essential force for social and political reform. Progressive women's campaigns for temperance, social purity, improved public welfare, the franchise, and urban renewal meshed with the evangelical impetus to rid society of its imperfections.[24] Reformers were also joined by businessmen who supported a moral reform movement that would increase the respectability of their cities and so promote expansion and investment in them.[25]

Irene Parlby (1868–1965), Alberta feminist, suffragist, rural reformer, and politician.

Source: Glenbow Archives NA-273-1

The Manitoba Political Equality League's success in attracting male support and involvement is aptly illustrated in the most famous of the mock parliaments, the one staged at the Regina Walker Theatre in Winnipeg in 1914. Men were not only well represented in the audience but also participated in the entertainment itself. Presented the day after Manitoba Premier R. P. Roblin had rejected the suffrage petition of a women's delegation to the legislative assembly, the mock parliament was entitled *How the Vote Was Not Won*. To the tremendous amusement of all, this mock parliament, like its predecessors, forcefully exposed the sanctimonious and contradictory arguments used by male politicians to deny female suffrage. The curtain parted to reveal the women sitting at desks, posing as legislators receiving a deputation of vote-seeking men who were pushing a wheelbarrow full of petitions. The "Premier," the witty and well-known Nellie McClung, congratulated the men on their "splendid appearance" but told them that "man is made for something higher and better than voting":

> Men were made to support families. What is a home without a bank account? . . . In this agricultural province, the man's place is the farm. Shall I call man away from the useful plow and harrow to talk loud on street corners about things which do not concern him! Politics unsettle men, and unsettled men mean unsettled bills—broken furniture, and broken vows—and divorce. . . . When you ask for the vote you are asking me to break up peaceful, happy homes—to wreck innocent lives. . . .
>
> It may be that I am old-fashioned. I may be wrong. After all, men may be human. Perhaps the time will come when men may vote with women. . . . the man who pays the grocer rules the world.[26]

She was echoing the words and tone Premier Roblin had used when speaking to the suffragists the day before, and the crowd roared in recognition.

THE PUBLIC DEBATE

Mock parliaments were but one vehicle used by supporters of the suffrage cause to get their message across to the public. They—along with their opponents—also expounded on their views in lectures, sermons, books, magazines, and newspapers. One of the earliest and least-known contributors to the debate was Ontario schoolmaster Donald McCaig, who published in the United States a yawn-inducing 241-page attempt to rebut John Stuart Mill's *On the Subjection of Women*.[27] Better known was the Toronto journalist and former academic Goldwin Smith. In an essay entitled "Woman Suffrage" published in 1893, Smith acknowledged that some women's reform work was a logical extension of their mothering role, but argued that the exercise of political rights was men's business and quite inappropriate for women. Woman's enfranchisement would, he suggested, lead to "national emasculation" and the disruption of home lives, as spouses supported different candidates and fought over politics. Smith, who prior to coming to Canada had resigned his Cornell University post in protest against that institution's decision to admit women, claimed that women did not need the vote. They already had, he maintained, equal access to education and equal opportunities in the professions.[28]

Physician, former soldier, literary critic, and professor of the history of medicine at McGill University, Sir Andrew Macphail, too, worried about the consequences of women's inappropriate ambitions, writing in 1910 that "the fall of the race always comes through the woman. Tempted by the 'subtle beast' towards ambition and away from her appointed task, she puts forth her hand to attain a knowledge which is forbidden, and brings the disaster of obliteration. This is the curse of Eve."[29]

Half a dozen years later, Canadian economist and humorist Stephen Leacock expressed his own opposition to women's suffrage. He argued that woman's true and only role was motherhood, and that society should recognize and uphold women in this role. The problem was that society did not truly value or support women's work in the home or deal adequately with the visible fact of women's necessary dependency in a harsh and frequently uncaring world:

> Women need not more freedom but less. Social policy should proceed from the fundamental truth that women are and must be dependent. If they cannot be looked after by an individual (a thing on which they took their chance in earlier days) they must be looked after by the State. To expect a woman, for example, if left by the death of her husband with young children without support, to maintain herself by her own efforts, is the most absurd mockery of freedom ever devised.[30]

Many Quebec intellectuals also opposed female suffrage. Alarmed by the threats to family life posed by industrialization and urbanization, Henri Bourassa, a vocal and articulate French-Canadian nationalist and founder of the influential Montreal newspaper

This pro-suffrage postcard was reproduced in the *Grain Growers' Guide* on July 8, 1914.
Source: From *Grain Growers' Guide* (July 1914).

Le Devoir, condemned anything that ostensibly drew women's attention from the home, including the vote. The "woman-elector," claimed Bourassa in 1918, would soon give way to the "woman-conspirator," the "woman-who-illegally-votes-in-the-place-of-someone-else," the "woman-vote-buyer," then the "woman deputy," the "woman senator," the "woman lawyer," and finally the "woman-man," a "hybrid and repugnant monster" who would kill the "woman-mother" and the "woman-woman."[31]

Male anti-suffrage writers were not alone in their views. Their theories and arguments were echoed across the country and struck a chord not only in the minds of anxious men, but also in those of concerned women. Adelaide Hoodless was one of the women who were never persuaded that the vote was the answer to women's problems. She believed that women exerted their most effective influence on government through the education of their sons. Although she admitted a possible role for unmarried women in municipal affairs, she maintained that the role of the married woman was essentially domestic. She was convinced that "any girl or woman who has been brought face to face with the great truths presented through a properly graded course in domestic science or Home Economics in its wider interpretation" would never be found "in the ranks of the suffragettes."[32] Another notable female anti-suffragist was Clementina Fessenden, a Hamilton, Ontario, woman who devoted much of her life to her work for the British Empire. The founder of Empire Day, first celebrated in Ontario in 1898, Fessenden also established a chapter of the Imperial Order Daughters of the Empire, wrote histories of the Union Jack, and campaigned to raise monuments to the heroes of the War of 1812. In 1909 and 1910, she wrote a newspaper column entitled "Anti-Suffrage Notes"—possibly the only newspaper column in the country specifically dedicated to opposing the vote for women. In 1909, Fessenden attempted to create a Canadian branch of the British Women's National Anti-Suffrage League; it is unclear, however, whether she managed to recruit any members. She also sent countless letters to newspaper editors denouncing woman suffrage bills before the legislature. However, like many British anti-suffragists, Fessenden was not opposed to women exercising the municipal vote. Widowed in 1898, she herself voted in local elections, arguing that municipal affairs were essentially an extension of women's work in the home, involving matters such as public health and education. Her opinion thus differed from that of male anti-suffragists, such as Goldwin Smith, who saw the municipal franchise granted to unmarried women and widows as "the thin edge of the wedge."[33]

Advocates of the vote for women, like their opponents, could be found in all provinces. In general, the progressive press was supportive, and in some cases ran separate women's columns addressing the need for improving women's status. The *Manitoba Free Press*, for example, devoted articles to these concerns from at least 1890. The existence of separate women's columns facilitated both the debate on women's issues and the emergence of women journalists, such as Francis Beynon and Isabel Graham, who tended to be strong advocates of reform. Labour, farm, and socialist newspapers also provided a forum for discussing the unequal treatment of women. The *Grain Growers' Guide* actively promoted suffrage, along with a host of other feminist reforms, including reformed dower law and improved homesteading, property, and guardianship rights for women.

Men in western Canada appear to have been relatively sympathetic to the suffrage cause. Dissatisfaction with government policies toward farmers was strong, and female suffrage would have strengthened the farm vote: this motivation probably affected both men and women in the Prairie provinces. It is also possible that western men were aware of the pioneering efforts of their spouses, regarding them as equal partners entitled to the vote. It seems more likely that some men, at least, were responding to women's perceived role as moral and spiritual guardians of the home, who would use the vote for reforms essential for the maintenance of a stable social order. Certainly, this was the motivation of the supporters of temperance and, more widely, of the Social Gospellers.

The possible influence of the massive and relatively recent immigration into the Prairie provinces should also be noted. The experience of resettlement may itself have played some liberating role, as may have the fact that a significant number of western settlers came from those American states where women had already won the vote. Finally, there is the less positive influence of nativism. There was growing prejudice against the non–Anglo-Saxon immigrants, accompanied by concern about purchase and manipulation of votes. Some were offended that illiterate foreign men could vote, while relatively well-educated Anglo-Saxon women could not. But whatever their motivation, many rural western men, individually and collectively—through such organizations as the United Farmers of Alberta and the Saskatchewan Grain Growers' Association, and through newspapers like the *Grain Growers' Guide*—vigorously supported the suffragist efforts.[34] At the same time, some of these men adamantly opposed granting equal property rights to women; dower right, for instance, had been abolished in the Northwest Territories in 1886.

For its part, organized labour was ambivalent in its support for suffrage. And when it was supportive, it generally equated the franchise with workers' rights. Labour newspapers emphasized the need to increase the power of labour generally, and also hoped that working-class women might help elect a labour government and bring about reforms that organized labour endorsed. Beginning in 1916, constant support for women's rights generally and female suffrage in particular was to be found in the Trades and Labour Congress–affiliated *Le Monde Ouvrier*, in which Montreal feminist journalist Éva Circé-Côté published a weekly column under the masculine pseudonym Julien Saint-Michel. For over 20 years, Julien Saint-Michel reiterated "his" support for female suffrage at the federal and provincial levels, buttressing "his" position with both equal rights and maternalist arguments.[35]

Socialist writers, too, discussed a variety of women's issues in the press. *Cotton's Weekly*, a socialist newspaper published in the eastern townships of Quebec, included columns in its first year (1908–1909) on the problems of working women, as well as on what it called women's emancipation and the problems of women in the home. Its columns addressed prostitution, sexuality, and even free love. The paper strongly supported suffrage, and advocated both socialist and feminist activism to bring it about. On the other hand, the Socialist Party of Canada and its newspaper, the *Western Clarion*, displayed considerable reluctance regarding both suffrage and the so-called woman question, arguing that the task of replacing capitalism should take precedence over addressing women's issues.[36]

Socialist Party women did, however, press their issues and interests. At the first convention of the Ontario section in 1908, delegates brought the question of women's suffrage to the floor. One of the women present was Sanna Kannasto, whom the party approved as its first paid organizer for the Finnish Socialists. Although still in her twenties at the time, Kannasto already had an established reputation as a speaker, writer, and organizer in the United States. Touring northern Ontario, she tirelessly recruited members in the distant mining towns, rural villages, and lumber camps. Where possible, she arranged additional separate meetings for women, at which she encouraged and facilitated the formation of women's groups, explored questions on women's role in socialism, and provided information and opinion on marital concerns and birth control. Sanna Kannasto's efforts met with some success. By the summer of 1913, 562 women had become members of the party, while many others had been influenced by Kannasto's tours and the resultant women's groups. One measure of the influence exercised by Kannasto is the attention she attracted from the RCMP. Officers closely monitored her activities, labelled her a "dangerous radical," and recommended her deportation. In 1920, following her arrest while on a speaking tour in western Canada, Kannasto wrote from jail: "I am not nervous, I am made of iron, I have not shed a single tear, although I have been in cruel cross-examinations. Despite everything, I am happy and I try to joke and keep up the humour with my prison guards."[37]

The gruelling pace of organizational work, agitation, and travel took its toll on the woman made of iron, however, contributing to the end of her common-law relationship. Increasing police harassment, added to the time and attention demanded by motherhood, led Kannasto to reduced activity after the birth of her children and eventually to retirement.[38]

The development of a separate women's press heightened publicity for the causes espoused by women. *Le coin du feu*, for instance, was founded by well-known Montreal feminist and *femme de lettres* Joséphine Marchand-Dandurand in 1893. Although the publication lasted only three years, it enjoyed considerable success and an enthusiastic female readership. *Le Journal de Françoise*, founded by Montreal journalist Robertine

Finnish women in Northern Ontario march for voting rights.

Source: Lakehead University Library Archives

Barry, was a bimonthly newspaper published between 1902 and 1909, aimed at female readers and consisting of news, features, regular columns, poetry, and literature.[39] Likewise, the Icelandic women's paper *Freyja*, and British Columbia's *The Champion*, produced by and for women, were completely devoted to an examination of the major issues facing women. In addition, most of the women's organizations had papers, bulletins, or reports that were widely distributed.

Female supporters of suffrage continued to move easily between various reform causes. Nellie McClung worked for Prohibition, factory laws for women, compulsory education, prison reform, and changes to the existing laws affecting women and children; it was to effect reforms in these areas that she and other feminists fought so hard to get the vote. Born in Ontario's Grey County in 1873, McClung participated in the Ontario migration to the west, moving with her family to Manitoba in 1880, and later as an adult to Alberta and British Columbia. By the time she reached her forties, McClung, the mother of five children, had become a bestselling author of socially conscious novels, and a rip-roaring public speaker.[40] Rooting her approach in social feminism, McClung explained women's public role in terms of their special capacity as women. Addressing the argument that politics were too corrupt for women, she retorted,

> What would you think of a man who would say to his wife: "This house to which I am bringing you to live is very dirty and unsanitary, but I will not allow you—the dear wife whom I have sworn to protect—to touch it. It is too dirty for your precious little white hands! You must stay upstairs, dear. Of course the odor from below may come up to you, but

Robertine Barry (1863–1910), also known as "Françoise," a well-known Quebec writer, journalist, and feminist.

Source: Public Domain

use your smelling salts and think no evil. I do not hope to ever be able to clean it up, but certainly you must never think of trying."

. . . Women have cleaned up things since time began; and if women ever get into politics there will be a cleaning-out of pigeon-holes and forgotten corners, on which the dust of years has fallen, and the sound of the political carpet-beater will be heard in the land.[41]

McClung was similarly comfortable advocating women's right to participate equally with men in the political realm, and frequently voiced the equal rights appeal to plain justice:

We went there to the Manitoba Legislature asking for plain, common justice, an old fashioned square deal, and in reply to that we got hat-lifting. I feel that when a man offers hat-lifting when we ask for justice we should tell him to keep his hat right on. I will go further and say that we should tell him not only to keep his hat on but to pull it right down over his face.[42]

Nellie McClung saw no contradiction between arguments based on women's special attributes and arguments appealing to simple justice. Women and men, she believed, were

Left to right: suffragists Nellie McClung, Alice Jamieson, and Emily Murphy. Jamieson was one of Canada's first women judges.
Source: Image HP39854 courtesy of Royal BC Museum, BC Archives.

different but equal. A particularly vibrant personality, McClung has come to epitomize both the strengths and weaknesses of what historians have long called the "first wave" of Canadian feminism. Her devotion to the rights of women was tireless; yet like many of her contemporaries, she espoused racial stereotypes and eugenic concerns.[43]

WORKING FOR LEGAL CHANGE

The campaign for legal reform gained momentum in the second decade of the twentieth century. The laws relating to property continued to be a concern everywhere, but were particularly in need of reform in the Prairie provinces, where women were still largely excluded from homesteading rights. No longer protected by dower law, they had no control over the disposal or use of family property, and widows had no legal guarantee of inheritance. The *Grain Growers' Guide*'s women's section articulated and actively promoted the public demand and campaign for dower laws. The first success came in 1910, partly through the efforts of writer and reformer Emily Murphy: Alberta legislators passed the Married Women's Relief Act, which entitled a widow to receive through the courts some part of her husband's estate if he had not adequately provided for her. However, dower law supporters intensified their campaign, insisting that women's claims to family property be legally recognized as rights not subject to the discretionary decision of a husband or judge. Farm women's concern for this question brought many of those who sought property and homesteading reform to support the right to vote; farm women's and suffrage organizations worked in common. When travelling on the Prairies in 1913–14, Scottish suffragist Elizabeth B. Mitchell described the link between the two issues, observing that the

> special trouble which has turned the prairie women's minds to politics is connected with the land. The woman so obviously shares with her husband in making the "improved farm" . . . that it is felt to be an injustice that this product of their joint labour becomes the sole property of the man.[44]

Between 1910 and 1919, all three Prairie provinces passed legislation guaranteeing wives' inheritance rights and restricting a husband's ability to sell or mortgage property without his wife's consent.[45] It seems clear, however, that the purpose of this legislation was to regularize credit relationships, rather than to recognize wives as equal partners with their husbands. Consent was not required for the husband to sell or dispose of farm equipment, livestock, seed, furniture, or any item other than the family home. Nor did the law acknowledge the contributions of separated or divorced wives who were forced to leave the farm.[46]

The law governing homesteading was an even harder nut to crack. The Homestead Act provided that all men, but only some women—widows and deserted, separated, and divorced women with dependants under the age of 21—had the right to homestead, entitling them to free legal title to frontier lands when they met specified conditions. The movement for reform to allow wives and unmarried women homestead rights began as sporadic, uncoordinated protests in a number of communities. The issue was eventually taken up by two influential activists, Georgina Binnie-Clark and Isabel Beaton Graham. Graham, who emigrated west from Ontario with her husband in 1885, was a founding member of the Winnipeg Women's Press Club, honorary secretary of that city's Women's Canadian Club, and women's editor of the *Grain Growers' Guide* from 1909 to 1911. Her November 1909 column featured a theoretical and practical discussion with Georgina Binnie-Clark on women's right to homestead. Binnie-Clark, a British journalist turned prairie wheat farmer, was the most prominent advocate of equality in homestead laws, and through her two books, *A Summer on the Canadian Prairie* and *Wheat and Woman*, the major publicist of this cause.[47] Although some western men supported the extension of homesteading rights to wives and unmarried women, the campaign for this reform encountered strong, highly organized, and politically influential opposition. In 1912, for example, delegates to the annual meeting of the Saskatchewan Grain Growers' Association rejected a motion to extend homesteading privileges to women. The battle continued unresolved until the 1930s, when control of public lands passed from the federal to the provincial governments. Manitoba and Saskatchewan then eliminated homestead rights for everyone; Alberta drew up its own legislation allowing "every person" who met specific conditions the right to obtain a homestead.

Important legal battles were also fought in the early twentieth century in British Columbia. Such leaders as Helen Gregory MacGill studied, discussed, and lobbied for improvements in family law affecting the lives of women. Born to an elite family in 1864 in Hamilton, Ontario, Helen Gregory graduated from Toronto's Trinity College with Bachelor of Music, Bachelor of Arts, and Master of Arts degrees. She became a journalist, and while travelling across the Prairies met and married her first husband. Pregnant and with a broken leg, she continued to Japan on her own to complete a newspaper assignment. After her return, she lived with her husband in San Francisco and subsequently Minnesota. When her husband died, she was left to support two young sons and her mother. Two years later, Helen married lawyer James MacGill, and by 1901 they had settled in Vancouver. There, as she had in San Francisco and Minnesota, she involved herself in women's organizations, including the Women's Musical Club, the Vancouver Women's Press Club, and, most important, the University Women's Club. In working with and for other women, Helen Gregory MacGill followed a family tradition established by her mother and grandmother. Her daughter and biographer, Elsie MacGill, recalled this: "In each new society [i.e., community] a compulsion forced her to work toward a particular goal of her own, the radix of the force being that disturbing thrust of intellect that had pushed her into Trinity, over to Japan, into writing, publishing, crusading."[48] In British Columbia, that goal came to be the protection and improved status of women and children. In 1912, with the backing of the Vancouver University Women's Club, MacGill produced a booklet outlining the inequities women faced before the law. British Columbia became the first province to enact an equal guardianship and custody law in 1917, giving mothers the same rights as fathers with respect to their children. Later the same year, the province established a juvenile court and appointed MacGill as one of its first two magistrates.

The plight of paid women workers was another focus of attention in British Columbia. Low wages, long hours, and miserable working conditions motivated suffrage and labour activist Helena Rose Gutteridge to work to unionize women and to demand improved conditions. This militant British suffragette, socialist, and Labour Party member arrived in Vancouver in 1911 and quickly immersed herself in reform activities. Gutteridge helped organize city laundry and garment workers, took a prominent role in the Vancouver Trades and Labour Council, and campaigned for the minimum wage for women as well as pensions for mothers left without other means of support. The passing of a 1918 law restricting hours of work for women was, in part, the result of her efforts. Similar campaigns to ameliorate women's working conditions were continuing in other provinces, and by 1920 a variety of further protective measures for female employees had been legislated in the Maritimes, Ontario, Quebec, and the Prairies.[49]

Hand-in-hand with British Columbia women's interest in legal and labour law reform went a renewed commitment to suffrage. From its founding in 1911, the provincial Political Equality League organized delegations, circulated petitions, and ran public meetings.[50] It garnered support from various men's and women's organizations, including the British Columbia Federation of Labour, the Local Option League, the WCTU, and the provincial opposition Liberal Party, but could not unite all political rights reformers. After 1911, a variety of more radical but short-lived suffrage associations appeared in the province. One in particular, Helena Gutteridge's British Columbia Woman's Suffrage League, objected to the Political Equality League on the grounds of its conservatism, its failure to involve working-class women, and its use of exclusively maternalist arguments. The aims of Gutteridge's group extended beyond obtaining the vote to dealing "with all matters connected with the interests of women, particularly those things that affect women out in the labour market."[51]

While support for women's suffrage in British Columbia appeared to grow, women activists in the Maritime provinces continued to struggle against a current of strong anti-feminist sentiment. Although sporadic attempts to raise the franchise question continued to come from WCTU or Local Council women in all three provinces, the separate suffrage associations floundered. Internal division apparently crippled the cause in New Brunswick, where there is no evidence of activity by the Women's Enfranchisement Association between 1903 and 1907. Revitalized in 1907, the Association began to work for the passage of a suffrage bill drawn up by one of its own members, Mabel French, New Brunswick's first female lawyer. In this effort and subsequent ones, the women met with increasingly overt mockery, insult, and even sexual harassment from some provincial legislators. The presence in 1909 of seven suffrage supporters at a hearing by the legislative Committee of the Whole on a bill to enfranchise unmarried women was responded to by catcalls of "Help" and "Police," the ringing of the division bells, and open laughter at a coarse "verse" directed at the women. Despite this public abuse, the Local Council of Women and the Sons of Temperance endorsed suffrage in 1910, and a well-publicized visit to Saint John was made in 1912 by British suffragette Sylvia Pankhurst.[52]

The same year saw the establishment of an Equal Franchise League in Moncton, and the publication by the Saint John *Globe* of a cogent letter to the editor, simultaneously rebuffing the abusive legislators and aggressively supporting equal political rights for women. The writer of the letter, Ella Hatheway, secretary-treasurer of the Women's

Enfranchisement Association and wife of a sympathetic member of the legislature, recalled the appalling treatment of the 1909 delegation, of which she had been part, and outlined the similarly uncouth reaction she had encountered when an attempt was made to introduce a bill in 1912. Insisting that women refused to be intimidated and would never abandon their just cause, she went on to outline her reasoning:

> The woman suffrage movement, the world over, has broadened and intensified during the past year. In no way is this shown more than in the growing demand from women that they shall no longer be regarded by men as sex beings, but as human beings; that they shall be recognized, politically and economically, as persons, not as females merely.[53]

In Nova Scotia, the local newspapers' prominent coverage and condemnation of the growing violence of the suffragettes in England inhibited overt suffrage support. Following the defeat of the suffrage bills in the 1890s, the movement's leaders had made a pragmatic decision to pursue other reform work through the Local Council of Women until some later date when, as leader Eliza Ritchie put it, "the time was ripe" for a return to explicit suffrage activities.[54] Certainly there was plenty to be done, and Local Council members had used their time and energy to advocate and advance a number of reform programs. Beginning in 1908, for example, they lobbied local and provincial authorities, and later the federal Royal Commission on Technical Education, for the establishment of a vocational school to train women for a variety of industrial occupations. Halifax Local Council women also engaged in a major public health campaign. They raised funds for the Victorian Order of Nurses through tag days, formed an anti-tuberculosis league, and educated the public about the causes and prevention of infant mortality. Through such activities they hoped to dispel public criticism of the women's movement, and particularly that coming from the city's Catholic clergy.[55]

The lack of separate suffrage organization and activity in Prince Edward Island during the first two decades of the twentieth century may have similarly stemmed from women's concentration on alternative reform work; or the winning of Prohibition may have taken the wind out of the reformers' sails. The only documented motion in favour of the franchise was passed in 1913 at the regional WCTU convention in Summerside. Otherwise, women activists in Prince Edward Island appear to have maintained a discreet silence on the subject. In Newfoundland, no separate suffrage activity existed until the founding of the Newfoundland Women's Franchise League in 1920.[56]

Like women in the Atlantic provinces, Quebec's female activists experienced a severe anti-feminist backlash prior to the Great War. At the turn of the century, French-Canadian lay and clerical elites increasingly responded to urban industrial growth, social dislocation, growing Anglo–American influences, and new public initiatives by women with an aggressive, conservative nationalism. In their blueprint for a better society there was no place for the "new woman." Yet, in fact, concerned nationalists, the leaders of the Catholic Church, and the emerging lay feminist organizations were all addressing, albeit in different ways, perceived threats to the social order and its basic unit, the French-Canadian Catholic family. In some cases, they cooperated in social, charitable, and educational action; but, with increasing frequency, both lay nationalists and church leaders allied themselves against feminism in any form. French-Canadian women's organizations nevertheless persevered.[57]

The founding of the *Fédération nationale Saint-Jean-Baptiste* (FNSJB) in 1907 provided francophone women's associations with a united voice and a public alliance with their sisters in the convents. By most standards, the FNSJB's feminism was not particularly radical; it adhered relatively closely to the tenets of the Christian feminism emerging in early twentieth-century Europe and its principles and activism are probably best described as "maternalist."[58] Nonetheless, it very successfully coordinated the efforts of Catholic women to improve Quebec society. Members' and affiliated groups' activities before the First World War were diverse. Some, for example, set up commercial, technical, and household science classes; others addressed the problems of factory women, establishing sickness and mutual aid funds, employment bureaus, and boarding houses for working women. Partly as a result of FNSJB work, by 1914 Quebec women teachers' pensions had improved, factory lighting had improved, pure milk depots or *gouttes de lait* had been established to reduce rampant infant mortality, and legislation had been passed making it mandatory to provide female store clerks with chairs. Perhaps the FNSJB's greatest contribution, however, was in uniting with the sisters of the *Congrégation de Notre-Dame* to achieve in 1908 the establishment of the *École d'enseignement supérieur*, the first institution in Quebec to offer higher education to francophone women.[59]

There was little explicit franchise activity in Quebec's francophone community prior to the First World War. It was the members of the anglophone Montreal Local Council of Women who founded the Montreal Suffrage Association in 1913. Their major efforts were educational, involving the distribution and sale of literature about suffrage and about the legal inequities affecting women.

WOMEN'S ORGANIZATIONS AND THE FIRST WORLD WAR

By the time the First World War broke out in 1914, Canadian women had organized around a remarkable number of social, political, cultural, and economic issues. Overlapping memberships in women's associations were common, and female voluntary organizations frequently adopted and supported each others' causes. Involvement in specific social reforms often seemed to lead individual women into a broad reform program.

Emily Murphy was an excellent example of this progression. The daughter of a well-to-do Ontario family, Murphy married a popular preacher. By 1910 she had settled with her husband in Edmonton and was beginning to find her niche as a journalist and popular novelist, known to her large public as "Janey Canuck." In addition to an active participation in the Canadian Women's Press Club, the effervescent Murphy lent her name, acumen, and energy to the cause of reform. She worked to establish a local Victorian Order of Nurses, police courts for female offenders, public playgrounds, and municipal hospitals, as well as the right for women to be elected as school trustees in Edmonton. Campaigns for a provincial dower law and tuberculosis prevention also occupied her attention, as did provincial and national drives for suffrage. During the war years she added to her list of activities the registration of female wartime volunteers, and participation in the War Council of Women. Like other social feminists, Murphy based her claim for equality on arguments about women's moral superiority. As an Edmonton magistrate, her treatment of young female offenders was sometimes unsympathetic. Her drive to control moral depravity also led Murphy to echo the racist sentiments of many other social reformers in questioning the advisability of admitting non-British immigrants to Canada—immigrants whom she saw as particularly prone to sexual precociousness and promiscuity.[60]

National commitment to the war effort provided many opportunities for individual and group endeavours. Spurred on in part by patriotic fervour, but especially by economic need, thousands of women entered the paid workforce, filling jobs vacated by enlisted men. Most of these women were young and unmarried.[61] Other women undertook a host of volunteer labours designed to aid the overseas campaign. They knitted socks, preserved foods, and salvaged clothing. Prominent Canadian women such as Lady Julia Drummond, the first president of the Montreal Local Council of Women and widow of the president of the Bank of Montreal, offered their English homes as hospitals and created an Information Department of the Canadian Red Cross Society, which became the main channel of communication between the soldier and his family. They also established Maple Leaf Clubs for soldiers on leave. Two Toronto women, Mary Plummer and Joan Arnoldi, formed the Canadian Field Comforts Commission to oversee the distribution of clothing and other supplies assembled by women throughout Canada to soldiers in England and on the Continent. Although some women worked separately, most joined existing, pro-British women's groups or reform organizations that adapted or enhanced their programs by emphasizing war service. Some suffragists persisted in their campaign but also established Suffragists' War Auxiliaries, which became involved in local recruitment drives and organized women to fill available jobs vacated by male service volunteers.[62] In some communities, suffrage activists planned future suffrage campaigns while they were involved in sessions for making soldier comforts and bandages for the Red Cross.

The visible, publicly acknowledged wartime work of women encouraged many reformers to press their more comprehensive demands. Despite the opposition of local employers, for example, the Halifax Local Council of Women created a women's employment bureau in order to promote better industrial career training, occupational access, and advancement.[63] In 1914, the Canadian Patriotic Fund, founded at the beginning of the century during the South African War, was reactivated and expanded in order to raise money for the families of enlisted men. Within months, the fund had become what can only be described as a national welfare service for those families. The money raised by individuals, including many women, for the Canadian Patriotic Fund was particularly crucial given that the state support available to soldiers' dependants was generally inadequate. Yet the recipients of this money, usually working-class families, were forced to endure home visits by middle-class women active in reform work, who scrutinized the household management and the personal comportment of soldiers' wives.

Social reformers, for their part, pointed to the improved living conditions for soldiers' dependent wives and children achieved by the Fund, and used these improved living conditions as an argument in favour of mothers' pensions, day nurseries, better housing, and health inspection.[64]

Wartime inflation and deprivation revived interest in the economy and domestic consumption, and Household Leagues, formed just prior to the turn of the century and affiliated with the National Council of Women of Canada, became particularly active and vocal in Victoria, Halifax, and northern Ontario. Members demanded government regulation of prices and quantities, the standardization of sizes in manufactured and canned goods, and the control of local food production and distribution. The Ottawa League, for example, investigated cooperative buying, while a similar association, the Calgary Consumers' League, put that idea into practice. Particularly concerned by high prices for the necessities of life in the fall and winter of 1914–15, the Calgary women brought carloads of flour and frozen fish into the city market, and sold them to members at substantial reductions. They also counteracted soaring fuel costs by arranging for discounted coal purchases.[65] Strategies such as these expanded in the later war years as the government launched thrift, food conservation, and what were called "self-denial campaigns." By 1917, the Quebec City Housewives' League had 10 000 members, and other leagues had expanded on a similar scale.[66]

More spontaneous and more radical responses to specific price increases also took place. In May 1917, for example, when Jewish bakers in Toronto announced a 12-cents a-loaf increase in the price of bread, the angry women of the Ward and Spadina Avenue community organized a committee and began a boycott of the bakeries. They canvassed neighbourhood homes and businesses for support, petitioned the federal government for the appointment of a food commissioner, and picketed all 15 bakeries, forcing their temporary shutdown. As the boycott grew, protesters broke bakery windows and damaged flour and bread. They disrupted and virtually halted bread delivery. *The Telegram* reported that "The bakers say the safety of their drivers was in danger and some were attacked by infuriated women, who pulled their hair and upset their bread baskets on the street." The women did not give up until the price of bread was lowered.[67]

Wartime patriotism directly benefitted many of the established women's organizations by attracting new members. The National Council of Women, the YWCA, the Women's Institutes, and the Imperial Order Daughters of the Empire (IODE) all experienced spectacular increases in membership. By 1915, the Women's Institutes had attracted 29 045 women to a total of 892 branches. During World War I, the Institutes spread beyond Canada's borders to England and eventually to other European countries.[68] The IODE's first chapters had been founded in 1900 in Fredericton and Montreal in response to the Boer War. This association aimed to mobilize women and children to support the British Empire and to appreciate British history, culture, and institutions, thereby cementing an Anglo-Canadian identity. The Great War was really the IODE's golden age: in just three years, 1915–1917, IODE membership increased by 10 000, and nearly 100 new chapters were formed. By the end of the war it had become one of the nation's largest women's voluntary associations. During the First World War, the IODE founded Red Cross branches, organized the Canadian Women's Hospital Ship Fund, sent gifts to soldiers overseas, assisted in recruitment, badgered those young men who had not enlisted, and organized material and emotional support for soldiers' families. By 1917 IODE members had collected more than $1.5 million to finance their efforts.[69] The success of these efforts depended upon extensive local fundraising and the unpaid labour of countless women, not all of whom were of British descent. Johanna Gudrun Skaptason formed the Jon Sigurdsson Chapter, IODE, in Winnipeg in 1916. Her daughter recalled, "Twice annually during those first war days our home became parcel packing-headquarters, with cartons, and cases of food, socks, etc., piled ceilingward and women working day after day, pausing only for coffee."[70]

Through their organized reform activities in the late nineteenth and early twentieth centuries, women had developed and refined the skills of organizing and fundraising. In the war years, when the government needed civilian assistance in drives to recruit men and to raise war funds, it found ready-made support in existing women's organizations. Prime Minister Robert Borden estimated in 1916 that Canadian women had raised the immense sum of between $40 and $50 million since the war began. In Newfoundland, as well, women had raised $205 614 in cash and supplies for the war effort by 1916.[71] Women also responded when wartime disaster struck. Already busy with various wartime causes, the time and energy of activist women were stretched to the limit by the Halifax explosion of December 6, 1917, which destroyed more than 2 000 homes, killed 1 600 people, and injured an additional 9 000. Women from all walks of life, including co-eds at Dalhousie University, participated in the rescue work under the leadership and initiative of prominent feminists and Local Council leaders. Leading women's movement activists such as May Sexton, Eliza Ritchie, and Agnes Dennis organized nursing care and coordinated the distribution of food and clothing.[72]

In 1918, the federal Cabinet War Committee convened a Women's War Conference, also known as the War Council of Women, in Ottawa. This largely symbolic gesture recognized the range and intensity of women's voluntary and emergency wartime efforts. The numerous resolutions adopted at the conference related to major unachieved reforms in the areas of health, welfare, education, and work that the National Council of Women of Canada and its affiliates and supporters had been espousing for over two decades.[73]

While the First World War had a positive effect on the image and prestige of organized women, it also accentuated old divisions and raised some new ones. For example, although its members were concerned about women's problems, the IODE's conservative patriotism and devotion to Empire—what some have called its "female imperialism"—occasionally put its members at odds with other women's organizations. The IODE protested, for example, the National Council of Women of Canada's affiliation with the International Council of Women, which, it argued, also included "enemy" affiliates.[74] In Winnipeg in 1918, the Local Council of Women, concerned about maintaining communications necessary to the war effort, acted as scab workers, replacing—and undermining the cause of—women telephone operators who were on strike.[75] Organized women also divided sharply on the issues of conscription and the Union government, the latter formed by federal Liberals and Conservatives in 1917 in order to pursue the national war effort. In Saint John, the refusal of Women's Enfranchisement Association members to endorse Prime Minister Borden's Union government sparked the resignations of its president and vice-president.[76] In Montreal, the issue of conscription split the Local Council of Women in two: in early 1918 its long-time president, Dr. Grace Ritchie-England, underwent an (ultimately unsuccessful) impeachment trial by the LCW for her criticism of Borden's wartime policies, notably the Wartime Elections Act and the Military Service Act, and for her supposed lack of patriotism.[77]

It was perhaps Canada's involvement in the war in the first place that presented the greatest challenge to female reformers. Central to the ideology of turn-of-the-twentieth-century feminism was a strong condemnation of violence, associated with men and male power. The Maritimes WCTU, for example, had been involved in the 1890s in a campaign for peace through international arbitration.[78] Flora MacDonald Denison was among the prominent women reformers who had written on the subject in the years before the war. Her *War and Women*, published by the Canadian Suffrage Association in 1914, blamed militarism on the domination of public life by men.[79] And Nellie McClung's *In Times Like These* (1915) included one of the most eloquent condemnations of all forms of war:

> But although men like to fight, war is not inevitable. War is not of God's making. War is a crime committed by men and, therefore, when enough people say it shall not be, it cannot be. This will not happen until women are allowed to say what they think of war. Up to the present time women have had nothing to say about war, except pay the price of war—this privilege has been theirs always.[80]

McClung and Denison were two feminists for whom the reality, as opposed to the abstraction, of war presented painful problems of personal conscience. Both had been against war; both had dearly loved sons who enlisted; both eventually came to support the Allied cause. Only a few Canadian women, in fact, sustained their pacifist opposition to violence. These included Winnipeg writer Francis Marion Beynon, British Columbia's Helena Gutteridge, and Toronto peace activist Laura Hughes, all of whom consistently and publicly condemned Canada's participation in the war. Beynon's refusal to alter her pacifist stance resulted in her forced resignation from her job as a respected journalist on the *Grain Growers' Guide*, and led to her self-imposed exile in the United States.[81] Early in the war, pacifism also inspired the president of the Toronto Business Women's Club, Mrs. C. R. Barker, to resign her presidency rather than share in the Club's war work. But these women and others who spoke or wrote publicly against the war found themselves increasingly isolated. Looking back in 1945, Nellie McClung recalled this:

> The fall of 1914 blurs in my memory like a troubled dream. The war dominated everything. Some of my friends were pacifists and resented Canada's participation in a war of which we knew so little. . . . Chief among the Empire's defenders among the women was Miss Cora Hind. Her views were clear cut and definite. We were British and must follow the tradition of our fathers. She would have gone herself if women were accepted. Miss Hind saw only one side of the question and there were times when I envied her, though I resented her denunciations of those who thought otherwise.
>
> The old crowd began to break up, and our good times were over.[82]

VICTORY

In spite of obstacles and disagreements, women continued to campaign for suffrage. The turning point in the long battle finally came in 1916, when the vigorous suffrage campaign waged by western women culminated in their enfranchisement in Manitoba, Alberta, and Saskatchewan. A year later, British Columbia and Ontario followed suit; women in Nova Scotia, New Brunswick, Prince Edward Island, and Newfoundland won the vote in 1918, 1919, 1922, and 1925, respectively. In all cases except New Brunswick and Ontario, the right to vote was accompanied by the right to hold office; New Brunswick women became eligible to hold office in 1934; and Ontario women, in 1919. Only Quebec held back and refused to grant the provincial vote to women until 1940.

At the federal level, women's franchise was achieved in three phases. The Military Voters Act in 1917 gave the vote to women nurses serving in the war. Later that year, the Wartime Elections Act extended the franchise to the wives, widows, mothers, sisters, and daughters of those, alive or deceased, who had served or were serving in the Canadian or British military or naval forces. This Act, designed to help re-elect Borden's Union government and endorse its mandate for conscription, drew both praise and outrage from suffrage advocates.[83] Support came primarily from people who, in the wartime context, believed in the superiority of the Anglo-Saxon race and saw the vote as a way of reshaping society according to their values. Opponents, like the Victoria and Regina Local Councils of Women, both of which passed resolutions protesting the law, objected to the act's discriminatory provisions, maintaining that valid change could be achieved only when all women acquired equal political rights with men.[84] Their political objective was finally met in 1918 with the passage of the federal Women's Franchise Act, which gave the vote to women who were over the age of 21 and British subjects, and who possessed the same qualifications that men required for the provincial franchise. Women of Asian descent, however, like male members of their families, could not vote because they were not eligible to become British subjects. The unrestricted right to the federal vote was also denied to Aboriginal women—who, along with Aboriginal men, remained disenfranchised under the terms of the Indian Act until 1960. Political participation in band politics had already been denied to Aboriginal women by the federal government in 1869 when band councils were established.[85]

Eligible Canadian women had achieved the franchise before women in Great Britain and, as far as the federal vote was concerned, before those in the United States as well. And in 1919, the federal government enacted legislation enabling women to be elected to the House of Commons.[86] The timing of these victories has generated considerable discussion among historians. Why did most of Canada's provincial governments acquiesce to the campaign for suffrage between 1916 and 1925? Why, in contrast, did Quebec not participate in the general trend?

The first question is perhaps the easiest to answer. Certainly, political motives are obvious major factors in the 1917 federal decision. Borden's Union government clearly had much to gain from the prospect of a loyal voting block of newly enfranchised women, at the height of bitterness over the conscription issue. In British Columbia and Manitoba, suffrage had become a partisan issue; newly elected Liberal governments were simply

This 1917 newspaper cartoon links military conscription, patriotism, and the need to defend the honour of womanhood.

Source: A.G. Racey, 1917, *The Montreal Daily Star.*

fulfilling their campaign promises. In Ontario, the incumbent Conservative government under Premier William Hearst gradually recognized the expediency of accepting female suffrage; in addition, Hearst was evidently pressured by Prime Minister Borden to adopt the cause. Concern about capturing women's votes undoubtedly motivated the Alberta and New Brunswick Liberal governments as well. In Newfoundland, the suffrage movement developed strong links to the international movement through its membership in the International Woman Suffrage Alliance.[87] International influences may also have played a part in other victories. After 1910 a revitalized feminist movement was sweeping Europe and North America, embodied in national associations but also in international organizations, such as the International Council of Women, the International Alliance of Women (formerly the International Woman Suffrage Alliance), the *Union internationale des ligues féminines catholiques,* and the Women's International League for Peace and Freedom, making it more difficult for Canadian legislators to justify women's continued exclusion.[88] A negative stance became even harder to defend in light of women's acknowledged and valued contributions to the war effort. Indeed, speeches introducing franchise measures often cited these contributions as a major rationale. It has also been suggested that the growth of a female labour market increased women's visibility as an independent force and gradually paved the way for the acceptance of equal political rights. Ultimately, the extraordinarily persistent efforts of the suffragist campaigners paid off. The campaign, after all, had taken some 60 years to win. From the time the fight for political rights began, thousands of women and hundreds of organizations had been involved. Even during periods of apparent inactivity and division, the movement never completely lost its focus or momentum.

Why did women in Quebec not secure the provincial suffrage in these years despite the presence in the province of dozens of female social reformers and many dedicated and tireless suffragists? One reason is certainly the strength of the opposition to woman suffrage in Quebec—an opposition to be found among intellectuals, journalists, politicians, jurists, physicians, and members of the Catholic Church hierarchy. Another reason is the fragility, in these years, of the Quebec suffrage movement outside the stronghold of Montreal; the Quebec City Local Council of Women, for example, quietly collapsed in 1900, only six years after coming into existence. The weakness of the WCTU and the lack of support for Prohibition in Quebec might also explain some of the lack of support for female suffrage. Finally, the vote was never the principal objective for Quebec feminists; many of these women, both anglophone and francophone, devoted a considerable amount of time and energy to efforts to reform the Civil Code and to eliminate, in particular, married women's legal incapacity.[89]

The reform movement that had claimed more than half a century of women's attention and that had contributed to winning female suffrage at the federal level and in almost all of the provinces could boast other important victories by 1920. Through their work aimed at counteracting the problems associated with urbanization and industrialization, improving the status and well-being of women in the workplace, and eradicating the inequities faced by women in family law, Canadian feminists never lost sight of the importance of family and children. They appear to have believed that a stable family life could both prevent and counteract social degeneration and promote moral regeneration. They thus called for greater state support for the family, particularly in matters of health and welfare. In the English-Canadian provinces, moreover, feminist reformers and their allies sought to counter the institutionalization of children by securing channels for legal adoptions, and in some provinces the establishment of Children's Aid Societies. By 1920, means-tested allowances for poor mothers were available in Manitoba (1916), Saskatchewan (1917), Alberta (1919), and British Columbia and Ontario (1920). Reform-minded women had also been involved over the years in the kindergarten movement and the founding of Home and School Associations. They had advocated and achieved separate courts, trials, and institutions for the group of children and adolescents increasingly identified as "juvenile delinquents." In addition, partly at least because of their efforts, various provinces gradually came to accept the need to provide separate facilities for female offenders.[90]

Reformers could take pride in all these accomplishments, but by far the greatest victory they achieved was the implementation of Prohibition throughout Canada during the war years. The spirit of sacrifice, the strong commitment to the reformation of society, and the growing acceptance of government intervention in the lives of Canada's citizens, all evoked by the war, created a climate of opinion extremely favourable to the Prohibitionists' cause. Supporters equated the corrupting liquor trade with the evil enemy, Kaiser Wilhelm, arguing that both were scourges of western civilization. Why sacrifice innocent young men to the Allied cause, only to have them frequent wet canteens and fall victims first to drink and then, in their vulnerable state, to prostitution and venereal disease? Moreover, Prohibition advocates argued that it was inefficient to use valuable grain for the manufacture of alcohol when it might better be sent to the starving Allied nations.

On the basis of these and similar arguments, the Prohibitionists' long-standing cry for the banishment of bottle and bar caught the attention and support of unprecedented numbers of Canadians, many of whom had previously been indifferent or overtly opposed to the temperance movement. Prohibitionist sentiment was strongest in the Prairie provinces, whose politicians were unable to ignore it. Newfound allies for the Prohibitionists included the Imperial Order Daughters of the Empire, the Orange Lodge, and the Anglican Church. Significant numbers of immigrants, who had previously been resistant to temperance overtures, were converted to the cause. Following the holding of provincial referenda, by the end of 1916 all three Prairie governments had enacted prohibitory legislation. Within a year, all other provinces, with the exception of Quebec, also endorsed Prohibition. In 1918 the Dominion government used its powers under the War Measures Act to apply Prohibition to that province also, and to stop interprovincial trade in liquor.

Victory was now complete, but was Prohibition the panacea that the WCTU and other supporters claimed it would be? Initially at least, they could take great satisfaction in the results: in Manitoba during the seven months following the introduction of Prohibition, arrests for drunkenness fell by 87 percent, and all other crimes by nearly one-third; in Alberta, arrests for drunkenness declined by 90 percent in 1917 and 1918. People also praised the effectiveness of the new legislation in creating a safer and more wholesome environment. One enthusiastic Saskatchewan farm wife proudly informed the provincial premier that her small community, "formerly a drunkard's paradise, since the banishment of the bars and dispensaries has assumed an air of thrift and sobriety."[91] But it was not clear to what extent other desired social changes had resulted.

The women's associations of the late nineteenth and early twentieth centuries addressed important needs. Accessible both to women who were able to make a full commitment and to those who could be involved only part-time, the women's movement reached out to a remarkable number of women in Canadian society in one way or another. By 1916, journalist Marjory MacMurchy could proclaim that one out of every eight women in the Dominion belonged to the network of women's societies.[92] Organized activity not only provided a sense of purpose for many women, but also prevented their personal isolation and—through exposure to and participation in the community of like-minded women—intensified their common identity. Through their clubs, members learned the organizational and public skills essential to their greater participation in the urbanized and industrialized world of the twentieth century. The lobbying skills and national and international networks that women developed enabled them to mobilize as the need arose. For example, in 1911, when Angelina Napolitano of Sault Ste. Marie, Ontario, faced the death penalty for killing her abusive husband, organizations including the WCTU, the NCWC, and various suffrage societies from outside Canada mounted a clemency campaign that resulted in the commutation of the death sentence to life imprisonment.[93]

Although Canadian women reformers personally claimed victory for many of the social, economic, and political reforms of this period, the extent to which these can be described as uniquely women's victories is debatable. In certain areas, such as the temperance and suffrage movements, a direct relationship between women's efforts and the reform in question can indeed be traced—although the efforts of male supporters of these causes clearly cannot be dismissed. In others, perhaps, men's and women's efforts were about equal. Male collaboration in feminist reform reflected the acceptance of women's movement goals by increasing numbers of Canadians. The thrust of the movement, with its emphasis on protecting the home and family life, perhaps posed no major threat to male supremacy. But it did call into question the exclusive nature of men's public power. Feminist thought challenged the supposed division of the world into men's and women's spheres by continuing to erode the boundaries between public and private activities. In the context of turn-of-the-century Canadian middle-class Christianity, the work of female reformers was genuinely radical. Ultimately, realistic appraisals of what was practical and generally acceptable guided women reformers. If their efforts fell short of social revolution, they nevertheless paved the way for increasingly revolutionary activity to come.

In the final analysis, although most historians identify maternal or social feminism as the dominant philosophy of this first-wave Canadian women's reform movement, the radical character of some aspects of the movement cannot be overlooked. From an early expression by the Toronto Women's Literary Club, the argument for equal rights evolved with, and often merged with, the idea of women's special maternal and nurturing role. Canadian middle-class women believed that, as mothers and as homemakers, they had knowledge and skills that were equal in worth to the knowledge and skills of men. In a just society, this value ought to be acknowledged and rewarded. These views challenged the unequal power balance both within and beyond the family unit. Between 1850 and 1920, a growing number of educated women were thus sensitized to the need for public action.

Notes

1. Éliane Gubin et al., eds., *Le siècle des féminismes* (Paris: Les Éditions de l'Atelier/Éditions Ouvrières, 2004); Johanne Daigle, "Le siècle dans la tourmente du féminisme," *Globe* 3, 2 (2000): 65–86.

2. National Council of Women of Canada (NCWC), *Women of Canada: Their Life and Work* (Ottawa: NCWC, 1900, reprinted 1975). Henrietta Muir Edwards's statement is found on page 51.

3. NCWC, *Women of Canada*, 14.

4. Conseil national des femmes du Canada, *Les femmes du Canada. Leur Vie et leurs Oeuvres* (Ottawa: Conseil national des femmes du Canada, 1900).

5. Beth Light and Joy Parr, eds., *Canadian Women on the Move 1867–1920* (Toronto: New Hogtown Press and OISE Press, 1983), 187–88.

6. Mary Kinnear and Vera Fast, *Planting the Garden: An Annotated Archival Bibliography of the History of Women in Manitoba* (Winnipeg: University of Manitoba Press, 1987), 209; W. J. Lindal, *The Icelanders in Canada* (Ottawa/Winnipeg: National Publishers/Viking Printers, 1967), 304; Marcia Koven, *Weaving the Past into the Present: A Glimpse into the 130 Year History of the Saint John Jewish Community* (Saint John, NB: Saint John Jewish Historical Museum, 1989), 26–27; Robin Winks, *The Blacks in Canada: A History* (Montreal and Kingston: McGill-Queen's University Press, 1971), 348; Sylvia Hamilton, "The Women at the Well," in Linda Carty, ed., *And Still We Rise: Feminist Political Mobilizing in Contemporary Canada* (Toronto: Women's Press, 1993), 189–203.

7. Jean Bannerman, *Leading Ladies Canada* (Belleville, ON: Mika Publishing, 1977, Rev. ed.), 67; P. R. Blakeley, "Anna of Siam in Canada," *Atlantic Advocate* (January 1967), 41–45; Ernest Forbes, "Battles in Another War: Edith Archibald and the Halifax Feminist Movement," in his *Challenging the Regional Stereotype* (Fredericton: Acadiensis Press, 1989), 71; Lois K. Yorke, "Anna Harriette Edwards" in the *Dictionary of Canadian Biography Online*,

http://www.biographi.ca/009004-119.01-e.php?&id_nbr=7355&interval=25&&PHPSESSID
=ulqghtg945nek75k0nqrtcd402

8. N. E. S. Griffiths, *The Splendid Vision: Centennial History of the National Council of Women of Canada, 1893–1993* (Ottawa: Carleton University Press, 1993), 91.

9. Catherine L. Cleverdon, *The Woman Suffrage Movement in Canada*, 2nd ed. (Toronto: University of Toronto Press, 1974), 29–33.

10. Deborah Gorham, "Flora MacDonald Denison: Canadian Feminist," in Linda Kealey, ed., *A Not Unreasonable Claim: Women and Reform in Canada, 1880s–1920s* (Toronto: Canadian Women's Educational Press, 1979), 47–70.

11. Karen Dubinsky, *Improper Advances: Rape and Heterosexual Conflict in Ontario, 1880–1929* (Chicago: University of Chicago Press, 1993), 140.

12. Gorham, "Flora MacDonald Denison," 56–57.

13. Gorham, "Flora MacDonald Denison," 58–60; Cleverdon, *Woman Suffrage Movement*, 36; Deborah Gorham, "English Militancy and the Canadian Suffrage Movement," *Atlantis* 1, 1 (Fall 1975): 83–112; Carol Bacchi, *Liberation Deferred?: The Ideas of the English-Canadian Suffragists 1877–1918* (Toronto: University of Toronto Press, 1983), 37–38.

14. Veronica Strong-Boag, "Canada's Women Doctors: Feminism Constrained," in Kealey, ed., *A Not Unreasonable Claim*, 124–26; Kathleen McConnachie, "Methodology in the Study of Women in History: A Case Study of Helen MacMurchy, M.D.," *Ontario History* 75 (March 1983): 61–70; Angus McLaren, "The Creation of a Haven for 'Human Thoroughbreds': The Sterilization of the Feeble-Minded and the Mentally Ill in British Columbia," *Canadian Historical Review* 67, 2 (June 1986): 127–50; Terry L. Chapman, "The Early Eugenics Movement in Western Canada," *Alberta History* 25 (1977): 9–17.

15. Carol Bacchi, "Race Regeneration and Social Purity: A Study of the Social Attitudes of Canada's English-Speaking Suffragists," *Histoire sociale/Social History* 11, 22 (November 1978): 460–74; Mariana Valverde, "'When the Mother of the Race Is Free': Race, Reproduction and Sexuality in First-Wave Feminism," in Franca Iacovetta and Mariana Valverde, eds., *Gender Conflicts: New Essays in Women's History* (Toronto: University of Toronto Press, 1992), 15–21.

16. Stephen A. Speisman, *The Jews of Toronto: A History to 1937* (Toronto: McClelland and Stewart, 1987), 149–53; Luigi G. Pennacchio, "The Defence of Identity: Ida Siegel and the Jews of Toronto versus the Assimilation Attempts of the Public School and Its Allies, 1900–1920," *Canadian Jewish Historical Society Journal* 9, 1 (Spring 1985): 41–60; Irving Abella, *A Coat of Many Colours: Two Centuries of Jewish Life in Canada* (Toronto: Lester and Orpen Dennys, 1990), 153.

17. Marilyn Färdig Whitely, "'Allee Sammee Melican Lady': Imperialism and Negotiation at the Chinese Rescue Home," *Resources for Feminist Research/Documentation sur la recherche féministe* 22, 3/4 (Fall/Winter 1993): 45–50.

18. *Census of Canada* (1901), Table 11, "Origins of the People." It is likely that census takers underestimated the size of the community.

19. Carrie Best, *That Lonesome Road* (New Glasgow, NS: Clarion Publishing, 1977), 189.

20. Georgina M. Taylor, "'A Splendid Field before Us': Violet McNaughton and the Development of Agrarian Feminism in Canada, 1909 to 1926," paper presented to the Canadian Historical Association, Ottawa, 1993, 5. For a published study of McNaughton, see Georgina M. Taylor, "'Let Us Co-operate': Violet McNaughton and the Co-operative Ideal," in Brett Fairbairn, Ian MacPherson and Nora Russell, eds., *Canadian Co-operatives in the Year 2000: Memory, Mutual Aid, and the Millennium* (Saskatoon: Centre for the Study of Co-operatives, University of Saskatchewan, 2000), 57–78.

21. Taylor, "'Splendid Field,'" 5.

22. Taylor, "'Splendid Field,'" 25.

23. Catherine C. Cole and Ann Milovic, "Education, Community Service, and Social Life: The Alberta Women's Institutes and Rural Families, 1909–1945," in Catherine A. Cavanaugh and Randi R. Warne, eds., *Standing on New Ground: Women in Alberta* (Edmonton: University of Alberta Press, 1993), 20–25.

24. Richard Allen, ed., *The Social Gospel in Canada* (Ottawa: National Museums of Canada, 1975), espec. Beatrice Brigden, "One Woman's Campaign for Social Purity and Social Reform," 36–62.

25. Paul Voisey, "The 'Votes for Women' Movement," *Alberta History* 23, 2 (Summer 1975): 17.

26. Candace Savage, *Our Nell: A Scrapbook Biography of Nellie L. McClung* (Saskatoon: Western Producer Prairie Books, 1979), 89; on the mock parliaments staged in British Columbia in 1910 and 1914, see Richard I. Bourgeois-Doyle, *Her Daughter the Engineer. The Life of Elsie Gregory MacGill* (Ottawa: NRC Research Press, 2008), 37, and Sylvie McClean, *A Woman of Influence. Evlyn Fenwick Farris* (Victoria, BC: Sono Nis Press, 1997), 96, 98.

27. Donald McCaig, *A Reply to John Stuart Mill on the Subjection of Women* (Philadelphia: J. B. Lippincott, 1870).

28. Goldwin Smith, "Woman Suffrage," in his *Essays on the Questions of the Day, Political and Social* (New York, 1893).

29. Andrew Macphail, "The American Woman," in *Essays in Fallacy* (New York, 1910), 24, cited in Veronica Strong-Boag, "Independent Women, Problematic Men: First- and Second-Wave Anti-Feminism in Canada from Goldwin Smith to Betty Steele," *Histoire sociale/Social History* 57 (May 1996): 14.

30. Stephen Leacock, "The Woman Question," in his *Essays and Literary Studies* (New York: John Lane, 1916).

31. Susan Mann Trofimenkoff, "Henri Bourassa and 'the Woman Question'," *Journal of Canadian Studies* 10, 4 (November 1975): 3–11; Henri Bourassa, "Le suffrage des femmes," in Michèle Jean, ed., *Québécoises du 20e siècle* (Montréal: Éditions du Jour, 1974), 195.

32. Terry Crowley, "Madonnas before Magdalenes: Adelaide Hoodless and the Making of the Canadian Gibson Girl," *Canadian Historical Review* 67, 4 (December 1986): 532.

33. Camille Soucie, "Thinking Imperially: Clementina Fessenden's *Anti-Suffrage Notes*," Paper presented to the Social Science History Association, St. Louis, Missouri, 2002; Smith, "Woman Suffrage," 186, cited in Strong-Boag, "Independent Women, Problematic Men," 15.

34. Carol Bacchi, "Divided Allegiances: The Response of Farm and Labour Women to Suffrage," in Kealey, ed., *A Not Unreasonable Claim*, 89–108; Christine MacDonald, "How Saskatchewan Women Got the Vote," *Saskatchewan History* 1, 3 (October 1948): 1–9; Voisey, "'Votes for Women,'" 10–23; Cleverdon, *Woman Suffrage Movement*, chap. 3; Nellie McClung, *In Times Like These*, introduction by Veronica Strong-Boag (Toronto: University of Toronto Press, 1972), 54–55.

35. Andrée Lévesque, "La citoyenne selon Éva Circé-Côté," in *Résistance et transgression. Études en histoire des femmes au Québec* (Montréal: Éditions du Remue-ménage, 1995), espec. 59–63.

36. Janice Newton, "Women and *Cotton's Weekly*: A Study of Women and Socialism in Canada, 1909," *Resources for Feminist Research*, 8 (1980): 58–61; Linda Kealey, *Enlisting Women for the Cause: Women, Labour, and the Left in Canada, 1890–1920* (Toronto: University of Toronto Press, 1998), espec. 123–25, 142.

37. Varpu Lindström-Best, *Defiant Sisters: A Social History of Finnish Immigrant Women in Canada* (Toronto: Multicultural History Society of Ontario, 1988), 151.

38. Lindström-Best, *Defiant Sisters*, 147–52.

39. Nancy Bourassa, "Joséphine Marchand-Dandurand (1861–1925)," and Line Gosselin, "Robertine Barry (1863–1910)," in Maryse Darsigny et al., eds., *Ces femmes qui ont bâti Montréal* (Montréal: Les Éditions du remue-ménage, 1994), 128–29, 147–48.

40. Veronica Strong-Boag, "'Ever a Crusader': Nellie McClung, First-Wave Feminist," in Strong-Boag and Anita Clair Fellman, eds., *Rethinking Canada: The Promise of Women's History* (Toronto: Copp Clark Pitman, 1986), 178–90; Mary Hallett and Marilyn Davis, *Firing the Heather: The Life and Times of Nellie McClung* (Saskatoon: Fifth House, 1993).

41. McClung, *In Times Like These*, 48.

42. McClung, *In Times Like These*, 87.

43. Janice Fiamengo, "A Legacy of Ambivalence: Responses to Nellie McClung," in Veronica Strong-Boag, Mona Gleason, and Adele Perry, eds., *Rethinking Canada: The Promise of Women's History*, 4th edition (Don Mills: Oxford UP, 2002), 149–63.

44. Margaret E. McCallum, "Prairie Women and the Struggle for a Dower Law, 1905–1920," *Prairie Forum* 18, 1 (Spring 1993): 28.

45. Linda Silver Dranoff, *Women in Canadian Life: Law* (Toronto: Fitzhenry and Whiteside, 1977), 49.

46. Alvin Finkel, "Populism and Gender: The UFA and Social Credit Experience," *Journal of Canadian Studies* 27, 4 (Winter 1992–93): 80–81.

47. Georgina Binnie-Clark, *Wheat and Woman*, introduction by Susan Jackel (Toronto: University of Toronto Press, 1979); and Binnie-Clark, *A Summer on the Canadian Prairie* (London: Edward Arnold, 1910).

48. Elsie Gregory MacGill, *My Mother the Judge: A Biography of Helen Gregory MacGill*, introduction by Naomi Black (Toronto: Peter Martin Associates, 1981), 115.

49. Susan Wade, "Helena Gutteridge: Votes for Women and Trade Unions," in Barbara Latham and Cathy Kess, eds., *In Her Own Right: Selected Essays on Women's History in B.C.* (Victoria: Camosun College, 1980), 187–204; Dranoff, *Women in Canadian Life: Law*, 70–73; Margaret E. McCallum, "Keeping Women in Their Place: The Minimum Wage in Canada, 1910–25," *Labour/Le Travail* 17 (Spring 1986): 29–56.

50. Michael H. Cramer, "Public and Political—Documents of the Women's Suffrage Campaign in British Columbia, 1871–1917: The View from Victoria," in Gillian Creese and Veronica Strong-Boag, eds., *British Columbia Reconsidered: Essays on Women* (Vancouver: Press Gang, 1992), 60–64.

51. Wade, "Helena Gutteridge"; Cleverdon, *Woman Suffrage Movement*, chap. 4.

52. Elspeth Tulloch, *We, the Undersigned: A Historical Overview of New Brunswick Women's Political and Legal Status, 1784–1984* (Moncton: New Brunswick Advisory Council on the Status of Women, 1985), 44–45.

53. Tulloch, *We, the Undersigned*, 47–48.

54. Ernest Forbes, "The Ideas of Carol Bacchi and the Suffragists of Halifax," *Atlantis* 10, 2 (Spring 1985): 121.

55. Forbes, "Battles in Another War."

56. Cleverdon, *Woman Suffrage Movement*, 201–2; Margot I. Duley, *Where Once Our Mothers Stood We Stand: Women's Suffrage in Newfoundland 1890–1925* (Charlottetown: Gynergy books, 1993), 78–95.

57. For an overview, see Susan Mann Trofimenkoff, *The Dream of Nation: A Social and Intellectual History of Quebec* (Toronto: Macmillan, 1982), chap. 6. On lay and religious women, see Marta Danylewycz, *Taking the Veil: An Alternative to Marriage, Motherhood, and Spinsterhood in Quebec, 1840–1920* (Toronto: McClelland and Stewart, 1987), espec. chap. 5.

58. Karine Hébert, "Une organisation maternaliste au Québec: la Fédération nationale Saint-Jean-Baptiste et la bataille pour le vote des femmes," *Revue d'histoire de l'Amérique française* 52, 3 (printemps 1999): 315–44; Karine Hébert, "Le maternalisme, une solution féministe à la Crise? La réponse de la Fédération nationale Saint-Jean-Baptiste," *Bulletin d'histoire politique* 9, 2 (2001): 52–62; Micheline Dumont, *Le féminisme québécois raconté à Camille* (Montréal: Les Éditions du remue-ménage, 2008), 30–47.

59. Marie Lavigne, Yolande Pinard, and Jennifer Stoddart, "The *Fédération nationale Saint-Jean-Baptiste* and the Women's Movement in Quebec," in Kealey, ed., *A Not Unreasonable Claim*, 71–88; Yolande Pinard, "Les débuts du mouvement des femmes à Montréal, 1893–1902," in Marie Lavigne et Yolande Pinard, eds., *Travailleuses et féministes: Les femmes dans la société québécoise* (Montréal: Boréal Express, 1983), 177–98.

60. Christine Mander, *Emily Murphy: Rebel* (Toronto: Simon and Pierre, 1985); Byrne Hope Sanders, *Emily Murphy Crusader* (Toronto: Macmillan, 1945); Rebecca Priegert Coulter, "Between School and Marriage: A Case Study Approach to Young Women's Work in Early Twentieth Century Canada," *History of Education Review* 18, 2 (1989): 26–27.

61. Barbara M. Wilson, *Ontario and the First World War* (Toronto: Champlain Society, 1977), lxxxv–xcv and 101–47.

62. Wilson, *Ontario and the First World War*, lxxxvi.

63. Forbes, "Ideas of Carol Bacchi," 121–22.

64. Veronica Strong-Boag, *The Parliament of Women: The National Council of Women of Canada 1893–1929* (Ottawa: National Museums of Canada, 1976), 323–24; Nancy Christie, *Engendering the State: Family, Work, and Welfare in Canada* (Toronto: University of Toronto Press, 2000), 46–93; Desmond Morton, *Fight or Pay: Soldiers' Families in the Great War* (Vancouver: University of British Columbia Press, 2004).

65. Strong-Boag, *Parliament of Women*, chap. 7.

66. *Canadian Annual Review* (1917), 432; Caroline Roy, "La Ligue des ménagères de Québec, 1917–1924" (M.A. thesis, Université de Montréal, 1995).

67. Speisman, *The Jews of Toronto*, 195–97.

68. Crowley, "Madonnas before Magdalenes," 520–47.

69. *Canadian Annual Review* (1915, 1916, 1917).

70. W. Kristjanson, "Johanna Gudrun Skaptason," *Icelandic Canadian* (Winter 1960), 39.

71. *Canadian Annual Review* (1916), 419; Duley, *Where Once*, 67–68.

72. Judith Fingard, "College, Career, and Community: Dalhousie Coeds, 1881–1921," in Paul Axelrod and John G. Reid, eds., *Youth, University and Canadian Society: Essays in the Social History of Higher Education* (Montreal and Kingston: McGill-Queen's University Press, 1989), 38, 41–42; and Forbes, "Battles in Another War," 82–84.

73. Strong-Boag, *Parliament of Women*, 324–25.

74. Strong-Boag, *Parliament of Women*, 329; Griffiths, *Splendid Vision*, 166–67; Katie Pickles, "Coffee, Tea, and Spinsters' Sprees: Female Imperialism in Sherbrooke and the Eastern Townships," *Journal of Eastern Townships Studies* 21 (Fall 2002): 73–97; Katie Pickles, *Female Imperialism and National Identity: Imperial Order Daughters of the Empire* (Manchester: Manchester UP, 2002).

75. Strong-Boag, *Parliament of Women*, 305, 329–32.

76. Tulloch, *We, the Undersigned*, 61.

77. Tarah Brookfield, "Divided by the Ballot Box: The Montreal Council of Women and the 1917 Election," *Canadian Historical Review* 89, 4 (December 2008): 474–501.

78. Forbes, "Ideas of Carol Bacchi," 122.

79. Flora Denison, "War and Women," in Ramsay Cook and Wendy Mitchinson, eds., *The Proper Sphere: Woman's Place in Canadian Society* (Toronto: Oxford University Press, 1976), 249–52; Deborah Gorham, "Vera Brittain, Flora MacDonald Denison and the Great War: The Failure of Non-Violence," in Ruth Roach Pierson, ed., *Women and Peace: Theoretical, Historical and Practical Perspectives* (London: Croom Helm, 1987), 137.

80. McClung, *In Times Like These*, 15.

81. R. R. Warne, "Nellie McClung and Peace," in Janice Williamson and Deborah Gorham, eds., *Up and Doing: Canadian Women and Peace* (Toronto: Women's Press,1989), 35–47; Barbara Roberts, "Women against War, 1914–1918: Francis Beynon and Laura Hughes," in Williamson and Gorham, eds., *Up and Doing*, 48–65.

82. Savage, *Our Nell*, 109–10.

83. Gloria Geller, "The Wartimes Elections Act of 1917 and the Canadian Women's Movement," *Atlantis* 2, 1 (Autumn 1976): 88–106.

84. *Canadian Annual Review* (1917), 428.

85. T. Bettel Dawson, *Relating to Law: A Chronology of Women and Law in Canada* (North York, ON: Captus, 1990), 36–37; Jo-Anne Fiske, "Child of the State Mother of the Nation: Aboriginal Women and the Ideology of Motherhood," *Culture* 13, 1 (1993): 18.

86. Cleverdon, *Woman Suffrage Movement*, chap. 5.

87. Duley, *Where Once*, 55, 77–78.

88. Forestell, "Mrs. Canada Goes Global"; Rupp, *Worlds of Women*.

89. Sylvie D'Augerot-Arend, "Why So Late? Cultural and Institutional Factors in the Granting of Québec and French Women's Political Rights," *Journal of Canadian Studies* 26, 1 (Spring 1991): 138–65; Andrée Lévesque, "Le Code civil au Québec. Femmes mineures et féministes," in *Résistance et transgression*, 24; Dumont, *Le féminisme québécois raconté à Camille*, 46–81.

90. Neil Sutherland, *Children in English-Canadian Society: Framing the Twentieth-Century Consensus* (Toronto: University of Toronto Press, 1976).

91. John Herd Thompson, *The Harvests of War: The Prairie West, 1914–1918* (Toronto: McClelland and Stewart, 1978), 98–106; Craig Heron, *Booze: A Distilled History* (Toronto: Between the Lines, 2003).

92. Marjory MacMurchy, *The Woman Bless Her* (Toronto: S. B. Gundy, 1916).

93. Karen Dubinsky and Franca Iacovetta, "Murder, Womanly Virtue and Motherhood: The Case of Angelina Napolitano," *Canadian Historical Review* 72, 4 (December 1991): 505–31.

PART THREE

LAND OF NEW OPPORTUNITIES?
FROM 1918 TO 1960

Employment office at women's reception centre for new immigrants, Toronto, circa 1947.

Source: Archives of Ontario, RG 9-7-4-5-61

On a moonlit evening in May 1918, Allied encampments near Étaples in France suffered a prolonged bombardment. By the time the seemingly endless attack was over, two Canadian field hospitals had been seriously damaged and four Canadian nursing sisters were dead or lay dying. Other nurses made heroic efforts to save the wounded: among them were the first nurses to receive the Military Medal for bravery. The activities of the Canadian nursing sisters overseas dramatically illustrates the new responsibilities Canadian women had assumed, and the sacrifices they had made for the war effort. Women's wartime contribution was one of the principal arguments used to justify the granting of the federal franchise to the majority of women in Canada, which occurred in May 1918.

More generally, the contribution of both women and men to the Allied cause enabled the Canadian government to claim a new, enlarged position for the Dominion within the British Empire. Prime Minister Robert Borden was one of the signatories to the Versailles Treaty at the end of World War I, the first Canadian representative to sign an international treaty in his own right. The subsequent gradual recognition of Canada as an entity with its own identity and interests laid the foundation for the evolution of the British Empire into the Commonwealth. In 1931, the Statute of Westminster officially confirmed Canada's transformation from a dependent colony into a sovereign state.

World War I, then, was a turning point for Canada as a nation. The Canada of 1919 was profoundly different from the Canada of 1914 in several fundamental aspects—demographic, economic, political, and social. Wracked internally by divisions between French and English, east and west, labour and capital, and plunged into a serious recession, the emerging nation stood poised on the brink of an uncertain future. Most Canadians could scarcely imagine that only 20 years later they would be at war again, or that many would welcome war's arrival as a way to escape the grinding poverty and unemployment produced by the Depression of the 1930s.

The Canadian inter-war experience can best be described as turbulent. The transition from a wartime to a peacetime economy was a painful one, particularly for women workers; jobs generated by wartime production ceased, and both unemployment and inflation rose during the post-war recession. In this difficult economic climate, labour militancy intensified, as working men and women sought to protect or improve their standard of living. Radical new organizations, such as the One Big Union, brought together industrial workers regardless of their trade or skill, and led many Canadians to fear that Bolshevism, recently triumphant in Russia, was about to wreak havoc in their own backyard. Thus, when workers initiated massive walkouts across the nation in the spring of 1919, the full weight of the Canadian state was ranged against them. The ensuing defeat of labour precipitated a rapid decline in union membership throughout the 1920s, and left the labour movement dispirited as well as depleted.

The expanding economy of the middle and late 1920s, particularly buoyant in central and western Canada, did result in new job opportunities and unprecedented prosperity for some segments of the Canadian population. The most significant economic growth occurred in the resource-related industries, especially in pulp and paper and in mining. However, these industries provided few employment opportunities for women. Public officials had urged women to give up their paid employment at war's end, but, pressured by economic need, poor women and women from ethnic and racial minorities paid no heed. With the return of prosperity, young single white women were once again actively recruited into the workforce, mainly in the growing clerical and service sectors. In the manufacturing sector, owners and managers used new technologies and scientific-management techniques to rationalize their operations and to reduce labour costs. Many skilled jobs were eliminated and replaced by repetitive assembly work; skilled workers were often pitted against unskilled workers, female workers against male workers.

In many areas of Canada, the improved economic conditions of the mid-1920s did make it briefly possible for some male workers to support their families on their own wages—the family wage was finally becoming a reality. Conversely, the traditional family economy, to which all able-bodied members of the family were expected to contribute, was under attack. Smaller families, and legislation in most provinces extending compulsory school attendance, reduced the number of children in the paid labour force and reinforced married women's roles as mothers and consumers. Indeed, married women's participation in the economy as paid workers was increasingly criticized as unnecessary and ill-advised.

Yet with the onset of the Great Depression in 1929, few families could rely on one male wage earner. Among the western industrialized countries, Canada was one of the most adversely affected by the economic downturn since its economy was so dependent on the export of commodities. Between 1926 and 1933, the price of wheat fell from $1.09 to $0.35 cents per bushel, and that of newsprint from $70 to $41 per ton. Entire single-industry towns were abandoned as families moved, usually to the larger urban centres, in a frenzied attempt to find jobs. In many families, only wives and daughters were able to find employment. As unemployment soared, married and single women were blamed for contributing to the nation's problems by taking jobs away from men. The Depression deepened, and women also found it extremely difficult to keep their paid work. Thousands of men, and some women, jumped on freight trains and travelled across the nation searching for jobs.

The wildly alternating cycles of bust–boom–bust from 1919 to 1939 created enormous fluctuations in population growth. Although the population increased from nearly 9 million in 1921 to 11.5 million by 1941, the pace of growth slowed and was at its lowest during the Depression years. For the first time since official records were begun in 1851, the number of births dropped during an intercensal period: between 1931 and 1941, there were only 2.29 million births, compared to 2.42 million during the previous decade. The most startling demographic change was the sharp decline in immigration after 1931 as economic conditions worsened and the Canadian government restricted immigration: a mere 149 000 immigrants arrived between 1931 and 1941, the lowest number recorded for any decade since 1851. Just as immigration plummeted during the Depression, so, too, did emigration, most notably to the United States. During the 1920s, 970 000 residents left Canada; but in the following decade, the United States tightened its immigration policies, and fewer than a quarter of a million Canadians left their native or adopted land to re-establish themselves elsewhere.

The impact of the Depression on population was most noticeable in Saskatchewan. The collapse of wheat prices, prolonged drought, and the plagues of grasshoppers that devoured the few existing crops overwhelmed many of the province's residents. Over 150 000 more people left the province than entered it, and in spite of natural increase, there were 25 000 fewer inhabitants in 1941 than there had been 10 years earlier. The pace of urbanization also slowed during the Depression: the proportion of all Canadians who resided in urban settings grew only 3 percent, reaching a level of close to 56 percent in 1941. As in the past, there were more women than men in the urban centres, especially in the 15–29 age group. In 1941, for the first time since the census began in 1851, there were also more female than male urban residents in the 30–34 age group, reflecting both the increased employment opportunities for women in this age group in the cities, and the departure of some of the men to perform military service.

Fluctuations in the nation's economy and population in the inter-war period created an atmosphere conducive to political change. Discontent with the Borden administration's wartime policies combined with the economic and social turmoil that enveloped the nation immediately after the war to produce new political movements and parties. Across the nation, farmers deserted the traditional parties to support emerging organizations, such as the Progressive movement in western Canada and the United Farmers in other provinces. Workers, returned veterans, and other disaffected groups variously sought to register their protest during federal and provincial elections by supporting socialist and labour parties, or independent candidates. The formation of the Communist Party of Canada, at a secret meeting held in a barn near Guelph, Ontario, in 1921, provided those on the left with yet another vehicle for political protest. These alternative political parties gave recently enfranchised women new avenues of political involvement. It soon became apparent, however, that both women and men voters preferred the two traditional parties, particularly the Liberal Party. For most of the 1920s, in fact, federal politics were dominated by the back-and-forth struggle for power between the bland but adroit Liberal leader, William Lyon Mackenzie King, and the brilliant but hapless Arthur Meighen, who had replaced Borden at the helm of the Conservative Party in 1920. With the exception of a few brief days, King managed to hold onto power for the Liberals by his skillful courting of the west and of Quebec.

Even King's political finesse, however, proved no match for the cataclysmic impact of the Great Depression, and in 1930 he was defeated by the Conservatives, now led by millionaire R. B. Bennett. Before King left office, however, Canadian women had the small satisfaction of seeing him name the first woman senator. The Liberal defeat was only a preliminary indication of a substantial political upheaval engendered by the Depression. At the federal level, the Co-operative Commonwealth Federation (CCF), formed in Calgary in 1932, and the Reconstruction Party, led by maverick Tory H. H. Stevens, offered new alternatives for voters in the election of 1935. Like most other leftist political organizations, the CCF officially endorsed the full participation of women and provided many women with a forum for involvement in the political process. Agnes Macphail, Canada's first woman MP, was among its founding members. Canadians, however, were in a cautious mood and preferred reinstating King and the Liberals to engaging in political experimentation. The advent of new parties and colourful leaders was more marked at the provincial level. Duff Pattullo and the Liberals in British Columbia, "Bible Bill" Aberhart and the Social Credit in Alberta, Mitchell Hepburn and the Liberals in Ontario, and Maurice Duplessis and the *Union Nationale* in Quebec all rode to power on a wave of protest against incumbents long ensconced in their respective legislatures.

There were a number of major technological innovations of the inter-war period that brought Canadians into closer contact. One of the new tools that this generation of politicians had at their disposal was the radio. Radio broke down much of the isolation that had been a hallmark of living in Canada, putting Canadians in contact not only with one another but also with the rest of the world. It often provided women at home with their only form of entertainment, and it served as a powerful instrument for the dissemination of information and mass culture. Other significant innovations were the automobile and the airplane. By 1930 there were more than 1.2 million motor vehicles registered in Canada. The car made it possible for workers to commute longer distances and so stimulated the growth of suburban areas. This one development alone had important ramifications for thousands of married women, whose own workplace, the home, was consequently changed. Households tended to become smaller and more private; increased emphasis was put on the nuclear family as a unit of consumption rather than of production, and on married women's role in making the home a haven in an increasingly complex society. As scientific-management principles were applied to the household, women were expected to save time and energy through more efficient home management, and spend more time with their children and husbands. The creation of the first national airline, Trans-Canada Airlines (TCA), by the federal government in April 1937 was followed two months later by the first dawn-to-dusk flight between Montreal and Vancouver, lasting some 17-and-a-half hours. Passenger service across Canada and to the U.S. developed quickly, and TCA recruited its first stewardesses, as flight attendants were then called, in 1938. While few women could aspire to this position since TCA hired only young, single, petite, registered nurses to attend to its passengers, the initiation of air travel and air mail service broke down regional isolation and made it possible for well-to-do Canadians to travel to distant places with an ease unimagined by previous generations. For Aboriginal women in remote communities, the advent of the airplane brought more mixed consequences. Although it made it possible for them to receive critical supplies and medicine more quickly, the same machine could also take their children or other family members away from them to distant residential schools or sanatoria.

Despite several indicators that the worst of the Depression was over by 1937, for hundreds of thousands of Canadians conditions did not improve until after Canada entered World War II in September 1939; when peace returned, the country enjoyed over two decades of continuous prosperity. Canadian participation in the war depended heavily on women's voluntary activities, as well as on their work in the paid labour force and, for the first time, in the armed services. When war ended, women were expected to leave their paid work and turn their attention to marriage and motherhood. Many did, giving rise to the baby boom generation of the late 1940s through the mid-1960s. The decline in women's labour-force participation immediately after the war, however, appears to have resulted less from the withdrawal of women from paid work and more from the lower participation rate of young women.

Canada's population increased from just over 11 million inhabitants in 1939 to 18.2 million in 1961. This population growth had three components: (1) high rates of natural increase (the baby boom and declining death rates), (2) the entry of Newfoundland into Confederation in 1949, and (3) a massive influx of immigrants—some two million in the period between 1941 and 1960. Population growth varied from region to region:

283

Ontario, Quebec, and British Columbia attracted the bulk of the immigrants, but the highest percentage increases in population after the war were recorded in northern and western Canada, where resource-based industries continued to grow and expand. By contrast, the proportion of the Canadian population located in the Atlantic region declined, despite the addition of Newfoundland.

Although the wave of immigration that began immediately after World War II was still overwhelmingly British and American in origin, by 1950 this was no longer the case. Immigrants made their way from war-torn countries, such as Italy and Holland, and from European displaced persons camps; subsequently, many fled internal upheavals, such as the Hungarian revolution. By 1951, seven out of every ten immigrants came from countries other than the United States and Great Britain. Initially, after the war, the majority of those arriving at Canadian points of entry were men, but after 1958 female immigrants outnumbered male immigrants in most years.

The female immigrant experience was remarkably unchanged from previous generations. Successive groups of young single women—Polish, German, Italian, then West Indian—were recruited for domestic service, and many suffered the same hardships of isolation and generally poor working conditions that British- and other European-born domestics had experienced in years gone by. The principal way for most women to enter Canada, however, was as family members, which meant that the majority of women immigrants were ineligible for the benefits and programs, such as government-sponsored language courses, that were available to adult male immigrants.

Immigrants of both sexes continued to prefer the cities to the country, and during this period the inexorable transformation of Canada from a rural and agricultural nation to an overwhelmingly urban and industrial society was completed. According to the 1961 census, nearly seven out of every ten Canadians lived in an urban setting. It is important to note, however, that the rate of urbanization varied considerably: Ontario remained the most highly urbanized province, while Prince Edward Island was the least urbanized at 45 percent. Increasingly, Canadians lived in very large centres, such as Montreal, Toronto, and Vancouver, and immigrants of both sexes preferred city to rural life. Within these internal migration patterns, there were some interesting cycles. During the 1950s, the greatest growth rates occurred in the suburban areas of the metropolitan centres: by 1961, 45 percent of all urban residents lived in the suburbs.

Changes in the composition and distribution of the population were in large part responses to the ebb and flow of economic life. In general terms, Canadian economic development followed that of other western industrial nations. The movement from an industrial to a post-industrial society was signalled in the 1950s by the declining importance to the national economy of primary (resource-based) industry and of secondary industry, such as manufacturing, and the continuous growth of the service and clerical sectors. By 1951 this latter area—known as the tertiary sector—comprised 48 percent of the labour force. This shift created employment opportunities for women so that despite widespread opposition to their working for wages, increasing numbers of married women entered the labour force in the 1950s.

Married women's labour-force participation was greatly stimulated by the renewed emphasis on the production and purchase of consumer goods at war's end. Increased consumer spending and the creation of a national social welfare system were integral parts of the plan developed by the federal government for Canada's post-war recovery. Industries converted their tremendous capacity for wartime production to the manufacture of automobiles, appliances, and other household goods. The advent of television in the 1950s provided yet another medium—an even more powerful one—through which advertisers could convince Canadians that such products were essential to an improved standard of living. For most families, the purchase of expensive consumer items was possible only if there was more than one wage earner in the family. This role was increasingly filled by wives since prolonged education for children, and legal restrictions on child labour, greatly reduced the number of young adolescents active in the full-time workforce.

The master plan of Mackenzie King's Liberal government for ensuring Canada's prosperity after the war also involved a massive development of the nation's natural resources, particularly in the west and north. To expedite this process, the government encouraged Americans to invest in such projects as the construction of a pipeline to carry gas and oil from Alberta to eastern Canada. As American investment in Canada grew by leaps and bounds, so, too, did concerns about the nation's sovereignty. Prominent Canadians like economist Harold Innis warned that the country was now in the process of becoming a colony once again, this time of an increasingly powerful American empire. In 1950 the Massey Commission, the royal commission appointed to report on the state of the arts and sciences in Canada, documented just how fragile Canadian culture was as a result of the pervasiveness of the American influence. For their part, Canadian women were actively involved in addressing this issue, well before the establishment of the Canada Council in 1957. Individually and collectively, they organized, financed, and administered significant projects in theatre, dance, and the visual arts, thereby making a vital contribution to the development of a distinctive Canadian culture. The negative impact of Canada's reliance on the United States was a favourite theme of the Conservative opposition leader, populist John G. Diefenbaker. After forming a minority government in 1957, and calling an election the following year, the Conservatives swept into power in 1958 with the largest parliamentary majority up to that time in Canadian history. Just four years after his apparently decisive victory, however, Diefenbaker was defeated at the polls by the Liberals, now led by the internationally renowned diplomat Lester B. Pearson.

Capturing the essence of women's experience during this exciting phase of Canadian history is both easier and more difficult than for earlier periods. For this period, oral sources are available to feminist scholars; these can be used to supplement traditional written sources. New magazines directed chiefly at middle-class women made their appearance during the 1920s, and provide a fascinating window on women's domestic and public life. This period also saw the beginning of the welfare state; the implementation of selective means-tested programs, such as mothers' allowances and old age pensions, were the first tentative steps taken in the inter-war period, followed by unemployment insurance in 1940 and universal programs, including family allowances in 1944, old age security in 1951, and hospital insurance in 1957. The immigration influx promoted the expansion of existing social service agencies and the development of new ones aimed at helping newcomers adjust to Canadian life. As a result, voluntary organizations and government bureaucracies generated masses of documents on many aspects of women's lives. Because of the importance our culture assigns to public and political activities, the historical sources dealing with such activities are relatively abundant. When we turn to other aspects of women's activities and experiences, however, the material is harder to find. Autobiographical and biographical accounts of prominent women continue to be a valuable source, although the limits of such material are obvious. Fortunately, studies of immigrant, poor, and powerless women are now available to contribute significantly to our understanding of those women considered to have been on the margins of society. On the other hand, it is more difficult to locate personal letters and diaries for these years. Women probably wrote fewer letters because the telephone was more available, and new forms of entertainment took up their limited spare time. In any case, for immigrant and other marginalized women, paid and unpaid work left little time for the luxury of letter-writing. If personal documents, such as diaries and letters, exist, they are only beginning to be deposited in archives.

The time period from 1918 to 1960 has, until recently, received less attention from historians than that between 1850 and 1918. Even now, while women historians have turned their attention to many aspects of women's lives between 1918 and 1960, the study of women's organizations during the inter-war and post-war period remains less extensive than for the earlier period. This may explain the belief—now challenged—that the women's movement in Canada disappeared after the achievement of suffrage. Careful reconstruction of the activities and issues that mainstream women's organizations pursued from the 1920s through the 1950s is, however, beginning to reveal that, on the contrary, many groups continued to work actively for the transformation of Canadian society in accordance with their interpretation of feminist principles. During the inter-war years, for example, the movement to gain the provincial franchise for women in Quebec galvanized various francophone suffrage organizations and received support from other provincial women's groups. And, finally in 1940, legislation was passed enabling Quebec women to vote and hold office at the provincial level. Recent scholarship shows that the 1950s were not, as they have been labelled, a period of stagnation for women: rather, during this decade women increased their involvement in municipal politics, the proportion of married women working outside the household continued to increase, and equal pay for equal work legislation was enacted. Studies have also documented the roles played by women's magazines and women's groups to attain these positive advances for women. Why, then, are the 1950s frequently depicted as a time of little progress for Canadian women? Is it because our historical understandings and knowledge have been extrapolated from historical accounts of American women's experience in the 1940s and 1950s that have tended to cast the period as one of inactivity, if not regression for American women? It would appear that the same is not true for Canadian women, but the question remains as to why women's issues failed to generate the same attention they had attracted during the suffrage campaign.

Questions also persist over the long-term impact of the cataclysmic events of war, especially World War II, on women. The prevalent view among historians has been that government, industry, and society in general saw women's increased participation outside the home as an anomaly, justified only by the war-time state of emergency. As a result, there was a concerted effort to have women leave paid work. Other historians, especially those who have drawn on oral testimony, note that through their war-time experiences many Canadian women gained a new sense of confidence and autonomy that fuelled changes in their expectations for themselves and their daughters. Such historians argue that the war years laid the basis for subsequent changes in women's labour force participation and for the advancement of greater equality for women. Any debate on the impact of war must, however, also include a discussion of the negative war-time experiences of many women, especially those of marginalized groups, such as the Japanese, who were forced to leave their homes and live in internment camps.

Many other questions about women's lives arise from our documentation of this period. Studies of women during the Depression have raised questions about how major economic change affects the role and status of women over time. Other questions focus on technology. What was the impact, as far as women were concerned, of the changes that were introduced into the home and factory, beginning in the inter-war period, in the name of improved efficiency? How did the increased job opportunities in the service and clerical sectors help or impede women's career aspirations? New and improved appliances and products became available in the majority of middle-class urban households as the distribution of electricity widened. Their use significantly lightened women's load, but in what way did these changes also create new demands on women's time and energy? For the women living in the newly created suburbs of late 1940s and 1950s, were their lives fulfilled or were they eager to enter the labour force when circumstances permitted? And what factors in post-war Canada explain the reinvigorated women's movement that appeared in the 1960s?

CHAPTER NINE

Women in the Corporate Economy

> It is a natural conviction that enfranchised Canadian women will apply themselves intelligently and with energy to the basic economic problems of national existence. It is only through the help of women that the future can be made secure. The co-operation of Canadian women in industrial life and reconstruction is indispensable.[1]

So wrote Marjory MacMurchy, a well-known journalist, at the end of World War I. The gains women had made in the labour force during the war inspired considerable optimism; reformers like MacMurchy and Nellie McClung believed that women's invaluable war work and their new voting power would usher in an unprecedented era of social reform, including advancement for women. For them, *reconstruction* meant not the restoration of Canadian society as it existed prior to 1914 but, rather, its re-ordering into a more perfect society.

Many commentators focused on new opportunities for single, educated women to engage in work that was light, clean, and non-threatening to their womanhood. As a result, they stressed the importance of higher levels of education. If women were transient, low-wage workers, it was because they had failed to equip themselves adequately for the workplace. Writers therefore recommended occupations such as nutritionist, social worker, journalist, sales clerk, stenographer, and librarian for the educated woman.[2] It is important to note, however, that these optimistic messages were directed to Anglo-Celtic women and did not address the systemic racial and ethnic discrimination that blocked access to these new employment opportunities for Aboriginal, African-Canadian, Jewish, and many immigrant women. While there was a wider acceptance of single women in the labour force, a woman's paid employment was expected to span only a few years before she married. One writer typically opined that "no other work that a woman can do is as important to Canada as making a home and taking care of children."[3] Given the loss of 60 000 Canadian lives during the war, full-time motherhood acquired an enhanced national importance. Nonetheless, whatever their own views about becoming stay-at-home mothers, many women were unable to exercise this option. For those who had no male breadwinner on whom to rely, or for those whose spouses earned too little, paid employment was an absolute necessity.

THE MODERN WORKING GIRL, 1918–1929

When the hostilities ceased and the men returned, it was expected that women would cheerfully surrender their newly acquired positions in the workforce. To encourage them to do so, the federal government bombarded women with a poster campaign. "Do you feel justified in holding a job which could be filled by a man who has not only himself to support, but a wife and family as well?" one such poster demanded: "Think it over."[4] Women were urged to seek so-called feminine areas of employment where they would not threaten the position of male workers.

The tremendous social and economic dislocation the nation experienced at war's end reinforced the pre-war belief that women should not compete for men's jobs. Massive unemployment, labour unrest, and political ferment characterized the last years of the war and the immediate post-war era. By 1918, female unemployment had risen significantly; it was one of the issues discussed at the Women's War Conference in February of that year. Thousands of female workers suffered enormous hardships as jobs became scarce, wages were cut, and inflation soared. Although the Women's Department of the Reconstruction Association proclaimed that this was the age of the woman at work, it, too, counselled women to avoid direct competition with men for jobs. When women *could* secure employment, they often had to be content with traditional female jobs and inadequate wages. According to a sympathetic observer in Hamilton, Ontario, some were forced into prostitution to support themselves and their dependants:

> And they are all working girls! Here was the dressmaker's apprentice who could not live on nothing a week, there the worker in the jam factory who was out of work for three months and had to find her bread on the street.... Clerks, barmaids, factory hands, servants, laundry workers, every trade was represented in which women are over-worked and exploited.[5]

In 1921, according to the federal census, more than 17 percent of all Canadian women over the age of 15 were counted as members of the paid labour force, and they constituted 15 percent of all paid workers. (See Figures A6 and A7 in Appendix.) There was considerable regional variation: female labour-force participation rates were higher in the industrialized provinces of Ontario and Quebec (19 percent), and considerably lower in predominantly rural provinces, such as Prince Edward Island (13.5 percent), Saskatchewan, and Alberta (13 percent). As in previous decades, the majority of women who worked outside the home were young and single. Half of all female workers were under 25 years of age, compared to only one in four male workers.[6]

Photograph of a woman and girl working in "a room" on the Gaultois, Newfoundland, fishing docks, around 1920.

Source: The Rooms Provincial Archives Division, A 43-159 / G. A. England

The 1920s has often been portrayed as a period during which young people asserted their independence and challenged the moral and social dictates of their parents. In reality, however, the lives of working-class daughters throughout Canada largely replicated those of their mothers. Economic necessity still compelled thousands of girls under the age of 15 to go out to work, either on a part-time or a full-time basis. Most unmarried employed women continued to live at home or under the watchful eye of relatives or other surrogate parents and also continued to hand over a significant portion of their meagre earnings to their families.[7] Quebec textile workers in the 1920s, for example, reported that they kept only a small portion of their bi-monthly pay for themselves; in some cases this amounted to just a few cents. Single Jewish women working in Toronto's garment industry did the same, as did Chinese store clerks in British Columbia and Ukrainian daughters on the Prairies.[8] Because family was considered so important, young working women did not generally object to this custom. Even had they wanted to live away from home, their low wages would have prevented most of them from doing so.

For women living in small or remote communities, domestic service frequently continued to be the only form of paid employment available.[9] African-Canadian women, wherever they lived, often found that it was the only work they could secure. For all its constraints, live-in domestic service could have several positive features: steady employment, room and board, an opportunity to learn English or French and to become familiar with middle-class Canadian customs. Angelina, a Micmac of Prince Edward Island, escaped from a "terrible childhood" and left home at the age of 15 in 1919: "I did not want to live there [on the reserve]. I could only get three cents a quart for blueberries and I resented the fact that I could barely speak English, that I had no education, that all I could do was wash dishes and scrub floors." She left the reserve to take a domestic job in Springhill, Nova Scotia, that paid the relatively substantial amount of $5 a month.[10]

As most Canadian-born white women continued to reject the long hours, low wages, demeaning status, and lack of privacy of household service, the federal government increased its efforts to encourage the immigration of foreign-born domestics. The majority still came from Great Britain; in the decade after the war, some 80 000 British women, including nearly 24 000 girls under the age of 18 sponsored by the Salvation Army, entered Canada to be domestic servants. Domestic service was also still being advocated as a suitable occupation for British gentlewomen, who were provided accommodation in hostels such as the Queen Mary's Coronation Hostel in Vancouver, where they were also given six- to eight-week training courses to enable them to secure employment as "home helps." The promoters of this type of work, usually pursued in rural areas for $20 to $25 per month, claimed that it was appropriate for British "ladies" since they were to be placed with families of similar social standing to their own, and to be treated as one of the family. Since there was a great deal of racism in Canada at the time and prejudice particularly against Asians, some residents favoured these immigration schemes as a means to strengthening imperial ties with Britain while reinforcing the white population by replacing Chinese male domestics.[11]

There was a substantial increase in domestic servants from other parts of Europe as well. Finnish servants, who constituted 8 percent of all immigrant domestics in the 1920s, took great pride in their work; for them, to be a servant was to be far from servile. When conditions proved unsatisfactory, they reacted energetically and in a variety of ways, ranging from frequent changes of employer to collective organization. Indeed, during the 1920s Finnish maids' organizations were established in a number of urban centres.[12] In 1931, one-quarter of all immigrant domestics in Ontario were from continental Europe; those from Germany and the Scandinavian countries were preferred, since it was widely believed that they could be readily assimilated into Canadian society. Because the demand for domestics regularly outstripped supply, however, the newly created Woman's Branch of the Department of Immigration also recruited women from central and eastern Europe. All unaccompanied immigrant women were put under the supervision of federally appointed train conductresses, who were to prevent their charges from being enticed away with offers of employment before they reached their intended destinations. Yet escapes did occur. From one party of 25 women, for example, 3 ran away in Montreal, and another 2 were caught trying to climb through the window minutes before the train's departure.[13]

Although the federal government had enacted highly restrictive immigration laws designed to exclude Chinese, Japanese, South Asians, Jews, and blacks, willingness to work as a domestic could ease entry into Canada for some women. In fact, almost twice as many black women as men entered Canada via ocean ports between 1916 and

1928. Of the 411 black women admitted to the country, the vast majority (329) came as domestic servants. Some of these women arrived under the provisions of a domestic-recruitment agreement between Canada and Guadeloupe initiated in 1921, but the plan lasted only a short time. Most of those recruited returned home.[14]

In western Canada, immigrant husbands and wives were frequently employed together as agricultural labourers. When Helen Potrebenko's parents first arrived in Alberta in 1928, her mother "fed the pigs in the morning, milked five cows, separated the milk, washed the separator, then repeated the whole thing in the evening. In between, she picked roots on newly-broken land," all for $1 per day.[15] Even when women stooked grain all day long in the fields as efficiently as their husbands, they were paid less than the men. Women also constituted half the seasonal workers in the fruit-growing areas of Ontario's Erie and Niagara regions in 1930. Similarly, British Columbia farmers relied heavily on women workers. Some Chinese women have since recalled their experience of this work. "Ruth" remembered that "The women used to take me to the farms when I was four or five in the summers. My mom weeded for 10 cents an hour in the 1920s."[16]

Women workers in employment sectors other than domestic service and agriculture could usually obtain better wages and shorter hours than women who worked in those two areas. However, overall, women remained clustered in certain industries and confined to low-paying jobs. (See Tables A5 and A6 in Appendix.) Even in industries where they formed a significant proportion of the workforce, women rarely posed a direct threat to male employment, since jobs were generally assigned on the basis of gender as well as race or ethnicity. The clothing, textile, and food industries continued to rely heavily on female labour, and the expanding retail and service sector created a demand for store clerks, waitresses, hotel workers, and beauticians. In British Columbia, Aboriginal women, and those of Japanese and Chinese descent found seasonal work in the salmon canneries, while recently arrived Jewish women from eastern Europe were concentrated in certain jobs in the garment industry in Montreal, Toronto, and Winnipeg.

A striking example of the intersecting dynamics of race and gender can be seen in the intensification of efforts to keep white women from working for, or even with, Chinese men. In 1923, British Columbia enacted the Women and Girls Protection Act, similar to legislation passed in Saskatchewan in 1912, that made it illegal for Chinese businesses to hire white women. The law was a response to popular concerns about potential intimacy between races and working girls' morality. Many individuals and groups, however, did not think that the law went far enough, since white employers could continue to hire both Chinese men and white women. The next year in Vancouver, there was a sensational murder case in which a Chinese house boy was accused of killing a Scottish nanny working in the same home. In response, Mary Ellen Smith—the first woman elected to B.C.'s legislature—introduced legislation to prevent households from simultaneously employing Chinese men and white women. This legislation was publicly opposed by some female domestic servants who feared losing their jobs, and it was ultimately declared unconstitutional. The question of whether the nanny had committed suicide—as the police originally determined—or been murdered, went unresolved. Nonetheless, white waitresses in cities such as Vancouver, Regina, and Toronto lost their jobs because of the enforcement of laws making it illegal for Chinese employers, many of whom were naturalized British citizens, to employ white women.[17]

A complex interplay of factors continued to determine the sexual division of labour. In general, women were excluded from skilled positions or from exercising control over the work process or over other workers. "Foreladies" were rare, and exercised authority only over other female operatives. In any work resembling that done in the home, women were still relegated to positions with less control and fewer rewards than those held by men. In the clothing industry, for example, men had jobs that were more prestigious and better paying as cutters and pressers, while women lined, hemmed, and finished the garments. Increasingly, female garment workers were concentrated in the highly competitive women's dress industry, a sector characterized by large numbers of small, under-capitalized contract shops, widely fluctuating markets dictated by rapid changes in fashions, and high levels of seasonal unemployment. By contrast, men were more likely to be employed in the larger, more stable companies producing men's made-to-measure wear. In the few instances where women and men did the same work, they often worked on different shifts—the women during the day, the men at night. Most factory departments were, therefore, predominantly of one sex, thus enhancing solidarity among workers of the same sex but impeding a sense of common interest between the sexes. When women and men performed the same tasks and were paid on an hourly basis, the men were nearly always paid at a higher rate. In the Toronto garment industry, for instance, the average female wage was one-half to two-thirds of the average male wage.[18]

During the 1920s, industrial workers of both sexes had to contend with the consequences of an increased emphasis on efficiency and scientific management techniques. As a result of time studies and technological innovation designed to increase profits, operatives faced speedups and ever-mounting production quotas. On the whole, women workers were more vulnerable to the negative effects of technological change, since they were virtually excluded from the decision-making process and were more often paid piece rates. When workers consistently achieved their quotas, unscrupulous employers cut their piecework rates. The nervous strain created by the hectic pace of production in manufacturing took its toll on the workers' health. In one Winnipeg clothing factory, a labour newspaper reported that the "girls" were seated side by side on long benches, and all sewing machines were operated by a single motor. As a result, the individual operators could not leave their machines without causing all to fall behind. The only respite from this arduous regimen was the half-hour the workers were allowed for lunch, which they were required to eat in the workroom.[19]

Many of the worst injustices, however, were experienced by workers in individual households under the system of "sweated labour." Entire families, often recent immigrants, basted, hemmed, cut out appliqués, or sewed on buttons at wages well below those paid in factories. Such workers were generally at the mercy of the clothing subcontractors, and were not protected by legislation of any sort. Nor was such work confined to the garment trade; in Toronto one food company sent out bushels of onions to Italian women for peeling and washing, and then collected the onions for further processing at its plant. Home work, for all its problems, was nevertheless the preferred form of employment for many immigrant women, since it allowed them to work with other family members and to combine paid employment with domestic responsibilities.[20]

Given the difficult conditions, limited opportunities, and low status of women workers in the manufacturing sector, clerical work became an increasingly attractive option. However, by the early 1920s there was already a glut of stenographers and typists. Ironically, these women shared a common fate with their supposed social inferiors, the so-called factory girls. Some stenographers and secretaries continued to perform skilled work, but with the increased specialization that took place after 1920, many female office workers were relegated to subordinate positions that were routine, low-paying, and dead-end.[21] Other white-collar occupations generally regarded as appropriate for women were those of sales clerk and telephone operator. In these positions, too, women were subject to a rigid sexual division of labour, intense competition from other women workers, low wages, and long hours.

For visible-minority women, there was the added problem of racial discrimination. Businesses routinely refused to hire Chinese or black women with secretarial training and, as one observer noted in 1930 with respect to black women in Montreal, "unless they have no negroid features coloured girls cannot obtain work in offices and stores."[22] Although most people believed that employers preferred young, single, clerical workers, at least one study indicated that the reality was far more complex. In 1929 the Toronto Local Council of Women surveyed 300 stenographers and secretaries. It found that four-fifths of them lived with their employed husbands and well over half had children. The largest number (35 percent) said that they worked to support themselves and their families. Slightly more than half saw their work as long-term, giving responses such as "always" to a question about how long they intended to work.[23]

The influx of women into the federal civil service during the first decades of the twentieth century had been a source of great concern for male bureaucrats, who feared the large numbers of women in government employment would deter bright young men from pursuing careers in that sector. After 1910 the most important positions were explicitly reserved for men. In 1918 additional restrictions were placed on female employment, and by 1921 women were virtually excluded from all permanent positions in the federal bureaucracy. Female employees who married were required to hand in their resignations. These stringent measures achieved their goal: between 1921 and 1931 there was a 13 percent decline in the number of female civil servants working in Ottawa, while the number of male civil servants increased by more than 6 percent.[24]

Women's opportunities for advancement in the business world were also extremely limited. Deeply rooted misogynist views surfaced in articles such as "Woman in Business Is Still at Heart a Woman," in which the author pontificated, "A man can do business very successfully with someone he dislikes but I have never met a woman who could."[25] Since it was assumed that women were destined for marriage, it seemed a waste of time and money to train them for more responsible positions. Nevertheless, wives were often indispensable to the successful operation of small family businesses, such as restaurants, laundries, grocery stores, and shoeshine parlours. As one Canadian-born Chinese woman recalled, "My mother helped out for many long hours in the laundry. She did not even go out to shop. She worked the longest. My mother worked six days and also Sunday. . . . Sometimes she had to cook for thirteen."[26] Rosetta Amon Richardson, the Toronto-born daughter of an Underground Railroad refugee, owned and operated the city's first Soul Food Restaurant with her husband before setting up and running a lunch counter at the Canadian National Exhibition.[27]

Traditional skills continued to be valuable sources of family income. African-Canadian women sold baskets at Halifax's city market, as they had since at least the mid-nineteenth century. In 1928, at the age of eight, Edith Clayton of East Preston, Nova Scotia, made her first maple basket for sale, thereby maintaining a six-generation family tradition. Across the continent in British Columbia, grandmother Mollyann of the Sechelt band also wove baskets, using the cedar roots she collected. She traded these to clothe her 15 children and later her grandchildren. Micmac women of Prince Edward Island applied their traditional skills to resist government initiatives to keep them and their families as stationary farmers at the Lennox Island Reserve. Cash earned through selling baskets and other crafts supported the Micmac in maintaining, albeit at near starvation-level wages, the migratory way of life they had historically preferred. Flower-selling, fishing, and blueberry- and potato-picking supplemented the women's craft income. In the outports of Newfoundland, wives earned much-needed cash through their berry-picking, and their management of the complex, all-important processing of the cod catch on shore.[28]

Resourceful women everywhere capitalized on or created opportunities to generate income. For example, in some communities Finnish women bootleggers or *Koiratorpparit*

Inuit women cleaning walrus hides at Cape Dorset, Northwest Territories, in 1929. Cape Dorset is now known as Kinngait, Nunavut.

Source: Library and Archives Canada / PA-101304

("doghouse"/"blind pig keepers") controlled the illegal liquor trade.[29] Other women turned to prostitution rather than accept the low wages offered by industrial employment and domestic service. In some Montreal brothels, the women were said to service up to 40 clients a night, and they were able to keep half of the $1 each client was charged. The vast majority of Canadians, however, continued to view prostitutes as moral degenerates, and not primarily as workers providing sexual services. Given the social ostracism and the many dangers associated with sex work—sexually transmitted diseases, violence, unwanted pregnancies, drug addiction, police harassment, and arrests—few women lasted long in the trade, however lucrative it might be. For those who worked in western Canadian brothels, the continuation of wartime Prohibition in many localities led to a sharp downturn in business, since brothels generated much of their income from the sale of liquor. In fact, Prohibition spelled the demise of red-light districts in many urban communities.[30]

For its part, nursing enjoyed a new level of respectability during this period, attracting thousands of young women into its ranks. From just over 300 in 1901, the number of nurses in Canada rose to over 20 000 by 1921, and nursing became one of the primary occupations for Canadian women in the 1920s.[31] The public image of nursing was greatly enhanced by the extraordinary heroism of the nursing sisters who served overseas during the war, and the important role nurses played in combating the horrendous Spanish influenza epidemic of 1918–19, which resulted in 50 000 Canadian deaths. Attempting to capitalize on their enhanced reputation, determined nurses engaged in an intensified campaign to control their profession. In 1919, advocates succeeded in convincing the University of British Columbia to establish the first university degree program in nursing in the British Empire. Shortly after, the University of Toronto and McGill University created similar academic programs to meet the urgent need for nursing teachers, nursing administrators, and public health nurses. Thanks to the efforts of the Grey Nuns, the *Université de Montréal* established the first university nursing course for francophone women in 1922.[32]

These initiatives to upgrade nursing did not, however, win unanimous approval either outside or inside the profession. In 1920, for example, the College of Physicians and Surgeons in British Columbia stated that two years of training was quite sufficient for nurses and proclaimed that "the overtraining of nurses is not desirable and results largely in the losing of their usefulness."[33] In fact, most nurses could not afford to take the five-year degree course and opted instead for the two- or three-year apprenticeships offered by the hospitals. Even for those more accessible, hospital-based forms of nursing education, administrators gave preference to white high-school graduates to reinforce the image of nursing as a respectable, middle-class profession. Chinese women seeking training and employment as nurses in British Columbia hospitals, such as the Vancouver General, faced explicit exclusion under racist policies. Similar bans blocked women of other races. In 1937, a Nova Scotia woman named Marie gave up her dream of being a nurse and decided to train as a teacher because Nova Scotia hospitals barred black women from nurses' training until 1945.[34]

Nurses throughout the country did, however, achieve some success in gaining control over who could be a member of the profession. Like doctors, they embraced science-based medicine and scientific management techniques to enhance their professional status and to distinguish themselves from untrained caregivers. By 1922, all provinces had enacted legislation that set out education and training requirements for registered nurses and that invested the power of registration in the hands of provincial nursing associations. Nonetheless, nurses did not achieve a level of power to regulate their members comparable to that enjoyed by the male medical profession. In Quebec, religious and linguistic differences further complicated the regulatory process. There, the 1920 legislation that had given the predominantly anglophone registered nurses' association exclusive control over registration was amended two years later at the insistence of some francophone nurses and doctors. As a result, the criteria for registration were diluted and the association's control over registration was broken.[35]

A national survey of nursing education reported in 1929 that the raison d'être of the nursing schools continued to be the provision of cheap labour for the hospitals. Most student nurses put in a 12-hour workday (nine hours on the wards, and three hours of lectures and study). During their first year of training, in particular, they were required to perform many heavy housekeeping duties. Once trained, most of them were replaced in hospitals by a new group of unpaid student nurses. In 1929, 60 percent of graduate nurses continued to be employed as private-duty nurses in patients' homes, where domestic work was often expected of them. During times of economic crisis, private-duty nurses found it difficult to secure full-time employment and had to compete with untrained women who were willing to provide similar services for lower wages. Among the private-duty nurses who participated in the 1929 survey, 60 percent stated that they were not able to save for their retirement. Still, some nurses actually preferred private duty nursing to working in a hospital setting since it afforded them more variety and a greater degree of autonomy.[36]

During the 1920s, the general shortage of nurses was particularly keenly felt in the area of public health nursing. Provincial and municipal health services grew in response to an emerging consensus about the fundamental importance of healthy citizens to nation-building. Provinces either set up their own nursing services or worked with other organizations, such as the Canadian Red Cross Society (CRCS), to provide them. To meet the demand for public health nurses, the CRCS established post-graduate training programs at five universities across Canada. Many of the first nurses recruited for isolated communities had formerly served in the nursing service of the Canadian Army Medical Corps. They had the experience, skills, and personalities needed to surmount the many challenges they encountered, as they travelled in all seasons—including on foot, by horse, by dogsled, and by railroad handcar—throughout their large, under-resourced districts. By 1922 there were more than 1 000 public health nurses in Canada.[37] And industry as well as governments found the employment of public nurses beneficial. For example, the Metropolitan Life Insurance Company substantially reduced its payouts to policyholders arising from infant and maternal deaths by sending nurses on a regular basis to visit pregnant and postpartum working-class women in their homes.[38]

In addition to receiving higher wages than nurses who worked in hospitals or private homes, public health nurses also enjoyed a greater degree of autonomy from physicians, especially when they were posted to remote areas. The range of regular and emergency health services these specialized nurses were called upon to deliver was seemingly limitless, as Edith Macey, the nurse at the Fisher Branch station in rural Manitoba, soon discovered.

Nurses aboard a hospital ship visiting Bella Bella, British Columbia, in the 1920s.

Source: Image B-07085 courtesy of Royal BC Museum, BC Archives. Image has been altered.

In addition to attending births and treating a variety of human ailments, she performed major surgery on a cow and a horse, and also saved a flock of young turkeys by administering medication. Although only Alberta and Newfoundland officially sanctioned the practice of nurses acting as midwives, midwifery was a standard part of outpost nursing. As a result of the efforts of a group of St. John's women, Newfoundland had its own training program in midwifery and nursing, and also recruited trained nurse-midwives, primarily from the United Kingdom, through organizations such as the Newfoundland Outport Nursing and Industrial Association and the International Grenfell Association.[39]

Whether they worked in remote areas or in urban settings, public health nurses also acted as social service providers, transmitting the norms and values of white, middle-class society, especially to immigrant, Aboriginal, and Métis communities. These nurses sometimes met with hostility or indifference from doctors and other male community leaders when they sought to establish much-needed services that were aimed primarily at women and children. The fact that physicians were paid on a fee-for-service basis meant that the dispensing of medical services by nurses—for free or for a modest fee—could represent a threat to doctors' livelihoods, as well as to their professional authority.[40]

Teaching remained the other primary occupation for women; in 1921, four out of every five teachers in Canada were women. Despite efforts to professionalize teaching by increasing educational requirements and improving working conditions, female teachers continued to have less training, be more likely to teach in rural, one-room schools, and be paid considerably less than their male counterparts. They also continued to be over-whelmingly young and single, with most exchanging their schoolroom duties for mar-riage and motherhood after a few years of teaching. In 1930, for example, 83.5 percent of rural schoolteachers in British Columbia were female, and 92.5 percent of women teachers were single. A similar situation prevailed in Nova Scotia, where some 1 700 autonomous school sections, seeking to keep education costs to a minimum, routinely hired single young women who lacked proper qualifications and had little or no teaching experience. Ongoing problems for rural schoolteachers in most provinces included isola-tion, poor housing, primitive and ill-equipped schoolhouses, overwork, lack of commu-nity support, and the need to deal with students of diverse ages and ethnic origins. For Mabel Jones, the 20-year-old teacher at Nixon Creek, an isolated logging camp beside Lake Cowichan on Vancouver Island, the strain proved too much when parents of three of her students continued to criticize her. In November 1928, she wrote a note saying "There are a few people who would like to see me out of the way, so I am trying to please them . . . what they said about me almost broke my heart. They are not true. Forgive me, please," and then she killed herself with a .22 rifle. A much less drastic and more representative response to pressure from students' parents was that of Mary Williams, who made the following caustic entry in her diary upon leaving her teaching post: "This is some life. Believe you me. The person who considers it an a honour to be a school-teacher is a couple of centuries behind time." Nevertheless, with its tradition of calling on women's nurturing qualities, and its respectability, primary schoolteaching retained its place as the female profession of choice in the inter-war period. It was also relevant that wages for even the most poorly paid teacher in 1931 were well above the average weekly wage of $12.01 for Canadian women.[41]

With the graduation of more women from Canadian universities and the expansion of secondary school education in the 1920s, many more women were hired to teach in high schools. At the end of the decade, women accounted for 70 percent of the students preparing for high school teaching at the University of Toronto's Faculty of Education, and over half of Ontario's secondary school teachers were women. However, there con-tinued to be a differential wage scale, with women teachers receiving substantially lower wages than their male counterparts. The rationale for the higher wage scale for men was that they were supporting families, but even single male teachers benefitted from this regime. Promotions also depended on gender: regardless of experience or skill, female high school teachers were excluded from administrative positions at the school and board levels. There was, moreover, a bar to the employment of married women, unless they could prove that they bore the primary responsibility for the economic maintenance of their family, or that they had some skill that made it very difficult to replace them.[42]

Some female educators such as Dr. Donalda Dickie, who taught at all three Alberta normal schools, played a significant role in the advancement of progressive education in Canada during this period. However, in spite of advanced degrees and extensive expe-rience, their gender prevented women faculty members from holding senior positions in the educational hierarchy. The proportion of women hired as university faculty did increase during this decade; by 1931, women accounted for 19 percent of full-time uni-versity teachers. But, as studies of women employed at Dalhousie University and at the universities of Toronto and Manitoba show, most women with advanced degrees occupied the lower paid and less prestigious jobs of instructor or demonstrator. When women achieved administrative positions in universities, they usually did so as deans of women or in female-dominated academic areas, such as home economics, nursing, and social work.[43]

It was during the 1920s that social work emerged as a significant new female profession, following the establishment of state-funded bureaucracies to implement new laws respecting child welfare, housing, mothers' allowances, and minimum wages for women. University-trained social workers using modern casework techniques increasingly replaced middle-class female volunteers acting on behalf of religious and charitable organizations. By 1928, the University of Toronto, McGill University, and the University of British Columbia had established schools of social work. In an effort to consolidate their position as professionals, graduates of these programs formed the Canadian Association of Social Workers in 1926.[44] In Quebec, in keeping with the tradition long established in teaching and nursing, the Roman Catholic Church insisted on controlling social welfare work involving francophone Catholics. Marie Gérin-Lajoie, daughter of the feminist activist Marie Lacoste Gérin-Lajoie, and the first French-Canadian woman to receive a Bachelor of Arts degree, studied social work at New York's Columbia University in 1918. Upon returning to Montreal, she started to work with poor families. As a result of pressure from the Church, Gérin-Lajoie subsequently took holy orders, founding the Institut Notre-Dame du Bon-Conseil in order to continue her work. In 1931, she established her own social welfare school, and eight years later, she offered one of the first courses in the newly established social work program at the Université de Montréal.[45]

Other emerging professions for women rose from the pressing need to treat thousands of soldiers wounded during the war and to rehabilitate them for return to civilian life. During the war, health-care workers, most of whom were women, received specialized training in massage and medical exercise. In 1920 they created their own organization, which eventually became the Canadian Physiotherapy Association. The association pressed for the establishment of a university program in physiotherapy, a goal achieved in 1929 at the University of Toronto. Training programs for occupational aides developed during the war as well, and by 1919 there were three-month courses available at the University of Toronto and at McGill. Over the next decade, occupational therapists found employment in military hospitals, tuberculosis sanatoriums, general hospitals, and mental hospitals. Their first professional associations were formed in Manitoba and Ontario in 1920, and by 1926, the Canadian Association of Occupational Therapists had been established. The exigencies of war, and the need to attend to the dietary needs of soldiers, similarly stimulated the growth of dietetics as a female profession.[46]

The 1920s also saw the continued small-scale entry of women into some male-dominated professions. For the first time, the federal census of 1921 included women architects, and in 1925, Esther Hill became the first registered woman architect when she joined the Alberta Association of Architects. While only four other women across Canada formally registered as architects over the next decade, a larger number studied architecture and subsequently worked in areas related to home and interior design. In 1927, Elsie Gregory MacGill, daughter of feminist activist and judge Helen Gregory MacGill, was the first woman in Canada to graduate with a bachelor of electrical engineering degree; two years later, she became the first woman in North America to obtain a master's degree in aeronautical engineering. Another first for women and aviation in Canada occurred in 1928 when Eileen Vollick, a textile analyst from Hamilton, successfully completed the requirements for a professional pilot's licence. She subsequently demonstrated aerobatic flying throughout Canada and the United States.[47]

Clara Brett Martin had led the way for women's entry into the law profession by being called to the Ontario bar in 1897, but few women followed in her footsteps over the next three decades. According to the 1931 census, there were 54 women lawyers across Canada, representing under one percent of all lawyers. Traditional views that women were too frail or irrational to be good lawyers or that they would waste their education by marrying and withdrawing from the profession persisted well into the twentieth century. Jewish women and other women of non-Anglo-Celtic backgrounds found it especially difficult to gain admission to the profession. Those women who did get into law schools frequently encountered a hostile environment there, and many withdrew before completing their studies. Those who finished their studies often had great difficulty obtaining the articling positions they needed to complete their law education. For those who persevered, graduates generally found it easier to secure government positions than to break into private practice.[48] Although more women entered medicine than law, the numbers of women physicians in Canada scarcely increased between 1911 and 1931, rising from 196 to 203. The desire to work as a medical missionary in countries such as China and India continued to motivate some women to enter medical school in the inter-war period. Just as female law students struggled to find articling positions, female medical students had great difficulty securing internships since most hospitals had a quota of only one or two female interns. Another shared trait between the two professions was the apparent preference for public employment following graduation. A study of women physicians in Manitoba indicates that they were to be found in institutional settings, such as hospitals and government health services, rather than in private practice, presumably because they were more accepted in such surroundings.[49]

ATTEMPTS AT IMPROVEMENT: WORKERS AND GOVERNMENTS REACT

Given women workers' low wages and acute vulnerability to the ravages of postwar inflation, it is not surprising that they played an active part in the labour unrest that swept through many communities after the war. In the early spring of 1919, for example, nearly 200 Victoria schoolteachers staged the first teachers' strike in the British Empire to support their demands for improved wages to offset spiralling inflation rates. Women were also the first to walk out in the Winnipeg General Strike on May 15, 1919. When some 500 telephone operators left their jobs shortly after dawn, hundreds of confectionery workers and sales clerks subsequently joined them. One of the most visible strike organizers in the General Strike was Helen Armstrong, president of the city's Women's Labor League (WLL). The WWL brought together unions representing an array of women workers in the retail, hotel, food, laundry, and garment industries, and even some in domestic service. During the strike, Armstrong was arrested several times and on one occasion jailed for several days for urging workers to walk off the job as well as allegedly inciting strikers to violence. Under her direction, the WLL provided up to 1 500 meals daily to women strikers and others in need. In addition, it gave cash grants to women who were on strike to cover the cost of their rent. Merchants or their agents who sought to carry on business as usual incurred the wrath of women who supported the strike; one company had three delivery wagons destroyed, and its drivers assaulted. A detective sent out to investigate warned that a strike-breaker should not go to that district for "his life is in danger if these women find out that he is at work, or had been working during the strike." The local mainstream press devoted significant coverage to the verbal and physical violence of some women supporting the strike, portraying the transgressors of respectable ladylike behaviour as rough and profane foreigners. Much less offensive to prevailing social norms were the dances and socials organized by the women's unions, which generated considerable revenues to add to the strike fund. Not all women, however, supported the strike; indeed, some worked to undermine it by crossing picket lines to provide what they considered essential services.[50]

The telephone operators in Vancouver played a visible but costly role in the general strike called there to support the Winnipeg workers. They did not join the initial walkout, since they were classified as essential workers by the strike committee, but 300 operators left their jobs at the peak of the strike in the middle of June. Although the Vancouver General Strike came to an end on July 3, the operators remained on strike until the middle of the month to protest the telephone company's policy of replacing striking supervisors and senior employees with strike-breakers. In the end, however, the operators had to return to work on the company's terms, and within a year the telephone operators' union disappeared. More successfully, by the end of 1919, hundreds of women telephone operators in Toronto had secured substantial improvements in their working conditions through unionization. Also in Toronto, a newly established union of bank employees claimed that over half of all bank clerks, many of whom were women, had joined its ranks. Other groups of women who had traditionally been considered unorganizable, such as domestic servants and waitresses, also joined unions. During the sympathy strike called in mid-May to support Toronto metal workers, approximately 2 000 garment workers joined in a show of solidarity.[51]

Responding in part to pressure from women's groups to improve the position of female workers, provincial governments extended their protective legislation by passing minimum wage laws that applied to women only. Organized labour, mainly because such laws limited female competition for male workers, also supported them. In 1917, Alberta became the first province to adopt a minimum wage law for women. Most provinces followed suit: British Columbia and Manitoba did so in 1918, Saskatchewan and Quebec in 1919, and Nova Scotia and Ontario in 1920. By the end of the decade, only New Brunswick and Prince Edward Island still had not passed such laws. But it took Alberta until 1924 to set up a permanent wage board, and minimum wage legislation was not actually put into force until 1927 in Quebec and until 1930 in Nova Scotia.[52]

A number of reasons motivated the proponents of these new legislative measures. The stated purpose of Ontario's minimum wage laws was not only to ensure "the right of the worker to live from her work," but also "to preserve the health, morals and efficiency of that large class of women dependent on their daily wage for a living."[53] As the number of young, Canadian-born women entering the labour force continued to mount, so did concern over the future of the Anglo-Saxon race: those very same women who toiled in industry, it was pointed out, would one day be the mothers of the nation. Some prominent feminists, such as British Columbia's Helen Gregory MacGill, served on provincial wage commissions while others were firmly opposed to minimum wage laws, and the pros and cons of protective legislation for women became the focus of vigorous debate. Maud Petitt Hill, a middle-class journalist and reformer, declared that protective legislation was highly desirable because women workers were even less unionized than men. She also argued that working "girls" had to be protected from themselves; otherwise, they might "overwork with the mere ambition of owning silken hose and patent pumps" and subsequently "produce an inferior race." Further, it was undesirable to have women working night shifts and "walking the streets alone at night."[54]

Other supporters of minimum wage laws for women, such as the British Columbia union activist Helena Gutteridge, were more clearly motivated by concern for the female worker's economic status. They firmly believed that such laws would result in improved wages and a better standard of living for women. Gutteridge also urged the organization of unions and championed equal pay for equal work.[55] Some concerned women, however, criticized protection as unwarranted privilege and a poor substitute for equality. They also pointed out that protective laws would render women less competitive, so that the principal beneficiaries of the maximum hours and minimum wages that applied only to women would be male workers. Moreover, the argument that such legislation would help preserve their morality was insulting to the women workers.

Minimum wage commissions began their work by establishing the basic weekly amount a single female worker required to keep herself in a respectable, if somewhat impoverished, state. In a number of provinces, the highest recommended amount was $12.50 per week. There was no acknowledgment that many female wage earners had dependants to support, nor was there provision for retirement savings or vacations. The budget that the commissioners invented was based on a full year's employment, an unattainable goal for many women. A third highly questionable assumption was that only a few unscrupulous employers were paying unconscionably low wages. Minimum wage rates varied from province to province and from industry to industry, and a separate order had to be issued to cover women in each trade. Within a province, the rate for women in the same type of employment might differ according to the size of community in which the worker resided, her age, and her experience. By the end of the decade, the majority of provinces had set minimum wages for most large groups of female employees. The exceptions, however, were notable: all those engaged in agriculture, domestic service, banking, teaching, and nursing. Initially, the wage commissions had no authority to regulate hours, a situation that many employers exploited by simply offsetting mandatory higher wages with longer hours. Eventually, however, this power was conceded to all provincial commissions except the one in Quebec.

Unfortunately, the minimum rate rapidly became the maximum most women could earn—and even these low wages were not guaranteed to all workers. There were exemptions for employers, for example, with respect to inexperienced workers or minors under the age of 18, as well as for "handicapped" workers and the elderly. In the case of piece workers, only 80 percent had to attain the minimum rate.[56] In addition, the problems created by the regulations were exacerbated by those related to enforcement. There were few inspectors, and the fines for contravening the law were paltry. Employers frequently claimed ignorance of the law, and many employees were unaware of its existence or were too intimidated to invoke it. In the needle trades, those piece workers who were furthest from earning the minimum wage at week's end were subject to layoffs or dismissal. When, in December 1924, the King Edward Hotel in Toronto posted an increase in chambermaids' weekly hours from 54 to 69, without any pay increase, 25 women struck and took their case to the Ontario Minimum Wage Board. Their employer, however, refused to deal with with any organized labour representation; the Board closed the file without any improvement to the chambermaids' pay.[57] Several other methods employers used to contravene the legislation included having more than one employee punch in on the same time card, switching workers from job to job, firing and rehiring them so that they could continue to be classified as inexperienced, or using so many different piecework rates that it was virtually impossible for workers and inspectors to discern how the wages had been calculated. Although wage commissions continued to claim that employers who resorted to such practices were rare exceptions (and primarily of foreign origin), many respectable and well-known establishments, such as the T. E. Eaton Company and the Robert Simpson Company, were among the offenders. The Minimum Wage Boards had initially reassured nervous employers that female wages would not rise drastically, and they were right; women workers continued to earn on average 54 to 60 percent of what men earned.

Was there a better alternative to government intervention to improve the lot of women workers? Many believed that there was: unionization. Outspoken female champions of working women, such as Communist activists Annie Buller, Becky Buhay, Bella Hall Gauld, and Florence Custance, argued that only by recognizing the class origins of their exploitation and then organizing themselves could working women effect significant changes in their lives. Buller, who had been sent at the age of 13 to work in a Montreal tobacco factory, worked her way up from sales clerk to department store buyer; in the end, however, she turned her back on what appears to have been a highly desirable position and devoted herself to Marxist politics and labour activism. She and her friends Buhay and Gauld were instrumental in setting up the Montreal Labour College in 1920 to promote the study of Marxism and to provide a meeting place for workers. Florence Custance was similarly involved in the Ontario Labour College, and in 1926, she established *The Woman Worker,* a newspaper representing the Canadian Federation of Women's Labor Leagues, then a network of 10 organizations scattered across the country. It was the first socialist publication in Canada devoted entirely to politicization of "all working women, whether they work in the factory, at home or in the office." Until its demise following Custance's death in 1929, the paper explored issues such as labour conditions, unionization, domestic labour, housing, protective legislation, birth control, and militarism. Jeanne Corbin, a young francophone woman from northern Alberta, was another important activist. Recruited by Buhay and Buller in 1929 to contribute to Communist labour publications in both Ontario and Quebec, Corbin became an organizer among miners and bush workers in northern Ontario and Quebec, and was later imprisoned for her involvement in the 1934 miners' strike in Noranda, Quebec.[58] Through their writings, their speaking tours, and their participation in various important strikes—and in some cases through their arrests—socialist women worked on behalf of both female and male workers.

During the 1920s, however, few Canadians of either sex embraced Communism or unions; after 1923, only one out of every eight non-agricultural paid workers was a union member. According to one estimate, fewer than one percent of female wage earners were unionized.[59] Employers had a variety of tactics at their disposal for discouraging unionization, including threatening workers with dismissal, moving their factories, and establishing shop unions that were pro-management. Craft unions representing mostly skilled male workers continued to dominate the Canadian labour scene, confining their activities to industrial settings in which there were few women. In any event, they had a tradition of excluding women. Many male unionists still considered female workers unlikely and undesirable union members; one concluded that because women did not have a long-term commitment to paid employment, and because they did not "possess that spirit of solidarity, characteristic of men in industry," female workers were "the most difficult workers to organize."[60] Even when women did join unions, many male leaders continued to regard the presence of women in the labour force as symbolic of an unhealthy industrial order in which a man could not earn enough to support his family. Once the family wage was secured, they argued, there would be no reason for daughters and wives to desert hearth and home. Such arguments ignored the continuing economic contribution made by working women, their right to work for wages outside the home, and the fact that many women workers had no male breadwinner to rely on.[61]

Reacting to male unionists' indifference or overt hostility, and their failure to deal with issues of importance to women, such as sexual harassment or unhygienic working conditions, many women in fact spurned unions. In the 1920s, unions made little effort to eliminate the pay differential between male and female workers, and by insisting on across-the-board raises they effectively increased the wage gap. As well, union halls were primarily male clubs. When, occasionally, women were hired by the international unions to act as organizers in industries with large numbers of female workers, they, too, suffered the familiar inequities in pay. In the early 1920s, for example, Mary McNab was hired as an organizer by the Amalgamated Clothing Workers in Hamilton, and was paid half the salary typically given to male organizers. In unions where women workers dominated the membership rolls, leadership roles did sometimes become available. Women delegates, however, remained a minority on urban Trades and Labour Councils.[62]

In Quebec the *Confédération des travailleurs catholiques du Canada* (the Canadian and Catholic Confederation of Labour) formed in 1921 under the aegis of the Catholic Church. This organization sought to protect Catholic workers not only from the exploitation inherent in unfettered capitalism, but also from what many French Canadians perceived as essentially atheistic, foreign-controlled international unions. By 1921 there were eight women's locals of the Catholic Confederation in Hull and one in Montreal; in addition, other female workers were organized along with their male co-workers into mixed locals. All told, approximately 2200 women belonged to exclusively female Catholic unions, and another 600 to the mixed Catholic unions; but together they accounted for only 3 percent of all the women workers in Quebec industry and commerce.[63]

Women workers, whether unionized or not, were far from passive. As individuals, they reacted to unsatisfactory work situations by changing jobs or getting married; collectively, they helped each other meet production quotas or engaged in militant activities such as slowdowns, walkouts, and strikes. In August 1921, hosiery workers in Stratford, Ontario, set up picket lines to try to win union recognition and improvements in wages. As in most labour–management disputes, the full force of the law was used against the strikers: 15 were arrested, of whom two had to be tried in juvenile court. Despite widespread local support, after two months the strike failed. In 1924, female workers at the E. B. Eddy match factory in Hull, Quebec, walked off the job to protest the firing of their female supervisors and management's attempts to force the workers to sign what were called "yellow dog" contracts renouncing union membership. They were more successful in pummelling the plant manager into temporary submission, however, than in achieving their long-term goals. Although a settlement was reached and the workers were rehired, the company refused to reinstate the female supervisors or to permit ongoing union activities. In yet another example of women's militancy, female spinners at the Canadian Cotton Mills in Hamilton led a walkout of some 600 workers in 1929 to protest an increase in their workload. Three of the six-person strike committee were women, and women were instrumental in their support of the five-week-long strike. In the end, however, they, too, failed to achieve their demands.[64]

Among women in the clerical and retail trades, both unionization and strike activity were even more rare. Managers often pre-empted attempts at organization by providing employee welfare schemes, such as company cafeterias, recreational facilities, pensions for loyal long-term workers, and piecemeal benefits for the "deserving." In Montreal the associations for women in white-collar occupations that had been created by the *Fédération nationale Saint-Jean-Baptiste* before World War I continued to operate. But total memberships never exceeded a few hundred women, and the major objective of these associations remained the educational and moral betterment of their members rather than fighting for better working conditions or pay. In several provinces, secretaries, stenographers, bank clerks, and other white-collar women workers formed local clubs that joined together to form the Canadian Federation of Business and Professional Women's Clubs in 1930. This development is evidence of the importance of mutual support and a sense of belonging among this group of workers.[65]

Other groups of female white-collar workers were able to record considerable progress in union organizing during this decade. In 1918 local women teachers' organizations had formed the Federation of Women Teachers' Associations of Ontario, which assigned priority to equal pay for equal work and also to contract protection. Within a year, more than one-third of the province's women teachers had joined the Federation. The militancy of some women teachers was demonstrated in 1922, when several in Owen Sound threatened strike action to support their demands for a decent wage. The local Board of Education conceded by raising the minimum annual salary for female teachers to $1 200.[66] In western Canada, female teachers also sought to improve their position by joining forces. Many Calgary teachers joined the Dominion Labour Party. Between 1918 and 1936, their support helped elect and maintain a Labour woman on the school board. Trustees such as Amelia Turner pressed teachers' collective bargaining rights and equality for female teachers. The Saskatoon Women Teachers' Association continued to campaign for better contracts, equal pay for equal work, and the retention of married women as teachers.[67] This activism notwithstanding, women in the teaching profession were still treated as second-class citizens. Their salaries lagged significantly behind those of men teachers; those who married generally lost their permanent contracts or were dismissed, while their male counterparts received bonuses. Furthermore, enrollment in the women teachers' associations remained strictly voluntary, and only a minority of rural teachers belonged, a fact that restricted both financial stability and bargaining power.

Similarly, nurses continued to press for better working conditions and a greater degree of professional recognition and self-regulation. In 1928, student nurses at Guelph General Hospital reacted to the heavy workload and the regimentation by launching a strike that lasted for two days. Although it appears to have resulted only in the departure of some of the nurses involved, the strike demonstrated that even the most powerless of women were prepared on occasion to strike back at the system.[68]

Women's militancy in the 1920s was not confined to those who worked for wages. In several instances workers' wives, mothers, and daughters lent both immediate and longer-term support to their male family members' labour struggles. In coal-miners' strikes in Nova Scotia (1922) and Alberta (1923), the militancy of the miners' wives was a significant factor in the collective demonstration of solidarity the men were able to mount. One Ukrainian woman in Edmonton recalled her first involvement in a labour dispute: "In 1921 there was a strike. We walked the picket line. We left at four in the morning. The police prevented us from going and pushed us with rifle butts. I was afraid. There I met other women, and we went to the Labour Temple for meetings." In Cardiff, Alberta, women armed with sticks engaged in a pitched battle with police and strike breakers or "scabs," and some were subsequently arrested and convicted of disturbing the peace.[69]

A MOST DEPRESSING DECADE

If the 1920s were difficult years for women workers, the 1930s were disastrous. Wages plummeted, working conditions deteriorated, union membership declined, and women's right to work was even more seriously challenged. For women who were not already working for pay, there was enormous pressure to replace unemployed family members in the labour force, to supplement the reduced wages of those still working, and to intensify their domestic labour in order to make ends meet. As the Depression deepened, millions of Canadians experienced unprecedented deprivation and an immeasurable loss of dignity. Although governments clumsily attempted to attenuate the worst effects of the economic crisis, they directed most of their efforts toward aiding men. Once again it was assumed that the vast majority of women would be looked after by their families, and women who had no one able or willing to support them were initially left to fend for themselves. Yet, while it is difficult to assess the actual numbers, we know that a large percentage of women in the labour force were supporting themselves, and many were responsible for the support of dependants.[70]

At first the worldwide economic crisis that began in October 1929 appeared to stimulate the entry of women into the labour force. In many families the role of breadwinner was initially transferred from men, who lost their jobs in the hard-hit resource and construction industries, to daughters and wives able to retain or find work in traditionally female areas of employment, such as domestic and personal service and food processing. Thus, the increase in the numbers of employed women was a response to male unemployment and to the segmentation of the labour force along gender lines, rather than a move by employers to replace more highly paid male workers by cheaper female labour, as was often claimed. It was young women who most dramatically increased their labour force participation rate: the proportion of women under the age of 20 who worked for wages rose from 16 percent in 1921 to 25 percent in 1931. By the latter date, one out of every five manufacturing operatives was a young woman under 18.[71] Given the tendency of the decennial federal censuses to consistently under-report the numbers of gainfully employed women, there were undoubtedly thousands more women working for wages for at least some part of the year. Evidence presented in 1934 before the Royal Commission on Price Spreads emphasized the vital role women were playing:

> Of 30 women from one non-union shop, practically all of whom were earning less than $12.50 per week, . . . 21 were married and were the sole providers for the family or were happy to support them; eight were single, but were helping to support their families, while only one girl had no dependents and no family obligations.[72]

As the crisis grew and the national unemployment rate mounted to almost one-third of all workers, resentment against wage-earning women increased. The deep-seated prejudice against married women working outside the home intensified, and the appropriateness even of single women working for wages, widely conceded during the 1920s, was now called into question. These convictions transcended regional, ethnic, class, and, to some extent, gender boundaries. Whether it was the westerner who counselled Prime Minister R. B. Bennett to end unemployment by firing all single young women, or the leaders of the Canadian and Catholic Confederation of Labour, including those representing female textile workers, who petitioned the Quebec government to bar all women from working for wages except in cases of absolute necessity, the message was the same: get the women out of the paid labour force. Men contended that they were being replaced by unskilled female workers. Women in business and the professions were also accused of taking away men's jobs. Stories abound of women who had to be content with lengthy engagements, clandestine relationships, or secret marriages in order to retain their jobs. For Aboriginal, ethnic, and visible-minority women, the discrimination encountered in securing employment was exacerbated by pervasive prejudice. Anti-Semitism was especially rife during the 1930s: one woman in Winnipeg was able to obtain and keep an office position only because, since she was tall and blond, her employers did not realize that she was Jewish.[73]

Despite the widespread perception that women posed a threat to male employment, there is incontrovertible evidence that, as economic conditions deteriorated, desperate male workers were undercutting female worker's wages and supplanting women in several industries. In the garment, textile, and leather industries, the practice of giving preferential treatment to male workers was common. Married female operatives, some with many years' experience, were dismissed so that their work could be re-allocated to male workers, often at rates of pay below the minimum required for women workers. Thus the minimum wage legislation that had been intended to protect women often proved their undoing. At one textile mill in Valleyfield, Quebec, a group of female apprentice weavers signed a petition imploring the provincial government not to apply minimum wage legislation to them so that they could keep their jobs.[74] The substitution of lower-paid male for female workers became so widespread that, in order to maintain male wage levels, the provincial governments of Ontario and Quebec extended their minimum wage legislation to include men. British Columbia had already made a similar move in 1934. In spite of these initiatives to protect all workers, the situation of women industrial employees continued to worsen as the Depression deepened. Professional women also suffered setbacks. Between 1932 and 1934, Winnipeg city council reduced the amount available for teachers' salaries by 20 percent; however, a new pay scale provided an even larger pay differential between male and female teachers so that the women bore the brunt of the decreases. Among high school teachers in that city, the women lost an average of $355 yearly while their male colleagues experienced an average reduction of only $100.[75]

When women were successful in securing or maintaining positions, they routinely experienced drastic wage cuts and deteriorating working conditions. In Ontario, the Factory Act was amended to allow the implementation of a double shift for women and youths between 6:00 a.m. and 11:00 p.m. The fact that so many of Canada's female wage earners were concentrated in industries characterized by low capital investment and intense competition rendered them all the more vulnerable to exploitation. However, even large companies such as the T. E. Eaton Company cut wages, reduced the number of employees, and increased production quotas. Mrs. Annie Wells, who began making dresses at Eaton's in 1916, testified before the Royal Commission on Price Spreads that she was not allowed to sit down during her eight-hour shift, and that after 1931 she was not able to make the minimum wage because the piece rates had been so greatly reduced. The price for sewing a dozen dresses was cut from $5 per dozen before 1929 to $3 by 1934. The resulting physical and nervous exhaustion of the workers led another witness, Miss A. Tucker, to declare that "the girls were just about insane. In fact it got to such a climax that they were threatening to commit suicide and even I myself was contemplating the same thing." Another employee revealed that she had gone out just once in 1934—to celebrate her birthday—the only time she attended a movie in three years. Once again, however, home workers were the ones who suffered the most. According to other testimony presented to the Royal Commission, in one Quebec home, a woman and her daughter produced a dozen pair of boys' short pants for 30 cents minus 5 cents for the thread they used. Their average daily production was one dozen pairs of pants.[76]

For many women workers there was only downward mobility into domestic service; between 1921 and 1931, there was a 7 percent increase in female wage earners employed as domestics, and a 6 percent decline in those engaged in manufacturing. Here was another effect of the Depression: for Canadians with fixed or steady incomes, the standard of living improved as prices dropped, and many families found they could afford a domestic helper. Local relief officers encouraged young women without jobs or families that could support them to become servants, and governments' only major initiative to reduce female unemployment was the development of domestic training programs. Young, healthy unemployed female workers could not receive relief as long as domestic service jobs at any wage continued to be available. At the end of 1936, only an estimated 400 single women had met government relief requirements in Vancouver; two-thirds of them were over 50 years old.[77]

Municipalities did not initially provide relief at all for single women; their first priority was to try to provide what limited assistance they could afford to married men. Municipal relief for single men was often poorly organized and inadequate, but usually some attempt was made to provide food and hostel accommodation. By contrast, responsibility for single women was generally relegated to their families or to private charitable organizations.[78] Unlike the roaming bands of unemployed young men who "rode the rods," women were not perceived as posing a serious threat to the social order, in spite of the fact that "girl hoboes were frequently encountered."[79] Even when women might qualify for financial assistance, relief officers could be sexist and insensitive. Some women were told that "with figures like theirs" they did not need relief. According to C. G. MacNeil, the Member of Parliament for Vancouver North, relief payments to women were so inadequate that "they are compelled to live in only the most disreputable parts of the city, denied any chance to dress respectably . . . ready material for prostitution in its most sordid forms."[80] For some women, prostitution was the only way they could eke out a livelihood during the Depression. Immigrants who could not get jobs faced double jeopardy: if they had been in Canada less than five years, they could be deported if they went on relief.

Women's ability to adapt to changing economic circumstances can be seen in the experience of Wet'suwet'en women in British Columbia. Before World War I, the development of settlements, railroads, and highways displaced the fur trade, and Wet'suwet'en men moved in increasing numbers into the paid labour force. Women continued their responsibility for fishing, farming, trapping, and berry-picking, and families of wage earners relied on this supplemental work. When the Depression virtually eliminated male wage opportunities, the women's work became even more vital. One woman recalled her experience of the 1930s with pride: "We stayed put while the men went all over for work. We did the fishing, had our big gardens in them days too. You bet, them days we fed the men. They sure were glad for us women. It was our catches that kept their bellies full." Not only did they feed their families and their own community, but Wet'suwet'en women also sold or traded their goods in town for clothing, fabric, flour, tea, and sugar. They shared fish and meat with neighbouring indigent white farm women. Within their communities, the Wet'suwet'en women enjoyed increased prestige as a result of these activities and their consequent control of wealth. Their experience was shared by other Aboriginal women. Letwammen women on Vancouver Island contributed to their family's subsistence through berry and hop-picking and by adding the production of hand-knit sweaters to their household activities. Similarly, since the men "were without a speck of work," Celina Amyotte Poitras, a Métis woman living in Lebret, Saskatchewan, provided a livelihood for her family by sewing for others at night by the light of a coal lamp.[81]

Wives of men who had lost their jobs strained to cope with the financial, social, and psychological repercussions of living with an unemployed breadwinner. Finnish immigrant wives frequently turned their household skills to domestic service and may have gained status and power by having money to spend.[82] Married women in other ethnic groups, such as the Ukrainian community in Sudbury, opened their homes to boarders to augment their family's income so that mortgage payments could be met and food put on the table. And in urban areas such as Montreal, owners of small family-run grocery stores relied on the unpaid labour of wives and children for up to 16 hours per day to keep their enterprises afloat.[83] Some husbands left their families to search for work elsewhere, and sometimes deserted them altogether rather than face the humiliation of failing to provide. The number of female heads of households in Edmonton, for example, rose from 978 in 1921 to 2 653 10 years later.[84]

The social stigma associated with being "on the dole" was crushing, and the regulations made the situation even worse: the relief authorities confiscated all possessions that might be considered luxuries, such as cars, radios, and jewellery. Persons receiving relief had to hand in their liquor permits, and if they owned a telephone it was removed. The limited financial assistance successful applicants received usually took the form of vouchers for food and rent; no provision was made for the replacement of clothing or for the sundry items most Canadians considered essential. When their silk stockings wore out, women powdered their legs and drew a black line down the back. They made clothing from flour bags, and mended, patched, and darned until the cloth disintegrated; sometimes women and children became virtual prisoners in their homes because they lacked suitable clothing to go out. Women also often lacked the cooking facilities and fuel they needed to prepare what little food they had. They substituted chicory or roasted grain for coffee, used game instead of butcher's cuts, and invented an endless variety of mock dishes. To obtain additional milk and clothing for her children, one woman consented to have sexual relations with her relief officer.[85]

When their myriad and continuous efforts to sustain the family failed, a few women appealed directly to the prime minister for help. Their letters reveal not only the pathetic state to which many had been reduced, but also their habit of putting husbands and children first, and their unshakable faith in God and country. The moving entreaty from Mrs. C. L. Warden of Lambert, Saskatchewan, written in the winter of 1934, speaks for itself:

> Your Honor:
> I am writing you regarding Relief. Will you please tell me if we can get Steady Relief and how much we should be allowed per week we have three children, 2 of school age. . . . There are times we are living on potatoes for days at a time. . . . I am five months pregnant and I haven't even felt life yet to my baby and its I feel quite sure for lack of food . . . the two oldest children and I are suffering from abscess teeth can we get them out and have the town pay for the Dental Bill.[86]

For some women even the opportunity to appeal to public authorities was denied. When Ukrainian immigrant Stepan Chiruk was imprisoned for three months for killing a moose and her calf in order to feed his family of six, his wife was told that she must agree to have him sterilized or the entire family would be deported. Zosya Chiruk refused, distributed her children among the neighbours, and went into hiding in the bush in northern Alberta. Eventually Zosya hired a lawyer, who advised her to return home with her children; this she did, only to find the police at her doorstep. Possibly because there were many neighbours present, the police promised Zosya that the family would not be deported, and that her husband would be allowed to return. Later that same night, when the neighbours had all gone, the police returned and took away Zosya and the children; the entire family was sent back to the Ukraine.[87]

Life during the Depression was especially harsh for older women who were separated, divorced, or widowed. Their sex and age combined to reduce their chances of employment. One particularly poignant story involved a needy and resourceful 77-year-old English widow, who advertised for a pensioner husband to supplement her small income. Although she did find a husband by this means, he was under 70 and therefore not yet a pensioner. His son reneged on a promise to provide his father with $20 a month until he reached pensionable age, and, ironically, the woman's financial situation became even more precarious.[88]

Women of all ages and regions fought back against indignities and deprivations with whatever limited means they possessed. In Vancouver, the *Unemployed Worker* reported groups of white and sometimes Asian women pressing a variety of demands at local relief offices. Among the reported results of political community action in 1933, the newspaper listed the provision of milk for women with babies; relief for ailing single women; clothing allowances for mothers and their children; medical care during pregnancy; and relief for destitute Japanese and Chinese families. Radical working-class women belonging to the Single Women's Protective Association in Vancouver launched a campaign in 1936 to achieve equal relief rates with men but were ultimately unsuccessful.[89] In 1932, Jewish women in Toronto, including labour militants, factory workers, and housewives, organized a boycott of kosher butchers, who were charging exorbitant prices for their products: "Every butcher was picketed each morning by small groups of women, often starting at 6:00 A.M. They tried to prevent anyone from going in, and often ripped the meat out of the hands of those who did buy, and threw it into the street."[90] Rural women on the Prairies, who confronted drought, dust, grasshoppers, sheriffs' writs, and bank foreclosures, found support in women's organizations and new political parties, such as the CCF (Co-operative Commonwealth Federation) and Social Credit.

As for unions, membership fell sharply during the worst years of the Depression as competition for jobs intensified. Workers were afraid to join unions for fear of losing their jobs, and they often could not afford to pay union dues. Nonetheless, there were some significant organizational initiatives. In 1936, Laure Gaudreault, who had started teaching 30 years earlier at the age of 16, formed an association of female rural school-teachers in the Chicoutimi area of Quebec. Created to protest the provincial government's failure to implement a promised salary increase, this group developed within a year into the *Fédération catholique des institutrices rurales*. Under Gaudreault's leadership, it undertook a vigorous campaign to improve the desperately low salaries and primitive working conditions that francophone women teachers in rural Quebec schools had so long endured.[91] Rural teachers in British Columbia also reached the limit of their patience. Frustrated by the lack of action by government and the Department of Education and angry over low salaries, poor housing and working conditions, and lack of bargaining power, the women formed the Rural Elementary Teachers' Association in 1938. Throughout the Depression, in aggressively pressing the right to work, to relief, and to equality in pay regardless of marital status, militant Vancouver women began to express an enlarged feminist consciousness and to challenge prevailing social and economic assumptions. Vancouver waitresses, for example, engaged in 10 separate strikes during the 1930s and emerged as one of the most militant groups of organized women. Significant gender-based pay differences fuelled their activism. The waitresses insisted on their agenda for equality: equal pay for waiters and waitresses became a union and strike demand for the first time in 1933.[92]

In Montreal and Toronto, leftist activists such as Léa Roback and Pearl Wedro worked to attract garment and fur workers into unions. The only unions to demonstrate any increase in membership during the early 1930s were those affiliated with the Workers' Unity League, which had been organized in 1929 by the Communist International and the Communist Party. In 1934 alone, the Workers' Unity League organized 109 strikes involving some 50 000 Canadian workers. Prominent among its affiliates was the Industrial Union of Needle Trades Workers, which was involved in the Toronto dressmakers' strike in February 1931 and the Montreal garment workers' strike of August

Miners' wives barricade the entrance to the community hall in Flin Flon, Manitoba, to stop a back-to-work meeting during the 1934 strike.

Source: Provincial Archives of Manitoba (N17230).

1934. In the latter, thousands of young women, primarily of Jewish and French-Canadian origin, took to the streets; when attacked by mounted police, the women fought back by stabbing the horses with pins.[93] It was surely no coincidence that, during the course of this violent strike, which lasted more than six weeks, the Quebec Minimum Wage Commission announced a slight upward adjustment of wages for female operatives in the garment industry, and reduced the workweek from 55 hours to 48 hours. When the workers returned to work, however, the battle for union recognition was lost, and within a year the Workers' Unity League had been disbanded.

Cross-class solidarity among women was vividly illustrated in 1934 during a strike in the Eaton's dressmaking department by workers who belonged to the International Ladies' Garment Workers' Union. Members of the Toronto Local Council of Women and other middle-class women's organizations raised funds for the strikers, lobbied government officials to force a settlement, and even joined the picket line. When the strike failed, the Local Council provided funds to help some of the strikers set up their own cooperative dressmaking shop. The organized women's movement's willingness to help the largely Anglo-Celtic workers at Eaton's in 1934 contrasted with the general lack of support from this sector for the mostly Jewish women garment workers during their 1912 strike against the same company.[94]

In April 1937 it was the International Ladies' Garment Workers' Union that led yet another strike of Montreal women garment workers, popularly called *midinettes*. Among the first to join the union was Yvette Charpentier. Sent to work at the age of 10, she became an active organizer among workers in the dress industry, and eventually the union's director of educational services. After four weeks of picketing involving 5 000 to 8 000 workers, the strikers won a general wage increase of 10 percent, a 44-hour workweek, and, more important, the "closed shop"—that is, only workers belonging to the union could be engaged by those companies that signed the collective agreement. Subsequently, further significant improvements in salary were established through arbitration, but the workers' victory was short-lived. Many employers simply reneged on the terms of the agreement.[95] Four months later, in August 1937, even more women were on strike in Quebec as a result of a province-wide walkout in the textile industry. This strike, led by the Canadian and Catholic Confederation of Labour, lasted more than a month. It ended with an agreement, arbitrated by Cardinal Villeneuve, Archbishop of Quebec, that won only minor improvements for the workers. The same year, female workers at two Peterborough textile mills were among the most militant participants in a strike called by the United Textile Workers, a union affiliated with the American-based Congress of Industrial Organization (CIO).[96]

After long and bitter conflicts, the immediate gains of these strikes were either negligible or minimal, but such confrontations constituted important demonstrations of female workers' solidarity. The strike of the *midinettes* in Montreal was especially significant, for it demonstrated the militancy of women previously considered unorganizable and also proved their ability to transcend the ethnic and linguistic divisions that employers had previously exploited to keep workers from uniting. Moreover, a new generation of female organizers, such as Léa Roback and Yvette Charpentier, emerged from the strike to carry on what would become a successful struggle for unionization over the next two decades.

Les Midinettes, Quebec garment workers, gathered outside their union headquarters in Montreal.

Source: Federal Photos

WAR WORK, 1939–1945

In 1939, Canadians were still preoccupied with the agonizingly slow recovery from the devastating impact of the Great Depression, but on September 17, they found themselves yet again propelled into an overseas conflict not of their own making. And once more Canadian women played a key role in the war effort through their multifaceted work in the nation's homes, fields, factories, and voluntary organizations. In addition, they were recruited for the first time into the ultimate bastion of male power, the armed forces.

From the beginning of the war, the Department of National War Services ran an extensive publicity campaign in both French and English aimed at involving Canadian housewives in the war effort. One advertisement, entitled "From the Frying Pan to the Firing Line," depicted three women pouring a panful of grease, which magically turned

315

into bombs, over an enemy ship. "Work at munitions production in your own kitchen," the accompanying copy exhorted.[97] In response, thousands of women and children collected fats, paper, glass, metals, rubber, rags, and bones for recycling into munitions and other war materials. The government's management of the war economy depended heavily on women, since Canadian homemakers were responsible for more than 80 percent of the nation's retail purchases.[98] The federal government also relied on women to support its rationing system and wartime savings program, and to maintain the nation's nutritional standards. In addition, hundreds of thousands of women planted victory gardens, knitted and sewed articles of clothing for the troops, made up parcels for prisoners of war, ran hospitality centres and canteens for members of the armed forces, organized blood banks, practised civil defence procedures, or served as spotters of enemy aircraft. All of this volunteer activity led to an unprecedented amount of news coverage of civilian women and a recognition by at least some observers that community work was essential war work.[99]

Across the nation wives and daughters supplemented the declining male agricultural workforce, as men signed up for military service or gravitated to more attractive industrial work. For some farm wives, the war years brought not only an increased burden of work and responsibility, but also new opportunities for personal growth and accomplishment. "Dorothy," for example, tackled the heavy farm work during her husband's absence overseas, maintained the equipment, looked after the house and children, taught Sunday school, and still found time for curling and hunting. On her husband's return, she handed him the family bankbook and proudly declared, "There is more money in there than we ever had in our lives."[100]

Recruitment of women for agricultural production was included in a federal government campaign to manage the wartime labour force and cope with labour shortages. Initially little government intervention was required, for there were some 900 000 unemployed Canadians when the war broke out. By 1942, however, this labour pool had been depleted as both industry and the armed forces expanded. In March of that year, Mackenzie King's government established the National Selective Service agency to oversee the recruitment and allocation of labour. Two months later, it created the Women's Division of the agency and placed it under the direction of Fraudena Eaton of Vancouver. In September 1942, the Women's Division undertook a national registration of women aged 20 to 24 in order to identify single women who could be recruited into war industry. Married women in this age category were also required to register, although the federal government hoped that, if it created a pool of single workers, wives could stay at home. Once the registration exercise was complete, the National Selective Service initiated massive publicity campaigns and arranged for the relocation of single women from the Prairies and the Maritimes to central Canada to work in war industries. In British Columbia, white women increasingly replaced male Asians in industries such as food, lumber, pulp and paper, and coastal shipping, particularly after the internment of Japanese Canadians.[101]

As the war progressed and workers of both sexes continued to be lured away by the higher wages offered by war industries, the demand for female employees rose, particularly in garment, textile, and service industries. Now there was no choice but to turn to married women to take up the slack. Throughout the summer of 1943, with the help of Local Councils of Women, Selective Service mounted ambitious drives to recruit married women for part-time work in the service sector, in establishments such as laundries and hospitals. Housewives were also asked to work evening shifts, created especially for them, in essential war industries. In July 1942, the Income Tax Act had been amended so that working wives were treated as full dependants no matter how much they earned. Previously, if a wife earned more than $750, her husband lost the "married status" exemption.[102]

The other major initiative was the provision, for the first time, of government-funded daycare services. In July 1942, the federal government acknowledged the need for institutional child care by introducing the dominion–provincial Wartime Day Nurseries Agreement. It provided for the two senior levels of government to share equally the costs of daycare services for children whose mothers were employed in war industries. However, only three provinces—Ontario, Quebec, and Alberta—signed the accord, and after further study Alberta decided not to implement the program. Eventually, 28 day nurseries were established in Ontario, and six in Quebec. These nurseries accommodated children between two and six years of age; in Ontario, home care was also arranged for children under the age of two, and after-school daycare, for those between the ages of six and sixteen. In keeping with the government's commitment to provide such services strictly to cope with the wartime emergency, only one-quarter of the available spaces were supposed to be given to the children of working mothers not employed in war industries. Public pressure, however, forced the government to amend the legislation to provide services for the children of all working mothers; priority was still assigned, however, to employees of war industries.[103]

In Quebec, the few day nurseries established under the program primarily served the anglophone population. French-Canadian Catholic leaders in that province denounced the employment of mothers. Part of this negative reaction was the result of opposition to the war itself, but in large measure it was a basic objection to women working outside the home. Religious leaders and nationalists in Quebec roundly condemned those married women who "deserted" their families for lucrative work in munitions plants, and articles published in the influential Jesuit publication *Relations* branded government-sponsored daycare facilities communistic and destructive of the family. In an impassioned speech, one member of the Quebec Assembly condemned all women's work outside the home. Such work, he claimed, created a dangerous desire for emancipation, thereby destroying the family and "sabotaging what is most precious to us."[104] Despite such vehement denunciations, thousands of French-Canadian mothers took on paid employment. Their primary reasons for doing so were economic. According to Florence Martel, Fraudena Eaton's Quebec assistant,

> We were coming out of the Depression. There were no longer sheets on the beds, the children had no shoes and there were no more kitchen utensils. . . . Women lacked everything for a long time and they did not go to work to buy luxuries, as certain people accused them of doing.[105]

Indeed, across Canada, many women indicated that an improved standard of living, not the call to loyalty and service, had drawn them into paid employment.[106]

As the labour shortage grew, women were admitted in increasing numbers into the dominion–provincial War Emergency Training Program and into non-traditional employment. Commentators frequently drew analogies between women's war work and their usual domestic tasks: running a lathe, for example, was even easier than operating a sewing machine.[107] By June 1943, about a quarter of a million women were working in war industries at such non-traditional jobs as welding, electronics, drafting, and industrial chemistry. But these apparent opportunities were of limited value. Government training programs for women were shorter than those for men, and most women received only two to six weeks' instruction. Consequently, there was little opportunity for women to secure the specialized training that would ensure long-term employment or upward mobility.

Visible-minority women, who had previously found it particularly difficult to secure waged employment other than domestic work, now found some job openings in industry and, to a limited extent, in clerical and retail settings. However, the positions they were able to secure were often the least desirable. When the Cape Breton steel company employed women as production workers for the first time during the war, it was slow to hire non-white women; and when they were hired, they were assigned the heaviest, dirtiest jobs—such as working at the coke ovens. Despite the special wartime conditions, securing employment in Southern Ontario's auto industry continued to prove impossible for African-Canadian women. As one observer noted, it was well known among "the coloured people of Windsor that their womenfolk were hardly ever sent to factories, stores, or offices" by the National Selective Service agency because employers would not accept them.[108]

Other women, however, did assume positions of authority, and immediately became the focus of media attention. They were held up as living examples of the emancipating effects of the war. Such was the case for Elsie Gregory MacGill, who had assumed the position of chief engineer of Canadian Car and Foundry Company's aircraft division in Fort William (Thunder Bay), Ontario. There she oversaw the production in 1940 of the Maple Leaf Trainer II, the first aircraft designed by a woman, and of all the engineering work for the approximately 2 000 Hawker Hurricane fighter planes manufactured in Canada. As well, Vancouver-born Molly Lamb Bobak became Canada's first woman official war artist in 1945, after spending three years working both within Canada and overseas to document the activities of the Canadian Women's Army Corps. Far more typical of war workers, however, were young women like Veronica Foster, the 1941 "Bren Gun Girl," who was chosen to glamorize work on the assembly lines.[109]

The image of the emancipated woman was further enhanced during the war by the entry of women into the armed forces; yet here, as in war industry, equality was never gained. Before the war began, thousands of women across the nation had organized themselves into paramilitary groups. Modelled on the women's auxiliary of the British army, these organizations taught their members military drill, first aid, map reading, signalling, and transport driving; some even included rifle practice. Shortly after their formation, the women's corps lobbied vigorously for official recognition from the Department of National Defence, but this approval was withheld. Only when the manpower shortage grew serious and pressure mounted from both home and abroad for Canada to use women in military support positions did the government decide to form the Canadian

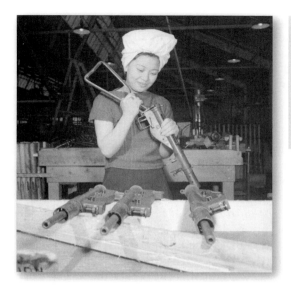

Agnes Wong of Whitecourt, Alberta, assembling a sten gun in an Ontario munitions plant in 1944. She was representative of the thousands of women who moved to Ontario to work in war industries.

Source: Ronny Jaques / National Film Board of Canada. Photothèque / Library and Archives Canada / PA-108043.

Women's Army Corps (CWAC). Established in August 1941, the new organization used the existing women's corps primarily as a source of recruits.[110.] Here was yet another case of women's war initiatives being taken over and directed by a male-dominated bureaucracy.

Initially, the CWAC was not incorporated into the army but, rather, constituted a separate organization. As a result, its officers did not enjoy the same ranks, authority, or insignia as men in the army did. Only in March 1942 was the CWAC integrated into the Canadian armed forces, and its members entitled to use the usual military titles and insignia. In 1941, the federal government also established the Canadian Women's Auxiliary Air Force, largely as a result of British inquiries about recruiting women to assist at Commonwealth Air Training Plan centres. In February 1942, the auxiliary was transformed into the Women's Division, Royal Canadian Air Force. In July 1942, the Women's Royal Canadian Naval Service was created. As the recruiting proceeded, issues arose concerning race, ethnicity, and language. One CWAC recruiting officer in Toronto considered it necessary to ask her superiors if a young Aboriginal woman who was the top student in her drafting class was admissible. In this case, the answer was an unequivocal yes. On another occasion, an Indian agent representing two women in their late teens who wished "to do their share for the Country," including overseas service, was advised that they were not suitable. However, if they "had a little training they would experience little difficulty in getting positions as domestics." While the total number of Aboriginal women who served in the armed forces is not clear, according to one account, there were at least 72. The first to volunteer was Mary Greyeyes of the Muskeg Lake Reserve in Saskatchewan.[111] Initially, only bilingual French-Canadian women were recruited; however, after English-language training facilities were established in the latter half of 1942, unilingual francophones were accepted. Once inducted, they were dispersed among the various basic training camps so that they might be more readily absorbed into the predominantly anglophone military organization.[112]

Women who entered the armed forces encountered many of the same obstructive attitudes and practices that confronted women in civilian life. In all ranks, they received only two-thirds of the basic pay of men with equivalent rank. Confronted with vehement protests by servicewomen themselves and by the National Council of Women, and with the negative impact the poor pay was having on female recruitment, the Department of National Defence raised women's basic pay to 80 percent of that received by men of similar rank. Job segregation on the basis of gender also remained a fact of life in the armed forces. It was understood that only the war emergency and the need to release able-bodied men for active duty justified the creation of the women's services. From the beginning, military authorities intended to use female recruits to replace support personnel, such as clerks, cooks, telephone operators, and drivers. In all areas, men remained firmly in charge. In the CWAC, the vast majority of recruits worked at typically female jobs: only 50 percent of army trades were open to them. Of nearly 6 000 CWACs surveyed in March 1945, 62 percent were working as clerks. In comparison, the situation of recruits in the Women's Division of the RCAF (WDs, as they were called) was definitely better: by 1945, 65 percent of the trades in that service were open to women. Pay scales were also higher in the air force, so although WDs also received only four-fifths of an airman's basic pay, they were better paid than their army counterparts.[113]

Most women who enlisted hoped to satisfy their spirit of adventure through an overseas posting, but with the exception of the nursing sisters, only one in nine servicewomen served outside Canada. We can well imagine the anger and disappointment felt by one group of WDs in training at Ottawa's Rockcliffe base, who found themselves scrubbing the floors in the governor general's residence. When they did manage to make it overseas, most CWACs found themselves assigned as clerks, laundry workers, and cooks; in fact, the first call for Canadian servicewomen to serve overseas came when Canadian Headquarters in London was unable to find sufficient laundry staff, and requested 150 CWACs to make up the shortfall.[114]

By the war's end, more than 43 000 women had enlisted in the armed forces: 21 000 in the Women's Army Corps, 16 000 in the Women's Division of the air force, and 6 600 in the Women's Naval Service. They came from all regions of the country, and from all walks of life. Some were underage, reportedly as young as 14; others were older women whose own sons were in the service. Some signed up out of a sense of adventure, while others did so for patriotic reasons. According to one study, more than 70 percent of female recruits were employed at the time they enlisted. Evidently, many left their civilian jobs for the superior remuneration, benefits, and training offered by the women's branches of the armed forces.[115]

These same factors seem to have motivated the more than 4 000 graduate nurses who signed up for duty with the Canadian armed forces. So large were the initial numbers volunteering that thousands had to put their names on waiting lists, and many more joined other Allied nursing services. The vast majority of those who enlisted were of Anglo-Celtic background, and in their late twenties, although women up to the age of 45 (the age was raised to 55 years in September 1943) were eligible to apply. Only single women and widows without children were recruited, but a small number of nurses who married while in service were kept on. Since nursing sisters automatically gained officer rank, with its associated privileges and higher pay, the military authorities expected them

Members of the Canadian Women's Army Corps disembarking at Naples, Italy, in June 1944.
Source: Canada. Dept. of National Defence / Library and Archives Canada / PA-108177

to conduct themselves as ladies and to serve primarily in a helping role to male doctors. Nonetheless, as the conflict dragged on, nursing sisters often found themselves close to the hostilities, and considered themselves central players in the war effort. They expanded their skill sets as they were called upon to utilize new medical technologies, and, to a degree, they successfully pushed the boundaries of what constituted nursing practice. At war's end, most found themselves in the same situation as other women in the military, with no choice other than a return to civilian life. In the end, the armed forces retained the services of only 80 nurses. Although there was a civilian nursing shortage, many military nurses found regular hospital nursing too confining, and left the profession for marriage, used their veterans' entitlement to obtain more education, or pursued public health nursing or other forms of nursing outside of hospitals. There were also 38 women doctors who served in the armed forces, as well as an undetermined number of women who worked as dieticians, physiotherapist aides, occupational therapists, and home sisters (living quarter managers).[116]

Despite the limitations and discrimination that women in the services frequently encountered, for many their wartime experience was exhilarating. "When you passed your exams and you received your flags," one member of the Women's Naval Service recalled, "it was like getting your degree. It had a big effect on our lives. We were proud of ourselves as individuals as well as women, for we succeeded under the same conditions as the men, and for many this changed our outlook toward our place within society."[117]

Nonetheless, the official mottoes of the women's services—"We are the women behind the men behind the guns"; "We serve that men might fly"; and "We serve that men might fight"—cast them in a subsidiary role. Although the women's naval and military units played a crucial role in the war effort, and considerable pressure was exerted on the government to maintain them as part of Canada's reserve forces, once the hostilities ceased they were promptly disbanded.

Even before peace was achieved, most Canadians expected women, especially those who were married, to re-dedicate themselves to work in the home. Many feared a resumption of the severe recession and massive unemployment of the 1930s, or of the inflation and social unrest of the years immediately following World War I. Spurred on by these concerns, in March 1941 the Liberal government named an Advisory Committee on Reconstruction, consisting of six prominent men. Almost immediately, women began to petition for female representation, on the basis of women's important contribution to the war effort. Finally, in January 1943, the government established a new subcommittee with the limited mandate of dealing with the problems that women in war industry were likely to encounter once the war ended. This subcommittee, whose terms of reference were soon expanded to allow it to report on postwar problems for all Canadian women, was headed by Margaret McWilliams—a journalist, Winnipeg councillor, and prominent women's organization activist—and included nine other women from across the nation.[118]

At its initial meeting, the subcommittee adopted as its first principle the strongly feminist precept that women had a right to postwar employment with equal remuneration and the same opportunity for advancement as men. Nevertheless, the subcommittee's final report was a mixture of old and new. It recommended that women be able to access training and retraining programs on the same basis as men, but that most be trained for distinctive women's occupations, such as domestic service, nursing, teaching, and social work. Somewhat radically, the subcommittee proposed that "household workers" be included in any national labour code that might be forthcoming so that they would be covered by minimum wage legislation, unemployment insurance, and workmen's compensation. Further, the subcommittee members proposed that married women in the home be viewed as economic partners with their husbands, be included in social security schemes such as health insurance, receive family allowances, and have access to government-funded morning nursery schools. Hoping to arrest the wartime exodus of women from rural areas, it urged governments to extend electricity to more rural areas, to supply household appliances at cost, to improve communication networks, and to expand rural educational, health, and recreational facilities. Some journalists described the report as a "charter of rights" or a "bill of rights" for Canadian women.[119] Yet despite its innovative character, the report received little public attention—apart from a few press accounts, which were usually consigned to the women's pages. The federal government ignored most of the report's recommendations, as it did most of the recommendations of the Advisory Committee's other subcommittees. It would take another quarter century before the feminist ideas contained in the report would be taken up by another government-appointed body, the Royal Commission on the Status of Women in Canada.

A Gallup poll conducted in 1944 indicated that 75 percent of the Canadian men polled, as well as 68 percent of the women, believed men should be given preference in postwar employment.[120] Given the physical and emotional strain endured by those among them who had combined paid employment with domestic labour—not to mention the aggravation of wartime shortages and the anxiety caused by the absence of loved ones—many Canadian women looked forward to a return to full-time home life at war's end. "When the Johnnys and Joes come marching home," a woman journalist noted, "just shopping for ham to cook ham and eggs—if she can get eggs—is apt to be important to a woman . . . even if she drops an odd pay envelope along the way."[121]

THE POST-WAR YEARS

If a return to normalcy was a highly touted goal, there could be no such return for women whose families were forced by the Canadian government to leave their homes. More than 22 000 Japanese Canadians, most of whom had been born in Canada, spent the war years in detention camps in the interior of British Columbia or working on sugar beet farms in Alberta and Manitoba.[122] After the war, most were resettled east of the Rocky Mountains, far away from their original homes. Other women, who had seen their husbands or close male relatives shipped off to remote internment camps for allegedly being Nazi sympathizers, Italian enemy aliens, or Communists, also experienced the anguish of separation.

And there were yet other victims of war: the nursing sisters serving in Hong Kong, who were raped, tortured, and confined to prisoner-of-war camps; and the thousands of Canadian women who lost sons, husbands, or lovers. When husbands did return from active duty, they were often virtual strangers, and the ensuing marital strains led to a dramatic increase in divorce. For Aboriginal women, there was often a sense of loss as their traditional lifestyles were disrupted by the rapid economic and social changes brought about as a result of wartime activities. Under the War Measures Act, the federal government expropriated Stony Point reserve lands on Lake Huron from the Chippewa (Anishnaabeg) in order to create the Camp Ipperwash military base. Affected families were moved to much smaller holdings on nearby reserve holdings with a promise that the band's Stony Point lands would be returned at war's end, but they never were.[123]

In contrast to inaction on the restoration of Aboriginal property, as the war came to an end, the federal government quickly put in place policies and practices to strongly influence women to stay at home. In 1944 Dorise Nielsen, the MP from North Battleford, Saskatchewan, gave Parliament a sardonic summary of men's attitudes toward women's appropriate role: "Well, girls, you have done a nice job; you looked very cute in your overalls and we appreciate what you have done for us; but just run along; go home; we can get along without you very easily."[124] The federal government withdrew its support for day nurseries, and amended its income tax regulations. After January 1, 1947, if a wife earned more than $250—not even the pre-war $750—her husband could no longer claim the full married status exemption. Subsequently, there were reports that existing shortages of trained nurses and other types of women workers were exacerbated by this policy, since married women were quitting work once they had earned $250.[125] There

Dining area for children at Hastings Park facility in Vancouver, British Columbia, 1942. Hastings Park served as the clearing station for Japanese Canadians sent off to internment camps.

Source: Library and Archives Canada / C-026386

was a deliberate effort as well to limit women's employment in the public service. The prime minister went so far as to make a request that his cabinet ministers not employ female secretaries, to which the minister of agriculture is reported to have responded, "To —— with him. I couldn't get along without her."[126] Within the public service, the married women who had been implored to help run the burgeoning wartime bureaucracy were now discharged, and married women continued to be barred from the federal civil service until 1955.

By September 1945, nearly 80 000 women in war industry had been laid off and thousands of servicewomen discharged.[127] At the peak of wartime employment in 1944, one-third of all women over the age of 15 had been in the paid labour force. Two years later, only one-quarter were working for pay. In fact, not until 1967 did women's participation rate surpass the 1944 level. During the war, cadres of bureaucrats and experts—educational and industrial psychologists, managerial consultants, and vocational counsellors—had worked diligently to mould women into a productive workforce to achieve victory. These same functionaries now turned their attention to convincing Canadian women that their future and that of the nation would be best served by devoting themselves full-time to the roles of wives and mothers. Single women or married working class women who needed to work to supplement the family income were to be redirected from manufacturing, where their continued presence might constitute a threat to male employment, into domestic service, where there was a dearth of workers. For those with better education, clerical work was considered an appropriate choice. Despite the existence of a Veterans Charter that endorsed equality of the sexes, ex-servicewomen also experienced differential access to post-war programs and services. Vocational counsellors sought to convince most to select post-war training programs for what were considered suitable occupations, such as stenography, homemaking, dressmaking, and nursing. Once again, the federal government developed a dominion–provincial short training program in domestic service—this time labelled the Home Aide program—to absorb unemployed women. And once again, Canadian women, whether industrial workers or veterans, responded by virtually ignoring the program.[128]

Despite the suffering of specific groups of women during the war, and the tendency to use women as a reserve army of labour during wartime and then keep them out of male-dominated sectors of the economy in peacetime, the impact of the war was not entirely negative for Canadian women. For many, the wartime opportunity to expand their activities produced positive, long-term results. According to one woman,

> The war killed all this servant business, being a maid, and I think it did a lot to finish off the idea that a woman's place and her only place was in the home. . . . The war and working in plants so changed me I became an entirely different person. I wish I'd kept a diary.[129]

It is important to note that the decline in women's labour force participation immediately after the war was much less pronounced in Canada than it was in the United States. There, women's labour-force participation rate reached even higher levels during the war, only to drop by 19 percent between 1945 and 1947.[130] In Canada, by comparison, the decline was less than 9 percent during the same period and appears to have been caused less by the withdrawal of women already in the workforce than by the lower participation rate of younger women. Prolonged education and earlier age for starting a family combined to keep younger women at home. By the mid-1950s, women's labour-force involvement was on the rise once again, and even the armed forces reversed their policy and started to accept women recruits back into all three services. (See Figure A.7 in Appendix.)

Indeed, the proportion of married women among paid female workers continued to increase. In part, this change was owing to the lower age at marriage and the growing acceptance of young married women working, providing that they did not have children; in part, it stemmed from the presence in the labour force of older women with school-age or older children. In 1941, only slightly more than 10 percent of all employed women were married; by 1951 the national percentage had tripled, although it was lower in some regions, such as Montreal, where only 21 percent of the female workforce was married.[131] Over the next 10 years, there was yet another significant increase: nearly half of women working for wages in 1961 were married. This change can also be measured by looking at the proportion of wives who were in the paid labour force: from only 1 in 25 in 1941, the figure had changed in 20 years to a remarkable 1 in 5. The increase in married women's labour force participation was already obvious by 1954, when the dominion chief statistician declared, "The woman's place is no longer in the home, and the Canadian home is no longer what it used to be."[132]

Canadians' strong desire to improve their material situations, following years of economic depression and war, was not to be denied. In the 1950s, television revolutionized mass advertising techniques, stimulating the demand for major consumer items, such as cars, appliances, and furniture. To purchase these objects, which most Canadians now considered essential, and to ensure access to higher education and better health care for their children, many married women, especially those who were new immigrants, had to augment family income by taking on paid employment. As in previous generations, immigrant women often worked as domestic servants or as factory operatives in the garment, textile, and other light industries. In one highly controversial case, a member of parliament from Quebec got permission in 1947 to recruit approximately 100 Polish women from European Displaced Persons camps to work in his rayon spinning mill in Beauce County. In return for their passage to Canada, the women contracted to work for two years in the mill, for minimum wage with any additional amounts they earned through piece-work bonuses to be paid to them only at the end of the two-year period.[133]

Some immigrant women, particularly those who knew little or no English, found it preferable to operate boarding houses or to perform piece work in their own homes so that they could combine child-rearing with generating income. Taking in boarders became a common activity for many recently arrived Italian women for there was a ready market of young, single Italian male workers looking for lodgings, meals, and other domestic services. The *padrona* ("boarding house operator") routinely shopped for and prepared three meals a day for her family and several boarders; washed, ironed and mended their clothing; cleaned the house and tidied the boarders' rooms; and grew her own garden. As one woman recalled of her time as a boarding-house keeper, "I arose and went to bed with the moon."[134]

The increased importance of women's labour force participation for efforts to sustain national economic growth led the federal government in 1954 to create a specialized women's department within the department of labour. Women's organizations had long demanded such an agency, so not surprisingly, veteran activist and former World YWCA staff secretary Marion Royce became the bureau's first director. The increasing numbers of mothers working outside the home had become the source of much controversy; consequently, one of the first projects the bureau undertook was a survey of employed married women in eight Canadian cities. More than 50 percent of those interviewed had dependent children, and some 80 percent worked full-time. They had evidently taken jobs for economic reasons: only 15 percent of their husbands earned a relatively high income of $4 000, but when the wives' wages were included, more than half the families reached this income level. Reflecting the high levels of postwar immigration, one-third of the workers in the department of labour survey were born outside Canada.[135]

Women workers with preschool children had to make their own child-care arrangements, and generally preferred family or friends. Royce persistently argued that there was a need for better daycare facilities and more part-time work for married women with children.[136] However, no level of government felt an obligation to provide such facilities, and most Canadians continued to believe that married women with young children should not be employed outside the home. It was still assumed that the vast majority of women could not successfully combine work and family. In 1955 one woman who tried but failed concluded vehemently,

> I don't care who you are or how well organized you are, you can't be a good wife and mother, hostess and housekeeper and also do a good job for your employer all at the same time. When you try, someone is bound to get cheated—your husband, your child or your boss—and in most cases, all three.[137]

Her solution: quit the job to save the marriage. But most married women in the paid labour force could not choose to quit their jobs. It was essential for them to work in order to maintain their families' standard of living in an increasingly consumer-oriented society.

The pronounced emphasis on consumption may also have increased the workload of most homemakers. As the standard of living rose and the volume and diversity of consumer goods increased, the tasks associated with household management became more complex. Managing the family budget and trying to balance family income against family needs was even more difficult in the new suburbs that mushroomed on the fringes of Canadian urban communities. These suburbs provided good places to raise young families, with green space and modern, well-equipped schools. However, suburban housewives were often isolated and without transportation, and so they had little opportunity to engage in comparison shopping and to buy at the lowest prices. Shopping plazas—the first in Canada was constructed in Toronto in 1946—were somewhat helpful, but they provided only a limited choice of shops. Women were also responsible for dealing with the countless salesmen, repairmen, public officials, and community representatives who showed up on their doorsteps.[138] Cut off from traditional women's support systems, young suburban housewives found it difficult to gain access to the experience and advice of older women. Their response was to seek female companionship and support networks with women of their own age group through coffee klatches, bridge clubs, home and school associations, and mixed volunteer groups.

Women who could afford domestic help frequently engaged immigrant women. Under the federal government's Assisted Passage Loan Scheme, single women without children and between the ages of 18 and 45 could receive assistance to pay their transportation costs to Canada, provided that they signed a contract to perform one year of domestic service. Between 1951 and 1961, some 80 000 women took advantage of this plan, with over half coming from only two countries—Germany (25 000) and Italy (18 000).[139] However, few remained in domestic service beyond the required year. In an effort to meet the ongoing shortage of domestics, to establish stronger commercial ties with the West Indies, and to counteract growing pressure for Canada to end its near exclusion of black immigrants, the federal government launched the West Indian Domestic Scheme (WIDS) in 1955. Under this legislation, an employer could sponsor a woman who was hand-picked and trained in domestic service in her own country before departing for Canada. The Canadian deputy minister of citizenship and immigration was so impressed by the training facilities set up in Barbados and Jamaica that he suggested that someone be sent from Indian Affairs "to study their organization, as it could be very useful in the training of [Canadian] Indian girls for this type of employment." Most of the women who came to Canada under this scheme were relatively well educated and previously held positions as teachers, nurses, or clerks. Once their year of service to their employers concluded, they could apply to stay in Canada. Unlike European women, however, most West Indian women were not included in the Assisted Passage Loan Fund that was available to other immigrants. Initially, the WIDS was limited to a total of 100 women a year from Jamaica and Barbados, but at the request of other West Indian governments, by 1966 it had grown to incorporate an annual quota of 500 women from more than 10 islands. As the numbers grew, however, so too did Canadian authorities' concerns that the women were not staying in domestic service and that they were seeking to sponsor their children and unskilled male partners or other relatives. The federal government increasingly took the view that its immigration policies should give preference to skilled workers and professionals. As a result, it cancelled the program in 1968.[140]

Domestic workers were isolated and of little interest to most unions, but for industrial workers, there were some significant attempts at organization. The labour militancy generated during World War II continued. During the war, as the demand for workers expanded, so did workers' bargaining power; union membership soared, especially with the expansion of industrial unionism, which sought to bring together all groups of workers in a given establishment.[141] Even the more conservative international unions became involved in organizing semiskilled and unskilled workers, within whose ranks were to be found thousands of women. In the textile industry, Madeleine Parent and her future husband, Kent Rowley, made impressive inroads. Parent graduated from McGill in 1940 and became a labour activist while still a very young woman. In 1942 she and Rowley started to organize Quebec cotton mill workers in Valleyfield and Montreal. They faced formidable odds, for they had to confront not only the might of the textile cartel headed by Dominion Textile, but also the overt hostility of the Roman Catholic Church and the provincial government, which denounced them as Communists.

Because of the wartime ban on strikes, it was only after the war ended that workers could walk off the job to back up demands for union recognition, a shorter workweek, and improved benefits. In June 1946, some 3 000 workers at Dominion Textile's Montreal mills and an additional 3 000 workers at the Valleyfield mill staged a walkout; approximately one-third of the workers were women. The blatantly pro-business government of Maurice Duplessis declared the Valleyfield strike illegal, and in fact not all the bargaining procedures required by law had been followed. The authorities made a concerted effort to break the strike, using the provincial police to protect strike-breakers and intimidate the workers. The Valleyfield strike was long, bitter, punctuated by violence, and marked by the arrest of the union leaders, including both Parent and Rowley. However, when it finally ended in September, the result was a first contract, improved wages, and other benefits for the workers.[142]

The importance of women's support for the trade union movement grew during and after World War II, as production workers saw many of their material gains threatened by the rising cost of living, and as women's consumer roles expanded. Some women's auxiliaries were also involved in the bitter internal struggles between local Communist union leaders and their international leadership that bedevilled many unions after the war. Such a situation occurred in Lake Cowichan, British Columbia, where the ladies' auxiliary supported the local "red" faction of the International Woodworkers of America. The political activities of this auxiliary also led it to support the so-called rolling pin brigade—a protest movement largely composed of housewife consumers—which culminated in a march on Ottawa after the war to demand price and rent controls, low-cost housing, and the establishment of a peacetime agency to regulate prices.[143]

Married women's work both inside and outside the home became even more important during the severe recession from 1957 to 1961 that resulted in high rates of male unemployment. As in the early 1930s, the clerical and service sectors of the economy were less severely affected by the economic downturn than traditional areas of male employment, such as construction, mining, and forestry. As a result, many wives found it easier to find work than was the case for their husbands. Noting the importance of married women's wages to the family economy during this period, a *Financial Post* reporter aptly summarized one of the most significant and enduring changes in postwar Canadian society: "This is a woman's world all right and getting more so. More and more married women are going to work and they are quickly being snapped into jobs. . . . Keep your eye on Mom."[144]

Notes

1. Marjory MacMurchy, *Women and Reconstruction* (Toronto: Canadian Reconstruction Association, n.d.), 9.
2. Ontario, Department of Labour, *Vocational Opportunities in the Industries of Ontario*, 1 (1920), iii; *What Shall I Do Now? How to Work for Canada in Peace* (Toronto: Canadian Reconstruction Association, Women's Department, 1919), 7.
3. *What Shall I Do Now?*, 3.
4. Ceta Ramkalawansingh, "Women during the Great War," in Janice Acton, Penny Goldsmith, and Bonnie Shepard, eds., *Women at Work: Ontario, 1850–1930* (Toronto: Canadian Women's Educational Press, 1974), 288.
5. Juliet Stuart Poyntz, "Problems of the Working Woman," *The New Democracy* (May 29, 1919).
6. Cynthia Comacchio, *The Dominion of Youth: Adolescence and the Making of Modern Canada, 1920–1950* (Waterloo, ON: Wilfrid University Press, 2006), 137.
7. Comacchio, *Dominion*, 130.
8. Gail Cuthbert Brandt, "'Weaving It Together': Life Cycle and the Industrial Experience of Female Cotton Workers in Quebec, 1910–1950," *Labour/Le Travail* 7 (Spring 1981): 164–66; Ruth A. Frager, *Sweatshop Strife: Class, Ethnicity, and Gender in the Jewish Labour Movement of Toronto, 1900–1939* (Toronto: University of Toronto Press, 1992), 166; Rebecca Coulter, "Teen-Agers in Edmonton, 1921–1931: Experiences of Gender and Class," University of Alberta, Ph.D. Thesis, 1987, 56; Tamara Adilman, "A Preliminary Sketch of Chinese Women and Work in British Columbia, 1858–1950," in Gillian Creese and Veronica Strong-Boag, eds., *British Columbia Reconsidered: Essays on Women* (Vancouver: Press Gang, 1992),

327; Frances Swyripa, "Nation Building into the 1920s: Conflicting Claims on Ukrainian Immigrant Women," in Manoly R. Lupul, ed., *Continuity and Change: The Cultural Life of Alberta's First Ukrainians* (Edmonton: University of Alberta Press, 1988), 140.

9. See, for example, Elizabeth Goudie, *Woman of Labrador* (Toronto: Peter Martin Associates Limited, 1975).

10. Olga McKenna, *Micmac by Choice: Elsie Stark—An Island Legend* (Halifax: Formac,1990), 164.

11. Comacchio, *Dominion of Youth*, 142; Marilyn Barber, "The Gentlewomen of Queen Mary's Coronation Hostel," in Barbara Latham and Roberta Pazdro, eds., *Not Just Pin Money: Selected Essays on the History of Women's Work in British Columbia* (Victoria: Camosun College, 1984), 141–58; Lindsey McMaster, *Working Girls in the West: Representations of Wage-Earning Women* (Vancouver: UBC Press, 2008), 145–47.

12. Varpu Lindström-Best, "'I Won't Be a Slave!': Finnish Domestics in Canada, 1911–30," in Jean Burnet, ed., *Looking into My Sister's Eyes: An Exploration in Women's History* (Toronto: Multicultural History Society of Ontario, 1986), 33–53; Varpu Lindström-Best, *Defiant Sisters: A Social History of Finnish Immigrant Women in Canada* (Toronto: Multicultural History Society of Ontario, 1988).

13. Helen Potrebenko, *No Streets of Gold: A Social History of Ukrainians in Alberta* (Vancouver: New Star, 1977), 180.

14. Adilman, "Preliminary Sketch," 309–39; Mahinder Kaur Doman, "A Note on Asian Indian Women in British Columbia 1900–1935," in Latham and Pazdro, eds., *Not Just Pin Money*, 99–104; Dorothy W. Williams, *Blacks in Montreal 1628–1986: An Urban Demography* (Cowansville, QC: Éditions Yvon Blais, 1989), 117; Ruth L. Harris, "The Transformation of Canadian Policies and Programs to Recruit Foreign Labour: The Case of Caribbean Female Domestics, 1950's—1980's," Ph.D., Sociology, Michigan State University, 1988, 80.

15. Potrebenko, *No Streets of Gold*, 186.

16. Joy Parr, "Hired Men: Ontario Agricultural Wage Labour in Historical Perspective," *Labour/ Le Travail* 15 (Spring 1985): 102; Adilman, "Preliminary Sketch," 329.

17. McMaster, *Working Girls,* 147–67; James W. St. G. Walker, "A Case of Morality: The Quong Wing Files," in Franca Iacovetta and Wendy Mitchinson, eds., *On the Case: Explorations in Social History* (Toronto: University of Toronto Press, 1998), 214–16; Constance Backhouse, "White Female Help and Chinese-Canadian Employers: Race, Class, Gender, and Law in the Case of Yee Clun 1924," in Wendy Mitchinson et al., eds., *Canadian Women: A Reader* (Toronto: Harcourt Brace,1996), 280–99.

18. Margaret E. McCallum, "Separate Spheres: The Organization of Work in a Confectionery Factory—Ganong Bros., St. Stephen, New Brunswick, 1900–1945," *Labour/Le Travail* 24 (Fall 1989): 69–90; Mercedes Steedman, *Angels of the Workplace: Women and the Construction of Gender Relations in the Canadian Clothing Industry, 1890–1940* (Toronto: Oxford University Press, 1997), 114–19; Frager, *Sweatshop Strife*, 121; Gail Cuthbert Brandt, "The Transformation of Women's Work in the Quebec Cotton Industry 1920–1950," in Bryan D. Palmer, ed., *The Character of Class Struggle: Essays in Canadian Working-Class History, 1850–1985* (Toronto: McClelland and Stewart, 1986), 115–37; Joy Parr, *The Gender of Breadwinners: Women, Men, and Change in Two Industrial Towns, 1880–1950* (Toronto: University of Toronto Press, 1990).

19. Jack Gregg, "Girls Live Only to Create Profits for a Boss," *The Young Worker* (May 1926), 2.

20. Steedman, *Angels of the Workplace,* 112–13; Franc Sturino, "The Role of Women in Italian Immigration to the New World," in Burnet, ed., *Looking into My Sister's Eyes*, 27–28.

21. Graham S. Lowe, "Women, Work and the Office: The Feminization of Clerical Occupations in Canada, 1901–1931," in Veronica Strong-Boag and Anita Clair Fellman, eds., *Rethinking Canada: The Promise of Women's History* (Toronto: Copp Clark Pitman, 1986), 116. See also Lowe, *Women in the Administrative Revolution: the Feminization of Clerical Work* (Cambridge: Polity, 1987).

22. Women's Book Committee, Chinese National Council, *Jin Guo: Voices of Chinese Canadian Women* (Toronto: Women's Press, 1992), 146; Dionne Brand, "'We Weren't Allowed to Go into Factory Work until Hitler Started the War': The 1920s to the 1940s," in Peggy Bristow, co-ord., et al., *"We're Rooted Here and They Can't Pull Us Up": Essays in African Canadian Women's History* (Toronto: University of Toronto Press, 1994), 177; as quoted in Adrienne Shadd, "300 Years of Black Women in Canadian History: Circa 1700–1980," *Tiger Lily* 1, 2 (1987), 10.

23. N. E. S. Griffiths, *The Splendid Vision: Centennial History of the National Council of Women of Canada, 1893–1993* (Ottawa: Carleton University Press, 1993), 186–87.

24. Veronica Strong-Boag, "The Girl of the New Day: Canadian Working Women in the 1920s," *Labour/Le Travail* 4 (1979): 146; Strong-Boag, *The New Day Recalled: Lives of Girls and Women in English Canada, 1919–1939* (Toronto: Copp Clark Pittman, 1988).

25. M. E. Clark, "Woman in Business Is Still at Heart a Woman," *Canadian Magazine* 69 (January 1928), 27.

26. Dora Nipp, "'But Women Did Come': Working Chinese Women in The Interwar Years," in Burnet, ed., *Looking into My Sister's Eyes*, 189.

27. Rella Braithwaite and Tessa Benn-Ireland, *Some Black Women: Profiles of Black Women in Canada* (Toronto: Sister Vision, 1993), 35.

28. Sylvia Hamilton, "Our Mothers Grand and Great: Black Women of Nova Scotia," *Canadian Woman Studies/Les cahiers de la femme* 11, 3 (Spring 1991): 46; Theresa M. Jeffries, "Sechelt Women and Self-Government," in Creese and Strong-Boag, eds., *British Columbia Reconsidered*, 91; McKenna, *Micmac by Choice*, 4, 50–51, 53; Marilyn Porter, "'She Was Skipper of the Shore-Crew': Notes on the History of the Sexual Division of Labour in Newfoundland," *Labour/Le Travail* 15 (Spring 1985): 112–16.

29. Lindström-Best, *Defiant Sisters*, 102–3.

30. Andrée Lévesque, "Le bordel: Milieu de travail contrôlé," *Labour/Le Travail* 20 (Fall 1987): 13–31; Lévesque, *Making and Breaking the Rules: Women in Quebec, 1919–1939*. Translated by Yvonne M. Klein (Toronto: McClelland and Stewart, 1994), 117–35; James Gray, *Red Lights on the Prairies* (Toronto: Macmillan, 1970).

31. Barbara Keddy and Dianne Dodd, "The Trained Nurse: Private Duty and VON Home Nursing (Late 1800s to 1940s)," in Christina Bates, Dianne Dodd, and Nicole Rousseau, eds., *On All Frontiers: Four Centuries of Canadian Nursing* (Ottawa: University of Ottawa Press and the Canadian Museum of Civilization, 2005), 44–45.

32. Diana Mansell and Dianne Dodd, "Professionalism and Canadian Nursing," in Bates et al., eds., *On All Frontiers*, 201–8.

33. Margaret M. Street, *Watch-Fires on the Mountains: The Life and Writings of Ethel Johns* (Toronto: University of Toronto Press, 1973), 128–29.

34. Kathryn McPherson, "The Nightingale Influence and the Rise of the Modern Hospital," in Bates et al., eds., *On All Frontiers*, 82–83; Adilman, "Preliminary Sketch," 323; Hamilton, "Our Mothers," 47.

35. Diana Mansell and Dianne Dodd, "Professionalism" in Bates et al., *On All Frontiers*, 197–211; Kathryn McPherson, *Bedside Matters: The Transformation of Canadian Nursing,*

1900–1990 (Toronto: Oxford University Press, 1996); McPherson, "Science and Technique: Nurses' Work in a Canadian Hospital, 1920–39," in Dianne Dodd and Deborah Gorham, eds., *Caring and Curing: Historical Perspectives on Women and Healing in Canada* (Ottawa: University of Ottawa Press, 1994), 71–101; Johanne Daigle, "Devenir infirmière: Les modalités d'expression d'une culture soignante au XXe siècle," *Recherches féministes* 4, 1 (1991): 67–86; Yolande Cohen et Louise Bienvenue, "Émergence de l'identité professionnelle chez les infirmières québécoises (1890–1927)," *Bulletin canadien d'histoire de la médecine* (août 1994); Yolande Cohen, *Profession infirmière: Une histoire des soins dans les hopitaux au Québec* (Montréal: Les presses de l'Université de Montréal, 2000).

36. Judi Coburn, "'I See and Am Silent': A Short History of Nursing in Ontario," in Acton, Goldsmith, and Shepard, eds., *Women at Work*, 142–47; Keddy and Dodd, "The Trained Nurse," 43–55; Mary Kinnear, *In Subordination: Professional Women, 1870–1970* (Montreal and Kingston: McGill-Queen's University Press, 1995), 107.

37. Linda Quiney, "'Suitable Young Women': Red Cross Nursing Pioneers and the Crusade for Healthy Living in Manitoba, 1920–30," in Jayne Elliott, Meryn Stuart, and Cynthia Toman, eds., *Place and Practice in Canadian Nursing History* (Vancouver: UBC Press, 2008), 91–110; Marion McKay, "Public Health Nursing," in Bates et al., *On All Frontiers*, 107–23; Dianne Dodd, Jayne Elliott and Nicole Rousseau, "Outpost Nursing in Canada," in Bates et al., 139–52.

38. Denyse Baillargeon, "Care of Mothers and Infants in Montreal between the Wars: The Visiting Nurses of Metropolitan Life, Les Gouttes de lait, and Assistance maternelle," in Dodd and Gorham, eds., *Caring and Curing*, 164–67.

39. Quiney, "Suitable Young Women," 91; Cecilia Benoit and Dena Carroll, "Canadian Midwifery: Blending Traditional and Modern Practices," in Bates et al., *On All Frontiers*, 35–36.

40. McKay, "Public Health Nursing," 118–19; Meryn Stuart, "Shifting Professional Boundaries: Gender Conflict in Public Health, 1920–1925," in Dodd and Gorham, eds., *Caring and Curing*, 49–70; Jayne Elliott, "(Re)Constructing the Identity of a Red Cross Outpost Nurse: The Letters of Louise de Kiriline, 1927–36," in Elliott et al., eds., *Place and Practice*, 144.

41. J. Donald Wilson and Paul J. Stortz, "'May the Lord have Mercy on You': The Rural School Problem in British Columbia in the 1920s," in Jean Barman, Neil Sutherland and J. Donald Wilson, eds., *Children, Teachers and Schools in the History of British Columbia* (Calgary: Detselig Entreprises Ltd., 1995), 21; George Perry, "'A Concession to Circumstances': Nova Scotia's 'Unlimited Supply' of Women Teachers, 1870–1960," *Historical Studies in Education/ Revue d'histoire de l'éducation* 15, 2 (2003): 327–60; Penelope Stephenson, "'Mrs. Gibson Looked as if She Was Ready for the End of Term': The Professional Trials and Tribulations of Rural Teachers in British Columbia's Okanagan Valley in the 1920s," in Barman et al., eds., *Children, Teachers and Schools*, 235–57; J. Donald Wilson, "'I am ready to be of assistance when I can': Lottie Bowron and Rural Women Teachers in British Columbia," in Barman et al., 285.

42. Susan Gellman, "The 'Feminization' of High Schools: The Problem of Women Secondary School Teachers in Ontario," in Sharon Anne Cook, Lorna R. McLean, and Kate O'Rourke, *Framing Our Past: Canadian Women's History in the Twentieth Century* (Montreal and Kingston: McGill-Queen's University Press, 2001), 172; Kinnear, *In Subordination*, 123–32.

43. Rebecca Priegert Coulter, "Getting Things Done: Donalda J. Dickie and Leadership Through Practice," in Elizabeth M. Smyth and Paula Bourne, eds., *Women Teaching, Women Learning: Historical Perspectives* (Toronto: Inanna Publications and Education Inc., 2006), 23–44; Dianne Hallman and Anna H. Lathrop, "Sustaining the Fire of 'Scholarly Passion': Mary G. Hamilton (1883–1972) and Irene Poelzer (1926–)," in Smyth and Bourne, eds., *Women Teaching*, 45–64; Judith Fingard, "Gender Inequality at Dalhousie: Faculty Women before

1950," *Dalhousie Review* 64 (1984–5): 687–703; Alison Prentice, "Bluestockings, Feminists, or Women Workers? A Preliminary Look at Women's Early Employment at the University of Toronto," *Journal of the Canadian Historical Association*, New Series 2 (1991): 231–61; Mary Kinnear, "Disappointment in Discourse: Women University Professors at the University of Manitoba before 1970," *Historical Studies in Education* 4, 9 (1992): 269–87.

44. Sara Z. Burke, *Seeking the Highest Good: Social Service and Gender at the University of Toronto, 1888–1937* (Toronto: University of Toronto Press, 1996), 100–14.

45. Hélène Pelletier-Baillargeon, *Marie Gérin-Lajoie* (Montréal: Boréal Express, 1985); Marie-Paule Malouin, *Entre le rêve et la réalité: Marie Gérin-Lajoie et l'histoire du Bon-Conseil* (Montréal: Bellarmin, 1998).

46. Ruby Heap, "Training Women for a New 'Women's Profession': Physiotherapy Education at the University of Toronto," *History of Education Quarterly* 35 (Summer 1995): 135–58; Nadia Fahmy-Eid et al., *Femmes, santé et profession: Histoire des diététistes et des physiothérapeutes au Québec et en Ontario, 1930–1980* (Montréal: Fides, 1997).

47. Annmarie Adams and Peta Tancred, *"Designing Women": Gender and the Architectural Profession* (Toronto: University of Toronto Press, 2000), 14–19, 37–43; Pamela Wakewich, "'The Queen of the Hurricanes': Elsie Gregory MacGill, Aeronautical Engineer and Women's Advocate," in Cook, MacLean, and O'Rourke, *Framing Our Past*, 396; "Eileen Vollick", Canadian 99s, http://www.canadian99s.org/articles/p_vollick.htm.

48. Kinnear, *In Subordination*, 78–89; Appendix 1, table 15, 179.

49. Kinnear, *In Subordination*, 53–62; Appendix 1, table 10, 177.

50. Benjamin Issit, "Searching for Workers' Solidarity: The One Big Union and the Victoria General Strike of 1919," *Labour/Le Travail* 60 (Fall 2007): 18–19; Mary Horodyski, "Women and the Winnipeg General Strike of 1919," *Manitoba History* 11 (Spring 1986): 28–37; J. M. Bumsted, "The Winnipeg General Strike Reconsidered," *The Beaver* 74, 3 (June/July 1994): 37–39; McMaster, *Working Girls in the West*, 134–44.

51. Elaine Bernard, "Last Back: Folklore and the Telephone Operators in the 1919 Vancouver General Strike," in Latham and Pazdro, eds., *Not Just Pin Money*, 279–86; James Naylor, "Toronto 1919," *Historical Papers/Communications historiques* (1986): 44, 50.

52. Margaret E. McCallum, "Keeping Women in Their Place: The Minimum Wage in Canada, 1910–1925," *Labour/Le Travail* 17 (Spring 1986): 29–56.

53. Ontario, *Sessional Papers*, Annual Report of the Minimum Wage Commission (1920), 5.

54. E. M. Murray and Maude Pettit Hill, "Do Women Want Protection? Yes and No," *Chatelaine* 1, 6 (August 1928): 7; Alice Klein and Wayne Roberts, "Besieged Innocence: The 'Problem' and Problems of Working Women—Toronto, 1896–1914," in Acton, Goldsmith, and Shepard, eds., *Women at Work*, 211–12.

55. Susan Wade, "Helena Gutteridge: Votes for Women and Trade Unions," in Barbara Latham and Cathy Kess, eds., *In Her Own Right: Selected Essays on Women's History in B.C.* (Victoria: Camosun College, 1984), 196–97; McCallum, "Keeping," 37.

56. Ontario, *Sessional Papers*, Annual Report of the Minimum Wage Commission (1921), 14.

57. McCallum, "Keeping," 54.

58. Louise Watson, *She Never Was Afraid: The Biography of Annie Buller* (Toronto: Progress Books, 1976), 1–11, 82; Margaret Hobbs and Joan Sangster, *The Woman Worker, 1926–29* (St. John's: Canadian Committee on Labour History, 1999), 7–12; Andrée Lévesque, *Red Travellers: Jeanne Corbin and Her Comrades* (Montreal and Kingston: McGill-Queen's Press, 2006).

59. Joan Sangster, "The Communist Party and the Woman Question, 1922–1929," *Labour/Le Travail* 15 (Spring 1985): 34.

60. H. A. Spencer, "Minimum Wage Laws for Women," *Canadian Congress Journal* 4 (March 1925): 37.

61. Frager, *Sweatshop Strife*, 135; Gillian Creese, "The Politics of Dependence: Women, Work, and Unemployment in the Vancouver Labour Movement before World War II," in Creese and Strong-Boag, eds., *British Columbia Reconsidered*, 372.

62. Creese, "The Politics of Dependence," 365; Margaret Hillyard Little, *"No Car, No Radio, No Liquor Permit": The Moral Regulation of Single Mothers in Ontario, 1920–1997* (Toronto: Oxford University Press, 1998), 20–25; Margaret Hobbs, "Equality and Difference: Feminism and the Defence of Women Workers during the Great Depression," *Labour/Le Travail* 32 (Fall 1993): 20–23.

63. Soeur Marie Gérin-Lajoie, "Le syndicalisme féminin," in Michèle Jean, ed., *Québécoises au XXe siècle* (Montréal: Éditions Le Jour, 1974), 104–6.

64. Strong-Boag, "The Girl of the New Day," 155–56; Michelle Lapointe, "Le syndicat catholique des allumetières de Hull, 1919–1924," *Revue d'histoire de l'Amérique française* 32, 4 (mars 1979): 603–28; Ruth Frager and Carmela Patrias, *Discounted Labour: Women Workers in Canada, 1870–1939* (Toronto: University of Toronto Press, 2005), 133–34.

65. Gérin-Lajoie, "Le syndicalisme féminin," 107; Joan Sangster, "The Softball Solution: Female Workers, Male Managers and the Operation of Male Paternalism at Westclox, 1923–1960," *Labour/Le Travail* 32 (Fall 1993): 167–200; Hobbs, "Equality and Difference," 210–13.

66. Pat Staton and Beth Light, *Speak with Their Own Voices: A Documentary History of the Federation of Women Teachers' Associations of Ontario and the Women Elementary Public School Teachers of Ontario* (Toronto: FWTAO, 1987), chap. 3; Doris French, *High Button Bootstraps* (Toronto: Ryerson Press, 1968), 43.

67. Patricia Roome, "Amelia Turner and the Calgary Labour Women, 1919–1935," in Linda Kealey and Joan Sangster, eds., *Beyond the Vote: Canadian Women and Politics* (Toronto: University of Toronto Press, 1989), 89–117; Apolonja Kojder, "In Union There Is Strength: The Saskatoon Women Teachers' Association," *Canadian Woman Studies/Les cahiers de la femme* 7, 3 (Fall 1986): 82–84.

68. Registered Nurses' Association of Ontario Foundation, *1987 Appointment Book* (Toronto: RNAOF, 1986).

69. Stephen Penfold, "'Have You No Manhood in You?': Gender and Class in the Cape Breton Coalmines, 1920–1926," *Acadiensis* 2 (Spring 1994): 21–44; Potrebenko, *No Streets of Gold*, 169; Anne B. Woywitka, "A Pioneer Woman in the Labour Movement," in Strong-Boag and Fellman, eds., *Rethinking Canada*, 196–97.

70. Creese, "The Politics of Dependence," 369.

71. Eric W. Sager, "Women in the Industrial Labour Force: Evidence for British Columbia, 1921–53," *BC Studies* 149 (Spring 2006): 44–47; Creese, "The Politics of Dependence," 365–70; Comacchio, *Dominion of Youth*, 137; Lara Campbell, *Respectable Citizens: Gender, Family and Unemployment in Ontario's Great Depression* (Toronto: University of Toronto Press, 2009), 42–46; Katrina Srigley, *Breadwinning Daughters: Young Working Women in a Depression-Era City, 1929–1939* (Toronto: University of Toronto Press, 2009).

72. Canada, House of Commons, Special Committee on Price Spreads and Mass Buying, *Proceedings and Evidence* (1934) vol. 1, 113.

73. Sybil Shack, *Saturday's Children: Canadian Women in Business* (Toronto: Faculty of Education, University of Toronto, 1977), 29.

74. Cuthbert Brandt, "The Transformation of Women's Work," 128.

75. Kinnear, *In Subordination*, 136–37.

76. Canada, Royal Commission on Price Spreads, *Minutes of Proceedings and Evidence* (1935), 4410, 4433, 4569, 4554, 110.

77. Creese, "The Politics of Dependence," 308.

78. Hillyard Little, "*No Radio,*" 76–106.

79. L. Richter, ed., *Canada's Unemployment Problem* (Toronto: Macmillan, 1939), 118.

80. "Single Women on Relief," *Canadian Forum* 16, 15 (March 1937).

81. Jo-Anne Fiske, "Gender and Politics in a Carrier Indian Community," University of British Columbia, Ph.D. Thesis, 1989, 89, 87–90; Fiske, "Carrier Women and the Politics of Mothering," in Creese and Strong-Boag, eds., *British Columbia Reconsidered*, 203; John Lutz, "Gender and Work in Lekwammen Families, 1843–1970," in Kathryn McPherson, Cecilia Morgan, and Nancy Forestell, eds., *Gendered Pasts: Historical Essays in Femininity and Masculinity in Canada* (Toronto: Oxford, 1999), 80–106; Sherry Farrell Racette, "Sewing for a Living: the Commodification of Métis Women's Artistic Production," in Myra Rutherdale and Katie Pickles, eds., *Contact Zones: Aboriginal Women and Settler Women in Canada's Colonial Past* (Vancouver: UBC Press, 2005), 40.

82. Lindström-Best, *Defiant Sisters*, 91.

83. Stacey Zembrzycki, "'There Were Always Men in Our House': Gender and the Childhood Memories of Working-Class Ukrainians in Depression-Era Canada," *Labour/Le Travail* 60, (Fall 2007): 77–105; Nancy Forestell, "The Miner's Wife: Working-Class Femininity in a Masculine Context, 1920–1950" in McPherson, Morgan, and Forestell, eds., *Gendered Pasts*, 139–57; Sylvie Taschereau, "'Behind the Store': Montreal Shopkeeping Families between the Wars," in Bettina Bradbury and Tamara Myers, eds., *Negotiating Identities in 19th- and 20th-Century Montreal* (Vancouver: UBC Press, 2005), 237–45.

84. Campbell, *Respectable Citizens*, 79–83; Rebecca Coulter, "Teen-Agers in Edmonton," 36.

85. Campbell, *Respectable Citizens*, 23–42; Denyse Baillargeon, *Ménagères au temps de la crise* (Montréal: Les Éditions du remue-ménage, 1991), 131–89; Barry Broadfoot, *Ten Lost Years, 1929–1939: Memories of Canadians Who Survived the Depression* (Toronto: Doubleday, 1973), 280, 74–75.

86. L. M. Grayson and Michael Bliss, eds., *The Wretched of Canada: Letters to R. B. Bennett 1930–1935* (Toronto: University of Toronto Press, 1971), 75–77.

87. Potrebenko, *No Streets of Gold*, 250–52.

88. James Gray, *The Winter Years: The Depression on the Prairies* (Toronto: Macmillan, 1966), 63–66.

89. Creese, "The Politics of Dependence," 380–81.

90. Dorothy Kidd, "Women's Organization: Learning from Yesterday," in Acton, Goldsmith, and Shepard, eds., *Women at Work*, 340.

91. Le Collectif Clio, *L'histoire des femmes au Québec depuis quatre siècles* (Montréal: Le Jour, 1992), 299–300.

92. Donald Wilson, "Lottie Bowron and Rural Women Teachers in British Columbia, 1928–34," in Creese and Strong-Boag, eds., *British Columbia Reconsidered*, 357–58; Creese, "The Politics of Dependence," 372, 383.

93. Steedman, *Angels of the Workplace*, 169–89; Evelyn Dumas, *The Bitter Thirties in Quebec* (Montreal: Black Rose Books, 1975), 49.

94. Ruth A. Frager, "Class, Ethnicity, and Gender in the Eaton Strikes of 1912 and 1934," in Franca Iacovetta and Mariana Valverde, eds., *Gender Conflicts: New Essays in Women's History* (Toronto: University of Toronto Press, 1992), 189–228.

95. Steedman, *Angels*, 241–52.

96. Cuthbert Brandt, "The Transformation of Women's Work," 129; Sangster, *Earning Respect*, 172–90.

97. Geneviève Auger et Raymonde Lamothe, *De la poêle à frire à la ligne de feu* (Montréal: Boréal Express, 1981), frontispiece [our translation].

98. Auger et Lamothe, *De la poêle à frire*, 53.

99. Jeff Keshen, "Revisiting Canada's Civilian Women During World War II," *Histoire sociale/Social History* 30, 60 (November 1997): 243–46.

100. Barry Broadfoot, *Six War Years, 1939–1945: Memories of Canadians at Home and Abroad* (Toronto: Paperjacks, 1974), 355–56.

101. Sager, "Women in the Industrial Labour Force," 54.

102. Ruth Roach Pierson, *"They're Still Women after All": The Second World War and Canadian Womanhood* (Toronto: McClelland and Stewart, 1986), 48.

103. Pierson, *"They're Still Women,"* 50.

104. Magda Fahrni, *Household Politics: Montreal Families and Postwar Reconstruction* (Toronto: University of Toronto Press, 2005), 57–59; Auger et Lamothe, *De la poêle à frire*, 128 [our translation].

105. Auger et Lamothe, *De la poêle à frire*, 128 [our translation].

106. Pierson, *"They're Still Women,"* 47–48.

107. Pierson, *"They're Still Women,"* 71.

108. Dorothy W. Williams, *Blacks in Montreal 1628–1986: An Urban Demography* (Cowansville, QC: Éditions Yvon Blais, 1989); Beth Light and Ruth Roach Pierson, eds., *No Easy Road: Women in Canada, 1920s–1960s* (Toronto: New Hogtown Press, 1990), 297; Dionne Brand, "'We Weren't Allowed to Go into Factory Work until Hitler Started the War': The 1920s to the 1940s," in Bristow, et al., *"We're Rooted Here,"* 171–91; Pamela Sugiman, "Privilege and Oppression: The Configuration of Race, Gender and Class in Southern Ontario Auto Plants, 1939 to 1949," *Labour/Le Travail*, 47 (Spring, 2001): 90–91.

109. Wakewich, "Queen of the Hurricanes," 397; Carolyn Gossage, *Double Duty: Sketches and Diaries of Molly Lamb Babok, Canadian War Artist* (Toronto: Dundurn Press, 1992).

110. This discussion of women in the armed forces relies extensively on Pierson, *"They're Still Women,"* chap. 3.

111. Grace Poulin, "Aboriginal Women: Invisible Servicewomen in Canada's WW II," 12–13; http://library.uvic.ca/site/spcoll/military/GPoulin.pdf; see also "Invisible Women: Aboriginal Servicewomen in Canada's Second World War," in *Aboriginal Peoples and the Canadian Military: Historical Perspectives* (Kingston 2007); Poulin, *Invisible Women: WWII Aboriginal Servicewomen in Canada* (Thunder Bay, ON: n.p., 2007).

112. Carolyn M. Gossage, *Greatcoats and Glamour Boots: Canadian Women at War, 1939–1945* (Toronto: Dundurn Press, 1991), 40, 44–46.

113. Barbara Winters, "Canadian Servicewomen in the Second World War: A Revisionist Approach," paper presented to the Canadian Historical Association, Charlottetown, 1992, 16–17.

114. Gossage, *Greatcoats*, 94, 150–52.

115. Winters, "Canadian Servicewomen," 26.

116. See Cynthia Toman, *An Officer and a Lady: Canadian Military Nursing and the Second World War* (Vancouver: UBC Press, 2007).

117. Paul Ward, "Women in World War II: Focus on the Women's Royal Canadian Naval Service," unpublished paper, April 1987, 27.

118. The other members included Margaret Mackenzie (Fredericton), Thaïs Lacoste-Frémont (Quebec City), Margaret Wherry (Montreal), Dr. A. Vibert Douglas (Kingston), Helen Smith

Agnew and Marion Findlay (Toronto), Susan Gunn (Lloydminster), Grace MacInnis and Evelyn Lett (Vancouver); see Gail Cuthbert Brandt, "'Pigeon-Holed and Forgotten': The Work of the Subcommittee on the Post-War Problems of Women, 1943," *Histoire sociale/ Social History* 15, 29 (March/mars 1982): 239–59; Mary Kinnear, *Margaret McWilliams: An Interwar Feminist* (Montreal and Kingston: McGill-Queen's University Press, 1991), 143–47; Jennifer A. Stephen, *Pick One Intelligent Girl: Employability, Domesticity and the Gendering of Canada's Welfare State, 1939–1947* (Toronto: University of Toronto Press, 2007), 105–12.

119. *Saturday Night* (June 24, 1944), 6; *Halifax Herald* (February 2, 1944), 8.

120. Clare Boothe Luce, "Women Can Win the Peace," *Chatelaine* (February 1944), 3.

121. R.M. Farquharson, "Will Women Go Back to the Kitchen?" *Canadian Home Journal* 40, (January 1944), 3.

122. Pamela Sugiman, "'These Feelings That Fill My Heart': Japanese Canadian Women's Memories of Internment," *Oral History*, 34 (Autumn 2006): 69–84; Sugiman, "Passing Time, Moving Memories: Interpreting Wartime Narratives of Japanese Canadian Women," *Histoire sociale/Social History*, 37, 73 (May/mai 2004) 51–79; Sugiman, "'Days You Remember': Japanese Canadian Women and the Violence of Internment," in Maroussia Hadjukowski-Ahmed, N. Khanlou and H. Moussa, eds., *Not Born A Refugee Woman: Contesting Identities, Rethinking Practices* (Oxford & New York: Berghan Books, 2008), 113–34.

123. Jo-Anne Fiske, "Gender and Politics," 138; Joan Holmes & Associates, Inc., "Ipperwash: General Historical Background." A report prepared for the Ipperwash Inquiry. www. attorneygeneral.jus.on.ca/inquiries/ipperwash, 19–23.

124. Canada, House of Commons, *Debates* (1944), 2629.

125. Pierson, *"They're Still Women,"* 49.

126. Library and Archives of Canada, MG 28, I–10 vol. 104, file 777, 1947.

127. Pierson, *"They're Still Women,"* 77.

128. Stephen, *Pick One Intelligent Girl*, 124–25, 179–84, 202–4; Ruth Pierson, "'Home Aide': A Solution to Women's Unemployment after World War II," *Atlantis* 2, 2 (Spring 1977): 85–96; *"They're Still Women,"* 90.

129. Broadfoot, *Six War Years*, 358.

130. Alice Kessler-Harris, *Out to Work* (New York: Oxford University Press, 1985), 277.

131. Fahrni, *Household Politics*, 39.

132. Omer Leroux, "All This and Suffrage Too," *Financial Post* (September 4, 1954), 22.

133. Joan Sangster, "The Polish 'Dionnes': Gender, Ethnicity and Immigrant Workers in Post-Second World War Canada," *Canadian Historical Review* 88, 3 (September 2007): 469–500.

134. Alexander Freund and Laura Quilici, "Exploring Myths in Women's Narratives: Italian and German Immigrant Women in Vancouver, 1947–61," *Oral History Review* 23, 2 (Winter 1996): 36. See also Franca Iacovetta, *Such Hard-Working People: Italian Immigrants in Post-War Toronto* (Kingston and Toronto: McGill-Queen's Press, 1992); Iacovetta, "From *Contadina* to Worker: Southern Italian Immigrant Women Working in Toronto, 1947–62," in Burnet, ed., *Looking into My Sister's Eyes*, 209–11; and Giovanna Del Negro, *Looking Through My Mother's Eyes. Life Stories of Nine Italian Immigrant Women in Canada* (Toronto: Guernica Editions Inc., 1997).

135. Canada, Department of Labour, *Married Women Working for Pay in Eight Canadian Cities* (Ottawa: 1958), 52.

136. Canada, Department of Labour, *Gazette* (1954), 1513.

137. Dorothy Manning, "I Quit My Job to Save My Marriage," *Chatelaine* (June 1955), 16.

138. John Kenneth Galbraith, *Economics and the Public Purpose* (New York: New American Library, 1973), 29–37.

139. Freund and Quilici, "Exploring Myths," 22–25.

140. Harris, "The Transformation of Canadian Policies." 82, 71–139.

141. See, for example, Julie Guard, "'Fair Play or Fair Pay,' Gender Relations, Class Consciousness, and Union Solidarity in the Canadian UE," *Labour/Le Travail*, 37 (Spring 1996): 149–77; Pamela Sugiman, *Labour's Dilemma: The Gender Politics of Workers in Canada, 1937–1979* (Toronto: University of Toronto Press, 1994).

142. Cuthbert Brandt, "Solidarity under Siege: The Valleyfield Strike of 1946," paper read at the Canadian Historical Association Annual Meeting, Halifax, June, 2003.

143. Sara Diamond, "A Union Man's Wife: The Ladies' Auxiliary Movement in the IWA—The Lake Cowichan Experience," in Barbara K. Latham and Roberta J. Pazdro, eds., *Not Just Pin Money: Selected Essays on the History of Women's Work in British Columbia* (Victoria: Camosun College, 1984), 287.

144. Michael Barkway, "Save Your Tears: Watch the Girls," *Financial Post* (November 16, 1957), 1.

CHAPTER TEN

Testing the Boundaries

In the years from 1918 to 1960, Canada experienced an exceptionally challenging series of events: a difficult recovery after World War I, the Great Depression, World War II, and then yet another period of major post-war adaptation. These global economic and social events caused major disruptions in the lives of Canadians and their families. For many, the uncertainty that accompanied these periods of change and stress led to a strong desire for a return to traditional lifestyles, including a reaffirmation of women's established roles as wives and mothers. Ironically, such calls occurred during times when increased educational and job opportunities appeared to offer women more choices than ever before. Canadians therefore had to try to reconcile the image and reality of the modern woman with deeply seated beliefs about women's nature and appropriate roles in society. Concepts such as femininity, domesticity, and female dependence were formulated and reformulated as economic, political, and social circumstances seemed to dictate. The print media, educational institutions, sports bodies, and government agencies all contributed to the creation of new ideals and standards for women. For the most part, they aimed at preserving what they considered the best of the old attitudes and assumptions about proper female roles while at the same time accommodating new understandings.

DEMOGRAPHIC PATTERNS

In the aftermath of World War I, whether or not women wanted or expected a return to pre-war normalcy, social, economic, and demographic changes were shifting what was considered normal. For thousands of women, the death of a fiancé or a husband in the trenches of Europe dramatically altered the contours of their lives as they faced the future as women on their own. Nonetheless, the marriage rate increased throughout the

1920s to a high of 7.7 per 1 000 population in 1927, as the economy expanded and jobs became plentiful. With the onset of the Depression, however, the marriage rate dropped quickly as the financial independence required by most couples to set up their own households became much more difficult to achieve; indeed, in 1932 the rate reached a low of 5.9. While there was a gradual recovery in the marriage rate throughout the rest of the decade, it would take the prosperity of the war and post-war periods to boost it to new levels. In 1942 and again in 1946, the marriage rate reached its highest rate of approximately 11 per 1 000 inhabitants.[1]

If there was considerable variation in inter-war and war-time marriage rates, the same was true for the mean age at first marriage (see Figure A.1 in the Appendix.) Indeed, as the marriage rate declined, the average age at which Canadians exchanged vows rose. In 1921, the average age for first marriage was 24.5 years for women and 28 for men. For the rest of the decade, it declined slightly for both sexes, only to rise again by 1931. The adverse economic circumstances of the 1930s and the initial war years led large numbers of individuals to postpone marriage, and by 1941, both women and men marrying for the first time were slightly older than they had been in 1921. The age at first marriage for women in that year was 25 years, and for men, just over 28 years.[2]

Delaying marriage usually resulted in smaller completed families since older brides had fewer years of marriage in which to bear children. Older women had also avoided starting married life at the time when they were most fertile—that is, their late teens and early 20s. The average number of children that a Canadian woman might be expected to bear during her lifetime fell from 3.2 in 1930 to 2.7 during the Depression decade, in large part because of delayed marriages. The average surpassed the 1930 level only in 1946, when it reached 3.3[3] (See Table 10.1.)

Another major determinant of family size in this period was whether the family lived in a rural or an urban setting, with rural families being larger on average than those of city dwellers. As urbanization continued to increase after World War I, average family size declined, particularly among members of the working class. Analysts of 1931 census data suggested that working-class couples were making a conscious decision to limit the size of their families in order to escape poverty and to improve their social position.[4]

Table 10.1   AVERAGE NUMBER OF CHILDREN BORN TO EVER-MARRIED WOMEN, BY MOTHER TONGUE, 1921–1946

Period of Birth of Women (Approx.)	English	French	Other	All Languages
1921–1926	3.11	4.14	3.17	3.37
1926–1931	3.25	3.82	3.22	3.39
1931–1936	3.21	3.40	3.09	3.24
1936–1941	2.84	2.77	2.81	2.81
1941–1946	2.37	2.23	2.52	2.36

Source: A. Romaniuc, *Fertility in Canada: from Baby-Boom to Baby-Bust* (Ottawa: Statistics Canada, 1984), p. 16; Statistics Canada, *Fertility*, Cat. No. 93-321 (Ottawa: Minister of Industry, 1993), Table 4, pp. 113–16.

Changes in the general fertility rate—the annual number of births per 1 000 women between the ages of 15 and 49—further indicate the significant changes in women's childbearing (see Table A.3 in the Appendix). In 1921, the rate of 120 was considerably lower than the 144 births recorded for the comparable female population 10 years earlier, and it continued to decline to only 87 by 1941. While the general fertility rate fell in all provinces, the decline was less dramatic in Quebec, which had a rate of 102 in 1941. In the same year, Nova Scotia also reported a relatively high general fertility rate of 98 per 1 000.[5] As a result of these changes in the fertility rate, the size of completed families fell. (See Table 10.2.)

Because women had fewer children and received improved pre-natal and post-natal care, fewer of them died as a result of childbirth. (see Figure A.3 in the Appendix). Therefore, the death rate for Canadian women fell from 12.4 per thousand in 1921 to 10.3 in 1941, a decline of 16 percent.[6] Better public health practices altered the life expectancy of both men and women, primarily by reducing infant mortality—although mortality rates remained unconscionably high among Aboriginal children, with 21 percent dying before their first birthday.[7] A Canadian woman born in 1931 who survived infancy could expect to live to 62 years of age, and a man, to 60 years; a woman born a decade later had a life expectancy of 66, while that of a man was 63[8] (see Figure A.5 in the Appendix). And longer life expectancy increased the average length of marriages. This phenomenon, combined with smaller family size, extended the time between children's leaving home and the death of the husband or wife. Couples who married in 1920, for example, could expect this post-parental period to be almost seven years longer than it had been for those who had married in 1900.[9]

The demographic patterns of women immigrants to Canada during this inter-war period were often different from those of Canadian-born women. While the total numbers of Canadian men and women between the ages of 25 and 34 were nearly equal, this was not the case for the Chinese, Japanese, and South Asian populations. Immigration restrictions on women belonging to these groups meant few of their men were able to

Table 10.2   SIZE OF COMPLETED FAMILIES, FOR WOMEN BORN BETWEEN 1922 AND 1946

Period of Birth of Women (Approx.)	0	1	2	3	4	5	6+	Average Number of Children per Married Woman
1922–1926	9.59	11.26	22.00	19.62	13.96	8.45	15.12	3.315
1927–1931	8.35	9.43	21.23	20.80	15.43	9.47	15.29	3.407
1932–1936	7.20	8.98	22.8	22.89	16.53	9.30	12.22	3.260
1937–1941	8.03	10.02	28.89	25.36	14.39	6.81	6.50	2.814
1942–1946	9.38	12.56	38.08	24.08	9.90	3.43	2.58	2.356

Source: A. Romaniuc, *Fertility in Canada: From Baby-Boom to Baby-Bust* (Ottawa: Statistics Canada, 1984), p. 31; Data for 1937–1946 calculated from Statistics Canada, *Fertility*, Cat. No. 93-321 (Ottawa: Minister of Industry, 1993), Table 1, p. 7.

bring wives or potential marriage partners to Canada. The Chinese Immigration Act of 1923, subsequently dubbed the Chinese Exclusion Act, prohibited the entry of wives and children of Chinese men already resident in Canada, although some senators proposed allowing entry to those wives who were aged 50 or older—that is, women past their childbearing years. As a result, Chinese males outnumbered Chinese females throughout the inter-war period by a ratio as high as 15 to 1. By 1941, the imbalance in the sex ratio declined as the percentage of the Chinese population born in Canada increased, but there were still 785 Chinese men for every 100 Chinese women. When wives and families forced to remain in China were unable to receive remittances from their male relatives in Canada during the Second World War, many of them experienced great hardship, including starvation. Even after the repeal of the exclusionary legislation in 1947, the volume of Chinese immigration remained small as Canada maintained a policy of favouring immigrants from Europe and the United States. As a result, in 1951 there were 17 155 married Chinese men compared to only 2 842 married Chinese women in Canada. It would take another two decades before the sex ratio for the married Chinese Canadian population became balanced.[10]

The sex ratio imbalance in the Japanese population, however, was less striking than it was among the Chinese; thanks to the arrival of the so-called picture brides after 1908, women accounted for just over one-third of all Japanese in Canada in 1921. Still, this proportion was strikingly low at a time when the overall numbers of women and men in Canada were nearly equal. In 1928, the federal government announced a modification of the so-called gentleman's agreement between Canada and Japan that had already limited the number of Japanese immigrants to 400 per year since 1908. A reduced annual quota of 150 Japanese immigrants was set, and this number now included women and children. The picture bride system was terminated; consequently, very few Japanese women entered Canada as immigrants during the inter-war period. Nor was there significant immigration from Japan following the wartime internment of west coast Japanese-Canadian families and their subsequent forced relocation across Canada. In fact, close to 4 000 individuals from that community were repatriated to Japan by order of the Canadian government, or with strong encouragement; over half of them had been born in Canada and one-third of them were children under the age of 16.[11]

By contrast, at the conclusion of the war Canada opened its gates to a flood of war brides and displaced persons from Europe. Although Canadian military authorities tried to discourage marriages of servicemen during the war, some 48 000 such marriages did take place. The vast majority of these unions were with British women, with a few thousand involving women from other areas of Europe, most notably the Netherlands. The Canadian government subsequently arranged for the passage of the war brides and their 22 000 children to Canada in converted troop ships and luxury cruise liners. Many arrived through Pier 21 in Halifax, and then climbed aboard special trains that took them on yet another long journey until they reached their final destination. In 1947, the federal government began to liberalize its immigration policies in order to accept some of the one million Europeans officially declared displaced persons (DPs) and refugees. By the following year, the government had authorized the entry of 50 000 such individuals. Initially, immigration officials who visited the DP camps gave preference to ". . . strong young men who could do manual labour and would not be encumbered by aging relatives." Some women were recruited as part of domestic labour schemes, while others came as a result of having Canadian relatives who could sponsor them. The broadening of the previously restricted category of "close relative" to include widowed daughters or sisters and their dependants under the age of 18, for example, enabled a significant number of female-headed Mennonite families who had escaped from the Soviet Union to emigrate to Canada.[12]

As the hardships of the Great Depression and the sacrifices of World War II gave way to the prosperity of the immediate post-war period, individuals who had postponed marriage began to establish new households and new families. Increased marriage rates—especially among young women—lower average age of brides marrying for the first time, and larger completed families were important signs of the significant changes in the economic and social context in which Canadians now found themselves. For young women, aged 15 to 19, the marriage rate more than doubled, climbing from 30 per 1 000 in 1937 to 62 per 1 000 in 1954.[13] And the average age at first marriage for women dropped from just over 24 years in 1941 to about 23 years in 1961 while for men, the average shifted from just under 28 to about 26.[14] The decline in age at first marriage was related to the general prosperity of the post–World War II years, to the growing acceptability of married women without children working outside the home, and to easier access to credit. The growing affluence of Canadians, moreover, meant that fewer parents needed to rely on supplementary income earned by their young adult children. Indeed, more parents were in a position to give financial support to young people who, a generation earlier, would have been considered too dependent to marry.[15]

Canadian women were also having more children, and having them earlier than had been the case for their mothers' generation. There was a sharp increase in the number of births per 1 000 inhabitants, which rose from 20 in 1937 to 29 in 1947.[16] Three trends—earlier age at first marriage, earlier births of first children, and larger completed families—combined to produce the renowned post-war baby boom. Between 1950 and 1959, the average birth rates in Canada exceeded those of the United States and all of the major European nations.[17] It is important to note, however, that significant increases in the birth rate were recorded only among married women under 30, and most strikingly

Arrival of a group of war brides and their children in Halifax, 1946. The federal government arranged for the passage to Canada of some 40 000 war brides and 22 000 children of Canadian servicemen.

Source: H.B. Jefferson fonds, 1992-304 no. 31 (N-082). Nova Scotia Archives and Records Management

among those under 25. As one observer pithily commented, "Young girls are more interested in raising families than jobs; not-so-young girls like jobs better than children."[18] In the younger groups of married women, birth rates continued to climb until 1956, a year in which nearly half of all live births consisted of third or later children. For women over 40, however, birth rates declined continuously and significantly compared to those established by women in the same age category during previous generations. Then, after 1956, declines in birth rates were recorded for women in all age groups.[19]

EDUCATION

As Canadian society became more urbanized and families grew smaller, young people generally spent more of their formative years in school. Accordingly, educational institutions became increasingly responsible for training adolescents for their adult roles. School-leaving age varied from province to province, and even within provinces, depending on whether children lived in a rural or an urban area. The age ranged from 14 in New Brunswick and Manitoba to 16 in cities in Ontario, Alberta, British Columbia, Saskatchewan, and Nova Scotia. Attendance requirements responded to specific realities and economic conditions—legislation allowed exemptions if children were required during the fishing and fruit-picking seasons, for other seasonal labour on farms, for necessary household duties such as the care of siblings, or for what was referred to as personal maintenance to support themselves or their families. In two jurisdictions, such exemptions were not needed because there was no compulsory attendance law in Quebec until 1943 or in the colony of Newfoundland until 1944.

A girl's ability to get an education, and the quality of her schooling, continued to vary according to class, race, ethnicity, religion, and rural or urban residence. Nevertheless, by their early teens, nearly all Canadian girls had received some formal schooling: by 1931, they were on average spending almost 10 years in the classroom.[20] Some girls living in remote areas could participate through correspondence courses, which were introduced across the country during the 1920s, and through the school radio broadcasts that began in the 1930s.[21] For most girls in such circumstances, however, instruction was still frequently interrupted by seasonal farm or domestic labour. The letters of 12-year-old Edna Snyder of Ashcroft, British Columbia, to her correspondence teacher provide a typical example. In the first month of 1927, she wrote to her teacher, explaining, "I have only been to school for three years. I have gone since I was nine years old and only had one whole year, [as] the others were only parts. I am also teaching my brother." Two months later Edna had to abandon her lessons to help her father haul hay.[22]

School curricula emphasized basic literacy skills and the development of vocational skills designed, in the case of girls, to prepare them for marriage and motherhood and for careers that complemented these roles. Throughout the 1920s and 1930s, provincial departments of education, often at the behest of women's organizations, expanded domestic science programs in the public elementary and secondary schools. These programs now reached greater numbers of girls and were available for longer periods of time.

For girls in Quebec, domestic science classes frequently replaced academic subjects, such as science, in the province's secondary and normal schools.[23] British Columbia appointed its first director of home economics in 1926. At that time, 55 home economics teachers were employed in elementary and secondary schools, teaching some 12 000 students, or close to 25 percent of the girls enrolled in the province's schools. In keeping with the application of scientific principles to household management, British Columbia's home economics courses stressed order, cleanliness, and the use of good equipment. Classroom visitors and reporters remarked on the regimentation and attention to detail. After visiting a class, one commentator noted that the teacher gave her students "a thorough training in systematic methods, the work of her classes being performed with almost military promptness and precision, each dish in each girl's cupboard being in its exact place, and even the knives, forks and spoons being ranged like a row of little soldiers."[24]

For Aboriginal girls, domestic training was an even more central component of their schooling. The principal of the Lejac Residential School in central British Columbia, for example, did not question the limitations of an education that predominantly stressed domestic skills—what more could Aboriginal girls expect or want? In fact, they received more classroom learning than did boys, who spent most of their time farming.[25]

Parents and taxpayers sometimes criticized domestic science programs as a waste of time and money. Some complained about the lack of attention to practical activities and the overemphasis on order and theory embodied in prescribed lectures on hygiene and nutrition. Others worried about students' possible frustration and dissatisfaction when they were unable to apply the prescribed classroom theories and practices in their own homes. In class, girls cooked on modern electric stoves and ironed with electric irons, but rural and working-class girls went home to the reality of wood or coal stoves and flat-irons. Teachers stressed standardization of recipes, a practice impossible in a home without measuring utensils, and at odds with family recipes handed down from generation to generation and calling for a "handful" of this and a "pinch" of that. Interviews with students exposed to domestic science training in British Columbia's schools during the 1920s suggest that most school-taught practices and recipes were rejected in favour

A classroom in St. Mary's School on the Blood Reserve, Carston, Alberta, 1933.
Source: Missionary Oblates, Grandin Collection at the Provincial Archives of Alberta, OB10558.

of the training received at home.[26] The tension between home and school created by the content of the domestic science curriculum was exacerbated by the perception of many immigrant and working-class mothers that such classes undermined their authority and denigrated their personal role in educating their daughters.

Proponents of domestic science, on the other hand, continued to stress its role in training working-class girls, particularly those from ethnic and racial minorities, both to ensure better-run working-class households and to provide a supply of trained servants for middle- and upper-class households. This latter rationale became particularly important in the 1920s, when the women who once might have gone into service increasingly opted for factory or other jobs outside the household. Another consideration was the growing awareness of the reality that many girls, including those from middle-class homes, now spent their formative years in classrooms and moved directly from school into the working world.

As a result, it was believed that many girls lacked sufficient opportunity to learn household skills from their mothers. In cities, single professional women, such as teachers, nurses, and secretaries, lived away from home, some in shared accommodation in apartments but most in boarding houses or similar settings. Without school-based instruction, domestic science advocates maintained, these women would lack the necessary skills in scientific homemaking when they needed them. Paradoxically, such arguments implicitly accepted women's increased participation in the workforce while simultaneously reinforcing attitudes about the primacy of women's domestic role.[27]

Between 1920 and 1950, in the English-speaking provinces, young women accounted for a higher proportion of high school enrollments than did young men.[28] Full educational equality, however, remained an elusive goal. Even at the elementary-school level, the experiences and expectations of young girls and boys continued to differ, and sex-role stereotyping was pervasive in the materials that students used well into the 1960s, as was to be noted in the 1970 *Report of the Royal Commission on the Status of Women in Canada*. In the American reading series *Fun with Dick and Jane*, for example, which was widely used in some provincial school systems, Dick engaged in active play, running and jumping, while Jane played with her dolls. Their father was away at work all day, and drove home in his late-model automobile just in time to eat the dinner that had been prepared by his smiling, aproned, stay-at-home wife. In Quebec, *Guy et Yvette* conveyed the same message of female subordination.[29] Nevertheless, women's work during the World War II years did have an impact in that there was an increased recognition that women had non-domestic responsibilities in addition to homemaking duties. For example, in 1945, the teaching of home economics, as domestic science was now called in Ontario schools, had as one of its primary objectives the fostering of "a conception of homemaking as an undertaking in which all members of the family co-operate." Ten years later, home economics teachers were advised that their students would be pursuing "two future careers—wage-earning employment, and marriage with the establishment of families and homes of their own." Suggested class topics included "Fathers as wage-earners and homemakers" and "Mothers as homemakers and frequently wage-earners too."[30]

In post-war Quebec, where the state played a very limited role in education until 1964, the Catholic church continued to stress the necessity to educate women differently from men; indeed, papal instructions issued in 1957 rejected co-education for Catholic secondary education. While acknowledging the financial necessity of educating adolescent females with males in some instances, the guidelines set strict conditions for the mingling of the sexes. The church's preferred option for educating francophone Catholic women in Quebec was the *institut familial*, organized around instruction in *la vocation féminine*—marriage and motherhood. Domestic science education was compulsory both in Quebec and in convent schools serving the francophone minority outside Quebec, such as the *Pensionnat Assomption* in northern Alberta. In Quebec, even the building, maintenance, and staffing of the *instituts familiaux* were entrusted to the female religious orders, who were given financial assistance by the provincial government. An anglophone woman journalist who produced a detailed study of the *instituts* could not contain her enthusiasm for this particular type of education for women: it promised them "real freedom and happiness," whereas women's quest for equality with men gave them, in her view, only higher wages, more career choices, and dissatisfaction. More categorically, an Oblate priest reminded the graduates of one convent school in May 1956 that a woman achieved greatness through kneeling. But the *instituts* had their detractors and the 1950s witnessed a vigorous debate between those who supported this kind of education and those who decried its single-minded focus on women's future roles as wives and mothers. Opponents called for the recognition of other career options for women, such as that of dietician, a profession open to women graduates of home economics programs offered by universities in other parts of the country. Even at the height of their popularity, however, the *instituts* attracted only 10 percent of female students in Quebec studying at the higher secondary level.[31]

While the church was promoting domestic science education for francophone women, the Quebec government was providing other options. After the introduction of compulsory education by the Liberal government in 1943, the number of normal schools for francophone Catholic women grew rapidly. The implementation of compulsory education also resulted in the extension and reform of secondary schools, including the provision for free secondary education. By 1959, most young francophone women, regardless of class, could acquire some secondary schooling.

If gendered curricula and expectations remained a substantial issue for most girls, poverty and racism posed additional problems. For Aboriginal girls in remote communities, in particular, residential schools were often the only form of formal education available. Attending such schools caused irreparable damage for many of the children. Often forcibly removed and cut off from their families, they were punished for speaking their own language, and were all too often the victims of physical and sexual abuse. In black communities, educational opportunities were frequently limited to poorly equipped and overcrowded schools that were in reality, if not by law, racially segregated. Women leaders, however, worked assiduously to open up career opportunities for young women, opportunities taken for granted by young white women. For example, as a result of a campaign in Nova Scotia led by Dr. Pearleen Oliver, schools of nursing began to accept young black women. The first two black graduates from the Children's Hospital in Halifax received their diplomas in the fall of 1948. Four years later, Addie Aylestock was the first African-Canadian woman to be ordained when she was named a pastor in the British Methodist Episcopal (BME) church. Then, in 1958, she was appointed to the position of general secretary of the BME conference.[32]

Enrollment of women undergraduates in universities during the inter-war period reached its peak in 1930, when almost one in four of all undergraduate students were women (see Table A.8 in the Appendix). The ratio of female to male undergraduates declined slightly throughout the 1930s, although in absolute numbers, undergraduate female enrollment increased (from just over 7 400 in 1930 to some 8 100 in 1940). The proportion of women in the total graduate enrollment also dropped during this decade, from one-quarter in 1930 to one-fifth in 1940. In contrast to undergraduates, the actual number of women graduate students declined slightly, from 352 in 1930 to 326 a decade later.[33] Within the universities and colleges, moreover, women continued to be channelled into "female" departments: home economics, nursing, and such courses as secretarial science (first offered at the University of Western Ontario in 1925). In the prestigious faculties of medicine, law, and engineering, however, women remained a tiny minority. In 1920–21, 18 percent of National Research Council grant holders were women; in 1930–31, women constituted only 10 percent of recipients.[34]

During World War II, women represented a larger proportion of the student body than previously, in part because they were keeping places for men to occupy once the war was over.[35] A prime example of this trend occurred in the University of Toronto's Faculty of Medicine. During the war, women as young as 16 and 17 found it relatively easy to gain admission. The resulting increase in female students facilitated the Women's Medical Society's successful petition in 1948 to have the yearly quota for female interns at Toronto's largest hospital doubled—from one to two.[36]

Once the veterans returned, their educational needs were assigned top priority. Although ex-servicewomen, such as future cabinet minister Judy LaMarsh, used the veterans' programs to acquire a university degree, only 2 600 of the approximately 50 000 ex-servicewomen joined her. The actual numbers of women attending university did increase, but their percentage dropped slightly from comprising 23 percent of all full-time undergraduates in 1940 to 21 percent in 1945. Moreover, most continued to enroll in traditionally female courses of study: humanities, nursing, household science, and physical and occupational therapy.[37] Between 1954 and 1962, the establishment of an additional 15 classical colleges for women in Quebec increased the possibility of continuing studies up to the university level. The formal recognition of women's full rights to practise as lawyers (1941) and notaries (1956) in the province reflected a growing demand that at least a few exceptional women be provided with the same educational and career opportunities as men.

KEEPING GIRLS OUT OF TROUBLE

Although the vast majority of young women did not go on to postsecondary education, most spent more time in school than in previous decades, especially after authorities raised the school leaving age to 16 in most provinces. Adolescence now became defined as the time young people spent in high school, leaving them with free time only outside of school hours.[38] And monitoring this time was no longer the parents' duty alone. Social reformers and professionals railed against unchaperoned co-educational activities and idleness, promoting instead protected, supervised home or group cultural pastimes.[39] Concerned that increased leisure time would create a generation of idle and potentially delinquent youth, adults oversaw a range of new and old, structured, and carefully supervised recreation activities. Youth clubs established their own educational programs, and organizations such as the Girl Guides of Canada added new objectives to their earlier goals of developing moral, upstanding citizens.

While emphasizing domestic activities related to their members' future roles as wives and mothers, girls' organizations also encouraged female independence and autonomous decision-making. The Canadian Girls in Training (CGIT), founded in 1917 by the Young Women's Christian Association (YWCA) and the Protestant churches, exemplified these goals. Initially, the YWCA had sponsored Girl Guide companies, but its dissatisfaction with what it perceived as the Girl Guides' secularism, imperialist and competitive spirit, and lack of opportunity for girls to participate in decision-making convinced the YWCA that a different organization was necessary. Canadian Girls in Training was the result. Groups met with their leaders at Sunday school and at mid-week sessions. Their activities reflected progressive educational theories that emphasized research and discussion, cooperation, and independent thought. Adolescent girls from 12 to 17 were encouraged to participate in physical, religious, intellectual, and service activities, not for reward but for their intrinsic value. The enthusiastic response to the movement can be measured by its numbers; in 1925 there were 30 000 members from Vancouver Island to Newfoundland. During the Depression, numbers peaked at 40 000 in 1 100 communities. Although the organizers assumed that marriage and motherhood were the ultimate goal for women, CGIT groups also urged girls to pursue their education. The Boys and Girls Clubs of Canada (reconstituted as 4H Clubs in 1952) also provided girls in rural areas with many opportunities for self-realization. During the Depression, for example, some 1 200 4-H Club girls in Manitoba independently organized and ran their own clothing and food projects. Although there was no prize money, they set up competitions and sold homemade goods, using the profits to assist themselves and their families.[40] The 4-H Clubs' emphasis on the development of both domestic skills and independence was in keeping with Canadian society's expectations for adolescent girls once they left school, for it was increasingly assumed that nearly all girls, whether working-class or middle-class, would seek employment. Organizations like the YWCA, business girls' clubs, and settlement houses continued their educational and support services for single working women living away from home, attempting to re-create a family atmosphere by fostering individual and group morality as well as homemaking skills.

Services provided by such organizations were regarded as essential in the 1920s in a society alarmed by the media image of the flapper—the girl who indulged in so-called immoral pursuits, such as drinking, smoking, wild dancing, and party-going. The author of the 1922 *Maclean's* magazine article "Is the Flapper a Menace?" confirmed society's worst fears, even though she admitted that the majority of young Canadian women followed more chaste lifestyles. Three flappers, aged 17, 18, and 20, all from middle-class homes, had described to the author a motoring outing where such large quantities of bootlegged liquor were consumed that one of the flappers declared, "It was a wonder we got back without an accident." Another told of "fussing" parties, "where each girl sits

Meeting of Canadian Girls in Training, 1919.

Source: Canadian Girls in Training/Library and Archives Canada/PA-125872

on a boy's knee and lets him kiss her all he wants to do. Sometimes the kissing goes on for hours." According to these flappers, unchaperoned parties were commonplace, and mothers were too innocent to know what was going on at them.[41] In her book *The Black Candle*, Magistrate Emily Murphy combined anecdotes from her courtroom experience with national and international statistics to link contemporary evidence of youthful women's moral laxity to drug trafficking, prostitution, and the white slave trade (as trafficking in women was then called). Interracial intimacy was also deemed cause for alarm. In 1930 in Oakville, Ontario, when it appeared that a white girl was going to marry a black man, masked Ku Klux Klan members reportedly burned a cross on the woman's lawn, forced her to return to her parents' home, and threatened her fiancé.[42]

A particularly strong media campaign in the 1920s linked the social immorality of modern life and the problems of youth to parental failure in rearing and supervising their sons and, particularly, their daughters. In contrast, one 1926 study of delinquent girls actually managed to identify a form of parental culpability ignored by most experts in this period: sexual abuse in the home.[43] Such concerns and moral panic over the real, perceived, or potential moral impropriety of young women persisted well into the 1950s, by which time the term *teenager* had become commonplace. Adults continued to respond by organizing and supervising activities aimed at providing healthy recreational pursuits to keep young people off the streets, and out of pool halls, cinemas, and dance halls.

Well into the post-war years, the programs for teenage girls run by the Girl Guides, the Canadian Girls in Training, 4-H clubs, and the YWCA continued to flourish. In addition, newly developed and adult-supervised teen clubs proliferated across the country, mainly in urban areas where they were extolled as safe havens from the dangers and immorality of the outside world. In addition to attempting to control adolescent sexuality, most programs continued to inculcate middle-class Canadian values among the nation's youth.[44]

Young girls and women who were deemed serious transgressors of accepted norms of behaviour were incarcerated in training schools and reformatories, where they spent more time in domestic training than in any other activity. In Ontario, working-class girls and women made up the majority of the occupants of training schools and reform institutions. Throughout the 1940s, the percentage of inmates who were of Aboriginal origin also increased when growing numbers of Aboriginals migrated to Ontario's urban centres following the disruption of their home communities by resource development.[45] Female delinquency was usually considered synonymous with sexual delinquency, and what were considered crimes were overwhelmingly related to moral rather than to criminal offences. For example, in 1942, 16-year-old Amélie was brought before the juvenile court in Winnipeg for stealing a purse containing $15 from a customer at the Eaton's department store. When it was discovered that she had been away from home without permission, she was subjected to a gynecological examination and found to have a ruptured hymen as well as syphilis. Subsequently, Amélie was sentenced to two years in a reform institution for delinquent girls, not for the theft but for her offence of sexual immorality.[46]

One proposal for combating problems caused by idle time was to convince school and municipal authorities to allow young people to use school equipment and playground facilities after hours and during vacations for activities organized by trained instructors.[47] Another, more successful proposal suggested organizing athletic clubs and youth sport groups. Participation in sporting activities promoted healthy alternatives to evil temptations, it was argued, not only during the school years but also into adulthood. Organized physical activity and games for girls and young women had the additional advantage that participants were supervised and therefore kept out of mischief. As a result, the number of athletic clubs expanded greatly and provided women with opportunities to participate not only as players but also as coaches, fundraisers, and administrators. Indeed, the 1920s and 1930s have been labelled the "Golden Age of Sports" for young women, in contrast to the previous generation. School athletic programs also expanded, and team activities, such as basketball and baseball, were popular, although after 1930, in eastern Canada, these games were usually played using "girls' rules" that restricted physical contact and limited physical exertion.

Women's sports caught the imagination of spectators and the press; businesses sponsored them to an extent that has only recently been matched. Female amateur hockey teams were particularly popular in many parts the country; on the Pacific coast, some played between periods of early professional hockey games. Perhaps the most famous team accomplishment was that of the Edmonton Grads. Formed from students and graduates of an Edmonton high school, this basketball team amassed 502 wins and only 20 losses from 1915 to 1940. Recognized four times as world champions at international tournaments, the Grads were forced to disband at the beginning of World War II because the military took over their practice facilities.[48]

At the international level, Canadian women competed for the first time at the 1928 Olympic Games in Amsterdam and achieved remarkable success. Ethel Catherwood, known as Saskatoon Lily, set a new world record while winning a gold medal in the high jump event. The team of Bobbie Rosenfeld, Ethel Smith, Myrtle Cook, and Jane Bell won gold in the 4 x 100 metre relay; Rosenfeld and Smith also won silver and bronze, respectively, in the 100-metre race. Rosenfeld, who excelled at a dazzling array of sports, including hockey and basketball, was named Canada's Female Athlete of the Half-Century in 1950. As well, Phyllis Dewar of Moose Jaw, Saskatchewan, became the first Canadian woman competitor to win four gold medals for swimming at the 1934 British Empire Games, a record that stood until 1966.[49]

At universities, women's sports thrived as well, although there was a significant difference in levels of support for men's and women's activities. While the number of women students had increased, campus facilities for women generally remained non-existent or pitifully inadequate. As early as 1911, female students at the University of Toronto had petitioned for a gymnasium. When Hart House was finally built in 1919 for sports and extracurricular activities, however, women were excluded. Although women at McGill had their own athletic facilities at Royal Victoria College, these were crowded and inadequate for the compulsory physical education program. The new Currie Gym, built on the McGill campus in 1939, assigned last priority to women's space requirements and accepted women only "on sufferance."[50]

Despite women's athletic and sporting achievements, physical education teachers and medical authorities continued to debate their biological fitness for physical activity, but most generally agreed that suitable types of exercise programs were beneficial.

A 1925 portrait of a champion ladies curling team from the South Peace region, Alberta.

Source: South Peace Regional Archives, 2002.57.32

Sports for girls were, therefore, encouraged as long as they were neither too aggressive nor too competitive. Organizers were cautioned in particular about the possible adverse effects of strenuous activities during puberty. Because menstruation continued to be viewed as a disabling time, during which girls were excused from gym classes and other sporting events, care was to be taken to ensure that normal menstruation patterns were established and maintained, and that no damage occurred to the female reproductive system. Gentle calisthenic exercises were promoted as a relief for menstrual pain and as a contribution to the development of good posture in young women.[51] For those young women able to afford them, sanitary napkins and tampons made it easier for them to participate in sports activities even when they were menstruating. Others continued to depend on rags, which they either threw away when finished or washed to be used again. Some Aboriginal women continued to use moss, which was both hygienic and convenient.

One parent's acceptance of the experts' views concerning the limitations that should be placed on girls' physical activities cost a young Maritimer the opportunity to compete in the 1928 Amsterdam Olympic Games. Gertrude Phinney, Canadian champion in the 220-yard dash, qualified for the Games but did not participate because her father believed "that strenuous exercise such as that demanded of a track athlete would most certainly have adverse effects on child bearing and cause perhaps 'irreparable harm' to the mysterious workings" of her female body.[52] Other parents and their daughters were not so concerned: Corinne Cooper revelled in the joy of physical exertion and became, in the late 1930s, the best female sprinter in the country.[53]

During World War II, Canadians became more aware of women's physical capabilities and strength as they went to work in the war industry, underwent basic training for entry into the armed forces, or proved their stamina in battlefield hospitals. However, medical experts continued to reinforce the belief that marriage and motherhood were the normal destiny for women, to the detriment of most of their other roles and activities, including sports. During the war, professional and semi-professional athletics for both women and men had a low priority, and when international competition resumed after the war, women's involvement in both competitive and recreational sport remained limited. Although a few women continued to win medals at international meets, they did so in individual events that were considered appropriate female activities, such as figure skating, swimming, skiing, and gymnastics. In contrast to the years when the Edmonton Grads made headlines, during the post-war period the media provided little coverage of women's athletics, and thus helped perpetuate the view that women's sports were of little importance. Nevertheless, the Canadian media and public did idolize a few outstanding female athletes who participated in individual sports, including Barbara Ann Scott, who won the Olympic, World, and European figure skating titles in 1948; and Marilyn Bell, who made history in 1954 at the age of 16 by being the first person to swim across Lake Ontario. They were admired, however, not just for what they did but also for the image they projected. The media were captivated by the petite blond skater whom they saw as epitomizing feminine grace and beauty. Bell, on the other hand, was the wholesome "girl next door."[54] These media-created images of Scott and Bell never challenged what were still seen as women's proper roles—namely marriage and motherhood.

MARRIED LIFE

Given the low pay women typically earned, their social and economic status usually improved with marriage—an improvement that reflected their husband's position, not their own. A number of factors helped ease the transition from a limited form of independence, where women had some money of their own to spend, to marital dependence. First of all, in the inter-war years, most young, single women from the working class continued to reside at home and to contribute a significant portion of their wages to their families. If a woman left her family before marriage, she usually went to live with either another family or with other young adults in a supervised setting, such as a boarding house or boarding school. As a result, her life was still carefully monitored.

After the Second World War and throughout the 1950s, it did become more common and more acceptable for young women to live on their own or independently with people their own age while working or completing their education. Still, they continued to be socialized from their earliest years for their wifely role, and many preferred this role to the alternative of poorly paid work and the frequently denigrated status of "spinster."

In the 1920s and 1930s, the expanding cosmetics industry emphasized the important role of physical attractiveness in finding and keeping a husband. The industry promoted the use of face creams, cosmetics, mouthwashes, and deodorants to produce and maintain an acceptable body image. Beauty parlours proliferated as new shorter hairstyles required the attention of trained hairdressers. In fact, employment opportunities for women in this industry increased even during the severe unemployment of the Depression. Advertising downplayed the relationship between beauty and sexuality in favour of more acceptable campaigns stressing the retention of a youthful appearance and enhanced femininity. This theme was echoed in women's magazines, in articles in the popular press, and in books. For example, in *Margaret Currie—Her Book*, the author, a columnist for the *Montreal Star*, devoted a chapter to "Beauty," outlining methods for skin care, weight loss, and hairstyling.[55]

The focus on weight loss reflected another aspect of the contemporary preferred body image—slimness. World War I had had a liberating effect on women's clothes: short, loose dresses that de-emphasized breasts and hips became fashionable, encouraging the pursuit of a slim, boyish look. Corsets had earlier been discarded by young women in favour of bras and girdles. Now women were advised to maintain a trim figure through careful diet and exercise programs as well. For the plump or big-breasted woman, these fashion prescriptions translated into painfully binding her breasts and starving herself into the fashionable silhouette. Aging or even mature women were out of style in the heyday of the cinema vamp.

Then, during World War II, those responsible for recruiting women into the labour force and the armed forces felt compelled to reassure the public that the new tasks women were undertaking were short term and did not constitute any real threat to existing gender roles. Emphasizing the attractive uniforms and homey atmosphere of the women's barracks, military authorities undertook a massive educational and publicity campaign to reassure Canadians that the femininity of the women recruits was not being jeopardized. Female recruits were allowed to wear makeup, encouraged to be attractive and feminine,

It makes you less on the tummy and less on the waist. But we call it the Little X-Plus!

Plus excitement. Plus freedom. Plus whatever it is that makes a woman more of a woman. It's all in the Little X Plus High-line Girdle. A new invention that has the specially firm cross-over front panel of the Little X Girdle but rising taller to do the same slender things for your waist.

This Plus panel is less than an ounce of very special fabric. It doesn't stretch sideways so it holds your tummy *flat*. But the unique slight down-stretch means that you get all the comfort and freedom you expect from Little X.

Get your Little X Plus High-line in black, white or pink in your size from small to extra large. It's part of a whole range that also includes a waist-high Girdle, Pantee Girdle and Corselet—all with the new, Plus panel in front.

The Little X Plus High-line Girdle by Silhouette is 63/-.
The Little X feeling is free.

1953 advertisment for a girdle.

Source: Antiques & Collectables/Alamy

and reminded "at all times to act in a becoming and lady-like manner."[56] On the civilian side, print media advertisements also stressed the importance for women of continuing to look feminine and glamorous even when they entered into masculine work environments. There was, nonetheless, some recognition that female roles were changing. Slacks were, at least temporarily, considered to be an acceptable form of dress for women, and the shoulder pads that featured so prominently in women's wartime clothing gave women a stronger, more masculine appearance. In keeping with efforts to reduce the amount of material consumed by the civilian population, skirts and dresses were kept at knee length.

The fashion images of the immediate post-war period, however, were markedly different, with a reassertion of femininity even sexuality. The 1950s were the decade of French designer Yves Saint Laurent's New Look, of the sweater girl, and of U.S. film star Marilyn Monroe. Saint Laurent designed clothes, he said, "for flowerlike women, clothes with rounded shoulders, full feminine busts, and willowy waists above enormous spreading skirts."[57] For many women, achieving such an appearance required encasing themselves in padded bras, crinolines, and waist-cinchers.

Another essential requirement for the proper feminine image was impeccable personal hygiene. Advertisements for soaps, deodorants, and sanitary napkins were numerous: one deodorant advertisement showed a tearful young woman under the caption "She lost her man because of *that*." It was not enough, however, to be clean and odour-free; a woman's chances of romantic success depended on improving her appearance by using the plethora of products the cosmetic industry had to offer her. Then, once she had used her beauty to effect the desired change in marital status, it was a woman's duty to continue to be sexually attractive to her husband. An advertisement for a disinfectant showed a distraught wife whose husband was walking out the door, suitcase in hand; if only she had used Lysol disinfectant in her douche to keep herself fresh and dainty!

But physical and sexual attractiveness were not all that was required of a wife. While it was acceptable for married women who could afford it to engage in hobbies like bridge, golf, and tennis, and cultural pursuits like piano playing, amateur acting, and painting, most free time was to be devoted to being a loving, supportive companion for their husbands. Of special concern were women who gambled or who played bingo to the detriment of their families. Women's magazines frequently exhorted their female readers to take up their husbands' interests and to educate themselves in order to augment their wifely roles.[58]

The idea of the wife as a husband's best friend became increasingly popular; young people were counselled to seek marriage partners whose interests, education, and values reflected their own. In Quebec, the clergy stressed the importance of friendship and companionship within marriage. Newly implemented marriage preparation courses used these ideas to reinforce the old prohibition against marriage outside the faith. A powerful demonstration of Catholic marriage occurred in 1939 when 105 francophone, working-class Catholic couples, the *Cent Mariés*, were married in a Montreal baseball stadium in the presence of 25 000 observers, including local dignitaries, public officials, and numerous reporters from both the print and film media. These marriages were commemorated and celebrated throughout the 1940s and 1950s at five-year intervals. Public coverage of these events noted the couples' happiness and fertility, giving credit to their Catholic faith and to the marriage preparation courses they had taken.[59] Other churches also provided marriage preparation courses but were usually less explicit about condemning mixed-faith marriages. Many religious groups did, however, encourage marriage within the fold by sponsoring chaperoned activities for young adults. Mennonite leaders, for example, organized church-related functions so young, single Mennonite women from the city could meet young, rural Mennonite men. In some communities, in fact, such as the Inuit and Armenian, arranged marriages were still the norm.[60]

Family-planning advocates and birth control advocates suggested that reduced family size would lead to improved marital happiness. Removing the fear of unwanted pregnancy, could, moreover, lead to more satisfying sexual relations. Indeed, books and birth control advice frequently included counselling aimed at enhancing the sexual aspect of marriage. *Sex, Marriage and Birth Control*, a 1936 Canadian guidebook written by an Anglican clergyman, stated as a fact that "in the life of love that marriage implies, satisfactory sexual intercourse is the prime factor."[61] Intuition and instinct were no longer sufficient to ensure that couples would achieve the desired sexual relationship; they were now expected to study marriage manuals in order to learn about the workings of their bodies and the correct sexual responses. Expression of sexuality outside of marriage, however, was still unacceptable, and heterosexuality remained the only accepted standard. The respectability of romantic, same-sex friendships had eroded earlier in the century and relationships between women that went beyond close friendships were deemed pathological.[62]

The strengthening ideal of companionate marriage may in part have been a response to demographic factors. As longevity for both sexes increased, it became more likely that couples would spend a substantial time together after their children had grown up. The view of marriage as an equal partnership was also supported somewhat by changes that improved the legal status of wives in relation to marriage. These included provincial equal guardianship laws and the 1925 federal Divorce Act that finally allowed a woman to obtain a divorce on the same grounds as a man—namely, simple adultery. Some women came close to attaining the ideal marriage. Newfoundland suffragist Fanny McNeil found in her husband a supportive friend and companion. When pressured by the government to curb his wife's political activities, his response was "Go to the devil."[63] Yet for other women, marriage often meant support of, and submission to, husbands who continued to be the heads of families both in theory and in fact. In another example, in the 1930s, one Japanese woman in Vancouver recalled envying the unmarried Anglican missionary women who worked in her community: "One thing I noticed about the missionaries is that women usually lived alone and they were independent and they were so wrapped up in what they were doing. In most Japanese families the women had to obey and serve the man. I remember thinking, it must be nice to be able to do what you want to do."[64]

Husbands were rarely encouraged to take up their wives' interests, though, and women continued to be responsible for the home. According to editorials in *Chatelaine*, it remained a wife's duty to create a smoothly run haven for her hard-working husband. And when problems arose, it was her responsibility to solve them.[65] Throughout the Depression, in fact, the press exhorted women to budget wisely, and to provide emotional support for unemployed husbands. Self-sacrifice and restraint of selfish desire were the hallmarks of the good wife in the ideal family setting. Frugal living and careful management of family finances were, however, a way of life for many women even before the onset of the Depression so the challenges presented during those years were not new ones.[66] Fearing possible rising divorce rates after the enactment of the 1925 divorce law, the popular press constantly reminded women that it was their duty, honour, and privilege to preserve family stability for the benefit not only of the family but also of the nation. Divorce rates did rise substantially after 1945 as war-time separations and experiences took their toll on marriages, reinvigorating media attention on women's role in nurturing and maintaining happy families.[67]

For many working-class, rural, or immigrant women, who had to cope with difficult living conditions that left little or no time for anything but domestic chores, the ideal companionate marriage was hard to put into practice. Gwen Lefort, a 16-year-old World War I war bride, discovered as much on her arrival in Canada in 1918. Her French-Canadian husband had told her "glowing stories" about Canada, none of which prepared her for life in Cheticamp, Cape Breton, where she spent 15 years before moving to the nearby town of New Waterford. In Cheticamp she raised nine children and, as she later recalled, "I cooked meals and scrubbed floors and washed my kids clothes on the scrubbing board you know. And drew water from the well—there was no indoor plumbing or anything."[68]

Later on, some war brides from the Second World War encountered similar circumstances. As Edith Matchett in New Brunswick recollected of her arrival from England to a small town in New Brunswick, "I just never thought that people lived this way. I had never seen a wood stove or how they carried in the wood, going outside to carry in water from a well, using an outside toilet because there was no bathroom."[69]

Many of the basic amenities lacking in rural and small town Canadian home were ones these women had taken for granted while growing up in English cities. Their experiences were not unique: many Canadian women coped with similar conditions. In 1941, almost all rural families still used outhouses and depended on outside water supplies.[70] And even those Canadian women who did enjoy comfortable material surroundings had little time for reading the experts' advice on being an ideal wife, let alone following it.

Throughout the inter-war period, the media bombarded women with pronouncements on the virtual impossibility and, above all, the undesirability of combining marriage with a career. Short stories telling of independent young women happily trading their jobs for marital bliss appeared frequently in widely read magazines like the *Canadian Home Journal* and *Maclean's*. Sometimes the stories related the unhappy lives of married women who attempted to be both housewives and paid workers but who eventually found true happiness by staying at home. Given that the circulation figures for these magazines were relatively high, the impact of such stories was potentially significant.[71] Canadian women's interest in having their own magazine was illustrated by the fact that in 1928 70 000 entries were submitted in a contest to name a new magazine. The winner, Mrs. Hilda Paine of British Columbia, received a cheque for $1 000. Her suggestion, *The Chatelaine*, was chosen because it "seemed to have about it a feminine grace. . . . In one word, it expressed women and Canada."[72]

Beginning in the 1920s, the burgeoning household technology industry and the mass media increasingly defined homemakers as new "professionals"; household management itself was touted as a "career." The customary, supposedly haphazard, approach to housework and child care was to be replaced by the principles of science and business. The promises of the new technology were especially appealing to those middle-class women who either could not find or afford to employ domestic servants. Furthermore, the growth in the number of families with disposable income coincided with the application of new technologies developed during World War I to domestic uses. Such products as instant coffee, tinned goods, and rayon were aggressively advertised in the mass media; increasingly, such ads were directed toward women, reflecting a recognition of the family's growing role as a unit of consumption, and that a woman's job was buying.[73] The key to the new domestic technology was electricity, which became available in the majority of built-up areas by the end of the 1920s. According to the 1941 census, nearly all urban homes had electricity. (See Table 10.3.) And while some 60 percent of rural non-farm homes used electricity, only one in five farm households had it. After the 1949 Rural Electrification Act was passed, farm households began to get electricity. However, for many farming women, it was the late 1950s before the new domestic technology replaced the many labourious tasks they had continued to perform by hand.[74]

Table 10.3 AMENITIES PRESENT IN CANADIAN HOUSEHOLDS, 1941

	% Electric Lighting	% Inside Running Water	% Telephone	% Refrigeration	% Flush Toilet (Private)
Rural					
Farm areas	20.2	12.2	29.3	22.2	8.1
Rural non-farm	59.5	41.0	27.8	35.9	32.8
Urban					
,1 000	75.0	35.0	24.7	35.0	27.7
1 000–5 000	94.1	81.6	34.0	56.3	66.5
5 000–15 000	97.2	94.4	45.0	66.1	82.8
15 000–30 000	98.7	96.4	53.8	67.4	85.2
.30 000	99.4	98.5	57.3	79.2	88.9
Canada Total	69.1	60.5	40.3	50.9	52.1

Source: Adapted from Statistics Canada, Eighth Census of Canada 1941, Volume IX, Housing, 1949.

Electricity meant a clean, safe, and efficient method of lighting and cooking. The electric stove not only cooked food but also made hot water readily available; the electric refrigerator preserved food more efficiently than iceboxes, and made less mess; the electric washing machine, in conjunction with the new easy-care fabrics, alleviated many heavy and time-consuming laundry chores. Women greeted these appliances with enthusiasm: they greatly decreased the physical effort involved in household labour, a fact much appreciated by housewives, most of whom now worked alone. But rising standards of housekeeping meant that they won little free time as a result.

Acquiring all these appliances made it necessary to reorganize the kitchen, and a new art of kitchen planning developed. Based in industrial organization, it stressed convenience and efficiency. For the minority of families able to afford such renovations, built-in cupboards replaced movable cabinets and open shelves, thereby providing increased storage space. Cupboards, countertops, and appliances were positioned to minimize unnecessary walking, bending, and climbing. Articles and intensified advertising in women's magazines and local newspapers praised the advantages of the changing technology and the streamlined kitchen.

Most working-class women could only dream of the new kitchens and home appliances. Middle-class women's access to them was, of course, limited by their economic dependence and their ability to persuade husbands to spend the money. This was clearly demonstrated in the advertising campaign by the Dominion government in connection with its 1936 Home Improvement Plan. Designed as a means of promoting employment within the depressed construction industry, and clearly directed at middle-class men, the plan provided low-interest loans to property owners for repairing and modernizing homes. The government also recognized women's vital importance to the plan's success, however. Supported by the media, and by manufacturers of household equipment, the government urged women to convince their husbands to take out loans to create new kitchens, bathrooms, dens for men, so-called rumpus rooms for children, or recreation rooms. After meeting the needs of husbands and children, and only then, it was suggested that women plan rooms entirely for their own use, perhaps a sewing room in the attic.[75] Consumer credit companies such as Household Finance Corporation also promoted the idea of borrowing money for household improvements.[76]

During World War II, the Canadian government put in place a massive campaign to encourage women—eventually including wives—to enter the labour force and military service. The government, accordingly, used newspapers, periodicals, radio, and the newly created National Film Board to modify the image of Canadian women. Those working on the home front were portrayed wearing coveralls and bandannas, swinging their lunch pails as they strode off to perform industrial war work. Household imagery was used to make the work more attractive: welding, for example, was compared to sewing. There were also many pictures and photographs of women in military and paramilitary uniforms, as they joined the armed forces, the Red Cross Corps, or Voluntary Aid Detachments, but those presentations were carefully crafted to stress the importance of women retaining their femininity.

At war's end, married women's labour-force role was played down, and domestic duties once again became the central feature of the idealized woman's life. For the most part, the Canadian media stereotyped women in the post-war years as happy homemakers and dedicated stay-at-home mothers, living in newly developed suburban housing. The cramped living conditions of many families in over-crowded flats and basement apartments were generally ignored.[77] Expert advice on how women should perform their domestic duties proliferated, much of it directed at newly arrived immigrant and refugee women. Reception and settlement agencies provided newcomers with advice about food purchases and preparation, designed to help them learn about improving nutrition and diet but with a subtext aimed at teaching them how to "eat Canadian."[78]

As well, women's role as consumers was generally re-emphasized. National Film Board films extolled the wonders of new conveniences such as electric stoves and refrigerators, mail-order shopping, department stores and supermarkets. In *Maclean's* magazine between 1939 and 1950, the proportion of all advertisements that directly appealed to women as homemakers rose from about 40 percent in the period 1939–1943 to more than 70 percent in 1950. And the emphasis shifted. No longer did the advertisements merely offer to free the housewife from the drudgery and boredom of her work; now they promised her a life of personal fulfilment—provided she wisely purchased the right products.[79] The francophone media followed a similar pattern, but adopted an even more traditional version. The ideal French-Canadian woman was a fervent Catholic as well as a devoted wife and mother, and she was still attached to the rural way of life.[80] During the 1950s in particular, articles dealing with women and the family thoroughly reflected the ideas of the Catholic Church: that nature destined women to perform domestic work, and that women's paid employment outside the home was to be deplored.

The time women supposedly saved from domestic toil, thanks to improved household technology, was to be reinvested in caring for husbands and children. In general, the media continued to present the view that the normal and desired fate of most women was marriage and motherhood. An advertisement for Weston's Bakery issued in 1951 paid tribute to the Canadian mother as the "heart of her home," responsible for the moral and civic training of her children.[81] The message of this advertisement was remarkably similar to that delivered by Dr. Hilda Neatby, Canada's pre-eminent woman historian of the 1950s. A professor at the University of Saskatchewan and a member of the Massey Commission on cultural affairs, Dr. Neatby never married. However, she confidently assured other women that the establishment of "a moral tone and moral practices in her family is a woman's first obligation to society. . . . Women, gifted and otherwise, are the individuals who in the present state of society have a large, perhaps the largest share in determining the cultural atmosphere of the home."[82]

Not all women married, however. Spinsterhood was not a highly regarded state, although an occasional editorial in *Chatelaine* did champion a woman's right to remain single. Some articles in Canadian mass-circulation magazines, such as *Saturday Night*, also strongly advocated education for women that would enable them to pursue certain "women's careers." Moreover, increasing numbers of Canadian women could not or did not conform to the powerful and pervasive image of women as stay-at-home mothers. Many working-class, immigrant, and refugee mothers had to enter the labour market in the post-war years to supplement their husbands' inadequate wages. And not all of the women who could afford to purchase the new household goods were passive consumers or mindless shoppers. They evaluated their options carefully, ignoring high-powered advertising campaigns and, as some letters to the editor of *Chatelaine* indicate, resisted the image of the "happy homemaker" promoted by the magazine.[83] The very vigour with which this image was promoted by the media in general may well have been a reaction to women's growing involvement in activities outside the home and, in some cases, their resistance to conventional heterosexual roles.[84]

MOTHERHOOD

During the 1920s and 1930s, medical and other experts bombarded women with popularized versions of new theories about childbirth and child care. They recommended that scientific approaches replace instinct, intuition, and informal advice. The new methods of child-rearing required more time and attention, but smaller families meant that the mother could pay more attention to each child. High maternal and infant mortality rates had worried late nineteenth- and early twentieth-century social reformers, and the loss of life in World War I motivated a renewed and systematic campaign to ensure "the production of future generations of healthy Canadians."[85] The campaign was fuelled by the findings of a number of studies on maternal and infant mortality by Dr. Helen MacMurchy, perhaps the best-known publicist of the infant welfare movement in Canada. Appointed by the Ontario government in 1910 to study and make recommendations on the problem of infant mortality, Dr. MacMurchy produced reports that brought her to national prominence as a doctor, writer, lecturer, and government official. Then, when the federal government created the Child Welfare Division of the Department of Health in 1919, MacMurchy became its head.

In a 1926 report, MacMurchy confirmed the extent of maternal mortality but did not address solutions. A number of women's organizations, medical associations, and government agencies then studied the problems of infant and maternal mortality and recommended ways to combat them. Three major needs emerged: (1) formalized pre-natal education and care, (2) increased medical competence, and (3) improved socio-economic conditions. Government and other appropriate agencies directed their efforts toward the first two areas but, for the most part, ignored the low standard of living that jeopardized the health of many pregnant women and their babies.

Reformers adopted the strategy of educating and supervising women, and providing them with what was perceived as the correct information. Health-care authorities advised that women should improve their physical health long before they became pregnant. Pregnant women, they recommended, should be monitored by a doctor or through medically supervised pre-natal clinics. Government and public health agencies published and distributed brochures written by doctors. The most famous of these, *The Canadian Mother's Book*, available in English or French from the Child Welfare Division of the federal Department of Health, had more than 200 000 copies in print by 1922. Childbirth itself was to be supervised by a doctor, preferably in a hospital. It was not long before half of all births took place in hospitals in the more populous provinces: in British Columbia, by 1929; in Ontario, by 1938; and in Quebec, by 1945. By 1961, Canada-wide, 97 percent of babies were born in hospitals.[86] (See Figure A.4 in the Appendix.) After the 1940s, midwifery and home birthing continued to be practised in some Mennonite, Hutterite, and Aboriginal communities as well as in Newfoundland and remote parts of Northern Canada. But even neighbourhood women who continued to act as midwives were influenced by modern medical techniques; for example, some in Newfoundland began to insist that during labour, women should no longer take whatever position they found comfortable but rather remain in bed, preferably on their backs.[87]

For many women the hospital experience was a positive one, providing them with a chance to rest and be looked after before returning home to normal household activities,

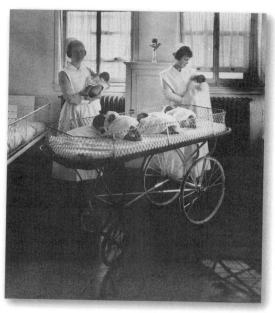

Nurses, cribs, and baby trolley, Montreal Maternity Hospital, 1925–26.
Source: McCord Museum MP-1973.1.7

care of the new baby, and, in most cases, other children. Leila Middleton's March 29, 1930, diary entry expressed this fact. After one miscarriage, one stillbirth, and two home deliveries, she gave birth to her third and fourth children in the hospital in Clinton, Ontario. Since she also had three stepchildren at home, it is not surprising that she wrote, "I enjoyed my hospital stay."[88] The drawback was that doctors increasingly treated the process of giving birth not as a natural event but as a medical one. Caesarean section rates increased from 2 percent of hospital obstetrical rates in the inter-war years to 5 percent by the late 1940s—a rate that some physicians believed was too high but that was to continue to rise.[89]

The inter-war years also saw a virtual explosion of expert advice from the fields of psychology, education, and social welfare, all of whom prescribed correct methods for mothering. It was generally the mother's responsibility to administer the experts' prescriptions for the proper physical, mental, and social adjustment of children; as a result, the ultimate responsibility for a child's success or failure remained with her. Popular articles, well-baby clinics, radio talks to mothers, pamphlets produced by governments and businesses, visits by public health nurses, and lectures to women's organizations—all ensured that more and more Canadian women received instruction in approved child-rearing practices. Motherhood was promoted as a woman's patriotic and moral duty, as well as her lifelong profession. As Dr. Helen MacMurchy put it in 1922,

> being a mother is the highest of all professions and the most extensive of all undertakings. Nothing that she can know is useless to a mother. She can use it all. The mother reports for special duty about 250 days before the baby is born and she is never demobilised until she meets the Bearer of the Great Invitation. Mother, at ninety years, is still Mother.[90]

Fearing the harmful effects of feminist politics on Quebec families, Monseigneur Georges Gauthier, archbishop and coadjutor of the Montreal Diocese, used his 1930 New Year's Eve sermon to stress the moral aspect of women's proper role "as queen of the home, creator of the race." Monseigneur Gauthier concluded that, "through their noble maternal functions," women held in their hands "the education and moral formation of the future generation."[91]

No aspect of infancy, childhood, or adolescence remained untouched by the new scientific authorities. In the inter-war years, these experts recommended a highly controlled and controlling approach. Beginning at birth, prescribed feeding times, especially for bottle-fed babies, allowed for no deviation. Breastfeeding was preferred, but for those who could not or would not, the correct methods of formula preparation were widely publicized. Unless there was a good reason to the contrary, weaning was to take place at nine months of age. Age (rather than the baby's state of readiness) also determined the timing for toilet training. Regimented sleep and exercise patterns rounded out the infant's schedule. Strict adherence to all these methods, mothers were told, would promote not only physical but also emotional health. Anything that detracted from the formation of appropriate regular habits was frowned upon. Indeed, behavioural and other problems in later life were attributed to the mother's failure to establish the discipline required by industrial society.

While the literature urged parents to love their babies, it advised against outward signs of affection, such as hugging and kissing, on the grounds that this behaviour would be likely to produce spoiled, nervous, and irritable children. Furthermore, medical experts suggested that excessive handling of infants could lead to a variety of physical problems, including bone deformities and spinal curvatures.[92] The mothers of school-age and older children also received instruction about how to oversee their physical, emotional, and intellectual development. Children's prompt and regular school attendance, their cleanliness and health, and their attitudes toward school and learning all demanded the mother's cooperation with, and support of, the educational and public health professionals' efforts. Overall, the authorities insisted on their right to intervene in the parent–child relationship by virtue of their scientific approach.

Responses by mothers varied. Not all followed the advice they were given. In rearing her first-born infant, Phyllis Knight, for example, a working-class woman who had immigrated to Canada in the late 1920s, rejected "silly psychological books," preferring instead instinct, tradition, and observation.[93] By contrast, others actively participated in disseminating the experts' views and values. A major expansion of Canadian Home and School Associations—the first of which had been established by women in Baddeck, Nova Scotia, in the 1890s—occurred during the 1920s and 1930s, when both local groups and provincial federations flourished. A national federation, devoted to the training and guidance of children and youth both during and after their school years, was established in 1929. The federation's growth during the inter-war period indicates a degree of acceptance of the partnership between parents—usually mothers—and educational experts. The fact that recommendations for changes in the school curriculum frequently originated with parents shows, however, that their involvement was not purely passive. Music and home economics, for instance, were two subjects vigorously promoted and actively organized by parent members of Home and School groups. Rural mothers also became involved in the education of their children through women's organizations. Thus, the United Farm Women of Alberta's Education Committee sought to improve rural education both inside and outside the classroom by emphasizing educational experiences that were both social and practical.[94]

Following World War II, feature articles and regular columns appearing in women's magazines offered vast quantities of advice—frequently conflicting—about how to deal with the myriad problems inherent in raising a child. The expansion of the middle class in the prosperity of the post-war years created an enlarged audience of prosperous, well-educated parents receptive to guidance about child-rearing. Child-care experts emphasized the emotional bonds between mother and child, and as infant mortality rates for the general population continued to decline, most mothers could be increasingly confident that this emotional investment would not be destroyed by the untimely death of their children.

Many mothers were anxious about their abilities as parents, increasingly so with the popularization of the work of child psychologists, such as Dr. John Bowlby. Bowlby was the British psychologist who, in the early 1950s, coined the phrase "maternal deprivation." It was a concept central to his book *Child Care and the Growth of Love*, discussed widely in women's magazines in North America. On the dubious basis of a study of orphaned children who had to be cared for in institutional settings or foster homes, Bowlby argued that irreparable damage was done to young children when they were separated from their mothers for a prolonged period. He counselled mothers not to leave children under three years of age in the care of others except for the most urgent reasons. Even "the holiday whilst granny looks after the baby" was "best kept to a week or ten days." Many mothers interpreted Bowlby's dictum about the "absolute need of infants and toddlers for the continuous care of their mothers" as meaning they should always be on call for their children.[95]

The conflicting advice that mothers of infants received further complicated their lives: should they feed the baby according to a strict time schedule, as earlier recommended so strongly, or when the baby demanded it? Although infant-care experts did point out the advantages of breastfeeding, and counselled mothers to try it, they assigned an inordinate amount of space in the literature to describing the procedures to be followed in bottle-feeding. Given the overwhelming importance accorded motherhood, and the confusion about how best to meet the demands of this role, it is small wonder that Canadian women relied on books such as the free government publication *The Canadian Mother and Child* (1940) and Dr. Benjamin Spock's *Baby and Child Care* (1946) for authoritative answers. By 1953, Canadian public health nurses had handed out to new mothers more than two million copies of the government book.[96] Once children reached school age, parent–teacher associations, popular magazines, and newspaper articles promoted the ideal of the normal family as espoused by the influential Canadian educational and child psychologists, Dr. William Blatz of Toronto and Dr. Samuel Laycock of Saskatchewan. According to these and other experts on school-aged children, the normal family consisted of a stay-at-home mother with well-adjusted, intelligent, and disciplined children and an attentive father.[97]

The experts who extolled the virtues of the scientific, informed approach to motherhood promised that, if their advice was followed, it would reduce the time involved in raising children. Little cognizance was taken of the contradiction in these arguments. In reality, acquiring, updating, and applying this information took more time than mothering had in the past. Mothers were now expected to read books, pamphlets, and relevant articles in the popular press; to attend baby and child health clinics; and to participate in mothers' clubs and parent–teacher associations, and the running of youth activities. Mothering, if one followed the experts, was becoming a full-time job. At the same time, experts ignored the economic reality of many women's lives. For most Canadians, the husband's wages, even if supplemented by a wife's or children's pay or by other household economic strategies, were barely enough to provide housing, food, and basic necessities.

By 1928, it was for the first time theoretically possible for the average male manufacturing worker to earn sufficient wages to provide for a family on his own. But in reality, in 1929, 60 percent of Canadian working men and 82 percent of working women earned less than the minimum necessary for the support of a family of four.[98] As late as the mid-1950s, only 14 percent of families had annual incomes over $4 000; when wives' income was taken into account, the percentage increased to 51 percent.[99] The concept of the family wage was, therefore, unrealistic at the best of times and, when strikes or unemployment hit, many women faced debilitating hardships. Following her 1925 visit to inspect conditions during the Glace Bay coal miners' strike, Canada's first woman MP, Agnes Macphail, criticized the federal government for its "neglect of humanity," particularly its failure to address the problems of the emotional and physical effects of this strike on women: "I could not help but be struck by the tragedy of womankind in the place. Their youth is brief. Some young women are hotly resentful . . . but for the most part, especially if they have many children, their attitude is subdued and apathetic."[100]

For some women, the demands of mothering proved too much to bear. One Winnipeg immigrant woman's inability to cope had a particularly tragic ending in December 1934. Despondent over her husband's continual lack of work and the prospect of a poverty-stricken Christmas, according to a newspaper account,

> she had just completed the hanging of Christmas decorations in her little home. Then with the home bravely adorned and spotlessly clean, she strangled one child, drowned the other in the bath, and killed herself by drinking a powerful germicide. There had not even been enough money in the house to buy the poison that killed her. She left a farewell note on the kitchen table bearing this out. "I owe the drug store 44 cents; farewell," it said.[101]

For the many wives who worked outside the home, or who raised livestock or took in boarders to make family ends meet, the time required to achieve the ideal household, children, or marriage was simply not available. Most, as a result, continued their traditional modes of child-rearing. The contrast between the old and the new is vividly illustrated in the 1957 account of one European woman, Mena Orford, who, with her doctor husband and children, spent time in an Inuit community. Initially she, like many other outsiders in the Canadian North, was highly critical of the lack of discipline among Inuit children. Before long, however, she was praising the children's good behaviour and the intense love of their parents. Orford went on to declare that the Inuit aversion to physical punishment was "more compassionate" than her own view on spanking children, and she began to question her own ideas on child-rearing.[102]

While the role of fathers was neither as circumscribed nor as scrutinized as that of mothers, it, too, was subjected to considerable attention. Preparation for perfect fatherhood, as with motherhood, was to begin long before the birth of children. The ideal father was physically and morally fit, and a good provider. While mothers were assigned primary responsibility for child care and for character and personality development, the father's role was to be supportive in every way possible. The literature accepted that men lacked their wives' patience, understanding, and time to study the new training methods, but suggested that they use their own business skills of efficiency and understanding to develop friendly relations with their children. The age of the tyrant father was over; instead, a father should have a positive influence on his children. This responsibility meant taking time from his busy schedule for such activities as ball games, fishing expeditions, and visits to the zoo or the circus. However, although experts did not assign a father's role the importance of a mother's with regard to the daily child-care responsibilities, they clearly recognized the father as the final authority and head of the family. "Bringing up children is a two parent job," commented one writer, "and almost always father sets the pace."[103]

Even when their childbearing and child-rearing years were coming to an end, women continued to be inundated with advice from various experts. Cultural taboos still shrouded the subject of sexual activity during menopause, and the attitudes of medical authorities toward menopausal problems remained ambivalent. By the end of the inter-war period,

Group of Inuit women sewing in Pangnirtung, NWT, (now Nunavut) August 1945.

Source: George Hunter/National Film Board of Canada/Library and Archives Canada/PA-166462

synthetic estrogen began to be manufactured and given to women during menopause—despite the fact that early studies were already reporting its possible carcinogenic effects. Articles in popular magazines depicted menopause as the end of women's reproductive life rather than as a time of freedom from pregnancy.[104] Menopause continued to be seen as a crisis in a woman's life, and many doctors and their female patients continued to consider it a medical and social problem. Writing in 1957, Dr. Marion Hilliard expressed a typical view of menopause and its treatment:

> Work is the wonderful antidote to the blues of menopause. This is a period when a woman's sense of uselessness is so acute that she can, literally, be driven to drink, dope, or mental illness. Her family is grown, her childbearing years are ending, her husband often could do just as well with a hired housekeeper. If she has some consuming occupation, . . . she isn't in as much danger of being shattered by what is happening to her physiology.[105]

HELP FOR WIVES AND MOTHERS

Meeting the new standards of motherhood was particularly difficult for women with large families, who were also more likely to be poor. While a growing number of Canadians were convinced that smaller families equalled healthier and happier families, the Criminal Code of Canada rendered both the distribution of family planning information and the sale of birth control devices illegal. Moreover, for the women themselves the subject was often embarrassingly taboo. Throughout the 1920s, desperate Canadian women seeking contraceptive advice wrote to *The Birth Control Review,* a journal published in New York by Margaret Sanger, founder of North America's first birth control clinic. The following letter from a Saskatchewan woman was typical:

> I am a young married woman nineteen years old and I have a dear little baby boy five and a half months old, and I am expecting another baby in four months. Now, we are not in a position to support more than two children as my husband and I both work hard for a living. I love my baby and I want to give him a fair chance in life. I have a good husband and he don't want to see a big family in want any more than I do. I have good health at present, but oh! Mrs. Sanger, how long would it be good if babies came to me that fast, and once health and happiness are gone, what is the use of asking help then? Now is the time, and if you could only tell me how to prevent conception you would make me the happiest woman in Canada.[106]

The pleas came from across Canada, from working-class and middle-class women and also from men. A college-educated woman related in a letter how, after three pregnancies, she had followed a neighbour's totally inadequate advice about birth control and given birth to two more children. Her health deteriorated, she had decided "not to go back to my husband unless I can know of an absolutely certain contraceptive." Physical separation was the best advice that some doctors were willing to give, and a few still warned that mechanical methods of birth control were dangerous as well as disreputable. Most doctors, however, maintained a public silence on the issue.[107]

Women did use a variety of contraceptive measures. But as letters to *The Birth Control Review* illustrate, their knowledge was limited and often incorrect, and such information had to be passed privately from one woman to another. Whenever the question of limiting family size moved from the private to the public arena, it was surrounded by controversy. Believers in the superiority of British stock continued to argue that the practice of family limitation among the Anglo-Celtic middle class would gradually lead to "race suicide" because their sort of people would eventually be outnumbered by the larger immigrant and working-class families. A similar argument was put forward by French-Canadian nationalists, who feared for the survival of their culture should the francophone population decline. Their message was reinforced by the Catholic Church, which proclaimed that marriage existed for procreation and that any artificial attempt to thwart this purpose constituted a sin. On the other hand, for its part, the United Church of Canada emphasized the use of contraception by married couples as essential for the promotion of companionate Christian marriages, but members of fundamentalist religions condemned the use of birth control as immoral and likely to contribute to sexual promiscuity.

Nevertheless, birth control advocates worked tirelessly to educate women. Particularly influential were American birth control leaders like Margaret Sanger and the anarchist Emma Goldman—who, during her exile in Canada, expounded on her view that birth control was an individual woman's right, part of the right to control her own body, and also a necessary weapon in the workers' struggle against capitalism. This latter argument found favour among some Canadian socialist groups, who were convinced that the capitalist system encouraged large working-class families in order to have a cheap source of labour for its factories and cannon fodder for its armies. In response, in 1924, British Columbia socialists founded the Canadian Birth Control League to educate the working class about these matters. Equally concerned about the physical and mental toll of unwanted pregnancies on farm and working-class wives, the women's branch of the United Farmers of Canada's Saskatchewan section passed the first public resolution on the matter at a 1929 convention. Calling on the government to rescind the ban on the distribution of birth control information, delegates asked for the establishment of birth control clinics staffed by trained doctors.[108]

It was evident that the motives for supporting family limitation were mixed. Eugenic arguments became increasingly popular in the1930s, when the ranks of the unemployed caused rising relief costs and deteriorating economic conditions raised fears of social unrest. A birth control clinic founded in British Columbia in 1932 counted among its objectives the need for "good breeding" and recommended the sterilization of the "unfit." And it was during this decade that both British Columbia and Alberta passed bills permitting the forcible sterilization of the "mentally ill and the retarded."[109] In the same decade, birth control clinics were established in at least three provinces: Ontario, Manitoba, and British Columbia. Rising relief costs also concerned Dr. Elizabeth Bagshaw, the pioneering medical director of a clinic in Hamilton, Ontario, from 1932 to 1966. But her main motivation—like Sanger's in the United States—was her genuine concern for the plight of working-class women facing repeated unwanted pregnancies. Founded and largely financed by Mary Hawkins, a wealthy Hamilton widow, the clinic was a godsend to many women, some of whom were given the contraceptive devices they were unable to pay for. This clinic also supported sterilization as a means of family limitation, and its dependence on doctors contributed to the medicalization of birth control.[110]

The debate about family limitation received national attention in 1936, when Dorothea Palmer was charged under the Criminal Code for distributing birth control information and devices to women in Eastview, a working-class French-Canadian suburb of Ottawa. Palmer was employed by Alvin R. Kaufman, the wealthy owner of the Kaufman Rubber Company in Kitchener, Ontario. Inspired by a growing personal conviction that limiting family size was essential for maintaining social order in a depressed economy, Kaufman had established a Parents' Information Bureau in his city in 1929. The Bureau hired married women as field workers in many parts of Canada; at the time of Palmer's arrest, it employed 53 such field workers to visit the homes of poor women and counsel them about birth control. During the Palmer trial, experts testified that it was "in the public good" to provide contraceptive information in areas like Eastview, with its large French-Canadian families and population of unemployed who were receiving public relief. More telling still were the 20 Catholic francophone women who testified that Palmer's work was appreciated and that they saw nothing wrong with the contraception methods that the Parents' Information Bureau promoted. The defence was successful: Palmer was acquitted on March 17, 1937, and an appeal of the verdict was dismissed. Yet, although the trial provided a platform for both opponents and advocates of birth control and had an undoubted effect in educating public opinion, the law regarding the distribution of birth control information and devices was not rewritten.[111]

In the face of the unequivocal evidence that many of their parishioners were consciously limiting their family size, the Catholic clergy in Quebec were compelled to publicly acknowledge natural forms of birth control, such as the rhythm method and the thermometer method, both of which relied on identifying women's periods of fertility. While the Roman Catholic hierarchy remained firm in its conviction that the primary function of marriage was procreation and in its condemnation of all artificial means of preventing conception, priests began to acknowledge that factors such as poverty and illness might place unbearable burdens on a marriage if there were too many unwanted pregnancies. By the 1940s, by organizing marriage preparation courses in which these methods were discussed, the clergy and groups under its supervision, such as the *Jeunesse ouvrière catholique féminine* (JOCF), played a key role in the dissemination of information about some forms of natural family limitation that would allow couples to space their births. However, Catholics were still expected to use abstinence as their primary means for controlling family size.[112]

During the inter-war years, governments in most provinces gave limited recognition to the economic hardships suffered by some families by introducing mothers' allowances. Mothers who, through no fault of their own, were left alone with the responsibility of raising children, were eligible for the allowances, which were to be short-term supplements, not regular income. Both the eligibility requirements and the amounts provided varied from province to province. Widows, however, were eligible recipients in all provinces; some provinces also paid allowances to deserted wives, wives whose husbands were physically and mentally handicapped, or wives of prisoners. Mothers with one dependent child qualified in certain provinces but not in others, and the maximum age of dependency varied from 15 to 16. In all provinces except Alberta and Saskatchewan, to qualify for assistance the mother had to be a married British subject, or the widow or wife of a British subject. This restriction resulted in the disqualification of unwed mothers and women who lost their status as British subjects upon marriage, as well as many immigrant women. Many mothers fell through the minimal safety net provided by the allowances. Heartrending ads in newspaper "Personal" columns show that some felt they had no alternative but to put their children up for adoption. All recipient mothers were encouraged to earn additional income when they could do so without neglecting their family responsibilities. Applicants were scrupulously scrutinized, especially if they were Aboriginal or from a racial or ethnic minority, and recipients were supervised to ensure that they were truly deserving. In the 1940s and 1950s, rates and eligibility increased and recipients began to receive free dental and medical services. The allowances remained below subsistence levels, however, and the moral regulation of recipients intensified, especially in the case of deserted and unwed mothers whose sexual behaviour was routinely monitored. Additionally, mothers from ethnic minority groups were required to take classes in child-rearing and household management. When mothers' allowances were approved for Aboriginal women, they were placed under the control of the Indian Agent or local missionary, whose main concern in this context was controlling Aboriginal women's sexuality. Mothers accused of sexual impropriety could not only lose their allowances, but were denied treaty interest payments and might have their children taken away and placed for adoption with non-Aboriginal parents.[113]

Mothers' allowances, like compulsory school attendance laws and child labour legislation, represented an example of direct state intervention in family life in support of a particular middle-class model of the family. The inadequacy of the family wage was finally recognized in 1944 when the federal government introduced the family allowance, a monthly sum to be paid for each child, with a decreasing allowance rate after the birth of the fourth child. Elite Quebec nationalists opposed this federal program on the grounds that it interfered with provincial autonomy and penalized large families. As the debate surrounding its passage showed, this was a controversial measure but one that was justified on the need to supplement the wages of the male breadwinner. Underlying the initiative was the assumption that married women were responsible for child care and ought not to be wage earners, except in emergency situations. Family allowance cheques were to be made out directly to mothers, except in Quebec, where the cheques were initially to be made out to the fathers. It was Quebec feminist and politician Thérèse Casgrain who discovered this extraordinary exception and managed to stop it before the first cheques were issued. After a delay of three weeks, Quebec women also received the family allowance cheque in their name. Although the sums involved were small, family allowance legislation did benefit families in all provinces—and it was important that the money was controlled by women. At the same time, the scheme reinforced the traditional view that the man was the wage earner and that the woman's proper role was a domestic one.[114]

The replacement of voluntary philanthropy with state assistance reflected the growing eagerness of the English-speaking middle class to enlist the state in the campaign to support Canadian family life. Institutions like orphanages, refuges, and training and reform schools, and even foster families, were increasingly under attack for their failure to produce good results. It was best, it was now argued, to use means that encouraged mothers to remain at home and keep their families together. During the Depression, relief was granted to women on the basis of their respectability as women, not on their willingness to work (which was the criterion for men). There was no recognition or financial support for women who were responsible for elderly or handicapped adult dependants. Single elderly women were particularly vulnerable. In 1949, maximum federal government payments under the means-tested old-age pensions scheme increased from $20 to $40 a month, an amount insufficient to provide even the very basic necessities. Single, widowed, and divorced elderly women vastly outnumbered their male counterparts and were most likely to be impoverished. A 1955 report in Winnipeg on the single elderly, who lived on their own enumerated 5 000 men and 11 000 women. These single elderly persons comprised 33 percent of all aged men and about 60 percent of all aged women in that city.[115]

An astonishing case of state intervention in an individual family occurred in Corbeil, Ontario, in 1934 with the birth of the famous Dionne quintuplets. The poor, rural French-Canadian parents of these children were completely "relieved" of the responsibility for raising their five girls, implying quite clearly that provincial authorities disapproved of the parents' values and lifestyle. Within two months of the birth, in fact, the provincial government placed Yvonne, Annette, Cécile, Émilie, and Marie Dionne under the control of a board of guardians, which did not include their parents. In September of that year, the five-month-old babies were moved from the family farmhouse to a separate, specially equipped hospital-like building, and placed under the care of Dr. Allan Roy Dafoe, the doctor who had delivered them. Dafoe instituted what he called, in the foreword to his mothers' guidebook, "medical control," characterized by rigorous monitoring of every aspect of the quints' lives and environment.[116] Although their parents might visit the girls, Elzire and Oliva Dionne could not interfere in their care, despite Elzire's protests in favour of her own cultural practices and her desire for an active role. In 1936 Dr. William Blatz, Canada's leading child psychologist, took control, introducing his own system of disciplined scientific routine and child study. Only in 1938 did the Dionne parents' arguments, combined with those of Catholic and Franco-Ontarian nationalists, succeed in restoring the parents' authority. But the damage had been done. It was too late to heal the rift that had developed between the quints and their family. The saga of the Dionnes represented more than intervention on the part of the government. The experts involved made their reputations and fortunes, and all Canadian women were treated to yet another campaign designed to convert them to perfect, germ-free child-rearing.

TRANSGRESSING THE NORMS

Some women did not or could not conform to the idealized maternal role, with its emphasis on self-effacing femininity or on scientific child-management. However, they frequently paid a high price for their non-conformity, as righteous moral indignation and shame haunted their lives. Unwed mothers, for example, were seen as "weak and ignorant, strong-minded and wicked, or simple-minded." The only exceptions tended to be those who were the victims of sexual abuse. The nuns who ran Montreal's *Hôpital de la Miséricorde* shielded their inmates from the outside world, but expected them to perform domestic duties both for their keep and as atonement for their transgressions. Wherever possible the unwed mother was encouraged to marry, even if the prospective husband was unsuitable, because marriage was seen as the only means of achieving a respectable living other than entering the convent. In Nova Scotia, the high level of births outside legal marriages in the 1940 and 1950s was attributed to blacks, Newfoundlanders, and the "retarded." Babies born to unwed mothers were often placed in care and, as recent research shows, many were sold to adoptive families, without the birth mother's knowledge or consent, while others died in infancy from neglect.[117] A more direct response to illegitimacy, in this case among women deemed mentally ill or feeble-minded, was sterilization. Between 1935 and 1945, 57 of the 64 patients sterilized at a British Columbia hospital were women. Of these, 46 were single women—mothers to a combined total of 33 illegitimate children.[118]

Provided that they did not get pregnant, little or no attention was paid to the situation of those women who, for reasons of choice or circumstance, did not marry. Yet some women challenged society's right to control their sexuality and restrict it to marriage. As knowledge of birth control spread, some women separated their sexuality from procreation. As early as 1928, a female Canadian university student questioned the assumption that she would marry, arguing that women should have the option to remain independent but not necessarily celibate. Introducing her discussion as a "protest and an explanation," this anonymous critic noted that she was not against marriage as a social institution, but rather was against having it thrown in her teeth as an "inevitable goal" or as "the simple panacea for all one's difficulties and ambitions."[119] A few women even chose to fulfill a desire for motherhood and children despite their single status: some Finnish women who had come to Montreal as domestic servants seem to have consciously chosen to have children despite their unmarried state.[120]

Most people, however, believed that the only respectable lifestyle for an unmarried woman was celibacy. Although by the 1940s the role of the religious celibate had declined in importance in Quebec, many women still chose life in a Roman Catholic or Anglican religious order, and the number of sisters and the number of female orders continued to expand both inside and outside Quebec. As well as offering a spiritual role, the convent still represented an important form of economic security and the possibility of self-development and a career. For some, it even provided a certain degree of independence.[121] The vast majority of Catholic women did not join a religious order, and of course for most non-Catholic women, this option did not exist.

In both French and English Canada, independent unmarried women constituted an important group. Some of them were poor working-class women, but not many of their occupations could adequately support separate households. In Paris, Ontario, a woman-centred textile town, some single and widowed women maintained shared households.[122] Since most professions still barred married women, the few women professionals were likely to be unmarried, and some combined economic and emotional resources, often for substantial periods of their lives. Charlotte Whitton, a social worker and later executive secretary of the Canadian Council on Child Welfare (who gained further renown and some notoriety as mayor of Ottawa during the 1950s) lived with Margaret Grier, another federal civil servant, for almost 30 years. The closeness of their relationship can be seen in the 96 letters that Whitton wrote to Grier demonstrating her grief after Grier's death in 1947. However, when marriage was so ardently promoted, close or lasting relationships between unrelated adult women were increasingly likely to attract social disapproval, and establishing joint households was suspect. Some women who recognized themselves as lesbians felt obliged to conceal their identity behind a façade of celibate friendship (the so-called old-maid companions); in the 1950s, some lesbians enjoyed meeting like-minded women at carefully screened and discreet house parties.[123]

Even some married women flagrantly contravened the conventional ideal of the housewife and mother depicted by the glossy magazines. The New Glasgow, Nova Scotia, temperance inspector Clifford Rose ran into a number of women who made ends meet for themselves and their families in ways that hardly accorded with the ideal. He recalled the notorious women, known as "mothers," who ran the "worst dives" in town. One, whose name was Delores, "was a mite of a woman [but] . . . her obscene and profane tongue was feared by friend and foe." Delores escaped prosecution for running an illegal tavern by smashing her rum bottles in the sink while the inspector was hammering on the door. The most famous of the women rumrunners, known as "the Queen," was the object of veiled admiration. A former nurse, horsewoman, and part-time movie actress in the United States, the Queen had returned to her native Nova Scotia with her husband in order to care for her aging parents. Attracted by the money to be made in smuggling rum, she used her commercial acumen and her ability to bribe highly placed government officials to create a business that even the inspectors had to admit was successful. Delores and the Queen were not entirely atypical in their involvement with the illegal trade in alcohol during Prohibition—the Prohibition that other women had fought hard to obtain. In Peterborough, Ontario, arrests of women for making and selling alcohol increased markedly in the 1920s.[124]

Many other women did not have husbands, but nonetheless had children or other dependants to support. For example, among post-war Mennonite immigrants and refugees, there was a high percentage of female-headed families whose husbands had been arrested, exiled, killed, or lost during the war years. Many faced not only the same social stigma as other unmarried mothers but also the suspicion and disapproval of the Mennonite church and community. These women frequently resisted communal efforts to regularize their situations through marriage with single or widowed Mennonite men. As one woman put it, when asked why she refused to marry a man who made frequent visits to the family home, "If I married him, I would have to sleep with him. Oh No!" Instead she preferred her single status, as did many others in the same situation. They raised their families alone despite frequent rejection and discrimination by their communities.[125] These Mennonite women demonstrated, yet again, that the ideal of a family in which the mother stayed at home to look after her children while her breadwinner husband supported the entire household, was increasingly just that—an ideal.

Notes

1. Warren E. Kalbach and Wayne W. McVey, *The Demographic Bases of Canadian Society* (Toronto: McGraw-Hill, 1971), 265.
2. Zheng Wu, "Recent Trends in Marriage Patterns in Canada," *Policy Options*, September 1998, 3. http://www.irpp.org/po/archive/sep98/wu.pdf.
3. Roy H. Rogers and Gail Whitney, "The Family Cycle in Twentieth Century Canada," *Journal of Marriage and the Family* 43, 3 (August 1981): 734.
4. John Herd Thompson with Allen Seager, *Canada, 1922–1939: Decades of Discord* (Toronto: McClelland and Stewart, 1985), 3; A. J. Pelletier, F. D. Thompson, and A. Rochon, *The Canadian Family*, Census Monograph no. 7 (Ottawa: J. O. Patenaude for the Dominion Bureau of Statistics, 1938), 19.
5. Jacques Henripin, *Tendances et facteurs de la fécondité au Canada* (Ottawa: Dominion Bureau of Statistics, 1968), 21.
6. Kalbach and McVey, *The Demographic Bases*, 46–47.
7. Canada, Dominion Bureau of Statistics, *Origin, Birthplace, Nationality and Language of the Canadian People* (Ottawa: King's Printer, 1929), 219.

8. Canada, Dominion Bureau of Statistics, *Vital Statistics 1964* (Ottawa: Queen's Printer, 1966), L2, 212.

9. Rogers and Whitney, "The Family Cycle," 729.

10. Tamara Adilman, "A Preliminary Sketch of Chinese Women and Work in British Columbia, 1858–1950," in Gillian Creese and Veronica Strong-Boag, eds., *British Columbia Reconsidered: Essays on Women* (Vancouver: Press Gang, 1992), 324; Enakshi Dua, "Racializing Imperial Canada: Indian Women and the Making of Ethnic Communities," in Marlene Epp, Franca Iacovetta and Frances Swyripa, eds., *Sisters or Strangers? Immigrant, Ethnic and Racialized Women History* (Toronto: University of Toronto Press, 2004), 71–85; Peter S. Li, *The Chinese in Canada. 2nd ed.* (Toronto: Oxford University Press, 1998), 65, 70.

11. Ken Adachi, *The Enemy That Never Was: A History of the Japanese Canadians* (Toronto: McClelland and Stewart, 1976), 91, 138, 318; Midge Ayukawa, "Japanese Pioneer Women: Fighting Racism and Rearing the Next Generation," in Epp, et al., eds., *Sisters or Strangers,* 236; Ayukawa, *Hiroshima Immigrants in Canada, 1891–1941* (Vancouver: University of British Columbia Press, 2008); Valerie Knowles, *Strangers at Our Gates: Canadian Immigration and Immigration Policy, 1540–1998,* rev. ed. (Toronto: Dundurn Press, 1997), 124.

12. Melynda Jarratt, *War Brides: The Stories of the Women Who Left Everything Behind to Follow the Men They Loved* (Toronto: Dundurn Press, 2009); Linda Granfield, *Brass Buttons and Silver Horseshoes: Stories from Canada's British War Brides* (Toronto: McLelland and Stewart, 2002); Knowles, *Strangers,* 130–34; Marlene Epp, *Women without Men: Mennonite Refugees of the Second World War* (Toronto: University of Toronto Press, 2000), 85–86.

13. Ruth Roach Pierson, *"They're Still Women after All": The Second World War and Canadian Womanhood* (Toronto: McClelland and Stewart, 1986), 216.

14. Monica Boyd, Margrit Eichler, and John R. Hofley, "Family: Functions, Formation, and Fertility," in Gail Cook, ed., *Opportunity for Choice: A Goal for Women in Canada* (Ottawa: Statistics Canada, 1976), 18.

15. John R. Miron, *Demographic Change, Household Formation and Housing Demand: Canada's Postwar Experience* (Toronto: Centre for Urban and Community Studies, University of Toronto, 1985), 7,18, Table 7.3.2.

16. *Canada Yearbook, 1976–77, Special Edition* (Ottawa: Supply and Services Canada, 1977), Table 4.35.

17. Kalbach and McVey, *The Demographic Bases,* 59.

18. "You'll Hire Older Women, Miss Giggles Will Marry," *Financial Post* (May 4, 1957), 1.

19. Boyd et al., 32

20. Rebecca Coulter, "Rhetoric and Reality: The Experience of Teenagers in Edmonton," paper presented to the Canadian Historical Association, Vancouver, 1983, 14; Coulter, "The Working Young of Edmonton, 1921–1931," in Joy Parr, ed., *Childhood and Family in Canadian History* (Toronto: McClelland and Stewart, 1982), 146; Joy Parr, "Introduction," in Parr, ed., *Childhood and Family,* 14; Neil Sutherland, *Children in English-Canadian Society: Framing the Twentieth-Century Consensus* (Toronto: University of Toronto Press, 1976), 165; Frederick Elkin, *The Family in Canada* (Ottawa: Vanier Institute of the Family, 1964), 113.

21. Beth Light and Ruth Roach Pierson, eds., *No Easy Road: Women in Canada, 1920s–1960s* (Toronto: New Hogtown Press, 1990), chap. 1; J. Donald Wilson, Robert J. Stamp, and Louis-Philippe Audet, eds., *Canadian Education: A History* (Scarborough: Prentice-Hall, 1970), 364–65.

22. Light and Pierson, eds., *No Easy Road*, 39.

23. Marta Danylewycz, Nadia Fahmy-Eid, et Nicole Thivierge, "L'enseignement ménager et les 'home economics' au Québec et en Ontario au début du 20e siècle: Une analyse comparée," in J. Donald Wilson, ed., *An Imperfect Past: Education and Society in Canadian History* (Vancouver: Centre for the Study of Curriculum and Instruction, University of British Columbia, 1984), 72.

24. Barbara Riley, "Six Saucepans to One: Domestic Science vs. the Home in British Columbia 1900–1930," in Barbara K. Latham and Roberta J. Pazdro, eds., *Not Just Pin Money: Selected Essays on the History of Women's Work in British Columbia* (Victoria: Camosun College, 1984), 168.

25. Jo-Anne Fiske, "Gender and the Paradox of Residential Education in Carrier Society," in Christine Miller and Patricia Churchryk eds., *Women of the First Nations: Power, Wisdom* (Winnipeg: University of Manitoba Press, 1996), 167–82; Margaret Blackman, "The Changing Status of Haida Women: An Ethnohistorical and Life History Approach," in Donald A. Abbott, ed., *The World as Sharp as a Knife: An Anthology in Honour of Wilson Duff* (Victoria: British Columbia Provincial Museum, 1981), 75.

26. Riley, "Six Saucepans to One," 172.

27. Riley, "Six Saucepans to One," 159–94; Danylewycz, Fahmy-Eid, et Thivierge, "L'enseignement ménager," 65–119; Richard Dennis, "'Home Suite Home'? Women and Apartment-Living in Early Twentieth-Century Toronto," paper presented at the Canadian Association of Geographers, Ottawa, 2009.

28. Donald Kerr et al., eds., *Historical Atlas of Canada* (Toronto: University of Toronto Press, 1990) vol. III, plate 33.

29. *Report of the Royal Commission on the Status of Women in Canada* (Ottawa: Information Canada, 1970), 174–75; Le Collectif Clio, *L'histoire des femmes au Québec depuis quatres siècles,* 2nd ed. (Montréal: Le jour, 1992), 439.

30. Ontario, Department of Education, *Courses of Study Grades IX, X, XI and XII, Home Economics, General and Commercial and Vocational Courses,* 1945; *Courses of Study in Grades XI and XII, The Home Economics Option of the General Course, the Commercial Course and the Art Course,* 1955.

31. Light and Pierson, eds., *No Easy Road,* 25; Basil Frison, *Coeducation in Catholic Schools: A Commentary on the Instruction on Coeducation* (Rome: Commentarium Pro Religiosis, 1959); Anne Gagnon, "The *Pensionnat Assomption*: Religious Nationalism in a Franco-Albertan Boarding School for Girls, 1926–1960," *Historical Studies in Education/Revue d'histoire de l'éducation* 1, 1 (Spring 1989): 95–117; Evelyn M. Brown, *Educating Eve* (Montreal: Palm, 1957), xiv–xv, 92–115; Micheline Dumont and Nadia Fahmy-Eid, *Les Couventines* (Montreal: Boréal, 1986), 160–61; Micheline Dumont, *Girls' Schooling in Quebec, 1639–1960* (Ottawa: The Canadian Historical Association Historical Booklet No 49), 18–19.

32. Jean Barman, Yvonne Hébert, and Don McCaskill, eds., *Indian Education in Canada,* 2 vols. (Vancouver: University of British Columbia Press, 1986–87); Wanda Thomas Bernard and Judith Fingard, "Black Women at Work: Race, Family and Community in Greater Halifax," in Judith Fingard and Janet Guildford, eds., *Mother of the Municipality: Women, Work and Social Policy in Post-1945 Halifax* (Toronto: University of Toronto Press, 2005), 191; *Nova Scotian Black Women of Distinction, Past and Present 1990—A Calendar* (Black Cultural Centre for Nova Scotia); Leo W. Bertley, *Canada and Its People of African Descent* (Pierrefonds, QC: Bilongo, 1977), 158.

33. F. H. Leacy, ed., *Historical Statistics of Canada*, 2nd ed. (Ottawa: Statistics Canada, 1983), W340–438; Paul Axelrod, *Making a Middle Class: Student Life in English Canada During the Thirties* (Montreal and Kingston: McGill-Queen's University Press, 1990).

34. Marianne Gosztonyi Ainley and Catherine Miller, "A Select Few: Women and the National Research Council of Canada, 1916–1991," *Scientia Canadensis* 15, 2 (1991): 109.

35. Nancy Kiefer, "The Impact of World War II on Female Students at the University of Toronto, 1939–49," University of Toronto, M.A. Thesis, 1984.

36. W. P. J Millar and R. D. Gidney, "'Medettes'; Thriving or Just Surviving? Women Students in the Faculty of Medicine, University of Toronto, 1910–1951," in Elizabeth Smyth, Sandra Acker, Paula Bourne, and Alison Prentice, eds., *Challenging Professions: Historical and Contemporary Perspectives on Women's Professional Work* (Toronto: University of Toronto Press, 1999), 215–23; Interview with Dr. Marjorie Moore, Toronto, April 16, 1987.

37. Leacy, ed., *Historical Statistics*, 2nd ed., W340–57.

38. Cynthia R. Comacchio, *The Infinite Bonds of Family Life: Domesticity in Canada, 1850–1940* (Toronto: University of Toronto Press, 1999), 88.

39. Coulter, "Rhetoric and Reality."

40. Margaret Prang, "'The Girl God Would Have Me Be': The Canadian Girls in Training, 1915–39," *Canadian Historical Review* 66, 2 (1985): 154–84; *4-H Clubs in Manitoba* (Winnipeg: Historic Resources Branch, Manitoba Department of Cultural Affairs and Historic Resources, 1983), 8; for a discussion of the variety of recreational activities provided for adolescents, see Cynthia Comacchio, *The Dominion of Youth: Adolescence and the Making of Modern Canada, 1920 to 1950* (Waterloo, ON: Wilfrid Laurier University Press, 2006), chap. 7.

41. Gertrude E. S. Pringle, "Is the Flapper a Menace?" *Maclean's* (June 15, 1922).

42. Emily F. Murphy, *The Black Candle* (Toronto: Thomas Allen, 1922; reprinted Toronto: Coles Canadiana Collection, 1973); Joan Sangster, "'Pardon Tales' from Magistrate's Court: Women, Crime, and the Court in Peterborough County, 1920–50," *Canadian Historical Review* 74, 2 (1993): 182; James W. St. G. Walker, *A History of Blacks in Canada* (Ottawa: Supply and Services Canada, 1980), 89; Allan Bartley, "A Public Nuisance: The Klu Klux Klan in Ontario, 1923–27," *Journal of Canadian Studies* (Fall 1995): 12.

43. Murphy, *The Black Candle*; Pringle, "Is the Flapper a Menace?"; Tamara Myers, "Women Policing Women: A Patrol Woman in Montreal, 1918," paper presented to the Canadian Historical Association, Ottawa, 1993, 19.

44. Comacchio, *The Dominion of Youth*, espec. chap. 7.

45. Joan Sangster, "Domesticating Girls: The Sexual Regulation of Aboriginal and Working-Class Girls in Twentieth-Century Canada," in Katie Pickles and Myra Rutherdale, eds., *Contact Zones: Aboriginal and Settler Women in Canada's Colonial Past* (Vancouver: University of British Columbia Press, 2005), 179–204.

46. Tanya Woloschuk, "A Promise of Redemption: The *Soeurs du Bon Pasteur* and Delinquent Girls in Winnipeg, 1911–1948," *Manitoba History* 51 (February 2006): 17–18; for a discussion of public concerns over female sexuality and delinquency, see Joan Sangster, *Regulating Girls and Women: Sexuality, Family, and the Law in Ontario, 1920–1960* (Toronto: University of Toronto Press, 2001); Sangster, *Girl Trouble: Female Delinquency in English Canada* (Toronto: Between the Lines, 2002); Carolyn Strange, *Toronto's Girl Problems: The Perils and the Pleasures of the City, 1880–1930* (Toronto: University of Toronto Press, 1995); Carolyn Strange and Tina Loo, *Making Good: Law and Moral Regulation in Canada, 1867–1939* (Toronto: University of Toronto Press, 1997); Tamara Myers, *Caught: Montreal's Modern Girls and the Law, 1869–1945* (Toronto: University of Toronto Press, 2006).

47. Lola Martin Burgoyne, *A History of the Home and School Movement in Ontario* (Toronto: Charters, 1934), 27.

48. M. Ann Hall, *The Girls and the Game: A History of Women's Sport in Canada* (Peterborough, ON: Broadview Press, 2002); Helen Lenskyj, *Out of Bounds: Women, Sport and Sexuality* (Toronto: Women's Press, 1986); Lenskyj, "We Want to Play . . . We'll Play: Women and Sport in the Twenties and Thirties," *Canadian Woman Studies/Les cahiers de la femme* 4, 3 (Spring/May 1983): 11–18; Wayne Norton, *Women on Ice* (Vancouver: Ronsdale Press, 2009).

49. Ron Hotchkiss, "'The Matchless Six': Canadian Women at the Olympics, 1928," *The Beaver* (October/November 1993): 23–42.

50. Anne Rochon Ford, *A Path Not Strewn with Roses: One Hundred Years of Women at the University of Toronto 1884–1984* (Toronto: Governing Council, University of Toronto, 1985), 65–72; Margaret Gillett, *We Walked Very Warily: A History of Women at McGill* (Montreal: Eden Press, 1981), 245–46; Helen Gurney, *A Century to Remember 1893–1993: Women's Sport at the University of Toronto* (Toronto: University of Toronto Women's T-Holders Association, 1993).

51. Coulter, "Rhetoric and Reality," 12; Helen Lenskyj, *Out of Bounds: Women, Sport and Sexuality* (Toronto: Women's Press, 1986), 33–53.

52. *Women at Acadia University: The First Fifty Years, 1884–1934* (Wolfville, N.S.: Acadia University, 1984), 12.

53. Leo W. Bertley, *Canada and Its People of African Descent* (Pierrefonds, Que.: Bilongo, 1977), 330.

54. Cochrane et al., *Women in Canadian Life*, 54, 56.

55. Margaret Currie, *Margaret Currie—Her Book* (Toronto: Hunter-Rose, 1924).

56. Carolyn Gossage, *Greatcoats and Glamour Boots: Canadian Women at War, 1939–1945* (Toronto: Dundurn Press, 1991), 123; T. Davidson, "'A Woman's Right to Charm and Beauty': Maintaining the Feminine Ideal in the CWAC," *Atlantis* 26, 1, 2001: 45–54.

57. Susan M. Hartmann, *The Homefront and Beyond: American Women in the 1940s* (Boston: Twain, 1982), 203.

58. See, for example, "How to Be a Good Wife," *Chatelaine* 13, 2 (February 1940); Suzanne Morton, "Winning under Capitalism: Luck, Bingo and Lotteries in Canada, 1919–1939," paper presented to the Canadian Historical Association, Charlottetown, 1992, 14–24.

59. Magda Fahrni, *Household Politics: Montreal Families and Postwar Reconstruction* (Toronto: University of Toronto Press, 2005), chap. 4.

60. Light and Pierson, eds., *No Easy Road*, chap. 1; Marlene Epp, *Mennonite Women in Canada: A History* (Winnipeg: University of Manitoba Press, 2008), 45; Janet Mancini Billson, "New Choices for a New Era," in Mary Crnkovich, *"Gossip": A Spoken History of Women in the North* (Ottawa: Canadian Arctic Resources Committee, 1990), 47; Isabel Kaprielian-Churchill, *Like Our Mountains: A History of Armenians in Canada* (Kingston and Montreal: McGill-Queens Press, 2005), chap. 9.

61. A. H. Tyrer, *Sex, Marriage and Birth Control* (Toronto: Marriage Welfare Bureau, 1936), xiii.

62. Karen Duder, "The Spreading Depths: Lesbian and Bisexual Women in English Canada, 1910–1965," Ph.D. Thesis, University of Victoria, 2001, 111.

63. Margot Iris Duley, "'The Radius of Her Influence for Good': The Rise and Triumph of the Women's Suffrage Movement in Newfoundland, 1909–1925," in Linda Kealey, ed., *Pursuing Equality: Historical Perspectives on Women in Newfoundland and Labrador* (St. John's: Institute of Social and Economic Research, Memorial University, 1993), 38.

64. Norman Knowles, "A Selective Dependence: Vancouver's Japanese Community and Anglican Missions, 1903–42," paper presented to the Canadian Historical Association, Calgary, 1994, 20.

65. Inez Houlihan, "The Image of Women in *Chatelaine* Editorials March 1928 to September 1977," University of Toronto, M.A. Thesis, 1984, 31–32.

66. For a discussion of how working-class women in Montreal coped during the Great Depression, see Denyse Baillargeon, translated by Yvonne Klein, *Making Do: Family and Home in Montreal during the Great Depression* (Waterloo, ON: Wilfrid Laurier University Press, 1999).

67. Cook, *Opportunity for Choice*, 22.

68. "Gwen Lefort, War Bride in WW I," *Cape Breton's Magazine* 35 (1984), 49.

69. Melynda Jarratt, *Captured Hearts: New Brunswicks' War Brides* (New Bruswick: Goose Lane Editions, 2008), 9.

70. A full 89.2 percent of farm families used outhouses, compared to only 11.9 percent of urban dwellers; 57.1 percent of farm households depended on outside water pumps, versus 7 percent of households in urban areas. *Census of Canada* (1941) vol. 9, Table 16, 73, and Table 14, 66.

71. Mary Vipond, "The Image of Women in Mass Circulation Magazines in the 1920s," in Susan Mann Trofimenkoff and Alison Prentice, eds., *The Neglected Majority: Essays in Canadian Women's History* (Toronto: McClelland and Stewart, 1977) vol. 1, 118–24.

72. Marjorie Harris, "Fifty Golden Years of *Chatelaine*," *Chatelaine* 51, 3 (March 1978), 43.

73. Christine Foley, "Consumerism, Consumption and Canadian Feminism 1900–1930," University of Toronto, M.A. Thesis, 1979, 23, 58–59.

74. Sandra Bassendowkski, "The Power of Electricity to Change Rural Women's Work in Post-War Saskatchewan," *Saskatchewan History* Fall 2005: 29–34.

75. Margaret Hobbs and Ruth Roach Pierson, "When Is a Kitchen Not a Kitchen?" *Canadian Woman Studies/Les cahiers de la femme* 7, 4 (Winter 1986): 71–76.

76. Cynthia Wright, "'Feminine Trifles of Vast Importance': Writing Gender into the History of Consumption," in Franca Iacovetta and Mariana Valverde, eds., *Gender Conflicts: New Essays in Women's History* (Toronto: University of Toronto Press, 1992), 242; Linda M. Ambrose, "Cartoons and Commissions: Advice to to Postwar Rural Youth in Ontario," in Cynthia R. Comacchio and Elizabeth Jane Errington, *People, Places, and Times: Reading in Canadian Social History Volume 2: Post-Confederation* (Toronto: Thomson Nelson, 2006), 278–93.

77. Yvonne Mathews-Klein, "How They Saw Us: Images of Women in National Film Board Films of the 1940s and 1950s," *Atlantis* 4, 2 (Spring 1979): 26; Joy Parr, *The Material, the Moral, and the Economic in the Postwar Years* (Toronto: University of Toronto Press, 1999).

78. Franca Iacovetta and Valerie J. Korinek, " Jell-O Salads, One Stop Shopping, and Maria the Homemaker: The Gender Politics of Food," in Epp, et al., eds., *Sisters or Strangers*, 190–230; Franca Iacovetta, *Gatekeepers: Reshaping Immigrant Lives in Cold-War Canada* (Toronto: Between the Lines Press, 2006).

79. M. Susan Bland, "Henrietta the Homemaker, and Rosie the Riveter: Images of Women in Advertising in *Maclean's* Magazine, 1939–50," *Atlantis* 8, 2 (Spring 1983): 70.

80. For one of the most consistent formulations of this nature, see *La terre et le foyer*, 1945–1962; see also Micheline Dumont-Johnson, "La parole des femmes: Les revues féminines, 1938–68," in Fernand Dumont, Jean Hamelin, et Jean-Paul Montminy, eds., *Idéologies au Canada français, 1940–1976* (Québec: Presses de l'Université Laval, 1981) vol. 2, 5–45.

81. *Maclean's* (June 15, 1951).

82. Hilda Neatby, "Are Women Fulfilling Their Obligations to Society?" *Food for Thought* 13 (November 1952), 20–21.

83. Joan Sangster, "Doing Two Jobs: The Wage-Earning Mother, 1945–70," in Joy Parr, ed., *A Diversity of Women: Ontario 1945–1980* (Toronto: University of Toronto Press, 1995), 98–134; Franca Iacovetta, " Remaking Their Lives: Immigrants, Survivors, and Refugees," in Parr, ed., *A Diversity*, 135–67; Joy Parr, "Shopping for a Good Stove: A Parable about Gender, Design, and the Market," in Parr, ed., *A Diversity*; Valerie J. Korinek, *Roughing It in the Suburbs* (Toronto, University of Toronto Press, 2000), espec. chap. 7, "'How to Live in the Suburbs': Editorials and Articles in the Fifties," 257–307.

84. See, for example, Line Chamberland, "Remembering Lesbian Bars: Montreal, 1955–1975," in Wendy Mitchinson et al., eds., *Canadian Women: A Reader* (Toronto: Harcourt Brace, 1996), 352–79; Elise Chenier, *Strangers in our Midst: Sexual Deviance in Post-war Ontario* (Toronto: University of Toronto Press, 2008).

85. Suzann Buckley, "Efforts to Reduce Infant Matern[al] Mortality in Canada between the Two World Wars," *Atlantis* 2, 2, part 2 (Spring 1977): 76.

86. Norah L. Lewis, "Reducing Maternal Mortality in British Columbia: An Educational Process," in Latham and Pazdro, eds., *Not Just Pin Money*, 344; Jo Oppenheimer, "Childbirth in Ontario: The Transition from Home to Hospital in the Early Twentieth Century," *Ontario History* 75, 1 (March 1983): 36; France Laurendeau, "La médicalisation de l'accouchement," *Recherches sociographiques* 24, 2 (mai/août 1983): 204; Veronica Strong-Boag and Kathryn McPherson, "The Confinement of Women: Childbirth and Hospitalization in Vancouver, 1919–1939," *BC Studies* 69–70 (Spring/Summer 1986): 142–74; F. H. Leacy, ed. *Historical Statistics of Canada*, 2nd ed. (Ottawa: Statistics Canada, 1983), B1–14.

87. Margaret MacDonald, "Tradition as a Political Symbol in the New Midwifery in Canada," in Ivy Lynn Bourgeault, Cecilia Benoit and Robbie Davis Floyd, eds., *Reconceiving Midwifery* (Montreal and Kingston: McGill-Queen's Press, 2004), 48; Wendy Mitchinson, *Giving Birth in Canada, 1900–1950* (Toronto: University of Toronto Press, 2002), chap. 3, "Midwives Did Not Disappear," 69–103; Janet McNaughton, "Midwifery, Traditional Obstetric Care and Change in Newfoundland," paper presented to the Ethnobotany/Ethnomedicine Group, Memorial University, December 1989, 8–9.

88. Diary of Leila Middleton, March 29, 1930, courtesy of her granddaughter Sharon Trewartha; Katherine Arnup, *Education for Motherhood: Advice for Mothers in Twentieth-Century Canada* (Toronto: University of Toronto Press, 1994).

89. Mitchinson, *Giving Birth*, 233–34.

90. Katherine Arnup, "Education for Motherhood: Government Health Publications, Mothers and the State," paper presented to the Canadian Sociology and Anthropology Association, Winnipeg, 1986, 21.

91. *La Presse* (2 janvier 1930), 1 [our translation].

92. Veronica Strong-Boag, "Intruders in the Nursery: Childcare Professionals Reshape the Years One to Five, 1920–1940," in Parr, ed., *Childhood and Family*, 160–78; Norah L. Lewis, "Creating the Little Machine: Child Rearing in British Columbia, 1919–1939," *BC Studies* 56 (Winter 1982–1983): 44–60; Cynthia Comacchio, *Nations Are Built of Babies: Saving Ontario's Mothers and Children, 1900–1940* (Montreal: McGill-Queen's Press, 1993); Denyse Baillargeon, *Babies for a Nation: The Medicalisation of Motherhood in Quebec, 1910–1970* (Waterloo, ON: Wilfrid Laurier University Press, 2009).

93. Phyllis Knight and Rolf Knight, *A Very Ordinary Life* (Vancouver: New Star, 1974), 165.

94. Charles Vincent Madder, *History of the Canadian Home and School and Parent–Teacher Federation 1895–1963* (Toronto: Canadian Home and School and Parent–Teacher Federation, 1964), n.p.; Kari Dehli, "For Intelligent Motherhood and National Efficiency: The Toronto

Home and School Council, 1916–1930," in Ruby Heap and Alison Prentice, eds., *Gender and Education in Ontario: An Historical Reader* (Toronto: Canadian Scholars' Press, 1991), 147–64; L. J. Wilson, "Educational Role of the United Farm Women of Alberta," in David C. Jones, Nancy M. Sheehan, and Robert M. Stamp, eds., *Shaping the Schools of the Canadian West* (Calgary: Detselig, 1979), 124–35.

95. Ruth Adam, *A Woman's Place, 1910–1975* (London: Chatto and Windus, 1975), 165–67.

96. For a full discussion of advice literature on child-rearing during this period, see Katherine Arnup, *Education for Motherhood: Advice for Mothers in Twentieth Century Canada.*

97. Mona Gleason, *Normalizing the Ideal: Psychology, Schooling and the Family in Postwar Canada* (Toronto: University of Toronto Press, 1999); Denyse Baillargeon, "We Admire Modern Parents: L'École des parents du Quebec and the Post-war Quebec Family, 1943–1955," in Nancy Christie and Michael Gauvreau, eds., *Cultures of Citizenship in Post-war Canada, 1940–1955* (Montreal and Kingston: McGill-Queen's Press, 2003), 239–76.

98. Bryan D. Palmer, *Working-Class Experience: The Rise and Reconstitution of Canadian Labour, 1800–1980* (Toronto: Butterworths, 1983), 192–93.

99. Patricia Connelly, *Last Hired, First Fired: Women and the Canadian Work Force* (Toronto: Women's Press, 1978), 69.

100. Margaret Stewart and Doris French, *Ask No Quarter: A Biography of Agnes Macphail* (Toronto: Longmans, Green, 1959), 92.

101. *Winnipeg Free Press* (December 18, 1934), as quoted in Canada, House of Commons *Debates* (January 22, 1935), 84–85.

102. Joan Sangster, "Constructing the 'Eskimo' Wife: White Women's Travel Writing, Colonialism, and the Canadian North, 1940–60," in Magda Fahrni and Robert Rutherdale, eds., *Creating Postwar Canada: Community, Diversity and Dissent, 1945–75* (Vancouver: University of British Columbia Press, 2008), 38.

103. Mabel Crews Ringland, "What about Father?" *Maclean's* (August 1, 1928), 59–61. See also Stella E. Pines, "We Want Perfect Parents!" *Chatelaine* 1, 7 (September 1928), 12–13.

104. Margaret Lock, *Encounters with Aging: Mythologies of Menopause in Japan and North America* (Berkeley: University of California Press, 1993), 341–42; Wendy Mitchinson, "No Longer the Same Women: Medical Perceptions of Menopause, 1910–1950," *Canadian Bulletin of Medical History* 23, 1: 2006, 7–47.

105. Marion Hilliard, *A Woman Doctor Looks at Love and Life* (Garden City, N.Y.: Doubleday, 1957), 112.

106. Light and Pierson, eds., *No Easy Road*, chap. 2.

107. Angus McLaren and Arlene Tigar McLaren, *The Bedroom and the State: The Changing Practices and Politics of Contraception and Abortion in Canada, 1880–1997* (Toronto: Oxford University Press, 1997), 67.

108. Angus McLaren, "'What Has This to Do with Working Class Women?': Birth Control and the Canadian Left, 1900–1939," *Histoire sociale/Social History* 14, 28 (November 1981): 435–54; McLaren and McLaren, *The Bedroom and the State*, chaps. 3 and 4; Angus McLaren, "The First Campaigns for Birth Control Clinics in British Columbia," *Journal of Canadian Studies* 19, 3 (Fall 1984): 50–64.

109. McLaren and McLaren, *The Bedroom and the State*, 64, 84.

110. Marjorie Wild, *Elizabeth Bagshaw* (Toronto: Fitzhenry and Whiteside, 1984), 97; Catherine Annau, " Promoting Prophylatics: The Birth Control Society of Hamilton's Very Public Profile," *Ontario History* 90, 1, Spring 1998: 49–68.

111. Le Collectif Clio, *L'histoire des femmes au Québec*, 250–51; Diane Dodd, "The Canadian Birth Control Movement on Trial, 1936–1937," *Histoire sociale/Social History* 16, 32 (November 1983): 411–28.

112. McLaren and McLaren, *The Bedroom and the State, 132–33;* Michael Gauvreau, *The Catholic Origins of Quebec's Quiet Revolution. 1931–1970* (Montreal and Kingston: McGill-Queen's University Press, 1995), 194–200; Michael Gauvreau, "The Emergence of Personalist Feminism: Catholicism, and the Marriage-Preparation Movement in Quebec, 1940–1966," in Nancy Christie, ed., *Households of Faith: Family, Gender, and Community in Canada, 1760–1969* (Montreal and Kingston: McGill-Queen's Press, 2002), 319–47.

113. Library and Archives Canada, Canadian Council on Social Development, MG 28, I10 vol. 13, file 497, *Aid to Dependent Mothers and Children in Canada: Social Policy behind Our Legislation*; Suzanne Morton, "Women on Their Own: Single Mothers in Working-Class Halifax in the 1920s," *Acadiensis* 21, 2 (Spring 1992): 95; Margaret Hillyard Little, *No Car, No Radio, No Liquor Permit: The Moral Regulation of Single Mothers in Ontario, 1920–1997* (Toronto: Oxford University Press, 1997), chaps. 1–5; Marie-Paule Malouin, *L'Univers des enfants en difficulté au Québec entre 1940 et 1960* (Saint Laurent, QC: Bellarmin, 1996); Robin Jarvis Brownlie, "Intimate Surveillance: Indian Affairs, Colonization, and the Regulation of Aboriginal Women's Sexuality," in Pickles and Rutherdale, eds., *Contact Zones,* 179–204.

114. Brigitte Kitchen, "The Introduction of Family Allowances in Canada," in Allan Moscovitch and Jim Albert, eds., *The Benevolent State: The Growth of Welfare in Canada* (Toronto: Garamond, 1987), 222–41; Dominique Marshall, translated by Nicola Doone Danby, *The Social Origins of the Welfare State: Quebec Families, Compulsory Education, and Family Allowances, 1940–1955* (Waterloo, ON: Wilfrid Laurier University Press, 1998); Thérèse F. Casgrain, *A Woman in a Man's World*, translated by Joyce Marshall (Toronto: McClelland and Stewart, 1972), 112–14.

115. Theresa Healy, "Resisting State Sanctioned Violence—Women's Strategies versus State Policy: Vancouver Relief Programmes in the 1930s," paper presented to the Canadian Historical Association, Calgary, 1994, 7; James Struthers, "Grizzled Old Men and Lonely Widows: Constructing the Single Elderly as a Social Problem in Canada's Welfare State, 1945–1967," in Nancy Christie and Michael Gauvreau, eds., *Mapping the Margins: The Family and Social Discipline in Canada, 1700–1975* (Montreal and Kingston: McGill University Press, 2004), 361.

116. Pierre Berton, *The Dionne Years* (Toronto: McClelland and Stewart, 1977), 81; Mariana Valverde, "Representing Childhood: The Multiple Fathers of the Dionne Quintuplets," in Carol Smart, ed., *Regulating Womanhood: Historical Essays on Marriage, Motherhood and Sexuality* (London: Routledge, 1992), 119–46; Allan Roy Dafoe, *Dr. Dafoe's Guidebook for Mothers* (New York: Julian Messner, 1936), xii; Gaétan Gervais, *Les jumelles Dionne et l'Ontario français, 1934–1944* (Sudbury, ON: Prise de parole, 2000).

117. Suzanne Morton, "Nova Scotia and Its Unmarried Mothers, 1945–1975," in Christie and Gauvreau, eds., *Mapping the Margins;* Andrée Lévesque, "Deviant Anonymous: Single Mothers at the *Hôpital de la Miséricorde* Montreal, 1929–39," *Historical Papers/Communications historiques* (1984): 175; see also Lévesque, *Making and Breaking the Rules: Women in Quebec, 1919–1939*, translated by Yvonne M. Klein (Toronto: McClelland and Stewart, 1994); Karen Balcom, "Scandal and Social Policy: The Ideal Maternity Home and the Evolution of Social Policy in Nova Scotia, 1940–1951," *Acadiensis* XXXI, 2 (Spring 2002): 3–37.

118. Angus McLaren, "The Creation of a Haven for 'Human Thoroughbreds': The Sterilization of the Feeble-Minded and the Mentally Ill in British Columbia," *Canadian Historical Review* 67, 2 (June 1986): 146.

119. Light and Pierson, eds., *No Easy Road*, chap. 3; see also Nicole Neatley, "Preparing for the Working World: Women at Queen's during the 1920s," in Heap and Prentice, eds., *Gender and Education*, 329–51; and Gwethalyn Graham, "Women, Are they Human?" *Canadian Forum* 16, 1 (December 1936): 21–23.

120. Varpu Lindstrom-Best, "'I Won't Be A Slave!': Finnish Domestics in Canada, 1911–30," in Jean Burnet, ed., *Looking into My Sister's Eyes: An Exploration in Women's History* (Toronto: Multicultural History Society of Ontario, 1986), 35.

121. Nicole Laurin et al., *A la recherche d'un monde oublié: les communautés religieuses de femmes au Québec de 1900 à 1970* (Montreal: *Le Jour,* 1991); Heidi MacDonald, "Entering the Convent as Coming of Age in the 1930s," in Elizabeth Smyth, ed., *Changing Habits: Women's Religious Orders in Canada* (Ottawa: Novalis, Saint Paul University, 2007), 99; Smyth, ed., 7; "Micheline Dumont-Johnson, "Les communautés religieuses et la condition féminine," *Recherches sociographiques* 19, 1 (janvier/avril 1978): 90; Marta Danylewycz, *Taking the Veil: An Alternative to Marriage, Motherhood, and Spinsterhood in Quebec, 1840–1920* (Toronto: McClelland and Stewart, 1987), 17.

122. Joy Parr, *The Gender of Breadwinners: Women, Men, and Change in Two Industrial Towns 1880–1950* (Toronto: University of Toronto Press, 1990).

123. The Lesbians Making History Collective, "People Think This Didn't Happen in Canada—But It Did," *Fireweed* 28 (Spring 1989): 81–86; Duder, "The Spreading Depths," 403–6, 290–92; Patricia T. Rooke, "Public Figure, Private Woman: Same-sex Support Structures in the Life of Charlotte Whitton," *International Journal of Women's Studies* 6, 5 (November/December 1983): 412–28.

124. E. R. Forbes and A. A. Mackenzie, eds., *Four Years with the Demon Rum 1925–1929: The Autobiography and Diary of Temperance Inspector Clifford Rose* (Fredericton: Acadiensis Press, 1980): 32–34, 42–43; Sangster, "'Pardon Tales,'" 167.

125. Marlene Epp, *Women without Men*, 149.

CHAPTER ELEVEN

Proving Themselves in Public Life

Speaking to the Canadian Federation of Business and Professional Women's Clubs in 1933, Josephine Dauphinee of Vancouver challenged the members to "study, read, discuss, . . . and learn to draw conclusions from your thinking. The men will welcome you to their councils and with equal rights, men and women will confer together over the problems of the day."[1]

This hopeful and confident attitude was typical of activist women in the inter-war period. These were not inactive "doldrum years", as some analysts depicted them. Buoyed by their achievements and by the recognition they had received during World War I, women's organizations were determined to solidify their gains and extend their social, economic, cultural, and political influence. Once the federal and provincial franchises had been achieved for most women, however, women's suffrage was no longer a shared goal. Temperance had also ceased to be a major issue with the introduction in many provinces of government regulations controlling liquor distribution and sales. In addition, new secular agencies took over many functions from evangelical-based organizations, such as the YWCA. The child welfare and public health programs long advocated by women's groups gradually moved forward with the establishment of the Federal Department of Health and its Child Welfare Division (1919), and the development of similar provincial and municipal agencies. Staffed in some cases by former activists from the women's reform movement, these agencies also opened up career opportunities for women as professional social work gradually replaced voluntary efforts.[2]

Nonetheless, there was still much work to be done, and through their public involvement, women continued to work for and on behalf of women. The exigencies of the Great Depression and World War II focused their efforts, and they put the skills they had honed through work in professional, volunteer, and religious organizations to use in a variety of ways. And once peace returned, many women's organizations renewed their efforts to achieve the equality with men for which their predecessors had worked for almost a century.

ORGANIZED WOMEN

In the 1920s, large numbers of women, mostly single and from the middle-class, joined career-related organizations that sought to establish women's equality with men.[3] One example was the Federation of Medical Women of Canada, established in 1924 to provide women doctors with a forum in which to meet, exchange ideas, and discuss problems. A founding member was Dr. Elizabeth Bagshaw, who was later responsible for founding a birth control clinic in Hamilton. A year after its creation, the federation had 65 members, drawn from all provinces. Another example of a separate organization for professional women was the Canadian Women's Press Club, which by the 1920s had branches in Winnipeg, Edmonton, Toronto, Vancouver, Ottawa, Halifax, and Saint John. These and other groups, such as the Federation of Women Teachers' Associations of Ontario and the Canadian Nurses' Association, were now able to launch vigorous campaigns aimed at enhancing the status of their members as professionals and assisting them in an increasingly difficult labour market. During the 1930s, the Canadian Federation of University Women, for example, worked hard to find teaching positions for those few academic women who were in the job market. Women doctors, teachers, nurses, and journalists worked to improve their salaries and to develop special training and career opportunities.[4]

Local Business and Professional Women's Clubs (BPWs) had started before the war, beginning in Toronto in 1910; in 1930 they joined together in the Canadian Federation of Business and Professional Women's Clubs. Their chair was Dorothy Heneker of Montreal, then the only Canadian woman to hold both Bachelor of Civil Law and Bachelor of Common Law degrees. Active in business, and working as a subordinate in her father's law firm because Quebec regulations would not allow women to practise law, Heneker was keenly aware of the disadvantages endured by women working in white-collar occupations. Others shared her concern, and by 1937 there were more than 2 000 members in Business and Professional Women's Clubs in urban centres across Canada.[5] From their inception, the BPW clubs were committed to equality between men and women and sought to improve the social and economic conditions of middle-class career women by promoting training and advancement for women in their chosen fields. Armed with their own survey on unemployment, in 1933 the Federation's National Board endorsed the principle of unemployment insurance, but added the proviso that "any legislation which might be introduced in respect thereof shall apply equally to men and women."[6]

The local BPW clubs provided opportunities for women with similar jobs to meet socially as well as to discuss issues of common interest. In the Montreal club, for example, bi-weekly talks covered topics ranging from parliamentary procedure to industrial working conditions for women in China and Australia. The club worked to establish a national health insurance scheme; lobbied the Quebec government for provincial and municipal political rights for women; provided funding and volunteers for other groups, such as the Big Sisters' Association and the Montreal Girls' Association; and, during the Depression, cooperated with the YWCA in registering unemployed women and locating jobs for them. During the Depression, the Federation also protested the dismissal of female bank clerks.[7]

While career-oriented groups sought equality for women with men, older established organizations such as the National Council of Women of Canada (NCWC) continued to focus on motherhood and the protection of home life, which they saw as necessary stabilizing factors after the upheavals of war. The NCWC largely ignored female career aspirations when it did not criticize them as a threat to the home, and it approved of only a limited range of occupations, such as domestic service, nursing, and teaching, and then only for unmarried women. The Council's conservative orientation discouraged many young professional women's groups from joining, and even antagonized former supporters. The Canadian Women's Press Club, for instance, ended its affiliation with the NCWC in 1925, and 23 local councils made the same choice within the next five years. During the Depression, when jobs were scarce, the NCWC joined those Canadians who argued that working women should not be competing with men for employment. Both the national and local councils did debate the plight of unemployed women, however, and they undertook relief work in many localities. Council discussions were pervaded, however, with concern that jobless women would turn to prostitution and with suspicion that they preferred relief to domestic service jobs. To counteract these perceived problems, the NCWC endorsed the creation of self-help groups where unemployed women could come together to knit, sew, or quilt; it also endorsed the upgrading of domestic work. Member associations were encouraged to establish domestic training courses, and the Council adopted a Code for Household Workers, designed to improve working conditions and combat women's reluctance to accept jobs as domestics.[8]

In spite of its conservative stance on women's paid employment, NCWC membership grew from 150 000 in 1919 to half a million by 1940. Most of the increase came from new group affiliates at the local level in the growing towns and cities of Ontario, and these enlarged local councils increasingly came to dominate national policy formation.[9] Continuing its tradition of family-focused reform, the National Council backed and monitored mothers' allowance legislation, and continued to address the issue of child welfare in the home, in institutions, and in schools. Concerned with marriage breakdown, it urged equal treatment for male and female divorce petitioners, the establishment of divorce courts in all provinces, an increase in the age of consent for marriage (then as low as 12 years for girls with parental permission), the treatment of adultery as a criminal offence, and enhancement of legal remedies for deserted wives. To safeguard the financial position of wives and mothers, it also proposed amendments to the provincial dower laws. However, although local councils on occasion became involved in consumer issues, such as boycotts to eliminate large commercial and industrial profits on some products, the NCWC's consumer policy generally resembled that of the Canadian Manufacturers' Association (CMA). For example, it endorsed the CMA's "Made-in-Canada" campaign and generally accepted the promotion of consumer goods. The pro-manufacturing and central Canadian outlook of the national organization had its impact, alienating many rural and western affiliates; by the late 1920s, in fact, the major organized farm women's associations had left the NCWC. Still, by the outbreak of World War II, National Council members had reason to feel that their work had helped to achieve considerable improvement in the quality of life enjoyed by Canadian women. Thanks at least in part to the NCWC's efforts, the care of the old and the sick had improved; women had benefitted from mothers' allowances; infant mortality and tuberculosis rates had declined; new urban parks served children's recreational needs; and in some regions innovative education programs had been put into place.[10]

For members of the Woman's Christian Temperance Union (WCTU) the primary focus remained alcohol abuse, but they expanded their activities to a variety of other fronts. Some sections concentrated on prison reform and during the 1930s a number of western locals were involved in the Canadian women's peace movement. After the defeat of Prohibition in various provinces in the 1920s and the introduction of government liquor control, the WCTU directed even more attention toward educating the public about the dangers of alcohol. Members continued their campaigns for temperance textbooks and courses in schools, held essay contests, and encouraged teachers to inculcate the virtues of temperance in their classrooms. Their gains are hard to assess. Drunkenness may have become less publicly visible in Canada as a result of the organization's efforts, but a ban on alcohol consumption was impossible to achieve. Prohibition was increasingly out of step with a society that no longer regarded the use of alcohol as a major social evil.[11]

Other organizations, notably the rural-focused United Farm Women of Alberta (UFWA) and the Women's Institutes, expanded both their influence and their programs. Established in 1915 as an auxiliary to the United Farmers of Alberta (UFA), the United Farm Women of Alberta aimed both to educate members for self-realization and to improve rural health services and education. Directed by a provincial board, the UFWA encouraged its member groups to undertake local projects, such as promoting the construction of libraries, to which the provincial body donated books. Local groups also organized lectures and study groups on topics including literature, music, immigration, rural health care, and schooling. Irene Parlby, first president of the UFWA, was elected under the United Farmers of Alberta banner as a member of the provincial legislature in 1921. She recognized the constraints of rural life and saw the farm women's organization as a vehicle for a lifetime learning process and as a practical outlet for her idealism and that of her peers. One of those very active and visionary peers was Susan Gunn, a former teacher, president of the United Farm Women of Alberta from 1924 to 1929, and a dynamic member throughout the 1920s of the Education Committee of both the UFWA and the UFA. Parlby and Gunn were dedicated to progressive educational reform, and through their countless speeches and writings did much to promote improvements in the province's rural schools. Speaking of her involvement in the agrarian movement during the inter-war period, Susan Gunn recalled the following:

> I was caught up in the work of the UFA and the UFWA. It was like a crusade, through co-operative effort we envisaged a new Heaven and a new earth, co-operative stores were started, municipal hospitals, the great wheat pools.
>
> . . . Then along came the devastating thirties and we were flat on our backs. It took us a long and weary time to get on our feet.[12]

As Alberta's Minister without Portfolio from 1921 to 1935, with responsibility for matters relating to women and children, Parlby continued to support and encourage farm women to think beyond domestic questions and to broaden their horizons. One of the many ways that the United Farm Women promoted this objective was to organize, in conjunction with the provincial Department of Agriculture, annual conferences known as "Farm Women's Week" at the University of Alberta. Efforts to make this event as accessible as possible included the provision for preschool children to attend at no extra cost.[13]

The provision of continuing education for rural women and close cooperation with provincial departments of agriculture were also central characteristics of the Women's Institute (WI) movement that flourished after the war. The Institutes, or Homemakers' Clubs as some local groups were called, engaged paid lecturers to speak about household science and agriculture, and these proved extremely popular. Although the development of domestic skills remained a primary concern, many local Institutes broadened their interests. The British Columbia Women's Institutes, for example, included business methods for young women as well as health care among the many other topics studied. When the province's Department of Health decided in the late 1920s to establish provincial health centres, it called on the WIs for support of its plan. The Alberta Women's Institutes undertook a wide range of community projects, including hot-lunch programs for schoolchildren, the establishment of public libraries, and relief work during the Depression. Other initiatives, such as those taken up by many Ontario Institutes, included rural school medical inspections and the establishment of community halls, parks, and skating rinks. Contrary to critics' view of the WIs as conservative and concerned only with reinforcing the status quo, membership empowered many rural women who, by the 1920s, were campaigning for positions on school boards and lobbying local and provincial governments for public health and education reform.[14]

In Quebec, the convergence of government, clerical, and rural women's interests in strengthening rural life had fostered the development and growth of French-Canadian Women's Institutes, called *Cercles de fermières* (farm women's clubs). In 1919 there were already 34 locals amalgamated under a provincial council, and the *Cercles* were among the founding members of the Federated Women's Institutes of Canada established in that year. Through their magazine, *La bonne fermière*, and through lectures, study groups, and exhibitions, the *Cercles* promoted the upgrading of homes and the development of farm skills.[15] Like the Women's Institutes, the *Cercles* were encouraged and subsidized by the state; also like the WIs, they reinforced the philosophy of separate spheres. They nevertheless provided opportunities for female organization and self-development. Perhaps more important, the Institutes and the *Cercles* opened new economic ventures for their members. By publicizing rural women's traditional activities through exhibitions and sales of farm produce and handicrafts designed for both domestic use and the tourist industry, they validated farm women's work and attempted to professionalize it. Théodora Dupont, the vice-president of the Saint-Denis *Cercle*, established in 1921, recalled the economic advantages of her membership:

> The Minister of Agriculture gave us two hives of bees per circle. Selected by lot, I was the happy winner of one of the hives with all the necessary operating equipment. . . . The first beneficiaries of these gift-hives had to give their first swarm to another farm woman who did not have one,

in my opinion an excellent idea. After that, an inspector came several times in the season, without charge, to give us the required instructions. The following spring, each farm woman received fourteen Plymouth Rock chicken eggs . . . for us to incubate, which gave us the chance to improve our flock.[16]

During the 1920s, Canadian rural women's organizations served as a model that women from other countries copied; in 1933, women from around the world met to create the Associated Country Women of the World.

Women belonging to Canada's racial, ethnic, and religious minorities also continued to organize and expand their own associations. Most of these had three related objectives: (1) to preserve and enhance their group culture, (2) to help members of their communities adjust to Canadian life and overcome prejudice, and (3) to maintain contacts with and assist members of their group outside Canada. Women's organizations, like the Eureka Club of Toronto, focused on promoting black culture and welfare activities. By 1920, the existence of various religious, charitable, and educational groups organized by African-Canadian women in Nova Scotia prompted the holding of the first Convention of Coloured Women in Halifax. Another group, the Hour-A-Day Study Club, was established in Windsor, Ontario, in 1934 to bring African-Canadian women there together for self-improvement, to organize cultural programs, to promote the study of black history, and to foster mutual understanding through involvement in the Windsor community. Club members were also involved with mixed-sex organizations, such as the Windsor Coloured Citizens' Association, formed at the beginning of the Depression, to fight discrimination in all aspects of life for the local African-Canadian population. The Universal Negro Improvement Association benefitted as well from the significant contributions of Afro-Canadian women, and many wives of Afro-Canadian porters became active in auxiliaries of the Brotherhood of Sleeping Car Porters.[17]

Some Jewish women, mainly of western European origin, worked together in the 1920s and during the Depression in the National Council of Jewish Women and in other Jewish women's groups. Through fundraising and volunteer work they supported schools, scholarships, orphanages, care for the aged, and summer camps. In 1913, Mrs. Slova Greenberg founded the Ezras Noshim, a mutual benefit organization for Toronto's Jewish immigrant women, for the purpose of visiting sick members and assisting with housework during illness. As the organization matured, it enlarged its welfare mandate. Prompted by the case of a pious 90-year-old woman living in a home for incurables who could not communicate her requirements for kosher food in English, Ezras Noshim organized the establishment of the Jewish Old Folks Home, completed in 1920. The following year, with other women, this association mobilized its members' considerable experience at door-to-door fundraising to the task of establishing a Jewish Hospital. Another group, the Zionist Hadassah, formed during World War I and dedicated to providing social services to Jews in Palestine, attracted more recently arrived eastern European Jewish women. This increased social action by Jewish women resulted not only from the growth of the community but also in reaction to the often blatant anti-Semitism of the period. Assimilationist pressures were strong. Following a number of complaints in 1919, the Toronto Board of Education successfully demanded that Ida Siegel's Mothers' Club at

Hester How School discontinue the use of Yiddish at its meetings and ordered that only English be used.[18]

Other women's groups were organized around the national identity of immigrants. There were many examples. Ukrainian women, for example, formed organizations that reflected the political and ideological orientation of their members. Under the auspices of the Communist-related Association of United Ukrainian Canadians, women members formed a Women's Section in 1922, and set up branches in many localities. Ukrainian Orthodox women formed their own association, the Ukrainian Women's Association of Canada, in Saskatoon in 1926. Its objectives were to promote the Ukrainian Orthodox faith, to preserve Ukrainian culture and traditions, and to provide moral and financial assistance to the citizens of the Ukraine. For their part, women in the Ladies' Section of the Macedonian Political Organization, founded in Toronto in 1927, dominated church and community social life. They raised funds and animated the community to support the achievement of a free and independent Macedonia while at the same time promoting and maintaining awareness of the Macedonian culture. Armenian women joined the Armenian Relief Society, which had Canadian branches even before World War I. As survivors of the Turkish massacres arrived during the 1920s, membership and activities expanded to include assisting Armenians internationally and locally; supporting Armenian choirs, theatre, poetry, and lectures; and expanding knowledge of the Armenian language. In addition, Syrian women in Montreal founded a non-sectarian Ladies Aid Society in 1930. The Society's mission—to provide financial and other relief to needy Syrian families—met initially with opposition from the clergy, who claimed that no poor Syrian families existed. The women had amassed facts and figures, however, and eventually won support.[19]

As shown by these various examples, women made vital contributions to the maintenance of communal identity and adaptation. Moreover, not all women's groups were content to play merely supportive roles. Leaders of the various Zionist women's organizations that emerged after 1900, such as the Daughters of Zion or the Herzl Ladies Society, actively sought roles in Zionist politics. The Pioneer Women's Organization, a Jewish socialist group composed mainly of working-class women born in eastern Europe, left the male-dominated Labour Zionist movement in 1925 because the women were disenchanted with their exclusion from the decision-making process. This independent group pursued overtly feminist goals, supporting programs in Palestine and North America aimed at increasing women's and children's political and social awareness.[20]

Women's clubs and organizations were the training ground for many of the women who were eventually to become active in public life. One notable example was Florence Bird, later head of the Royal Commission on the Status of Women in Canada, who gained organizational experience in Montreal and Winnipeg during the 1930s and early 1940s. In her autobiography, she gives credit to the associations in which she participated, not only for their many tangible achievements but also for their role in developing individual women's potential.[21] For many women, this potential became fully realized when women's organizations were mobilized for public service during World War II and responded enthusiastically to the patriotic call for their selfless, unpaid efforts. As had been the case during World War I, the work that involved the greatest number of Canadian women was volunteer work. This time, however, through the Women's

Ukrainian women's convention, Saskatoon, 1957.
Source: Glenbow Archives NA-3386-13

Voluntary Services Division, created in the autumn of 1941, the federal government sought to coordinate and control their activities. Some women's organizations resented this intervention, since they had already begun their own programs.[22]

As wartime production expanded, employment levels soared, and the average Canadian's purchasing power grew rapidly. At the same time, there were fewer civilian goods available, and as a result there were shortages, a sharp increase in the cost of living, and the threat of an uncontrollable price–wage spiral. To control inflation, the federal government created the Wartime Prices and Trade Board to establish production quotas and maximum prices for many civilian goods. Various women's organizations, such as the National and Local Councils of Women, made it their responsibility to see that the Board's price guidelines were followed. Impressed by their price-monitoring activities, the board moved to create a Consumer Branch with the well-known editor of *Chatelaine*, Byrne Hope Saunders, as its head. Subsequently, 14 regional committees coordinated the efforts of more than 10 000 liaison officers supplied by women's voluntary organizations; these women informed consumers of the board's regulations, policed prices, and laid the basis for the establishment of the Canadian Consumers' Association when the war ended. In rural areas the Women's Institutes were especially active in promoting women's war services, and in mobilizing women for agricultural production. In British

Columbia and Ontario, dominion–provincial programs were established to mobilize farm labour; by 1943 nearly 13 000 farm women, urban working women, teachers, and students were enrolled in Ontario's program.[23]

In addition to providing the personnel needed to implement many of the government's wartime civilian programs, some women's organizations continued their efforts to influence social conditions and public policy. For example, in 1941 the Provincial Council of Women of Ontario started intensive efforts that 10 years later produced women's eligibility for jury service in the province.[24] After the war, women's voluntary organizations turned with renewed energy to their own social and political agendas. The media-generated image of the happy housewife engrossed in her domestic life belied the reality of many women's active participation in public life.[25] When wartime-imposed price controls were lifted, consumer activism mobilized wives from different class and ethnic backgrounds to organize Canada-wide protests over rising food costs. For example, in 1947–48, Montreal housewives boycotted grocery and butcher stores and lobbied the provincial government to allow for the sale of margarine, a cheaper substitute for butter.[26] Most established groups continued to engage in traditional service activities, but also paid sustained attention to issues ranging from taxation and the status of Aboriginal Canadians to urban planning, peace, and the arts. Unfortunately, contemporary media comments were often patronizing and dismissive, identifying the groups as outlets for the idle rich. "Like most club women everywhere," read one typical account, members of the National Council of Women of Canada are "great hands for passing resolutions." Their "resounding outcries against strong drink, atomic warfare and the traffic in Chinese slave girls," the report went on, "come in for some gentle kidding." Such descriptions trivialized the important social issues—such as alcohol abuse, militarism, and the international sex-trade in women and children—with which the members of the NCWC were grappling. Critics also ignored the NCWC's goals in relation to women's status, as outlined in its 1943 policy document "Women in the Post-War Period." It called for more female representation in the political and public arenas, equal pay for equal work, and the elimination of discrimination against the employment of married women and against women more generally in various lines of employment. Nor were contemporary commentators aware of the extraordinarily diverse membership of the Local Councils of Women, which in 1953 included several women's auxiliaries of the United Mineworkers of America and the Locomotive Engineers and Firemen. And, along with its core of Protestant groups, the NCWC had both Jewish and Catholic member organizations.[27]

In the period following World War II, the National Council of Women and the Canadian Federation of Business and Professional Women's clubs lobbied the federal cabinet annually, and played a significant role in advancing the social, political, and economic status of women. In the late 1940s, for example, the BPW protested a federal government employment posting that limited applications for the position of Regional Director of Family Allowances for New Brunswick to male residents of the Maritimes. As a result of the BPW protest, the job went to its nominee, Muriel McQueen Fergusson, a New Brunswick lawyer who was later appointed a senator; in 1972 she became the first woman Speaker of the Senate. The BPW also succeeded in having the federal Civil Service Commission drop the wording "for men only" from advertisements for many positions, and also petitioned the federal government to open the competition for diplomatic appointments to women. Similarly, the BPW inundated the cabinet with requests to place women on the Civil Service Commission, the Unemployment Insurance Commission, the Board of the CBC, the Board of Broadcast Governors, and various royal commissions, as well as calling for the appointment of a woman senator from each province. Since these requests were invariably accompanied by an up-to-date list of qualified women candidates, the BPW was sometimes successful. Nor was the private sector neglected, for the BPW called for the appointment of women to the boards of corporations, including chartered banks. But women's groups extended their campaigns well beyond the appointment to prominent positions of a few token women from their own class or from their own organizations. Concerted lobbying resulted in 1954 in the creation within the federal Department of Labour of the vitally important Women's Bureau, which was devoted specifically to gathering and disseminating information on all facets of women's employment.

Another significant achievement of women's groups was the passage of "equal pay for equal work" legislation by the federal government and nearly all the provinces. In Ontario, women's groups showed how they worked together. The Women's Committee of the Ontario CCF was instrumental in having a bill introduced in 1949 that would have banned sex-based employment discrimination and required equal pay, but the proposed legislation was defeated.[28] One year later, 21 YWCAs set up public affairs committees to promote anti-discrimination employment laws. It was against this background that Margaret Hyndman, the national president of the BPW, led a delegation in 1951 to meet with Ontario's provincial premier, Leslie Frost. She argued for inclusion of the principle of equal pay in the forthcoming Fair Employment Practices law. Despite the growing pressure from women's organizations, Frost expressed his reservations; but he invited the women to present a brief outlining what the likely impact would be. Since Hyndman was a lawyer, he also asked her to draft an equal pay bill. Within a week, not only had these submissions been delivered, but every member of the provincial legislature had been lobbied and supplied with a copy of the Universal Declaration of Human Rights, with the appropriate sections dealing with discrimination on the basis of sex and equal pay underlined. Co-sponsored by Agnes Macphail, who was now a member of the Ontario legislature, and communist Rae Lucock, the other woman MPP, the Female Employees Fair Remuneration Act was introduced on the symbolically significant date of March 8—International Women's Day—and on January 1, 1952, Ontario became the first province to put equal pay legislation into effect. The BPW subsequently lobbied other provincial governments to enact similar legislation; by 1960, with the exception of Quebec and Newfoundland, all had passed equal pay laws.[29] In 1955, the BPW asked one of its own members, Ellen Fairclough, the Conservative labour critic, to introduce in the House of Commons a private member's bill requiring equal pay for equal work. Although the bill was defeated, the Liberal government took up the cause. According to the federal minister of labour, the government's 1956 decision to implement equal pay legislation to cover more than 70 000 women working under federal jurisdiction was made largely because of the pressure exerted by the BPW and by representatives of the National Council of Women, including the minister' own wife.

Other large national groups, such as the Federated Women's Institutes of Canada (FWIC), also expanded their activities. The FWIC's membership alone numbered 95 000 by 1958. At the national level, this organization, too, lobbied for the introduction of equal pay for equal work. In conjunction with universities and provincial departments of agriculture, local institutes offered evening courses specifically designed for married women in paid employment. As noted by Gladys Manness, a woman from a small rural community in Manitoba, membership in the WI was important because it provided the opportunity to discuss national and international issues: "It's broadened our outlook." Stories abound of the extraordinary lengths to which rural women went to attend WI meetings, especially in wintertime. One devoted New Brunswick member, Mrs. J. D. Ross, found herself "snowbound at home atop a hill and unable to persuade her husband to shovel her out." Undaunted, she climbed aboard her son's "flying saucer" sled. "With a half-knitted afghan in one hand and a fresh pie in the other she sped downhill and thumbed a ride" to the Institute meeting; by the time she arrived home, the path had been shovelled.[30]

By 1940, the *Cercles de fermières* in Quebec had organized their 645 clubs (with 28 000 members) into district federations that were still funded by the provincial government and not under the institutional control of the Catholic Church. In 1944, some 80 percent of the club's members resisted Church attempts to incorporate them into a new, church-dominated auxiliary of the Catholic farmers' union. This assertion of autonomy was not easy for practising Catholic women, for the Church went so far as to deny the sacraments in its attempts to control organizational affiliation; 15 years later, it was reported that some priests would still refuse to celebrate Mass at conferences sponsored by the *Cercles*.[31] Despite clerical opposition, the *Cercles*' membership had grown to 50 000 by 1945, and the provincial organization developed a program that included a larger emphasis on public policy. In 1947, for example, it drew attention to the economic value of work performed by women in the home, and in 1955 its annual congress urged committees working on the reform of the Quebec Civil Code to increase their efforts to improve the situation of married women in the province. It was in large part due to the concerted efforts of women's groups that the antiquated Family Code was finally reformed in 1964, under the sponsorship of Quebec's first elected woman provincial legislator, Claire Kirkland-Casgrain.[32]

As the farming population decreased in size and social importance in Canada, members of rural women's groups were less likely to be women directly involved with farm production; their interests accordingly widened. For example, in the 1940s and 1950s, Ontario WIs researched, wrote, and published an important series of local histories, the *Tweedsmuir Histories*, that are still widely used. In 1957 the Church-controlled group of Quebec farm women changed its name to the *Union catholique des femmes rurales* (UCFR) so that it could recruit women who lived in rural areas and small communities, regardless of their connection to agriculture. The UCFR, which was about the same size as the *Cercles*, stressed its independence of state funding; topics discussed in its study groups included feminist issues like contraception.[33]

Professional organizations such as the Federation of Women Teachers' Association of Ontario and the Canadian Women's Press Club focused their post-war efforts on enhancing the working conditions and status of their members: for teachers this meant seeking equal pay with male colleagues, while for women journalists it involved working to obtain access to traditional male assignments.

Women's organizations with more specialized membership also continued to be active. In 1951, African-Canadian women formed the Canadian Negro Women's Club, through which they raised money for scholarships and promoted work on the history of blacks in Canada. And Mennonite women doubled their fundraising efforts to assist fellow immigrants and refugees living in displaced person's camps. The well-established organizations of Ukrainian women also responded to the plight of compatriots in displaced persons' camps in Europe, with particular attention given to single mothers, widows, and orphans. As well as sending relief parcels of food, medicine, and clothing, the women's groups protested forced repatriations, lobbied for admission of refugees, and sponsored kindergartens in the camps. Many of the Ukrainian refugees who then made their way to Canada were strongly anti-Communist, and a new Women's Association emerged within the nationalistic Canadian League for the Liberation of the Ukraine.[34] The National Council of Jewish Women had a continuing commitment to promote social legislation and create social services, especially for the elderly. In addition to assisting Jewish refugees and supporting many projects in the newly created state of Israel, the Council gave considerable financial support to the Canadian Mental Health Association, the Canadian Red Cross, and other volunteer groups. Like other federated women's organizations, the Council forwarded to federal and provincial politicians the resolutions passed at regular national meetings; in the postwar years, the topics of these resolutions included a Canadian bill of rights, family planning, and equal pay for equal work.[35]

The Canadian Negro Women's Club 10th Anniversary Banquet and Ball, October 1961, King Edward Hotel, Toronto.

Source: Ontario Black History Society

RELIGION

Religion remained a central focus in most Canadians' lives, and women continued to provide essential support to their religious denominations in myriad ways. And, whether they worked in volunteer organizations or in poorly paid positions as was the case for missionary work, women gained self-confidence in their abilities and, for some, access to careers frequently denied to them elsewhere.[36] Major Protestant women's groups had originally included the conversion and assimilation of the country's immigrant and Aboriginal female populations in their home mission mandates. By the 1920s, however, they began to alter their policies in light of resistance from the targeted communities as well as evolving notions of missionary work. For example, the Methodist and Presbyterian Woman's Missionary Societies that operated residential school homes for the daughters of Alberta's Ukrainian settlers gradually widened their training programs to emphasize service to the wider community. As the school homes closed in the inter-war period, medical and community missions occupied increasing amounts of the missionary societies' time and resources; then, as government and Ukrainian-led community services grew, these activities also declined. Although early efforts directed to conversion and acculturation failed, by providing essential medical, educational, and other services to neglected outlying communities, the religious societies met important needs.[37] Sometimes the services these religious societies provided unintentionally subverted the missionaries' aims. This was certainly the case for the young Wet'suwet'en girls who attended the Lejac Residential School in British Columbia during the inter-war period. Run by the Oblates of Mary Immaculate, the school's basic curriculum was designed to train future farm wives. Not only did the school's students resist efforts to eradicate traditional Aboriginal practices, but in the 1940s they used the literacy skills they had developed at the school to spearhead community action and protests against harsh conditions at Lejac. And, after the ban against Aboriginal women's participation in band politics was lifted in 1951, some of the former students became the first women to stand for and win elected band office.[38]

As with secular society, women from different ethnic and racial groups worked in their own religious organizations. Mennonite church women, for example, organized sewing circles to support charitable work at home and abroad. The scope of the work undertaken by the sewing circles was impressive, and they raised significant amounts of money to support the work of the Mennonite Central Committee. For example, in the 1920s the sewing circle in the village of Mannheim near Kitchener, Ontario, crafted quilts and comforters, knitted clothing, made soap, canned produce for use in various Mennonite institutions, carried out home visits to the elderly and the sick, prepared and served meals at church events, bought books for a reading circle, and raised funds to support mission workers. Funds generated by these sewing circles supported relief efforts for fellow Mennonites still living in the Soviet Union and suffering from disease and famine. With the onset of the Depression, the sewing circles expanded their activities to raise money and donate clothing to needy Mennonite families and others within their local communities.[39] Within Afro-Canadian churches, in another example, women continued to play central financial and spiritual leadership roles: "Missionary work was women's work . . . women . . . visited the sick, raised money for those in need here and in Africa and organized the social life of the Black community."[40]

Overseas missionary work continued to attract women moved by a deep sense of Christian duty. These women were also keen to take advantage of opportunities to develop professional careers in education and medicine, which were not readily available to them in Canada. In the 1920s and 1930s, some embraced modern concepts of missionary work—that is, they no longer focused on conversion. Nor did they see their activities as women's work for other women but, rather, as contributing to the advancement of host societies by fostering education and culture, and by building hospitals and schools of medicine and nursing. For example, Florence Murray, a Canadian Presbyterian woman missionary doctor in Korea from the 1920s through to the 1960s, insisted on professional training and standards for both male and female students. She saw herself as a doctor first and an evangelist second.[41]

Murray decided to become a medical missionary only after she discovered that she could not enter the ministry itself. In universities and normal schools many young women who had a deep sense of Christian duty joined the Student Christian Movement (SCM), which was formed in 1920 from the student departments of the YWCA and YMCA. An offshoot of the Social Gospel movement, this Christian reform association organized study groups on most Canadian campuses during the 1920s and 1930s to re-examine traditional notions of Christianity and to address pressing social problems. The SCM became an outlet for spirituality and idealism as well as a training ground for students interested in social change and international cooperation. At some universities, the SCM was co-educational; at others, men and women met separately.[42]

Through their Student Christian Movement activities, many young women sharpened the interpersonal and organizational skills that would prove useful for their future successful participation in public life. Mary McGeachy went from active participation in SCM activities at the University of Toronto in the 1920s to an international career as a diplomat and humanitarian for more than 50 years.[43] Another SCM member, Marion Royce, was a driving force in the YWCA at both the national and the international levels during the 1930s and 1940s, and in 1954 became the first director of the federal Department of Labour's Women's Bureau. The applied Christianity learned in the SCM also led some women into political activism. Both Marjorie Mann and Avis McCurdy, for example, later active members of the Co-operative Commonwealth Federation (CCF), credited the student organization, at least in part, for their later political perspective. McCurdy, who came from a middle-class Maritimes family, recalled in a 1982 interview, "I came straight to the CCF because I was convinced I had to be my brother's keeper. It was right out of my religious background—CGIT and SCM. I had also worked in business in my summers, and was overcome with the injustice and inequality."[44]

Women's experiences and activities through their missionary work and SCM membership sharpened their desire for equal participation in church life, particularly within the major Protestant churches. Beginning in the 1890s, both the Methodist and Presbyterian churches had commissioned single women as deaconesses, giving them an opportunity to participate in church life in a manner that mirrored their separate sphere: deaconesses visited the poor and the inmates of prisons, workhouses, and hospitals, and nursed the sick. Although some undertook managerial work—for example, those who oversaw the daily activities of the Jost Mission for the poor in Halifax—their limited training and lack of financial compensation reflected the churches' continuing perception that women's role was of a volunteer nature. Despite some improvements in training and salary by the 1920s, the female diaconate continued to be relegated to an inferior status within the church hierarchies. When a shortage of ordained ministers developed during and immediately after World War I, deaconesses were called upon to take over many ministerial duties and responsibilities, but were prohibited from administering the sacraments or performing marriages. Dissatisfaction with these limitations in role and status caused many deaconesses to leave, taking jobs in the expanding fields of nursing and social work—areas where their skills were clearly welcomed. By 1925, the year of the Methodist, Presbyterian, and Congregational union as the United Church of Canada, there remained only 67 Presbyterian and 47 Methodist deaconesses in Canada.[45] During World War II, there was a renewed demand for more deaconesses, needed to serve as supply ministers when significant numbers of male clergy left their congregations to serve as chaplains in the Canadian armed forces or to take up other forms of employment. Deaconesses were also involved in providing services to the burgeoning populations in war production centres, to newly arrived war brides, and to women in the armed forces. Nonetheless, they were not allowed the same rights as male clergy for decision-making within the Church. In addition, the seemingly insatiable demand for women church workers led the United Church to create attractive, short-term training programs for university women. These programs undermined the deaconesses' attempts to professionalize their vocation and to raise both its status and remuneration.[46]

For Protestant women, separate auxiliaries and charitable associations within their churches remained the avenue for most of their achievements. Like the Women's Missionary Society of the United Church, Mennonite women's organizations provided an example of how women's strength could be perceived as a threat to the male establishment. The Mennonite Women's Missionary Society, which had been established by a woman in Ohio in 1918, was essentially dissolved in 1927 by the church's male-controlled missionary board when it created a committee to coordinate the mission and relief work of the local sewing circles. Occasionally, women were allowed to attend the meetings at which male church members elected leaders of the female sewing groups, but the women could not vote. The 1920s also saw the introduction of strict new dress regulations among Canadian Mennonites, which were much more prescriptive and restrictive for women than for men.[47]

Other church women were involved directly in the fight for equality in their denominations. The slowly growing campaign for equal status within the Protestant churches realized one goal when the Methodist Assembly admitted women delegates for the first time in 1922. Nellie McClung, the seasoned women's rights activist, was instrumental in pushing forward this reform. She also urged that women be ordained as part of the regular clergy. After the 1925 founding of the United Church of Canada, she devoted a major part of her energy to lecturing and writing on expanding the role of women in the church. The impetus for McClung, as for other women who advocated female ordination, was personal spiritual conviction as well as the quest for women's rights.[48]

The standard response of the United Church leaders—that they were willing to consider female ordination only if and when there was a candidate seeking it—was first put to the test when a request for ordination was received from Lydia Gruchy in 1926. Gruchy, a theology graduate and preacher, served three large Saskatchewan congregations. Her acceptance by the congregations, and her endurance of the physical exertions involved in tending to their spiritual needs ought to have defused the usual arguments against women ministers: i.e., that they were unacceptable to church members and could not withstand the hardships of the extensive travel that was necessary in many rural areas. Still, Gruchy's application was refused by the 1926 meeting of the United Church's General Council, which instead recommended a new diaconate to which women could be ordained. This compromise was rejected by both Gruchy and her employer, the Saskatchewan Conference, which required a fully ordained minister capable of performing all the functions of that role. Continued requests for Gruchy's ordination were made by the Saskatchewan Conference, backed by Nellie McClung and a small but forceful group of supporters.[49] The campaigners were disappointed by the lack of support from the United Church's Women's Missionary Society. This society—which was created, supported, and administered by women—raised and controlled a million-dollar budget in the 1920s, and maintained nearly 300 female missionaries in Canada and overseas. Perhaps the Society perceived that competition with the ordained ministry for female recruits would have an adverse effect on its membership and work. The Society may also have opposed female ordination because it believed that its own expanding organization provided sufficient career opportunities for capable, well-educated church women.[50]

The fact that the very strong Women's Missionary Society remained outside the control of the male church leaders certainly engendered feelings of anxiety, if not outright hostility, in at least some men. The eventual reluctant acceptance of female ordination by the 1934 General Council has been attributed to the church leaders' determination to assimilate women's growing strength into the male-dominated church structure rather than tolerate it outside. Even after the ordination of Lydia Gruchy in 1936, the fight for equal rights in Protestantism was only beginning. Although in 1946 married women were also accepted as United Church ministers, most other Protestant churches remained closed to the idea of women assuming genuine leadership roles, whether married or single.

Women's lack of access to equal roles in the established Protestant churches may partly explain women's numerical dominance in the various new Protestant religious groups that mushroomed, particularly in western Canada before World War II.[51] One well-known example was the International Church of the Foursquare Gospel and its charismatic leader. Born on a dairy farm near Ingersoll, Ontario, in 1890, Aimee Semple McPherson was exposed to popular religion as a child through her mother's involvement in the Salvation Army and in evangelical camp meetings. By age 19 she had completed elocution lessons, won numerous medals in WCTU public-speaking contests, and married a Pentecostal preacher, Robert Semple. She travelled with him to China; after he died, she returned to North America, penniless and with an infant daughter. Several years later, after an unsuccessful marriage to New York grocer Harold McPherson, Aimee returned with her children to Ingersoll to preach. Now known as Sister Aimee, she launched a continent-wide religious campaign that combined evangelism and drama. By the mid-1920s she had established a church, the Angelus Temple, in California. Her ability to attract followers was enhanced by her use of the media—which were infatuated with all aspects of her life, particularly her mysterious disappearance in 1926, and the numerous court cases related to her marriages and her church's finances. In western Canada, McPherson founded and ran several churches and a Bible school. During the Depression, she became as well-known a radio preacher as the Social Credit premier of Alberta, William Aberhart.[52]

Within Roman Catholicism, it was difficult for women to move beyond the separate, subordinate roles that church authorities ascribed to them. In 1920, the Catholic Women's League was established to federate diverse groups of Catholic laywomen organized at the local diocesan level. League members responded to the needs of Catholic immigrants and working women, and supported the cause of Catholic education. By 1939, the League had 50 000 members in 554 divisions across Canada.[53] However, the Church reserved service roles in public health and education for the female religious orders, as it assigned similar roles to women within the family. In Quebec, this view of the appropriate activities of lay and religious women solidified in the 1920s and 1930s, as the perceived threat to French-Canadian nationalism that was posed by urbanization and industrialization intensified. The male church hierarchy continued to view equal political, social, and economic rights for women with horror. Some Quebec women did, however, establish roles for themselves through their involvement in *Action catholique*, a Church-sanctioned movement of lay Catholics, including such groups as *Jeunesse ouvrière catholique* (JOC) and *Jeunesse agricole catholique* (JAC), which sought to re-Christianize and socially reconstruct Quebec society during the 1930s. Particularly important for married women, in the postwar period, was the opportunity to lead Church-sanctioned marriage preparation courses, organized by the JOC. Under their leadership these courses, while essentially conservative in emphasizing women's primary roles as wives and mothers, did become increasingly focused on the emotional and sexual needs of women within marriage.[54]

For unmarried Catholic laywomen, however, clerical insistence on the maternal role left few respectable career alternatives. Such attitudes may have contributed to the remarkable increase in the number of nuns and the expansion of the Church's female orders. Between 1921 and 1931 the number of nuns in Canada increased by nearly 50 percent, from some 21 000 to 31 000. An additional 10 000 women joined religious orders during the 1930s, and the numbers continued to increase steadily throughout the 1940s and 1950s. They reached their zenith in 1965, when there were 183 congregations with close to 66 000 members, a number equal to almost 7 percent of Canada's female population.[55]

After experiencing a loss of membership during the war years, Protestant lay-women's groups also flourished during the early 1950s. In the United Church, between 1942 and 1955, the combined membership of the Women's Missionary Society and the Women's Auxiliary rose from just under 278 000 to just over 400 000, but membership subsequently started to decline again. In 1962 the two organizations were amalgamated into the United Church Women, as the General Council, composed overwhelmingly of men, argued that the merger would prevent duplication of work. Unfortunately, the change also meant an end to the autonomy that the influential Women's Missionary Society had always exercised in relation to its missions; because the WMS was now subordinate to the national mission boards, men assumed control of what had previously been women's work and women's financial resources.[56]

ARTS AND CULTURE

During the inter-war years, women worked both individually and collectively to provide support for the arts as they had done in previous decades. However, rather than organize their own groups, women in the arts tended to join men, including helping to found mixed-sex societies dedicated to the promotion of their members' work. Possibly their limited numbers, along with the struggle for recognition and acceptance that all artists experienced—male and female alike—encouraged collective strength. A number of female writers participated in the founding convention of the Canadian Authors' Association, held in 1921, and women artists were among the founders and active members of the Canadian Group of Painters. In 1933, nearly one-third of the members belonging to the latter group were women; six years later, landscape artist Isabel McLaughlin was elected the organization's first female president. Women painters participated as founders of nearly all the major artistic organizing efforts of the inter-war years. In the 1920s, the Beaver Hall Hill group in Montreal brought together 10 female and 8 male artists who not only shared studio space but also contributed to the development of a cooperative modernist movement. Several women artists were invited by the all-male Group of Seven to include their works in its exhibitions and, in 1924, 54 works by 30 women artists were selected to represent modern Canadian art at the prestigious British Empire Exhibition held in England. Among Canada's internationally acclaimed visual artists were sculptors and long-time companions Frances Loring and Florence Wyle. Together with colleague Elizabeth Wyn Wood and two men, they established the Sculptors' Society of Canada in 1928 (chartered in 1932). Women sculptors had benefitted from the postwar enthusiasm for municipal and other patriotic memorials, and for the first time they competed equally with men to produce major public pieces.[57]

The apparent breakdown of society during the Depression along with the emergence of new forms of political and social activism challenged some women artists to address the question of the relationship of their work to social change. Such consciousness stirred poet Dorothy Livesay, who, with 34 others, began the Progressive Arts Club in 1932 to link writers and the left. Committed to social action in both her poetry and her life,

Internationally acclaimed sculptors and lifelong partners Frances Loring and Florence Wyle.

Source: FLAHERTY, Robert J. Canadian 1884–1951. Portrait of Frances Loring and Florence Wyle (Church Street, Toronto), 1914. Bromide print, toned on paper. 21.7 × 16.2 cm. ART GALLERY OF ONTARIO. Gift of the Estates of Frances Loring and Florence Wyle, 1983.

Livesay described the summer of 1932, after her return from Paris, as "a crucial one for friendship and love. . . . My political convictions became the dominating obsession of my life. This lost me friends, split me away from parents, disrupted my relationship with my lover."[58] Similarly arguing for political involvement, painter Paraskeva Clark wrote, "those who give their lives, their knowledge and their time to social struggle have the right to expect help from the artist. I cannot imagine a more inspiring role than that which the artist is asked to play for the defense and advancement of civilization."[59]

Other women worked within the community to advance culture and art through both existing and new organizations of women. The Women's Art Association of Canada carried on the tradition of promoting public interest in art; among its varied activities, it encouraged the work of women artists. By the 1920s it had branches in large and small urban centres throughout the nation, and in 1927 it arranged the first meeting between Emily Carr and the Group of Seven. Local groups like the Heliconian Club in Toronto sponsored a variety of cultural activities; others, like the Hawthorn Women's Club (established in Winnipeg in 1923), worked to foster the study of the arts. In Montreal, Lillian Rutherford organized the Phyllis Wheatley Art Club in 1922 for other African-Canadian women and, in the mid-1930s, this club was reconstituted as the Negro Theatre Guild of Montreal. Women's auxiliaries provided funding and promotion for many theatrical companies, musical organizations, art galleries, and schools of art. In 1936, Antonia Nantel, wife of Senator Athanase David, organized the first Montreal Music Festival. Many of the local literary clubs, Shakespearean societies, and musical societies of the later nineteenth century that had been organized by women continued, or new ones were formed.[60]

Few women made a living through the arts, however, even when their works received national and international acclaim. Among those who did receive accolades were the writers Gabrielle Roy, Gwethalyn Graham, and Phyllis Brett Young. Roy won the Governor General's Award twice during this period: first in 1947 for *The Tin Flute* (the English translation of her novel *Bonheur d'occasion*) and again in 1957 for *Street of Riches* (the English translation of *Rue Deschambault*). In 1947, Roy became the first woman to be admitted to the Royal Society of Canada; she has since been widely recognized as one of the major figures in Canadian literature. Gwethalyn Graham also won the Governor General's Award twice: for her first novel, *Swiss Sonata*, in 1938; and for *Earth and High Heaven* in 1944. *Earth and High Heaven* became the first Canadian book to reach number one on the *New York Times* best-seller list. Phyllis Brett Young's success came later with the publication of her critically acclaimed novel, *The Torontonians* (1960), which depicted the life of a discontented housewife in the Toronto suburbs of the 1940s and 1950s.[61]

In 1950, the federally appointed Royal Commission on National Development in the Arts, Letters and Sciences (the Massey Commission) reported that the precarious state of cultural life in Canada might easily be further undermined by the all-pervasive American influence. American radio and television did not recognize the existence of the 49th parallel, and, for many Canadians, it was hard to distinguish between what was Canadian and what was American. It was in this difficult environment—before the establishment of the Canada Council in 1957—that women initiated some of the most important projects in theatre, dance, and the visual arts. As artists, organizers, fundraisers, and administrators, they made a vital contribution to nearly all aspects of Canadian culture. At art galleries throughout the country, women organized their own committees. Through their fundraising, pioneering of picture loan programs, encouragement of young artists, and pressure exerted on gallery boards to make new acquisitions, they indeed had a major impact. As one noted art critic pointed out, "these women, perhaps more than any other group . . . consciously pioneered the public acceptance of contemporary art."[62] Women's committees also played a vital role in the development and support of the performing arts, especially opera, music, and ballet. Without their enthusiasm and extensive fundraising efforts, the nation's cultural life would have been greatly diminished.

In English Canada, Dora Mavor Moore played the role of "theatre's fiery godmother." Beginning in the 1920s, she organized amateur theatre productions and gave drama lessons in Toronto, but her most important contribution to the dramatic arts came in 1946 when she formed the New Play Society. Planned as a permanent, professional, non-profit company, it scored a number of theatrical firsts, including the first performance of a Canadian play at the Royal Alexandra Theatre in Toronto. Moore's role in the success of the New Play Society was central: "A classic diva, she begged, browbeat, improvised, scrimped, borrowed, wheedled and worked for years to keep theatre alive. . . . Moore used to put on classical productions costumed entirely in crepe paper and, when there was no money for crepe paper, presented Shakespeare in modern dress."[63] Dora Mavor Moore was also one of the moving spirits behind the establishment of the Stratford Shakespeare Festival in 1952.

In Montreal, Yvette Brind'amour developed *Le rideau vert*, a permanent professional theatre company that gave its first performance in1949. It subsequently commissioned several new plays by French-Canadian playwrights, including Françoise Loranger's Encore cinq minutes, which won a Governor General's Award.[64] Another innovative organizational project was the establishment of the Montreal Women's Symphony, founded by Ethel Stark in 1940. Stark, the first Canadian to hold a scholarship at the Curtis Institute of Music in Philadelphia, was a violinist and conductor. In 1947 this critically acclaimed group became the first Canadian orchestra to play in New York's Carnegie Hall. Despite its success, it was a short-lived venture, mainly because of the lack of financial resources: ironically, unlike many symphonies of the period, the Montreal Women's symphony did not have a supporting women's committee to raise funds.[65]

Women also founded three major ballet companies in Canada in the postwar era. In 1949, Gweneth Lloyd and Betty Farrally organized the Royal Winnipeg Ballet, the country's first professional dance company; two years later, it received its royal charter. At the same time, ballet enthusiasts in Toronto engaged Celia Franca, a principal dancer with the Sadler's Wells Company in Britain, to found a national company. The National Ballet of Canada gave its first performance in Toronto in 1951, but struggled throughout the decade to establish itself as a truly professional and permanent company. Funds were initially so scarce that its director, Celia Franca, had to work part-time in a department store.[66] Nor was Montreal to be denied its own ballet company: thanks once again to the vision and energy of a determined woman, *Les grands ballets canadiens* became a reality in 1957. It was founded by Latvian-born Ludmilla Chiriaeff, who had trained with the Bolshoi Ballet and came to Canada in 1952.

As creative artists and performers in the 1950s, women faced special obstacles. The attitudes of the day did not support intense dedication to their arts. In particular, for most women in the performing arts, it was extremely difficult to combine motherhood with the demands of their careers. A notable exception was Maureen Forrester, the famous contralto, who later became the first woman head of the Canada Council. A mother of five, she delighted in telling people, "I can sing the morning I'm giving birth, and even during. It doesn't bother me. It's just the conductors who get nervous."[67] Few artists, especially in the days before Canada Council grants, could support themselves by their artistic endeavours; and even when government grants became more widely available, they were not always designed to meet the needs of women artists. In the visual arts, in particular, female applicants were not well served by the funding system established by the Canada Council after 1957. If their work borrowed techniques associated with women's traditional handicrafts, it was likely to be dismissed as merely craft. The artificial distinction between art (male) and craft (female) served to devalue women's artistic endeavours and diminish their chances of securing financial assistance. Ironically, the agency established in the 1960s to promote greater support and recognition for the crafts was named the Canadian Crafts*men*'s Association.

Despite the obstacles they encountered, women played an activist role, both individually and collectively, in the development of the visual arts in the post-war period. In English Canada, for example, Hamilton's Hortense Gordon was one of the first painters in Canada to experiment with abstraction and to promote non-representational art. Her work was displayed, along with that of more than 70 other women painters, in the Canadian Women Artists exhibition that opened to critical acclaim in New York in April 1947. The idea for the exhibition had come from Edna Breithaupt, chair of the Arts and Letters Committee of the National Council of Women. Funding was secured from the federal government to defray the shipping costs, the first example of the government's cooperation with a voluntary organization to support the arts. In the words of one commentator, the exhibition "carved a niche for Canada's artists in one of the most important art centres of the western world."[68]

In Montreal in 1948, the arts world was stunned by the publication of *Le refus global*, a ringing manifesto that called on all artists to reject the fetters of the past and to "break out of the walls of the common mould." Written by abstract painter Paul-Émile Borduas, it was signed by 15 other *Québécois* painters, no fewer than 7 of whom were women.[69] Quebec became a centre for abstract art, and with artists such as Rita Letendre, Suzanne Bergeron, Marcelle Ferron, and Lise Gervais, it had what one critic described as "more active women painters of the first rank than any other arts centre in the world."[70]

These young artists were encouraged by such women as Agnes Lefort of Montreal, who, in 1950, opened the first Quebec art gallery committed to displaying contemporary work. Another important locus of artistic activity, Cape Dorset in the Northwest Territories, drew heavily on women's talents, in this case Inuit women. Printmaker Pitseolak Ashoona was one of the best-known members of the artists' cooperative established there in 1959, and she enjoyed a high level of commercial success. Similarly, Jessie Oonark of the Baker Lake cooperative achieved international recognition by portraying Inuit themes in her cloth pictures.[71]

POLITICS

Although most women in Canada were able to vote in federal and provincial elections following World War I, there remained notable exceptions. While women in Quebec were eligible to vote and hold office at the federal level at the same time as women from other provinces or territories, they were permitted to do so at the provincial level only in 1940. Over the years, women in various minority communities suffered the same exclusions as the men from those communities. Chinese-Canadians, Japanese-Canadians, and other East Asians had access to the full range of federal and provincial franchises only by 1951. For the Aboriginal communities, there were even greater delays: the last gender-based electoral regulation ended in 1951, when status Indian women ceased to be barred from participating in band elections, but they had to wait until 1960 before getting the right to vote federally. The Inuit were given the right to vote in 1950. In 1969, Quebec became the last province to finally extend its provincial vote to status Indians. Canada finally had an electoral system that did not make exclusions based on gender, race, or ethnicity.[72]

For the women who had fought for the vote, a key question of the 1920s was how women's suffrage would influence the political process. Initially, politicians were eager to court the new female electorate, for they accepted suffragists' arguments that women would vote as a bloc to reform society. It became apparent within the decade, however, that regional, class, cultural, and other differences divided women's political allegiances just as they did men's. In 1918, a group of Ontario women from the National Equal Franchise Union attempted to form a non-partisan Woman's Party working through the National Council of Women of Canada. Their efforts were strongly opposed, especially by western Council members; the result was an ineffective and short-lived organization.[73] More pragmatic was the practice that the National Council began of adopting a Canadian Women's Platform to identify women's issues to be pursued through the established political parties. The 1920 platform incorporated reform positions on the political equality of the sexes, equal pay for equal work, equal child guardianship, and a female minimum wage. The Council also continued to mount campaigns to educate women about their political responsibilities and to encourage their participation in partisan politics. In Alberta, the UFWA adopted its own political education agenda—which included disseminating knowledge about public institutions and services, providing training in parliamentary procedure and the conduct of meetings, and helping women develop public-speaking skills.[74]

Such activities were more important than might be thought at first, for many women still found it very difficult even to cast their ballots. According to Elsie Inman, a founder of the Women's Liberal Club in Prince Edward Island and later a senator, when Island women finally did get the provincial vote in 1922, many had to overcome their husbands' opposition in order to use it. In one case that she recalled, the woman "was scared to vote because her husband threatened her if he saw her at a poll." Working on the assumption that the man would not recognize his wife if she were attired differently, Inman took the woman home, dressed her in Inman's own clothes, coat, and veil, and successfully conducted her to the polling station. When Inman went to accompany another woman to vote, she was met by the irate husband, who accused her of trying to lead his wife astray.

He sternly admonished her, "You're from a nice family, and have a good husband, you should be ashamed of yourself."[75]

Although a number of local women's auxiliaries to the two major political parties existed as early as 1906, they were not formally integrated into party structures. This situation changed in 1928, however, when the Liberal Party formed a national women's auxiliary, the Federation of Liberal Women of Canada, to attract women to the party. The Conservative Party followed suit shortly after. Both women's organizations were established to bring women to the parties as voters, with no intention of integrating them into strategic or leadership roles. Within the party organization, they were expected to carry out the essential day-to-day tasks of party maintenance, serving as the staffers who raised small-scale party funds, stuffed envelopes, distributed literature, answered telephones, and "minded" campaign offices. During elections, they became indispensable as canvassers, poll clerks, and scrutineers. In riding associations, they became secretaries and occasionally treasurers.[76] Valuable as these activities were, they were unlikely to provide opportunities for women to gain the skills, reputation, or political contacts necessary for party or public office. Legal equality, then, did not bring inclusion as equals in political processes and organizations.

Many of the third parties that emerged or grew into prominence in Canada after World War I were relatively receptive to having women participate; these included the United Farmers' parties in Alberta, New Brunswick, Nova Scotia, and Ontario, and the Progressive Party at the national level. Leftist third parties, such as the Co-operative Commonwealth Federation (CCF) and the more radical Socialist Party and Communist Party of Canada, embraced social and economic issues, such as equal pay, protective labour legislation, and birth control—issues that had long been dear to reform-minded women.[77] In their quest for members and for citizens willing to stand for office when there was little hope of winning, the newer parties actively recruited women. Agnes Macphail, Canada's first woman MP, was among the founders of the CCF, and the party relied heavily on women like Louise Lucas, another founder who became known as the Mother of the CCF in Saskatchewan due to her indefatigable organizational efforts. Another Saskatchewan resident, Gladys Strum, became the first woman president of a Canadian political party when she was chosen to head up the CCF party in her home province in 1944. Many women also worked at the local level for the CCF, as did Nellie Fraser. Fraser was widowed at the age of 32 in 1919. Her husband, who had been an agent with the Great West Life Company in Saskatchewan during the wheat boom, left her enough money to live on and to support their three children. In 1938, with her family grown up, she sold her home in Winnipeg, moved to Toronto, and became involved with the party, speaking on its behalf on local radio. A commitment to peace activism led her to work with the Women's International League for Peace and Freedom, eventually becoming president of its Toronto branch. Unlike their male colleagues, however, women organizers were not always paid. The UFWA president, for example, received only a reimbursement of expenses up to $500 per year and no salary, while the UFA president received an annual salary of $4 000 and a $750 expense account.[78]

Even the leftist parties' support of women's issues was limited. In the 1920s, the Communist Party of Canada took up the so-called woman question; by the middle of the decade, the party had inaugurated a women's department with the object of advancing communism among women, established a women's column in its newspaper, and formed a national organization of working-class women. The Women's Labour Leagues, led by Florence Custance, numbered 37 by 1937. Finnish, Jewish, and Ukrainian leagues predominated, reflecting the party's important ethnic connections. These leagues focused on the economic exploitation of women and attributed their subordination to the capitalist system. Despite this activity, women's issues never became a major priority for Canadian Communists; like other organizations, the party reflected structures of inequality in the larger society.[79] The more influential CCF was also committed to the emancipation of women but had similar difficulty living up to its promise. Concerned primarily with overcoming class inequality and getting candidates elected, the party relegated the cause of equal rights for women to the background.

During the Depression years, when unemployment and economic problems dominated political life, socialist and communist women cooperated with each other and with women of other political persuasions on social and economic issues. In 1935, for example, when relief camp internees in British Columbia went on strike and occupied the Vancouver post office, women from various local groups—including the Vancouver Communist Party, the CCF, the Local Council of Women, and the WCTU—joined together to form a Mothers' Council. It passed a resolution urging the federal government to provide genuine work and a living wage for the strikers. Led by women from the CCF and the Communist Party, the Mothers' Council participated in rallies and demonstrations supporting the unemployed, and organized the distribution of food and clothing, and the provision of shelter to the destitute. Similar groups in Saskatchewan and Alberta established women's committees to aid the On-to-Ottawa Trek of unemployed workers in the summer of 1935. After the Trek ended in a violent riot provoked by police action in Regina, interest in the Mothers' Council waned, although Communist Party of Canada involvement remained strong. In 1936 the Mothers' Council affiliated with the Local Council of Women and became the socialist voice on the latter's Unemployment Relief Committee.[80]

After 1921 women had another, more direct avenue to making their views known: they could be elected to legislative office federally and in most provinces. A small number of women, many of whom had cut their political teeth in women's organizations, then entered the provincial legislatures. Despite their limited presence, they did have some

Members of the Winnipeg Women's Labour League prepare relief bundles to support striking Nova Scotia coal miners in 1925.

Source: Provincial Archives of Manitoba (N-9343).

success in furthering the social and welfare legislation that the newly enfranchised members of women's groups supported. There were many hurdles to be overcome, however.[81] The first woman seated in the House of Commons, Agnes Macphail, faced discrimination during all stages of the political process. When she won the United Farmers of Ontario federal nomination over 10 men at the South-East Grey convention in September 1920, protests against her candidacy flooded the riding executive. Called before the executive and under pressure from some quarters to resign, she refused, arguing that she had been duly selected by the accredited delegates. During her election campaign, opponents attacked her religion—the Church of Jesus Christ of the Latter Day Saints—her sex, and her "mannish" behaviour, but on December 6, 1921, Macphail was duly elected. As the only woman member of the Commons, Macphail was an alien novelty, commented upon and scrutinized by other MPs, by the public, and by the press. Her first session, she herself admitted, was "miserable. . . . I was intensely unhappy. Some members resented my intrusion, others jeered at me, while a very few were genuinely glad to see a woman in the House. Most of the members made me painfully conscious of my sex."[82]

But Macphail did not shrink from the responsibility she had accepted, taking it so seriously that she rejected several marriage proposals in order to continue her work. Sensitive over being a spinster in an era when marriage was highly valued, Macphail took pains to announce the marriage offers publicly. She sat as the South-East Grey

Agnes Macphail portrait, circa 1922.

Source: Kelsey Studio / Library and Archives Canada / C-006908

member from 1921 until 1940. While she never lost sight of the interests of her agrarian constituency during her years in Parliament, Macphail also came to see herself as representing and acting for the women of Canada. In her day she was regarded, and criticized, as a feminist. She supported the struggle for women's suffrage in Quebec; fought successfully for the Archambault Royal Commission on prison reform and then for the implementation of its findings; and worked for peace and social welfare provisions, including unemployment insurance, family allowances, and pensions for the old, the blind, and the disabled. Defeated in the federal election of 1940, partly because of her pacifism, Macphail later served as one of the first two women to sit in the Ontario legislature.[83]

Only five women were elected to the federal Parliament before 1950. Like Macphail, Gladys Strum and Dorise Nielsen, both from Saskatchewan, represented third parties; both were elected for the CCF, Nielsen in 1940 and Strum in 1945. Nielsen, an avowed Communist, used the more acceptable "front" of the CCF party to run, but once elected she became acknowledged as the first Communist elected to the House of Commons. She was also the only woman elected in 1940.[84] The other two of the five elected to Parliament, who sat for the major parties, were both cases of widow's succession—replacements for previously elected husbands (although in Black's case her husband was ill, not deceased). However, both Cora Taylor Casselman, who was elected in an Alberta by-election following her Liberal husband's death, and Martha Black, who represented her Conservative husband's Yukon riding for five years when he was incapacitated by poor health, turned out to be excellent parliamentarians in their own right.[85] Black, an American immigrant who was estranged from her first husband, had walked across the Chilkoot Pass in 1898 while pregnant with her third child. She settled near Dawson City and became a successful sawmill owner and operator. In 1904 she married George Black, who later became the territory's commissioner and, in 1921, its Member of Parliament. When 69-year-old Martha ran in his place in 1935, she faced a hard battle. Despite her husband's popularity, her victory was far from assured, and she won by only 134 votes. In her autobiography she recalled how she had had to confront her hecklers: "There were the younger women who said, 'What can this damned old woman do for us at Ottawa?' That was hard to take, yet I hurled back, 'You'll be lucky when you reach my age if you have my sturdy legs, my good stomach, my strong heart, and what I like to call my headpiece.'"[86] Once in the Commons, she concerned herself with pensions and unemployment, and supported both cadet training and the imperial tie with Britain. When her husband was well enough to replace her in 1940, Black retired.

For many women with an interest in politics, their role continued to be support of husbands in electoral politics. In many such cases, these efforts were crucial to their spouses' successes. John Diefenbaker, MP and prime minister, had the good fortune to have two wives who were essential to his career. His first wife, née Edna May Brower, a gregarious charmer who humanized and worked with the dour "Chief," had been a primary school teacher in Saskatchewan before her marriage. When she died in 1951 after 22 years of marriage, she was the first non-parliamentarian to receive recognition in the House of Commons. The Canadian Press's Douglas How wrote, "Parliament has lost its unelected Member of Parliament." He added, "Lake Centre [Diefenbaker's riding at that time] was a rarity, a riding with two members."[87] His better-known second wife, Olive

Palmer, was a widow when Diefenbaker married her two years after Edna's death; for 26 years she gave him unquestioning support, on which he greatly depended.

It is clear that women who actually made the decision to seek elected office did so for a variety of reasons. A feminist consciousness evolved during the post-suffrage era as women recognized the continued presence of systemic barriers to their equal participation in public life. The inter-war political development of Margaret McWilliams is a case in point. The first woman to receive a degree in political economy from the University of Toronto, McWilliams actively participated in Winnipeg's Canadian Women's Club, Local Council of Women, and University Women's Club. Her belief that educated women had a responsibility to influence and lead in their local and national communities encouraged her to serve as the first president of the Canadian Federation of University Women in 1919. In 1933, with the considerable support of the Local Council of Women, she successfully ran in the municipal election in South Winnipeg and remained a city councillor for four terms.[88]

Margaret McWilliams was just one of 11 Winnipeg women who stood for aldermanic office between 1918 and 1939. During the same period, 19 different women candidates ran for school trustee. By contrast, the numbers of male candidates were 443 and 258, respectively. Like the men, the women politicians represented the range of class and ethnic politics in the city, but they also focused on gender issues and consciously identified with other women as a social group in their campaigns and political behaviour. Ida Siegel of Toronto was an excellent example of this ability to combine class, ethnic, and gender politics. In addition to founding several Jewish organizations, many of which provided services for Jewish women and children, Siegel served as the first treasurer of the Children's Welfare Council of Toronto. In 1931, she was elected trustee to the Toronto Board of Education, but was unsuccessful in her attempt to be elected to city council two years later. In the anti-Semitic, anti-feminist climate of the 1930s, her defeat was not surprising. In 1934, Nora Frances Henderson, women's editor of the *Hamilton Herald* and an advocate for a greater role of women in public life, was the first woman in Canada elected to a city board of control—the executive committee of city council. She was subsequently re-elected to this position 16 more times. In the focus that female municipal politicians put on women's issues, we can see continuity with the pre-war women's movement and the seeds of the renewed feminist activity in the 1960s. Although few in number, women entered municipal politics more frequently than at other political levels.[89] Being involved locally did not necessitate moving away from family and allowed women to have an impact in areas of life—such as education, public health, and community services—that were of immediate concern to them. In addition, once women had the vote, they also assumed a civic housekeeping function, watching over the performance of the elected (male) politicians. Toronto's Association of Women Electors (AWE) was founded in 1938, and until the mid-1980s, the volunteer group closely monitored and reported on the Toronto City Council and its standing committees. AWE activist June Rowlands went on to be elected city councillor and, then, in 1991, the first female mayor of the City of Toronto.[90]

At the provincial level, only 49 women managed to win legislative seats between 1920 and 1970. All of those elected prior to 1950 were from Ontario and the west; none were elected from the Maritime provinces or Quebec. Lady Helena Squires, wife of the Liberal premier of Newfoundland, which was not yet a part of Confederation, was elected to the colony's legislature in 1930, and thus became the first woman to be elected to a legislative assembly in the Atlantic region.[91] Most of this first generation of women in provincial legislatures represented parties with no chance of forming a government. For instance, the CCF sponsored a number of female candidates, two of whom, Dorothy Steeves and Laura Jamieson, were elected during the 1930s to the British Columbia legislature.[92] Steeves's primary commitment was to socialism rather than women's issues, but Laura Jamieson, like many of the early women's activists, associated herself with a broad range of feminist causes and groups, including suffrage, the women's peace movement, the British Columbia Parent–Teacher Association, the Business and Professional Women's Club, and the Women's School for Citizenship. Before her election in 1939, Jamieson had served for 11 years as a magistrate in a Burnaby juvenile court.[93]

The United Farmers of Alberta was one of the few third parties to form a provincial government in this period, and therefore also one of the few to gain the opportunity to legislate on women's issues. After its election in 1921, the UFA appointed Irene Parlby as minister without portfolio. Aided and endorsed by the United Farm Women of Alberta, she became a spokesperson for women's issues, such as the provision of a minimum wage for women, married women's property rights, mothers' allowances, and children's welfare. She found support on these issues from Nellie McClung, who had also been elected to the legislature in 1921, but as a Liberal. The United Farmers of Alberta government passed 18 acts that positively affected the welfare of women and children during its term. However, efforts by Parlby and some UFWA members to make wives co-equals with their husbands in the disposition of farm assets, and to recognize women's economic contributions in cases of separation and divorce, failed in face of opposition by both the UFA and conservative women in the UFWA. Similar forces combined to defeat a UFWA campaign to legalize contraceptive devices and to provide government funding to disseminate birth control information.[94]

During the 1920s women also initiated and brought to successful conclusion a campaign to obtain Senate appointments for women. At issue was the exclusion of women from the upper house; some reform-minded women also believed that the Senate could be used as a platform from which to exert influence on public policy. In 1919 the first conference of the Federated Women's Institutes of Canada, presided over by Magistrate Emily Murphy, passed a resolution requesting that the prime minister appoint a woman senator. Surely women, now voters and eligible for election to the House of Commons, ought to be among those persons who, if qualified, could be summoned to serve in the Senate. The National Council of Women and the Montreal Women's Club renewed the request, settling on Murphy as their candidate. But the governments of both Arthur Meighen and Mackenzie King stalled, apologetically pointing out that women were ineligible under the terms of the British North America Act of 1867.

After eight years of requests, refusals, and a lack of progress, Murphy and four other prominent women, including Nellie McClung, Louise McKinney, and Irene Parlby, all of whom had served in the Alberta legislature, joined together to mount a legal challenge. The fifth petitioner, Henrietta Muir Edwards, was very well known in women's organizations for her many years of service as convenor of laws for the National Council of Women. These women (now known as the Famous Five) used an obscure section of the

Meeting of United Farm Women of Alberta, accompanied by their families, at Bredin, Bear Lake, 1924.
Source: South Peace Regional Archives, 177.053

Supreme Court Act to petition the government for an Order-in-Council directing the Supreme Court to rule on the constitutional question of whether the term "qualified persons" in Section 24 of the BNA Act included women, and therefore whether women were eligible to be summoned to the Senate. The Supreme Court ruling in April 1928 held that the term "qualified persons" did *not* include women. The five petitioners then asked the government to allow an appeal of the judgment to the Judicial Committee of the Privy Council in England, at that time the highest court of appeal on questions related to Canadian law. The government agreed and the appeal was heard. On October 18, 1929, the Judicial Committee unanimously reversed the judgment of the Supreme Court of Canada and held that the word "persons" in Section 24 of the BNA Act *did* include women as well as men.[95]

Emily Murphy was never invited to sit in the Senate; being a well-known Conservative, she was passed over by Mackenzie King in favour of Liberal Cairine Wilson, who was appointed the first woman senator in 1930. The Montreal-born Wilson had not achieved the same recognition from the general public and the women's movement as Murphy, but she had devoted her married life to social and charitable reform causes, and (more importantly, from the point of view of the Senate appointment) to Liberal Party politics after 1921. An active volunteer with the Red Cross, the Victorian Order of Nurses, the Presbyterian Woman's Missionary Society, the Salvation Army, the YWCA, and the Ottawa Welfare Bureau, Wilson was a founder of the national Federation of Liberal Women. As a senator, she involved herself in divorce legislation, immigration, and the League of Nations. She was also president of the Canadian League of Nations Society,

Unveiling of bronze tablet commemorating the victory of the "Famous Five" in the lobby of the Canadian Senate, Ottawa, June 11, 1938. Prime Minister Mackenzie King, centre; Nellie McClung, extreme right. Also included are Mrs. J. C. Kenwood (daughter of Judge Emily Murphy); Doctor E. M. Douglas (president of Professional Women's Clubs); Senator Cairine Wilson; and Senator Iva C. Fallis.

Source: Glenbow Archives NA-3043-1

and one of the few Canadians to protest the restrictive immigration policies that prevented the entry into Canada of Jews fleeing Nazi persecution in the 1930s.[96]

Even when the Conservatives returned to office later in 1930, and a Senate vacancy was created in 1931 by the death of a Catholic senator from Edmonton, Murphy was once again not offered a seat, this time because she was a Protestant. Two years later, she died without achieving the appointment for which she had fought so long and hard. In 1935 a second woman, Iva Fallis of Peterborough, Ontario, was named to the Senate. Fallis, active in the campaign that resulted in the Conservatives' victory and a former vice-president of the Canadian Conservative Association, used her position in the upper chamber to advocate for women's rights, old age security, and human rights.[97]

In Quebec, women were still unable to vote provincially and ineligible to hold public office until 1940. Under pressure from the Roman Catholic Church, the *Fédération nationale Saint-Jean-Baptiste* (FNSJB) had abandoned its support for women's suffrage by 1920. For a short period there was no separate suffrage organization in Quebec, a situation remedied in 1922 by the formation of the *Le Comité provincial pour le suffrage feminin/* Provincial Franchise Committee (CPSF/PFC). It consisted of two sections, one English and one French; the heads of each shared the new organization's leadership. Marie Lacoste Gérin-Lajoie, president of the FNSJB, became president of the French section, and Anna Lyman headed the English section. The new suffrage association sent delegations to the provincial government, mounted education campaigns, and supported attempts to introduce the suffrage question in the province's Assembly.

Hopes for a continuing women's suffrage movement that would unite anglophones and francophones, Local Council of Women and FNSJB members were dashed in short order. When Archbishop Paul-Eugène Roy of Quebec City denounced suffrage in a 1922 pastoral letter, Gérin-Lajoie took her case and that of the women of Quebec to the International Union of Leagues of Catholic Women, hoping to win papal support. Although she was successful in getting the Union to pass two favourable resolutions—one encouraging enfranchised women to exercise their rights, and another approving the civic, moral, and religious education of women—a third resolution tied any new suffrage activities to prior approval of the Church in each country. When Gérin-Lajoie and the FSNJB attempted to interpret the clause as relating to a local authority—Archbishop Bruchéis, the relatively progressive bishop of Montreal—the international body responded that approval was required from all the province's bishops.[98] The position of the Quebec Church hierarchy was made clear by Cardinal L. N. Bégin in a letter supporting his auxiliary bishop, Archbishop Roy, and published in the newspaper *Le Canada* on March 19, 1922. "The entry of women into politics, even by merely voting," he emphasized, "would be a misfortune for our province. Nothing justifies it, neither the natural law nor the good of society."[99] This pressure forced the FSNJB to withdraw its support for the CPSF/PFC and Gérin-Lajoie to resign her presidency.[100]

After this serious setback, the CPSF/PFC marked time. In 1928 it was revitalized under the dynamic leadership of Thérèse Casgrain, and renamed *La Ligue des droits de la femme*/League for Women's Rights the following year. Casgrain, who was the daughter of an upper-class political family from Montreal (her husband served as Speaker of the House of Commons and as secretary of state in the Mackenzie King government), used her influence to campaign for political and professional rights for Quebec women throughout the 1930s. She was a tireless worker, championing the cause of Quebec women through her writings, lectures, and radio broadcasts.[101]

Meanwhile, in 1927 a separate suffrage organization, the *Alliance canadienne pour le vote des femmes du Québec*, had been formed under the leadership of Idola Saint-Jean, a language instructor at McGill University and an energetic social and political activist. A member of the original CPSF/PFC, Saint-Jean had resigned in January of that year to initiate her own campaign for the vote. The *Alliance* attracted working-class francophone women; it sometimes operated alone and sometimes in unison with other suffrage forces

Thérèse Casgrain, leader of the Quebec CCF, campaigning in the 1957 provincial election.

Source: The Canadian Press

to build what its founder called "a militant campaign."[102] Saint-Jean was at the heart of the struggle, writing for newspapers, magazines, and the group's own publication; lobbying the legislature; and presenting briefs to government commissions. By courageously running as an independent candidate in the 1930 federal election, she generated a great deal of publicity for the suffrage cause; although she lost, she did manage to win the support of nearly 3 000 electors. The work of the various Quebec suffrage organizations and the support of other provincial women's associations, including the Montreal Local Council of Women, culminated in the endorsement of women's franchise by the Quebec Liberal Party at its 1938 convention. Thérèse Casgrain had secured the admission of delegates from the Association of Liberal Women to the provincial congress and the placement of woman suffrage on the official program. When the Liberal party assumed power in 1940, it finally passed the necessary enabling legislation for women to vote and hold office at the provincial level.[103]

Quebec women were battling on a number of fronts during the inter-war period. Their inferior legal and economic status was also a major focus of organizational effort. Spurred on by improvements in the legal status of women in other provinces, both anglophone and francophone women sought similar reforms for themselves. In response to these demands and to divert attention from the suffrage issue, the Liberal government of Louis-Alexandre Taschereau set up the Commission on the Civil Rights of Women, headed by Judge Charles-Édouard Dorion, in 1929. The women who appeared before the Commission sought to lessen the severe restrictions on married women and to equalize authority within the marital relationship. Similar changes were under discussion in France at the same time. A particular change these women sought was the elimination of the double standard for legal separation. Under Quebec law, a husband could seek

Idola Saint-Jean, a leader of the campaign for the provincial franchise for women in Quebec.

Source: Library and Archives Canada/Garcia Studio/Catherine Lyle Cleverdon fonds/C-068508

a separation if his wife committed adultery, whereas to be granted the same right, she had to prove that her husband kept his "concubine" in the family home. The primary demand, however, was that married women be legally entitled to control their own earnings. Even though no more than 10 percent of Quebec wives earned wages, witnesses testified about the hardships caused to women and children by husbands who refused to provide the necessities of life for their families and who squandered their wives' earnings.

Most briefs presented by delegations were extremely moderate, stressing the need to limit a husband's right to dispose of community assets for frivolous purposes without consulting his wife. No individual or group appearing before the Commission seriously challenged the patriarchal structure of Quebec families. No one threatened the sacrosanct role of the husband as *chef de famille* by suggesting that he no longer be accorded his wife's obedience, or that mothers and fathers share responsibility for family affairs. Nevertheless, faced with the hostility of the Church, the legal profession, and the government, the Dorion Commission produced arguments for retaining the status quo, stating that "women themselves have not really evolved. Created to be the companions of men, women are always, and above all else, wives and mothers."[104]

In the light of such sentiment, it is not surprising that the minor changes recommended by the Dorion Commission affected few women. They did include giving women the right to control their salaries and any goods or property brought with them into a marriage. But no other changes in the law respecting legal separations were recommended. In fact, the Commission, like the clerical and nationalist forces that opposed Quebec feminists in the first four decades of the twentieth century, echoed the powerful view that women had to remain in subordinate and familial roles if the French-Canadian nation was to survive. Assessing the Commission in her autobiography, Thérèse Casgrain wrote that "while the Dorion report brought a few amendments to our Civil Code, it did not go very far." She also believed that in the report's arguments against change, it was easy to observe the "scornful and haughty attitude of our masculine elite towards women."[105] The feminists were deeply disappointed, even though the Commission's deliberations and reports did provide a forum for the discussion of women's rights.

On the eve of World War II and looking back over nearly two decades of women's active participation in domestic politics, some other observers also felt discouraged. Even the normally irrepressible Nellie McClung was disillusioned: "When women were given the vote in 1916–17 . . . we were obsessed with the belief that we could cleanse and purify the world by law. . . . But when all was over, and the smoke of battle cleared away, something happened to us. Our forces, so well organized for the campaign, began to dwindle."[106] Not all suffragists, however, concurred. Helen Gregory MacGill, the prominent B.C. feminist, wrote a 1936 article entitled "Canadian Women Have Not Failed in Politics." To prove her point, she cited a long list of important social and legal reforms—enacted at both the provincial and the federal levels—that were directly attributable to women's public involvement.[107]

If getting more women elected to public office was key to effecting positive change, then the postwar years proved very bleak. At the federal level, few women stood for election and fewer still were elected. The number of women MPs ranged from zero after the 1949 election to five after the 1962 election. (See Table A.11 in the Appendix.) Canada did get its first female Cabinet minister in 1957 when Ellen Fairclough became Secretary of State in John Diefenbaker's Conservative government; she remained the only female cabinet member until her defeat in 1963.[108] At the provincial level, few women were successful and some lost seats gained in earlier elections. Women were most successful in British Columbia, where five were elected to the provincial legislature in 1941 and two in 1945; the number crept back up to four only in 1960. However, Nancy Hodges, one of the women elected in 1941, made history in the British Commonwealth by becoming the first woman to hold the position of Speaker when she was appointed to that post in the legislature in 1950. The relative, if small, success of British Columbian women is attributed to a number of factors, including the strength of its social feminist organizations, its lack of ties to tradition, and its history of socialist and social democratic political parties that advocated equality.[109] In general, the obstacles to women's gaining entry to provincial legislatures remained manifold. In Prince Edward Island, for example, Elsie Inman sought a nomination to run for the provincial assembly in the early 1950s. On the night of the vote, an unexpected number of men turned up to challenge her nomination. She lost and, as she later recalled, "I heard afterwards that it [getting men to offer themselves] wasn't against me, but they didn't want a *woman* there, because they'd talk too much or go after things, perhaps for women. They didn't want women mixed up in it. It was a man's legislature."[110] Women did have more success at the local level, including the election of the first woman mayor in Canada, Barbara M. Hanley, who presided over Webbwood, Ontario (population 600), from 1936 to 1944. Then, in 1951, Charlotte Whitton, who championed the cause of child welfare across Canada, became mayor of Ottawa, the first female mayor of a major Canadian city. She was subsequently re-elected mayor four more times, and then served as a city councillor until 1972.[111]

The slowness and difficulty of changing policy from the outside motivated activist Aboriginal women to seek more direct involvement in their own government after they gained the right to participate in band elections in 1951. In 1954, Elsie Knott, of the Anishinabek Nation, was the first woman to be elected chief of a First Nations community in Canada. This 33-year-old mother of three served her community of Curve Lake near Peterborough, Ontario, as chief and councillor for 16 years. Chief Knott was an advocate for secondary and postsecondary education, Ojibwe language instruction, better housing, water, roads, and hydro. She is also fondly remembered for driving a school bus, initially a converted hearse, for over 30 years and seldom missing a day of work even in winter.[112]

INTERNATIONALISM

World War I had provoked for many an altered awareness of the nation's position in the world, and in the 1920s and 1930s some Canadian women developed and acted on a new international perspective. National organizations of farm, business and professional, and university women identified with like-minded women around the world and linked their associations in international bodies. Many of these groups sought to promote a world view and to eradicate racial prejudice and intolerance.

Their efforts were part of a larger movement of international cooperation among women and their organizations, which was by no means new. Connections between women's groups in Canada, the United States, and Great Britain were long-standing, as was the international outlook of the various Protestant missionary societies. Within the missionary societies, new theories of individual self-worth and cultural relativism began to replace old ideas about Christian superiority.[113] The National Council of Women did maintain its membership in the International Council of Women (ICW). Consequently, some women were able to contribute at the international level, while local groups gained access to information and strategies concerning global issues that affected women. At the 1920 meeting of the ICW, the delegates addressed women's rights as citizens, issues related to women's education, and concerns about health. International interests also frequently sparked national and local efforts on behalf of women. In 1936 an ICW request for information about the experience of older, unemployed Canadian women prompted the National Council of Women of Canada to undertake its own survey and subsequently to work to improve employment conditions for this group of women.[114]

Canada's involvement in World War I had not only highlighted the interdependence of nations but also produced a profound reaction against war itself. In the aftermath of the war, Canadian women and men established in 1921 a national organization to support the efforts of the League of Nations in Geneva. In Vancouver, the University Women's Club, led by its founder, Evlyn Fenwick Farris, voted in 1924 to become a corporate member of the League of Nations Society and supported the setting up of a Conference for World Peace. Four years later the club passed a resolution asking Parliament that "For every hundred dollars spent for national defence, one dollar be spent in the promotion of international goodwill." Members proposed that the money be used for courses in international relations at the university level and for scholarships for an exchange of students between Canada and other countries.[115]

Membership in the Canadian League of Nations Society reached a peak in 1929 as a result of the work of women's organizations such as the WCTU and the National Council of Women of Canada, especially in the west. Although initially dominated by a male elite, the Society owed its survival to the efforts of its many women members. By the 1930s it had become, in effect, a women's peace organization, led by Cairine Wilson. In addition to taking up the League of Nations Society's cause, Local Councils of Women sponsored lectures, study groups, and essay and speaking contests to promote the spirit of international understanding. Despite its tradition of avoiding controversial issues that could create tensions for some of its members, the National Council of Women of Canada lobbied Ottawa on peace issues, urging government support for the 1932 Disarmament Conference.

As individuals, Canadian women also participated in the work of the League of Nations. In 1929, for example, Agnes Macphail was a member of the Canadian delegation to the League of Nations. Rejecting pressure that she sit on the committee dealing with welfare, women, and children, Macphail successfully insisted on becoming the first woman delegate to sit on the Disarmament Committee. Charlotte Whitton, while serving as the executive secretary for the Canadian Council on Child Welfare, represented Canada on the League of Nations' Commission on the Protection of Women and Children, and later on the League's Advisory Committee on Social Questions. She also served as a member of the Advisory Committee of Experts on the Protection of Women created by the International Labour Organization. Nellie McClung was also one of Canada's delegates to the 1938 session of the League of Nations.

Even before the end of World War I, a group of women who were dissatisfied with the efforts of existing organizations had formed a separate peace party, the Canadian Women's Peace Party. It was one of the founding groups for the Women's International League for Peace and Freedom (WILPF). By the late 1920s, Canadian branches of the WILPF were active in Ontario and the west. More left-leaning than other peace organizations, WILPF did not involve a large number of Canadian members, but it did attract women of high calibre. Violet McNaughton, editor of the women's page of the *Western Producer*, became a spokesperson for the organization, and she is credited with creating strong support for its activities among rural women in the west. Laura Jamieson, aided by various women's organizations, organized peace conferences in Vancouver, Winnipeg, and Saskatoon, and together with Violet McNaughton and Agnes Macphail represented Canada at the International Congress of WILPF in Prague, Czechoslovakia, in 1929. Upon their return they determined to build a stronger movement in Canada, and in 1930, 17 locals of the United Farm Women of Alberta and the Alberta WCTU joined WILPF.

A major goal for women's peace groups was the reorientation of Canadian education. They campaigned to replace cadet training in schools with physical education and to change textbooks and curricula that glorified the military and war. They also tried with some success to get their own members elected as school trustees in Winnipeg and Toronto in the 1930s. Although WILPF members cooperated with the League of Nations Society, the WCTU, and Local Council of Women branches, for the most part they found these groups unwilling to adopt the pacifist positions they promoted.

The increasing sympathy for radical social change among the members of WILPF accelerated during the Depression. McNaughton became active in the League for Social Reconstruction; Jamieson joined the Co-operative of Unemployed Workers and later the CCF. Pacifists faced a dilemma at the outbreak of the Spanish Civil War when commitment to non-violence conflicted with support of a legitimate leftist government attacked by local and international fascism. Their dilemma intensified as aggressive right-wing dictators became more powerful in Germany and Italy. Sharp divisions occurred within the membership of the Women's International League, with some persisting in their opposition to all war, while others concluded that war against the Nazis and Hitler was a regrettable necessity. Perhaps for this reason, by the late 1930s the organization had lost its base across the country and ceased to attract younger women.[116]

For Canadian women, as for all Canadians, peace and international understanding were elusive goals. The optimism that characterized the women's peace movement faltered during and following World War II. At the same time, the achievement of international peace, always a major concern of Canadian women's groups, assumed a new urgency in the light of Cold War anxieties about nuclear war. In the post-war period, Canadian women and their associations took a special interest in international affairs, and particularly in the work of the United Nations. Mildred Osterhout Fahrni, a political and social activist from British Columbia who spent time at Mahatma Gandhi's ashram in India in the 1930s, attended the founding conference of the United Nations in 1945. Three years later, she was named national secretary of the International Fellowship of

Reconciliation, an organization dedicated to world peace.[117] The Women's Institutes and other women's voluntary associations mounted vigorous campaigns to have the federal government ratify the Declaration of Human Rights, which was passed by the United Nations General Assembly in 1950. Many of the national women's organizations were affiliated to long-established international federations that acquired formal participatory status in the functional agencies of the United Nations. Women who were prominent in these associations, such as Mary McGeachy and Marion Royce, served as Canadian representatives to the United Nations and its affiliated organizations, largely as a result of pressure from women's groups on the Canadian government to make such appointments. In addition, at various levels both the National Council of Women and the Business and Professional Women's Clubs included, belonged to, or actively supported the United Nations associations within Canada. The familiarity of the executive members of the BPW with events at the United Nations led them, in 1954, to petition the federal government for ratification of Convention 100 of the International Labour Organization, requiring equal pay for work of equal value, and of the United Nations Convention on Political Rights of Women.

Between 1919 and 1960 women's organizations rooted in the first women's movement provided the transition to the resurgent feminism of the late 1960s. Addressing issues that ranged from the local to the international, they continued to provide a vital arena in which women of different classes, ethnicities, and religions could meet, learn, and act. Often ahead of governments, pushing for a thorough restructuring of public policies in key areas, they established and maintained innovative programs until governments were ready to assume responsibility. In so doing, they helped effect tangible improvements in the lives of Canadians, especially for children, women, and the elderly.

Notes

1. Elizabeth Lamont Forbes, comp., *With Enthusiasm and Faith: History of the Canadian Federation of Business and Professional Women's Clubs . . . 1930–1972* (Ottawa: Canadian Federation of Business and Professional Women's Clubs, 1974), 7.

2. Dorothy Sue Cobble, "Reassessing the 'Doldrum Years': Working Class Feminism in the 1940s," Paper presented to the Eighth Annual Berkshire Conference on the History of Women, Douglass College, Rutgers University, June 1990; Diane Crossley, "The BC Liberal Party and Women's Reforms, 1916–1928," in Barbara Latham and Cathy Kess, eds., *In Her Own Right: Selected Essays on Women's History in B.C.* (Victoria: Camosun College, 1980), 229; Diana Pedersen, "Providing a Woman's Conscience: The YWCA, Female Evangelicalism, and the Girl in the City, 1870–1930," in Wendy Mitchinson et al., eds., *Canadian Women: A Reader* (Toronto: Harcourt Brace, 1996), 194–210.

3. Gail Brandt, "Organizations in Canada: The English Protestant Tradition," in Paula Bourne, ed., *Women's Paid and Unpaid Work: Historical and Contemporary Perspectives* (Toronto: New Hogtown Press, 1985), 89.

4. Marjorie Wild, *Elizabeth Bagshaw* (Toronto: Fitzhenry and Whiteside, 1984), 57–58; Marjory Lang, *Women Who Made News: Female Journalists in Canada, 1880–1945* (Montreal and

Kingston: McGill-Queen's University Press, 1999), chap. 3; Doris French, *High Button Bootstraps* (Toronto: Ryerson Press, 1968), 48; Pat Staton and Beth Light, *Speak with Their Own Voices: A Documentary History of the Federation of Women Teachers' Associations of Ontario and the Women Elementary Public School Teachers* (Toronto: FWTAO, 1987); Marion V. Royce, *Eunice Dyke, Health Care Professional* (Toronto: Dundurn Press, 1983), chap. 7.

5. Judi Cumming, "The Canadian Federation of Business and Professional Women's Clubs," *The Archivist* 14, 1 (January/February 1987): 4–5; Forbes, comp., *With Enthusiasm and Faith*, 15–32.

6. Forbes, comp., 29.

7. Forbes, 28–29, 15–17.

8. Veronica Strong-Boag, *The Parliament of Women: The National Council of Women of Canada 1893–1929* (Ottawa: National Museums of Canada, 1976), 444; National Council of Women of Canada, *Yearbook* (1935, 1936).

9. N. E. S. Griffiths, *The Splendid Vision: Centennial History of the National Council of Women of Canada, 1893–1993* (Ottawa: Carleton University Press, 1993), 11, 162–3.

10. Strong-Boag, *Parliament of Women*, 357–58, 364–67; Christine Foley, "Consumerism, Consumption and Canadian Feminism 1900–1930, University of Toronto, M.A. Thesis, 1979; Anne Leger Anderson, "Regional Identity and Women's History," paper presented to the Canadian Historical Association, Calgary, 1994, 17; Rosa L. Shaw, *Proud Heritage: A History of the National Council of Women of Canada* (Toronto: Ryerson Press, 1957).

11. Nancy M. Sheehan, "Temperance, Education and the WCTU in Alberta, 1905–1930," *Journal of Educational Thought* 14, 2 (August 1980): 108–24; Sheehan, "'Women Helping Women': The WCTU and the Foreign Population in the West, 1905–1930," *International Journal of Women's Studies* 6, 5 (November/December 1983): 395–411; Sheehan, "The WCTU and Educational Strategies on the Canadian Prairie," *History of Education Quarterly* 24, 1 (Spring 1984): 101–19; Sheehan, "The WCTU on the Prairies, 1886–1930: An Alberta–Saskatchewan Comparison," *Prairie Forum* 6, 1 (1981): 17–33; Sharon Anne Cook, *'Through Sunshine and Shadow': The Women's Christian Temperance Union, Evangelicalism, and Reform in Ontario, 1874–1930* (Montreal and Kingston: McGill-Queen's University Press, 1995), chap. 7.

12. L. J. Wilson, "Educational Role of the United Farm Women of Alberta," *Alberta History* 25, 2 (Spring 1977): 35.

13. Wilson, "Educational Role of the United Farm Women," 30.

14. Alexandra Zacharias, "British Columbian Women's Institutes in the Early Years: Time to Remember," in Latham and Kess, eds., *In Her Own Right*, 69; Catherine C. Cole and Ann Milovic, "Education, Community Service, and Social Life: The Alberta Women's Institutes and Rural Families, 1909–1945," in Catherine A. Cavanaugh and Randi R. Warne, eds., *Standing on New Ground: Women in Alberta* (Edmonton: University of Alberta Press, 1993), 28–29; Linda M. Ambrose, *For Home and Country: The Centennial History of the Women's Institutes in Ontario* (Erin, ON: Boston Mills Press, 1996), chaps. 4 & 5; Linda M. Ambrose and Margaret Kechnie, "Social Control or Social Feminism? Two Views of the Ontario Women's Institutes," *Agricultural History* 73, 2 (Spring 1999): 222–37.

15. Le Collectif Clio, *L'histoire des femmes au Québec depuis quatre siècles* (Montréal: Le jour, 1992), 307–9; Yolande Cohen, *Femmes de parole: L'histoire des Cercles de fermières du Québec 1915–1990* (Montréal: Éditions Le Jour, 1990).

16. Nathalie Hamel, "Coordonner l'artisanat et le tourisme," *Histoire sociale/Social History*, 67 (May 2001): 334; Naomi Black and Gail Cuthbert Brandt, *Feminist Politics on the*

Farm: Rural Catholic Women in Southern Quebec and Southwestern France (Montreal and Kingston: McGill-Queen's Press, 1999) 29; Beth Light and Ruth Roach Pierson, eds., *No Easy Road: Women in Canada, 1920s–1960s* (Toronto: New Hogtown Press, 1990), chap. 5.

17. Sylvia Hamilton, "Our Mothers Grand and Great: Black Women of Nova Scotia," *Canadian Woman Studies/Les cahiers de la femme* 11, 3 (Spring 1991): 47; Dionne Brand, *No Burden to Carry: Narratives of Black Working Women in Ontario, 1920s–1950s* (Toronto: Women's Press, 1991), 16–17, 19; "History of Hour-A-Day Study Club," *Impetus—The Black Woman: Proceedings of the 4th National Congress of Black Women in Canada* (1977), 8; Peggy Bristow, "The Hour-A-Day Study Club," in Linda Carty, ed., *And Still We Rise: Feminist Political Mobilizing in Contemporary Canada* (Toronto: Women's Press, 1993), 145–72; Peggy Bristow, "A Duty to the Past, A Promise to the Future: Black Organizing in Windsor— The Depression, World War II, and the Post-War Years," *New Dawn: The Journal of Black Canadian Studies*: http//aries.oise.utoronto.ca/dawn/journal.

18. Stephen A. Speisman, *The Jews of Toronto: A History to 1937* (Toronto: McClelland and Stewart, 1987), 305–7, 319–20; for an overview of Jewish women's activities outside Toronto, see Norma Baumel Joseph, "Jewish Women in Canada: An Evolving Role," http:/ www.bnaibrith.ca/institute/millennium/millenium12.html.

19. Mary Prokop, "Looking Back on Fifty Years," *Ukrainian Canadian* (March 1972): 7–14; Lillian Petroff, "Macedonian Women in Toronto in 1940," *Polyphony* 8 1–2 (1986): 24–28; Isabel Kaprielian, "Armenian Refugee Women and the Maintenance of Identity and Heritage," *Polyphony* 8, 1–2 (1986): 33; Baha Abu-Laban, *An Olive Branch on the Family Tree: The Arabs in Canada* (Toronto: McClelland and Stewart, 1980), 146. For a discussion of these and other ethnic organizations, see Jean Burnet, ed., *Looking into My Sister's Eyes: An Exploration in Women's History* (Toronto: Multicultural History Society of Ontario, 1986); Robert F. Harney, ed., *Gathering Place: Peoples and Neighbourhoods of Toronto, 1834–1934* (Toronto: Multi-cultural History Society of Ontario, 1985).

20. Paula J. Draper and Janice B. Karlinsky, "Abraham's Daughters: Women, Charity and Power in the Canadian Jewish Community," in Burnet, ed. *Looking into My Sister's Eyes*, 75–90; Irving Abella, *A Coat of Many Colours: Two Centuries of Jewish Life in Canada* (Toronto: Lester and Orpen Dennys, 1990), 153–54.

21. Florence Bird, *Anne Francis: An Autobiography* (Toronto: Clarke, Irwin, 1974), 119.

22. Ruth Roach Pierson, *"They're Still Women After All": The Second World War and Canadian Womanhood* (Toronto: McClelland and Stewart, 1986), 36–37.

23. Pierson, *"They're Still Women,"* 33.

24. Vivien R. Kerr, A *Flame of Compassion: The History of the Provincial Council of Women of Ontario* (Toronto: T. H. Best, 1967), 37, 57.

25. Judith Fingard, "Women's Organizations: The Heart and Soul of Women's Activism," in Judith Fingard and Janet Guidford, eds., *Mother of the Municipality: Women, Work, and Social Policy in Post-1945 Halifax* (Toronto: University of Toronto Press, 2005), 25–48.

26. Julie Guard, "Canadian Citizens or Dangerous Foreign Women? Canada's Radical Consumer Movement, 1947–1950," in Marlene Epp, Franca Iacovetta and Frances Swyripa, eds., *Sisters or Strangers? Immigrant, Ethnic, and Racialized Women in Canadian History* (Toronto: University of Toronto Press, 2004), 161–89; Magda Fahrni, *Household Politics: Montreal Families and Postwar Reconstruction* (Toronto: University of Toronto Press, 2005), chap. 5.

27. N. E. S. Griffiths, *The Splendid Vision: Centennial History of the National Council of Women of Canada, 1893–1993* (Ottawa: Carleton University Press, 1993), 231–32, 251–54; David MacDonald, "Powerful Woman's Lobby in Canada," *Chatelaine* 29, 6 (June 1957), 57–58.

28. Dean Beeby, "Women in the Ontario CCF, 1940–1950," *Ontario History* 74, 4 (December 1982): 275–76.

29. Elizabeth Forbes, comp., *With Enthusiasm and Faith*, 56–111; David MacDonald, "The Most Powerful Woman's Lobby in Canada," *Chatelaine* (June 1957), 58.

30. Robert Collins, "The Biggest Country Club in Canada," *Maclean's* 10, 7 (July 5, 1958), 48; Helen F. Morton, "Women on the Land," *Food for Thought* 10, 7 (April 1950), 7; Ambrose, *For Home and Country*, chap. 7.

31. Yvonne Rialland Morrissette, *Le passé conjugé au présent: Cercles de fermières au Québec, Historique 1915–1989* (Montréal: Éditions Pénélope, 1989), 151; *La terre et le foyer* 12, 1 (janvier 1955), 25; Yolande Cohen et Suzanne Marchand, "Les relations entre les Cercles de fermières et l'État à travers leur correspondance (1920–1968)," unpublished paper, 18.

32. Le Collectif Clio, *L'histoire des femmes au Québec depuis quatre siècles*, second edition, (Montréal: Le jour, 1992), 442.

33. Linda M. Ambrose, "Ontario Women's Institutes and the Work of Local History," in Beverly Boutillier and Alison Prentice, *Creating Historical Memory: English-Canadian Women and the Work of History* (Vancouver: University of British Columbia Press, 1997), 75–100; Le Collectif Clio, 417–19; Jocelyne Lamoureux, Michèle Gélinas, et Katy Tari, *Femmes en mouvement: Trajectoires de l'Association féminine d'éducation et d'action sociale, 1966–1991* (Montréal: Boréal Express, 1993).

34. Pat Staton and Beth Light, *Speak with Their Own Voices*, chap. 5; Marjory Lang, *Women Who Made the News*, chap. 3; Marcia Wharton-Zaretsky, "Black Women Organizing," *Atlantis* 24, 2, 2000: 61–71; Frances Swyripa, *Wedded to the Cause: Ukrainian-Canadian Women and Ethnic Identity 1891–1991* (Toronto: University of Toronto Press, 1993), 183–84; Marlene Epp, *Mennonite Women in Canada: A History* (Winnipeg: University of Winnipeg Press, 2008), 155–56.

35. Ethel Vineberg, *The History of the National Council of Jewish Women of Canada* (Montreal: National Council of Jewish Women of Canada, 1967), 58; Eliane Leslau Silverman, "Women in Women's Organizations: Power or Pouvoir" in Lorraine Radtke and Henrikus J. Stam, eds., *Power/Gender: Social Relations in Theory and Practice* (London: Sage, 1994), 270–86.

36. Elizabeth Gillian Muir and Marilyn Fardïg Whitely, eds., *Changing Roles of Women within the Christian Church in Canada* (Toronto: University of Toronto Press, 1995), 3–16.

37. Michael Owen, "'Lighting the Pathways for New Canadians': Methodist and United Church WMS Missions in Eastern Alberta, 1904–1940," in Cavanaugh and Warne, eds., *Standing on New Ground*, 1–18; Frances Swyripa, "Nation Building into the 1920s: Conflicting Claims on Ukrainian Women," in Manoly R. Lupul, ed., *Continuity and Change: The Cultural Life of Alberta's First Ukrainians* (Edmonton: University of Alberta Press, 1988), 125–51.

38. Jo-Anne Fiske, "Gender and the Paradox of Residential Education in Carrier Society," in Christine Millerand Patricia Churchry, *Women of the First Nations: Power and Wisdom* (Winnipeg: University of Manitoba Press, 1996), 167–82.

39. Marlene Epp, *Mennonite Women*, 161–63; "Mennonite Women's Groups in Waterloo Region: Pioneer Leaders for More than a Century," Mennonite Heritage Portrait, http://www.mennoniteheritageportrait.ca/Report.php?ListType=Documents&ID=1844.

40. Dionne Brand, *No Burden to Carry*, 18.

41. Ruth Compton Brouwer, *Modern Women Modernizing Men: The Changing Missions of Three Professional Women in Asia and Africa* (Vancouver: University of British Columbia Press, 2002.)

42. Paul Axelrod, "Moulding the Middle Class: Student Life at Dalhousie University in the 1930s," *Acadiensis* 15, 1 (Fall 1985): 117; Marget Gillett, *We Walked Very Warily: A History*

of Women at McGill (Montreal: Eden Press, 1981), 231–32; Ruth Compton Brouwer, "Transcending the 'Unacknowledged Quarantine': Putting Religion into English-Canadian Women's History," *Journal of Canadian Studies* 27, 3 (Fall 1992): 53–54; Doris McCarthy, *A Fool in Paradise: An Artist's Early Life* (Toronto: Macfarlane, Walter and Ross, 1990), espec. chaps. 5 and 6; Catherine Gidney, *A Long Eclipse: The Liberal Protestant Establishment and the Canadian University* (Montreal and Kingston: McGill-Queen's Press, 2004), 48–63.

43. Mary Kinnear, *Women of the World: Mary McGeachy and International Cooperation* (Toronto: University of Toronto Press, 2004).

44. Joan Sangster, "'Women and the New Era': The Role of Women in the Early CCF, 1933–1940," in J. William Brennan, ed., *"Building the Co-operative Commonwealth": Essays on the Democratic Socialist Tradition in Canada* (Regina: Canadian Plains Research Center, University of Regina, 1985), 72.

45. Christina Simons, "'Helping the Poorer Sisters': The Women of the Jost Mission," in Veronica Strong-Boag and Anita Clair Fellman, eds., *Rethinking Canada: The Promise of Women's History*, 2nd ed. (Toronto: Copp Clark Pitman, 1991), 286–307; Diane Haglund, "Side Road on the Journey to Autonomy: The Diaconate prior to Church Union," in Shirley Davy, ed., *Women, Work and Worship in the United Church of Canada* (Toronto: United Church of Canada, 1983), 206–27; John D. Thomas, "Servants of the Church: Canadian Methodist Deaconess Work, 1890–1926," *Canadian Historical Review* 65, 3 (September 1984): 371–95.

46. Mary Anne Macfarlane, "Faithful and Courageous Handmaidens: Deaconesses in the United Church of Canada, 1925–45," in Muir and Whiteley, *The Changing Role of Women*, 238–58.

47. Marlene Epp, *Mennonite Women*, 157–58.

48. Randi R. Warne, *Literature as Pulpit: The Christian Social Activism of Nellie L. McClung* (Waterloo, ON.: Wilfrid Laurier University Press, 1993).

49. Mary E. Hallett, "Nellie McClung and the Fight for the Ordination of Women in the United Church of Canada," *Atlantis* 4, 2 (Spring 1979): 2–16; Valerie J. Korinek, "No Women Need Apply: The Ordination of Women in the United Church, 1918–65," *Canadian Historical Review* 74, 4 (December 1993): 473–509.

50. Shelagh Parsons, "Women and Power in the United Church of Canada," in Davy, ed., *Women, Work, and Worship*, 172–88.

51. William E. Mann, *Sect, Cult and Church in Alberta* (Toronto: University of Toronto Press, 1955), 40.

52. Janice Dickin, "Pentecostalism and Professionalism: The Experience and Legacy of Aimee Semple McPherson," in Elizabeth Smyth, Sandra Acker, Paula Bourne, and Alison Prentice eds., *Challenging Professions: Historical and Contemporary Perspectives on Women's Professional Work* (Toronto: University of Toronto Press, 1999), 25–43.

53. Valerie J. Fall, comp., *"Except the Lord Build the House . . .": A History of the Catholic Women's League of Canada 1920–1990* (Winnipeg: Catholic Women's League, 1990).

54. Michael Gauvreau, "The Emergence of Personalist Feminism: Catholicism and the Marriage-Preparation Movement in Quebec, 1940–1966," in Nancy Christie, ed., *Households of Faith: Family, Gender, and Community in Canada, 1760–1969* (Montreal and Kingston: McGill-Queen's University Press, 2002), 319–47.

55. Diane Bélanger et Lucie Rozon, *Les religieuses au Québec* (Montréal: Libre Expression, 1982), annexe 2, 294–319; Heidi Mac Donald, "Entering the Convent as Coming of Age in the 1930s," in Elizabeth Smyth, ed., *Changing Habits: Women's Religious Orders in Canada* (Ottawa: Novalis, Saint Paul University, 2007), 86–102; Smyth, ed., Changing Habits, 7.

56. Davey, ed., *Women, Work and Worship*, 54.

57. Clara Thomas, "Women Writers of the Twenties: the Dynamics of Community," paper presented to the York University Women's Studies Colloquium, November 1978; Joan Murray, "Isabel McLaughlin," *Resources for Feminist Research/Documentation sur la recherche féministe* 13, 4 (December/January 1984/5): 17–20; Natalie Luckyj, *Visions and Victories: Ten Canadian Women Artists 1914–1945* (London, ON: London Regional Art Gallery, 1983), 3–14; Barbara Meadowcroft, *Painting Friends: The Beaver Hall Women Painters* (Montreal: Véhicule Press, 1999); Frances Rooney, "Frances Loring and Florence Wyle, Sculptors," *Resources for Feminist Research/Documentation sur la recherche féministe* 13, 4 (December/January 1984/85): 21–23; Rebecca Sisler, *The Girls: A Biography of Frances Loring and Florence Wyle* (Toronto: Clarke, Irwin, 1972); Elspeth Cameron, *And Beauty Answers: The Life of Frances Loring and Florence Wyle* (Toronto: Cormorant Books, 2007).

58. Dorothy Livesay, *Right Hand, Left Hand* (Erin, ON: Press Porcepic, 1977), 48.

59. Luckyj, *Visions and Victories*, 16.

60. Luckyj, *Visions and Victories*, 109; Maria Tippett, *Emily Carr: A Biography* (Toronto: University of Toronto Press, 1979); Robin Winks, *The Blacks in Canada: A History* (Montreal and Kingston: McGill-Queen's University Press, 1971), 417; Adrienne Shadd, "300 Years of Black Women in Canadian History: Circa 1700–1980," *TigerLily* 1, 2 (1987): 11; Jean Bannerman, *Leading Ladies Canada* (Belleville, ON: Mika Publishing, 1977, Rev. ed.), 309.

61. Gabrielle Roy, Biography, http://www.maisongabrielleroy.mb.ca/en/biography.php; Phyllis Brett Young, with an introduction by Nathalie Cooke and Suzanne Morton, *The Torontonians* (Montreal and Kingston: McGill-Queen's Press, 2007); Coral Ann Howells and Eva-Marie Kroller, eds., *The Cambridge History of Canadian Literature* (Cambridge: Cambridge University Press, 2009), 294, 318, 333.

62. Sandra Gwyn, *Women in the Arts in Canada* (Ottawa: Information Canada, 1971), 21.

63. Barbara Moore, "Canadian Theatre's Fiery Godmother," *Maclean's* 71, 4 (February 15, 1958), 19.

64. Gwyn, *Women in the Arts*, 31.

65. Frances Rooney, "The Montreal Women's Symphony," *Atlantis* 5, 1 (Fall 1979): 70–82.

66. Gwyn, *Women in the Arts*, 36.

67. Gwyn, *Women in the Arts*, 13.

68. Maria Tippett, *By a Lady: Celebrating Three Centuries of Art by Canadian Women* (Toronto: Viking, 1992), 109–11.

69. Paul-Émile Borduas, "Refus global," in Ramsay Cook, ed., *French-Canadian Nationalism* (Toronto: Macmillan, 1969), 280; Patricia Smart, *Les Femmes du Refus Global* (Montréal: Boréal, 1998).

70. Gwyn, *Women in the Arts*, 18.

71. Tippett, *By a Lady*, 150–51.

72. Elections Canada, "The Evolution of the Federal Franchise," http://www.elections.ca/content. asp?section=gen&document=ec90785&dir=bkg&lang=e; Ken Adachi, *The Enemy That Never Was: A History of the Japanese Canadians* (Toronto: McClelland and Stewart, 1976), 344–46.

73. Carol Bacchi, *Liberation Deferred? The Ideas of the English-Canadian Suffragists 1877–1918* (Toronto: University of Toronto Press, 1983), 129–30; Georgina M. Taylor, "'A Splendid Field before Us': Violet McNaughton and the Development of Agrarian Feminism in Canada, 1909 to 1926," paper presented to the Canadian Historical Association, Ottawa, 1993, 28.

74. Strong-Boag, Parliament of Women, 438–39; Ramsay Cook and Wendy Mitchinson, eds., *The Proper Sphere: Woman's Place in Canadian Society* (Toronto: Oxford University Press, 1976), 324–27; Nanci Langford, "'All that Glitters': The Political Apprenticeship of Alberta Women, 1916–1930," in Cavanaugh and Warne, eds., *Standing on New Ground*, 73–6; Sheila McManus, "Gender(ed) Tensions in the Work and Politics of Alberta Farm Women, 1905–29," in Cavanaugh and Warne, eds., *Telling Tales*, 123–46.

75. Douglas Baldwin, *Abegeweit: Land of the Red Soil* (Charlottetown: Ragweed, 1985), 328.

76. M. Janine Brodie and Jill McCalla Vickers, *Canadian Women in Politics: An Overview*, CRIAW Papers No. 2 (Ottawa: Canadian Research Institute for the Advancement of Women, 1982), 6; Patricia A. Myers, "'A Noble Effort': The National Federation of Liberal Women of Canada, 1928–1973," in Linda Kealey and Joan Sangster, eds., *Beyond the Vote: Canadian Women and Politics* (Toronto: University of Toronto Press, 1989), 39–62.

77. Joan Sangster, "The Communist Party and the Woman Question, 1922–1929," *Labour/Le Travail* 15 (Spring 1985): 25–56; John Manley, "Women and the Left in the 1930s: The Case of the Toronto CCF Women's Joint Committee," *Atlantis* 5, 2 (Spring 1980): 100–19; Sangster, "The Role of Women in the Early CCF, 1933–1940" in Kealey and Sangster, eds., *Beyond the Vote*, 118–38.

78. Georgina M. Taylor, "Gladys Strum: Farm Woman, Teacher and Politician," *Canadian Woman Studies/Les cahiers de la femme* 7, 4 (Winter 1986): 89–93; J. F. C. Wright, *The Louise Lucas Story* (Montreal: Harvest House, 1963); Nellie Fraser's life story was told by her son, Craig Fraser, 1987; Alvin Finkel, "Populism and Gender: The UFA and Social Credit Experiences," *Journal of Canadian Studies* 27, 4 (Winter 1992–93): 79.

79. Sangster, "The Communist Party and the Woman Question," 27.

80. Irene Howard, "The Mothers' Council of Vancouver: Holding the Fort for the Unemployed, 1935–1938," *BC Studies* 69–70 (Spring/Summer 1986): 249–87.

81. Langford, "'All That Glitters,'" 71–85.

82. Margaret Stewart and Doris French, *Ask No Quarter: A Biography of Agnes Macphail* (Toronto: Longmans, Green, 1959), 74.

83. Terry Crowley, *Agnes Macphail and the Politics of Equality* (Toronto: James Lorimer, 1990); Doris Pennington, *Agnes Macphail Reformer: Canada's First Female MP* (Toronto: Simon and Pierre, 1989).

84. Faith Johnston, *Great Restlessness: The Life and Politics of Dorise Nielsen* (Winnipeg: University of Manitoba Press, 2006).

85. Sylvia B. Bashevkin, "Independence versus Partisanship: Dilemmas in the Political History of Women in English Canada," in Veronica Strong-Boag and Anita Clair Fellman, eds., *Rethinking Canada: The Promise of Women's History* (Toronto: Copp Clark Pitman, 1986), 258.

86. Martha Louise Black, *My Ninety Years* (Anchorage: Alaska Northwest Publishing, 1976), 137.

87. Simma Holt, *The Other Mrs. Diefenbaker* (Toronto: Doubleday, 1982), 320, 321.

88. Mary Kinnear, *Margaret McWilliams: An Interwar Feminist* (Montreal and Kingston: McGill-Queen's University Press, 1991), 3–6.

89. Mary Kinnear, "Post-Suffrage Politics: Women Candidates in Winnipeg Municipal Elections, 1918–1939," *Prairie Forum* 16, 1 (Spring 1991): 41–57; Michael Brown, " Ida Siegel," *Jewish Women: A Comprehensive Historical Encyclopedia,* http://jwa.org/encyclopedia/article/siegel-ida; Dawn E. Monroe, "Famous Firsts—Politicians and Public Servants," *Famous Canadian Women,* http://famouscanadianwomen.com/famous%20firsts/politicians%20

and%20public%20servants.htm; Patricia Roome, "Amelia Turner and the Calgary Labour Women, 1919–1935," in Kealey and Sangster, eds., *Beyond the Vote*, 89–117.

90. Sylvia Bashevkin, *Tales of Two Cities. Women and Municipal Restructuring in London and Toronto* (Vancouver: University of British Columbia Press, 2006), 323–34.

91. *Report of the Royal Commission on the Status of Women in Canada* [RCSW] (Ottawa: Information Canada, 1970), 339; Monroe, *Famous Canadian Women*.

92. Susan Walsh, "The Peacock and the Guinea Hen: Political Profiles of Dorothy Gretchen Steeves and Grace MacInnis," in Alison Prentice and Susan Mann Trofimenkoff, eds., *The Neglected Majority: Essays in Canadian Women's History* (Toronto: McClelland and Stewart, 1985) vol. 2, 144–59.

93. Linda Louise Hale, "Votes for Women: Profiles of Prominent British Columbia Suffragists and Social Reformers," in Latham and Kess, eds., *In Her Own Right*, 294.

94. Finkel, "Populism and Gender," 81–84; Catherine A. Cavanaugh, "Irene Marryat Parlby: An 'Imperial Daughter' in the Canadian West, 1896–1934," in Catherine A. Cavanaugh and Randi R. Warne, eds., *Telling Tales: Essays in Western Canadian Women's History* (Vancouver: University of British Columbia Press, 2000) 100–22.

95. Olive M. Stone, "Canadian Women as Legal Persons," *Alberta Law Review* 17, 3 (1979): 370–71; Catherine L. Cleverdon, *The Woman Suffrage Movement in Canada*, 2nd ed. (Toronto: University of Toronto Press, 1974), 143–55; Robert J. Sharpe and Patricia I. McMahon, *The Persons Case: the Origins and Legacy of the Fight for Legal Personhood* (Toronto: The Osgoode Society for Legal History, University of Toronto Press, 2007).

96. Valerie Knowles, *First Person: A Biography of Cairine Wilson, Canada's First Woman Senator* (Toronto: Dundurn Press, 1988); Franca Iacovetta, "The Political Career of Senator Cairine Wilson, 1921–1961," *Atlantis* 11, 1 (Fall 1985): 108–23.

97. "Biographical Sketch," Senator Iva Campbell Fallis Fonds, Peterborough Centennial Museum and Archives, http://archeion-aao.fis.utoronto.ca/cgi-bin/ifetch?DBRootName=ON&Record Key=42&FieldKey=F&FilePath=ON00226f/ON00226-f0000045.xml.

98. Luigi Trifiro, "Une intervention à Rome dans la lutte pour le suffrage féminin au Québec (1922)," *Revue d'histoire de l'Amérique française* 32, 1 (juin 1978): 3–18.

99. Thérèse F. Casgrain, *A Woman in a Man's World*, translated by Joyce Marshall (Toronto: McClelland and Stewart, 1972), 54.

100. Marie Lavigne, Yolande Pinard, and Jennifer Stoddart, "The Fédération nationale Saint-Jean-Baptiste and the Women's Movement in Quebec," in Linda Kealey, ed., *A Not Unreasonable Claim: Women and Reform in Canada, 1880s–1920s* (Toronto: Canadian Women's Educational Press, 1979), 79; Marie-Aimée Cliche, "Droits égaux ou influence accrue? Nature et rôle de la femme d'après les féministes chrétiennes et les antiféministes au Québec 1896–1930," *Recherches féministes* 2, 2 (1989): 101–19.

101. Susan Mann Trofimenkoff, "Thérèse Casgrain and the CCF in Quebec," *Canadian Historical Review* 66, 2 (June 1985): 125–53; Casgrain, A Woman in a Man's World.

102. Cleverdon, *Woman Suffrage Movement*, 232.

103. Diane Lamoureux, "Féminisme de charme et féminisme du choc," in Anita Caronet and Lorraine Archambault, eds., *Thérèse Casgrain: Une femme ténace et engagée* (Sainte-Foy: Presses de l'Université du Québec, 1993), 49; Micheline Dumont, *Le féminisme racontée à Camille* (Montréal: Remue-ménage, 2008), ch. 13.

104. Jennifer Stoddart, "Quebec's Legal Elite Looks at Women's Rights: The Dorion Commission 1929–1931," in D. H. Flaherty, ed., *Essays in the History of Canadian Law* (Toronto: Osgoode Society, 1981) vol. 1, 342.

105. Casgrain, *A Woman in a Man's World*, 62–63.

106. Candace Savage, *Our Nell: A Scrapbook Biography of Nellie L. McClung* (Saskatoon: Western Producer Prairie Books, 1979), 171.

107. Elsie Gregory MacGill, *My Mother the Judge: A Biography of Helen Gregory MacGill*, introduction by Naomi Black (Toronto: Peter Martin Associates, 1981), 218–19.

108. Ellen Louks Fairclough, *Saturday's Child: Memoirs of Canada's First Female Cabinet Minister* (Toronto: University of Toronto Press, 1995).

109. Lynda Erickson, "Parties, Ideology, and Feminist Action: Women and Political Representation in British Columbia Politics" in Jane Arscott and Linda Trimble, eds., *In the Presence of Women: Representation in Canadian Governments* (Toronto: Harcourt Brace and Company, Canada, 1997), 106–27.

110. John Crossley, "Picture This: Women Hold Key Posts in Prince Edward Island," in Arscott and Trimble, 281–82.

111. James Doyle, "Barbara M. Hanley, First Woman Mayor in Canada," *Ontario History* 84, 2 (June 1992): 130–40; P. T. Rooke and R. L. Schnell, *No Bleeding Heart: Charlotte Whitton A Feminist on the Right* (Vancouver: University of British Columbia Press, 1987).

112. Cora J. Voyageur, *Firekeepers of the Twenty First Century: First Nations Women Chiefs* (Montreal and Kingston: McGill-Queen's University Press, 2008), chap. 3.

113. Owen, "'Lighting the Pathways.'"

114. Griffiths, *Splendid Vision*, 167–69, 196–97, 212–13.

115. Sylvie McLean, *A Woman of Influence: Evlyn Fenwick Farris* (Victoria, BC: Sono Nis Press, 1997), 174.

116. Donald M. Page, "The Development of a Western Canadian Peace Movement," in S. M. Trofimenkoff, ed., *The Twenties in Western Canada,* Mercury Series, Paper No.1 (Ottawa: National Museum of Man, 1972), 81–89. Thomas Paul Socknat, *"Witness against War": Pacifism in Canada, 1900–1945* (Toronto: University of Toronto Press, 1987); Veronica Strong-Boag, "Peace-Making Women: Canada 1919–1939," in Ruth Roach Pierson, ed., Women and Peace: *Theoretical, Historical and Practical Perspectives* (London: Croom Helm, 1987), 169–90.

117. Nancy Knickerbocker, *No Plaster Saint: The Life of Mildred Osterhout Fahrni* (Vancouver: Talonbooks, 2001).

PART FOUR

1960 TO THE PRESENT

Muriel Duckworth and the Halifax Raging Grannies celebrate the signature of the Land Mines Treaty, 1999.

Source: CP Photo/Halifax Chronicle Herald-Peter Parsons

The 1960s were for most Canadians a time of great hope and confidence. Canadian arts and cultural activities were booming in spite of fears about the pervasive influence of the United States on Canada's economy, politics, and media. Quebec's Quiet Revolution and the wider sexual and social changes of the era were also in full blossom. In 1966, universal medical insurance crowned the achievement of a welfare state that promised to care for the needy and deprived. A year later, Canada marked its hundredth anniversary with an ambitious national celebration. Feminists were pleased to note that the second woman to be a Cabinet member in Canada, Judy LaMarsh, had been called on to organize these festivities. A hugely popular new prime minister, Pierre Elliott Trudeau, elected in 1968, promised a "Just Society," and his government offered support and funding for oppositional and marginal voices, including many women's groups.

However, others in Canadian society felt that change was neither as fast nor as sweeping as it should be. Beginning in the late 1960s, Quebec nationalists, Aboriginals, students, and many different groups of women struggled to transform society, sometimes cooperatively but most often on parallel or even conflicting courses. A resurgent women's movement that called itself the Second Wave of feminism launched public actions on behalf of women themselves. Some Canadian feminists were socialist feminists, who believed they could bring about change for women only by dismantling both capitalism and patriarchy. Other women, so-called radical feminists, sought transformation of society through a complete overhaul of its gender relations. "Our revolution is the most important revolution in the history of human beings," wrote "Dorothy," a self-identified radical feminist, writing in 1971 for the journal *The New Feminist*. Commenting on the sweeping recommendations of the Royal Commission on the Status of Women that had reported the previous year, she expressed the desire for more fundamental change.

At the same time, the social and political ferment of the sixties puzzled and distressed other Canadians, leading them to long for the good old days when people seemed to know their place. Then, everyone appeared content to bask in unprecedented national prosperity, and to pursue single-mindedly the good life. After the Depression and the war, it had been good to have a home of one's own, a car in the driveway, a fridge in the kitchen, and 2.5 kids in the rec room watching *Les Plouffes* or *Father Knows Best*.

But it was too late to go back. Canada grew and changed dramatically in the last decades of the twentieth century and the first decade of the twenty-first. In 1961, Canada's population was just over 18 million; by 2007, it had surpassed 33 million. Immigrants contributed two-thirds of population growth, since the average number of children born to Canadian women was in decline. By 1971 this number had already dropped to the reproduction level of 2.1, and in the 2000s Canadian women averaged only 1.5 children. The drop in fertility was especially swift and striking in Quebec from the 1960s; in this part of Canada the change was closely connected to the other major social transformations that constituted the Quiet Revolution. In general terms, however, the decline in Quebec's fertility was the acceleration of a trend that was visible in industrialized nations worldwide. Similarly, Canada was an aging society; it was estimated in 2008 that Canada would soon have more people leaving the labour force than entering it. The flow of immigrants that sustained national productivity and growth increasingly came from non-European sources. In 1971, just over 60 percent of immigrants came from Europe; by 2006, by contrast, almost 70 percent came from Asian locations, including the Middle East. Canada was not only a multicultural society but also a multi-racial one with significant visible minorities. The majority of immigrants settled in the larger cities, and Toronto became the most multiracial city in the world, with half of its residents born outside the country.

For women, the experiences that comprised immigration did not change in any significant way until well into the twenty-first century. Most women still came as family members. Only in the late 1980s was it recognized that many of these women were entering the paid labour force and needed to be eligible for work-related programs, such as language courses, that the government provided for male immigrants. Groups of younger women—Italian, West Indian, then Filipina—were recruited for the household service scorned by women born in Canada. Working conditions continued to be poor for the domestics isolated in private homes, even though new organizations now emerged to further their cause. In addition, women were disadvantaged as Canadian governments increased their emphasis on the economic components of immigration as opposed to social ones, favouring investors and skilled workmen over family-class immigrants.

Changes in the composition and distribution of the population were in large part responses to changes in economic life. The greatest growth continued to occur in the suburban areas of the metropolitan centres: while in 1961 fewer than half of all urban residents lived in the suburbs, by 1991 the majority of them did. In the late 1960s and the early 1970s, however, a back-to-the-land movement sparked a small but not insignificant shift of population to rural areas beyond the cities and their suburbs, especially among the urban middle class. Then, within a decade, middle-class Canadians, sometimes even the same individuals, were turning to the inner city for housing. Many of these were affluent yuppies—young urban professionals—who played a role in the transformation of the inner cores of the larger metropolitan centres during the 1970s and 1980s. By 1981, Toronto had replaced Montreal as the nation's largest metropolitan centre. Movement west, especially to British Columbia and Alberta during the years of great prosperity for the resource industries, then resulted in extremely rapid growth for Calgary, Edmonton, and Vancouver. The 1991 census indicated that nearly eight out of every ten Canadians lived in an urban setting, even though these areas comprised only 4 percent of Canada's terrain. By 2006, almost half of the Canadian population was located in the six largest metropolitan areas—Toronto, Montreal, Vancouver, Ottawa-Gatineau, Calgary, and Edmonton. The Atlantic provinces, on the other hand, in part because they did not have any large metropolitan area with employment opportunities that would draw immigrants and generate growth, declined in share of the population. The largest metropolitan centre in the area, Halifax Regional Municipality, had fewer than 400 000 inhabitants by 2006. At the time of Confederation in 1867, more than one in five Canadians had lived in the Maritime provinces; by 1991, only one in twelve was located in the Atlantic region.

The prosperity that most Canadians were still enjoying in the late 1960s began when World War II brought the Great Depression to a close. After the 1960s, the economy experienced a series of slowdowns and mini-booms often characterized by inflation, rising unemployment, and skyrocketing interest rates. In the early 1980s, and again in the early 1990s, most regions of the country were fighting a full-fledged recession. Recovery followed, but governments at all levels struggled with budget deficits. By the 1990s,

Canada was looking more like a neo-liberal than a welfare state, although national health insurance had become an untouchable icon of Canadian identity. Many women's organizations had become dependent on the financial support of the federal government; they reeled and protested under policies of funding only projects, not ongoing costs, and a new refusal to fund advocacy. Even service groups such as transition houses, now very numerous, felt the pressure of the deficit reduction strategies of all levels of government.

As Canada moved from an industrial to a post-industrial society, resource-based industries and other related sectors, such as manufacturing—which mainly employed male workers—became less important for the labour force. At the same time, the service and clerical sectors, where the majority of workers were women, experienced steady growth. In 1951, this latter area, known as the tertiary sector, accounted for just under half of the labour force. In 1991, by comparison, it comprised almost three-quarters. Fifteen years later, the 2006 census showed that more than three out of four employed Canadians worked in the service industries alone. Two incomes were necessary for most couples, many of whom were now cohabiting rather than marrying. Involvement in the paid labour force on the part of most women, even those with small children, was accepted as an economic and personal necessity. Then, at the end of the first decade of the twenty-first century, a world recession threatened Canada. Oil prices dropped, the resource and manufacturing sectors—including the critical North American automobile industry—encountered devastating drops in sales, and global trade slowed. Workforces in Alberta, Quebec, and Ontario suffered along with those in the traditional have-not provinces. Unemployment was higher for men than for women, and women's wages averaged nearer to men's because men's wages had fallen. Although Canada was not as hard hit as many other industrialized nations, economic conditions dominated national politics and deflected attention from other policy issues, such as those relating to the environment and to gender equality.

Canadian economic development was much like that of other western industrial nations, as the world moved from Sputnik to the information highway. The rapid pace of technological change was epitomized by the development of computers: from bulky constructions taking up the space of a large room, they evolved into ever-smaller personal computers that transformed the ways in which many Canadians lived, thought, and communicated. By December 2004, 71 percent of Canadian households owned computers—in 1998, by way of comparison, that figure had been only 49 percent. Later, cell phones acquired many of the capabilities of small computers. Younger people in particular used the multiplying forms of electronic devices for entertainment and socializing, as well as in education from elementary to postsecondary levels. Few technological changes had so much impact on the lives of women, both at work and in terms of the resources available for personal and activist communication.

In politics, the five decades beginning in 1960 saw profound changes in both federal–provincial relations and party politics. In 1962, Lester B. Pearson's government was the first of a series of Liberal governments lasting until 1984, except for a brief Progressive Conservative interval of nine months in 1979 when Albertan Joe Clark headed a minority government. Quebec rapidly became a secularized, modern, dynamic society that was uncomfortable in the Canadian federation as it then existed. Among the Quebecers, political structures and public opinion shifted toward support of autonomy and possibly sovereignty. The year 1963 saw the formation of the small *Front de libération du Québec* (FLQ), which in the next few years carried out about 200 terrorist acts, including bank hold-ups, bombings, and shootings. By 1973, the sovereigntist social democratic *Parti Québécois* (PQ), founded in 1967 by ex-Liberal René Lévesque, had won enough seats in the provincial Parliament to form the official opposition, and the party grew steadily in popularity. A major impetus to its success was the federal government's 1970 invocation of the War Measures Act against the FLQ, a step highly resented in Quebec. The FLQ had kidnapped the British Trade Commissioner and then abducted and murdered a Quebec Cabinet minister. This was the last attempt to use extra-legal means to change Quebec's status.

Under Trudeau, the Liberals formulated a firmly federalist vision of a bilingual, bicultural, and also multicultural Canada. The west was unenthusiastic, while sovereigntist pressures grew in Quebec. The PQ formed a majority provincial government in 1976 and made French into Quebec's official language the next year. Canada had become officially bilingual in 1969, but this and other concessions came too late. In April 1980, the PQ started a campaign leading up to a referendum on a new concept, "sovereignty association," which responded to the fact that most Quebecers wanted Quebec to be recognized as a nation but did not want to leave Canada. Women were active on both sides of the question, and in Quebec the pro-federalist "Yvettes," led by well-known feminists including Thérèse Casgrain, played a significant role. After sovereignty association was defeated by a 60–40 vote in May 1980, the PQ returned to electoral politics, seeking to win the confidence of the electorate and to create conditions for winning another referendum. Trudeau's response to Quebec nationalism was to "patriate" the Canadian Constitution, which accordingly in 1982 shed the imperial veto and acquired a new Charter of Rights and Freedoms. As a result of feminist efforts, the Charter included substantive as well as procedural guarantees of gender equality. However, the negotiations leading to the new Canadian constitution left Quebec isolated and even more alienated.

Conservative governments with a western base and a vision of decentralized federation—Brian Mulroney's majorities, 1984–1993, and Stephen Harper's minorities, beginning in 2006—made major concessions to Quebec nationalism, without apparent success. Two elaborately negotiated constitutional plans attempted in vain to satisfy both the aspirations of Quebec and the demands of other groups, including the Aboriginals seeking self-government. In 1990, the Meech Lake Agreement prepared by the provincial premiers and the federal government failed for lack of ratification by Manitoba and Newfoundland, and in 1992 the Charlottetown Accord was narrowly defeated in a national referendum. Some women's groups and many individual women opposed the two projects, fearing the loss of federal social programs and a weakening of the gender equality guarantees under the Charter of Rights. Some of them had also opposed the movement toward continental free trade that became part of Canadian politics in 1987. North American trade agreements threatened to open up Canada to cheaper competition that would harm industrial areas, such as garment and textile manufacturing, that still employed large numbers of women.

From 1990 a federal sovereigntist party, the *Bloc Québécois*, a Quebec breakaway from the Progressive Conservatives, voiced nationally the dissatisfaction of Quebecers with their position. In 1993 the federal Progressive Conservatives were reduced to only two seats, one held by a woman and one by a man. The catastrophic defeat had been under the leadership of Canada's first female prime minister, Kim Campbell, who paid the price for the Mulroney government's unpopularity, losing even her own seat. The incoming government, Jean Chrétien's majority Liberals, concentrated on dealing with the alarming federal deficit that had developed by the 1990s. This government failed to respond effectively to a second referendum organized by the PQ in 1995. Federalist forces prevailed, but just barely: 50.7 percent to 49.3 percent with an astonishing turnout of 93.5 percent of eligible voters. Under Chrétien's successor, Paul Martin, the Liberals foundered between 2003 and 2006, suffering from a complacency produced by their many years in office as well as a referendum-related scandal in the Liberal Party of Quebec. Western alienation generated a new regional conservative party—Reform, founded in 1987—that managed finally in 2003 to merge with the remnants of the venerable Progressive Conservative Party. The new Conservative Party came into office in 2006, determined to reduce the size and role of the federal government. Its version of federalism accelerated the hand-over to the provinces and to individual Canadians of federal social welfare programs cherished by women activists. There would be neither the ambitious reforms promised by the previous government to the Aboriginal peoples nor any sort of national program for daycare. Nor would there be federal support of feminist activism—women were considered just another interest group.

As always, international affairs set the wider context for Canadian politics and society. During the postwar period, this country had done its best to position itself as a "middle power" that could mediate among the American and Soviet blocs and the neutral grouping of ex-colonies and their allies. As governments composed almost entirely of men succeeded each other in Canada, women moved slowly toward greater participation in both conventional and protest politics. Led by the first new postwar national women's group to emerge in Canada, the Voice of Women for Peace, Canadian women were central in the protests against the American war in Vietnam. They also played a key role in the wider anti-nuclear and peace campaigns in Canada that reacted to the Cold War politics of military expansion and the nuclear arms race.

The Cold War that defined postwar international relations effectively ended in 1989 with the fall of the Berlin Wall that had divided Germany. Neither conventional nor nuclear wars seemed likely to threaten the North America continent. However, regional wars continued elsewhere, and Canadian women participated in Canada's peacekeeping missions as well as in combat zones, beginning with the Gulf War of 1991. At the same time, other Canadian women continued to organize to protest all forms of militarism. New threats emerged, including pandemics such as HIV-AIDS and new varieties of influenza; a good deal of the national response relied on the women who formed the larger part of the health-care sectors. Newly militant Islamic extremists used the virtually unstoppable weapon of suicide bombings, targeted initially against the state of Israel and then spread to the territories of other nations perceived as opponents of fundamentalism. On September 11, 2001, a group of hijackers succeeded in flying two loaded passenger planes into the World Trade Center in New York City, causing almost 3 000 deaths; a third hijacked plane hit the Pentagon; a fourth was downed by passengers and crew before it reached its target. Canada joined the U.S.-led coalition that in 2001 invaded Afghanistan, home base of the terrorist group Al Qaeda that was responsible for what came to be called 9/11. In this war, women soldiers, who were about 15 percent of Canada's armed forces, played a significant role in combat. The Canadian engagement in Afghanistan became very unpopular, but it dragged on under NATO control; it was justified as an effort to create a free nation that would, as well as denying a haven to terrorists, also provide autonomy and basic rights for Afghan women.

Women were increasingly aware of the complexity of their goals and struggles. It was clear, however, that they had interests to defend. By the 2000s women made up about one in five of elected officials, hardly adequate representation for over half of the population. A major project of feminists was increased access to decision-making positions in both the private and the public sectors. Their traditional attempts to exert pressure from outside the system were not enough; they needed a more meaningful level of participation inside it. Women and women's groups continued to press for change, including peace and disarmament and a new resistance to globalization. A younger generation of women, born after the 1970s, announced that they were the Third Wave of feminism, one that was more aware than their foremothers of the multiple intersections of gender, race, ethnicity, religion, sexual preference, and bodily condition that could disadvantage women.

The many changes in women's lives affect our study of them as we move into the present. While the study of women's history began in earnest in the 1970s, the recent past has yet to be studied in detail. Consequently, secondary analyses are still relatively scarce. As to primary sources, it continues to be true that records of economic, cultural, and political activities—the public sphere—are relatively abundant. When we turn to other aspects of women's experience, however, and to women who were not in a position to leave a record in the public sphere, material is more difficult to find. As a result, many dimensions of women's lives in the period from 1960 onward remain unexamined. However, historians' attention has now begun to turn to the relatively unchronicled lives of poor and powerless women, including their associational life and their attempts to produce change. There is now material available relating to many previously neglected groups of women, such as immigrant and Aboriginal women, women of colour, lesbians, and transsexuals. In addition, social scientists, many of them feminists, are producing studies that historians like ourselves can use. The subjects of their work include the contemporary women's movement as well as such other topics as work and politics.

It remains difficult to capture the day-by-day experiences of women, and the perspectives of the majority of Canadian women. The task of locating sources for the most recent decades has been hampered by the fact that the telephone, e-mail, and online social networks such as Facebook and Twitter have essentially replaced the personal letter as the major means of communication. Even diaries are now often electronic. If written diaries exist, they are still relatively inaccessible, compounding the problem of understanding the private worlds of ordinary women. Unfortunately for historians, the newer women's organizations that emerged, beginning in the 1960s, were committed to informal procedures and non-hierarchical structures; as a result, they have generated fewer organizational records than traditional ones did. Newsletters and briefs are difficult to locate, even though several archival locations are collecting such documents. More autobiographical and biographical accounts of prominent women are now appearing; they continue to be a valuable, if limited source. In addition, we have found useful material in magazines and newspapers as well as online, supplemented by written and oral personal sources. Finally, more formal oral history has begun to provide documentation for the recent past, including for those groups of women who have traditionally been relegated to the margins of history.

In addition to the problem of sources, there are the challenges of interpretation. Historians venture into the realm of the present with considerable trepidation; the subjectivity involved in choosing personalities, events, and issues on which to focus is all too apparent. Here there is not yet an accumulated body of historical scholarship to use as a reference point nor any consensus on what should or should not be included. The treatment of the newer incarnations of the women's movement embodies these problems, as does the whole question of possible improvement in the lives of women. Can we assert that women are better off today in Canada than they were 50 years ago? There often seems to be an overload of roles and responsibilities as the majority of women combine duties in the family and in the workplace. Sexism and heterosexism continue to be powerful constraints on even those women most privileged by class and race. For Aboriginal and visible minority women, for elderly and disabled ones, for women who are unemployed or underemployed or just plain poor, there are multiple obstacles to equality.

Still, for those looking back over the recent decades in Canada, it is evident that women have made considerable progress. They are better educated and have access to more and better jobs than women in the increasingly remote 1960s. As a result, there are now fewer restrictions on young girls' aspirations. More young women than young men are now attending universities. Women do not yet have equal pay, but they do have legislation attempting to mandate pay equity. Views and practices relating to women's sexuality have become more progressive, including recognition and rights for those who are not heterosexual. Women rarely die in childbirth or in backstreet abortions as they so frequently used to. Violence against women has not much diminished, but public opinion no longer tolerates it. Women have a greater voice in politics and even in economic decision-making. And they now play a major, acknowledged role in culture and in the arts.

The gender revolution continues with new players emerging. Where will it be in another 50 years?

CHAPTER TWELVE

New Trends and Old Issues
in Women's Work

> They're labelled luxury-mad materialists. They're blamed for deliquency and divorce. They're accused of throwing men into breadlines. But the fact is, Canada's 700 000 working wives are merely unrecognized pioneers in a social revolution.[1]

So wrote distinguished journalist Christina McCall Newman in an article about women and work penned in 1961 for *Chatelaine*, Canada's popular women's magazine. McCall Newman was correct in identifying at the beginning of the 1960s both the importance of married women's rapidly increasing participation in the paid labour force, and the continued, widespread negative reactions to their working outside the home.

Over the next half century, a sea change occurred in the composition of the nation's workforce that both reflected and produced profound transformations in the lives of women and their families. By the 1990s, Canadian women earned the distinction of having one of the highest labour force participation rates in the world. An even more dramatic change that took place during that time period was the very strong involvement in paid work of married women with children. Who could have predicted in 1960 that seven out of every ten mothers with children under the age of 16 would be working for pay by the late 1990s? It was not only the numbers of women streaming into the paid workforce that drew attention in the 1970s and 1980s, but also the extent to which they challenged previous notions of what constituted women's work. A number of historic firsts were recorded as they took on roles as firefighters, police chiefs, military commanders, corporate executives, and university presidents. Even the sky no longer seemed to be the limit as Roberta Bondar, Canada's first woman astronaut and the first neurologist in space, filled the role of payload specialist aboard the space shuttle *Discovery* in 1992.

It was, however, the "glass ceiling" and the "pink-collar ghetto" rather than the frontiers of space or the expanse of the corporate boardroom that most Canadian women workers encountered.[2] Even in the early twenty-first century, women in the workforce were much more likely to be office workers or retail workers than skilled trades workers or senior corporate managers. Gender segregation along industrial and occupational lines, if somewhat more mutable than previously, was still strongly in evidence. Nor was there much progress in eliminating the significant gap between women's and men's earnings. Women also continued to grapple with other problems experienced by previous generations of female workers, including poor working conditions and sexual harassment in the workplace, and the need to balance their household work with their paid employment. The extent to which they were able to surmount these problems depended very much on the class, race, and ethnic group to which they belonged and the region of the country in which they resided. For all women, even the definition of *work* remained contested as their enormous contributions in the form of household labour and volunteer work remained largely unrecognized. And all too frequently, when economic downturns occurred, the stereotypes re-emerged of egotistical women working for luxuries and taking jobs from men, and of mothers damaging their children and families by their reduced presence in the home. These were the same stereotypes McCall Newman had so succinctly captured in the early 1960s.

WOMEN AND THE WORKPLACE: THE NEW REALITY

After an initial decrease immediately following World War II, women's labour force participation rate—the percentage of women over the age of 15 who were working for pay or who met the official definition of being unemployed—increased significantly in the 1950s. Rising from 24 percent in 1951, it was 30 percent 10 years later. After 1960 women's participation rate continued its upward trend, moving to nearly 40 percent in 1971. (See Figure A6 in Appendix.) By 1981 over half of Canadian women were in the workforce. By this time, government statisticians were routinely using another measure—the employment rate—to track labour force trends, and we show both rates in Figure 12.1. Unlike the labour force participation rate, the employment rate did not include the unemployed, but only those Canadians over the age of 15 who had paid jobs.

Figure 12.1 LABOUR FORCE PARTICIPATION AND EMPLOYMENT RATES, WOMEN AND MEN 15 YEARS OF AGE AND OVER, 1961–2006

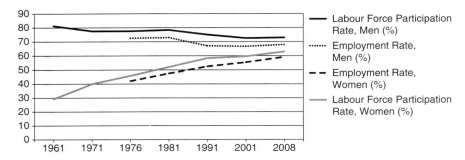

Sources: Adapted from Statistics Canada, *Women in Canada: A Gender-based Statistical Report* 89-503-XIE 2005001, 2005, released March 13, 2006; and the Statistics Canada CANSIM database http://cansim2.statcan.gc.ca table 282-0002.

In the early 1990s, for the first time, women's employment rate actually fell—from nearly 54 percent in 1990 to just over 51 percent in 1993. However, men's employment rate fell even more during the same period, from 70 percent to 65 percent. The decline in both cases was attributable to the loss of jobs brought on by the severe recession Canada experienced in the early 1990s.[3] Subsequently, women's labour force participation and employment rates both increased steadily, while the rates for men underwent little change. As a result, there was an increasing convergence in the employment trends of Canadian women and men.

Another dramatic shift occurred within the population of female workers, as a significantly larger percentage of older, married women engaged in paid employment. In 1976 younger women—those between the ages of 15 and 24—had the highest level of employment within the female population (see Figure 12.2), but by 2008, it was women between the ages of 45 to 54 who were the most involved in the workforce. These data reflect a generational shift; younger women were postponing entry into the workforce in favour of more education, while older women embraced paid employment to help improve their families' economic situation and also for their own satisfaction.

Not surprisingly, a woman's education level also had a strong influence on whether or not she was employed. Only 14 percent of women who had not proceeded beyond primary school held jobs in 2008, while 58 percent of those who completed high school did so. For women with a postsecondary certificate or diploma, the employment rate was nearly 70 percent, and it was over 75 percent for those with an education beyond the bachelor's level.[4] A woman's chance of being employed also varied according to where she lived. In 2008, women in Alberta had the highest employment rate (almost two-thirds), while women in Newfoundland and Labrador had the lowest (just under half).[5] Having a disability also affected the likelihood that a woman would be employed; 46 percent of women with disabilities were employed in 2006 compared to 65 percent of women without disability. Nonetheless, women with disabilities were more likely than

Figure 12.2   PERCENTAGE OF WOMEN EMPLOYED BY AGE, 1976–2008

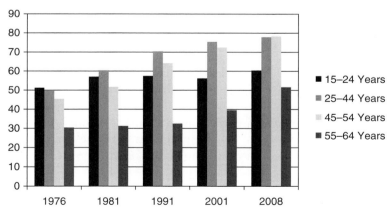

Sources: Adapted from Statistics Canada, *Women in Canada: A Gender-based Statistical Report* 89-503-XIE 2005001, 2005, released March 13, 2006; and the Statistics Canada CANSIM database http://cansim2.statcan.gc.ca Table 282-0002.

able-bodied women to be the main income recipient for their family; income in this case would include disability payments.[6]

Aboriginal women were far less likely to work for wages than non-Aboriginal women: in 2006, they had an employment rate of 51 percent compared to nearly 60 percent for all Canadian women. Within the Aboriginal population, however, there were some noticeable differences. While Métis women had a similar rate of employment to non-Aboriginal women, fewer than half of all Inuit women (49 percent) and status Indian women (46 percent) were employed. The last statistic reflected the generally low levels of educational attainment of First Nations' women as well as the scarcity of job opportunities available in reserve communities, where female employment was just under 40 percent in 2006.[7] For off-reserve women, who formed the majority of Indian women, discrimination continued to contribute to their difficulties in finding and keeping paid employment. All too common were situations such as that experienced by Irene Desjarlais when she entered nursing: "My first day at Brandon General I was so scared I felt like turning around and running down the steps and home. This was the first time away from my people. I heard someone say that I'd be just like the rest of the Indians and quit, wasting the government's money."[8] For Desjarlais, these racist remarks only strengthened her resolve: she went on to establish a very successful career in nursing.

In 2006, with an employment rate of 56 percent, visible minority women were also somewhat less likely to be working for pay than their non-visible minority counterparts. While they were better educated on average than Canadian-born women, many were recent immigrants who found it harder to secure employment. There was, however, considerable variation among the various female populations that made up this heterogeneous grouping. For instance, less than half of the Korean, West Asian, and Arab women had jobs, compared to nearly 72 percent of Filipinas and 60 percent of black women. In the case of the Korean women, these figures reflect the fact that many were unpaid workers in family businesses; by contrast, many Filipina and black women worked for pay as domestics and elsewhere in the service sector.[9]

By far the most striking aspect of the growth in women's paid work was the large-scale entry of married women into the paid workforce, as their labour-force participation rate tripled between 1951 and 1971.[10] By the latter date, for the first time more than one-third of all married women were working for pay. These employment trends reflected the fact that increasing numbers of women now completed their families by age 30 and, once their few children were in school, had reduced child-care responsibilities. In previous decades, a woman's adult life typically had two distinct phases: paid work before marriage, and then permanent withdrawal to the domestic realm. Now, for a relatively brief period lasting until the middle 1980s, a woman's life cycle had three distinct phases: paid employment until the birth of her first child, child-rearing at home, and re-entry into the paid workforce once all of her children reached school age.

By 1985, just over half of all Canadian women were working for pay, and a new pattern had emerged. By this time, for the majority of Canadian women, adult life was no longer divided into separate phases of employment and child-rearing; rather, most women typically combined the two. As Figure 12.3 shows, by 2006 nearly 70 percent of women

Figure 12.3   PERCENTAGE OF WOMEN WITH CHILDREN AND EMPLOYED, BY AGE OF YOUNGEST CHILD, 1976–2006

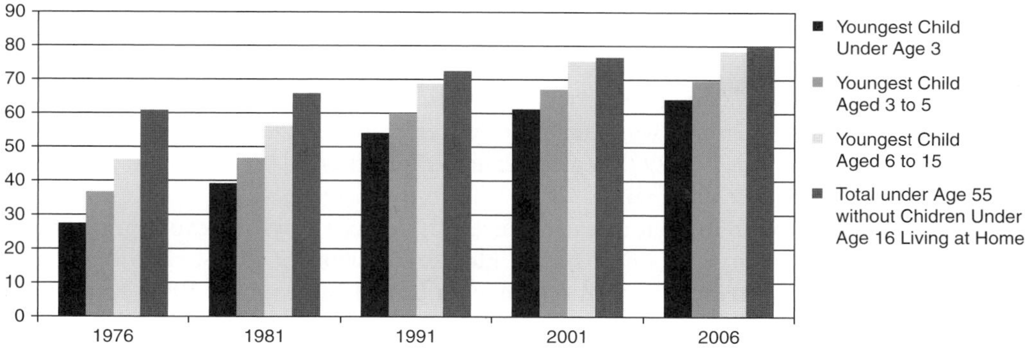

Sources: Statistics Canada, *Women in Canada*, 5th ed., 121, Table 5.5; *Women in Canada: Work Chapter Update*, Catalogue 89F0133XWE, Table 5.

with children under 6 years of age at home were employed, compared to just over a third in 1976.

In the 1970s and 1980s, when the female labour participation rate was growing fastest, the majority of working mothers with young children had to fend for themselves to arrange child care, which was often either prohibitively expensive or of dubious quality. In 1991, there were more than 3.1 million mothers with children under the age of 13 in the workforce, but there were only 333 082 licensed child-care spaces, and the number of new spaces was growing at the slowest rate since 1978. Over the next two decades, the number of licensed child-care spaces did rise significantly, and in 2007, there were 837 923 such spaces. But much of the increase was due to the Quebec government's adoption of a universal child-care program in 1997, which resulted in the addition of a large number of spaces for school-aged children in that province. Despite the increases, working parents across Canada continued to find it very difficult to access affordable, high-quality child care. In 2006, there was regulated child-care space available for only 17 percent of children under the age of 12, and for just 19 percent of infants and children under the age of six. A 2007 study reported that the growth in licensed child-care spaces slowed significantly between 2004 and 2006.[11]

The importance of married women's contribution to family income through paid employment increased substantially from the late 1950s on; it became the principal reason for women with young children to continue to participate in the labour force. In 1971, nearly six in ten of all families derived income from a single-earner husband; 20 years later, only two in ten did so. Wives' paid labour was especially crucial for low-income families: the lower the husband's earnings, the more likely it was that the wife would be in the labour force. In the early 1980s, a Portuguese textile worker married to a seasonally employed construction worker explained her role proudly: "That's life. I need money. I go to the factory. . . . The wife help, is good because I buy the house, need to pay . . . need the money." A farmer's wife in Saskatchewan gave a similar explanation: "Sometimes we have bills that we can't meet. . . . That's why I started working in the first place. . . . Grain sales were so low that we couldn't make ends meet and I had to get a job."[12] Despite married women's increased economic contribution, the average family income in 1991 was roughly the equivalent of what it had been in 1980, after adjustment for inflation but without taking into account higher levels of taxation. One of the effects of the recession of the early 1990s and the attendant decline in male earnings was that more wives earned either as much as or more than their husbands did. In 1992, nearly a quarter of all employed wives were in this category.[13]

Although this severe recession was replaced by relatively strong economic growth from the late 1990s until the onset of the global recession of 2008, the importance of married women's wages for family income continued to grow. In 2003, two-thirds of married and common-law couples were dual-earner families, and wives' earnings accounted for just over a third of such families' incomes. In fact, the proportion of wives who earned more than their husbands almost tripled between 1967 and 2003, rising from 11 percent to 29 percent. Even more notable was the fact that two-thirds of them earned more than twice as much as their husbands. The earning capacity of these wives was related to their generally higher levels of education and resulting greater tendency to be in professional and managerial positions compared to wives who were secondary earners. Wives' earnings were also important in keeping family income from falling below Statistics Canada's low-income cutoff line: the percentage of dual-income families below this line in 2003 would have risen from the recorded 3 percent (just over 120 000) to 9 percent (over 400 000), had it not been for the added income contributed by the female spouse. A study done in 2008 confirmed that some married women increased their employment income to offset their husbands' loss of income due to layoffs. Overall, it was women's wages that largely protected family incomes from decreasing.[14]

From 1969 until 1989, the jobless rate was usually higher among Canadian women than among men. The highest rates of female unemployment after 1976 occurred during the economic downturn between 1982 and 1985 when they averaged around 11 percent. After 1990, with the exception of the early 1990s—another recessionary period—women's unemployment rates fell steadily and were consistently lower than men's.[15] (See Table 12.1)

Table 12.1   UNEMPLOYMENT RATES, WOMEN AND MEN, 1976–2008

Year	Women	Men
1976	8.2	6.4
1981	8.3	7.2
1991	9.7	10.8
2001	6.9	7.5
2008	5.7	6.6

Sources: Adapted from Statistics Canada, Women in Canada: A Gender-based Statistical Report 89-503-XIE 2005001, 2005, released March 13, 2006; and the Statistics Canada CANSIM database http://cansim2.statcan.gc.ca table 282-0002.

Then the global recession unleashed in late 2008 sent general unemployment rates up in Canada to almost 9 percent in June 2009. Once again, women over the age of 25 were less adversely affected than men in the same age category: 6.1 percent of those women were classified as unemployed compared to 8.4 percent of men of the same age group. As in the early 1990s, this difference was the result of the loss of manufacturing jobs, held in large measure by men, and the relative stability of public sector employment, where significant numbers of women found employment. Between June 2008 and 2009, the percentage increase in part-time employment was almost twice as high for men as for women (7.3 and 4.1 percent, respectively). For both women and men under the age of 25, the recession was particularly painful; youth unemployment mounted to 16 percent, the highest rate in over a decade. On the other hand, the employment rate for workers over the age of 55 actually rose, especially for women. These statistics indicated once again the extent to which the gender and age dynamics of labour force participation had changed over the course of 50 years. It was now older women, rather than those under the age of 25, who were holding down paid jobs. And their levels of employment were increasingly similar to those of men.[16]

THE CHARACTERISTICS OF WOMEN'S WORK

Women performing paid work in Canada after 1960 experienced many situations similar to those encountered by their mothers and grandmothers. Two problems were particularly persistent: the continued assignment of most work according to gender and the lower rewards that accompanied work classified as female. From 1951 until the late 1980s, the massive influx of women into the paid workforce occurred primarily in clerical and retail jobs, expanding areas where the demand for their services was already highest. In 1991, more than 85 percent of all working women were in service industries, compared to 62 percent of all men. Furthermore, five occupational groupings—clerical, sales, retail, teaching, and health care—accounted for seven out of every ten female workers. During the early 1990s, as a result of widespread downsizing and restructuring programs in both the public and the private sectors, there was a decrease in the proportion of full-time women workers who did clerical work. The recession, global competition, free trade arrangements with the United States, government deficits, and technological change all contributed to increased unemployment and underemployment. Although women accounted for less than one-third of manufacturing workers in the early 1990s, between 1990 and 1992 they lost more manufacturing jobs—171 000—than did their male counterparts, who lost 149 000. Although there was a net employment increase between 1989 and 1997, most of it was the result of increased rates of self-employment and part-time work.[17]

By the end of the 1990s, the worst of the economic turbulence subsided, and between 2001 and 2006 Canada experienced the highest annual increase in total employment (1.7 percent) among all of the Group of Seven industrialized nations. Nonetheless, in a context of intense global competition and a very strong Canadian dollar, manufacturing

English women recruited by the agency Office Overload arrive in Toronto in 1966.
Source: York University Libraries, Clara Thomas Archives & Special Collections, Toronto Telegram fonds, image no. ASC02614

shrank. Ontario lost jobs in the automotive industry, and Quebec, in the clothing and textile industries. By 2006, the textile industry alone recorded a loss of over 18 000 sewing machine operators, representing nearly one-third of the individuals, mostly women, employed in this occupation in 2001. On the other hand, the generation of healthy surpluses by the federal and provincial governments led to a re-investment in the public sector, including health, social services, and education, sectors that were prime areas of female employment. Health care and social service employment grew by an annual rate of 2.6 percent, a pace well above the national average growth. The retail sector also experienced above-average growth; retail salespersons and sales clerks increased the most of all occupational groups.[18]

During the 1990s, media accounts trumpeted the entry of women into so-called male areas of employment, pointing to such women as Maureen Kempston Darkes, the first woman president of General Motors of Canada; Dr. Wendy Clay, the first woman major-general in the Canadian armed forces; or Lenna Bradburn, whose appointment by the city of Guelph in 1994 made her the first woman chief of a municipal police force in Canada. While there is no doubt that women made important strides in moving into male-dominated industries and occupations, evidence of the persistence of the sexual division of labour was readily available. For example, in 2006, women accounted for 96 percent of early child educators and 84 percent of elementary schoolteachers, but for less than 2 percent of plumbers, carpenters, and electricians. Also in 2006, 56 percent of all Canadian women workers were employed in just five sectors. In descending order

444

of importance they were health care and social assistance, retail, education, accommodation and food services, and manufacturing. By comparison, the top five sectors for Canadian men in 2006 were industry, construction, retail, professional, scientific and technical services, and transportation, which together accounted for half of male workers.[19]

In terms of occupational distribution, there was some convergence in the characteristics of the female and male labour forces. For the first time in 2006, the single most common occupation for both was retail salesperson or sales clerk. For women, the next most frequent jobs were cashier and registered nurse, while for men they were truck driver and retail trade manager. Women did increase their representation in senior management occupations, especially within the public sector, where they accounted for over 40 percent of senior managers and officials. Overall, women held just under a quarter of senior management positions, but only 7 percent of the executive positions of the top 100 publicly traded Canadian companies.[20]

Teaching and nursing continued to account for the largest numbers of female professionals—nearly 700 000 or close to one in ten of all women workers. Within the teaching profession, while the pattern of women being underrepresented in the upper echelons continued, there was notable progress. By 2000, for example, 44 percent of secondary school principals in Ontario were women.[21] Women also increased their representation in a number of traditionally male-dominated professions, comprising by 2006 half of all veterinarians and optometrists, and nearly 60 percent of all pharmacists. The surge of women into these lines of work occurred within a context of significant changes to how these professions were practised. In what was now an overwhelmingly urban society, most veterinarians made a living from small animal practices, rather than from caring for large animals such as cows and horses. The resulting lighter, cleaner work was more attractive to women. In optometry and pharmacy, the predominance of women coincided with the demise of small optical outlets and drug stores owned by individual professionals, and the expansion of large chains in which the optometrist or pharmacist became a salaried employee.[22]

Women also made significant gains in the traditional male professions of medicine and law. But in both cases, access to positions of higher prestige and higher income continued to be elusive. In 1996, women comprised just under a third of general practitioners and family physicians, and almost as many of specialist physicians. Ten years later, with women accounting for six of ten medical students and for over half of practising physicians under the age of 35, it appeared that the increased presence of women in medicine would continue, especially as male baby-boomer doctors began to retire. But in 2009, when women doctors accounted for nearly half of all family physicians and for over 45 percent of obstetricians/gynecologists and pediatricians, they made up only 20 percent of all surgical specialists.[23] The trajectory of increase for women in the legal profession was quite similar to that in medicine, as they went from representing 31 percent to 39 percent of all Canadian lawyers and Quebec notaries. Women lawyers, however, were less likely than their male counterparts to be in sole practice (42 percent versus 60 percent), earned only half as much on their hourly billings, had less chance to be made partners in large firms, and were two to three times more likely to leave private practice altogether. In recognition of the latter problem, the Law Society of Upper Canada struck a committee in 2008 to recommend measures to keep more women in the practice of law. The committee's report concluded that the most frequent cause of women leaving the profession was the difficulty in combining the long hours demanded by many firms with their parental responsibilities. As one woman lawyer commented,

> I feel that one issue which is not addressed at all by the legal profession is providing flexibility for parents of young children, especially female parents who end up with most of the responsibility. Maternity leave policies at most firms are ridiculous and draconian.[24]

Progress was also slow for women who wished to move into non-traditional occupations in the nation's mines, forests, steelworks, and rail yards. Companies like Stelco in Hamilton, Ontario, and Cominco in Trail, British Columbia, which had hired women as production workers during World War II, dismissed them when male workers became available after the war. While Alberni Plywoods in Port Alberni, British Columbia, did allow single women to remain in production jobs after 1945, it dismissed married women and imposed a hiring freeze on all women between 1958 and 1972. Faced with negative publicity from feminist coalitions, such as "Women Back into Stelco," and court challenges under human rights legislation for their failure to hire female production workers, in the late 1970s companies began to accept female applicants for blue-collar jobs. However, the several hundred women who did secure employment at Stelco never represented more than one percent of the workers and were often isolated; many became the objects of sexual harassment by male co-workers. One woman, Joanne Santucci, told of the sexual harassment, which commonly took the form of pornographic pinups, but also told how it could be combatted:

> There was a really gross picture, eh? I saw it one day, and the next night I went in again and looked, and there was this little paper bikini taped to the girl's crotch . . . and up on her top. . . . Later BJ said she did it. The guys thought that was hilarious. Instead of ripping it down, she added to it. Turned it into something different.[25]

By the early 1990s, the newly hired women, lacking seniority, were among the first workers to be laid off when the economy slowed down and layoffs in the steel industry became commonplace. As one of those workers explained in 1996, "We were all part of the Women Back into Stelco campaign in the late 1970s. When we won, we were all hired on at Stelco, but when the lay-offs happened, well, you know what happens to women—last hired, first fired. We've all lost our jobs there."[26]

Publicly owned enterprises were also slow to accept women into non-traditional occupations. It was 1981 before the Halifax Transit Commission hired its first permanent female bus driver, and only in 1987 did Air Canada hire a female cargo-handler in the Atlantic region.[27] In the case of Canadian National Railways, it took a 10-year legal battle initiated by a small Montreal women's group—*Action travail des femmes,* dedicated to finding jobs for women on welfare—to force the company to hire more women in non-traditional jobs.[28] In June 1987, the Supreme Court ruled that the Human Rights Commission could require companies to hire a specified percentage of women. Many of the blue-collar positions that women were fighting for were jobs involving hard physical labour and sometimes danger as well. However, the wages and benefits paid for such jobs were generally twice those paid for so-called women's work. Some women also relished the physicality and challenges of work in industry and the trades. "Office work never appealed to me," explained one such worker. "I don't know, it just didn't seem interesting. It wasn't for me."[29] Yet the office continued to be the milieu in which most women would earn their paycheques: by 2006, women still accounted for only 7 percent of employees with occupations in trades, transport and equipment operations.[30]

In response to the fundamental restructuring of the Canadian economy in the 1980s and 1990s and the disappearance of various forms of stable, full-time employment, many women created their own businesses. In 1994, for example, the women of Ahousat Initiative and Nuu'chah'nulth Business Association developed an ecotourism project that provided visitors a unique opportunity to observe Aboriginal culture on British

A woman working in a non-traditional occupation as a heavy equipment operator.

Source: Lisa F. Young/Shutterstock

Columbia's Flores Island.[31] Despite the lower bankruptcy rate among female owners of small businesses, however, women generally experienced more difficulty than men in securing the credit they needed to start up their enterprises. In one telling incident, Elizabeth Tower, who headed her own company, was asked to get her husband to co-sign a loan when, in fact, he was her employee.[32]

Between 1990 and 1997, the rate of increase in the numbers of women who were self-employed was greater than that for men. The trend toward self-employment for both sexes continued to grow, but less dramatically, and by 2002 women accounted for just over one in three of the self-employed.[33] For analysts, the growth of self-employment generated a debate about whether it was primarily "push factors"—the disappearance of standard employment opportunities offering full-time work and benefits—or "pull factors"—the desire for more flexibility and personal control—that motivated Canadian women and men to opt for this work situation. While working for oneself might offer greater flexibility for women with family responsibilities, for self-employed women engaged in full-time work, it meant longer hours on average spent generating an income. Self-employed women with no employees of their own also had lower average wages than non-self-employed women. Given that the most common activities pursued by independently employed women in 1991 were child care, sales, and hairdressing/barbering, their lower average earnings are not surprising. Self-employed workers typically could not access unemployment insurance (renamed employment insurance in 1996), and lacked company-sponsored benefits, such as health insurance, drug plans, parental leave, and retirement pension plans.[34] Norah Spinks, who established an agency to counsel other organizations and their employees about how to balance work and family, found it impossible to take any time off when her daughter was born. Because she was self-employed, she was not eligible for the maternity leave benefits provided for by unemployment insurance. Nor did she want to put her nine employees out of a job by suspending operations, although they could have collected unemployment benefits if she had done so.[35]

Among visible minority women, there were varying rates of self-employment. In 2001, one-third of all Korean women were self-employed, no doubt reflecting the large number of small businesses, such as convenience stores, owned by Korean families in which they laboured, often without wages. By contrast, for black women and Filipinas, the self-employment rate was less than 5 percent.[36] Even the category "black" may well mask important differences in the degree to which African-born women relied on self-employment to make a living, compared to women of African descent born in Canada or the Caribbean. A study conducted among black women in Edmonton in 1999, for example, found that a number of African-born women resorted to self-employment because they had difficulty getting their educational credentials recognized by Canadian employers. As one Nigerian woman commented, "Hopefully, people will begin to know more about Nigeria or about Africa and begin to see that when you come in with a bachelor of science degree, it's the same thing as a bachelor of science degree from Canada, and it's not inferior. But a lot of it is ignorance."[37]

For visible minority women in general, employment discrimination continued to be a concern. A 2005 study revealed that discrimination related to employment was a problem reported by just over one in ten visible minority women.[38] This number was undoubtedly an underestimation of the problem, since it represented only the most overt forms of discrimination and depended on the willingness of individual women to identify and report discriminatory practices.

Middle-class black women with professional training in education and nursing frequently encountered discrimination in employment. In 1964, for example, Gloria Baylis, a Barbadian who had trained in England and had two years' nursing experience in Montreal, responded to an advertisement placed by the Queen Elizabeth Hotel for a part-time nurse. When Baylis arrived for the interview, she was told that the position was already filled. Subsequently, she discovered that this was not true; with the assistance of the Negro Citizenship Association, she laid charges against the Hilton management for discrimination in hiring practices. The company was found guilty and fined the derisory sum of $25. But the case did not end there: the hotel chain appealed the decision through all levels of the Quebec court system, and it was only in 1977 that the case was finally decided (with the original verdict being upheld).[39] Successive groups of visible-minority immigrant women continued to encounter similar situations. "It was so disappointing," said Ziddah, a young Palestinian woman hunting for a job in the 1980s. "I went around and made all these applications and no one called. I felt so badly because they hired Canadians after me, that I was too dark. Then K-Mart called me and I was so excited and so happy."[40] Women like "Ziddah" continued to be overrepresented among low-status, low-paid employees, such as domestic servants; hospital, restaurant, and laundry workers; and garment and textile workers.

During the severe recession of the 1990s, women who had recently immigrated to Canada found it especially difficult to find employment: in 1996, only 51 percent of those who were between the ages of 25 and 44 and who had arrived in Canada in the previous five years had jobs, compared to 58 percent of their counterparts 10 years earlier. With 73 percent of all Canadian women employed in 1996, the difference in the employment situation of recent immigrant women was particularly stark.[41] Moreover, as global competition undermined the Canadian garment and textile industries, there was a decrease in the better-paying unionized positions, and a greater tendency to contract work out to home workers. One source estimated that 26 000 of the 36 000 garment workers in Quebec in the early 1990s were so-called underground workers. In Montreal, Haitian, Greek, Portuguese, and other immigrant women were paid by the piece to sew clothes at home. Their wages were often below the legislated minimum, and they had to pay for their own sewing machines and thread. Unprotected by labour legislation and isolated from other workers, home workers expressed frustration over the constant tension they experienced as they struggled to meet their employers' strict deadlines while juggling child-care responsibilities and household duties.[42] The daily routine of a Vietnamese worker who made garments at home in London, Ontario, was typical:

> I get up around 6 am, sometimes earlier, work until 7.30 when get children up, get breakfast, etc., and see everyone out of the house. Work from 9 until 11.30, get lunch for children, work from 1 to 4 when children come home from school, and start supper. Start work again around 7 and work until 9, or 10 or 11.[43]

In 2001, 11 percent of immigrant women and 12 percent of visible minority women with jobs were employed in the manufacturing sector, a rate nearly triple that of women born in Canada. In the Southeast Asian population, nearly one in four women were so employed.[44] Certain groups of immigrant women also continued to be overrepresented among domestic workers. By the 1990s, the largest numbers of domestic workers came from the Philippines and the Caribbean nations. Debt-ridden governments in the Southern hemisphere encouraged their citizens to find jobs outside their own countries and send some of their foreign-currency wages back home in the form of remittances. On the demand side, as has already been noted, more Canadian women were entering higher-paid professions and were looking for assistance with child care, elder care, and other domestic duties, assistance generally no longer available from extended family members. It should be noted that, from the federal government's perspective, it was financially advantageous to continue programs that facilitated the entry of foreign domestics, who would be paid by individual employers, rather than provide public child care. Under the Live-in Caregiver Program, Canadian employers could apply to Citizenship and Immigration Canada to offer a position to a foreign worker to take care of children, the elderly, or persons with disabilities. As indicated by the name of the program, the temporary worker was obligated to live in the home of the sponsoring family and to be employed on a full-time basis. After the caregiver had worked in Canada for 24 months within a 36-month period, she could apply for a permanent resident visa.[45]

By 2009 live-in caretakers were covered by provincial employment standards, and from an international perspective, Canada's program for foreign household workers appeared quite progressive. Nonetheless, as was the case for indentured servants of past centuries, live-in caretakers were compelled to live in the employer's residence. And, like domestic servants in previous generations, they were isolated and vulnerable to exploitation by unscrupulous employers, who might include members of their own extended family. Such was the case for one domestic worker sponsored by her cousin:

> I looked after my cousin's two children. I prepared meals, I looked after the children, I did the laundry and the housework. She paid me thirty-five dollars a week. I got up early at 5 o'clock . . . I didn't have time to rest, even on Saturday and Sunday, I went to bed only at midnight. They [my cousin and her husband] never took me anywhere, and I couldn't leave. What's more, I couldn't eat what I wanted. If I took something from the fridge, my cousin would get angry when she returned.[46]

In 2007–08, over 5 000 individuals, most of whom were workers in the Live-in Caregiver Program, sought assistance from INTERCEDE, a Toronto-based non-profit support organization for domestic workers and other temporary workers. The issues the workers raised most often were those related to employer violations of the Ontario Employment Standards Act, including failure to pay overtime, holiday, and vacation pay; failure to issue a record of employment and pay slips; and failure to remit taxes deducted from the caregiver's salary.[47] The continued challenges associated with domestic work were apparent, despite constant improvements in household appliances that made the work less physically taxing.

For women in other sectors of the economy, such as sales and service, new workplace technologies were more problematic. Beginning with the recession of the early 1980s many managers promoted the use of micro-technology in order to reduce the size of their staffs;

with computerized inventories, for example, far fewer clerks were needed. For women who managed to retain their jobs, there were other threats: a dilution of skills required to perform the work, increased use of monitoring devices to record their rate of work, more shift work, alienation from other workers, and health problems such as backache, eye strain, and high levels of stress. The office worker hired to do word processing for other employees she did not even know, or the grocery store clerk pulling items over optical scanners while the electronic cash register at her counter monitored her speed and sales volume, illustrated the dehumanizing effects of micro-technology. Conditions like these led one researcher to coin the phrase "the electronic sweatshop."[48]

In the 1990s, the increased use of computers and the Internet, coupled with downsizing and contracting out in both the private and public sectors, created an environment that was seemingly conducive to having more employees work from home. However, the proportion of Canadian workers who reported doing some or all of their work from home scarcely changed between 1971 and 2005, remaining at about one in ten. Moreover, two-thirds of such individuals did so for fewer than 10 hours per week. And there were no significant gender differences in these patterns.[49]

Where women did continue to be overrepresented was as part-time workers. The percentage of women who worked part-time increased during the 1980s; by 1993, more than a quarter of the women in the labour force worked part-time, compared to only a tenth of the men. In fact, women accounted for more than seven out of every ten part-time workers. Over the next decade, this situation remained virtually unchanged. In 2004, 27 percent of all women workers were employed on a part-time basis, compared to just 11 percent of all male workers, and women continued to account for nearly 70 percent of part-time workers. For women, taking care of family members or other personal responsibilities remained an important reason for seeking part-time work: among those between the ages of 25 and 44 who were working part-time, more than one in three gave this rationale. All the same, more than 25 percent of such women indicated that they would prefer full-time work, but were unable to secure it. This rate was close to that for male part-time workers, 28 percent of whom would have preferred full-time positions.[50]

Woman working at a computer in an office.
Source: Photos.com

Most part-time workers were not covered by pay equity, unemployment, or maternity leave legislation, and this situation caused considerable concern among many labour-force analysts. A large number of major employers in the service sector, such as multinational fast-food firms, successfully combined franchising, computerized work processes, and reliance on a predominantly part-time workforce to generate impressive profits. The high rate of turnover among most part-time workers made it extremely difficult for such workers to organize. A telling example of how difficult it was occurred in Orangeville, Ontario, in 1993, when 17-year-old Sarah Inglis attempted to organize a union at the local McDonald's. Had she succeeded, it would have been a landmark in North American labour history; however, the determined teenager and the Service Employees International Union proved no match for the giant McDonald's Restaurants of Canada organization. Five years later the Canadian Autoworkers Union did manage to unionize a McDonald's restaurant in Squamish, British Columbia. The first union at a Starbucks franchise in North America was put in place by the same labour organization in Vancouver in 1996. Workers there organized to protest the implementation of Starbucks' computerized labour scheduling process that tracked sales and forecast labour needs. Using this tool, the owners had begun to replace experienced workers with lower paid, new employees. The collective agreement signed in August 1997 contained provisions for work to be allocated on the basis of seniority. In August 2004, workers employed at a Wal-Mart in Jonquière, Quebec—many of whom were women working on a part-time basis—were the first to unionize one of the company's stores in North America. However, their success was short-lived. Just as the union and the company began mandatory arbitration, the company announced that it was closing the store for economic reasons. Subsequent workers' suits against Wal-Mart alleging that it had closed the store to punish workers for their union activities eventually made their way to the Supreme Court of Canada. In November 2009, the Court ruled that the company did have the right to close the store.[51]

A worrisome trend for both women and men was the rapid expansion of another form of nonstandard employment—temporary work. In the 1960s, the temporary employment industry had focused on placing women in clerical positions: those women were mostly white and middle-class, married, and wishing to supplement their husband's income. However, by the 1980s, as a result of major economic trends, including increased global competition, privatization, contracting out, and just-in-time delivery, Canadian businesses increasingly turned to employment agencies to meet new and different workforce needs. Temporary workers therefore came to include workers of both sexes with widely varying skill sets, from assembly workers to computer programmers and managers. Employers could reduce their costs by not having to provide the level of benefits accruing to full-time workers. They could also off-load to employment agencies many of the functions previously performed by in-house human resource departments, traditionally a major source of employment for women. With significant reductions in government expenditures during the 1990s, public sector agencies as well as privately owned companies increasingly relied on temporary workers. This trend had particularly serious consequences for female employment in areas such as health services. By the turn of the twenty-first century, labour analysts around the world were referring to the growth of temporary work in many economic sectors as further evidence of the feminization of paid employment, and the replacement of good jobs—permanent full-time positions with benefits—with what were considered bad jobs—part-time or temporary jobs with minimal or no benefits.[52]

A more traditional form of temporary work was the taxing seasonal work women performed in agriculture; in fish, vegetable, and fruit processing; and in retail establishments. Working conditions under these circumstances tended to be extremely trying because of the long hours necessary during short-season employment, and the lack of job security. "You work for the season, however long it lasts," explained Gina Vance, who worked in a Nova Scotia seafood plant:

> This year it was only ten weeks; they didn't do any crab. But my first season was six months, six days a week, nine, ten hours a day. . . . During the season you only get Sunday off, but even Sunday is geared towards the factory because of washing uniforms, aprons and gloves.[53]

In that plant in the late 1970s, workers stood on concrete floors in rubber boots up to 10 hours a day with their hands submerged in cold water for most of their shift, unable to talk with co-workers because of the noise of the machinery and the oppressive discipline imposed by management. In many communities, it was women's wage labour in fish-processing plants during the summer that enabled them to claim the unemployment benefits needed to support their families during the rest of the year.

The east-coast fishing industry underwent dramatic changes following the closing of the cod fishery by the federal government in 1992. Greatly diminished in size, the fisheries continued to rely to a great extent on women's paid and unpaid labour. In 2006, when women accounted for fewer than one in five fishing vessel skippers and deck hands, it was estimated that they accounted for six out of every ten fish processors.[54] As a result, the continuing closure of fish plants had a very strong impact on women in Atlantic fishing communities.

Conditions for agricultural workers, many of whom were Aboriginal or immigrant women, were often even worse than for fishery workers. The backbreaking toil, long hours, very low wages, and deplorable living quarters provided on some farms ensured

Workers, applauded for their "remarkable eyesight," separate peas for freezing or canning according to their colour.

Source: Photo: At the factory, peas pass inspection on belt that takes them to canning line or to freezing plant 11 July 1959 © Government of Canada. Reproduced with the permission of the Minister of Public Works and Government Services Canada (2010). *Source:* Library and Archives Canada/Canada. Dept. of Manpower and Immigration collection/PA-205814

that people became agricultural labourers only as a last resort. Particularly vulnerable were women admitted to Canada after 1989 as part of the Seasonal Agricultural Workers Program (SAWP). Under this program, the federal government allowed migrants from certain countries entry into Canada to perform seasonal farm work. The employer could request workers on the basis of nationality and gender, and could even specify individual workers. In 2006, there were just under 400 women participating in the SAWP in Ontario, representing about 2.5 percent of all migrant workers in that province. Three of every four of these women came from Mexico, with the remainder originating from Caribbean countries. According to a study of migrant women agricultural workers in Canada, many of these women were their family's primary breadwinners, and they had to cope with separation from their children for several months. In addition, migrant women often faced more constraints than their male counterparts, with some employers insisting on curfews for the women, prohibiting them from receiving visitors, or even forbidding them to leave the farm. A small minority of farm labourers, they often encountered sexual harassment from their fellow workers. As in the case of domestic workers, the migrant worker's work visa was valid for only one designated employer. The opportunity to be re-engaged in the SAWP in subsequent years depended on a positive evaluation from the employer; unlike the much larger Live-in Caregiver Program, this one did not hold out the possibility of workers remaining in Canada and acquiring permanent residency. In fact, some women were arbitrarily sent home for becoming pregnant, for being injured on the job, or for having visitors, with no right of appeal.[55]

WAGES AND BENEFITS

After social class, gender had the biggest effect on differences in wages and salaries. The persistence of segregation of workers by gender was a major cause of the continuing wage gap between women and men. In the retail sales sector, for example, women had lower average wages because they were often assigned work based on commissions. Selling lingerie, however, did not carry the same financial rewards as selling refrigerators or automobiles.

Overall, as Figure 12.4 indicates, there was a steady, if slow, decrease in the gender-based income gap between 1970 and 1991. The average annual income of full-time female workers rose from approximately 60 percent to nearly 70 percent of the average annual income of full-time male workers. Over a decade later, the earnings ratio remained virtually unchanged.

The wage differential continued to exist despite the enactment, between 1951 and 1973, of equal-pay-for-equal-work legislation. The primary weakness of these laws was that they applied only when women performed work that was the same as, or very similar to, work done by men in the same establishment, a situation frequently precluded by the existence of female work ghettos. In fact, equal pay laws sometimes actually reinforced the sexual division of labour, since employers in industries highly reliant on female labour could benefit from employing only women and paying them low wages.[56] Studies prepared for the Royal

Figure 12.4 WOMEN'S AND MEN'S ANNUAL EARNINGS FOR FULL-TIME, FULL-YEAR WORKERS, 1971–2003*

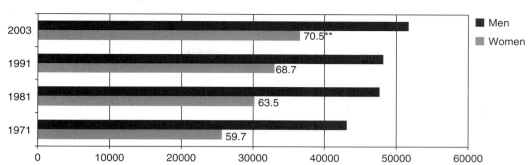

*Expressed in constant 2003 dollars.
**Women's earnings as a percentage of those of men.

Source: Women in Canada, 5th ed., 152, Table 6.9 "Average annual earnings of women and men, by employment status, 1967–2003."

Commission on the Status of Women in Canada (1967–1970) and for the various status of women groups that formed in the 1970s clearly demonstrated these flaws in the equal pay laws. As a result, members of the Commission and other women activists demanded legislation implementing "equal pay for work of equal value."[57] Under this approach, endorsed by the International Labour Organization in 1951 and ratified by Canada in a 1972 international treaty, jobs were to be evaluated according to a number of criteria. Most often those criteria included "skill," which meant qualifications required, along with the amount of effort needed to perform the job, the level of responsibility, and the working conditions. Proponents of this evaluation method argued that it was possible objectively to compare predominantly female job classes (such as clerical) with predominantly male job classes (such as trades), and identify when work was of equal value. Similarly rated jobs were then to receive equal wages regardless of the gender or classification of the worker. In Canada, such equal value provisions are usually referred to as pay equity.

In 1977, the federal government passed pay equity legislation for all workers under its jurisdiction, which meant mainly those working in the federal public service, Crown corporations, interprovincial transportation and communication, and chartered banks. Although this legislation did not immediately have a major impact, its potential usefulness for female workers was demonstrated on a number of occasions. For example, in 1978, librarians working for the federal government, who were mostly female, had their salaries raised to the level of those of historical researchers, who were mostly male. Quebec passed similar pay equity legislation in 1976, covering both the private and the public sectors, as did Ontario in 1987.[58] Manitoba's legislation, passed in 1985, affected only the public sector. Even with the new legislation, however, old problems persisted and new ones arose. Women who worked for small employers were usually excluded from coverage—for example, in Ontario, only employers with more than 10 employees were included in the legislation. The strict requirements that were established regarding which job classes could be compared, along with the difficulty of establishing gender-neutral job evaluation schemes, continued to hamper efforts to achieve equity.[59]

Pay equity legislation was significant, however, for it formally recognized the systemic discrimination that women encountered in the paid labour force, and demonstrated that feminists—who had been instrumental in bringing about the legislation—could influence state policy.

In addition, pay equity was an essential part of the more comprehensive programs given the name of "employment equity" by Judge Rosalie Silberman Abella in her Royal Commission report in 1984. Employment equity related to women, visible minorities, Aboriginals, and persons with disabilities, all of whom were badly hampered by workplace rules and expectations that had been developed historically for white, male, able-bodied workers. For women in particular, positive or affirmative action was needed, not just to deal with pay disparities and workplace segregation, but also to provide the training and support services, such as daycare, necessary for them to participate as equals in the paid labour market.[60] The federal government passed the Employment Equity Act in 1986, and initiated modest equity programs for the public service and for institutions or businesses that had federal government contracts. A revised Employment Equity Act that extended and strengthened the original law was legislated in 1995. In 1993, the NDP government of Bob Rae in Ontario was the first provincial government to introduce employment equity legislation; the law applied to all but small workplaces. This legislation was repealed in 1995, however, by the Conservative government of Mike Harris, which was ideologically opposed to the concept of systemic discrimination and to employment equity programs. In its place, the Conservatives established an equal-opportunity policy that emphasized the importance of individual merit-based assessment procedures free of discrimination. Their actions left British Columbia as the only province with employment equity legislation, passed in 1994. By 2000, eight provinces had some sort of employment equity policy, but these policies were not enshrined in law. The following year, Quebec passed employment equity legislation that covered many public-sector employees in the province. In 2009, only Newfoundland and Alberta did not have formal employment equity programs, which in Canada typically set goals or targets—not quotas—for hiring, promoting, and paying members of the four designated groups in the relevant workforce.[61]

In spite of all the progressive legislation of the 1970s and 1980s, women's lower wages remained a central fact of their working lives, affecting their standard of living and that of their children, and dooming many to an impoverished old age. Women's increasing life expectancy, together with low wages, produced a distinct class of poor people in Canada: widows and elderly single women. Existing pension plans, such as the Canada Pension Plan, were calculated on the basis of earnings accumulated through a continuous, lifelong involvement in the labour force. But what if the retired worker had taken years out of the labour force to raise children, as so many women had? Pensions for housewives became a major issue in the 1970s and 1980s, although some considered it a discriminatory measure, since by this time only the well-to-do could afford to have wives full-time in the home for their entire adult lives.

As child-care alternatives became more limited in the 1980s, and many mothers wrestled with the dilemma of how to balance paid employment and child-rearing, a growing percentage of those who could afford to do so stepped out of the labour force. Such pauses, however, were expensive: one federal study estimated that women who interrupted their employment for a decade or more, and then resumed employment, forfeited on average $80 000 of career earnings. In addition, they would also have significantly lower pensions at retirement. Men, by contrast, appeared to enjoy a 30 percent increase in their earning potential as a result of being married.[62] Responding to lobbying by women's organizations, provincial governments gradually agreed to a drop-out provision, which meant that up to seven years could be dropped from Canada (or Quebec) Pension Plan calculations on account of absence from the workforce to care for children.[63] These measures, in addition to other factors, such as the significantly increased percentage of women who were employed and paying into both public and private pension plans, had a beneficial impact: by 2003, the inflation-adjusted annual average income of women over the age of 65 was nearly one-third higher than it had been in 1981.[64]

By the end of the 1980s, there were just beginning to be legal requirements that pro-rated benefits be provided to part-time workers. Another hopeful sign was the employment lawsuit won by Edna Cronk in 1994. Cronk, a 29-year clerical employee of a Hamilton insurance company, was let go with a nine-month severance pay package when the company restructured. This settlement was less than half the number of months' salary paid to managers who were dismissed at the same time. In a groundbreaking decision, she was awarded 20 months' severance pay, on the basis that her job had been as important to her as the managers' had been to them, and that she had suffered as much from the loss of her employment as they had from theirs.[65] Nonetheless, as late as 2005, fewer than half of all part-time workers received non-wage benefits from their employers, and fewer than one quarter had access to any of the following employer-sponsored plans: pension, group-registered retirement savings, life/disability insurance, supplemental medical insurance, or dental. Since women continued to account for 70 percent of all part-time workers, they clearly were at a disadvantage.[66]

For most women workers, maternity leave was made available in the 1960s and 1970s under provincial legislation that entitled pregnant employees to leave and then resume their jobs without loss of position or seniority; payment to partly replace wages was given separately under the federal unemployment insurance program. Initially, a longer qualifying period was required than for cases of unemployment on other grounds, apparently on the assumption that women who were already pregnant might take jobs just to get support. In the 1970s, those provisions had paradoxical implications, as Stella Bliss discovered.

In 1976 Bliss was unemployed, having been fired. She had at that point worked long enough to be eligible for normal benefits but did not apply for them because she was pregnant and did not intend to seek work until after the baby was born. Then, ready and eager to work but unable to find a job, she was refused benefits on the grounds that, having been pregnant when she became jobless, the only unemployment benefits she was entitled to were the pregnancy ones—for which she had not worked long enough to be eligible. This decision, she claimed, discriminated against women. The Supreme Court of Canada disagreed in 1978, arguing that Bliss was denied benefits not because she was a woman but because she was pregnant. The discrimination was made not by law but by nature, which decreed that only women became pregnant. This situation got a certain amount of public attention. With the assistance of pressure from women's organizations, two changes occurred in 1983: an amendment to the Unemployment Insurance Act so that it was no longer necessary to be in the workforce longer for pregnancy than for other unemployment benefits, and an amendment to the Canadian Human Rights Act so that discrimination because of pregnancy was no longer allowed.[67]

Over the next two decades maternity leave provisions were ensconced in provincial employment standards legislation, and new provisions were added in most jurisdictions regarding additional paid and unpaid parental leave. In 2001, the federal government extended to one year the length of time for which mothers could take combined maternity and parental benefits. However, many women—including the self-employed and students—were still not covered, and the highest Employment Insurance benefit in 2007 was 55 percent of wages, up to a maximum of $423 per week. As a result, depending on province or territory, some 30 to 50 percent of all new mothers did not participate in the federal/provincial maternity leave programs. Quebec provided the most generous support under its parental insurance plan, inaugurated in 2006, and was unusual in including self-employed workers as well as employees. In November 2009, the federal government announced its intention to introduce new legislation to enable the self-employed to make voluntary employment insurance payments so that they could obtain maternity and parental leave benefits along with sickness and compassionate care benefits.[68]

Given all of the legislative initiatives mentioned above, as well as women's increased educational attainment and movement into higher-paid occupations in the late 1990s and early 2000s, one might have expected to see a substantive narrowing in Canada of the gender gap in wages. In fact, the proportion of wages earned by women who worked full-time and full-year to those of their male counterparts remained almost unchanged, dipping to 68 percent in 1997 but settling at 72 percent in 2006.[69] Compared to the situation in a number of other countries, the ratio of women's earnings to men's in Canada continued to remain noticeably lower. In 2004, among the 21 industrialized nations belonging to the Organisation for Economic Co-operation and Development (OECD), Canada was among the six countries (along with the United States, Switzerland, Germany, Japan, and Korea) where men's median earnings surpassed women's by more than 20 percent. By contrast, the difference was under 10 percent in New Zealand and Belgium.[70]

Even when workers' education was taken into account, Canadian women earned less than male workers with an equivalent level of education. In 2003, women with a university degree who worked full-time earned on average $53 400 compared to $77 500 earned by their male peers. Even more surprising, the earnings gap between university-educated women and men actually increased between 1995—when such women's earnings were 75 percent of those of men with equivalent education—and 2005, when they earned just 69 percent as much.[71] Jobs associated with women's work in the home, in particular, remained woefully undervalued: in New Brunswick in 2003, the more highly paid child-care workers—usually professionals with postsecondary training—were earning only $7 to $8 an hour, a wage "so low" that they were "finding it difficult to build a career."[72]

Evaluating the causes of the gender gap in wages is difficult. Nearly all analysts who have studied this gender gap agree that half or more of the wage differential between women and men is left unexplained by obvious objective factors, such as education and major field of study, work experience, or withdrawal from the workforce.[73] It is possible, however, that in the future the wage gap may be reduced as a result of new factors, such as the replacement of baby-boom generation women by their more highly educated daughters, who may choose less traditional career paths. In 2003, for example, women between the ages of 16 and 24 had an earnings ratio of 81 percent of wages earned by men in the same age group, and women aged 25 to 34 earned just under 75 percent of what men in their age category did. By contrast, women over the age of 45 earned on average less than 70 percent of the income of men in their age group.[74] It is also possible that the gender gap in pay may be reduced by a continued decline in male wages. With the disappearance of high-paying, unionized jobs in manufacturing, growing numbers of men have had to resort to part-time, temporary jobs—the type of jobs that have traditionally composed such a significant part of women's employment—with a resulting drop in wages. If one takes into account all earners, women's annual average earnings increased by over 18 percent between 1992 and 2006, while the equivalent increase for men was only 13 percent. This process of "harmonizing down," according to some analysts, began to manifest itself in Canada starting in the 1990s and has already played a role in narrowing the wage gap in some other countries, such as Australia and France.[75] In other words, it is not so much that women's paid employment situation as a whole has improved but, rather, that men's has deteriorated.

WORKING FOR THE FAMILY

For the many women who worked long hours without pay in family businesses, arguments about the size of the gender-based wage gap were of little relevance. In 1981, more than 52 000 Canadian women laboured as unpaid workers in family enterprises. While nearly 60 percent worked on family farms, others staffed small retail establishments. Although amendments to the federal Income Tax Act in 1981 permitted the payment of salaries to spouses working in unincorporated family businesses, thereby entitling them to contribute to the Canada Pension Plan, many women were unable to take advantage of the change, since financially hard-pressed family businesses could not afford to pay them wages.[76]

For farm women, the 1980s were particularly difficult. Ownership of land by large agricultural enterprises increased, and the proportion of family-owned farms declined. Squeezed by rising interest rates and production costs, and by declining commodity prices, farmers' incomes plummeted and bankruptcies soared. While there were 623 000 farms in Canada in 1951, by 1981 there were fewer than 319 000. In many instances, farm families survived precariously, thanks to the income that wives obtained from paid employment off the farm. A 1982 survey of farm wives in Ontario's Grey and Bruce counties reported that 60 percent of them had had off-farm employment during the previous 10 years. Many farm women were thus compelled to work what could be termed a triple day. Not only did they hold down full-time jobs and perform the bulk of the household work, but they also did their share of the farm chores.[77]

Given the economic crisis confronting many farm families, rural women coped with high levels of stress, and with little access to support services such as daycare centres or health clinics. In spite of the idyllic image of rural life, domestic violence, intergenerational conflict, and medical problems, such as alcoholism, heart disease, and ulcers, were increasingly frequent. "Jane's" story was typical. She was married to a full-time Ontario farmer, but in 1986, in order to pay the bills, the family of four depended on the $200 weekly salary she earned as an office worker. Her marriage was strained, and she was under medical care for stomach trouble.[78] Women in several provinces organized to save the family farm. These groups included Ontario's Women for the Survival of Agriculture (1975) and Concerned Farm Women (1981), and the Saskatchewan Agricultural Women's Network (1985). The continued migration of the rural population to urban centres also resulted in a reduction in the community services and facilities that past generations of farm women had fought so hard to obtain. As rural post offices, stores, schools, and churches disappeared from the countryside, women were active in such groups as Rural Dignity for Canada, created to protest the closing of rural post offices.

Between 1986 and 2006, the number of farms continued to decline, from over 290 000 to just under 230 000, and those that remained became larger as the average size increased from 310 to 456 acres. While there was a growth in the number of corporate farms, the proportion of those that belonged to families who incorporated into larger multi-generational businesses also increased. By 2006, women represented just over one-quarter of all farm operators, and women's work, both on and off the farm, continued to represent a major economic contribution to the agricultural enterprise. A 2001 study found that fewer than half of farming couples with sales in excess of $10 000 followed the traditional pattern of working only on the farm; for the majority, at least one spouse performed paid work off the farm. Since the percentage of farm women with post-secondary education continued to increase, it was often easier for them to find such employment compared to their husbands, who tended to have less education. Another study found that farm women were more likely to have jobs than women in general: "There aren't more farm women," it concluded, "but more farm women are working off the farm."[79]

Work on the farm continued to be divided along gender lines, with women performing a much larger share of the household labour than their male partners and men performing significantly more agricultural work. However, a study conducted for the National Farmers Union in 2001–2002 showed that women were more active in agricultural work, such as operating machinery, caring for animals, and running farm errands, than they had been 20 years before. Given the decline in the number of farms reporting the use of paid agricultural labour, to 39 percent in 2006, farm wives' unpaid agricultural work became increasingly important to the success of many farm operations. Women were more involved in farm management as well, and were largely responsible for the maintenance of farm records. While farm husbands, especially those who were younger, increased the time they spent performing household tasks, wives continued to be the primary caregivers, looking after children and elderly relatives. Farm women also spent more hours on average compared to non-farm women in volunteer and community activities. Clearly, the time needed to perform all of the various forms of work in which they were involved greatly diminished the amount of available leisure time, and contributed to the stress they experienced.[80]

Farm women's situation with regard to household work was typical, since women everywhere in Canada continued to perform the bulk of domestic labour. Such work, however, still went largely unrecognized and unrewarded. Government statisticians estimated that if the unpaid services Canadian women provided in the home were assigned a value, they would account for one-third to one-half of the Gross Domestic Product. It was reported in 2003 that unpaid household work had a value of between $235 and $374 billion, depending on the method of calculation.[81] For full-time housewives, there were none of the usual benefits of full-time employment—salary, vacation, sick leave, social security provisions—and, in spite of the introduction of labour-saving devices, the time women spent performing domestic duties was not significantly reduced. The absence of full-time domestic help and the constantly rising standards of performance intensified the homemaker's responsibility for housework, and for the management of consumption and of the family in general.

For many wives, housework continued to be rendered more difficult by the fact that their husbands worked shifts so that they had to juggle different schedules in order to accommodate the conflicting needs of husband, children, and household. As one Flin Flon, Manitoba, wife explained, "Those changing shifts are awful. It's a constant reminder that his work comes first over any other needs this family might have. We can never get ourselves organized into any regular pattern because our lives are always being turned upside down."[82]

In Inuit communities, as a result of government relocation schemes that forced people to move into larger permanent settlements, men who participated in hunting expeditions had to go farther away and be absent for extended periods in order to secure game. Child-rearing, traditionally shared by parents, became predominantly women's work. Sewing machines and camp stoves made women's household tasks easier, but also represented increased work as the women assumed responsibility for maintaining

Mrs. Lillian Dick pickets the Super S Drugs store in Calgary, Alberta, in March 1970 to protest its signage belittling wives. The sign read "Next to no wife, a good one is best."

Source: Glenbow Archives NA-2864-5209

and repairing these items. In some cases, women stopped making traditional clothing altogether and so lost touch with an important aspect of Inuit women's handicrafts and culture. Acculturation also seems to have exacted a physical price for Inuit women: according to a long-term study of one group of Inuit, the women were on average nearly 2.5 cm shorter in 1990 than they were in 1970. Scientists attributed this height loss to the fact that the women, who had traditionally carried children and other heavy loads on their backs (an activity that strengthens muscles and increases bone mass), no longer did so. Consuming purchased food items, which were low in vitamin D and calcium, was also cited as a likely cause of the change.[83]

The importance of household labour was not lost on the women who performed it. In 1991, Saskatchewan homemaker Carol Lees defied the law and refused to complete the existing Census Canada forms that would have required her to insert a zero for the number of hours she worked. Her protest was supported by an Ottawa feminist organization called Mothers Are Women, and in 1996, for the first time, the Canadian census collected data on unpaid work.[84] Two years later, the federal government's budget included a tax credit for unpaid work provided by caregivers. As the labour force participation of women increased in the late 1990s and early 2000s, there was some re-alignment of activities as the number of hours spent on housework went up somewhat for men and down slightly for women. By 2005, nearly 70 percent of men between the ages of 25 and 54 were performing household chores, compared to only 54 percent some 20 years earlier. On average, men were spending 2.5 hours each day on household duties, up from 2.1 hours in 1986. Nonetheless, in spite of their increased involvement in paid work, women were still spending an average of over 12 more hours a week on household tasks than men were. In most cases, women also were the ones who assumed overall responsibility for ensuring that the work got done. Small wonder, then, that female members of dual-wage families were likely to report being more time-stressed than their partners, no matter whether they had children or not. Only half of women who had children and who were part of couples with long workdays expressed satisfaction with their work–life balance, compared to over 70 percent of men in the same circumstances. Despite the many demands made on them, women were also slightly more likely to volunteer their services in 2005 than were men, with respective volunteer participation rates by gender of 16 and 13 percent, respectively.[85]

LABOUR ACTIVISM

As awareness of their specific economic problems grew, so did the efforts of Canadian women to resolve them. In the workplace, women increasingly used their collective strength to improve wages and working conditions, and to address other issues such as daycare and sexual harassment. As Figure 12.5 indicates, between 1966 and 2004, union membership doubled among female workers, while the rate for men declined significantly so that the rate for both sexes became virtually the same. Most of the increase in women's union membership occurred among public-sector workers, a large proportion

Figure 12.5   UNIONIZATION RATES, FEMALE AND MALE WORKERS, 1966–2007

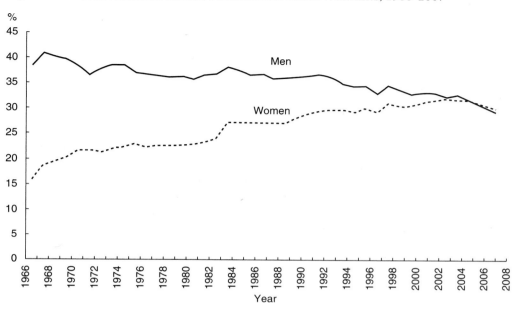

Sources: Adapted from Statistics Canada, Women in Canada: A Gender-based Statistical Report 89-503-XIE 2005001, 2005, released March 13, 2006, 112. Stats Can. "Unionization" in Perspectives on Labour and Income, August 2007, Table 1, "Union membership and coverage by selected characteristics."

of whom were women. By 2007, 71 percent of workers in public administration, which incorporated all levels of municipal, provincial, and federal government administration, belonged to unions. Women workers were also actively courted by large industrial unions, such as the United Auto Workers (the Canadian Auto Workers after 1985) and the United Steelworkers of America. These unions sought to maintain their numerical strength in the context of a shrinking manufacturing sector by organizing workers in the clerical and service sectors. [86]

In unions, special women's committees and women's caucuses were influential in defining issues and developing policies of importance to women in relation to topics such as maternity leave, child care, equal pay, occupational health and safety, sexual harassment, and the elimination of discrimination against women workers. The success of these groups was especially noteworthy within the militant, nationalist trade union movement in Quebec.[87] In 1979, Quebec public sector unions were the first to succeed in obtaining fully paid maternity leave (20 weeks) for their female members in place of the partly paid leave available under the federal unemployment insurance plan. A year later, after a lengthy strike, the Canadian Union of Postal Workers (CUPW) won the right to fully paid maternity leave of 17 weeks for its members. These two victories soon led to the provision of maternity benefits with full pay for most public sector employees in Canada.[88] Trade union feminists were also successful in making connections across union boundaries by means of such organizations as Saskatchewan Working Women,

Union Sisters in Vancouver, Organized Working Women in Ontario, and the Women's Bureau of the Canadian Labour Congress, and established ties to the broader-based contemporary women's movement.

Union women, both as leaders and as rank-and-file activists, assumed a more visible role during the 1970s and 1980s. Madeleine Parent worked with her husband Kent Rowley to establish the nationalist Canadian Confederation of Unions in 1969. Grace Hartman, a mother of two who began work as a typist in 1954 to help supplement her husband's wages, rose through the ranks to become by 1985 the head of the largest national union, the Canadian Union of Public Employees. The links between the union movement and the women's movement were illustrated by Parent and Hartman, both of whom were actively involved with the National Action Committee on the Status of Women, the largest grouping of women's organizations in Canada in the late twentieth century. In fact, Hartman served as the second president of this new organization, founded in 1972. In 1986, a historic moment occurred when Shirley Carr became the first woman president of the influential Canadian Labour Congress. One year later Gwen Wolfe, a laboratory technologist, became president of the Nova Scotia Federation of Labour, making her the first woman to head a provincial labour organization in Atlantic Canada.[89]

On the picket lines, by their determination and courage, militant rank-and-file women won a grudging new respect from their employers, along with substantial public support. In a number of bitter strikes characterized by employer intransigence and marred by picket-line violence, working women fought to improve their situation. Among the most well-known of these disputes were the 1978 strike at the Fleck automotive parts factory (in Centralia, Ontario), the 1979–80 Radio Shack electronics warehouse strike (in Barrie, Ontario), the 1981 B.C. Telephone strike, and the 1984–85 Eaton's department store strikes (in six Ontario locations).[90] In these disputes, workers were seeking union recognition, first contracts, equal pay, and improved wages and working conditions. Each dispute lasted for several months, and each constituted a remarkable demonstration of women's solidarity, not only among the workers themselves but also within the women's movement. Women of many different social and ethnic backgrounds walked the picket lines with the strikers and gave them financial support. Frances Lankin, later a Cabinet member in the Ontario NDP government, underlined the importance of the "Women's Solidarity Picket" for the Fleck strike:

> As we climbed aboard the yellow and black school bus we could feel the excitement. There was an electric charge in the air—the kind of thing that occurs when you sense something important is happening. . . . The growing alliance between women's movement activists and trade union women activists was making an impression on the labour movement.

She noted with satisfaction that "Fleck was a woman's strike."[91] Women's solidarity pickets were also organized during the Radio Shack and Eaton's strikes, and additional support for the Eaton's workers was demonstrated on March 9, 1985, when the International Women's Day march made its way into Eaton's showplace store in downtown Toronto.

During the Fleck and Radio Shack strikes, public support was also generated by managements' heavy-handed attempts to use strikebreakers and police to break the strikes. During the Fleck dispute, which lasted just over five months and involved 75 female strikers, 7 000 police days were logged at a cost of more than $2 million.[92]

Less dramatic but of equal significance were the first partly successful attempts to organize clerical and retail workers into small independent unions operating along feminist principles. In 1972 the Service, Office, and Retail Workers' Union of Canada (SORWUC) was created to organize workers in banks, offices, and restaurants, and subsequently made news by setting up unions in some bank branches. Unfortunately, SORWUC did not have the experience or financial resources necessary to wait out the lengthy periods involved in first-contract negotiation. In this instance, the interests of the women's movement and those of the trade union movement did not coincide, since the Canadian Labour Congress opposed the independent union and was running its own organizational campaign among bank workers.[93] In the end, SORWUC was no match either for the nation's most powerful financial institutions or for its largest labour federation, and by 1978 many of its locals had been decertified. A small but successful organizing drive undertaken by the United Steel Workers in 2005 resulted in a first contract covering bank workers in five Sudbury area branches of the Canadian Imperial Bank of Commerce (CIBC). Three years later, just over 60 workers belonging to this local walked

Women on the picket line during a strike at the Uniroyal tire factory in Kitchener, Ontario, June 1973.

Source: University of Waterloo Library. Record Photo.

the picket line for nine months in a dispute over wages and benefits. The strike ended with workers winning substantially higher salaries for all workers rather than the small selective increases originally proposed by bank managers. Organized workers within the financial industry remained a small minority, however. A 2003 report noted that only 9 percent of all workers in the finance and insurance industry were unionized.[94]

In contrast, unionization made major inroads among professional women, especially nurses and teachers. In several provinces, they exchanged their goal of developing traditional professional associations in favour of trade union affiliation and a more militant approach. An important change occurred for teachers when membership in teachers' associations became compulsory. In Ontario, the Federation of Women Teachers' Associations of Ontario had become the official bargaining unit for all female elementary teachers in the public-school system in 1944. By the 1960s, the Federation was playing a leading role in addressing issues of importance to all women, such as sex-role stereotyping and affirmative action. In 1998, it joined with the existing provincial male teachers' organization to form the Elementary Teachers Federation of Ontario (ETFO). In Quebec, starting with the *Corporation des instituteurs et institutrices catholiques* (CIC), which grew out of an association of rural women teachers formed by Laure Gaudreault in 1946, female and male teachers belonged to the same professional association. By 1960, union membership was required for teachers in Quebec, and by 1972 the CIC had evolved into the secular *Centrale des enseignants du Québec* (CEQ); it was one of the most militant of all teachers' organizations and cooperated closely with other trade unionists in that province. The CEQ played a central role in the formation of the *Front Commun* of some 210 000 union members who took part in a 10-day general strike in Quebec in 1972, and in subsequent major labour actions over the next decade. The CEQ's leftist orientation enabled its women members to win support for a comprehensive and radical feminist agenda. Its call for equality extended well beyond the workplace and included such demands as the recognition of a woman's right to decide if and when to have children, and the reorganization of housework along egalitarian lines.[95]

Businesswomen also realized the benefits to be gained from mutual support; new organizations (such as the Canadian Association of Women Executives and Entrepreneurs) sprang up, and directories (such as Montreal's *Bottin des femmes*) emerged to facilitate networking among their members. Contacts between women in the corporate and business world were extremely important, because women often lacked the role models and mentors that male executives found so important. As one female vice-president commented, "There's still that old-boys' network when you're reaching above middle management." Similarly, women lawyers set up women lawyers forums under the umbrella of their national and provincial bar associations to promote the advancement of women in their profession.[96]

By the 1990s, the growing convergence in the employment patterns of Canadian women and men was reflected in union membership trends. In 1997, women accounted for 45 percent of all unionized workers, and in three provinces—Prince Edward Island, Saskatchewan, and Alberta—they accounted for more than half. Beginning in 2004, the rate of union membership among women surpassed that of men and by 2007, 30 percent of female workers were unionized compared to just over 29 percent of male workers. The rapid growth in union membership among women workers can be accounted for by a number of factors, including women's increased and men's decreased labour force participation; the expansion of the unionized public service sector, which was a major source of female employment; and the contraction of the unionized, male-dominated manufacturing sector. Indeed, workers in the public sector were over four times more likely to belong to a union in 2007 than those employed in the private sector.[97]

Union membership had a significant impact on women's wage-earning capacity, particularly for part-time workers. Part-time women workers belonging to unions earned an average hourly rate of $19.85 in 2006, while their non-unionized counterparts averaged just $12.20 an hour. Because part-time women workers who were unionized also worked more hours per week than those who did not belong to unions, their average weekly earnings were nearly double. For full-time unionized women workers, the average hourly wage was $22.54 compared to $17.58 for non-unionized workers. While much of the difference in average wage can be explained by the fact that unionized workers tend to have characteristics linked to higher earnings, such as being older, more educated, and working in larger enterprises, according to one study, there was still an 8 percent union wage premium. In addition, the average hourly wage gap for unionized, full-time female employees with their male counterparts was only 6 percent, while unionized women working part-time actually earned 12 percent more than male part-time workers. However, only one in four part-time workers was represented by a union compared to one in three full-time workers.[98]

Labour militancy, as measured by strikes and lockouts, declined dramatically in the late 1990s and early 2000s, falling from over 1 000 such incidents annually in the early 1980s to fewer than 300 annually following 2002.[99] However, many of these disputes involved thousands of women, as public sector workers reacted to attempts by governments to make significant cuts to their expenditures. Walkouts occurred over issues such as the contracting out of services and job losses, wage freezes or reductions, or the erosion of hard-won benefits. Among the most notable struggles were the nurses' strikes in Saskatchewan and Quebec in 1999, the hospital workers' strike in British Columbia in 2004, and the British Columbia teachers' strike of 2005. The case of the hospital workers' dispute in B.C. was especially noteworthy since 85 percent of the 43 000 members of the Hospital Employees Union (HEU) were women; many were over the age of 45; and individuals who were members of visible minorities accounted for nearly one-third of the membership. Despite their marginalized position as workers, the hospital workers were able to win considerable support from community groups and other unions opposed to measures taken by Gordon Campbell's government to reduce some health-care services and to privatize others. Such moves were estimated to result in some 6 000 job losses. Just four days into the strike, the government passed back-to-work legislation imposing a new collective agreement that increased the workweek, retroactively reduced wages 11 percent, weakened contract language, and reserved the right to contract out work to the private sector. The hospital workers refused to obey the legislation, and hundreds of other unionized workers walked off the job to support them in what was now an illegal strike. A province-wide general strike appeared imminent, but was averted when representatives of the government, the health employers, the British Columbia Federation of Labour, and the union leadership reached a tentative agreement that limited the loss of jobs to the equivalent of 600 full-time workers but imposed pay cuts of 15 percent and lengthened hours. For many of the HEU workers, there was a strong feeling that they had been sold out by their leadership. Susan Barron, a laboratory technician at the Royal Jubilee Hospital in Victoria and a single mother who could ill afford the substantial wage cut she faced, succinctly summarized the feelings of many: "I feel betrayed." Others felt that the union leadership had done the best it could, and had managed to put the government on notice about the political cost of any additional health cuts.[100]

The global recession of late 2008 resulted in more bitter public sector strikes, such as the lengthy walkouts of civic workers in Windsor and Toronto that occurred in the spring and summer of 2009. While it was the mostly male garbage workers' absence from work, and the resulting rotting mountains of garbage that grabbed media attention, it was largely female office workers, public health nurses, child-care workers, and social workers who walked the picket lines in an effort to maintain existing benefit packages. In both disputes, women labour leaders played a key role, with Ann Dembinski, president of the CUPE local representing Toronto inside workers, acting on behalf of its 18 000 members, and Jean Fox, president of CUPE's inside worker local in Windsor, acting on behalf of an additional 1 400 workers.[101]

Like previous generations of women workers, those who remained outside of unions engaged in their own forms of militancy. A widely publicized dispute between Newfoundland women and the federal bureaucracy occurred in the late 1970s when "squidjigging" women were denied unemployment insurance benefits because government officials refused to believe that these women actually performed the heavy physical labour involved in the catching and preparation of squid. "Well, the men got their unemployment [benefits]," said Betty Burt, one of the leaders of the group, "and the women who had a man's name, such as Georgie, Frances, they got their money." When confronted by an angry deputation of "squid women," a Revenue Canada representative hastily declared that one of the women qualified for unemployment benefits—after he felt the muscles in her arm! In the end, about four-fifths of the women were deemed to qualify on the basis of their previous season's work, but the criteria for receiving unemployment benefits in subsequent years were made more restrictive.[102]

As earlier, women also played an important role in supporting the men in their families during the trying circumstances of prolonged strikes. When the workers at Inco in Sudbury went on strike in 1979, a group of local feminists and workers' wives set up a special committee to support the strikers by mobilizing community resources and promoting solidarity among the workers' families. Like the traditional union ladies' auxiliaries, "Women Supporting the Strike" organized clothing drives, community dinners, and Christmas parties for the strikers' families. They also raised money and travelled widely to win public support. However, unlike traditional trade union women's auxiliaries, the wives' committee sought to assert its financial and political autonomy from the union, an objective that led to frequent tension within the committee itself and with the striking local of the United Steelworkers of America. The wives' committee not only demonstrated the importance of mobilizing women's support for the strike, but also underlined the connections between wage work and domestic work by demonstrating the extent to which women were directly affected by the strike. Cathy Mulroy, a woman who worked in the Inco plant, reported with admiration the way "the wives of workers got together":

> I liked that these women were interested in what their husbands were doing. I went to a meeting about bargaining, and these women were at the door giving out pamphlets saying "come to the bean supper." . . . This man behind me says to one of the women, "What are you doing here? You have no business in the union hall." I turned around and said, "Of course they have. They're on strike just like their husbands are. They're going to have to go through a lot too."

Mulroy was invited to the wives' group and found that "it was exciting! All these women. Really huffing and puffing. Now *this* was a union meeting."[103] After the strike was successfully concluded, several of the women involved in the wives' committee became active in the local women's movement.

The experience of the Sudbury wives was very useful to the women who formed the United Miners' Wives Association during the 1981 miners' strike in Cape Breton. Once again it was striking workers' wives and local feminists who organized to represent women's interests. As in Sudbury, the activities of the wives' group had a transforming effect at both an individual and a collective level. As one participant pointed out, it "seemed like a new thing, women holding a bake sale to raise money to send themselves, not their husbands, to the Labour Day rally in Sydney."[104] During the lengthy and extremely bitter strike waged by the Canadian Association of Smelter and Allied Workers in Yellowknife, Northwest Territories, against Royal Oak mines in 1992–93, striking miners' wives also created their own organization to help families get through the strike. For most of these women, it was their first foray into political activism, as they travelled extensively on behalf of the strikers and promoted their "Adopt a Family" fundraising efforts.[105] Such efforts were not new; they were merely part of the tradition of Canadian women helping themselves as well as others.

There were many other examples of women taking the initiative to protect the economic interests of their families and communities. In Nova Scotia, women came together in 1995 to form Women's FishNet to give women a stronger voice in decision-making affecting the fishing industry, in promoting alternative employment opportunities, and in enhancing the sustainability of coastal communities. One of the group's affiliates, the Shelburne County Women's FishNet, joined with the Canadian Research Institute for the Advancement of Women (CRIAW) to investigate the effect of the decline of the fisheries on women's health, supported the opening of two women's resource centres, lobbied for change in policies that discriminated against women, and established Harmony Bazaar, an annual outdoor women's music festival.[106] In New Brunswick, Mi'kmaq women on the Burnt Church reserve took part in protests against federal restrictions on lobster fishing that they considered violated their treaty rights and threatened their survival. Some joined the men in their community in setting lobster traps in defiance of the fishing ban. The dispute was finally resolved in 2002 when an agreement was signed between the band and the federal government that recognized the band's right to continue to fish for subsistence purposes.[107] Sometimes disputes over control of dwindling fish stocks pitted fishing communities' interests in one province against those in another. In 2003, women in Prince Edward Island formed Women for Environmental Sustainability with the express purpose of keeping New Brunswick herring trawlers out of waters along PEI's shores, and four years later, they led a publicity campaign to have the Department of Ocean and Fisheries rescind licences for two such boats.[108]

The resolution and creativity of individual women—whether working for pay outside the home, for no pay at home or in a family enterprise, or volunteering their time to improve their communities—had a significant impact not only on the economy, but also on Canada's social and political life. Indeed, it was often issues associated with work that captured the attention of the contemporary women's movement and served as a rallying point for meaningful change.

Notes

1. Christina McCall Newman, "Working Wives Are Here to Stay," as quoted in Valerie Korinek, *Roughing it in the Suburbs: Reading Chatelaine Magazine in the Fifties and Sixties* (Toronto: University of Toronto Press, 2000), 327.

2. The "glass ceiling" is a phrase commonly used to describe the combination of invisible but real barriers to the career advancement of women and minorities; the "pink-collar ghetto" refers to the continued concentration of women in relatively low-paying, low-status areas of the labour force, such as the clerical and service sectors.

3. Penny Basset, "Declining Female Labour Force Participation," *Perspectives on Labour and Income* 6, 2, Summer 1994 (Statistics Canada, Cat. no. 75-001E).

4. Statistics Canada, "People Employed by Educational Attainment," http:// www40.statcan. gc.ca/101/cst01/labor62-eng.htm.

5. Statistics Canada, "Labour Force, employed and unemployed, numbers and rates by province, 2008," http://www40statcan.gc.ca/101/cst01/labor07a-eng.htm.

6. Diane Galarneau and Marian Radelesku, "Employment among the Disabled," *Perspectives on Labour and Income* 10, 5, May 2009 (Statistics Canada, Cat. no. 75-001-X).

7. Statistics Canada, 2006 Census of Population, Cat. no. 97-559-XCB2006008.

8. "Irene Desjarlais," in Canada, Department of the Secretary of State, *Speaking Together: Canada's Native Women* (Toronto: Hunter-Rose, 1975), 46.

9. Statistics Canada, 2006 Census of Population, Cat. no. 97-562-XCB2006017.

10. Pat Armstrong and Hugh Armstrong, *The Double Ghetto: Canadian Women and Their Segregated Work*, 3rd ed. (Toronto: McClelland and Stewart, 1994), 191, Table 20.

11. Punam Khosla, "Review of the Situation of Women in Canada," National Action Committee on the Status of Women (July 1993), 18; Margaret Philp, "Money Crisis Blocks Ontario Child-Care Reform," *The Globe and Mail* (March 31, 1994), A8; Martha Friendly, Jane Beach, Carolyn Ferns and Michelle Turiano, *Early Childhood Education and Care in Canada 2006*, "Child Care Space statistics 2007," Childcare Canada, http://www.childcarecanada. org/pubs/other/spaces/index.html.

12. As quoted in Pat Armstrong and Hugh Armstrong, *"A Working Majority": What Women Must Do for Pay* (Ottawa: Canadian Advisory Council on the Status of Women, 1983), 36.

13. "Two-Earner Families Decline," *The Globe and Mail* (June 3, 1993), A6; Bruce Little, "In Recession, Women's Wages Pay the Way," *The Globe and Mail* (May 16, 1994), A11.

14. Statistics Canada, *Women in Canada: A Gender-based Statistical Report*. 5th ed. (Ottawa: Ministry of Industry, 2006), 140, 142; Statistics Canada, *The Daily*, "Study: Wives as Primary Breadwinners" (August 23, 2006); Statistics Canada, *The Daily*, "Study: Hours and Earnings of Dual-Earner Couples" (April 24, 2009); Statistics Canada, *The Daily*, "Study: How Families Respond to Layoffs" (February 21, 2008).

15. *Canada Year Book: 2008 Edition* (Ottawa: Statistics Canada), 269; *Women in Canada*, 5th ed., 114; Statistics Canada, "Labour Force, Employed and Unemployed, Numbers and Rates by Province," http://www40.statcan.gc.ca/101/cst01/labor07a-eng.htm.

16. Statistics Canada, *The Daily*, "Latest Release from the Labour Force Survey" (July 10, 2009).

17. Pat Armstrong, "The Feminization of the Labour Force: Harmonizing Down in a Global Economy," in Isabella Bakker, ed., *Rethinking Restructuring: Gender and Change in Canada* (Toronto: University of Toronto Press, 1996), 35; Deborah Sunter, "Demography and the Labour Market," *Perspectives on Labour and Income* 2, 2, February 2001 (Statistics Canada, Cat. no. 75-001-XPE).

18. Statistics Canada, *The Daily*, "2006 Census: Labour Market Activities, Industry, Occupation, Education, Language of Work, Place of Work and Mode of Transportation" (March 4, 2008); Statistics Canada, *The Daily*, "Study: Recent Changes in the Labour Market, 1991 to 2004" (March 18, 2005); *Canada Year Book 2008*, 270.

19. Statistics Canada, 2006 Census of Population, Cat. no. 97-559-XCB2006010.

20. Statistics Canada, 2006 Census of Population, Cat. no. 97-559-XCB2006012; Rosenzweig & Company Inc., *The Annual Rosenzweig Report on Women at the Top Levels of Corporate Canada, January 2009* (Toronto, 2009), 2.

21. "Census Snapshot: Canada's Changing Labour Force, 2006 Census," *Canadian Social Trends*, June 3, 2008, (Statistics Canada, Cat. no. 11-008-X); Cecilia Reynolds, Robert White, Carol Brayman and Shawn Moore, "Women and Secondary School Rotation/Succession: A Study of the Beliefs of Decision Makers in Four Provinces," *Canadian Journal of Education*, 31, 1 (2008): 34.

22. Linda Muzzin, Patricia Sinnott and Claudia Lai, "Pawns between Patriarchies: Women in Canadian Pharmacy," in Elizabeth Smyth et al., eds., *Challenging Professions: Historical and Contemporary Perspectives on Women's Professional Work* (Toronto: U of T Press, 1999), 296–314. The feminization of pharmacy in Quebec is discussed in Johanne Collin, *Changement d'ordonnance—mutations professionnelles, identité sociale et féminisation de la profession pharmaceutique au Québec* (Montréal: Boréal, 1995). For information on women and chartered accountancy, see Cyndy Allen and Margaret Conrad, "Who's Accounting? Women Chartered Accountants in Nova Scotia," in Smyth et al., *Challenging Professions*, 255–76.

23. Canadian Medical Association, CMA Masterfile, January 2008, http://www.cma.ca/index.cfm/ci_id/16958/la_id/1.htm#prov-spec.

24. Vesna Jaksic, "Canada Seeks to Retain Women Lawyers," *The National Law Journal*, June 30, 2008, http://www.law.com/jsp/law/careercenter/lawArticleCareerCenter.jsp?id=1202422614723; John Hagan and Fiona Kay, *Gender in Practice: A Study of Lawyers' Lives* (Oxford University Press: New York, 1995), 184–85, 202.

25. Jeanette Easson, Debbie Field, and Joanne Santucci, "Working Steel," in Jennifer Penney, *Hard Earned Wages: Women Fighting for Better Work* (Toronto: Women's Press, 1983), 200, 211; Meg Luxton and June Corman, *Getting By in Hard Times: Gendered Labour at Home and on the Job* (Toronto: University of Toronto Press, 2001), 84–94; Susanne Klausen, "The

Plywood Girls: Women and Gender Ideology at the Port Alberni Plywood Plant, 1942–1991, *Labour/Le Travail*, 41 (Spring 1998): 219–28.

26. Luxton and Corman, *Getting By*, 4.

27. *Today's Woman* [supplement to *The Halifax Chronicle–Herald* and *The Mail–Star*] (March 10, 1987), 8, 14.

28. Ann Rauhala, "Job Quota for Women Is Upheld," *The Globe and Mail* (June 26, 1987), A1, A2; Doris Anderson, "How a Tiny Women's Group Defeated a Corporate Giant," *The Toronto Star* (July 18, 1987), K1.

29. Solange de Santis, *Life on the Line; One Woman's Tale of Work, Sweat, and Survival* (New York: Anchor Books, 2000); Luxton and Corman, 125.

30. Statistics Canada, 2006 Census of Population, Cat. no. 97-559-XCB2006010.

31. Judith Lavoie, "Women Combine Aboriginal Culture with Eco-tourism," *The Globe and Mail* (June 25, 1994).

32. Ellen Roseman, "More Women Entering the Business World, Determined to Overcome Cautious Attitudes," *The Globe and Mail* (May 29, 1987), C7.

33. Statistics Canada, "Self-employment, Historical Summary," http://www40.statcan.gc.ca/l01/cst01/labor64-eng.htm.

34. Arthur Gardner, "Their Own Boss: The Self-employed in Canada," *Canadian Social Trends. Volume 3* (Toronto: Thompson Educational Publishing, 2000), 188–91; Melissa Cooke-Reynolds and Nancy Zukewich, "The Feminization of Work," *Canadian Social Trends,* Spring 2004 (Statistics Canada, Cat. no. 11-008): 27; Gary L. Cohen, "Women Entrepreneurs," *Perspectives on Labour and Income* 8, 1, Spring 1996, (Statistics Canada, Cat. no. 75-001-XPE): 26–28.

35. Alanna Mitchell, "Others Enjoy Benefits Unheard of in Canada," *The Globe and Mail* (January 24, 1994).

36. *Women in Canada*, 5th ed., 252.

37. Adenike O. Yesufu, "The Gender Dimensions of the Immigrant Experience: The Case of African-Canadian Women in Edmonton," in Wisdom J. Tettey and Korbla P. Puplampu, eds., *The African Diaspora in Canada: Negotiating Identity and Belonging* (Calgary: University of Calgary Press, 2005), 137.

38. *Women in Canada*, 5th ed., 255.

39. "Queen Elizabeth Hotel Fined for Anti-Black Bias," *The Oracle* (February 3, 1977), 7.

40. Catherine W. Warren, *Vignettes of Life: Experiences and Self Perceptions of New Canadian Women* (Calgary: Detselig Enterprises, 1986), 48.

41. Jane Badets and Linda Howatson-Lee, "Recent Immigrants in the Workforce," in *Canadian Social Trends Vol. 3*: 16–17.

42. Khosla, "Review," 15; Micheline Labelle et al., *Histoire des immigrées: Itinéraires d'ouvrières colombiennes, grecques, haïtiennes et portugaises de Montréal* (Montréal: Boréal Express, 1987), 141, 197.

43. Belinda Leach, "Behind Closed Doors: Homework Policy and Lost Possibilities for Change," in Bakker, ed., *Rethinking Restructuring*, 211.

44. *Women in Canada*, 5th ed., 225, 250, 255.

45. Human Resources and Skills Development Canada, "Temporary Foreign Worker Program: Live-In Care Giver Program," http://www.hrsdc.gc.ca/eng/workplaceskills/foreign_workers/lcpdir/lcpone.shtml.

46. Labelle et al., *Histoire des immigrées*, 180. Our translation.

47. INTERCEDE, "Annual Report, 2007-08," http://www.intercedetoronto.org/Annual_Report_April_2007_To_March_2008.

48. Judith Gregory, "The Electronic Sweatshop," in Joan Turner and Lois Emery, eds., *Perspectives on Women in the 1980s* (Winnipeg: University of Manitoba Press, 1983), 99–112; Heather Menzies, *Women and the Chip: Case Studies of the Effects of Informatics on Employment in Canada* (Montreal: Institute for Research on Public Policy, 1981).

49. *Canada Year Book 2008*, 272; Ernest B. Akyeampong and Richard Nadwodny, "Evolution of the Canadian Workplace: Work from Home," *Perspectives* Winter 2001, (Statistics Canada, Cat. no. 75-001-XPE): 32.

50. Armstrong and Armstrong, *Double Ghetto*, 3rd ed., 48; *Women in Canada*, 5th ed., 109–10.

51. Kenneth Kidd, "Big Mac Meets the McUnion Kid," *Report on Business Magazine* 10, 12 (June 1994): 46–53; Dan Glenday, "Off the Ropes/New Challenges and Strengths Facing Trade Unions in Canada," in Dan Glenday and Ann Duffy, eds., *Canadian Society: Meeting the Challenges of the Twenty-First Century* (Toronto: Oxford University Press, 2001), 16–17; Anthony Bianco, "No Union Please, We're Wal-Mart," *BusinessWeek,* February 13, 2006, http://www.businessweek.com/print/magazine/content/06_07/b3971115.htm?chan=gl; CBC News, "Wal-Mart Wins at Supreme Court," November 27, 2009, http://license.icopyright.net/user/viewFreeUse.act?fuid=NzU4MjY3NA==A.

52. Leah F. Vosko, *Temporary Work: The Gendered Rise of a Precarious Employment Relationship* (Toronto: University of Toronto Press, 2000), espec. chap. 4–6.

53. Gina Vance and Anne Bishop, "No More Lobsters for Lizmore," in Penney, *Hard Earned Wages,* 42–43.

54. "Fishing Industry," Women in Resource Development Committee, http://www.wrdc.nf.ca/wrdc/fishery/index.htm.

55. Kelly Preibisch and Evelyn Encalada, *Migrant Women Farm Workers in Canada,* University of Guelph—Rural Women Making Change, July 2008, http://www.rwmc.uoguelph.ca.

56. Armstrong and Armstrong, *The Double Ghetto*, rev. ed. (Toronto: McClelland and Stewart, 1984), 45.

57. Lorna R. Marsden, "The Role of the National Action Committee on the Status of Women in Facilitating Equal Pay Policy in Canada," in Ronnie Ratner Steinberg, ed., *Equal Employment Policy for Women: Strategies for Implementation in the United States, Canada, and Western Europe* (Philadelphia: Temple University Press, 1980), 242–60.

58. Pat Armstrong, *Labour Pains: Women's Work in Crisis* (Toronto: Women's Press, 1984), 59.

59. Pat Armstrong and Hugh Armstrong, "Lessons from Pay Equity," *Studies in Political Economy* 32 (Summer 1990): 29–54.

60. Rosalie Silberman Abella, *Equality in Employment: A Royal Commission Report* (Ottawa: Supply and Services Canada, 1984).

61. Abigail B. Bakan and Audrey Kobayashi, *Employment Equity Policy in Canada: An Interprovincial Comparison* (Ottawa: Status of Women Canada, 2000), 11–34; Human Resources and Skills Development Canada, "Employment Equity Act Review," December 2001, http://www.hrsdc.gc.ca/eng/lp/lo/lswe/we/review/report/main/.shtml.

62. Jeff Sallot, "Career Pause Expensive for Wives," *The Globe and Mail* (July 7, 1992), A6.

63. Dennis Guest, *The Emergence of Social Security in Canada,* 3rd ed. (Vancouver: UBC Press, 2003), 197, 205–7.

64. *Women in Canada,* 5th ed., 278.

65. Michael Valpy, "The Wrong Way to Say Goodbye," *The Globe and Mail* (July 22, 1994).

66. Statistics Canada, *Workplace and Employee Survey Compendium*, (Cat. no. 71-585-X), 50, Table 4.4, 2005.

67· Leslie A. Pal and F. L. Morton, "*Bliss v. Attorney General of Canada*: From Legal Defeat to Political Victory," *Osgoode Hall Law Journal* 24, 1 (Spring 1986): 141–60; Mary Eberts, "Sex-Based Discrimination and the Charter," in Anne F. Bayefsky and Mary Eberts, eds., *Equality Rights and the Canadian Charter of Rights and Freedoms* (Toronto: Carswell, 1985), 198.

68. *Trends and Analysis: Early Childhood Education and Care in Canada, 2006, 1.4*, http://www.childcarecanada.org/pubs/other/TandA/Trends_Analysis07.pdf; Ian Marlow, "Bill Would Extend EI Benefits to the Self-Employed," *The Toronto Star* (November 4, 2009).

69. *Canada Year Book 2008*, 286, Table 21.11.

70. Organisation for Economic Co-operation and Development, "*Gender Wage Gaps*," http://www.oecd.org/dataoecd/19/14/38172488.pdf.

71. *Women in Canada*, 5th ed.,153, Table 6.10; Sue Calhoun, "Wage Gap Widest for University-Educated Women," http://www.bpwcanada.com/english/images/stories/about/incomequity/universitywomen_%20wage_gap.pdf.

72. Tracy Carr, "Poll Shows Child-Care Program Needed, Group Says," *New Brunswick Telegraph-Journal*, January 29, 2003.

73. Heather McIvor, *Women and Politics in Canada* (Peterborough, ON; Broadview Press, 1996), 112–14; Marie Drolet, *The "Who, What, When and Where" of Gender Pay Differentials* (Ottawa: Statistics Canada, 2002).

74. *Women in Canada*, 5th ed., 154, Table 6.12.

75. *Canada Year Book 2008*, 286, Table 21.11; Cooke-Reynolds and Zukewich, 28; Armstrong, "Feminization of the Labour Force," in Bakker, ed., *Rethinking Restructuring*, 29–52.

76. Armstrong and Armstrong, *The Double Ghetto*, 3rd ed., 45.

77. Gisele Ireland, *The Farmer Takes a Wife* (Chesley, ON: Concerned Farm Women, 1983), 14–15.

78. Muriel Lush, "The Family Farm Is Dying," *Women's Concerns*, Division of Mission in Canada of the United Church in Canada, 31 (Winter 1986): 8.

79. Statistics Canada, "Characteristics of Farm Operators, Canada and Provinces: Census Years 1991 to 2006," http://www.statcan.gc.ca/pub/95-632-x/2007000/t/4129760-eng.htm; Greg Hymes, "Farm Women Head to Work off the Farm—More or Less," Statistics Canada, http://www.statcan.gc.ca/kits-trousses/agric/edu04_0050a-eng.htm.

80. Naomi Black and Gail Cuthbert Brandt, *Feminist Politics on the Farm; Rural Catholic Women in Southern Quebec and Southwestern France* (Montreal and Kingston: McGill-Queen's University Press, 1999), 64–74; Diane Martz and Ingrid Brueckner, "The Canadian Farm Family at Work: Exploring Gender and Generation," National Farmers Union, March 2003, http://www.nfu.ca/epff/documents/The_Canadian_Farm_Family_at_Work.pdf; Cynthia Silver, "From Sun-up to Sundown: Work Patterns of Farming Couples," *Canadian Social Trends*, Summer 2001, (Statistics Canada, Cat. no. 11-008): 15; Statistics Canada, *Selected Historical Data from the Census of Agriculture* (Cat. no. 95-632-XWE), 2007.

81. Alanna Mitchell, "Unpaid Housework Valued to $319 Billion, Statscan Says," *The Globe and Mail* (April 7, 1994), A7; "Women and Unpaid Work—Milestones in Canada," Unpaid Work Press Conference, January 2003, PEI Advisory Council on the Status of Women, 2, http://www.gov.pe.ca/acsw/index.php3?number=70137&lang=E#women.

82. Meg Luxton, *More Than a Labour of Love: Three Generations of Women's Work in the Home* (Toronto: Women's Press, 1980), 48.

83. Stephen Strauss, "Inuit Shorter; Snowmobiles Blamed," *The Globe and Mail* (July 1, 1994), A1.

84. Meg Luxton and Leah F. Vosko, "Where Women's Efforts Count: The 1996 Census Campaign and 'Family Politics' in Canada," *Studies in Political Economy,* 56 (Summer 1998): 56.

85. Statistics Canada, *The Daily,* "General Social Survey: Paid and Unpaid Work" (July 19, 2006); Statistics Canada, *Overview of the Time Use of Canadians,* Cat. no. 12F0080XWE.

86. Linda Briskin, "Women and Unions in Canada: A Statistical Overview," in Linda Briskin and Lynda Yanz, eds., *Union Sisters: Women in the Labour Movement* (Toronto: Women's Press, 1983), 28–43; Heather Jon Maroney, "Feminism at Work," in Bryan D. Palmer, ed., *The Character of Class Struggle: Essays in Canadian Working-Class History, 1850–1985* (Toronto: McClelland and Stewart, 1986), 160–75; Statistics Canada, "Unionization," *Perspectives on Labour and Income* (August 2007): 3, http://www.statcan.gc.ca/pub/75-001-x/commun/4211933-eng.pdf.

87. Martine Lanctôt, "La genèse et l'évolution du mouvement de libération des femmes à Montréal, 1969–79," Université du Québec à Montréal, Thèse de maîtrise, 1982.

88. Ann Porter, *Gendered States: Women, Unemployment Insurance and the Political Economy* (Toronto: University of Toronto Press, 2003), 143.

89. "Shirley Carr," *The Canadian Encyclopedia,* http://www.thecanadianencyclopedia.com/index.cfm?PgNm=TCE&Params=A1ARTA0001429.

90. Lynda Yanz and David Smith, "Annotated List of Women's Strikes," *Resources for Feminist Research/Documentation sur la recherche féministe* 10, 2 (July 1981): 77–83; Linda Briskin and Patricia McDermott, eds., *Women Challenging Unions: Feminism, Democracy and Militancy* (Toronto: University of Toronto Press, 1993).

91. Frances Lankin, "Foreword," in Carole Conde and Karl Beveridge, *First Contract: Women and the Fight to Unionize* (Toronto: Between the Lines, 1986), 6–7.

92. Conde and Beveridge, *First Contract,* 72.

93. Laurell Ritchie, "Why Are So Many Women Unorganized?" in Briskin and Yanz, eds., *Union Sisters,* 208–9.

94. Janet Gibson, "CIBC Workers Vote to Accept Deal with Bank," October 20, 2008, NorthernLife.ca., http://www.northernlife.ca/News/LocalNews/2008/102008-cibc.aspx.

95. Maroney, "Feminism at Work," 162.

96. Rona Maynard, "Why Women Still Fail to Reach the Top," *Report on Business Magazine* 1, 5 (May 1985): 80–85; Canadian Bar Association, http://www.cba.org/CBA/conf_women/Women_Lawyers/default.aspx.

97. Glenday, "Off the Ropes" in Glenday and Duffy, eds., *Canadian Society: Meeting the Challenges,* 19; Gillian Creese and Brenda Beagan, "Gender at Work: Strategies for Equality in Neo-Liberal Times," in Edward Grabb and Neil Guppy, eds., *Social Inequality in Canada: Patterns, Problems, and Policies,* 5th ed. (Toronto: Pearson Prentice Hall, 2009), 232; Labour Canada, "Union Membership in Canada, 1997–2007, http://www.hrsdc.gc.ca/eng/lp/wid/union_membership.shtml; Statistics Canada, "Unionization," *Perspectives on Labour and Income* (August 2007), http://www.statcan.gc.ca/pub/75-001-x/commun/4211933-eng.pdf.

98. "Unionization," 7.

99. "Unionization," 8.

100. David Camfield, "Neoliberalism and Working-Class Resistance in British Columbia: The Hospital Employees' Union Struggle, 2002–2004," in Bryan D. Palmer and Joan Sangster, eds., *Labouring Canada: Class, Gender and Race in Canadian Working-Class History* (Don Mills, ON: Oxford University Press, 2008), 444–60; Roger Annis, "Drawing the Lessons

of the HEU Strike," *Seven Oaks: A Magazine of Politics, Culture, and Resistance* 1, 12 (May 10, 2004).

101. CUPE, "Tentative Deals to End Toronto Strike, http://cupe.ca/strikes/toronto-strike-tentative-agreements; Doug Schmidt, "Windsor Waits for CUPE Votes to Be Counted," *The Windsor Star*, July 16, 2009.

102. Betty Burt and Loretta Burt, "Squidjigging Women," in Penney, *Hard Earned Wages*, 229–34.

103. Cathy Mulroy, "Miner's Daughter," in Penney, *Hard Earned Wages*, 182.

104. Luxton, "From Ladies' Auxiliaries to Wives' Committees: Housewives and the Unions," in Meg Luxton and Harriet Rosenberg, eds., *Through the Kitchen Window: The Politics of Home and Family* (Toronto: Garamond, 1986), 63–81.

105. Erin Mullen, "Women in the Strike," *Kinesis* (December 1992/January 1993), 8.

106. "Women's Organizations Anchor Fishing Communities," *Gulf of Maine Times*, 1, 4, Winter 1997, http://www.gulfofmaine.org/times; "Shelburne County Women's FishNet," http://www.women's fishnet.com.

107. "Native Women Join Men to Set Lobster Traps," CBC News, November 10, 2000, http://www.cbc.ca/canada/story/1999/10/11/fish_dispute991011.html.

108. "Women's Group Resurfaces to Battle Trawlers," CBC News, October 19, 2007, http://www.cbc.ca/canada/prince-edward-island/story/2007/10/19/women-trawlers.html.

CHAPTER THIRTEEN

Changing Lives in a Changing Society

Throughout the last half of the twentieth century and continuing into the twenty-first, there were striking shifts in the patterns of women's lives, for the experiences of most women surrounding marriage, childbearing, child-rearing, and aging were very different from those of previous generations of women. Individual women's choices produced dramatic changes in the timing of such events as entering marriage and starting a family. The trends that had produced the postwar baby boom of the late 1940s and early 1950s—earlier age at first marriage, earlier births of first children, and larger completed families—all changed during the rest of the century. At the same time, massive numbers of women of all ages and circumstances entered areas of activity previously defined as male. Women attained unprecedented levels of autonomy and equality. However, tension persisted between the reality of women's personal experiences and the social constructions of what it was to be a woman. In sports and recreational activities, in educational institutions, and in culture and the arts, girls and women made steady progress, but a deeply ingrained sexism—sometimes blatant, but more often subtle—still moulded and frequently constrained their choices.

DEMOGRAPHIC AND LIFE CYCLE PATTERNS

To understand the changes in the large demographic patterns of Canadian women's lives from the 1960s through the first decade of the twenty-first century, it is useful to track them through the cycle of Canadian women's adult lives. For younger women in general, beginning with the period after the war but accelerating as the century wore on, an important change was the greater degree of independence they enjoyed. As time went on, more young women spent a substantial period of their lives living outside their parental homes while they pursued postsecondary education or worked for pay—in the latter case, with a growing expectation that, even after marriage, they would continue in their jobs. The boom in apartment construction, in particular between 1961 and 1970, was related to this trend. During the five-year period from 1966 to 1971, the total number of households in Canada grew by 17 percent and at the same time the number of households with single, never-married heads almost doubled. However, the trend for young adults to live on their own decreased in the 1980s and 1990s and it was down sharply by 2006 as a result of decreased job opportunities for young people and the much higher cost of both housing and postsecondary education. In that year, 60 percent of those aged 20 to 24 lived with their parents, compared to about half 20 years earlier.[1] Since a substantial number of these young people had left the home and then returned, they were sometimes called the boomerang generation. The French term, *le phénomène Tanguy,* referred to Tanguy Goetz, the main character in the 2001 film *Tanguy;* at the age of 28 he still had never left home.

The increased economic, social, and sexual freedom enjoyed by the generations of young Canadian women who came of age after 1960 was reflected in the way in which the practice of two persons living together as a couple without marriage (cohabiting) became more acceptable. Beginning to be significantly popular in the 1970s, this way of life for young adults became even more common in the 1980s and 1990s, with common-law couples increasing from 6 percent of families in 1981 to 16 percent in 2006. The change in family forms was most striking in Quebec. In that province, which had no tradition of common-law marriage, such relationships were called *unions de fait* or de facto unions. For many Quebec couples, long-term cohabitation, often with children, apparently was becoming a substitute for marriage. As shown in Figure 13.1, by 1991, one in five of all couples in Quebec was cohabiting, and by 2001 it was almost one in three. As

Figure 13.1 PERCENTAGE OF COUPLES COHABITING BY REGION OF RESIDENCE, 1981, 1991, AND 2001

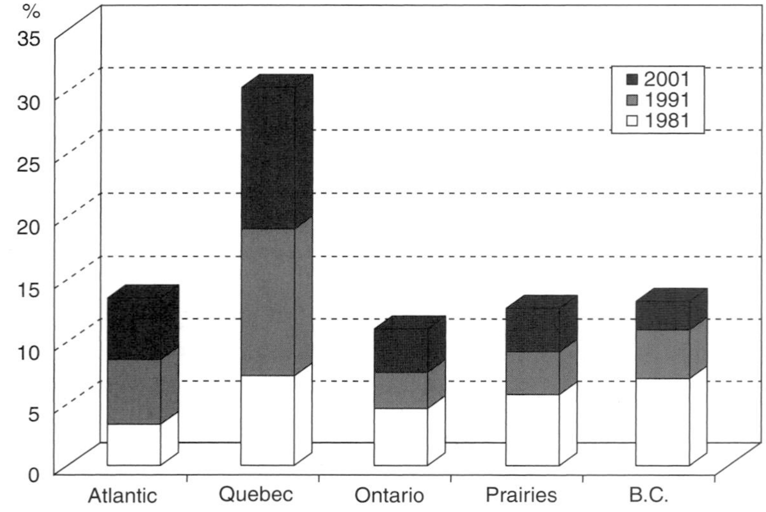

Source: Céline Le Bourdais and Evelyne Lapierre-Adamcyck, "Changes in Conjugal Life in Canada: Is Cohabitation Progressively Replacing Marriage?" *Journal of Marriage and Family,* 66, 4 (November 2004). Copyright © 2004 Blackwell Publishing Ltd. Reproduced with permission of Blackwell Publishing Ltd.

early as 1997–1998, almost half of all births in Quebec were to cohabiting parents, while in the rest of Canada three-quarters of births were still to married couples. Outside of Quebec and the territories, cohabitation was sometimes just a new way of going steady, but it was most likely to be a childless prelude to marriage, a way of testing out the stability of a relationship. Nationwide, of women born in the 1960s, no less than 42 percent were in common-law relationships as they started to live in a couple. Younger people were most likely to be in non-formal unions, but by 2006 cohabitation of persons in their forties or older was increasing even more rapidly than among those aged 25 to 29, apparently at least in part because divorced persons were choosing not to remarry. Couples in the territories particularly frequently opted for informal arrangements; in 2002, almost a third of all couples in Nunavut, and only a slightly lower percentage in the Northwest Territories and the Yukon, were common-law unions. These figures reflected the significantly greater tendency for Aboriginal women—and especially Inuit women—to remain outside of formal marriage, at a rate more than double that of non-Aboriginal women. By contrast, in the same year, only a tiny fraction of visible minority women aged 15 and over (3 percent) were living with a common-law spouse.[2]

As cohabitation became more common and accepted all over Canada, Ontario in 1990 became the first province to approve legislation regulating common-law marriage. Although some who preferred a less constraining arrangement were not pleased, in most parts of Canada common-law relationships of a specified duration now acquired the same obligations as those of more formally sanctioned arrangements, especially as regards children, both natural and adopted. In 1999 the Supreme Court decision in the case of *M. v. H.* (concerning rights of lesbian partners on dissolution of a relationship) applied the Charter of Rights to require that common-law arrangements be open to same-sex couples. Henceforth, such couples were able to form common-law relationships in Ontario, and they also acquired some entitlements federally; other provinces also accordingly adjusted their regulations. De facto unions in Quebec already had some consequences under several provincial and federal statutes but they had no standing under the Civil Code of Quebec: the provincial government wished to retain an option for those who did not choose to take on marriage-like obligations to their partners and children. There continued to be only limited protection to persons in such relationships in Quebec, apart from any specific contractual arrangements a couple might make. Women were well-advised to examine the implications of whatever form of union they chose; when relationships broke down, the consequences differed. Even though there was no longer any legal difference related to the situation of children's parents nor any stigma attached to children born out of wedlock, problems could follow when cohabiting ended. A case in Quebec created something of a sensation in 2009, when it turned out that the former companion of the billionaire founder of the Cirque du Soleil had no legal right even to the support he was paying to her and their three children, let alone a share in his immense wealth. He had apparently avoided any form of marriage for just that reason. Sympathy for Guy Laliberté's ex-partner was muted by the revelation that she was receiving payments of $35 000 a month, which she wanted increased. Had she been living in any other province or territory, she would automatically have been entitled to a share of his property.[3]

Despite the increasing range of options open to them, over the years the majority of Canadian women continued to opt for a traditional form of marriage. (See Table A.1

in Appendix.) In 1996, when only 7 percent of census families were common-law, married couples comprised 80 percent of census families; 10 years later, married couples still accounted for 69 percent of all census families (the remainder were single-headed or common-law). However, there was an uninterrupted decline in marriage rates after 1972. From 9 marriages per 1 000 inhabitants in the early 1970s, the rate went down to less than 5 per 1 000 by 2002. Prince Edward Island had the highest marriage rate in 2002, with 6.6 marriages per 1 000 people while Quebec with just 3 and Nunavut with only 2.5 marriages per 1 000 population recorded the lowest rates. Clearly, the much higher frequency of *unions de fait* (de facto) or common-law relationships in the latter jurisdictions had affected marriage rates. By the year 2000, less than two out of five women in Quebec were likely to marry; in the rest of Canada it was still three out of five. Furthermore, as marriage became less popular, it also tended to be postponed longer. The average age of women at first marriage rose to a significant degree, remaining at about two years younger than for grooms. (See Figure A.1 in Appendix.) In 1971, the average age at first marriage for brides was 22 years; by 2004, it was almost 29 years, while for first-time grooms the average age rose from 24 years in the early 1970s to almost 31.

Nor was marriage any longer limited to heterosexuals. Lengthy campaigns by gay and lesbian activists had the result that eight provinces and one territory approved same-sex marriages. Ontario retroactively recognized in 2003 two same-sex marriages that had taken place on January 14, 2001; these were the first such in the world to be given legal standing. After a series of lower court decisions, the federal government obtained in 2004 a Supreme Court opinion permitting it to redefine marriage so as to include same-sex couples. Aloysius Cardinal Ambrozic, Archbishop of Toronto, was among those who requested without success that the Liberal government use the constitution's notwithstanding clause to override the Charter of Rights to bar same-sex marriage. In 2005, Bill C-38 made same-sex marriage legal throughout Canada. This legislation referred to civil marriage; no religion was to be obliged to marry same-sex couples. By the end of 2009, Canada was one of eight countries worldwide to legislate same-sex marriage. In 2006, same-sex marriages comprised less than 1 percent of all marriages in Canada, while married same-sex couples accounted for 17 percent of all such couples. Nearly half of these married couples were made up of women, who were more likely than male couples to have children (16 percent to 3 percent).[5]

Other features of marriage changed, in ways that often provoked considerable inter-generational conflict. In both Inuit and other Aboriginal societies and also in some immigrant groups, those young people who had been expected to enter into marriages arranged by their parents more often chose their own partners instead. While not all older Aboriginal women felt they had been well served by arranged marriages, many associated the new, "white" custom with increased marital problems, domestic violence, and marriage breakdown. Some South Asian parents also found love marriages problematic and sometimes sought to ward them off by arranging for marriage partners from their original homeland to come to Canada. By the millennium, though, the issue was not so much whether marriages would be arranged as whether they would remain within racial groups. Mixed unions were rising steadily, reported at a peak of 13 percent in Vancouver among those in their twenties in the 2001 census. Nationwide, Japanese, black, and Latin American Canadians were the most likely to marry out.[6]

Whatever their official marital status, women had fewer children than in previous generations. The Canadian birth rate dropped substantially in the years between 1959 and 1971. Quebecers experienced the most dramatic changes in their birth rate; in only one decade—1959 to 1969—the birth rate per 1 000 population in that province was cut in half. By 1970 Quebec had the lowest birth rate in Canada. Quebec women, who averaged 3.7 children in 1961, had 1.88 in 1971, while the average number of children born to Ontario women went only from 3.74 to 2.22 during the same period.[7] The transformation in Quebec of marriage patterns and fertility rates was an integral part of the Quiet Revolution, the amalgam of demographic, economic, social, and political transformations that began in the 1940s and reached full impact in the 1960s. The rapid rate of urbanization and the modernization of Quebec agriculture during the 1950s rendered irrelevant the traditional arguments of French-Canadian nationalists in favour of an increased population. Mechanization of farms reduced the need for abundant labour; even in rural areas, the benefits of larger family size evaporated. (See Table A.2 in Appendix.)

In Quebec and elsewhere, the decline in fertility was facilitated by increased knowledge of and access to birth control methods, including the newer technologies. Nationwide, the birth control pill was available by the early 1960s in the larger urban centres, though only by prescription; in most instances, physicians limited its use to married women. Indeed, legal penalties for displaying and selling contraceptive devices remained in force until 1969. It was in part the conviction and jailing of a Toronto pharmacist in 1960 for selling condoms that motivated Barbara and George Cadbury to organize the Planned Parenthood Association of Toronto one year later. By 1963 they had succeeded in establishing both the Planned Parenthood Federation of Canada and the Canadian Federation of Societies for Population Planning. In Quebec, the decline in the social power and moral authority of the Roman Catholic Church translated into an increasing willingness on the part of Catholics to ignore church doctrine. Like other Catholic women throughout North America, women in Quebec adopted the birth control pill and other methods of contraception officially condemned by the Vatican, thereby asserting more effective control over their lives. When Pope Paul VI explicitly and strongly condemned the use of artificial means of birth control in his 1968 encyclical, *Humanae Vitae*, Canadian Catholic bishops took a nuanced official position. In a collective statement, they declared that the use of birth control was a matter of individual conscience, which was to be informed by careful consideration of divine law and traditional church teachings.[8]

By 1981, the Canadian birth rate was at 15.3 per 1 000 population and by 1991 it was down to 14.3. Paradoxically, a small increase in the birth rate now took place in Quebec, where the government moved aggressively to counter the fall in fertility. In 1988 the provincial government offered its citizens attractive allowances for newborn children: $500 per year for each of the first two children and $3 000 for each subsequent child. In 1997, however, this baby bonus was terminated; it was estimated that it had cost the government more than $15 000 for each baby who would not otherwise have been born. Larger families were also promoted in Quebec by exceptionally generous parental leave programs as well as, beginning in 1997, daycare for $5 a day (later raised to $7), regardless of family income.[9]

Between 2001 and 2008, the national birth rate rose slightly from just over 10.5 per 1 000 population to 11.1. However, regional contrasts continued to be striking. In 2007/2008, Nunavut had the very high birth rate of 25.2 per 1 000 population, with the Northwest Territories and Alberta recording the next highest rates at 16.0 and 13.6, respectively. Also above the national average were Manitoba and Saskatchewan, each with rates above 12.0.

In all of these cases, it was the presence of significant numbers of Aboriginal women of childbearing age that accounted for the higher birth rates. It also appeared that Quebec's child-friendly social policies were continuing to pay dividends, as by 2009 that province's rate of 11.2 births per 1 000 people slightly surpassed the national average.[10] The lowest birth rate at that time occurred in Newfoundland and Labrador, where it was just 8.7. In response to the province's loss of population, in 2008 the government of Newfoundland and Labrador provided for a payment of $1 000 for every newborn or adopted child plus a supplementary monthly payment of $100 for the year of parental leave, in order to "nurture family growth." "I look at it as something to help young couples raise their children. We do things for seniors," said the Finance Minister, Tom Marshall.[11]

A different kind of analysis of the changing fertility rates between 1960 and 2006, based on looking at the fertility rate of groups of women, reveals considerably more about changing reproductive behaviour than do the crude birth rates (calculated per 1 000 population) previously cited. Age-specific fertility rates are calculated by dividing the number of live births in each age group by the total female population (in thousands) in each age group. The simplest measure of all is the total fertility rate. It represents the number of children an imaginary woman would have—if she were subject to all the age-specific fertility rates for women between the ages of 15 and 49 recorded for a given year. By 1971, the average number of births per woman had already dropped below the minimum rate of 2.1 that was needed to replace the population. This average continued to decline throughout the 1980s, rising again briefly in 1990. The temporary slight increase was due to a number of factors, including the tendency of baby boomers who had postponed having children to now start families.[12] (See Table A.3 in Appendix.)

In addition to regional differences, a number of other qualifications must be made to generalizations about fertility rates. The mother's age, for example, had a substantial impact. In the 1960s and 1970s women over 30 shared in the decline in the birth rate. Then, in this segment of the population, and this one alone, birth rates started to rise. Between 1975 and 2002, the rates rose hugely: from 64 to 91 per 1 000 women aged 30 to 34, and from 21 to 36 for those aged 35 to 39. Although at this time women between the ages of 25 and 29 still had the highest birth rate—97.5 births per 1 000 women of that age—even that number was nearly a quarter lower than it had been in 1975. More strikingly, the fertility rates for women under the age of 25 fell to less than half of what they had been in 1975. These changes in age-specific fertility rates resulted in a noticeable increase in the mean age of a mother giving birth to her first child. In 2002, such a woman was on average slightly more than 27 years old, compared to only 23 in the late 1960s; by 2008 she was 29 years old. Later age of marriage and the postponement of child-bearing for career reasons seemed to be among the most obvious explanations. By 2006, the fertility rate of women aged 30 to 35, which was still increasing, was more than that of women aged 25 to 29, and the fertility rate of women aged 35 to 40 was also continuing to rise.[13]

Fertility rates among Aboriginal women remained higher than those of Canadian women in general. The total number of children that an Aboriginal woman might expect to bear during her lifetime did fall from 5.5 children in the 1960s to 2.6 children by the beginning of the next century. But such a woman's fertility rate was still well above the national average of 1.5 children; both figures were unchanged in 2006. The fertility rate for Inuit women remained the highest, at 3.4 children in 2001.[14]

The significant changes that were occurring with regard to marriage and births had important effects on the size and nature of Canadian households. (Again, see Table A.2.) The average number of family members per household fell from 3.7 in 1971 to 3.0 in 2006. More specifically, one-person households came to outnumber households of five or more persons by a ratio of three to one; by the latter date, less than a fifth of families had three or more children. In the same period, the frequency of one-parent or sole-support families stabilized at just under 16 percent of Canadian families. Within this group, there was a substantial increase in the percentage of lone parents who had never been legally married; it rose to 30 percent in 2006 from only 2 percent in 1951. Widows headed two-thirds of lone-parent families in 1951 but by 2006 only about a fifth. Cultural differences mattered here, too: in 2001 it was reported that 24 percent of black women aged 15 or over, 19 percent of Aboriginal women, and 15 percent of Latin American women were heading families of their own, while the frequency for Canada overall was only about 8 percent. As in previous decades, in 2006 four of every five lone-parent families were headed by women.[15]

Ever larger numbers of Canadian women simply did not have children at all. In 1991, 12 percent of women aged 35 to 44 who were or had been married did not have children, compared to less than 8 percent 20 years earlier. According to one expert, about half of such women were childless by choice; some of them preferred to call themselves "child-free." Analysis of data gathered in 2001 suggested that among childless women aged 20 to 34 about 7 percent did not intend to have children at all (the number for men was 8 percent).[16] A small survey conducted partly in Canada between 2004 and 2006 supported the suggestion that many childless women were so deliberately. Its author wrote this:

> I . . . saw similarities between my survey and surveys of the childfree that had come before mine, which suggested that the top motives people cited in the '70s and '80s—such as marital satisfaction and the freedom to pursue opportunities, which respondents felt were important for their happiness and sense of fulfillment—are as compelling today as they were thirty years ago.[17]

For women who never married or had children, new patterns of family size and style that could mean independence in youth and middle age also implied absence of family support in illness and old age. An example is Susan Dick, a single woman without a partner who had a long and happy career as a professor of English at Queen's University in Kingston. Dick wrote movingly in 1991 about her extended, damaging experience of hospitalization for a rare nerve disease. During the worst of the ordeal, she wondered whether she "would recover the health and independence and simple joys of life" she had experienced. "Friends played a crucial role," she wrote. Friends, for her, replaced distant family. When Dick's elderly widowed mother moved up from the States to join her daughter, hired caregivers were needed for both of them. Dick was unable to teach, but she continued to do research.[18]

The declining role of the extended family and of communal involvement in women's lives is also reflected in the decline of the traditional practice of customary adoptions in Inuit society, even in Nunavut, where it is legally recognized. In certain circumstances, birth parents had been able to place one or more children with members of their extended family or with friends. There was no stigma attached to the practice of adoption, no reference to "giving up" or "giving away" the child; instead, the Inuktitut word describing the child in question translates as "the one we took" or "my adopted." This system had traditionally provided a mechanism for ensuring that all children were looked after and for helping to keep sex ratios within families in balance. The children knew who their birth parents were, and frequently remained in close contact with them. But such arrangements became less common. Furthermore, with increased intrusion of modern governmental bureaucracies into their lives, Inuit practising customary adoption outside of Nunavut were on occasion forced to set aside their own customs and hire lawyers to work through the new system.[19]

As Canadian women moved through their years of potential childbearing, the choice about whether and when to have children expanded as abortion ceased to be illegal. The widespread use of family limitation practices, along with the stand taken by the Catholic bishops in 1968, made it politically possible the following year for the federal government to amend the provisions of the Criminal Code dealing with contraception and abortion. Contraception was taken out of the Code completely, but abortion remained limited by a requirement for medical approval by a hospital committee. The urgent need for changes in the existing abortion laws was all too obvious: between 1954 and 1965, there were an estimated 50 000 to 100 000 illegal abortions. In British Columbia, abortion-related deaths accounted for one in every five maternal deaths occurring between 1946 and 1968. When the Supreme Court ruled in 1988 that Criminal Code provisions concerning abortion contravened the Charter of Rights, abortion was entirely decriminalized. The number of now-legal abortions performed in Canada peaked at 110 000 in each of the years 1996 and 1997 and then decreased to 105 000 (in 2002). It should be noted that the abortion rate remained fairly constant following 1970, at about 15 per 1 000 women between the ages of 15 and 44. As of 2002, there was about one abortion for every three births in Canada, a rate which dropped to one in four by 2006. Women between the ages of 18 and 24 were the most likely to have abortions. The most striking change was the increasing percentage of those procedures performed in clinics rather than hospitals: one in 20 in 1986, almost one in three by 1996, and just under half in 2004. (See Table 13.1.) However, access to abortion services remained wildly uneven across the country.[20]

Table 13.1   INDUCED ABORTIONS 1975–2002, NUMBER PER 100 LIVE BIRTHS TO WOMEN AGED 15 TO 44

	Performed in Hospital	Performed in Clinics
1975	13.7	—
1980	17.7	1.3
1985	16.7	1.0
1990	17.5	5.0
1995	18.7	9.4
2000	19.4	12.7
2002	17.8	14.2

Source: Adapted from *Canadian Women* 5th edition 84, Table 3.15.

Birth control and abortion were controversial issues in the twentieth century, with a significant influence on how women progressed through their lives; so was divorce. The divorce rate rose steadily during the 1960s, from 36 per 100 000 population at the start of the decade. It was nearly 55 per 100 000 by 1968, even though at that time neither Quebec nor Newfoundland and Labrador yet had any provincial divorce legislation in place to supplement federal provisions. Then, after the enactment of a federal divorce law in 1968, the rate rose sensationally, more than doubling in a year; it was up to 124 per 100 000 by 1969. The new legislation provided for divorce on the grounds of marriage breakdown, as well as on the previously existing basis of matrimonial offences, such as adultery. By the end of the 1960s, divorce was becoming a familiar occurrence in Canadian life; it was a factor in the increased labour-force participation of women who had to support themselves and in many cases their dependent children, after their marriages had ended.

The most significant rise in the divorce rate took place in the 1970s. By 1981 it had reached 278 divorces per 100 000 Canadians. A revision of the legislation in 1986 simplified the rules about jurisdiction for divorce, removed the element of fault in divorce, and abridged the process for actually granting a divorce; it led to a further increase, with the highest rate of 362 being recorded in 1987. (See Figure 13.2.) The divorce rate then gradually declined, and it was down to 224 by 2002. By the standards of the early 1960s, the rate was nonetheless significantly high. Indeed, about two out of every five marriages ended in divorce. However, only 30 percent of first marriages ended in divorce, and many people remarried. There were significant regional variations in the rates of divorce also: in 2003, when the national rate was still 224 per 100 000 population, the Yukon, with 285 divorces, and Alberta, with 252, had the highest rates, while Newfoundland and Labrador had just 128. More striking was the extraordinarily low rate of only 14 divorces per 100 000 people in Nunavut. This last figure once more reflects the much lower marriage rate and the higher frequency of common-law

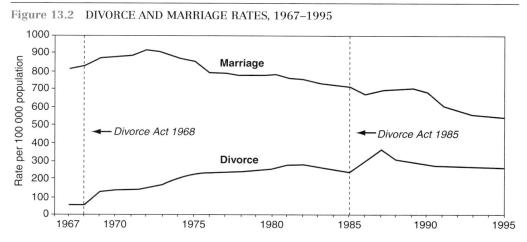

Figure 13.2 DIVORCE AND MARRIAGE RATES, 1967–1995

Source: Statistics Canada, *Marriage and Conjugal Life in Canada,* 91-534-XPE 1991001, 1991 April 23, 1993.

relationships in that territory. In general, formal marriages that followed common-law relationships were the ones most at risk for divorce, possibly because those involved remained skeptical about marriage itself. Higher rates of divorce contributed to the significant increase in women raising families on their own. While the courts still continued to give preference to mothers over fathers in custody disputes, shared custody of children became much more common. Whereas in 1980 custody was awarded to mothers in over three-quarters of cases, by 2003 custody of children was awarded to mothers in only just under half of cases; it went jointly to both parents in 44 percent and to fathers in 8 percent of cases.[21]

While such trends as abortion and divorce stabilized in the twentieth century and into the twenty-first, there was by contrast a pronounced increase in life expectancy for all Canadians. (See Figure A.5 in Appendix.) In 1921 the relevant statistics were 61 years for women and 59 for men, rising to 83 for women and 78 for men in 2005. The age gap in life expectancy at birth for the two sexes increased from less than two years in 1921 to over six years by 1991, although it then shrank slightly again, to under five by 2005. The precise reasons for this gender-related longevity gap were not clear but the phenomenon was evident worldwide.[22] The most significant cause of extended life expectancy for both sexes was the reduction of infant mortality: the infant death rate—the number of deaths of children under two years of age per 1 000 live births—was just about halved between 1951 and 1971, going from 38.5 per 1 000 live births to 17.5. From about 10 such deaths in 1981 it continued to drop, reaching a continuing level of just over five infant deaths per 1 000 live births in 1996. Aboriginal infant mortality rates, however, continued to be shockingly high. At the end of the 1960s, among status Indians, eight times as many children aged two years and under died as did other Canadian children in the same age category. Consequently, in 1970 life expectancy was only 37 years for Indian women, and 34 years for Indian men. In 2006, looking at all Aboriginal populations, the infant mortality rate per 1 000 live births was still estimated to be about four times higher than in the non-Aboriginal population. In Nunavut, with an 85 percent Inuit population, infant mortality also decreased but remained relatively high, at 10 per 1 000 births in 2005 (the national rate was 5.4). Aboriginal women were also far more likely to suffer from many health problems, including chronic diseases, such as type two diabetes; one Saskatchewan study found that between 1990 and 2005, the diabetes rate for Aboriginal women was about four times higher than among non-Aboriginal women. Despite subsequent significant improvements in their longevity, it was estimated that Aboriginal women born in 2001 still had relatively low life expectancies; they could anticipate living five years fewer than their non-Aboriginal counterparts, that is, 77 years. For Aboriginal men in 2001, the figure was 71 years, so there was also a larger gender-based gap than among non-Aboriginals. For the Inuit population, both life expectancy and the gender-based gap remained even more unfavourable: 72 years for women and just over 60 years for men. In 2004 Inuit women had a life expectancy more than 14 years lower than the average for all Canadian women; their infant mortality rate was two to three times the Canadian level.[23]

As a result of increased longevity, the age composition of the whole population changed markedly over the second half of the century, and the impact was greater for women. A larger proportion of Canadians were over the age of 65: in 2006, such seniors accounted for 13 percent of the population, compared to 11 percent in 1986 and only 7 percent in 1941. Women's longer life expectancy resulted in Canada's having significantly more senior women than senior men: the older women accounted for almost three out of every five seniors in 2004. In fact, women over the age of 65 were the fastest growing group within the female population, increasing at twice the rate for women under the age of 65. In 2004, there were 2.3 million senior women in Canada—an increase of over 70 percent from 1981. Government statisticians projected that, with the aging of the baby boom generation and increased longevity, women over 65 years of age would account for one of every four Canadian women by 2031. More importantly, within the senior group, the proportion of women over the age of 85 was growing the most rapidly. This was the group of women most likely to face serious health, economic, and social challenges. They were also the senior group most likely to live on their own: about six out of ten of them did so compared to three out of ten women aged 65 to 74. In all senior age categories, women were twice as likely to live on their own as were senior men.

Of course, generalizations about the Canadian population's age structure and life expectancy do not apply uniformly. For example, by 2001 there was a higher proportion of seniors among foreign-born women, with one in five of them over the age of 65, compared to just over one in ten among women born in Canada. On the other hand, for the separate but overlapping category of visible minority women, some of whom were born in Canada to very long established but often still marginalized population groups, only a small percentage were seniors (7 percent). As a result of the much higher fertility rates of most Aboriginal women, the female Aboriginal population remained much younger than the female non-Aboriginal population. In 2001, nearly one of every three Aboriginal women was younger than 15 years of age whereas only one in five non-Aboriginal women was. Among the Inuit female population, nearly 40 percent were in this youngest category. It was therefore not surprising that only 4 percent of Aboriginal women were seniors, compared to 14 percent of the non-Aboriginal female population.[24]

REPRODUCTION: CHILDBIRTH AND MOTHERING

Even though motherhood was no longer the central, continuing, and defining feature of women's lives, it remained the one physical and social event that differentiated women as a gender. Men could certainly "parent," and they did more of it as time progressed, but they could not give birth. Even after birth, primary responsibility for nurturing— "mothering"—remained with women, as a responsibility most often assumed gladly. During the last quarter of the twentieth century, almost every aspect of maternity— pregnancy, delivery, and child-rearing—was subject to radical change from what it had been even a generation earlier.

For the majority of childbirths, there was increased medical intervention and control of women's bodies. The incidence of Caesarean sections (C-sections) increased to an unprecedented level. C-sections had a very long history as a drastic but effective solution to some types of problematic births, and modern technology had made them much safer than in earlier days. However, the persistent high level of occurrence was troubling in an age when nearly all women had access to pre-natal care and ample medical facilities. (See Figure 13.3.) Sometimes C-sections were performed for the convenience of physician or patient or in response to the doctor's possible legal liabilities. More often, they reflected technological advances in tracking fetal distress by use of devices such as fetal heart monitors. And it was possibly relevant that older mothers were now more likely to be giving birth. In any case, the percentage of births by C-section per 1 000 live births rose after 1970 from 6 percent to just under 20 percent in 1988. The frequency of C-sections varied by regions and even by institutions. In one hospital, nearly one-third of all babies born live in 1994 were by Caesarean delivery, at a time when the national rate was just under 18 percent. In 2005–2006, just over a quarter of all Canadian babies were delivered by C-section. The following year, the C-section rate was over 30 percent in the three provinces and territories with the highest rates.[25]

As early as the 1980s, there was official medical approval for VBACs (vaginal birth after Caesarean caesarean) so that succeeding babies could be born naturally in the absence of new risk factors. Nevertheless, in spite of campaigns by women activists, the incidence of VBACs actually declined between 1997 and 2005, going from 35 percent to 20 percent of eligible mothers. This may in part explain the persistently high level of C-sections in Canada. In 2009, the Society of Obstetricians and Gynaecologists of Canada (SOGS) announced that C-sections were no longer recommended even for breech births.[26] Training doctors to handle such births vaginally, which had been virtually discontinued, would be renewed, and the general goal would be "promotion of natural childbirth," spontaneous labour without use of forceps, vacuum, or C-section. "Our primary purpose is to offer choice to women," said a representative of SOGS.[27]

Figure 13.3   CAESAREAN SECTION RATES, 1979–2002

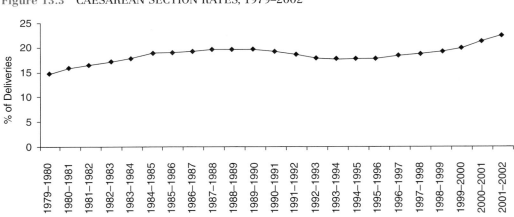

Source: Canadian Institute for Health Information, *Giving Birth in Canada: Providers of Maternity and Infant Care* (Ottawa, Ont.: CIHI, 2004), p. 9.

Improved medical techniques were saving more premature babies, including ones far younger than in previous generations. Risks decreased for mothers, too. As a result of improved nutrition, and better pre-natal and postpartum care, fewer women died in childbirth: the likelihood of a Canadian woman dying this way fell from one in 150 in the 1930s to one in 3 000 by the 1960s. (See Figure A.3 in Appendix.) By 2001, 97 percent of new mothers had pre-natal care, mostly from physicians (88 percent).[28]

Monitoring of pregnancies, and particularly of those seen as at risk, was aided by an expanding panoply of new techniques. Even as late as the 1990s, at a time when the birth rate of older women was increasing, any first pregnancy after the age of 30 continued to be seen as risky; pregnant women who were seen as older provoked increased medical supervision. By the turn of the century, the age of 35 was seen as marking the point at which abnormalities and infertility in attempted pregnancies became statistically probable. Doctors warned about abnormalities such as Down syndrome, although even women over 40 had only approximately 1 chance in 60 of bearing a chromosomally abnormal child. The biological impact of older fathers was overlooked in discussions that in effect put all the blame on women. Wendy Lill, who had a Down syndrome child when she was 34, wrote angrily, "Instead of buying the theory about maternal age hook, line and sinker, I think we should be demanding more investigation on links between radiation, environmental pollutants, and all sorts of birth defects."[29] A study reported in 2006 that the genetic quality of sperm did in fact decline as men aged, increasing the risk of infertility and failed pregnancies, as well as, possibly, birth defects.

Since it was more difficult for older women to become pregnant, and older pregnancies were likely to be somewhat more complicated for both mothers and babies, women acquired a whole new range of anxieties and stresses, beginning with the feeling of a "biological clock" ticking away during childless years. Mapping of the human genetic code, beginning in the 1970s, opened important but alarming possibilities of detecting genetic abnormalities in children while they were still in the womb, including the presence of severe hereditary diseases or disabling physical conditions. Decisions about whether or not to abort an abnormal fetus were no less agonizing now that diagnostic procedures were more developed.[30]

By the 1980s, researchers had learned how to flush out human eggs, fertilize them outside the body (in vitro fertilization, or IVF), and implant them, sometimes in a different woman's womb (surrogacy). Canada's hundredth test-tube baby was born in 1987; a year later, the nation's first test-tube quintuplets—only the third set in the world—appeared. This practice and other related processes were costly, as well as subject to decisions by doctors about who was considered a fit subject for the procedures. The new reproductive technology alarmed feminists because it implied treatment of the female body as a baby-making machine. The complex health and ethical issues surrounding many of the scientific and medical innovations in the area of human reproduction became the focus of general public concern. Many were disturbed by the increase in certain practices, such as the fertilization and then implantation of numerous eggs. For women employing what were now referred to as Assisted Reproductive Techniques (ART), multiple births or relatively premature or small, immature babies were, very likely, placing an added strain on the health system. A report in 2007 noted that chances of success in ART declined with age: for women under 35 years of age, the live birth rate was about a third per cycle of fertility treatments, while for women over 40 the rate was only just over a tenth. In addition, the practice of surrogacy seemed to imply renting the wombs of impoverished women. The federal Royal Commission on New Reproductive Technologies released its controversial report in November 1993, after four years of exhaustive study, marked by serious internal rifts within the Commission. The Commission recommended that the government introduce legislation to ban some procedures, such as surrogacy, and impose limits on the use of others. Federal legislation that was proclaimed in 2004 incorporated most of these recommendations, and in 2006 a regulatory and licensing body was established. However, by 2009 the right of the federal government to act in these areas was under constitutional challenge and exactly one section had reached the stage of regulations. But the year 2009 also saw a number of other related developments: Quebec introduced for a second time a law proposing more generous support of IVF; an expert panel in Ontario reported with far-reaching recommendations on the subject; and the government of Manitoba promised new tax credits for infertility treatments.[31]

Artificial insemination was the one reproductive technology amenable to self-help. By the 1980s, some lesbians had conceived in this way with the assistance of male friends. Such cases separated sexuality and reproduction in the most extreme way yet, and also seemed to reassert women's claim to define the identity of both children and families. As lesbianism became more accepted, key questions related to sexuality and to family composition were raised again from a different perspective. In 2007 the Ontario Court of Appeals ruled that a child could have three legal parents. The case of *A.A. v. B.B.* concerned the biological parents of a child and the woman who was the lesbian partner of the mother; the three adults and the child lived amicably together in the same household. The court accepted the argument that all of the adults were in a parental relationship with the child. This case was a clear indicator of the shifts in the definition of a family.[32]

Women's increased autonomy was also expressed in demands for less mechanized childbearing, and these efforts had some success, in spite of the two-edged consequences of some initiatives. In the 1960s, women turned to partial anaesthesia, such as spinal blocks, which could relieve the pain associated with childbirth but left them conscious and able to apply some of the lessons of the widely attended pre-natal classes held for both mothers and fathers. By the next decade, fathers were encouraged to be present during labour and delivery; babies were allowed to be bigger and were considered less fragile; babies rooming in with their mothers had become a routine practice in hospitals. However, partly for financial reasons, medical administrators drastically reduced the hospitalization period for healthy mothers and their babies, removing a respite often valued by busy women. By the 1980s, a small but significant number of women were once again opting for home births, childbirth without medication, or the assistance of midwives in either hospital or home births. The ancient profession of midwifery, accepted in all industrialized areas except North America, began to be revived. By 2009 midwifery was fully covered in the provincial health plans in British Columbia, Manitoba, Quebec, and Ontario; all of the other provinces and territories were at various stages in the process of regulation and coverage. A program evaluation in Ontario in 2003 showed that midwife-assisted births had a 30 percent lower rate of C-sections, as well as generally a lower rate of complications and a much higher level of cost-effectiveness, as compared to those assisted by obstetricians and family doctors. Another study completed in 2009 found that, for low-risk births, planned home births assisted by registered midwives were as safe as those that took place in hospitals, while both the need for interventions and the risk of complications were lower. In spite of the growing popularity of home births and birthing centres, however, at the turn of the century 99.7 percent of births were hospital births. (See Figure A.4 in Appendix.)[33]

After women gave birth, conditions for most new mothers had also improved, though changes in family structure often meant reduced support from their own mothers and other relatives. The energetic efforts of volunteer moms of La Leche League helped promote breastfeeding as the preferred form of infant feeding. By 2005 the League was recommending breastfeeding for at least one year and preferably two; the World Health Organization and the Canadian Pediatric Society also advised that children not be given solid food before six months, while breastfeeding could continue even beyond two years. Modern baby bottles and disposable bottle liners, as well as better formulas and baby food, did make child care easier for those who could not or would not breastfeed, and all mothers were helped by relaxation of earlier regimes of either total permissiveness or comprehensive regimentation in child care. New, more flexible, and less sexist editions of the iconic *Dr. Spock* appeared. The eighth edition, revised and updated in 2004, included "all the information you need to meet the changes and challenges of childrearing in the new millennium—including entirely new chapters about international adoption, coping with terrorism and disasters, college planning, autism. . . ." Other topics included blended families and gay and lesbian parenting. By the late twentieth and early twenty-first centuries, however, younger parents were looking less to Dr. Spock than to publications such as Heidi Murkoff's bestselling books on pregnancy, childbirth, and child-rearing that began with *What to Expect When You're Expecting*. Spock had continued the traditional pattern of expert advice to women. Murkoff, by contrast, was a young mother with no medical training, though she did have assistance from her mother and a nurse.[34]

The reassertion of traditional, woman-controlled patterns in medicine and family life was real, but it should not be overstated. For many Canadian women, the advice literature on mothering and changes in practices surrounding childbirth and child-rearing were irrelevant, given the cultural and material contexts in which they found themselves. Some women continued to find breastfeeding "unappealing" or "disgusting" or felt that bottle-feeding was simply easier. In 2003, some 85 percent of Canadian mother initially breastfed their babies —up from 25 percent in the mid 1960s—but only 17 percent were doing so exclusively at six months, as recommended. Poverty and isolation frequently limited the availability of medical facilities and services. Aboriginal women in particular did not have access to services that most Canadian women came to count on routinely for assistance in delivering and raising healthy children. In Inuit communities, for example, the practice of flying pregnant women out of their own communities to hospitals in larger centres remained widespread, and those women often had to give birth far away from family and friends. In response, Aboriginal women also organized to restore traditional practices of birthing. The Indian Homemakers' Association in British Columbia began running courses on traditional mothering. In addition, community-based health centres were established, including, beginning in the 1980s, in seven remote Inuit communities at Nunavik, Quebec, on the eastern shore of Hudson Bay.[35]

WOMEN'S BODIES: HEALTH, SPORTS, AND PHYSICAL FITNESS

The last half of the twentieth century was an era when, for many Canadian women, their physical selves were less constrained than ever before. To start with, attitudes about sexuality experienced great changes. In the 1950s, premarital sex was still socially unacceptable for respectable young women. However, by the late 1960s, sexual intimacy outside of marriage became less scandalous, as the student movements of the period adopted the peace movement slogan "make love, not war" and promoted both freer discussion and freer practice of sexuality. Despite the greater freedom, it seems likely that at this time most single young women limited their sexual relationships to the men whom they intended to marry. At the same time, they were far more likely than in earlier periods to be living with their lovers, even having children, without immediate marriage plans. General acceptance of enduring common-law relationships was, however, still in the future.

As the 1970s turned into the 1980s, heterosexual women became aware that sexual liberation had some major flaws for them. The Pill meant decreased fear of pregnancy. However, sex separated from procreation represented greater advantages for men than for women, for it often provided men with the possibility of greater access to physical intimacy accompanied with reduced responsibility. Pregnancy, including pregnancy due to contraceptive failure, was still very much women's business. Furthermore, specific, unexpected health hazards emerged as a result of the new sexual mores. The number of sexually transmitted diseases increased, and they affected women particularly severely. The old curses of syphilis and gonorrhea were now more easily diagnosed and treated, but genital herpes, chlamydia, and pelvic inflammatory disease (PID) were increasingly common, likely to interfere with a woman's fertility, and likely also to be transmitted to children.

By the middle of the 1980s, acquired immune deficiency syndrome (AIDS) had appeared, with no known cure. Women's vulnerability to AIDS was initially underestimated by public health authorities, who seemed aware of women mainly as potential carriers of the disease who could infect men and children. In 1994, the Canadian Society of Gynaecologists and Obstetricians recognized that women could be infected via heterosexual intercourse as well as by blood transfusion and the use of infected needles. Ten years later, women comprised approximately 9 percent of the cases testing positive for AIDS in Canada and 16 percent of those with the prior condition of human immunodeficiency virus (HIV). As AIDS occurrence became less frequent in Canada, women made up an increasing proportion of adult cases reported; young women aged 15 to 19 went from one in ten of cases reported before 1994 to two in five in 2004. Although there was still no vaccine, by the twenty-first century it became possible to live with AIDS; that is, new antiretroviral drugs were able to hold the condition sufficiently in check to permit a fairly normal life.[36] Lynn Kampf, a retired nurse living in Pickering, Ontario, was typical. She had been infected by tainted blood received during surgery in 1981 before the Red Cross put rigorous safeguards in place. She described herself as "a healthy, active grandmother who happens to have AIDS." "I take one pill a day to heal my condition and a couple of others to deal with side effects," she said. "The picture is not so bleak as it was 15 years ago—thank God."[37]

In 2007, the panoply of public, free preventive medicine in all provinces and territories came to include the vaccination of girls against the human papilloma virus (HPV), which can cause cervical cancer and genital warts. Vaccination began as early as grade four (in Quebec); although males also spread HPV through sexual contact and could also be inoculated against it, there was little or no suggestion that boys should have the injections. Some feminists read this as a continuation of the age-old double standard and were also concerned about the intensive campaign in favour of the program by the drug company that had developed the vaccine. The Catholic Church and many traditional parents believed that the vaccinations encouraged sexual activity in the young; about half of Alberta's Catholic schools refused to allow the vaccinations. At this time, the Church and some parents also opposed the movement toward modernizing and expanding sex education in the school curriculum.[38]

The continuing patterns of male initiative and domination in sexual matters were difficult to counter. Because men often expected that women would take responsibility for contraception, women were under increased pressure. Coercive sex, including so-called date rape, was alarmingly common, even among highschoolers. Media highlighted a reported increase in the frequency of oral/genital sex among young people; it was non-procreative although it entailed the familiar risks of sexually transmitted infection, male dominance, and the destruction of young women's reputations.[39] Oral contraception now entailed a smaller dose of hormones, but many women distrusted such substantial chemical intervention into their bodies over a period of fertility that might span more than 30 years. Side effects ranged from depression and obesity to such potentially fatal conditions as blood clots and heart disease.

The use of the intrauterine device (IUD) also proved to be dangerous, sometimes producing ectopic pregnancy or sterility; it was used infrequently in Canada, even before a health disaster in the 1970s with one particular form, the Dalkon Shield. Tubal ligation to sterilize women remained a surgical operation involving a hospital stay whereas, for men, vasectomy was a simple procedure that could be carried out in a doctor's office. Despite this difference, for a considerable period female sterilization continued to be more common than male sterilization. A 1984 study showed that, of the 68 percent of women between 18 and 49 years of age who used some form of birth control, 35 percent had been sterilized, compared to only 13 percent of their partners. Sterilization became less popular over the years, however, especially among women. According to 2004 figures, of women who had experienced intercourse, only 8 percent had been sterilized, as opposed to 15 percent of men. Oral contraceptives were the method most frequently used by these women, at 32 percent, followed by use of a condom at 21 percent. Condoms, now much improved, had a revived popularity, but younger people and those in ongoing relationships were less likely to use condoms, thus putting their health seriously at risk. Progress on the development of a male contraceptive was unnoticeable. Some women returned to such earlier contraceptive devices as sponges, diaphragms, or douches; if safer in one sense, these approaches were still unreliable as contraceptives. Health Canada began in 2005 the process of approving the sale through pharmacies of Plan B (levonorgestrel), the effective morning-after emergency contraceptive that could be used in case of rape, contraceptive failure, or other unprotected intercourse. In 2008, Plan B was federally approved for over-the-counter sale at pharmacies, as was already occurring in most provinces; only Quebec maintained a system of intervention by pharmacists. In 2009, Plan B One-Step made available an even simpler process of self-medication.[40]

As the baby boom generation reached middle age in the later years of the twentieth century, menopause became a much more widely studied and discussed phenomenon. A youth-oriented society found it difficult to accept the physical changes that occurred in aging women. Artificial hormones—estrogen and progestin—helped to relieve such disagreeable menopausal symptoms as hot flashes, night sweats, and dry vagina. In addition, pharmaceutical companies campaigned aggressively to persuade women that artificial hormones were necessary to replace the natural ones lost at menopause. In 1991, in Canada as a whole, 15 percent of post-menopausal women were on hormone replacement therapy (HRT), while the rate reached 30 percent in Quebec. Medical authorities who endorsed this therapy often cited research on what was believed to be the efficacy of hormones in producing significant reductions in the incidence of osteoporosis and heart disease among post-menopausal women. In 2002, however, a very substantial American study of the effect of HRT on women's health, scheduled to run until 2005, was discontinued when it began to show persuasively that such treatments actually increased the risk of breast cancer, strokes, and heart attacks. Further studies suggested in 2009 that HRT also created an increased likelihood of mental impairment. The findings of such studies were not unambiguous but there was a marked decrease in the use of the therapy. Now more appropriately designated as "menopausal hormone therapy," it focused more narrowly on the actual undesirable symptoms of menopause experienced by some but by no means all women.[41]

As menopause became a politicized issue, so, too, did breast cancer, which was estimated in 1992 to strike one in nine Canadian women. Activists pointed to the thousands of Canadian women who died each year from this disease, and the relatively small amount of financial and human resources devoted by governments and the medical establishment to developing effective prevention and treatment strategies. Pat Kelly, who founded a self-help group for women with breast cancer, noted that in 1989 there were 333 AIDs-related deaths in Ontario, and 1814 attributable to breast cancer. That same year, the provincial Ministry of Health spent $37 million for AIDS research and community education programs, but nothing on breast cancer research or education. Kelly flatly declared, "No more daffodils, no more lunches. We want a cure."[42] In 1992, the House of Commons Subcommittee on the Status of Women undertook a major review of breast cancer and its treatment and produced recommendations for research and treatment. Even by the 2000s, however, some aspects of research and even treatment were still heavily dependent on volunteer fundraising. "Run for the Cure" (of breast cancer) events became common in Canada. Ex-MP Belinda Stronach, after recovering from a mastectomy, started fundraising for a $27 million Comprehensive Breast Cancer Research Centre to be opened in 2010. She also donated $1 million and pledged to raise matching funds for the creation of an academic chair in reconstructive breast surgery at the University of Toronto. By 2007 the death rate for breast cancer for Canadian women had fallen 25 percent since 1986. But it was still the leading cancer cause of death for young women, with psychological consequences for body image and self-esteem that outweighed its incidence.[43]

Lung cancer, though not so much noticed, was by 2001 the fastest growing cancer among women, causing more deaths than breast cancer. The death rate from it almost doubled from 1976 to 1985, and increased a third more over the next 10 years; in 2004 the growth rate continued but somewhat more slowly. These trends reflect changing smoking patterns. Women started smoking in considerable numbers only after World War II and there was a lag before the impact on health became visible. In later years, the frequency of smoking began to drop, as the health risks became known. In 1970 almost two in five women over 15 were current smokers, but in 1991 the number was fewer than one woman in three, and by 2003 the number had dropped to just over one in five. Presumably, in the future rates of lung cancer would reflect this change. In 2005, 18 percent of Canadian males and 15 percent of females over the age of 12 were daily smokers. A small note of cheer was the fact that in 2009 a study of OECD countries showed that Canadian teenagers were smoking the least of 15-year-olds there. But Canadian girls smoked more than boys did: 10 percent and 7 percent, respectively, had smoked at least one cigarette in the previous seven days).[44]

For many women, the quest for the perfect body became obsessive. Anorexia or self-starvation became recognized as a serious health hazard, especially for younger women, as did bulimia, characterized by binge eating, with each binge followed by a purge (self-induced vomiting). As the Internet became widely used in Canada, some websites encouraged this sort of self-destructive behaviour. Increasingly, fat women were made to feel like outcasts, morally defective persons who lacked self discipline. In the 1970s, a movement for Fat Liberation announced that "fat is a feminist issue;" social pressure for some ideal body size was seen by these activists as a central part of the objectification of women.[45] Fat was also a cultural and generational issue, particularly for women, as standards of some recent immigrant groups were rejected in favour of an Anglo-Celtic and commercial model. "In my time, fat women were honoured. . . . Truly, I don't understand present-day fashions at all. . . . Anywhere a man touches, he can feel bones," lamented "Hannah," an 89-year-old Morocco-born woman who lived in Montreal in the 1980s.[46] When obesity became a major public health concern in the 1980s, it increased the stigma of being even moderately overweight. But in the twenty-first century, a small but possibly significant counter-movement promoted more realistic models of normal or even plus-size feminine beauty.[47]

Clothing was now expected to display women's contours without assistance from the substantial foundation garments that had helped earlier generations of women conform to a womanly ideal. Women's clothing became blatantly eroticized, and many were concerned to see teenaged and then even preteen girls in close-fitting, seductive clothing

Young woman in pantsuit, Calgary, Alberta, 1970.

Source: Glenbow Archives NA-2864-6835a

promoted by massive advertising campaigns. For adult women of all ages, fashion continued to stress the value of youthfulness and to make women feel compelled to present a physically, even sexually attractive appearance. Far fewer such demands were made on men. In a 2007 poll, 27 percent of the women respondents said that if they could afford it, they would have cosmetic surgery, compared to only 13 percent of men.[48]

For an increasingly sedentary society, concern about appearance led to concern about the need for some form of exercise. Regular participation in physical activity was recommended by the medical profession for prevention and cure of such ongoing health concerns as anorexia and obesity. Exercise was also recognized as important for dealing with major diseases, such as diabetes and cancer, as well as with menopause and aging. Popular, widely available activities for women included classes in swimming, yoga, tai chi, and various forms of aerobics. From the 1960s on, women also became more active and successful in both recreational and competitive sports. A growing number of Canadian girls and women were thus challenging the stereotypes of what constituted appropriate female behaviour. A renewed women's movement facilitated such changes as it produced significant alteration in attitudes as well as in laws and regulations concerning sports and sports funding.

Nonetheless, women's participation at all levels of sports continued to be eclipsed by that of men, for reasons both structural and attitudinal. Working women with families found it difficult to take time from their hectic schedules to take part in sports, and few evening sports programs offered child care. Participation levels were directly related to income, and on average women had less money than men. Moreover, for many years some girls and women continued to believe it was unladylike to sweat or to develop muscles, even when the female ideal began to incorporate the trimmer body of the woman who worked out. There were also proportionately fewer female coaches and physical education teachers than in the past, and women continued to be woefully underrepresented among sports administrators and executives. For instance, as women's inter- and intra-collegiate sports received more attention and funding, women coaches and sports administrators were often replaced by men.[49]

In the 1960s, women's team sports had to contend with second-class status. Professional team sports, geared to men's interests and needs, siphoned off most of the financial support and public interest previously given to amateur athletics. As well, young girls usually had less opportunity than boys to play such sports as hockey or baseball. Only occasionally could exceptional girls, such as future Olympic runner Abby Hoffman, register for a boys' hockey team; she was able to do so in 1956 only by giving her name as A. Hoffman and because she was slight and boyish. The few team sports that girls were encouraged to play were carefully redesigned to preserve their femininity. Baseball was made less dangerous by the institution of a "no-sliding" rule, and women's basketball was allowed to play by so-called men's rules only in the late 1960s. The view that active participation in sports was somehow incompatible with femininity was reinforced in some cases by female physical educators themselves. One university instructor, writing in 1961, suggested drawing attention to "the most charming looking students through the election of baseball queens, field hockey queens and archery queens." The idea was to counteract the unattractive image of female athletes: the successful candidates were to be photographed in non-sports clothes, and to have their pictures prominently displayed.[50]

The issue of whether women and girls should be allowed on men's teams in competitive amateur sports was technically settled in 1986, although attitudes and expectations were slow to change. Justine Blainey, who had been 12 when she wanted to play on a boys' hockey team, obtained a Supreme Court ruling that entitled her to do so, while leaving the girls' teams in place.[51] In 2002, Justine Blainey Broker commented, "Today I am a doctor of chiropractic and a mother, and every day I yearn for the swish of the ice and the rough and tumble of top-level competitive hockey."[52] But she was badly treated when she was a hockey player, enduring opposition including death threats, pornographic graffiti on the walls of arenas where she was playing, and strangers in the subway yelling invective. In 2008, Jessie and Amy Pasternak, aged 17, had to go to mediation through the Manitoba Human Rights Commission to get permission to compete in high school hockey tryouts along with boys. "Wouldn't it be lovely if the Pasternak decision finally rid us of this too-many-women-on-the-ice paranoia?" wrote one commentator.[53]

Women, as such, were still not usually thought of as athletic or, even more, as team players. The few high achievers were dismissed as exceptions, and feminine success in competitive contexts continued to be associated with individual sports, such as skating, skiing, and swimming. Skier Nancy Greene became a superstar in the 1960s, winning more World Cup victories than any other skier, male or female, as well as Olympic gold and silver; she was eventually voted Canada's female athlete of the twentieth century and in 2009 she was appointed to the Senate. But opportunities for women to compete in team events at the Olympic level lagged. It was not until 1964 that the first such event for women, volleyball, was added to the Olympic roster. Still, despite the relative lack of opportunities and support, Canadian women athletes' overall performance at international events managed to remain on a par with that of Canadian men and, as time went on, their achievements increased. At the 1992 Summer Olympics in Barcelona, Spain, women athletes captured the majority of the gold medals won by the Canadian team: four out of seven. From the 1990s, the Canadian women's national hockey team dominated world events, winning the women's world championship for the seventh successive time in 2001. In the same year, the University of Winnipeg women's basketball team equalled the North American university and college record for the largest number of consecutive victories by either a women's or men's team. But even for such dazzling performances, media coverage remained discouragingly sparse. When the Canadian men's hockey team failed to place in the first three at the 1998 Olympic games, sports columnists lamented that Canada had never won a medal in hockey, not noticing that the women's team had won silver that same year. Captains Cassie Campbell-Pascall and Hayley Wickenheiser then led the team to gold medals in 2002, 2006, and 2010.[54]

There continued to be far fewer women's events in all Olympic categories, however, and fewer than half as many women as men on Canadian Olympic teams. Nevertheless, Canadian women won as many medals as the men in 2002, and from then on they won more. By 2009, only one Olympic winter sport remained closed to women: ski jumping. It was in Canada that the exclusion was challenged. Looking to the 2010 Olympics, which were scheduled for Vancouver, women ski-jumpers sued the Vancouver Olympic Committee (VANOC). Opposition to the women's demand included allegations that women's bodies could not stand the impact of landing: one official warned that women's uteruses might break and their spines snap upon impact. Dick Pound, himself a Canadian Olympian and former vice-president of the International Olympic Committee, told the ski-jumpers they were making a "huge and hideous mistake" by turning the dispute into a gender issue. Canadian competitor Zoya Lynch responded, "They want us to just sit and look pretty and not speak our mind. Well, we are speaking our mind, and we are trying to do something for women's sport at the 2010 Olympics."[55] Madam Justice Lauri Ann Fenelon of B.C.'s Supreme Court found that the women had indeed been discriminated against, but the Charter of Rights did not apply to the International Olympic Committee in Geneva. The B.C. Court of Appeal agreed, and in December 2009 the Supreme Court of Canada refused to hear a further appeal. In August 2009 it was

Carol Huynh, 2008 Olympic gold medallist in wrestling.

Source: Toronto Star/GetStock.com

announced that boxing would be opened to women in the 2012 Olympics, leaving sprint canoe as the only remaining all-male sport in the summer games.[56]

Sexuality and sexual and gender identity remained central issues for women athletes. Even as the Canadian women's hockey team won silver at the 1998 Olympics in Nagano, Japan, the team and especially coach Shannon Miller were assailed with hostile rumours of lesbianism: how could a real woman be an expert at a men's sport? And if she was a lesbian, could she be a role model for young girls? Although public homosexuality was more tolerated by the turn of the century, in Canada most female athletes still felt obliged to present conventionally feminine images.[57] Overall, the reactions to women's achievements in sports remained somewhat mixed. Some observers deplored lost femininity, while others regretted the tendency for attitudes to change among women and girls from the pursuit of autonomy and recreation to a fierce, masculine focus on competition. But in 2003 a commentator was cautiously optimistic, writing that although stereotyping and financial differentials persisted, women athletes were now less inhibited by them: "Fitness and femininity are now compatible."[58]

EDUCATION

Views about appropriate, distinctive roles for women continued to shape all aspects of Canadian culture, including education. In 1964, guidelines unequivocally restated the identification of the wife and mother as the nucleus of the family; she bore the principal responsibility for achieving either "an organized and artistic way of living or a chaotic and unattractive existence within the home."[59] Canadian parents tended to reinforce the messages implicit in the textbooks. An "Attitude Study" undertaken in 1966 by the Federation of Women Teachers' Associations of Ontario reported that parents considered nursing, teaching, and social work to be the best occupations for their daughters, but favoured medicine, engineering, science, architecture, the law, and business for their sons. To a surprising degree, gender stereotyping in textbook materials remained unchanged, despite the massive changes taking place in the lives of women. In 1975, for example, seven of every ten people portrayed in Quebec school texts were male. Gone were the references to the outstanding women of the past that had been in the old manuals, especially those used by the teaching nuns in previous generations. The earlier images were not replaced: women simply disappeared.[60]

Feminist educators' efforts to achieve gender equality in elementary and secondary schooling throughout the next decades met with some success, though far more limited than they hoped. In the 1970s and 1980s, provincial ministries of education and teachers' unions set up committees to examine gender issues in education. These committees gathered data and established guidelines and incentives for equal participation of girls in the schools, as well as for equal representation of women on the staffs of schools and as administrators. Curricula and textbooks were mandated to include the experience and activities of both genders. However, classroom materials continued to lack meaningful representation of girls and women; in Ontario, for example, few schools implemented the Ministry of Education's 1984 sex-equity policy. By the 1990s, provincial restructuring projects combined with attention to diversity and to the many forms of discrimination to lessen the focus on gender equality.

By contrast, a new gender gap in education received substantial public attention: by many measures, boys were falling behind in school. Girls had always done better in literacy (reading and writing), and graduated from high school in greater numbers. Now they were catching up in science and mathematics, partly due to new affirmative action programs including science camps for girls. Some observers suggested that single-sex (i.e., sex-segregated) classes and schools, as in previous days, would better allow for differences in learning styles. Boys, it was claimed, were typically aggressive and restless while girls were calmer and more group-minded. Other commentators charged that feminists had succeeded in producing a high school curriculum that was too female-centred and therefore drove boys to perform below their capacity. It was also possible that too much attention was being paid to corporate-driven test scores, while gender analysis, along with concern for class and race, was being sidelined. The Toronto District School Board released in 2009 a proposal for the first all-boys public elementary school in Canada; there were already a few all-girls schools and all-girls and all-boys classes in the public education system, and many single-sex schools in the private one.[61]

In 2004, four young women in the women's studies program at the University of Western Ontario felt that high school teaching was still so sex-role stereotyped that something had to be done. Their "Miss G_ project," named after an unfortunate, anonymous young woman whom nineteenth-century educators believed had been killed in 1873 by too much studying, attempted to get women's studies into the secondary school curriculum in Ontario. The members of the group attracted a good deal of public attention through media-savvy lobbying, including stunts like a croquet game on the grass at Queen's Park with participants wearing sashes with the words "Miss Education." In 2009 they succeeded in getting a pilot gender studies course into the Ontario curriculum for grades 11 and 12.[62] Generally, however, the integration of women's perspectives and history into high school courses continued to depend on the teachers involved. Textbooks nodded to feminism, but tended to substitute visual material (that is, pictures of women) for substantive text about women's experiences and activities.

While sex-role stereotyping and lack of interest in women remained substantial problems for women's education in general, poverty, racism, and geographical isolation multiplied their effects. It was not until 1969 that the federal government finally decided to close residential schools for Aboriginal children, with all their history of physical and sexual abuse and exploitation; the last one, in Saskatchewan, was closed only in 1996. It took another 12 years for the federal government to issue a formal apology for forcing Aboriginal children to attend these schools. For the status Indians and Inuit—the groups who had been subjected to the residential school system—the Department of Indian and Northern Affairs Canada (INAC) adopted the policy of First Nations local control of education in 1973. An INAC document reported that, by the year 2000, 98 percent of the schools on reserves were administered by First Nations themselves, including high schools in some cases. INAC also provided financial support for postsecondary education, although never enough to match the continually increasing number of young Aboriginals seeking higher education. Despite these positive changes, a smaller percentage of Aboriginal women continued to complete secondary school than did non-Aboriginal women. In 2001, 60 percent of Aboriginal women aged 25 or more had graduated from high school, compared to 71 percent of non-Aboriginal women. The Inuit, in particular, had low rates of high school completion; less than a third of Inuit students completed grade 12 in 2007–2008.[63]

After 1960, there was a significant increase in the numbers of women across Canada attending postsecondary institutions, described by one study as "an eventual explosion of [women's] participation and degree completion."[64] By 1970, women accounted for 37 percent of full-time university undergraduates. However, women continued to be concentrated in certain areas considered appropriate to their sex, a pattern that was to persist. In 1969–1970, more than 95 percent of the students enrolled at Canadian universities in undergraduate programs in household science, nursing, secretarial science, and physical and occupational therapy were female but only 1 percent of those enrolled in applied science and engineering were. (See Table A.8 in Appendix).[65]

In Quebec, women had to wait for reforms in the provincial educational system, undertaken in the wake of the comprehensive Parent Commission report (1964), before it became common for them to attend university. Among the results were the abolition of the domestic science schools and the creation of co-educational CEGEPs (*Collèges d'enseignement général et professionnel*). By 1970, women accounted for one-third of all full-time undergraduates in the province, and for nearly half of all part-time university students, figures comparable to those in other provinces. Unfortunately, while the secularization of the Quebec educational system in the 1960s created many new opportunities, it also had negative consequences for those women who had overseen the education of girls and young women for three centuries. With the closing of normal schools and the transfer of responsibility for teacher training to the universities, large numbers of nuns lost their teaching positions.[66]

By 1982–1983, women students were already in the majority in community colleges. In 1987 they reached parity in full-time university undergraduate populations, and in 1988, more than half of all BAs or first professional degrees were awarded to women. At this time, women's university participation rate increased most rapidly among those pursuing studies on a part-time basis; in 1988, 65 percent of all part-time students were female. Overall, women's share in postsecondary education increased so rapidly that, by 2009, women undergraduates outnumbered men three to two. The percentage of males with university degrees in 1971 was more than double that for women, but by 2001 more than half of Canadians with bachelor's or first professional degrees were women. (See Table A.8 in Appendix.)[67]

Women continued to be largely clustered in traditionally female fields, those that did not require scientific or mathematical training at the pre-university level. In 2001, over three-fifths of undergraduate students enrolled in social sciences and humanities, as well as in visual and performing arts, communications, and technology were women; in education, women comprised nearly four-fifths. Beginning in 2001, Statistics Canada put in place new classifications of fields that made comparisons over time difficult and obscured the slowness of changes. However, in 2001, only just about a quarter of all undergraduate students in "Mathematics, Computer and Information Sciences" were

Mariam Bhabha, *Québécoise* and Muslim, at her daughter's graduation from Queen's University, 1998.

Source: From Sadia Zaman, ed., *At My Mother's Feet*, for the Canadian Council of Muslim Women (Quarry Women's Books, second printing, 2001), 109

female, and the same was true for "Architecture, Engineering, and Related Technologies." In 2006–2007 the figures were largely unchanged (See Table A.9 in Appendix.)[68]

At the graduate level in Canadian universities, there was also a steady increase in the number of female students. By 1970, women accounted for just over a fifth of graduate students, a substantial increase but still a slightly smaller fraction than in 1921. Women earned about one-fifth of the master's degrees and less than one-tenth of the doctorates awarded in 1969–1970. By 1988, however, women received 45 percent of the master's degrees awarded and a third of the doctorates. The gender balance in the higher levels of higher education shifted even more decisively at the turn of the century. (See Table A.10 in Appendix.) By 2004–2005, women were receiving almost half of the Ph.D.s awarded. If male foreign students receiving that degree had been subtracted from the calculation, Canadian women receiving doctorates would have been a slightly larger fraction—just over half. However, the historic concentrations in subject matter continued, with very few fields showing gender parity even in undergraduate enrollment. It seemed likely that gender polarization in postsecondary education was a major explanation of women's lesser income and influence in the labour market.[69]

For the on-reserve status Indian population, disadvantages continued, and along with them the difference in educational achievement between males and females. In 1996 just under a third of the Indian women who went to university received their degrees; this was a rate 10 percentage points above their male counterparts. However, only 6.3 percent of Indian women aged 25 or more had a university degree, compared to 16 percent of non-Aboriginal women in the same age group. Figures from 1996 also showed that Inuit women had the lowest levels of university education, with only 5 percent of them having even attended university, let alone graduated. In 2001, when almost a fifth of non-Aboriginal women had completed university (17 percent), only 7 percent of Aboriginal women aged 15 and over had done so. Only the figures for community college certificates and diplomas were about the same for Aboriginal and non-Aboriginal women—just under 20 percent—while for Aboriginal men the comparable rate was 11 percent. By 2010 policy analysts were citing statistics that showed 14 percent of Aboriginal women had university degrees, exactly half of the 28 percent for non-Aboriginal women. These university degrees represented substantial economic advantages for Aboriginal women, who, for reasons that were not clear, were earning considerably more than non-Aboriginal women with the same level of education.[70]

It was generally acknowledged that the greatest obstacle to progress for the territory of Nunavut, largely Inuit in population, was the shortage of trained Inuit specialists to run its affairs. In July 2009, after completing a special three-year part-time program, 21 Inuit women earned the degree of Master of Education; this was the first graduate degree program specifically offered to students residing in the territory. The traditional woman's knife, the *ulu*, served as symbol for the program, and students were allowed to complete their assignments in Inuktitut. Maggie Kuniliusie, a graduate who was scheduled to become a school principal in the fall of 2009, explained, "In our program, right from the beginning, we have had this motto that we are here to enhance and sharpen our *ulus*. We were there to sharpen our skills and it was a wonderful feeling."[71] Each graduating student was presented with an *ulu* for a reminder.

Education, the field from which these Inuit women graduated, had long been dominated by women. At the postgraduate level that produced university faculty members, by 2001–2002, seven of ten doctoral students enrolled in education were women, but women still represented fewer than three in ten of the doctoral candidates in science and engineering. One possible reason for the reluctance of women to pursue studies in less traditional areas, especially at the graduate level, was the lack of female role models.

Women rejoicing on receiving their M.Ed., Nunavut, 2009.

Source: Steve Simon - Photographer. Women in the photo are Maggie Kuniliusie and Saa Pitsiulak.

In the mid-1960s only slightly more than one in ten university teachers in Canada were women, and only a very few of them were in technical or science-based departments.[72] Their role was symbolized in some universities by a continuing exclusion from full faculty club privileges. At McGill, in the 1970s, a few determined women faculty fought to eliminate the rules that prevented their use of the faculty club's dining room, a battle they finally won in 1976 over the objections of one-third of the Club's members. Virginia Douglas, one of the principal organizers of the campaign, recalled meeting an elderly colleague at the faculty club a few weeks after the vote: "Placing a fatherly hand on her shoulder, he said, 'Dr. Douglas, it is such a pleasure to see you here, although I must admit I voted against having ladies in this dining room. But Dr. Douglas, I didn't mean you.'"[73] Douglas's experience of condescension and unwilling acceptance exemplifies the "chilly climate"—the attitudes and assumptions that made many places uncomfortable for women even when they were no longer formally barred. Beginning in the 1980s, this term was used to describe an important factor in slowing women's integration into such masculine workplaces as postsecondary education.[74]

By 1991, women represented a fifth of university faculty. They had their highest representation—30 percent—in education, but only 4 percent of the faculty members in engineering and applied sciences were women. Beginning in the 1990s, however, women steadily increased their share of university hires even in non-traditional fields, rising to 34 percent in 1990–1991 and 39 percent in 2002. Between 1991 and 2003, at least in part because of affirmative action programs in hiring, the number of female full-time university teachers grew by over 50 percent. Because, at the same time, the number of male full-time faculty members decreased, women increased their portion of full-time faculty from 20 percent to over 30 percent. More important, by 2002 just over a quarter of faculty with tenure—permanent university employment—were women, almost double 1990's 14 percent; they also held 38 percent of positions leading to tenure. Nonetheless, women still remained significantly underrepresented as faculty members in non-traditional fields, such as engineering and applied sciences, mathematics, and physical sciences. In all fields, female faculty members continued to be less likely than their male colleagues to hold the rank of full professor. However, there was change in this area as well. From fewer than 1 in 20 full professors in 1984, women increased their share to almost 4 in 20 by 2004. Similarly, the proportion of associate professorships held by women more than doubled to over one in three.[75]

By 2003, a full quarter of Canadian academics were men aged 55 or more; the majority of them could be expected to retire in the next decade, even though retirement rules were highly variable in Canadian universities. Certainly the pool of women with doctorates was growing. Women could hope to do well in university hiring and advancement, once the recession-fuelled freezes on university hiring ended.[76] The sex ratios in university teaching guaranteed, however, that it would be a long time before parity was reached. And other differentials persisted. The pessimistic conclusion of a study published in 2009 was the following: ". . . in terms of such major issues as rank, discipline, pay, prestige, work-life balance, working conditions, and equity activism, women's realities in post-secondary education continue to differ significantly from men's."[77] The solutions, the authors concluded, would come from political and social rather than educational factors.

CULTURE AND THE ARTS

In the 1960s, women's efforts to achieve equality with men appeared to require a denial of a separate female identity. By the end of the decade, however, awareness of the value of that identity began to re-emerge. As the century progressed into the next one, women recognized, once again, how necessary and desirable it was for women to draw upon their own experiences to bring about the changes they sought. Their contributions to Canadian culture asserted yet again the feminist commitment to the creativity of women and their essential role in making life more humane and enjoyable.

In the 1970s, Canadian women's contributions to the arts often explored simultaneously nationalist and feminist themes. A prime example was Joyce Wieland, whose 1971 show at the National Gallery was the first solo exhibition of the work of a living Canadian woman. An extraordinarily versatile artist, at home in a variety of media from collage to film, she drew inspiration from women's history and daily experiences, especially in her quilt works. Wieland's 1971 show, with its interwoven themes of nationalism, ecological concerns, and women's issues, was an important early statement of feminist aesthetics. In 1987, the Art Gallery of Ontario mounted a major retrospective of Wieland's works, describing her as "Canada's foremost woman artist;" it was the first major retrospective exhibit there of a living Canadian woman artist.[78]

Like Wieland, Newfoundland contemporary realist artist Mary Pratt turned to the world of women for much of her subject matter. Many of her best-known paintings had as their subject items from her own kitchen, such as *Eviscerated Chickens*, raw and ready for cooking, and *Jelly Shelf,* which became a 52 cent stamp in the 2007 series of Art Canada stamps. Sculptors, too, drew from their own female experience. Toronto sculptor Maryon Kantaroff, a proud member of Toronto's New Feminists, began to question the male aesthetics she had tried so hard to apply to her early sculptures. From strident, angular shapes she moved to rounder, softer, and more fluid ones. Characteristic of her attempt to reconnect her work with the female experience was the appearance of the egg in her works, a form she described as "a symbol of the beginnings of life, the essence of life, the seat of all potential, awareness."[79]

Yet in spite of these and other individual success stories, the work of many women artists remained unknown. In 1984, a number of women artists formed the Women's Art Resource Centre (WARC) in Toronto, started a curatorial library, and initiated a wide range of activities, including forums, a journal, and a gallery. As a tenth anniversary project, WARC undertook a study of the National Gallery in order to measure the status of women in the arts. Its findings were disturbing: there had been little improvement from 1970 to 1993 in the proportion of acquisitions budgets and gallery space devoted to women's art, and there was a "continuing effacement of Canadian women artists."[80] In 1998, Joyce Zemans, the first woman to be appointed Dean of the Faculty of Fine Arts at York University and first woman director of the Canada Council, re-examined the situation of Canadian women artists. She looked at the presence of women artists in the National Gallery, in commercial galleries, among the teaching and especially studio staff in educational institutions, and as jurors and recipients of grants, and concluded that they "remained under-represented in most of the situations critical to their success."

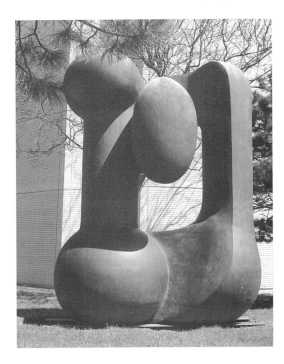

"Song of Deborah," 1979 statue by Maryon Kantaroff (Baycrest Hospital, Toronto).

Source: Courtesy of Maryon Kantaroff

By 2009, when she had started updating her study, she felt that the situation could only be said to be "somewhat" improved.[81]

It was as creators of literature, however, that women made their best known and most widely recognized contributions to Canadian cultural life. By the 1960s, issues related to women's lives and experiences were explicitly woven into women writers' work. Those writers were centrally important in the 1960s and 1970s, the time when Canada's culture became an established area of academic study inside and outside of the country. In their presentation of a diversity of powerful central women characters, Canadian women's fiction, it has been suggested, generally reflected resistance to any overriding national narrative and to their own status as a "colonized gender."[82] Many of these writers were self-identified as feminists; they and other women writers dealt with themes closely related to issues of gender and sexuality. Important and highly regarded women authors who exemplified such a focus on women's lives and experiences in the 1960s and 1970s included Marie-Claire Blais, Nicole Brossard, and Antonine Maillet; Maillet's widely read novel about an Acadian woman, *Pélagie-la-Charette*, won the Prix Goncourt in 1979. In 1976 Louky Bersianik (Lucile Durand) published *L'Euguélionne*, a feminist and fantastic novel that had a substantial influence among Quebec women. Margaret Laurence, Margaret Atwood, Alice Munro, Mavis Gallant, and Marian Engel all wrote importantly—and very popularly—on topics that could be summed up by the title of Munro's prize-winning first collection of linked short stories: *Lives of Girls and Women* (1971).

By the 1970s and 1980s and on past the turn of the century, new generations of women began to publish literary works exploring issues surrounding the ethnic, racial, and sexual identities of women who, like them, were either immigrants or from long-established but traditionally non-literary Canadian communities. Thus, Maria Campbell drew a disturbing picture of contemporary Métis women's experience in her autobiographical work *Halfbreed* (1973). The poetry of Dionne Brand represented and interpreted black women's experience in Canada, while poet and novelist Joy Kogawa recounted in the semi-autobiographical *Obasan* the experiences of a Japanese-Canadian family forcibly uprooted during World War II; its sequel *Itsuka* (1992; rewritten in 2005 as *Emily Kato*) told of the campaign for redress and reparations in which Kogawa herself was involved. Other examples of women whose works epitomized the country's regional and cultural diversity were Manitoba Mennonite writers Di Brandt and Miriam Toews. In addition, the renowned women writers of the 1960s and 1970s (with the exception of Marian Engel and Margaret Laurence, who died in 1985 and 1987, respectively) continued to be active in the twenty-first century. Alice Munro's remarkable short stories regularly appeared in the *New Yorker*, and her collections were reviewed internationally. When she was awarded the Man Booker International Prize for lifetime achievement in 2009, a *New York Times* reviewer wrote that Munro "has a strong claim to being the best fiction writer now working in North America."[83] Munro was just one of many Canadian women writers who over the years earned an amazing number of national and international literary awards in Canada, including a very large number of Governor General's Awards. Lorna Crozier, Denise Desautels, Madeleine Gagnon, Anne Hébert, Gwendolyn MacEwan, Carol Shields, and Jane Urquhart were among the female novelists and poets who, like Atwood, Gallant, Laurence, and Munro, attained such recognition.

Explicitly feminist plays and companies also attracted considerable attention by the 1970s. The all-female *Théâtre des cuisines*, active from 1974 to 1976 and again from 1980, presented two plays, the pro-choice *Nous aurons les enfants que nous voulons* and *Môman travaille pas, a trop d'ouvrage*, about housework. In Toronto, Nightwood, an alternative, feminist women's theatre established in 1978, also created new opportunities for female playwrights; it was still active in 2009. By the early 1980s, women dramatists such as Sharon Pollock, Judith Thompson, and Jovette Marchessault had built up an impressive body of work, much of which explored explicitly feminist themes. Subsequently, Djanet Sears, Colleen Wagner, Carole Fréchette, and other women playwrights powerfully reflected the regional, racial, and ethnic diversity of Canada in their work.[84]

In film as well, Canadian women made their mark. Anne Poirier described her filmmaking as "political, committed to the most important liberation movement of our time. . . . always from the women's point of view."[85] In 1968 she was the first woman in Quebec to make a feature film. *De mère en fille (Mother-to-Be)* explored the physical and emotional experience of pregnancy. With Jeanne Morazain, Poirier wrote in 1971 a report that urged the National Film Board of Canada/Office national du film du Canada (NFB) to set up a separate film program coordinated by women; she then headed, between 1972 and 1975, the series *En tant que femmes (As Women)*. Studio D, the English-language women filmmakers' group at the NFB, was set up in 1974, headed by Kathleen Shannon, the first woman to lead an NFB film unit since the Second World War.[86] A French counterpart, *Regards de femmes (Women's Gaze)*, was established under Josée Beaudet in 1968. These two very successful programs were expressly mandated to produce feminist films. The women filmmakers at the NFB directed a number of impressive, prize-winning documentaries, including Cynthia Scott's *Flamenco at 5:15,* which won an Academy Award in 1983 for Documentary Short Subject. Bonnie Sherr Klein's *Not a Love Story: A Film About Pornography* (1981) had a huge impact in its investigation of the pornography industry and its social and economic consequences, and *If You Love This Planet* (Terri Nash, 1982) addressed global ecological issues from a feminist perspective. Klein's later NFB film *SHAMELESS: The ART of Disability* (released 2006), was made after Klein herself had partially recovered from two catastrophic brain stem strokes; the film featured, among other creative artists with disabilities, Klein herself, poet and writer Catherine Frazee, and sculptor Persimmon Blackbridge.[87] Studio D and *Regards de femmes* were both closed in 1996 as a result of governmental budget cuts.

Women made other notable documentary films. One example was Christine Welsh, a Métis whose *Keepers of the Fire* (1994) recorded the strength of Native women across Canada. In *Finding Dawn* (2006), she examined the fate of the approximately 500 Aboriginal women, many living on the streets in British Columbia cities, who disappeared beginning in 1991 and were presumed to have been murdered. African Nova Scotian Sylvia Hamilton explored the history and contribution of black women in her province in her films. *Black Mother, Black Daughter* (1989) combined historical and biographical approaches, while her 2 000 film *Portia White: Think on Me* recorded the career of Halifax contralto Portia White. Hamilton's *No More Secrets: A Two Part Series About Violence Against Black* Women (1992), made for the Women's Commissions of the African United Baptist Church in Nova Scotia, examined the delicate issue of violence against women in the African Nova Scotian community, and in 2007 her film *Little Black School House* told the tale of black schools and racism. Some women filmmakers, such as Patricia Rozema (*I've Heard the Mermaids Singing,* 1987; *Mansfield Park,* 1999; *Kit Kittredge: An American Girl,* 2008) succeeded in breaking into the commercial North American market. In 2002 Winnipegger Nia Vardalos produced one of the biggest indie hits of all time, *My Big Fat Greek Wedding,* based on her own experience of marrying a non-Greek.

In the many fields of classical music, women achieved new standards of creativity in performance and composition, contributing to the explosion of Canadian culture in the postwar era. Avant-garde composer and music educator Barbara Pentland, born in Winnipeg in 1912, explored new techniques of abstract structuring in her works, which were performed throughout the world. The text of her "Disasters in the Sun" (1976) was written by Dorothy Livesay; in this work, Pentland expressed her struggle against male domination. Innovative women composers, such as Alexina Louie in British Columbia, also influenced the development of contemporary Canadian music. The Canadian Music Council, which instituted a composer of the year award in 1977, bestowed that honour on Louie in 1986. Still active and much honoured in the new millennium, in 2002 Louie was one of three recipients of the National Arts Centre Composer Awards, a grant of $75 000 that required creation of three new orchestral works and continuing close work with the NAC Orchestra. Opera singers Portia White, Teresa Stratas, Lois Marshall, and Maureen Forrester established themselves as stars, followed by younger women such as sopranos Liping Zhang, Isabel Bayrakdarian, and African-Canadian Measha Brueggergosman. In

2008, in a cross-genre initiative that resonated with the literary traditions of Canadian women, City Opera Vancouver commissioned a chamber opera about the Aboriginal poet and performer Pauline Johnson as "a signature role" for mezzo-soprano Judith Forst, born in B.C. Its libretto would be written by Margaret Atwood.[88]

In other areas of the performing arts as well, women contributed to a growing sense of Canadian achievement. Dance flourished as Canada consolidated its companies and performers. The National Ballet School (NBS) trained many of Canada's outstanding dancers, including Veronica Tennant and Karen Kain. After Betty Oliphant, the NBS's first artistic director, retired in 1984, Mavis Staines moved up from the position of associate artistic director. In 2005, Karen Kain crowned her career by becoming artistic director of the National Ballet of Canada. By 2009 a second generation of Canadian classical principal dancers was reaching retirement. Thus, at the age of 40, Chan Hon Goh, known as the "iron butterfly," performed her final *Giselle*; she saw herself as a role model for immigrant children.[89] In the field of modern dance, now less estranged from classical styles than it once had been, Peggy Baker was the recipient in 2009 of a Governor General's Lifetime Artistic Achievement Award. Starting in 1992, she was the first artist-in-residence at the National Ballet School. "This lady never fishes in muddy waters," declared celebrated ballet dancer and choreographer Mikhail Baryshnikov, who had worked with her. "She propels herself in all things from deep within and the result is always amazing."[90] Remarkable female instrumentalists included cellist Ofra Harnoy, classical guitarist Liona Boyd, pianist Angela Hewitt, and violinist Jeanne Lamon, who directed the Tafelmusik Baroque Orchestra from 1981.

Generations of non-classical women singers also established highly successful careers that helped to shape Canada's national consciousness. In the 1950s and 1960s, they included such stars as Gisèle McKenzie, "Juliette," Catherine MacKinnon, Sylvia Tyson, Ginette Reno, and Pauline Julien, as well as "Canada's songbird," Anne Murray. Among the well-known artists of the late 1970s were the highly influential Joni Mitchell as well as Angèle Arsenault, Ferron, and the sisters Kate and Anna McGarrigle. Then came the beginning of the careers of feminist folksinger Heather Bishop, Saskatchewan's Connie

Dancer Peggy Baker with a student, 2002.
Source: Courtesy of Canada's National Ballet School. Photo by Jeannette Edissi-Collins.

Kaldor, Nova Scotia's Rita MacNeil, and lesbian and animal rights activist k.d. lang, as well as folksinger Loreena McKennitt, Inuit singer Susan Aglukark, and the wildly popular Céline Dion. The turn of the century saw the rise to fame of a new, highly successful generation of singers and musicians, including singer and jazz pianist Diana Krall and singers Avril Lavigne, Shania Twain, Alanis Morissette, and Nelly Furtado, all born after 1960 and most after 1970. Sarah McLachlan's Lilith Fair, an all-female travelling festival, ran from 1997 to 1999 and raised nearly $10 million for women's charities across North America. Its return as Lilith 2010 was announced in December 2009.[91] Sarah and Tegan, Bif Naked, Feist, and Ottawa-born hip hop artist Eternia were also among the newer Canadian women singers and bands in the indie pop stream. Eternia's participation in the "Girls' Rights are Human Rights Too" campaign was an example of the involvement of some of these performers with issues of concern to women. She focused on the issue of sexual assault of teenage women, saying. "I've been through it." She added, "I want girls to never, ever feel ashamed."[92]

With the evolution of Canada into a more diverse society and the heightened awareness of the need to preserve and promote more than mainstream culture, thousands of women contributed to the cultural mosaic that was closely associated with Canadian identity. Along with the high culture and popular culture contributions already mentioned, there was, as always, a panoply of community-based volunteer contributions. Within their ethnic communities, women were prominent in the organization of language classes, choirs, theatre and dance groups, and cultural festivals. Among others, Jeni Le Gon in Vancouver, Anne Packwood in Montreal, and Grace Price Trotman in Toronto worked to preserve and reinforce black culture through drama, music, dancing, and fashion design. Aboriginal women such as Anne Anderson, a Cree living in Edmonton, devoted themselves to writing and teaching their ancestral language and to passing on their customs. There were many such women whose life-work was related to artistic and cultural work drawing on their particular group traditions. For instance, in Nova Scotia there was Teresa Marshall, a Mi'kmaq sculptor and filmmaker and, in New Brunswick, Shirley Bear of the Maliseet Negootiook First Nation, elder and herbalist, multimedia artist and writer.[93] It became widely recognized that, whatever their racial or ethnic community, women played a leading role in preserving and transmitting their particular group's history and cultural heritage.

Women's tasks of cultural preservation and transmission became increasingly important as many of the old patterns and rituals that had formerly characterized the lives of women disappeared in the last half of the twentieth century. Women's roles were no longer ordered sequentially (work–marriage–family) but instead became intertwined and interactive. Marriage became a less significant event, since it no longer involved the end of employment and almost immediate initiation into motherhood. As the role of wife became more and more separable from that of mother, it was possible and even common to be one but not the other. Moreover, there was less physical separation of the sexes. Canadian women no longer spent most of their lives in the female-oriented space of the household. At the same time, the non-domestic workplace was no longer exclusively inhabited or defined by men. Neither did the traditionally male-dominated public spheres of sports, education, and the arts any longer lack women's major achievements and influence.

Notes

1. John R. Miron, *Demographic Change, Household Formation and Housing Demand: Canada's Postwar Experience* (Toronto: Centre for Urban and Community Studies, University of Toronto, 1985), 7.18, Table 7.3.2 ; *Canada Year Book: 1976–1977 Edition* (Ottawa: Statistics Canada), 169; *Canada Year Book: 2008 Edition* (Ottawa: Statistics Canada), 52.

2. Céline Le Bourdais and Evelyne Lapierre-Adamcyck, "Changes in Conjugal Life in Canada: Is Cohabitation Progressively Replacing Marriage?" *Journal of Marriage and Family*, 66, 4 (November 2004): 931, 935; Anne Milan, Mireille Vézina, and Carrie Wells, *2006 Census, Family Portrait: Continuity and Change in Canadian Households in 2006* (Ottawa: Statistics Canada, 2007), cat. no. 97-55-XWE2006001, Figure 8, Figure 9, Table 1; *Women in Canada: A Gender-based Statistical Report*, 5th ed. (Ottawa: Statistics Canada, 2006), Cat. no. 89-503-XIE, Chart 2.2, 189, 243.

3. Robert Leckey, "Families in the Eyes of the Law: Contemporary Challenges and the Grip of the Past," *IRRP Choices* 18, 8 (July 2009): 15; Droit-In.com, "Jugement sur les conjoints de fait: Un déni des droits pour les enfants nés hors mariage!" (July 7, 2009) http://www.droit-inc.com/tiki; Sue Montgomery, "Quebec Billionaire's Ex Loses Common-law Case," *The Gazette* (July 30, 2009); and see comments on Soundoff, *MontrealGazette.com* (posted July 16, 2009), http://communities.canada.com/montrealgazette/blogs/soundoff/archive/2009/07/16/314799.aspx.

4. Le Bourdais and Lapierre-Adamcyck, 930–31; *Canada Year Book 2008*, 171, 176, Table 14.3; *Women in Canada*, 5th ed., 37.

5. Miriam Smith. "Political Activism, Litigation and Public Policy: The Charter Revolution and Lesbian and Gay Rights in Canada, 1985–99, *International Journal of Canadian Studies*, 21 (2000): 81–109; CTV.ca News Staff, "Chronology: Same-sex Marriage in Canada," (Feb. 15, 2005), http://www.ctv.ca/servlet/ArticleNews/story/CTVNews/1102628108228_98037308; Susan Smith, "Gay Rights Advocate Set an Example Simply by Being Who He Was; Obituary of Norman Carter," *The Globe and Mail* (February 1, 2010), 9; BBC News, "Same-sex Marriage Law Backed in Portugal's Parliament," (January 8, 2010), http://news.bbc.co.uk/2/hi/8448640.stm; Milan, Vézina, and Wells, Table 2; *Canada Year Book 2008*, 172.

6. Erin Anderssen et al., *The New Canada: A Globe and Mail Report on the Next Generation* (Toronto: McClelland and Stewart, 2004), 29, 30; *Canada Year Book 2008*, 161; Lauren La Rose, "Mixed-race Taboo Drops Away," CBC.ca, (April 2, 2008), http://www.cbc.ca/news/background/census/mixed-marriages.html; *Canada Year Book 2008*, 161.

7. Angus McLaren and Arlene Tiger McLaren, *The Bedroom and the State: The Changing Practices and Politics of Contraception and Abortion in Canada, 1880–1997*, 2nd ed (Don Mills: Oxford University Press Canada, 1997), 125; Jacques Henripin, *Naître ou ne pas être* (Quebec: Institut québécois de recherche sur la culture [IQRC], 1989), Collection: Diagnostic, no. 10, 26, 27.

8. McLaren and McLaren, 132–33; Michael W. Higgins and Douglas R. Letson, *My Father's Business: A Biography of His Eminence G. Emmett Cardinal Carter* (Toronto: Macmillan, 1990), 101–13.

9. *Canada Year Book:1978–1979 Edition* (Ottawa, Statistics Canada), 167; *Canada Year Book: 1985 Edition* (Ottawa, Statistics Canada), 67, Table 2.34; Statistics Canada, *Births and Birth Rate, by Province and Territory* (February 4, 2010), CANSIM Tables 0551-004, 051-001 and Cat. no. 91-215-X; CTV.ca News Staff , "Quebec Sees Biggest Birth-rate Hike Since 1909,"

(January 27, 2007) http://www.ctv.ca/servlet/ArticleNews/story/CTVNews/20070126/quebec_babyboom_070126/20070127?hub=TopStories; Kevin Milligan, "Backgrounder—Quebec's Baby Bonus: Can Public Policy Raise Fertility?" (Toronto: C.D. Howe Institute, January 24, 2002), http://www.cdhowe.org/pdf/Milligan_Backgrounder.pdf.

10. Statistics Canada, *Births and Deaths (*1995), 40, Table 3.2; Statistics Canada, *Births and Birth Rate, by Province and Territory* (2010), Cat. no. 91-215-XWE.

11. "Budget: It's A Bouncing Baby Bonus," *The Telegram*, St. John's NL (April 29, 2008), 1.

12. *Canada Year Book 1978–1979*, 167; *Canada Year Book 1985*, 67, Table 2.34, Table 3.8; Statistics Canada, *Canadian Vital Statistics, Marriage Database* (August 14, 2009), http://www40.statcan.gc.ca/l01/cst01/famil04-eng.htm; Statistics Canada, *The Daily*, "Births" (September 26, 2008); *Women in Canada*, 5th ed., 40; Statistics Canada, *The Daily*, "Births" (September 22, 2009); Stephen Strauss, "Baby Boomlet Continues, Statistics Canada Reports," *The Globe and Mail* (May 31, 1992), A6.

13. *Women in Canada*, 5th ed., 51: Table 2.9, 42, 43: Chart 2.7; Erin Anderssen, "Babies on Hold," *The Globe and Mail* (May 9, 2009), A6; Adriana Barton, "The Hot-flash Clash," *The Globe and Mail* (July 13, 2009), L3.

14. *Women in Canada*, 5th ed., 189–91; R. Stout and R. Harp, *Aboriginal and Maternal Health in Canada: Review of On-Reserve Programming* (British Columbia Centre of Excellence for Women's Health, Prairie Women's Health Centre of Excellence: April 2009), 6, http://www.pwhce.ca/pdf/AborigMaternal_programmes.pdf.

15. *Canada Year Book 2008*, 171; *Women in Canada*, 5th ed., 244, 189, 45: Table 2.1.

16. Janice Turner, "Childless by Choice," *The Toronto Star* (January 25, 1994), B5; Susan Stobert and Anna Kemeny, "Childfree by Choice," *Canada Social Trends* (Ottawa, Statistics Canada, 2003), http://www.statcan.gc.ca/kits-trousses/pdf/social/edu04_0030a-eng.pdf.

17. Laura Scott, *Two is Enough: A Couple's Guide to Living Childless by Choice* (Berkeley: Seal Press, 2009), 110.

18. Susan Dick, "Being Ill/Being Well: Reflections on an Illness, " *Queen's Quarterly* 99, 4 (Winter 1992): 813, 808.

19. Lee Guemple, "Men and Women, Husbands and Wives: The Role of Gender in Traditional Inuit Society," *Études/Inuit/Studies* 10, 1–2 (1986): 13; Mary Crnkovich, *"Gossip": A Spoken History of Women in the North* (Ottawa: Canadian Arctic Resources Committee, 1990), 47–49; Julie Cruikshank, "Becoming a Woman in Athapaskan Society: Changing Traditions on the Upper Yukon River," *Western Canadian Journal of Anthropology* 5, 2 (1975): 11; Inuit Community Centre—Tungasuvvingat Inuit, "Inuit Customary Adoption," http://www.ontarioinuit.ca/html/children.htm.

20. McLaren and McLaren, 136, 52–53, 145; *Women in Canada*, 5th ed., 72, 87: Table 3.16; AbortioninCanada.ca, "Abortion Clinics," http://www.abortioninCanada.ca/facts/abortion_clinics.html; Statistics Canada, *Report on the Demographic Situation in Canada* (2005 and 2006); Statistics Canada, *Fertility* (November 2009), Cat. no. 91-209-XWE; Statistics Canada, *Induced Abortions per 100 Live Births* (June 2010) http://www40.statcan.ca/l01/cst01/health42a-eng.htm.

21. DivorceRate.org, "Divorce Rates in Canada," http://www.divorcerate.org/divorce-rates-in-canada.html; Milan, Vézina, and Wells, 15; Leckey, 24; *Women in Canada*, 5th ed., 40, 50: Table 2.8; Dr. Anne-Marie Ambert, "Divorce: Facts, Causes and Consequences," Vanier Institute of the Family, Virtual Library (2005) http://www.vifamily.ca/library/cft/divorce_05.html#True.

22. *Canada Year Book 2008*, 211, 212: Table 17.a, 372: Table 28.3; *Women in Canada*, 5th ed., 57, 72: Table 3.4.

23. James S. Frideres, *Canada's Indians: Contemporary Conflicts* (Scarborough: Prentice-Hall, 1974), 19; *Women in Canada, 5th ed.*, 190, 191: Chart 8.10; The Source, Women's Health Data Directory, "Life Expectancy," http://www.womenshealthdata.ca/category. aspx?catid=91&rt=2; CBC News, Saskatchewan, "Diabetes on Rise Among Young Aboriginal Women," (January 18, 2010), http://www.cbc.ca/canada/saskatchewan/story/2010/01/18/ diabetes-aboriginal.html; Statistics Canada, *The Daily*, "Deaths" (January 14, 2008); Stout and Harp, 192, 193: Chart 8.10; *Overview of Inuit Health*, http://www.naho.ca/inuit/e/ overview/; *Canada Year Book 2008*, 58: Table 5.5, 22.

24. John Robert Colombo, ed., *The 1995 Canadian Global Almanac* (Toronto: Macmillan, 1994), 61; *Women in Canada*, 5th ed., 265, 268, 219, 243, 186; Milan, Vézina, and Wells 2007, Figure 12.

25. *Women in Canada*, 5th ed., 93: Table 14, 189; Gene Allen, "MDs Urged to Reduce Cesarean Operations," *The Globe and Mail* (July 17, 1991), A5; Canadian Institute for Health Information, *Giving Birth in Canada: Providers of Maternity and Infant Care*, Ottawa (April 21, 2004), 23, http://dsp-psd.pwgsc.gc.ca/Collection/H118-25-2004E.pdf; Canadian Institute for Health Information, News Release, "Canada's Caesarean Rate at Record High" (July 26, 2007), http://www.sources.com/Releases/ICAN01-CaesareanRate.htm; Sharon Kirkey, "Canada's C-Section Rate at Record High," Canwest News Service (June 25, 2008), http:// www.canada.com/life/Canada+section+rate+record+high/796939/story.html.

26. *The Source*, Women's Health Data Directory, http://www.womenshealthdata.ca/category. aspx?catid=108&rt=3; "Vaginal Delivery of Breech Presentation," SOGC Practice Guidelines No. 226, (June 2009), http://www.sogc.org/guidelines/documents/gui226CPG0906.pdf; Society of Obstetricians and Gynaecologists of Canada, Media Advisory, "No More Automatic C-section for Breech Births, Says Ob/Gyn Society," http://www.sogc.org/media/ advisories-20090617a_e.asp.

27. Carla Wintersgill, "C-section Not Best Option for Breech Birth," *The Globe and Mail* (June 18, 2009), L1, L6.

28. McLaren and McLaren, 44.

29. Wendy Lill, "Celebrating Sam's Birth," *Herizons* 4, 8 (December 1986): 20.

30. Lawrence Livermore National Laboratory Public Affairs, Press Release, "Study Shows that Quality of Sperm Deteriorates as Men Age," (June 5, 2006) https://publicaffairs.llnl.gov/news/ news_releases/2006/NR-06-06-01.html; David Devore, "Genetic Screening and Ethics, An Overview," Woodrow Wilson Biology Institute (1992), http://www.woodrow.org/teachers/ bi/1992/gen_screen1.html.

31. Royal Commission on New Reproductive Technologies, *Proceed with Care* (Ottawa: Government of Canada, Political and Social Affairs Division, April 22, 1994), http:// dsp-psd.communication.gc.ca/Collection-R/LoPBdP/MR/mr124-e.htm; Francesca Scala, "Feminist Ideals versus Bureaucratic Norms: The Case of Feminist Researchers and the Royal Commission on New Reproductive Technologies," in Yasmeen Abu-Laban, ed., *Gendering the Nation-State: Canadian and Comparative Perspectives* (Vancouver: UBC Press, 2008), 97–119; Health Canada, "Publication of Proposed Assisted Human Reproduction Regulations Delayed Until Supreme Court Appeal is Decided," http://www.hc-sc.gc.ca/hl-vs/reprod/hc-sc/legislation/ delay-interruption-eng.php; CBCNEWS.ca, "Ottawa, Quebec fight for jurisdiction over fertility treatments," (April 23, 2009), http://www.cbc.ca/canada/montreal/story/2009/04/23/ montreal-fertility-scoc-cp-0423.html; Caroline Alphonso, "Fertility Treatments, Older Mothers Leading to Rise in Premature Births," *The Globe and Mail* (January 30, 2009), A4; *Raising Expectations: Report of the Expert Panel on Infertility and Adoption* (Ontario: Ministry of

Children and Youth Services, August 2009), http://www.children.gov.on.ca/htdocs/English/ infertility/index.aspx; Steve Lambert, "Manitoba Plans New Tax Credits, Social Housing," *The Globe and Mail* (December 1, 2009), A10.

32. Miriam Smith, "Political Activism, Litigation and Public Policy: The Charter Revolution and Lesbian and Gay Rights in Canada, 1985–99," *International Journal of Canadian Studies* 21 (2000): 81–109; CTV.ca News Staff, "Chronology: Same-sex Marriage in Canada," (February, 15, 2005), http://www.ctv.ca/servlet/ArticleNews/story/CTVNews/1102628108228_ 98037308; *A.A. v. B.B.* 2007 ONCA 2.

33. Statistics Canada, *National Longitudinal Survey of Children and Youth* (2006), Table 3-2; Association of Ontario Midwives, "Benefits of Midwifery to the Health Care System," (May 2007), http://www.aom.on.ca/Communications/Government_Relations/Benefits_of_ Midwifery.aspx; ScienceDaily, "Planned Home Birth With Registered Midwife as Safe as Hospital Birth, Canadian Study Shows," (September 1, 2009), http://www.sciencedaily.com/ releases/2009/08/090831130043.htm; Statistics Canada, *Live Births by Weeks of Gestation and Sex, Canada, Provinces and Territories, Annual,* Table 102-4512. http://cansim2.statcan. ca/cgi-win/CNSMCGI.PGM?&Lang=E&ArrayId=102-4512&Array_Pick=1&Detail=1&Res ultTemplate=CII/CII___&RootDir=CII/&C2SUB=HEALTH

34. La Leche League International, "How Long Should a Mother Breastfeed?" http:// www.llli.org/FAQ/bflength.html; CBC News, "Canadian Pediatricians Suggest New Breastfeeding Guidelines," (March 12, 2005), http://www.cbc.ca/health/story/2005/03/08/ Breastfeed_050308.html; Amazon.com, "Dr. Spock's Baby and Childcare, 8th Edition," http:// www.amazon.com/Dr-Spocks-Baby-Childcare/dp/0743476670; http://www.whattoexpect. com/home/about-the-author.aspx; Arlene Eisenberg, Heidi Eisenberg Murkoff, and Sandee E. Hathaway (New York: Workman Publishing Company Inc., 1984), new editions into 2009.

35. Wayne J. Millar and Heather Maclean, "Breastfeeding Practices," *Health Reports* 16, (March 18, 2005): 25, http://www.statcan.gc.ca/studies-etudes/82-003/archive/2005/7787-eng.pdf; D. Meemee Lavell-Harvard and Jeannette Corbiere Lavell, ed. *"Until Our Hearts Are On the Ground": Aboriginal Mothering, Oppression, Resistance and Rebirth* (Toronto: Demeter Press, 2006); "Inuit Bring Births Back to Community," *Ryerson University News and Events* (July 11, 2008), http://www.ryerson.ca/news/news/Research_News/2008Archive/20080711_ VanWagner.html.

36. *Women in Canada*, 5th ed., 65; Susan McWilliam, "Ontario Women and HIV/AIDS Working Group Literature Review: HIV Prevention and Women," (February 2006), 10, http://www. health.gov.on.ca/english/providers/pub/aids/reports/ontario_women_hivaids_working_group_ literature_review_hi.pdf.

37. "I Wonder What's Going to Get Me, But I Don't Think it's Going to Be AIDS," *The Globe and Mail* (April 23, 2009), A13.

38. André Picard, "Church Has No Place in Vaccinations," *The Globe and Mail* (November 6, 2008), L4; *Santé et Services Sociaux Québec*, "HPV Vaccination Program" (2010), http://www.msss.gouv. qc.ca/sujets/santepub/vaccination/index.php?programme-de-vaccination-contre-le-vph-en.

39. Sharlene Azam, *Oral Sex is the New Goodnight Kiss*, 2008 paperback and film; but see Bob Altemeyer, *Sex and Youth* (Lulu Press, 2009), on actual studies related to this issue, chap. 5, and his conclusion on p. 115.

40. Statistics Canada, *Weekly* 32, 17 (May 6, 1983), 1; *Women in Canada: A Statistical Report*, 2nd ed. (Ottawa: Statistics Canada, 1990), 139; Amanda Black et al., "Canadian Contraception Consensus," *SOGC Clinical Practice Guidelines*, No. 143, Part 1 of 3 (February 2004), 146, http://www.sogc.org/guidelines/public/143E-CPG1-February2004.pdf; Statistics Canada,

The Daily, "Early Sexual Intercourse, Condom Use and Sexually Transmitted Diseases," (May 3, 2005), Canadian Women's Health Network, "Emergency Contraception in Canada," (April 20, 2008,) http://www.cwhn.ca/resources/cwhn/ec.html.

41. Pauline Couture, "Québécois Voices," *The Globe and Mail* (November 16, 1991); National Heart, Lung, and Blood Institute, National Institutes of Health, "NHLBI Stops Trial of Estrogen Plus Progestin Due to Increased Breast Cancer Risk, Lack of Overall Benefit," NIH news release (July 9, 2002), http://www.nhlbi.nih.gov/whi/pr_02-7-9.pdf; Richard N. Fogorous, M.D., "Is HRT Really Safe Again?" *About.com: Heart Disease* (July 2, 2007), http://heartdisease.about.com/od/womenheartdisease/a/HRT3.htm; Anne Harding, "Hormone Therapy Linked to Brain Shrinkage in Older Women," CNN Health, (January 12, 2009), http://www.cnn.com/2009/HEALTH/01/12/healthmag.hormone.therapy/index.html; Caroline Alphonso, "Women Shocked by Rise in Hormone-drug Costs; Makers Say Lowered Demand for Premarin is to Blame," *The Globe and Mail*, (June 4, 2009), A7; Natasha Singer and Duff Wilson, "Menopause, as Brought To You by Big Pharma," *The New York Times* (December 13, 2009), 7.

42. Pat Kelly, "Breast Cancer Epidemic Is a Crime," *Kitchener-Waterloo Record* (March 13, 1992), A7.

43. Lisa Young, "Fulfilling the Mandate: Women in the Canadian House of Commons," in Jane Arscott and Linda Trimble, ed., *In the Presence of Women: Representation in Canadian Governments* (Toronto: Harcourt Brace Canada, 1997), 97; Sarah Hampson, "Belinda Stronach: Ex-politician, Breast Cancer Survivor: Her New Side," *The Globe and Mail* (March 30, 2009), L1, L4; Canadian Cancer Society, media release, "Canadian Cancer Statistics 2007: Breast Cancer Death Rate Dropping," (April 11, 2007) http://www.cancer.ca/Canada-wide/About%20us/Media%20centre/CW-Media%20releases/CW-2007/Canadian%20Cancer%20Statistics%202007%20Breast%20Cancer%20Death%20Rate%20Dropping.aspx?sc_lang=en.

44. *Women in Canada*, 5th ed., 58, 59: Chart 3.9, 61; *Canada Year Book 2008*, 212; Organisation for Economic Co-operation and Development, *Society at a Glance—OECD Social Indicators* (2009), *Key Findings: Canada*, http://www.oecd.org/dataoecd/27/53/42671752.pdf; *Canada Year Book 2008*, 212–13.

45. L. Schoenfielder and B. Wieser, eds., *Shadow on a Tightrope* (Iowa City, Iowa: Aunt Lute Book Company, 1983); C. M. Donald, *The Fat Woman Measures Up* (Charlottetown: Ragweed, 1986).

46. Marie Berdugo-Cohen, Yolande Cohen, et Joseph Lévy, *Juifs marocains à Montréal: Témoignages d'une immigration moderne* (Montréal: VLB Éditeur, 1987), 109 [our translation].

47. The Judgment of Paris Forum, "A Forum for Discussing Topics Related to Plus-Sized Beauty," http://www.judgmentofparis.com/board/index.php?.

48. Zosia Bielski, "Lolita at 5?" *The Globe and Mail* (June 9, 2009), L1, L3; Jay Teitel, "The Liberation Generation Gap," *More* (November 2007): 104–7, 142; "One in Five (20%) Canadians Say that If They Had the Means and Ability, They'd Have A Nip and Tuck . . ." Ipsos Reid News Center Press Release, (December 28, 2007), http://www.ipsos-na.com/news/pressrelease.cfm?id=3772.

49. Jean Cochrane, Abby Hoffman, and Pat Kincaid, *Women in Canadian Life: Sports* (Toronto: Fitzhenry and Whiteside, 1977); Ann Richardson, *Fair Ball: Towards Sex Equality in Canadian Sport* (Ottawa: Canadian Advisory Council on the Status of Women, 1982); Patrick J. Harrigan, "Women's Agency and the Development of Women's Intercollegiate Athletics, 1961–2001," *Historical Studies in Education*, 15,1 (2003): 65–66, 45–46.

50. Helen Lenskyj, *Out of Bounds: Women. Sport, and Sexuality* (Toronto: Women's Press, 1986), 84–85.

51. Lenskyj, *Out of Bounds*, 70.

52. Justine Blainey-Broker, "Someone's Gaining on You Boys," *The Globe and Mail* (October 7, 2002), A19.

53. Laura Robinson, "Skating in Circles: Dumb and Dumber," *The Vancouver Sun* (September 29, 2008).

54. Lenskyj, *Out of Bounds*, 84–85; Richardson, *Fair Ball*, 38–48; Laura Robinson, *Black Tights: Women, Sport, and Sexuality* (Toronto: HarperCollins, 2002), 90, 92, 93–94.

55. Rod Mickleburgh, "Strong-willed Ski Jumpers Take on the Mighty Olympic Establishment," *The Globe and Mail* (April 21, 2009), A1, A8.

56. Laura Robinson, "Why Can't Women Ski Jump at the Games?" *The Globe and Mail* (April 17, 2009), A13; Rod Mickelburgh, "Judge Reserves Decision in Women Ski Jumpers' Case," *The Globe and Mail* (April 25, 2009), A5; CBCNEWS.ca, "Female Ski Jumpers Lose Olympic Battle," (July 21, 2009), http://www.cbc.ca/canada/british-columbia/story/2009/07/10/bc-olympic-women-ski-jump-decision.html; in the Supreme Court of British Columbia, *Sagen v. Vancouver Organizing Committee for the 2010 Olympic and Paralympic Winter Games,* (November 20, 2009), http://www.courts.gov.bc.ca/jdb-txt/CA/09/05/2009BCCA0522.htm; Court of Appeal for British Columbia, *Sagen v. Vancouver Organizing Committee for the 2010 Olympic and Paralympic Winter Games,* (November 20, 2009), http://www.hrlrc.org.au/year/2009/sagen-v-vancouver-organizing-committee-for-the-2010-olympic-and-paralympic-winter-games-2009-bcca-522-20-november-2009/; CBC, Vancouver Now, "Supreme Court Spurns Women Ski Jumpers, (December 22, 2009), http://www.cbc.ca/olympics/skijumping/story/2009/12/22/bc-oly-women-scoc.html; BBC Sport Olympics, "Women's Boxing Gains Olympic Spot," (August 13, 2009), http://news.bbc.co.uk/sport2/hi/olympic_games/8196879.stm; JustCanoeIt! "What is Sprint Canoe?" http://www.justcanoeit.com/content/what_is_sprint_canoe.asp.

57. Robinson, *Black Tights*; M. Ann Hall, *A History of Women's Sport in Canada* (Peterborough, Ont: Broadview Press, 2002), 92–200; Christie Blatchford, "Frankly, Gay Rumors a Bust," *Canoe Nagano 1998,* (February 6, 1998), http://www.canoe.ca/SlamNaganoColumns/feb6_blatchford.html; Helen Jefferson Lenskyj, *Out on the Field: Gender, Sport and Sexualities* (Toronto: Women's Press, 2003), 146; Paul Walder, "Faster, Higher, Stronger: How Female Athletes Rose to the Top," *The Globe and Mail* (February 26, 2010), A8.

58. Harrigan, 70.

59. Ontario, Department of Education, *Home Economics, Intermediate Division,* 1964.

60. Shirley Stokes, *The Shortest Shadow: A Descriptive Study of the Members of the Federation of Women Teachers' Associations of Ontario* (Toronto: FWTAO, 1969), 3; Le Collectif Clio, *L'histoire des femmes au Québec depuis quatres siècles,* 1st ed. (Montréal: Quinze, 1982), 439.

61. Linda Eyre and Jane Gaskell, "Gender Equity and Education Policy in Canada, 1970–2000," *Orbit* 34, 2 (2004): 6–8; Bernie Froese-Germain, "Are Schools Really Shortchanging Boys? Reality Check on the New Gender Gap," *Orbit,* 34, 1 (2004): 13–15; Sarah Boesveld, "Boys' Schools Foster 'Achievement Culture,'" *The Globe and Mail* (October 22, 2009), L1, L5.

62. Michelle Miller, *Branding Miss G_: Third Wave Feminists and the Media* (Toronto: Sumach Press, 2008), 44; Shannon Mills, "A Room of One's Own: Women's Studies in High Schools," and Paulette, "Account by Student who took Ms. Mills' Course," *The Miss G_ Project* (February 15, 2006), http://www.themissgproject.org/about/; "Miss G Project Sees

Success," *Herizons* 23, 1 (Summer 2009): 6, 7; Victoria Bromley and Aalya Ahmad, "Wa(i)ving Solidarity: Feminist Activists Confronting Backlash," *Canadian Woman Studies/Les cahiers de la femme* 25, 3, 4 (September/fall 2006): 68.

63. Native Women's Association of Canada, *Situation of Aboriginal Women in Canada Requires Improvement,* (January 16, 2009), http://www.turtleisland.org/discussion/viewtopic. php?f=15&t=6497; Indian and Northern Affairs Canada, *Post-Secondary Education for Status Indians and Inuit* (December 2000); *Canada Year Book 2008,* calculated from 7: Table 1.2, 122: Table 10.

64. Lesley Andres and Maria Adamuti-Trache, "You've Come a Long Way, Baby? Persistent Gender Inequality in University Enrolment and Completion, 1979–2004," *Canadian Public Policy/Analyse de politiques* 33, 1 (2007): 97.

65. Jill Vickers and June Adam, *But Can You Type? Canadian Universities and the Status of Women* (Ottawa: Canadian Association of University Teachers, 1977), 59, 32.

66. F. H. Leacy, ed. *Historical Statistics of Canada,* 2nd ed. (Ottawa: Statistics Canada, 1983), W389–94, W405–8, W436–42; Thérèse Hamel, "L'enseignement d'hier à aujourd'hui: Les transformations d'un métier 'féminin' au Québec," in *Questions de culture 9: Identités féminines: Mémoire et création* (Quebec: Institut québécois de recherche sur la culture, 1986), 51–70.

67. *Women in Canada,* 5th ed., 90; *Canada Year Book 2008,* 122–123; Elizabeth Church, "Who's in the Know: Women Surge, Men Sink in Education's Gender Gap," *The Globe and Mail* (December 7, 2009), A5, A1.

68. *Women in Canada 1985,* 32, 33, 25, 90; Canadian Congress for Learning Opportunities for Women, *Decade of Promise: An Assessment of Canadian Women's Status in Education, Training and Employment, 1976–1985* (Toronto: Avebury Research, 1986), 36–37; Vivian Smith, "Unwilling to Keep Taking It Like a Man," *The Globe and Mail* (April 24, 1993), A1, A4; *2006 Census: Educational Portrait of Canada,* Figure 2; *Canada Year Book 2008,* 118, 119; Statistics Canada, Cat. no. 97-560-X.

69. Andres and Adamuti-Trache, 113.

70. Indian and Northern Affairs Canada, *Post-Secondary Education for Status Indian and Inuit* (December 2000); INAC, *Aboriginal Women—A Profile from the 1996 Census,* 2nd ed. (2001); *Women in Canada,* 5th ed., 196; Joe Friesen, "Aboriginal Women Do Better by Degrees," *The Globe and Mail* (April 8, 2010), http://www.globecampus.ca/in-the-news/article/aboriginal-women-do-better-by-degrees/.

71. CBC News, "21 Nunavut Women Graduate with UPEI Education Degrees," (July 2, 2009) , http://www.cbc.ca/canada/north/story/2009/07/02/nunvaut-ed-grads.html; Elizabeth Church, "Nunavut's Educational Ambitions Bear Fruit," *The Globe and Mail* (July 1, 2009) A9.

72. *Women in Canada, 5th ed.,* 92; Garth Williams, "Doctoral Education in Canada 1900–2005," Canadian Association for Graduate Studies, (September 2005), 11, http://www.cags.ca/media/docs/cags-publication/doctoral_education_canada_1900-2005.pdf; Vickers and Adam, 114.

73. Margaret Gillett, *We Walked Very Warily: A History of Women at McGill* (Montreal: Eden Press, 1981), 404.

74. The Chilly Collective, *Breaking Anonymity: The Chilly Climate* (Waterloo: Wilfrid Laurier University Press, 1995); Elena Hannah, Linda Paul, and Swani Vethamany-Globus, eds., *Women in the Canadian Academic Tundra: Challenging the Chill* (Montreal and Kingston: McGill-Queen's University Press, 2002).

75. *Women in the Labour Force: 1994 Edition* (Ottawa, Statistics Canada), 37; Statistics Canada, *The Daily,* "Study: The Rising Profile of Women Academics" (February 24, 2005); Canadian

Association of University Teachers, "Narrowing the Gender Gap: Women Academics in Canadian Universities," *CAUT Equity Review*, (March 2008), 2, 1–3, http://www.caut.ca/uploads/2008_2_Staff.pdf.

76. Statistics Canada, "The Rising Profile of Women Academics," *Perspectives on Labour and Income*, 6, 2 (February 2005); Christopher Worswick, "Mandatory Retirement Rules and the Retirement Decisions of University Professors in Canada," (Statistics Canada Analytical Studies Branch Research Paper Series, December 2005), Cat. no. 11F0019MIE-No.27.

77. Wendy Robbins and Vicky Simpson, "Pyramids of Power: A Statistical Snapshot of Women in Post-Secondary Education in Canada and Some Ideas for Making Change," *Atlantis* 33, 2 (Spring 2009): 13.

78. Marie Fleming, "A Tribute Whose Time Has Come," *Art Gallery of Ontario News* 9, 4 (April 1987): 1; Joyce Zemans, "A Tale of Three Women: The Visual Arts in Canada," *Revue d'art canadienne/Canadian Art Review* 25, 1–2 (1998): 106.

79. Maryon Kantaroff, "Breaking Out of the Female Mould," in Gwen Matheson, ed., *Women in the Canadian Mosaic* (Toronto: Peter Martin Associates, 1976), 287.

80. Women's Art Resource Centre, WARC Gallery, Linda Abrahams, "Who Counts?—and Who's Counting?" *Matriart*, 5, 1 (1994), http//warc.net/v.3/english.html.

81. Zemans, 104; personal communication from Zemans (July 2009); see also, for periods before 1967, the Canadian Women's Art History Initiative at Concordia University, http://cwahi.concordia.ca/.

82. Coral Ann Howells, *Private and Fictional Words: Canadian Women Novelists of the 1970s and 1980s* (London: Methuen, 1987). See also Janice Williamson, *Sounding Differences: Conversations with Seventeen Canadian Women Writers* (Toronto: University of Toronto Press, 1993).

83. Simon Houpt, "Munro 'Amazed' to Win Man Booker International," *The Globe and Mail*, (May 9, 2009), A5; for a list of winners of the Governor General's literary awards, see http://www.canadacouncil.ca/NR/rdonlyres/CCA1B1A6-59E5-4748-BFEE-B64313E92624/0/CumulativeWinners2008.pdf.

84. Cynthia Zimmerman, ed., *Taking the Stage: Selections from Plays by Canadian Women* (Toronto: Playwrights Canada Press, 1994); Zimmerman, *Playwriting Women: Female Voices in English Canada* (Toronto: Simon and Pierre, 1994).

85. NFB Profiles, "Anne Claire Poirier," Canadian Women in Film, (January 1, 2010), http://www.onf-nfb.gc.ca/eng/portraits/anne_claire_poirier/.

86. Canadian Women in Film, "Kathleen Shannon (1935–1998)," (April 12, 2005). http://www.collectionscanada.gc.ca/women/002026-714-e.html.

87. National Film Board of Canada, "SHAMELESS: The Art of Disability," http://www.onf-nfb.gc.ca/eng/collection/film/?id=51620.

88. CBC News, "New Vancouver Opera Focuses on Poet Pauline Johnson," (March 21, 2008), http://www.cbc.ca/canada/toronto/story/2008/03/11/pauline-opera.html.

89. Paula Citron, "The National Ballet Loses Its 'Iron Butterfly,'" *The Globe and* Mail (May 27, 2009), R1, R2;

90. Mikhail Baryshnikov, "Introduction," in Carol Anderson, *Unfold: A Portrait of Peggy Baker* (Toronto; Dance Collections Press/Danse Presse, 2008), iv.

91. Kate Harper, "Lilith Fair's 2010 Return," *CHARTattack*, (April 24, 2009), http://www.chartattack.com/news/68930/lilith-fair-returns-in-2010; "Lilith Fair 2010 Announces Lineup," *The Globe and Mail* (December 11, 2009), R3; J. Maki Matopanyane, "The Black Female

Body and Artist in Canadian Hip Hop: The Question of Femini(st)ne Space," *New Dawn: The Journal of Black Canadian Studies* 1,1 (Spring 2006): 32–34.

92. Errol Nazareth, "The Kids are All Right," *Toronto Sun,* http://www.urbnet.com/eternia/tour-torontosun.html.

93. Rella Braithwaite and Tessa Benn-Ireland, *Some Black Women: Profiles of Black Women in Canada* (Toronto: Sister Vision, 1993), 37, 48; Joan Acland, "Elitekey: The Artistic Production of Mi'kmaq Women," *Revue d'art canadienne/Canadian Art Review* 25, 1–2 (1998): 5–10; also see Shirley Bear bio at http://shirleybear.banff.org/bio.html.

CHAPTER FOURTEEN

Reorganizing for Change

The 1960s and 1970s witnessed a resurgence of feminist ideas and activity in many parts of the world. In Canada, old organizations supported and assisted newer ones in what has come to be identified as the Second Wave of feminism. The newly active feminists of the late 1960s liked this marine image, and the media picked it up. They were making the point that the women's movement had worked its way through something like the trough between two waves, so that the tide of change was ready to move further up the shore. Later feminist theorists pointed out that the idea of two discontinuous periods of feminism was modelled on the American example, a pattern that did not fit Canada very well. Furthermore, even when the highest tides of the first women's movement had receded, the advances in women's autonomy had not. Perhaps feminism was more like underground lava flow and then volcanic eruption, or the movement of tectonic plates that produces continental change. Such images implied change that was sometimes fiery, often slow, but massive and irreversible.[1]

WOMEN AND PEACE

It was around the issue of peace, long a concern of women's groups, that the first significant new postwar national women's organization was born. The Voice of Women for Peace was usually called just the Voice of Women (VOW); its members often referred to themselves as "Voices." VOW's immediate forerunners were informal local discussion groups formed by women at the end of the 1950s, as they became aware of the dangerous fallout from nuclear tests. The earliest recorded is the Mothers' Committee on Radiation Hazards, founded in West Vancouver in 1958 by Marion Kellerman, who "just wanted safe milk for her children"; other small radiation hazards committees soon appeared across the country.[2] When the Paris Summit Conference on disarmament broke up in May 1960, Canadians were appalled. "We all believed we were on the brink of nuclear war," recalled Kay Macpherson, future leader of VOW.[3] *Toronto Star* columnist Lotta Dempsey was the catalyst, in a column lamenting the Summit Conference's failure and asking what women could do. The response to her article was overwhelming, and at the suggestion of veteran peace activist Helen Tucker, a hugely successful mass meeting of women led to the formation of a new peace organization for women. VOW effectively replaced the old Women's International League for Peace and Freedom (WILPF), strong in Canada and internationally in the inter-war period, which had virtually ceased to function, though it was to revive in a small way later in the Cold War. Voice of Women, founded in July 1960, had a membership of 5 000 by 1961. Most members were politically inexperienced young women, but they were joined by former members of the socialist and peace movements and by women long active in traditional women's organizations. Macpherson, previously active in Toronto's Home and School Association and Association of Women Electors, was one of the earliest and most prominent Voices and became its third president in 1963, after Helen Tucker and Thérèse Casgrain. Exemplifying the recruitment patterns of the women's movement, 22-year-old Michèle Jean became secretary of the Quebec branch after her aunt, Mariana Jodoin, the first woman senator from Quebec, took her to an organizing meeting at the home of Thérèse Casgrain. Jean went on to a distinguished career as a feminist journalist, historian, and civil servant in Quebec and then with UNESCO.[4]

The non-partisan organization initially won general acceptance from the Canadian public and even the Canadian government listened politely to its representatives. However, when the Voice of Women aggressively criticized the decision of the newly elected Liberal government to accept nuclear weapons in Canada, it lost many early members who were active in the Liberal Party, including Maryon Pearson, the wife of the prime minister. The group received substantial publicity in 1964, when Thérèse Casgrain and Kay Macpherson, to their delight, were arrested by the Paris police as a VOW delegation attempted to deliver a letter to the secretary-general of NATO. However, the media soon insinuated that the group was soft on Communism, possibly even a Communist-front organization. Such smears, reminiscent of the red-baiting of the inter-war period and very much part of the McCarthyism of the early postwar years, were encouraged by the fact that several of VOW's most active members, including Casgrain and Macpherson, had close connections with the NDP, the CCF's successor as of 1961.[5]

Throughout the 1960s, Voice of Women actively pursued its goal of fostering peace through a wide variety of activities familiar to women's volunteer groups, such as writing briefs, sending delegations to international conferences, and sponsoring its own conferences inside Canada. Its members' activities in search of peace led them to question Canada's relationship with the United States, especially in the area of foreign policy. VOW thereby placed itself in the forefront of the Canadian nationalist movement of the 1960s. Recalling the Cuban Missile Crisis of 1962, External Affairs minister Howard Green later stated that the vigorous lobbying led by VOW had contributed to the government's decision to delay putting Canada's portion of the North American aerial defence system on the alert requested by the United States. Voice of Women also helped inspire the United Nations to declare 1965 International Co-operation Year, and played a significant role in organizing Canadian opposition to the war in Vietnam. Innovative and highly visible campaigns drew on women's specific experience. For example, Dr. Ursula Franklin, professor of metallurgy at the University of Toronto, organized the collection of thousands of children's baby teeth in order to demonstrate concretely how the radioactive fallout from bomb tests moved through the food chain into children's bones.

As it pursued its primary goal of the prevention of war, Voice of Women became involved in a number of other issues. Its early commitment to bilingualism and biculturalism was fuelled when its 1962 Peace Train delegation to Ottawa, led by Thérèse Casgrain and including many francophone women, was met by the unilingual Howard Green. Voice of Women activists were also prominent in many other progressive causes of the 1960s involving the environment, human rights, science policy, and the status of women. For example, Halifax Voice of Women supported the anti-discrimination movement by carrying out a study of bias against African Nova Scotians. Muriel Duckworth, a long-time member and national president, summed up the connections:

> Somehow we're always having to make these choices of how to separate what is strictly the Peace Movement and what is the Women's Movement, what is the Ecology movement and what is the Human Rights movement. I think these movements are alive and effective because more and more of us see these things as interrelated.[6]

Although its continuing membership soon declined to about 1 000 activists and later dropped even further, VOW did not cease to be a source of protest. The national organization and one regional chapter—Nova Scotia—remained active. At the turn of the century, that chapter was among the more visible protesters challenging war and militarism in general and, specifically, the Canadian participation in NATO's post 9/11 action in Afghanistan and then the subsequent American invasion of Iraq.[7]

VOW was of lasting importance, not least because of the many women who combined it with other areas of feminist activism and politics; Macpherson and Duckworth were among those who ran for provincial and federal office. Other women preferred involvement in the support groups for women interested in electoral politics that appeared later, such as Toronto's Women for Political Action (1972) and Committee for '94 (1984) as well as Newfoundland's 52% Solution (1987). A successor group, Equal Voice, was founded in 2001 to help get more women elected both nationally and provincially; the new organization encouraged and monitored the percentage of women nominated by the political parties in Ontario and then federally. It also inaugurated a variety of activities, including an online campaign school, that effectively drew attention to the need to have more women present where political decisions were made.[8] "'Equal voice' means 'fair representation,'" declared Equal Voice founder Rosemary Speirs. [9]

TOWARD A NEW AGENDA FOR WOMEN

Although in the postwar period the larger public and the media had little interest in women's activism, some women journalists continued to play a role that was "quietly subversive."[10] By the early 1960s, they were already discussing many of the topics that were to preoccupy the re-emerging women's movement. Doris Anderson, editor of *Chatelaine* from 1957 to 1977, wrote editorials on topics including married women's paid employment and the dearth of women in public life. Anderson's editorials became more feminist, and more explicitly so, and the magazine published articles on controversial subjects such as abortion, birth control, and lesbianism. Rona Maynard, who edited *Chatelaine* in the last years of the twentieth century, described Anderson as "an eagle in the dovecote" of Cold War–era magazines for women.[11] Anderson refused an offer to publish chapters of Betty Friedan's influential *Feminine Mystique*: Canadian women, she felt, had already seen such material in *Chatelaine* and her editorial board found the future bestseller's presentation "turgid" and "heavy-footed."[12]

Two surveys conducted by *Chatelaine* among its readers demonstrated how much mainstream Canadian women had changed in the time from the beginning of the 1960s, when the revived women's movement had not yet had any impact, to 1968 when it was in full swing. The stated goal of the first, relatively small 1961 survey was to "find out whether the stereotype of the harassed North American housewife— tense, frantic, and frustrated—was fact or myth." Although the very fact of the survey suggested concern about the mood of housewives, the answers were cheery and positive: 87 percent of respondents wanted their daughters "to grow up to be housewives rather than working wives." Only about 6 percent said they themselves would prefer to "work" if they had affordable or adequate child care; another 43 percent said that part-time employment would be acceptable. Seven years later, in a far larger and more representative survey administered to 11 000 *Chatelaine* readers across the country, the majority of those answering agreed that "marriage with children and a career would be their preference." They supported by large majorities—in most cases by over three-quarters—a whole list of what were soon to become women's movement demands, including government-supported daycare, legislation enforcing equal pay, equal access to employment, government-financed birth control clinics, and wider grounds for abortion and divorce.[13]

In Quebec as well, there was a subtle yet significant shift in the orientation of the women's press after 1960. With the appearance in 1960 of the French version of *Chatelaine*, and the appointment of Francine Montpetit as the new editor of Montreal's 50-year-old magazine *La revue populaire*, Quebec women were offered more realistic appraisals of their situation. However, an article on birth control published in *La revue* in September 1962 created a storm of controversy that resulted in the firing of Montpetit and the eventual demise of the magazine. *Châtelaine* remained as the sole commercial publication directed to Quebec women. However, although English-Canadian general-interest magazines contained a declining proportion of articles about women and work during the 1960s, *Chatelaine/Châtelaine* and the *Canadian Home Journal* continued to direct their readers' attention to women's changing roles.[14]

Over time, the editors of *Chatelaine* moved away from Doris Anderson's self-assumed role as the vanguard of feminism. Less militant than Anderson, Maynard's feminism reflected the new appreciation of women's culture and experience. When she became editor of *Chatelaine* in 1994, she wrote, "This magazine will be the meeting place where busy women can kick off their shoes and tell the untold stories of their lives the way they do among friends, when kids and husbands aren't around. . . . "[15] As earlier, post-1960s Canada saw many remarkable and feminist journalists, such as Penny Kome and Michele

Landsberg. Under editor Sally Armstrong (1988–1999) *Homemakers'* magazine added a substantial amount of attention to feminism in Canada and to women's rights internationally, interests that continued after her departure. Armstrong made documentary films and was the author of books including *Veiled Threat: The Hidden Power of the Women of Afghanistan* (2002); she went on to work for *Chatelaine* and *Maclean's*.

From the 1960s, the women's movement became infinitely more active and also more visible. All over Canada, old organizations were revitalized and new ones proliferated; together they mobilized an unprecedented number and variety of women who espoused new labels and even new ideologies. Moreover, millions of women who identified with no particular group or ideology became more aware of their identity as women and their need for autonomy and recognition. Looking back over her experiences in the women's movement, one young woman writing in 1980 raised a fundamental issue, using the prevalent water images: "How to measure the ripple effect generated when one person in transition touches another who touches another, the ripples colliding, intersecting, overlapping and causing further ripples?"[16]

The foundation of Voice of Women in 1960 is a useful marker, but the beginning of the public process of change can best be dated to 1966. This was when existing francophone and anglophone women's organizations began to regroup and reorganize in a way that they had not done for over a generation. In Quebec, after the celebration of the twenty-fifth anniversary of enfranchisement, representatives of women's groups called together by Thérèse Casgrain agreed to found a new coalition. The result, the *Fédération des femmes du Québec* (FFQ), was the first substantial, enduring new feminist organization of Quebec women since the formation of the suffrage leagues in the 1920s. The FFQ was an umbrella group modelled on the *Fédération Nationale Saint-Jean-Baptiste* and the Councils of Women. Like them, it was limited by the need to reach consensus among its member groups. By 1980, the FFQ's diverse membership included 35 affiliates, among which were at least five anglophone groups and Quebec's Native Women's Association; in 2009 its 36 member groups included one for Iranian women and another for lesbian mothers. Unlike its predecessors earlier in the century, however, the organization had no religious ties. This important change reflected the reduced influence of the church in Quebec, especially its decreasing importance for women. Becoming more radical, in 1975 the FFQ took a public position in favour of removing abortion from the Criminal Code. On into the next century, it was to maintain a vanguard position in Quebec feminism, focusing on violence against women as well as a host of other social and economic issues.[17]

The year 1966 also saw the founding of the *Association féminine d'éducation et d'action sociale* (AFEAS), which combined two established church-sponsored women's organizations that had been cautiously moving toward union for some years: the *Union catholique des femmes rurales* and the *Cercles d'économie domestique*. Although clerical interest in reasserting control over the Catholic laywomen's organizations had been the immediate impetus for the merger, the influence of Church representatives steadily declined over the years; in 1975, the AFEAS overruled its chaplains and prepared a carefully worded statement that supported the current Canadian system of approval of abortions. Focusing on housewives, the organization pointed out that all women worked, even though a high proportion of them did not get paid. It developed a special interest in women who worked in family businesses and it produced an important study of women's work in the home, *Pendant que les hommes travaillaient, les femmes elles . . .*, updated in 1984 by the AFEAS's daughter group, the *Association des femmes collaboratrices*. In 2009 the AFEAS claimed 13 000 members in 300 groups; policies they supported included the long-gun registry and publicly funded midwifery services, as well as environmental projects such as promotion of reusable bags for groceries and other purchases. Other activities related to violence against women and the AFEAS's continuing campaigns, the ninth in 2009, to have women's unpaid, "invisible" work in the home adequately included in national accounting.[18]

The first president of the AFEAS, Germaine Goudreault, was also a member of the FFQ's first executive, and the two organizations worked closely together. The new coalitions of Quebec women's groups produced a surge of reform activity, which by the end of the 1960s included major revisions of Quebec family law. The *Cercles de fermières* were among those becoming more interested in public policy, passing resolutions and initiating programs to deal with such widely divergent issues as ecology and sexually transmitted diseases. They remained unaffiliated, however, celebrating their fiftieth anniversary in 1965. One study of a regional federation of the *Fermières* found that in 1997 their central policy concerns were environmental issues and domestic violence. In 2009 the group's website claimed 38 000 members and had developed working files on topics including addiction, women's poverty, and how to be environmentally active in daily life. A dossier on reconciling career and home used as its central example the tale of a young woman soldier. Continuing interest in crafts and cooking was accompanied by explicit attention to married women and the family but none to rural life.[19]

In the new stage of organizational activity, Aboriginal women were among the first to come together. In British Columbia an Indian Homemakers' Association was in place as early as 1960; the group was still active in the 2000s, working on family education and counselling about addiction as well as offering classes in traditional mothering and a Healing Circle. On the more militant side, it was in 1968 that Mary Two-Axe Early from the Kahnewake Reserve in Quebec drew together a group of Indian women who had lost entitlements under the Indian Act because of marriage to husbands who were not status Indians. Calling themselves "A Group of Women from a Canadian Indian Reserve," they made an influential submission to the Royal Commission on the Status of Women. They became Indian Rights for Indian Women (IRIW), Aboriginal women's first recorded feminist group although, typically, they did not use the feminist label. One of the notable examples of cooperation among women's groups was the continuing support that non-Aboriginal women's groups gave over the years to the campaigns to amend the Indian Act to remove its blatant sexism.[20]

The Royal Commission on the Status of Women in Canada (RCSW) itself was what marked the later 1960s as crucial for the renewed women's movement in Canada. The RCSW came into being in 1967 as a result of a coordinated campaign on the part of national women's organizations. There had always been communication and cooperation among the large national women's groups, if only because of the overlapping memberships of many of the women involved. In the 1960s, a loosely organized Canadian Committee on the Status of Women (CCSW) explicitly coordinated action, as when its member organizations testified before the Special Joint [Parliamentary] Committee on

Divorce in 1966. As vice-president of the Canadian Federation of University Women (CFUW), Laura Sabia was active with the CCSW.[21] In 1966, as president of the CFUW, she formally called together representatives of some 30 national women's organizations to discuss their common concerns. Among the group were the Woman's Christian Temperance Union, Young Women's Christian Association, the National Council of Women, the National Council of Jewish Women of Canada, the Imperial Order Daughters of Empire, and the Canadian Federation of Business and Professional Women's Clubs; all except the WCTU were still active in Canada in 2009. The women present, calling themselves the Committee for the Equality of Women in Canada (CEW), agreed to send the prime minister a brief supporting a request for a royal commission. As editor of *Chatelaine*, Doris Anderson supported the call for such an inquiry. Reluctant to suggest that "one more be added to the groaning shelfful of past Royal Commissions," she justified the request by referring to the rising level of women's participation in education and the workforce. "What we don't need in a commission, is an all-woman witch-hunt," she wrote. "We do need a forward-looking commission composed equally of impartial men and women prepared to take a cool twentieth-century approach to our problems."[22]

Laura Sabia, who spearheaded the push for the royal commission, was far less temperate. Educated in a Montreal convent school, she told an interviewer that the nuns' obsequious deference to the priests had been an early cause of her own "revulsion towards a male-dominated society." In later years, she attributed her independence to the strength of her parents, but also to having been an outsider in Canadian society: "As a child, I hated being 'Italian.' I resented the 'dirty-dago-wap syndrome' of the twenties and early thirties."[23] When she graduated from McGill University, instead of following her plan to go to law school, she married, raised four children in St. Catharines, Ontario, and plunged into community activities. With no daycare available when she was a municipal councillor in St. Catherines, she took along her son Michael as she did such constituency work as examining flooded basements. She later led a long fight for gender equality at Bell Canada. "There are 25 000 women in Bell Canada and you can't tell me they are all stupid," was her comment on the dearth of women in management positions there.[24] A $104 million pay equity settlement to telephone operators was overseen in 2006 by her son Michael, described in *The Globe and Mail* business magazine in 2007 as "one of the few Canadian CEOs who pay more than lip service to gender equality."[25]

The committee that Sabia drew together in 1966 consisted of the heads of the large continuing women's federations, including groups that had earlier been among the most vocal and consistent campaigners for woman suffrage. Their feminism can be inferred from their ready response to Sabia's appeal; in the same year, similar organizations in the United States had rebuffed suggestions that they publicly support issues related to women's equality. In addition, the six-year-old Voice of Women was actively involved. The leaders of the *Fédération des femmes du Québec* shared the Committee's concern that the women of Canada should appear united by having representation from both francophone and anglophone women's groups. As a result, Thérèse Casgrain, along with future judge Réjane Laberge-Colas, then president of the FFQ, joined the CEW's delegation to Ottawa. Women's groups from all three federal political parties also supported the brief calling for a royal commission, as did a considerable number of well-established women's professional and service groups.[26]

Laura Sabia, networking, 1969.
Source: CP PHOTO

The Pearson government ignored the request from the Committee, provoking Laura Sabia into what *The Globe and Mail* described as an "ultimatum to the Government: establish a royal commission or face the consequences."[27] Sabia's son, Michael, recalled the incident:

> Picture, if you will, a typical scene from our household in the 60s. Mother is preparing dinner. Father, a surgeon, and his 10-year-old son are waiting to be fed. The phone rings, and a brief discussion ensues, mother calmly saying: "Tell the Prime Minister that I will lead an uprising of Canadian women."[28]

She said that she would march two million women on Ottawa, the combined memberships of the groups that had supported the appeal to the government. Afterward, Sabia noted repeatedly that she would have been lucky to mobilize *two* women for an actual march.

This gesture has become legendary, with Sabia and others convinced that it produced the Royal Commission on the Status of Women, which was formally established in February 1967. Certainly, Sabia's bravado captured the headlines. In terms of specific timing, it seems clear that the Committee's activities served as a catalyst for the commission that had been sought in vain by Judy LaMarsh, who had followed Ellen Fairclough as the second solitary woman in the federal Cabinet. More generally, the explanation for the commission is probably to be found in the interrelated patterns of education and work that characterized women's lives in the 1960s, patterns that also explain women's renewed responsiveness to feminism. Strains had developed as a result of the combination of unchanged social attitudes with major changes in women's employment and education. The revived women's movement was to articulate the grievances that resulted.

At this time, an expanding economy required a vast infusion of labour. Sylva Gelber, head of the Women's Bureau of the federal Department of Labour, was concerned that the failure of Canada "to utilize our human resources" (meaning women) to their full capability was "to deny to the nation the productivity essential for the maintenance of a high standard of living."[29] Ten industrialized nations, including the United States, had already begun to look into the problems and economic possibilities represented by the status of women. In Parliament, where the Liberal government lacked a majority, the New Democratic Party, which held the balance of power, used the issue of a women's commission as yet another handy weapon against the government; the NDP was urged on by Grace MacInnis, the only woman in its caucus. By 1965 Canadian women were voting at the same rate as men, and participating in election campaign activities almost as frequently.[30] The CEW's specific request—for a royal commission—was ideally suited to the double purposes of getting the necessary information about fully integrating women into the workforce while also appeasing and, if necessary, defusing feminist complaints.

The general mandate of the commission, announced early in 1967, was "to inquire and report upon the status of women in Canada, and to recommend what steps might be taken by the Federal Government to ensure for women equal opportunities with men in all aspects of Canadian society."[31] The presidency of the commission was handed over to the first woman to head a royal commission in Canada. Professionally known as Anne Francis and appointed under her husband's name as Mrs. John Bird, for the rest of her life, including when she was appointed to the Senate, she was known as Florence Bird; in French the RCSW is referred to as *la Commission Bird*. Bird was then a broadcaster at the CBC specializing in the history of working women; she was known to Prime Minister Pearson through the Canadian Institute for International Affairs, for which she had written a pamphlet on the rights of women at the early date of 1950. The usual regional and political concerns dictated the composition of the seven-member commission, which included two men, one of them from Quebec. Quebec academic Jeanne Lapointe was selected because of her experience with the influential Parent Commission on education in her province (1963–65). All the same, women's groups were heeded, and members also included Lola Lange, active in the Alberta Farm Women's Union, as well as juvenile court judge Doris Ogilvie from New Brunswick. Elsie Gregory MacGill was effectively the Commission's vice-president. An informed and persuasive third-generation feminist, she was representative of many groups of women: a westerner, the first woman aviation engineer in Canada, past president of the Canadian Federation of Business and Professional Women's Clubs, and partly disabled from polio. The young executive secretary, also responsible for "sociological" research, Monique Bégin, was a protégée of Thérèse Casgrain. An activist in the Montreal Catholic school board, the University Women's Clubs, and the FFQ, she was later to be an MP and a Cabinet minister.[32]

LaMarsh had unsuccessfully recommended appointing more women who were not middle-aged and married. Nor were there were any women of colour, immigrant, Aboriginal, working-class, or even young women on the commission. However, the diverse concerns of Canadian women were set out in the 468 briefs and approximately 1 000 letters received, and, above all, in the extensively announced public hearings that were held in 14 cities in all 10 provinces as well as in the Territories. The Commission deliberately used its unprecedented wide-ranging public sessions as a device for public education, and also commissioned the first systematic studies of the situation of Canadian women.

Initial media responses were skeptical if not frivolous. They provided "a field day for some cartoonists," Elsie MacGill recalled:

These were so out of touch with reality about women's shapes and styles that they depicted women in the audience as simpering, large, bosomy, and wearing hats, although simpering had gone out with Queen Victoria, the popular fashion model was the very thin, very narrow, very flat-chested Twiggy, and hats had vanished from daily wear.[33]

But the media and public alike moved to a grudging interest and respect. "The petitioners weren't just strident suffragettes in garden-party hats," wrote one woman journalist who went to the commission's first Ottawa meeting as a self-described "lapsed feminist," nor were they merely women preoccupied with "female neuroses." Indeed, they included "the dispossessed of Canadian society . . . The Other Canada." In Yellowknife, a Métis girl asked if the chairman of the Commission could come to her prison cell; 18 years old, pregnant and in despair, she'd been jailed for trying to kill herself by swallowing hairspray.[34]

The RCSW reported in 1970, having expanded its mandate to cover the many relevant areas of policy such as health, education, and family law that were under provincial jurisdiction. In addition, the Commission singled out for attention a number of particularly disadvantaged groups of women, such as mothers who were the sole support of their families. "We were liberal, and pragmatic feminists," Monique Bégin reflected 20 years later, "yet parts of the report were, and still are, purely utopian in the eyes of the Canadian state, although these sections appeared to the commissioners as plain common sense."[35] Deliberately published as a single, inexpensive volume, the

Senator Florence Bird, previously chair of the Royal Commission on the Status of Women, 1982.
Source: THE CANADIAN PRESS/Peter Bregg

report was a bestseller. In addition, the NCWC and the FFQ prepared shorter digests in English and French that were widely distributed through women's organizations. After a careful reading of the 167 recommendations it contained, a *Toronto Star* columnist told his readers that the report was nothing less than "a bomb already primed and ticking . . . packed with more explosive potential than any device manufactured by terrorists" and represented "a call to revolution."[36]

The established women's organizations had produced the Royal Commission and its report through a familiar process of coalitions and pressures on government. Impatient when the government did not respond quickly to the Commission's report, Laura Sabia led the Committee on Equality for Women as it evolved into the National Ad Hoc Committee on the Status of Women in Canada. It met during 1971 and early 1972 before it became the ongoing National Action Committee on the Status of Women (NAC). The Ad Hoc Committee presented a substantial brief to the government, incorporating three priority goals: expansion of daycare, insertion of "sex" as a prohibited basis of discrimination under Canadian human rights provisions, and decriminalization of abortion.[37] The adoption of the third priority lost it the support of Catholic groups, but brought on board several groups that supported freedom of reproductive choice. By 1988, two of the three goals had been achieved. However, a study released by UNICEF 20 years later showed that in 2008 Canada was seriously deficient in terms of early-childhood care, compared to other OECD countries; it shared with Ireland the last place in achievement of benchmarks.[38]

The "Strategy for Change" conference that inaugurated NAC in the spring of 1972 set a pattern of cooperation among widely differing feminist groups, more than 40 of them represented by the some 500 women who attended. In a uniquely Canadian way—like the FFQ—NAC incorporated representatives of older and more conventional women's organizations as well as newer ones, including Voice of Women and women's liberation groups. Socialist feminists, radical feminists, status of women committees, and many small service organizations were also there at the start. Laura Sabia was the obvious choice for the new organization's first president.[39]

NAC's initial program was, basically, the Report of the Royal Commission on the Status of Women in Canada. Its first move to extend that agenda to wider issues of national policy occurred in 1974. Under the leadership of its second president, trade unionist Grace Hartman, the group objected to wage and price controls because they made it difficult to raise women's pay to make it equal to men's. June Menzies, a founder of the Manitoba Action Committee on the Status of Women, itself a founding and continuing member of NAC, was vice-chair of the board that imposed the controls. This was an early taste of the problems that would emerge as more women became participants in formal structures of power.[40]

In the 1970s and 1980s, NAC grew into an effective lobbying group, a coalition that operated on a basis of consensus among its widely differing components. It was generally accepted as speaking for Canadian women on a variety of issues, ranging from the situation of what were then called stewardesses at Air Canada to the wider issues of pay equity, violence against women, daycare, and access to abortion. In 1984 NAC listed almost 500 member groups and claimed to represent indirectly some five million Canadian women. At its peak in 1992, with a total of 737 affiliates, it included 489 different Canadian women's groups, along with a large number of progressive, mixed-gender organizations, such as unions, that were supporters of women's equality. The venerable National Council of Women of Canada did not join NAC; its national, provincial, and local federations continued to bring together many of the older anglophone and ethnic women's community and service organizations. Many women's groups declined to join any coalition at all, staying outside of NAC, the National Council, and the *Fédération des Femmes du Québec*. The FFQ itself moved in and out of NAC membership. The many unaffiliated women's organizations drew on the larger coalitions for information and for support in times of need. Some feminist analysts were hopeful in the 1980s that NAC was evolving toward some sort of new national "parliament of women."[41] Moving into the 1980s, NAC showed increasing interest in mainstream politics, though it was careful to avoid alignment with any political party; for the 1984 election the group succeeded in arranging a public leaders' debate in which all three major federal parties participated. However, under the influence of its more radical members, NAC then moved from lobbying the government to a more confrontational or protest approach. In 1987 it vehemently opposed the emerging engagement of Canada in international free trade agreements, and it became deeply involved in constitutional disputes, as discussed in chapter 15.[42]

After the publication of the RCSW's report in 1970, one of the central projects of many women's groups was to have governments set up official, state-funded advisory bodies on the status of women. The federal council, chaired by Katie Cooke, was founded in 1973; it was eventually joined by provincial counterparts. Laura Sabia soon left the first federal Advisory Council on the Status of Women in order to head the Ontario Council. Many of these governmental groups did important, innovative work. In New Brunswick, LES FAM (*Liberté, Egalité, Sororité: Les Femmes acadiennes de Moncton*), the first explicitly feminist group in the province, pushed the government into appointing an advisory council in 1977; two years later, that council produced the first Canadian publication on family violence.[43] In spite of such accomplishments, however, the advisory councils often encountered bureaucratic resistance, and they risked co-optation. Sabia finally resigned from the Ontario council in response to a frustration shared by many women activists, exploding in her *Toronto Sun* column:

> From "Royal Commission" to "Councils" we have been kept busy pushing paper. "Do advise us," say the astute politicians, "we're such numbskulls, tell us what to do." And we fell for it, God Help us, hook, line, and sinker.[44]

She underestimated the achievements of her own council, which included prodding the Ontario government into significant reforms in family property law. Eventually every province except British Columbia put in place some sort of status of women council, with Alberta's Advisory Council on Women's Issues established only in 1986.[45]

New non-governmental status-of-women organizations oriented specifically to the RCSW's report soon also appeared to press for provincial-level implementation of the Commission's recommendations. By the end of the 1970s, most provinces had such volunteer groups. They varied so greatly that it is difficult to generalize about them, but status-of-women committees (sometimes calling themselves action committees or councils) tended not to include men. Usually small and informally structured, they were sometimes completely unsubsidized, as was the case for the Ontario Committee on the Status of Women (OCSW), founded in 1971. Concentrating on lobbying provincial cabinets and civil servants, they provided a policy-focused form of feminist activism for younger professional women who did not have explicit ideological commitments. In general, the professional competence and expertise of these volunteer groups seem to have given them access to governments, especially to bureaucracies, and some degree of actual influence on policy. Their members honed political skills as they lobbied government and officials; some developed political ambitions and moved on to electoral and appointive positions in government. One example was Lynn Verge, one of the women who founded Newfoundland's five volunteer Status of Women Councils. Elected to the House of Assembly in 1979, she served as Minister of Education (1979–1985) and Justice (1985–1989), and was then Leader of the Progressive Conservative Party of Newfoundland and Labrador for a year until 1996, when she left the House of Assembly. Another woman who followed a similar route into electoral politics was Aideen Nicholson, a founding member of the OCSW. A social worker who had been administrator of Ontario's Reformatories for Women and then headed a child-care agency, Nicholson defeated a sitting MP to become one of the first to raise women's issues as a backbencher in the House of Commons (1974–1988). Later, she served on an Immigration and Refugees Board (1989–1995).[46]

In Quebec, no volunteer status-of-women committee developed, in part because of the effectiveness of the exceptionally well-funded provincial *Conseil du statut de la femme*, which in 1978 published a comprehensive document entitled *Pour les Québécoises: Égalité et indépendance*. Volunteer pressure activism in Quebec also tended to be pre-empted by the nationalist, social-democratic *Parti Québécois* (PQ), formed in 1968, which had an active women's committee and included influential women, nearly always feminist. When the PQ took office in 1976, Lise Payette, the first woman Cabinet minister in Quebec and the first person to have responsibility in Quebec for the status of women, pushed hard for change and helped to produce major improvements in areas like family law. Finally, in 1980, Quebec civil law finally broke with the old Napoleonic Code and recognized women as "complete human beings" equal to their spouses. Symbolic of this change, from 1981 on Quebec women were not just permitted to retain their birth names after marriage, as all Canadian women were, but actually required to do so.[47]

WOMEN'S LIBERATION AND RADICAL FEMINISM

"Women's liberation" came to Canada at about the same time as the RCSW was carrying out its ground-breaking but more conventional activities. The most important part of this new strain of feminism was the changed perspective it brought to women. Beginning in the last years of the 1960s, many individual women carried out a painstaking, sometimes painful reappraisal, of their lives as women. Women had always been aware of their condition, but if things were wrong they tended to blame themselves. Now a different way of looking at women's lives emerged. A new slogan proclaimed that "The personal is the political." That is, the political world outside the family—society and the state—shaped the personal lives of individuals, and personal relationships themselves were political because they involved power. Women's difficulties, many of them came to understand, were systemic rather than merely the result of individual bad luck or incompetence. The most routine and unlikely incidents could produce a "click" of understanding, a shared awareness of what women had in common. One account told of how it could happen:

> . . . checking neurotic hostess reflexes when a male dinner guest complains there are no serviettes on the table: knuckles white with the effort not to jump up when he could more easily reach them, we mystify him with roars of laughter at our shared struggle.[48]

The formal term for the process, derived from Marxist praxis, was "consciousness-raising." Whether or not it was based on the organized meetings of small discussion groups, consciousness-raising was central to what defined feminism in the 1960s and 1970s; it motivated many women to work for public and political solutions to their personal situation.

The women's liberation movement (WLM), initially a product of the international student movement of the mid-1960s, became publicly visible toward the end of the decade. Most militant were the young women university students who shared their dissatisfaction with the treatment of women in the politically-oriented and influential student movement of the 1960s, and also with that movement's failure to take seriously the problems of women in the larger society. The events that unfolded at a conference held in Montreal in 1969 to protest U.S. involvement in Vietnam were typical. As participant Naomi Wall recalled,

> On the final day . . . all hell broke loose. Women refused to discuss the resolutions or the war until every woman present who had something to say about the conference was heard. The men went wild. How could these women insist on addressing their concerns as women when men were dying in Vietnam? . . . Who gave a damn whether they were listened to?[49]

Eventually, the women's caucuses broke away from their mixed-sex origins. But they kept their vocabulary—the liberation of women echoed the liberation of colonized peoples. They brought with them to the women's movement much of the 1960s counterculture, including a preference for openness and self-expression and the rejection of conventional standards of dress and sexuality. Furthermore, the members of women's liberation groups kept the analytic and organizational preferences of the student movement. Unlike the majority of Canadian women's groups, which inclined to relatively formal structures and to the conventional tactics of lobbies and pressure groups, women's liberation, whose goal was systemic change, relied on consciousness-raising through small, unstructured cells and through demonstrations. And whereas the older feminists had a perspective that combined women's maternal and family concerns with a liberal concern for equality, the beliefs of the younger feminists tended to be closely connected to Marxist or other forms of socialism. By the end of the 1960s, many of Canada's women activists were committed to socialist belief systems that saw capitalism as the root cause of women's situation.

In 1967 a women's caucus at the University of Toronto rebelled against the male chauvinism in a student organization, the New Left Committee. As a result, Toronto's was one of the first five women's liberation groups existing in North America. In 1968 Toronto Women's Liberation was followed by developments on the west coast, beginning with the Women's Caucus in Vancouver. At Simon Fraser University, two students rewrote the Communist Manifesto as the "Feminine" Manifesto (they thought the word *feminist* was too confrontational), ending "women of the world unite, you have nothing to lose but your apron strings." By September 1968 a Women's Caucus at Simon Fraser's Student Society was offering abortion counselling and referral, and by 1969 they had their own office and organization. Montreal Women's Liberation, centred in the anglophone universities, followed much the same route and time frame, growing out of the student movement and the concern for women's autonomy that produced McGill's 1968 *Birth Control Handbook*. The media were fascinated by the "libbers" and their more or less outrageous street demonstrations, often about such seemingly novel and certainly sensational issues as abortion and sexuality. The movement's members were happy to be described in the inflammatory language of revolution, and they distrusted the cooperation with government in which the rest of the Canadian women's movement still had confidence.[50]

The first public action by Toronto Women's Liberation was a protest against a wintertime outdoor bikini contest in January 1969. In the words of one TWL member,

> A beautiful sister . . . stunned the organizers and onlookers by emerging fully clad under her borrowed furs, with a sign: "I Have A Mind." . . . The winner, a McMaster University philosophy student, was asked to comment on the incident. She was uncomprehending. Disgusted with being treated as a sex object? "That's what a girl wants most."[51]

By the end of the 1960s, additional women's liberation groups had been started in Regina, Saskatoon, Winnipeg, Ottawa, Guelph, Hamilton, Halifax, Sudbury, Thunder Bay, and Edmonton. In 1970, the RCSW was told there were 16 "local units of the Women's Liberation Movement" in Canada. Some apparently drew membership not just from students, but also from women who were members of other radical groups.[52]

In Quebec, francophone women's liberation groups grew out of the Quebec student groups committed to Quebec nationhood. Montreal's *Front pour la libération des femmes du Québec* (FLF) dated its own start to a public protest in Montreal in 1969 by women calling themselves the *Front commun des québécoises*. A response to the fact that the Montreal city administration had banned all demonstrations after a wave of trade union and other leftist activity, the street action used classic suffragist tactics: the women chained themselves together, and the fire department had to be called out to cut them free. The demonstration was initially an attempt to exploit possible police chivalry toward women, but it suggested to some of those involved that women could, and should, move out of a passive role in politics. The FLF's 1971 manifesto focused on colonization and on the experience of women in the Quebec independence movement, including the absence of any mention of women in the earlier manifesto of the *Front de libération du Québec*. The FLF's members described themselves as *esclaves des esclaves* (slaves of slaves). Their Cellule X carried out a series of feminist *action-chocs*. The first was a demonstration on Mothers' Day in 1970 in support of free access to abortion. The next year they disrupted the trial of FLQ activist Paul Rose in protest against the continued exclusion of women from juries in Quebec. Francophone women's liberation supporters also translated and somewhat altered the widely distributed and influential McGill *Birth Control Handbook*. The French version (1970), equally well received, which focused on Quebec, did its best to reconcile the desire for an increased population for a new nation with the need of women to control their own bodies. Along with members of the anglophone Montreal Women's Liberation, the FLF initially participated in the abortion referral service that was started at McGill. Before the end of the decade, however, the anglophone and francophone WLM groups in Quebec had permanently ceased to cooperate.[53]

The Canadian women's liberation movement made its first significant public appearance on the national level with the 1970 Abortion Caravan, probably the most innovative of a wide range of activities and organizations that responded to the failure of the 1969 legislation to remove abortion from the Criminal Code. The three-vehicle caravan took 17 women across the country from Vancouver to Ottawa in two weeks, stopping along the way for street theatre, demonstrations, and meetings. Hundreds more women joined en route and helped disrupt the House of Commons on the Monday after Mother's Day by chaining themselves to the Visitors' Galley. Two days earlier, they had left on the prime minister's doorstep a coffin symbolizing the victims of backstreet abortions. The Abortion Caravaners who disrupted Parliament recognized that they were using tactics that militant suffragists had previously used in the United States and Britain. But the Canadian movement was at the same time significantly different, even though some of its early leaders were American immigrants to Canada. For one thing, the Abortion Caravan was modelled on the On to Ottawa Trek that took place during the Great Depression. Acting explicitly in a tradition of women's activism in Canada, Winnipeg Women's Liberation turned Nellie McClung's play *Votes for Women* into a musical.[54] Feminists of the last part of the century often consciously placed themselves within the traditions of Canadian feminism, embracing leaders like Nellie McClung as heroes for the movement. Thus, in a 1988 interview, Muriel Duckworth of Voice of Women said she traced her "feminist roots" to her mother, "who read Nellie McClung," and "turned her china cabinet into a bookcase to start up a community library. . . ."[55] Before long, while recognizing the achievements of their foremothers, feminists would be critical of the way many of them shared the race, class, and heterosexist biases of their times.[56]

In Quebec, most elements of women's struggles were squarely aligned with sovereigntist politics. In 1970 the *Front pour la libération des femmes* declined an invitation to join the Abortion Caravan. The FLF was uninterested in federal politics. Its goal, it said, was to challenge the existing Quebec government and the future Quebec nation to be more responsive to women than the federal government was. Such a project made collaboration with anglophone women's liberation groups virtually impossible, even when linguistic barriers could be surmounted. In addition, relatively few young francophone women wished to join separate women's organizations that might divert energy away from a political struggle based on class as well as nationalist interests. The Marxist and nationalist feminists who were the majority in Quebec soon came to concentrate on action through the women's committees of the powerful trade union organizations and in the *Parti Québécois*.[57]

Outside Quebec, pan-Canadian nationalism was crucial to the women's movement, accounting to a large degree for the cooperation and even convergence between the supporters of women's liberation and other women activists. Anti-Americanism played a significant role, since the closest threat to Canadian national identity had always been from the United States. Within the student movement, there was increasing hostility to the American war resisters who had come to Canada expecting to lead the left. Women's liberation groups shared the concerns of the student organizations. "The problem the Canadian left faces is not the draft," stated a 1969 Toronto Women's Liberation pamphlet, "it is American imperialism."[58] Those who founded the Canadian women's liberation movement also shared with Voice of Women, as well as the surviving first-wave groups, the Canadian feminist conviction that women were better able than men to protect Canadian values. Central issues included the equal treatment of women as well as active resistance to American influence. The latter concerns led directly to the anti-globalization activism that drew many younger women to mixed-sex organizations and protest movements in the years following 1980.[59] Student- and community-based women's groups turned toward providing direct services for poor and minority women. The services they provided often focused on issues related to women's bodies and sexuality: abortion referral and counselling, rape crisis centres, and transition houses and other facilities for battered women, usually organized according to a consensual model deliberately designed as a contrast to male-style hierarchy. The motive was certainly new, for it included a political attempt to sensitize women to the abuses of the patriarchal, capitalist state. The result, which some found dismaying, was familiar—once again, women volunteers were providing social services the state neglected.

Soon, however, the undifferentiated groups that called themselves women's liberation in Canada were experiencing breaks and schisms. The majority of their members came to define themselves as "socialist feminists," to describe their focus on the ways in which capitalism and patriarchy were mutually reinforcing as systems of oppression for women. A key slogan was "A socialist who is not a feminist lacks breadth. A feminist who is not a socialist lacks strategy."[60] Saskatoon Women's Liberation seems to have been the first to define itself as socialist-feminist, in the late 1960s; it was to survive until 1981. Socialist-feminist groups including Bread and Roses of Vancouver and the International Women's Day Committee in Toronto now became a significant element of the women's movement in English Canada. Attention to women in the industrial labour force produced an emphasis on workplace activism, including attempts to start women's or feminist unions. Socialist feminists also devoted major attention to child care, considered necessary to facilitate women's paid labour; cooperative daycare centres were among their earliest projects in both Vancouver and Toronto.[61]

Other women opted for a feminism that considered gender rather than class structures to be central to women's oppression. Those who identified themselves as "radical feminists" chose "to concentrate exclusively on the oppression of women as women and not as workers, students, etc."[62] Bonnie Kreps, who had been active in radical feminism in New York, appears to have started the first radical-feminist group in Canada: Toronto's New Feminists. In 1969 she walked out of a Toronto Women's Liberation meeting that refused to accept that "women were oppressed in the household."[63] She was followed or later joined by women who were likely to be somewhat older than the liberationists. Female faculty members or faculty wives, or sometimes professional women, they felt uncomfortable with both the youth and the Marxist orthodoxy of women's liberation. Radical feminism did not grow out of any existing form of mainstream theory; its relationship to the other sorts of feminism became a major theoretical problem for feminists.[64]

For radical feminists an early goal was the obliteration of gender roles as a basis of oppression. This logic produced efforts to get permission for girls to wear jeans instead of skirts to school, as well as major attention to sex-role stereotyping in literature and teaching materials. Over time, radical feminists moved to a focus on the importance of women's specific unique experience and values. If patriarchy was the oppressor, as embodied in men's attitudes and behaviour, it was reasonable to conclude that female values and practices were preferable. Such feminists tended to be unconventional, explicitly theoretical, and insistent on consciousness-raising. For them, the personal and the political were particularly closely connected, and some women moved from radical feminism to personal or political lesbianism and separatism. Such characteristics made them very different from non-liberationist women's groups, while their rejection of class analysis separated them from descendants of the original women's liberation movement. Toronto New Feminists voluntarily dissolved in 1973, agreeing that their raised consciousness ought now to be applied in their daily work, which was mainly in academic and artistic circles. Other radical-feminist groups seem to have existed in Sarnia, Oshawa, and Saskatchewan; as well, one anglophone group in Montreal, the Feminist Communication Collective, issued a newsletter aimed primarily at immigrant women.[65]

In Quebec, women's liberation produced a succession of small autonomous action groups and a series of feminist newspapers, best described as radical-feminist. Several of these publications were widely read and influential in spite of their short life spans. Best known were *Québécoises deboutte!* and *Les têtes de pioche* (March 1976–June 1979), the latter a project of experimental writers who included the well-known author Nicole Brossard. *Pluri-elles* was founded in 1977 in an attempt to coordinate the many small feminist groups; it was soon renamed *Des luttes et des rires des femmes*. The successive names suggest their creators' movement toward pluralism, greater diversity, and mutual tolerance. English-language feminist groups also produced a proliferation of movement publications that were more in the nature of newsletters or broadsides, mostly socialist-feminist, less visible outside the movement than the radical-feminist francophone material. A number of more substantial feminist publications in English, such as *Broadside,* emerged in the late 1970s and 1980s; most were short-lived, but *Herizons*, after a hiatus, survived into the twenty-first century. In the same period, presses such as gynergy press in Charlottetown and Press Gang, SisterVision, and The Women's Press in Toronto provided a less ephemeral form of publication, an outlet for the growing flowering of literature by women. Of these early feminist presses, only Montreal's *Editions du remue-ménage* (founded in 1975) was still publishing in 2009, though the feminist publishing mission was continued then by Sumach and Green Dragon presses as well as two others housed at York University—Inanna and Demeter.[66] Other expressions of radical feminism continued in the twenty-first century. In Montreal, the group called *Les Sorcières*, started in 2000, was still in existence in 2009, as were *les Cyprines*, *les Féministes radicales de l'UQAM* (FRU), and *Némésis*.[67]

Nation-wide, the influence of radical feminism can, in general terms, be traced in groups organized around women's specific experience and values. Women Against Violence Against Women (WAVAW), which started in Canada in 1977 to carry out "spontaneous street action," had a clearly radical-feminist orientation. Its member groups, including especially active ones in British Columbia, protested snuff movies, sadistic pornography for which the women being filmed were beaten, tortured, or even murdered. Vancouver WAVAW started a rape crisis centre in 1982. The activities of WAVAW included Take Back the Night marches, beginning in 1981, calling for streets safe from violence against women. Such marches continued to be frequent, especially in large urban centres but also in smaller towns, such as Prince Rupert, B.C. Many organizers, over the years, respectfully asked men and boys not to participate in the march because it was felt to make a far more powerful statement for women to be marching through the streets at night without any men to protect them. Other marches, such as the 2008 march in Edmonton, chose to include men as allies. Similarly inspired marches focused on the approximately 500 Aboriginal women murdered or missing since the first such death was recorded in 1991 in Victoria, B.C. Thus, on February 14, 2008, university students and student groups from the University of Victoria and Camosun College organized their eighteenth march, now called the Stolen Sisters Memorial March, one of many such marches organized in Winnipeg, Toronto, Calgary, Edmonton, Thunder Bay, London, Sudbury, and Vancouver. In the fall of 2009, 70 rallies demanding action on violence against native women were planned in 68 cities.[68]

The newer versions of feminism had a major impact on women's studies as the field developed in Canada, beginning in the late 1960s and early 1970s. Many of the first generation of instructors were women's movement activists who brought their theoretical perspectives with them. Socialist feminists and their analysis of women's paid and unpaid work played a strong role. Thus, an important paper originating in the discussions of the socialist-feminist Vancouver Women's Caucus and written by Margaret Benston in 1969 identified housework as a significant category of labour. From this beginning, Canadian socialist-feminist analysts developed interpretations of reproductive labour as a parallel to productive labour. Sociologist Dorothy Smith's critiques of conventional social science attracted international attention, especially her argument that the everyday world was the best starting point for theorizing about women's lives. Radical-feminist theorist Mary O'Brien, a former midwife who came to university late in life, coined the term "malestream" to highlight the androcentricity—the focus on men and masculinity—of mainstream political philosophy.[69] More widely, the radical-feminist emphasis on women's difference or specificity served as an intellectual justification for study and research focusing on women. By the 1980s, the academic field of women's

A 2008 badge showing support for Aboriginal women who had disappeared and had been murdered.

Copyright: Amnesty International Canada. "No More Stolen Sisters" button created for annual Sisters in Spirit vigils calling for an end to violence against Indigenous women and girls in Canada.

studies was well established in a large number of Canadian universities, supported by three journals—*Atlantis, Canadian Woman Studies/Les cahiers de la femme, Resources for Feminist Research/Documentation sur la recherche féministe*—and by five regional women's studies chairs endowed by the Department of the Secretary of State.

Integrating women's experiences and perceptions into existing academic disciplines proved to be a painfully slow process. For faculty members—mostly male—who were already ensconced in the university, women's studies' insights were unpersuasive and its (female) instructors threatening. Alison Prentice, a pioneer in women's history, recalled that in 1973 she had difficulty proving at her comprehensive examinations for her doctorate in history that "women are a social class": ". . . I was angry. Sweeping an accusing hand around the room, I said what was obvious at least to me: '*You* are all men. . . . Down the hall the secretaries are all women. Are you trying to tell me that women aren't a social class?'" The men were not convinced, but concluded that she "clearly had a bad day;" they passed her. Prentice also recorded unwelcoming male responses that were less academic, "arising from the mere fact of being with other women faculty":

> The most disturbing challenge happened when five women instructors at York University's Atkinson College, who met once a month for lunch, were sitting together in the far corner of the otherwise empty faculty lounge. "Aha," crowed the dean as he looked in the door. "If I shot all of you, that would finish the women's movement at Atkinson, wouldn't it?"[70]

The field of women's studies became less popular with undergraduate students in the new century; although graduate programs continued to draw large numbers of enrollments, some undergraduate programs contracted or closed. Responding to concerns, including the newer notions of the fluidity of gender identities, some programs and departments changed the politically militant title of Women's Studies to titles such as

Gender and Women's Studies or even simply Gender Studies.[71] Although it was feminist theorists who had directed attention to the social construction of gender, surviving radical feminists were not happy with this shift away from a focus on women's social and political position.

Finally, radical feminism was influential in the development of feminist separatism in Canada, both in its cultural dimensions and in the form of radical lesbianism or lesbian separatism. Radical-feminist attention to male dominance encouraged the analysis of heterosexism and of lesbians' situation in a society dominated by heterosexual values. Many lesbians, including lesbian feminists, started their associational lives in women's groups or feminist organizations, or in mixed-sex gay ones. Over the years, the same processes as led women to form their own organizations produced explicitly lesbian social or service organizations as well as lesbian-feminist groups. Such organizations tended, however, to be short-lived. The earliest recorded, Gay Sisters in Vancouver, existed only briefly from 1971. Under the auspices of the YWCA, the first national lesbian conference was held in Toronto in 1973 and, shortly afterward, members of the group Montreal Gay Women (later called Labyris) started *Long Time Coming*, the first lesbian newsletter in Canada (1973–1976). Many lesbian groups were primarily social, though some of these also ran lesbian phone lines. Most were to be found in urban centres, such as the Lesbian Organization of Southern Saskatchewan, based in Regina and featuring alcohol-free events (1983 to the mid-1990s). Other lesbian groups combined functions; the collective *coop-femmes* that was started in Montreal in February 1977 established a social centre for francophone lesbians, held arts and music events, and also engaged in some political action on issues relating to abortion and child care. More centrally activist and political groups included Wages Due Lesbians, founded in Toronto in 1974, which sought to get wages for caring work in order to enable women's choices, including about sexual orientation; later in 1974 it became a national Lesbian Mothers' Defense Fund that for some 10 years supported women threatened with loss of child custody because of their sexual orientation.[72] One atypically long-lived group was Edmonton's Womonspace, founded in 1981 to provide "a strong and supportive lesbian presence in the community;" in July 2009 it was able to boast that it was "financially viable" though run entirely by volunteers.[73]

In Canada, the different sorts of women's organizations managed to cooperate on specific projects, in spite of their different ideological perspectives. Voice of Women's orientation toward maternity—as reflected, for example, in its continuing campaigns against war toys—aligned VOW with radical feminists in the effort to eliminate the consequences of sex-role stereotyping. Socialist-feminist interest in the economic dimension of domestic labour was an additional basis of possible agreement among women's groups, for the household, central for traditional women's organizations, was also crucial to the analyses made by radical feminists. The result was often joint action on specific issues, however much socialist-feminist theory condemned the concept of "sisterhood" as apolitical and inimical to class analysis.[74] In the 1970s, campaigns to include "sex," "sexual harassment," and "sexual preference" in human rights codes mobilized groups ranging from women's auxiliaries of the industrial unions to the most extreme radical feminists. A similar spectrum of groups protested sexism in advertising, in textbooks, and in the media more generally. Persistent coalitions responded to the violence and hostility to women expressed in widely distributed, sadistic, hard-core pornography.

Reproductive choice as symbolized by access to abortion was a key issue that generated joint action among women in Canada, including many who had found the rhetoric of the women's liberation movement daunting. "Here was something I could support unequivocally," wrote Cerise Morris, a student at that time. "The right of a woman to legal abortion affects me personally—affects women of all classes and political beliefs."[75] Before the Royal Commission on the Status of Women reported, its relatively liberal recommendations were pre-empted by the 1969 revisions of the Criminal Code. The new regulations permitted abortions but only when performed by a doctor in an accredited hospital under specified conditions that could add up to a tortuous and lengthy process. Among these requirements was certification by a three-doctor therapeutic abortion committee (TAC) that continuation of the pregnancy would threaten the life or health of the mother; the pregnant woman was not allowed to appear before the TAC to present her own case. The 1969 reforms disappointed many, and women and sympathetic men mobilized across Canada in a lengthy struggle to make abortion legal. Much of the activity focused around the figure of Dr. Henry Morgentaler, a Holocaust survivor who defined himself as a humanist and became the chief symbol of the

A pro-choice march in Montreal in 1979. The banner announces sponsorship by the national (Quebec) coalition for unrestricted abortion.

Source: Courtesy of Claudine Kurtzman

pro-choice movement. Morgentaler performed abortions in defiance of the law, announcing that he was carrying on legitimate acts of civil disobedience. Although he was repeatedly arrested and brought to trial, three Quebec juries and one in Ontario refused to find him guilty.[76]

Beginning in 1974, CARAL (initially the Canadian Association for the Repeal of the Abortion Laws and then the Canadian Abortion Rights Action League) led a coalition that also included more radical groups, such as the British Columbia and Ontario Coalitions for Abortion Clinics. In 1971 proactive groups opposing the right to abortion became publicly visible under the rubric of pro-life in response to pro-choice activities; that year saw the first of what would become annual demonstrations in Ottawa calling for an end to all abortions. A different approach was taken by the pregnancy crisis service, Birthright, which was started in 1968 in Toronto by a Catholic laywoman, Louise Summerhill, to provide support for unmarried mothers. The world's first such service, it eventually comprised more than 600 centres in Canada, the United States, South Africa, and Colombia. Birthright consistently refused any sort of active opposition to abortion.[77] But other activists, supported by the Catholic Church as well as by fundamentalist and right-wing organizations, systematically picketed the abortion clinics that Morgentaler established, first in Ontario and Manitoba, harassing both the staff and the women who came to have abortions.

The Canadian Charter of Rights and Freedoms made it possible, on January 28, 1988, for the Supreme Court to strike down the federal law on abortion as unconstitutional, although its decision did not draw on the equality provisions of the Charter. The judges found that the law interfered with women's security of person, a right guaranteed by the Charter. The Court's first woman justice, Bertha Wilson went further, characterizing the Criminal Code provisions on abortion as "forcing a woman, under threat of criminal sanction, to carry a foetus to term unless she meets certain criteria unrelated to her own priorities and aspirations. . . ."[78] Even Madam Justice Wilson, however, agreed that it would be acceptable for the state to legislate about abortion in order to restrict terminations at an advanced stage of pregnancy.[79] A compromise bill for recriminalization that satisfied no one was finally defeated by a tie vote in the Senate on January 31, 1991. Women senators voted as a bloc against the measure; Mira Spivak, a Conservative senator, was quoted as saying, "It's a step forward for women in being able to control their own destiny and choose what to do with their bodies."[80]

Groups opposed to abortion continued their attack. Morgentaler's Toronto clinic, which had been bombed and partly destroyed in 1983, was completely burned down in 1992; in November 1994 a Vancouver doctor who performed abortions was shot and seriously injured while he was eating breakfast in his kitchen; and early in 1995, after receiving death threats, two of the four doctors who were performing abortions at the Victoria General Hospital decided to stop providing the service. Other Canadian doctors providing abortion were subsequently threatened or wounded, but without significantly reducing the availability of the service.[81]

After the 1988 Supreme Court decision, the issues of costs and more generally of access became central. Abortion was now basically a provincial matter, but with a federal interest that could be enforced through the central government's role in the national system of health insurance. From 1995 on, the federal government required all provinces to pay the costs of abortions in hospitals, although in Prince Edward Island it had to be in a hospital outside of the province and New Brunswick set extremely restrictive conditions. Most provinces also arranged to fund abortions in clinics, which now were agreed to be safer and less expensive, but in 2009 there were no clinics in Prince Edward Island, Nova Scotia, Saskatchewan, or the territories. In 2008 Dr. Morgentaler was given permission by the provincial justice system to sue the province of New Brunswick for denying repayment of the approximately $750 cost of an abortion in his clinic there.[82]

Although not as central or polarizing an issue as in the United States, abortion continued to provoke strong feelings in Canada. Canadians generally accepted women's right to choose abortions. By 1992, according to a nation-wide poll, 79 percent of those surveyed agreed that "an abortion is a medical decision that should rest with the woman in consultation with her physician." In a 2008 survey 49 percent of respondents agreed that abortion should be legal under any circumstances. Though most of the other respondents wanted to set some conditions, such as limiting when in a pregnancy the procedure should be allowed, by this time only 5 percent wished to make it illegal again. It was clear, though, that there was some reluctance to provide public funding for abortions not seen as "medically required." In practice, government and medical practice now defined medical necessity very broadly.[83] What was described as a "secretive, parliamentary anti-abortion caucus" still existed in 2009, and sporadically produced Private Member's bills that were designed to limit access to abortion.[84] They were provoked by the fact that Canada was one of the very few countries in the world that placed no legislated restrictions on abortions.

THE WOMEN'S MOVEMENT: GENDER PLUS

Many women who came together for joint action in the last years of the twentieth century rejected identification with feminism or with the women's movement, but their actions often contradicted their words. "I'm not a feminist," they would say, "but . . ." And then they would go on to say that women should get equal pay, or be treated fairly, or simply be listened to. Women's caucuses or committees attached to mixed-sex institutions such as unions and churches represented one form of collective action. Such groups multiplied in the 1970s and 1980s, as did a new generation of separate women's organizations; the process continued into the 1990s, with more groups focused on multiple identity, particularly women's various racial, religious, and ethnic affiliations. The recently mobilized members of these organizations were often newly militant, but they continued long-established traditions of women organizing within and for those communities marginalized by Canada's white, European, and Christian mainstream populations. By contrast to earlier women's groups, the newer ones tended to be more unstructured—abjuring the formal machinery of constitution and by-laws—and more focused on relatively narrow and specific goals.

Among the earliest to mobilize were Aboriginal women. Among the Haudenosaunee, women justified their right to participate in policymaking on the basis of "the matriarchal roots of the Six Nations Iroquois Confederacy."[85] But their impetus for collective action was usually related to the everyday situations that they encountered. A Maliseet of the Tobique Reserve in New Brunswick, Caroline Ennis, explained how many Indian women got started in political activism:

> When I got involved in the demonstrations and lobbying, it wasn't for the non-status thing; it was purely a women's thing—because of the kinds of things they were doing to women like my mother—to women like Yvonne who used to get beat up by her husband all the time.[86]

Native women organized to deal concretely with problems, including violence, disease, abuse of alcohol and drugs. They began to challenge the assimilationist systems of education and welfare that had shipped children off to residential schools or placed them for adoption with white families and condemned tuberculosis patients to long hospital stays away from home. "Aboriginal women must provide the direction that encourages the Nation's warriors to respond as is appropriate to protect our children," stated the Ontario Native Women's Association, founded in 1971 in Thunder Bay.[87] In 1974, 13 Aboriginal women's groups came together to form the Native Women's Association of Canada (NWAC), and in 2009, Pauktuutit, the very active Inuit women's organization, celebrated 25 years "of advocacy and succcess.[88]

These women's groups did not draw the support of all of the women in their communities, however. As Aboriginal women attempted to assert their claims, they sometimes feared that it was a betrayal of cultural autonomy to appeal to white women, white women's organizations, and the white man's government over the heads of their own leaders. Consequently, some of them chose to act within the existing male-dominated Aboriginal organizations even in respect to women's issues. Concern about the identity and survival of their people even led some to oppose not just inter-racial marriage but also birth control and abortion.

An issue of both symbolic and practical importance even for those women it did not affect directly was Section 12(1)(b) of the Indian Act. This provision gave Indian status to all wives of status Indians and their children but took it away from status Indian women and their children if the women married non-status men. Some Indian women's organizations simply supported the men's groups that, unwilling to revise the Indian Act, successfully appealed a Federal Court of Appeal decision that would have restored Indian status to Jeannette Corbiere Lavell of the Wikwemikong Band in Ontario. Others argued persuasively that sexist components of the Indian Act came from white legislators who were attempting to assimilate the Indian population, rather than from Indian men. In 1973 the Supreme Court of Canada confirmed that Lavell had forfeited her status by marrying a non-Indian; the same decision was given in the case of Yvonne Bedard of the Six Nations Reserve. The Court found that Indian women were entitled only to "equality in administration and enforcement of the law." The Bill of Rights enacted in 1960 did not forbid "inequality within a group or class by itself, by reason of sex."[89]

With the court route blocked, Indian women who had lost their status turned to lobbying, sit-ins, and appeals to international organizations. They were supported in

Métis Elder Edith McLeod and Jeannette Corbiere Lavell at a demonstration in support of Aboriginal women's rights after the Supreme Court decision of 1973.

Source: Archives and Special Collections, University of Ottawa (P-X10-1-1282) / photographer unknown

these endeavours by a number of women's groups, including NAC and VOW. The most widely publicized case was that of Sandra Lovelace, a Maliseet of the Tobique Reserve in New Brunswick, who finally took her case to the Human Rights Committee of the United Nations. Lovelace's action generated substantial publicity for the cause of Indian women; in 2005 she was named a senator. Additional publicity and public pressure were generated when the Tobique women's group organized a 100-mile walk of women and children from the Oka Reserve, near Montreal, to Ottawa in July 1979. In 1981 the United Nations committee found Canada in breach of the International Covenant on Civil and Political Rights. The federal government, reluctant to provoke the hostility of male Indian leaders, professed itself helpless. Indian status had significant economic and political implications; along with the right to free medical treatment and free education, status made possible a share in what were sometimes substantial resources, as well as a voice in First Nations self-government.[90]

It was not until 1985 that the discriminatory clauses of the Indian Act were revised, restoring Indian status to those women who had lost it by marrying out, as well as granting it to their children. However, Bill C-31 separated Indian status from the band membership that was a precondition for residence on reserve, a distinction that created difficulties for some of those reinstated women and children who wished to live on reserves but could still be barred by band regulations. An additional, new grievance was the so-called second generation cut-off, which meant that the reinstated children could not pass on their status as other status Indians could. Jeannette Lavell's own family constituted an example of what could happen under Bill C-31, even when band councils were supportive. Lavell's daughter Meemee and her son Nimke had their Indian status restored with their mother's. Each had a child whose other parent was a status Indian. Each also had a child whose other parent did not have Indian status. The result:

> My daughter has two daughters, Autumn Sky and Eva. Only Autumn Sky has status; her sister does not. My grandson, Neeganwhedung, has full status, but Nimke's daughter Kyana has no status. . . . Autumn Sky and Neeganwhedung are both members of Wikwemikong, while their siblings, living under the same roof, are not.[91]

In 2007 Sharon McIvor, a leader of NWAC, was successful in her attempt to show that, under 1985's Bill C-31, women were still discriminated against. If women had lost Indian status, even when it was restored, their grandchildren were treated differently than the grandchildren of male status Indians. Such discrimination extended backward historically to the establishment of the Indian Act's gender-linked definitions of status. In 2009, the B.C. Court of Appeal gave the government one year to come up with a new, non-discriminatory definition of status Indians. Bill C-31 had added approximately 175 000 people to the Indian register and produced a flood of women and children wishing to be housed on reserves often ill-prepared to sustain the accompanying costs. Nevertheless, acting rather differently than in the past, the Assembly of First Nations (AFN) supported the McIvor case, including its allegations of discrimination based on gender. With probably more than half of all children of status Indians having non-Indian parents, the second-generation cut-off was likely soon to reduce the Indian population seriously, threatening extinction of some groups. The government responded that NWAC as well as the AFN would be involved in the process of developing new regulations.[92]

Aboriginal women's rights continued to be entangled in the problem of whether the federal government or the various Aboriginal organizations, including NWAC, should design regulations for the different First Nations. Arrangements about matrimonial real property for women when relationships ended by death or divorce had been legislated for non-Aboriginal women by the provinces, but the issue had been neglected for Aboriginal women, who were subject to federal jurisdiction. In 2008, after inconclusive consultations with NWAC and the AFN, the Conservative government tabled a bill settling the situation in a way that disregarded Aboriginal preferences and would have undercut traditional practices related to both divorce and communal ownership of property. After this bill died on the order paper, it was reintroduced in February 2009 in spite of vigorous Aboriginal protests, including those of NWAC. The bill was reintroduced again in May of the same year but died on the order paper when Parliament was prorogued in December.[93]

For many other women's groups as well, the revival of feminism meant a new movement toward nationwide, coordinated action. In 1971, television actor and host Kay Livingstone led the revitalisation of the 20-year-old Canadian Negro Women's Club as an Association (CANEWC/CANEWA). In 1971 CANEWA drew together the many black women's organizations across the country. Two years later, under the presidency of Aileen Williams, the groups were ready to organize the first national Conference of

Black Women. After seven annual meetings, they established the Canadian Congress of Black Women "to provide a network of solidarity for Black Women in Canada, and to be a united voice in the defence and extension of human rights and liberties for Blacks in Canada." Projects carried on by the national and local sections of the Congress included research on health issues and the establishment of health support groups in relation to those diseases particularly affecting black women and their families. By 1994, they were actively involved in overtly political activities, such as the support of black women against police harassment. The National Congress of Black Women Foundation was set up as a charitable institution, explicitly including all immigrants of African origin in its mandate; its Umoja Society in British Columbia stated in 2007 that it "stood as Canada's African-Caribbean-Canadian organization working to address the needs of people living with and at risk of HIV/AIDS and/or Hepatitis C."[94]

Ethnic identification combined with shared needs also generated many new women's groups in an increasingly multicultural nation. The immediate problems of women in their communities often included issues that had been specific to women in their countries of origin. For example, the India Mahila Association (IMA), founded by three women in Vancouver in 1973 shortly after South Asian women began to arrive on the west coast in large numbers, started with orientation services for new women immigrants. By the late 1970s, the group had become publicly visible around the issue of violence toward women. Then the problem of what has been labelled "feticide" emerged in Canada as it had in India. When an American doctor targeted South Asian community newspapers to advertise a service for determining the sex of fetuses, often the first step to abortion of a female, IMA led protests. In the 1980s, the group recruited a younger generation of South Asian women who had some involvement with the broader women's movement. IMA was still active some 20 years later, still on a volunteer basis, operating out of members' houses. Similarly, issues connected to their homeland were among the motivations in 1973 for founding the Rally of Haitian Women in Montreal (RAFA); this was one of the groups that participated in the first congress of black women in Canada. RAFA was established to provide services for women in Montreal's large Haitian community but also to testify and work against the brutally repressive Duvalier regime in Haiti; in 1979, it became *Neges Vanyan* (Valiant Women). With regime change in Haiti in 1986, many of these activists returned to promote new feminist groups there.[95]

The political tensions of the twenty-first century made the Canadian Council of Muslim Women (CCMW) a conspicuous participant in public debates; it had been organized at the early date of 1982. Its mandate was articulated in the first issue of the CCMW newsletter: the group would focus on "the special needs, concerns, interests, talents, successes and frustrations of Canadian Muslim women," and they would hope to work with other women's groups. CCMW founders included granddaughters of the women who had made possible the historic Al Rashid Mosque in Edmonton, and they were the centre of the coalition that saved the mosque when it was threatened with demolition in 1988. The group's goals expanded over the years. Like so many other women's organizations, in 2000 the CCMW highlighted young women. In the same year, founder and first president Lila Fahlman was appointed chaplain for the Muslim students at the University of Alberta. In 2005–2006, the group was able to prepare a needs assessment based on a survey of Muslim women and a series of focus groups, and to prepare a report directed at increasing the integration of Muslim women into Canadian society. The CCMW was particularly concerned with a tendency toward "self-imposed segregation" of Muslim women, and the acceptance of the situation by some parts of Muslim society in Canada.[96]

As always, most new women's groups began when a small number of women who shared an identity felt the need for joint action on immediate, shared problems. Wives of members of the Canadian military came together, claiming the right to meet and discuss their needs, a right denied under the blanket prohibition of political activity on armed forces property. Such groups tended to be absorbed into the armed forces' welfare sections, but as late as 2006 a new, apparently short-lived support group called the Military Wives Sisterhood emerged in the wake of the Afghan War.[97]

The DisAbled Women's Network (DAWN), founded in 1985, was different and distinctive, for it was not community-based. Its membership was, on the face of it, a specific, limited category of women, one often targeted by legislation, particularly employment equity legislation. At the same time, all women were potential members; as DAWN pointed out, every woman was only "temporarily able-bodied," liable to be disabled at any time by disease, injury, or old age. Surveys of DAWN's membership showed that women with disabilities found it especially difficult to get education and jobs and that they were frequently victims of sexual or other abuse. Jill Summerhayes summed up the self-image of women with disabilities: "we all felt sexually inadequate, incapable, elderly, weak, dependent at various times, more so because we thought of ourselves as less than complete."[98] Summerhayes's osteoarthritis, a common ailment that seriously reduced mobility and stamina, forced her to give up a managerial job in newspaper advertising as well as community activities connected with the Family Crisis Centre, the Cancer Society, and the United Way. From her home in Cambridge, Ontario, she generated a very successful business, making and marketing fashion canes for women with disabilities like hers. In 2009, the national organization of women with disabilities had its headquarters in Montreal and the bilingual name of DAWN-RAFH Canada (*Réseau d'action des femmes handicapées du Canada*). It was engaged in the second stage of an ambitious survey of the state of access and accommodations in transition houses for "disAbled women."[99]

The groups formed in the 1970s and 1980s often initially benefitted from government encouragement and funding. In many cases they endured into the twenty-first century even when public funding was reduced and then entirely eliminated for those groups that were engaged in advocacy, as most were. Such was the case with the National Organization of Immigrant and Visible Minority Women of Canada (NOIVMWC), founded in 1986 to coordinate and voice the concerns of the approximately 500 "world majority" women's groups that existed by that time. It succeeded in establishing links among a large number of groups, despite doubts about whether immigrant women shared the perspectives of women of colour from long-established ethnic communities in Canada. In 2009 the organization concluded its "Livelihood Project," that included designing and delivering training for leadership for women in the immigrant and black communities.[100]

The end of the twentieth century was not an easy time for women activists. Many women who attempted to move beyond the perspective of their own situation found

Bonnie Sherr Klein, filmmaker and disability activist, receiving an honorary degree, 2000.

Source: © Ryerson University. Reproduced with the permission of Ryerson University. nlc-8971

themselves accused of taking over the products and messages of those they attempted to help, while "help" itself was seen as condescension. One early example was Anne Cameron, whose 1981 book *Daughters of Copper Woman* played a major role in making white women aware of the rich tradition of the Aboriginal women of Canada. Cameron had lived for many years in Haida communities, where women elders had given her permission to publish the creation legends they controlled. Her children, whose father was Métis, were accepted as First Nation members. She was nevertheless criticized for appropriating the voice of Indian women and for using her resources as a white woman to publish material that Aboriginal women could not get into print. "The guys in suits are hoping that we will divide so they can once again conquer," she responded in 1990. She pleaded for communication and cooperation among women for the sake of the tasks that still faced them, appealing eloquently to a tradition that she traced to diverse foremothers:

> We promised if ever the time came when The Grandmother, the Earth, needed us, the Children of her daughter First Woman, who became First Mother, would come together again and learn to live as a Rainbow Family, in love and in balance.

> "I think that's what feminism is," she said. "The coming together of all the colours of sisters and cousins."[101]

Notes

1. Verta Taylor and Leila J. Rupp, "Preface," in Sandra Grey and Marian Sawer, ed., *Women's Movements: Flourishing or in Abeyance?* (London: Routledge, 2008), xii–xvi; Karen Offen, "'Eruptions and Flows': Thoughts on Writing a Comparative History of European Feminisms, 1700–1950," in Anne Cova, ed., *Comparative Women's History: New Approaches* (New York: Columbia University Press, 2006), 55–57.

2. Barbara Roberts, "Women's Peace Activism in Canada," in Linda Kealey and Joan Sangster, eds., *Beyond the Vote: Canadian Women and Politics* (Toronto: University of Toronto Press, 1989), 196.

3. Kay Macpherson with C. M. Donald, *When in Doubt Do Both: The Times of My Life* (Toronto: University of Toronto Press, 1994), 89–90, 101.

4. Christine Ball, "The History of the Voice of Women/*La voix des femmes*: The Early Years," University of Toronto, Ph.D. Dissertation, 1994; Michèle Jean, "Idola Saint-Jean, Féministe" (1880–1945)" in Pol Pelletier, ed., *Mon héroïne* (Montréal: Éditions du remue-ménage, 1981), 119.

5. Thérèse F. Casgrain, *A Woman in a Man's World*, translated by Joyce Marshall (Toronto: McClelland and Stewart, 1972), 166–67; Macpherson, 106–8.

6. Muriel Duckworth, "Voice of Women Dialogue," *Atlantis* 6, 2 (Spring 1981): 172.

7. Kay Macpherson and Meg Sears, "The Voice of Women: A History," in Gwen Matheson, ed., *Women in the Canadian Mosaic* (Toronto: Peter Martin Associates, 1976), 71–89; Keith Louise Fulton and Ann Manicom, ed., "Peace Work in Process," *Atlantis* 24, 1 (Fall/winter 1999): 71–78; Frances Early, "'A Grandly Subversive Time': The Halifax Branch of the Voice of Women in the 1960s," in Judith Fingard and Janet Guildford, ed., *Mothers of the Municipality. Women, Work, and Social Policy in Post-1945 Halifax* (Toronto: University of Toronto Press, 2005), 253–80.

8. Sylvia Bashevkin, *Tales of Two Cities. Women and Municipal Restructuring in London and Toronto* (Vancouver: UBC Press, 2006), 34; Mary Eberts. "'Write It For the Women' Doris Anderson, the Changemaker," *Canadian Woman Studies/Les cahiers de la femme* 26, 2 (Summer/fall 2007): 7; Lisa Young, "The Canadian Women's Movement and Political Parties, 1970–1993"; Manon Tremblay and Caroline Andrew, eds., *Women and Political Representation in Canada* (Ottawa: University of Ottawa Press, 1998), 197–98, 201–2; Rosemary Speirs, "Presentation to Equal Voice's Annual General Meeting, Nov. 08."

9. Amanda Reaume, "Changing the Face of Politics: An Interview with Rosemary Speirs," *Antigone* magazine, Issue 4 (n.d.), 14, http://www.equalvoice.ca/.

10. Valerie J. Korinek, *Roughing It in the Suburbs: Reading Chatelaine Magazine in the Fifties and Sixties* (Toronto: University of Toronto Press, 2000), 26.

11. Rona Maynard, *My Mother's Daughter. A Memoir* (Toronto: McClelland & Stewart, 2007), 234.

12. Korinek, 331.

13. Korinek, 97–98.

14. Micheline Dumont-Johnson, "La parole des femmes: Les revues féminines, 1938–68," in Fernand Dumont, Jean Hamelin, et Jean-Paul Montmigny, eds., *Idéologies au Canada français, 1940–1967* (Québec: Presses de l'Université Laval, 1981) vol. 2, 5–45; Gertrude Joch Robinson, "The Media and Social Change: Thirty Years of Magazine Coverage of Women and Work (1950–1977)," *Atlantis* 8, 2 (Spring 1983): 87–111.

15. Maynard, 235.

16. Patricia Carey, "The Personal Is Political," *Canadian Women's Studies/Les cahiers de la femme* 2, 2 (1980) : 6.

17. Cécile Coderre, "La Fédération des femmes du Québec. Fille cadette de Thérèse Casgrain?" in Anita Caron et Lorraine Archambault, ed., *Thérèse Casgrain: Une femme tenace et engagée* (Québec: Presses de l'Université du Québec, 1993), 68, 69; Le Collectif Clio, *L'histoire des femmes au Québec depuis quatre siècles,* 2nd ed. (Québec: Le Jour éditeur, 1992), 464–67.

18. Azilda Marchand, "Les femmes au foyer: Hier et demain," *Canadian Women's Studies/Les cahiers de la femme* 2, 2 (1980): 46–48; Yolande Bédard, "Quand le coeur et la tête des collaboratrices sont en affaires," in Voice of Women, Canada, and Women for a Meaningful International Summit, *First World Summit:"Women and the Many Dimensions of Power,"* Report of a conference to celebrate the 50th anniversary of women's right to vote in Quebec (held in Quebec, June 3–8, 1990), 34–37; Jocelyne Lamoureux, Michèle Gélinas, et Katy Tari, *Femmes en mouvement: Trajectoires de l'Association féminine d'éducation et d'action sociale, 1966–1991* (Montréal: Boréal Express, 1993), 88–90; L'Association féminine d'éducation et d'action sociale, "L'AFEAS: Qui sommes-nous?" http://www.afeas.qc.ca/qui-sommes-nous/.

19. Naomi Black and Gail Brandt, *Feminist Politics on the Farm: Rural Catholic Women in Southern Quebec and Southwestern France* (Montreal and Kingston: McGill-Queen's University Press, 1999), 30; "Les CFQ en action" (1998–2009), http://www.cfq.qc.ca/a_propos_des_cfq/les_cfq_en_action/.

20. Joanne Arnott, "Dances With Cougar: Learning from Traditional Parenting Skills Programs," in D. Meemee Lavell-Harvard and Jeannette Corbiere Lavell, eds., *"Until Our Hearts Are On the Ground": Aboriginal Mothering, Oppression, Resistance and Rebirth* (Toronto: Demeter Press, 2006), 94–104; Indian Homemakers' Association of B.C., "Description," http://vancouvercommunity.net/multicultural/140.html; Janet Silman (as told to), *Enough is Enough: Aboriginal Women Speak Out* (Toronto: The Women's Press, 1987), chapters 5 and 6, "Lobbying" and "Retrospective," 223–48.

21. Lorna R. Marsden and Joan E. Busby, "Feminist Influence through the Senate: The Case of Divorce, 1967," *Atlantis* 14, 1 (Spring 1989), espec. 79, n. 2.

22. *Chatelaine* 39, 7 (July 1966); Cerise Morris, "'No More Than Simple Justice': The Royal Commission on the Status of Women and Social Change in Canada," McGill University, Ph.D. Thesis, 1982, 114.

23. Laura Sabia, "'You Are Not One of Us': The Roots of My Militant Feminism," *Canadian Woman Studies/Les cahiers de la femme* 8, 2 (Summer 1987): 36, 32.

24. Sylvia Fraser, "Laura Sabia: Not Exactly Mom and Apple Pie," *Chatelaine* 48, 11 (November 1975): 100; "How Laura Built a Lobby," *Saturday Night* 90, 6 (September 1978): 4; Judy LaMarsh, *Memoirs of a Bird in a Gilded Cage* (Toronto: McClelland and Stewart, 1969), 316.

25. Sinclair Stewart, "That Was Intense," Report on Business, *The Globe and Mail* (November 2007), 57.

26. Cerise Morris, "'Determination and Thoroughness': The Movement for the Royal Commission on the Status of Women in Canada," *Atlantis* 5, 2 (Spring 1980): 1–21; Penney Kome, *Women of Influence: Canadian Women and Politics* (Toronto: Doubleday, 1985), 76–87. The brief was presented by Sabia, Laberge-Colas, Margaret Hyndman for the Canadian Federation of Business and Professional Women's Clubs, Julia Schwartz for the National Council of Jewish Women of Canada, and Margaret MacLellan for the National Council of Women of Canada. Morris, "'Determination and Thoroughness,'" 121.

27. Barry Craig, "Women's March May Back Call for Rights Probe," *The Globe and Mail* (January 5, 1967), 1.

28. Michael Sabia, "Growing Up Feminist," *Chatelaine* 59, 5 (May 1986): 44; LaMarsh, 301–2.

29. Department of Labour, "Text of an Address Prepared for Delivery by Miss Sylva M. Gelber, Director, Women's Bureau, Canada Department of Labour," News Release (December 8, 1969).

30. John Terry, *Male–Female Differences in Voting Turnout and Campaign Activities, Canada and Ontario* (Ottawa: Library of Parliament, Research Branch, Political and Social Affairs Division, 1982), 4.

31. *Report of the Royal Commission on the Status of Women in Canada [RCSW]* (Ottawa: Information Canada, 1970), vii.

32. Monique Bégin, "The Royal Commission on the Status of Women: Twenty Years Later," in Constance Backhouse and David H. Flaherty, eds., *Challenging Times: The Women's Movement in Canada and the United States* (Montreal and Kingston: McGill-Queen's Press, 1992), 25; Anne Francis, "The Rights of Women," *Behind the Headlines* 10, 4 (September 1950); Florence Bird, *Anne Francis: An Autobiography* (Toronto: Clarke, Irwin, 1974); Richard I. Bourgeois-Doyle, *Her Daughter the Engineer: The Life of Elsie Gregory MacGill* (Ottawa: NCR Research Press, 2008), 236; Florence Bird, "Reminiscences of the Commission Chair," in Caroline Andrews and Sanda Rogers, eds., *Women and the Canadian States/Femmes et l'Etat Canadien* (Montreal and Kingston, McGill-Queen's University Press: 1997), 185–97.

33. Elsie Gregory MacGill, "Legalist Feminism," presentation to a conference on the Canadian Women's Movement (held at York University, September 1977), 6–7.

34. Christine Newman, "What's So Funny about the Royal Commission on the Status of Women?" *Saturday Night* 84, 1 (January 1969): 22, 24.

35. Bégin, "The Royal Commission on the Status of Women: Twenty Years Later," 29.

36. Anthony Westell, "Report Is More Explosive Than Any Terrorist's Time Bomb," *The Toronto Star* (December 8, 1970), 13.

37. Submission of the National Ad Hoc Committee on the Status of Women to the government of Canada, February 1972.

38. UNICEF, Innocenti Research Centre, *The Child Care Transition: A League Table of Early Childhood Education and Care in Economically Developed Countries,*" Report Card #8 (December 2008).

39. Susan Crean, "Introduction: Daring the Dance," in Susan Crean, ed., *Twist and Shout: A Decade of Feminist Writing* in *This Magazine* (Toronto: Second Story, 1992), ix–x; Collectif Clio, 1992, 476.

40. Ustün Reinart, "Three Major Strands in the Women's Movement in Manitoba, 1965–1985," in James Silver and Jeremy Hull, eds., *The Political Economy of Manitoba* (Regina: Canadian Plains Research Center, University of Regina, 1990), 166, n. 2.

41. Jill Vickers, Pauline Rankin, and Christine Appelle, *Politics As If Women Mattered: A Political Analysis of the National Action Committee on the Status of Women* (Toronto: University of Toronto Press, 1993).

42. Leslie A. Pal, *Interests of State: The Politics of Language, Multiculturalism, and Feminism in Canada* (Montreal and Kingston: McGill-Queen's University Press, 1993), 226; Alexandra Dobrowolsky, *The Politics of Pragmatism. Women, Representation, and Constitutionalism in Canada* (Toronto: Oxford Canada, 2000); Lisa Young and Joanna Everitt, *Advocacy Groups* (Vancouver: UBC Press, 2004), 48–55; Anne Molgat, with an addition by Joan Grant-Cummings, 1997, "'An Action That Will Not Be Allowed to Subside': NAC's First

Twenty-five Years," NAC History Project, n.d., http://nac-cca/index_e.html; Sylvia Bashevkin, *Women on the Defensive: Living Through Conservative Times* (Chicago: University of Chicago Press, 1998), 38–40; Lisa Young, "The Canadian Women's Movement and Political Parties, 1970–1993," in Manon Tremblay and Caroline Andrew, eds., *Women and Political Representation in Canada* (Ottawa: University of Ottawa Press, 1998), 196–217; Judy Rebick, *Ten Thousand Roses: The Making of a Feminist Revolution* (Toronto: Penguin Canada, 2005), espec. 179–94. Membership figures were calculated from NAC's own membership lists, subtracting groups such as male or mixed-member unions that are not women's groups and counting multiple-branch groups, such as the YWCA, only once.

43. Micheline Piché, "Les acadiennes font entendre leur voix," *La gazette des femmes* 16, 1 (mai/juin 1994): 24.

44. Laura Sabia, "Liberation from the Women's Movement," *Toronto Sun* (July 7, 1976), 43.

45. For Ontario, Jonathan Malloy, *Between Colliding Worlds: The Ambiguous Existence of Government Agencies for Aboriginal and Women's Policy* (Toronto: University of Toronto Press, 2003), 191, n. 7; for Alberta, Lois Harder, *State of Struggle: Feminism and Politics in Alberta* (Edmonton: University of Alberta Press, 2003), 66–67; for Nova Scotia, Janet Guildford, "A Fragile Independence: The Nova Scotia Advisory Council on the Status of Women," in Judith Fingard and Janet Guildford, eds., *Mothers of the Municipality: Women, Work, and Social Policy in Post-1945 Halifax* (Toronto: University of Toronto Press, 2005), 281-304.

46. Canadian Research Institute for the Advancement of Women, "Women's Involvement in Political Life: A Pilot Study," research report submitted to the United Nations Educational, Scientific, and Cultural Organisation (April 1986), 24–29; Harder, 2003, on Alberta Women's Action Committee; Brown, 95–99, on Vancouver Status of Women Council and the Status of Women Action Group (SWAG) in Victoria; for Manitoba, Reinart, 153, also Menzies in Rebick, 23–25; for the Ontario Committee on the Status of Women, M. Elizabeth Atcheson and Lorna R. Marsden, eds., *White Gloves Off: Ontario Committee on the Status of Women* (Toronto: Feminist History Society, forthcoming 2011), http://www.Feministhistories.ca; for Newfoundland, Ann Bell, "Commentary," in Naomi Black and Louise Carbert, eds., *Women's Exercise of Political Power: Building Leadership in Atlantic Canada, Atlantis* 27:2 (Spring 2003): 100; "1996 Alumna of the Year: Lynn Verge," *Luminus—MUN Alumni News* (n.d.) http://www.mun.ca/munalum/luminus5/2.html.

47. Diane Lamoureux, *Fragments et collages: essai sur le féminisme québécois des années 70* (Montréal: Éditions du remue-ménage, 1986), 73; Mariette Sineau and Evelyne Tardy, *Droits des femmes en France et au Québec 1940–1990* (Montreal: Les Éditions du remue-ménage, 1993); Jackie F. Steele, "Republican Liberty, Naming Laws, and the Role of Patronymy in Constituting Women's Citizenship in Canada and Québec," in Yasmeen Abu-Laban, ed., *Gendering the Nation-State: Canadian and Comparative Perspectives* (Vancouver: UBC Press, 2008), 230–3l.

48. Carey, "The Personal Is Political," 6.

49. Naomi Wall, "The Last Ten Years: A Personal/Political View," in Maureen Fitzgerald, Connie Guberman, and Margie Wolfe, eds., *Still Ain't Satisfied! Canadian Feminism Today* (Toronto: Women's Press, 1982), 16.

50. Frances Wasserlein, "A Twenty-Five-Year-Old Herstory: The Women's Caucus," *Kinesis* (December 1992/January 1993): 18–19; *Women Unite! An Anthology of the Canadian Women's Movement* (Toronto: Canadian Women's Educational Press, 1972); Sara Evans, *Personal Politics: The Roots of Women's Liberation in the Civil Rights Movement and the New Left* (New York: Vintage, 1980), 208; Francie Ricks, George Matheson, and Sandra

W. Pyke, "Women's Liberation: A Case Study of Organisations for Social Change," *The Canadian Psychologist* 13, 1 (January 1972), 31–40.

51. Satu Repo, "Are Women Necessary?" *Saturday Night* 84, 8 (August 1969): 30.

52. Nancy Adamson, Linda Briskin, and Margaret McPhail, *Feminist Organizing for Change: The Contemporary Women's Movement in Canada* (Don Mills: Oxford University Press, 1988), 70; Rebick; RCSW *Report*, 2.

53. Véronique O'Leary et Louise Toupin, eds. *Québécoises deboutte! Vol. 1: Une anthologie de textes du Front de libération des femmes (1969–1971) et du Centre des femmes (1972–1975)* (Montréal: Les Editions du remue-ménage, 1982), 1, 53; Un groupe de femmes de Montréal, *Manifeste des femmes québécoises* (Montréal: Éditions l'étincelle, 1971), 52; Michèle Lamont, "Les rapports politiques au sein du mouvement des femmes au Québec," *Politique* 5 (hiver 1984), 75–106; Micheline Dumont, *Le féminisme québécois raconté à Camille* (Montréal: Les éditions du remue-ménage, 2008), 123–28; Christabelle Sethna, "The Evolution of the *Birth Control Handbook*: From Student Peer-Evaluation Manual to Feminist Self-empowerment Text, 1968–1975," *Canadian Bulletin of Medical History/Bulletin canadien d'histoire de la médecine* 23, 1 (2006): 107–10.

54. Krista Maeots, "Abortion Caravan," *Canadian Forum* 50, 594–95 (July/August 1970): 15; Phyllis Waugh, "Movement Comment: Choice Description," *Broadside* 9, 2 (November 1987), 6; Wasserlein, "A Twenty-Five-Year-Old Herstory," 19; Reinart, "Three Major Strands," 155.

55. Marion Kerans, "Muriel Duckworth: The Peace Movement's Best Friend," *Peace Magazine* 4, 5 (October-November 1988): 8, http://archive.peacemagazine.org.

56. Gwen Matheson and V. E. Lang, "Nellie McClung: 'Not a Nice Woman,'" in Matheson, ed., *Women in the Canadian Mosaic*, 1–22; Gloria Geller, "The Wartimes Elections Act of 1917 and the Canadian Women's Movement," *Atlantis* 2, 1 (Autumn 1976): 88–106; Linda Kealey, ed., *A Not Unreasonable Claim: Women and Reform in Canada, 1880s–1920s* (Toronto: Canadian Women's Educational Press, 1979).

57. Diane Lamoureux, "Nationalism and Feminism in Quebec: An Impossible Attraction," in Heather Jon Maroney and Meg Luxton, eds., *Feminism and Political Economy: Women's Work, Women's Struggles* (Toronto: Methuen, 1987), 51–68; Pierrette Bouchard, "Féminisme et marxisme: Un dilemme pour la Ligue communiste," *Canadian Journal of Political Science* 20, 1 (March 1987): 57–78; Simonne Monet-Chartrand, *Pionnières québécoises et regroupements de femmes d'hier à aujourd'hui* (Montréal: Les Editions du remue-ménage, 1990); Micheline de Sève, *Pour un féminisme libertaire* (Montréal: Boréal Express, 1985); Dumont, *Le féminisme*, 88, 159–61; Madeleine Parent, "Fifty Years a Feminist Trade Unionist: An Interview," in M. Patricia Connelly and Pat Armstrong, eds., *Feminism in Action: Studies in Political Economy* (Toronto: Canadian Scholars' Press, 1992), 47–65.

58. Toronto Women's Liberation Group, "Is Feminism Necessary for Women's Liberation?" (Canadian Union of Students, 1969), 3.

59. Rebick, 253–57; Judy Rebick and Kiké Roach, *Politically Speaking* (Vancouver/Toronto: Douglas & McIntyre: 1996).

60. Cited as an epigraph in Peggy Morton, "Women's Work Is Never Done," *in Women Unite!*, 46.

61. Linda Briskin, "Socialist Feminism: From the Standpoint of Practice," in Connelly and Armstrong, eds., *Feminism in Action*, 286; Adamson et al., 70.

62. Bonnie Kreps, "Radical Feminism," in *Women Unite!* 74.

63. Letter from Bonnie Kreps, November 1986; Bonnie Kreps, *Guide to the Women's Movement, Canada: A Chatelaine Cope Kit* (Toronto: n.d.).

64. Sherill Cheda, Johanna Stuckey, and Maryon Kantaroff, "New Feminists Now," *Canadian Women's Studies/Les cahiers de la femme* 2, 2 (1980): 27–31; Naomi Black, *Social Feminism* (Ithaca, N.Y.: Cornell University Press, 1989).

65. Lanctôt, "La genèse," 119.

66. Phylinda Masters, "Women, Culture and Communications," in Ruth Roach Pierson, Marjorie Griffin Cohen, Paula Bourne, and Philinda Masters, eds., *Canadian Women's Issues*, vol. I: *Strong Voices: Twenty-Five Years of Women's Activism in English Canada* (Toronto: James Lorimer, 1993), 407–9; May Lui, "Riding the Roller Coaster of Feminist Publishing in Canada," section 15.ca, Rebels without a Clause (May 16, 2007), http://section15.ca/ features/reviews/2007/08/16/riding_the_roller_coaster/; http://www.herizons.ca/faq; http:// www3.sympatico.ca/equity.greendragonpress/; http://www.sumachpress.com/.

67. Geneviève Pagé, "Variations Sur Une Vague," in Maria Nengeh Mensah, ed. *Dialogues sur la Troisième Vague Féministe* (Montréal: Les éditions du remue-ménage, 2005), 45; Eve-Marie Lampron, "A nos crayons, à nos pancartes: quelques débats actuels en théorie féministe," *Le Féminisme en bref*, Numéro spécial (2008); Marie-Hélène Côté, "De nouvelles Sorcières," *A Babord!* (nov.–déc. 2003), http://www.ababord.org/spip.php?article507.

68. "WAVAW Demands," *Broadside* 3, 2 (November 1981): 19; "Celebrating 20 Years 1974–1994," *Kinesis* (March 1994): 11, 20; "In Women's Interests: Feminist Activism and Institutional Change," (Vancouver: Women's Research Centre, 1988); "Take Back the Night," *Kinesis* (September 1994): 5; "Prince Rupert Women Take Back the Night," *Kinesis* (December 1994/January 1995): 9; Shannon Philips, "Take Back the Night: Women, Men Alike Welcomed to Challenge Violence Against Women," *Vue Weekly*, Edmonton, 649 (March 27, 2008), http://www.vueweekly.com/article.php?id=8163; Danielle Pope, "Stolen Sisters Honoured in March," *The Martlet*, University of Victoria, (February 12, 2009); Amnesty International Canada, "Stolen Sisters: A Human Rights Response to Discrimination and Violence Against Indigenous Women In Canada," (March 3, 2004), http://www.amnesty.ca/ campaigns/resources/amr2000304.pdf; Sue Bailey, "Failure to Curb Violence Against Native Women 'Shocking,'" *The Globe and Mail* (October 1, 2009), A12.

69. Margaret Benston, "The Political Economy of Women's Liberation," *Monthly Review* 21, 4 (September 1969): 13–29; Linda Briskin, "The Women's Movement: Where Is It Going?" *Our Generation* 10, 3 (Fall 1974): 23–34; Roberta Hamilton and Michèle Barrett, eds., *The Politics of Diversity: Feminism, Marxism and Nationalism* (Montreal: Book Center, 1986); Dorothy Smith, *The Everyday World as Problematic* (Toronto: University of Toronto Press, 1987); Mary O'Brien, *The Politics of Reproduction* (London: Routledge and Kegan Paul, 1981).

70. Alison Prentice, "Moments in the Making of a Feminist Historian," in Wendy Robbins, Meg Luxton, Margrit Eichler, and Francine Descarries, eds., *Minds of Our Own: Inventing Feminist Scholarship and Women's Studies in Canada and Québec, 1966–76* (Waterloo, ON: Wilfrid Laurier University Press, 2008), 100, 101.

71. Canadian Women's Studies Association, "Academic Women's Studies and Women's Studies Organisations," http://www.yorku.ca/cwsaacef/womens_studies_academic.html.

72. M. Julia Creet, "A Test of Unity: Lesbian Visibility in the British Columbia Federation of Women," in Sharon Dale Stone, ed., *Lesbians in Canada* (Toronto: Between the Lines, 1990); Dorrie, "Creating Communities," in Nym Hughes, Yvonne Johnson, and Yvette Perreault, *Stepping Out of Line: A Workbook on Lesbianism and Feminism* (Vancouver: Press Gang, 1984), 161; Becki Ross, *The House That Jill Built: A Lesbian Nation in Formation* (Toronto: University of Toronto Press, 1995); "The LMDF is Three Years Old! An Interview with

Francie Wyland," *Grapevine* (Spring 1981), 1–2; Katherine Arnup, "Lesbian Mothers and Child Custody," *Atkinson Review of Canadian Studies* 1, 2 (Spring 1984): 35–39; Arnup, ed., *Lesbian Parenting: Living with Pride and Prejudice* (Charlottetown: gynergy books, 1995); communications from Tom Warner, 2009.

73. Womonspace Home Page, http://www.womonspace.ca/golf.htm.

74. Julie McLean, "Militantly Impotent: Has the Women's Movement Come to This?" *Branching Out* 3, 2 (April/June 1976): 9.

75. Cerise Morris, "Diary of a Feminist," in Margret Anderson, ed., *Mother Was Not a Person* (Montreal: Content Publishing/Black Rose, 1972), 182, 184.

76. Eleanor Wright Pelrine, *Abortion in Canada* (Toronto: New Press, 1972); Pelrine, *Morgentaler: The Case That Rocked Canada* (Toronto: Gage Educational Publishing/ Signet–New American Library, 1976); Anne Collins, *The Big Evasion: Abortion, The Issue That Won't Go Away* (Toronto: Lester and Orpen Dennys, 1985).

77. "Louise Summerhill" [obituary], *The Globe and Mail* (August 14, 1991), D7.

78. Christine Overall, "Feminist Philosophical Reflections on Reproductive Rights in Canada," in Backhouse and Flaherty, *Challenging Times*, 243.

79. Shelley A. M. Gavigan, "Beyond *Morgentaler*: The Legal Regulation of Reproduction," in Janine Brodie, Shelley A. M. Gavigan, and Jane Jenson, eds., *The Politics of Abortion* (Toronto: Oxford University Press, 1992), 117–46; F. L. Morton, *Morgentaler vs. Borowski: Abortion, the Charter, and the Courts* (Toronto: McClelland and Stewart, 1992).

80. "Federal Abortion Bill Defeated," *Pro-Choice News* (Spring 1991), 1.

81. Robert Matas and Miro Cernetig, "B.C. Doctor Hit by Sniper," *The Globe and Mail* (November 9, 1994), A1; "Death Threats Aimed at Halifax Doctors," *The Globe and Mail* (February 3, 1995), A4; http://www.prochoiceactionnetwork-canada.org/abortioninfo/history.shtml

82. AbortionInCanada.ca, "Where do Canadians Obtain Abortions?" (2004), http://www.abortionincanada.ca/facts/abortion_clinics.html; *Women in Canada: A Gender-based Statistical Report, 5th ed.* (Ottawa: Statistics Canada, 2006), Cat. no. 89-503-XIE, 70.

83. Richard Mackie, "Public-Opinion Poll Results Fuel Fight for Abortion Pill," *The Globe and Mail* (July 22, 1992), A4; AngusReidStrategies, "Canadians Uphold Abortion Policy, Split on Health Care System's Role" (June 20, 2008), http://www.angus-reid.com/uppdf/2008.06.20_Abortion.pdf.

84. Gloria Galloway, "Fate Unclear for Liberals Backing Anti-Abortion Cause," *The Globe and Mail* (December 30, 2008), A6; Paul Tuns, "Pro-Life Chair Boldly Speaks Out," *The Interim* (February 2009), http://www.theinterim.com/2009/feb/03caucus.html.

85. Marlene Pierre-Aggawamay, "Native Women and the State," in Joan Turner and Lois Emery, eds., *Perspectives on Women in the 1980s* (Winnipeg: University of Manitoba Press, 1983), 67; The Mohawk Women of Caughnawaga, "'The Least Members of Our Society,'" *Canadian Women's Studies/Les cahiers de la femme* 2, 2 (1980).

86. Silman, *Enough Is Enough*, 94.

87. Daryl Webber, "The Women's Movement in Northern Ontario: Its History, Growth and Current Affairs," (Glendon College, York University, Women's Studies Honours Thesis, 1986), 16–22.

88. Government of Canada, Aboriginal Canada Portal, "Women—National Aboriginal Organisations" (June 12, 2009), http://www.aboriginalcanada.gc.ca/acp/site.nsf/en/ao04362.html; http://www.nwac-hq.org/en/nwacstructure.html; http://www.pauktuutit.ca/home_e.htm.

89. Kathleen Jamieson, *Citizens Minus: Indian Women and the Law* (Ottawa: Canadian Advisory Council on the Status of Women, 1978), 82; Paula Bourne, *Women in Canadian Society* (Toronto: OISE, 1976), 111–31; Elizabeth Atcheson, Mary Eberts, and Beth Symes, *Women and Legal Action: Precedents, Resources, and Strategies for the Future* (Ottawa: Canadian Advisory Council on the Status of Women, 1984), 14–15.

90. Silman,155; Atcheson, Eberts, and Symes, *Women and Legal Action*, 17–18; Caroline Lachapelle, "Beyond Barriers: Native Women and the Women's Movement," in Fitzgerald, Guberman, and Wolfe, 257–64; D. Meemee Lavell-Harvard,"Thunder Spirit: Reclaiming the Power of Our Grandmothers," in Lavell-Harvard and Lavell, 8–9.

91. D. Meemee Lavell-Harvard and Jeannette Corbiere Lavell, "Aboriginal Women vs. Canada," in Lavell-Harvard and Lavell, 191.

92. Sally Weaver, "First Nations Women and Government Policy, 1970–92: Discrimination and Conflict," in Sandra Burt, Lorraine Code, and Lindsay Dorney, eds., *Changing Patterns: Women in Canada*, 2nd ed. (Toronto: McClelland and Stewart, 1993), 92–150; Peter Sero, "Blood Lines Cross Mohawk Country," *NOW* magazine (October 6–12, 1994), 15; Joyce Green, "Balancing Strategies: Aboriginal Women and Constitutional Rights in Canada," in Alexandra Dobrowolsky and Vivien Hart, ed., *Women Making Constitutions: New Politics and Comparative Perspectives* (London: Palgrave Macmillan, 2003), 45–47; Bell Curry, "B.C. Ruling 'Opens Floodgates' for Native Status," *The Globe and Mail* (June 16, 2007), A8; "AFN Praises Sharon McIvor on October 6th, First Nations Women's Day," *NationTalk* (June 2, 2009). http://www.nationtalk.ca/modules/news/article.php?storyid=13976

93. "Legislations Lost: The 36 Bills that Died," *The Globe and Mail* (January 22, 2010), http://www.theglobeandmail.com/news/politics/prorogation/the-36-bills-that-died/article1441162/; Elizabeth Bastien, "Matrimonial Real Property Solutions," *Canadian Woman Studies/Les cahiers de la femme* 26, 3, 4 (Winter/spring 2008): 90–104.

94. Reports of the fifth and sixth conferences of the Congress of Black Women of Canada, 1982, 1984; Status of Women Canada, *Canada's National Report to the United Nations for the Fourth World Conference on Women*, September 1995, Beijing, China (Ottawa: August 1994), 38; Linda Carvery, "Congress Has Ambitious Goals for Black Women," *Pandora* 4, 1 (September 1988): 27; Rosemary Sadlier, *Leading the Way: Black Women in Canada* (Toronto: Umbrella Press, 1994); Rudy Platiel, "Judge Halts Strip-Search Inquiry," *The Globe and Mail* (September 20, 1994), A6; National Congress of Black Women Foundation/Umoja (June 25, 2007), http://www.nationalcongressofblackwomenfoundation.org/donate.html; Marcia Wharton-Zaretsky, "Foremothers of Black Women's Community Organizing in Toronto," *Atlantis* 24, 2 (Spring/Summer 2000): 67–71. *Umoja* is the Swahili word for unity.

95. Manisha Singh, "A 19-Year Old Herstory: India Mahila Association," *Kinesis* (March 1993); Sunera Thobani, "More Than Sexist . . ." *Healthsharing* 12, 1 (Spring 1991): 10, 11, 13; Aruna Papp, "A Matter of Gender," *Healthsharing* 12, 1 (Spring 1991): 12; communication from IMA, 2009; Carolle Charles, "Gender and Politics in Contemporary Haiti: The Duvalierist State, Transnationalism, and the Emergence of a New Feminism (1980–1990)," *Feminist Studies* 21, 1 (Spring 1995): 150–51.

96. Sheila McDonough and Sajida Alvi, "The Canadian Council of Muslim Women: A Chapter in the History of Muslim Women in Canada," *The Muslim World*, 92 (Spring 2002): 79, 93; "Amina and Rikia" and "Lila," in Sadia Zaman, ed., *At My Mother's Feet: Stories of Muslim Women* (Kingston: Quarry Women's Books, 2001), 37–38, 66–67; Nuzhat Jafri, "The Canadian Council of Muslim Women: Engaging Muslim Women in Civic and Social Change," *Canadian Woman Sudies/Les cahiers de la femme* 25, 3, 4 (Summer/fall 2006): 98.

97. Deborah Harrison and Lucie Laliberté, *There's No Life Like It! Military Wives in Canada* (Toronto: James Lorimer, 1994); defunct website accessed in 2009.

98. Jill Summerhayes, *Supporting Myself in Style: Confessions of the Cane Lady* (Cambridge, ON: Imp Press, 1990), 58.

99. Pat Israel and Fran Odette, "The Disabled Women's Movement 1983 to 1993," *Canadian Woman Studies/Les cahiers de la femme* 13, 4 (Summer 1993): 6–8; DAWN-RAFH Canada, (April 27, 2009), http://www.dawncanada.net.

100. Carmencita R. Hernandez, "The Coalition of Visible Minority Women," in Frank Cunningham et al., eds. *Social Movements/Social Change: The Politics and Practice of Organizing* (Toronto: Between the Lines, 1988), 157–68; Roxana Ng, "Finding Our Voices: Reflections on Immigrant Women's Organizing," in Jeri Dawn Wine and Janice L. Ristock, eds., *Women and Social Change: Feminist Activism in Canada* (Toronto: James Lorimer, 1991), 184–97; Linda Carty and Dionne Brand, "'Visible Minority' Women: A Creation of the Canadian State," in Himani Bannerji, ed., *Returning the Gaze: Essays on Racism, Feminism and Politics* (Toronto: Sister Vision, 1993), 169–81; Awha Al-Buasidy, "Generic Term More Accurate," *Quota Magazine* (February 1994), 5–6; NOIVMC, "Welcome to NOIVMC," "Projects" (2006–2008), "Graduation of the Project" (March 7, 2009), http://www.noivmwc.org/noivmwcen/overview.php.

101. Christine St. Peter, "'Woman's Truth' and the Native Tradition: Anne Cameron's *Daughters of Copper Woman*," *Feminist Studies* 15, 3 (Fall 1989): 499–523; Anne Cameron, "The Operative Principle Is Trust," in Libby Scheier, Sarah Sheard, and Eleanor Wachtel, eds., *Language in Her Eye: Views on Writing and Gender by Canadian Writers Writing in English* (Toronto: Coach House, 1990), 70, 71.

CHAPTER FIFTEEN

The Personal Becomes Political

In the aftermath of the radical changes that began in the late 1960s, women moved, both individually and collectively, to make society and politics respond to women's shared personal agendas. This enterprise involved sustained efforts to alter attitudes to take more account of women and to alter social structures accordingly. It therefore also entailed more attempts to influence public policy and government and to participate directly in public life. Organized religions, which had traditionally been major influences in most women's lives, attempted to adjust to women's increasing demands for a voice. Along with significant feminist successes in the 1970s and 1980s, the increased number and diversity of women's organizations generated serious tensions that were further exacerbated by the growing strength of anti-feminism and of more overt backlash. Nevertheless, it seemed clear that the energy of women's actions was not abating, in spite of less propitious economic times and successively less supportive governments. New generations of young women grew up with feminism as a familiar part of their environment, even though many rejected a feminist identification. By the end of the century, a new cohort of activists, who clearly shared their foremothers' concerns, proudly called themselves the Third Wave.

LAW, THE LEGAL SYSTEM, AND JUSTICE

An early, important example of the politicization of individual women's situations was the case of Irene Murdoch, whose private problems started a process that produced major changes in family property law. Murdoch was an Alberta farm wife who could represent the many wives who worked only "in the home." When her jaw and her marriage were broken in 1968, she claimed a share of the family ranch on the basis of her contributions to it. Urban feminists were stunned to learn that Murdoch was regularly involved in "haying, raking, swathing, mowing, driving trucks and tractors and teams, quietening horses, taking cattle back and forth to the reserve, dehorning, vaccinating, branding," that she ran the ranch single-handed for about five months out of each year, and that her husband felt she did no more than what was expected of "any ranch wife." The Supreme Court justices did not believe that such customary labours "would give any farm or ranch wife a claim in partnership."[1]

In 1973 Murdoch was finally granted a lump-sum maintenance payment, but it implied no recognition of her role in the economic unit of the household. The assumptions of the law remained the same: women were entitled to support during marriage and to appropriate maintenance after its breakup, with return obligations of domestic duties and sexual availability on an exclusive basis for the duration of the marriage. The Murdoch case helped alter both law and attitudes about family property in the common-law provinces, for it mobilized women and women's groups to press for change. Beginning in 1977 with Manitoba, the provinces and territories approved legislation giving concrete recognition to the fact that domestic activities, usually carried out by women, were what made it possible for wage earners to acquire money and property for the family. The Supreme Court completed the process of legal change when it established, in the Beblow case in 1993, that wives in enduring common-law as well as formal marriages were entitled to half the household assets when the relationship ended. In striking contrast to the Murdoch decision, the Supreme Court found that Catherine Peter was entitled to compensation for the 12 years during which she had lived with William Beblow, cared for his two children and her four, built a pigpen, tended and slaughtered chickens, and worked part-time as a cook.[2] Although the new legislation and court decisions concerning family property did not apply to Quebec's unique system of de facto unions, they incorporated the feminist insistence that domestic work was as valuable as work in the paid labour force. In addition, the federal government responded to women's complex dual role by adding maternity leave to the Unemployment Insurance (subsequently Employment Insurance) system in 1971 and providing both a child-care tax expense deduction as well as tax deductions for non-earning parents. The system was later expanded (1990) to include parental leave, for which both parents are eligible.

The law related to rape was another area in which attitudes and law changed, if slowly, as a result of individual action backed up by women's organizations. Rape crisis centres were among the services earliest provided and most energetically supported by the women's movement in the 1970s. Changes in legislation were a major goal, for, despite modifications in the law in 1976, victims of rape were doubly victimized by their treatment in court, where women's sexual history could be presented and there were very demanding requirements for demonstration of resistance. In 1977 a groundbreaking feminist book, Clark and Lewis's *Rape: The Price of Coercive Sexuality,* showed the extent to which rape was underreported, under-prosecuted, and unpunished in Canada—in part because of the very severe penalties that made juries reluctant to convict. The book's authors also articulated an argument increasingly adopted by feminists: rape was a crime of violence against women, rather than one of sexuality. In response to persistent lobbying by women's groups, in 1983 the federal government enacted new legislation that redefined rape as assault. With less extreme jail sentences possible, successful prosecution would be more likely. This change was accompanied by the rape shield provision, which banned consideration of the alleged victim's sexual history; perhaps women would now be less reluctant to report rape or attempted rape. In the same legislation, marital rape was defined as a crime. These changes in law were regarded by feminists as among the most promising legal changes their activities had produced. But some women began to have doubts about whether rape was in fact merely assault as the new laws implied, since it was so often used as a way to control and punish women.

In any case, the law's protection turned out to be fragile, requiring continual scrutiny and action. In 1991 the Supreme Court found some of the rape shield provisions unconstitutional on the grounds that they unfairly limited efforts at defence, so that new legislation was required. Feminist lawyers, along with representatives of sex workers and other diverse women's groups, then participated in the discussions that produced new provisions popularly known as "No means no." This modification of the Criminal Code and the accompanying programs of public education stressed the importance of explicit consent on the part of those involved in sexual activity, so that signs of physical resistance would no longer be required to establish that a woman had been sexually assaulted. Insistent opposition from some members of the legal profession and also from supporters of free speech, who were concerned about the rights of those accused of crimes, made it clear that the law implicitly required major changes in sexual behaviour and attitudes. Over time the law itself contributed to such changes. However, it was not possible to have the new legislation include recognition that certain groups of women—members of visible minorities, disabled women, lesbians, prostitutes—were at particular risk for forced sex.

In 1994, the Supreme Court appalled many by its decision in the Daviault case. They ruled that a new trial would be allowed for a 72-year-old man convicted of raping a semi-paralyzed 65-year-old woman confined to a wheelchair; his extreme drunkenness was allowed as a defence. Within weeks, an Alberta man accused of beating his wife was acquitted on the same grounds. Federal legislation (Bill C-72) then responded to limit the use of extreme intoxication as a defence; this 1995 bill had a preamble stating explicitly that it was directed against crimes of violence, and particularly crimes of violence against women and children.[3]

Feminist activity concerning legal matters relating to women was vigorous and effective. After the Charter of Rights and Freedoms was added to the Canadian constitution in 1982 feminist lawyers who had been active in the constitutional struggles beginning in 1980 organized an ambitious legal aid fund dedicated to fighting significant cases. The Legal Education and Action Fund (LEAF) was able from 1982 to 1992 and again from 1994 to 2006 to take advantage of a federal program that funded Charter challenges in the courts; it raised the rest of the substantial amounts needed for proactive litigation from individual donors as well as through various women's groups. LEAF's initial cases were symbolic of all women's needs for autonomy and status. The first concerned married women's names: living in the Yukon, Suzanne Bertrand wanted to retain her birth name because it reflected her French-Canadian ancestry. The second case attacked the regulation that welfare recipients, most of whom were women, would lose assistance if there was a "spouse in the house" who might support them, or even a friend who carried out activities thought to be typical of a spouse. By 1993 LEAF was able to boast quietly about having supported "more than 100 legal test cases," singling out for mention the areas of "pregnancy discrimination, sexual harassment, violence against women, pension inequities and sex bias in welfare regulations." By 2009 the Fund had 150 extremely diverse cases to its credit, as well as a range of other activities related to women's legal, political, and social situations. In February 2009, LEAF was granted leave to intervene in a case dealing with issues related to affirmative action under Section 15 (2) of the Charter (*Micmac Nation of Gespeg v. Canada*). Its activities the same year included public evaluation of the federal budget in terms of its impact on women. LEAF presented submissions to the Human Rights Commission on a prototype for a Canadian human rights report card and to the House of Commons Status of Women Committee on proposed changes that would limit the effectiveness of pay equity processes in the public service.[4]

As women graduated from law schools in increasing numbers, some of them began to be appointed judges. First-wave magistrates Emily Murphy, Alice Jamieson, and Helen Gregory MacGill had lacked formal legal training, but Helen Kinnear, Canada's first woman barrister to be appointed a judge (in 1943), was also the first woman honoured as King's Counsel in the British Commonwealth. In 1969 Canada had its first woman Superior Court judge when Réjane Laberge-Colas ascended to the bench in Quebec; in 1982 Bertha Wilson was appointed to the Supreme Court of Canada. She was joined there four years later by Quebec's Claire L'Heureux-Dubé and then, in 1989, by Albertan Beverley McLachlin. By 1985 women constituted about 13 percent of all judges and magistrates, and they were beginning to represent the diversity of Canadian women. When Maryka Omatsu was appointed to the Ontario Court of Justice in 1993, she was the first woman of East Asian descent to be made a judge. Active in the movement that obtained a small degree of financial redress for the survivors of the Japanese-Canadians who were interned during World War II, Omatsu initially found it difficult as a young woman, even though she was a fully qualified lawyer, to obtain respect in either her own ethnic community or the wider legal system.[5]

In February 1990, Madam Justice Bertha Wilson surprised her audience at Osgoode Hall Law School when she stated publicly her view that the law was a male and masculinist profession. After she retired from the Court, she was appointed to head a task force on sex equality set up by the Canadian Bar Association. Her report documented a high level of attrition of female lawyers—in part because firms would not accommodate child-rearing obligations. It also revealed widespread sexual harassment and discrimination against female judges and lawyers. These charges were confirmed by the 1993 Ontario inquiry into the conduct of the "kissing judge," who humiliated two young women Crown attorneys with deep kisses, groping, and sexual innuendo. Wilson's report recommended that law schools should adopt affirmative action programs, that the law societies should monitor law firms, and that judges should receive mandatory training programs concerning both racism and sexism. The public apparently shared Wilson's doubts about judges: a 1993 poll found that only 40 percent of Canadians felt that courts were fair to women. In March 2009 another panel looked back to Wilson's 1990 talk. The distinguished participants—who included the Hon. Justice Micheline Rawlins, the first black woman appointed to the bench in Ontario—pointed to the important cases affecting women where women judges had been influentially involved: the Morgentaler case that decriminalized abortion in 1988; *Tremblay v. Daigle*, the 1989 case that ruled that the father of a child could not prevent an abortion; and *Lavallee*, the 1990 case allowing

Supreme Court of Canada, 2009, with Chief Justice Beverley McLachlin third from the left.

Source: Philippe Landreville, photographer. Supreme Court of Canada Collection. Reproduced with the permission of the Minister of Public Works and Government Services, 2010.

women the battered wife defence for killing an abusive spouse. The panellists concluded that a bench that was diverse in respect to both gender and race would be the most desirable because it would draw on varied experience, while possible biases would be counteracted; it would also inspire more confidence in the public.[6] Appointed Chief Justice in 2000, the Right Honourable Beverley McLachlin presided in 2009 over a court of which three of the remaining eight justices were women. By this time, women judges made up 32 percent of the entire federally appointed bench. Justice Ruth Bader Ginsburg, then the only woman in the Supreme Court of the United States, commented approvingly in 2009 on the gender composition of the Canadian Supreme Court. "In Canada, where McLachlin is the chief, I think they must have a different way of hearing a woman's voice if she is the leader."[7] Problems continued inside the legal profession, however. In B.C. and Ontario, Law Society working groups once more recommended attention to work–life balance.[8] But women lawyers seemed to feel more was going on. One of them, partner in a large firm, was quoted as saying about gender discrimination, "We're invisible. They don't even think about us!"[9] In 2008, Diane LaCalamita sued the prominent Toronto firm of McCarthy Tétrault, who had recruited and then dismissed her. She charged that the firm was "plagued by systemic gender-based discrimination and a culture of discrimination." LaCalamita had refused an offered $200 000 settlement and was asking $12 million. A Master of the Ontario Superior Court of Justice (Commercial List) ordered that LaCalamita's lawyers be given access to confidential personnel records.[10]

At the other end of the justice system, women emerged horrifyingly into public attention when, in a period of less than two years beginning in 1989, six Aboriginal women killed themselves in the federal prison for women (P4W) in Kingston, Ontario. Echoing the 1938 findings of the Archambault Commission instigated by MP Agnes

Macphail, every investigation of the federal penal system (16 between 1968 and 1981 alone) recommended closing the women's prison and redistributing the very few federally convicted women to locations near their homes. In 1981 the Canadian Human Rights Commission found that women prisoners were discriminated against in terms of sex, since in virtually every dimension of program and facilities they were worse off than men. The disproportionate incarceration of Aboriginal women was scandalous; they made up almost a quarter of the population of the federal prison, and even larger proportions of those incarcerated in the provinces and territories. In 1990, a unique federal task force consisting almost entirely of women, including representatives of the Native Women's Association of Canada (NWAC) and the Canadian Association of Elizabeth Fry Societies as well as two former prisoners, recommended replacing the single federal facility with five regional ones. In addition, a specially designed healing lodge was to be created for Aboriginal women who preferred that alternative; it would be closely integrated with a First Nations community, have elders and other spiritual healers always available, and be staffed by Aboriginal people. The other non-Aboriginal facilities were to be similarly linked in a holistic way to supportive networks of women's groups. However, economy rather than principle seemed to dictate the placement of the new facilities.[11] By 1994 some progress had been made in developing regional correctional facilities for women. But 142 federally sentenced women were still in the Kingston facility, where in April 1994 a prison riot resulted in what was later described as "cruel and humiliating," treatment of inmates, including strip searches by male members of a prison security unit. A videotape of the proceedings was leaked and shown on national television. A deeply flawed internal inquiry was followed by a more effective one conducted by the Honourable Louise Arbour, who made extensive procedural recommendations, including a number specifically relating to the treatment of Aboriginal women prisoners. She began the preface to her report, "The history of women and crime is spotted with opportunities most of which have been missed. We hope that history will not dictate our future."[12] P4W was finally closed in 2000. But the correctional system, designed for and dominated by men, continued to deal inequitably with women, particularly Aboriginal women. During the period 1998 to 2008, the number of federally incarcerated female Aboriginal prisoners increased by 131 percent. As a result, in 2007–2008, Aboriginal women, who made up two percent of Canada's overall population, constituted 33 percent of the women in federal prisons. The promised culturally specific programming for them remained infrequent. In particular, although by 2009 there were 81 healing lodges in the system for Aboriginal men, there were none for women. Nor were the problems only federal. In the summer of 2009, more than three dozen Manitoba women were transferred to a converted adult unit in the Brandon Correctional Centre; a new female correctional centre, to be completed in 2011, would replace the facility built in 1893.[13]

For the majority of women who were not personally involved with the formal machinery of law and justice, court decisions were of indirect but still substantial importance. The continuing issue of pornography was a particularly noteworthy example because of everyday issues relating to freedom of speech and women's possibilities for self-expression. Pornography was also an issue about which women disagreed vehemently. In 1992 the Butler case established for Canada a new interpretation of pornography that attracted considerable international interest. Obscenity would no longer be interpreted to mean "offensive to conventional morality." Instead, material could be seized and its producers, importers, or distributors charged by either Customs or police if the material exploited sex in such a way that there was a tendency to promote harm to women or children. In particular, both child pornography and combinations of sex with violence were to be prohibited. Most women were uncomfortable with pornography that involved violent or degrading portrayals of women and still more uncomfortable with sexual material portraying children or models who looked like children. Indeed, radical-feminist groups, including Women Against Violence Against Women (WAVAW), had long opposed such publications and films. But the risks of censorship remained great, as many other feminists and feminist organizations pointed out. In particular, lesbians predicted that the new definitions would be used against homosexual erotic material rather than the widely distributed hard-core heterosexual pornography.

Such fears were supported the first time the Butler case's decision was applied: in 1993 Customs officers seized copies of a lesbian erotic magazine, *Bad Attitude*, ordered by a gay and lesbian bookstore in Toronto. "It's our material—our books, our magazines, our voice—a voice that we're learning to speak with louder and louder," protested the manager of Little Sister's, a lesbian bookstore in Vancouver that, since 1986, had been regularly affected by delay and confiscation of material. In 1994, Little Sister's challenged Canada Customs in court about the legality of such action under the Charter of Rights. A trial judge and then the B.C. Court of Appeals agreed that the behaviour of the Customs officers was discriminatory but ruled that it was justified under section 1 of the Charter: this limitations clause permits government to curtail individual rights in order to prevent objectionable conduct, such as obscenity. However, the federal Supreme Court backed Little Sister's in 2000 and ruled that only legislatively defined obscene material could be seized. The reverse onus section of the Customs Act—which obliged book importers to prove that material was not obscene—was unconstitutional. Arbitrary seizures continued, however, and Little Sister's again went to court in 2002, this time trying to make a case that systemic discrimination was at issue. Two years later, the bookstore was unable to obtain from the court system the "advance funding" that is sometimes available for long and costly legal battles, such as this was proving to be, and the case was dropped. The moral and feminist implications of Little Sister's situation remained significant even after pornography of every sort became increasingly available on the Internet.[14]

In other areas, the federal government was more readily responsive to women's needs. For example, Canada became the first nation in the world to allow women to achieve refugee status for gender-related reasons, on the basis of guidelines issued by the Immigration and Refugee Board in 1992. The guidelines provided shelter for women who feared persecution from severe forms of discrimination because they were unwilling "to conform to discriminatory precepts or practices arising from religious or customary laws." Thus, refugee status was granted to a Zimbabwean forced against her will into a polygamous marriage, a Chinese woman resisting sterilization, and a Guinean woman who did not want her two-year-old daughter to suffer genital mutilation; domestic violence by partners or spouses was also grounds for refugee status for women under circumstances where a state was unable or unwilling to protect them.[15]

The mixed results of Canadian government initiatives were reflected in international statistics, which, beginning in the last years of the twentieth century, started to compare systematically the position of women in the different nations of the world. Canada scored well in general terms of economic development and overall quality of life, measured in terms of education, life expectancy, and income. Nonetheless, many Aboriginal women, older widows, and single mothers did not enjoy these high standards; some were living under conditions approximating those in countries in the global South. In 1992 the United Nations' Development Program (UNDP) rated this country number one in Human Development, and it was number three in 2005. However, as measures were developed internationally to estimate the differences in the situation of men and women—gender gaps—Canada's ranking was depressed by features of its economic and political structures, including the relatively large difference between male and female wages, and the relatively low number of women in legislatures and in ministerial positions. Many Scandinavian and other European countries at Canada's level of economic development had higher scores. In Canada, the situations that created the gender gap were changing only very slowly, which indicated areas of concern for twenty-first century activists.[16]

THE CONSTITUTION

Constitutional battles dominated national politics in Canada in the period beginning with the 1960s. The modernization of Quebec fuelled calls for independence, while economic and political change strengthened regional calls for devolution of powers. At the same time Aboriginal groups actively pursued land claims and self-government. Feminism and the action of women's groups became part of the mainstream in the *Parti Québécois's* 1980 referendum in Quebec about a proposed new constitutional arrangement, sovereignty association. Lise Payette, the first woman to serve in a Quebec Cabinet, had responsibility for the status of women (along with consumer affairs, cooperatives, and financial institutions). A popular broadcaster, both a feminist and a committed sovereigntist, she caused a commotion by accusing federalist *Québécoises* of being "Yvettes." Guy and Yvette were the Dick and Jane of Quebec schoolbooks, and Payette used the name to stand for the traditional submissive wife-and-mother who does what her husband and father tell her. Women active in the Quebec Liberal Party responded vigorously, organizing first a "brunch" and then a series of public meetings, ending with a vast session in the Montreal Forum. There, more than 14 000 women cheered federalist feminists, including Monique Bégin and Thérèse Casgrain, who talked about the role of women in building Quebec and Canada and the way future generations in Quebec would benefit from federally provided opportunities and social services. Polls showed a significant shift in women's votes, and analysts agreed that women played a role in federalism's 10 percent victory in the referendum. Some journalists interpreted the whole episode as a rejection of feminism in favour of traditional values, while others saw it as manipulation by the Liberal Party of Quebec.[17] In response, some feminist political scientists pointed to the key role played by women members of the Liberal Party: one described the "Yvettes" campaign as "a brilliant political strategy thought up by women."[18] A third, wider-ranging interpretation was that many women had made a rational policy choice related to their own interests.

During the referendum, the federal government had promised redress of Quebec's persistent grievances about the structure of Confederation. After the defeat of sovereignty association, it accordingly pressed for a reformulated and patriated constitution that would include a Charter of Rights and Freedoms, entailing, for the first time, a formal judicial review of law in terms of basic principles. As many cases had shown—including those of Bliss, Lavell, Bedard, and Murdoch—the 1960 Bill of Rights was virtually useless for women. It was clear by the end of the 1970s that, generally speaking, unequal laws would be upheld by Canadian courts, the only remedy being the slow process of legislative change. Many women's organizations accordingly reacted with enthusiasm to the suggestion that women's rights to equality might be enshrined in fundamental law. Individual legislative or administrative acts could then be challenged directly and possibly ruled unacceptable.

For anglophone women, the 1980–1981 campaign for the inclusion of women's rights in the constitution became a landmark similar to the Persons Case of 1929, an icon of feminist effectiveness. According to a feminist journalist, "a political earthquake occurred in Canada in 1981, dramatically changing the foundation for government policy making."[19] The reality, however, was less clear-cut. In 1980, anglophone women's organizations lobbied intensively in connection with the proposed constitution, focusing particularly on getting adequate references to gender equality into the Charter of Rights and Freedoms. It was partly in response to their efforts that, in January 1981, the justice minister announced a revision of the proposed Section 15 of the Charter, to read, "Every individual is equal before and under the law and has the right to equal protection of the law and equal benefit of the law." The experience of many women was behind that seemingly clumsy formulation, which attempted to ensure not just that laws were equally enforced, but also that they would have no discriminatory provisions and no discriminatory impact.

That same January, a national conference on women and the constitution, scheduled for the next month by the federal Advisory Council on the Status of Women, was cancelled. The Council's chair, former journalist and editor Doris Anderson, resigned dramatically with the charge that the cancellation had been ordered by the minister responsible for the status of women. A small, Toronto-centred group of feminists moved in as a self-appointed ad hoc committee to hold the conference as and when originally scheduled. They surprised themselves and many others by conducting in February 1981, without government funding, a successful three-day meeting of more than 1 300 women from across Canada. Anderson's resignation and the bitter accusations and counteraccusations within and around the council attracted considerable publicity, as did the counter-conference. Then, in April, after continued lobbying spearheaded by members of the ad hoc committee, the guarantees of equality in Section 15 were backed up by Section 28, which states that "notwithstanding anything in this Charter, the rights and freedoms referred to in it are guaranteed equally to male and female persons."[20]

The drama was not over, however. That fall, a federal–provincial conference bypassed Quebec to work out an override arrangement that would allow provinces to pass special limited-term legislation in any area, "notwithstanding" any guarantees in the Charter. It was several days before it was clear to the public and to politicians that the override applied also to the hard-won Section 28. Edythe MacDonald, a federal civil servant present during the negotiations about the override, recalls that she burst out in rage that "the women of Canada would not put up with this treachery."[21] Nor did they. After an angry, intensive campaign of public meetings, letters, and telegrams, and private lobbying by women's groups and individual women, the provincial premiers agreed to exempt Section 28 from the override. Pierre Trudeau, the prime minister who was responsible for the patriated constitution, was to observe years later that "the women were very clever when they made us put it in that form—notwithstanding. . . ."[22] He thus recognized the role of women—and women's groups—in shaping their constitutional rights, and also how important those rights were.

Many anglophone women were jubilant: thanks to their efforts, Canada now had the equal rights provisions that the United States had failed to acquire. But Marilou McPhedran, a well-known feminist lawyer who played an important role in the ad hoc committee, summed up the results as follows: "To make any lasting change you have to participate in the workings of the institution and that's not what the ad hoc committee did; we assaulted the institution and forced it to respond."[23] Many women felt pride for precisely that reason: the assault, the assumption and use of power, and the visible, if limited, success.

Quebec women and Quebec women's organizations were not involved in these campaigns. They were convinced that the Quebec Charter of Rights already provided all the protection needed, and they did not wish to grant legitimacy to the federal government even by challenging it. Both federally and in the provinces, governments now modified a considerable number of items of law and public policy in anticipation of obligations under the equality provisions of the Charter that came into effect in 1985. In applying the principles of the Charter, the Supreme Court explicitly referred to the Persons Case conception of the Constitution as "a living tree," a document that was "drafted with an eye to the future" that must be "capable of growth and development over time to meet new social, political and historical realities unimagined by its framers."[24]

Constitutional negotiations continued, and the next round began in 1987, with the preparation of the so-called Meech Lake agreement, a renewed attempt to find some way of reconciling Quebec's nationalist demands with the maintenance of federalism. Many women were alarmed at the possibility that the resulting constitutional changes would nullify Charter guarantees that were important for all women but especially for Aboriginal women; it would, they thought, also threaten national social programs. However, speaking on behalf of Quebec's francophone women, both the *Conseil du statut de la femme* and the *Fédération des femmes du Québec* supported the Meech Lake agreement. As before, they expressed confidence in the Quebec government and its institutions: "In the Province of Quebec, the respect of women's rights is more and more becoming part of political culture. . . . The progress we have made with regard to the status of women is linked to the concept of a distinct society."[25]

In 1990, when the Meech Lake agreement was discussed by elected national and provincial leaders in the unsuccessful attempt to complete its ratification, no women were present at the negotiating table. But in 1992, women and women's organizations became, for the first time and in a way not repeated since, publicly recognized players among those dealing with a possible constitutional settlement. In preparation for a nation-wide referendum on new constitutional arrangements, the federal government consulted widely with many citizens' forums and public action groups, including women's. Once again the main issue for many women activists was that the referendum document—the Charlottetown Accord—seemed likely to allow communal rights, particularly Quebec's and those of the Aboriginal peoples, to overrule the Charter of Rights and its protection for women and other so-called minority groups. The National Action Committee on the Status of Women had earlier opposed the proposed Meech Lake Agreement, without drawing much public attention. It now experienced its most visible role in public policy, getting excellent media coverage for its outspoken opposition to the agreement. By contrast, NDP Leader Audrey McLaughlin and many other politically active women supported the accord. All three major federal parties also favoured it, as did many individual women, feminist or not. Three Aboriginal women were conspicuous among the representatives of the four national Aboriginal organizations that helped develop the text for the referendum: Nellie Curnoyea was government leader of the Northwest Territories; Mary Simon was president of the Inuit Circumpolar Conference that served as a voice for the Inuit from Canada, Alaska, Greenland, and Siberia; and Rosemarie Kuptana was the elected head of the national Inuit organization, the Inuit Tapirisat of Canada (later known as the Inuit Tapiriit Kanatami of Canada).[26]

Some Aboriginal women had organized in support of their belief that their specific concerns were not fully served by the national association of chiefs. The Native Women's Association of Canada (NWAC) went to court to oblige the government to give direct funding and equal voice to their group as the representative of Aboriginal women in the constitutional discussions. NWAC's case was based on the possible loss of Charter

Opponents to the Charlottetown Accord during the pre-referendum debates in 1992. From left to right: Preston Manning (Reform Party), Lucien Bouchard (*Bloc Québécois*), former prime minister Pierre Elliott Trudeau, Jacques Parizeau (*Parti Québécois*), and Judy Rebick of NAC.

Source: Estate of Duncan Macpherson. Reprinted with permission - Torstar Syndication Services.

protection for Aboriginal women, but its continuing concern was over the absence of persons who would speak to women's issues in the processes leading to Aboriginal self-government. In 1992, the Charlottetown Accord was rejected by both Quebec and the rest of Canada in a national referendum. The Supreme Court found against NWAC in 1994; however, by that time the federal government seemed to be accepting it as a legitimate participant, along with the four other national-level Aboriginal associations, in the ongoing talks about Native self-government. NWAC was a full participant in drawing up the 2005 Kelowna Accords—never implemented—that pledged the federal government to substantial investment in ending Aboriginal poverty. The group was also present by invitation in 2008 when the federal government apologized for the shame of the residential schools.[27]

The impact of the Charter on women was massive, as laws and regulations were changed to conform with the requirements of Section 15. For example, at a time when Canada once again became engaged in military missions overseas, it was significant that full access to the Canadian Armed Forces had been opened up for women. By 1989, women could be part of almost all occupations in the Canadian Armed Forces, including combat roles; service in submarines, previously exempted, was added in 2000. The Canadian Forces were unsuccessful in obtaining an exemption from Charter requirements in respect to sexual orientation; a series of legal suits by lesbians who had been dismissed from the military ended in 1992 with a settlement of $100 000 to former 2nd lieutenant Michelle Douglas. Canadian women served in the combat zones of the 1991 Gulf War and as part of the Canadian military that went into Afghanistan under NATO auspices in 2001. Captain Nichola Goddard was the first of three Canadian women in the Armed Forces who had died in service by June 2009 in the difficult struggle in Afghanistan. By then, women made up about 2 percent of Canadian regular force combat troops and 15 percent of Canadian Forces personnel overall. Women were also acting as war correspondents, and in December 2009 Michelle Lang's name had to be added to the list of Canadian women killed in the Afghanistan war.[28]

POLITICS

Canadian women continued to be active in the many mixed-sex movements and organizations that attempted to influence public policy, such as the anti-American nationalist groups that were vocal after 1960. Maude Barlow was a conspicuous voice in this cause and, beginning in the 1990s, in the environmental movement. So also was Inuit activist Sheila Watt-Cloutier. For some women, however, the slowness and difficulty of changing public policy from the outside led them to seek more direct involvement in government. Thus, in 2006 Elizabeth May went from executive director of the Sierra Club to leader of a new Green Party of Canada; the same year, and again in 2008, she ran unsuccessfully for the federal Parliament. In the process, she attracted substantial attention to her party's policies—often a significant motive for women standing for office under obviously unfavourable conditions.

Judy LaMarsh, Secretary of State for Canada, elected most newsworthy woman of 1967, with Bobby Gimby, composer of the Centennial theme song "Ca-na-da."

Source: Courtesy of The Niagara Falls Review

Even in the last half of the twentieth century, women were slow to make their mark in elected office. After status Indian women gained the right to participate in band elections in 1951, there were no longer legal barriers to any woman holding office on account of her sex. However, status Indian women, like status Indian men, could not vote or hold office federally until 1960 and it was only in 1969 that Quebec became the last province to admit them to the provincial franchise. In the 1960s and 1970s those few Canadian women who became directly involved in electoral politics were most often elected as so-called political widows, replacing ailing or deceased husbands; this was true of two out of the four women who were in the House at the time when the Royal Commission on the Status of Women was put in place in 1967. Similarly, the first woman elected to Quebec's *Assemblée Nationale*, Claire Kirkland-Casgrain, entered the legislature in 1961 through a by-election to fill the seat left vacant by her father's death. Attitudes and expectations were slow to change. A 1966 publication of the Department of Citizenship and Immigration stated flatly that "winter weather is a limiting factor" to Canadian women's political activity.[29] As late as 1975, a national survey showed that Canadians tended to believe that "the average man" would make a better politician than the "average woman."[30] The 1968 election saw only one woman returned to the federal Parliament, Grace MacInnis of the NDP. The next federal election, in 1972, was a turning point in terms of national electoral office, as Progressive Conservative Flora MacDonald and Liberals Jeanne Sauvé, Albanie Morin, and Monique Bégin were returned, the latter three Quebec's first women MPs. These four women joined Grace MacInnis to multiply by five the number of women MPs. (See Table A. 11 in Appendix).[31]

Bégin, MacDonald, and Sauvé all became Cabinet ministers, holding some very powerful ministries that were not conventionally associated with women—MacDonald, for example, served as secretary of state for External Affairs from 1979 to 1980. Sauvé was later the first woman to be Speaker of the House and also the first woman to be governor general, in 1980 and 1984, respectively. Younger women also began to be elected. Sheila Copps, for example, moved from the Ontario to the federal legislature in 1984 and provided two landmarks for women in Parliament: she was the first woman Member of Parliament to get married while in office and in 2009 was still the only MP to have given birth while in office. Possibly more significant, at least in conventional political terms, was the fact that Copps served as Jean Chrétien's deputy prime minister, as did Anne McLellan after her. Subsequent federal governments did not appoint women to such a truly powerful position, although the number of female Cabinet ministers slowly increased.

There continued to be a glass ceiling, however, for those women attempting to acquire a major share in power. In 1975, Rosemary Brown was the first woman and also the first black person to contest the leadership of a national party: the NDP. As well, as a member of the B.C. legislature, she had been the first black woman to sit in any legislative body in Canada. She came in a strong second, but the delegates at the convention selected Ed Broadbent, the son of an Oshawa auto worker. Brown was not a conventional politician, but one of those women who came to politics through volunteer activities, in her case both anti-racist and anti-sexist. Founder and board member of the Vancouver Status of Women Council, she stood for office at that group's urging and carried those concerns into her 14 years as an MLA. An obituary in 2000 quoted her saying, "Conservative women and women on the right continually told me that I didn't speak for them. However, I did work for them. I have never lost sight of the fact that I was the women's candidate, that they nominated me, worked for me, and elected me."[32] Brown went on to head MATCH, a Canadian group that sponsored development projects for women in the global South; in 1993 she became chair of the Ontario Human Rights Commission.[33]

In 1976, Flora MacDonald, the former secretary of the Progressive Conservative Party who had worked her way up through her party's ranks, then a popular MP from Kingston and the Islands, was resoundingly defeated in an attempt at the party's leadership. Public-opinion polls had shown that 86 percent of the public would be willing to vote for a party with a woman leader and many convention delegates had publicly pledged support to MacDonald before apparently reneging, to produce a disappointing showing in secret ballot votes. It was not surprising that the party, with its base in the West, finally preferred an Albertan, but it was evident that MacDonald's gender had been a major element in the outcome.[34]

It was 1989 before a woman became leader of a federal party. Audrey McLaughlin, a former social worker who had represented the Yukon in Parliament for two years, was picked as national leader by the NDP. Soft-spoken and a strong feminist, she inclined toward consensus-building. In the summer of 1993, Kim Campbell won a Progressive Conservative Party leadership convention, where she was presented by Ellen Fairclough, the first woman federal cabinet minister (1957–1963), and endorsed by Flora MacDonald. Since her party was in power, Campbell automatically became prime minister, but only until the Conservatives lost the next election. 132 days later she was defeated in her own riding, and the party was reduced to two seats. Although two of the major federal parties had women leaders, issues such as women's rights had been reduced in importance during the 1993 campaign. Many observers felt that both McLaughlin and Campbell, though qualified for the party leaderships, won them mainly because no male politician wished to take on the task at the time when their party was non-competitive.[35] The same situation existed when Alexa McDonough of Nova Scotia, an experienced provincial politician, followed McLaughlin as federal NDP leader in 1995. As the party began to look more competitive, largely due to McDonough's efforts, the next leader, in 2003, was the far more aggressive Jack Layton. McDonough retired from politics in 2008. At the time when she was making the decision to step down as federal NDP leader, she reflected on her career in politics. "In my experience, women actually do have a kind of humanising, a feminising, a civilising effect within . . . political parties," she told a workshop of feminist academics and women politicians. McDonough also felt that governments with more women in them were more likely to produce policies that helped women, partly because women's presence helped make elected men more sensitive to women's concerns.[36]

At the provincial level, British Columbia's Rita Johnston was the first woman to head a government, serving as premier from April to October 1991 after the sitting premier resigned because of a scandal; along with her Social Credit party, Johnston was then defeated at the polls. Two years later, Catherine Callbeck in Prince Edward Island became the first woman—and by 2009 the only one—to lead a provincial party to victory and head the subsequent government. A formal portrait made the summer after the election showed what the PEI Women's Network described as "History in the Making": the lieutenant governor, premier, (acting) Leader of the Opposition, Speaker, and Deputy Speaker were all women.[37] After Callbeck, no more women were premiers until Eva Aariak became premier of Nunavut in 2008; she headed a non-partisan legislature that chooses its leader by consensus.

In the 1990s, women significantly increased their share of legislative seats both federally and provincially.[38] Voters showed increasing hostility to incumbents, and the much-increased number of women candidates often benefitted from the resultant dramatic changes of government. The 1993 Parliament included 53 women—18 percent—a good proportion of women by international standards, at that time second only to the Scandinavian countries. Among the new MPs were two women of colour, Jean Augustine and Hedy Fry (who had defeated Prime Minister Kim Campbell in her B.C. riding). Augustine, who had been put into Toronto's Beaches–Woodbine riding by the Liberal leader as part of his party's affirmative action for women candidates, had come from Grenada as a domestic at the age of 22 and later became a school principal, a leader in the Canadian Congress of Black Women, and head of the Metropolitan Toronto Housing Authority. She felt that she brought a special point of view to politics: "It's the perspective of an immigrant woman raising two daughters. . . . It's knowing something about, say, the issue of day care because you have had to take children on a bus to day care." Augustine, who was immediately appointed parliamentary secretary to the prime minister, identified as one of her constituencies "the community of black and ethnic women."[39] The increased presence of women in Parliament also had a concrete if small impact on the Parliament building itself, which had been erected the year before Agnes Macphail set foot there. In 1994, after one rookie woman MP missed a vote because the women's washroom was so remote from the main chamber of the House of Commons, women MPs finally got a new washroom close to the legislative action. In 2008, there were 68 women elected to Parliament (22 percent).

Although women were initially slower to increase their legislative representation provincially than federally, women's share of seats in the provincial legislatures also crept up from about 5 percent in the 1960s and 1970s.[40] An NDP majority government in Ontario (1990–1995) resulted in a rise in the proportion of women in that legislature to 26 percent, and Premier Bob Rae appointed 11 women to a 27-member Cabinet; both were records at that time. Although the constraints, especially fiscal, on that government meant limits on social programs, the Rae government did put many women-friendly policies in place, and not all of them were undone by the Conservative government that followed. However, NDP women reported that the climate of the provincial Parliament was distinctly worse in reaction to the increased presence of women. Marion Boyd, who held ministerial posts in the Rae government, wrote a report on behaviour in the House, noting "verbal attacks and manipulation of tone . . . and other forms of behaviour," including examples of male Opposition MPPs "significantly increasing the volume—that is, more heckling, coughing and hissing when a woman rises to speak, introducing a wall of sound before she has even started her words, blowing kisses across the floor of the House, and mocking the higher-pitched voices of female members."[41]

Quebec's *Assemblée Nationale* also had a steady high level of women MNAs; it reached 30 percent women in 2003 and stayed around that level, where it was in 2009. Quebec finally had a woman leader of a major party when long-time *péquiste* Pauline Marois was chosen as head of the *Parti Québécois* in 2008. However, she was elected at a time when the PQ was in Opposition and its sovereigntist cause was not doing particularly well.

By 2006, the percentage of legislators at the provincial level who were women was roughly equivalent to what it was federally—about 20 percent—with Manitoba, Quebec, and B.C. higher and the Atlantic provinces lower. Observers were distressed to note that the proportion of women elected to political office seemed to platform out at all levels of government at about one-fifth, a percentage too low for a so-called critical mass that would enable women to produce legislation favourable to women or to at least moderate the aggressive and impolite behaviour characteristic of politics. The result in Canada was a big push by feminists to increase the number of women nominated as candidates for office, with feminists working within the parties and through new organizations, such as Equal Voice and Quebec's *Groupe Femmes, Politique et Démocratie*. The vastly increased nominations, most notable in the NDP, the first party to adopt affirmative action for women and minority candidates, tended to be for ridings not likely to be won by the nominating parties. Still, once nominated, women were elected at the same rate as men, and numbers increased, if slowly. Manitoba in 2009 had the highest percentage of women in a provincial Parliament at that time: 32 percent.

The plateauing of women's representation at provincial and federal levels seemed to be related to the fact that they were relatively less often elected outside Canada's largest cities. The shortfall in elected women was now apparently part of public consciousness: a poll conducted in the fall of 2008 showed that 63 percent of Canadians thought women were underrepresented in Parliament and no fewer than 85 percent said they supported efforts to get more women elected.[42] As late as 2009, however, a judge of the Ontario Superior Court refused to accept the evidence of a young woman MPP on the grounds that she was commuting to Queen's Park in Toronto, "leaving her husband and children in Ottawa." "I didn't know that truth had a gender," responded 34-year-old MPP Lisa MacLeod.[43]

It was initially at the municipal level, for so long a target of women's organizations, that women most rapidly increased their participation. From the end of the 1970s, women became more numerous as mayors of cities and towns, while also increasing their representation on city councils and school boards. In 88 of the larger municipalities, where women constituted 15 percent of city councillors in 1984, the level grew to about a quarter in 1993. Ottawa had several women mayors after 1951's pioneer, Charlotte Whitton, and in 1994 Barbara Hall followed June Rowlands as the second woman in a row to become mayor of Toronto, responsible for a budget larger than that of many nations. Hazel McCallion, who was first elected mayor of Mississauga, Ontario, in 1968, became the longest-serving mayor in that borough's history, serving her eleventh successive term in 2009. But by 2009 representation of women at this level was also seemingly stalled, at just under one-fourth of councillors and only 15 percent of mayors of all municipalities.[44]

Smaller towns did sometimes have women at the helm. A typical example was Makkovik, Labrador, which had 395 citizens in 1987, when Ruth Flowers advanced from deputy mayor to mayor. "I got involved in municipal politics because I wanted to see things change around for us up here," said Flowers. "Things that the rest of Canada takes for granted like a safe home for women, daycare, more social services and police protection."[45] In 1984 Daurene Lewis, a descendant of Rose Fortune, Annapolis Royal's famous pioneering policewoman and porter, was the first black woman mayor, not just in Canada but in North America. She was also Nova Scotia's first black woman candidate for Parliament. Campaign schools and other proactive attempts to engage and equip interested women for municipal politics became common after the first campaign school for women in Canada was initiated by the B.C. Canadian Women Voters Congress in 1999. Some campaign schools were provided by status of women sectors of the provincial governments, others by the Union of Canadian Municipalities or by volunteer feminist groups.[46]

Reserves were rather like the smaller municipalities, although they were dependent mainly on the federal government rather than on the provinces. In 2000 about 90 women were chiefs (15 percent), a number which rose to 107 (18 percent) nine years later. In February 2007, a national conference of women chiefs was held in Vancouver. At it, an unidentified woman chief was quoted as saying something women activists might have said at almost any time in Canada's history: "We are the women and we know where the dirt is. The community expects us to clean it up. That is our job as leaders."[47]

Most reserves were likely to be poverty-stricken. But some controlled considerable resources and developed substantial businesses that needed managing. In other cases, band chiefs had the additional role of leading negotiations about land claims with provincial and federal governments. In 2009 Kim Baird, who had become chief of the 358-person Coast Salish Tsawwassen First Nation at the age of 29, concluded the first land claims treaty negotiated between the B.C. government and an urban reserve. Women candidates were unsuccessful in attempts to be elected head of the Assembly of First Nations (originally the Indian Brotherhood), but in September 2009 Chief Betty Ann Lavallée, New Brunswick Aboriginal Council president, was elected national chief of the Congress of Aboriginal Peoples, representing Canada's Métis, off-reserve, and non-treaty Indians. A member of the Mi'kmaq people, Chief Lavallée had a long history of advocacy for Aboriginal causes as well as experience in development, and 17 years of service in the Canadian Armed Forces.[48]

Governor General Michaëlle Jean inspects RCMP recruits in Saskatchewan, 2006.

Source: © Her Majesty the Queen in Right of Canada represented by the Office of the Secretary to the Governor General of Canada (2008). Photo credit: Ssgt Eric Jolin, Rideau Hall. Reproduced with the permission of the Office of the Secretary to the Governor General.

Women were more frequently found in political positions that were appointive. Some of these were almost entirely ceremonial, such as governor general, a position held successively by Jeanne Sauvé, Adrienne Clarkson, and Michaëlle Jean. This position was, however, of considerable symbolic importance since, as the Queen's representative, the governor general served as Canada's head of state. All the above women were appointed in part for gender reasons. In addition, Sauvé was chosen by a Liberal government anxious to demonstrate that Quebecers could play a role in the federal government. Both Clarkson and Jean were non-Anglo-Celtic immigrants, Hong Kong Chinese and Haitian, respectively, and they were understood to be representative of the importance of both immigrants and women in Canada. By 2000, already over one-third (37 percent) of the appointed senators were women. Although the impact and future of the Senate were disputed, by 2009 a number of well-known feminist activists had served in the Red Chamber, including Thérèse Casgrain, Florence Bird, Lorna Marsden, Lucie Pépin, Nancy Ruth, and Sandra Lovelace Nicholas.

Other positions to which women were appointed were unarguably powerful. In the twenty-first century, Canadian governments came to fear the annual reports generated by Auditor-General Sheila Fraser. Julie Dickinson was "the most powerful woman in Canadian Banking" as head of the Office of the Superintendent of Financial Institutions. Louise Arbour was appointed to the High Court of Justice of Ontario and then the Court of Appeals for Ontario and later (1999–2004) served on the federal Supreme Court. In addition, she served as chief prosecutor of war crimes for the International Criminal Tribunals for Rwanda and the former Yugoslavia, as well as the UN's high commissioner for human rights. In August 2009, Privacy Commissioner Jennifer Stoddart, previously a feminist historian, forced the social networking giant Facebook to agree to changes that would restrict the sharing of personal data to third-party users; it was a decision with massive implications.[49]

Numbers and firsts were useful if sometimes discouraging indicators, but more important were the reasons and results of women's increasing involvement in electoral politics. Women candidates for political office at every level were likely to have policy issues rather than ambition or career advancement central to their motivation for political action, and sometimes, though not always, party affiliations were less important to them. Thus, Claudette Bradshaw, active on behalf of disadvantaged children, felt that the non-governmental organizations she worked with, such as Big Brothers and Big Sisters

Club, were limited in impact; she became a Liberal MP and, in 1997, a federal Cabinet minister. In 2009, Susan Huntingdon managed the rare feat of getting elected to the B.C. legislature as an Independent, voicing community concerns in her riding of Delta South.[50]

RELIGION

As the twentieth century passed away, analysts noted the dramatic decline in the membership in Canada of the mainline Christian churches from their peak in the 1960s, and some attributed it to the withdrawal of women, especially young women. "As the young women go, so go the country's Christian communities," wrote one commentator in 2007 when the trend was clear. "Future mothers have proved to be the key to the churches' future as organized, living bodies."[51] At the most extreme, some women actively rejected traditional religious institutions. For them, the churches were among the most powerful institutions of patriarchy; they turned away, unsatisfied by what they interpreted as co-option. The search for a spirituality responsive to women led some of them toward religions more compatible with feminism, including groups that drew on ancient traditions of witchcraft. By the 1980s, Canadian women had available an eclectic range of goddess cults made up of women only. For such women, the problem of conflict between male standards and female autonomy was solved; their separate organization asserted their legitimate interests as women. It was also estimated that some 60 to 70 percent of the participants in neo-paganism were women, apparently because of the prominent role of goddesses and of female celebrants in such versions of spirituality.[52]

Within the established religions, women worked for change, but progress varied. In all the mainstream religions, the 1960s and 1970s saw a flowering of discussion and activism among women determined to infiltrate and reform from within. An especially long-lived example was *L'autre parole*. Started in 1976 by a collective of the same name and still lively in 2009, it was a Christian and feminist publication. "*Notre théalogie parle de Dieue*," it announced, using the tactic of feminizing French typical of feminists in Quebec.[53] Most commonly, attempts to transform the churches subsided as women were more accepted into existing church hierarchies. In Canada, Protestant churches had a long history of women's active participation. The largest Protestant denomination in the country, the United Church of Canada, was increasingly responsive to women, and in 1982 peace activist Lois Wilson was elected moderator. She later recalled that she "thrived on the demands of the job." She added, "Since as a woman I had no role models, I was free to innovate."[54] Wilson went on to become the first woman president of the World Council of Churches and was active within a wide range of groups, including Amnesty International and the Canadian Civil Liberties Union; her memoirs ended with an account of her support of the Innu women who were campaigning against low-level NATO training flights in the area of Goose Bay, Labrador. For Lois Wilson, and for many other women, religion was still a major motivator for feminism and for activism.

For its part, the Anglican Church of Canada made reforms more speedily than its counterpart in the United Kingdom, starting to ordain women ministers in 1976. Sixteen years after the first ordination of women, Victoria Matthews was elected Canada's first female suffragan bishop, one of five women bishops in the worldwide Anglican communion. She described herself as a feminist but "not a strident one": "I am a woman and have a woman's perspective," she said, "but I don't bring womanhood to the House of Bishops, I bring myself."[55] Individual churches and parishes were not necessarily as speedy or positive in response. Thus, although the Cathedral Church of St. James in Toronto began to incorporate women into the substantial lay governance structures of the cathedral in the 1960s, there was reluctance in some quarters to admit women to a sacramental role. The historian of the Cathedral writes, "By 1988 the question of the role of women permeated parish life," and "the tensions ran high." After a parish weekend conference, a taskforce, and some negative reactions—including accusations of heresy and a lawsuit—attention turned to appointing a woman priest. Carol Langley, admitted to the ministerial staff as a deacon in 1990 and then a priest in 1991, was warned when she was first hired, "You will need the heart of a dove and the skin of a rhinoceros."[56] In 2007, women made up one-quarter of the active Anglican clergy, and by that time three women had served as bishops. Still, most top positions in the Church remained firmly in the hands of men, a phenomenon that some commentators labelled "the stained-glass ceiling." Bishop Anne Tottenham, the second woman bishop in Canada, commented, "It's the same in all the professions. There is still a whole issue of acceptance."[57] Nonetheless, by 2006 women accounted for one out of every five Anglican ministers, and in 2010 they comprised one of every three in the United Church of Canada.[58]

The Roman Catholic Church, the religion that still claimed the largest number of adherents among Canadians—43 percent in 2001—remained resistant to recognizing women's possible contributions in other than the age-old, limited ways. Devoted Roman Catholic laywomen were essential to the everyday operations of a faith that, like all mainstream religions, was losing adherents. Questioning long-established practices, some Catholic women began discussion groups and feminist activism designed to reform practices and doctrines so that they might remain within the communion. But they had little or no impact. Opposition to contraception and abortion continued, even though already by the 1980s most Canadian Catholics were almost as permissive as the rest of the country on these issues. There was still no possibility of ordaining women or even allowing laywomen a larger official role in the church. In Toronto, in 1987, an 11-year-old girl, Sandra Bernier, who had regularly been serving at the altar, was barred from doing so during a special celebratory Mass. The prohibition against female altar servers was repeated in 1994 for the 150th anniversary of the diocese of Toronto. Later in 1994, the Vatican formally permitted such access, but in the same year the Pope himself repeatedly and categorically ruled out any possibility of women being accepted into the priesthood. Two thousand prominent Quebec women signed a statement of dissent, but shortly after his installation in November of the same year, Jean-Claude Cardinal Turcotte, Archbishop of Montreal, explicitly supported the Pope's position.[59] When, in 2008, abortion reformer Henry Morgentaler was awarded an honorary degree by the University of Toronto, and then, in the next year, the Order of Canada, the Church led the small but vocal protests. Cardinal Turcotte resigned from the Order, as did two other Catholic notables, and two more threatened to follow suit. Supporters of Morgentaler, delighted to see him recognized, said wryly that they had thought there would be "a flood of medals to be returned." A 2008 poll showed that 65 percent of Canadians approved of Morgentaler's honour.[60]

Ironically enough, the appeal of the religious life declined for women even while feminist historians were illuminating the importance of the nuns as representing alternative, valuable roles for women outside of marriage, and Marguerite Bourgeoys and Marguerite d'Youville were canonized as the first female Canadian saints. Entry into the orders dwindled, and many nuns broke their vows. By 1991, there were only 152 religious communities of women in Canada, down almost half from the high point of 1967. The decline had been rapid: between 1966 and 1971, the number of women in religious orders declined by two-thirds and in the same period the number of women entering the religious life decreased by 80 percent. Though so much smaller, the remaining communities mostly adapted to the changing environment. By 2009, there were only 94 members in Canada of the 400-year-old Institute of the Blessed Virgin Mary, more often known as the Sisters of Loretto. The order, with 1 000 members worldwide, had been active in Vatican II and the first to adopt lay dress. Its mission expanded to include "outreach to the poor, ministry to prisoners, retreat work and spiritual direction, work with refugees, parish ministry, education by correspondence, and collaboration with local bishops in the work of religious education" as well as concern for the rights of women. In Canada, it was still carrying out teaching functions (for example, in Toronto's Loretto College School) and it also became active around the relationship between ecology and spirituality. In 2009, the Sisters carried through an exemplary "green" renovation of the women's residence they ran at the University of Saint Michael's College, making it into one of the first sustainable buildings in Toronto.[61]

The other Abrahamic religions varied in receptivity to changes driven by those feminists who wished to remain within the community. Such a one was Elyse Goldstein, 13 years old in 1968 when she shocked everyone present in the synagogue for her bat mitzvah by announcing that she wanted to become a rabbi and not a *rebbetzin* (rabbi's wife): "let my husband be the *rebbetzin*."[62] After she was ordained in 1983, she served in two congregations and then in 1991 became head of Kolel: The Adult Centre for Liberal Jewish Learning in Toronto. Reconstructionist and Reform Jewish congregations as well as some Conservative ones responded to an increasingly strong voice coming from women. They instituted bat mitzvah ceremonies for girls, arranged mixed seating in synagogues, began to modify God language liturgy, and finally allowed women full participation in the public aspects of religion. By 2009, there were 16 women in Canada who had been ordained as rabbis, though fewer than half of them presided over congregations. But Orthodox women saw relatively few changes; there were no Orthodox women rabbis. Orthodox women continued to have to supplement legal divorce with their ex-husbands' permission (the *get*) if they wished to remarry inside their religion. However, Canadian Jewish women led an international campaign for legal change and, as a result of pressure started by volunteer committees, Canadian divorce legislation was altered in 1990 so that the *get* could no longer be used as a bargaining chip in divorce settlements.[63]

For their part, Muslim women found personal and spiritual decisions about religion and the related social practices particularly difficult as issues relating to the role of women in Islam became politicized. A good deal of attention focused on what might seem a trivial problem—dress codes for women. Muslims reformers had since the early twentieth century advocated westernization in family law and practices, including the wearing of European clothing by both men and women. But in the second half of the century some Muslim women returned to observing the traditional *hijab*. The code of modesty and chastity was prescribed for girls and women by Muslim religious law, and it was interpreted to require women to wear garments that concealed the hair and obscured the body or, in the most radical versions, all of the face. Muslim women and, even more, Muslim feminists disagreed about the *hijab*. "Feeling that one has to meet the impossible male standards of beauty is tiring and often humiliating," wrote Naheed Mustafa, a young Canadian-born college graduate. For her, the *hijab* was a way "to give women ultimate control of their own bodies."[64] By contrast, for secularized Muslim feminists, such as Fauzia Rafiq, a member of the editorial committee of *Diva*, a magazine for South Asian women, the effort of some Canadian Muslim men to "enforce Islamic law pertaining to family life" amounted to "consolidating male power . . . in the name of religion, cultural diversity and hereditary rights."[65] In 1994, some schools in Quebec attempted to forbid girls to wear the headscarf that was the commonest version of the *hijab*, but the Quebec Human Rights Commission ruled that a school could intervene only if a student was wearing the scarf against her will. In the interest of supporting women's autonomy within marriage and the family, in 2005 the government of Ontario rejected an attempt to set up *Shari'a* (Islamic family law) courts and then removed authority from the pre-existing religion-based Jewish and Christian arbitration tribunals.[66]

Muslims in Canada comprised a small but rapidly growing group. Two percent of the population in the 2001 census, which was more than double the percentage in 1991, they were expected to increase another 160 percent by 2017.[67] In the period following the attacks on the World Trade Center in New York in September 2001, identifiable Muslims were liable to be viewed with distrust—and the women wearing the *hijab* were the most obvious members of that group. Sixteen-year-old Sultana Yusufali was one of the Canadian Muslim women who wore a headscarf by her own choice. In 2001, she wrote of the hostile reactions she encountered: "Perhaps the fear is that I am harbouring an Uzi underneath." She described herself as "Veiled Not Silent."[68] In 2007, at the time of three federal by-elections in Quebec, Muslim women became symbols of anxiety about potential terrorism, as the federal government created a bogus crisis about the possibility that fully veiled women could not be properly identified if they refused to uncover their faces to male poll officials. It was estimated that while just over two-fifths (42 percent) of Muslin women wore some sort of head covering, only 3 percent wore the face-concealing *niqab*, all of them so orthodox that it was unlikely they would participate in electoral politics. In 2009 the federal government quietly dropped plans to make the few women affected unveil if they chose to vote.

Canada's participation in the war in Afghanistan was partly supported by references to the improvements being made in the condition of Afghan women. Freedom from the *burq'a*, the all-enveloping robe traditionally worn by Afghan women, was the visible proof of liberation, and many believed that the same argument should apply in Canada. Some Canadian Muslim women felt themselves in an untenable position, torn between religious, family, and Canadian and peer group social pressures. Populations living in areas of Quebec where few immigrants were to be encountered voiced concern about excessive accommodation to the preference of minority groups; such views shaded alarmingly into nativism, Islamophobia, and anti-Semitism. In response, Quebec set up in 2007 a provincial royal commission to examine the issue of reasonable accommodation. The Bouchard-Taylor Commission found that most Quebecers and Quebec organizations were quietly making adaptations to what were the social rather than the religious concomitants of life for the devout in a diverse and, in principle, tolerant society. It was not difficult, for example, to provide women-only swimming arrangements for the women of the Orthodox Jewish or Muslim faiths. The Commission also recommended a more thoroughgoing secularization of public life and in particular of publicly provided services. The issue reignited after 2009 when a *niqab*-wearing woman filed a human rights complaint when, after significant attempts at accommodation by the woman teacher, the Quebec government expelled her from a class in French conversation intended to integrate immigrants into a society that, among other things, placed high value on gender equality.[69]

Women in many religions did manage to combine women's rights and concern for social conditions with a continuing commitment to their faiths. One example was among the Sikhs who formed a sizeable community in Surrey, B.C., where they supported one of the largest Sikh temples in North America. Here, in 2009, a youth slate, mostly born in Canada and including three women, decisively defeated the long-established management committee of the Guru Nanak Sikh Gurdwara temple. Their 19-year-old leader, Gursimran Kaur, a mathematics student at Simon Fraser University, ran on a platform of traditional customs, including women's rights. "In our religion, the first guru told us equality for women is very important because . . . she is the creator," she said. Gender equality and fighting domestic violence were at the top of her agenda.[70]

THE WOMEN'S MOVEMENT: BACKLASH, DISAGREEMENT, DIVERSITY, INNOVATION

Although many Canadians responded enthusiastically to the changes in women's lives and to feminism, others, including some women, reacted with suspicion, hostility, and organized opposition. The anti-feminist Federation of Women United for the Family was founded in Alberta in 1981, and played a significant role in Alberta politics from that date.[71] In the mid-1980s a national group headed by women prominent in the organized opposition to reproductive freedom began to get media attention. Established in 1983, the organization called itself REAL Women, an acronym for Real, Equal, Active, for Life. It claimed that other activist women's groups represented only a small number of "radical feminists." By contrast, although it lacked any sort of geographical reach and concealed its funding and membership, it claimed to speak for the real women of Canada who were silent. "What are we? plastic women?" responded Judy Erola, previously the federal minister responsible for the status of women.[72] REAL Women opposed abortion, universality of social services, the equality clauses of the Charter of Rights and the Court Challenges program supporting related litigation, no-fault divorce, legislation on equal pay for work of equal value, publicly funded daycare, affirmative action in employment, and legal protection of the rights of homosexuals.[73] Given the dependence of Canadian women's groups on public funding, REAL Women represented a genuine threat, since it opposed such support, and many members of the media were happy to counterpoise REAL Women against large, well-established feminist organizations, such as NAC and LEAF. In 2009, REAL Women's website welcomed cuts in government funding and support for women's programs. Feminists, its president declared, were just "one special-interest group."[74]

Anti-feminist women's groups responded in part to the persistent inequities in the treatment of women. There could be no disagreement among feminists with the wish to adapt the workplace to the needs of the family. Even in their defence of an idealized traditional family, anti-feminist women were attempting to obtain recognition and reward for the distinctive abilities and activities of women. But such groups seemed unable to accept the alterations or diversity in values or lifestyles that the multi-faceted women's movement spoke for. Florence Bird, who had chaired the Royal Commission on the Status of Women and was now a senator, summed up the problem in 1987:

> REAL Women wants to recreate the beautiful and happy society of the '50s ads—the happy mother, the beautiful, shining kitchen and the three happy children who never get sick. . . . It's nostalgia for the good old days that were never very good.[75]

Similar ideologies motivated parliamentarians who blocked national funding for daycare and formed what they called a family caucus in 1989. The caucus, whose members had also supported the Conservative government's unsuccessful attempts to recriminalize abortion, had delayed insertion of protection for lesbians and gay men into the federal Human Rights Act. In addition, the group generated legislation that would have prevented granting family-defined benefits to same-sex couples, however long-lasting or well-established their relationship. That bill on same-sex couples died on the order paper before the 1993 election, but not before it had shown the strength of conservative forces in Canadian life.[76]

Some individual men also reacted with hostility to both the reality and the rhetoric of the second wave of women's activism. The most shocking example, the Montreal Massacre of December 6, 1989, became symbolic of opposition to feminism and also, more generally, of violence against women.[77] Catherine Bergeron traced the events that led to the death of her sister, Geneviève, who had hoped to become an engineer like their father. Christmas break was near and Geneviève was in the cafeteria with her friend Marco, at a polytechnic institute that was part of the *Université de Montréal*. Afterward, Marco told Catherine what happened:

> They were just sitting in the upper level of the cafeteria chatting about an essay which was nearly due. Geneviève heard noises and ran down the stairs to the main floor. She thought the man holding a gun was a joke, a carnival trick.[78]

Plaque on the exterior wall of École Polytechnique, Montreal, commemorating the victims of the massacre, December 6, 1989.

Source: Bobanny/Public Domain

It was not a trick, or a robbery, as some of the young men thought when the man with the gun ordered them to leave. Geneviève tried to run and hide, but she was cornered behind the stereo speakers and shot twice, from so close that the spent cartridges from the bullets were found on her chest. She died instantly. Thirteen other young women students were also killed by the gunman, who then shot and killed himself. He had failed to be admitted to an engineering program at the *École polytechnique*. "I hate feminists," he screamed at his victims, and he left a letter listing other targets, all of them successful women whom he identified as feminists.[79] "We are not feminists," Natalie Provost told him, insisting she was just an engineering student. Shot four times, she survived and completed a degree in mechanical engineering; in 2009 she was the head of a strategic planning department in the Quebec government. "At the time, I thought to be a feminist meant you had to be militant," said Provost on the twentieth anniversary of the shooting. "I realized many years later that in my life and actions, of course I was a feminist." Her four children "have always known that when she was young, Maman was injured by a gun."[80]

Women's groups organized vigils and marches, and attempted with some success to focus the widespread feelings of grief and shock upon the more routine domestic violence committed by men against women. Some journalists helped to produce an improved understanding of the fear that constrained the lives of many women, while polls showed increasing public awareness that the courts failed to protect women from violent men. In one national survey four years after the massacre, 67 percent of respondents felt that violence against women had become worse in recent years; many blamed unemployment and economic hardship for the increased domestic tensions. By the 1990s, in contrast to the past, women were as likely as men to be victims of violent crime; for women, however, in four out of five cases, the attacker was someone they knew. A study released by Statistics Canada at the end of 1993 showed that more than half of a representative group of women had been physically or sexually assaulted by men at least once in their adult lives; another StatsCan study reported that more than 78 000 women and children had used battered women's shelters in 1991–1992. Support for educational programs and resources to diminish violence against women increased, with both federal and provincial governments making some commitment. In 2007–2008 nearly 62 000 women were admitted to one of 569 shelters across Canada—there had been only 18 shelters in 1975. Several provinces had also established special family violence courts. These programs seemed to be having some impact: although violence and particularly sexual assault continued to be vastly underreported, spousal homicide against women (and men) declined, and it seemed that non-lethal attacks on women were less severe. But if violent incidents by spouses had decreased, such attacks by boyfriends had increased.[81]

In 1991, December 6 was proclaimed a National Day of Remembrance and Action on Violence Against Women, which was widely observed by "memorial services in cities, towns and villages, in universities and colleges, in churches and community centres, in hospitals and legislatures, in libraries and parks." This was a list given in 2009, by Stevie Cameron, a journalist who had this account of how she had reacted when she heard about the massacre 20 years earlier: "I heard the news on the radio as I drove home. . . . I pulled over in shock and wept. My two daughters were students just like these girls."[82] Cameron lamented the continuing lethal violence against women, pointing to the examples of the mass murder of women from Vancouver's Eastside, the Aboriginal women who disappeared on the "highway of tears" in northern British Columbia, and the others missing and murdered in Edmonton and Winnipeg, as well as the appearance in Canada of honour killings by Islamic fundamentalists.

Most men shared in the horror provoked by the massacre. Pressed by activists to respond, Parliament approved a gun registry that agents of policing recommended in order to reduce the risk of inappropriate use of weaponry; it was put in place in 1995. Working to oppose violence against women, male support groups emerged, including the White Ribbon Campaign of men that became an international movement. But some objected to women-only ceremonies mourning the victims of the massacre, which they felt implied that all men were potentially violent. More generally, many men—and some women—became resentful of the continuing demand for changes in attitudes and policies relating to women. The resulting anti-feminism joined with a wave of anger about something labelled "political correctness," often abbreviated to "P.C." Apparently coined by socialists joking among themselves about the pressure to toe an orthodox party line, the phrase was widely adopted to describe those who rejected the assumption that European, white, male, heterosexual, and able-bodied added up to a norm to which all others should defer. Objections focused on events like the cancellation of the Miss Canada pageant under feminist pressure (in 1992), policies barring sexual or racial slurs or other forms of harassment, insistence on gender-neutral language, and even the increasing disapproval and legal restriction of smoking. All of these changes related to what the majority of Canadians had, in the past, found acceptable, but that many now found sufficiently offensive to bar legally. In addition, especially during economic hard times, employment equity programs seemed threatening to white, able-bodied men endangered by the constricting job market. They were made profoundly uneasy by targets for hiring and promoting women, visible minorities, Aboriginals, and the disabled. Critics raged about what they saw as the politicization of sex, race, class, and language. On occasion, feminists were labelled professional zealots or even "feminazis." Such reactions exaggerated the power of women, minorities, and their supporters.

Ironically, by the end of the twenty-first century, attacks on an allegedly aggressive, powerful feminism co-existed with insistence that feminism was irrelevant in a post-feminist era.[83] There were also accusations that young women were repelled by feminism because it treated women as victims: "whining, poor-little-me feminists have turned women, especially young ones, off."[84] Perhaps the success of the second wave of feminism was overestimated by young women growing up in a formally equal but less prosperous world. Some feminists suggested, optimistically, that even the opposition to women's goals was evidence that women's concerns were now being taken more seriously. "I see the backlash as a sign of success," said Lorna Marsden, then president of Wilfrid Laurier University. "People are now paying more attention to gender issues. In the past, these issues were marginalized and trivialized."[85] In the year 2000, a poll found that 32 percent of the women respondents considered themselves feminists, and about the same time another poll reported that 65 percent of all those answering were either somewhat sympathetic or very sympathetic to "the feminist movement."[86]

By this time, the structure of the women's movement had changed. Identity politics were now highlighted in Canada, as various population groups mobilized to an unprecedented degree around shared characteristics, such as race, ethnicity, or sexual orientation. The 1980s and 1990s saw the birth of many new organizations comprising women with multiple identities; such groups spoke for populations as specialized as Asian Lesbians of Toronto, or potentially as inclusive as immigrant domestic workers (International Coalition to End Domestic Exploitation—INTERCEDE). Women who were not part of Canada's historically white and Christian majority voiced anger at the way that government, media, and the established feminists had felt entitled to define women's goals. As resources diminished because of recession and neo-conservatism, voluntary groups became increasingly competitive. Substituting the term *diversity* for the confrontational and relativist concept of *difference* did little to allay tensions.

There were clearly issues that affected women in general. Foremost among these were those related to bodily conditions: abortion and contraception, incest and rape and other forms of violence against women, pregnancy and birthing, child-rearing, and the varieties of female sexuality. Paradoxically, these very issues provoked the most heated disputes among women and women's groups, for it was around such questions that loyalty to community and gender interest clashed most emphatically. One example was the question of domestic violence. When this topic was first raised as a subject of public policy in 1982 in a report presented to Parliament by MP Margaret Mitchell, male MPs felt free to respond with jeers and catcalls. Both attitudes and policy swiftly changed, but not without difficulty. In the 1970s, women involved with the shelter and transition house movement recognized that police forces were reluctant to intervene in what were seen as merely family quarrels. In addition, battered women were often so dependent on their partners, both psychologically and economically, that they were reluctant to take legal action against them. Women's groups accordingly urged, with some success, that police practice be changed so that officers would automatically lay charges when called in because of family assault, whether or not the victim requested it. London, Ontario, was the first of many municipalities to adopt such a policy, in 1981. However, abused women in minority communities showed increasing reluctance to call on the police for help. Because their partners were likely to be treated in a discriminatory fashion, such women were under pressure from relatives and friends not to seek assistance from public authorities. The women "have to choose one kind of violence over another," said Shelley Das, executive director of the National Organization of Immigrant and Visible Minority Women of Canada (NOIVMWC).[87] In 1994 NOIVMWC joined with the Elizabeth Fry Society and the National Association of Women and the Law to urge that ethnic communities set up councils responsible for supporting the women in question and for disciplining and educating their partners. Both citizens and law enforcers had mixed responses to these suggestions.[88]

For women activists, the racial and ethnic composition of women's groups sometimes seemed more important than their beliefs. An example that related to public policy was the Canadian Panel on Violence Against Women set up by the federal government in 1991 in collaboration with a diverse network of women's organizations. The panel's 1993 report, which comprised almost 500 recommendations, mostly targeted at the federal government, argued that violence against women would not end until women obtained fair and equal treatment in all areas of life: "a fundamental restructuring of society," in the words of panel chair Pat Marshall.[89] Under other circumstances it might have been recognized that the report was a far-ranging successor to the Report of the Royal Commission on the Status of Women in Canada, highlighting problems and groups of women not given sufficient attention in the initial assessment. However, both NOIVMWC and NAC savaged the panel's report because of the virtual absence of women of colour from the panel and the relatively brief discussion of those women's particular problems. Aboriginal women, by contrast, noted that the panel's research constituted the first major study of the violence they endured. Statistics Canada reported that in 1999 Aboriginal women suffered levels of spousal and other abuse at a rate three times that of non-Aboriginal women, a differential that remained true as late as 2004. There was also evidence that the spousal violence they endured tended to be more severe and damaging.[90]

Other issues of special concern to Aboriginal women began to arise as Aboriginal organizations acquired power over social services, including areas such as adoption and foster care. The interest of the Aboriginal communities in controlling such services was obvious; for example, the disproportionate placement of Aboriginal children in foster care had reached a scandalous level. However, the new agencies were often controlled by men. In 1991, Winnipeg Aboriginal women's groups went to the media, against the orders of the Assembly of Manitoba Chiefs, to publicize cases like those of a young Ojibwe woman who brought her children to a Winnipeg shelter, saying they had been beaten by their father—who was on the board of the Aboriginal child welfare society that decided to return the children to his care. Marilyn Fontaine-Brightstar, a member of the Aboriginal Women's Unity Coalition, presented such groups' views in *Weetamah*, Manitoba's Aboriginal newspaper:

> Abuse and exploitation of women and children is a political issue of equal importance to achievement of our inherent right to govern ourselves. Given that our elected aboriginal leadership is reluctant to stand up for this part of our community, we have no other choice.[91]

For women in Quebec, the tensions between Quebec nationalism and women's issues continued. In 1990, Lise Payette, who had returned to broadcasting, was asked by the provincial government to head an official commemoration of the fiftieth anniversary of the enfranchisement of Quebec women. She now compounded her earlier remarks about "Yvettes" with what was heard as a statement that immigrant women, as newcomers, were not entitled to participate in the event. Some immigrant women's groups accordingly refused to contribute to the celebration and exhibits. The *Fédération des femmes du Québec* (FFQ) also encountered problems in 1992, when the group set in motion extensive consultations for a project titled *Pour un Québec féminin pluriel*. Sovereigntist women blocked the formulation of what was intended to be a non-partisan feminist blueprint that would apply whether independence took place or not.

Over time, the FFQ was able to adapt. The wide consultation drew together representatives of many categories of women who had previously had little involvement with the umbrella group. The next year, the *Fédération* redefined its mandate to focus on those women who were economically disadvantaged and also those who suffered multiple discrimination, such as immigrants, Aboriginal women, lesbians, those with disabilities, or members of visible minorities. In 2004, the FFQ updated its platform to recognize the inter-related and global dimensions of its continuing feminist mission. By this time, the coalition had been greatly affected by participation in the 1995 Bread and Roses Women's March in Quebec and the UN's Beijing Conference on women later in the same year. Subsequently it took part in two worldwide Marches of Women against poverty and violence in 2000 and 2005 and in planning another for 2010. The FFQ also added to its activities a significant element related to young women, facilitating a pan-Canadian conference in October 2008, with follow-ups, under the rubric *Toujours RebELLES* (Waves of Resistance).[92]

Media regularly highlighted the confrontations now occurring inside women's organizations. Disagreement around issues of women's diversity had been going on longer than most remembered, however. In a 1993 interview, well-known lesbian author Jane Rule recalled an episode in the "early 70s":

> I can remember sitting in one of the first women's movement consciousness raising groups when somebody brought in an article from a magazine about lesbians and said she thought this would corrupt kids, and I said, you know, up to now, we've been talking about everything as I or we, and I think if you want to talk about lesbians, you have to do the same thing. You can't talk about them. And I am willing to start by saying that I am a lesbian and I am ready to talk about it. Dead silence.

Rule recounted that within two or three more years, everyone in the group was talking about "a range of sexuality." They developed a women's studies program and "saw to it that there was lesbian content in all the things we did."[93] But few women were as outspoken and brave as Rule, and few women's groups adapted as hers did. As a result, by the 1980s lesbians and also women of colour had become increasingly resentful of what they perceived as the insensitivity of white, heterosexual women, including feminists, to other women's particular needs. In addition, women with disabilities and older women reacted to the failures of able-bodied younger women to accommodate the contingencies of bodily condition. It also became clear that some women felt excluded by the pervasive Christian culture of Canada, with its sense of superiority to all other religions. Although women in non-mainstream categories had developed their own organizations, they now began to demand that those groups that claimed to speak for women respond to the differences of situation and experience among their membership.

Much of the friction among organized women resulted from the failure of long-hoped-for reforms to improve women's lives substantially, particularly for those whose disadvantages were multiple. Many groups split up or went out of existence. Service-providing groups and cultural media were the most vulnerable to the particularisms of identity politics, and the cross-pressures of race and sexual orientation were often excruciating for the women involved. The oldest feminist press in Canada, founded in 1972, went through a wrenching process of change after women of colour protested that they had been asked to participate in a lesbian fiction anthology only after the contents and procedure were set. As a result, many of the original members of The Women's Press left in 1988 to form a new feminist press, Second Story.[94]

Some women's organizations adopted policies of affirmative action themselves. NAC hired a black movement activist as executive director and acclaimed as president in 1992 a South Asian immigrant originally from Tanzania, Sunera Thobani. Thobani was a resident of Vancouver, where she had been active with the India Mahila Association and the B.C. Coalition for Abortion Clinics. Her election represented the first time that NAC's leadership came from outside of Toronto, which should have enhanced the organization's claim to be nationally representative. But Thobani's women's movement credentials were eclipsed for the public by the way in which she spearheaded NAC's growing focus on anti-racism as well as an anti-Americanism not much welcome in Canada after the tragedy of 9/11.[95]

There was increasing uncertainty about the role and scope of the large national women's organizations, especially NAC. In July 1993, following the publicity related to the involvement of NAC in the constitutional battles, a national poll asked respondents to identify an organization that represented the interests of Canadian women; half of those polled said that there was no such thing, and only 14 percent mentioned NAC, although numerous other groups were listed.[96] Contact and cooperation among women's groups of all kinds were in fact ongoing, and NAC was best understood as one of the major intersection points. NAC could feel pride in some real if modest successes. For several years, it managed to bring together disparate groups in a shared focus on lobbying for common goals. Most important, it had strengthened the network of women across regions and interests, providing a communications link in the form of annual meetings as well as newsletters and visits by officers. Like all social networks, however, the web of women's groups was a fragile one. By the 1990s the connections were weakening, and by the early years of the next century, the web pretty much fell apart. By 2006, NAC had basically ceased to exist. Funding of social programs was increasingly shifting to the provincial and even municipal levels of government, and the attention of activists shifted accordingly, although some still yearned for a pan-Canadian organization that could speak for women's equality.[97]

As Canada moved into the end of the twentieth century, more information emerged about the many extraordinary women in Canada's diverse racial, ethnic, and religious traditions. History collectives and individual researchers started to uncover, for example, the rich inheritance of lesbians and women of colour. Publications and films made visible the strength and coherence of ethnic and religious traditions, potentially freeing women to criticize their own communities with less defensiveness: even those disadvantaged because of ethnicity or religion or sexual orientation might have their own prejudices that needed to be combatted. Women of blended racial background pointed out the exclusionary effect of defining individuals by race or national origin. Few people in Canada were not of multiple ancestry, regardless of how they might identify themselves or be identified. For example, Elizabeth Goudie, who was born in Mud Lake, Labrador, in 1902, and who raised 10 children as the wife of a Labrador trapper, began her memoirs with the following sentence: "In approximately the year 1806, our great-great-grand-mother, who was an Eskimo orphan, ran away from down Rigolet Eskimos." Marriages over the generations produced "quite a mixture—Eskimo, English, French, Scottish and Indian," she said, adding that her children "are proud of their Indian and Scotch blood."[98] Almost a century after Goudie's birth, Anne Vespry, of even more complex ethnic background, reflected in 1993 that

> few of us identify as mixed race. It is easier to choose sides, identifying with one race over another, assimilating. Perhaps we are the heroes of the race wars, learning from the best that our ancestry has offered and disdaining the close-minded prejudice or xenophobia that lurks in our cultural closets.

When asked what her parents are, she replies, "librarians;" when pushed as to where they are from, she says "They're Canadians."[99]

As women learned more about one another, they found it easier to recognize some shared bases of disadvantage. Ageism, for example, became an issue at the end of the 1980s, only partly because feminist activists, youthful in the 1960s, were becoming aware of their own mortality. Although Canada's component cultures differed somewhat in their respect for the aged, most Canadians considered older women sexually worn out and irrelevant, unemployable, and virtually invisible. Older women of a variety of backgrounds were noteworthy, nevertheless, for their energy and imaginativeness. Some were able to resist ageism by insisting on maintaining their independence and their continuing engagement in professional and physical activity. In 1992, Carrie Best, then aged 91, restarted the *Nova Scotia Clarion*, which had discontinued publication in 1956. Ivy Granstorm of Vancouver was a world record holder in the "70 plus" category in track and field, with a repertoire ranging from 100 to 10 000 metres.[100] In 2009, sculptor Artis Lane, born in 1927 in North Buxton, Ontario, dedicated first her sculpture of Sojourner Truth (the first black woman to be recognized in the Rotunda of the U.S. Capitol) and then one of Mary Shadd Cary in Chatham, Ontario. "Mary Shadd Cary is my heroine, she is my voice of protest that I pour into my visual imagination," said Ms. Lane. She had gone from a segregated school in North Buxton to be the first black student chosen as the queen of the Beaux Arts Ball of the Ontario College of Arts, followed by a notable career as painter and sculptor.[101]

Some older women who were active in the peace and anti-nuclear movements sought a distinctive mode of protest. Troubled by "sexism and ageism in the local peace movement," in Victoria, B.C. , on Valentine's Day, 1987, a group of these women presented an "un-valentine" to the local MP who was chairman of the parliamentary Defence Committee, deploring inaction on issues such as the visits of nuclear-powered submarines to a base near Victoria. The Raging Grannies, as they called themselves, were wildly successful in drawing public and media attention to what became a substantial international movement (including at least 30 "gaggles" in Canada by 2008 as well as many others in the United States, the U.K., Australia, Israel, Greece, and Japan). Decked out in pink running shoes and outrageous hats, singing satirical versions of popular songs, they deliberately made themselves ridiculous in order to get their messages heard. Many were members of Voice of Women who had now found a new way to oppose militarism and sexism. They continued to oppose nuclear submarines, war toys, environmental pollution, and pornography, but added new targets such as the Charlottetown Accord and the North American Free Trade Agreement and then the twenty-first-century wars in Afghanistan and Iraq. Like many women activists by the last decades of the century, the Grannies explicitly saw themselves as feminists, and they also consciously valued the comradeship that came of women working together.[102] Linda Siege summed it up: "I want to live in a principled way but still have fun." Doran Doyle, who named the group, described herself as "Catholic and feminist" and commented, "We came together as older women at the peak of experience who would not be shunted aside. We're raging for peace. A wonderful paradox."[103] More traditionally, older women who would not have called themselves feminists organized to support those grandmothers in sub-Saharan Africa who were caring for their orphaned grandchildren whose parents had died of HIV-AIDS. Using imaginative events such as Scrabble tournaments and African meals, more than 220 groups of Canadian "grannies" raised consciousness and funds—over $7 million between 2006 and 2009—to support the heroes of the HIV-AIDS epidemic. After the first few groups developed spontaneously, their volunteer efforts were coordinated by the Stephen Lewis Foundation; they continued the charitable intent of the women's missionary societies of earlier days but without their condescension or proselytizing mission.[104]

One factor that facilitated both acknowledged and unrecognized feminism, including projects such as the Grandmother-to-Grandmother support groups, was the ubiquity of the electronic media, especially social networking. The price of personal computers declined rapidly, inexpensive laptops were produced, and their use became widespread. Cell phones rapidly acquired multiple computer capacities, including the ability to take and share instant photos of everything encountered. By 2008, 65 percent of Canadians had mobile phones and many young people did not even have—or want—access to land lines. Instant text messaging, using a stylized and reduced vocabulary, went back and forth constantly among them. The Generation Xers who followed the Boomers grew up in an environment where just about everyone was connected electronically, and online social networks such as Facebook and Twitter formed a major part of their social life.[105]

Online open diaries became popular in approximately 1994; they were followed by blogs (a contraction of *weblog*) and online affinity groups, which became a major source of information and opinion on every imaginable subject. Women were soon drawn to the Internet for creative and social uses, which sometimes became political ones. One outstanding example of a woman who made creative use of the Internet was Stephanie Pearl-McPhee. Lactation consultant, doula, and knitter, jobless when barred from Toronto hospitals because of the SARS epidemic of 2003, she became the "Yarn Harlot." Under that name, she wrote and published six books about knitting and her life as a knitter and, most important, she started a blog. With thousands of active users, it was named Best Blog by the Canadian Blog Awards in 2008. Initially responding to the December 26, 2004, Indian Ocean tsunami, the Yarn Harlot founded *Tricoteuses Sans Frontières*/Knitters Without Borders as an ongoing fundraising effort for *Médecins Sans Frontières*; by July 2009 she had raised over $600 000.[106]

Thanks to the Internet, activists could now inexpensively and quickly contact one another both trans-Canada—important in Canada's vast expanses—and internationally. Most feminist or women's service organizations and all relevant government agencies had websites through which they could communicate, while individual women had their own online diaries or blogs. For women who were restricted by home demands, and even more for women who were in abusive relationships, access to the Internet was transformative; the arrival of the radio and television had been breakthroughs in terms of information, but now even extremely isolated women of all ages had the possibility of making contacts in an entirely new way. It seems likely that electronic virtual groups filled the gaps in communication and sociability left by the fragmentation and decline of membership that affected both old and newer women's organizations.[107]

Confident in the use of the new electronic media and seeking to do feminism in a new way, younger women carried forward the struggle for women's autonomy and for influence on the world. Often, they called themselves the "Third Wave." Their situation was, indeed, a new one. Lisa Bryn Rundle, born in 1974, noted in 2001 that she had "grown up in a society already infused with feminism."[108] Another young woman, Emily Pohl-Weary, described how, like her peers, she felt she led a double life:

> In high school, I was pretty and vapid, wore pink miniskirts, teased my curled bangs and dated the football quarterback. After school I went to anti-war demos with Mom, read Germaine Greer's *The Female Eunuch* and cared for my whip-smart, bitchy, second-gen (at least) feminist grandmother.[109]

Pohl-Weary published in 2004 a collection of stories and accounts called *Girls Who Bite Back: Witches, Mutants, Slayers and Freaks*. She was responding to her generation's fascination with pop culture, providing superheroines for the young women who were, like her, granddaughters rather than daughters of the feminists of the 1960s and 1970s.[110] The TV program *Buffy the Vampire Slayer* became an icon for some of these young women: Buffy was a heroine with "strength, ability, courage, and cleavage."[111] A new generation was trying to revalidate feminism and women's identity in a new age, convinced that their earnest elders had fallen short.

Many young women, though often considering themselves feminists, were pessimistic about the effectiveness of both mainstream politics and single-sex activism; they preferred the radical, oppositional groups that dedicated themselves to protests against such institutions of globalization as the International Monetary Fund and various world economic summits. Conspicuous among them was the daughter of filmmaker Bonnie Sherr Klein; Naomi Klein became a well-known representative of what one observer called "the anarchic formlessness of the anti-corporate protests."[112] Her activist, feminist mother's strokes and the Montreal Massacre together made her decide to identify herself as a feminist, although all her work was in mixed-sex groups. Author of books analyzing global capitalism and a frequent and effective public speaker, Klein became something of an icon for the left, especially in the United States. Many other young women opted for direct service in environmental and anti-poverty groups in Canada or overseas. All of this was squarely in the tradition of Canadian women's activism, which had always included radical protest, concern with worldwide problems, and a tradition of service both at home and abroad.

It was not easy to characterize the self-styled Third Wave, apart from the age of the participants, who tended at any time to range from about 14 to 35. They were appreciative of pop culture (including fashion and music), and insistent on the value of all versions of female sexuality. At the same time, they were aware of the complexity of the situation of women, with its cross-cutting dimensions such as race, class, ethnicity, and gender. All this, they felt, was new. Theorists of the Third Wave often rejected the bifurcation of gender into male/female, especially in Quebec, where some declared that the Third Wave was fundamentally "queer." Here an English term was being used in Quebec to encompass a broad understanding of the fluidity of gender identity. Such third-wavers considered themselves feminists although they deconstructed in a post-modern fashion even the now accepted formulation of gay/lesbian/bisexual/transsexual (GLBT). For instance, *Les Panthères roses* of Montreal, founded in 2002, had in 2003 what they identified as a feminist project of disrupting Montreal's gay pride parade in order to protest its commercialization.[113] Others among the younger feminists continued to be interested in more conventional pressure and electoral politics. This was the route followed by Amanda Reaume, who was a 21 year-old UBC English major in 2006 when she started *Antigone* magazine with the slogan of "A magazine about women, politics, women in politics, and the politics of being a woman." *Antigone* was deliberately designed and produced to resemble the homemade cut-and-paste "zines" popular among the young. It was also the very seriously intended journal of the Women in Legislative Leadership Association (WILLA), started by students at Simon Fraser and UBC in 2005 to get other young women involved in both formal and informal politics. Reaume's project prospered, generating an Antigone Foundation, a blog, and numerous other activities, including plans for a magazine for even younger women.[114]

Canadian women's activism showed no signs of dying out, even under conditions of economic stress and reduced government support of volunteer groups. Older organizations persisted with some, such as the YWCA, dating back even to the nineteenth century, and others, such as the VOW and FFQ, dating from what in retrospect looked like the halcyon 1960s and 1970s. More ephemeral groups came and went, changing with the times, but with no indication that they were becoming less numerous. After the

Lavinia Crawley of East Preston, Nova Scotia, with her second husband. A descendant of a family that immigrated to Canada during the War of 1812, she was 88 when this photo was taken in 1982.

Source: Black Cultural Centre for Nova Scotia.

"Pan-Canadian Young Feminist Gathering" in 2008 called Waves of Resistance (Toujours RebELLES), a manifesto protested, "In this so-called post-feminist world, our roles in society are still defined by traditional views on gender." The participants acknowledged their foremothers generously—including their mother organization, the FFQ. Situating themselves in historical tradition, they called for both ambitious international projects and smaller dispersed and local ones. At the same time, they recognized in a thoroughly modern way the variety that had always existed among women. "We are women of diverse abilities, ethnicities, origins, sexualities, identities, class backgrounds, ages and races," the RebELLES declared.[115]

For Canadian women, sisterhood was not dead or forgotten. But it would now resemble life in the blended families of the new millennium.

Notes

1. Linda Silver Dranoff, *Women in Canadian Life: Law* (Toronto: Fitzhenry and Whiteside, 1977), 52–53.

2. Lissa Geller, "Common Law Spouse Ruling," *Kinesis* (May 1993) 7; for rural women and feminism see Louise I. Carbert, *Agrarian Feminism: The Politics of Ontario Farm Women* (Toronto: University of Toronto Press, 1995).

3. Lorenne M. G. Clark and Debra Lewis, *Rape: The Price of Coercive Sexuality* (Toronto: Women's Press, 1977); Paula Bourne, "Women, Law and the Justice System," in Ruth Roach Pierson, Marjorie Griffin Cohen, Paula Bourne, and Philinda Masters, eds., *Canadian Women's Issues* vol. 1 *Strong Voices* (Toronto: James Lorimer, 1993), 331–33; Isabel Grant, "Second Chance: Bill C-72 and the Charter" (1996), http://www.ohlj.ca/archive/articles/33_2_grant.pdf.

4. F. L. Morton, "The Political Impact of the Canadian Charter of Rights and Freedoms," *Canadian Journal of Political Science* 20, 1 (March 1987): 41–42; Doris Anderson, "Women Need Money to Test Charter," *The Toronto Star* (May 23, 1987), G1; Eleanor Wachtel,

"'The Day Daddy Died and Nancy Got Rich,'" *Financial Post Moneywise* (March 1989), 67; Michael Mandel, *The Charter of Rights and the Legalization of Politics in Canada* (Toronto: Thompson Educational Publishing, 1994); Sherene Razack, *Canadian Feminism and the Law: The Women's Legal Education and Action Fund and the Pursuit of Equality* (Toronto: Second Story, 1991), 48, 65, 128–30; advertisement on the back of *Herizons* 6, 4 (Winter 1993); Women's Legal Education and Action Fund/*Fonds d'action et d'éducation juridique pour les femmes* (2009), http://www.leaf.ca/legal/reform-analysis.html#target.

5. Dranoff, *Women in Canadian Life: Law*; Ann Rhodes, "Women Judges: A New Breed," *Chatelaine* 59, 5 (June 1985): 52, 87–90; Canadian Advisory Council on the Status of Women [CACSW] *Work in Progress: Tracking Women's Equality in Canada* (Ottawa: 1994), 108; "*Bittersweet Passage Gets Award*," *Kinesis* (February 1994), 8; Maryka Omatsu, *Bittersweet Passage: Redress and the Japanese Canadian Experience* (Toronto: Between the Lines, 1992).

6. Madam Justice Bertha Wilson, "Will Women Judges Really Make a Difference?" text of speech delivered at Osgoode Hall Law School, York University, February 8, 1990; Donn Downey, "Humiliated by Judge's Kiss, Crown Attorney Testifies," *The Globe and Mail* (September 14, 1993), A18; Downey, "The Strange Case of [the] Kissing Judge," *The Globe and Mail* (September 29, 1993), A17; Geoffrey York, "Most Feel Courts Unfair to Women," *The Globe and Mail* (July 29, 1993), A1; The Law Society of Upper Canada/*Barreau du Haut-Canada*, "International Women's Day Looks at Whether Woman Judges Have Made a Difference" (April 8, 2009), http://www.lsuc.on.ca/latest-news/b/archives/?C=1029&i=16057; Office of the Commissioner for Federal Judicial Affairs, *Number of Federal Judges on the Bench as of June 1, 2009*, http://www.fja.gc.ca/appointments-nominations/judges-juges-eng.html.

7. Emily Bazelon, "The Place of Women on the Court: An Interview with Judge Ruth Bader Ginsburg," *The New York Times Magazine* (July 12, 2009), 25.

8. The Law Society of Upper Canada, *Retention of Women in Private Practice Working Group, Final Report* (May 2008), http://www.lsuc.on.ca/about/b/equity/retentionofwomen/; Law Society of British Columbia, *Report of the Retention of Women in Law Task Force* (June 30, 2009).

9. Margaret Wente, "The Higher A Woman Climbs . . ." *The Globe and Mail* (September 22, 2009), A13.

10. Oliver Bertin, "McCarthys Ordered to Produce Confidential Financial Data," *The Lawyers Weekly* (August 28, 2009), http://www.lawyersweekly.ca/index.php?section=article&articleid=984.

11. Ellen Adelberg and the Native Women's Association of Canada, "Aboriginal Women and Prison Reform," 92 n. 19; Sheelagh Cooper, "The Evolution of the Federal Women's Prison"; Margaret Shaw, "Reforming Federal Women's Imprisonment"; Carol LaPrairie, "Aboriginal Women and Crime in Canada: Identifying the Issues," all in Ellen Adelberg and Claudia Currie, eds., *In Conflict with the Law: Women and the Canadian Justice System* (Vancouver: Press Gang, 1993); John Edwards [Commissioner, Correctional Service Canada, Ottawa], "Women's Prisons," *The Globe and Mail* (February 14, 1995), A22.

12. Public Works and Services Canada, *Commission of Inquiry Into Certain Events at the Prison for Women in Kingston* (1996); *Federally Sentenced Aboriginal Women Offenders*, an Issue Paper by the Native Women's Association of Canada, June 2007.

13. Michelle M. Mann, "Good Intentions, Disappointing Results: A Progress Report on Federal Aboriginal Corrections (Office of the Correctional Investigator, November 2009), http://

www.oci-bec.gc.ca/rpt/pdf/oth-aut/oth-aut20091113-eng.pdf ; "Female Prisoners to Go to Men's Jail," *The Globe and Mail* (June 15, 2009), A4.

14. Catherine Creede, "Lesbian Erotica in Porn Net," *Herizons* 6, 4 (Winter 1993): 4; Chris Dafoe, "Little Sister v. Big Brother," *The Globe and Mail* (October 8, 1994), C1; Brenda Cossman, "Little Sister's Shipments Routinely Detained," *Xtra!* (November 11, 1994), 24; Stuart Blackley, "Little Sister's on Trial," *Xtra!* 263 (November 25, 1994), 17; Nancy Pollak, "Business as Usual," *Ms.* (May/June, 1995), 11–15; SGM, *Notable Cases: Charter Litigation, Little Sister's Book and Art Emporium v. Canada* (Minister of Justice, 2009), http://www.sgmlaw.com/en/about/LittleSistersBookandArtEmporiumv.CanadaMinisterofJustice.cfm; Marcus McCann, "Little Sister's Declares Defeat in the Wake of 7–2 Supreme Court Ruling," *Xtra*, national (January 19, 2007), http://www.xtra.ca/public/viewstory.aspx?AFF_TYPE=1&STORY_ID=2583&PUB_TEMPLATE_ID=2.

15. Shannon e. Ash and Theresa McCarthy, "Female Circumcision Refugee Accepted," *Kinesis* (September 1994), 6; Michael Valpy, "The Women Persecuted for Being Women," *The Globe and Mail* (March 11, 1993), A2; Valpy, "Many Answers Needed on Domestic Violence," *The Globe and Mail* (March 25, 1993), A2; "195 'Gender' Refugees in 1994," *The Globe and Mail* (March 10, 1995), A4; Ingrid Peritz, "Deportation Revoked for Woman, Daughter," *The Globe and Mail* (June 9, 2007), A10; Dr. Emily F. Carasco, "Claiming Refugee Status in Canada Because of Gender-Related Violence" (July 2008), http://www.owjn.org/owjn_2009/index.php?option=com_content&view=article&id=105&Itemid=67.

16. Canadian Advisory Council on the Status of Women, "Work in Progress: Tracking Women's Equality in Canada," (June 1994), 6–7; John Stackhouse, "Women Everywhere Still Trail in Wages, Power, UN Reports," *The Globe and Mail* (August 17, 1995), A12; UNDP, *Human Development Indices* (2008), http://hdr.undp.org/en/media/HDI_2008_EN_Tables.pdf; Ricardo Hausmann, Laura D. Tyson, and Saadia Zahidi, World Economic Forum, *Global Gender Gap Report 2008*, http://www.weforum.org/pdf/gendergap/report2008.pdf Table #11.

17. Evelyne Tardy, "Les femmes et la campagne référendaire," in Guy Lachapelle, ed., *Québec: Un pays incertain* (Montréal: Éditions Québec-Amérique, 1980), 183–203; Michèle Jean et al., "Nationalism and Feminism in Quebec: The 'Yvettes' Phenomenon," in Roberta Hamilton and Michèle Barrett, eds., *The Politics of Diversity: Feminism, Marxism and Nationalism* (Montreal: Book Center, 1986), 322–38; "Les Yvettes douze ans après: Essais d'interprétation," in Anita Caron et Lorraine Archambault, eds., *Thérèse Casgrain: Une femme ténace et engagée* (Sainte-Foy: Presses de l'Université du Québec, 1993), 163–95; Le collectif clio, *L'histoire des femmes au Québec depuis quatre siècles* 2nd ed. (Québec: Le Jour, éditeur: 1992), 480.

18. Evelyne Tardy, "Le caractère paradoxal de l'engagement des Québécoises," in Caron et Archambault, 182.

19. Penney Kome, *The Taking of Twenty-Eight: Women Challenge the Constitution* (Toronto: Women's Press, 1983), 23.

20. Walter Tarnopolsky, "The Constitution and Human Rights," in Keith Banting and Richard Simeon, eds., *"And No One Cheered": Federalism, Democracy and the Constitution Act* (Toronto: Methuen, 1983), 272; Beverly Baines, *Women, Human Rights and the Constitution* (Ottawa: Canadian Advisory Council on the Status of Women, 1980); Chaviva Hosek, "How Women Fought for Equality," in Banting and Simeon, 280–300; Sandra Burt, "Women's Issues and the Women's Movement in Canada," in Alan Cairns and Cynthia Williams, eds., *The Politics of Gender, Ethnicity and Language* (Toronto: University of Toronto Press, 1986),

156–58; *Canadian Woman Studies/Les cahiers de la femme* "Celebrating Doris Anderson," 26, 2 (Winter/spring 2007), esp. Carolyn Bennett, "Which Way to Ottawa," 42–54.

21. MacDonald's recollection, in a 1988 speech cited by Donna Greschner, "Meech Lake: Constitution-Making as Patriarchal Practice," in Dawn H. Currie and Brian D. MacLean, eds., *Re-Thinking the Administration of Justice* (Halifax: Fernwood, 1992), 59, n. 13.

22. *Senate Debates,* (March 31, 1988), 3002.

23. Anne Collins, "Which Way to Ottawa?" *City Woman* (Holiday, 1981), 30.

24. Mr. Justice Brian Dickson in 1984, in *Hunter v. Southam Inc.*, cited in Robert J. Sharpe and Patricia I. McMahon, *The Persons Case: The Origins and Legacy of the Fight for Legal Personhood* (Toronto: University of Toronto Press, 2007), 203.

25. *Fédération des femmes du Québec*, "Are Women's Rights Threatened by the Distinct Society Clause?" in Michael D. Behiels, ed., *The Meech Lake Primer: Conflicting Views of the 1987 Constitutional Accord* (Ottawa: University of Ottawa Press, 1989), 296–97.

26. Beverly Baines, "Gender and the Meech Lake Committee," in Clive Thompson, ed., *Navigating Meech Lake: The 1987 Constitutional Crisis* (Kingston: Institute of Intergovernmental Relations, Queen's University, 1988), 43–52; Ad Hoc Committee of Women on the Constitution, "We Can Afford a Better Accord: The Meech Lake Accord," *Resources for Feminist Research/Documentation sur la recherche féministe* 17, 3 (September 1988), 143–64; Lawrence Leduc and Jon H. Pammett, "Referendum Voting: Attitudes and Behaviour in the 1992 Constitutional Referendum," *Canadian Journal of Political Science* 28, 1 (March 1995), 9, 15, 21; Marianne Stenbaek, "Mary Simon: Walking in Two Worlds but in One Spirit," in Mary Crnkovich, *"Gossip": A Spoken History of Women in the North* (Ottawa: Canadian Arctic Resources Committee, 1990), 261; Martha Greig, "Constitutional Notes," *Suvagunq* 7, 2 (1992); Judy Rebick, *Ten Thousand Roses: The Making of a Feminist Revolution* (Toronto: Penguin Canada, 2005), 179–96.

27. Miro Cernetig, "Resetting the Unity Table," *The Globe and Mail* (August 24, 1992), A1; Supreme Court of Canada, *R. v. Native Women's Association of Canada*, espec. Jeannette Corbiere Lavell, *Affidavit*, March 3, 1994.

28. The Canadian Lesbian & Gay Archives, "Armed Forces, What We Got: The Details," (June 27, 1997), http://www.clga.ca/Material/Records/docs/details/caf.htm; CBCNews in Depth, "Women in the Canadian Military" (May 30, 2006), http://www.cbc.ca/news/background/cdnmilitary/women-cdnmilitary.html.

29. Rosamonde Ramsay Boyd, "Women and Politics in the United States and Canada," *Annals of the American Association of Political and Social Science* 375 (January 1968), 56.

30. Decision Marketing Research, *Women in Canada* (Ottawa: Office of the Co-ordinator, Status of Women, 1976), 120.

31. Penney Kome, *Women of Influence: Canadian Women and Politics* (Toronto: Doubleday, 1985), Appendix I; Sherill MacLaren, *Invisible Power: The Women Who Run Canada* (Toronto: Seal Books, 1991), 213, n. 11, 226; Sydney Sharpe, *The Gilded Ghetto: Women and Political Power in Canada* (Toronto: HarperCollins, 1994).

32. Penny Kome, "People Activist, Rosemary Brown," Section 15.ca, Rebels Without A Clause (June 2, 2000), http://section15.ca/features/people/2000/06/02/rosemary_brown/.

33. Rosemary Brown, *Being Brown: A Very Public Life* (Toronto: Random House, 1989).

34. In one survey, 73 percent said it would make no difference to their support if a party had a woman as leader, and 13 percent said they would be more likely to support such a party: Canadian Institute of Public Opinion, Poll No. 382; Val Ross, "The Honorable Flora," *Chatelaine* 53, 1 (January 1980): 36; Edward Greenspoon, "Tories Ready—Finally—to Accept Woman Leader," *The Globe and Mail* (June 14, 1993), A9.

35. Sylvia Bashevkin, "'Stage' versus 'Actor' Barriers to Women's Federal Party Leadership," in Bashevkin, ed., *Opening Doors Wider: Women's Political Engagement in Canada* (Vancouver: UBC Press, 2009), 115: Table 7.1.

36. Alexa McDonough, "Commentary," in Black and Carbert, 141.

37. John Crossley, "Picture This: Women Politicians Hold Key Posts in Prince Edward Island," in Jane Arscott and Linda Trimble, eds., *In the Presence of Women: Representation in Canadian Governments* (Toronto: Harcourt Brace & Company, 1997), 280.

38. Donley T. Studlar and Richard E. Matland, "The Growth of Women's Representation in the Canadian House of Commons and the Election of 1984: A Reappraisal," *Canadian Journal of Political Science* 17, 1 (March 1994): 53–80; MacLaren, *Invisible Power*, 218–19.

39. Rick Haliechuk, "Augustine First Black Woman in House," *The Toronto Star* (October 26, 1993), B6; Patricia Orwen, "Surge in Female MPs Raises Activists' Hopes," *The Toronto Star* (October 28, 1993), A11.

40. Parts Two–Four in Arscott and Trimble, 108–337; Manon Tremblay and Réjean Pelletier, "Feminist Women in Canadian Politics: A Group Ideologically Divided?" *Atlantis* 28, 1 (Fall/automne 2003): 80–90.

41. Lesley Byrne, "Making A Difference When The Doors Are Open," in Bashevkin, *Opening Doors Wider* 102–3, 98, 101,

42. Louise Carbert, "Are Cities More Congenial? Tracking the Rural Deficit of Women in the House of Commons" in Bashevkin, *Opening Doors Wider*, 71: Figure 5 and general argument; Equal Voice Canada, "Canadians Support Efforts To Elect More Women, Poll Shows" (June 18, 2009), http://www.equalvoice.ca/speaks_article.cfm?id=75.

43. Jane Taber, "'I Didn't Know Truth Had a Gender," *The Globe and Mail* (August 11, 2009), A1.

44. Sylvia Bashevkin, *Tales of Two Cities. Women and Municipal Restructuring in London and Toronto* (Vancouver: UBC Press, 2006), 44; Linda Trimble, "Politics Where We Live: Women and Cities," in James Lightbody, ed. *Canadian Metropolitics: Governing Our Cities* (Toronto: Copp Clark Ltd, 1995), 94; Federation of Canadian Municipalities, "Female-Male Municipal Statistics" (January 2009), http://www.fcm.ca/CMFiles/Female-Male%20Municipal%20Statistics-January%2020091OQD-2182009-3386.pdf; see also Elizabeth Gidengil and Richard Vengroff, "Representational Gains of Canadian Women or Token Growth?" *Canadian Journal of Political Science/Revue canadienne de science politique* XXX, 3 (September/septembre 1997): 513–537.

45. Interview by Marian Frances Wright in *A Woman's Almanac: Voices from Atlantic Canada* (St. John's, NL: Creative Publishers), 78–81.

46. Louise Carbert, "Making it Happen: Recruiting and Training Rural Women for Leadership," in Barbara Pini, ed., *Representing Women in Local Government: An International Comparative Study* (New York: Routledge, forthcoming 2010).

47. Cora Voyageur, *Firekeepers of the Twenty-First Century: First Nations Women Chiefs* (Montreal and Kingston: McGill-Queen's University Press, 2003), 111, 11, 156; communication from Voyageur.

48. Yvon Gauvin, "NBer Elected National Chief," *Times and Transcript* (September 16, 2009), http://timestranscript.canadaeast.com/news/article/793291.

49. *Still Counting: Women in Politics Across Canada*, Table 2.5 (2008), http://stillcounting.athabascau.ca/table2-5.php; Tony Fouhse, "Nobody's Saviour," *Report on Business, The Globe and Mail* (May 2009), 40; Karim Bardeesy, "Facebook Makes Friends With Privacy Czar," *The Globe and Mail* (August 28, 2009), A3.

50. Louise Carbert and Naomi Black, Introduction, "Building Women's Leadership in Atlantic Canada," Black and Carbert, 74; Gary Mason, "For Citizens, B.C. Women Symbols of Hope," *The Globe and Mail*, (May 30, 2009), A1.

51. Michael Valpy, "Churches Come Tumbling Down," *The Globe and Mail* (December 22, 2007), http://www.theglobeandmail.com/news/opinions/churches-come-tumbling-down/article805237/.

52. Michael W. Higgins and Douglas R. Letson, *Women and the Church: A Sourcebook* (Toronto: Griffin House, 1986), espec. 142–208; Mary Jo Leddy, Bishop Remi de Roo, and Douglas Roche, "Women in the Church: The Unfinished Revolution," in Michael Creal, ed., *In the Eye of the Catholic Storm: The Church since Vatican II* (Toronto: HarperCollins, 1992), 44–54; Joanna Manning, "A Personal Challenge for the Empowering of the Laity," *Grail* 8, 3 (September 1992): 67–92; Naomi R. Goldenberg, *Changing of the Gods: Feminism and the End of Traditional Religions* (Toronto: Fitzhenry and Whiteside, 1979), 85–114; Bob Harvey, "Proud to Be Pagan," *Ottawa Citizen* (December 21, 1991), 16.

53. "L'autre parole: La Collective des femmes chrétiennes et féministes," http://www.lautreparole.org/accueil.html.

54. Lois Wilson, *Turning the World Upside Down* (Toronto: Doubleday, 1989), 132.

55. Jack Kapica, "A Woman Joins the Men's Club," *The Globe and Mail* (December 7, 1993), A1.

56. C. T. McIntire, "Women and the Life of St. James' Cathedral, Toronto, 1935–1998," *Journal of the Canadian Church Historical Society* 40, 2 (Fall 1998): 144, 146, 14.

57. Leanne Lamordin, "Where Are the Next Examples of Women in Leadership," *The Anglican*, (September 4, 2007).

58. The United Church of Canada, "Organization Statistics" (January 28, 2010), http://www.united-church.ca/organization/statistics.

59. Statistics Canada, *Selected Religions, for Canada, Provinces and Territories—20% Sample, 2001 Census*, http:www12.statcan.ca/census01/products/highlight/religion; Reginald Bibby, "Religion à la Carte," *The Globe and Mail* (September 12, 1987), D2; Linda Aisenberg, "Crusading Kids," *Chatelaine* 61, 3 (March 1988): 58, 135, 138–139; Jack Kapica, "Vatican to Allow Women at Altar," *The Globe and Mail* (April 13, 1994), A10; Kapica, "Altar Girl Has Forgiven, Not Forgotten," *The Globe and Mail* (April 27, 1994), A10; Richard Mackie, "Quebec Catholics Face Debate Over Women's Role," *The Globe and Mail* (January 3, 1995), 16.

60. Les Perreaux, "Three Resign from Order of Canada Over Appointment of Morgentaler," *The Globe and Mail* (June 2, 2009), A8; "Two Thirds (65%) Approve Dr. Henry Morgentaler's Appointment to the Order of Canada," Ipsos News Centre, Press Release (July 9, 2008).

61. Elizabeth Smyth, "Professionalization among the Professed: The Case of Roman Catholic Women Religious," in Elizabeth Smyth, Sandra Acker, Paula Bourne, and Alison Prentice, eds., *Challenging Professions: Historical and Contemporary Perspectives on Women's Professional Work* (Toronto: University of Toronto Press, 1999), 248; Loretto Sisters in Canada, http://www.ibvm.ca/about/history/canada; Carolyn Girard, "Loretto Sisters Meet Need of Their Community for 400 Years," *The Catholic Register* (January 8, 2009), http://www.catholicregister.org/content/view/2639/858/; Anthony Reinhart, "And the Sisters Said, Let There Be Light," *The Globe and Mail* (September 17, 2009), A5.

62. Rabbi Elyse Goldstein, "Introduction," in Goldstein, ed., *New Jewish Feminisms: Probing the Past, Forging the Future* (Woodstock, Vt.: Jewish Lights Publishing, 2009), xix.

63. Sarah Silberstein Schwartz and Margie Wolfe, eds., *From Memory to Transformation: Jewish Women's Voices* (Toronto: Second Story Press, 1998); Norma Baumel Joseph, "Jewish

Women in Canada: An Evolving Role," section 12 in B'nai Brith Canada, *From Immigration to Integration: The Canadian Jewish Experience: A Millennium Edition* (2000), http://www.bnaibrith.ca/institute/millennium/millennium12.html; communications from Norma Baumel Joseph, 2010; information on number of rabbis from Dr. Susan Landau Chark; Sara Hurwitz, "Orthodox Women in Rabbinic Roles," 144–54 in Goldstein; F. Lisa Rosenberg, *Jewish Women Praying for Divorce: The Plight of the Agunot in Contemporary Judaism*, unpublished Ph.D. thesis, Women's Studies, York University, 2000.

64. Huda Khattab, *The Muslim Woman's Hand Book* (London: TA-HA Publishers, 1993); Naheed Mustafa, "My Body Is My Own Business," *The Globe and Mail* (June 29, 1993), A26.

65. Sadia Zaman, "Canada's Muslim Women Set Gaze beyond the Veil," *NOW* magazine (May 21–27, 1992), 25.

66. Amber Nasrulla, "Educators outside Quebec Mystified by Hijab Ban," *The Globe and Mail* (December 13, 1994), A1, A4; André Picard, "Hijab in Schools Supported," *The Globe and Mail* (February 15, 1995), A4; Women Living Under Muslim Laws, "Canada: Support Canadian Women's Struggle Against Shari'a Courts," http://www.wluml.org/node/69; CTV News, "McGuinty Rules Out Use of Sharia Law in Ontario, (September 12, 2005), http://www.ctv.ca/servlet/ArticleNews/story/CTVNews/1126472943217_26/?hub=TopStories; Janice Gross Stein, "Religion, Culture, and Rights: A Conversation about Women," prepared for The Conference on Identity and Polarization, The Sheldon Chumir Foundation (October 3–4, 2008) http://www.chumirethicsfoundation.ca/files/pdf/Religion%20Culture%20&%20Rights_Stein.pdf.

67. Statistics Canada, Population Projections of Visible Minority Groups, Canada, Provinces and Regions, 2001–2017, Cat. no. 91-541-XIE, Table 6, Table 7.

68. Sharlene Azam, *Rebel, Rogue, Mischievous Babe: Stories About Being A Powerful Girl* (Toronto: HarperCollins, 2001), 14, 13.

69. Michael Adams, *Unlikely Utopia: The Surprising Triumph of Canadian Pluralism* (Toronto: Viking Canada, 2007), 89; Lysiane Gagnon, "Read My Lips: There's No Veil Issue," *The Globe and* Mail (November 12, 2007), A13; John Bryden, "Ottawa Won't Push Plan to Make Voters Lift Veil," *The Globe and Mail* (June 26, 2009), A6; *Echanger pour s'entendre: Commision de consultation sur les pratiques d'accomodement reliées aux différences culturelles*, Final Report (Gouvernment du Québec, 2008), http://www.accommodements.qc.ca/index-en.html; CBC News, "Quebec to Address Niqab Issue," (March 3, 2010), http://www.cbc.ca/canada/montreal/story/2010/03/03/montreal-woman-with-niqab-feels-treated-unfairly.html.

70. Robert Matas, "The New Face of Canada's Sikhs," *The Globe and Mail* (November 17, 2009), A1, A12.

71. Ellen Long, "Traditionalist Women's Groups in the 1980s: A Case Study of the Alberta Federation of Women United for the Family," University of Alberta, Honours Thesis, 1986; Lois Harder, *State of Struggle: Feminism and Politics in Alberta* (Edmonton: The University of Alberta Press, 2003), 53–57, 123–24.

72. Judy Erola speaking at York University, *The Second Decade/La deuxième décennie* 1, 2 (December 1986).

73. Karen Dubinsky, *Lament for a "Patriarchy Lost"? Anti-Feminism, Anti-Abortion and REAL Women in Canada* (Ottawa: Canadian Research Institute for the Advancement of Women, 1985); Leslie A. Pal, *Interests of State: The Politics of Language, Multiculturalism, and Feminism in Canada* (Montreal and Kingston: McGill-Queen's University Press, 1993), 143–47; Sylvia Bashevkin, *Women, Power, Politics: The Hidden Story of Canada's Unfinished Democracy* (Toronto: Oxford, 2009), 172–74.

74. Cecilia Forsyth, National president, REAL Women of Canada, letter to *The Globe and Mail* (January 12, 2010).

75. Val Sears, "Will the Real Women Please Stand Up?" *The Toronto Star* (January 3, 1987), B4.

76. Katherine Teghtsoonian, "Neo-Conservative Ideology and Opposition to Regulation of Child Care Services in the United States and Canada," *Canadian Journal of Political Science* 26, 1 (March 1993): 97–121; Geoffrey York, "Tory Politicians Form Family Compact," *The Globe and Mail* (June 3, 1992), A1; Shannon e. Ash, "Human Rights and Lesbian Rights: Pissed Off, No Surprise," *Kinesis* (December 1992/January 1993): 5; Ash, "Canadian Human Rights Amendments: Not a Pleasant Package," *Kinesis* (March 1993): 5.

77. Liam Lacey, "A Sensitively Made Film Still Raises Doubts," review of *Polytechnique*, *The Globe and Mail* (March 20, 2008), R1.

78. Colleen Turner, "Sister of Massacre Victim Remembers Music and Laughter," *The Gazette*, Montreal (December 6, 1993), 1, 6.

79. "Text of Marc Lépine's Suicide Letter," in Louise Malette and Marie Chalouh, eds., *The Montreal Massacre*, translated by Marlene Wildeman (Charlottetown: gynergy books, 1991), unpaged appendix.

80. Catherine Porter, "Lessons of the Montreal Massacre: Why Women Must Fight to be What They Want," The Star.com (December 5, 2009), http://www.thestar.com/news/canada/article/734817--lessons-of-the-montreal-massacre.

81. Gillian Walker, "The Conceptual Politics of Struggle: Wife Battering, the Women's Movement, and the State," *Studies in Political Economy* 33 (Autumn 1990), 63–90; Timothy Appleby, "Women As Likely As Men to Be Victims of Violence, Study Finds," *The Globe and Mail* (November 19, 1992), A11; Alanna Mitchell, "50% of Women Report Assaults," *The Globe and Mail* (November 19, 1993), A1; Agnes Huang, "Beyond Surveying the Violence," *Kinesis* (December 1993/January 1994): A1, A6; Sange de Silva [Executive Director, Canadian Centre for Justice Statistics, Ottawa], "Dimensions of Violence against Women," *The Globe and Mail* (December 3, 1994), D7; Holly Johnson, *Measuring Violence Against Women: Statistical Trends* (Ottawa: Statistics Canada, 2006), 44, 30–31, http://www.statcan.gc.ca/pub/85-570-x/85-570-x2006001-eng.htm; Statistics Canada, *The Daily*, "Violence Against Women: Statistical Trends" (October 2, 2006); Statistics Canada, "Violence Against Women . . . By the Numbers 2009," http://www42.statcan.ca/smr08/smr08_136-eng.htm.

82. Stevie Cameron, "Have We Forgotten the Dead?" *The Globe and Mail* (December 4, 2009), A17.

83. Rick Salutin, "Loose Canons," *Saturday Night* 106, 10 (December 1991): 20, 22, 74, 76; Alanna Mitchell, "Sponsor Cancels Miss Canada Pageant," *The Globe and Mail* (January 4, 1992), A1; Barry Brown, "A Message to Feminist Fanatics: Get Real," *The Globe and Mail* (January 9, 1992), A16; Amy Friedman, *Nothing Sacred: A Conversation with Feminism* (Toronto: Oberon, 1992); Ray Conlogue, "Feminism: A Presumption of Guilt," *The Globe and Mail* (October 16, 1993), D5; Deanne Rexe, "Feminism's Lost Generation," *The Globe and Mail* (May 17, 1993), A16.

84. Kate Fillion, "Avoiding the Victim Syndrome," *The Globe and Mail* (March 16, 1994), C1.

85. Geoffrey York, "Street Fighting Woman," *The Globe and Mail* (September 26, 1992), D4. Marsden had been an active member of the Ontario Committee on the Status of Women, president of NAC, and a senator. She was later president of York University.

86. Environics Focus Canada 2001; Canadian Election Study 2000.

87. Sean Fine, "End Sought to Mandatory Charges in Wife-Abuse Cases," *The Globe and Mail* (January 27, 1994), A1.

88. Sean Fine, "Black Policemen Support One Policy for All Wife Assault Cases," *The Globe and Mail* (February 1, 1994), A3; Dawn H. Currie and Brian D. MacLean, "Women, Men, and Police: Losing the Fight against Wife Battery in Canada," in Currie and MacLean, eds., *Re Thinking the Administration of Justice*, 251–75; Neil Bissoondath, *Selling Illusions: The Cult of Multiculturalism in Canada* (Toronto: Penguin Canada, 1994), 135–44.

89. Agnes Huang, "Canadian Panel on Violence against Women: Some Things Never Change," *Kinesis* (September 1992): 3.

90. Vivian Smith, "Equality Called Key to Ending Violence," *The Globe and Mail* (July 30, 1993), A1; Sandra Harder, *Violence Against Women: The Canadian Panel's Final Report* (February 1994), http://dsp-psd.pwgsc.gc.ca/Collection-R/LoPBdP/MR/mr122-e.htmt; Statistics Canada, *Measuring Violence Against Women, Statistical Trends* (2006), 65.

91. Stevie Cameron, "Chiefs to Speak Out on Family Violence," *The Globe and Mail* (December 16, 1991), A4.

92. Forum pour un Québec féminin pluriel, *Pour changer le monde* (Montréal: Les Editions Ecosociété, 1994), 119; Fédération des Femmes du Québec, "Qu'est-ce que la FFQ?" "Plate-forme politique de la FFQ," http://www.ffq.qc.ca/presentation/index.html; Fédération des Femmes du Québec, "Dossier Spécial, "Le rassemblement pancanadien des jeunes féministes," *Le Féminisme en bref* (2008), 1–21.

93. Keith Louise Fulton, "Bending the Rules: An Interview with Jane Rule," *Herizons* 6, 4 (Winter 1993): 30.

94. Chris Gabriel and Katherine Scott, "Women's Press at Twenty: The Politics of Feminist Publishing," in Linda Carty, ed., *And Still We Rise: Feminist Political Mobilizing in Contemporary Canada* (Toronto: Women's Press, 1993); May Lui, "Riding the Roller Coaster of Feminist Publishing in Canada," section 15.ca, *Rebels without a Clause* (May 16, 2007), http://section15.ca/features/reviews/2007/08/16/riding_the_roller_coaster/; Ayanna Black, "Working with Collectives," *Tiger Lily* 1, 2 (1987): 30–33, and 1, 3 (1987), 29–32.

95. Deborah Wilson, "Heir to NAC Stung by Attack," *The Globe and Mail* (May 10, 1993), A1; Angela Gogga, "From Rebick to Thobani: NAC Gets New Head," *Kinesis* (May 1993): 3; Patricia Elliott, "Feminism's New Face," *Canadian Living* 19, 8 (August 1994): 63–66; Mary-Jo Nadeau, "Rebuilding the House of Canadian Feminism: NAC and the Racial Politics of Participation," in Bashevkin, *Opening Doors Wider*: 33-48; Sylvia Bashevkin, *Women, Power, Politics: The Hidden Story of Canada's Unfinished Democracy* (Toronto: Oxford University Press, 2009), 166–169.

96. Geoffrey York, "Most Feel Courts Unfair to Women," *The Globe and Mail* (July 29, 1993.), A1.

97. Susan Phillips, "Meaning and Structure in Social Movements: Mapping the Network of National Canadian Women's Organizations," *Canadian Journal of Political Science* 24, 4 (December 1991): 765–766; 56; Bashevkin, *Women, Power, Politics*.

98. Elizabeth Goudie, *Woman of Labrador* (Toronto: Peter Martin Associates, 1973), 3, 4.

99. Anne Vespry, "Coming Home: A One Act Play," *Xtra!* (August 20, 1993), 186.

100. Rosemary Sadlier, *Leading the Way: Black Women in Canada* (Toronto: Umbrella Press, 1994), 28, 32; Patricia Vertinsky, "Sport and Exercise for Old Women: Images of the Elderly in the Medical and Popular Literature at the Turn of the Century," *International Journal of the History of Sport* 9, 1 (April 1992): 83; Jane Taylor, "On Being Older and Wiser," in Pierson et al., eds., *Canadian Women's Issues* vol. 1, 222.

101. Mary Ann Colihan, "Canadian Who Has Lived a Life of Firsts Makes History Again," *The Globe and Mail* (April 29, 2009), A1, A7.

102. Toronto Raging Grannies flyer n.d.; Allison Gardner, "The Grannies Are Coming, Watch Out, Watch Out!" *Maturity* 13, 2 (March 1993); Raging Grannies International, "Gaggles" (March 20, 2008) http://raginggrannies.org/gaggles; Carole Roy, *The Raging Grannies: Wild Hats, Cheeky Songs, and Witty Actions for a Better World* (Montréal: Black Rose Books, 2004), 10, 5, 29–30.

103. Karen Skowron, "Go, Granny, Go!" *Earthkeeper* (1993), 42, 44.

104. *Grandmothers to Grandmothers*, Stephen Lewis Foundation (2009), http://www. stephenlewisfoundation.org/grandmothers.html.

105. "Nearly Four-In-Ten Canadian Adults (37%) Have Visited Online Social Networks and Three-In-Ten (29%) Have a Personal Profile on One," Ipsos News Centre Press Release (October 4, 2007), http://www.ipsos-na.com/news/pressrelease.cfm?id=3664; Omar El Akkad, "The Medium is No Longer the Message," *The Globe and Mail* (March 10, 2009), A3; "What? You Don't Have a Social Network Profile? You Are Now in the Minority," Ipsos News Center Press Release (June 19, 2009), http://www.ips; na.com/ news/pressrelease.cfm?id=4436; "Globalive Arrives," *The Globe and Mail* (December 12, 2009), A6.

106. Yarn Harlot, http://www.yarnharlot.ca/blog; Diane Peters, "Confessions of a Yarn Harlot," *Metro iPhone*, http://iphone.metronews.ca/Calgary/columns/columnslist/article/162130.

107. C. J. Rowe, "Cyberfeminism in Action: Claiming Women's Space in Cyberspace," in Sandra Grey and Marian Sawer, eds., *Women's Movements: Flourishing or in Abeyance?* (London and New York: Routledge, 2008), 128–39; Lisa Campbell, "Grrls Plugged In: How Canadian Rural Young Women are Using the Internet," *Canadian Woman Studies/Les cahiers de la femme* 24, 4 (Summer/fall 2005): 167–70; Michèle Ollivier and Wendy Robbins, "Electronic Communications and Feminist Activism: The Experience of PAR-L," *Atlantis*, 24, 1 (Fall/ winter 1999): 39–53.

108. "Introduction: A Conversation with Allyson, Lisa and Lara," in Allyson Mitchell, Lisa Bryn Rundle and Lara Karaian, *Turbo Chicks: Talking Young Feminisms* (Toronto: Sumach Press, 2002), 19.

109. Emily Pohl-Weary, "The Mutant Generation: Shaping Stronger and Wiser Superheroines," in Pohl-Weary, ed., *Girls Who Bite Back: Witches, Mutants, Slayers and Freaks* (Toronto: Sumach Press, 2004), 14.

110. Jennifer Harris, "Betty Friedan's Granddaughters: *Cosmo*, Ginger Spice & Other Marks of Whiteness," in Mitchell, Rundle, and Karaian, 195.

111. Carly Stasko, "How to Be Your Own Superhero: A Chronicle of Experimentation," in Pohl-Weary, 77.

112. Larissa MacFarquhar, "Outside Agitator: Naomi Klein Reboots the Left," *The New Yorker* (December 8, 2008), 64.

113. Geneviève Pagé, "Variations Sur Une Vague," Les Panthères roses, "Récit d'un retour dans le placard public," both in Maria Nengeh Mensah, ed., *Dialogues sur la Troisième Vague Féministe* (Montréal: Les éditions du remue-ménage, 2005), 42–48, 113–19; Diane Lamoureux, "La réflexion 'queer:' apports et limites," in Mensah, 92; Patricia Elliot, "Who Gets to Be A Woman?: Feminist Politics and the Question of Trans-inclusion," *Atlantis* 29, 1 (Fall/winter 2004): 13–20; Eve-Marie Lampron, "A nos crayons, à nos pancartes: quelques débats actuels en théorie féministe," *Le Féminisme en bref*, Numéro spécial (2008), 6.

114. http://antigonemagazine.wordpress.com/about/; Mayan Kreitzman, "Amanda Reaume, Editor of Antigone Magazine: This Is What a Feminist Looks Like," *UBC Insider: Separating the Truth from the Chaff* (May 16, 2007), http://ubcinsiders.blogspot.com/2007/05/amanda-reaume-editor-of-antigone.html.

115. *Manifesto of the Pan-Canadian Young Feminist Gathering* (March 8, 2008), http://www.rebelles.org/en/manifesto.

Appendix

Table A.1 MARITAL STATUS OF MALES AND FEMALES, AGES 15 AND OVER, 1911–2006 (PERCENT)

Census Year	Single[a]		Married[b]		Widowed		Divorced	
	M	F	M	F	M	F	M	F
1911	45.0	34.9	51.5	56.9	3.4	8.2	0.1	0.1
1921	39.2	32.0	56.7	59.2	4.0	8.6	0.1	0.1
1931	41.0	34.0	54.9	57.4	4.0	8.5	0.1	0.1
1941	39.8	33.0	56.1	58.0	4.0	8.8	0.2	0.2
1951	32.1	25.7	63.9	64.5	3.8	9.4	0.3	0.4
1961	29.9	23.7	66.4	66.8	3.6	9.7	0.4	0.5
1971	31.6	25.0	65.0	63.8	2.5	9.8	1.0	1.3
1981	31.3	24.5	64.3	62.4	2.2	10.0	2.2	3.1
1991	34.1	27.4	58.2	55.6	2.3	10.4	5.3	6.6
2001	49.5	43.1	43.1	41.9	1.9	8.2	5.5	6.8
2006	45.2	38.5	48.6	48.2	1.9	7.6	4.3	5.7

[a] Never Married

[b] For 1971, 1981, 1991, 2001, and 2006, figures include those married, living common-law, or married and separated.

Sources: Roy H. Rodgers and Gail Witney, "The Family Cycle in Twentieth Century Canada," *Journal of Marriage and the Family* 43, 3 (August 1981), 732; Statistics Canada: *Women in Canada: A Statistical Report, 1985; Age, Sex, and Marital Status*, Cat. no, 93-310, Table 5, Cat. no. 95F0407XCB2001004; CANSIM Table 051-0010.

Figure A.1 AVERAGE AGE AT MARRIAGE, BRIDES AND GROOMS, 1921–2004

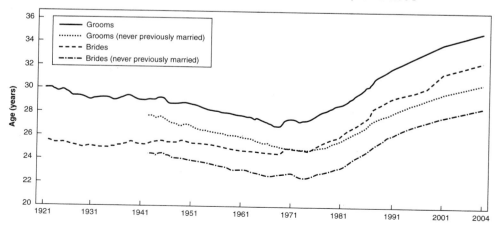

Sources: Statistics Canada: *Health Reports 1992*, Cat. no. 82-003, Chart 2, 409; CANSIM Table 101-1002.

Table A.2.   AVERAGE NUMBER OF PERSONS PER HOUSEHOLD, 1881–2006

Year	Total	Rural	Urban
1881	5.3		
1891	5.3		
1901	5.0		
1911	4.8		
1921	4.6	4.7	4.5
1931	4.4	4.6	4.3
1941	4.3	4.5	4.2
1951	4.0	4.2	3.9
1961	3.9	4.2	3.7
1971	3.5	3.9	3.4
1981	2.9		
1991	2.7		
2001	2.6		
2006	2.5		

Sources: Statistics Canada: *Historical Statistics of Canada*, Series A248-253; Cat. no. 97-554-XCB200603.

Figure A.2   DIVORCE RATES, 1921–2005

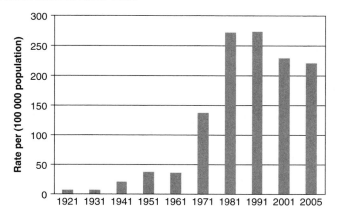

Sources: Statistics Canada: *Historical Statistics of Canada*, Cat. no. 11-516-XWE, Series B75-81; *Divorce in the 1990s*, Cat. no. 82-003-XPB; *Women in Canada*, 5th ed., Table 2.5; CANSIM Table 101-6501.

Table A.3 AGE-SPECIFIC AND TOTAL FERTILITY RATES, 1926–2007

Year	Fertility Rates by Age of Mother[1]							Total Fertility Rate[2]
	15-19 yrs	20-24 yrs	25-29 yrs	30-34 yrs	35-39 yrs	40-44 yrs	45-49 yrs	
1926	29.0	139.9	177.4	153.8	114.6	50.7	6.0	3.4
1931	29.9	137.1	175.1	145.3	103.1	44.0	5.5	3.2
1941	30.7	138.4	159.8	122.3	80.0	31.6	3.7	2.8
1951	48.1	188.7	198.8	144.5	86.5	30.9	3.1	3.5
1961	58.2	233.6	219.2	144.9	81.1	28.5	2.4	3.8
1971	40.1	134.4	142.0	77.3	33.6	9.4	0.6	2.2
1981	25.9	91.4	123.2	66.7	19.1	3.2	0.2	1.6
1991	26.0	77.5	120.3	83.6	28.3	3.9	0.2	1.7
2001	16.3	56.1	97.9	89.9	35.5	6.1	0.3	1.5
2007	14.0	52.6	101.7	106.0	48.5	7.9	0.4	1.7

[1] Number of live births per thousand women for specified group

[2] The number of children a woman would have in her lifetime based on age-specific fertility rates that year.

Sources: Statistics Canada: *Historical Statistics*, Series B1-14; *Women in Canada*, 5th ed., Table 2.9; *Births—2007*, Cat. no. 84F0210X, Table 4.

Figure A.3 MATERNAL DEATH RATES, 1921–2000

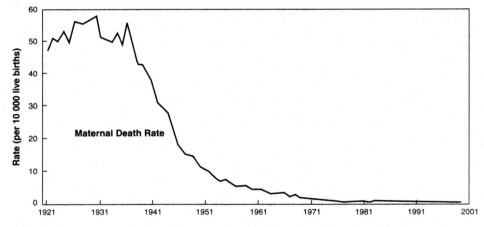

Sources: Statistics Canada: *Selected Infant Mortality and Related Statistics, Canada, 1921–1990.* Cat. no. 82-549, Chart 7; World Health Organization, *Making Every Mother and Child Count-World Health Report, 2005* (Geneva, 2005), 2.

Figure A.4 PERCENTAGE OF BIRTHS OCCURRING IN HOSPITALS, 1931–2006

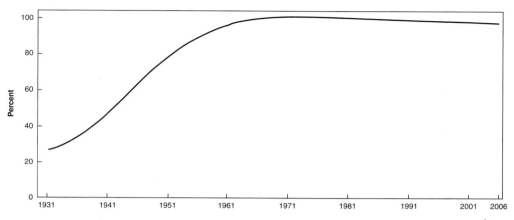

Sources: F-.H. Leacy, ed, *Historical Statistics*, 2nd ed. (Ottawa: Statistics Canada, 1983), Table B 1–14; Statistics Canada, CANSIM Table, 102-4516.

Figure A.5 LIFE EXPECTANCY AT BIRTH BY SEX, 1920–2007

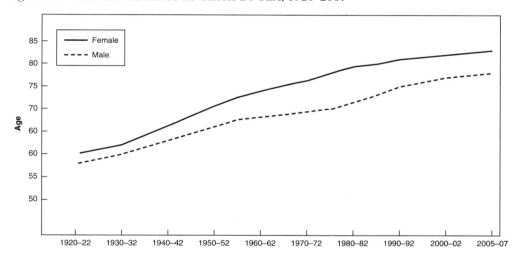

Sources: Statistics Canada: *Deaths, 1992*, Cat. no. 84-211 (Ottawa: Minister of Industry, 1995), Table 14; Cat. no. 84-537-XIE; CANSIM Table 102-0512.

Figure A.6 LABOUR FORCE PARTICIPATION RATES OF WOMEN AND MEN, 1921–2006 (PERCENT)

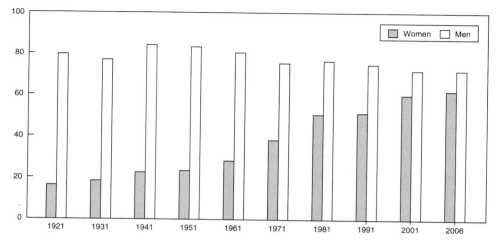

Sources: F.H. Leacy, ed., *Historical Statistics of Canada*, 2nd ed. (Ottawa: Statistics Canada, 1983); Statistics Canada: Cat. no. 71-201; *Women in the Labour Force 1994*, Cat. no. 75-507E, Table 1.1; CANSIM Table 282-0002.

Figure A.7 WOMEN AS A PERCENTAGE OF THE LABOUR FORCE, 1921–2006

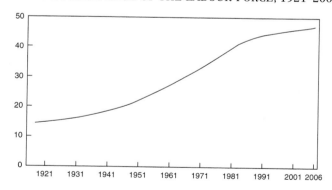

Sources: F.H. Leacy, ed., *Historical Statistics of Canada*, 2nd ed. (Ottawa: Statistics Canada, 1983); Statistics Canada: Cat. no. 71-201; *Women in the Labour Force 1994*, Cat. no. 75-507E, Table 1.1; CANSIM Table 282-0002.

Table A.4a WOMEN'S PARTICIPATION IN THE LABOUR FORCE BY AGE, 1921–1991
(PERCENT)

Year	1921	1931	1941	1951	1961	1971	1981	1991
Age Category	Percentages							
15–24	29	33	41	42	41	49	61	65
25–34	17	24	25	24	30	44	66	77
35–44	11	13	16	22	31	44	64	78
45–54	11	13	13	20	33	44	56	70
55–64	10	13	10	14	24	34	42	36
Total%	18	20	21	24	30	39	52	58

Sources: Canadian Congress for Learning Opportunities for Women, *Decade of Promise: An Assessment of Canadian Women's Status in Education, Training and Employment, 1976–1985* (Toronto: Avebury Research, 1986), 61; Statistics Canada, *Labour Force Annual Averages, 1991,* Table 1.

Table A.4b WOMEN'S PARTICIPATION IN THE LABOUR FORCE BY AGE, 2001 AND 2006
(PERCENT)

Year	2001	2006
Age Category		
15–24	63	66
25–44	80	82
45–64	63	68
65 and over	3	5
Total%	60	62

Source: Statistics Canada, CANSIM Table 282-0002.

Table A.5   WOMEN AS A PERCENTAGE OF THE LABOUR FORCE, BY OCCUPATION, 1901–1991

Occupation	1901	1911	1921	1931	1941	1951	1961	1971	1981	1991
Managerial	3.6	4.5	4.3	4.9	7.2	8.9	10.3	15.7	25.7	39.5
Professional	42.5	44.6	54.1	49.5	46.1	43.5	43.2	48.1	48.0	55.3
Clerical	22.1	32.6	41.8	45.1	50.1	56.7	61.5	68.4	77.3	81.7
Sales	10.4	20.2	25.6	26.0	32.1	38.3	40.3	30.4	36.9	44.4
Service	68.7	64.8	58.6	62.1	65.0	47.8	50.0	46.2	53.7	57.3
Primary	1.1	1.5	1.6	1.9	1.5	3.1	9.2	16.4	19.6	23.0
Blue Collar	12.6	10.2	10.1	8.5	11.0	11.5	10.6	12.0	–	–
All Occupations	13.4	13.2	15.4	17.0	19.9	22.0	27.3	34.3	38.3	44.5

Figures for 1901 are for women 10 years of age and older,

Figures for 1911–1971 are for women 15 years of age and older

Figures for 1981 and 1991 are for women 25 years of age and older.

Sources: Rosalie Silberman Abella, *Research Studies of the Commission on Equality in Employment* (Ottawa: Supply and Services Canada, 1985), 525; Statistics Canada, *Labour Force Annual Averages, 1993*, Cat. no. 71-220, Table 1.

Table A.6   DISTRIBUTION OF WOMEN IN THE LABOUR FORCE BY LEADING OCCUPATIONAL GROUPS, 1901–1981 (PERCENT)

Occupational Group	1901[a]	1911	1921	1931	1941[b]	1951	1961	1971	1981
Personal Service	42.0	37.1	25.8	33.8	34.2	21.0	22.1	22.3	18.3
Manufacturing and Mechanical[c]	29.6	26.3	17.8	12.7	15.4	14.6	9.9	11.2	9.9
Professional	14.7	12.7	19.1	17.8	15.7	14.4	15.5	17.5	19.8
Clerical	5.3	9.4	18.7	17.7	18.3	27.5	28.6	32.7	34.3
Commercial and Financial[d]	2.4	6.8	8.5	8.3	8.8	10.5	10.2	8.3	10.1
Managerial[e]	—	—	—	—	—	—	—	3.9	5.5
Other[f]	6.0	7.8	10.1	9.6	7.7	11.9	13.6	3.8	3.3
Total[f]	100.0	100.1	100.1	99.9	100.1	99.9	99.9	99.7	101.2

[a] 10 years of age and over in 1901, 15 years of age and over in 1911–1981

[b] not including active service, 1941.

[c] includes stationary enginemen and occupations associated with electric power production

[d] includes saleswomen

[e] figures for 1901 to 1961 are unavailable; before 1971, this category was included under "other."

[f] includes armed forces

Sources: Janice Acton, et al., eds., *Women at Work: Ontario, 1850–1930* (Toronto: Canadian Women's Educational Press, 1974), 280; Labour Canada, Women's Bureau: *Women in the Labour Force, 1971: Facts and Figures*, Table 14; *Women in the Labour Force, Part 1: Participation 1983*, Table 9b; *Women in the Labour Force, 1990–91*, Table 5.

Table A.7　DISTRIBUTION OF EMPLOYMENT, BY OCCUPATION, 1987, 1996, AND 2006

	1987			1996			2006		
	Women	Men	Women as a percentage of total employed in occupation	Women	Men	Women as a percentage of total employed in occupation	Women	Men	Women as a percentage of total employed in occupation
	percentage								
Managerial									
Senior management	0.3	0.8	21.0	0.3	0.7	27.2	0.3	0.8	26.3
Other management	5.7	9.7	30.7	7.8	10.9	37.5	6.7	10.2	36.9
Total management	6.0	10.5	30.1	8.2	11.6	37.0	7.1	11.0	36.3
Professional									
Business and finance	1.9	2.3	38.3	2.8	2.7	46.9	3.3	2.8	51.6
Natural sciences/engineering/mathematics	2.3	7.0	19.6	2.3	8.0	19.1	3.2	10.1	22.0
Social sciences/religion	4.3	2.0	61.4	6.0	2.3	68.8	6.7	2.4	71.3
Teaching	3.8	2.6	52.3	5.1	2.8	60.1	5.6	2.8	63.9
Doctors/dentists/other health	0.9	0.9	43.1	1.2	1.1	48.1	1.4	1.0	55.3
Nursing/therapy/other health-related	8.3	0.9	87.1	8.3	1.0	87.0	8.9	1.1	87.4
Artistic/literary/recreational	2.7	2.1	48.4	3.1	2.4	51.5	3.4	2.6	54.1
Total professional	24.1	18.0	50.4	28.8	20.3	54.2	32.5	22.9	55.9
Clerical and administrative	29.7	7.9	73.9	25.6	7.2	74.9	24.1	7.1	75.0
Sales and service	30.0	18.4	55.2	28.6	19.2	55.4	28.6	19.3	56.8
Primary	2.3	7.2	19.7	2.1	6.5	20.9	1.5	5.3	20.5
Trades, transport and construction	2.1	28.9	5.2	2.1	26.4	6.1	2.1	26.3	6.5
Processing, manufacturing and utilities	5.8	9.1	32.4	4.7	8.8	30.6	4.1	8.1	31.1
Total[1]	100.0	100.0	43.0	100.0	100.0	45.4	100.0	100.0	47.1
Total employed (thousands)	5,307.7	7,025.3	…	6,099.0	7,322.4	…	7,757.2	8,727.1	…

[1] Includes occupations that are not classified.

Source: Statistics Canada, *Women in Canada: Work Chapter Updates,* Cat. no. 89F0133WE.

Table A.8   FEMALE ENROLLMENT AS A PERCENTAGE OF FULL-TIME UNIVERSITY
UNDERGRADUATE ENROLLMENT, SELECTED FIELDS OF SPECIALIZATION,
1891–1991

Field of Specialization	1891	1920	1930	1945	1961	1971	1981	1991
Agriculture	–	1.3	1.1	4.0	4.2	13.1	36.6	45.5
Arts, Science, Letters	21.8	31.6	32.6	26.6	29.3	40.6	49.1	56.8
Commerce and Business Administration	–	3.0	14.3	8.9	7.0	13.9	38.7	45.9
Dentistry	0.0	1.8	1.3	1.2	4.5	7.5	22.7	40.3
Education	–	61.8	64.4	48.0	48.1	55.8	69.2	67.1
Engineering and Applied Sciences	0.0	0.1	0.2	0.6	0.7	2.4	10.6	17.6
Fine and Applied Arts	–	–	91.7	80.6	66.4	53.9	62.2	61.7
Health Professions (misc.)	–	–	–	100.0	82.6	72.7	82.8	61.4
Household Science	–	100.0	100.0	100.0	100.0	98.9	97.2	90.8
Law	0.4	3.7	3.4	4.4	5.3	14.9	39.9	51.2
Mathematics and Physical Sciences	–	–	–	–	–	–	28.1	29.7
Medicine	3.1	4.6	4.2	7.3	9.8	20.3	38.5	45.2
Nursing	–	100.0	100.0	100.0	99.8	97.9	97.4	93.4
Pharmacy	0.0	5.9	6.1	25.9	27.3	52.5	64.2	61.5
Religion and Theology	–	1.9	1.9	2.4	1.3	28.7	30.9	41.1
Veterinary Medicine	0.0	0.0	0.0	2.3	5.9	16.1	48.8	64.3
Unclassified	0.0	–	–	–	55.2	34.0	48.1	53.9
Female % of Total Undergraduate Enrollment	11.6	16.3	23.5	20.8	26.2	37.7	46.7	53.1

Sources: F.H. Leacy, ed., *Historical Statistics of Canada*, 2nd ed. (Ottawa: Statistics Canada, 1983), W439–455; Statistics Canada: *Universities: Enrolment and Degrees, 1981,* Table 8; *Universities: Enrolment and Degrees, 1991*, Cat. no. 81-204, Table 8, 44–45.

Table A.9   FEMALE ENROLLMENT AS A PERCENTAGE OF FULL-TIME UNIVERSITY
UNDERGRADUATE ENROLLMENT, 2001–2007

	2001/02	2006/07
Education	78.3	77.9
Visual and Performing Arts, Communications Technologies	66.1	66.5
Humanities	62.9	62.4
Social and Behavioural Sciences and Law	65.9	65.8
Business, Management and Public Administration	54.8	50.4
Physical and Life Sciences and Technologies	58.4	57.3
Mathematics, Computer and Information Sciences	27.1	26.2
Architecture, Engineering and Related Technologies	22.9	20.2
Agriculture, Natural Resources and Conservation	55.9	58.0
Health, Parks, Recreation and Fitness	70.4	71.7
Personal, Protective and Transportation Services	52.3	55.4
Other Programs	60.1	60.4
Female % of Total Undergraduate Enrollment	57.7	57.9

Source: Statistics Canada, CANSIM Table 477-0013.

Table A.10   PERCENTAGE OF DEGREES GRANTED TO WOMEN BY CANADIAN
UNIVERSITIES, 1920–2006

Academic Year	Bachelor and first professional degrees[a]		Master and licence[b]		Doctorates	
	Total	% Earned by Women	Total	% Earned by Women	Total	% Earned by Women
1920–21	3 627	18.3	218	22.0	24	1.0
1930–31	5 290	25.3	468	21.4	46	7.0
1940–41	6 576	24.1	673	10.6	75	5.0
1950–51	15 754	20.3	1 632	13.9	202	5.5
1960–61	20 240	25.8	2 447	19.0	305	8.5
1970–71	67 200	38.1	9 638	22.0	1 625	9.3
1980–81	86 243	49.5	12 432	37.4	1 738	23.0
1990–91	114 815	56.5	18 038	47.3	2 947	31.6
2001	129 240	60.2	24 906	52.3	3 708	42.7
2006	160 998	61.7	34 107	52.9	4 449	43.4

[a] Includes equivalent diplomas (as, for example, in Theology) and Honours degrees

[b] The licence in the French-language universities is the next degree after the Bachelor, as the Master's
Degree is in the English-language universities. This category excludes Master's and Licence Degrees (e.g.,
in Law, Optometry) that are in reality the first professional degree. Those are included under that heading.

Sources: Daniel Kubat and David Thornton, *A Statistical Profile of Canadian Society* (Toronto: McGraw-Hill
Ryerson, 1974), 124; Statistics Canada: *Education in Canada: A Statistical Review for 1980–81*, Cat. no.
81-229, Tables 31–33; *Education in Canada: A Statistical Review for 1992–93*, Cat. no. 81-229, Tables 37,
39, 41; CANSIM Table 477-0014.

Table A.11 WOMEN CANDIDATES IN FEDERAL ELECTIONS, 1921–2008*

YEAR AND PARTY	CANDIDATES	ELECTED	PERCENTAGE ELECTED
1921			
Progressive	1	1	100%
Total	**4**	**1**	**25%**
1925			
Progressive	1	1	100%
Total	**4**	**1**	**25%**
1926			
Progressive	1	1	100%
Total	**2**	**1**	**50%**
1930			
Progressive	1	1	100%
Total	**10**	**1**	**10%**
1935			
Independent Conservative	1	1	100%
United Farmers of Ontario-Labour	1	1	100%
Total	**16**	**2**	**12.5%**
1940			
Unity	1	1	100%
Total	**9**	**1**	**11%**
1945			
CCF	6	1	16%
Total	**19**	**1**	**5%**
1949			
Total	**11**	**0**	**0%**
1953			
Progressive Conservative	10	3	30%
Liberal	3	1	33%
Total	**47**	**4**	**8.5%**
1957			
Progressive Conservative	5	2	40%
Total	**29**	**2**	**7%**

YEAR AND PARTY	CANDIDATES	ELECTED	PERCENTAGE ELECTED
1958			
Progressive Conservative	3	2	67%
Total	**21**	**2**	**9.5%**
1962			
Progressive Conservative	7	3	43%
Liberal	6	2	33%
Total	**26**	**5**	**19%**
1963			
Progressive Conservative	12	1	8%
Liberal	6	3	50%
Total	**40**	**4**	**10%**
1965			
NDP	16	1	6%
Liberal	8	2	25%
Progressive Conservative	8	1	12.5%
Total	**37**	**4**	**11%**
1968			
NDP	21	1	5%
Total	**36**	**1**	**3%**
1972			
NDP	28	1	4%
Liberal	10	3	30%
Progressive Conservative	6	1	17%
Total	**71**	**5**	**7%**
1974			
Liberal	20	8	40%
Progressive Conservative	11	1	9%
Total	**137**	**9**	**7%**
1979			
NDP	47	2	4%
Liberal	21	6	29%
Progressive Conservative	14	2	14%
Total	**195**	**10**	**5%**

YEAR AND PARTY	CANDIDATES	ELECTED	PERCENTAGE ELECTED
1980			
NDP	33	2	6%
Liberal	23	10	44%
Progressive Conservative	14	2	14%
Total	**218**	**14**	**6%**
1984			
NDP	64	3	5%
Liberal	44	5	11%
Progressive Conservative	23	19	83%
Total	**214**	**27**	**13%**
1988			
NDP	84	5	6%
Liberal	53	13	24.5%
Progressive Conservative	37	21	57%
Total	**302**	**39**	**13%**
1993			
NDP	113	1	1%
Progressive Conservative	67	1	1.5%
Liberal	64	36	56%
Reform Party	23	7	30%
Bloc Québécois	10	8	80%
Total	**476**	**53**	**11%**
1997			
NDP	107	8	8%
Liberal	84	37	44%
Progressive Conservative	56	2	4%
Reform Party	23	4	17%
Bloc Québécois	16	11	69%
Total	**408**	**62**	**15%**
2000			
NDP	88	5	6%
Liberal	65	39	60%
Progressive Conservative	39	1	3%
Canadian Alliance	32	7	22%
Bloc Québécois	18	10	56%
Total	**373**	**62**	**17%**

YEAR AND PARTY	CANDIDATES	ELECTED	PERCENTAGE ELECTED
2004			
NDP	96	5	5%
Liberal	75	34	45%
Conservative	36	12	33%
Bloc Québecois	18	14	78%
Total	**391**	**65**	**17%**
2006			
NDP	108	12	11%
Liberal	79	21	27%
Conservative	38	14	37%
Bloc Québecois	23	17	74%
Total	**380**	**64**	**17%**
2008			
Liberal	113	19	17%
NDP	104	12	11.5%
Conservative	63	23	36.5%
Bloc Québecois	20	15	75%
Total	**445**	**69**	**15.5%**

* Information provided only for parties who were successful in electing women candidates.

Source: Parliament of Canada, *Women Candidates in General Elections, 1921 to Date,* http://www2.parl.gc.ca/Sites/LOP/HFER/hfer.asp?Language=E&Search=WomenElection.

Aboriginal Names and their European Equivalents

Aboriginal Name	European Equivalent
Denesuline	Chipewyan
Haudenosaunee	Iroquois
Innu	Montagnais/Naskapi
Inuit	Eskimo
Mi'kmaq	Micmac
Nuu'chah'nulth	Nootka
Ojibwe/Anishinaabeg	Ojibway/Ojibwa
Salish	Flathead
Wendat	Huron
Wet'suwet'en	Carrier

List of Acronyms for Organizations

AFEAS	*Association féminine d'éducation et d'action sociale*
AFN	Assembly of First Nations
AWE	Association of Women Electors
AWIs	Alberta Women's Institutes
BPWs	Business and Professional Women's Clubs
CACSW	Canadian Advisory Council on the Status of Women
CAMC	Canadian Army Medical Corps
CANEWC/ CANEWA	Canadian Negro Women's Club/Canadian Negro Women's Association
CARAL	Canadian Abortion Rights Action League (initially Canadian Association for the Repeal of Abortion Laws)
CBC	Canadian Broadcasting Corporation
CCF	Co-operative Commonwealth Federation
CCMW	Canadian Council of Muslim Women
CCSW	Canadian Committee on the Status of Women
CEGEP	*Collège d'enseignement général et professionnel*
CEQ	*Centrale des enseignants du Québec*
CEW	Committee for the Equality of Women in Canada
CFBPWC	Canadian Federation of Business and Professional Women's Clubs
CFUW	Canadian Federation of University Women
CGIT	Canadian Girls in Training
CIC	*Corporation des instituteurs et institutrices catholiques*
CMA	Canadian Manufacturers' Association
CPSF/PFC	*Comité pour le suffrage féminin*/Provincial Franchise Committee
CRIAW	Canadian Research Institute for the Advancement of Women
CTCC	*Confédération des travailleurs catholiques du Canada*
CRCS	Canadian Red Cross Society
CUPE	Canadian Union of Public Employees
CWAC	Canadian Women's Army Corps
DAWN-RAFH	DisAbled Women's Network/*Réseau d'action des femmes handicapées*
DWEA	Dominion Women's Enfranchisement Association

ETFO	Elementary Teachers Federation of Ontario
FFQ	*Fédération des femmes du Québec*
FLF	*Front pour la libération des femmes du Québec*
FLQ	*Front de libération du Québec*
FNSJB	*Fédération nationale Saint-Jean-Baptiste*
FWIC	Federated Women's Institutes of Canada
FWTAO	Federation of Women Teachers' Associations of Ontario
ICW	International Council of Women
IMA	India Mahila Association
IRIW	Indian Rights for Indian Women
INAC	Indian and Northern Affairs Canada
INTERCEDE	International Coalition to End Domestic Exploitation
IODE	Imperial Order Daughters of the Empire
JAC	*Jeunesse agricole catholique*
JOC	*Jeunesse ouvrière catholique*
JOCF	*Jeunesse ouvrière catholique féminine*
LCW	Local Council of Women
LEAF	Legal Education and Action Fund
LES FAM	*Liberté, Egalité, Sororité : Les femmes acadiennes de Moncton*
NAC	National Action Committee on the Status of Women
NCWC	National Council of Women of Canada
NBS	National Ballet School
NDP	New Democratic Party
NFB	National Film Board/Office national du film du Canada
NOIVMC	National Organization of Immigrant and Visible Minority Women of Canada
NWAC	Native Women's Association of Canada
OCSW	Ontario Committee on the Status of Women
PQ	*Parti Québécois*
RAFA	Rally of Haitian Women
RCAF (WD)	Royal Canadian Air Force (Women's Division)
RCMP	Royal Canadian Mounted Police
RCSW	Royal Commission on the Status of Women
REAL Women	Realistic, Equal, Active, for Life Women of Canada
RNAO	Registered Nurses' Association of Ontario
SCM	Student Christian Movement

SGGA	Saskatchewan Grain Growers' Association
SORWUC	Service, Office, and Retail Workers' Union of Canada
TWL	Toronto Women's Liberation
TWLC	Toronto Women's Literary Club
UCFR	*Union catholique des femmes rurales*
UFWA	United Farm Women of Alberta
VAD	Voluntary Aid Detachment
VANOC	Vancouver Olympic Committee
VON	Victorian Order of Nurses
VOW	Voice of Women for Peace
WAVAW	Women Against Violence Against Women
WCTU	Woman's Christian Temperance Union
WILLA	Women as Legislative Leaders
WILPF	Women's International League for Peace and Freedom
WIs	Women's Institutes
WLL	Women's Labor League
WLM	Women's Liberation Movement
WMS	Woman's Missionary Society/Women's Missionary Society
YWCA	Young Women's Christian Association

Index

NEL